COMPUTERS IN EDUCATION

Dedicated to the memory of Donovan Tagg, who for 25 years worked untiringly for the cause of Education and Computers. He edited many volumes for IFIP, of which this proved to be the last, since he died on the eve of this Conference.

COMPUTERS IN EDUCATION

Proceedings of the IFIP TC 3
1st European Conference on Computers in Education - ECCE 88
Lausanne, Switzerland, 24–29 July, 1988

edited by

Frank LOVIS
Computing Discipline
Faculty of Mathematics
The Open University
U.K.

and

E. D. TAGG†

1988

NORTH-HOLLAND – AMSTERDAM · NEW YORK · OXFORD · TOKYO

ISBN: 0 444 70483 3

Published by:
ELSEVIER SCIENCE PUBLISHERS B.V.
P.O. Box 103
1000 AC Amsterdam
The Netherlands

Sole distributors for the U.S.A. and Canada:
ELSEVIER SCIENCE PUBLISHING COMPANY, INC.
52 Vanderbilt Avenue
New York, N.Y. 10017
U.S.A.

PRINTED IN THE NETHERLANDS

PREFACE

In order to bridge a gap of 14 years without a major TC-3 Conference in Europe, IFIP encouraged the organisation of a regional event in between two WCCEs, namely, Norfolk 85 in the USA and Sydney 90 in Australia. It took little effort to convince the Swiss Federation of Informatics to propose Lausanne for a remake of WCCE 81 and TC-3 to accept the suggestion, because so many fond memories were attached to the 1981 venue. (Readers who wish to know the meaning of the acronyms appearing in this preface are kindly referred to Prof. Brauer's article in this volume on the TC-3 25th anniversary.)

The substance of a Conference, however, consists of the contributions of the authors who deserve full credit for the scientific quality of these proceedings. There were more valuable papers than we could possibly accomodate and the selection work of the Programme Committee was not an easy task. Fortunately, each European country provided a number of specialists in the various areas of interest who agreed to act as reviewers and whose invaluable contribution I must here acknowledge. Each paper was sent to 3 independent reviewers, one from the same country as the paper's author, one from another country and, the chairperson of the paper's specific area. I want to thank all these reviewers, whose names are nowhere to be found in this book, for the precise and timely job they did. Without their selflessness and dedication, it would have been impossible to maintain the high standards which have been the trademark of such IFIP events in the past.

The final program is the work of the Programme Committee who endorsed the selection of papers prepared by a sub-group composed of the TC-3 Working Group chairmen, the Swiss members of the PC and the two editors, F. Lovis and D. Tagg. They also proposed the invited speakers: J. Hebenstreit as keynote speaker, S. Larsen and J.I. van Deursen as invited speakers for the Tuesday and Wednesday and T. Stonier to contribute to the concluding remarks, with E. Brunswick from UNESCO. Each author received a typing kit directly from North-Holland and comments from the editors for possible improvement of their earlier draft. Most of the authors were thoughtful enough to send their papers to Frank Lovis before the imposed deadline. Only a few papers had to be completely retyped but a good many, which were sent also on a diskette, were reprinted using Frank's laser printer. The good appearance of this book must be credited to the relentless efforts of Frank Lovis.

Of course, none of this could have been accomplished without the excellent support from the Organizing Committee, headed by M. M.-H. Cuendet. They looked after all the printed materials, collected the necessary financial support and worried about the Conference premises, hotel accomodation, the exhibition and social events. Working with them is always a pleasure which, I hope, will be shared by every participant in ECCE 88.

Last but not least, I want to express special thanks to three persons without whom our sophisticated organizations would have collapsed long ago: G. Roberts runs the IFIP Secretariat in Geneva, R.-M. Fabbiani works for the Organizing Committee and L. Noël tries to prevent all the papers that end up on my desk from burying me. Secretaries don't get academic recognition or even credit for organizing major events, but without their constant and efficient pushing, things like ECCE 88 would simply not happen. For every Conference, there is a lot of hard and obscure work to be accomplished, anguished times to be survived. There are also good times and satisfactions and I hope that examining the final result, which is this book, will provide a sufficient motivation for other people to devote their time and energy to do it again.

B. Levrat
(Chairman, Programme Committee, ECCE 88)

EDITORIAL

The papers in these proceedings are grouped under the following headings, in accordance with the decision of the Programme Committee:

— Informatics Across the Curriculum and Informal Education
— Formal and Informal Learning and Teaching Environments
— New Technologies and their Educational Potential
— Social and Psychological Aspects
— Local, Regional, National and International Projects
— Educational Aims, Policies and Curriculum
— Courseware Development
— Long Term Educational Research and Evaluation

All the papers accepted for presentation at ECCE 88 are included here, although in some instances it proved a close-run thing. Not every country seems to welcome the importation of North-Holland typing kits and some authors actually proved impossible to contact. Thus, in a few cases, the Editors have had to work from the drafts which were originally submitted and we can only hope that we have produced final versions which properly realise these authors' intentions.

The media employed by the authors ranged from vintage mechanical typewriters to the latest laser printers. Moreover, a wide selection of the 300 or so available fonts was used — not always proving suitable for the purpose. At present, editors of conference proceedings probably receive a more diverse input than ever before, which certainly leads to an exciting experience. Soon, however, it should be reasonable to insist that all papers are submitted as ASCII files: this we heartily commend to our successors. Electronic mail will also prove a boon: we were seldom able to use it in this task, but it was marvellous when we could.

In his Preface, Bernard Levrat thanks some of those who have helped us greatly: we warmly endorse his comments. In addition, we record our gratitude to Val Kirby, of the Open University (UK), who went well beyond the call of duty in solving some of the trickiest problems. At North-Holland itself, Stephanie Smit and Janet Mitchell were soothing, patient and invariably helpful.

F. Lovis and E.D. Tagg
(Editors)

TABLE OF CONTENTS

2. FORMAL AND INFORMAL LEARNING AND TEACHING ENVIRONMENTS

Tools for Language Learning II
Chairperson: S. Wills

CAL In Biology
Chairperson: Bl. Sendov

Computers in Mathematics Teaching
Chairperson: J. Moonen

8. LONG TERM EDUCATIONAL RESEARCH AND EVALUATION

CONCLUDING PRESENTATIONS

A View of the Development and Activities of TC3

Wilfried Brauer   (D)

(Chairman, TC3)

At the first European Conference on Computers in Education (ECCE '88), the Technical Committee for Education (TC3) of IFIP is happy to celebrate its 25th anniversary. This gives me the opportunity for a personal interpretation of the development and the activities of TC3.

Soon after the invention of the computer, one realised that computers could not only be used for mathematical calculations, but that they could also serve for a wide variety of purposes in information processing, that special education on computers for a wide range of people was needed and that the general public had to be informed about the many possible uses of computers. Therefore, to support and coordinate national and international activities in developing curricula and producing education material, and to have a forum for discussion and exchange of ideas and information, IFIP established, as early as 1963, a Technical Committee for Education as its third Technical Committee (after the committees on terminology and on programming)

Administrative data processing (ADP) was already considered as one of the most important applications of computing and also as a field where special training was particularly needed. Thus, the first major activity of TC3 (at the beginning, in cooperation with the International Computing Centre in Rome, later with several other institutions) was the creation and organization of ADP seminars, which reached people from all over the world, from industrialized as well as from developing countries.

The art of computer programming developed rapidly into an independent new science with deep theoretical foundations, with its own principles, methods and techniques, and with a broad spectrum of applications. Moreover, it offered new tools, new ways of working and new kinds of thinking to other disciplines and thus became a basic science of a fundamental character similar to that of mathematics, physics or chemistry. Anticipating this trend, TC3 started very early to discuss the question of teaching informatics at school and set up in 1966, as its first Working Group, WG 3.1, on "Informatics Education at the Secondary Education Level". Naturally, one of its main concerns is teacher training.

The achievements in computing enlarged the field of ADP considerably; the area of information systems especially became one of great importance and also of great complexity. To answer the demand for training in this quickly growing area, TC3 founded a separate Working Group for "Organization of Educational Seminars" (WG 3.2) in 1968. The group soon realized that there was also need for a model curriculum on information system design education. Because of the importance of informatics for many other disciplines, the scope of WG 3.2 was again enlarged in 1981. Its title is now "Advanced Curriculum Projects in Information Processing".

The emerging fundamental character of informatics, the great versatility and the increasing availability of computers, together with new educational theories (in particular, those based on Skinner's theory of behaviorism) stimulated, in the late sixties, many projects on the creation of computer-based tools for teaching and learning, even including ideas on replacing teachers by computers. Naturally, TC3 joined this movement and formed its WG 3.3 on "Instructional Use of Computers" in 1971. Since a few years ago, this group has not been active, because several of its activities fit better into the specific framework of other working groups of TC3. But it is probable that it will soon be revived with a broader scope, which will also encompass the use of other communication media in education.

In the sixties, the number and the size of computer centres grew enormously. Programming and operating computers was no longer restricted to a small number of people with higher education. This necessitated systematic education on computers at the post-secondary level and vocational training. So, in 1971, TC3 also created Working Group 3.4 on "Post-Secondary Education and Vocational Training" which, after a revision in 1983, is now called "Vocational Education and Training".

The advent of microcomputers caused new educational problems. Computers became part of daily life and even children could use them. Many parents bought micros for their children; many others were not able to do so. To avoid misuse of the computer because of lack of guidance, and to give all children the opportunity to learn how to play and to work with the computer in a sensible way, knowledge of the use of computers in daily life has to be taught as early as elementary school. This also creates a problem of teacher training. TC3 therefore formed a new Working Group (WG 3.5) on "Informatics in Elementary Education".

Knowledge of computers and their use, of informatics and its applications, is by now a necessity for almost everybody. This asks for mass education. The new communication technologies on the other hand make mass education possible via teleteaching, distance learning, or remote education. And thirdly, this type of education is more and more influenced by the use of computers. The world-wide interest in this new form of teaching has led TC3 to form, in 1987, a Working Group on "Distance Education" (WG 3.6).

Thus, TC3, in its past 25 years, has always taken a leading position in detecting new trends and new demands and in converting these insights into appropriate actions.

The main activity of TC3 and its Working Groups has been and will be the organisation of seminars, conferences and workshops, and the publication of their results.

TC3 is proud that it was and is able to organize successfully its own series of World Conferences on Computers in Education (WCCE): Amsterdam (1970), Marseilles (1975), Lausanne (1981), Norfolk/Virginia (1985). The next WCCE will be held in 1990 in Australia.

TC3 also co-sponsored an important regional conference: "The Rio Symposium on Computer Education for Developing Countries" (Rio de Janeiro, 1972). Recently, we started again on the organization of regional conferences: 1986:"Microcomputers in Secondary Education" in Tokyo and now ECCE '88. Also, in 1986, we co-sponsored another symposium in a developing country: the first ICOMIDC Symposium on "Informatics and the Teaching of Mathematics in Developing Countries", Monastir/Tunisia.

Of particular importance and of special character are the many Working Conferences of TC3, in which a small group of carefully selected experts presents and discusses new scientific results, educational methods, teaching experiments, and tools for teaching and learning. The papers presented and the discussions are edited with great care and are published in the North-Holland series of IFIP Proceedings, in order to make the results available to a wide public.

TC3 workshops have produced a number of other publications: a series of booklets for teachers in secondary schools; "An International Curriculum for Information System Designers";"A Modular Curriculum in Computer Science".

Results from other meetings and workshops of TC3 and its Working Groups were spread simply by the multiplying function of its members.

Therefore, to work successfully in TC3 or its W G's needs serious engagement, particular motivation, special expertise, as well as a good knowledge of and close relations to all relevant activities in one's own country. We are always glad to find new active members. TC3 and its W G's can only be as good as their members are - it is the individual persons who have the ideas and who do the work.

It is impossible to list here all those persons who have been particularly active in connection with TC3; let me list only the officers of TC3 and its Working Groups.

TC3 Chairmen

N I Bech (DK) (preparatory: 1962)
R A Buckingham (GB) (1963-73)
D H Wolbers (NL) (1974-78)
J Hebenstreit (F) (1979-84)
W Brauer (D) (1985-)

Vice-Chairmen

W F Atchison (USA) (1971-72)
J Hebenstreit (F) (1973-78)
Atchison/Brauer (USA/D) (1979-84)
Atchison (USA) (1985-86)
P Bollerslev (DK) (1987-)

Secretaries

M Shader (USA) (1964-72)
B Penkov/Atchison (BG/USA) (1973-78)
Penkov/T Brattvag (BG/N) (1979-80)
G Wiechers (ZA) (1981-)

W G 3.1 Chairmen

D Chevion (IL) (1966/67)
W F Atchison (USA) (1968-77)
F Lovis (GB) (1978-83)
P Bollerslev (DK) (1984-)

W G 3.2 Chairmen

R A Buckingham (GB) (1968-78)
W F Atchison (USA) (1983-)

W G 3.3 Chairmen

Sylvia Charp (USA) (1973-79)
R Lewis (GB) (1980-)

W G 3.4 Chairmen

A Berger (A) (1973-78)
P G Raymont (GB) (1979-84)
B Z Barta (IL) (1985-)

W G 3.5 Chairman

F Lovis (GB) (1984-)

W G 3.6 Chairman

G Kovacs (H) (1987-)

TC3, in its past, has cooperated with a large number of international and national organizations; I should like especially to mention UNESCO, because there have been good contacts there for a long time, which have intensified in recent years, and there are good prospects for further cooperation.

In the future, TC3 will continue to be of great importance and will have lots to do, if it goes on being innovative in detecting new problems and possibilities, since informatics is still a rapidly growing discipline which will produce many new things of importance for education - either as knowledge to be learnt or as tools to be used. Moreover, more and more people all over the world - children and adults - need more education about informatics and its uses. Based on my experience in TC3, I am optimistic that IFIP's Technical Committee for Education and its Working Groups will meet this challenge.

(Note: A quite comprehensive account of TC3's past activities will be found in the anthology compiled on the occasion of its 25th anniversary: R Lewis & D Tagg (eds): "   ", North-Holland, Amsterdam, 1988.

Keynote Address

COMPUTERS IN EDUCATION, F. Lovis and E.D. Tagg (eds.)
Elsevier Science Publishers B.V. (North-Holland)
© IFIP, 1988

Computers and education

An encounter of the third kind

by Jacques HEBENSTREIT

ESE - Plateau de Moulon

91190 GIF-sur-YVETTE - FRANCE

Abstract

In the late forties, when the first computers were built, nobody thought that these machines had any future outside a few big military laboratories who had the money to buy them and the competence to use them.

The first attempts to use computers in education go back to the early sixties and at that time, because of the price of computers, the main effort was to prove that replacing teachers by computers would decrease the cost of education while improving the quality.

The advent of the microcomputer in the late seventies has brought a dramatic change in the image of computers, who suddenly changed their status from the ominous "Big Brother" to the gentle "user friendly pet", also called "personal or domestic or home computer".

This started an increasingly optimistic view of the role of microcomputers, based on arguments like "Children like computers", "Computers amplify the child's intelligence", "Give a child a computer and he starts becoming creative", etc... which led governments to the decision to put computers in schools and, because nobody really knew what to do with them, to the devastating wave known as "computer literacy" or "computer awareness".

Ten years were necessary to recover from that wave and it is not yet the case in all countries.

Because of the huge commercial interests involved and also because the use of computers has in most cases been imposed on the teaching community, great efforts have been made to "prove" the advantages of the use of available commercial hardware and software, based on the axiom "Computers are good for you", whereas very little fundamental research has been made in cognitive psychology to evaluate how, when, where and how much the use of computers can improve education.

Informatics in the eighties

The history of technology shows with evidence that the form and initial use of a new product is strongly conditioned by the past (the first cars looked like horse-carriages and the electric engine, first designed to replace steam engines, had to wait 50 years before finding its place in vacuum cleaners, washing machines, typewriters and electric shavers).

This general statement is of course true for computers.

Since the beginning and up to a few years ago, a company could not afford to buy a computer because of its price, unless the machine was to replace a large quantity of manpower which means that the main use of computers was the replacement of people by computers for large applications in big companies (printing payrolls, management of orders and invoices, etc) exactly along the line of the first industrial revolution.

To speak of children and computers at that time would have been pure nonsense.

However, for the last 10 years or so, because of the massive decrease of the price of computers, due to the advent of the microprocessor, the whole philosophy of use of computers has changed drastically.

In big companies, analysts are studying today the content of the job of each person from the worker up to the chairman of the board to find out which part or parts of each job can be automatized, and each person receives a micro-computer or a terminal to assist him by automatizing such or such a part of his job, either to save time, or to allow him to do better, or to do more in his work.

We are entering the era of **computer assisted activities** (Computer Aided Design, Computer Aided Manufacturing, Computer Aided Drafting, Computer Aided Management, Computer Aided Medical Diagnosis, Computer Aided Office, etc) which is also called CAX, where X stands for any activity.

Ten years ago, computers were used to replace people along the line of taylorism where hundreds of people did punch cards to feed the machine. Today, we are entering a period where computers are becoming personal tools, sitting on the desk of each professional and allowing him not only to save time by asking the computer to take over all the tedious parts of his task, but allowing him also to do much more and attack more difficult and more complex problems than he could before.

The fast increase in the number of computers used in all professions and at all levels of activities (the production of microcomputers for 1986 was around 9 million units and is going to increase sharply this year) has already had a number of consequences.

The first consequence is a lack of professionals in informatics which are, by definition, those who design and manufacture the hardware and the software, which the users of computers will buy and use.

The second consequence is, at least in developed countries, a kind of growing awareness in public opinion of the key-role of informatics for the society of tomorrow, which has been initiated and strongly supported by all mass-media and official speeches.

This in turn has led governments in almost all developed countries to proposals or decisions to introduce computers in the whole educational system from kindergarten to university.

Moreover, because of the decreasing price of computers and the way manufacturers and computer-shops are advertising their products, an increasing number of parents are feeling more and more guilty if they do not buy a computer for their children.

Despite some dissimilarities in scope and methods, all proposals or projects to introduce computers in education, can be classified in what I shall call three scenarios.

First scenario : computer awareness/computer literacy

In that first scenario, children should be taught about computers, how they work, how they are used, their social impact, the way they change jobs and, last but not least, children should be taught programming (the British Micro-electronics in Education Project included even micro-electronics) and all this before the age of 12 or 15.

This scenario looks like a kind of emergency decision to face the massive arrival of microcomputers. It is over simplified because it does not make much sense to teach the state of the art of informatics to children who will be adults in 10 years from now, given that nobody is able to predict what informatics will look like in 10 years from now (who was able 10 years ago to predict 500 $ computers, computer networks, integrated service networks, electronic mail, extensive data-banks, multiple windows, pull-down menus, etc).

In my opinion, this scenario is not only useless, it is harmful because the time spent on these topics could be better used to teach much more fundamental subjects like mathematics, sciences or oral and written expression,

which are more than ever necessary to turn out the highly adaptive people needed by our modern and fast changing society.

In some places, it is suggested to go even further and to teach programming and/or algorithms.

The teaching of programming

Some people argue that it is necessary to be able to program a computer with two kinds of argument :

   a) if you don't know a programming language, you will be like an invalid in a computerized society,

   b) if you know a programming language, you will be able to find a well paid job.

These two arguments were valid years ago, but are not true any more :

   a) citizens of the computerized society will not write programs, they will use computers in the CAX mode with pre-written cheap software, because it will be sold by the hundred thousand copies (one should remember that LOTUS 1,2,3 has sold over 1 million copies in one year),

   b) if companies can afford to buy microcomputers, they cannot afford the cost of having their employees write programs instead of doing their work. Moreover, those people who will be hired to write programs will be required to be specialists in programming which has little to do with the simple knowledge of a programming language.

Other specialists argue that programming has intellectual virtues and they compare it to mathematics or even latin. Training in programming is supposed to teach children :

   a) to "think logically" (whatever this means),

   b) to formulate solutions in a clear, exhaustive and unambiguous way,

   c) to be careful and handle all details,

   d) etc.

Objectively, these people take their desire for reality.

The truth is that we should like future programmers to have the above qualities, but experience has shown that the teaching of programming, even intensively, has been unable to develop these qualities for people who did not have them beforehand.

The incredible large number of reports on the bad working methods and the low productivity of **professional programmers** are a proof of it, as well as the cruel anecdotes which are well known in professional circles.

I shall only give two of these :

> "if we could manage to allow programmers to write their software in natural language, we should notice that the majority of them cannot write",

> "in software, the first 90% of a job takes 90% of the time, the last 10% takes also 90% of the time".

Some people argue that this was true up to now because we were not able to teach "good" programming, but the "new" programming methods or such and such new "miracle-language" or "miracle-system" are going to change the situation.

It may well be possible but it remains to be proved, mainly because in many places, the current practice of teaching programming is not up to the level of the arguments. You may have seen, as I have, recent books on "Data structure and algorithms" where eating breakfast or peeling potatoes become algorithms like :

> BEGIN; DO eat a toast UNTIL no more hungry
> END;

> or
> BEGIN; WHILE potatoes in the basket DO peel a potato

> END;

which tend to "prove" that humans do everything in an algorithmic way and which, in the best case, can be considered as bad jokes and, in the worst case, as pure nonsense and in any case as deeply misleading.

Moreover, which language should be taught ? Programming languages have changed in the last 10 or 20 years; some have disappeared (JOVIAL, ALGOL60 etc) others have appeared or reappeared (BASIC, PL1, APL, ADA, PASCAL, LISP, etc) more are coming (PROLOG, SMALLTALK, OCCAM, etc) implying different styles and methodologies of programming. Which programming language and which style will be current practice in 10 or 20 years from now, when today's children will be adults? Will we have "intelligent machines" which will make today's "fundamental concepts" as obsolete as the Ptolemaic solar system or the stone axe ? Who knows ? Or will it finally be possible to write programs in a natural language and should we teach Japanese to all children ?

The teaching of problem-solving

Some experts argue that the ultimate goal of teaching programming is not programming but "problem-solving".

Now "problem-solving" is an interesting concept and one may wonder how it can be applied to various problems like :

- the problem of unemployment,

- the problem of coexistence between East and West,

- the problem of the financial debt of developing countries,

- the problem of the existence of God.

But even if we restrict the definition of the word "problem" to :

> "Any question having at least one solution which can be found by applying scientific methods"

it is well known that the concept of problem solving is almost as old as science itself and has little to do with programming.

Along the centuries, a number of great scientists like Hobbes, Leibniz, Boole, Turing and others have worked on the subject, but we have not made any real progress since the rules given by René Descartes in his "Discours de la méthode" published in 1636 except adding buzz-words like "top-down analysis", "divide to conquer", etc.

Fundamentally we should remember that in most disciplines, problem-solving as such is only the second act of the play, the first act and often the most difficult being to recognize what the problem really is and to formulate it properly, and for that purpose the computer is of no use.

Moreover, no computer will ever tell you whether your program is relevant to the problem you have in mind and whether the results you get make sense or not.

Most of the time when I look at my students trying to solve an already well defined problem through programming it always reminds me of that English humorist who said that "The invention of the computer is a real revolution in human history, because never, since man exists, has it been possible to print so much nonsense in so short a time".

In fact, what is common between the proposals of teaching programming and teaching problem-solving is the idea that there are "informatics methods" for solving problems and that the ultimate in problem-solving is writing a computer program that solves the problem.

This is a completely aberrant view of problem-solving in general and is nothing more than an attempt to make a theory out of what has been the practice of analysts and programmers for the last 20 years or so. The classical problem solved by analysts and programmers was to automatize a procedure or a set of procedures made by hand (like establishing payrolls or sorting files, etc) through the use of a computer program.

Unfortunately, the **general** activity of problem-solving is not reducible to that specific work of automation of procedures and therefore the teaching of programming and/or algorithms is of no use, except for professionals in informatics.

The real challenge lying before us is totally different. In our fast changing society new problems are arising all the time, and our role should be to prepare children to solve these problems which we don't even know today, first of all by developing insight, intuition and imagination based on a solid understanding of the basic paradigms of sciences, and second by helping them to analyse in a problem which part is relevant to their own intellectual effort and which part can be given to the computer, used as an assistant. As said

Terry Winograd, "Computers should not be regarded as a mathematical abstraction but as systems with which people interact".

It is my opinion that computers can be used in education towards that purpose and I shall come back to that subject later on.

Second scenario : the computer as an intelligence amplifier

Most psychologists believe that children learn about the world through their interaction with the world and Piaget goes even further by saying that children develop their "logico-mathematical tools" through abstraction from their daily experiments with the world.

If we accept the idea that children learn about the world by doing and that therefore their vision of the world depends on the variety of their experiments, then the use of computers raises a number of questions, because with computers children can make types of experiment which are completely impossible without computers. What are these new experiments and do they (if at all) change the way children perceive the world ?

a) there are simple drawing-softwares with which it is possible to make drawings on a screen with a light pen. In its simplest form such a software draws a straight line through any two successive positions of the lightpen. How do children use that possibility ? How do they explain the automatic drawing ?

b) a bit more sophisticated are icon-driven drawing softwares where 2 points can define either a rectangle or a square or a circle, depending on the icon chosen. Moreover, a drawing or a part of it can be moved all over the screen, can be made larger or smaller, etc. All these possibilities do not exist on paper. How do children use these possibilities ? How much do they like it ? How do they explain what they see ?

c) if having drawn a closed line, the computer is able to fill-in the enclosed surface with any colour, what are the experiments children make to find out how it works (filling a non-closed curve, superposing two surfaces with different colours, contour and surface in different colours, etc) ?

d) if different basic drawings are available through icons in a menu (houses, trees, flowers, ships, windmills, boys, girls, animals, etc) do children use the icons separately or together to draw a landscape? After having used this drawing-software, do they still draw on paper and if so, what is the influence of the software on their future drawings ?

e) what is the impact of a text processing package on the speed of learning of writing and spelling ? What is kept and what is lost when children switch to handwriting ? Is there a transfer between both activities ?

f) the description of an action to be executed by a device later on upon request, can be done either by pressing functional keys, as in the case of the toy called "Big track" or by typing instructions on a keyboard. Which way is the easier for children ? Why ?

g) what difference do children see between a mobile executing a list of instructions by moving on the floor and a mobile in the form of a triangle simulating a real mobile and moving on a screen (generally vertical) ? What kind of relationship do they see between the mobile and its simulation ?

h) the possibility to prescribe (in symbolic form) a set of actions to be executed later on by a device is given by the use of computers. How does that possibility change (or not) the notion of flow of time (past, present, future) for children ?

i) to make a drawing on a screen, storing it in memory and calling it again at a later time, is one level of abstraction higher than drawing on a piece of paper and storing it in a physical location where it can be found again. How does this different approach change the way a child conceives the concept of storing for later access ? What difference does he/she make between storing in a computer and storing in a physical location ? How does he/she understand the necessity of naming an object before storing it in memory ?

j) Piaget has insisted on the fact that the child becomes progressively conscious that he is an actor, as compared to outside objects. A robot with a program can become an actor while being an object. Does this change the way a child understands the outside world and his relationship to that world ?

There are many more questions along these lines and they are all open questions, mainly because little research has been done on these and other fundamental problems.

There is a historical reason for that lack of fundamental research.

Years ago, some computer scientists developed various pieces of software and/or hardware aimed at the child-computer interaction and promoted these (mostly for commercial reasons) as **the** only tools for interaction. Psychologists and pedagogues were not sufficiently competent in computer science to define their own hardware/software tools for investigating the child-computer interaction in terms of psychology and pedagogy; therefore the only research they did was to investigate the properties and possibilities of the products designed by the computer scientists, with a tendency to draw universal conclusions as if these products were the only possible ones.

Recently, as more and more psychologists and pedagogues have become familiar with computers, an increasing number of psychologists and pedagogues are defining by themselves their subjects of research in the area of child-computer interaction and are developing by themselves the hardware/software tools they need for their specific investigations.

This will hopefully bring to a stop wonder stories about "Children love computers", "They cannot stop typing on the keyboard", "They take the computer to bed" which may be true for some children but hide the fact that counter examples of children completely reluctant to computers can be mentioned as well and in equal number.

Statistically, children do not love or hate computers; when they can access one, they play a while with it and then they change to other games.

It will also hopefully bring to a stop stories about the wonderful properties of miracle-programming-languages like LOGO, which are supposed to make children become creative and explore and find out lots of things by themselves, as opposed to the use of software packages which are accused of "programming the child". To believe that the use of any specific programming language can make people become creative is either a naïve view or an overoptimistic view of mankind in general and of children in particular, which reminds one of Jean Jacques Rousseau's "gentle savage" corrupted by civilization.

That so many optimistic assertions about the psychological impact of using LOGO, made without any element of proof as to their general validity, have been accepted by psychologists and pedagogues and that nobody ever mentioned a single drawback or dared raise an objection, can only be explained by the dominant social status of computer scientists and the complete lack of competence in computer science of psychologists and pedagogues.

Third scenario : Computer assisted activities

In this scenario, the role of the computer is the role of an assistant which will be used as a set of resources and services. In other terms, the future user of a computer will not be more concerned by computers "per se" than the citizen of our "electronified" society is concerned by electronics.

What he will be interested in is the quality and variety of services available at his terminal, which will be an outlet of a complex network system for communication, information and processing and the use of such a terminal will be socially accepted if, and only if, its use is sufficiently simple, which means compatible with the usual behaviour of people in our society.

The history of informatics of these last twenty years shows with evidence that a considerable effort has been made by professionals to simplify the use of computers, so as to put the machine at the service of man, instead of obliging people to learn a complex set of relevant details of the machine, which in fact was putting man at the service of the machine. We have still to go further in that direction to accomplish the statement of Arno Penzias (Nobel Prize in 1978), "We must teach computers to understand people".

The computer as a source of services and resources is going to play a major role in education and in many countries there are now projects in progress to use computers in education.

In the early sixties, the main role of computers in education was to replace teachers. It was the so-called tutorial mode which simulated as well as possible the role of the teacher in the classroom, giving lectures, asking questions, correcting answers and so on. Witness of that tendency are the numerous publications of that time trying to show that computer based education was cheaper than institutional education.

The reason for the promotion of the tutorial mode was the high price of computers which made their use economically feasible in education only if they were able to replace teachers.

The tutorial mode is not bad in itself. It may be very useful in a number of circumstances (children who have to stay away from school for a given period, rehearsal for the less gifted, learning check-list-type of activities like maintenance, control, etc), but it is by no means **the** solution, because it is just ridiculous to try to reduce all pedagogical processes with all their complexity to that kind of rudimentary mechanism, which is much more likely to develop conditionned reflexes in children than anything else. The fact that it is put to work through advanced technology and with reference to Socrates does not change the problem.

If we consider on the contrary that education is a complex process where the aim of teaching is to help each child to acquire knowledge, not for the purpose of memorizing it and becoming able to answer questions, but with the purpose to help each child to build for himself a coherent mental representation of the world around him, so as to become able to act on this very world with increasing chances of success in his actions, then there is a wide variety of possible uses of computers at each step of the pedagogical process and not only for the child but also for the teacher.

We have already mentioned the growing tendency of using computers in the CAX mode. If we apply this to education, than we have two actors : the teacher and the child, and each of them can be assisted by computer in their activity.

Computer Aided Teaching

Very little has been done in this direction up to now and therefore very few software packages (which I shall call "teachware") are available to help teachers to improve their teaching in the classroom.

One interesting application is the "electronic blackboard" where the teacher uses the keyboard to show texts and pictures. Many different uses are possible :

- increasing the number of examples,

- simulation of experiments,

- presentation of cases where an unknown rule is applied and asking the class to find the rules, etc.

Some experimental teachware has been developed in France under the name "Pictureware" and has given extremely interesting results.

In one of these experiments (age 13-15), the teacher shows a triangle where two points are fixed and one of the points can be moved through the keyboard. He asks how this last point should be moved to get a triangle having the same area as the original one.

After discussion between the pupils, a move is proposed.

If the area of the new triangle is equal to the original one, the proposed point appears green and the computer gives a "beep"; if it is not the case, the new point appears red and nothing happens. New discussion, new point, etc, until a line of green points, parallel to the fixed side, appears on the screen which properly commented on by the teacher allows him to introduce the formula of the area of the triangle, which at the same time justifies and explains what is shown on the screen.

What this factual description is unable to describe is the excitement in the classroom, the vividness of the discussions between pupils before making a decision and the pleasure of those who, in the meantime, guess that all the points lie on a straight line. What is important here is the emergence of a new type of pedagogy where the computer, in the hands of the teacher, plays an active role. What is also important is the change introduced in the relationship between the teacher and the pupils, where the teacher is not the one who teaches the truth and gives bad marks for a wrong answer. On the contrary, he is encouraging the

intuition, the imagination and the creative thinking of the pupils and leaves it to the computer to show if a pupil's proposal is wrong or right with the subsequent demonstration which helps to understand why some ideas were right and others not. This example gives only a slight idea of the wide range of possible uses of the computer by the teacher and much more research is necessary in this direction.

Another possible use of the computer to assist the teacher in the classroom is "guided discovery" which is the teacher's version of a game called "Microworld".

For that purpose, the teacher uses a software package simulating an experimental phenomenon (physics, chemistry, biology, demography, geography, etc). Pupils work in groups on a terminal where they can change the parameters of the phenomenon and make experiments and are asked to discover the laws governing the phenomenon, whereas the teacher goes from one group to another.

There are many different objectives :

- to put children in a research situation, i.e. construction of an explanatory model of what has been observed. This is a real inductive way of reasoning and requires creative thinking at a rather high level of abstraction (children are working on a symbolic representation of a real event),

- to verify that children apply correctly the experimental method : experiment, hypothesis, verification of the hypothesis through experimentation, new hypothesis, etc, with examples and counter examples,

- to verify that children apply a strategy to make their experiments converge towards a conclusion and are not gaming around through trial and error,

- to help children to become autonomous in a situation which requires constructive thinking in the search for a solution.

Another interesting possibility for the teacher is the use of small data-banks which can be used in many disciplines, the main purpose being to show that there are methods for asking the right questions and for refining these progressively and that there are also methods for making a distinction between relevant and non-relevant facts in the answers given by the computer.

Computer Aided Learning

Here, we are interested in the assistance a computer can give to the pupil.

I shall only just mention video-games or the so-called educational games because, apart from what I have said previously about the psychological impact of the specific properties of the computer, they have on the whole little pedagogical value.

Besides these, the tutorial mode or the drill and practice mode can help the less gifted children at home to improve their results provided their parents pay attention to it, because I don't know many children who volunteer for working after class-hours even on a computer, when it becomes daily practice.

More interesting is a text processing system with dictionary look-up which can be used to improve spelling or can encourage children to write, either because it comes out neatly printed or it can be sent directly through electronic mail.

Dictionaries or encyclopedias on computers, including video-disks, are much more likely to be used by children, because they are no longer heavy books accessed through alphabetical order, but give immediate answers with moving pictures on the screen, to any question.

Simulation has already been mentioned as a possible teaching tool in the hand of the teacher. It has an even greater role to play as a learning aid. It is often said that simulation is useful in education because it allows experiments which would be too expensive or too dangerous or just impossible to make in the laboratory.

While this is true, it is only a very partial view of simulation and it is missing the main point.

What the user is acting upon during simulation is neither the real **concrete** phenomenon or system which is simulated, nor the **abstract** (mathematical) model which has been implemented on the computer and which is not visible to the user.

The "object" on which the user is acting during simulation is "concrete", in the sense that it reacts to the actions (on the keyboard) of the user as do real objects, but is still "abstract" because its behaviour can be seen on a screen, but it cannot be seen or touched as would be the case of a real object. Therefore, the thing with which the user interacts is somewhere between abstract and concrete, at a level which does not exist outside of simulation : an "abscrete" object.

The very original nature of any "simulated object" implies a new type of intellectual activity when such a "simulated object" is used, manipulated or studied.

Moreover, through simulation, the user can investigate the behaviour of the model in a number of ways which are not directly possible in the real phenomenon :

- no moving body can materialize its trajectory, whereas it is easy to do so on a screen,

- no moving body will display, on request, a graph showing its speed or acceleration as a function of time or position,

- no real phenomenon will contract or expand time to allow detailed investigation,

- no real system will ever answer **instantly** to the question "what happens if ?", but will request lengthy procedures to change the conditions of an experiment, thereby discouraging the user tfrom continuing his investigations.

The main interest of simulation lies in the pedagogical value of that intermediate level of abstraction between the real phenomenon and the abstract model, in the form of a set of relations describing the behaviour of that phenomenon, and that level is not accessible without the use of computers.

The pedagogical value of that intermediate level of abstraction has however received very little attention up to now.

Long term implications

The use of computers as an assistant with the variety of techniques which have been described is aiming at the improvement of present education by giving children more autonomy, more critical thinking, more possibilities to become creative.

Moreover, by having children working with computers, they become familiar with their future environment in the society of tomorrow and with the variety of tools which they will have at their disposal.

That computerized society is no science fiction; it is already a reality in an increasing number of places in the form of CAX tools.

Because these tools give their users an increasing power over their environment by allowing them to solve problems which they would have been unable to solve, by allowing them to master more and more complex problems, it is indispensable to familiarize children with these tools, not by giving them lectures on computers or programming, but by giving them the opportunity to use these tools in the widest possible variety of situations.

To reach this objective, knowledge about computers and programming is generally useless because writing a program of 50 or 100 instructions does not allow the understanding of anything about what a data-bank is, how to access it and how to use it; in the same way as knowing how to pilot a plane is totally irrelevant to what one has to know to fly from Paris to Lausanne on a commercial airplane.

In the first case, one has to learn how to control a plane with its problems in mechanics and aerodynamics, with its take-off and landing procedures, etc. In the second case, there are specialists to pilot the plane but the passenger is not concerned by these problems; what the passenger has to know is how to read a flight schedule, how to plan flight connections, how to make a seat reservation, the address of the air terminal, the duration of the ride to the airport, the maximum weight of his luggage, etc.

The image of the user in front of his computer with a programming language as his only resource is an image of the past. More and more computers are integrated in complex systems of information, communication and processing, ranging from the local working station with dozens of sophisticated software packages, where instructions are by the hundred thousand, to local, regional and international networks. Each user will therefore be linked to thousands of other computers with access to information and software packages available all over the world, which he will be able to down-load in his own station for further use. This multiplication of more and more sophisticated software tools, which will be accessible from any professional or private terminal, is the major characteristic of the computerized society, which is the society our children will live in and for which we have to prepare them.

The invention of printing made it possible to put at the disposal of everybody, in book form, the knowledge accumulated by past generations and therefore contributed to the general progress of knowledge.

The advent of information, communication and processing systems represents a radical change, because these allow not only a faster and easier access to that accumulated knowledge, but they allow, moreover - and this is completely new, to put methods and techniques to work by executing software packages written by others.

Up to now, we had to learn in books the description of the methods and techniques and try to apply step by step these memorized methods to each problem encountered.

By adding the information, communication and processing systems to the printed knowledge we are, without being always clearly conscious, leaving the era of **discursive information** (description of what we have to do to solve a problem), to enter the era of **operational information** (how to choose the software package which, when executed by a computer, will give the solution of the problem).

If we analyse the implications of this radical change, some remarks are in order :

a) it is absurd to believe that there will one day exist software packages which will solve all the problems or answer all the questions which men will ask,

b) the software packages which are massively developed today are packages which will **assist** men in the solution of problems by giving an aid to process automatically **certain parts** of his problems,

c) the use of these software packages is not trivial. It implies first of all learning how to use them and it implies also that the user has sufficiently mastered the domain of the problem to be able to make a critical appraisal of the results given by the computer (no software will ever allow a specialist in biology to design a new machine-tool, and no computer will ever allow a TV-repair man to design a building).

The contents, the techniques and the methods of all present-day educational systems, from elementary school to university, are based implicitly on the hypothesis that for solving the problems which are given or will be given to the student, the student will have at his disposal his brain, a sheet of paper, a pencil and eventually some books. This very hypothesis is never explicitly stated but it is the very basis of **all** educational systems.

If, as I do believe, in the very near future any pupil or student will have permanent access to systems of information, communication and processing, where thousands of software packages will be available to help him to solve his problems, then it is clear that the preceding hypothesis is no more valid.

In other terms, the generalized access to systems of information, communication and processing will progressively put in question the methods, the techniques and the contents of all systems of education from elementary schools to university, because that very access puts in question all the knowledges and all the know-how's, as we define them today.

The next step

There is a Chinese proverb saying that "Prophecies are extremely difficult, mainly when it concerns the future". This being so, I take the risk to predict that before 10 years from now, each child will have a powerful and cheap computer in its pocket, which it will use intensively in the classrooom as well as out of the classroom.

This means a considerable change to the present use of computers by children, where it is the teacher who chooses the courseware and the teacher who decides how and when the computer will be used.

To get prepared for the consequences of that most significant change in the way computers will be used by children, I strongly believe that it is urgent to start working in three directions :

1.- Increase considerably the research efforts in cognitive psychology, so as to be able to specify guidelines on how, when and where to use computers for the optimal improvement of education.

2.- Set up experimental teams of courseware authors to specify and design, in various disciplines, simultaneously a text-book and its accompanying courseware as a single integrated learning unit using a coherent pedagogical strategy based on the optimal (synergetic) use of both media. My prophecy is that in ten years from now no text-book will sell if it does not come with its accompanying courseware and that today's marketing of courseware in bits and pieces has no future.

3.- Set up a small number of experimental classes with one computer for each pupil with well chosen and motivated teachers, having defined beforehand the new pedagogic strategies to be used in the classroom and produced or chosen the relevant courseware to make the best possible use of that one-computer-per-student environment, which will be the rule in ten years from now.

Conclusion

It has often been said that informatics was going to bring deep changes in our intellectual habits because of its intrinsic logic and, to accelerate these changes, it was urgent to teach the techniques of informatics to everybody and mainly to children. The implicit hypothesis was that we could prepare our society for the unavoidable changes by teaching algorithms to everybody through top-down analysis, data-structures, rigorous logical thinking, iteration loops, recursion and proofs of programs.

The generalized use of computers **is** going to change our mental habits but not because of the afore mentioned reasons.

What is going to happen is that, through the effect of economic competition or because of the simple necessity of survival of industrialized countries, more and more sophisticated informatics tools will be introduced everywhere.

What is going to happen is that everybody will have to use in his professional life first, and in his private life afterwards, such powerful tools that they would have been properly inconceivable 10 or 20 years ago.

This will lead us unavoidably, through daily practice, to formulate all problems differently because they will be solved through the use of much more powerful tools and this will lead people quite naturally to think differently (long distance travel problems are considered differently today from what they were before the invention of the rail road, the car or the airplane, and this has changed deeply the way we look at the world in general).

The advent of CAX tools and their generalized use in the next ten years is going to put in question all our know-how's, and the teaching of computers and programming is by no means an answer to that question. What is in question is much deeper, it is the question of how we are going to change our whole systems of education so as to take into account the existence of these powerful tools and how we are going to integrate these in a new set of coherent curricula at all levels so as to educate everybody to make the most efficient use of these tools, starting at the elementary school and up to university.

Terry Winograd has said that "There is one thing which computers cannot do and which people do quite naturally : "think";" but it has also been said that the way we think is to a considerable extent conditioned by the nature and the kind of tools we use.

The advent of CAX tools is therefore opening a whole new era where men will be relieved from a considerable amount of routine intellectual activities and mechanical thinking and this gives us for the first time in history a unique occasion for using education to develop insight, imagination and creativity, which are more than ever necessary to make the best use of these tools.

Dr Hamming has said that "The purpose of computing is insight and not numbers" and I should like to paraphrase his statement by saying that the ultimate purpose of computing should not be to turn people into servants of the computer but to develop in people those qualities which are unique to men; in other terms, the ultimate purpose of computing should be to help people to become more human.

Invited Papers

COMPUTERS IN EDUCATION, F. Lovis and E.D. Tagg (eds.)
Elsevier Science Publishers B.V. (North-Holland)
© IFIP, 1988

NEW TECHNOLOGIES IN EDUCATION: SOCIAL AND PSYCHOLOGICAL ASPECTS

STEEN LARSEN

The Royal Danish School Of Educational Studies, 101 Emdrupvej, DK-2400
Copenhagen N.V., Denmark.

It is argued that simply transferring information to the students is
not identical to giving them knowledge. It is necessary to
understand this difference if one's theory of teaching and learning
shall not be reduced to what is called a simple theory of teaching.
In accordance with these considerations, a three-stage theory for the
use of information technology in education is presented, based on the
fundamental view that explicit information can be transformed into
personal knowledge through so-called socio-cognitive restructuring in
social learning situations. Therefore, our schools should be changed
from auditories of isolated listeners into laboratories of active
cooperation.

1. INTRODUCTION

The current fast development and wide-spread use of new technologies in education creates a need for a corresponding development of our educational theories and philosophy. This renewed thinking must take its point of departure in the fact that these new technologies are more heavily based on handling of information than ever before. Therefore, it is important to understand what information actually is, and what it is not, if the new technologies shall not lead to a simplification and degeneration of our educational systems. If this is not realized, we risk bringing up a generation of students who have access to more information than any earlier generation in history, but in spite of this have less knowledge.

Does this sound like a contradiction? It is not. It is only a contradiction to those who think that giving students information is identical to giving them knowledge. The aim of the present paper is to discuss this problem and to present a theory for the use of information technology in education.

2. SIMPLE AND DEVELOPED THEORIES

Concerning the quality of education, we can distinguish between simple and developed theories of teaching and learning. Inexperienced teachers frequently use analogies that fall into the category which can be called "the t r a n s f e r theory of teaching" (Fox, 1983). From this attitude the students' minds are seen as containers into which the relevant information has to be transferred.

This theory is simple because no distinction is made between information and knowledge. It is simply taken for granted that transferring information to the students is identical to giving them knowledge. Educational problems are generally reduced to problems of how to make good materials for instruction, how to develop and refine the methods of transfer, and how to elaborate teaching aids and finally inject the relevant information accurately into the receiving container. This simple transfer theory is the one on which most of today's computer-assisted education is based.

Once it is considered, however, that the student is also a subject and not just an object for transferrence, and it is thus realized that the student has to build up his own personal knowledge from the obtained information, then the simple transfer theory turns into a more complicated and developed theory.

The first step in this transition from a simple to a developed theory of education is to consider the difference between knowledge and information. This difference belongs to the process of communication, which is generally associated with the idea of transferring a message from one person to another. However, the root of the word communication is "common", that means something which is subject to general use, as language. The prerequisite for the communication of one's inner thoughts is to form them according to the common semantical and syntactical rules. This process, however, where one's inner thoughts are trans— formed according to the common linguistic formulas must take place inside the person before any message can be transferred to other persons. This means that communication consists of two processes: (1) the process where the subjective and personal knowledge is transformed into common linguistic formulas, and (2) the process by which this linguistic message is transferred to others and made public.

```
personal        c        public
                o
                m
                m
            -->u-->
            -->n-->
KNOWLEDGE   -->i-->    INFORMATION
            -->c-->
                a
                t
                i
                o
                n
```

Thus knowledge is something personal, pre-conceptual and non-linguistic in origin, which through the process of communication can be turned into public information. Correspondingly, information can be defined as personal knowledge which has been transformed through the process of communication.

These arguments have two important implications: First, knowledge does not exist outside human beings because of its subjective, pre-conceptual dimension, which means that knowledge contains more than mere information. It is a conglomerate also including non-linguistic aspects as previous experience, feelings, episodic memories, imaginations, expectations, etc.

From this follows the second implication that knowledge can not be transferred directly from one person to another, without first being transformed into information. Information can be transferred directly because it consists of separate and well-defined elements, whereas knowledge due to its coherent and implicit character must be induced (Larsen, 1986c).

3. THE DEVELOPED THEORY OF EDUCATION

On this background the developed theory of education can now be described in three stages. The first stage of the educational process is the teacher's transformation of his implicit personal knowledge into explicit information. This process consists of functions such as defining concepts, choice of terminology, parting the subject material into clear and well-arranged subsections, formulation of text, etc. This stage where the implicit personal knowledge is turned into explicit information is the initial one in all educational processes. It can be the teacher's preparing himself for the next lesson, the planning of a new textbook, or the initial stage in implementation of educational software.

When this transformation has been carried out, the educational process moves into its second stage: the transfer of the produced information to the students. This process includes all the well-known media for transfer of information: speech, script, radio programs, television, computer software, etc. In this stage the problem is to ensure that the relevant information is transmitted as effectively as possible to the students, without disturbing noise or interruption.

In these two first stages we are still in the domain of the simple theory of the educational process. It is not until the third stage is considered that the simple theory is turned into a developed theory. Thus, considering this third stage is to realize that the students are individual subjects who have to develop their own personal knowledge from the information which has been transmitted to them. This means that in stage three a process must take place in the student, which in some respect is the reverse of the teacher's transformational process in stage one: the transformation of the obtained public information into personal knowledge. Through this process the received information is "digested" so to say; it loses its character of being a pattern of separate and well-defined elements, which are gradually assimilated and integrated into the student's already existing knowledge.

The final aim in education is to create expertise, and this is not just build up from explicit information and formal logical thinking. Real experts do not, however, in concrete life situations, work according to explicit rules or facts. True experts have exceeded the stage of formal logic and informational self-regulation and work more automatically, directed by experience, intuition and personal knowledge.

This difference between formal-logic and commonsense thinking has been described by Minsky (1983):

"Why was it easier...to make programs expert at calculus or chess than to make infant-level block-building and scene-analysis programs? The apparent answer is almost paradoxical: the procedures we so admire in specialized human experts, however difficult they may be to discover or learn, are often quite clear and simple in the final analysis...The expert knowledge required to work on a particular kind of mathematical structure seems much more uniform and homogeneous.

It has been astonishingly hard to see what commonsense knowledge is composed of...no one has ever been able to write down good formal logical axioms and rules of inference for any substantial body of commonsense knowledge."

But we cannot be knowledged! Each of us must acquire knowledge for ourself."

How are, however, the received information in stage three transformed into personal knowledge and expertise?

This tranformation is taking place when the students are engaged in activities like co-operation, social interaction, discussion, explanation, recollection of previous experience, and solving of real-life problems. The restructuring of the student's knowledge is facilitated by the regular appearance of so-called socio-cognitive conflicts in these activities.

Stage 1: TRANSFORMATION

The expert's transformation of personal knowledge into explicit information.

ANALYSIS
DEFINITION
EXPLANATION
DISPOSITION
SEPARATION
FORMULATION
SCHEMATIZING
VISUALIZATION
ETC.

Stage 2: TRANSMISSION

Transmission of information to the learner.

SPEECH
SCRIPT
PICTURES
RADIO
TV
VIDEO
COMPUTERS
EXPERT SYSTEMS
ETC.

Stage 3: INDUCTION

The learner's transformation of explicit information into personal knowledge.

PERCEPTION
UNDERSTANDING
INTEGRATION
RECOLLECTION
DIALOGUE
DISCUSSION
COOPERATION
EXPERIMENTATION
ETC.

And why? Because personal knowledge and common-sense thinking are not based exclusively on rule-governed processes. Logical functions are strictly rule-governed and can be called "monotonomous" in the sense that from given premises they lead to distinct and predictable conclusions. Through practice and experience this logic and monotonomous way of thinking is so to speak gradually "foreshortened", leading to the real expert's more personal, automatized and intuitive thinking. The advanced expertise is through its non-monotonomous aspects closer to common-sense thinking than to formal-logic thinking. As stated by Daniel Boorstin (1980), chief librarian in the American Congress:

"It is a cliché of our time that what this nation needs is an "informed citizenry"..."I suggest, rather than what we need - what any free country needs- is a knowledgeable citizenry. Information, like entertainment, is something someone else provides us. It really is a service! We expect to be entertained, and also to be informed.

4. SOCIO-COGNITIVE CONFLICTS AND COGNITIVE RESTRUCTURING

According to Piaget (1950), cognitive development is closely related to engagement in actions and operations which are both individually and socially organized. He states that it is by a constant interchange of thought with others that we are able to decentralize ourselves, to coordinate internal relations deriving from different viewpoints. According to Piaget cooperation is the first of a series of forms of behaviour which are important for the constitution and development of thinking.

Learning theorists such as Murray (1974) and Bandura (1977) explain the child's acquisition of new skills by processes of imitation, in particular imitation of superior models. However, both Mugny and Doise (1978) and Weinstein and Bearison (1985) have shown that subjects who interacted with less advanced partners showed as much progress as subjects who interacted with more advanced partners. Therefore, the conception that imitation is the fundamental mechanism in social learning must be modified.

Thus Marion, Desjardins and Breante (1974) observed that "interaction among participants increases when a cognitive conflict is felt by all". According to this, Doise, Mugny and Perret-Clermont (1975) established a socio-cognitive conflict model of development in children, based on the hypothesis of "cognitive conflict experienced and resolved socially". In a number of experiments they have shown that when children are working together in dyads and thus have the opportunity to generate socio-cognitive conflicts, they are able to solve problems at a more advanced level compared to children working individually on the same problems. Furthermore, it has been shown by Mugny and Doise (1978), that in dyadic combinations where subjects who functioned at different levels of mastery worked together, both the less and the more advanced partners progressed.

Apparently, cognitive restructuring is stronger in groups than in individual work because the social interaction brings different views into opposition which leads to cognitive conflicts between the subjects. And as stated by Piaget (1975), "the most pro- ductive factors in acquisition (are) the disturbances brought about by conflict".
Such conflicts oblige the subjects to coordinate their actions, which brings about an accomodation in the encounter with other points of view which can only be assimilated if cognitive restructuring takes place. According to Perret-Clermont (1980), cognitive conflicts of this kind

"brings about the disequilibrium which make cognitive elaboration necessary, and in this way cognitive conflict confers a special role on the social factor as one among other factors leading to mental growth. Social-cognitive conflict may be figuratively likened to the catalyst in a chemical reaction: it is not present at all in the final product, but it is nevertheless indispensable if the reaction is to take place."

Concerning the importance of social interaction in learning, it can thus be concluded that a child, when working alone on a certain task, might more easily remain inclosed in an egocentric approach compared to children working together. In this last case, the socio-cognitive conflicts, due to different points of view, makes cognitive restructuring necessary in the subjects.

5. COMPUTER-ASSISTED INSTRUCTION AND SOCIAL INTERACTION

Until now there has been only little systematic investigation of the character of social interaction between students working with computers. Some more or less anecdotal descriptions have been published concerning students sharing ideas when using text editing programs (Rubin, 1980; Collins, Bruce and Rubin, 1982; Zacchei, 1982) and of computer programming in group settings (Jabs, 1981).

A few systematic studies, however, have been carried out which enlighten the difference between individual and collective work with computers. Thus Reid, Palmer, Whitlock and Joner (1973) observed that some children solved problems more effectively in a group than they did when working alone. Furthermore, Cheney (1977) found that students who worked in pairs on learning computer programming did much better on an exam compared to those who had worked individually. In accordance with this, Klaus and Grau (1976) in a study where 48 7th-graders below the performance median in arithmetics worked both individually and in groups with computer-controlled tasks of increasing difficulty, found that on the average 60% less time was required in group work as compared to individual work.

It could be suggested that students of high mastery will dominate and even passivate their lower achieving peers when working together in small groups. Apparently, this is not necessarily the case. Thus Webb (1984) in a study of learning to program microcomputers in small groups, found that the number of turns and the amount of time at the keyboard had almost no relationship with computing outcomes. The students not at the keyboard seemed to be at least as involved with the material as the students at the keyboard. Furthermore, the cooperation in the groups seemed to be less based on verbalization as compared to normal classroom settings:

"In group work in the typical classroom setting, students can verbally explain how to do the work or can show another student the solution, for example, by writing the solution to a mathematics problem on paper or on the blackboard. Even while "showing" the work, students often rely on verbal cues when the written solution is not complete. With a computer, however, the strategies or approaches to solving a problem (the program) and the results are clearly seen by everyone because they appear on the screeen in standardized fashion. In this way, students can learn from what other group members do as well as from what they say."

6. STAGE 3: A LABORATORY FOR COGNITIVE RESTRUCTURING

From the presented 3-stage theory of education it follows that the use of new information technology must be seen in a wider perspective than just as a device for effective transmission of information.

Knowledge can not, like information, be transferred to the students, but must be induced in learning settings which make the transformation from information into knowledge possible. As pointed out, such learning settings must be based on social activities which create the regular socio-cognitive conflicts that facilitate the cognitive restructuring. Because the initial stages in the teaching process are more or less devoted to transfer of information, our educational institutions are at present dominated by auditories. If the importance of stage 3 is not considered, the new technology will simply be prolongation of this traditional and simple way of teaching. What is needed, however, in an information age, is not just more complicated and electrified "auditories", but laboratories for cognitive restructuring.

Brown (1983) suggests that computer technology will give learning-by-doing a renaissance in the schools:

"I believe that technology will fundamentally change both the use and content of learning-by-doing. In particular, it will make possible a wider range of learning-by-doing scenarios as well as extending the kinds of knowledge that can be taught. Namely, it will facilitate the learning and improvement of metacognitive skills -- skills for thinking about thinking, learning, remembering, and diagnosing."

This vision, however, does not relate to the original educational philosophy behind learning-by-doing. Due to the lack of authentic, practical work in the schools, reality is replaced by artificial and abstract scenarios. Learning is closely connected to problem solving, and the computer is a powerful tool for this purpose. But what kind of problems does the learner actually solve when the computer is used in education? It is seldom used as a tool for solving authentic problems, but rather as a generator of artificial problems.

In fact it all seems to end in a paradox: In the schools we now have a powerful tool for problem solving, but what are the problems to be solved with it? Due to the isolation of the schools from the rest of societal life, most problems the children are dealing with in the school are still of an artificial and abstract character.

7. A SOCIETY WITHOUT SCHOOLS?

According to some educational philosophers, the solution to this paradox could be a society without schools. Illich (1972), for example, has described the vision of a de-schooled society. Currently this idea of society without schools has been related to the new information technology. Papert (1983), the constructor of the computer language LOGO, states it in this way:

"The presence of the computer is what will make a de-schooled society possible and even necessary, because if my vision of the way computers will be used is realized, it will come into conflict with the rational structure of schools on every level, from the epistemological to the social".

Accordingly, other researchers in this field have argued that the microcomputers will give new life to the home as workshop, studio, and laboratory, that they will accelerate the spread of alternative modes of education and thus the process of "de-schooling" society. Present educational systems have been developed as a result of social, historical, and economic factors that are now changing. Current education will be still less able to meet today's needs, which may lead to either abolition of educational institutions or at least extensive de-emphasis of their role in a more widely-based, less formal educational system, (Ross, 1982).

A development like this will according to Papert turn the present public education into a private act:

"The next few years will see an explosion in the number of privately owned computers. Much more significantly, they are about to cross a power threshold that will support the LOGO-like use of them. When this happens, there will be for the first time a viable alternative to schools and the possibility that education will once more become a private act...it is a plausible, even very likely scenario that over the coming decade a significant number of families will come to see the private computer as a viable alternative to public school", (Papert, 1983).

This vision is close to dreams that have also occupied educational thinkers like Rousseau and Dewey. Back to the natural way of learning and learning by doing. But like everything else also educational methods have their preconditions which must be present if the dream shall not be turned into a nightmare. And what are the prerequisites for the natural way of learning by doing? The answer is simple: That there is something to do in the social reality of the child. Something which is authentic and necessary. Something which the child is forced to learn by a social necessity in its daily life. Why do most children learn to talk without organized instruction? Because it is a social necessity in their daily life. Why do most children n o t learn to read and write without organized instruction? Because it is n o t a social necessity in their daily life. This means that natural learning by doing depends on how strongly necessity is represented in the child's social reali- ty. What is necessary will be learned automatically and without organized instruction. In the pre-industrial society the social necessity was high and correspondingly the need for organized instruction was low. The world was small and static and could in an almost literal sense be overviewed by the child.

In the high-technological society this relationship is changed. Due to the technological development things become easier and social necessity is corre- spondingly reduced. One of the most common statements to be heard when a new technological device is introduced is: "It will no longer be necessary to...". For instance wash your clothes or do your dishes by hand, go to the bank, to the library, shopping, and perhaps not even go to school.

For adults this can mean more personal freedom because there will be less to do. But what are the consequences for the children when there is less societal necessity and less to do? It means that there is less natural learning and less learning by doing. Then we must organize tasks and situations which are necessary to the children. Organized necessity, or I would prefer to say artificial necessi- ty: Simulation. Where social necessity goes out, simulation and motivation moves in. "As if ...", becomes the keyword.

The immediate presentation is replaced by the mediated re-presentation, a gradual and unnoticed process which makes educa- tion still more abstract and inauthentic, (Larsen, 1986b).

It must be realized, however, that educa- tion is not identical with instruction and therefore the schools are not solely occupied with teaching and instruction, but have also important social purposes. If education is changed into a private act, for instance carried out by the computer in the home, some very important social dimensions in education can possibly be lost (Larsen, 1986a).

Thus the interaction between the child and the computer forms an artificial dyad which immediately seems to be parallel to that between teacher and pupil. However, effective learning is not solely a matter of establishing teacher-pupil relation- ships. Such relationships can be effec- tive in initial stages of a new learning process where much instruction and new information is necessary. But when the educational process moves into stage 3, this instructional relationship becomes less important as the student begins to use his skills and knowledge in a larger social perspective in co-operation with others. However, in obtaining this social extension of the learning processes, the private computerized instruction in the home could be counter-productive due to its individual character.

8. CONCLUSION

Since most of today's computer-based education is based on the transfer theory, it generally concentrates the attention on stage 1, the teacher's transformation of his personal knowledge into public information, and stage 2, the transmission and distribution of infor- mation to the child.

In the implementation of educational software (Larsen, 1987), these two stages are well-known, and much time and effort is used on developing programs and data- bases which can present all the relevant information to the students. However, the third stage, where the obtained information so to say is digested by the student, is often overlooked. This is a serious mistake which simplifies the educational situation according to the principle of a mere transfer of infor- mation. Thus to transform the obtained information into personal knowledge demands two important functions, namely that the objective and explicit information gets subjective and personal references, and that it is integrated into already existing coherent patterns of knowledge in the student's mind.

However, due to their subjective character, these functions can not be built into the software, but must be stimulated from other parts of the situation in which the learning takes place. This is the reason why knowledge can not simply be transmitted, but must be induced through activities as co-operation, social interaction, restructuring of knowledge due to socio-cognitive conflicts, discussions and solving of real-life problems. Therefore, education must be based on both communication, transmission and personalization, and the use of information technology should never be seen in isolation but as part of a much broader educational situation. It is a tool, not an end in itself.

When we work with this new technology in education, we should have this 3-stage model in mind and be especially aware of the activities in stage 3. Thus, for example, when we introduce new educational software we must ask ourselves: what are the necessary pedagogical activities which are needed to complement my software to be sure that the presented information is digested into knowledge in my pupils?

The further integration of new information technology in education therefore implies the understanding that education is not merely a matter of instruction. The new technology will then no longer be regarded as teaching machines, for which qualified software must be developed, but as devices which, controlled by the learner, can be a powerful tool for the development of personal knowledge. In this perspective, however, the information technology is just an aspect of the social setting in which education is taking place. Thus what is needed now is not more sophisticated technology or stronger interest and attention toward its characteristics and use, but a revised "educational sociology" (Larsen, 1988). The principles, on which the present educational systems are based, are more in accordance with thoughts belonging to the former century than with the possibilities inherent in the new technology.

The new technology will expand the educational possibilities, partly because an overwhelming amount of information will be at hand for the students, and partly because the computers apparently open a more practical kind of learning activity

than the mental operations which dominate most traditional learning in the classroom.

In the educational perspective, however, the advantages of the new information technology can be turned into disadvantages if this is not used according to an explicit and well-defined educational philosophy. Thus the new information technology can be used as a powerful tool to bring almost any kind of information into the classroom. But this is no reasonable educational strategy. Our schools must be changed from auditories of isolated listeners into laboratories of active cooperation. The present challenge is to investigate how the new information technology can be used in the realization of this necessary change.

REFERENCES

Bandura, A. 1977. Social Learning Theory. New Jersey: Prentice-Hall, Englewood Cliffs.

Boorstin, D. 1980. Remarks by Daniel Boorstin, the Librarian of Congress, at White House Conference on Library and Information Science. Journal of Information Science, 111-113.

Brown, J.S. 1983. Learning by Doing Revisited for Electronic Learning Environments. In M.A.White (ed.), The Future of Electronic Learning. New Jersey: Hilldale.

Cheney, P.H. 1977. Teaching computer programming in an environment where collaboration is required. AEDS Journal, 11, 1-5.

Collins, A., Bruce, B.C. and Rubin, A. 1982. Microcomputer based activities for the upper elementary grades. Proceedings of the Fourth International Learning Technology Congress and Exposition. Warrenton, VA: Society for Applied Learning Technology.

Doise, W., Mugny, G. and Perret-Clermont, A.-N. 1975. Social interaction and the development of cognitive operations. European Journal of Social Psychology, 5, 367-383.

Fox, D. 1983. Personal Theories of Teaching. Sudies in Higher Education, 8, 151-163.

Illich, I. 1972. De-Schooling Society. New York: Harper and Row.

Jabs, C. 1981. Game playing allowed. Electronic Learning, 1, 5-6.

Klaus, F. and Grau, U. 1976. Soziale Anregungsbedingungen als Motivations-faktor in einen Ubungsprogramm. Zeit-schrift fur Entwicklungspsychologie and Padagogische Psychologie, 8, 37-43.

Larsen, S. 1986a. Computerized instruc-tion in the home and the child's development of knowledge, Education and Computing, 2, 47-52.

Larsen, S. 1986b. Computers in Education: A Critical view. In: B. Sendov and I. Stanchev (Eds.), Children in an Infor-mation Age. New York: Pergamon Press.

Larsen, S. 1986c. Information can be transmitted but knowledge must be induced. Programmed Learning and Educational Technology, 23, 331-336.

Larsen, S. 1987. Psychological and Pedagogical Considerations in Relation to Implementation of Educational Software. In: J. Moonen and T. Plomp (Eds.), Developments in Educational Software and Courseware. New York: Pergamon Press.

Larsen, S. 1988. How should new techno-logies be used in education? In: D. Harris (Ed.), World Year Book of Education (in press).

Marion, A., Desjardins, C. and Breante, M. 1974. Conditions experimentales et developpement intellectuel de l'enfant de 5-6 ans dans le domaine numerique. In Pourquoi les echecs dans les premieres annees de la scolarite? Recherches Pedagogiques (C.R.E.S.A.S., Ed) No.68 INRDP, Paris.

Minsky, M.L. 1983. Computer Science and the Representation of Knowledge. In: M.L. Dertouzos and J. Moses (Eds.), The Computer Age: A Twenty-Year View. Cambridge, Massachusetts: The MIT Press.

Mugny, G. and Doise, W. 1978. Socio-cognitive conflict and structure of individual and collective performances. European Journal of Social Psychology, 8, 181-192.

Murray, J.P. 1974. Social learning and cognitive development: modelling effects on children's understanding of conser-vation. British Journal of Psychology, 65, 151-160.

Papert, S. 1983. Computers and Learning. In: M.L. Dertouzos and J. Moses (Eds.), The Computer Age: A Twenty-Year View. Cambridge, Massachusetts: The MIT Press.

Perret-Clermont, A.-N. 1980. Social Interaction and Cognitive Development in Children. London: Academic Press.

Piaget, J. 1950. The Psychology of Intelligence. Routledge and Kegan Paul, London.

Piaget, J. 1975. L'equilibration des Structures Cognitives. Probleme central du developpement. Etudes d'Epistemologie genetique, Vol XXXIII, P.U.F., Paris.

Reid, J., Palmer, R., Whitlock, J. and Joner, J. 1973. Computer-assisted instruction performance of student pairs as related to individual differences. Journal of Educational Psychology, 65, 65-73.

Ross, J. 1982. Home computer based learning systems. In: The Computer: Extension of the Human Mind. Proceedings, Annual Summer Conference, College of Education, University of Oregon.

Rubin, A. 1980. Making stories, making sense. Language Arts, 57, 285-298.

Webb, N.M. 1984. Microcomputer learning in small groups: cognitive requirements and group processes. Journal of Educa-tional Psychology, 76, 1076-1088.

Weinstein, B.D. and Bearison, D.J. 1985. Social interaction, social observation, and cognitive development in young children. European Journal of Social Psychology, 15, 333-343.

Zacchei, D. 1982. The adventures and exploits of the dynamic storymaker and textman. Classroom Computer News, 2, 28-30.

COMPUTERS IN EDUCATION, F. Lovis and E.D. Tagg (eds.)
Elsevier Science Publishers B.V. (North-Holland)
© IFIP, 1988

Computers in Dutch Education: results and analysis of a stimulation plan.

Drs J.I. van Deursen
Head of the Education and Information
Technology Project Staff (PSOI) of the
Ministry of Education and Science,
the Netherlands

1. INTRODUCTION

In 1984, in the period in which a number of the surrounding ECC-countries were also taking action, the Dutch government launched a national plan which had as its aim the stimulation of the introduction and use of information technology on a grand scale. This plan was called the Information Stimulation Plan (INSP). In this paper we offer a review of the original aims and the ultimate results of this stimulation plan. We also consider future activities which have arisen as a result and in continuation of the INSP.

The reader should look upon the following as a case history. It is an impressionistic record of the experiences gained from the INSP. We have kept close to the practicalities and have not aimed at producing a report which is either scientifically accountable or methodologically interesting. Neither is it a political scientific analysis. The paper is a report of the experiences of those directly involved and the aim is to share these experiences with the reader. In approaching the matter in this way the paper is held up as a mirror to the reader, in which certain elements may be recognizable.

2. THE INFORMATICS STIMULATION PLAN

2.1 Motivation and aim

Over a period of five years (from 1984 through 1988) a great impulse was to be given to the introduction of computers in the worlds of industry, science and education by means of all types of infrastructural measures and divergent projects. In order to achieve all this a budget of 1.7 billion guilders (approx. 870 million $) was made available. Of this sum, 270 million guilders (approx. 140 million $) was earmarked for measures in the field of regular education. At the same time funds were made available for the stimulation of research, special education, the

marketing sector and the government. The willingness of the government and parliament to make such an extensive investment - in a period when budgets were being drastically cut - stemmed from the concern about the economic position of the Netherlands among the great industrial powers like the USA, Japan and a few EEC countries. There was a general consensus that the Netherlands were in danger of being left behind at the starting post. For a country like the Netherlands which has traditionally been extremely dependent on its export and service sector this was reason enough for reflection. Of course education has a part to play in that type of situation - it is part of the solution. It is obvious that a well-educated professional corps, and adequate preparation of the ordinary citizen in information technology (IT), may have an important influence in the process of a country's adjustment to the new demands. Education, when considered as a sector of society, was in dire need of a positive monetary injectione from the government after having born the brunt of cuts in the education budget for a number of successive years. The schools reacted enthusiastically to the educational component.

Now we have reached the last of the five project years, we can draw our conclusions about the educational component.

2.2. The educational component in the INSP

The INSP, when regarded in terms of education, had an unusually wide range of influence: all sectors from primary education right through to higher education, were subject to the plan. Only the universities were beyond its scope, at least as far as the educational section was concerned.

The main goals of the INSP for education were:

1. improving the quality of the 'human capital', the school-leavers;

2. preparing ordinary citizens for IT as a social phenomenon. During the process Computer Assisted Learning and Computer Managed Instruction attracted more attention as means of improving the quality of the educational learning process and making education more efficient. This all took place, it should be noted, without any impairment to the aims first mentioned.

The budget of 270 million guilders was earmarked for the various sectors of education and for a number of activities which would create the necessary conditions to carry it out. In line with the main aims of the policy, most of the money was made available for training schemes in the vocational education sector: 46%, or 125 million was reserved for secondary and higher vocational education. For the remaining educational sectors there was a joint sum amounting to 73 million guilders; for a number of sections like in-service training, research, and an infrastructure for programme development - which were prerequisites for the proper running of the project.

At the beginning of the period covered by the plan there was a smaller amount allowed each year than in the final year. In 1988 there was 2.2 times as much as at the start.

Illustrative of the motives of the INSP, was the fact that the ministry of Economic Affairs also provided a share of the 270 million. This budget of 85 million was earmarked for projects in vocational education.

2.3 How does it function?

The INSP had a completely new aura when it came to the handling of large-scale innovation. The project model was introduced at all levels. It was not just the activities at school that had a project-like character, but the new structures for consultation and the realization were to function temporarily as a project, that is until the end of the plan's period.

Another new feature was that use was made of project managers who were outside the normal innovation structures and institutions, and who were in many cases from industry or from the universities. The organizations which had till then been appointed to prepare and instigate educational innovations were not involved when it came to taking initiatives. They were increasingly involved in the actual carrying out of the projects.

A key position was held by the COI, the Centre for Education and Information Technology. A number of project managers was installed in this specialized institute. The staff of the COI made a considerable contribution in the development of the methodology for the development of the programmes.

Another new factor (also temporary) was that the department installed a co-ordinating unit: the Education and Information Technology Project Staff, PSOI. These project staff members were forced to break through the normal civil service ranking and effectuate cooperation with another department, that of Economic Affairs. On the 31st of December 1988 the staff will no longer exist.

2.4 What does it result in?

The INSP is carried out along three channels:
-   the distribution of hardware
-   the production and distribution of software
-   the provision of in service training.

In the initial stage attention was directed towards the acquisition of hardware. Nearly all the applications to the project were for this purpose. As time went on it became clear that in service training and software development were indispensably linked to the hardware. From that point on no further projects were started which did not make use of an integrated approach.

We are now able to confirm that the realization of the chief operational aims for the differing sectors is in sight, as is the meeting of the conditions. Many teachers have been trained, most schools have a reasonable amount of hardware at their disposal, and a growing store of software is being developed.

What is even more important is that we can confirm that the INSP has played a stimulating role. There is, without doubt, a speeding up of the introduction and use of IT in education. Without INSP there would only be a handful of project schools (the opinion leaders), in full swing. In addition, the INSP has been a tremendous instigator of multiplication.

All sorts of initiators, in the field of education and beyond, followed in the footsteps of the INSP. The level of participation was high and the amount of activity shown was great.

Due to the fact that the IT theme had continuous good publicity, there was a willingness in all manner of groups to cooperate and finance the plans. The interest in the innovations remained great. We will name just a few examples:

- school boards bought computers from their own funds and sent their teachers on training courses;
- businesses gave donations in the form of hardware, courses, or cooperation in projects to individual schools in the region or to groups of schools;
- parents started up fund raising activities for the purpose of buying hardware for their children's schools;
- municipal councils provided schools in their area with hardware and organized courses;
- teachers joined together in so called subject working parties. They got together and made programmes, lesson models and organized information days;
- the central government supported large scale projects which had been thought up by industry like the NIVO-project, for all the secondary schools. For the unemployed with higher education qualifications the PION* was devised: 1500 academics and people with higher vocational training were re-trained to become information analysts.
- working from the other end the representatives of industry took up the government's ideas for the ISI project, in which, under the auspices of the Chamber of Commerce, (unemployed) school-leavers were trained to become microcomputer operators or programmers.

The government developed a number of related large scale projects which supported the aims of the INSP and/or extended the INSP. The project in question was NaBoNT, in which teachers from vocational educational institutions were given the opportunity to follow vocationally directed courses in the field of new technologies. And SURF which developed a proposal for a national network linking up the different institutions doing research and establishments of higher education and improved the local infrastructure.

In conclusion mention must be made of the fact that, in the meantime, the long term budget of the Ministry of Education provides for the replacement of hardware and the acquisition of software for all educational sectors. These measures ensure the continuation of the stimulus first given in the INSP. In total a sum of 51 million guilders a year is involved, which is booked as a definite cost factor in the budget of the Ministry of Education and Science. Parliament has agreed to the proposal to continue a number of activities in the period following the INSP (from 1989) where further support from government is called for.

3. THE PLAN IN PRACTICE

The INSP is still seen as an ambitious plan. This was also the case at the Ministry of Education. The grand scale and the somewhat unusual approach to this educational innovation are the reasons for this. Putting a plan into practice can, in this type of situation, lead to unexpected surprises. That is of course exactly what happened: the INSP lead to a number of unexpected plus points, and, in a few areas, to unexpected setbacks.

3.1 Plus points

Generally speaking, we may consider that the goals set by the INSP have, to a considerable extent, been attained. In some cases they even surpassed themselves. In particular where initiatives from businesses, school boards, schools and government were launched which were on the same line as the INSP, one sees a great deal more in the way of results than was first projected. This becomes clear from the reports which the school inspectors have produced on the basis of a complete inventory of the state of affairs in IT education. It then appears that there are now far more activities, material and knowledge available than just the projects introduced into schools by the government.

A number of factors and events were responsible for this stimulus.

1. It appeared that businesses were prepared to work in projects on a small or large scale. They contributed by means of their products (hardware, software) or their expertise (training programmes, project management, obtaining funds).

2. From the very beginning the individual willingness shown by teachers to take part in IT in service training was extremely great.

3. It was possible to compose working teams from all walks of life: educational experts, systems developers and programmers learnt to communicate with one another.

4. Generally speaking, those taking part in the project remained realistic and pragmatic when stating their aims. The norm was whether it was feasible given the existing educational situation. There was not the tendency in the IT project to attempt to make all sorts of technically perfect materials nor to develop extremely fundamental philosophies.

5. As already stated the support from parliament and society for the INSP at the outset in 1984 was great. The surprising fact was that the support was continuous. Proposals for allied projects were met by support. This was also translated in terms of financial priorities, and this at a time when the Government finances were not in such a healthy state.

It is worth considering for a moment the effects which these events had on the running of the INSP.

The contribution by trade and industry meant that more materials got to schools earlier. The result was that more teachers and pupils became acquainted with IT. This results in an important quantative effect. This can be seen most clearly in the NIVO project. The ministry was planning to introduce informatics, that is a computer literacy course, in every secondary school during INSP. The budget for this area of education was in fact insufficient to allow the purchasing of so much hardware. Due to the participation of three computer suppliers and contributions from sponsors in Dutch trade and industry, it proved possible to provide the schools with a basic set of hardware, software and courses.

In a qualitative sense it meant this support from the firms gave the schools professional hardware, which also meant that pupils learnt to use materials from the professional world. NIVO was the first instance in education of sponsoring on a grand scale. It goes without saying, that the firms were partly motivated by the need to serve their own long term interest. But the fact that education would most certainly benefit, meant that educational organizations and parliament welcomed the move.

Many teachers showed their willingness by signing up for all sorts of in service training courses involving IT. Due to this the courses were continuously over subscribed. In many cases it did not just mean participating in a course. Many trained teachers organized introduction courses for their colleagues at school. The effects of this are not yet known in terms of an increase in the use of IT by a greater group of teachers than were initially trained. Due to the fact that the in service training actually took place during the teachers' free time, the continuing enthusiasm has exceeded all expectations. At the same time we must bear in mind, that as a result of the falling school rolls, the motivation among teachers to learn a new skill is bound to be great.

Those working in education often have little experience of or affinity with sectors like trade and industry. This is particularly true of general education and primary education. Within the framework of the INSP it was certainly necessary for the development of the software to set up lines of cooperation and communication with professions in this sector. Of course it took some getting used to, on both sides. This has gradually become a more smooth running process. An increasingly large number of people from the educational field is capable of communicating with those in the programme development world, so that high quality courseware can be produced.

Had the educational reformers been more interested in ideology than in the reality of the everyday school situation, it would not have come as a surprise. This was however not the case in the INSP. As the project progressed, the requests from schools became more realistic and it was easy to keep to the specified project aims. This meant that little time was lost on unenforceable aims and inapplicable materials.

The continuing confidence in the INSP as a good project for the Netherlands had positive offshoots in two directions. It meant that there was a shared perspective for the INSP goals and it also meant the chance of adding a number of items to it.

New, large projects, brought about by the initiative of trade and industry or by the government, met with a good growing climate. Due to this fact, it was possible to start on a number of necessary activities which had not been allowed for in the design of the INSP. They have already been mentioned under 'participation by trade and industry'.

For the sustained success of the INSP it was very important that at an early date, namely in the proposed budget in 1986 and following years, budgets were reserved for the replacement of hardware and for the buying of software after 1988. In this way consolidation of the INSP project results was guaranteed beforehand. This stopped the risk of enthusiasm waning, and people giving up in the last one or two years of the plan's duration, and also meant that its true potential was realized as well as motivating extensions to the plan.

3.2 Set backs

Although there were unexpected favourable influences on the INSP project there were times when things did not go the way they had been planned. This meant that the policy items or the plans which had been arranged had to be revised.

1. Project organization

The likelihood of officially introducing the regulations for IT education through the project organization structure was greatly overestimated. Even for the project staff, armed with a specific policy plan and well defined areas of competence and authority, it was difficult to operate within an existing organization. Connections with the mainstream organization are essential, because as soon as the very first results appear, it is time to start thinking about measures which will make their introduction possible. What in fact happens, is that you are confronted with different people, different systems of financing and different arguments. It is then sometimes difficult and/or time consuming for the two organizational sectors to come to a consensus in the preparation of policy. A great deal of time is spent on 'missionary work', and solving communication problems.

Working within a project framework can from time to time present one with unpleasant surprises. The education sector may be viewed as a rigid organization. The feasibility of running experiments like projects is overestimated. Particularly the very first projects showed budgets which were overdrawn and time limits which were exceeded. In addition there was a tendency to stray from the original course. As the INSP project progressed, more attention was paid to the structure and content of the management of the projects, particularly the larger projects. That meant that more definite agreements were made on budgets and planning, and that the yield, in product terms, was defined beforehand. This definitely had a positive effect on its progress, but it cost a lot of money and extra effort.

2. Thought processes of the decision-makers

Particularly at the beginning of the INSP project, we were regularly confronted with thought processes from groups of decision makers and some opinion leaders which were difficult to attune to IT thinking. We mean here representatives of educational organizations, those running the initial teaching training and the performers of the in-service training.

a. Educational organizations

The problems with educational organizations came to light in discussions on the contents and in determining strategy.

The government had expected that the educational organizations would have realized the need for action like the INSP, and that they would see that the unusual form of innovatory organization was a good idea in this case. It took quite a while before they were prepared to work in accordance with the INSP rules. They did not try to obstruct procedures, they just took on a passive stance. They followed the INSP's movements from a distance. Half way through the INSP period matters began to improve. Then the cooperation resulted in an important contribution. When the NIVO project was set up (in 1985), it was decided that the organizations involved would be invited to actively participate. The NIVO hereby became a triumvirate organization: trade and industry, school boards and the government formed a management team which had control over the budgets. The organizations were given staff who, on the one hand, were to aid the representatives in the management team and, on the other hand, to channel the information to schools. The ice was broken thanks to the favourable way in which this project ran. In the second half of the INSP the cooperation went without a hitch and proved to be very favourable to the progress of the v NIVO project and for its overspill to other INSP activities.

As far as the contents were concerned, the objections were more a matter of principle. Educational organizations regarded the computer as a tool for learning just like any other. In the Netherlands the government has no say in learning materials; not on their production, nor about the individual school's choice and their use in the classroom. This vision manifested itself particularly in discussions where the standardization of hardware, uniformity in procuring software, and programme development were at issue. In the view of the INSP, computers and programmes are more technical tools, or didactic aids, which in themselves contribute little or nothing to the contents of the actual education. But they do demand a technical infrastructure and control from a certain methodology. It will take a lot of time and patience before these views on IT are harmonized where hardware and software are concerned.

b. Initial training

Experiences with the initial teacher training colleges fall into the same category of setbacks. Up to the present moment the level of activity at the initial training institutes is extremely low. The same institutes take care of the IT in service training with great energy, but, at the present moment, their day students still have to manage almost without lessons on computers. This may mean that in a few years the Netherlands will be confronted with difficulties in sustaining the attainments of the INSP. The money is there, there is an increasing supply of software, but the new generation of teachers are lacking in knowledge about the use of IT and are not convinced that computers are an integral part of education. In Robert Aiken's view there is little point in preparing the current older generation for IT. They will soon be leaving the field, and on the whole lack the mental agility to want to start on IT. The middle group will only start to play a significant role in this sense with regard to the use of IT for management purposes. The younger generation is most suited and the most

assessable group for the introduction of IT.

If this line of thought proves true, then the Netherlands is faced with a problem. We inform many young teachers about IT through in service training. In actual fact, due to the agreements on teachers seniority rating and order of dismissal, in a time like the present when rolls are falling, it is the younger teachers who have to leave first. This means that the knowledge and the spirit of enthusiasm for IT will disappear for a greater part too. Due to the same fall in the number of pupils, few recently graduated students manage to find jobs. Those which are available for the educational market have, in actual fact, a considerable backlog in their knowledge of IT in education.

c. In-service training

The teacher training colleges have a considerable influence on the in service training in their position as opinion leaders. There, the situation gives less reason for concern. Enough action is being taken thanks to the generous budgets and thanks to a small group of teachers who jumped at the chance, but the actual content was not always the most desirable. It remains difficult for trainers to design in service training courses in such a way that the teacher taking it is offered the practical knowledge and skills necessary to work with IT in the classroom. The first set of courses did not meet the requirements in this respect. It was not then really clear what the application of IT in the classroom would mean. But when that did become more clear, the problem of giving the course the right content remained.

Renewed attempts have been made to improve the connection with classroom practice. A number of effectivity evaluations have been carried out to measure the level of satisfaction and to get indications as to the ideal contents. In service training is also a part of a developmental project, in most cases, so the link can easily be made. Nevertheless the discrepancy remains. This may be due partly to the fact that those involved in education themselves form a very critical audience when it comes to being given courses. The reason for dissatisfaction must arise partly from the fact that the trainers at the teacher training colleges are of an older generation, because there too, the young ones have left as a result of the decreasing number of students. They fill the lessons 'quite naturally' with their own knowledge and offer the course which they find useful. IT finds itself in a poor starting position. The methodology used was also along traditional lines. The teacher training colleges continued to use the traditional form of in service training: the course, given by a teacher, is attended by a restricted group of teachers. There is little or no use made of new media for the provision of in service training.

In view of these opinions, shared by various decision makers and opinion leaders, it is remarkable that Parliament has shown more interest for the INSP and the idiosyncracies which accompany it. There too, the freedom of education is weighed up and balanced, but it has never come to a complete rejection of (technological) contents and strategies for these reasons.

3. Projects in higher vocational education

The project approach in which schools could put in requests, did not work at the higher education level. The requests required a budget that was a good tenfold of what was available for the INSP. Allocation of projects was only to take place on the grounds of merit. Then the top down method of work was substituted for the bottom up approach. The aim behind this was not just to be able to experiment more directly in certain areas, but to make more money available. We wanted to achieve this by getting firms to take part in the so-called 'spear-point projects'. Schools and school boards were enthusiastic and it appeared to be possible to get firms interested. Despite all this, it was difficult to get the joint venture off the ground. The school organizations were not prepared for a large, separate functioning project with the outside world. A lot of mistrust had to be overcome. For the firms it was also a new situation and some aspects were difficult. They shared a responsibility for the product, had to cooperate on the actual content and above all were bound to this continued cooperation for a number of years. This was a quite different prospect from that of donating hardware and getting on with their own jobs. They had to make large investments in the process coordination and in professional project management in order to ensure that everything went according to plan.

4. Autonomous developments in primary education

Primary education was thought to have a low priority due to its content. This is the reason why the accompanying budget was low and the decision was taken that during the INSP it would be sufficient just to look for openings for the use of IT in primary education. This was supposed to take place in the form of a number of in depth experiments. Nevertheless schools, school boards and parents started to purchase computers for their schools on a grand scale. Each school tried to find its own ideal. This process continued even after the in depth strategy chosen by the IT had been pointed out and after the lines on which IT in primary education would be run in the future had been made clear. This led to unbridled growth and to a maximum amount of variation in hardware at schools, with all the accompanying dispersion. When substantial arguments, which had been offered to explain the need for a restricted approach failed to make an impact, another strategy was tried. The ministry wanted to assemble a set of instructions. This was to include the steps which should be taken when considering purchasing hardware. If the instructions were properly adhered to the choice of hardware would become clear. The fact that the Netherlands enjoys freedom of learning materials (the computer is viewed in this category in the Netherlands) meant that the minister was unable to prescribe guidelines for the choice and purchase of computers. The request for a set of instructions was directed to the school boards' organization. They refused to comply, their reason being that this type of advice could be seen as a violation of the freedom of schools to arrange their own educational system. Eventually, it was left to organizations within the innovatory structure, the LPC, to come up with advice. In the meantime an increasing number of schools had gone ahead with their purchases. The government did try to influence the software policy at schools. For this purpose projects were set up which showed "exemplary" software plus indications as to how they could be used didactically. The production and distribution of this package was an occasion for much brain racking.

5. Production of courseware

A final point which causes us concern is the fact that we have still not managed to create a situation in which the continuity and quality of software development is guaranteed. We had realized from experience abroad that the development of software for the educational sector is difficult. It was also a well known fact that activating the production of software among the profit making sector is virtually impossible. Therefore, attempts were made continuously, in all ways, to create a certain structure and to create certain conditions whereby a number of barriers could be cleared away. The most important stimuli, due to their far reaching nature, were in order of their creation:

- the design of a standard methodology for courseware development;
- courseware development within the NIVO (fl 21 million);
- software coupons for all secondary schools to enable them to buy commercial programmes;
- Courseware Midden Nederland, in which about 90 teachers from the higher vocational sector were retrained to be courseware writers and whereby the production in the first years was subsidized (investment total fl 26 million);
- POCO, a project with the aim of making programmes which could be used frequently to illustrate ordinary lesson programmes (fl 24 million).

The group of people experienced in the making of software is an ever growing one, even today, and this is also true of the knowledge which exists on how the production process may best be tackled. However, we have not reached the stage where production lines have arisen, thereby releasing a continuous stream, which will be commercially interesting for the producers. The POCO (Project for Courseware Development for Computers in Primary and Secondary Education) has aroused the interest of the publishers to become involved in the production projects and to function as publishers in the distribution. This means a turnabout in the attitude shown by educational publishers, which gives us reason for hope.

In the case of the professional training schools the situation is quite different. The problem here is not the availability of software. There it is often possible to work with software typically used in the professional world. Particularly in secondary vocational education there is a need for adapted versions which the pupils can comprehend. Making these is no easy task. In vocational education there are a number of different problems to consider: the programmes are often expensive, the instructions are not always easily understood and, of course, instructions for educational purposes are lacking. Producing this material has led to a great deal of brain racking in vocational education. In addition to the production of courseware, an activity has been launched which serves the consumer. We have, in response to a request from Parliament, instigated a software evaluation project: Software and Courseware evaluation Nederland (SCEN). SCEN evaluates programmes for their user friendliness rating and their suitability for application in educational programmes, and publishes these reports in a publication produced every other month.

6. Working in a blinkered fashion

When a group with specific aims like the project staff becomes an integral part of another organization, there is a danger that the group will become less sensitive to signals from outside and get taken up by the regular procedures and rules instead. Their level of mental agility quickly declines. Once the INSP was well underway and the parties involved were used to their new role and method of work, we found ourselves working in a blinkered fashion now and again. That can prove to be at the expense of valuable suggestions, because these are then no longer valued as such.

5. PERSPECTIVES

The INSP may be considered a success. Not only because a good number of the operational aims have been realized, but particularly because of the impact the plan has had in the eyes of society and in a quantitative and qualitative sense. The absolute necessity of introducing computers into education and learning about them has become far more generally accepted. Many teachers already use them and will be followed in turn by their colleagues. The government's budget and school boards' budgets show the reservation of funds for the continuation of these activities. That is a good result.

Yet at the same time this good result is what gives us reason for concern for the future of the use of IT in education. The concern involves two matters:

1. Can we prevent the teachers and hardware from being confronted with a 'lack' of materials? That is to say: will we be able in the long term as well to keep producing lesson materials and trained

teachers? The situation as it stands in software development and in the initial training courses gives reason for concern.

2. Will we be successful in continuously convincing the decision makers, parliament and the educational organizations that the mental and financial offers for IT education are worthwhile ? A lot of money is tied up in IT, and the educational budget is constantly under pressure due to the constant need for economies. The moment is bound to come when the yield of IT education is questioned. For vocational education it will be easy to show the benefits. It will be more difficult for secondary and educational establishments to provide convincing evidence. Great expectations are always the most vulnerable, so whether the attainments of the INSP can be sustained in the long run remains too be seen.

Finally we would like to bring four matters to your attention through which we hope to withstand the test of time.

1. We advocate the principles of developing courseware: market research, user friendliness levels and standardization of the user interface. The only chance of courseware production being successful is when these principles are adhered to.

2. In association with this we repeat the argument of the EEC conference 'CAL for Europe' which put its case for an international approach to courseware development. Each country on its own is too small to realize commercially viable production. In addition, in a few years time, there will be a situation in which there is a joint market. Bringing together the scarce knowledge of each of the member states of the EEC, and combining schools from the different educational sectors, may lead to target groups which would be commercially viable.

3. It is important not to keep in service training, software development and hardware campaigns separate. These elements, when linked up together, hold enormous potential for education. They must not be allowed to disintegrate.

4. Even if we do have our hands full with the smooth running of the introduction of IT in education, we would still like to emphasize the importance of not focusing solely on information technology. Expansion towards New Technologies is well worth considering when it comes to increasing the relevance to education and society as a whole. The technology push in education holds great promise for adapting education to the new demands which a new Europe will make on it. It is, however, a truism to say that using new technology forces the teacher to make a synthesis between the ancient dichotomy between education and training, between 'Bildung' and 'Berufsvorbereitung'.

1. Informatics Across The Curriculum and Informal Education

COMPUTERS IN EDUCATION, F. Lovis and E.D. Tagg (eds.)
Elsevier Science Publishers B.V. (North-Holland)
© IFIP, 1988

A COMPUTER-ASSISTED APPROACH TO CHRONOLOGY IN THE HISTORY CLASS

G. COLOTTE, History and Geography teacher High Scool A. Mézières (Jarny FRANCE)
B. DUGAND, History and Geography teacher High School (Rombas FRANCE)
J. LOPPARELLI, History and Geography teacher High School (Rombas FRANCE)
M. MERCIER, History and Geography teacher High School Devant les Ponts (Metz FRANCE)

At a time when historical pinpointing is being reintroduced in French schools as a fundamental skill, the computer can become an important asset if it deals with this theme as a skill and not as abstract knowledge and gets rid of its reputation as a time-consuming device. By integrating computer-assisted teaching into a comprehensive pedagogical progression, our project describes the conditions for its success, both with teachers and students : chronology is studied through a series of computer-assisted sessions on four ancient civilizations, spread out over the whole year, while parallel activities include complementary work to satisfy official requirements.

1. THE STAKES INVOLVED IN THE PROJECT

Historical pinpointing and chronology are two fundamental elements in History : *"There is no History without dates (...); they are that without which History would disappear..." (Claude Levi Strauss, 1962)."*

This is without any doubt one of the basic skills aimed at in the teaching of History. The computer-assisted approach seems very promising ; yet a number of elements are at stake in this project.

1.1. On the institutional level

If it is now considered normal for this skill to hold an important place in the curriculum for the first grade of high school [1], this has not always been the case. The study of chronology had almost completely disappeared from official instructions [2], and its absence was a major handicap for the understanding of History ; nor was this absence unrelated with children's lack of interest in History.

Its return to the new curriculum for the sixth grade [3] shows an intention of filling this gap ; the new curriculum insists on the chronological framework of civilizations (prehistoric, Egyptian, Hebraic, Greek, Roman, of ancient India and China) and on its significance : "... *the student becomes acquainted with the different timeframes of History : short time of events and generations, the longer time of economic cycles and social changes, the still longer duration of civilizations..."* [4].

At a time when computer-assisted teaching is still looking for an audience, it seems a good opportunity to use it in fulfilling an official objective, i. e., integrating the chronological dimension in the study of economic, political, religious, artistic and social landmarks in ancient History. The problem of reading the objective then becomes more technical .

1.2. On the computer level

The chronological approach to History exhibited in the educational software available in French schools is still sadly 'obsolete' : the student is too often prompted to remember historical dates and events, and is only tested on his ability to memorize these, never to reflect or deduce. Exercises of the multiple choice or gap-filling types are liable to bore and discourage our young children from acquiring this skill.

The production of software in this field should abandon the purely cognitive and abstract approach for an intelligent learner-oriented one.

This is the kind of approach we have chosen, because it enables us to examine the best uses to which the computer can be put in acquiring fundamental skills in History ; for such is the ambition of the project described here. In this perspective, we allocated the computer three tasks :
- placing its attraction into the service of the study of History.
- using its technical assets : its ability to repeat, to let the student correct himself, to control and evaluate the work done, to work at the student's own pace and rhythm.
- integrating the study of chronology into that of each civilization, in order to avoid limiting this skill to one lesson at the beginning of the school-year, with the consequence that it is rarely acquired at the end of the sixth grade.

This last task will be difficult to fulfil, because of teachers' deep-rooted habits. The third point at stake is thus the adherence of teachers to this new approach to a fundamental skill.

1.3. On the pedagogical level

Our project's originality lies in its taking into account the teachers' needs . The least enthusiastic among them still question the real impact of the computer in their field ; many see it as a time-consuming device which hinders their yearly progression , because of the limited subjects treated by educational programs ("mere details", for most teachers) and of the necessary splitting of classes into two groups [5] . They think they could not possibly complete the syllabus defined by the official instructions.

Since we propose both computer-assisted and non-computer-assisted activities, we offer our colleagues an example of a complete teaching sequence.
Our aim in gambling on a computer-assisted teaching program is to gain teachers' adherence. This can only be obtained on condition that we prove the efficiency of the computer in the acquisition of a fundamental skill, without unduly hindering the teachers' yearly progression.

2. PEGAGOGICAL ENVIRONMENT

2.1. The objectives

The first point in our research was to establish a list of the skills that could enable a child aged 11 to 13 to "find his own way" in time. Five of them were agreed upon, the child having to achieve mastery in the following fields :
- construction of a time line starting from a given medium,
- vocabulary linked with chronology (date, century, millennium, period, duration, landmark, before, after, event, anterior, posterior, simultaneous, ...),
- mathematical notions linked with chronology (locating a date in a century, calculating duration, giving a date in a century, chronological classification),
- reading a time line,
- comparing several parallel time lines.

These objectives cannot be dissociated, for the above-mentioned reasons, from the general context of History and Geography teaching in the sixth grade. This is why each computer-assisted session is proposed to be in parallel with a number of other activities that follow the objectives given by official instructions [6].

2.2. Teaching strategies

The class distribution we used most often, both in computer-assisted and parallel activities, consisted of groups of two or three students. It answered the technical constraint linked with the hardware available in French schools, and it provided excellent ground for independent work. Indeed, students often reach sixth grade with very heterogeneous knowledge and know-how (see First results).

Moreover, learning is not a uniform process at this level. Putting students in this group-work position is one of the keys to success at school : everyone can learn at his own pace.

This formula was used in three of the six stages making up the teaching sequence. In the three other stages, each student was given a personal evaluation project.

2.3. Choice of software

Using the computer should not be regarded as a deontological problem : teachers must take advantage of all the resources offered by technological progress.

The problem lies in choosing the software, which must answer three demands :
- enabling both low-ability and good students to progress at their own pace, by offering repetitions for those who need it and further information for the others.
- being attractive enough to be used throughout the school year.
- offering a perfect illustration to the civilizations on the syllabus for the sixth grade.

None of the software available on the French market answered all these purposes . One of them, PICUS, distributed by the C.N.D.P. [7], was chosen because it met our first two demands. Other programs were created by the research group to answer the third requirement : EGYPTE for Pharaonic Egypt, ISRAEL for the Hebrew people, GRECE for Greek civilization and ROME for the Roman world.

2.4. Technical choices

Some choices were motivated by the hardware available, others by the difficulty for young children to assimilate certain mathematical notions.

Choices motivated by the hardware : the educational programs were created for use on the hardware most currently available in French schools, i.e. a network with an IBM compatible service center and Thomson MO5 or TO7 terminals. They were written in L.S.E. [8] or Microsoft BASIC. The graphic definition of screens (320 X 200) doesn't allow the pupil to pinpoint a date with good accuracy ; this is why we tolerate relative precision (± 12 years and a half). See document 1.

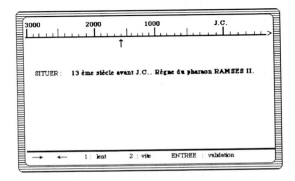

document 1 : procedure for building time-line (program EGYPTE).

Choices motivated by mathematical notions : their purpose was to make the learning of problematic notions easier ; the year 0 never existed, so the reference point is always mentioned by the event which characterizes it, i.e. the birth of Christ. At the beginning of the sixth grade, children don't know about negative numbers , which it is thus unwise to use for dates before Christ. Moreover, negative dates are meaningless : they show a progress in time, never a recession. Help is given in all cases when a student has to compute durations extending before or after the reference point. Incidentally, we are confronted here with the problem of school books. The year 0 and time lines with negative dates appear in most of them. The situation is serious, since the History manual is often bed-side reading material for the students, in whose minds such notions cannot but do harm.

3. THE TEACHING SEQUENCE

3.1. Overview

The six stages of the sequence cover the entire school year.

Each one both reinforces acquired notions and builds up new ones, in the following progression :
- at the beginning of the school year, the general aspects of chronology are covered, with an emphasis on the acquisition of vocabulary, and immediate checking through a series of exercises. The program PICUS is used throughout.
- the study of Egyptian and Hebraic chronologies reinforces acquired notions. The stress is put here on building and reading a time line.
- Greek and Roman chronologies are the next two stages, based on the interrelation of the time lines studied so far. Building new time lines strengthens acquired skills.

Remarks :

- additional computer activities are proposed for students who achieve the appointed task in less time than is alloted.
- each of the computer-assisted activities comes with a series of exercises for the half-class who are not currently working on the computers ; they deal with Egyptian, Greek and Roman cartography (stages 2, 4 and 5), or with individual evaluation.

3.2. The first stage

The implementation of chronological tools is achieved through the use of the program PICUS. The different parts of this program (notions of date and period, events in time, centuries, chronological order) all include a learning phase followed by an evaluation phase. The teaching method is never the same from one part to the other. The play activities which it proposes strongly motivate the young child : a face appears on the screen after each answer, gay or sad, according to whether the answer was right or wrong. The student has a capital of 1000 points at the beginning, which he must try to increase to a maximum of 18000 by giving right answers. At the end of the session, the student is asked to review the studied notions and to do exercises on paper.

The parallel activity aims at evaluating the knowledge and know-how acquired at the end of primary school. This test was built with the help of primary school teachers. It covers both History and Geography, and mostly aims at assessing skills, the objective being to draw the most accurate picture of the class that one will have to deal with for a whole year. Moreover, such a test is essential for anyone wishing to adapt his teaching to his students.

3.3. Egyptian and Hebraic chronologies (stages 2 and 3)

Students are asked to locate on the screen the essential chronological landmarks of both civilizations. Help is given when the answer is wrong. The student is allowed six attempts for each proposition. After correction by the computer, he has to write down each dated event on the paper time line witch he has been given at the beginning of the session. This document is the medium used for supplementary exercises, and will also be used in subsequent sessions.

Supplementary exercises review the basic notions applied to those two mediterranean civilizations ; for the brightest students, they will mean a strengthening of knowledge

acquired in the first stage, for the others, a complete review of basic notions, thanks to help sections (see document 2). At the end of each of these stages, students are given printed individual results.

The parallel activity to Egyptian chronology aims at building a map of the Egyptian world (see document 3). The student is asked to look for a number of historical and geographical locations in an atlas or his manual, to place them on a blank map previously provided, and to write down the captions. The application of a geographical skill to a historical subject can be justified by the simple environment of Ancient Egypt, a gift of the Nile in the middle of a sand desert.

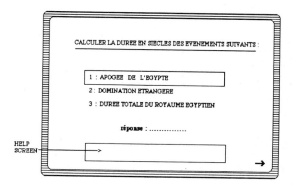

HELP SCREEN ≠ 1

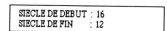

HELP SCREEN ≠ 2

SOLUTION

document 2 : reinforcement exercise with appropriate help (Program EGYPTE).

1 A l'aide de votre manuel (Nathan) pages 28 et 42, réaliser la carte de l'Egypte ancienne, en situant les termes suivants :

mer Méditarranée	Thèbes
Basse Egypte	2 ème cataracte
désert de Libye	Abou Simbel (temple
1 ère cataracte	désert d'Arabie
Haute Egypte	Tell el Amarna
Nil	Karnak (temple)
Sinaï	Memphis
mer Rouge	tropique nord
Louxor (temple)	Guizeh (pyramides).

2 Colorier en "bleu" les mers, en "jaune" les déserts, en "vert" la vallée du Nil.

3 Encadrer le nom des capitales.

4 Souligner le nom des villes célèbres par leurs monuments.

5 Compléter la légende de la carte.

6 Choisir parmi les trois le titre qui convieznt le mieux :t
    L'AFRIQUE,   L'EGYPTE ANCIENNE,
    LES PEUPLES ANTIQUES ET L'EGYPTE.
L'écrire dans le grand rectangle au dessus de la carte. Donner les raisons qui vous ont amené à refuser les deux autres.

7 En vous servant de l'échelle de la carte (2,5 cm sur la carte représentent 200 km sur le terrain), calculez la distance approximative depuis la 1 ère cataracte jusqu'au delta du Nil du territoire égyptien.

8 Quelle remarque générale faites-vous sur la cadre naturel de l'Egypte?

9 Que peut-on déduire quant aux activités des hommes ?

Document 3 : question-form on Ancient Egypt.

While half of the class is exploring the peregrinations of the Hebrew people during the two millenniums B.C., the other half writes a synthesis on Egyptian chronology. This is a good opportunity to assess the skills so far acquired : building a time line, text commentary, analysis of artistic or figured documents, logical re-ordering of a list of words, illustrating a historical map, using key-words in context.

3.4. Greek and Roman chronologies (stages 4 and 5)

During each of the two computer-assisted sessions, building the time line takes only a short time, the same device (computer + paper support) being used. Moreover, the landmarks are less numerous : we chose only five important landmarks in Roman History against ten for Pharaonic Egypt.

The fact that these two civilizations are studied at the end of the school year enables us to introduce a new problem , with the comparison of several time lines. The problems this approach could raise for children of heterogeneous level were taken into account in the two programs GRECE and ROME, which are multi-level . For the same subject, three different modes are provided, from the simplest (level 1) to the most complex (level 3) ; the choice of level is left to the computer after a set of initial questions, and is reassessed after each question, so that it can change from one to another (see document 4)

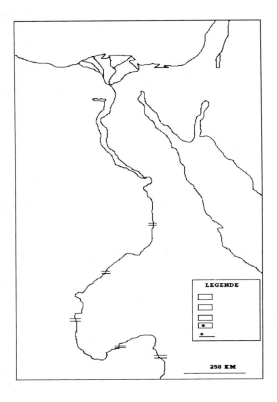

document 3 : map of Ancient Egypt.

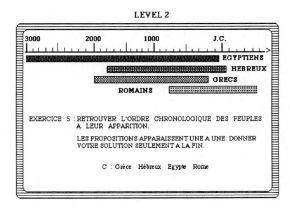

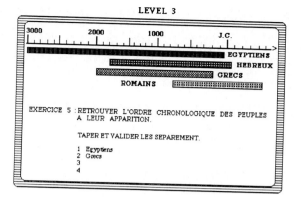

document 4 : diversised approach to one course item (Program ROME).

The parallel activities are still concerned with cartography, and aim at bringing out Greece's natural environment on the one hand, and the phases of Roman expansion from the Latium hills to the borders of Armenia or Scotland, on the other.

3.5. Final evaluation (stage 6)

It is not computer-assisted. Its double task is :
- measuring the acquired skills in historical pinpointing,
- comparing the yearly progression of the teachers who used the computer-assisted approach with that of the teachers who did not use it. A common assessment of the general know-how required at the end of the sixth grade, is also proposed

4. FIRST RESULTS

The sequence described here is being tried out in three schools ; three teachers are using the computer-assisted approach with five classes, with a total of 125 students ; seven other teachers are working together on the final evaluation test. A total of 458 students is thus more or less directly involved in the experimentation on chronology.

The first results are known : the first evaluation, conducted in September 1987 for the first year of experimentation, confirms that children arriving in sixth grade are of widely different levels, and gives quite a similar picture of the five classes. The figures given below illustrate this statement :
- 18 students average between 0 and 5 out of 20 (3.9%)
- 206 average between 5 and 10 out of 20 (44.9%)
- 201 average between 10 and 15 out of 20 (43.9%) .
- 33 average over 15 out of 20 (7.3%)

The age of the children involved ranges from 10 to 14, most of them being 11 or 12. The experimentation will be conducted over several years. Computerized results will be available each spring.

The computer-assisted approach to humanities (historical sciences) is very promising. We think we are on the right track in making its integration into a comprehensive pedagogical program the key to its success.

THANKS

Our sincerest thanks to Claire Maniez for her translation

(FOOT)NOTES

[1] Secondary education in France consists of four years in a first cycle and three years in a second cycle, with a final examination called Baccalaureat. The sixth grade is the first year of the first cycle (children aged 11 or 12).
[2] Bulletin Officiel de l'Education Nationale nx 22 of June 9th 1977
[3] Bulletin Officiel de l'Education nationale nx 44 of December 12th 1985
[4] Collèges : programmes et instructions. C.N.D.P. 1985 p.241
[5] The hardware found in most schools was provided through the State project "I nformatique pour Tous" (Computers for Everyone), February 1985. It usually includes a network system with six terminals, which can only accommodate part of a class at one time, with two or three students per terminal.
[6] Collège : programmes et instructions C.N.D.P. Paris 1985,, pp239-243
[7] PICUS was written by Mr P. Piboule, who teaches at Jean Moulin High Scool in Montmorillon (86).
[8] L.S.E. (Symbolic Language for Teaching) is a high level language which was developed in France to write educational programs.

REFERENCES

[1] Mataigne B. , l'évaluation des didacticiels, Direction des Politiques et Plans, Gouvernement du Québec (Québec 1984).
[2] Antrop M. and Vandenbossche E. , De computer, de leekracht en de leerling. Verlagboek van de werkseminaries voor de licentiaten aardrijkskunde schooljarr 1983-1984. (Interfacultair Centrum voor Lerarenopleiding, Riksuniversiteit Gent, Gand 1984).
[3] T. O'Shea, J. Self, Learning ad teaching with computers, (harvester press Brighton 1983).
[4] J. Nicol, J. Jean, Pupils , computers and history teaching in new horizons in educational computing,(ed. J. Ellis Harvood LTD Chichester 1984).

COMPUTERS IN EDUCATION, F. Lovis and E.D. Tagg (eds.)
Elsevier Science Publishers B.V. (North-Holland)
© IFIP, 1988

Information Technology in Danish School Libraries.

Educational Advisor Niels Tovgaard

Board of Education, Odense, Denmark
Bullerupvej 30,
5240 Odense NØ
Denmark
Phone +459107000

Information technology is getting more and more common in schools. It is used as an educational tool as well as an administrative tool. Computers are used in most subjects for wordprocessing, running databases, doing graphics etc.
But what about the school libraries? In 1986–87 a project was started in the city of Odense, Denmark. In this project the computer was used in the school library. It was running internal and external databases, wordprocessing and graphic software and students and teachers could preview educational software in the school library.
The conclusion of the first year of the project is that the computer gives many new opportunities for students and teachers in their daily work in school, and that computer software is now looked upon and used in the same way as books and other teaching aids in school.
It is now planned to equip school libraries in the city with computers.

1. THE DANISH ELEMENTARY SCHOOL

The Danish elementary school is different from most school systems in the world. The Danish elementary school is not divided into primary and secondary school, as you know from England, for instance. Danish students attend the same school from age 6 to age 16, and they have the same teachers too.
This means that teachers must be educated to cover the whole range from grade 1 to grade 10. In Danish elementary schools one or two teachers, called form masters, are specially related to a group of children.

2. DANISH SCHOOL LIBRARIES

Each school in Denmark has its own school library, and it is a very important place in the school. Many activities go on in this room, and many materials are kept here. It is especially important to stress that the school librarian is an advisor in many situations for teachers concerning teaching aids.

3. PURPOSE OF THE PROJECT

The purpose of the project is to seek new possibilities by using information technology in the student´s and teacher´s daily life in school.

This is done by

practical work with internal and external databases in school libraries, investigating their applicability.

comparing different database systems for the internal databases and the internal administration of the teaching aids and books of the school.

testing the applicability of existing wordprocessors. Both students and teachers took part in this test.

giving students and teachers the opportunity to preview educational software in the school library.

4. THE PROJECT

4.1 Schools

Three schools took part in the first year of the project:

The Hoejby School has 423 students in the age range from 6 to 16. The school library has 12,589 volumes in its fundamental book collection and 5,000 books in sets for use in classrooms.

The Sanderum School has 957 students in the age range from 6 to 16. The school library has 30,288 volumes in its fundamental book collection and 26,000 in sets for use in classrooms.

The Sct. Klemens School has 592 students in the age range from 6 to 16. The school library has 15,032 volumes in its fundamental book collection and 8,000 in sets for use in classrooms.

4.2 Computer Equipment.

For this project, each school library was equipped with a microcomputer of high performance, the RC Partner. It had 1024 KB RAM, two 1,2 MB disc stations, one 42 MB hard disk, one tape streamer, one modem, colour monitor and a quality printer.

As shown in fig. 1, this computer runs Concurrent DOS enabling it to run 4 consoles at the same time. In this way, the user is able to run 4 jobs at the same time, and it is possible for him to shift from one job to another. For instance, he can shift from running a database to computer graphics and back again without losing data.

4.3 Help from the local computer centre.

For technical assistance, the participating school librarians worked together with the local centre for computers in education.
At the start of the project, the librarians had some computer experience.

5. USE OF EXTERNAL DATABASES

5.1 Getting started

One of the problems in using external databases is that commands of the actual base logon and logout differ from base to base. This problem was solved using the function keys on the keyboard. Logon to any base is done by pressing just one key on the keyboard. The communication program then creates a connection to the host computer. This means that everybody at the school is able to search information in databases outside the house, without really knowing anything about computers.

The following functions can be done by function keys: logon, help, show next record, show previous record, make a screendump to the printer, and logout. This means that even if databases differ, the user can always use the function keys for these functions.

This kind of automatic logon, however, is problematic in one way. Anyone with access to

the machine can be connected to any base and without intending to, waste a lot of money!

5.2 Most used external database

The most used external database was the BASIS, which is a database for libraries in Denmark. BASIS is run as a professional base. It is possible to get information about all books, diskettes, slides etc., in Danish libraries. Search is possible on author, title, readability, topic, publisher and any word in the annotation. Search can be combined by ´and´ – ´or´ – ´not´. It is possible to download a search to diskette and print it out later. This base has been very much used by both students and teachers in all three schools.

5.3 Newspapers

At the start of the project, everybody was very excited to be connected to a database containing newspaper articles. Teachers and students have found the database good and a fine tool when working with actual topics. Using this database is extremely expensive, however. This has prevented using this base in a large scale.

5.4 Other external databases

As shown in fig. 2, a number of external databases have been accessed in the project.

Teledata – a Danish system containing information of various kinds, e.g. travel agencies. The system also contains an electronic encyclopedia.

CPI – a system containing some public domaine software and a bulletin board. It has not been used very much in this project.

RC Info – A database containing information about computer software. Gives access to a bulletin board.

The telephone company´s database with telephone numbers has been used as an example of an external database. You can dial this base directly and search it using your own computer.

LFU – A database on videoes. Gives access to a bulletin board.

In this project, no foreign database has been used. At a later stage, we have ideas about telecommunicating with other students somewhere in the world.

5.4 Bulletin Boards

At one of the schools in the project, the

librarian has started a bulletin board on his machine. This has been of great help for the project. All kind of information has been exchanged by using the mail function on the board. Although the schools in the project are within a distance of 30 km, this mail function has been used very much.

6. USE OF INTERNAL DATABASES

6.1 Teaching aids in the school library

The school library contains many different kinds of teaching aids: fiction, scientific books, fundamental book collection, sets of books for use in classrooms, teacher's guides, maps, tapes for sound and video, computer software, etc.

In most Danish schools, the librarian is responsible for the local guidance of teachers in combining and using these teaching aids. This has until now been mostly done by heart and by help of catalogues. Catalogues are often too old to contain all the information about materials at the school. The librarian often finds himself in the situation that he cannot answer these kinds of question.
Users of school libraries want to book materials for later use. This often creates quite a difficult situation for the school librarian. Here the computer comes in as a good administrative tool.

For this, the three school libraries in the project have used a professional database program. Their major demands were that it must be menu driven and must be capable of search using keywords, and the user must be able to run a reservation- and booking system.
The menu system is used by teachers and students in their work with the system. The school librarians have got a range of features, started by codes that does not appear on the screen.

As the librarians made a database containing all teaching aids at the school, it was possible for teachers and students to get information easily by using this system. For instance, it is possible to get a printout of all the materials for a certain subject or topic. Using the computer, it is likewise possible for teachers to book sets of books or other materials for use in the classes.

6.2 Fundamental book collection

As described earlier, it is possible to search in the external base called BASIS. Especially when students use this opportunity, it might be rather expensive. The goal here is a local search in the school's own book collection by help of an easy self instructing program. Such programs are now being developed for use in

school libraries. With such programs it will be possible to download information from the external base BASIS to the school's own hard disk and the search will then be done locally. This is a much cheaper way of searching and the students can use it for all the time they need.

7. PREVIEW OF EDUCATIONAL SOFTWARE

It is essential that a teacher without any computer knowledge is able to preview educational software in the school library. All educational software must be so prepared that it can be started from a menu.
Thus, one of the consoles on the microcomputer placed in the school library is reserved for software previews and diskette copying. The system is so designed that the user can place his disc in the disc drive and press RETURN, whereupon the program on the actual disc will start and be executed. This means that the teacher or student does not need to know anything about computers in order to examine a piece of software.
The system with 4 consoles on the microcomputer means that while doing the preview, the computer can, at the same time, download data from an external database.

8. USE OF WORDPROCESSING

The school libraries in the project have all been using a wordprocessor for their daily work. It has been used for writing letters, reports, lists of books and editing of downloaded information from databases. It has been a great help not only for the school librarians, but also for teachers and students.

9. USE OF GRAPHIC SOFTWARE

The school libraries in the project have all made use of graphics software. It has been used for making plates and overhead transparencies. This has been done not only by the librarians, for both students and teachers have used these opportunities to give their creations a professional lay-out.

10. CONCLUSIONS

Conclusions from the first year of the project:

- the basic version of the system must be easy to use.

- the computer must be of high performance, with at least 1 MB of internal memory and not less that 30 MB external memory (hard disk).

- the computer must be able to communicate by modem.

- the monitor must be able to show colours.

- computer software for school libraries must be reasonable in price.

- a communications program must be able to make automatic contact with the host computer.

- wordprocessors must be well documented and with built-in help, so that students and teachers can use them with little instruction.

- graphic software must also be well documented and easy to use.

- the school library must give teachers possibilities for previewing educational software.

- additional training in computer use and computer software must be offered to school librarians.

- rates for using external databases must be lowered.

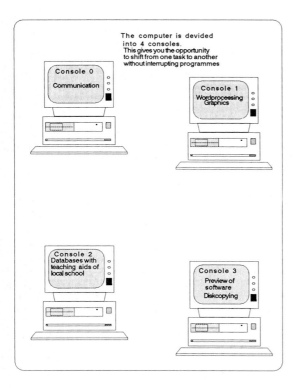

Figure 1

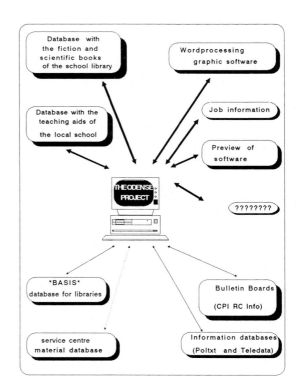

Figure 2

COMPUTERS IN EDUCATION, F. Lovis and E.D. Tagg (eds.)
Elsevier Science Publishers B.V. (North-Holland)
© IFIP, 1988

LEARNING GEOGRAPHY WITH COMPUTERS - an inservice resource pack

Deryn M Watson

Educational Computing Unit, King's College, University of London, 552 Kings Road,
London SW10 OUA.

After the initial flurry of computer awareness courses, it became apparent that for IT to
be delivered successfully across the curriculum, it needs to be properly incorporated in
the curriculum of the main subjects taught in schools. Despite considerable efforts to
provide hardware and geography software, the use of computers in geography classrooms is
still rare. It would seem that the concern of the teachers, and in particular a
re-appraisal of their teaching strategies and classroom organisation, needs to be included
in inservice courses. A resource pack of materials has been devised with this approach,
in an attempt to bridge the gap between the potential and reality of use in the classroom.

1. INTRODUCTION

At the time of WCCE, Lausanne, July 1981, there
was relatively little hardware in schools, and
certainly not much software for use by subjects
across the curriculum. Many papers at that
conference addressed the philosophy and structuring of computer awareness courses, and there
was debate as to whether programming, and in
which language, should be an integral part of
any such course (1). By 1988, seven years
later, the issues have changed and diversified.
This paper sets out to analyse the philosophy
behind the development of a major computer
based learning resource for geography teachers
in the UK, as an illustration of these changes.

2. THE SITUATION IN THE UK

The concerns at WCCE, 1981, were also reflected
in UK schools. It has been estimated that in
the 1970s, 5% of secondary schools had access
to some form of computing power, usually linked
to a mainframe. In 1980, with the introduction
of microcomputers, some Local Education
Authorities (LEA) had begun purchasing a
variety of hardware and a large number of
computer studies or computer awareness courses
were devised for schools. Most schools however
had no computers.

By 1988, there has been a significant shift in
both the hardware and software scene in schools.
The Department of Trade and Industry (DTI)
instituted a series of hardware purchasing
schemes; all secondary and primary schools now
have micros. There are thought to be at least
16 per secondary and 3 per primary; while this
is not nearly enough, it is clearly a healthy
base. Because of the DTI scheme, these machines are one of two types: the RM 380/480Z and
the BBC Model B. This standardisation has been
most important to the development of software.
The only deviation from this is a reflection

of recent purchases of 16 bit MSDOS based hardware.

In parallel, during 1980-86, there has been a
major initiative from the Department of Education and Science (DES), a national Microelectronics Education Programme (MEP). The director of
MEP announced that "the aim of the Programme is
to help schools to prepare children for a life
in society in which devices and systems based
on microelectronics are commonplace and pervasive" (2). The programme was structured into
three categories - a national information and
resource network, teacher training and software
development, and was operated through 14
regional centres. The teacher training element
concentrated on inservice needs and was divided
into 4 domains: computer studies, microelectronics, information systems and computer based
learning. Training was to take place at different levels, from short 1-3 day "awareness and
familiarisation" courses, to longer specialist
courses for teachers wishing "to expand their
knowledge of electronics or to develop computer
based learning materials". A cascade process
for the passing on of skills from course attend-
ees to other colleagues in schools, was envisaged.

After 6 years, at the close of MEP, it was
recognised that while much work had been
achieved with respect to raising the level of
awareness and developing a range of materials,
there was much more work to be done if the aims
were to be fully accomplished (3). One area of
concern was that in 1980 there was not much
educational software - software which, for
instance, historians, biologists, or modern
linguists would be happy to use. Hence the MEP
strategy that included software development. By
1986 a large quantity of software had been
developed for use in both primary and secondary
schools. It appeared, however, that it was not
often being used in the classroom, and some
schools and LEAs were still not aware of the

range of materials and devices available.

So two further initiatives emerged. The DTI launched another scheme, for the purchase of educational software. A total of £6 million was put into the system, over a three year period 1986-9, to boost sales of educational software. And there is no doubt that the cost of software, during the period of local and central financial restraint, was one cause of the problem. The DES responded by setting up the Microelectronics Education Support Unit (MESU), to continue the MEP work in this field, but with a clearer focus specifically on the problem of encouraging a full and wide-ranging use of applications in schools. Thus, their task was to consolidate rather than initiate. As John Foster, the Director of MESU, said in 1986; "There has never been an educational idea that has been taken up so quickly and so widely as has the use of the computer in our schools. However, they are too rare and too special" (4).

3. THE CASE FOR GEOGRAPHY

Geography provides a useful example of the nature of this problem. Geographers in the UK had been in the forefront of developments in the 1970s; by 1980 there was already a small but active body of geography software developers and users (5). As a result, Geography was one of the subjects, along with mathematics and science, named in the MEP policy document as the focus for development and inservice work. Geographers' interest has not waned (6) particularly in the appropriate use of computers within the curriculum (7, 8) and the amount of activity in software development compares favourably with that in other countries (9). By 1986, there were at least 50 titles of Geography software in publishers' catalogues. Geographers were the subject teachers, after science, who most actively went on the 2 and 4 day inservice courses mounted by the MEP. The Geography Association produced a booklet, New Information Technologies and Geography (10). Yet the amount of geography software being used in schools was patchy in the extreme, and the HMI report indicated considerable concern at the gap between the provision of hardware and software and even some inservice courses, and the reality of this filtering through to regular practice in the classroom.

Something was still clearly wrong.

4. THE PERSPECTIVE OF TEACHERS

It seemed that too many simplistic assumptions about the nature of the inservice teacher training provision had been made. The technology provides opportunities for problem solving and decision making, discovery learning, investigations, testing hypotheses, and new forms of communication which themselves may result in a re-appraisal of teaching strategies in the

classroom. Simply introducing the hardware and software to teachers was not enough; more often than not, this added to the concerns of the average classroom teacher, by opening up problem areas without strategies for their solution. These could be identified as follows:

Hardware:

Where is the computer/s?
How do I have a chance to explore the micro and feel confident with it?
Who is available to help, but not patronise me, while I learn?
Do I have to move the class to the micro, or can I move the micro(s) to my geography room?

Software:

What geography software is there?
How can I evaluate it?
Will it fit into, and enhance my existing curriculum?
What do I need to remove or change to make room in the curriculum for the software?

Classroom:

How do I physically arrange and manage the classroom if I have 1 or 3, or even a network of computers?
Is there a printer?
Is there a large monitor?
How do I arrange access by the pupils to the micro?
What do pupils do while they do not have access?

Teaching and learning:

Will using the micro reinforce my style of teaching, or will it have to change?
What learning outcomes can I expect from using the software?
Are these new outcomes and how can I assess them?
What change will all this mean and who can support me during this period of change?

An inservice strategy that takes teachers out of their classrooms for a quick "Cook's tour" of the hardware and available software does not address these issues. A new approach was needed.

5. THE SCHEME

A scheme was needed that would tackle head-on the problems outlined above. Accordingly, a Geographer Computer Based Learning panel was set up in November 1985, funded initially by the MEP, as an offshoot of their national CBL panel for teacher training. The panel consisted of educators from both university institutions and colleges of education, and advisers from LEAs and HMI, as well as software developers. Not all members were actively involved in CAL, but all were active in Geography Education. There was significant agreement as to the nature of the problem. Putting on more and longer courses was not the answer; materials were desperately needed by both the advisers and trainers to act as the basis upon which inservice education could take place.

The following proposal was drawn up to seek funds which outlined the scope of the Project.

A proposal for a Geography CBL Inservice Pack

Proposal: To produce a substantial inservice pack of materials to support the use of computer based materials in the geography curriculum. This would:

1) reflect the variety and scope of geography syllabuses;
2) be modular in structure, reflecting any key aspects of geography – e.g. mapwork, data interrogation, modelling and simulations;
3) link software with each module;
4) explore the issues that teachers need to consider when using the new technology; e.g., teaching styles, classroom organisation;
5) report on known case studies/publications reflecting a variety of current use in geography classrooms;
6) refer to other inset materials, sources of information, etc., that will help the teacher to maintain an ongoing understanding of the topic.

It is hoped to be able to negotiate with some publishers for the inclusion of published software in the pack.

Method: It is aimed to employ two full-time editors of material – ideally each for one year, preferably on a DES pooled fellowship arrangement. These will work closely with the Geography Panel, which consists of key names in the field. These fellows would be based in a higher education institution for the duration of their work. The completed pack of modules and software would be published, and 'launched' at special inservice days with LEA advisers and teacher trainers.

Audience: The pack is aimed for use by three groups:

1) LEA advisers responsible for geography as part of a substantial inservice course.
2) Geography teachers within their schools, as a basis for long-term consideration of the incorporation of educational computing materials in their schools.
3) Teacher trainers in institutions of higher and further education.

It is anticipated that such a pack would act as a sound basis for the formulation of opinion of geography teachers about software and its potential, and thus their purchasing policy. Its practical nature should ensure that software once acquired is used in the classroom, not left on a shelf in the stock cupboard.

Funds were raised from MEP, and the Group drew up the criteria for selection for the 2 school-teacher fellows.

Selection Criteria for Editors to work on Geography Inset material

- Expertise in curriculum development
- Knowledge and practice in modern geography.
- Awareness and experience of the wide range of applications of computers for the geography curriculum.
- Experience in a managerial or advisory role.
- To have carried out inservice training in a school or an LEA.
- Have current or recent classroom experience.

Note the emphasis on geographical education rather, than on just CAL awareness. Rather than advertise, the committee drew up a list of 18 people whom they knew might fulfill these criteria and approached them. Seven expressed a definite interest, 4 were shortlisted and 2 were appointed. Unfortunately, one of the schoolteacher fellows was subsequently unable to take up the post. The fellow who did, Mike Milton, was seconded for 1986/7 from his post as a Head of Humanities department, in a large secondary school in Bromley, South East London.

6.   PRODUCING THE MATERIALS

The schoolteacher fellow, working closely with the active members of the panel, then set about a series of tasks.

Advice: The first task was to seek out and meet as many key people as possible, for advice. These people were from the CAL and Geography community, Geography Education departments, LEA advisers and the inservice training world.

Software: The second task was to call in and view as much geography software as possible, to prepare recommendations for inclusion in the pack. It was essential that the teachers, when using the pack, would put their hands on and try out geography software immediately as part of their learning experience. Thus, some software from existing catalogues had to be chosen; no attempt was made to write software for inclusion in the pack, though data sets were created later for use with a chosen data handling package.

The chairwoman of the group had to persuade the new national funding body, MESU, both to continue to support the work, at a time when they had not yet worked out their national strategy and programme, and to underwrite, to the tune of tens of thousands of pounds, the capital required to bulk purchase/license the software from commercial suppliers, for inclusion in the pack.

Geographical Ideas: The material was to be constructed around geographical themes, which would act as self-contained modules in a pack. Material labelled "Population" or "Climate" would attract Geography teachers more than sections labelled "Simulations" or "Spread-sheets". A search was made of all the major Geography syllabuses, to pick out common themes. Five themes emerged - Population and Settlement, Development Studies, Physical Processes, Field-work and Economic Understanding. A matrix was then drawn up, with these themes set against styles of specific software, such as data hand-ling, spreadsheets, simulations, wordprocessing. Software names were then placed in various spaces in the resulting matrix.

Completing the matrix: Completing the matrix was not just a question of matching different software styles to geography topics. The panel had to consider the availability of the soft-ware in versions for the two main micros in the schools, to ensure that we had chosen from as wide a range of developers and publishers as possible, and to limit our choice to the number that it was feasible to underwrite. Thus, the choice was both pedagogic and political. In the end, 8 pieces were chosen, 1 for each Theme, 2 for the introduction and 1 to be used with all themes. All but one of the pieces of software ran on both machines; most already also had 16 bit MSDOS versions.

Case studies: The schoolteacher fellow then set about finding teachers for the case studies, a number of which were to illustrate the use of one of the 8 pieces of defined software. A large number of schools were approached, usually based on earlier contacts made during the advice phase. As with the software choice, the decisions were complicated; we wanted to cover the 9-19 age range and different styles of school. We wanted the schools to reflect both urban and rural environments, as well as a proper geographical spread from north to south, east to west, of the country.

Structured routes and questions: At the same time, it became apparent that case studies were not enough. The case studies written reflected a variety of uses of software; teachers may read these, but how does this help them actually to put the software in, and to plan how to use it themselves? It was decided that as an intro-duction, a structured route, rather like a flow chart, would be drawn, taking teachers step by step through the software in the pack, indicat-ing one way in which they could organise the class or lesson aims, at different stages. This flow chart was to be supported by a series of small 'snippets' of help, advice or questions for the teacher.

A Reader: There were also some general issues to be drawn out, that would not emerge with just a collection of flowcharts, 'snippets' and case studies. A variety of articles were commissioned from teachers, advisers, and others in the field, to tackle some of the more general themes to be included in each module, for instance, progression in fieldwork. During the commissioning of these articles and case studies, it became apparent that some of the ideas expressed were more far reaching and less appropriate to the specific themes. So these and others were drawn together to form a separate Reader.

Collation and editing: By the end of the year, a vast mass of materials had been collected. Each theme which was to form a module, now contained a flowchart to use with a specified piece of software, a data set, case studies using a variety of software, and one or two articles. The Fieldwork module was thinner than the others and sat uneasily with the rest; these were geography topics, whereas Fieldwork was a methodology to support topics. So this was scrapped and the material incorporated into the remaining four. On an initial reading and first editing of the mass, it became apparent that yet another module was required - on the different strategies and routes through the resource modules that the users could take. The penalty for producing a pack with no fixed linear route for its use, is an investment in material to help explain the flexibility. Thus the final resource pack, Learning Geography with Computers (10), consists of the following parts:

- An introductory module to geography and computers, including how to set up and use a data file, a simulation and a simple news-paper simulator.
- The four modules of Geography themes:
  - Economic Understanding
  - Development Studies
  - Population and Settlement
  - Physical Processes
- A Reader consisting of 16 papers, to support the materials.
- A "how to use" module, including various teaching and inservice strategies.
- The 8 packs of software and notes that accompany the software.

The following section headings, taken at random from various modules, illustrate the implement-ation of a philosophy of using geography learn-ing as a focus.

'Using STARS in Aberavon school'
'Strategies for change in the classroom'
'Using SLOPES to investigate variations between North and South facing slopes of a sub-glacial meltwater channel in the North Cheviot Hills'
'Social and political literacy'
'Using CHOOSING SITES to explore office location in Bromley'
'What will pupils learn from using SANDHARVEST?'
'Using GRASS for an enquiry on urban inequality'.

At the end of the academic year, the school-

teacher fellow returned to his school, and from
September 1987 to April 1988, the chairwoman of
the group collated and edited the pack. Just
as during the development, this was a team
effort. An editorial board, made up of the
working members of the panel, was formed to
help. At the same time, MESU undertook to
produce and publish the material themselves,
and the group was very concerned that the style
of presentation should reflect the professional
approach to Inset that the material was intended
to embody. The final pack was published in late
Spring 1988.

<u>A Video</u>: Throughout the development period,
the group was very keen to make a video to be
included in the pack. Because there was only
1 schoolteacher fellow, and not 2 as planned,
it was difficult to fit this in. At the same
time, the funders were reluctant to invest
further before they could see an end product.
At the time of writing the paper, however, it
looks as though some funding might be available.
The group has already drawn up the criteria for
the video. In essence, the value of a video is
to support the pack by illustrating aspects that
are difficult to communicate by other means.
The obvious area, in this instance, is the
actual realities of a geography classroom in
operation while using a computer. The storyboard for the video would detail specific
aspects of classroom organisation, teaching
strategy and learning that the pack highlights.

7. THE DISSEMINATION

While it is hoped that the production of this
material will contribute towards solving the
major problems outlined, it is not in itself
enough. How will advisers and teachers become
aware of it? Will they buy it? Who will
support them in their use of it?

Throughout the operation of this scheme, the
panel regularly distributed information leaflets
about the production of the pack and its aims.
The publication of the pack was timed deliberately to coincide with the annual Geography
Association Conference, and a major presentation
on the material was included in the conference
programme. Articles were submitted to 'Teaching
Geography' and other relevant publications. The
committee has also regularly reported back to
the funders on the need for a dissemination
policy and programme to ensure that the material
is used.

Planning and maintaining dissemination that
takes cognisance of 104 different LEAs and a
variety of teacher inservice training schemes,
is a nightmare. In this instance, the situation
has been considerably eased by a further
national initiative. The DES announced in 1987
a scheme to fund, for the next 3 years, advisers
based in LEAs who are to coordinate and train
teachers for the use of IT across the curriculum

in schools. These IT advisers will be supported
in their LEAs by the MESU. Thus this pack,
Learning Geography with Computers, is perfectly
timed to provide materials for these new IT
advisers and to act as one basis upon which
they can set up the training of their teachers.

8. CONCLUSION

It took from October 1985 to April 1988 to plan,
set up, collate and publish this resource pack
for geographers. The cost breaks down at:

1 man year for schoolteacher fellow;
Materials and expenses for schoolteacher fellow;
0.50 man year for editing;
Committee meeting expenses (18 in toto);
Honoraria for 30 case studies and 25 articles;
Capital to bulk purchase/licence software packs
from publishers;
and Capital to finance publication process.

The many hours of work and advice given by the
key panel members cannot be counted in financial
terms.

The value of the pack lies in the fact that it
was being conceived and developed at a time
when there was growing awareness for such a
need; this is reinforced by its completion
which coincided with a national initiative
which will depend upon the availability of such
materials for success. It is hoped that the
philosophy that lies behind the development of
this pack can act as a model for others in
different subjects. The success of the Geography materials will only be measureable in the
early 1990s.

If pupils are to feel at home with technology
in their adult world, then they have to be
confident and critical users. Giving them
separate CAL awareness or IT courses, will not
achieve this. But using computers, for the
posing and testing of hypotheses, solving
problems and making decisions in the Geography
curriculum, makes this subject one of the main
delivery agents for IT. To enable this to
happen, there has to be a realisation that it
is the curriculum basis, not the technology
basis, which has to be the focal point. To
deliver such a realisation requires a teaching
force that are also confident and critical
users of the technology. This can only be
achieved by the development of materials that
focus on the teachers' curriculum requirements.

REFERENCES

1 Lewis, R. and Tagg, E.D., Computers in
  Education, North Holland, Amsterdam, 1981.
2 Fothergill, R., Microelectronics Education
  Programme - The Strategy. Department of
  Education and Science, London 1981.
3 HMI Inspectors - Aspects of the work of the

Microelectronics Education Programme,
Department of Education and Science, London,
1987.

4   Microelectronics Education Support Unit -
Introductory booklet, MESU, Warwick, 1986.

5   Shepherd, I.D.H., Cooper, Z.A., and
Walker, D.R.F., Computer Assisted Learning
in Geography, Council for Educational
Technology in association with the Geographical Association, London, 1980.

6   Kent, A., (ed) Geography Teaching and the
Micro, Longman, Harlow, 1983.

7   Watson, D.,(ed) Some implications of micros
on curriculum development. In Lewis, R. and
Tagg, E.D., Involving Micros in Education,
North Holland, Amsterdam, 1982.

8   Watson, D., (ed) Exploring Geography with
Microcomputers, Council for Educational
Technology, London, 1984.

9   Graves, N.J., (ed) Computer Assisted
Learning in Geographical Education,
University of London, Institute of Education
for the International Geographical Union,
London, 1984.

10 Fox, P., and Tapsfield, A., (eds) The Role
and Value of New Technology in Geography,
Council for Educational Technology, London
1986.

11 Watson, D., (ed) Learning Geography with
Computers. Microelectronics Education
Support Unit, Warwick, 1988

COMPUTERS IN EDUCATION, F. Lovis and E.D. Tagg (eds.)
Elsevier Science Publishers B.V. (North-Holland)
© IFIP, 1988

FACTORS AFFECTING THE USE OF COMPUTERS BY UNDERGRADUATE PHYSICS STUDENTS

Dr. E. Boyes
Department of Education
University of Liverpool
England

This paper discusses the use of a network of IBM PC's in the Department of Physics of the University of Liverpool, England. The network has been used mainly with "content-free" software and the use by first year undergraduate physics students has been carefully monitored. Associations between the use of the network and the students' previous experiences with, and their present attitudes towards, computers have been noted. Despite there being considerable differences in the previous experience of male and female students, there is inconclusive evidence that gender had any real effect on their use of the system. The main determining factors appear to be the quality, rather than quantity, of their previous experience, and the attitude they have towards computers at the start of their course.

1. INTRODUCTION

In 1985 a grant was obtained from the Computer Board of Great Britain to install a network of IBM PC's in the Department of Physics of the University of Liverpool. The grant submission emphasised that there would be a formal element of evaluation to which the network would be exposed. To this end, the design of the net-working system was carefully thought out; in particular, it was considered important that the use of the network by students should be auto-matically monitored. The system will be briefly described.

In order to ascertain their computing background, questionnaires were issued to the first year undergraduate students (aged between 18 and 19) when they first entered the University. Using this instrument, it was hoped to ascertain their previous experience, their present awareness and attitudes, and their future expectations, reservations and intended use of the system. Part of the evaluation process also involved the interviewing of students, and also the close monitoring of their progress within certain software packages, using a tape recorder and taking notes of the screen output. A question-naire was also issued after their first year of using the system.

This paper considers particularly the factors affecting the students' use of the system, rather than the evaluation of particular soft-ware packages.

2. THE LIVERPOOL SYSTEM

A network to which students would be able to "log on", using their own password, was felt to be important; this would give the possibility of monitoring the student use in the central filestore, and also enable software security, particularly important with licensed software, to be ensured. As the Physics Department at Liverpool is in two adjacent buildings, this meant that a network capable of extending to over 1000 m was required.

A total of 30 IBM PC's and 6 printers were initially installed in public areas within the Physics Department. The networking system used is the Corvus Omninet, and on top of this runs the MENUGEN menu package from Microft Ltd. When students log on, they only see the MENUGEN system; this shows a series of menus, at different levels, which include all the choices open to the students. Even after running a particular piece of software from the menu system, the students cannot break out into the network/machine operating system; instead, control is automatically taken over by the MENUGEN software. As they make their choices on the different levels of menus on offer, a log file is kept both of their choices and of the time spent in each.

At the beginning of their first term at Liverpool, students were given their passwords and a short lesson on how to use the system. They were then encouraged to use the packages available, particularly the content free packages, such as word processing and symbolic algebra, by giving them credit for set exercises which they completed; students who completed these exercises gained exemption from other parts of the course. This, indeed, is intended to be the general policy: that software which is to be used should, as far as possible, be formally incorporated into the course, either by setting tutorial problems which require the software to be used, or by making the software part of the laboratory practicals. During the first year, a number of computer-linked laboratory practicals were devised; these take

data directly from experimental situations and
assist the students in its analysis. Other
tutorial computer assisted learning packages
were also developed but these were not available
until late in the year. This paper deals mainly
with the content-free software which students
were encouraged to use.

3.   USE BY STUDENTS

The extent to which the network has been used by
the 54 first year students can be easily seen
from examination of the log file for the academic
year 1986/87. Two important indicators of overall use by the students are: the number of times
each student logged on to the network, and the
total time spent logged on to any of the various
software packages.

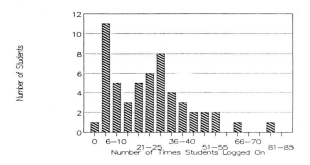

Figure 1

Figure 1 shows the profile for the number of
times each student logged on to the network for
whatever reason; the mean number of occasions is
22.6, and the mode is 22. Clearly, some students
made a great deal of use of the system with over
50 "logons" recorded, while others made very
little use; one student did not attempt to use
it at all. The time spent by students using
the network can be seen in *Figure 2*. Over the
time period during which they were encouraged to
use the system (from Christmas to Summer), the
mean time spent logged on was 7.2 hours, with a
median of 6.3 hours. A minority of students
spent over 20 hours, in total, using the various
software packages. Much of this time was spent
word processing and using the Symbolic
Mathematics package to solve the tutorial
problems which had been set.

4.   FACTORS AFFECTING STUDENT USE

It had been felt for some time that physics
students at Liverpool had not been as enthusiastic towards using computers as one might
have expected. It seemed, to some members of
staff, that students had deliberately "anti-
selected" computing in choosing to study
physics, and although most of them recognised

the need for the use of computers in physics,
few seemed keen to take on final year projects
which involved the use of computers.

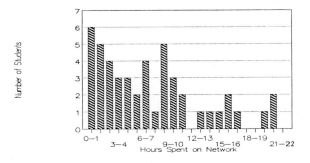

Figure 2

In order to try to gauge the reasons for this,
it was decided to look at the student use of the
network, as it varied for different groups within the total cohort. A significance level of
p < 5% was considered acceptable. So that, if
there was greater than a 5% chance of any
measured difference being due to random error,
the difference would be considered not to be
real.

4.1. Ownership

It was thought that where students had previously
owned a personal computer, this might give them
confidence to use the system more. Indeed, the
ownership of personal computers by undergraduate
Physics students has been increasing over the
past few years. *Figure 3* shows the recent trend
in the percentage of first year Liverpool
Physics students owning computers. Within the
present cohort, there are 64% who own computers,

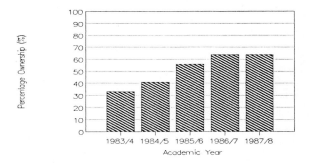

Figure 3

and one might expect that these would be more
likely to make use of the network in the
Physics Department. However, no significant
difference could be seen between the owners
(31 of them) and the non-owners; the t-test for

example gave the chance probability, for the slight differences seen, as 37%.

4.2. Previous Experience

In the pre-course questionnaire, students had been questioned as to their previous experience with computers, both in terms of the quantity, i.e., the extent of that experience, and also its quality. The latter involved questioning the students with items, using a Likert-type scale, as to whether their previous computing experience was difficult, useful, daunting, etc. The scores on the items were summed to give an overall score for "quality" of previous experience.

(i) Quantity

As with the ownership of computers, no significant trend was noticed between the amount of previous experience students had had on computers and the extent to which they used the network.

(ii) Quality

There appears to be a highly significant association between the measure of the quality of experience before the university course began, and the amount students used the network. As one might expect, the more positive the previous experience, the greater use was made of the system. The Kendall correlation between the number of occasions logged on and the measure of the quality of previous experience was 0.37 (p << 1%), and the time spent on the system showed a similar dependence.

4.3. Welcoming Attitude

The pre-course questionnaire had also questioned students regarding their desire to work further with computers; again, a score for each student was obtained from the Likert-type scales used. As one might expect, those with a more positive welcoming attitude tended in all respects to use the system more. For example, the Kendall correlation for the time spent on the system with this welcoming attitude measure was 0.26 (p < 3%).

4.4. Gender

The rather small number of students (54) for this particular year makes any statistical comparisons difficult, particularly with regard to gender, as there were only 8 females. Indeed, no consistently significant differences were noted between the ways in which the different sexes used the network. The Kendall correlation coefficient (0.21) for the sex of the student with the number of logons was only significant at the 7% level, as was a t-test. In this regard, the males appeared generally to "log on" to the system more than the females. An analysis of variance estimated the reality of this difference at the 3% level.

The total time spent on the system, however, showed no difference between males and females; for example the t-test estimated any slight difference at the 94% level.

It should be pointed out that a significant association was noted between the quality of the previous experience with computers and the gender of the student, the male students indicating a more positive previous experience. The Kendall correlation coefficient was given as 0.28 (p. < 3%).

4.5. Maths, Physics and General Ability

No significant association could be seen between students' grades in pre-university examinations and their overall use of the system, although use of the mathematics packages showed a considerable link with previous mathematical ability. The least insignificant link with overall use was a slight association with the general ability of the student (p < 6%) in the negative direction (i.e., the more able may have tended to use the system less).

5. CONCLUSIONS

Most Physics educators would agree that the use of computers is extremely important for the physicist. Indeed, when asked about this, 90% of the students in this study felt that computers were an important part of scientific work. Despite this, however, there were many students who, possibly because of previous daunting experiences, were hesitant to use computer facilities which were available to them.

At all levels in education, we must beware of thrusting the use of computers on to students without **serious** pedagogical thought. True, there is a proportion of students in most disciplines which seems to take to computers rather easily, possibly through playing games, or via electronics and control. Nevertheless, there is also a large proportion for whom the use of computers, at least in the initial stages, is a chore. These students are easily "put off", and the experience at Liverpool in previous years, with students who have little or no computing background, bears this out.

Clearly, the mystique of the computer, and those who have mastery of it, is somewhat daunting to such students. This means that their introduction to different computer packages must be carefully thought out, and that students must perceive the need to use such packages. This is why the use of the computer network at Liverpool will continue to be a required part of the course, using, amongst other things, software of a "service" nature, and for which the students will receive some credit. The evaluation of the network will continue, so that student needs may be identified and software packages introduced accordingly.

COMPUTERS IN EDUCATION, F. Lovis and E.D. Tagg (eds.)
Elsevier Science Publishers B.V. (North-Holland)
© IFIP, 1988

HIGH-SCHOOL OPTICS WITH MICROCOMPUTERS

David Singer and Uri Ganiel

Department of Science Teaching
The Weizmann Institute of Science
Rehovot 76100, ISRAEL

Our approach to the use of microcomputers in science teaching is to integrate
them into the teaching-learning sequence as an additional tool. Following this
approach, we developed four modules which are integrated into the course on
Optics taught in Israeli high-schools. The modules are: Romer's Experiment,
Hide and Seek in Mirrors - a game, Fermat's Principle, and Thin Lenses. The
packages emphasize aspects of the material which are difficult or impossible to
deal with satisfactorily by conventional, non computer-based, means. The
modules promote an interactive mode of learning, utilizing the advantages of
the microcomputer, such as animation, formula driven graphics, and the choice
of random events.

1. INTRODUCTION

In recent years, microcomputers have become
commonplace in many schools, and their use is
expanding every day. As the hardware is
becoming more and more powerful, it is clear
that educational software is lagging behind.
Turning our attention to physics education, we
find that there is a very large variety of
educational software available [1,2]. However,
by and large, computers have not transformed
the physics classroom.

A. Bork, one of the pioneers of the use of
computers in physics education wrote in 1980:
"The computer will over the next twenty five
years become the major delivery system for
learning physics... It will largely replace
lectures and may even replace textbooks..."[3].

There is no indication that physics education
is moving in such a direction. Indeed, it
seems that such far reaching predictions are
now met with much scepticism. There is a very
long way that research on learning and
artificial intelligence will have to go before
a computer, even with very sophisticated
software, will replace the teacher - if that
will ever happen at all. This does not exclude
very exciting possibilities which the computer
presents, and which are being explored by
educational software developers. However,
teachers and educators are still searching for
the optimal uses of computers, and will
probably be doing so for years to come.

Our view on the use of microcomputers in
science teaching is based on the general
concept that such use should be integrated into
the teaching-learning sequence as an additional
tool, rather than as a replacement of any
particular method. The teacher should maintain
a central role as lecturer, director of group
activities, or leader of laboratory activities.
Computer based modules give the teacher an
additional tool, which adds new dimensions to
the activities he directs, thus broadening the
scope of his possibilities.

Following this approach, we have developed a
number of modules, which are intended to be
integrated into the course on optics taught in
Israeli high-schools. In general, the topics
covered emphasize aspects which are difficult
or impossible to deal with satisfactorily by
conventional means (i.e. lecture, textbook, or
laboratory activity).

More details and some "screens" from each
package are described in the following pages.

2. ROMER'S EXPERIMENT

Following a series of observations, the Danish
astronomer Romer showed for the first time
(1676), that the speed of light is finite
(light requires time to travel from one point
to another).

In his experiments, Romer studied the times of
eclipses of one of Jupiter's moons (Io). This
moon has an average period of revolution of 42
hr, 28 min, 16 sec, which was determined from
the average time between two successive
emergences of Io from the shadow of Jupiter.

From a long series of observations, Romer found that the *measured* period of Io around Jupiter was not constant but changed periodically during a year. Since Romer was convinced that the *real* period was constant, he concluded that the changes in the measured period were due to the changing distances between the Earth and Jupiter. Since light travels with finite velocity, the changes in the *observed* period represent the variations in the time required by light to travel the different distances.

It is obvious that it is impractical to conduct an experiment such as Romer's in high-school. Also, a clear explanation of the experiment and its interpretation is somewhat elaborate, and is either lacking or even wrong in many textbooks. It is therefore a natural example where a computer-simulation can be very useful.

In the first part of the program, the student is shown a simulation of the astronomical events, leading to Romer's observations. The simulated motions on the screen enable the student to follow in a few seconds events that take many days in reality. It also reduces astronomical distances to the size of the screen. Such scaling down of time and distance makes the description of astronomical phenomena easy and understandable.

In order to interpret these observations, the student is guided through a series of simulated experiments. From these simulations, which describe the same dynamics as occurs in the astronomical events, he learns that the *observed* period of a periodic phenomenon can change because of the motion of the observer.

Only after a stepwise exposure to the necessary elements of information does the student return to Romer's observations. He can now find the connection between these observations and reach the conclusion that the speed of light is finite.

A few "screens" from this program are shown in Figs. 1, 2, 3.

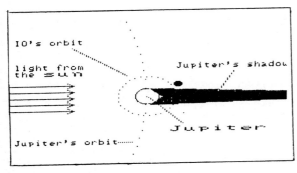

Figure 1. A screen from the sequence demonstrating Romer's observations.

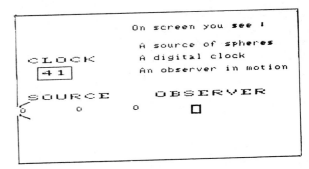

Figure 2. A screen from an explanatory sequence: the source emits spheres at constant time intervals. The user records the times at which the spheres hit a moving observer. The observed intervals depend on the velocity of the observer.

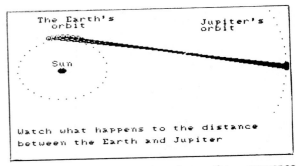

Figure 3. A screen from the sequence explaining Romer's observations and conclusions.

3. HIDE AND SEEK IN MIRRORS - A GAME

One of the basic principles in Geometrical Optics is the law of reflection. The law itself is simple, and with its use the formation of images in mirrors can be easily understood. In a plane mirror, the image is located "behind" the mirror at a location which is symmetric with the source with regard to the plane of the mirror.

Many studies show that students have difficulties with the concept of an image and its location "behind" the mirror: Many students think that the image is located on the plane of the mirror. Our package enables the student to broaden and consolidate his understanding of image formation in plane mirrors.

The program includes two parts: a tutorial and a game. In the tutorial, a cross section of a plane mirror appears on the screen. The location and size of the mirror change randomly. Two random points appear in front of the mirror. The student has to decide whether a person located in one of the points can see the image of the other point in the mirror (Fig. 4). Utilizing the graphic representations which appear on the screen, the student can develop a strategy for making this decision (Fig. 5).

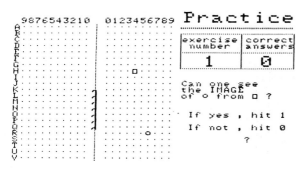

Figure 4. A screen from the tutorial preceding the game.

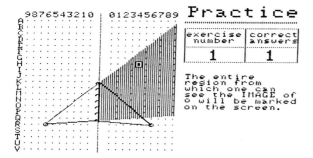

Figure 5. An explanatory screen following the previous screen.

This tutorial prepares the student for the game. In the game, the computer "hides" at a random location in front of a plane mirror. The student has to find this location in an optimally small number of steps. In each step, the student locates himself in one of 220 possible points in front of the mirror. In response, the computer "tells the student" whether or not he "sees" the student's image in the mirror. After each step the student receives some feedback. Using this feedback, the student can develop an intelligent strategy to proceed in the game successfully. This strategy is based on the law of reflection and the various symmetry properties which follow (Figs. 6, 7).

The instant feedback that the student receives, the possibility to play the game repeatedly, where each time a new situation - and therefore a new challenge - is presented, are some of the important advantages of the computer. Integrating this game into the learning sequence will hopefully improve students' motivation, interest, and understanding of the subject. These questions are presently being investigated during our implementation and evaluation activities.

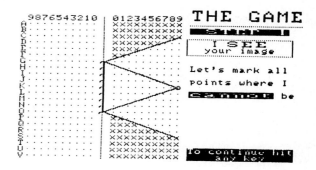

Figure 6. A screen from the game; after the user chooses a location, he receives feedback from the computer.

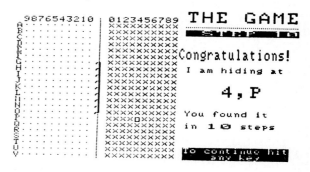

Figure 7. Final screen appearing after a successful game.

4. FERMAT'S PRINCIPLE

The laws of reflection and refraction can be derived from a general principle, known as Fermat's principle. It states that the time light takes to travel between two points, has a stationary value, and usually it is simply a minimum.

While in the case of reflection the proof of the principle is easy, in the case of refraction it is too complicated for young students. Because of the mathematical complexities, it is usually avoided at the high-school level. However, the principle is important, and its introduction is of great didactical value.

In this module, the student is engaged in a simulated experiment which leads him to the principle through trial and error. The program starts with an everyday problem, represented in Figs. 8, 9. To find the answer to the problem the student is guided through a simulated sequence, where he tries to "enter the water" in different locations on the beachline. Through trial and error he finds the answer and then the law that describes the requested path (Figs. 10-13).

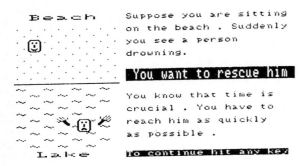

Figure 8 Introductory screen from the module on Fermat's principle.

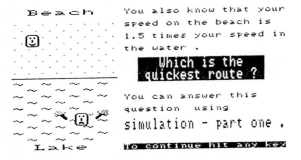

Figure 9.   The screen following   the previous screen.

In   the   second   part   of   the   simulation   the student   learns   about   reversibility,   i.e.   the shortest   time   to   travel from point A to point B is obtained by the same   path as for the travel from point B to point A.

Having established the rule   by which the paths of minimum travel time are determined,   the law of refraction (Snell's law)   can be introduced in a more meaningful way than by simply stating it.

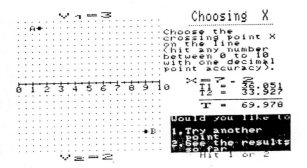

Figure 10.   Screen   shown   after   choosing   a crossing point.

Some   important   aspects   of   the   use   of microcomputers   in   science   teaching   are exemplified in this package: the demonstration of   phenomena   which   cannot   be   realized   in   an actual   laboratory   experiment,   as   well   as   the clear   representation   of   solutions   to   problems which are conceptually simple   but need a level of mathematical   ability that most   students do not possess.

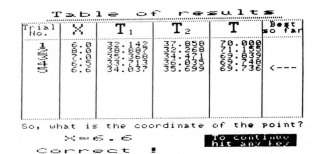

Figure 11.   Summary screen shown to   the user upon request.

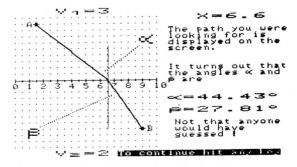

Figure 12.   Screen shown after the correct path has been found.

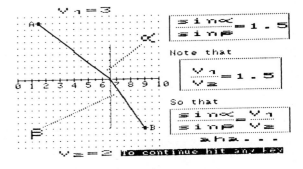

Figure 13.   Screen leading to   "discovery" of the law of refraction.

5. THIN LENSES

This package is basically a tutorial, which emphasizes elements that are sometimes neglected in lecture textbook presentations.

The program enables the student to examine any type of thin lens, choose its parameters and study any variety of image formation situations. Thus, the student controls the size of the lens, its focal length and the distance between it and any object. Performing such a variety of experiments in a real laboratory is practically impossible.

Another feature of the package is that it deals with *beams* of light rather than rays, as is usually done. In reality, light sources emit beams of light, but for reasons of convenience most textbooks deal with rays, and usually only a few special rays. Working with this package the student engages in situations which are closer to reality, and consequently serious misconceptions are avoided.

There are six parts to this package:
a. *Classification of thin lenses*
   In this part, the student learns how to distinguish between converging and diverging lenses.
b. *Focal lengths of different lenses*
   In this part, the student learns about the focal length and its dependence on the shape of the lens (Fig. 14).
c. *The image of a point source in a converging lens*
   Here the student observes the behaviour of different beams of light emerging from point sources located on the axis of a converging lens and passing through the lens. The program enables the student to change the focal length of the lens, the size of the lens and the location of a point source along the axis (Fig. 15, 16).

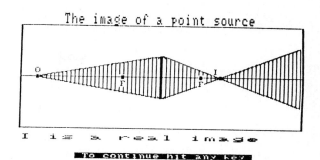

Figure 15.   One of the screens demonstrating image formation of a real image.

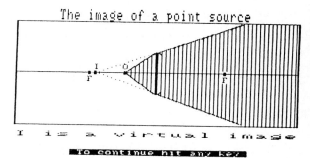

Figure 16.   One of the screens demonstrating image formation of a virtual image.

d. *The image of a point source in a diverging lens*
   This part is similar to the previous one, but deals with diverging lenses.
e. *The image of an extended object in a converging lens*
Here the student observes beams of light emerging from different points on an object which is perpendicular to the axis of a converging lens. By choosing different points on the object he observes how the image (real or virtual) of the object is constructed (Fig. 17-20).

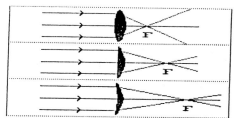

Figure 14.   Focal lengths of different converging lenses.

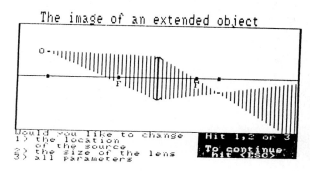

Figure 17.   One of the screens demonstrating image formation of an extended object.

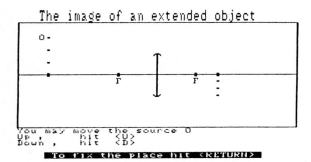

Figure 18.   One of the screens demonstrating image formation of an extended object.

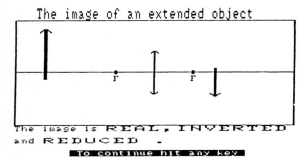

Figure 19.   Final screen showing the image of an object.

f. The image of an extended object in a
*   diverging lens*

It should be emphasized that although this package deals with standard material which can be found in any textbook on geometrical optics, the approach is different than the one found in most books.   Focii of difficulty are treated specifically (such as the ray-beam confusion, the effect of lens-size,   the use of "special" rays to construct images, etc.).

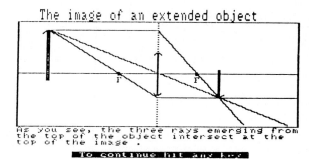

Figure 20.   Constructing the image with three special rays.

The dynamics   of computer   simulations are utilized, e.g. in simulating the motion of the source approaching a lens and observing how the image moves as a consequence. Such simulations help students to internalize the topic of image formation and magnification and they are much more   transparent   than   the mathematical representations by formula.

REFERENCES

[1] Fuller, R.G.   "Resource letter CPE-1: Computers in physics education", Am. J. Phys. 54, 782 (1986).
[2] Taylor, E.F., "Comparison of different uses of computers in teaching physics", Physics Education 22, 202 (1987).
[3] Bork,   A.   "Physics in the Irvine Educational Technology Center", Comput. & Educ. 4, 37, (1980).

COMPUTERS IN EDUCATION, F. Lovis and E.D. Tagg (eds.)
Elsevier Science Publishers B.V. (North-Holland)
© IFIP, 1988

A N.M.R. SPECTRUM ANALYSIS : A PROBLEM SOLVING PARTNER BASED ON THE STUDENT'S APPROACH

RABINE Jean-Pierre, ROUILLARD Michel, CABROL Daniel (*), DUBREUIL Françoise (**)

(*)   Centre de Recherche Pédagogique et de Rénovation Didactique en Chimie
      Université de NICE - Parc Valrose - F 06034 NICE CEDEX - France
(**) Laboratoire Informatique de l'Ordinateur Pour l'Enseignement
      Université PARIS 7 - Tour 23 - Rez de Chaussée - F 75251 PARIS CEDEX 05 - France

This paper presents an example of a novel approach in C.A.L., using the computer as an interactive partner in solving a particular problem in N.M.R. The student is given a molecular formula and its hydrogen N.M.R. spectrum and is asked to derive the structure of the compound. Different commands are displayed, depending on the student's state of knowledge. As the system keeps track of what the student has already established and discovered, the system always individualizes the session. This approach could be applicable to other domains where the student learning would be facilitated by practising problem-solving with the help of an expert.

1. INTRODUCTION

This paper presents a new approach which we developed to provide a supportive environment for interpretation of nuclear magnetic resonance spectra.

Analysing a NMR spectrum is a complex process which mingles stages of analysis with stages of hypothesis, deduction and synthesis. There is no known systematic and unique method of spectrum analysis. Experts and beginners, for example, approach the problem in very different ways. The expert often takes shortcuts, globally identifies more important fragments, takes many factors into account simultaneously, and this enables him immediately to eliminate certain structures. In order to succeed, the beginner has to learn what is to be observed, and what can be deduced from different kinds of data.

The classical approach for beginners :

A number of educational products have been developed so far in order to help beginners. Ingham and Herson [1] have "devised flow charts which successfully assist the beginner to become proficient"; in 1975, Ayscough and the CALCHEM project [2] had already produced complex computer programs in which the computer was able to "accommodate a variety of strategies, keep a record of the interpretation of different clues, suggest reasonable alternatives, and provide appropriate hints based on the information which the student has already acquired". "Information fed back to the student was designed to enable him to locate any errors or misconceptions and to correct these" [3].

In some of our computer educational software, we developed the same kind of approach, except that we wanted to help the students along their interpretative activity without imposing on them a unique strategy. We first designed a teaching material on proton NMR, aimed at individual students working without the constant presence of a teacher. This document combined audiovisual resources (a slide projector driven by an audiotape) [4], and micro-computer facilities [5] which could train students on prediction of spectra. We offered the students simulation programs [6], and wanted them to have an opportunity to interpret a number of spectra which we considered as quite typical [7]. We wanted to make it clear to the student that there was not just one way to solve NMR problems ; each new spectrum could illustrate a different way of attacking the problem, as an expert would, taking advantage of what a particular spectrum looked like. With such pieces of software, we thought the students would in the end be able to build up in their own mind some of the criteria which are helpful in solving a spectrum analysis problem.

This kind of program which assists the student in each step of the resolution and gives him a particular methodology based on the author's approach proved useful for the beginners, even though they were not placed in "real situations".

Designing a solver partner :

Because "real problems rarely come with the necessary information in a convenient package" |2|, we decided to create learning situations which were closer to the real thing. We had to imagine a way to interpret input messages from students who were not answering a precise question (See infra : The proposal option). We wanted the student to select the proper information and find out his own path to the solution. We had thought of a non-directive "solving-environment", somewhat similar to those found in C.A.D. packages or those found in the micro-worlds described by Papert |8|. Such an environment was interesting because the student could then attack the problem in many different ways and construct original solutions which did not have to be anticipated by the author. The problem in a learning environment is precisely that the student is not an expert of the domain under study, and thus, he cannot react properly when he is faced with difficulties, whether related to the next step of the solving process, or related to the interpretation of some kind of data.

The most appropriate strategy seemed to be to develop a kind of problem solving partner based on the student's approach, which provides a lot of resources especially designed to help the student when needed ; the idea being that the student is not guided along if he thinks he can manage without guidance.
These resources can be accessed on request, and deal with all types of difficulty or misconception the student can encounter in solving the problem. In our approach, the student's sequence of proposals or deductions is stored, so that he can get useful advice.
The system we use comments on the student's behaviour, makes remarks and gives advice when asked, but does not ask the student for a complete sequence of reasoning such as in Sleeman |9|.

This paper describes some characteristics of the non-directive learning environment we have thought of.

2. THE NATURE OF THE PROBLEM

Nuclear Magnetic Resonance is used by chemists as a tool to probe the structure of chemical compounds. As the techniques are changing very fast, the gap between the specialist and the occasional end-user is widening. In Chemistry, the NMR technique is one of the most thorough and effective technique of structural investigation. Training sessions about N.M.R. are therefore quite in demand.

The analytical approach toward a N.M.R. first order spectrum consists of decomposing the spectrum into its characteristic elements and of assigning each of those elements a part of the molecular structure. The fragments which have thus been identified are then combined together, taking the unidentified atoms into account, and respecting the rules of stereochemistry. Every possible combination must be considered when constructing the plausible structures. One then looks for other details in the spectrum (the shape of signals, the value of chemical shifts, for example), or in the results delivered by other spectroscopic methods, so as to eliminate all the structures which do not fit and thus finally reach a precise determination. Assigning a pattern rarely excludes all forms of ambiguity and so the chemical structure is progressively elaborated, in a series of hypotheses (pattern assignments and structures), which must all be cross-compatible and also compatible with the other physical and chemical data.

Thus, experience with teaching analysis of N.M.R. spectra has led us to identify the following learning goals for the students :

- develop skills in recognising typical spectral patterns associated with particular structural features

- decompose the spectrum into the characteristic elements

- elaborate a series of hypotheses and make logical deductions from the integration, chemical shifts and multiplicity of the peak

- assign each of those elements a part of the molecular structure

- combine separate structural features to obtain information about the structure of the compound

- recognize the limits of this spectroscopic technique and identify what kind of information could be gained using other spectroscopic techniques.

Before being able to face this kind of problem solving task, the student must have understood some basic principles of the technique (i.e he must have a sufficient theoretical knowledge), he must be able to estimate the main values of some typical chemical shifts and coupling constants (factual knowledge) and must know how to use correlation tables (operational knowledge). These prerequisite skills can be gained by using other teaching materials [4-5 6].

3. GENERAL ARCHITECTURE OF THE PROGRAM

Since we wanted the student to gain expertise in interpreting spectra, we created an environment in which he was asked to solve the problem by himself. The student is faced with interpreting the spectrum shown in figure 1.

Your task is to establish the structure of the compound whose hydrogen NMR spectrum is displayed.

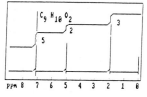

Your choice : Summary   Eureka
              Advice   Tables
              Expert   Quit
              Proposal

Fig. 1. Example

Communication within the program is achieved through a menu selection. A friendly user interface allows the student to skip from one resource to another through the control of a supervisor which makes it possible to take into account new facts, attempts or deductions made by the student and to adapt the displays to individual student's needs and state of knowledge. Figure 2 presents the architecture of the program and shows what are the available resources. The learning environment is composed of six different resources. They can be activated at any time, and what has been done in any of the proposed modes is recorded in such a way that the supervisor is able to adjust help comments, advice or guidance to each situation.

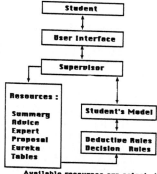

Available resources are selected at a given time by the supervisor.

Fig. 2. Architecture of the program

3.1. The PROPOSAL option

The student can describe, step by step, all the facts he discovers and what can be deduced from them. He is in no way guided in this task. Each proposal is assessed.

Examples of student inputs :

"The integrated intensity 3 of the peak at 2 ppm indicates there is a methyl group" (fact)

"Since there is no coupling, the methylene and methyl groups are not directly connected" (deduction)

igure 3 gives the kind of comment delivered in case of an inadequate proposal.

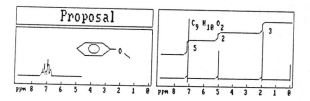

Your proposal : there is a phenoxy group at 7.2 ppm

No. If there were a *phenoxy* group, the protons of the aromatic group would not be equivalent. Compare the display on the left with the experimental spectrum.

Fig. 3. Proposal

3.2. The TABLES option

This option illustrates one of the facilities the student can take advantage of when he wants to access extra information, i.e. the tables of δ chemical shifts. This kind of personal investigation is necessary to find out the possible chemical environments of the compound under study.

3.3. The SUMMARY option

This facility gives the student a good summary of what he has already found out (facts, deductions, impossibilities). The summary is constructed dynamically by the supervisor and depends on what has been done before (fig. 4).

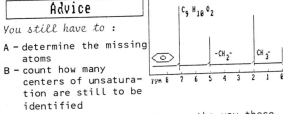

```
┌─────────────────┐     ┌──────────────────────┐
│   Summary       │     │ C₉ H₁₀ O₂            │
└─────────────────┘     │                      │
```

You identified :

a phenyl group at
7.2 ppm
a methylene group at
5.2 ppm
a methyl group at
2.3 ppm

You noticed :

a phenoxy group is impossible here

Fig. 4. Summary

3.4. The ADVICE option

The ADVICE option makes suggestions on what to do next, or on the hypotheses to check. Additional information can be obtained, on request, on one of the possible following steps of the problem solving process.

```
┌─────────────────┐     ┌──────────────────────┐
│   Advice        │     │ C₉ H₁₀ O₂            │
└─────────────────┘     │                      │
```

You still have to :

A - determine the missing
atoms
B - count how many
centers of unsatura-
tion are still to be
identified

Enter A or B if you want to see the way these results can be produced

Fig. 5. Advice

3.5. The EXPERT option

The user can ask "EXPERT" to help him in solving the problem. As above, the user can specify the kind of help he requires. With that option, the student can follow the reasoning of an expert analysing the same spectrum (questions are then adressed to him).

3.6 The EUREKA option

The EUREKA option tells the student whether or not his solution is correct.

(i) When the solution is correct, the system can ask for justification. The student is asked for a justification when there is a matching with a decision rule that means that the student did not make all the necessary checks on hypotheses or conclusions.

(ii) When the solution is not correct, the system displays the available information which is contradictory with the student's conclusion.
The advisor tries to match his decision rules with its model of the student. If there is evidence that the student found out all the pieces of information required to construct the structure of the compound, he is then offered two new resources : PASTE and FORMULAE options.

(iii) The PASTE option
When activated, all the parts of structure are displayed and the student can paste them together to built the final structure of the compound, as in [9]. This option can help the student to eliminate some structural arrangements which are not compatible with all the data extracted from the spectra (multiplicity of the signals and chemical shifts).

(iv) The FORMULAE option
This option displays a set of possible structures of the compound. If the student chooses a wrong structure, he can compare the experimental spectrum of the compound under study, which is displayed on the left of the screen, to the one of the selected compound displayed on the right (or characteristic parts of the spectrum of the compound chosen by the student). From the graphics, he can then evaluate peaks positions, the multiplicity, the chemical shifts, the effect of neighbouring groups on the spectrum, etc.

4. TECHNICAL ASPECTS

The program has been developed with the "LEGATO system" (*) available on IBM-PC compatibles, equipped with 640K RAM.

(*) LEGATO is a system created by the Laboratoire Informatique de l'Ordinateur Pour l'Enseignement, Université de PARIS 7, Tour 23 - Rez de Chaussée, F 75251 PARIS CEDEX 05.

4.1. The user interface

LEGATO offers resources that facilitate the design of this solver partner :

(i)   There is a built-in resource which detects whether the student is making a menu selection, or making a natural language entry (all input passes through a kind of filter which is able to recognise requests).

(ii) For each type of data base request, it is possible to restore automatically what was displayed on the screen prior to the request.
For example : a request for TABLES, ADVICE or SUMMARY will lead to the desired displays, automatically followed by a return to the previous screen (either PROPOSAL, or EXPERT, or EUREKA mode of interaction).

(iii) There are facilities for the analysis of open ended messages and of numerical values

(iv) Proposals, requests for help can be easily commented upon locally.

(v)   Access to a wordprocessor and a graphics editor is possible through two user-friendly editors, so colour graphics can be displayed easily.

(vi) A fixed logical structure makes it possible to store vital information for subsequent research activity and a relatively sophisticated record keeping is included, together with sorting, printing and statistic procedures.

4.2. The student's model

Each interaction with the student during our program updates a list of facts and deductions, describing part of the student's state of knowledge. The lists of facts will be exploited by the supervisor each time a summary or a piece of advice is required, and to decide the following step in the problem solving process in the EXPERT and EUREKA modes.

The rules applied by the supervisor refer to stored lists including :

- The list of hydrogen containing groups found out by the student ; (methyl, methylen, phenyl) ;

- The list of groups thought to be absent by the student (carbonyl, phenoxy, ethyl...) ;

- The number of centres of unsaturation in the molecule ;

- The number of centres of unsaturation still to be assigned ;

- The multiplicity (no multiplets) ;

- The molecular assymetry ;

Some of the facts describe the student's use of the resources :

- The student accessed the TABLE resource

- Such and such pieces of advice have been displayed, etc.

4.3. The supervisor

Decision rules can be handled by LEGATO. The rules refer to the student's state of knowledge (as inferred by the supervisor), and to the patterns to identify in the stored lists.
A stack of comments can be associated to each rule, which may produce new facts concerning the student each time a decision rule is applied.
The system keeps a record of each rule which has been applied.

Examples :

When a student has got all the needed elements to construct the structure of the compound, a decision rule of the supervisor will lead to this first comment :

"You know all the structural elements allowing you to build the structure of the compound".

A second deductive rule makes it possible to construct a new fact that will possibly be exploited in a comment : out of the 11 plausible structures, only 2 are still possible if the student found that there were one phenyl group, one methylene group, one acetyle group, one carbon atom and one oxygen atom, to be placed.
The supervisor will note that conclusion.

5. CURRENT DEVELOPMENT AND CONCLUSION

This work is related to chemical spectroscopy, but the method can be applied to other fields where students can learn-by-doing under the guidance of an expert. It is a first step towards the design of more general problem-solver partners which are not tools for research, but are intended to help students gaining experience in interpreting spectroscopic data. Our experience in this area shows that the design of such products must rely on the analysis of specific examples, in order to build the decision and deductive rules. This prototype is one of these examples.

Many interesting challenging problems have been encountered in developing this prototype. They are related to the design of the student's model, the selection of events which have to be taken into account - the definition of the decision and deductive rules.

In the present stage of development, we have made a series of choices concerning the above mentioned problems and we are now faced with the following questions :

- are the student's model and selected events accurate enough to provide the basis of an adaptative response of the supervisor ?
- what will be the attitude of the student using the system ?
- does the student use all the resources of the system or only some of them ?
- are these resources efficient in helping the students ?

We are now planning a field investigation with students from different universities, in order to collect data to answer these questions.

One advantage of the LEGATO system we are using is the provision of automatic record-keeping of the student-system interaction. The files created during experimentation can be merged and analyzed automatically.
Moreover, the fundamental choices made in the initial stage of this project concerning the student's model, the recorded events, and the rules are not incorporated in the code of the program but, on the other hand, are separated modifiable objects. This important aspect allows us to improve the system continuously.

REFERENCES

[1] A.M.Ingham and R.C.Henson, Interpreting Infrared and Nuclear Magnetic Resonance Spectra of Simple Organic Compounds for the Beginner, J.Chem.Educ., vol.61, no.8, August 1984, 704-707.

[2] P.B.Ayscough, Project case study. CALCHEMistry. Br. J. Educ. Technol., vol. 8, no.3, October 1977, 201-213.

[3] P.B.Ayscough, H.Morris and J.A.Wilson, Application of computer-assisted learning methods in the teaching of chemical spectroscopy, Comput. and Education, vol.3, 1979, 81-92.

[4] J-P. Rabine, M.Rouillard, D.Cabrol et R.Luft, Initiation pragmatique à la R.M.N. du proton : une expérience d'autoformation basée sur des techniques audiovisuelles et informatiques, Actualité Chimique, Mars 1984, 23-27 (French).

[5] J.P.Rabine, M.Rouillard, D.Cabrol, REMANO - A self-training on N.M.R. spectroscopy prediction of spectra. Programs AP 713 and AP 714 distributed by the SERAPHIM PROJECT. NSF - Science Education.

[6] P.Schatz, RACCOON. Program IB 716 distributed by the SERAPHIM PROJECT. NSF - Science Education.

[7] J-P.Rabine, M.Rouillard, D.Cabrol, F.Dubreuil, Didacticiel de formation à l'analyse des spectres R.M.N. Une méthode respectant la démarche des étudiants. Proceedings of the "Forum E.A.O. 84", September 1984, 79 (French).

[8] S.Papert, Mindstorm, Basic Book, New York (1980).

[9] D.H.Sleeman, R.J.Hendley, ACE : a system which analyses complex explanations, Intelligent tutoring systems, Academic Press Inc, London, 1982 99-118.

[10] R.D.Draper, B.R.Penfold, Nuclear Magnetic Resonance Interpretation with graphics. J.Chem.Educ., vol.61, no.9, Septembre 1984, 789-790.

COMPUTERS IN EDUCATION, F. Lovis and E.D. Tagg (eds.)
Elsevier Science Publishers B.V. (North-Holland)
© IFIP, 1988

TEACHING FILE ORGANISATION METHODS AT A DISTANCE

P.A.LEADBETTER & H.M.ROBINSON

The Open University, Computing Discipline, Faculty of Mathematics, Walton Hall, Milton Keynes. MK6 7AA ENGLAND.

Two of the main problems of teaching file organisation methods in an introductory computing course at degree level are the time available to cover the extensive subject matter and the 'dryness' of the material itself. These problems need to be addressed because, at whatever level a student studies information systems, he will need to have grasped the fundamentals of file organisation as carried out daily in data processing installations. Our aim was to devise teaching materials based on practical exercise work which would overcome the above problems, and provide a sound and understandable exposition for novice computer students.

1. INTRODUCTION

This paper describes the approach taken in the Open University course M205 - Fundamentals of Computing - in order to provide adequate coverage of the file organisation techniques traditionally encountered in commercial data processing. M205 serves as a foundation course in the software aspects of computing and is a prerequisite for the study of courses of a more specific nature.

The course comprises thirty units, divided into 6 blocks, each of 5 units. Each block has a specific theme which is developed in the constituent units, and each unit should consume about 10 hours of student study time. Broadly speaking, the software life cycle and its management are central themes that run through the course as its intellectual and pedagogic framework. Within this framework a top down design methodology for program construction and a study of data structures enables students to develop appropriate solutions to particular problems. The programming language used for the final stage of the software life cycle (that is, implementation) is UCSD Pascal which is supplied to students, along with all Course Team developed software, on floppy disks. The University expects every student to have access to a stand-alone home computing facility, using an industry standard PC.

Our interest lies in Block V, whose theme is Information Systems, which deals with file and database systems. The first three units look at *serial*, *direct* and *index sequential* file organisations, and contain the final significant practical computing work in the course. The last two units of this block explore data modelling and data bases and for a variety of reasons, which need not concern us here, involve no practical computing work.

2. PRACTICAL WORK PRIOR TO BLOCK V

The course entails a significant amount of practical work in the form of practical exercises. For very small problem areas students are expected to provide the whole design and/or implementation of complete programs. For larger problems, especially those later in the course, the students are only expected to complete certain allocated portions of problems and write only part of a design or program which we call a 'program fragment'. These program fragments can then be embedded in the program template supplied on the course disk, provided with each block, to yield an executable program. This approach alleviates the burden of too much mundane coding and also exposes students to dealing with larger problems and solutions.

3. PRACTICAL WORK IN BLOCK V

3.1 Background

This block is the last in which students will be exposed to significant practical work and as such one might expect students to be given fairly considerable practical exercises. The problem we encountered was that of giving the students practical work that was realistic both in terms of complexity and in terms of the study hours allocated to each unit. The notional amount of 10 hours study per unit over a one week period, resulting in 300 hours of work over the 32 week course, constrains the amount of practical work since the student first has to read and assimilate approximately 35 pages of single spaced text. The course, being at the foundation level, is intended for novice computing students: it is most important for the well-being of the students that these 10 hours per unit study periods are not exceeded.

In more detail, we were faced with the problem of practical work associated with the teaching of *serial*, *direct* and *index sequential* file organisations. Serial files, in fact, presented no real problem. The teaching concentrated on serial file concepts through the facilities available in UCSD Pascal and it was natural that the same style of practical work as that used in the rest of the course should be employed. The major problem was posed by direct and index sequential files. We wished to concentrate our teaching on the central issues of *insertion*, *retrieval* and *deletion* within such file organisations methods, rather than the detail of how they may be realised in UCSD Pascal. We quickly realised that, unlike serial files, we could not articulate our teaching in terms of the facilities of UCSD Pascal: the absence of direct support for such files made for a very artificial approach. Attempts to incorporate practical work in this fashion quickly degenerated into a tedious explication of lengthy Pascal code rather than an illumination of the essential features.

3.2 Adopted Strategy

Our strategy for developing practical work, therefore, centred around the idea of using as much common material as possible among all the four practical sessions, while expecting the students to compose very little design or program code. First thoughts turned to the use of a common scenario with the same source data file - in this case, a lady credit broker and her file of customer debtor records. The lack of student development work suggested a number of *simulation* programs, each of which was developed with a similar menu-driven system. In order to test their understanding, each of the simulation runs has a number of self-assessment questions which must be tackled by students, and has answers close on hand. Finally, it was decided that as the processing became more involved (from self-indexing, through hashing to index sequential and finally, to a fully inverted file system) it would no longer be sufficient from a teaching point of view, to have the students just compare the original input file against the final processed output file for each run. They must become involved during the actual processing. Rather than follow sterile annotated diagrams [1] and be involved in the tedium of 'dry run' situations, we recognised that more life could be injected into the learning process if explanatory tracing type comments were generated as the processing proceeds. This strategy was prompted as a result of both authors' face-to-face teaching of this material in various polytechnics and their first hand industrial experience of information systems. In short the educational objectives have to be achieved by making the teaching interesting enough to help overcome the disadvantages suffered by students who are taught at a distance.

3.3 Direct files

The second unit [2], deals with direct files, and describes the techniques of self-indexing and hashing. Previously the practical work had been designed to exhibit and explain certain aspects of the Pascal language; for example, in the manipulation of serial files. It was felt that, the language having been mastered, now was not the time to concentrate on the code or implementation of hashed files, but on the techniques and underlying reasons for choosing a particular organisation. Even though the self-indexing mechanism and its implementation are fairly straightforward, we felt that an important aspect of the practical was to illustrate realistically the *retrieval , insertion* and, in particular, the *deletion* of records. Once the groundwork of such file maintenance activities had been practically demonstrated in the very simplest of situations, then students would be able to appreciate the rationale of similar operations in hashed files and, later, in index sequential files.

As a vehicle for demonstrating the techniques for different file organisations, students were introduced to a credit broker scenario where the initial requirement of immediate access was to a data file taking up only 50% of the available storage space. Having completed study of the self-indexed system, the credit broker then decides she needs a hashed file organisation. This is implemented within the same high level menu-based program control structure, providing the same facilities as for self-indexing, using the same data file, storage area and variable names. Both systems are as identical as possible, with the exception of the method of file organisation. The only significant differences being those that are important to the teaching.

3.4 Index sequential files

By the time we reach the index sequential practical work in Unit 3 [3], our credit broker decides in favour of an index sequential organisation. Again, for the reasons mentioned above, the implementation is as close to the previous two systems as possible, making use of the *same data file*(supplied on the block disk), *storage area* and *variable names*. Apart from the different file organisation method, the only modifications are extensions to the top-level menu and inclusion of extra variable names, to accommodate more complex processing. This more complex processing takes the place of relatively straightforward numerical transformations as used previously, and involves a multi-level index file organisation. In order to make sure that the students will be able to understand and follow the running of this *simulation* program; it generates *explanatory tracing comments* during the required processing of debtor records against the supplied test data file.

3.5 Inverted files

The final practical exercise again comprises a simulation program that demonstrates a fully inverted file system and contains explanatory tracing comments as the processing proceeds. It also is a menu-based system (similar to the aforementioned three systems), but has three levels of menu instead of one, to accommodate the type of query that such a system can handle. The supplied data file has to be different from that used earlier, because of the difficulty of creating an inverted index for each and every secondary key (field) in the file.

4. STUDENT TASKS

4.1 Self-indexing

In this practical section the students run a *simulation* program and are not required to design or code any programs. The task undertaken is the maintenance of the credit broker's customer account file.

The students are instructed to copy the self-indexing simulation program and the customer accounts file to their user disk, and hence, obtain a printer listing of both files. They can then refer to the source text file of the program code and may read a brief description of the procedures in the course unit. After compiling and executing the source text file, students are confronted by a screen menu which has seven options:

Menu for the Simulation of a Self Indexing file system

Choose an option in the range 1 - 7
Note - file must be opened prior to access

<1>	Open file
<2>	Retrieve record
<3>	Insert record
<4>	Delete record
<5>	Display file
<6>	Print file
<7>	Close file

Figure 4.1 Screen contents for top level menu.

After choosing option 1 to open a file and being prompted for a file name, the students are then expected to *retrieve*, *insert* and *delete* several records of their own choice, keeping a record of the outcome of each of their operations. On completion of their file processing operations, the students then use the print menu option 6 to obtain a revised listing of the account file and are told to compare it with the original so that they understand exactly how and why the program works. Their next task is to answer a range of comprehensive questions and so exhibit their understanding of the self-indexing program. If the students' own choice of test data for this practical exercise did not help them answer the questions written in the unit text, then we suggest that they re-execute the self-indexing program, but this time with a more comprehensive range of data and operations.

4.2 Hashing

In this practical exercise, we revert temporarily to the accustomed format of using program templates. The students have been previously exposed to the theory of hashing and overflow in the text of the unit preceding the practical exercise section. Their task here is to write and insert two missing procedures in the *program template*

supplied by the Course Team. Both of the two procedures use the same hash function and progressive overflow technique and must take into account logically deleted records. Before embarking on this task, however, the students are asked to copy the program template file and the data file to their user disc, print them out and study them. They must then answer a number of assessment questions which should help them understand the program template and assist them in writing the two missing procedures. The screen menu contents are similar to Figure 4.1, apart from a different header line.

The students must now design and code the two missing procedures, insert them in the template program and then compile and execute the completed program with data of their own choice. As in the previous practical, they are told to make a note of the record operations that they undertake as the running of the simulation program proceeds, and on completion, to print the updated version of the account file. The difference between this and the original account file should be solely as a result of the inclusion of successful hashing procedures run with their chosen data. If necessary, or simply for comparison purposes, the students can access an *answer* file which provides a solution with the two missing procedures.

4.3 Index sequential

In this practical session the students run a simulation program that generates *explanatory tracing comments* during the program's processing cycles. There are no design or coding exercises in this session - only a number of questions to test the students' understanding of the way in which this index sequential system has been implemented. The top level menu has been extended, and now contains 10 options which can be seen in Figure 4.2.

The students are asked to copy the index sequential source text file and the two data files containing the first and second level indexes to their user disk. They then obtain a printer listing of the source text file and may refer to the brief descriptions of each of the procedures as described in the unit. There is also a diagrammatic representation of the multi-level file organisation in the unit, which shows the relationships between each of the indexes and the buckets of records in the customer account data file. As previously, they compile and execute the source code and on seeing the screen menu, print the original data file and then retrieve, insert, delete and update several records of their own choice. As each operation proceeds, the students follow screen-based explanatory comments that are generated at each stage of the processing. These comments should act as a guide to the processing cycle, and thereby help the student understand exactly how and why the program works. Typical commentary for a record *insertion* and *deletion* can be seen in Figures 4.2 and 4.3 respectively.

Menu for the Simulation of an Index Sequential file system

Choose an option in the range 1 - 0
Note that files must be opened prior to access

     <1>   Open files
     <2>   Retrieve record
     <3>   Insert record
     <4>   Delete record
     <5>   Update record
     <6>   Display first level index
     <7>   Display second level index
     <8>   Display data file
     <9>   Print data file
     <0>   Close data file and terminate run

Choice is ? **3**
Inserting one record
account number (1....9999) ? **4247**
searching first level index, accno = 4247
    4247 > 3133 at flindtb[0]
    4247 <= 5693 at flindtb[1], end of first level index search
searching second level index, accno = 4247, bucket no = 1
    4247 > 4244 at slindtb[3]
    4247 <= 4737 at slindtb[4], end of second level index search
searching the data file, accno = 4247, bucket no = 4
    acctfile^.accountno = 4432, record no = 40, end of bucket
search
shuffling down   0 from location 48 to location 49
shuffling down   0 from location 47 to location 48
shuffling down   0 from location 46 to location 47
shuffling down 4737 from location 45 to location 46
shuffling down 4640 from location 44 to location 45
shuffling down 4579 from location 43 to location 44
shuffling down 4568 from location 42 to location 43
shuffling down 4530 from location 41 to location 42
shuffling down 4432 from location 40 to location 41

account number = 4247
      name = ? **Mr Leadbetter**
      balance = ? **100.40**

Record inserted

Figure 4.2 Example commentary for a record insertion

In the example of Figure 4.2, after choosing to insert a customer record with account number 4247, the first, and then the second level indexes are searched, which leads us to bucket number 4 in the data file. In order to maintain the sequential order of this file, record number 4247 needs to be inserted in record location 40, but record number 4432 already occupies this position. Record 4737 is shuffled downwards into the first local overflow area (location 46), and so each of the preceding records are shuffled one place down to accommodate the record insertion in its rightful place.

A similar process takes place in the deletion example of Figure 4.3, except that once the record has been deleted from the bucket, each of the succeeding records must be shuffled up one location. Having run the simulation program a number of times, the students are then asked to test their understanding of the system by attempting to answer some self-assessment questions.

Menu for the Simulation of an Index Sequential file system

Choose an option in the range 1 - 0
Note that files must be opened prior to access

     <1>   Open files
     <2>   Retrieve record
     <3>   Insert record
     <4>   Delete record
     <5>   Update record
     <6>   Display first level index
     <7>   Display second level index
     <8>   Display data file
     <9>   Print data file
     <0>   Close data file and terminate run

Choice is ? **4**
Deleting one record
account number (1....9999) ? **5430**
searching first level index, accno = 5430
    5430 > 3133 at flindtb[0]
    5430 <= 5693 at flindtb[1], end of first level index search
searching second level index, accno = 5430, bucket no = 1
    5430 > 4244 at slindtb[3]
    5430 > 4737 at slindtb[4]
    5430 <= 5693 at slindtb[5], end of second level index search
searching the data file, accno = 5430, bucket no = 5
    5430 > 4765, record no = 50
    5430 > 4875, record no = 51
    acctfile^.accountno = 5430, record no = 52, end of bucket
search
shuffling up 5431 from location 53 to location 52
shuffling up 5432 from location 54 to location 53
shuffling up 5693 from location 55 to location 54
shuffling up   0 from location 56 to location 55

Record deleted

Figure 4.3 Example commentary for a record deletion

4.4 Inverted files

As mentioned before, we depart from our credit broker scenario. A data file containing a number of book details is supplied. There are four fields in each record and for each field an ordered index file is supplied.

The simulation program file, book data file and four index files are all copied to the student's user disc. The student lists the source code file, may refer to the procedure descriptions in the unit, and then compiles and executes the program. He will then test the program with simple and compound queries of his own choice, follow the screen commentary and finally, answer a number of questions regarding the program.   One example of the output generated from the query "Do Collins publish any biography books costing 10.95 ?" is:

Top level - Menu for the Simulation of an Inverted file system

Choose an option in the range 1 - 8
Note - file must be opened prior to query

<1>   Open files
<2>   Display file
<3>   Print file
<4>   Display indexes
<5>   Print indexes
<6>   Query database
<7>   Close files
<8>   Help

Choice is ? **6**

2nd level - Query menu. Choose an option in the range 1 - 6

<1>   Book name
<2>   Publisher
<3>   Class
<4>   Price
<5>   End of query
<6>   Help

Query menu choice is ? **2**

3rd level - Query menu to select Publisher

<1>   Collins
<2>   Longman
<3>   Pan

Choice is ? **1**

The following data records were selected: 0 4 7 8 10 14 16 19

2nd level - Query menu. Choose an option in the range 1 - 6

<1>   Book name
<2>   Publisher
<3>   Class
<4>   Price
<5>   End of query
<6>   Help

Query menu choice is ? **3**

3rd level - Query menu to select Class

<1>   Biography
<2>   Fiction
<3>   Cookery
<4>   Sport

Choice is ? **1**

The following data records were selected: 8 13 14 15 16

Merging records from the previous selection: 0 4 7 8 10 14 16 19
with records from the current selection: 8 13 14 15 16
give the intersected records: 8 14 16

2nd level - Query menu. Choose an optioon in the range 1 - 6

<1>   Book name
<2>   Publisher
<3>   Class
<4>   Price
<5>   End of query
<6>   Help

Query menu choice is ? **4**

3rd level - Query menu to select Price

<1>   5.95
<2>   6.25
<3>   7.50
<4>   9.95
<5>   10.95
<6>   11.50

Choice is ? **5**

The following data records were selected: 6 14 15 16

Merging records from the previous selection: 8 14 16
with records from the current selection: 6 14 15 16
give the intersected records: 14 16

2nd level - Query menu. Choose an option in the range 1 - 6

<1>   Book name
<2>   Publisher
<3>   Class
<4>   Price
<5>   End of query
<6>   Help

Query menu choice is ? **5**

The following records were selected

| 14: | Nancy Fordmit | Collins | Biography | 10.95 |
| 16: | Alan Turning | Collins | Biography | 10.95 |

Figure 4.4   An example run of the inverted file system

The top level menu has eight options. Option 6 'Query database' generates a second level menu of six options and each of the first four choices gives a third level menu listing the various possibilities within each index. It can be seen from Figure 4.4 that whenever a query involving multiple secondary keys is made, the first two indexes are searched and sets formed of successful hits. A set interaction operation is performed on these two sets producing a third result set. If necessary, other indexes are searched producing a new set which is then merged with the previous result set to form the final output set. In Figure 4.4 there are two books 'Nancy Fordmit' and 'Alan Turning' that satisfy the query objectives.

5. SUMMARY

In the early and middle parts of the course, the composition of simple, small programs and/or the use of program templates have provided the basis around which most practical activities have been centred. In the final practical exercises of the course, the use of a different teaching vehicle has been employed - that of simulation programs. Four have been written as demonstrations of self-indexed, hashed, index sequential and fully inverted file systems. All four programs have the same menu-based control structure. The first three use a common data file. The third and fourth programs contain built-in explanatory tracing messages to help in the educational aspects of teaching at a distance.

It is our contention that this hands-on experience of small simulation systems, with built-in commentary, provides a clear and understandable exposition of some of the most important concepts of file organisation in data processing. This approach is dictated by the time constraints imposed on student study periods and by the quintessential nature of the material.

The course, which contains these materials, runs for the first time in 1988, and only at the end of its first year will we be able to judge whether our approach in using these simulation programs has been successful.

ACKNOWLEDGEMENTS

We would like to express our thanks to Gordon Davies (M205 Course Team Chairman) for his advice and support and also to Adam Gawronski of the Academic Computing Service within the Open University for his help in implementing the above systems.

REFERENCES

[1] Martin, J., Computer Data-Base Organisation (Prentice-Hall, Englewood Cliffs, N.J., 1977)
[2] M205 Fundamentals of Computing, Block V Information Systems, Unit 2 Direct Files, The Open University Press 1988.
[3] M205 Fundamentals of Computing, Block V Information Systems, Unit 3 Indexed Files, The Open University Press 1988.

COMPUTERS IN EDUCATION, F. Lovis and E.D. Tagg (eds.)
Elsevier Science Publishers B.V. (North-Holland)
© IFIP, 1988

TEACHING INFORMATION RETRIEVAL SKILLS: HOW INSTRUCTIONAL METAPHORS INFLUENCE THE EFFECTIVENESS OF INTERACTION

Frances M.T. Brazier

Henk C. Trimp

Department of Cognitive Psychology
Vrije Universiteit, De Boelelaan 1115
1081 HV Amsterdam, the Netherlands

Centre for Educational Geography
Vrije Universiteit, De Boelelaan 1105
1081 HV Amsterdam, the Netherlands

The optimal use of computer systems depends upon the quality of interaction. This in turn is influenced by instruction and interface variables. Theoretical and empirical methods are used (1) to compare the effectiveness of the use of a metaphor in instruction concerning two information retrieval systems and (2) to determine the influence of interface variables on the interaction.

1. INTRODUCTION

The number of programs with which students are confronted, increases continually. Psychological variables no doubt influence the process of interaction [1,2] with which individuals engage, but to what extent is the quality of the interaction influenced by instruction and interface variables?

Payne [3] emphasizes the importance of the analysis of the mapping required between the actions required in a known situation and those required in an automated situation. Waern [4] indicates the necessity of similarity in metaphors at the level of actions, for instruction purposes. The quality of the instruction(al) sequence may be expected to affect the quality of the image users form of the system with which they are confronted (the mental model).

The influence of metacommunication on the quality of the mental model has been discussed in Van der Veer [5]. The language itself is only one element which characterizes the interaction. Information on the state of the system, for example, can influence the interaction to a large extent.

In this paper, the effects of instruction, based on a metaphor, in two systems, on the quality of the models users form and on the strategies employed, will be addressed on the basis of both theoretical and empirical data.

2. INFORMATION HANDLING SYSTEM

Two information handling packages which have found their way into the British educational system have been employed within this study. Both systems were designed for educational use, to provide children and teachers with a relatively powerful tool for information handling activities. QUEST [6] is a command-driven system, GRASS [7] a menu-driven system.

The knowledge that the systems had been designed for the same purposes, formed the basis for this project. The conceptual worlds [8] with which users are confronted are therefore comparable; the systems were designed for (nearly) identical (1) tasks, (2) systems, and (3) user groups. The human-machine interfaces are, however, outwardly totally different. Theoretical con-

sideration of the extent of this difference was the first step taken in the comparison of these two systems.

3. THEORETICAL COMPARISON OF GRASS AND QUEST - TASK ANALYSIS

Moran's [9,10] Command Language Grammar provided a framework for the theoretical task analysis of the two systems. The four levels of interaction defined in this grammar: task level, semantic level, syntactic level and key-stroke level, were elaborated and compared. At the highest level, task level, the systems were completely identical (the use of graphical forms of representation and statistical manipulations were not considered in this project). The explicitation of the tasks distinguished, necessary for the purpose of comparison, provided a basis for analysis at the following level, the level of semantics. The elements and structures employed for the execution of the tasks, namely the selection, retrieval and sorting of data, were specified at this level. The objects, attributes and actions involved in both systems were again identical. An example of part of the results of the analysis at this level is shown in fig. 1. The object *file* has the attributes *file name, header*. The object *condition* (logical expression) has as attributes *a truth value, operators* (relational, logical, numerical and alpha-numerical), and *variables* (attributes of fields and information).

Object	Attribute
FILE	- file name
	- header
FIELD	- description
	- field name
CONDITION	- truth value
	- operators (relational, logical, (alpha-) numerical
	- variables (attributes of fields information)

Fig. 1. An example of the semantic level of the task analysis

The differences between the two systems became obvious at the level concerning the translation of the semantics into syntax. The use of the command name *print* for the selection of fields (hence *not* for sending something to the printer or screen), is an example of a semantic conflict which can occur at syntactic level. The use of the logical operator *Or* for the union of sets in a condition, is another idiosyncratic example of semantic origin, found in QUEST.

The most striking differences between the two systems concern the form of interaction with the system, the visible part of the interaction. At syntactic level, the actual (sequences of) commands/menu-options involved in the execution of an action, are defined. In GRASS, the execution of an action involves the presentation of a series of menus from which an option must be chosen. The specification of the contents of a field is, for example, requested as a result of one of the menu-choices. In QUEST, in contrast, the specification of actions occurs directly through the execution of commands. The *values* command in QUEST provides an overview of the state of the system (unnecessary in GRASS). The syntax of the QUEST-commands is predefined and quite rigorous, but consistent.

The lowest level, key-stroke level, is the level at which the physical interaction is defined. Not only the functions of keys are specified, but also the function of switches, knobs, etc. GRASS and QUEST differ considerably at this level.

4. EMPIRICAL COMPARISON

Given the similarities and differences described above, empirical comparison was warranted. The practical consequences of learning to work with both systems were examined by integrating instruction and exercise into a course on the use of information technology in Geography education.

The effectivity of the instruction was examined. Observation of the difficulties students (in principle, novice users) encountered and the quality of the image the students formed of the systems (their mental models), were considered.

4.1 Method

(i) Subjects. Twenty-two teacher training college students majoring in Geography participated in the study; participation was obligatory. The students were divided into two comparable groups on the basis of intelligence scores concerning spatial ability and analogies.

(ii) Procedure. Both groups of students were confronted with both systems. The sequence of confrontation differed. In the first phase of the experiment, Group I learned to work with GRASS, Group II with QUEST. In the second phase, Group I worked with QUEST, Group II with GRASS.
In both phases of the experiment (a) instruction, (b) training, and (c) tests were administered.

a. Instruction. The instruction the students received consisted of two parts: (1) a general introduction on databases and (2) demonstration and explanation of the two database programs used in this project, GRASS and QUEST. The general introduction was given to the whole group once (in the first phase of the experiment), the demonstration and explanation were given twice in each phase: once for the group of students being taught QUEST and once for the group being taught GRASS.

General introduction. The use of databases in society was the first topic considered in the introduction: mailing lists, personnel

administration, public databases such as Viditel, Prestel, etc. From that moment on, a metaphor was used to illustrate the structure of a database: the *card filing system*. During the course of their studies, students all make some use of the Institute's Resource Centre's catalogue. This catalogue consists of a hand-operated system of title descriptions with two entries: *alphabetical* (titles and authors) and *systematic* (subject matter area and subdivisions of subject matter areas). Consideration was given to the fact that one of the two entries has to be chosen in order to look up an article. The choice of the entry used depends on the accuracy of the retrieval specification. If the author and/or the title of a publication is known the alphabetical entry is chosen; if one or more publications on a certain subject are the object of search the systematic entry is most appropriate.

The basic concepts of file organisation were reviewed. The card on which the details of a publication are listed is the unit of research: a *record*. Each element of information on the card, for example, the title of the publication, is a characteristic: a *field*. A search operation is based on a known field (for example, a title or subject) to find other field value(s) of one or more records (for example the book index number). The use of an electronic file was described on the basis of assumptions. Each field in a record can be used for searching purposes. Whereas at least three cards (for title, author, one or more subjects) are needed for each publication in the hand-operated system, an electronic file has only one copy of each publication.

Finally, the possibility to substitute 'publication', as the object of search, by any other arbitrary unit, was explained. A second metaphor was shortly employed in this context: the table. Within geographical literature and school books, the table is a form of presentation often used. In this case, the rows (most often) represent a record and the columns a field, see table 1.
As (1) the table is closely related to the structure of the electronic database, as often presented to the user, and (2) searching within

Table 1: The table metaphor, used shortly during instruction

field record			
	population figure	population density	GNP
the Netherlands			
Belgium			
etc.			

a table can be easily compared to searching within a database program, the table can be seen as an applicable metaphor.

Demonstration and explanation. One microcomputer, a monitor (for the teacher) and a large screen (for the students) were used for the demonstration. The data file employed for this purpose contained information at ward-level from a census in the Greater London Council. The tasks for which information retrieval systems can be utilized, were covered systematically. The sequence of instruction was based on the level of complexity of retrieval specifications, starting with the most simple form of interaction.

Each retrieval specification (known as a 'query' in QUEST, and initiated by 'search data' in GRASS) was explained. The relation between the retrieval specification and the steps needed actually to retrieve the sought data, was closely examined. The students followed the process as it was being described on the screen in front of the class. The sequence of instruction was predefined and consisted of

1. finding a characteristic of a given unit: What percentage of houses is in residential ownership in the ward Camden?,

2. finding one or more records with a given characteristic: Which wards belong to the Inner City?

3. finding one or more records with two given characteristics (requiring an intersection): In which wards in the Inner City do more than 10% of the households have more than one person per room?

4. finding a record with the highest value for a given characteristic (sorting): Which ward has the highest percentage of male unemployment?

5. finding a relation between two characteristics: Is there a relation between the percentage of unemployed and the percentage of households without a car? (searching and sorting).

Each exercise was covered completely, including the steps needed to display the relevant data on the screen (the PRINT command in QUEST, the option 'DISPLAY RECORDS' in GRASS). The demonstration took approximately 25 minutes in total, independent of the system.

b. Training. Having received instruction, the students were given 22 exercises to complete individually. A timetable was made for supervised access to the computers in the computer laboratory. Completion of the exercises was considered a sufficient condition for mastery of the system. The time required for completion was recorded. Incorrect answers to exercises were marked as such by the supervisor, in between sessions. Students were required to correct mistakes at the beginning of the next session, before continuing. The supervisor was present during all sessions and available for answering questions. The metaphor of the card filing system was used consequently as the basis for response. Answers were most often return questions on the meaning of what the student had just attempted, or on the meaning of the question posed in the exercise. What do you know? What do you want to know? How can you let the system know what you mean?

The 22 exercises were divided into 3 sets, each set pertaining to a different domain. The first set was on volcanoes (name, area, height, status, etc), the second on horses (race, height, colour, strength, etc). The exercises were of the same types as those presented during instruction, with the exception of those concerning the discovery of relations. All important forms of interaction were thus considered. The students received an overview of the structure of the domain with each set of exercises.

One of the major obstacles in learning to work with command-driven systems is the necessity to know the required commands and syntax before being able to do anything. A one page overview of the command syntax was given to QUEST users. GRASS users were not provided with additional material as the syntax of the menus was obvious.

c. Tests
Mental model test. The mental model students formed of the systems was investigated using the mental model test. This test was designed in accordance with the methodology described in Van der Veer [11], and contains two parts: the representation test and the knowledge test. The primary purpose of the representation test is to obtain information about the representation the user has formed of the system. The user is asked to explain how the system works at different levels. The way in which this is instigated is by asking the user to provide descriptions for two types of users: (1) a college student who has *never* worked with a computer system, but who has had experience with card filing systems, and (2) a college student who *has* had experience with both types of card filing system. The exact formulation of the first task is shown in fig. 2.

---

1. Explain to a fellow-student who has had experience with the card-index system in the school library, but who has *never worked with a computer*, how to use QUEST to retrieve information from a file and how to change the order of the data.

Use the rest of this page and write in telegram style and/or with sketches and/or diagrams, etc.

Fig. 2. The first task in the representation test

The second part of the mental model test, the knowledge test, will not be considered in this context.

Experimental task. In the experimental task the students are asked to solve a few geographical questions concerning the city of Leeds, by making use of an information retrieval system. This task was only assigned in the first phase of the experiment, after completion of the mental model test. The questions related to the distribution of ethnic minorities in the city. The datafile consisted of data on 18 variables for each of the 33 wards of Leeds, see fig. 3.

The first question was relatively simple, requiring retrieval of the average values of (1) the percentage of inhabitants born in the New Commonwealth (NEWCOM), (2) the percentage of households with more than one person per room (CROWD) and (3) the percentage of households living in a residence with more than 7 rooms (SPACE). In the second question, the students were asked to find out which wards had a more than average percentage of inhabitants from the New Commonwealth, and to shade these wards on the map (spatial distribution). The hypothetical (positive) relation between the distribution of ethnic minorities and 'over-populated' residences, was the topic addressed in the third question. The students were asked to find out which of the wards with a high percentage of ethnic minorities (the result of the previous question) had a more than average percentage of households with more than one person per room, and which did not. Question four concerned the hypothetical (negative) relation between the distribution of ethnical minorities and large residences. The students are asked to test this hypothesis without any further instructions on how to do so.
The interaction between the user and the system was registered on video, the students' answers were written on paper. The protocols of the interaction were extracted from the tapes to enable further analysis.

4.2. Results

The effect of instruction on the learning process can be judged by examining the observations made during the training process, the time involved in mastering the systems, the representations the students formed of the system, and the protocols registered.

(i) Training
Time. The average times required for the completion of the three sets of exercises were identical for both groups. For both groups, it holds that the time required in Phase 2 was significantly shorter than in Phase 1.

Observations. The number of times the supervisor provided assistance differed for the two groups. The QUEST group in the first phase of the experiment required the most assistance. Both groups, however, were confronted with the same initial

Description of the data-file Leeds

This file contains data (census 1981) on the wards in the English town of Leeds. For purposes of comparison Leeds has been included as a unit (averages!). (This means that Leeds is a "record").

Fieldnames	Description	Fieldnames	Description
WARD	ward identifier (code)	TOTRES	total number of residents
NAME	name of the ward	NOWCBATH	% permanent households lacking inside WC or bath
AREA	areas in hectares	NOCAR	% households without a car
MALES	total number of males	CROWD	% permanent households with >1 person/room
FEMALES	total number of females	SPACE	% permanent households with >7 rooms
MIGR1Y	% residents who were 1 year migrants	PHOUSEH	total number of permanent households
MIGRWA	% residents who were working migrants	ADULTS	total number of adult residents
NEWCOM	% residents born in New Commonwealth	MUNEMPL	% male adult residents 'seeking work'
NOTUK	% residents not born in UK	FUNEMPL	% female adult residents 'seeking work'

Fig. 3. Description of the Leeds datafile

difficulties in encoding the problem into terms which could be employed in the information retrieval system. A few examples should clarify this point, see fig. 4.

(1)	print mikeno
(2)	print names
(3)	query country ident "Guatemala"
	print gt 4000

Fig. 4. Examples of encoding problems

The difficulties encountered emphasize the difference in the problem domain in which the student is used to solving problems as such, and the task domain imposed by the information retrieval system. The students are used to referring to a volcano by its name, the volcano is known by its name and is not seen as a volcano with a tag on. This causes the confusion which results in commands such as *print mikeno* instead of *print name ident "mikeno"*. The use of plural forms of fieldnames was also encountered more than once in the specification of the fields to be viewed, as in *print names*. Having created a set, the most obvious way of finding out which volcanoes are higher than a certain height, is by going through them again and looking at certain fields. The translation to system commands was not automatically understood. *query country ident "Guatemala"*, *print gt 4000* is a good example of what can go wrong. The correct sequence entails the use of an intersection in the retrieval specification in which both limitations are specified: *query country ident "Guatemala" and height gt 4000*. The fields to be viewed can then be specified with a *print* command.

The thought processes observed above were just as obvious for GRASS users. In that system, however, users were often faced with a screen full of menu options which meant very little to them. The sequence was frequently stopped abruptly by the escape key.

In both systems, the formulation of logical expressions caused problems, as did the combination of complex statements and other restrictions. In fig. 5 a number of such complex queries are displayed.

(1)	query status sub ("dormant" or "believed extinct") gt 4000
(2)	query area sub "Africa" and status "believed extinct"
(3)	query colour sub "BL" and "BR" and "CH"

Fig. 5. Examples of problems encountered in complex queries

It is assumed that the system knows that the only numerical value must refer to the height of the volcano in *query status sub ("dormant" or "believed extinct") gt 4000*. Again, the necessity of the use of an intersection in which the field name *height* is included, has not been realized. The omission of a relation (between status and "believed extinct") in *query area sub "Africa" and status "believed extinct"* is another example of assuming the system is capable of understanding more than is provided. The difference between the logical operators *AND* and *OR* caused many a problem. Black, brown and charcoal horses in natural language cannot be translated as *query colour sub "BL" and "BR" and "CH"*. The correct formulation is *query colour sub ("BL" or "BR" or "CH")*. The confusion was made even greater in GRASS by the names of the entries: *add to the search (OR)*, which is the first entry encountered in the menu, followed by *narrow down the search (AND)*.

Typing mistakes and syntax errors (missing brackets, quotation marks), were made frequently, especially in QUEST. In GRASS, strings were accidentally ended with a space character, causing problems which could not be traced (a space is not identifiable as such in the retrieval specification displayed).

(ii) Mental model test. The responses to the two questions posed in the representation test, were diverse. Not only did the didactic quality of the explanations vary, but also the level at which they were formulated.

Levels of representation. Moran's four levels were employed to analyse the data thus acquired. Reference to the tasks involved, (selection, sorting and presentation of data), were classified as descriptions at task-level. The inclusion of information on objects, attributes and actions (records, fields, relations, retrieval specifications), was seen to refer to a semantic-level representation of the system. Descriptions in which the exact commands and/or menu choices needed to complete certain (sub-)actions were specified, were classified as syntactic-level descriptions. Specification of the keys and switches involved, indicated key-stroke level representation.

The assumption behind the classification of the descriptions is that the student will, in at least one of the two situations, try and provide a more general view of the system - if the mental model the student has formed is complete enough to do so. All students have some knowledge at syntax level. They have been trained to work with systems and have completed the exercises satisfactorily. Knowledge at a higher level, however, is more general and requires abstraction from the concrete experience gained. This knowledge is most likely more transferable than knowledge at a lower level.

The major difference between the two questions in both phases of the experiment is that none of the students provided a description at task level for a colleague with information retrieval system experience. QUEST subjects provided more complete descriptions of the system in both phases. The number of descriptions which included a syntactic element was also greater.

Use of metaphor. Further examination of the descriptions the students provided shows that QUEST subjects were more inclined to refer to the use of card-filing systems and/or libraries. The exact frequencies are shown in table 2.

Table 2: The number of descriptions which included references to the metaphor

	Phase 1	Phase 2
QUEST	10 (11)	2 (11)
GRASS	6 (11)	3 (10)

10 of the 11 QUEST-subjects referred to the metaphor in their descriptions, as did 6 of the 11 GRASS subjects.

The use of the metaphor decreased in the second phase of the experiment. 3 of the 10 subjects who had initially worked with QUEST (and thus worked with GRASS in the second round), and 2 of the 11 subjects in the other group, referred to the metaphor.

(iii) Experimental Task. Both the domain and the sequence of the questions in the task are comparable to those used during instruction. The first two questions concern specific retrieval specifications, using one dimension at a time. Although the sequence of retrieval specifications (strategies) differed between students, the distribution of the strategies between the two systems was identical. 4 of the 11 subjects considered each question individually (at least in the interaction), re-typing the same retrieval specification (name = leeds) for each variable. The rest of the subjects showed that they had noticed the relation between the three sub-questions by entering the retrieval specification only once.

Only one strategy was used for the second question, namely the relevant retrieval specification, and selection of the names of the associated wards to be displayed. These wards were then marked on the map provided. Both of the first two questions were completed correctly by all subjects.

The third and fourth questions concerned the relation between two characteristics of the wards. In the third question, the completion of the task required the use of retrieval specifications. The strategy demonstrated during instruction in which an intersection was used, was employed by 9 of the 22 students. 12 students used only one of the dimensions known in their retrieval specification, determining the value on the second dimension after the relevant records had been presented. One student did not limit the number of records viewed by defining a retrieval specification, but examined the records by viewing all 34.

The fourth question differs greatly from the previous three in that the students are asked to *test* a relation between two characteristics. It is worth noting that the method of sorting on one dimension and then (visually) comparing the values presented (demonstrated during instruction), was used by only one subject with success. Most (15 out of 22) students limited their comparison to the six wards found in question 2. The general preference shown in question 3, for selecting records on the basis of one dimension instead of two, was also found to hold here. The strategy employed entailed: (1) selecting the wards with a more than average % inhabitants from the New Commonwealth, (2) viewing the value of % large residences (SPACE), (3) comparing these values with the average for Leeds (found in question 1), and (4) counting both the number of wards with a *more* than average and a *less* than average % large residences. The result was that 3 wards had more, and 3 wards less than the average % large residences. The conclusion of most subjects was that the hypothesis should be rejected.

Only five subjects considered more than 6 wards in their solution. The method known to geographers of plotting results on a map to discover spatial associations, was used by only one subject. By marking the wards with relatively large percentages of (1) inhabitants from the New Commonwealth and (2) large residences, on the map provided for question 2, a marginal overlap in the transition zone of Leeds (the zone between the deprived centre and the more prosperous north) was found.

4.3. Discussion

Contrary to the current assumption that menu-driven systems are easier for novice users to learn, both in time and in effort (e.g. [12]), than command-driven systems, we have found the time needed to master the systems to be identical. The fact that supervision was available is no doubt an important factor which should not be forgotten, but nevertheless the initial complexity of the command-driven system (QUEST) did not result in longer learning times. Both groups needed assistance in the interpretation of the tasks, independent of the system with which they were confronted. The card filing system metaphor was used consequently in the assistance provided. The mapping of task domains, from the task domain in which students were used to working, to a task domain in which the form of interaction is determined by the system, required time. The translation of task domains was not necessary in the second phase of the experiment, resulting in shorter learning times. The amount of assistance required decreased accordingly.

In the mental model test, QUEST users provided a more complete description of the system than did the users of GRASS. The exclusion of task-level descriptions in the second question, proves that the differentiation required was achieved. The frequency of reference to the metaphor also differed between the systems, especially in the first phase of the experiment. The users initially confronted with QUEST, referred to the card-filing system (or library) more often than their counterparts, even in the second phase of the experiment. The similarity the students experienced between learning environments may well be the cause of this. In normal card-filing systems, the student decides what to do and when. In command-driven systems, the user is fully responsible for the interaction, for the initiation of all forms of interaction. In menu-driven systems, the user is given a more passive role: the system decides which actions are appropriate and when. The comparison with the real-life metaphor of a card-filing system is more difficult to conceive.

Examination of the strategies used in the experimental task and their relation to the applicability of the metaphor, is warranted. The strategy most often employed in the last two questions, involved the retrieval of a number of records, on the basis of one dimension, and the examination of the second dimension, once the data were presented. This is actually what probably happens in hand-operated card filing systems. The first three questions were relatively simple, the fourth required more precise analysis, using extra information available within the system. Only five subjects made use of this information, whilst only one subject thought of using other available information (the map). There are a number of possible reasons for this self-imposed restriction: (1) *The halo-effect* of the questions: the way in which questions 2 to 4 are posed suggests the necessity of a 'narrowing down' approach, in contrast to the necessity of broadening the field of interest for question 4. (2) *The card-filing system metaphor*: the metaphor does not provide the support needed for the required data manipulation within the field of Geography, possibly resulting in a limited scope of search. (3) '*Imprisonment*' *by the system*: working extensively with a system for a period of time narrows the scope of attention, excluding consideration of external sources.

5. INSTRUCTION BASED ON METAPHORS - conclusions

Metaphors are used in instruction to stimulate transfer of prior knowledge. The discussion between the authors of this paper focused on the following question: *Did the card-filing metaphor contribute to positive or negative transfer?* In other words, *Did reference to the card-filing system facilitate or hinder learning to work with information retrieval systems?*

Transfer research [17,4] suggests that positive transfer will arise when the actions to be performed (and not only the prevailing goal and conditions) in the new situation are similar to those in the earlier situation. Transfer will slow down learning when goals and conditions are similar, but the required actions are different.

The students who participated in this experiment were familiar with (1) the card filing system and (2) the problem domain used in both the initial instruction and the experimental task (both concerned spatial distribution in urban areas). Reference to the metaphor in the representation test, especially by QUEST subjects, shows it was somehow integrated in the mental model formed. This is also reflected in the results of the experimental task, in which a preference for a translatable sequence of actions was shown. In the more complex task (question 4), this strategy no longer sufficed. The students, however, continued to apply card-filing system strategies. Negative transfer caused by discrepancies between the two types of tasks, is found. This is most likely due to the fact that the card-filing system is not meant to support comparisons of large sets of data, but to support literature search.

The use of metaphors in teaching information retrieval requires (1) similarity of actions, (2) familiarity and (3) validity in the problem-domain. The first two criteria were met reasonably, the third only partially. The experimental task brought a few problems to light, even though it has been adapted to fit into the experimental set-up.

Does this imply that the use of metaphors in teaching information retrieval systems should depend on the quality of the metaphor as a metaphor for information retrieval, or on the specific types of tasks for which the systems are to be employed?

The authors differ in opinion as to the function of teaching information retrieval.

If the aim is to teach Geography, the choice of metaphor should depend on the domain in which the system is to be employed. The table metaphor used shortly during instruction meets the second and third criteria in combination. The students are well acquainted with the form of notation and are accustomed to using it in their field of work. The combination of criteria may be the determining factor for the applicability of metaphors.

If the aim to is teach the more general skill of information retrieval, however, this should be done as such. The card filing system is certainly valid in the *domain* of information retrieval, similar to the goals, actions and conditions required, and it scores highly on familiarity. The domain in question is namely that of information retrieval and not the domain of the data stored. The use of the information found for further processing, may well prove the necessity of other (types) of metaphors. This has little to do with information retrieval, and can therefore be addressed in a different phase.

REFERENCES

[1] Jos J. Beishuizen and Frances M.T. Brazier, Search strategies in internal-external memories, *Proceedings of the Third European Conference on Cognitive Ergonomics*, September 15-19, 1986.

[2] Jos J. Beishuizen, Leren opzoeken van informatie, Dissertation, Vrije Universiteit, Amsterdam, 1986.

[3] Stephen J. Payne, Complex problem spaces: modelling the knowledge needed to use interactive devices, *Proceedings of the Second IFIP Conference on Human-Computer Interaction*, September 1-4, 1987, 203-214.

[4] Y. Waern, Information used and users' models of a computer supported task. *Paper presented at the MACINTER meeting, IAAPs*, Jerusalem, 1986.

[5] Gerrit C. van der Veer, M. Tauber, Y. Waern and B. van Muylwijk, On the interaction between system and user characteristics, *BIT*, vol. 4, nr. 4, 1985, 289-308.

[6] QUEST, Edition 3, AUCBE, Hatfield, 1984.

[7] GRASS, Graphics Searching and Sorting. An information handling package from Newman College, Newman Software, Birmingham, 1985.

[8] D.A. Norman, Some observations on mental models. In: *Mental Models*, D. Gentner and A.L. Stevens (eds.), Lawrence Erlbaum, London, 1983.

[9] T.P. Moran, The command language grammar: a representation for the user interface of interactive computer systems, *International Journal of Man-Machine Studies*, vol. 15, 1981, 3-50.

[10] T.P. Moran, Getting into a system. External-Internal task mapping Analysis, *CHI '83 Proceedings*, 1983.

[11] Gerrit C. van der Veer and Frances M.T. Brazier, Users representations of systems: a methodological approach, *to appear in Proceedings of MacInter Symposium, Stuttgart, 1987*.

[12] I. Sommerville, Software engineering, International Computer Science Series, Addison Wesley Publishing Co., London, 1982.

[13] D.E. Kieras and P.G. Polson, An approach to the formal analysis of user complexity, *International Journal of Man-Machine Studies*, vol. 22, 1985, 365-394.

COMPUTERS IN EDUCATION, F. Lovis and E.D. Tagg (eds.)
Elsevier Science Publishers B.V. (North-Holland)
© IFIP, 1988

E D U B A S E - AN EDUCATIONAL FILE MANAGEMENT SYSTEM

DR. S.H. VON SOLMS

Rand Afrikaans University
P.O. Box 524
Johannesburg 2000, South Africa.

EDUBASE is a graphics-driven file management system using the principle of analogy to introduce beginners to the basic ideas of data management. EDUBASE is designed using a tiered approach. This means that students are only provided with a limited amount of new knowledge at every level, and can therefore assimilate all this knowledge before proceeding to the next level. This prevents the student from being swamped by a lot of technical information about the package, most of which is not relevant or important at that specific stage.

1.   INTRODUCTION

Any person exposed to a micro computer, or any other type of computer, very soon experiences the need for some data management tools and facilities. This fact is borne out in classrooms where children want to store data in their computers, in houses where housewives want to store personal information, in offices where secretaries are expected to use computerized files, etc., etc.

A very large number of data management packages are available on the market, but the beginner often finds the complexity and facilities of these packages overwhelming. Firstly he does not yet understand the basic concepts involved in data management, like files, records and fields, and secondly he does not know which of the many facilities available in his data management package to use.

A data management package which introduces the beginner to these concepts in an environment which he understands, and exposes him to the facilities of the packages in a controlled way, may therefore be a big help.

EDUBASE is such a packet.

2.   EDUBASE - An Educational Tool

EDUBASE uses the analogy of cabinets and drawers to introduce the ideas of files, records and fields to beginners. Operations such as retrieve, edit, save and select are performed within this cabinet/drawer environment.

In EDUBASE a file is graphically represented by a cabinet, with a framed wall sign indicating its name. (FIG. 1). Drawers in a cabinet represent records in a file. Each drawer name can be seen as the record key or record name. Sections in a drawer represent fields in a record. (FIG. 2).

Retrieving data is represented graphically by looking inside a drawer of a cabinet, editing data by changing something in a drawer, saving data by building a new computer cabinet, and selecting data by graphically comparing data in different drawers.

During all these operations, students graphically open and close drawers of computer cabinets. They can physically see the data inside the drawers and they can modify it. If they modify it incorrectly, they will see their mistakes. In this way the idea of user responsibility for data is introduced right from the beginning.

Apart from being an educational tool, EDUBASE is also a fully functional system which can be used in a live environment for data processing, though with very limited facilities at present.

3.   The Design of EDUBASE

One of the most interesting aspects of EDUBASE concerns the way in which it was designed. EDUBASE uses a tiered approach, meaning that the package is segmented into four different 'levels', each one providing more powerful

*EDUBASE was developed while the author was a visitor to the Program Product Research and Development Centre of Burroughs Canada in Montreal. Financial assistance from the Council for Scientific and Industrial Research and the Ernest Oppenheimer Memorial Trust in South Africa is acknowledged.

facilities than the previous one. These levels are distinctly separated. Students working on Level 1 cannot use any facilities on a higher level, in fact they are not even aware that other levels exist . Students on Level 3 can use all facilities on Levels 1 to 3, but not on Level 4. This prevents students from experimenting, and getting confused, with facilities not yet introduced to them. The progression from one level to the next is explicitly controlled by the instructor. Only two cabinets are displayed on the screen at the same time. A 'scroll' facility allowes the user to view the next/previous two cabinets. (*FIG. 3*).

The limitations and facilities on the four levels are as follows:

Level	Limitations	Operations
1	* Two pieces of data per drawer (one on the front of the drawer and one inside the drawer)	* retrieving data from existing drawers
		* editing data in existing drawers
	* maximum of eight drawers per cabinet	* building new cabinets
	See *FIG. 4.*	
2	* Three pieces of data per drawer	* as on level 1, except that the building of new cabinets includes the division of drawers
	* maximum of eight drawers per cabinet	
	See *FIG. 2.*	

(NOTE: Two pieces of data per drawer means that the drawer itself contains one piece of data, because one piece of data is always written on the 'front side' of the drawer, indicating the drawer name. Three pieces of data per drawer therefore means two pieces of data inside the drawer itself, implying that the drawer is divided into two sections. Drawer sections can be given names, introducing the idea of field names within a record (drawer).)

3	* as on level 2	* as on level 2
		* selecting and comparing data

(NOTE: The selection and comparison of data i graphically simulated by 'weighing' values retrieved from drawers.)

See *FIG. 5.*

Level	Limitations	Operations
4	* 5 pieces of data per drawer	* as on level 3
	* Maximum of 100 drawers per cabinet.	

(NOTE: Only eight drawers can be represented graphically on the screen at the same time. A cabinet containing more than eight drawers can be scrolled to display the next/previous eight drawers. Only two sections in a drawer can be displayed at the same time. A drawer containing more than two sections can be scrolled to display the next/previous two sections.)

See *FIG. 6.*

Levels are designed in such a way that a student will discover the limitations of the specific level by himself. Well-chosen exercises by the instructor will support this discovery. At that stage the instructor can advance the student to the next level, where he can use the more powerful facilities provided on the specific level.

4. Manipulating EDUBASE

EDUBASE is written in PASCAL and implemented on the UNISYS ICON micro computer. The package makes full use of the graphic facilities on the ICON. All operations and selections are made by choosing the relevant graphic image on the screen. A graphic image is selected by moving the cursor, using the build-in trackball, to the relevant image. The keyboard is only used to input user data. Manipulating the package itself needs no keyboard input at all.

Extensive use is made of pop-up windows, simplifying the use of the package.

The icons appearing on the top of the screen, has the following meaning:

1. Scroll left to see previous two cabinets.

2. As above for scrolling right.

3. Door icon for leaving EDUBASE. On selecting this icon, a pop-up window may prompt for the relative action. (*FIG. 7*).

4. Build icon, allowing the construc-
    ting of new cabinets.

5. Write icon, allowing the editing of
    existing cabinets.

6. Look icon, allowing the user to
    "look at" (retrieve) data from
    existing cabinets.

7. Scale icon, used in selecting and
    comparing data from existing cabi-
    nets.

    The user selects a criterion, which
    is placed on an enlarged scale.
    Successive drawers from the selected
    cabinets are automatically opened,
    and the selected field placed on the
    other side of the scale. The scale
    reacts, and if the criterion is
    satisfied, the value is placed in
    the list area.

    (FIG. 5).

5. Conclusion

The tiered approach to the development of EDUBASE
is very significant. A learning path for students,
staying within a well-known environment, therefore exists, and progression within this learning
path can be explicitly controlled by the instructor. The four levels summarized above form the
first version of EDUBASE, and are operational.
Further levels will expand the facilities of the
package, adding more and more powerful features,
until eventually a fully-fledged data base management system exists. In this way students can
start with a very simple and limited package and
progress up to a full data base management
system, always staying within a well-known
environment making use of well-known terminology.

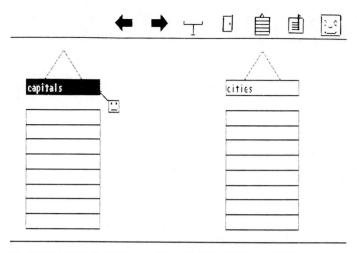

USE <SCROLL> ICONE TO SCROLL WALL SIGNS AND THEN SELECT A CUPBOARD
USE <DOOR> ICON TO EXIT

FIG. 1

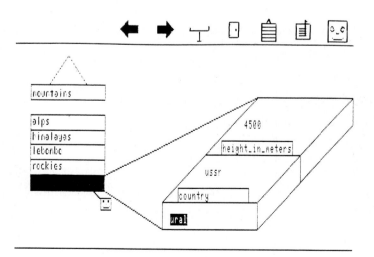

SELECT NEW DRAWER FROM CUPBOARD OR EXIT THROUGH <DOOR> ICON

FIG. 2

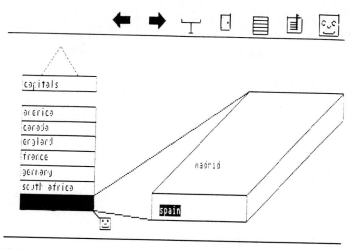

SELECT NEW DRAWER FROM CUPBOARD OR EXIT THROUGH <DOOR> ICON

FIG. 3

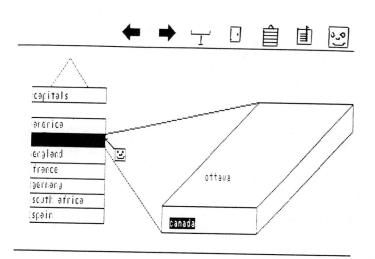

SELECT NEW DRAWER FROM CUPBOARD OR EXIT THROUGH <DOOR> ICON

FIG. 4

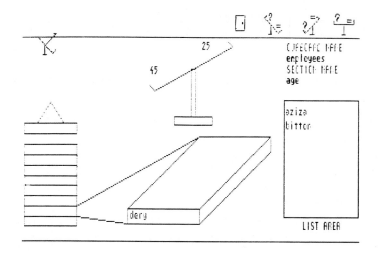

FIG. 5

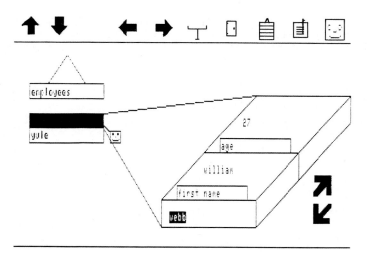

SCROLL CUPBOARD, SELECT A DRAWER OR SCROLL DRAWER
EXIT THROUGH THE <DOOR> ICON

FIG. 6

COMPUTERS IN EDUCATION, F. Lovis and E.D. Tagg (eds.)
Elsevier Science Publishers B.V. (North-Holland)
© IFIP, 1988

CERTAINTY AND DOUBT: THE PEDAGOGY OF RELATIONAL DATABASES

Hugh ROBINSON

Computing Discipline, Faculty of Mathematics, The Open University,
Milton Keynes, MK7 6AA, United Kingdom

This paper discusses the development of relational database technology and the manner in which this development is reflected in the curriculum. The development is seen as a process of transition from a monotheistic unity to a state where there are several competing paradigmatic claims for the characterisation of the technology. The influence of other database technologies is also seen as factor in this move away from a central dogma. The paper discusses the implications of this account for teaching practice and argues that maturity in the technology is indicative of maturity in the curriculum, with an emphasis on the acquisition of competencies.

1. INTRODUCTION

This paper offers an account of the development of relational database technology as manifested in the associated curriculum. The central thesis explored is that the degree of consensus amongst practitioners over the characterising features of the technology determines the extent of agreement amongst teachers on the nature of the curriculum. In particular, the problems posed for curriculum development when there is strong divergence amongst practitioners are examined. It should be emphasised that the paper discusses the development of a technology and its pedagogic consequences: it does not in any way offer a critique of that technology.

2. CERTAINTY

A decade ago, the nature of any university or polytechnic curriculum concerning relational database technology was seen as unproblematic. By common consent, a missionary, sometimes messianic, stance was taken on relational databases and an agreed liturgy existed for the pedagogic celebration of the virtues of such systems. The metaphysics of this liturgy had three central tenets:

- The world was tabular: a relational database provided a natural, obvious and simple way of representing reality.
- The world was canonical: normalisation provided a means of making this representation stand in a direct correspondence to reality.

- The world's foundations were mathematical: languages based on a relational algebra or calculus offered a concise and direct way of expressing the required manipulation of reality.

Indeed, if God had not intended the world to be relational, why should He have given us a canonical form for data and a calculus of manipulations?

Teaching relational databases meant teaching, in a variety of ways, this liturgy, be it in the classroom or via the textbook. For example, Deen (1977: 131) stated

> A basic feature of the relational model is its simplicity ... providing the simplest possible data structure which can be used as the common denominator of all data structures. ... The concepts of the relational model are founded on mathematics ...[this author's ellipses]

In the same vein we have ' *... the relational model tends to represent data as it exists.'* (Kroenke 1977: 194) and *'There is a simpler and more elegant method - the use of* relational *databases.'* (Martin 1976: 95, original emphasis). *Simpler* and *more elegant* were predicates asserted in comparison with the so-called *Data Base Task Group (DBTG) proposals* (this seemed to be the preferred term, even though this group had been superseded by the Data Description Language Committee in the early 1970's). DBTG database systems were *not* natural, obvious and simple; they allowed un-normalised records; and they even required manipulation of a database to be expressed in a procedural and occurrence-based fashion.

This brief retrospection is, of course, simplistic. However, it aims to capture the directness of purpose and paradigmatic agreement that was so very evident to anyone teaching the topic at the time.

3. DOUBT

Clearly, it is the contention of this paper that matters are not quite so simple; that the curriculum is problematic and worthy of attention. Kent was one of the first people to question persistently the early monolithic relational database theology (see Kent 1978, for example) and, in the spirit of his work, a series of dilemmas are now outlined that justify a serious appraisal of teaching practice for relational systems. This paper adheres to the belief that the explication of the dilemma is an illuminating task in its own right. It does not pretend to burden the reader with the specific resolutions that the author would prescribe in the context of his own teaching.

3.1 Liturgical schisms

It is very clear that, whilst adhering to the articles of faith, there are, in practice, at least two distinct schools of thought concerning their evangelisation. *First,* there is the tradition which emphasises the naturality and simplicity of the relational approach. Martin in his series of charismatic texts (see Martin 1977 and 1980, amongst others) embodies this tradition, as does, in a more thoughtful fashion, Date (see Date 1983, for example). *Second,* there is a tradition that emphasises the perceived rigorous and formal assumptions behind, and consequences of, such a simple way of representing data. Ullman (1980) and Maier (1983) are typical examples of such a formal approach. The correspondence between Kent and Ullman on the *universal relation assumption* can be seen as the two traditions in conflict (see Kent 1981, 1983a and Ullman 1983).That there is a conflict, over and above the tendency of theory to obfuscate, is clear to any undergraduate who examines Date's (1983) *Database: A Primer* only to move onto Maier's (1983) *The Theory of Relational Databases*.

3.2 The dilemma of normalisation

Normalisation to third normal form (3NF) can be taught in an intuitive and non-formal fashion that has a direct appeal and application. Such teaching can be done without recourse to the mathematics of relational technology: dependency theory and the basis of reduction through *project* and reconstruction through *join*. However, there are *practical*, albeit untypical, problems which require the generality of a 'higher' normal form: Boyce-Codd Normal Form (BCNF). Yet the teaching move to BCNF has one minor and one major problem. The minor problem is that some relations are clearly better left in 3NF: this is not an issue of great significance but it does detract from the pedagogic impact of introducing a 'higher' normal form. The major problem is that BCNF really requires a level of comprehension beyond that needed for 3NF: functional dependencies and candidate keys are not now something that can be tacitly avoided (Kent 1983b notwithstanding).

And once such a comprehension has been grasped, there is an overwhelming desire for a teacher to recount his own intellectual efforts and to complete the story of *non-loss decomposition and join* with fourth and fifth normal form (4NF and 5NF) and the arcane reaches of dependency theory. This is all a very right and proper exercise of an undergraduate's intellectual capacity, but the world inhabited by join dependencies all too readily seems to be one of contrived pathology rather than practical normality. The higher normal forms do indeed finish the story but at the expense of a sense of loss for the experiential revelation of 3NF. Undergraduates are easily convinced of the need to view the world through the lens of normalisation: they are also likely to deduce that the clarity of practical focus fades beyond BCNF.

3.3 The challenge of EAR modelling

The use of an entity-attribute-relationship (EAR) conceptual data model in the development of an information system is now accepted practice, at least in the United Kingdom. The use of EAR models presents a challenge to the purity of vision ascribed to relational databases on two counts. *First,* an EAR model is usually regarded as a higher level of abstraction than any corresponding relational data model: the EAR model bears, in some, albeit ill-defined sense, a more direct relationship to the portion of reality being modelled. The EAR model incorporates the notion of reality consisting of *things, properties of things and associations between things:* a metaphysical scheme that is open to debate but, *prima facie,* seems richer than any offered by relational data models. Indeed, attempts to incorporate the metaphysical scheme of EAR modelling into relational systems, such as that of Codd (1979), seem singularly unsuccessful in the sense that they have dismally failed to generate the catholic appeal that the early work on relational systems so vividly inspired. *Second,* the EAR model focused (some) attention on the design of relational systems using EAR models.This attention was, and remains, a largely United Kingdom pre-occupation, as witness the recent *An Integrated Approach to Logical Design of Relational Database Schemes* of Beeri and Kifer (1986) where a reliance is placed on functional and multi-valued dependencies as the major design tool. Focusing on design quickly reveals how complex a relational database can be in representing a simple EAR model. Consider the following short example, based on a (fairly well known) sheep breeding EAR model. The EAR data model diagram is given as *Figure 1:* (some of) the attributes involved are as follows.

        FLOCK (FlockId, FlockName)
        SHEEP (SheepId, SheepName, SheepSex, DateOfBirth)
        MATING (DateOfMating, MatingDetails)

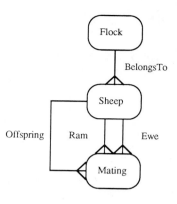

Figure 1

For reasons of brevity, no attempt is made to give a complete conceptual data model, with formal definitions of the meaning of the features just introduced. It is assumed that their likely intuitive meaning for the reader will suffice. It should, however, be clear that, in order to represent the sheep breeding data model as a relational database the following relations are needed.

FLOCK   (<u>FlockId</u>, FlockName)
SHEEP   (<u>SheepId</u>, SheepName, SheepSex, DateOfBirth, InFlockId,
             SheepIdOfMother, DateOfConception)
MATING (<u>SheepIdOfEwe</u>, <u>DateOfMating</u>, SheepIdOfRam,
             MatingDetails)

with attributes defined over domains as follows,

FlockId, InFlockId *domain* IdOfFlock
FlockName *domain* NameOfFlock
SheepName *domain* NameOfSheep
SheepId, SheepIdOfMother, SheepIdOfRam, SheepIdOfEwe *domain* IdOfSheep
SheepSex *domain* SexOfSheep
DateOfMating, DateOfBirth, DateOfConception *domain* Date
MatingDetails *domain* ResearchText

This relational data model is by no means simple and easy for students (or even practitioners, for that matter) to understand and use. In particular, the relationships (Ram, Ewe, etc) that are being represented are difficult to perceive, despite the *strong* domaining (*weak* domaining, using only standard data types, would make the situation more chaotic). Indeed, it would appear that one putative relationship - that represented by the pairing of (SheepIdOfMother, DateOfBirth) values in the Sheep relation with (SheepIdOfEwe, DateOfMating) values in the Mating relation is spurious and has no semantic meaning. This uneasy handling of relationships is evinced further when the mechanisms proposed to capture the semantics of relationships in relational databases (that is, the semantics of the pairing of attributes which represent relationships between relations) are examined, as in Date's (1981) work on referential integrity, for example. Students can be forgiven for making an unfavourable comparison with the corresponding features in DBTG systems.

3.4 The contribution of standardisation

A *de facto* standard for relational systems exists with the SQL language and this is in the process of becoming a *de jure* standard (see ISO 1987, for example). Standardisation is a business beset with its own problems and difficulties, but the SQL standard is, nevertheless, disappointing in its failure to capture many of the essential features of a relational database. For example, there is no concept of a relational key or of the central importance of domains. Yet, clearly, SQL represents the generic form with which undergraduates will be working as information system practitioners. But is SQL taught at the expense of the illumination of the algebra and the calculus, even if the latter have rarely, if ever, been fully implemented?

3.5 Coda

Of course, all the above has **not** tried to show that any **one** dilemma raises tremendous pedagogic problems but that, by a process of attrition, the innocence of the early days has been lost, and, with this loss has come a lack of clear direction as to what should and should not be taught and emphasised about relational databases on a degree level course. Parenthetically, it should be remarked that this transition from a central dogma to several competing paradigmatic claims is by no means atypical in the development of a technology.

4. MATURITY

These dilemmas will not be resolved by awaiting an edict or encyclical from the relational establishment. Such a resolving edict will not arrive, for no relational establishment exists, and, in any case, its use reduces the teacher's role to one of mere reportage. The resolution lies in the recognition that teachers do not merely passively reflect an intellectual tradition: they interpret, structure and make manifest that tradition. In the spirit of such an academic egalitarianism, this paper emphasises that the study of relational databases at degree level implies the study of an *intellectual discipline* **and** that the study of *this* intellectual discipline should equip the undergraduate with a set of *competencies* that will enable her to bring order and sense to the vagaries of a technology that will *inevitably* progress, in the manner outlined, further away from any monotheistic unity.

Two examples of such competencies are: *assessing and using the relational features of a particular system* and *designing a relational database*. At the risk of stating the obvious, the acquisition of the former does not involve the incantation of the current version of Codd's (1985: 19) *'eight important features of the relational model'* against some born-again relational system. Rather, the acquisition of these competencies will involve a range of discrete and specific skills involving at least some of the following:

- the over-looked importance of domains in both defining the relational data structure and proscribing unacceptable manipulations;

- the importance of relational views and the problems of their provision and manipulation;

- what the declaration of a key asserts;

- the efficacy of BCNF and the avoidance of problems requiring 4NF and 5NF by an appeal to the wider concerns of EAR modelling;

- an emphasis on the importance of relationships and a correct understanding of what can and what cannot be expressed about relationships in a relational system;

- the utility of an algebra in formulating the manipulation of relations;

- the expression of integrity constraints.

This is not an exhaustive list nor in any way a comprehensive resolution of the problems as presented in this paper. It is, however, an indication of the programmatic concerns involved in producing a course that claimed to teach relational databases at degree level.

ACKNOWLEDGEMENTS

An earlier version of this paper was read by Mike Newton of the Faculty of Mathematics, the Open University. The author is grateful for his comments.

REFERENCES

Beeri C & Kifer M 1986, An Integrated Approach to Logical Design of Relational Database Schemes, *Transcations on Database Systems,* **11**, 2.

Codd E F 1979, Extending the Database Relational Model to Capture More Meaning, *Transcations on Database Systems,* **4**, 4.

Codd E F 1985, The State of Database Management, in D Iggulden (ed), *The corporate database,* Pergamon Infotech, Oxford.

Date C J 1981, Referential Integrity, *Proc. 7th International Conference on Very Large Data Bases.*

Date C J 1983, *Database: A Primer,* Addison-Wesley, Reading, Massachusetts.

Deen S M 1977, *Fundamentals of Data Base Systems,* Macmillan, London.

ISO 1987, ISO TC97 SC21 WG3, *Database Language SQL,* ISO 9075-1987(E).

Kent W 1978, *Data and Reality,* North-Holland, Amsterdam.

Kent W 1981, Consequences of Assuming a Universal Relation, *Transcations on Database Systems,* **6**, 4.

Kent W 1983a, The Universal Relation Revisited, *Transcations on Database Systems,* **8**, 4.

Kent W 1983b, A Simple Guide to Five Normal Forms in Relational Database Theory, *Communications of the ACM,* **26**, 2.

Kroenke D 1977, *Database Processing,* SRA, Chicago.

Maier D 1983, *The Theory of Relational Databases,* Pitman, London.

Martin J 1976, *Principles of Data-Base Management,* Prentice-Hall, Englewood Cliffs, New Jersey.

Martin J 1977, *Computer Data-Base Organization,* Prentice-Hall, Englewood Cliffs, New Jersey.

Martin J 1980, *An end user's guide to database,* Savant Research Studies, Carnforth.

Ullman J D 1980, *Principles of Database Systems,* Computer Science Press, Rockville, Maryland.

Ullman J D 1983, On Kent's 'Consequences of Assuming a Universal Relation', *Transcations on Database Systems,* **8**, 4.

COMPUTERS IN EDUCATION, F. Lovis and E.D. Tagg (eds.)
Elsevier Science Publishers B.V. (North-Holland)
IFIP, 1988

ACTIVE PROGRAMMING AND ITS USE IN EDUCATIONAL
PRACTICE

Bogdan I.Jankovic

Center for Multidisciplinary Studies University of Belgrade
Slobodana Penezica-Krcuna 35
11000 BEOGRAD, YUGOSLAVIA*

The new concept of active programming has been introduced and defined.
The special language for active programming has been designed and the
syntax of the language has been described. The possibilities for
implementation of active programming on mini and microcomputers were
shown. Also, it was pointed out how this concept could be used in
practice for computers in education.

1. INTRODUCTION

In some cases a user wants to change the course of a
computer program or to modify it. In other cases, he wants
just to change the value of a program parameter. In a
conventional use of a computer, a user ought to prepare a
program previously. If one wants to change a parameter
value, then a special dialogue (menu) should be
programmed. However, in some applications, one cannot
predict all possible situations which could occur. Even, if
this could be done, a program may be excessively large for
most small machines (mini and microcomputers for
example).

The idea of active programming was originated in
application of computers in research laboratories. The
problems of the complexity of research experiments are
twofold. The first type of complexity could be named
predictable complexity, because situations and events that
could occur in an experiment are predictable in advance.
The second type is named unpredictable, or random
complexity. Here, in an experiment, quite new events and
situations arise, which could not be predicted in advance.
For instance, many physiological experiments have this sort
of complexity, owing to complex and stochastic processes
and nonstandard behaviour of the objects investigated [1].

The proposed method is used for overrunning the
unpredictable type of complexity by active interaction
between user and small computer during its running.

2. ACTIVE PROGRAMMING

2.1 DEFINITION

A possibility of changing of an implemented algorithm on a
computer during its running, through some action of user,
is named active programming.

For successful active programming the following
conditions should be fulfilled:

1. A user ought to know not only the semantics of the
program, which is running on a computer, as a whole, but
also the semantics of the current program action.

2. The computer system ought to provide permanent
information for the user about the current program action.

3. Independent input of a user's action (message), during
program running, has to be provided.

4. Appropriate and immediate interpretation of the message
received.

Basically, active programming consists of three phases,
which successively take place in the following schedule:

1. Catching sight of a new situation - decision for action.

2. Announcement of a message to the computer.

3. Interpretation of a message received.

The first and the second phases involve action by the user -
and the third one is provided by computer. Considering
these facts it could be concluded that the efficiency of active
programming is dependent upon the duration of these
phases. Accordingly, the majority of the time spent in
performing active programming is realised by phase 1
(from several seconds to more minutes), and phase 2 (up to
several seconds), while the activation of the third phase is
negligible compared with the previous ones. Considering
the total duration of the procedure, it could be concluded
that active programming, as a method, could be used
efficiently for changing the strategy of the program, during
its running according to the estimation and judgement of
user.

2.2 LANGUAGE FOR ACTIVE PROGRAMMING

Language for active programming (LAP) is provided for the
non-computer-specialist, so its syntax is simple. On the
other hand it could be easily modified to a particular user's
application.

A user communicates with the computer in this language,
by inserting messages and data, typing on the keyboard of a
terminal. A message is a string of characters and represents
a syntax unit (a statement) in the language LAP. Each
message, or data is terminated with a carriage return (CR),

or RETURN key. If the inserted message has syntax errors, an immediate report about error is printed on the terminal. So, the user has a chance to insert again a correction message. The same message could be inserted in a mode of program preparation and inspection, or during program running, in active programming mode. In this later case, a special control character should be activated (CTRL/P in this implementation), preceding the message insertion. In this mode of operation, an inserted message is not echoed on the terminal (not visible), until the current statement is finished.

2.2.1 SYNTAX OF LANGUAGE LAP

Syntax of language LAP is described in modified Bachus notation [2], as series of metalinguistic equations:

$$\langle \text{user's message} \rangle ::= [\text{CTRL/P}] \ \langle \text{line} \rangle \ \langle \text{end of line} \rangle \tag{1}$$

$$\langle \text{line} \rangle ::= \langle \text{unlabelled line} \rangle \ | \ \langle \text{program line} \rangle \tag{2}$$

$$\langle \text{unlabelled line} \rangle ::= \langle \text{command} \rangle \ | \ \langle \text{instruction} \rangle \ | \ \langle \text{procedure} \rangle \tag{3}$$

$$\langle \text{program line} \rangle ::= \langle \text{label} \rangle \ \langle \text{unlabelled line} \rangle \tag{4}$$

$$\langle \text{program} \rangle ::= [\langle \text{program line} \rangle]_1^N \tag{5}$$

$$\langle \text{command} \rangle ::= \langle \text{general command} \rangle \ | \ \langle \text{procedure command} \rangle \ | \ \langle \text{program command} \rangle \ \langle \text{zone command} \rangle \tag{6}$$

$$\langle \text{general command} \rangle ::= \text{INIT} \ | \ \text{BYE} \tag{6.1}$$

$$\langle \text{procedure command} \rangle ::= \text{ANP} \ | \ \text{ERAS} \ | \ \text{LISTZ} \tag{6.2}$$

$$\langle \text{program command} \rangle ::= \text{START} \ | \ \text{LIST} \ | \ \text{MEMO} \ | \ \text{CALL} \tag{6.3}$$

$$\langle \text{zone command} \rangle ::= \text{NULZON} \ | \ \text{SETZON} \ | \ \text{LISTZ} \ | \ \text{CHANGE} \ | \ \text{DELETE} \tag{6.4}$$

$$\langle \text{instruction} \rangle ::= \langle \text{input} \rangle \ | \ \langle \text{output} \rangle \ | \ \langle \text{jump} \rangle \ | \ \langle \text{cycle} \rangle \ | \ \langle \text{stop} \rangle \tag{7}$$

$$\langle \text{input} \rangle ::= \text{INPUT} \ \langle \text{variable} \rangle \tag{7.1}$$

$$\langle \text{output} \rangle ::= \text{OUTPUT} \ \langle \text{variable} \rangle \tag{7.2}$$

$$\langle \text{jump} \rangle ::= \text{GOTO} \ \langle \text{label} \rangle \tag{7.3}$$

$$\langle \text{cycle} \rangle ::= \text{REPEAT} \ \langle \text{variable} \rangle, \ \langle \text{label} \rangle \tag{7.4}$$

$$\langle \text{stop} \rangle ::= \text{STOP} \tag{7.5}$$

$$\langle \text{procedure} \rangle ::= \langle \text{name of procedure} \rangle \tag{8}$$

$$\langle \text{name of procedure} \rangle ::= \langle \text{letter} \rangle \ [\langle \text{letter} \rangle \ | \ \langle \text{digit} \rangle]_0^5 \tag{8.1}$$

$$\langle \text{label} \rangle ::= [\langle \text{digit} \rangle]_0^4 \tag{9}$$

$$\langle \text{variable} \rangle ::= \langle \text{letter} \rangle \ [\langle \text{letter} \rangle \ | \ \langle \text{digit} \rangle]_0^1 \tag{10}$$

$$\langle \text{letter} \rangle ::= A \ | \ B \ | \ C \ | \ \ldots \ X \ | \ Y \ | \ Z \tag{11}$$

$$\langle \text{digit} \rangle ::= 0 \ | \ 1 \ | \ 2 \ | \ 3 \ | \ 4 \ | \ 5 \ | \ 6 \ | \ 7 \ | \ 8 \ | \ 9 \tag{12}$$

2.2.2. HOW TO USE THE LAP LANGUAGE

It was pointed out that various users could use their own versions of the LAP language. So, a user at first forms the version of the LAP language, e.g. a creation of a library of a suitable set of procedures. With the help of the procedure commands (6.2), the user can create the library of procedures (command ANP - Adaptation of New Procedure), get a list of procedures in the library (ERASE). After that the user could form his program using instructions, or procedures from the library. On Figure 1 is shown a sample of this opening session.

Figure 1 An opening Session of Active Programming

The user could store a program file with the help of command MEMO, and afterwards call it by command CALL. The set of instructions is very modest and it generally used for the users' procedures interconnections. A procedure is, generally, a program or a suitable device, which is previously prepared, and a user could utilize it as an algorithmic step in his program. Several procedures, in one program could share the common zone. This zone is permanently settled in operative memory, and consists of values of different types (integer, real, string and logic), and tables of corresponding names of variables. Zone commands (6.4) are used for initiation, setting, or changing the contents of the common zone.

As was already pointed out, all commands, instructions and procedures, from the corresponding library, could be used in program immediate mode, or during program running, e.g. in a mode of active programming.

2.3 IMPLEMENTATION OF ACTIVE PROGRAMMING

A computer system is acceptable for implementation of active programming, if it could perform, besides its current program, the following actions simultaneously and independently:

1. Inform the user about the current action of a running program.

2. Acceptance of user's message.

3. Interpretation of received message.

In order to perform these functions a computer system ought to have certain hardware-software facilities. First of all, a computer ought to perform independent processes in parallel. This possibility could be successfully provided by an appropriate interrupt system. On the other side, the communication between the user and the computer system, is supposed to be done in a problem-oriented language (one is described in 2.2). In order to communicate in a high level language, a compiler, or an interpreter should be present as an interface between a man and a machine. The basic request is that the user should be informed continuously about the current action of a source program during its execution, and at the same time the user's message should be immediately interpreted. Then, obviously an interpreter is the only acceptable solution - not a classical compiler.

Therefore, a computer system should contain an interrupt system, as a hardware facility, and an interpreter for an appropriate problem-oriented language, as a software facility. The interpreter should be unique for interpretation of received messages and algorithmic steps of the source program as well.

These demands could be fulfilled by all contemporary mini and microcomputer systems.

Active programming was implemented on a DECLAB-11/40 computer system. The interpreter was designed for the LAP language. The interpreter was written in source FORTRAN IV language. An additional subroutine in assembly language (MACRO-11), was written for receiving users' messages during program running, in order to support an active programming mode. As the interpreter was written in the FORTRAN language, it could be relatively easily transferred to another computer system with the FORTRAN IV compiler. The procedures which the user utilizes for compiling his program, are also, originally written in FORTRAN IV. The course of programme processing is so organized, that the interpreter, procedures, and majority commands are swapped from internal memory and disc store (by chain possibility in the RT-11 operating system). So, one routine (the interpreter, a procedure, or a command), at a time, is alone in all available internal memory (except the common zone and assembly routine for receiving of a user's message, which are permanently stored in the operating memory). In such a case, rather complex and extensive procedures could be included as algorithmic steps in the user's programs. So, the whole system was implemented on only 32 kbytes of internal memory. the adaptation of this system on microcomputers with floppy and hard discs (RM380Z and IBM PC) have been done as well. Also, an attempt has been made to design a specialized computer system, based on microprocessor technology.

3. APPLICATION IN EDUCATION

It was pointed out, that active programming originated in considering computer applications in research laboratories. It was successfully used in physiological and neurophysiological laboratories [1]. One user, a neurophysiologist for instance, could use this system effectively for guiding his experiments in an appropriate direction according to the current circumstances.

In an analogous situation is the teacher, who is using the computer as an assistant during a lecture. A small computer system (such as IBM PC, or similar), could be used successfully not only for running a computer education program, but also to control other education devices, such as slide and film projectors, videodiscs and even real educational experiments. In such circumstances a lot of unexpected events could arise, moreover if communication with an audience is informal and friendly, many questions and comments may be expected. Then a lecturer would like to change the course of his lecture, which was previously prepared as a program and which is now running on the computer, or just wants to add or withdraw some program parts from the program running. Such appropriate reactions a lecturer could have, partly with the help of an active programming technique. Because an appropriate program module library has been prepared previously, the lecturer can use this for program modifications at the time.

On the other side the active programming technique could be used individually by students themselves in computer assisted education. The active programming could be used in an interactive simulation, which is very important for computer applications in education. A student could combine different program modules for the purposes of education, either preparing a program for themselves, previously, or using them "ad hoc" in the mode of active programming. it was mentioned that procedures (educational program modules) could share a common zone, which is permanently in internal memory. This common zone could contain the values of the parameters of educational modules. So, students could also change their values in an appropriate time, attaining different behaviours and effects of running educational modules, which are embedded in the user's program.

The problem, which exists for programming of user - computer dialogue, which, as a rule, is present in educational modules, is well known [3]. It could be substantially reduced with the help of active programming. On the other hand, active programming "stimulates" the student to think and take part, not only in preparing an educational program as an entity, but also in modifying it and playing with it during its running. In such cases, one of the main reasons for using a computer in education, e.g. to activate a student in the learning process, is achieved.

REFERENCES

[1] Janković, B., The Active Programming of Neurophysiological Experiments, Proc. of DECUS Europe Symposium, Amsterdam, Sept. 1980., pp. 61-67.

[2] Janković, B., Parezanović, N., The Generative Grammars of Metaprogramming Languages, Matematicki Vesnik, Vol. 13, No. 3, 1976., pp. 273-278.

[3] Parezanović, N., Description and Production of Interactive Programs, Involving Micros in Education, pp. 133-138, North-Holland Publ.Comp. IFIP, 1982.

COMPUTERS IN EDUCATION, F. Lovis and E.D. Tagg (eds.)
Elsevier Science Publishers B.V. (North-Holland)
© IFIP, 1988

EDP CURRICULUM FOR AN APPLICATION-ORIENTED INFORMATION PROCESSING COMMUNITY

Douglas S. Tung

Department of Computer Science
The Chinese University of Hong Kong
Shatin, Hong Kong

In Hong Kong, the manpower shortage problem for the computer profession has existed for a decade. Recent surveys show that this problem will persist for the coming years. A curriculum aimed to train EDP practitioners was proposed by the Vocational Training Council to provide the professional knowledge for entry to different jobs within EDP. An EDP Training Centre was established to offer courses based on the curriculum. The relationship between the curriculum and the professional certification programs is close, because the latter is a meaningful measure of educational and experienced-based knowledge for entrants to the profession, as well as a self-motivating tool for career development. (Keywords: curriculum, certification.)

1. THE ENVIRONMENT

Hong Kong exists as a financial centre and by international trade — textile, plastic toys and consumer electronics. There are minimal natural resources other than people, hence there is no heavy manufacturing industry. Since late 1970's growth in data automation has been astounding in Hong Kong. The number of computer installations in the local commerce, industry, government and educational organizations has grown steadily in the recent years, as shown in Table 1. The term "computer installation" refers to an in-house installation comprising one or more computers, irrespective of whether they are purchased, leased, rented, borrowed or donated.

Table 1: Growth of Computer Installations
in Hong Kong (1978-1986)

Year	Number of installations
1978	276
1979	461
1980	551
1981	684
1982	918
1983	1005
1984	1209
1985	1442
1986	1431

The large applications are in the obvious areas of banking, transportation, utility companies and government administration. Medium sized systems and minis cover all business areas. In micros, there are in excess of 40,000 illegitimate machines believed to exist, mostly at homes. There are around 22,000 legitimate 16-bit microcomputers being used in commercial organizations and educational institutes.

2. MANPOWER SURVEYS

The expansion in the use of computer facilities in the local industry and business has created the staffing requirements for a decade. People with the necessary skills of programming, systems analysis and design have to be imported to satisfy the needs. The Committee on Electronic Data Processing Training of the Vocational Training Council (hereafter, the Committee) conducted surveys in 1983 and in 1985 on the manpower situation and training needs to cope with the steady growth of the EDP industry in Hong Kong [5, 7].

2.1 Manpower situation

These manpower surveys of all computer installations and education institutions enabled projections be made on the demand and supply of computer personnel for the next several years. The demand was provided by each installation giving two estimates, one on the high end, and the other on the low end. The means of these estimates were then calculated. The supply figures are rather deterministic. They were provided by the universities, polytechnics, technical institutes and post-secondary colleges. In 1983, there were 4,477 systems development staff, i.e. EDP managers, analysts and programmers. This is tabulated in table 2. The 1985 findings confirmed that the 1984 and 1985 projections broadly agreed with the results of the 1983 survey.

Table 2: Demand and Supply of Systems Development Staff
in Hong Kong for 1983–1989

	83	84	85	86	87	88	89
Demand							
High end	4477	5290	6251	7386	8731	10320	12199
Low end	4477	5114	5709	6304	6900	7495	8091
Mean	4477	5202	5980	6845	7816	8908	10145
Estimated increase in demand based on mean		725	778	865	971	1092	1237
Actual demand (R.E.)		5423	5857	(6749)			
Actual increase in demand/ (R.E.)		946	434	(892)	(1067)		
Supply							
Estimated supply from universities & polytechnic		153	302	330	618	701	745
Supply as % of demand		21	39	38	64	64	60
Actual/(R.E.)		16	70	(37)	(58)		
Taking into account supply from post-secondary institutes		243	392	480	788	881	945
Supply as % of demand		34	50	55	81	80	76
Actual/(R.E.)		27	90	(53)	(74)		

(R.E.) = (Revised estimates)

The surveys showed that the higher learning institutions, i.e. universities and polytechnics, will produce only about 60% of the required trained manpower. The rest of the supply will depend on the post-secondary institutions either funded by the Government or by the private sector. However, in the recent years, there have been serious outflows of skilled computer personnel, estimated to be about 200 of the work force. Although the figure would appear to be relatively low, it should be noted that the majority of these emigrants have between five and ten years working experience. The consequence of a large emigration is potentially serious and damaging in terms of the EDP profession as a whole and the quality of EDP work done, not only now, but in the future.

2.2 Need for practical-oriented training curriculum

The traditional computer science/studies curricula in the higher learning institutions have always been criticised for being irrelevant to the needs of the computing community. However, these institutions hold the opinion that any narrow vocational curriculum would not be appropriate for the academic standard. They are concerned with the education of the whole person, not just the tailoring of his/her mind to fit for one particular kind of occupation. There is more to education than training in one or more useful skills.

Other finding of the surveys showed that the EDP training provided by the public and private institutes were mainly of an introductory nature. It was estimated that 58% of the courses, 70% of the students and 75% of the student course hours were involved only in basic elementary training [6]. Further, the Committee felt that it was necessary to develop and publish a curriculum for courses to be taken before entry to an EDP career, and as prerequisite for advancement within an EDP career.

3. ELECTRONIC DATA PROCESSING TRAINING CURRICULUM

The Committee undertook to determine a comprehensive assembly of the professional knowledge required by EDP practitioners in Hong Kong if they are to be properly equipped to contribute to the promotion and installation of EDP systems in Hong Kong's commerce and industry. This author was on the Committee. In drafting the curriculum, a number of computing curricula have been referenced [1, 2, 3, 4]. Each curriculum prepares students for different career paths after graduation.

3.1 The curriculum

It comprises a two-year full-time course. There are 126 modules incorporating at least 500 topics. Various combinations of modules are suitable for entry to different jobs within EDP. The durations of the modules range from 2 hours to 54 hours, consisting of lectures, practicals, or a mixture of these.

The curriculum is a mixture of "common sense" applications with emphasis on good documentation and user-friendliness, and the technically demanding topics such as relational databases and networking. An additional feature is the stress on product knowledge which needs to be possessed by anyone claiming to be a competent EDP practitioner. This curriculum serves as a reference for conducting courses in the EDP Training Centre, and the technical institutes of the Hong Kong Vocational Training Council.

Though a precise categorisation of modules is not practical, due to the overlapping nature of the topics, the following represents a convenient break-down [8].

(i) An introduction to Electronic Data Processing

This category consists of 11 modules. They are: an introduction to organizations and the role of EDP; organization of the EDP functions; an introduction to the project orientation of EDP; basic structure of a modern digital computer; input and output devices, memory elements of a computer; assembling, compiling, linking, interpreting and running programs; various computer languages, their uses and differences; an introduction to data communications; an introduction to local area networks; and the terminology of system software.

(ii) Programming

This category consists of 19 modules. They are: flowcharting; programming, testing and debugging techniques; structured programming techniques, program segmentation, overlay, branching and looping, subroutines; arrays, vectors and matrices; output formats, layouts and editing; program documentation; module testing; system testing; programmer productivity aids, data dictionaries and program/data independence; COBOL; RPG; BASIC; PL/1; TP monitors; optimising software; an introduction to data management; database administration; data analysis and data dictionary.

(iii) Systems analysis and design

This category consists of 33 modules. They are: systems concepts; the role of the systems analyst; current approaches to systems analysis; human issues associated with data processing; systems investigations; feasibility studies (including cost-benefit analysis); analysis of systems; decision tables; systems outline design (including Fourth Generation Systems Design); structured analysis and design techniques; presentation techniques; report writing; systems input design; forms design; forms appearance; systems output design; screen design; computer processing design; computer output to microfilm; file design; simple forecasting methods; documentation standards; requirements specification; feasibility report/management proposals; systems specification; program specification; user procedures; organizational impact of information systems; system security; Fourth Generation Languages; query facilities; sizing for new applications/installations; O and M methodologies; and brainstorming.

(iv) Project Management

This category consists of 3 modules. They are: project planning; controlling project performance; and systems implementation.

(v) The Elements of Business

This category consists of 7 modules. They are: types of business in Hong Kong; the basic functional areas of business; accounting; financial modelling; management information systems; decision analysis; and decision support systems.

(vi) Computer Applications

This category consists of 3 modules. They are: computer graphics; CAD/CAM; and office automation.

(vii) Computer Science

This category consists of 19 modules. They are: addressing methods; input and output devices; assembling, compiling, linking, interpreting and running programs; instruction formats; basic structure of a modern digital computer; memory elements of a computer; system software; developments in empirical management-oriented systems software; international standards; data transmission systems; local area networks; real time issues; elements of data communications networks; principles of data communications lines; network design; network management; computer performance evaluation and capacity planning; sorting; and technical aspects of microcomputers, including personal computers.

(viii) EDP Management

This category consists of 19 modules. They are: introduction to management; installation standards manuals; the administrative functions; managing people; increasing personal effectiveness; holding effective meetings; skills for project managers; EDP training; budget preparation; distributed processing; communications facilities and services; current trends in information systems; negotiating hardware procurement contracts; negotiating software application package procurement contracts; negotiating software procurement contracts; negotiating consultancy procurement contracts; migration strategies; overview of major hardware and software suppliers and their products; and EDP security, auditability and privacy.

(ix) Systems development management

This category consists of 7 modules. They are: systems programming/addressing methods; systems and programming team supervision; managing the systems analysis function; managing the programming function; managing the programming function; control and monitoring of program problem correction; quality assurance; and software application packages.

(x) EDP operation management

This module consists of 5 topics. They are: managing the operations function; contingency planning; reliability/maintenance service measurement and control; capacity planning and performance improvement; and capacity planning to handle increases in transaction volumes.

3.2 EDP Training Centre

In April 1986, the Hong Kong Vocational Training Council established an EDP Training Centre with a set-up budget of US$0.64 million and approximately the same amount as annual recurrent cost for the initial years. The objectives of the Centre are to provide intensive follow-up training for fresh graduates who have finished their tertiary education but are not yet fully experienced to take on specific projects in their employments, and to conduct a Career Entry Training programme for people who are just starting their careers in the EDP field and a Professional Development programme for those who are already in the profession but wish to improve and upgrade themselves. It is also a testing field for the Training Curriculum.

The current plan of the Centre is to produce an additional 120 trained personnel available to the EDP industry each year. Since May 1986, over 1000 people have enrolled in 80 courses offered by the Centre.

4. COMPUTER CERTIFICATION PROGRAMMES

Though certification is not a panacea for the problems of developing more competent personnel or enhancing the competence of the existing staff, yet it is one meaningful measure of educational and experience-based knowledge for entrants to the profession as well as a self-motivating tool for career development. The curriculum can gain support from the industry and commerce if it is to meet the guidelines of the professional bodies. In fact, in designing the Curriculum, this factor has been considered. Thus, the courses could be taken as studies or reviews for professional examinations, or for recertification of professional qualifications.

In Hong Kong, there is a Basic Course in Computer Programming Certificate Examination, jointly sponsored by the National Computing Centre and the City and Guilds of London Institute. The examination provides an entry qualification for trainee and junior programmers who are seeking employment in computer areas.

The Institute for Certification of Computer Professionals, U.S.A. (ICCP) holds examinations for the Certificate in Data Processing (CDP), the Certificate in Systems Professionalism (CSP), the Certificate in Computer Programming (CCP), and Associate in Computer Processing (ACP) twice each year.

The British Computer Society Examination is a popular computer certifying examination in

Hong Kong. A few private schools claim to offer courses geared to it and some correspondence schools offer home study courses for part of the Examination. Likewise, the Institute of Data Processing Management UK. conducts examinations twice each year.

These professional qualifications can provide a valid standard to help potential employers and the general public to identify knowledgeable practitioners in the application-oriented computing career.

5. CONCLUDING REMARKS

New technology requires new knowledge, new expertise and new skills. In the future, Hong Kong is likely to remain as a user of high technology rather than a producer or creator of high technology. Hong Kong must continuously upgrade its technologies in order to maintain its competitive position in world markets.

By 1989, the projected output is 745 graduates from the universities and the polytechnics, but the demand in industry will also have risen to over 10,100. It is important that some vocational training institutes should address the problem regarding the quantity of training required to produce enough staff to meet the likely demands.

At the moment, Hong Kong is going through a transitional phase in which information technology will play an increasing role. Hong Kong's position as a financial centre and international trade market does require the support of its high-quality information processing capabilities.

To provide the right education and training for the local milieu is a challenge, particularly when there is a worldwide shortage of qualified people to work in the profession or to teach the programmes. With the establishment of the EDP Training Centre and the implementation of the application-oriented curriculum, there will be more knowledge personnel who can harness the new technologies in innovative uses to achieve improved productivity in commercial and industrial organizations.

REFERENCES

[1] Association for Computing Machinery, Curriculum Committee, Curriculum Recommendations for Undergraduate Programs in Information Systems. Comm. ACM, vol. 16, no. 12, December 1973, 727-749.

[2] Association for Computing Machinery, Curriculum '78: Recommendations for Undergraduate Program in Computer Science. Comm. ACM, vol. 22, no. 3, March 1979, 147-165.

[3] British Computer Society, Examination Syllabus, Parts I and II, London, 1983.

[4] Institute of Electrical and Electronics Engineers, A Curriculum in Computer Science and Engineering, Committee Report, IEEE, California, Long Beach, 1977.

[5] Strickland, John E., EDP Training in Hong Kong, Hong Kong Computer Society, Yearbook 1983, Hong Kong, 1984, 3-4.

[6] Vocational Training Council, Report on the 1983 Survey of Establishments offering Training in Electronic Data Processing, Hong Kong, 1984, 14-15.

[7] Vocational Training Council, Electronic Data Processing Training Curricula, Hong Kong, 1985.

COMPUTERS IN EDUCATION, F. Lovis and E.D. Tagg (eds.)
Elsevier Science Publishers B.V. (North-Holland)
IFIP, 1988

EDULAN, A TOOL FOR SOFTWARE EDUCATION

Koenraad O.M. De Bosschere

Laboratory for Electronics, State University of Ghent
St.-Pietersnieuwstraat 41, B-9000 Ghent, Belgium °

Software education institutions face the challenge to educate and train people capable of producing and maintaining ever larger and more complex software systems. Appropriate software tools are needed to expose students to a proper balance of size, breadth, and complexity.
In this paper, an integrated package **EDULAN** is presented, aimed at providing hands-on experience in various aspects of computer science and software technology. **EDULAN** combines a well-chosen mix of interesting aspects of very diverse programming languages and machine architectures in one package. It is easy to use; a two-year use in several courses of a computer science curriculum has demonstrated its effectiveness.

1. INTRODUCTION

Computer applications are becoming more complex and sophisticated at an extremely high rate. High demands are put on new software systems with respect to performance, user friendliness, integration with other systems, cost, etc. Complex applications have very diverse aspects: operating systems, languages and language implementations, numerical and graphical methods, real-time aspects, debugging, concurrency aspects, etc. Large software packages are made by teams of programmers, not by individuals. Lifespan support of software packages typically involves more than one programmer. Reading and modifying programs written by others is therefore as important as writing new programs.

Good software education should reflect these requirements. However, very often the educational system lags behind on the requirements of society. This is also the case in software education. Most of the above aspects are treated in separate courses, in a rather theoretical way, and not providing experience in problem solving. Hands-on experience and insight in the interrelation between those seemingly unrelated topics are however indispensable.

In principle, the diversity of computer science and software engineering aspects can be illustrated using existing systems and tools such as Turbo Pascal, MODULA-2, Ada, MsDOS on real microprocessors. However there are a number of disadvantages to that approach.

In the first place, the complexity of practical software systems is unnecessarily large, due to a lot of details that are mostly irrelevant to illustrate the software principles being taught.

Secondly, sources of compilers and operating systems are not readily available, and are generally not useful for educational purposes because they are too technical, too detailed and, again, far too complex.

Thirdly, the existing processor architectures are also too complex to master in a sufficiently short time. Most modern microprocessors possess a large number of very sophisticated instructions. There are no simple but complete models of contemporary microprocessors for use in education. This was also the prime motivation for the development of Knuth's MIX machine [14].

Fourthly, debugging at the machine level is an important technique in building systems software. However, debugging is very difficult for concurrent programs. It is therefore much easier to learn to debug in a shielded environment, with a symbolic debugger and an easy-to-trace language.

What is needed in an educational environment is a proper balance between size, complexity, and accessibility so as to allow meaningful experiments. This paper presents the software support package EDULAN, aimed at filling the above requirements.

EDULAN is an abbreviation of *EDUcational LANguage* and was designed to give students in computer science some experience in fields like

° This work has been done in the context of a masters thesis at the Computer Science Laboratory of the State University of Ghent.

(a) software engineering;

(b) compiler construction and operation;

(c) operating system aspects like memory management, process scheduling and address translation, multitasking and concurrency principles;

(d) debugging tools;

(e) machine representations and support of compiled high-level languages;

(f) reading programs written by others.

EDULAN is a workbench of modest complexity, consisting of

(a) a language definition in extended BNF, very simple, yet complete;

(b) a compiler written in a modern high-level language (Turbo Pascal), available in source form;

(c) a minimal intermediate language definition, replacing modern extensive instruction sets;

(d) a run-time system, providing most modern operating system concepts such as memory management, multitasking, symbolic debugging facilities and program statistics.

The main advantage of this workbench is that it is an integrated package. Students don't have to study multiple systems superficially, but they can study one system in detail.

EDULAN is a new language. Although one might argue that there are already enough programming languages, there are several reasons to define and implement a new language instead of using an existing one.

(a) Implementing an existing language creates the obligation to strictly implement an (ad hoc) standard or a subset thereof. Any deviation from the standard creates a new version of an existing language. In [15], a BASIC interpreter is extended with a real time multitasking kernel. The drawback of that approach is that it tries to elucidate concepts that are alien to the language and that all known disadvantages of BASIC are retained;

(b) Implementing an existing language restricts our freedom to add new interesting aspects from an educational point of view. Interesting concepts derived from several languages can be included in the new language;

(c) Creating a new language gives the freedom to use the same uniform terminology throughout the whole course.

In the following sections we will briefly describe some aspects of the EDULAN language, its environment, and its uses. The complete description of the language can be found in the appendix.

2. THE LANGUAGE EDULAN

Modules, Procedures and Processes

As in MODULA-2 [9], an EDULAN program consists of one main program and perhaps a number of separate modules. In contrast with the main program, a module does not contain a main body of directly executable code. It can only contain and export certain objects (identifiers and types). Objects in modules are accessible by other modules, including the main program, only if they possess the export attribute. The execution of a program always starts with the directly executable code of the main program. A **MONITOR** module looks like an ordinary module, but only one **PROCEDURE**, **PROCESS** or **FUNCTION**, exported from this module, can be executed at any time in a multitasking environment.

As in Pascal [10], EDULAN instructions can be grouped into subprograms. **PROCEDURE** and **FUNCTION** subprograms cannot be lexically nested in EDULAN, but they can be called recursively. At the syntactic level, a **PROCESS** looks like a **PROCEDURE**. At the semantic level, a **PROCESS** is executed asynchronously with respect to its caller, while a **PROCEDURE** (as well as a **FUNCTION**) is executed synchronously with respect to its caller. Synchronism means that a caller waits for the termination of the called subprogram (fig. 1). Asynchronism means that a called subprogram proceeds independently of its caller. Once it has been started, a **PROCESS** leads its own life. If two processes want to synchronize, they must explicitly do so using synchronization primitives (semaphores, messages, shared variables). Processes are the only natural method of expressing parallelism in EDULAN.

```
PROGRAM Processes;

  PROCEDURE P1;
  BEGIN ... END P1;


  PROCESS P2;
  BEGIN ... END P2

  BEGIN            ┌─ execute P1
    CALL P1 ───────┘              │
                 ┌───────────────┘
    START P2  (* asynchronism *)
       │  └─────────────┐
  END Processes    execute P2
                        │
              terminate program
```

fig. 1   procedure and process execution

Decomposing a software system in smaller parts that can be compiled separately (modules) and can be debugged separately (subprograms and processes) is an important software engineering technique that can be illustrated by means of an EDULAN program.

Control structures

EDULAN possesses the three usual control structures [5]: sequencing, selection and iteration. sequencing is expressed using a semicolon symbol between two statements, selection is expressed using an **IF** statement, and iteration is expressed using a **WHILE** statement. These control structures can be nested to any depth.

In addition to the preceding control structures, there is also an **EXIT** statement. The **EXIT** statement serves as a structured replacement for the unstructured **GOTO** statement in other programming languages. Most **GOTO** statements can be replaced by a proper combination of subprograms with **EXIT** statements. An **EXIT** statement will always terminate the last called (and active) program or subprogram. When an **EXIT** statement is executed inside a complex control structure in a subprogram, the whole structure is left and control is returned to the caller of the subprogram. If the **EXIT** statement is executed in the main program, the program is terminated. In **FUNCTION** subprograms, the **EXIT** statement must be provided with a scalar value as a function return value. An example:

```
FUNCTION Double (i: INTEGER):  INTEGER;
  BEGIN
    EXIT i + i
  END Double;
```

Data structures

In EDULAN there are three simple scalar data types, each with their own operators. The **INTEGER** type is mainly used for indexing. The **BOOLEAN** type is used for keeping and expressing conditions and the **SEMAPHORE** type is used for synchronization.

The **ARRAY** structure is the only structured type. An array is a linear indexed sequence of scalar variables of the same type. The array index must be of the **INTEGER** type.

Besides type and structure, all variables in EDULAN have four additional attributes that supply information to the compiler and the linker, and that are visible to the programmer.

(i) The *Scope* Attribute

The scope attribute tells the compiler whether a variable is defined locally (in a subprogram), globally (at the outermost level) or as a subprogram parameter (neither globally nor

locally). The scope attribute is defined by the location of the declaration of a particular variable.

(ii) The *Lifetime* Attribute

The lifetime attribute tells the compiler whether a variable is stored in a static or a dynamic memory area (stack). Variables, local to subprograms are normally stored on the stack [5] at calling time of a particular subprogram and exist only during the execution of that subprogram. Global variables are stored in static memory and exist during the total execution time. The only significant use of the lifetime attribute is to make local variables static. This means that the scope of a local variable remains restricted to one subprogram, but that between two subprogram calls the value of that variable remains unchanged (Usually, these variables are called "own" variables).

(iii) The *Address* Attribute

The address attribute tells the compiler whether a variable will be stored by value or by reference. This corresponds to the R-value and L-value concepts of the programming language C [11]. Store by value is the default address attribute. It is obligatory to declare subprogram arguments by reference if information must be passed back from the called program to the caller. Imported variables must always be stored by reference because the linker must be able to substitute the address of the corresponding exported variable.

(iv) The *Link* Attribute

The link attribute provides the linker with information about the objects being exported or imported by each module. Imported variables must always be stored by reference in static memory. The header of imported subprograms must be redeclared in all importing modules.

Synchronization

Synchronization in EDULAN can be achieved in two ways [8]. Mutual exclusive program sections can be grouped as exported subprograms in one **MONITOR** module or synchronization can be explicitly coded using **SEMAPHORE** variables and P and V operations thereon. A semaphore in EDULAN is a variable, initialized to 1. A V operation increments this variable. A P operation decrements this variable, if its value is at least 1. If this variable is zero, the process is swapped out until the semaphore becomes positive, due to a V operation on the same semaphore by another process. The key point in testing semaphores is that the P and V operations are uninterruptible by other processes. **MONITOR** modules have a module semaphore to synchronize the execution of the different **MONITOR** subprograms [9].

3. THE EDULAN COMPILER AND RUNTIME SYSTEM

The EDULAN environment consists of 7 programs: the scanner, the parser, the E-code generator, the linker, the decoder, the lister and the E-code interpreter with the debugger. The communication between the programs is achieved by means of interpass files [1]. For example, the scanner reads the source, tokenizes it, and writes the results into the first interpass file. If the scanner was successful, the parser reads the first interpass file. Figure 2 shows the control flow in the compiler.

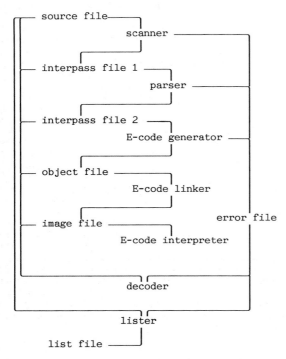

fig. 2 compiler and run time control flow

An important feature of EDULAN is that all interpass file formats are documented by means of their BNF description. Interpass files are ordinary ASCII files that can be printed, even edited.

We now presents a short description of the various programs in the environment.

(i) The scanner

The scanner is the front end of a compiler [2]. It reads the source, finds reserved words and converts them into special codes (tokens) for use in the next passes of the compiler. All identifiers are converted into entries in the symbol table. The scanner substitutes symbolic constants by their real values. The scanner output is written to the first interpass file.

(ii) The parser

The task of a parser is to verify the syntax of the tokenized version of the source. The output of the parser is an interpass file with all constructs checked against syntactic correctness, expressions in postfix notation and all variables assigned an address and attributes.

(iii) The code generator

The code generator reads the output of the parser and translates it into an object file. The output is in E-code format. E-code is the machine language of a virtual E-machine, described later on. Because E-code is of a relatively high level, it is called an *intermediate* code [12,13]. E-code is simpler to learn than most assemblers and E-code generation is easier to understand. Some E-code instructions have a two or three byte representation that allows the illustration of local code optimization. The code generator can also generate extra E-code instructions to check the array bounds at run time. The execution of E-code is obviously slower than machine code, but speed is not very important as EDULAN is not a production system.

(iv) The linker

The linker identifies all imported objects in the main program, asks for the module names of the unresolved externals, and puts all addresses at right places in the resulting image. The EDULAN linker performs type checking between modules at link time, akin to module version-control in most MODULA-2 implementations.

(v) The lister

When the scanner, the parser or the code generator detect errors, they create an error file. After each compiler pass, the error file is checked. When errors occur the compilation process is stopped and the lister is started. The lister takes the sources, the error file and a file with error messages and produces a listing with the error messages on the appropriate places between the source lines.

(vi) The decoder

The decoder is a program that produces a symbolic decode listing of all compiler-produced files. That listing is useful for inspecting the output of the compiler passes without decyphering.

(vii) The interpreter

The interpreter is able to load the E-code image, generated by the linker, and to start the execution at the entry point, the beginning of the executable code of the main program.

The E-machine is a simple stack machine (like the M-machine [12]). The E-code model has 9 registers and 53 operation codes such as: several load and store operations, P and V operations and input/output operations. There are no condition codes.

For lack of an E-code processor chip, E-code must be interpreted. In this context, interpretation has major advantages:

- the code generation can remain the same when porting the EDULAN environment to another computer.

- the E-code instruction set can be easily extended.

- E-code traces are more readable than most native code traces.

The interpreter is provided with a powerful *debugger* that allows a number of experiments during program execution. It can trace program execution, set break points, show and modify register and memory contents. It also can show some static and dynamic program statistics. It can ignore array bounds, semaphore operation, garbage collection, etc.

A program can be executed in a so called *monitor mode*. That mode shows a summary of the use of memory by the several processes. The distribution of memory among the active processes, the status of all processes, the current process, etc., are displayed repeatedly.

The interpreter is provided with a run time system that works as a kind of operating system for the scheduling of the concurrent processes. This run time system manages the distribution of the memory pages among the processes needing extra space, and collects the pages that are no longer needed by the processes, so as to use memory in an optimal way.

4. CURRENT STATUS AND POSSIBLE USES OF THE EDULAN ENVIRONMENT

Currently, EDULAN is implemented on an IBM PC/AT or compatible. It consists of about 8500 lines of Turbo Pascal. The manual (with tutorial) is about 250 pages long. EDULAN has now successfully been used for 2 years on several occasions in the computer science curriculum of the State University of Ghent. In particular it has been used to illustrate

(1) various aspects of software engineering, including the writing and documenting of readable programs; reading programs written by others through the analysis of the EDULAN environment itself. The environment is an example of a sizeable but well decomposed software package;

(2) the formal definition of programming languages;

(3) the study of compiler principles, their operation and implementation;

(4) operating system aspects like memory management, process scheduling and address translation, multitasking and concurrency principles, the nondeterministic or statistical behavior of multiple tasks in a concurrent environment;

(5) machine languages, automatic code generation, representations and support of compiled high-level languages, static and dynamic instruction frequency statistics;

(6) practical programming exercises by extending the existing system with, as an example
- additional parsing algorithms,
- additional synchronization mechanisms,
- macro processing capabilities in the scanner,
- a syntax sensitive editor,
- a program formatter to give EDULAN programs a standard layout;

(7) the demonstration of many software principles without having to go into detail. A number of eye-catching EDULAN demonstration programs can be set up to illustrate several aspects of modern high-level languages that are hard to explain in a theoretical way. It is much easier for a student to grasp the significance of a software error by means of a convincing demonstration than by reading an abstract explanation.

Although EDULAN covers language aspects in a fairly extensive way, it is clear that it lacks several concepts of modern high level languages, such as exception handling, string or list manipulation, heap variables, aids for software specifications and correctness proofs. It is equally clear that the current implementation of EDULAN can be extended to include most of the missing language characteristics.

Results

Currently, EDULAN is being used in two one-semester courses. In a course on compilers, the complete source of the EDULAN environment is used as a case study. The various parts of the compiler are discussed in class. Then the students are asked to write a small parsing application such as an interpreter for a mini language to evaluate algebraic expressions or a cross reference generator for real Pascal programs. In the operating systems course, EDULAN is used as an illustration tool. The students are asked to compile and run a number of existing parallel EDULAN programs and to trace their execution. Afterwards, the students are asked to write a number of small parallel programs themselves and to experiment with the available synchronization primitives. A two-year experiment with EDULAN indicates that students gain a deeper insight in the internal working of compilers and operating systems and in software engineering in general, after having studied the EDULAN environment.

5. CONCLUSIONS

In this paper we have presented EDULAN, an integrated system aimed at the support of software education. In its current form, EDULAN is a self-contained package, consisting of a MODULA-2 like language definition, a compiler, an intermediate language, and the associated interpreter. EDULAN thus provides realistic illustrations of varied topics such as language design, compiler design, language implementation, modularity, multitasking, debugging, etc. Students have full access to the internal organization of the package and are so allowed to extend the system. This ability provides nontrivial examples of good programming style, and an ideal training environment for team programming techniques. EDULAN has been in use for two-years in a computer science curriculum, with excellent results.

ACKNOWLEDGEMENT

The author wants to thank Prof. R. De Caluwe for her offer to provide the possibilities to experiment with the EDULAN package in several courses [16] and Prof. J. Van Campenhout for his thorough proofreading and the several valuable suggestions.

APPENDIX   A BNF DESCRIPTION OF EDULAN

```
<ProgDecl> ::= <ProgramType> <Identifier> ;
    [ <VarDecl> ]   { <ProcDecl> }
       [ BEGIN [ <Instructions> ] ]
    END <Identifier> .

<ProgramType> ::=  PROGRAM | MODULE | MONITOR

<VarDecl> ::=
    VAR <VariableDecl> { <VariableDecl> }

<VariableDecl> ::=
    <IdentDecl> [ ; <LinkAttr> ] ;

<IdentDecl> ::= <StorageAttr> <Identifier> :
    [ ARRAY <Range> OF ] <TypeSpec>

<StorageAttr> ::= [ VAL | REF ] [ STAT | DYN ]

<Range> ::= '[' [ - ] <UnsignedInteger> ..
                 [ - ] <UnsignedInteger>  ']'

<TypeSpec> ::= INTEGER | BOOLEAN | SEMAPHORE

<LinkAttr> ::= IMPORT | EXPORT

<ProcDecl> ::= <Proc> <Identifier>
    [ ( [ <FormalParams> ] ) ] [ : <TypeSpec>]
    [ ; FORWARD ] [ ; <LinkAttr> ] ;
    [ [ <VarDecl> ] BEGIN
      [ <Instructions> ] END <Identifier> ; ]

<ProcType> ::= PROCEDURE | FUNCTION | PROCESS

<FormalParams> ::= <IdentDecl> { , <IdentDecl>}

<Instructions> ::= <Instr> { ; <Instr> }
```

```
<Instr> ::= <AssignmentStat>  | <IfStat> |
    <WhileStat> | <ReadStat>  | <WriteStat> |
    <CallStat> | <ExitStat> | <PStat> | <VStat>

<AssignmentStat> ::= <Addressable> := <Expr>

<Addressable> ::=
    <Identifier> [ '[' <IntegerExpr> ']' ]

<Expr> ::= <IntegerExpr> | <BoolExpr>

<IntegerExpr> ::= <IntegerTerm>
    { <IntegerAddOp> <IntegerTerm> }

<IntegerAddOp> ::= + | -

<IntegerTerm> ::= <IntegerFactor>
    { <IntegerMulOp> <IntegerFactor> }

<IntegerMulOp> ::= * | DIV | MOD

<IntegerFactor> ::=
    <UnsignedInteger> | - <IntegerFactor> |
    <Addressable> | ( <IntegerExpr> ) |
    <Identifier> [ ( [ <ActualParams> ] ) ] |

<BoolExpr> ::=
    <BoolTerm> { <BoolAddOp> <BoolTerm> }

<BoolAddOp> ::= OR | XOR

<BoolTerm> ::=
    <BoolFactor> { <BoolMulOp> <BoolFactor> }

<BoolMulOp> ::= AND

<BoolFactor> ::= TRUE | FALSE |
    NOT <BoolFactor> | <Addressable> |
    <Identifier> [ ( [ <ActualParams> ] ) ] |
    ( <BoolExpr> ) |
    '{' <Condition> '}'

<Condition> ::=
    <IntegerExpr> <RelOp> <IntegerExpr>

<RelOp> ::= = | <> | >= | > | <= | <

<IfStat> ::=
    IF <BoolExpr> THEN [ <Instructions> ]
       [ ELSE [ <Instructions> ] ]
    ENDIF

<WhileStat> ::= WHILE <BoolExpr> DO
    [ <Instructions> ] ENDWHILE

<ReadStat> ::= READ ( <Addressable> )

<WriteStat> ::= WRITE
    ( <FormatString> [ : <IntegerExpr> ] )

<FormatString> ::= <String>

<CallStat> ::= <CallType>
    <Identifier> [ ( [ <ActualParams> ] ) ]

<CallType> ::= CALL | START

<ActualParams> ::= <Expr> {, <Expr> }

<ExitStat> ::= EXIT [ <Expr> ]

<PStat> ::= P ( <Addressable> )

<VStat> :: V ( <Addressable> )

<Identifier> ::= <Letter> {<Letter> | <Digit>}
<UnsignedInteger> ::= <Digit> { <Digit> }
<String> ::= ' { <Char> } '
<Comment> ::= (* { <Char> } *)
```

REFERENCES

[1] David Gries, *Compiler Construction for Digital Computers*, Wiley, New York, 1971.

[2] G. Goos and J. Hartmanis, editors, Lecture Notes in Computer Science, *Compiler Construction, An Advanced Course*, Springer Verlag, Berlin, 1974.

[3] A.V. Aho and J.D. Ullman, *Principles of Compiler Design*, Addison-Wesley, Reading, Mass, 1977.

[4] J. Lewi, K. De Vlaminck, J. Huens and M. Huybrechts, *A Programming Methodology in Compiler Construction*, North Holland, 1979.

[5] Henry Ledgard and Michael Marcotty, *The Programming Language Landscape*, Science Research Associates, Chicago, 1981.

[6] Maurice H. Halstead, *A Laboratory Manual for Compiler and Operating System Implementation*, Elsevier Computer Science Library, New York, 1974.

[7] Georg E. Maier, *Exceptionsbehandlung und Synchronisation, Entwurf und Methode*, Springer Verslag, New York, 1985 (German).

[8] Françoise André, Daniël Herman, Jean-Pierre Verjus, *Synchronization of Parallel Programs*, North Oxford Academic Publishing Company Limited, 1985.

[9] Niklaus Wirth, Modula-2, Tech. Report Institute for Informatics, ETH Zurich, 1980.

[10] Kathleen Jensen, Niklaus Wirth, *Pascal User Manual and Report*, Springer Verlag, New York, 1974.

[11] Kernighan and Ritchie, *The C Programming Language*, Prentice Hall, Englewoord Cliffs, 1978.

[12] Niklaus Wirth, *The Personal Computer Lilith*, Tech. Report Institute for Informatics, ETH Zürich, 1981.

[13] J.M. Van Campenhout, The Combination of Interpretation and Multiprocessing: A Marriage of Reason?, *Proc. Parallel Computing*, FU Berlin, 1985.

[14] D. Knuth, *The Art of Computer Programming: Fundamental Algorithms*, Addison Wesley, Reading, Mass., 1976.

[15] P.P. Dasiewicz, A Soft Real-time Multi-Tasking Basic Interpreter, *Proc. Software Engineering for Real Time Systems*, Cirencester, 1987, pp 173-177.

[16] K. De Bosschere, EDULAN, een didactisch softwarehulpmiddel bij de studie van systeemsoftware, *Masters thesis, State University of Ghent*, Ghent, 1987 (Dutch).

COMPUTERS IN EDUCATION, F. Lovis and E.D. Tagg (eds.)
Elsevier Science Publishers B.V. (North-Holland)
© IFIP, 1988

INTEGRATION OF TECHNOLOGY FOR SOCIAL SKILLS TRAINING

Malka Margalit, Israel.

School of Education, Tel Aviv University, Ramat-Aviv, 69978, Tel-Aviv, Israel.

Within the social-learning model, the project aimed at investigating computer integration into social skills training for adolescents with special needs. Two types of computer software were developed: An adventure game and simulations of social interactions. Content for the simulations was developed through (1) a literature review within the social-learning model, (2) analysis of critical social interactions (n=125) reported by teachers, counselors and social workers in 9 special schools; and (3) a survey of 165 adolescents' social skills. The comprehensive training procedure consisted of computer simulations, group discussions, role playing and homework tasks. Two cases demonstrate the program advantages and difficulties, directing future developments.

1. INTRODUCTION

1.1. The significance of social training

Individuals with special needs represent an heterogeneous group, differing widely in strengths and difficulties. However, regardless of the specific handicapping condition, social competence seems to be a central issue explaining aspects of present functioning, prospects for future adjustment, and directions for intervention planning. Among children with special needs, increased anxiety, passivity and a sometimes impulsive behaviour style seem closely related to a prolonged need for adult assistance and support [1]. Learning disabled and hyperactive youth experience difficulties in interpersonal relationships, and especially in perceiving and understanding others' affective states [2]. Ballar et al [3] stated that the high level of peer rejection in mentally retarded children has often been attributed to their social skills deficits. Difficulties in performing academic and nonacademic tasks, predicting sequences of events, and understanding complicated situations affect both current adjustment and future opportunities.

Individuals with special needs approaching adolescence may face more complicated dilemmas in the area of social relationships than do their nonhandicapped peers. They must not only cope with social dilemmas, but often they lack even the basic skills to deal effectively with the emerging age-related interactions with peers and authoritative figures. Skills such as self-control, the ability to postpone satisfaction, and the capacity to negotiate with authoritative demands have special meaning at this developmental stage.

A substantial number of studies has indicated that developmentally disabled children can be trained to be more proficient in problem solving and to develop more effective use of cognitive strategies, contributing to improved coping behavior [4, 5, 6, 7]. Computers may enable these individuals to explore and experience effective information processing within a controlled and structured environment.

1.2 Competence approach and social competence

The current conceptual definition of socially deviant behavior in adolescence reflects a theoretical change. Until recent years, the mental health approach has been dominated by defect approaches, such as the medical and the psychoanalytical models, which tune their users into the study of pathology. Conversely, competence and coping models, which focus on positive behaviors and capacities, lend themselves to planned interventions aimed at building skills and competencies rather than identifying, and eliminating defects. Young persons are seen as potentially capable of setting goals, identifying needs and developing skills that will enable them to cope more effectively with stress and to interact more effectively with environmental demands, as well as to lead fuller, more productive lives.

Competence models emphasize the ongoing mutually influencing interactions between individual and environment. The person-environment relationship has been described as fluid and changeable and as interdependent or transactional [8]. In terms of individual differences, the models usually emphasize, in combination with the effectiveness of overt behaviours, cognitive capacities such as response repertoires, coping skills, problem solving abilities, and capacities to generate behaviours appropriate to the situational requirements.

1.3 Social skills identification

The ability to cope with developmental tasks at the adolescent stage, requires an age-appropriate level of social competence. Social skills are defined as the ability to interact with others in a given social context in specific ways that are socially acceptable or valued and at the same time personally beneficial, mutually beneficial, or beneficial primarily to others [9]. At any given developmental level, social competence depends on adequate attention, information processing and motivation. In order to behave successfully in social interactions, the individual needs to have: (a) problem solving ability (b) empathy and perspective taking ability, and (c) the ability to control impulsive behaviors (self control). Therefore, any intervention program must consider these competencies, as well as the use of mediators.

Problem Solving: D'Zurilla and Goldfried [10] defined problem solving as a "behavioral process, whether overt or cognitive in nature, which (a) makes available a variety of potentially effective response alternatives for dealing with a problematic situation and, (b) increases the probability of selecting the most effective response among these various alternatives" (p.108). Thus, both a facility for generating alternatives and the ability to evaluate and select the most effective ones are necessary for efficient problem solving behavior [11].

Emphathy and perspective taking: The young person's ability to depart from the egocentric point of view, in favor of perspective taking and empathic feelings toward others, is usually viewed as developmental. Piaget [12] highlighted the developmental stage of egocentrism and the inability to perceive a situation from another person's point of view. However, this process is not an automatic one, and experience with peers seems to be an essential ingredient in its development.

Affective and cognitive elements were studied [13, 14] as interrelated parameters that must be carefully specified for research and intervention planning.

Self control: self control of impulsive behavior is a central issue in social skills training. In order to control impulsive behavior, the individual needs insight into his or her activity, motivation to monitor it, and mediators to delay and monitor his/her performance.

Mediators: The development of mediators which introduce a delay into the individual's automatic chain of responses, is often regarded as having considerable potential, particularly when the mediators are deliberately programmed as strategies for generalization. Mediators such as language (e.g., self-reporting, self-instructing), visual imagery and expectations have to be incorporated into the social training program. Bandura [15] pointed out that visual imagery is particularly important when verbal skills are lacking, and computers offer new possibilities in this area. A further cognitive mediator is that of expectations. "Efficacy expectations" [16] were defined as the convictions that one can successfully execute the behavior required in order to produce the desired outcomes. Computer activity may change self evaluation, affecting efficacy expectations.

The question of generalization or transfer is a crucial aspect [17], as is the question of maintenance of the trained skill. In order to enhance the generalization process, the trainee should be informed about the goals and advantages of training, and the training should involve different settings, such as school and work, free time with peers, and the family setting.

2. METHOD

The present paper will not address all aspects of this four-year project, but rather will focus on the pilot study, pinpointing the main issues in integrating technology and social skills training. This project consisted of the development of software and a training procedure for integrating computers into social skills training. Software was developed on the basis of a literature review, a social skills survey, and identification of problematic social interactions through content analysis.

2.1. Social skills identification

The structure of social competence among disabled adolescents and young adults in Israel was investigated via self assessment and teacher and parent reports of 165 adolescents with special needs, using the competence approach. In addition, the content analysis of 125 descriptions of social events, using the critical event approach, added validity to the identified social skills. Difficulties among adolescents from eight special schools were reported by their teachers, counselors and social workers. Three experienced special educators defined groups of difficulties and their sources.

2.2. Software development

In this project two types of software are being developed: (a) an adventure game and (b) simulations of social interactions. The latter are still being developed, thus only the former will be described. An adventure game was programmed on the Commodore 64, detailing the adventures of Prince Yoav, who is constantly confronted with tasks demanding social problem solving. The game was based on the social-learning model, using a projective framework. The skills were defined according to Goldstein's Structured Learning Approach which has recently gained considerable attention [18]. Prince Yoav must solve social problems and face stressful situations, authoritative demands, and insulting remarks. He must develop self-control, the ability to negotiate with others, and the capacity to plan his social interactions. The disabled adolescent was invited to advise Yoav on the best strategy in each of the different episodes, so as to avoid dangers and difficulties and to win the princess' love. Planned behavior was reinforced (by gaining points), and impulsive decisions were punished (by losing points).

3. PILOT STUDY

3.1. The sample

The training was performed in three different settings: (a) a rehabilitation center (4 males and 3 females), (b) a school for mentally retarded adolescents (4 males and 3 females) and (c) learning disabled youth club (2 males and 1 female). The 17 adolescents were students of special education, with an age range of 16 to 20 years.

3.2. Instruments

Goldstein's social competence questionnaire [18]: The Hebrew adaptation of the questionnaire was factor analyzed, and four factors were identified: interrelation competence, self-control competence, planning competence and control in stressful situations.
Social interaction questionnaire: The questionnaire consisted of 13 descriptions of socially stressful situations. The four solutions provided for each situation represent different levels of stress resolution: impulsive, passive, self-controlled, and avoidant responses.
Prince Yoav's adventure game (see 2.2)

3.3. Procedure

Before and after training on the computer, using the adventure game, the adolescents were interviewed individually, using the questionnaires. The students met with the trainer in small groups once or twice a week, for a total of 5 to 7 meetings. Each meeting lasted 45 to 80 minutes. The training included a group discussion before and after the game, pinpointing decision-making during the game situation and during the adolescents' real-life social interactions and conflicts. The adventure game was used as a projective simulation to elicit motivation for sharing personal experience and exploring a wide range of alternative solutions. Discussions of personal experiences and their relations to the projective plot were encouraged and explored.

3.4 Results

All participants enjoyed the procedure and the game, making personal comments and detailing social encounters. They viewed the situation as facilitating a discussion of their own difficulties. Most of the participants tended to "fail" the game at least twice in each session, regardless of the prolonged discussions. They continued to request additional chances to "win more points", insisting on repeating the same game at every meeting. The repeated activities enabled the adolescents to reach automaticity of the trained skill. Their main difficulties seemed to stem from their inability to control impulsivity. In some areas, such as providing help to friends in need, they did not demonstrate any difficulty, supporting the demand for a modular training procedure adaptable to individual needs and differences.

4. TWO CASES

4.1. Etti

Etti, a nineteen year old female, who was described as a learning disabled, impulsive adolescent, avoided any difficulty by running away from the stressful situation. She played the adventure game at four different weekly meetings, lasting 65 to 75 minutes each. She seemed very aroused by the game and related the adventures of Yoav and the princess to her own difficulties with her parents. She advised the prince to run away, and spontaneously spoke about her disagreements with her parents, in which she tended either to shout and weep uncontrollably, or to run away. She continually repeated that she knew running away would not solve anything, and that she always had to return home and be punished. However, she initially responded to every conflict in the game with a similar reaction. After two meetings, she expressed a wish to be able to cope less impulsively with stressful situations. In the third meeting she played more slowly, and spoke most of the time about how difficult it would be for a real prince to cope with such stresses and not run away.

Etti was also asked to write down episodes that occurred during the week, when she had felt like running away or reacting impulsively, and what had happened. Her self-report reflected a growing measure of self-control and planning. Her scores in the game gradually increased (from 210 to 240 to 300 and finally to 490). At the end of the training, she wrote to the counsellor who performed the training, "This game helped me to think before I do something, taught me what to do when unhappy things happen to me. However, I would like to be alone with the computer, to think about my behaviour all by myself. To try and see what will happen if I run away and if I stay, if I plan carefully and if I let it go." Etti's scores on the social skills questionnaire are presented on Table 1. After training she improved her scores in planning and self control, but no changes were noted on interpersonal relations. She demonstrated increased reflective thinking and decreased impulsive problem solving.

4.2. Gal

Gal, a nineteen year old, trainable mentally retarded adolescent, enjoyed the adventure game and played it six different times for 45 minutes each. He tended to relate personal problems and familial conflicts to the game, and he especially enjoyed increasing his scores. Gal relayed personal stories of being afraid in crisis situations (e.g., meeting a dog), and of how he began to plan in advance in order to avoid stress. Once, when the teacher was late to class, he took on her role, telling his classmates, "Let's pretend we're playing with computers. Who wants to be Prince Yoav and tell us a problem?" Very seriously he encouraged his friends to present difficulties and to list alternative solutions. As can be seen in Table 1, his scores revealed advancement in three areas: (a) self control, (b) planning ability, and (c) managing in stressful situations.

5. DISCUSSION

The purpose of the project was to facilitate change in social functioning among students with special needs through comprehensive social skills training. Computer programs were integrated in a problem solving procedure in order to reinforce explorations and experiencing of social alternatives. The pilot study demonstrated the value of computer programs in facilitating the learning of alternative responses and the exploration of new solutions within a protected environment. Two major areas for discussion were raised by the pilot study: individual differences and the role of teachers.

Individual differences, even in this small group of adolescents, were demonstrated not only in competence levels, but also in specific behavior styles (e.g., a preference to work alone). These variations accentuate the need for a modular program that can be easily adapted to individual needs and differences.

The teacher's role is central to developing the desired social strategies. Special attention should be devoted to the teacher's training, including an emphasis on understanding the concept of strategies and mediators, and sensitivity to students' individual needs. Teachers should learn to teach individuals (1) how to learn rather than only what to learn, and (2) to teach them to

Social Competence Questionnaire Scores

Skills	Etti Pre	Etti Post	Gal Pre	Gal Post
Planning	23	28	19	33
Self Control	22	35	29	32
Interpersonal	54	54	75	74
Stressful Situations	30	45	32	43

behave as successful learners who spontaneously plan, check and monitor themselves in their learning, performance and problem solving. The informed training approach adds an important aspect by providing trainees with a clear rationale of the strategy to be trained and the direct relationship between strategy use and its beneficial effects on learning. It has already been established that a trainee is likely to generalize a learned strategy to a new environment only if the application is clearly to his or her advantage. However, if the trainee considers the strategy application to involve excessive effort, and the benefit not matching the effort expenditure, he or she is unlikely to generalize the learned strategy. The integration of computers into training emphasized the growing recognition that the critical question lies not in what the computer will do to the disabled child, but rather what the child can do with computers [19].

ACKNOWLEDGEMENT

The contents of this report were developed under grants from the Israeli Ministry of Education, Rothschild Foundation and Nitzan Tel-Aviv.
The author would like to acknowledge the editorial assistance of Dee M. Bargteil.

REFERENCES

[1] Matson, J.L., Heinze, A., Helsel, W.J. and Kapperman, G. Assessing social behaviors in the visually handicapped: The MESSY, Journal of Clinical Child Psychology 15 (1986) 78.

[2] Bryan, T.H. Social relationships and verbal interactions of learning disabled children, Journal of Learning Disabilities 11 (1978) 107.

[3] Ballard, M., Corman, L., Gottlieb, J.R. and Kaufman, M.J. Improving the social status of mainstreamed retarded children. Journal of Educational Psychology 69,5 (1977) 605.

[4] Campione, J.C., Brown, A.L., and Bryant, N. R. Individual differences in learning and memory, in R.J. Sternberg, ed, Human abilities: an information-processing approach (Freeman, New York, 1985), pp.103-126.

[5] Margalit, M. The role of technology in the search of coherence of special needs children in Israel, Invitational FY87 Symposium on Special Education Technology (June 1987, Washington, DC).

[6] Margalit, M., Weisel, A., and Shulman, S. The facilitation of information processing in learning disabled children using computer games, Educational Psychology, 7(1) (1987) 47.

[7] Mayer, R.E. Thinking, problem solving, cognition (Freeman, New York, 1983).

[8] Wine, J.D. From defect to competence models, In J.D. Wine and M.D. Smye, eds., Social skills (The Guilford, New York, 1981),pp.3-35.

[9] Gresham, F.M. Conceptual and definitional issues in the assessment of children's social skills: Implications for classification and training, Journal of Clinical Child Psychology 15(1) (1985) 3.

[10] D'Zurilla T.J.and Goldfried, M.R. Problem solving and behavior modification, Journal of Abnormal Psychology 78(1) (1971),107.

[11] Shure, M.B. and Spivak, G. Interpersonal problem solving as a mediator of behavioral adjustment in preschool and kindergarten children, Journal of Applied Developmental Psychology, 1 (1980) 29.

[12] Piaget, J. The language and the thought of the child. (Routledge & Kagan Paul, London, 1926)

[13] Fesbach, N.D. Empathy in children: Some theoretical and empirical considerations. Counseling Psychologist 5(2),(1975) 25.

[14] Rotenberg, M.J. Conceptual and methodological notes in affective and cognitive role taking (sympathy and empathy): An illustrative experiment with delinquent and nondelinquent boys, Journal of Genetic Psychology 125 (1974) 177.

[15] Bandura, A. Self-Efficacy: Toward a unifying theory of behavioral change, Psychological Review 84 (1977) 191.

[16] Bandura, A. Social learning theory, (Prentice-Hall, Englewood Cliffs, N.J, 1977).

[17] Davies, R.R. and Rogers, E.S. Social skill training with persons who are mentally retarded, Mental Retardation 28 (1985) 186.

[18] Goldstein, A.P., Sprafkin, R.P., Gershaw, J.N. and Klein, P.A. Skillstreaming the adolescent. (Research Press, Illinois, 1983).

[19] Turkle, S. The second self: computers and the human spirit (Simon and Schuster, New York, 1984).

COMPUTERS IN EDUCATION, F. Lovis and E.D. Tagg (eds.)
Elsevier Science Publishers B.V. (North-Holland)
IFIP, 1988

CAN COMPUTER HELP COMBAT SCHOOL FAILURE* ?

Claude PAIR [+], Daniel CHARTIER [§], André FLIELLER [**], Michel GALLOY [**]
Jean-Marc GEBLER [+], Michelle PILLOT [++], Maryse QUERE [+]

The paper presents experimental work on the use of Computers in view of helping pupils aged 14 to 18 who have failed to achieve basic academic standards. We first endeavoured to identify the reasons for their failure, before utilizing informatics in various situations (class-room or autonomous access to computers) and for various activities (games, drawing, text processing, information retrieval, programming, use of courseware). The paper presents first results as to the pupils' progress, their problem-solving strategies and their attitudes towards the computer.

1. INTRODUCTION

The introduction of computers into French schools dates back to the early 1970's <13> ; only the upper secondary schools were then concerned, in other words the more successful pupils. Later on, all schools, including primary, were equipped with microcomputers <15>. But no clear objectives were defined. There is, therefore, a strong risk that only those already the most successful at school will draw the greatest benefit from informatics, which will widen the existing gap between them and the others.

Moreover it is remarkable that none of the 133 sessions of the 4th World Conference on Computers in Education <9> specifically dealt with the problem of how informatics can help remedy or reduce school failure. This does not mean that its contributions are not underlined in various lectures on LOGO, word-processing or the national experience of a country, but stresses how little this theme is taken into account in experimental and research work.

However think tank organisations and decision makers are concerned with this problem. For example, <20> states that the new information technologies are intended for children who make no progress in the educational system. The Ministry of Higher Education in Canada has created a research centre, one of whose themes will be the individualization of teaching, for under and over-achieving pupils <7>. But are these concerns being absorbed into reality ?

Some numerically significant experiences of introducing computers into the educational system show the advantages that problem pupils derive <8>. Outside the educational system, computers are valuable too in an active pedagogy which succeeds in doing away with the traditional emphasis on the teacher-learner relationship and creates a new way of evaluating standards <4> <5>.

The hypothesis on which our experiment is based is also that computers can be instrumental not only in avoiding school failure but also in remedying causes of it.

As a matter of fact, one of the major problems met by the French school system is what to do with pupils who, having repeated several classes at primary school level or at "collège" (i.e. lower secondary school) reach the age of fourteen or fifteen with poor prospects of achieving the collège terminal requirements. One of the possibilities offered to them until now has been to enter a vocational secondary school (lycée professionnel) ; but many of the corresponding jobs are on the way of disappearing and those which remain require higher skills. Therefore, it has been recently decided to create classes of a new type, called "technological", in these vocational schools <14> <1>. The aim of these new classes is not vocational training but, through different methods and particularly through the study of various technologies, to enable the pupils to reach, in two years, the standards in general skills expected from all pupils at the end of the collège.

This quite naturally led us to choose as a testing ground those technological classes, which moreover are still searching for the subjects, contents, techniques and methods enabling them to achieve their objectives.

The aims of this project are as follows:
- to improve the level of success in some of these classes ;
- to observe the conditions of setting up this new tool in classes ;
- to reflect on what such a "technological" class built around computing (a technique not yet established at this level, unlike mechanics or short-hand and typing) could be ;
- to research into the characteristics of this category of pupils, into their progress when engaged in various activities involving computing, and into the qualities of the courseware most likely to make them progress.

*"School-failure" is the direct translation of "échec scolaire", a recurring theme in all school debates in France. "Echec scolaire" refers both to the inability of the present school system to adapt itself to all pupils and to the fact that a great number of pupils cannot adapt themselves to it.
+ Centre de Recherche en Informatique de Nancy et Cellule de Formation des Maîtres de l'Université de Nancy I, BP 239, 54506 Vandœuvre Cedex, France.
§ Institut National d'Orientation Professionnelle, 41 rue Gay-Lussac, 75005 Paris, France
** Laboratoire de Psychologie Sociale (G. R. C.), Université de Nancy II, 54000 Nancy, France.
++ Centre Régional de Documentation Pédagogique, 99 rue de Metz, 54000 Nancy, France.

2. DESCRIPTION OF THE EXPERIMENT

2.1. Defining the experimental field

We worked with three vocational secondary schools on the outskirts of Nancy. Two of them have secretarial work and accountancy as main technical subjects : the majority of the pupils are girls. In the other one, subjects taught are industrial techniques (mechanics, electricity...) and the pupils are mostly boys. In each of these schools a group of pupils of the first year started taking part in the experiment in the autumn of 1986 (105 pupils in all) ; for them the experiment will, therefore, end in June 1988. These classes represent a first stage of the experiment and they are the subject of this article.

Each class has at its disposal a "nano-net" which is the hardware that was installed in every school of this level. In our case the net is constituted by eight home micro-computers (Thomson MO5's). This hardware supports educational software ; courseware on a variety of subjects, but also more general software (word-processor, graphics, information retrieval, spreadsheet...), as well as programming languages, in particular LOGO. The teachers of these classes had varying degrees of knowledge in computer science. Most had none but some of them already had a good working knowledge of computers.

2.2. Identifying the key problems areas

The first part of the work aimed at becoming familiar with the technological classes which constitute our research environment. This implied knowing the pupils and the objectives of their teachers, as well as identifying the problems encountered in achieving these objectives.

To know the pupils, we first of all had to compare them to others of a similar age who had stayed at the secondary school. This comparison was made with the help of tests in French and mathematics (to assess school work), in logical reasoning and in logical spatial reasoning. A questionnaire was also used and children were interviewed to know how they felt about school and school work.

On the other hand, workshops with teachers have made it possible to define their teaching objectives and to get to know their opinion on the nature and the origin of the difficulties encountered by the pupils.

The result of this first task, carried out both with pupils and teachers, has been the identification of four types of difficulties which seem to be part of the explanation of pupils' failure :
- a lack of motivation for school
- a lack of autonomy in their work and difficulties with problem solving
- an insufficient familiarity with written language
- a slowness in the development of logical capacities which prevents the acquisition of notions requiring the use of formal thinking (as understood by Piaget).

These difficulties lead pupils to have serious gaps in various subjects ; this shows up failure, increases lack of motivation and inhibits the capacities for autonomous work. So it is therefore clear that the difficulties are interdependent.

To these hypotheses founded on this first exploration, we have added another one, less obvious at first sight and which deals with the ways of presenting facts : some of the pupils who are behind in their educational development have an individual preference for a mode of presentation in the logic of facts generally associated to strategies of global resolution (an example of which is given by pictorial representations used in problems of a predominantly spatial nature) ; and they are behind partially because of this preference for which teachers have scant regard. Indeed, in teaching habits and in teachers' expectations, sequential representation generally holds a privileged place and analytical reasoning supported by a written text is preferred. So should one discover in pupils with learning difficulties a relative superiority in the field of spatial aptitudes, one could use them to overcome these difficulties.

2.3. The planning of activities

One soon realises how computer science can assist in resolving these difficulties. The computer is, and all researchers agree on this point, a powerful tool for motivation.

One may also hope that computing, and notably programming, is a tool for the development of logical capacities, in particular with regard to sequencing, to combinatorial thinking, type-setting and, more generally, passing from the "concrete" to the "formal" stage. It is true that in spite of much research work, particularly on LOGO [21], no definite proof seems to have been put forward regarding this topic, notably owing to the brevity of the experiments. Moreover, the work done is mostly about pupils younger than those with whom we are concerned.

Language difficulties reside not so much in the spoken word but rather in the written word [11]. Pupils who have reached an educational stalemate do not take sufficient distance from the written text, they do not consider it as an object upon which it is possible and interesting to work. In this respect the computer, especially with word-processing, has an important role to play and many experiments have already been carried out in this domain [12][16].

Finally, courseware, notably in mathematics and in grammar, is intended to facilitate the acquisition of certain notions and to fill up identified gaps.

But since the difficulties encountered by the pupils are not unrelated, it is impossible to deal with them separately. Moreover, one cannot hope that one or the other computing activity, necessarily limited in time, can by itself reverse a situation where the pupil's failure is deep-rooted and already long standing.

The originality of our experiment is that several forms of activity are being used concurrently. To begin with, games and graphic activities are presented in order to motivate the pupils and to enable them to become familiar with the machine. It is then possible to go straight from the purely gratuitous games to others of a more educational nature, then to courseware aimed at definite topics (particularly in Mathematics and French). When the pupils have mastered the use of the machine one can introduce information retrieval software and spreadsheets. The spreadsheet leads to a kind of programming in which nothing is concealed : this prepares pupils to go further in the procedural aspect when they come to use LOGO. Similarly, the use of word processing not only makes language exercises possible but also renews the presentation of educational documents and homework.

Indeed, an important idea is that it is not enough to use the computer during lesson time, for two main reasons : time is limited and it is not possible to restrict oneself to computing activities ; the development of the ability to be autonomous and to work alone cannot be achieved without periods set aside for independent work. We have, therefore, expressed the wish for pupils to have free access to computers outside lesson time.

2.4. Carrying out the experiment

This type of "action-research", which aims at embracing all the classroom activities, can never be carried out exactly as planned. We were confronted with several kinds of difficulties.

Problems of a technical nature limited the scope of our experiment : hardware not as reliable as had been hoped, especially the lightpens we had been counting on for drawing ; low quality courseware, insufficiently founded on an analysis of the causes of failure ; a word-processor not able to play its role to the full, uninviting as it was ; lastly, technological courseware hard to come by.

School organisation also limited our impact. For example, the fact that many pupils had to leave immediately after class to catch the school buses meant that the three schools concerned reacted unequally to autonomous work.

One can, however, ask oneself if this is not symptomatic of deeper causes. The fear of leaving often difficult and unpredictable children on their own undoubtedly made some teachers hesitant, though it must be said that, whenever such a risk was taken, fear proved to have been unfounded. The refusal of some teachers to let their pupils familiarize themselves with the computers through games did not help. It might also be that some teachers were worried that their pupils would become more skilled than they.

It was perhaps rash to work with teachers who were so unequally qualified. Some of them who had little training or who didn't have courseware relevant to their discipline didn't use computers and in effect withdrew from the experiment. On the whole the computers were used as planned, though it must be said that : word-processing played a lesser role than expected and so limited its use after school hours ; the organisation of autonomous work varied from one school to another ; it was almost non-existent in one, was timetabled in another albeit under the firm guidance of a tutor, it worked as planned in the third school even though the pupils chose to play games rather than do schoolwork. The total amount of time the pupils spent in activities involving computers varied from 120 to 200 hours over the year.

3. SOME RESULTS

The experiment is not yet at an end. It would therefore be premature to draw any conclusions, although we have already achieved some interesting intermediary results.

3.1. Tests on knowledge and on the development of logical capacities

Two ability tests were given, one at the beginning and the other at the end of the school year, following the test-retest procedure. The children were tested on their school work, on the development of their logical capacities and on their logical spatial reasoning.

The school work was appraised through adaptations of existing tests <29>. The level of logical thinking was assessed through a Piaget style test <6> divided into four parts, respectively based on logic of classes, propositional logic, combinatorial thinking and coordination of two reference systems. Subjects are graded into five levels: Preoperational, Concrete operational, Transitional, Formal operational level A, Formal operational level B. Spatial skills were assessed by means of two tests loading heavily on the spatial factor <25>.

The assessments aimed both at comparing pupils from technological classes to those in the lower secondary schools (first test and a sample group made up of pupils from neighbouring secondary schools), and assessing the pupils' progress during the year (second test and a twenty-nine pupil technology class not involved in the experiment).
The results of the first assessment revealed that :
- In schoolwork, secondary school pupils were greatly and uniformly superior in Mathematics ; in French, the experimental classes' pupils presented mixed results rather than globally worse ones.
- As to logical reasoning, the Transitional level is the most common among pupils of the technological classes, whereas a majority of secondary school pupils (who, it must be stressed, are on average one year younger) reached the Formal level A. One exception, however, should be noted which does not contradict the hypothesis made at the end of 2.2 : in the part of the test which required candidates to coordinate two spatial movements, the technological industrial class obtained relatively good results.
- The aptitude at logical spatial reasoning only marginally differentiated between the two educational types.

From the second evaluation at the end of the school year, it becomes apparent that the pupils in the technological classes involved in the experiment have on average made significant progress in Mathematics, in French and in the test in which the coordination of two systems of reference relies on spatial representation of the problem (mechanical curves). In Mathematics and two out of the three classes in French, their level remains, however, far below that of the pupils in secondary school classes at the beginning of the school year.

The most interesting result is found in the two parallel groups of the same vocational school one of which was a reference group. The comparison between the two tests does not give a very clear result in the tests of logical development. But as regards school work, the class which had had the advantage of a "computer bath" shows much greater progress : if one takes as a criterion the increase in the average score, it is of 46% in mathematics in the experimental class against 33% in the reference class, and of 48% in French against 9%. This result is quite encouraging, even if it is still fragile and would need to be confirmed by tests on greater numbers of pupils.

It is corroborated by a more qualitative yet interesting observation. In one of the schools, the second year experimental class comprises, for reasons of reorganisation, both pupils who have used computers in mathematics in the previous year as well as others who have not ; as the teachers worked in close collaboration, progression and work, apart from the use of computers, were very similar. A great difference, however, appears in the pupils' performance when they are interpreting and using graphics. This might bring an element of confirmation to the hypothesis expressed earlier concerning the pupils' perception of knowledge.

3.2. Evaluation by the teachers

As already mentioned, we first obtained from the teachers a list of stumbling blocks which, in their opinion, hindered their pupils' progress and differentiated them from those who had remained in the *collège* : a certain slowness in mastering abstract capacities and a lack of autonomy concerning schoolwork and problem solving were found to be at the root of the pupils' difficulties.

To enable teachers to clarify what these notions meant for them and carry out the observation, we have drawn up a reference list from their definitions. It describes the capacities which, once mastered, lead to abstract thinking and autonomy (e.g. finding information, working alone, analysing a document). We decided to make these capacities the object of our observation. What we try to discover is for which capacities computers can help pupils to show their ability and to set in motion their own learning strategies. Hence the capacities were evaluated at the end of the year in two situations, but only in one of them computers were used. This first stage led us to discover the capacities for which it was possible to note, with certain pupils, their mastery in a computer evaluation situation and not in the other situation, and inversely the mastery in a non-computer evaluating situation and not in the other one. In the first case it is possible to surmise that the "computer bath" has helped in the mastering of certain capacities, but without any transfer to other situations.

Parallel with this evaluation carried out on precise situations and according to previously defined criteria, the teachers provided conclusions on the attitude and motivation of the pupils. As has been the case in most other experiments, these evaluations are globally positive on motivation but less so on the results obtained in schools.

3.3. Pupils' opinions and representations of informatics

Analysing the educational value of computers leads one inevitably to consider how pupils view computers. Research has shown the importance of how knowledge is viewed <27>. Taking into account the pupils' views not only helped us to assess what importance they would give to computers in their training, but also enabled us to measure our impact. <2> underlines these considerations and proposes an attitude scale ; another proposal is <24>.

To study how pupils view the computers after a year's work, we questioned them in June 1987. They see the computer in a rather positive light, as an aid to learning for which you do not have to be particularly bright. A good many of them consider that the computer can help them in their jobs and in everyday life. This picture is confirmed by the fact that many of them wish to go on using computers. One notices, however, that in the group of those who did not go to the computer room outside lesson time, a proportionally greater number of pupils state that, in the future, computers will replace man and that they will cause unemployment.

3.4. Observations on problem solving by pupils

<21> presents LOGO programming as a powerful means to develop the structuring of thought as analysed by Piaget. However results in this field are disappointing since no measureable effect has been observed in the acquisition of structured thought <10> <22> <26>. Founded on "before and after" comparisons, this research, however, fails to study the activity of the pupil who is in training, so leaving aside an essential question if one wishes to elucidate the problem of the transfer of knowledge <19>. To understand the effects of programming one would have to stop turning it into a "black box"<23>.

One reaches the same conclusions regarding the possible role of social interaction resulting from the learning of LOGO in groups. Some authors refer to the concept of the socio-cognitive conflict <17> to theorize about the effect of these interactions. But most of the time, socio-cognitive conflicts are also studied through "before and after" comparisons, which deal with the interactions as with a "black box" <3> <28>.

Consequently, it was found opportune to plan some research work which would concentrate on the process of problem solving and on the processes of interaction in the course of programming with LOGO. As to the former, we took a special interest in the planning of the action on the one hand and in the exploitation of errors on the other. Concerning the latter, three hypotheses were made.
1. To explain the role played by interactions in the training, more than one process must be brought into play : socio-cognitive conflicts, but also explanations that the pupils mutually give each other (affecting both the giver and the receiver), and acquisition of solutions through observation.
2. The interactions have negative as well as positive effects.
3. The relative level of competence of the partners is an essential variable for the interpretation of these effects.

Data was collected by a method combining observation and experimentation. After twenty hours of initiation in LOGO, the thirty pupils of one of the experimental classes were systematically observed in ten weekly half hour sessions during which they were asked to make two drawings successively (a factory and then a locomotive), by following models provided by the experimenters. The pupils could use a manual but had to work entirely on their own and received no further training in LOGO during the whole observation period.

For the first drawing, the pupils were divided at random into two groups : one where they worked individually and the other where they worked in pairs. The situations were inverted for the second drawing so that each pupil worked alone in five sessions and with a partner in the other five. The pupils themselves chose their partners.

The pupils' activity was recorded by regular hard copies (one every twenty-five seconds) which, once put together, reveal all the validated orders as well as the successive stages of the completed drawing. The conversations of the pairs were recorded and the two types of records compared. A voluminous corpus resulted which is, as far as we know, unique. The collected material is now being analysed. The conversation will be studied from the point of view of thematic contents and the results examined in the light of the composition of the pairs (difference in the levels of competence). But we also intend to use the methods of conversational analysis developed by the linguists of the Geneva school <17>.

The observations made of the pupils at work already provide some indications as to how the pupils react in these circumstances. They do not attempt to think ahead. When drawing, they only take a quick glance at the picture they must reproduce and set themselves to work immediately, without taking time to either analyse possible problems or break down their work. In LOGO this attitude is hardly conducive to a correct use of procedures.

Pupils seemed not to acquire the capacity to learn from mistakes. Faced with a mistake, the pupils we observed would make successive attempts at correcting their work without taking time to analyse the problem. This might put into question the idea that pupils can progress without the help of a teacher.

As for interactions, hypotheses 1 and 2 seem verified ; mutual assistance is the result not only of one but of several processes, and interactions do not just have positive effects on the study of programming. Important differences between individuals and between pairs have also appeared ; the type of interactions changes a great deal with each pair and some pupils seem better adapted to one method of work than to the other.

4. CONCLUSION

We have attempted to conduct a relatively global experiment both as regards our objective (the fight against school failure) and our methods (the simultaneous use of all the aspects of computers). It is then clear that only a global evaluation can be envisaged.

This research, however, enables one to examine now certain more specific points such as the problem-solving strategies of this type of pupils, the interaction between them, the evaluation of their attitudes towards the computer,

and even the exploration of the characteristics of the software adapted to their needs.

In particular, the relative independence of the figurative aspects of knowledge and the opportunities of graphic representations offered by computers could help in the designing of courseware which would lead the pupils to the mastery of abstract logical and mathematical notions by the use of a variety of representations of knowledge. Negative numbers and powers of numbers, which we have noticed pupils find difficult, are possible examples.

REFERENCES

<1> G. Baloup, C. Delamare and A. Gendrot, Propositions pédagogiques pour aider les élèves à construire leur réussite scolaire, Cibles n° 12-13, 1986.

<2> G.G. Bear, H.C. Richards and P. Lancaster, Attitudes toward computers : validation of computer attitudes scale, J. Educat. Computing Res., vol 3, n° 2, 1987, 207-218.

<3> A. Flieller, La coéducation de l'intelligence, Presses Universitaires, Nancy, 1986.

<4> J.N. Gers and D. Poisson, Premier bilan de l'utilisation des ordinateurs en insertion jeunes, Cahiers d'études du CUEEP, Lille, 1986.

<5> Hermes, L'insertion, une transition dans le système éducatif : étude sur les usages de la micro-informatique, recherche d'ancrages et de déblocages. Equipe Hermes, Université de Provence, Marseille, 1986.

<6> J. Hornemann, Influence du contenu sur la résolution de problèmes logiques, Enfance, n° 1-2, 1974, 45-64.

<7> J.P. Hubac, Rapport de mission au Québec, Agence de l'Informatique, Paris, 1986.

<8> IBM, The Viksjö Project, final report, IBM, Stockholm, 1987.

<9> IFIP, Proceedings of the 4th WORLD Conference on Computers in Education, North Holland, Amsterdam, 1985.

<10> L. Krasnor and J. Mitterer, Logo and the development of general problem-solving skills, The Alberta Journal of Educational Research, vol. 30, 1984, 133-144.

<11> A. Lazar, Ecrire au tertiaire, Rencontres Pédagogiques, Institut National de Recherche Pédagogique, Paris, 1986.

<12> A.M. Le Corguillé, B. Michonneau and R. Collinot, Traitement de texte et enseignement du français, Cedic-Nathan, Paris, 1987.

<13> W. Mercouroff, L'expérience française d'introduction de l'informatique dans l'enseignement secondaire, Computers in Education, IFIP World Conference, North Holland, Amsterdam, 1976, 23-25.

<14> Ministère de l'Education Nationale, Participation des lycées d'enseignement professionnel à la rénovation du premier cycle : expérimentation en classe de quatrième de L.E.P., Bulletin Officiel de l'Education Nationale, n° 16, 1984, 1586-1588.

<15> Ministère de l'Education Nationale, Informatique pour tous, Mission aux Technologies Nouvelles, Paris, 1985.

<16> Ministère de l'Education Nationale, L'informatique dans les lycées : comparaison de différents modes d'approche et d'appropriation de l'informatique en seconds cycles long et court, Direction des Lycées, Paris, 1986.

<17> J. Moeschler, Argumentation et conversation : Eléments pour une analyse pragmatique du discours, Hatier, Paris, 1985.

<18> G. Mugny, Psychologie sociale du développement cognitif, Peter Lang, Berne, 1985.

<19> J. Mitterer and L. Krasnor, Logo and the development of problem-solving : an empirical test, Brock University, St. Catherines, Ontario, Canada, 1985.

<20> OECD, Information technologies and basic learning, CERI-OECD, Paris, 1986.

<21> S. Papert, Mindstorms : Children, computers and powerful ideas, Basic Books, New-York, 1980.

<22> R. Pea, Logo Programming and Problem Solving, Bank Street Technical Report 12, New York, 1983.

<23> R. Pea and M. Kurland, On the cognitive effects of learning computer programming : A critical look, Technical Report 9, New York Center for Children and Technology, 1984.

<24> P.M. Popovitch, K.R. Hyde, T. Zakrajsek and C. Blumer, The development of the attitudes toward computer usage scale, Educational and Psychological Measurement, vol. 47, 1987, 261-269.

<25> M. Reuchlin and E. Valin, Tests collectifs du centre de recherches, BINOP, vol. 3, 1953, 1-152.

<26> F. Robert, A propos des expériences de transfert dans le cadre des utilisations de Logo, Congrès Le fonctionnement de l'enfant à l'école, Université de Poitiers (France), 1987.

<27> M. Sanner, Représentation et obstacles épistémologiques, Aster 18, 1980, 88-96.

<28> A. Trognon, Sur la coréférence dans les groupes de travail, Colloque La psychologie sociale appliquée dans ses pratiques, Maison des Sciences de l'Homme, Paris, 1985.

<29> S.I.G.E.S., Evaluation pédagogique dans les collèges (Français-Mathématiques), Document de travail, SIGES, Ministère de l'éducation Nationale, Paris, 1982.

COMPUTERS IN EDUCATION, F. Lovis and E.D. Tagg (eds.)
Elsevier Science Publishers B.V. (North-Holland)
© IFIP. 1988

COMPUTER-ASSISTED ACQUISITION OF SEMANTIC CONCEPTS BY DEAF CHILDREN

An ad interim report on a research project

by Felix STUDER

Institut de pédagogie curative de l'Université de Fribourg/Suisse
21, rue St. Pierre Canisius, CH-1700 Fribourg, Switzerland

A computer program aimed to teach semantic concepts to deaf children is presented. The program has not been completed yet. More psychological knowledge of the process of learning is needed in order to improve present programs.

1. INTRODUCTION

The research project I will deal with stems from the fact that up to now the teaching programs used in schools are unsatisfactory from an educational point of view (cf O'SHEA, SELF [1]). The lack of flexibility and adaptability in these teaching programs makes them significantly inferior to human teachers. I believe these programs should be used only when they prove to be superior to human teachers, not only in consequence of their higher patience and emotionally neutral reactions.

For the past twenty years, what has been called artificial intelligence has been used to develop programs of higher quality. I will explain here that difficulties are still to be found in the development of such programs. In general it can be said that the problems lie less in the domain of data processing than in that of psychology because the procedures of learning and instruction are not understood well enough yet.

2. THE SUBJECT

Underlying this research project is the following problem:

The hearing impairment of deaf children is the cause of their inability to communicate verbally. This is the primary handicap. Because semantic concepts are learnt for the most part through verbal communication, there is a secondary handicap: an insufficient mastery of semantic concepts. The person who does not master concepts sufficiently is handicapped in his ability to communicate verbally. Diagram 1 illustrates how the limited ability to communicate verbally and the insufficient mastery of semantic concepts create a vicious circle.

My conversations with teachers led me to believe that the insufficient mastery of semantic concepts was the main handicap of deaf people. In general deaf adults are not able to understand an average newspaper article. Communication problems are still present even after the acquisition of the ability to speak and to lip-read. An impressive example of the inability of deaf children to master semantic concepts is cited by AFFOLTER and BISCHOFBERGER:

"In school deaf children learnt that every child, every adult and even dogs and cats had a name. This can be expressed

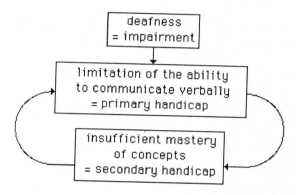

Diagram 1: Starting with a hearing impairment the limitation of the ability to communicate verbally and the insufficient mastery of semantic concepts create a vicious circle.

by the phrase 'are called'. One morning a girl brings to school a wonderful bunch of peonies. The teacher grabs the opportunity for a further example. X brings flowers... The flowers are called 'peonies'. Hearing this sentence the children begin to laugh, they shake their heads denying that flowers should be called any name at all. Where is the head? Where are their eyes? The mouth? The new meaning of 'are called' was obviously in conflict with what the children had learnt according to earlier experiences, namely that 'are called' is valuable for that which has a head, two eyes and a mouth." [2]

Considering the importance of the problems arising from the insufficient ability to master semantic concepts, one would expected diagnosis and treatment to be known in full detail. But it is not so. No one seems able to say exactly what semantic concepts are or are not mastered by deaf children. The acquisition of semantic concepts is encouraged by teachers of deaf children with such personal commitment that some success worthy of recognition is obtained, even though the explanation of the underlying didactic principles remains unsatisfactory.

During visits to classes I had the impression that the average deaf child could not learn most of the semantic concepts unless they were repeated over a long period of time. These were not only abstract semantic concepts, the insufficient mastery of which would be understandable, but very often concrete ones of everyday life.

3. THE AIM OF THE PROJECT

The aim of my research project is:

1. the development of a method for the acquisition of unknown semantic concepts and for the correction of wrongly and insufficiently mastered semantic concepts;

2. the implementation of this method by means of a computer program;

3. the application and evaluation of this method.

In view of the present state of my work I will deal with only the development and implementation of the method.

I would like to state that the use of a computer is justified by the complexity of the method and not by blind enthusiasm for it as a tool.

4. TO WHOM THE PROGRAM IS ADDRESSED

The program is addressed to deaf children who are of average intelligence and are able to read. The child should be no younger than nine years old. Communication within the program is guaranteed by the ability to read. The inputs are made by the "mouse".

Though the addressees are clearly defined, I think the program can be used more widely, since not only deaf children have an insufficient mastery of semantic concepts. More specifically I have children with learning disabilities in mind.

5. THE LEARNING OF CONCEPTS

A learning program that fits each learner can only be developed if there is a model to explain how the specific ability is acquired in the normal process of human development. Concepts are acquired through the child's experiences within his environment and through the generalisation of these experiences [3].

On the acquisition of a concept there is the perception of a concrete situation. Such a perception leads to a mental image, and it is the repetition of these perceptions that brings about an embedment of the mental image. The child hears an appropriate word and associates the word with a mental image. In the course of time the child abstracts criteria from the mental image: a concept is born. A mental model turns into a mental representation. The process of abstraction is achieved through assimilation and accommodation.

If a new perception of a situation is equal or nearly equal to the mental image and the word used by the environment (adults or other children) is the same, the new perception is assimilated to the mental image. This way the main criteria of the concept are learnt by the child.

If in spite of the difference between the new perception and the mental model the environment uses the same word, the child must accommodate his comprehension of the concept.

6. THE TEACHING OF CONCEPTS

The method for teaching the concepts used in the computer program is directed towards the acquisition of the concepts explained above. The process of acquisition is more quick than by the normal process and limited to an exactly defined set of concepts. The concepts in a set are related and in this way form a subject. These are the same procedures in the computer program as in the constructing process of concepts during the human development - namely the repeated confrontation with situations that leads to some perceptions by the trainee and the process of assimilation and accommodation that are in a logical point of view inductive conclusions.

7. THE STRUCTURE OF THE PROGRAM

The structure of the program is represented in diagram 2.

The instruction component contains examples of teaching concepts, that are shown to the trainee in form of pictures. He receives a statement for each example if it is a typical example for the concept, a near-miss example or an exceptional example. With this information he should be able to construct the concept by inductive process. The program is so unrestrictive that it enables the teaching of all concepts after an appropriate preparation. This preparation means that every example must be defined as an and/or-linkage of at the most ten criteria.

The expert model contains knowledge of the way concepts are ideally concluded from examples. Corresponding research runs under the name of "inductive learning", "inductive inference" or "learning from examples". MICHALSKI [4] has defined inductive learning as a process of acquiring knowledge by drawing inductive inferences from teacher- or environment-provided facts. Inductive inference has some differences in comparison to the deductive system:

1. there is no absolute certainty in inductive inference;
2. inductive inference never ends; new experiences can affect present conclusions;
3. the rules for inductive inference are not completely known and will never be known completely;
4. inductive inference has been considered of poor quality for a long time and as not worthy of exploration.

In contradiction to this lack of interest, the fact remains that people very often learn by inductive inference. Inductive inference is not only a logical problem but a psychological one. Conceptual inductive learning has a strong cognitive science flavor. It emphasizes inducing human-oriented rather than machine-oriented descriptions. [4]

With reference to MICHALSKI [4] and to WINSTON [5] I have established seven rules of inductive inference. Some of them can be explained only by logical reasoning, others by semantic knowledge as well. When the learner is con-

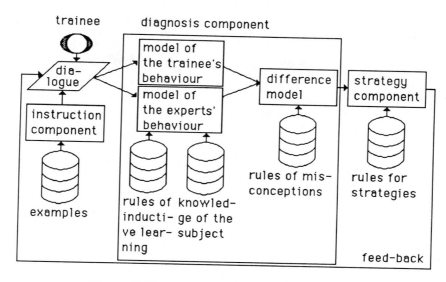

Diagram 2: The structure of the program.

fronted by a typical example the following five rules should be observed: 1.) the dropping condition rule, 2.) the adding alternative rule, 3.) the extending reference rule, 4.) the climbing generalization tree rule and 5.) the inductive resolution rule. There is a sixth rule, the required link heuristic rule, that deals with near-miss examples and a seventh rule, the exception rule, which deals with exceptional examples. (Cf MICHALSKI [4] and WINSTON [5] for more details.)

To examine if adults - who should know how to acquire concepts - really use these rules of inductive inference or not, I have tried to find out, in an experiment using the concepts "amphora" and "tank-car", how often they use them.This was with a small group of 8 adults who had higher education. Diagram 3 shows the results.

It is obvious that the rules for the most part are used correctly, with the required link heuristic rule (rule 6) being the sole exception. Thus one can say that people do acquire concepts according to these rules although they are not conscious of them.

The question of knowing if people think according to these rules is important to know whether the computer program has the behaviour of a glass-box or a black-box expert (cf BURTON, BROWN [6]). A glass-box expert imitates hu-

man ability to solve problems whereas a black-box expert cannot think in the same manner as human beings. The above-mentioned results prove that my concept-teaching program acts as a glass-box expert. It legitimates me teaching these rules to children who have an insufficient mastery of semantic concepts.

According to the characteristics of inductive inference, the construction of concepts never ends. If there are new experiences that do not conform to the present comprehension of the concept, an accommodation of concept-understanding is necessary. Of course, there is a moment when the meaning of the concept acquired by the learner adjusts to the one of average adults. The purpose of the program is not to examine a "correct" comprehension of the concept but the completeness of the conclusion drawn from the given examples. If a learner is confronted with a sufficient number of examples, comprehension corresponding to general meaning is automatically guaranteed.

If the trainee has the impression of having learnt the concept from the examples, he can feed his concept-definition into the computer (i.e., the criteria and their relations). The computer will compare the trainee's definition to the expert's solution. If there are mistakes, the strategy component creates an individual response as a feed-back to the trainee. There is still a lot of research to be done in order to

	Rule 1	Rule 2	Rule 3	Rule 4	Rule 5	Rule 6	Rule 7
Correct: Used where required	76.3%	77.8%	75.0%	66.7%	76.2%	12.8%	66.7%
Incorrect: Not used where required	15.3%	11.1%	12.5%	33.3%	23.8%	40.4%	22.2%
Incorrect: Used where not required	8.4%	11.1%	12.5%	0.0%	0.0%	46.8%	11.1%
Total:	100.0%	100.0%	100.0%	100.0%	100.0%	100.0%	100.0%

Diagram 3: The mastery of the rules of inductive inference by 8 adults.

know the possible mistakes and the best feed-back.

8. CONCLUSIONS

It is not more knowledge about computers but more use of psychological knowledge that is needed to improve instruction programs. Without the knowledge of

1. the learning process during human development
2. a teaching method that has been thoroughly analysed
3. a knowledge of possible mistakes

we shall be waiting for better programs for ever.

REFERENCES

[1] O'SHEA T., SELF J.: Lernen und Lehren mit Computern. Künstliche Intelligenz im Unterricht. (Basel: Birkhäuser, 1986).

[2] AFFOLTER F., BISCHOFBERGER W.: Psychologische Aspekte der Gehörlosigkeit. In: JUSSEN H., KROEHNERT O. (Eds.): Pädagogik der Gehörlosen und Schwerhörigen. Handbuch der Sonderpädagogik Band 3. (Berlin: Marhold, 1982), pp 605-630.

[3] SZAGUN G.: Bedeutungsentwicklung beim Kind. Wie Kinder Wörter entdecken. (München: Urban and Schwarzenberg, 1983).

[4] MICHALSKI R.S.: A Theory and Methodology of Inductive Learning. Artificial Intelligence, 1983, 20. 111-161.

[5] WINSTON P.H.: Artificial Intelligence. (Reading, Mass.: Addison-Wesley, 1984).

[6] BURTON R.R., BROWN J.S.: An Investigation of Computer Coaching for Informal Learning Activities. International Journal of Man-Machine Studies, 1979, 11. 5-24.

2. Formal and Informal Learning and Teaching Environments

COMPUTERS IN EDUCATION, F. Lovis and E.D. Tagg (eds.)
Elsevier Science Publishers B.V. (North-Holland)
© IFIP, 1988

Computer education for teachers

ROTHAN Bernard   CLERC Françoise   SIMONNET Françoise

Centre de Formation à l'Informatique et à ses Applications Pédagogiques
I.U.T. Département Informatique
2bis Boulevard Charlemagne
54000 NANCY

Abstract : The paper starts from the observation that up to now most computer training programmes for teachers have dealt mainly with technical aspects, whereas the use of computers in subject areas implies preliminary didactic and pedagogical thinking.

It describes a continuing teacher training experiment in the pedagogical uses of the computer in their subject areas ; it explains how the training team was constituted and organized to meet this objective and gives the main themes of the programme.

It also presents some of the documents used as an illustration of the underlying ideas.

Key-words : Educational informatics, learning, diversified teaching strategies, evaluation, pedagogical sequence, educational program, teacher education, program graph.

A word-processing program, six groups of fourth form[*] pupils in a mathematics "class". Files are circulated among the terminals of the nano-network[**] . The objective : being able to build the reciprocal of a theorem.

A class of sixth form[***] pupils in front of a monitor ; a teacher leading the debate, a pupil writing results on the blackboard, another one executing the group's decisions on the keyboard of the micro-computer. Step by step, a diagram of French population in 1980 is being built on the screen.

A nano-network with six terminals in the computer room. Six pupils are working on individual exercises of a reading development program.

---

[*]The third form in secondary education (pupils aged 13 - 14).

[**] A network where 6 or 8 home computers are connected to a professional computer which controls the drives, printer and communication between terminals.

[***] The first form in secondary education (pupils aged 11-12).

1. Introduction

Training teachers : what for ?

Since computers have been introduced into teaching, technical progress and pedagogical research have promoted the realization of two objectives : generalizing the teaching of informatics as a subject, and finding more and more relevant uses of the computer as a learning resource in all subjects.

In France, this introduction dates back to 1972, when the first hardware equipments appeared in some schools ; since then, two types of computer training have been offered : an in-depth one-year training programme, and a lighter programme (50 to 100 hours) carried out in schools equipped with hardware. Until very recently, the content of these programmes remained very technical. Problem solving and programming made up a significant part of the in-depth training, the objective then being the production of educational software, which was conspicuously lacking.

In spite of these efforts, there remains a gap between the few teachers who use educational or professional software and sometimes even write their own programs, and the wavering majority who still feel shivery at the idea of appropriating new technological tools.

In other countries as well, people in charge of computer training are pondering over the objectives and contents to be set for the necessary training in pedagogical uses of the computer, and stress the difficulty of maintaining any permanence in a field which is constantly upset by the rapid evolution of micro-computer technology and its uses at school.

2. Building the training project

2.1. Using computers in the classroom

Together with changes in the structure and organization of the schools, teacher training is a fundamental element in the evolution of the education system. An opportunity to act in this perspective appeared in the Académie* of Nancy-Metz, thanks to the combined actions of institutional officials and of teachers involved in general pedagogy and computer training. In 1986, a "Computer Resource Centre" (CRI) was created, whose members are at the head of research groups composed of teachers and/or computer trainers. Its -appointed tasks are producing pedagogical sequences using the computer in different subject areas, and proposing training programmes in pedagogical uses of the computer. During the school year 1986-1987, eight subjects were covered : German, English, History, Geography, French, Maths, Music, Technology. Three research groups also worked on transverse themes : low-ability pupils, reading, telematics.

2.2. Producing pedagogical sequences

The cohesion of the training team (CRI) was achieved through inter-training and group discussion to reach a common definition of a pedagogical sequence (see Appendix I), which was then used as a theoretical basis in the research groups dealing with subject areas. The problems and difficulties met with in the different groups were analysed to ensure a better effectiveness in future training programmes.

The uses of the computer in each subject being different, the approaches varied from one group to the other ; some chose a pedagogical or didactic entry point, while others built their sequences around one of the available educational programs. For each sequence, contents and objectives were defined, learning activities and a system of formative and prescriptive evaluation were proposed. In most cases, the computer is only used as a teaching resource, which both supposes and facilitates the adjustment of teaching methods to the learning processes of the pupils.

The assessment of the sequences is achieved through several stages : first, they are submitted for critical reading to the other members of the CRI, who are asked to make remarks and proposals (we called this process "milling") ; they are then referred to institutional or university "experts" for criticism, before being experimented in class situation by one or several teachers. The final stage involves writing and publishing the description of the sequences.

3. The training programme

3.1. Training in the pedagogical uses of the computer

The in-depth computer training offered in the Académie of Nancy-Metz during the school year 1986-1987, aimed at mastery of the hardware and software used in French schools and a competence in building pedagogical sequences using the computer, as well as a competence in acting as a trainer in computer education. Sixteen teachers were selected for this programme, representing primary, secondary and special education and covering nine subject areas.

The contents included general knowledge in both computer science (problem solving, programming in Pascal, Logo, LSE*, BASIC and Prolog, structure of computers, operating systems, robotics, telematics) and pedagogy, with the aim of integrating the computer as a tool in teachers' practice.

Twelve weeks of the one-year training were more especially devoted to this pedagogical aspect ; this part of the programme, which was under the responsibility of the CRI, is described below (see Appendix II).

---

* The university district which manages the education system at the local level : there are 28 Académies in France.

* Langage Symbolique d'Enseignement : this high-level language was created and used in France to write the first educational programs.

3.2. Learning with the help of the computer (Module II)

The first objective was concerned with identifying the underlying learning processes of an educational program. Observing the mental processes of pupils using these programs and pinpointing the underlying teaching objectives enabled the trainees, after they had been given some theoretical background, to formulate a classification of the uses of the computer : in tutorial mode (programs aimed at acquiring, strengthening or assessing knowledge and know-how) or in heuristic mode (programs based on simulation or information access which develop analysing and reflective abilities, creativity, problem solving and decision making capacities). Other aspects covered in this module were the different relationship of pupils to knowledge and to the group in computer-assisted teaching ; the possible contribution of the computer in mastering difficult notions in each subject ; the problems involved in the use of the computer in the different subject areas.

3.3. Devising the project for an educational program (Module III)

One week was devoted to devising and building the graph of an educational program. Besides developing the trainees' competence as software writers, this module enabled them to assess educational programs better both as users and future trainers.

After being given some theoretical background, the trainees had to analyse a program and discover its structure. Software writers were invited to talk about their practice. Then, with the help of a production guide, five groups set out devising the model for an educational program ; the different steps of the process were : choosing a subject, looking up the existing products in the field (documents, programs, etc.), writing the objectives, making a functional analysis of the project, drawing the graph, designing the screens. Communication, interactivity and computerization of the project were then dealt with. Five programs were produced during this week* .

3.4. Building pedagogical sequences using the computer in different subject areas (Modules IV and V)

These two modules were the core of the training programme. After analysing a few pedagogical sequences - those produced by the research groups of the CRI- in order to identify the different stages involved (see Appendix I), the trainees built two sequences in subjects imposed by the training team** . They were asked to write down the problems they met in the process, as well as the method they chose in their group work.

The next stage started with the elaboration of an observation grid ; the trainees were then sent out to observe the implementation of the computer as teaching aid in different schools*** . The data collected during the observation of some 30 pedagogical sequences in 10 different schools, was analysed and enabled the trainees to come to certain conclusions concerning the more or less appropriate manner in which some programs can be integrated into teaching strategies, and the contribution of the computer in the adjustment of teaching methods to the pupils' learning processes. These conclusions were of great interest to them, both as teachers and as future trainers/leaders.

One of the key points of this module was the reflection on the necessity to adapt teaching to the pupils' needs. In order to help the pupils build up their knowledge, the teacher must consider the diversity of their cognitive styles, use a variety of languages and teaching resources, diversify work organization in the classroom, build up a formative evaluation system, which enables the pupils to participate actively in the management of their appropriation of knowledge, and implement remedial activities to meet his objectives.

The trainees were then asked to build a pedagogical sequence in their subject area. Five sequences were produced, experimented and evaluated**** .

The last activities in this module dealt with the trainees' competence as leaders in their educational environment, with two main concerns : helping other teachers to build pedagogical sequences ; assessing the needs of a school district in matters of computer education and meeting these demands.

4. Evaluating the programme

Continuous evaluation was used throughout the training programme. This system enabled both trainers and trainees to get a picture of the group's progression from one module to the other, and also to place each trainee in relation to the group. Group discussion about the overall

---

* The five subjects chosen by the trainees were :
- firm managing (History-Geography class, sixth form : pupils aged 11-12)
- general assessment of pupils' knowledge and know-how at the end of primary school
- geometrical simulator on cones (Maths class, last form : pupils aged 17-18)
- simulation of an experiment in Chemistry (sixth and fifth forms : pupils aged 11-13)
- "puff pastry", project management for special education and low-ability pupils.

** Introduction to the word-processing program "Maxitexte" and training session for teachers on the uses of the reading development program "ELMO 0".
*** A synthetic account of the observation was sent to the schools visited.
**** The subjects of these sequences were :
- orthogonal symmetry (Maths, pupils aged 11-12)
- French population (History-Geography, pupils aged 14-15)
- proportionality and spreadsheet (Maths, pupils aged 11-12)
- vectors in the Euclidean plane (Maths, pupils aged 13-14)
- telematics and school correspondence

results of the evaluation and analysis of the answers to each question, allowed a better control of the programme. During the final evaluation activities, the problem of finding appropriate tools for assessing the effectiveness of a training project was raised and analysed.

In carrying out this training programme in the pedagogical uses of the computer, the training team tried to use the computer as much and in the most appropriate manner as possible : it was used in preparing documents, treating and representing evaluation data, and managing the training programme.

Such a training programme must necessarily be built according to the principles contained in its objectives : making a contract with the trainees, explaining the objectives, devising diversified learning activities. The choice of a production-based approach made it necessary for the training team to achieve great cohesion ; but the objectives could not have been met without the involvement of the trainees, whose requirements concerning the quality of their productions often exceeded those of the training team, and made them suitable for publication or use in subsequent training sessions. However, it is necessary to specify, while stating the objectives, that the aim of these productions is training and not publication.

5. Perspectives

In a society where daily life is increasingly affected by the various applications of computer science, the education system is forced to take this new reality into account and to adapt it to its own goals. The computerization of the socio-economical and cultural environments requires an evolution in teaching content and methods. But one cannot transform the education system without integrating computer education into continuing teacher training, in particular, through training sessions organized by teams including people with pedagogic, didactic and computer science competence. In implementing such a training programme, we discovered that the problems linked with the appropriation of a new technological tool were soon left behind to raise a more fundamental "pedagogical inquiry" : what knowledge ? What for ? How ?

Acknowledgements *The authors wish to thank Mrs Monique Grandbastien for having initiated the project and Ms Claire Maniez for translating the paper.*

Bibliography

BARBIER, J.-M., L'évaluation en formation (Paris PUF 1985)

BLOOM, B.S., Taxonomie des objectifs pédagogiques Tome 1 : domaine cognitif (Quebec Presses de l'Université 1975)

BOULET, A., CHEVRIER, J., Typologie des objectifs et des contenus des programme de formation des maîtres en A.P.O. (applications pédagogiques de l'ordinateur) (Paris Actes Colloque EAO Agde mars 87 ADI 1987)

HAMELINE, D., Les objectifs en Formation initiale et en Formation continue (Paris ESF 1979)

LA GARANDERIE, A.de, Pédagogie des moyens d'apprendre Les enseignants face aux profils pédagogiques (Paris Le Centurion 1985)

LANDSHEERE, V. de, Définir les objectifs de l'éducation (Paris PUF 1980)

LEGRAND, L., La différenciation de la pédagogie (Paris Scarabée 1986)

LHERMENIER, J. & All, Pratique du Logo, processus cognitifs, styles cognitifs (Paris Revue Enfance n° 2-3 1985 pp 159 - 163)

LOVIS, F. B., TAGG, E. D., (Eds) Informatics and teacher training (Actes I.F.I.P. 1984 Elsevier North Holland)

MAGER, R.F., Comment définir les objectifs pédagogiques ? (Paris Gauthier-Villars 1971)

MANIEZ, C., CALL me ELMO ! (Nancy CRDP Mémoires Vives 1987)

MEIRIEU, P., L'école mode d'emploi Des méthodes actives à la pédagogie différenciée (Paris ESF 1985)

MEIRIEU, P., Différencier la pédagogie Pourquoi ? Comment ? (Lyon CRDP 1986)

MEIRIEU, P., Apprendre... oui, mais comment (Paris ESF 1987)

O'SHEA, T., SELF, J., Learning and teaching with computer (Harvester Press Brighton 1983)

PAOUR, J.L. & All, Educabilité de l'intelligence dans un environnement micro-informatique à programmer (Revue Enfance n° 2-3 1985 pp 147 - 158)

POISSON, D. & All, Bilan et perspectives de dix années d'utilisation de l'informatique pédagogique au C.U.E.E.P. (Lille Les cahiers d'études du C.U.E.E.P. n° 6 janvier 86)

PAPERT, S., Jaillissement de l'esprit : ordinateurs et apprentissage (Paris Flammarion 1981)

PATUREAU, V., Former des auteurs et des réalisateurs de didacticiels Un enjeu pour le marché de l'E.A.O. (Paris Actes Colloque EAO Agde mars 87 ADI 1987)

WITKIN, H.A., Les styles cognitifs "Dépendants à l'égard du champ" et "Indépendant à l'égard du champ" et leurs implications pédagogiques (L'orientation scolaire et professionnelle Avr 1978 pp 299 - 349)

APPENDIX I

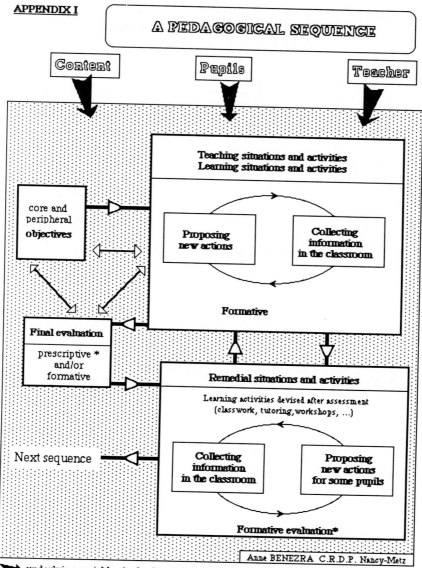

A PEDAGOGICAL SEQUENCE

Content   Pupils   Teacher

Teaching situations and activities
Learning situations and activities

core and peripheral **objectives**

Proposing new actions   Collecting information in the classroom

Formative

Final evaluation

prescriptive *
and/or
formative

Remedial situations and activities

Learning activities devised after assessment
(classwork, tutoring, workshops, ...)

Next sequence

Collecting information in the classroom   Proposing new actions for some pupils

Formative evaluation*

Anne BENEZRA C.R.D.P. Nancy-Metz

underlying variables in the dynamic system
chronological progress for the pupils
overall consistency

* Formative evaluation : leads to pedagogical decisions
* Prescriptive evaluation : leads to social decisions (average, guidance, ...)

APPENDIX II

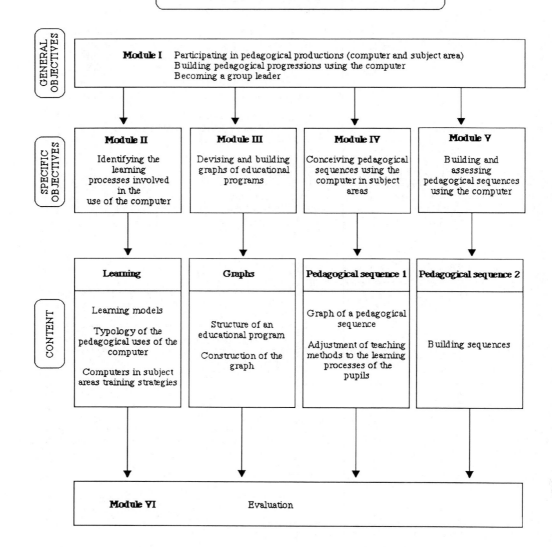

Graph of the Training Programme

GENERAL OBJECTIVES

Module I   Participating in pedagogical productions (computer and subject area)
Building pedagogical progressions using the computer
Becoming a group leader

SPECIFIC OBJECTIVES

Module II	**Module III**	**Module IV**	**Module V**
Identifying the learning processes involved in the use of the computer	Devising and building graphs of educational programs	Conceiving pedagogical sequences using the computer in subject areas	Building and assessing pedagogical sequences using the computer

CONTENT

Learning	**Graphs**	**Pedagogical sequence 1**	**Pedagogical sequence 2**
Learning models Typology of the pedagogical uses of the computer Computers in subject areas training strategies	Structure of an educational program Construction of the graph	Graph of a pedagogical sequence Adjustment of teaching methods to the learning processes of the pupils	Building sequences

Module VI   Evaluation

COMPUTERS IN EDUCATION, F. Lovis and E.D. Tagg (eds.)
Elsevier Science Publishers B.V. (North-Holland)
© IFIP, 1988

THE IN-SERVICE EDUCATION OF TEACHERS (INSET) IN INFORMATION TECHNOLOGY (IT) - A UK PERSPECTIVE

J. Gardner, J. Fulton and M. Megarity.

School of Education, The Queen's University of Belfast
Belfast, N. Ireland. BT7 1NN

In 1980 the UK Government took the first steps towards ensuring that every school should have microcomputers to enable children to be exposed to the new technology in the areas of learning and applications. From 1981-86 the Microelectronics Education Programme pursued a policy of encouraging a cross-curricular approach to the assimilation of information technology in the face of an unprecedented increase in the uptake of computer studies in schools. This paper examines the issues and, using findings from a number of recent surveys, reports on the ways in which the situation has developed over the past seven years.

1. THE NATURE OF IT INSET

Staff development is a priority in all professions and not least in teaching and training. Teaching skills are framed within a comparatively steady knowledge context but the methodology is constantly evolving and teacher educators face a recurring need to update and develop their courses in both the pre-service and in-service sectors of teacher education. In some organisational respects it is easier to incorporate information technology (IT) into courses for prospective teachers and some guidance for pre-service (initial) teacher education course planning does exist [1]. The IT problems in this area of teacher education, particularly with respect to resource levels, are still the focus of current debate [2] but the emphasis in this paper will be on the in-service education of teachers (INSET).

INSET is designed to update practising teachers in developments in their subjects and the statutory education authorities earmark considerable sums of money each year to fund in-service activities. The provision of INSET is often more expensive and much more difficult than pre-service owing to the fact that, in addition to the resourcing problems shared with the pre-service sector, high substitution costs may be incurred if teachers have to be relieved from normal teaching duties for the duration of courses.

In the UK-based Microelectronics Education Programme, MEP [3], in-service teacher education was one of three specifically funded activities drawing on £23M from the Department of Education and Science, DES, and indirectly supported by £20.5M in hardware subsidies to schools from the Department of Trade and Industry, DTI, [4]. The ultimate purpose of any in-service programme is to improve the education provided to pupils by the teachers concerned and in the case of the MEP the raison-d'etre was stated as helping schools to·

"to prepare children for life in a society in which devices and systems based on microelectronics are commonplace and pervasive" [3].

One of the most pervasive microelectronic devices is the computer and for some years arguments have raged on the merits of making it the basis of a subject in its own right or a tool for teaching across the curriculum. Hubbard [5] has observed that countries which are just beginning to consider the role of IT in education tend to choose the former model while those with experience in the field (he identifies the UK [3] and France [6]) choose the latter. Cerych [7] takes the view that the question has become somewhat blurred with the acknowledgement that the options can be complementary but there is evidence (see for example Frey [8]) that some States are remaining dogmatic on the issue. In the UK it can be argued that most schools actually adopt a "mixed-economy" approach to IT in their curricula although it is useful to view in-service work as being targeted at teachers in three distinct IT categories:

1.1 Academic IT;
1.2 Vocational IT;
1.3 Cross-curricular IT.

1.1 Academic IT

Academic IT is taken to comprise formal studies of the new technology per se in such subjects as GCSE Computer Studies or GCE Advanced-level Computer Science (for an explanation of terms see [9]). Although it can be argued that the emphasis on applications in the former contrasts sharply with the more conventionally academic approach to the science of computing in the latter, both represent a standard timetabled solution to a curricular development. The INSET activities in this category include updating the teachers involved in the use of new hardware and software, operating

systems, peripheral devices and so on and the opportunity to examine professional issues such as syllabus developments, assessment techniques and new teaching resources.

Computer studies/science has experienced a phenomenal growth in UK schools since the launch of the first central government initiative to equip schools with microcomputing resources [4]. Table 1 shows this growth in terms of examination entries in computer studies/science in Northern Ireland [10] and England and Wales [11]. Clearly both sets of figures indicate that the growth has peaked and is beginning to level off. The curricular impact of this development may be placed in perspective when viewed in the light of the overall examination entries listed in Table 2 [12]. It is interesting to note that those subjects which are often portrayed as being vulnerable to a growing technical/scientific emphasis in the curriculum (for example history or art and design) are retaining some measure of dominance over computer studies and its ilk in terms of pupil examination choices.

TABLE 1

Examination entries in Northern Ireland* and England ** (10,11)

Year	N. Ireland	Annual Increase	England	Annual Increase
1980	--	--	16812	--
1981	--	--	25306	8494
1982	1558	--	38424	13118
1983	3185	1627	50421	11997
1984	4353	1168	63777	13356
1985	5330	977	71807	8030
1986	5878	548	--	--
1987	6103	225	--	--

*   N. Ireland figures comprise CSE and "O" -level entries.
** England figures comprise "O" and "A"-level entries. Figures are not yet available for 1986 and 1987.

TABLE 2

Examination entries at "O"-level in England, 1985 (12)

Rank	Subject	Entries	Rank	Subject	Entries
1	Eng. Language	509684	7	Comp. Studies	153315
2	Mathematics	318625	8	French	147657
3	Eng. Lit'ture	236334	9	Art/Design	144933
4	Biology	218084	10	History	126609
5	Geography	191058	11	Rel. Studies	66996
6	Physics	183586	12	Comp. Studies	62485

1.2 Vocational IT

Vocational IT is taken to mean the incorporation of the relevant IT tools and techniques into those areas of the curriculum which have a vocational emphasis. One of the specific objectives of teaching such subjects as business studies or commerce at GCSE level is to contribute to the employability of the many pupils who choose to leave school at the end of compulsory education (approximately 16 years of age). Clearly it is desirable that such courses should help prepare pupils for a world of work in which information technologies are assuming ever increasing importance. IT applications such as wordprocessors, spreadsheets and databases are now everyday office tools and many schools are equipped to provide vocational tuition in their use.

1.3 Cross-curricular IT

This mode of information technology in schools is the least formally defined of the three categories. The overriding factor is the wish to assimilate IT techniques and applications into the everyday activities of the staff and pupils. The aim of this approach is to demistify IT and provide all pupils, irrespective of academic or vocational aspirations, with exposure to, and consequent familiarity with, standard IT hardware and applications. The approach is manifested in two ways.

Firstly each conventional (ie timetabled) subject is expected to incorporate appropriate IT applications in its delivery with computer assisted learning packages and subject-specific applications. Examples of the latter include the use of computers in such areas as data-logging in science experiments, composition in music classes, graphics in art and design classes, desktop publishing in English classes and databases in history classes. Secondly the staff is expected to use IT in a natural manner - turning to such applications as wordprocessing and databases in their daily administrative tasks. This is very much a "hidden curriculum" technique ie the education of pupils by example as opposed to pedagogy. The theory is that the pupils will experience meaningful and practical applications of IT without an overt instructional emphasis and will be more amenable as a consequence to exploiting them in their own everyday activities.

2. IT IN-SERVICE - AN OVERVIEW

In 1982 Burghes [13] was estimating that the computers in schools were being used for computer studies 90% of their usage time. In relation to the burgeoning examination entries noted above this is perhaps understandable but it should not be extrapolated to suggest a computer studies emphasis in teacher education. Indeed in the years succeeding this, the MEP took action to foster more cross-curricular use of the resources by deliberately targeting courses at teachers in the humanities and arts subjects. The Computer Based Learning domain of the Programme, with responsibility for IT applications and specifically computer assisted learning (CAL) throughout the curriculum, is a case in point and an estimated 41,000 teachers took part in courses during the period January 1982 to March 1986 [14]. The scale of the in-service problem is illustrated by the fact that the teachers in this group received an average of only 1.7 course days each.

With the benefit of hindsight it is now becoming clear that this level of in-service was insufficient to effect widespread use of computing across the curriculum. One of the last actions of the MEP was to commission reports from the various subject associations on the penetration of the technology into their teaching/learning domains. Many of the reports [15-21] highlight three main constraints on the progress of IT integration in their subjects: low hardware resource levels, poor software quality and insufficient in-service training. The problems have also attracted media attention [22,23] and a number of researchers have pinpointed weaknesses particularly in in-service. Bleach [24] for example, in a survey of 537 primary schools concluded that although 70% of the teachers involved had been on an in-service course, staff were only

"barely confident in wiring up machines and hardly likely to attempt the more adventurous skills such as databases and wordprocessing"

Other surveys [25,26] in the secondary sector have also shown that the in-service provision has not met the objective of effecting the use of computers in the support of teaching and learning. A DES survey in 1985 [27] indicated that only 20% of secondary headteachers could acknowledge that computers had made a

significant contribution to teaching in
their schools yet almost 60% of primary
headteachers did so. Bleach's survey sheds
some light on the meaning of this latter
statistic by recording that only 17% of the
schools involved in a similar survey were
making full use of the computers ie. using
them for most of the time.

It is not surprising, then, that the
situation is known to Government and in a
recent circular to Chief Education Officers
the DES states that IT

"is still not a part of the
teaching repertoire which all
teachers fully appreciate or feel
comfortable with; and for many
pupils access to IT is by no
means the commonplace activity
which it needs to be if the
greatest benefit is to gained"
[28]

Government has, however, recognised that
teacher education is

"...an important prerequisite of
the effective application of IT
in teaching and learning." [29]

and has provided £10.5M in Educational
Support Grants (ESG) for IT in the 1988-89
financial year for England and Wales with a
proportionate amount under the Vocational
Education Programme (VEP) in Northern
Ireland [30]. Much of these monies will be
used to fund IT coordinator posts for
schools' support in local authorities and
the training of these personnel will be
contributed to centrally by the successor
to MEP, the Microelectronics Education
Support Unit (MESU) [31].

The training of specialists to
support the general teaching body is a
conventional approach to staff-development
and in the field of IT it is well-
established. As long ago as 1972 an IFIP
Working Group produced a far-sighted
document [32] which advised policy makers
to pursue a two-pronged in-service,
computer literacy programme. The report
recommended the targeting of all teachers
in general awareness programmes with extra,
in-depth provision for specialists. The
need for specialists is still apparent but
the definition of their role varies from
school-based "responsible teachers" [33] to
personnel acting in support of schools such
as the "roving consultants" of Ellam and
Wellington [34].

Many countries have instituted
programmes similar to that proposed by
IFIP. For example, the concept of
specialist personnel found support in the
"train the trainers" or "cascade" approach
to in-service which MEP aspired to. The
reality of MEP, however, was that the
pressure from teachers and authorities
alike made the former short-term awareness
courses the main priority. MEP achieved
its "pump-priming" objectives, particularly
in creating an environment for enthusing
the general teaching community and
facilitating the development of
specialists, but the infra-structure for
continuing staff development, which could
exploit the gains made, was more or less
beyond the limits of its control. A
significant group in this infra-structure
(in addition to the local authority
advisory services and the Inspectorate) are
the institutional teacher educators.

3. TEACHER EDUCATORS - THE INSET PROVIDERS

In a recent postal survey of the
teacher education centres in the UK, the
authors achieved a 59% response to a
questionnaire which sought to identify,
amongst other things, the level of IT
penetration in teacher education. The
survey instrument was sent to named
personnel who had responsibility for
information technology courses in the
various institutions. Figure 1 presents a
brief digest of the respondents'
institutions and personal details.

The gender breakdown amongst IT
teacher educators is very pronounced with a
male/female ratio of approximately 6:1.
The age profile for the majority of the
respondents fell within the 41-50 years of
age range. Most IT teacher educators do
not have any formal background in computing
and of those who do (34%), just less than
half have a degree or diploma. This is not
surprising because such was the impetus of
IT development in education after the
Government interventions of 1980/1 [3,4],
that teacher education institutions, for
the most part, had to redeploy expertise
from other fields to cater for the sudden
rise in demand. While some institutions
may have been fortunate enough to have been
able to appoint new staff with the
necessary background, the majority of
courses continue to be provided by staff
who have expended much of their free time
in investigating and learning about the
role of IT in education for themselves.
The experience has been a frenetic one in

most institutions and the problems and implications associated with IT have been dealt with on a largely ad hoc basis. Indeed it is only recently that IT teacher educators have had the opportunities to reflect on their experiences [35] or to formulate a corporate and coherent approach to the issues of IT in education [36].

The situation has also been difficult in schools where computing courses are offered mainly by self-taught or re-trained teachers. Notwithstanding Government advice that all teachers should be qualified to degree level in their chosen subjects [37], the continuing lack of qualified personnel in the educational computing field is exemplified by the Universities Council for the Education of Teachers (UCET) survey of 1985 which showed that only 0.3% of the UK Post-Graduate Certificate in Education pre-service group (n=4223) were qualified as computer studies teachers [38]. With only media studies and Russian having less students (10 and 8 respectively) it is clear the deficit in experience and qualifications is not going to be rectified easily.

The official emphasis in UK education is, of course, on the cross-curricular assimilation of IT but the lack of formal technical training for cognate, supporting personnel, ie. the computer studies/science tutors and teachers within schools and teacher education institutions, is likely to continue to be a factor in inhibiting IT progress in education. Some consolation is provided by DES figures for 1987 [12] which show that although only 1300 teachers are designated as main subject computer studies teachers, 9400 teachers are teaching at least one class of computer studies per week. In some respects this indicates that expertise is beginning to spread, with computer studies being shared, if not throughout the curriculum then certainly to some extent throughout the staff.

Figure 2 shows that teacher educators are providing courses which should encourage a more cross-curricular assimilation of the technology. In-service courses which comprise computer studies/science topics alone, represent only 9% of the total provision while 77% have IT or CAL elements. The nature of the

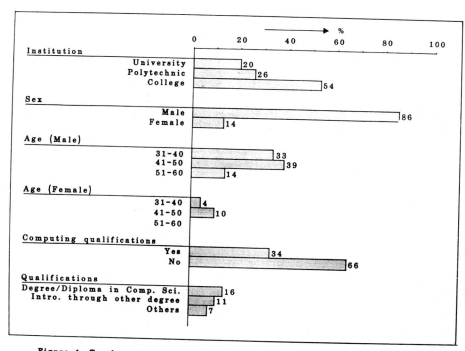

Figure 1. Teacher educator profiles. (n = 70)

intersection between the educational technology courses and computer studies/science (5%) is not clear but the systematisation of the learning objectives in CAL and other IT environments gives a sound basis for the overlap between these areas and educational technology. Table 3 confirms the likely cross-curricular emphasis in in-service courses with the conventional "content-free" applications (wordprocessing, databases and so on)

featuring high on the list of IT areas covered.

CONCLUDING REMARKS

In the seven years since the initial announcement which heralded the MEP, the hardware and software available to education has changed both in power and quality. Undoubtedly these changes will continue but there are signs that whereas previous changes have invariably caused

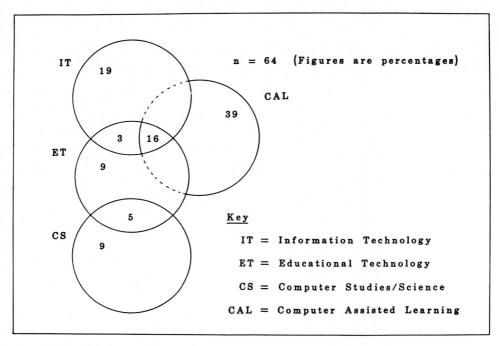

Figure 2. In-service course content

TABLE 3

IT areas represented in INSET courses (n=69)

IT Area	% of Respondents	IT Area	% of Respondents
Wordprocessing	96	Microelectronics	45
Databases	96	Robotics	42
Logo	86	Interfacing	42
Spreadsheets	71	Authoring Languages	35
Videotex	62	Expert Systems	29
Electronic Mail	58	Prolog	29
Computers in Society	55	Artificial Intelligence	21
BASIC, Pascal etc	54	Others	10

problems for in-service providers (new hardware, new operating processes, new emphases) it is likely that new developments in the future will ease many of the problems by improving the user interface. There is now much more commitment to portability in software and to providing sufficient power to enable more meaningful applications in the curriculum. The teaching community is also changing, with the general level of familiarity and confidence growing as the technology becomes ever more pervasive in society. For the next seven years the hope must be that teacher education in IT will break away from the current position of being dominated by considerations of hardware and software operation, to a more productive situation where the learner, the teacher, the curriculum and the pedagogy can re-establish their priority over the tools.

ACKNOWLEDGEMENTS

The authors gratefully acknowledge the role of the Economic and Social Research Council (Information Technology and Education Programme) and the Department of Education for Northern Ireland in supporting the research reported in this paper.

REFERENCES

[1] D. Hawkridge, Information technology in initial teacher training, Council for Educational Technology, London, 1984
[2] See articles by I. Birnbaum and S. Heppell in Educational Computing, vol. 8, no. 6, Sept. 1987
[3] R. Fothergill, Microelectronics education programme - the strategy, Department of Education and Science, London, 1981
[4] "Micros in schools" and "Supported software" schemes, Department of Trade and Industry, London
[5] G. Hubbard, Social and educational effects of technological change, Brit. J. Educational Studies, vol. 22, no. 2, June 1984
[6] Informatics for all, Ministere de l'Education Nationale, Paris, 1985
[7] L. Cerych, Problems arising from the use of new technologies in education, Eur. J. Education, vol. 20, no. 2-3, 1985
[8] K. Frey, Computer education in schools: the distribution model and the integration model in the Federal Republic of Germany, American Educational Research Association, San Francisco, April, 1986
[9] Note for non-UK readers: compulsory education stops at 16 years of age in the UK. Two types of examination are available at 16+: General Certificate of Education Ordinary-level and the Certificate of Secondary Education. The former (GCE)is usually viewed as being targeted at more able pupils while the latter (CSE) is usually aimed at the less able. In 1988 both examinations will be replaced by a common General Certificate of Secondary Education (GCSE) examination. GCE Advanced-level examinations, taken at approx. 18 years of age, remain part of the higher education selection process
[10] Statistics Department, Northern Ireland Schools Examination Council, Belfast
[11] Statistics Branch, Department of Education and Science, London
[12] Statistics Branch, DES, London but for comparison with 1984 figures see J. Wellington et al, Skills for the future, University of Sheffield, Sheffield, 1987
[13] K. Ruthven, Theory into practice, in D. Smith (Ed.), Information technology and education: signposts and research directions, 21-29, ESRC, London, 1985
[14] M. Aston, MEP computer based learning, 1981-1986, Advisory Unit, Hatfield, 1986
[15] R. Masterson and R. Phillips (Eds.), Information technology and science education, Association for Science Education, Hatfield, 1986
[16] M. Withers et al, The use of microcomputers in school chemistry, Royal Society of Chemistry, London, 1986
[17] F. Blow and A. Dickinson (Eds.), New history and new technology, The Historical Association, London, 1986
[18] J. Barker et al, Computers in school biology, Institute of Biology, London, 1986
[19] P. Fox and A. Tapsfield (Eds.), The role and value of new technology in geography, The Geographical Association, Sheffield, 1986
[20] A. Mathews et al, Information technology implications for craft, design and technology, Association of Advisers in Craft, Design and Technology, Aylesbury,1985
[21] S. Hurd et al, Survey of computer use in economics and business studies, Economics Association, Stoke on Trent, 1986
[22] A. Cane, An acorn for the teacher, Financial Times, June 21, 1986
[23] T. Ginn, A 55-second disaster, Guardian, February 26, 1987
[24] P. Bleach, The use of microcomputers in primary schools, Reading University School of Education, Reading, 1986
[25] J. Gardner, Computer assisted learning and in-service teacher training, Brit. J.

Educational Technology, vol. 15, no. 3, 175-182, 1984

[26] J. D'Arcy, Mathematics and the micro, Northern Ireland Council for Educational Research, Belfast, 1985

[27] Statistical Bulletin 18/86, DES, London, 1986

[28] B. Penfold, Baker to keep watch on value from micros, Educational Computing, vol. 8, no. 6, Sept. 1987

[29] Learning to live with IT - an overview of the potential of information technology for education and training, Cabinet Office, London, 1986

[30] Vocational Education Programme, Department of Education, Bangor, Northern Ireland

[31] Microelectronics Education Support Unit (MESU), University of Warwick, Coventry

[32] Computer education for teachers in secondary schools -aims and objectives in teacher training, International Federation for Information Processing, Technical

Committee for Education, 1972 available from Brit. Computer Society, London

[33] Microcomputers in Scottish schools - a national plan, Scottish Council for Educational Technology, Glasgow, 1985

[34] N. Ellam and J. Wellington, Computers in the primary curriculum, University of Sheffield Division of Education, Sheffield, 1987

[35] J. Gardner and M. Megarity, Information technology and in-service teacher education, ESRC Occasional Paper ITE/21/87, University of Lancaster, Sept. 1987

[36] R. Keeling et al, The in-service education of colleagues and self, in Information technology in teacher education -a discussion document, MESU (see [31] above), 1987

[37] Better schools, DES, London, 1986

[38] Employment of students completing courses of initial teacher training in Universities in 1985, Universities Council for the Education of Teachers, London, 1985

COMPUTERS IN EDUCATION, F. Lovis and E.D. Tagg (eds.)
Elsevier Science Publishers B.V. (North-Holland)
IFIP, 1988

OF THE LINGUISTIC PREREQUISITES OF COMPUTING LITERACY

Enrica Lemut (*) - Enrica Ferrero (**)

(*)   Istituto Matematica Applicata del C.N.R.
      Via L.B. Alberti, 4
      16132 Genova, Italy
(**) Circolo Didattico Piossasco
     Scuola Elementare "G. Ungaretti"
     Piossasco (Torino), Italy

The present paper deals with the problem of the linguistic prerequisites of computer literacy, on the basis of a diagnostic survey carried out among a large number of students (from the age of 13-14 years) and with respect to the elaboration and experimentation of appropriate approaches, with a view to using them with younger pupils as well.
The premises underlying the design and experimentation of the innovative teaching situations, aimed to develop the linguistic prerequisites deemed more important are also outlined.

1. INTRODUCTION

The present paper outlines the motivation and salient features of research activities which have been carried out for four years, designed to identify and develop the linguistic prerequisites needed in computer science literacy. On the basis of the experimental teaching activities and the research work conducted at school, proposals for teaching situations favouring the development of these prerequisites are advanced and specific learning difficulties illustrated.
This research is being carried out within the framework of a curricular project for linguistic, mathematic-scientific and technological teaching in elementary schools (6-11 year-old pupils); a curricular project for mathematic-scientific and technological teaching in Italian "scuole medie" (intermediate schools for 11-14 year-old pupils) and several experiences of computing literacy with pupils of various ages. These activities involves over 220 teachers under the coordination of the group we belong to.
In paragraph 2, emphasis is laid on the fact that linguistic deficiencies are associated to specific learning difficulties in the approach to computing science. The experience built up with 13-14 year-old or older students (even University ones) has demonstrated that attempting to remedy these deficiencies during the initial phase of computer teaching is neither economic nor productive. In fact, the difficulties arising in the approach to algorithms and computer programming are added to linguistic ones, at an age when students are less willing or no longer sufficiently flexible for a systematic, far-reaching attack on their linguistic competence. The linguistic

competence required should therefore be developed from the first years of elementary education when pupils are asked to learn to read and write. Work subjects and activities should therefore be devised in relation to the children's age and a competence to develop.
Paragraph 3 deals with the premises underlying our reasearch work. Paragraph 4 provides examples of teaching and working situations designed to develop the linguistic competence which is considered a fundamental requisite for computing literacy. The problems arising in the learning process of specific connectives ("while", "if", "until"), relevant in computer science literacy, are analysed in detail in paragraph 5. Finally, paragraph 6 concerns versatility and the critical comparision of different languages and working methodologies which are being experimented with in this respect.

2. LINGUISTIC PREREQUISITES IN COMPUTING LITERACY

Our experiences have revealed that linguistic deficiencies are usually associated with the crucial elements of computing literacy: the elaboration of algorithms, the understanding of the relations between algorithms and programs, assignment, the conditional jump and the distinction between the sequence of instructions of a program and the sequence of execution depending on specific input data. In some cases, a definite cause-effect relation between certain linguistic deficiencies and difficulties in mastering the above mentioned points can be identified. The difficulties in mastering "if-clauses" at linguistic level are a case in point. In fact, they affect the mastering of the conditional jump. On the other hand, linguistic deficiencies sometimes reveal the existence of more general logic and/or cultural difficulties which are the cause of problems in computer science literacy. In this respect, we should like to point out that several studies emphasize the importance of the development of linguistic skills in the logical and cultural process of maturation.

After this premise, a classification of the linguistic difficulties identified during our activities, is called for to facilitate the comprehension of the following paragraphs:

(i)   *difficulties related to the oral and written verbalization of one's thinking* in situations where its "logic" is strictly determined by the features of the problem to solve and/or the calculating system (resources, characteristics of the languages available..). In situations of this kind, teachers generally do not grasp the students' points of view and suppositions and are therefore unable to interact effectively with them and end up presenting them with solutions which often depart from the students' reasoning efforts. Moreover, what is most disquieting is that pupils easily lose the thread of their thinking.

On the other hand, when they translate their thinking into symbolic language, they are unable to manage it, together with the reference to the problem posed. Students whose capacity to produce texts of various kinds (invention of stories, comments on facts) is judged "sufficient" have demonstrated that they experience the same difficulties. The ability to produce a text exclusively on the basis of stylistic requirements and expressive needs is completely different from that required to produce a text on the basis of logic requisites, not depending on the person producing it.

(ii) *difficulties related to the mastering of specific connectives and linguistic structures* recurring in the verbal description of the conditional jump and the syntax and the semantics of the statements of programming languages. In dealing with the syntax of instructions, at least initially, the references to the theoretical framework systematizing the syntax of a given programming language can be reduced to the minimum. On the other hand, as far as the semantics of statements is concerned, pupils need to understand and actively master the *particular* meanings of connectives like "if", "while", and "until" in programming languages. The students taking part in our activities generally understand sentences from everyday language which include these connectives, but many of them are unable to use them effectively in the texts produced and are not aware of the large number of meanings they can acquire within and without the computing context.

(iii) *difficulties in mastering the variety of languages* which have to be managed, almost simultaneously, during the solution of a problem with the computer. In particular, when tackling numerical problems, the following factors have to be taken into account: the algebraic language, the language required to elaborate and describe the algorithm (for example, flow-chart) and the linguistic features of the programming language adopted. The flexibility required to move from one language to the other and, above all, to control the operations of "translations" and the meanings the same notations acquired in different languages, is not innate and can therefore be developed by means of appropriate activities.

The above mentioned difficulties emerge both in the activities strictly defined as "computer literacy" (approach to computer programming, solution of problems with the computer) and in those concerning the analysis of automated processes and the discovery and explication of the "logic" underlying the functioning of a programmed device (a calculator, a washing-machine). This consideration is of particular interest in the working out of a programme aimed at the elimination of these linguistic difficulties, since it suggests that this objective might be achieved on the basis of linguistic activities designed to encourage the "rationalising" of the automated processes and devices.

3. ELABORATION OF THE RESEARCH PLAN

The principles underlying our work, and outlined hereafter, are not completely original. They draw inspiration from theories of the acquisition of linguistic competence in which *semantics plays a fundamental role*, in keeping with tendencies which have gaining ground, within the framework of language sciences, since the 1970's (see [1], [2]). The originality of our approach lies in *the identification of experience fields* for the systematic development of linguistic competence from the very first years of school (6-7 year-old pupils).

(i)   Certain experience fields present no difficulty of access to children. Here, the activities of verbalization lead to the natural development of competence in *verbal representation of a kind of thought*, which is strictly determined by "logics" completely extraneous to the child's reasoning strategies, by developing the necessary syntactic complexity and an appropriate use of connectives. In particular, the analysis of the functioning and use of common machines (household appliances...), manual and automated production processes and the study of the procedures leading to the solution of the traditional arithmetic problems of elementary schools, are effective activities to this end.

(ii) The variety of linguistic forms which can be used for the representation of the thought related to these fields of experience, if governed by the verbal language, enables children to develop the capacity to make critical comparisions and master the *different meanings* which similar forms acquire in different contexts and the *different forms* which can be used to represent the same meaning.

(iii) During the teaching activities conducted on the basis of what has been stressed in the previous two points, the role played by the teacher is of fundamental importance and consists of three basic moments. The first concerns the formulation of the teaching situations on the basis of an a priori analysis of the linguistic potentials of a specific machine, or a process or procedure to verbalize. (During this phase we all work in groups, individually elaborate the texts in keeping with the instructions which will be given to children, and then compare the different texts produced). During the second phase, the linguistic structures necessary to rationalise the machine or the process chosen are introduced by the teacher, who *proposes* particular linguistic forms and individually *guides* the process of verbalization or non verbal representation with the children facing the greatest difficulties. The third phase centres on the management, in class, of the linguistic analysis of different texts and non-verbal linguistic representations produced by children (from the age of seven) to favour the understanding of the meanings acquired by certain connectives, expressive graphic forms, etc., in and outside the context examined.

To systematise the a priori analysis of the meanings of connectives and work out systematic processes of verification of acquisitions, we have relied on research into the acquisitions of connectives carried out over the last fifteen years within the framework of psycholinguistics (see [3], [4]).

Methods and work proposals advanced within the framework of the didactics of mathematics (cf. [5], [6], [7]) have also proved extremely useful, both with respect to the methodology adopted in the elaboration of the teaching situations and the specific teaching problems related to the mastering and linguistic explication of mathematical concepts and procedures.

With regards to the hypotheses previously illustrated and the references to research conducted by others, the authors would like to emphasise the importance of being able *to work within the framework of curricular, long-term projects,* with phases marked by increasing difficulties, moments of analysis of the difficulties encountered by children, proposals and experimental activities to overcome them. Our experience in the field of innovative,

experimental teaching methods within the framework of school curricula might provide a valuable contribution to other forms of research which, on the other hand, focus on children of a certain age in a socio-cultural and educational environment and on the existence or lack of specific linguistic skills.

The role of the teacher in class (cf. hypothesis iii) deserves special mention.

We think that, specially with children belonging to a poor socio-cultural environment, the teacher has to encourage children to organise their thoughts, provinding them with the linguistic structures which best suit their communicative efforts, through an individually tailored approach. In this respect, teachers have to enhance their capacity to analyse children's communicative efforts, while encouraging them to complete and organise their thinking. The teacher's task is therefore to help children to overcome the difficulties experienced in the verbalisation of their thoughts with activities concerning the children's processes of oral (more than written) verbalisation *when they take place.*

It should be recalled that these difficulties are due generally to the child's family environment and, in it, to the lack of effective verbal interaction.

The considerations hitherto illustrated rely on the convinction, corroborated by our experience in schools, that any child without brain lesions or serious mental handicaps can acquire the linguistic competence needed to understand the basic elements of computer literacy, as is borne out by widely endorsed theories on the linguistic potentials present in all children of our age (cf. Bernstein and Bruner). The most serious linguistic deficiencies encountered at school level or after school do not depend on children's intelligence but on educational deficiencies existing at school or family level.

4. DEVELOPMENT OF SYNTACTIC COMPLEXITY AND MASTERING OF CONNECTIVES OF RELEVANCE IN COMPUTER LITERACY: EXAMPLES OF TEACHING EXPERIENCES

A first example concerns activities which have been conducted for the last four years with children attending the first year of primary school on the subject "machines". The whole program, which requires more than one hundred hours of work in class during the first school-year, cannot be completely described here. Let us focus our attention on the analysis of the *use* and *functioning* of the most common machines. The child must verbalize, answering specific instructions: "how it is used", "how it functions".

We have decided to choose certain machines, considering that they basically fall into two classes: machines where *the description of the use cannot be clearly distinguished from that of the functioning* (i.e. usually traditional machines, such as bicycles) and machines where the description of the use *can clearly be distinguished* from that of the functioning, (for example, highly automated machines whose commands activate internal functioning, the mastering of which by the user is not essential to use the machine at an elementary level, such as some electric household appliances, calculators, etc.).

The distinction between "functioning" and "use" is of basic importance: the verbalisation of the use of an electric appliance such as a mixer or (at a higher stage of maturity) of a machine such a calculator, consists basically in instructions for the use with a very simple syntactic structure (subject-verb), expressing the actions to be performed on the machine to obtain the desired "product", and possibly, "controls" to be performed in order to regulate the times and modes of execution of the activity. The verbalization of the "functioning", on the contrary, shows (in many machines) a far higher syntactic complexity (contemporaneity, presence of several interacting subjects, etc.); we can summarize this by saying that the verbalization of the use is (mainly in modern machines) as simple as necessary to help the user, whereas the verbalization of the functioning can be very complex, since it is addressed to the designers of the machine. As a teaching choice, we believe that the children should try all kinds of verbalization. Obviously, the complexity of the required performance should be increased gradually.

As far as the use is concerned, it is interesting to note that, on a teaching level, the verbalization process can be related to the actual activity carried out with the machines: the child follows his verbalization on the machine in question and, in this way, he may discover that a certain "instruction" or a suitable control are lacking, that the order between two instructions is wrong, etc....

A second example concerns the verbalization of a class-activity with 8 to 9 year-old children (third year of school): it is possible to choose a sequence of class productions complying with criteria of growing complexity and gradually introducing iteration, contemporaneity, etc. Obviously, the various productions must also be chosen (linguistic potentiality being equal) on the basis of practical performance possibilities.

In each task, the children are asked to verbalize and formalize the process they have experienced directly through flow-charts. This is the most interesting activity, for several reasons:

(i) it lends itself to interesting comparisions between the linguistic expression used (correct? partially correct?....) and its meaning: if a child writes that "the eggs are broken and then the whites are separated from the yolks", the situation can be recreated....

(ii) it enables the teacher to observe the children's *variety of both verbal and non verbal expressive forms*, thus making it possible: to ascertain the active mastering of the syntactic structures achieved by the children; to identify the most difficult points, in order to program more systematic attacks on them; to start activities of linguistic analysis, both of the variety of forms which can be used to convey one meaning and of the variety of meanings of one expression or connective in different contexts.

A third example concerns the verbalization and formalization, by means of flow-charts, of an automated production process (10 year-old children). On the basis of the previous attitude, more advanced targets can be set, as regards the semantics underlying the various languages used and the syntactic structure of the adopted linguistic representations. In particular, the following is possible:

(i) interpreting a process as a sequence of work-phases, or as a sequence of "semi-finished products undergoing changes" or else, as a sequence of machines operating changes. As a result, the meanings of the flow-charts vary too.

(ii) analysing individual work-phases, underlining that, in some cases, flow-charts cannot be used to represent them correctly, because they cannot be split into simple, independent and successive actions (chocolate production is a case in point, since ingredient mixing occurs while the product is kept warm by an infrared lamp).

5. THREE EXAMPLES OF SPECIFIC STUDIES ON CONNECTIVES: "WHILE", "IF", "UNTIL"

This paragraph focuses its attention on management problems and learning difficulties connected with the mastering of the connectives "while", "if" and "until", in teaching situations of the type illustrated in the previous paragraph.

5.1. "while"

Teachers must be well aware of the variety of meanings of this connective, as well as of the variety of linguistic forms which can express each of these meanings. The analysis (first on the part of the teacher and then in the course of class-work) is not easy because, in order to identify the variety of meanings (distinction between the adversative "while" and the "while" expressing contemporaneity...), the context must usually be taken into consideration.

Furthermore, serious verbalization problems arise in the description of some of these meanings (i.e.: verbal explication of the different meanings of "while" in the following three sentences: "while one lever goes up, the other goes down", "while the vessel empties, the warning light is off", "while you make the mixture, I turn the oven on").

We have already seen that the work on "while" can be begun with seven-year-old children. Starting from the situations where it is used by some children, other sentences should be built where "while" occurs and attempts should be made to replace it with the adverb "contemporaneously", with the gerund... With 8-9 year-olds, the teacher can also start to *explicate* and verbalize the variety of meanings of "while". These activities entail considerable learning difficulties for about 20% of the children: in this respect, the children having difficulties in the *linguistic reflection* on "while" seem to be also unwilling to use it in contexts differing from those where its use has been introduced and "forced" by the teacher.

5.2. "if"

Six-year-old children starting elementary school have no difficulties in understanding sentences where "if" occurs, probably because the youngest children learn the meaning of the conditional "if" from the hierarchical relations of their educational context and because the semantics of the *dubitative* "if" and of the other meanings of "if" (exhortative, etc...) can be easily identified from the context.

The active use of "if", on the contrary, presents the children with considerable difficulties. In particular, they seem unwilling to use "if" in mathematical reasoning; they prefer to list the alternatives without linking them by means of "if...otherwise"; in some cases, however, it is difficult for them to point out the possible alternatives. As regards the analysis of production processes by means of controls, on the other hand, we have noted that their verbalization does not necessarily mean that the children, even when using "if", are aware of the different paths of the "product" units, in relation to the result of the control concerning these units (that is particularly evident when the control takes a product unit back to a work-phase preceding that of the control itself). Apparently the same difficulty arises here as that noticed in the activities of computer literacy with regard to the distinction between the sequence of program statements and the sequences of the step-by-step execution of the program.

5.3. "until"

The several protocols collected on "until" have given the following results:
- in verbalizing, the same child prefers the verbal form "I repeat.... until", or avoids it according to the context
- the children of the same age group and of the same class have very different behaviour patterns (they use or avoid "until") in the

same *given* situation.
It is therefore interesting to analyse:
(a) the situation where the children prefer, in average, to use "until" or to avoid it. Its specific semantics *seem* to play an important role: in some cases, the child's attention is raised by the *control* (and he states it and attaches less importance to iteration, thus resorting, for example, to the form "every time I control that..."); in other cases, on the contrary, his attention is raised by the *repetition* of a certain activity as long as certain conditions persist, and then it is more natural to use "I repeat... until".
(b) the strategies by means of which this connective is avoided, both at 8-9 years of age and later at 13-14 years, when we propose cases of iteration controlled by an arrest factor, which are very well verbalized by sentences such as "I repeat... until". The youngest children and the linguistically less-favoured ones usually explicate the repetition of the control; others state the control to be performed and explicate that this control is to be performed "every time" (this is the most mature form, which is present also in children with considerable linguistic skills). We have also seen that these interpretative criteria generally make it quite easy to foresee, on the basis of the a priori analysis of a productive process carried out in the class, whether its semantics will urge the children to use some forms to express iteration, or others (8-10 years).

We have noticed similar behaviour patterns in 13-14 year-olds and we have ascertained that interesting comparisions can be drawn (with classes adequately prepared from a linguistic point of view) between the expression "I repeat... until" and loops controlled by "if... then" in verbalizing automated processes (before turning to computer programming).

6. FLEXIBILITY AND AWARENESS IN THE USE OF DIFFERENT LANGUAGES

Beside comparing and reflecting on the variety of languages available to formalize production (or calculation) processes, as described in the previous paragraphs, we also regard the activities envisaged in our project *to explicate solving procedures for the typical arithmetic problems* of primary school (6-11 year olds), as important in order to reach the flexibility and awareness which are essential prerequisites to use different languages.

In this respect, we *introduce* graph language during the second year (7-8 year-olds), since it is a useful instrument to represent the process and the dynamics of the children's solving reasoning; we *require* the verbalization of problem solving reasoning as an account for the reasoning performed to attain the solution and *propose* the use of verbal language as a means to organize the thinking *during the solving procedure* of the most complex problems. Algebraic language, on the other hand, seems a suitable tool to provide a definitive and concise representation of the sequence of calculations to be performed to solve a certain problem, whereas we have noticed some difficulties in using it (before the age of 7-8) as a thinking instrument to solve problems, especially when the children have not yet mastered the meanings of the operations represented by the symbols "-" and ":". After outlining the linguistic activities concerning the solution of problems proposed during our class activities, we should like to point out the aspects more closely related to the linguistic competence involved in approaching computer science.

Firstly, we believe that, even in this case, the variety of expressive forms helps the child choose the most suitable one each time and master the different expressive modes of one concept. In our opinion, however, the most useful aspect is another one: i.e. passing from specific strategies to solve specific problems to general reasoning (e.g. written calculation techniques), applicable to any numeric situation similar to the considered one. In this way, for example, the technique of the written calculation of division can be devised with the direct participation of the children (aged between 8 and 9).

This work program is an important approach to algorithmic thinking and to the solution of problems with a computer. Moreover, it connects the development in linguistic competence and the comparison between different formalizations of the calculations to be performed with the learning process: the child verbally states (and formalizes through graphs, algebraically, or by means of special diagrams) his solving procedures; some of these procedures are pointed out by the teacher and proposed to the class as applicable and useful for a wider range of problems, and then the verbal statement of the general procedure and its formalization become important instruments in passing on to the standard algorithm which can be applied to any number.

REFERENCES

[1] Antinucci, F., Parisi, D., Early semantic development in child language, in: E. Lenneberg (eds.), Foundations of language development: a multidisciplinary approach (Academic Press, New York, 1975)

[2] Katz, J.J., Semantic Theory (Harper and Row, New York, 1972).

[3] French, L.A., Acquiring and using words to express logical relationships, in: Kuczaj, S.A. and Barret, M.D. (eds.), The development of word meaning (Springer-Verlag, New York, 1985) pp.303-338

[4] French, L.A., Nelson, K., Children's understanding of relational terms: some ifs, ors and buts (Springer-Verlag, New York, 1972).

[5] Brousseau, G., Actes de la Ecole d'ete' de Didactique des Mathematiques 1982 Orleans (1982) 35 (french)

[6] Douady, R., Jeux de cadres et dialectique outil-object dans l'enseignement des mathematiques, These Universite de Paris VII (1984) (french).

[7] Laborde, C., Deux codes en interaction dans l'enseignement matematique: langue naturelle et ecriture symbolique, These Universite de Grenoble (1982) (french).

[8] Nelson, K., Cognitive development and the acquisition of concepts, in: Anderson, R.C. and Spiro, R.J. and Montagne, W.E. (eds.), Schooling and the acquisition of knowledge (Hillsdate, New York Erlbaum, 1977)

[9] Nelson (ed), K., Children's Language (Gardner Press, New York, 1978).

[10] Schlesinger, I.M., Steps to Language (Lawrence Erlbaum Ass. Publishers, Hillsdale, 1982).

[11] Zammuner, V.L., La comprensione e il ricordo delle discontinuita' semantiche nelle storie dei bambini, Giornale italiano di Psicologia, no.12 (1985) pp.495-514 (italian)

COMPUTERS IN EDUCATION, F. Lovis and E.D. Tagg (eds.)
Elsevier Science Publishers B.V. (North-Holland)
© IFIP, 1988

TEACHERS HAVE BEEN GROWING UP[*]

Evgenia Sendova and Rumen Nikolov

Research Group on Education,
Bulgarian Academy of Sciences
Bd Vitosha 5, Sofia 1000, Bulgaria

This paper deals with the role of the informatics teachers in the experimental schools of the Research Group on Education (RGE), affiliated with the Bulgarian Academy of Sciences and the Ministry of Education. Different organization forms for stimulating the teachers in informatics are considered - teacher training courses and seminars, annual conferences, a bulletin *Informatics and Mathematics*, teacher research projects. The now five year experience of the RGE informatics team shows that only with the joint efforts of researchers and teachers can the teaching of informatics be successful.

To teach informatics is good
but to be good at teaching informatics
is still better...

1. INTRODUCTION

Today when the teaching of informatics still lacks traditions, it is both attractive and difficult to be a teacher of informatics. It would be good if he combined the spirit of Columbus, the universality of Da Vinci and Benjamin Spoke's love for children. We came to this obvious conclusion after a five-year experiment of teaching informatics in the schools of the Bulgarian Research Group on Education (RGE) [8,9,10]. Addressing the teachers the RGE leader pointed out what an awful mistake it would be to think that they could be replaced by good textbooks or by good educational software. Important as the quality and attractiveness of the software and textbooks may seem, nothing rates higher than the teacher's creative powers and selfconfidence. But these must be patiently cultivated. The traditional way to do this are the teacher training courses. And that is how we began.

2. THE FIRST STEPS

A two-week teacher training course in Logo was included in the course system of the RGE in 1982/1983 schoolyear [2]. And the problems began:

- not only was informatics a new subject for the teachers but also they had to work according to principles of education to which they were not accustomed e.g the integration of different school subjects and to teach how to learn by oneself. The majority of the teachers did not know the non-mathematical subjects (English, physics and musics) to the extent needed for such an integrated course;

- not all of the teachers have a university degree. Most of them are aged between 40-45. Only the younger ones have studied informatics;

- there were a number of psychological barriers regarding both the new techniques and the age-difference between them and their trainers.

During the first course the teachers acted as pupils - worked with the textbooks by themselves (as the RGE pupils are supposed to do) and entered an educational environment very near to that at school. The advantage of such an approach is that they would experience what their pupils would do later.

The main problems the teachers were faced with during the first two years were due not only to the lack of experience but also to the specific conditions - about 30 pupils per class with five computers on average. The teachers worked in isolation and received our consultations by phone. The only special books on the

---

* This project has been supported financially by the Committee for Science at the Council of Ministers under Contract No 554.

subjects available were the informatics textbooks [1,4]. Thus they hardly felt superior to their pupils.

3. GROWING UP

What steps did the section *Informatics* at RGE undertake to help the teachers?

3.1 The turtle learns to speak Bulgarian

A Bulgarian version of Logo was developed which not only made the teachers work easier but played a psychological role since both the children and the teachers felt that the computer is not a stranger. In the revised edition of the textbooks the Bulgarian version of Logo was adopted [5,6,7]. The greater part of the teachers' notes and recommendations have been taken into consideration - the number of topics was reduced, some of the more difficult ones were moved from the fifth to the sixth grade textbook.

3.2 Annual conferences

The annual conferences held every spring are very important events for the RGE-teachers. The section "Informatics" began functioning in 1986 and is getting very active - the number of the reports in 1987 was doubled. During the sessions as well as in organized discussions the teachers share ideas about how to overcome difficulties, argue, criticize, share experience. And although a discussion (by definition) is a debate where nothing is born, some good ideas came to life - to organize olympiade in informatics and to edit a bulletin.

The RGE directorate tends to stimulate the teachers. The best of them get special prizes at the annual conference, have their reports published in Bulgarian and English [13], participate in international conferences, meet specialists on a visit to RGE.

3.3 The first Logo-olympiade

In view of an old tradition in the Bulgarian educational system to organize contests in mathematics, physics, linguistics and lately - in informatics, we answered the wish of RGE-teachers to have our own olympiade in informatics. Stress was put though on the preparation - there were preliminary rounds in order to nominate the participants in the final one. This served as good motivation for work. The final round was reached by 50 pupils (between 11 and 13 years old). At the first stage the children worked on a sheet of paper and at the second one they checked their programs on a computer. The results are optimistic - a lot of pupils showed a good programming style. This event enabled both the teachers and the pupils "to see how

the land lies" and to establish further creative contacts.

3.4 The bulletin *Informatics and Mathematics*

The necessity of having a publication that would serve as a focus for the various teachers' activity has been felt for a long time. It was at the annual RGE conference (1987) that the project of the first issue of a bulletin under the title *Informatics and Mathematics* was shown to be discussed. The goals of such a bulletin are to react in time to the teachers' problems and questions, to make known their good ideas, to overcome the isolation in which they work, to enrich their knowledge in mathematics, informatics, psychology. Here are some of the headings:

- *We introduce to you* - acquaints the teachers with articles of well known specialists in informatics (published usually for the first time in Bulgarian);

- *What is your opinion?* - considers some debatable questions;

- *The teachers share* - most of the papers delivered at the annual conferences are carried here;

- *Our contribution* - teachers' papers rewarded at the annual conference as well as papers delivered by RGE-researchers at international conferences could be found here;

- *To appear* - parts of forthcoming textbooks, books and dissertations are put under this heading for preliminary discussion;

- *What, where, when?* - the most recent news concerning interesting events in our field (conferences, exhibitions, visits etc.) are put under this heading;

There are some other headings dealing with robotics, psychology, evaluation etc. Between the rubrics - challenging problems and of course - a lot of humour (the sense of which so many informaticians are lucky to possess).

Only two issues of the bulletin have appeared up to now but the first comments are very rewarding. The teachers (and we also) have been growing up.

4. MATURITY

After the first teacher training course more and more differential training was needed. Since the teachers were not specially chosen there were some who did not manage to make progress after the first course. These were only single cases though. The majority of the teachers approach their vocation with a sense of responsibility and show professional creativity. There is also creative work in the way teachers relate informatics to other subjects (mathematics, physics, music), in the way they adapt the existing textbooks to the teaching of younger pupils, and in the way they organize their work (in the not so favourable conditions). There were also teachers who have shown up with their research spirit. All this led us to the idea of organizing the teacher training courses in a different way.

4.1 Seminars - a new kind of teacher training courses.

A twenty days seminar was organized for the first time in the framework of the latest teacher training course (together with the usual ten days courses for beginners and advanced teachers). Ten teachers having shown both sufficient knoweledge in Logo for developing educational software and endeavour towards creative teaching took part in the seminar. The course consisted of two parts: a practical seminar *Educational software for fifth grade* and a method seminar *Teaching informatics in the fifth grade*.

4.1.1 The practical seminar

The goal of this seminar was to enable the teachers *to look with another eye* on the software assisting the textbooks [6,7] thus gaining selfconfidence in being not only users but also authors of educational software. In favour of such an idea was the circumstance that the educational programs under consideration are *transparent* [3], i.e. readable, relatively short and the execution of which could be traced on the screen. There were three kinds of classes:

- a lecture - the process of developing a program (already used by the teacher) is followed. The advantages of the step-wise refinement method are demonstrated, program-graphs are built, the possibilities for some projects modification are discussed and realized later;

- *reading* programs - the teachers read programs, represent their structure in the form of a graph. The classes again end with discussion;

- practical classes - the teachers work actively with a computer. There are demonstrations and discussions at the end;

- teachers' reports - educational software developed by teachers (not only in the seminar's framework) is discussed.

The discussions accompanying the classes turned out to be very fruitful and gave birth to interesting sugges-

tions, e.g. how to modify certain computer programs so that they could be used for different educational goals. There was a suggestion for example to turn a program similar to *Instant* into: *One-key Logo*, computer constructors, a text-editor in graphics mode, a graphical editors of electronic circuits and structural chemical formulas etc. It was discussed also how to modify the program *Animals* for it to be used in different subject areas: botany, history, geography, physics, chemistry, mathematics, languages etc. Some of the proposals have been developed. The course ended with challenge towards the teachers - to develop educational software in the framework of research projects. It was pointed out that the practical seminar could be used by the teachers as a model for their extra-classes teaching in school.

4.1.2 Method seminar

This seminar aimed at generalizing the five years experience of teaching informatics in fifth grade. One of the first tasks of the seminar was to determine and discuss the structure of the lesson from the method point of view. It was generally agreed that the teachers should not be told exactly what to do. (Even the Ten Commandments say only what one should not do.) What the teachers need are directions and recommendations. A possible methical development of a lesson could (not "should") include the following topics:

a) goals of the lesson;
b) basic notions to be introduced or used;
c) computer experiments, problems and possible solutions;
d) minimum level to be achieved during the lesson;
e) the most common mistakes and methods to deal with;
f) subject matter and problems suitable for extra-classes activity.
g) tests;
h) different form of organization - contests, collective work, exchange of programs etc.

Every participant in the seminar was supposed to develop a couple of lessons in the above style. After the discussion at the end of the course a second version of the method materials had been worked out taking into consideration the notes concerning the first one. The teachers have exchanged the materials. The discussion will continue on the pages of the bulletin *Informatics and Mathematics*, where the materials will be published together with the remarks. The final version of the materials will serve as a base of a teachers' handbook to be written by all the RGE teachers (together with the authors of the informatics textbooks).

5. CONCLUSIONS

Our experience shows that only with the joint effort of the RGE informatics team and the teachers can we hope to continue successfully the now five-year old experiment in the teaching of informatics. In favour of this the following projects are envisaged in the near future:

- to develop introductory courses in informatics on the base of different problem areas - e.g mathematics, physics, music;

- to develop methods for using new educational software tools (e.g *Plane Geometry System* [11,12]).

- to develop and edit teaching materials (teacher's handbooks, collections of problems, case-studies, tests etc.) with the active participation of teachers.

As for a further future we dream that every RGE school would become a real research laboratory.

No matter that a teacher in informatics is expected to be a philosopher as well as a psychologist, a technician, an organizer and eventually - an informatician, all the same the chance is there since there are few specialists in informatics able to work with children... We are greatly pleased to say that there are quite a number of teachers in the RGE schools deserving appreciation. It was no chance that during a visit to one of the RGE schools Seymour Papert was asked by a child: *"Do you have in the States such a good teacher as ours?"* The obvious answer was *"No"*.

REFERENCES

[1] Nikolov, R., Logo. An Experimental Textbook for the 5-th Grade (RGE, Sofia, 1983) (in Bulgarian).

[2] Nikolov, R., Teacher Training in Logo, in: Lovis, F. and Tagg, D., Informatics and Teacher Training, Proceedings of the IFIP WG 3.1 Working Conference (North-Holland, Amsterdam, 1984) pp 59-68.

[3] Nikolov, R., A Learning Environment in Informatics, Ph.D. Thesis (Sofia University, 1987) (in Bulgarian).

[4] Nikolov, R. and Sendova, E., Language and Mathematics. Logo for the 6-th Grade (RGE, Sofia, 1984) (in Bulgarian).

[5] Nikolov, R. and Sendova E., Informatics textbooks for Beginners, in: Proceedings of the First International Conference "Children in the Information Age" (Varna, Bulgaria, 1985) pp 621-629.

[6] Nikolov, R. and Sendova, E., Informatics-1. Logo (RGE, Sofia, 1985) (in Bulgarian, Russion and Spanish).

[7] Nikolov, R. and Sendova, E., Informatics-2. Logo (RGE, Sofia, 1987) (in Bulgarian).

[8] Nikolov, R., Sendova, E. and Dicheva, D., What to Teach in Informatics and How - a Bulgarian Experiment, this volume.

[9] Penkov, B. and Sendov, Bl., The Bulgarian Academy of Sciences Research Group on Education Project (BARGEP), Int. Conference in Math Education (UCSMP, Chicago, 28-30 March, 1985).

[10] Sendov, Bl., To the Heart of the Matter (RGE, Sofia, 1986) (in Bulgarian).

[11] Sendov, Boj. and Dicheva, D., Mathematical Laboratory in Logo Style, this volume.

[12] Sendov, Boj., Fillimonov, R. and Dicheva, D., A System for Teaching Plane Geometry, Proceedings of the Second International Conference "Children in the Information Age" (Sofia, Bulgaria, 1987) pp 215-225.

[13] Sendova, E., ed., Creative Teaching Informatics. Papers Delivered by Teachers at the RGE Conference (RGE, Sofia, May, 1986).

COMPUTERS IN EDUCATION, F. Lovis and E.D. Tagg (eds.)
Elsevier Science Publishers B.V. (North-Holland)
© IFIP, 1988

IN-SERVICE TRAINING OF TEACHERS OF COMPUTING: A CASE STUDY

Charles J V Murphy

Department of Information Systems, Institute of Informatics,
University of Ulster at Jordanstown, Newtownabbey,
County Antrim BT37 0QB, Northern Ireland

Northern Ireland has a population of approximately 1.5 million. There are 280 schools
and colleges providing secondary level education. Although part of the United Kingdom,
Northern Ireland has a separate Department of Education (DENI) which operates in
conjunction with five Education and Library Boards (ELBs).

The Institute of Informatics of the University of Ulster (previously the Department of
Computing Science of the Ulster Polytechnic) in Jordanstown, County Antrim has been
providing a programme of in-service courses for teachers of computing in secondary
schools since 1979. This paper contains an outline of the rationale and philosophy of
the courses, a brief historical account of the programme and a summary of the experience
gained. It should provide a useful case study for other education authorities facing the
same needs.

1. INTRODUCTION

A micro-computer specially designed for use in
schools was first demonstrated in Northern
Ireland in May, 1978 at the annual conference
of the Computer Education Group, a society of
computer enthusiasts who were trying to promote the teaching of computing in schools at
that time. The machine in question was the
RML 380Z, a Z80 based micro with a cassette
backing store.

The Department of Computer Science of the
Ulster Polytechnic took a leading role in
generating the initial response of Northern
Ireland's education system to the arrival of
the micro. Action was initiated on three
fronts:

(i)   provision of equipment: an Advisory
        Panel was established to advise the DENI
        and the ELBs on how best to implement
        the introduction of computers to schools;

(ii)   provision of examination syllabuses: a
        working party was set up to establish
        an examination in Computer Studies at
        Ordinary (16+) Level in the Northern
        Ireland GCE;

(iii)   provision of teacher training: the
        Polytechnic initiated a one year full-
        time in-service course in computing for
        teachers, leading to a Post-Graduate
        Diploma and obtained the support of DENI
        which agreed to grant one year's leave
        of absence with full salary to 12-15
        serving teachers each year to take the
        course. The first intake was in
        September 1979.

At the same time North-West College in
Londonderry approached the Polytechnic for
authorisation to offer the same Diploma course
over two years in a part-time, day-release
mode and persuaded their local ELB to allow
15 teachers leave of absence on one day per
week for two years to take this version of the
course.

2. THE COURSE - THE POST-GRADUATE DIPLOMA IN COMPUTER EDUCATION

2.1 Rationale

Prior to 1978 some computing had been taught
in a few of Northern Ireland's schools usually
by enthusiasts from the mathematics department.
Those involved in designing the course at the
Polytechnic were very much of the opinion:

(a)   that it would be essential to re-train
        existing teachers as few graduates in
        computing entered the teaching pro-
        fession, and that this situation was
        unlikely to change in the immediate
        future; and

(b)   that a substantial course was needed to
        provide the necessary in-depth training
        of teachers in this new subject area.
        Most traditional in-service training is
        in the form of short, 2-5 day, courses
        designed to refresh or update teachers
        who already have a basic training in
        their subject area. Very few teachers
        had any basic training in computing and it
        was felt that many typical short in-
        service courses merely served to confirm
        for teachers their feeling of being
        inadequately qualified.

2.2 Aims and Objectives

The primary aim of the course was to provide experienced teachers with the skills and knowledge of computing to enable them to teach the subject at all levels in secondary schools.

It was also accepted by the course designers that those who completed the Diploma would be expected to assist and advise other teachers who might wish to use computers in their work. Thus included in the course was a secondary aim of making the teachers aware of the potential of the micro as an educational aid across the curriculum.

The objectives of the course were that the teachers should be able to:

(i)   identify and justify the place of computing in the school curriculum;

(ii)   design and teach courses in computing at all levels in secondary schools;

(iii)   assist and advise school pupils and other teachers who might wish to use computers in their work.

Three aspects of the philosophy underlying the design of the course are worth mentioning.

Firstly the designers of the course felt strongly that there should be an effort to move the study of computing away from its traditional links with mathematics and towards a greater emphasis on problem solving and information processing.

Secondly it was decided that, as far as possible, those members of the Polytechnic staff chosen to teach on the course would themselves have experience of teaching at secondary level. In this way it would be possible for each lecturer, when teaching a particular computing topic, to include consideration of how that topic might best be presented to secondary school pupils.

Thirdly it was decided to consider the experience of the teachers attending the course as a resource, to be used in two ways:

(a) through their contributions to formal seminars and discussions on the development of the use of computers in schools; and

(b) in the way the teachers would interact informally and learn from each other in the periods between their timetabled classes.

This last consideration was a major factor in the decision of the Polytechnic to opt for a full-time rather than a part-time course. A counter argument in favour of the part-time day release approach was that teachers could enhance their study of the material of the course and examine the associated approaches to teaching by applying them to their own pupils.

2.3 Course Content

Syllabus	Hours
Programming and Problem Solving	140
Information Processing and its Applications	130
Architecture and Systems Software	70
Social Implications	20
Modelling Methods	40(*)
Curriculum Development in Computer Studies	40(**)
Computers in Education	40
Course Project	120
Total	600 hours

* - This was later reduced to 20 hours to allow the inclusion of a 30 hour course in Micro-processor Control of Devices.

** - In the day-release mode this syllabus was reinforced through practical work in each teacher's own school.

2.4 Syllabus Content

All of the syllabuses have been modified over the lifetime of the course in response to the rapid development of both hardware and software.

(i)   Programming and Problem Solving

This syllabus was designed to produce teachers who would be well qualified to teach programming and who would belie the criticism often expressed by those in third level education and in industry [1] that programming was taught so badly in schools that it often did more harm than good.

The syllabus emphasises (i) a structured approach to problem solving and program design and (ii) information processing rather than numerical and scientific computing. Inevitably it was necessary to teach BASIC as it was almost the only language available in schools at the time, but PASCAL is also taught, not only to give the teachers an appreciation of a language with advanced programming and data structures, but also to give them experience of programming with an editor and compiler.

This syllabus also includes programming in a typical micro-computer assembly language both to give a deeper appreciation of computer architecture and systems software and to make the point that good programming practice is necessary at any level of language.

(ii)   Information Processing and Applications

This syllabus was designed initially as a traditional course in Data Processing and

Systems Analysis through applications and case studies with some programming in COBOL to illustrate the topics being covered. It has changed over the years in keeping with developments in the subject area: eg it now includes a study of databases, while COBOL has been replaced by a database management system, dBASEIII [2].

(iii) Architecture and Systems Software

This is another mainstream computer science syllabus concentrating on the computer itself as a hardware and software system. It covers the traditional topics both in architecture, eg the CPU, data storage, machine logic and the hardware/software interface and in systems software, eg translation software, operating systems and utilities. The main development in this syllabus has been a change in emphasis away from mainframe and towards micro-computer systems.

(iv) Social Implications

Some observers consider this to be the most important single topic in a modern computing course for teachers [3],[4]. The development and application of micro-electronics is leading to far reaching technological and social changes. Schools will have to develop their curriculum both in content and in method to meet new demands and to avail of the new technology. Teachers must be made aware of the issues involved.

In this syllabus each member of the group chooses, or is assigned for special study, a relevant aspect of the social implications of computing. The findings of each study are submitted in an extended essay and presented to the rest of the group in a seminar paper. In this way a large area of the subject is covered while each student gains experience in private reading and research.

(v) Modelling Methods

Initially the emphasis in this syllabus was on statistical modelling and numerical methods as, even in the early 1980's, these topics were still on some examination board syllabuses in computing. As with other courses, however, the coming of the micro has led to a change in emphasis away from numerical mathematics and towards such topics as simulation and graphics leading to computer aided design.

(vi) Curriculum Development in Computer Studies

Computing is still a relatively recent introduction to the school curriculum and thus a widely accepted teaching methodology for the subject has not had time to develop. There are particular problems as the subject demands a wide range of skills: numerical/mathematical, analytical/problem solving and literary/descriptive. Few teachers are experienced in dealing with all of these and mathematicians in particular appear to have difficulty in adapting to those aspects of the subject which require a more discursive treatment.

The lecturers on this course are careful to avoid an authoritative approach and it is in this syllabus that the teaching experience of the students is most valuable. The course is presented through seminars and discussions. Each member of the group takes a topic from one of the schools' examination syllabuses and presents a discussion paper on its teaching.

Computing can be studied at a variety of levels: awareness, appreciation, literacy, studies and science [5]. This syllabus also considers the issues involved in designing and introducing appropriate courses in computing to an already overcrowded school syllabus.

(vii) Computers in Education

This syllabus examines the potential of the computer as an education aid as well as the issues and difficulties involved in promoting and developing its use across the whole school curriculum. The students also consider how the school curriculum may have to change both in content and in methodology in response to developments in information technology.

The syllabus deals with such issues as computer based learning and teaching, computer managed learning and the use of the computer in school administration. This is a rapidly developing field of study, application and research and the course has had to be adapted from year to year in an attempt to evaluate the advances in hardware, software and applications, eg in recent years this syllabus has included a study of newer languages such as LOGO and PROLOG as well as the potential educational uses of context free software such as databases, word-processors and spreadsheets.

(viii) Computer Control of Devices

When the Diploma course was first designed in the late 1970's this aspect of computing was not included. In more recent years, however, there have been developments in equipment and materials suitable for teaching and demonstrating the subject in schools and it was felt that teachers would not be properly qualified in computing if they did not have some understanding and experience of using micro-processors to monitor and control peripheral devices. As far as possible those teaching this syllabus try to avoid an over technical, electronics based approach. Instead they use a variety of "black-box" interface modules thus allowing the students to concentrate on the micro-processor control aspects of the topic.

TABLE I   Enrolments - Full-Time Diploma

Year	79/80	80/81	81/82	82/83	83/84	84/85	Total
Applications	22	47	64	85	85	72	*
Enrolment	12	15	16	15	15	16	89
Completions	9	16	16	12	15	17	81

* The total number of applications is not the sum of the applications for individual years as many teachers applied to join the course on more than one occasion.

3. COURSE EVALUATION

The course has proved extremely popular and successful. As is shown in TABLE I applications far outnumbered enrolment and it is interesting to note that out of 89 teachers enrolled over six years only 8 failed to complete the course, the most common cause being a failure to complete the course project. Obviously the teachers who enrolled were highly motivated since in order to get on the course they had:

(i)   to persuade their head teachers and boards of governors to release them from their teaching duties;

(ii)   to persuade DENI to award grant aid; and

(iii)   gain a place on the course in the face of stiff competition.

To supplement the evaluation based on assessment and informal feedback from students a formal evaluation was carried out in Autumn 1982. This took the form of a questionnaire sent to all those who had completed the full-time course in the previous three years. The feedback collected was concerned mainly with how the teachers felt about the relevance of various topics to their jobs as teachers.

Out of 41 diplomates 29 completed the questionnaire and of these 27 expressed a high degree of satisfaction with the content and presentation of the course, but in relation to their job as teachers of computing the responses showed that the diplomates divided into two main categories.

Group A expressed a high degree of satisfaction with the course and revealed a desire for further study in the subject. Group B tempered their general approval with reservations. The groups divided on two main issues.

The first of these issues centred on the inclusion in the course of computing topics which went beyond the immediate needs of some teachers, eg programming in PASCAL or COBOL, systems software, modelling methods, practical work on terminals to mainframes. Some took the view that as such topics were not needed

directly in the classroom they could have been omitted leaving more time devoted to increased practical work with micro-computer systems and languages available in schools. Other teachers saw such topics as relevant to a comprehensive study of the subject.

The second issue was concerned with the general area of teaching methodology. A minority did not feel comfortable with the discussion/seminar approach to this topic and expressed a preference for more authoritative direction on how to approach the teaching of the subject.

About the same time as the survey of the full-time course was being evaluated a comparable division was being observed among those teachers taking the part-time version of the course. There were, as in the full-time groups, a number of teachers who saw the Diploma as a valuable introduction to further study of computing but there was also a significant number each year who did not complete the course but who dropped out at the end of the first year expressing the view that they had acquired enough expertise in computing to meet their needs as teachers.

4. A THREE STAGE PART-TIME COURSE

In response to this accumulation of feedback the course development committee decided to redesign the in-service teacher training provision in two major ways.

Firstly the two year part-time version of the Diploma was subdivided into two stages:

Stage 1:   a one year part-time day release course leading to a Post-Graduate Certificate; and

Stage 2:   a second one year part-time day release course leading to the Post-Graduate Diploma.

Teachers with the Certificate should be able to:

(i)   teach computing in schools up to GCSE (16+) level; and

(ii)   use a computer effectively in their work.

Teachers with the Diploma should be able to:

(i)   teach computing in schools up to GCE Advanced (18+) level; and

(ii) assist and advise other teachers who might wish to use computing in their work.

In conjunction with the Department of Education it was decided to offer the Certificate at a number of Further Education Colleges thus making it available to a wider range of teachers. Only a small number from each Certificate group would then proceed to the University to take the Diploma. The Department agreed to grant day-release to teachers for both the Certificate and the Diploma. In response to demand, a provision was included so that a small number of teachers who had already acquired some expertise in teaching computing could enter directly to the Diploma stage.

Secondly, a Stage 3 was designed to permit those who had already taken the Diploma to up-grade their qualification to an MSc by taking a further part-time course. This consists of a number of advanced courses in computer science together with a detailed study of curriculum innovation.

Teachers with the MSc should be able to:

(i)   teach computing at all levels in schools and colleges; and

(ii) give continuing leadership in the use of computers in schools and in the associated development of the school curriculum.

The three stage part-time system came into effect in September 1984 and the full-time version of the Diploma was discontinued after August 1985. The new system provided a flexible multi-level course designed to meet the in-service training needs of all those teachers wishing to acquire an expertise in computing appropriate to their desired level of teaching.

The structure of the three-stage course is shown in TABLE II and the enrolment figures are shown in TABLE III.

TABLE II - Part-Time Course Structure (Contact Hours in Brackets)

POST-GRADUATE CERTIFICATE (210)	POST-GRADUATE DIPLOMA (180)	MSc (144)
Programming & Problem Solving (BASIC) (45)	Advanced Programming (PASCAL & Assembler) (45)	Programming Systems (36)
Information Processing 1 (52.5)	Information Processing 2 (45)	Information Systems (36)
Architecture & Systems Software 1 (37.5)	Architecture & Systems Software 2 (22.5)	Computer Organisation & Operating Systems (36)
Micro-Processor Control 1 (15)	Micro-Processor Control 2 (15)	
Curriculum in Computer Studies (27)	Curriculum in Computer Science (45)*	Issues in Curriculum Innovation (36)
Computers in Education 1 (18)	Computers in Education 2 (22.5)	
Social Implications (15)	Modelling Methods (15)	Course Dissertation
	Course Project	

* In day release mode this includes teaching practice

TABLE III (a)   Enrolments - Part-Time
                 Certificate

Centre	84/85	85/86	86/87	87/88
Jordanstown	13	14	14	8
Belfast	18	16	16	14
Portadown	19	16	19	11
Total Enrolment	50	46	49	33
Completions	44	45	49	-

TABLE III (b)   Enrolments - Part-Time Diploma

Year	84/85	85/86	86/87	87/88
Enrolment	-	18	18	14
Completions	-	15	16	-

TABLE III (c)   Enrolments - Part-Time MSc

Year	84/85	85/86	86/87	87/88
Year 1	15	12	11	12
Year 2	-	12	9	12
Extension	-	-	9	10
Completions	-	3	8	-

5. RECENT DEVELOPMENTS

With the continuous and rapid development in micro-computing and its applications there is a constant need to keep in-service training up-to-date and this has led to almost annual course revision and/or adjustment. Once again the course committee is being asked to review the course content and structure in light of current developments in the use of computers in schools. A number of new considerations are now emerging:

(i)   Although there is still a considerable need for in-service training of teachers of computing the demand for basic training is declining. Meanwhile the subject itself is changing as computing develops; eg the need for training in a third-level language is in process of being replaced by a need for experience in the use of context free packages and fourth generation languages. These changes have been so rapid that already there is a need for short, top-up, courses for those who were trained as recently as the early 80's.

(ii)   There is a growing need for a member of staff in each school to initiate, guide and support curriculum development in the area of Information Technology: the title Information Technology Co-ordinator has been suggested [6]. The member of staff concerned will require a certain level of expertise in computing together with considerable management and curriculum development skills. Although there would be considerable overlap between the expertise needed to teach the subject and that needed to promote its use across the curriculum, the type of course required for an IT Co-ordinator would require a different kind of emphasis from the existing Certificate/Diploma/MSc. Many teachers who take the existing course admit that their intention in so doing is not to teach computing but to use computers across the curriculum. They claim that although it does not meet their specific needs they come on the current course because it is the only one of its kind available.

(iii)   Whilst the Certificate and Diploma courses have been highly successful in achieving the primary, and relatively straightforward, aim of training teachers of computing, they have been less successful in the secondary aim of producing members of staff who can assist and advise other teachers who wish to use computers in their work. In many schools the same individual would be expected to carry out both roles and a teacher who successfully completes the MSc will be more than adequately qualified for both.

In attempting to respond to these considerations the current thinking of the course committee would be as follows:

Firstly, it should be possible to design a first stage Post-Graduate Certificate which would provide the necessary foundation for all those teachers who require in-service training in computing and its educational applications;

Secondly, such a Certificate could then be followed by a number of second stage Post-Graduate Diplomas (or options within a single Diploma) each designed to meet more specific needs. Such an arrangement would permit the design of Diploma courses which could focus more accurately on the needs of a homogeneous group. The Royal Society of Arts have devised a scheme along these lines [7]. A single Diploma is perhaps weakened by an attempt to meet a wider range of needs.

Thirdly, if the courses were to be re-designed as a set of relatively independent modules, teachers could pick those parts of the course which most directly meet their needs and build up each of the qualifications on a credit basis. At the same time each of the modules could also be offered as a stand-alone, short, course for teachers who do not wish to acquire qualifications.

6. CONCLUSIONS

(i)   In-service training in this field needs to be able to respond quickly to changes in the requirements of the subject, of the teachers and of education in general. For this purpose a newer institution such as a Polytechnic with its vocational and marketing approach to courses is possibly better equipped than the more traditional Universities and Colleges of Education.

(ii) The course leader should be someone with experience of teaching who can relate to special requirements of teachers. Teachers are frequently put off by the more technical approach of a highly trained expert in computing.

(iii) Courses must be multi-level and flexible to meet the varying demands of a variety of teachers. Some teachers object to course content which goes beyond their immediate requirements. Others are more ambitious but these tend to become highly qualified and are subsequently in a position to leave second level teaching. Teachers will frequently enrol on a course which does not exactly meet their perceived needs, but which is the only course of its kind available.

(iv) Teachers on in-service training courses are almost invariably highly motivated and are prepared to work hard to acquire the knowledge and expertise they require.

(v)   Many teachers do not have self-confidence in their own professional expertise and would like to be presented with clear teaching methods and lesson plans. This should be avoided and instead teachers should be encouraged to develop their self-confidence and professionalism.

(vi) The need for in-service training of teachers of computing as a subject should be relatively short term, say 10 years. Gradually the demand will shift, in fact it is already shifting, to in-service training in the application of computers across the curriculum. This is a more complex task

and is associated with the broader issue of curriculum innovation.

(vii) It is essential to have a good working relationship between the education authorities responsible for funding and the institutions responsible for course provision. Those responsible for funding must be sufficiently enlightened to realise that thorough training is required even if it is expensive. Computing in schools has suffered considerably from its reliance on poorly trained enthusiasts.

7. POSTSCRIPT

The MSc in Computer Science Education has just (October '87) been granted accreditation for both Parts I and II of the British Computer Society Examinations. It is the only course of its kind in the United Kingdom to be so recognised. However the accreditation is conditional on the academic level of the computer science content of the course being maintained. The BCS would not look kindly on any attempt to reduce the computing content to make way for more consideration of the broader educational issues. This is in direct contrast to the views expressed by the educational authorities in Northern Ireland who have suggested that more education and less computing would be appropriate. The discussion is continuing.

REFERENCES

[1]   British Computer Society Schools Committee, Curriculum for the Future, BCS, October 1984.

[2]   dBASE III, Relational Database Management System, Ashton-Tate, 1982.

[3]   Tagg, W., Change in Perspective, AUCBE, May 1985.

[4]   Dutton, Peter, Nicholls, Peter and Prestt, Brenda, All Change, Microelectronics Education Programme, 1984.

[5]   Stanley, Neil (Ed), Topics in Contemporary Computer Studies, Books I & II, Microelectronics Education Programme, 1984.

[6]   Report of a Task Group, Information Technology across the Curriculum: an INSET strategy, Vocational Education Programme (NI), May 1987.

[7]   The Royal Society of Arts Examination Board, Modular Information Technology Scheme for Teachers, RSA, 1985.

COMPUTERS IN EDUCATION, F. Lovis and E.D. Tagg (eds.)
Elsevier Science Publishers B.V. (North-Holland)
© IFIP, 1988

TEACHER EDUCATION AND TEACHER TRAINING - THE IDENTIFICATION OF IN-SERVICE REQUIREMENTS TO SUPPORT COMPUTER USAGE ACROSS THE CURRICULUM

JOHN MALLATRATT

School of Computing, Lancashire Polytechnic, Preston, PR1 2TQ, England.

Consideration is given to the way in which aspects of Government policy in the UK appear to be defining the in-service training needs of teachers in relation to introducing computing technology into the curriculum. The notion of training is contrasted with the concept of less directive in-service education and the difficulties in ascertaining teachers' needs for both types of provision are discussed. An endeavour to glean detailed information about needs in a particular locality is described and a course designed on the basis of this information is evaluated.

1. INTRODUCTION

1.1 Aspects of Government Policy

In the UK, the Government is currently embarking upon a strategy to take greater central control over the previously locally administered education service. A significant element of this programme is the introduction of a national curriculum [1], but many less dramatic manifestations prevail. For example, the regionally organised Microelectronics Education Programme has been replaced by the nationally administered Microelectronics in Education Support Unit. In addition, a scheme has been introduced which enables the Government to exert considerable influence over the nature of the in-service training and education opportunities available to teachers. This scheme, the Grant-related in-service training scheme (GRIST), delineated in [2], is motivated by a desire to more effectively manage the teaching force to ensure that its members have the capacity to deliver the curriculum that is required [3,4]. It functions by preferentially funding training which is supportive of Government designated key areas of the curriculum, and consequently marks the beginning of a period during which these curricular objectives form the basis for determining the professional development needs for teachers.

1.2 Models of in-service requirements

This curriculum-led model of staff development for school teachers follows the introduction of the system in the further education sector, where it has been increasingly applied over the last few years [5,6]. The beliefs upon which it is based are that it is both practicable and desirable to specify centrally the nature of the curriculum and how it should be delivered. Teachers, as the agents of implementation, need only to receive the appropriate training to make good any 'deficiencies' that they might have and the picture is complete. However, this view of how the education system operates has been criticised as being too simplistic, underestimating the difficulties concomitant with introducing innovation into such an organisation [7]. These were recognised by the Association of Educational Communications and Technology [8] when they referred to an earlier phase of technology:

'Educational technology is a complex, integrated process, involving people, procedures, ideas, devices and organisations, for analysing problems and devising, implementing, evaluating and managing solutions to these problems, in all aspects of human learning'.

In addition, the Government model fails to take account of the iterative nature of curriculum development. Strategies and objectives need to be refined, or even altered, during the implementation phase, a view advanced in [9] by Stenhouse when he stressed the critical role of teachers in the innovation process. That is, that they need to be able to actively shape a development as the ideas that it embodies gain a contextual meaning.

2. TEACHER TRAINING AND TEACHER EDUCATION

The consequences of these different analyses of the education system become critical when consideration is given to the nature of the 'training' support which should be given to teachers to facilitate curriculum innovation. The philosophy embedded in the UK Government strategy is that clearly discernable, curricular alterations are required, either affecting the content or its mode of delivery, and that teachers need to be <u>trained</u> to be able to execute them.

In contrast, there is the view promoted by advocates of increased teacher <u>education</u>. Their belief is that sound curriculum development will ensue as a consequence of expanding professional knowledge and understanding even though precise outcomes will not be so predictable [10]. Hence, teachers need to be supported to enable them to adapt to new roles [11,12] and should be prepared through an education which both encourages self analysis and challenges the premises of teaching [13]. The resultant knowledgeable and critical workforce would then be able to apply its theoretical understanding in real educational contexts, and as stated in [14], ´the individual agendas of the participants, (whether they be) conscious or sub-conscious, can be worked through´.

3. DIFFICULTIES IN NEEDS IDENTIFICATION

The conflicts in needs identification are further compounded by the multiplicity of actors involved in the task [15]. Government, the local authorities (the employers), schools and individual teachers all have legitimate interests in the process of their derivation, and mechanisms should be established to enable participation of all the partners.

Within the model favoured by the UK Government this is effected by a requirement upon local authorities to demonstrate that bids for central government funding key with locally derived curriculum development plans and respond to the demands for training expressed by their teaching force. Although at first sight this appears to grant significant roles to both the individual teacher and his employing authority, there are two reasons why this does not occur. Firstly, the local authority development plan has to be justified in terms of indicating how that authority is progressing towards the national objectives. That is, it relates to convergent strategy rather than being a separately conceived entity. Secondly, there are a series of doubts about the validity of the data collected from teachers. Some of these concerns relate to the administrative capabilities of local authorities and their capacity to collect the data accurately. Although not a trivial issue, it is reasonable to

expect that this will be resolved as systems develop to meet the demands of the scheme. More disturbing, however, is the fact that teachers might not be in a position to clearly identify their needs. Findings from [16,17] show that the usual response from teachers who have a perception of a need for some form of in-service support is to seek to meet that need by developing further subject expertise, even though this might not represent the most appropriate solution. Furthermore, according to [18], when set in a context of significant curricular innovation the situation is exacerbated, teachers´ perceptions of their needs becoming ´general inventories that focus on curriculum change (and) represent the dominance of curriculum programming over in-service teacher education´.

4. A LOCAL STRATEGY FOR IDENTIFYING AND MEETING NEED

The issues introduced above will now be considered in the context of the development of a two-year part-time in-service course for teachers administered by the School of Computing at Lancashire Polytechnic.

The course was first established in 1975 and was unambiguously constructed upon a training ethos. Teachers were perceived as having a need to develop computing expertise in order to be able to service examinable computer studies courses in their own institutions and a subject-driven course was provided.

By 1981, an additional ´training´ need had become apparent. This arose from the growing demand, predominantly from parents, that all children should leave compulsory education having developed some form of computer literacy, a movement catalysed by the Government announcement of the Micros in Schools scheme and the Microelectronics in Education Programme [19]. Secondary schools sought to offer computer appreciation/awareness courses and needed teachers competent to staff them. This needs situation was compounded by contemporaneous curriculum-led developments in the further education sector resulting in the inclusion of computer literacy elements in basic vocational courses.

The response of the designers of the Polytechnic course was to offer a subset of the main course, requiring two terms of study, to this new ´market´ of teachers and lecturers. Being just a collection of components from the original course, the new creation retained the training bias of its progenitor. It was advertised and recruited successfully.

By 1985, however, it was becoming clear that there was a mismatch between the course designers´ perception of needs and those of the students. (Ironically, this manifested itself in debate about the subject matter that had been chosen as being most appropriate for teachers' needs, although, after further analysis, this was recognised as a symptom rather than the cause of the ailment). During the period that it had been running, the nature of cohorts of students that the course had attracted had changed significantly. Originally these had comprised almost totally mathematics and science teachers aspiring to teach about computers but this had changed to a situation where such students were in a minority. Indeed, it was apparent that there was a multiplicity of motivations for people embarking upon the course; what was less clear was whether the course could meet their several demands.

In order to explore the needs situation more thoroughly a course advisory group was established. This was essentially a self-selecting body, although invitations were extended to the local authority, head teachers and college principals in the locality, as well as past and current students, and each category was represented.

As a result of their initial deliberations the group identified six categories of potential student for in-service:

1. Teachers/lecturers of computing/IT examination courses.

2. Teachers/lecturers of computer literacy/IT appreciation courses.

3. Teachers/lecturers of any discipline wishing to use the computer as a tool in the teaching/learning situation.

4. (Senior) school or college staff wishing to use the computer as an administrative aid.

5. School/college co-ordinators/ facilitators of computing/IT across the curriculum.

6. Previous course participants wishing to update their knowledge.

Although a crude analysis, it represented a considerable refinement upon the existing model under which recognition for just two categories of student has been made. Moreover, it established a basis from which further consideration of needs could be explored. As the course administrator, two aspects of the debate which was to ensue were of particular interest. Firstly, did each group identified have educational as well as training needs and, secondly, how great was the commonality of needs of the differing groups?

The answer to the first of the questions is clearly affirmative, given the arguments advanced above by the advocates of professional development. However, it had been possible to overlook this fact when students had been recruited predominantly from categories one and two and their _training_ needs had been so evident. What did ultimately focus attention on the issue was the increasing recruitment of teachers whose main objective was to use the computer as a tool in various areas of the curriculum. People from different subject disciplines could not be instructed about the best way a computer could be used in their fields because each environment would have its own characteristics which would determine the appropriateness of particular strategies. This is not to say, however, that such teachers have no training need. In [20] the extensiveness of this component is stressed, a view with which the author concurs. This returns consideration to the second of the questions above, namely determining how much overlap exists between these training needs and those of the members of the other groups. It is at this stage that the course advisory group adopted a pragmatic stance. Indeed, since the field of in-service education and training is one that suffers from ´theoretical impoverishment´, it is arguable that this was the only option available. Accordingly, the re-designed course includes a first year which is common to all students and a second which is dominated by an option system. Additional flexibility is afforded by its modular construction, and the opportunity that exists for any student (teacher) to elect to take his own pathway through a subset of the whole course.

5. COURSE EVALUATION

The revised course admitted its first cohort of students at the beginning of the academic session 1986-7. Feedback has been sought from this group, via a questionnaire and structured interviews, and the information collected will be considered alongside other course data below. However, firstly discussion of the function of evaluation seems appropriate.

In [21], evaluation is quoted as being the process of:

'delineating, obtaining and providing information useful for making decisions and judgements about educational programs and curricula'.

When an in-service course is being evaluated there will be a variety of perspectives on its worth. In the above case, these perspectives include the group of interests that were represented on the course advisory group as well as the views of members of each of the categories of student for which the course is designed. The evaluation process should encourage this community to be self-critical and to be able to refine plans in the context of experience.

The timing of the evaluation determines the criteria that can be applied and this has to be resolved within the context of each particular enterprise. Consider the polytechnic course which incorporates both aspects of training and education. Where a training ethos pervades, such as in courses operating under the aegis of the UK Government scheme, there is a clear expectation that observable outcomes will shortly ensue: a teacher's in-service experience. In contrast, on courses where the educational aspect is stressed, less obvious and less immediate outcomes are expected, and doubts exist about whether these can be measured. One reason is that the longer the delay between the staging of a course and the evaluation of its effect the more difficult it becomes to attribute the cause of an observed change to the in-service input; but it has also been suggested that it is inevitably the quality of the support environment for the change that is recorded in longitudinal experiments [22]. Further doubts about the viability of this form of evaluation arise when course objectives are considered. For example, one of the aims of the polytechnic course is that teachers will become competent at using computers appropriately in educational environments; that is, that they will apply their professional judgments as to when and how the computer should be deployed to enhance children's learning experiences. It seems unlikely that this can ever be objectively assessed.

Returning to consideration of the evaluation data available for this course, student opinion will now be presented. The most significant finding was the reaction to the modular construction of the course, which was favoured by nearly 90% of respondents. It was felt that this put the student in greater control of his educational experience, a view corroborated by the fact that some students have already elected to take individualised pathways through the scheme.

The nature of the subject content of the first year, however, was less well received. Three of the five modules designed for study at this stage were seen as appropriate to the needs of the majority, although the other two were not. Comments were also received about the nature of the subject matter within each module. An attempt had been made within the course design to achieve a blend between elements that were reactive in nature and those which were pro-active, since the obvious concern was that computing developments occur more rapidly than do teachers' opportunities for in-service education and training. Sixty four percent of students felt that this blend had been achieved whilst a further 27% felt that they had the resources to apply all aspects of their learning within the short-term.

One of the assumptions implicit in the revised course design was that a heterogenous cohort of students was desirable. It was felt by the course providers that the wealth and range of experience possessed by students coming from different needs categories would be beneficial to the learning environment and provide rich material that could be shared within the group. However, 19% of students felt that they would have benefitted from being a member of a more homogenous grouping.

The data reported above has been collected at a very early stage of the course's implementation and it will need to be supplemented in due course, both by further analyses of student opinion and by canvassing the views of participants in the design process. Also, recruitment patterns will need to be monitored. Although at present they are satisfactory, there is a concern that all the students on the revised course have identified themselves as belonging in one of the first four needs categories, although at this stage there is insufficient data to judge how significant a finding this is.

Ultimately, it is arguable, evaluation of the effectiveness of the course needs to incorporate information about the subsequent activity that takes place in classrooms, although this seems an area that is beset with difficulties. It is to be hoped that future research will help to provide insights into this field.

6. CONCLUSION

Teachers' needs for in-service training and education in the domain of computer use across the curriculum are difficult to determine. Government sponsored programmes which imply that curriculum-led strategies coupled with rational management provide the solution are misleading. Instead, the derivation of satisfactory courses requires that genuine collaboration and negotiation takes place between the parties involved.

In addition, it is critical that evaluation of experiences takes place and that this is used to refine course design, although precisely when and how this should be effected needs to be considered within the context of the course. Certainly there would appear to be a role for all the collaborators in this process and the author would also suggest that a wide variety of data types be utilised.

What is most essential is that the definition of need be recognised as an iterative process and that it be reviewed as the education system, and the roles of participants within it, evolve.

REFERENCES

[1] Department of Education and Science, The National Curriculum 5-16, consultation document, Department of Education and Science, 1987, 1-34.

[2] Department of Education and Science, Local Education Authority Training Grants Scheme circular 6/86, Department of Education and Science, 1986, 1-12.

[3] Department of Education and Science, Better Schools Cmnd 9469, HMSO, 1985, 1-20.

[4] J. Graham, Centralisation of power and the new INSET funding, British Journal of In-Service Education, vol. 13, no. 1, Winter 1986, 5-9.

[5] John Miller, Understanding and managing change: curriculum-led institutional development, Coombe Lodge Report, vol. 19, no. 4, 1986, 229-234.

[6] R. Challis, Political aspects of curriculum development, Coombe Lodge Report, vol. 17, no. 4, 1984, 541-546.

[7] William Evans, An investigation of curriculum implementation factors, Education (US), vol. 106, no. 4, 1986, 447-453.

[8] Association for Education Communications Technology, Educational technology: definition and glossary of terms, quoted in T. Plomp and J. van de Wolde, New information technologies in education: lessons learned and trends observed. European Journal of Education, vol. 20, nos. 2 and 3, 1985, 243-256.

[9] L. Stenhouse, An introduction to curriculum research and development, Heinemann, London, 1975.

[10] Janet Harland, The new INSET: a transformation scene, Journal of Education Policy, vol. 2, no. 3, 1987, 235-244.

[11] Terry Cicchelli and Richard Baecher, The use of concerns theory in in-service training for computer education, Computers and Education, vol. 11, no. 2, 1987, 85-93.

[12] Joan Bliss, Peter Chandra and Margaret Cox, The introduction of computers into a school, Computers and Education, vol. 10, no. 1, 1986, 49-54.

[13] L. Stenhouse, Innovation and stress, quoted in A. Ross, In-service and curriculum development, British Journal of In-Service Education, vol. 9, no. 2, Spring 1983, 126-136.

[14] Terry Brown, The need for a mixed INSET economy, British Journal of In-Service Education, vol. 11, no. 3, Summer 1985, 142-144.

[15] Yehuda Bien, Resistance to change in education, Research in Education, no. 35, 1986, 73-86.

[16] Roger Neil, Current models and approaches to in-service teacher education, British Journal of In-Service Education, vol. 12, no. 2, Spring 1986, 58-67.

[17] John Daresh, Research trends in staff development and in-service education, Journal of Education for Teaching, vol. 13, no. 1, 1987, 3-11.

[18] Richard Bents and Kenneth Howey, Staff development - change in the individual in Dillon-Peterson (eds), ASCD Yearbook, ASCD, Washington, 1981.

[19] Richard Fothergill, Microelectronics Education Programme - the strategy, Department of Education and Science, London, 1981, 1-11.

[20] P. Forcheri and M.T. Molfino, Teacher training in computers and education: a

two year experience, <u>Computers and
Education</u>, vol. 10, no. 1, 1986, 137-143.

[21] Curriculum Development Centre,
Curriculum evaluation: a CDC study group
report quoted in Stephen Kemmis, Seven
principles for programme evaluation in
curriculum development and innovation,
<u>Journal of Curriculum Studies</u>, vol. 14,
no. 3, 1982, 221-240.

[22] D Royce Sadler, Follow-up evaluation
of an in-service programme based on action
research: some methodological issues,
<u>Journal of Education for Teaching</u>,
vol. 10, no. 3, 1984, 209-218.

COMPUTERS IN EDUCATION, F. Lovis and E.D. Tagg (eds.)
Elsevier Science Publishers B.V. (North-Holland)
© IFIP, 1988

A COMPUTER AIDED APPROACH TO HIGHER SCHOOL SEMESTRIAL TIMETABLES

Stefan Ivanov Buchvarov, Ivan Petrov Ganashev

Union of the Mathematicians in Bulgaria
Acad. G. Bonchev str., bl. 8, P.O. Box 373, 1113 Sofia

The problem originating in the application of computers to the making of a semestrial type
timetable for the lessons in a higher educational establishment are discussed. The formal
treatment of the problem is given and its NP-completeness in shown.
Hereby is presented a heuristic algorithm with which a solution of the problem is found
for polynomial time.
A criterion for assessment of the solution quality is suggested. The iteration steps,
aiming at decreasing the value of the "defect of the timetable kernel", and a solution for
the automated lessons distribution among the lecturers is described.

1. INTRODUCTION

The making of the timetable in a higher educational establishment (HEE) is the last and the
most important stage of the educational process
planning. The timetable consists of: a kernel –
correspondence between lecturers, teaching
rooms, syllabi elements of the different groups,
and teaching time periods; an envelope – educational documentation ensuring the realisation
of the timetables – for the groups, for the lectures, for the teaching rooms. It summarizes
the results of all the other planning stages:
forming a structural-logical teaching scheme,
defining the necessary subjects, forming a curriculum and syllabi. The correctly made timetable should meet many methodical, organizational, and other requirements which, as a rule,
surpass several dozen in number. Simultaneously
with the educational process requirements, the
timetable should be in accordance with the conditions of other HEE systems, relevant to it,
as well as with the internal limitations of the
resources on which it is constructed. The question of the correct approach in the making of
such a timetable is investigated by many
authors. They come to the definite conclusion
that a timetable which meets all these requirements to a satisfactory extent could be only of
a semestrial type (the so-called "unique week"
type) [1].

The parameters of a HEE of average size, e.g.
an university or a technical institute, are
such that the making of a semestrial timetable
is not possible without a computer for two basic reasons:
- it is not possible to make a timetable in accordance with the whole system of requirements sufficiently close to the optimal one,
  for the time required by the schedule for organization of the educational process;
- the preparing of educational documentation,
  when the kernel of the timetable is ready, is
  also a labour-intensive process, and has many
  preconditions for mistakes.

2. ON THE COMPLEXITY OF THE PROBLEM

The application of computers requires the approach to the making of an algorithm which generates the timetable kernel, to be well grounded. For this purpose, it is necessary for the
corresponding problem to be formulated correctly.

2.1. Formulating the problem

It is given:
- set G of n educational groups;
- set H of the teaching time periods, $H = G \times H_o$,
  where H_o is the set of the physical teaching
  time periods for the semester;
- set C of the lecturers;
- set T of the educational elements, $T = G \times T_o$,
  where T_o is the nomenclature of the subjects;
  the educational element, $t = (g, t_o) \epsilon T$,
  $g \epsilon G$, $t_o \epsilon T_o$ represents the modification of the
  subject t_o studied by group g;
- for each $c \epsilon C$ – set $A_o(c) \subseteq H_o$ of the admissible
  teaching time periods for the lecturer c; in
  this way the compulsory preliminary occupation of the lecturers is taken into account;
- for each $t \epsilon T$ – set $A_t(t) \subseteq H_o$ of the admissible
  teaching time periods for the educational ele-
  ment t; thus it is possible to control the
  beginning, the end and the position in the
  days of the week for the lessons in a given
  subject in a given group;
- for each pair $(c, t) \epsilon C \times T$ – an integer number
  $R(c, t) \epsilon Z_o^+$, defining the number of lessons
  from the educational element t to be teached
  by lecturer c.

It is to be found a function $f: C \times T \times N \to \{0, 1\}$ ($f(c, (t_o, g), (h_o, g')) = 1$ means that lecturer c deals with subject t_o in group g in the moment h_o), which responds to the conditions:

- $(f(c, (t_o, g), (h_o, g')) = 1) \Rightarrow$

$$g = g' \wedge h_o \epsilon A_c(c) \cap A_t((t_o, g));$$

- for each $(h, c) \epsilon H \times C$ there exists no more than one $t \epsilon T$, such that $f(c, t, h) = 1$;
- for each pair $(c, t) \epsilon C \times T$ there exist precisely $R(c, t)$ meanings of h, for which $f(c, t, h) = 1$.

2.2. NP-completeness of the Problem of Making a Semestrial Timetable

Thus formulated, the problem is NP-complete, even in the special case of n = 1. Indeed, in this case it is equivalent to the problem of making a school timetable, described in [2, 3], for which it is proved in [3] that it is NP-complete.

3. ALGORITHM

The statement in 2.2 determines the application of a heuristic algorithm of nondeterministic type, which solves the following problem, a little more generalized than the one described above.

Let us have a set L of lessons. For each $l \epsilon L$, it is given:
- its subject $t(l) \epsilon T_o$;
- the set $g(l) \subseteq G$ of the groups taking part in the lesson together;
- the set $c(l) \subseteq C$ of the lecturers engaged with the lesson;
- the set $d(l) \subseteq H_o$ of the permitted time periods for the lesson.

A partial ordering relation "<" (">") may be defined upon the elements of L, $l_1 < l_2$ means that the lesson $l_1 \epsilon L$ should be teached before the lesson $l_2 \epsilon L$. The timetable kernel is assumed to be ready when for each $l \epsilon L$ a teaching time period $h(l) \epsilon d(l)$ is found in such a way that:
- for each $l_1 < l_2$: $h(l_1) < h(l_2)$;
- for each pair $(c_o, h_o) \epsilon C \times H_o$ there exists no more than one $l \epsilon L$ such that $h(l) = h_o$ and $c_o \epsilon c(l)$;
- for each pair $(g_o, h_o) \epsilon G \times H_o$ there exists no more than one $l \epsilon L$ such that $h(l) = h_o$ and $g_o \epsilon g(l)$.

An algorithm, consisting of the following two basic phases, is preferred to the several possible ones.

In the first phase, for each $l \epsilon L$ a subset $h_1(l) \subseteq N_o$ is defined, from which the value of $h(l)$ is to be chosen during the second stage. Generally $h_1(l)$ consist of one week of teaching time, thus for each lesson the corresponding semester week is chosen. In the definition of $h_1(l)$, some of the requirements have to be taken into consideration. They are ordered corresponding to their importance for the quality of the educational process. As an example, we can give the usual requirements for intervals between the different methodical forms, such as lectures and practical exercises, in a given subject, the requirements coming from the intradisciplinary thematic links, the requirements for combining more difficult and more easy methodical forms, the requirement for reasonable weekly occupation of the lecturers, and so on.

The second phase realizes the determination of the specific value of $h(l) \epsilon h_1(l)$ for each $l \epsilon L$, meeting as many requirements as possible. This is made by splitting H_o into sub-aggregates corresponding to the days of the week. The defining of a suitable value for $h(l)$ takes place when g is fixed, but the order for the fixing of the n groups is different for every day and is generated pseudo-accidentally. Another approach is to define the values of $h(l)$ by fixed g for the whole semester. This approach, however, puts some (the first ones) groups into privileged position and injures other ones, because after each g the available resources will decrease. That is why the first approach is chosen.

4. TIMETABLE QUALITY CONTROL

The making of the timetable kernel begins with some organizational and planning activities, which conventionally can be divided into two groups:
- activities whose way of performing is synonymously determined under the conditions of a HEE for a given period;
- activities whose way of performing is nonsynonymously determined, that is they have more than one possible variant.

In the first group, they are:
- to provide for the teaching-material base;
- to provide for lecturers;
- bringing up to date of the HEE organizational structure;
- specifying the actual contents of the curriculum for each group and the syllabus in each subject [4].

In the second group, they are:
- planning the educational process organization - groups having common lectures, schedule for the beginning and the end of the semester for each group, schedule for the beginning and the end of the studying of each subject for

the group, schedule for the common (for the whole HEE) activities during the semester;
- distribution of the lessons among the lecturers (when there is more than one group from a given speciality and respectively more lecturers with the same specialization and qualification, it is not synonymous);
- specification of the volume and the calendar time of the conditional preliminary resources occupation;
- defining the priorities system of the groups and the subjects in the group for the planning process (if such is used).

The information from the second group has a set of admissible values. The specific values of its different parts participate actively in the work of the algorithm for making the timetable kernel described in 3., that is, they are its parameters. This serves for controlling the semestrial timetable quality.

Let us divide the requirements for the timetable according to two basic indicators: importance and type. According to their importance they could be basic, primary and secondary: according to their type - organizational, methodical and ensuring the unaided work of the students. Let A_1, α_1 mean the number and the weight of the basic, A_2, α_2 - of the primary, A_3, α_3 - of the secondary organizational requirements; let M_1, μ_1 symbolize the number and the weight of the basic, M_2, μ_2 - of the primary and M_3, μ_3 - of the secondary methodical requirements; let S_1, σ_1 mean the number and the weight of the basic, S_2, σ_2 - of the primary and S_3, σ_3 - of the secondary requirements ensuring the unaided work of the students.

The concrete values of A_1, M_1 and S_1, $l = 1,2,3$, as well as the sense of the separate requirements are specific for each HEE and are defined by experts. The values of the weights α_1, μ_1, σ_1, $l = 1,2,3$ determine the degree of inadequacy of the lessons in a given subject as a consequence of non-performance of the respective requirements. They are also specific and could be determined by the method of expert estimates. They should vary in the $(0,1]$ interval.

Let us define the quantity "defect of the timetable kernel" for a given week, in the following way:

$$D_w = \sum_{l=1}^{3} [\sum_{i=1}^{A_1} \alpha_1 a_{i,1} + \sum_{j=1}^{M_1} \mu_1 m_{j,1} + \sum_{k=1}^{S_1} \sigma_1 s_{k,1}],$$
(1)

where:
- $a_{i,1}$, $i = 1,\ldots,A_1$, $l = 1,2,3$ is the number

of the cases of unmet organizational requirements of each type;
- $m_{j,1}$, $j = 1,\ldots,M_1$, $l = 1,2,3$ is the number of the cases of unmet methodical requirements of each type;
- $s_{k,1}$, $k = 1,\ldots,S_1$, $l = 1,2,3$ is the number of the cases of unmet requirements for ensuring the unaided work of the students.

Let N_w be the total number of the planned lessons for the week. Then the normalized measure K_w for "defect of the timetable kernel" for a given week, will have the following form:

$$K_w = \frac{D_w}{N_w}.$$
(2)

From this measure, one can easily define a measure for the "defect" totally for the semester:

$$K_{sem} = \frac{1}{F} \sum_{w=1}^{F} K_w,$$
(3)

where F is the number of the working weeks in the semester.

The formulae (1), (2) and (3) give an opportunity for assessment of the quality of the semestrial timetable kernel, both at the time of its making and as a complete result. The aim is for K_w and K_{sem} to reach values as close to zero as possible.

Thus the making of the timetable kernel is an iteration process in which the algorithm described in 3. is performed several times with different values of the non-synonymous parameters already mentioned.

5. AUTOMATING THE DISTRIBUTION OF LESSONS AMONG THE LECTURERS

As stated in 4., one of the parameters of this process is the distribution of lessons among the lecturers. Its making is a labour-intensive operation, with many preconditions for mistakes, which was responsible for the application of computers in this activity. In this way, a more complete automation of the iteration process of making a timetable kernel, close to the optimal one, is ensured.

The distribution of the lessons among the lecturers is done in an interactive mode, so that:
- for each group, in accordance with the syllabus of each curriculum subject, a lecturer suitable for the type and the specifics of the separate lesson is to be ensured;
- each lecturer is to be given lessons that he can, and is licensed to, teach;
- the produced distribution is to be formally correct, logically connected, and on a com-

mon information basis with the other input
data for making the timetable kernel.

The realization of this process is organized in
three dialogues.

By the first dialogue, the correspondence between the lecturers and the subjects they are
licensed to teach is defined. It is taken into
consideration that each subject syllabus contains a certain number of methodical forms of
lessons, which in general require different
qualification of the respective lecturers [4].
For example, the lectures are to be distributed
among lecturers who possess academic rank,
while the exercises and other practical lessons are distributed among those not having
academic rank. The information organization
permits this differentiation to be realized in
the form of conditional lecturers for the subject. In this sense, the first dialogue determines the relation "conditional lecturer - possible real lecturer (s)" for a subject.

The second dialogue interpretes the curriculum
of the group. The aim is to select from the
existing data base for each group and for each
subject, that it studies, a syllabus, corresponding to the curriculum in number of lesssons
and distribution of methodical forms.

The third dialogue realizes the actual distribution of the lessons among the lecturers. The
results of the first two dialogues are its information basis. It is used to determine the
relation "conditional lecturer - real lecturer"
for a given subject - group. The real lecturer
should be one of the possible ones, defined by
the first dialogue.

It is the third dialogue that permits non-synonymous solution, thus becoming one of the iteration process parameters for improving the
timetable kernel quality.

6. CONCLUSION

The described algorithm and the software for
its realization were made and have been used
in a HEE teaching transport specialists since
1984.

REFERENCES

[1] Savelyev, A.Y., Zubaryev, U.B., Kovalyenko,
    V.E., and Koloskova, T.A., Automating HEE
    Control, Radio i svyaz, Moscow, 1984 (in
    Russian).
[2] Garey, M.R., and Johnson, D.S., Computers
    and Intractability, W.H. Freeman and Co.,
    San Francisco, 1979.
[3] Even, S., Itai, A., and Shamir, A., "On the
    complexity of timetable and multicommodity
    flow problems", SIAM J. Computer, No. 5,
    1976, pp. 691-703.
[4] Jotev, G.B. und Buchvarov, S.I., "Mathema-
    tisches Modell einer Lehranstalt mit inte-
    grierter Struktur aus Bildungemodulen zur
    Kaderausbildung im Verkehr", Transport i
    kibernetika, No. 2, 1987, pp. 10-14 (in
    Bulgarian).

COMPUTERS IN EDUCATION, F. Lovis and E.D. Tagg (eds.)
Elsevier Science Publishers B.V. (North-Holland)
© IFIP, 1988

CHECKING ONESELF UP BEFORE ENTERING UNIVERSITY - A REAL SIZE EXPERIMENT WITH COMPUTERS

Gérard REBMANN et   Janine BRUNEAUX   (U.F.R. de Physique *)
Jacqueline ROBINET   (I.R.E.M. **)

Université Paris 7
2 Place JUSSIEU
75251 Paris Cedex 05, FRANCE

Incoming students are testing themselves for guidance towards special classes (level groups). Various stages of conception, development, running and analysis of results of the test are described and commented.
The target population is the incoming students (first year, first registration) in the "Sciences and Structure of the Matter " Department (Introduction to mathematics and physics).
More than 400 students underwent this evaluation for a week, on 32 personal computers set up in two rooms.
The test consists of two parts (mathematics and physics), and lasts about two hours. An author language Diane Arlequin especially designed for CAL applications has been used to write it.
A real time diagnosis was immediately given to the student while answers were collected as well as data connected to acquisition time, possible request for help and then stored in a data base form file.
This test turned out to be efficient and instructive. A majority of students followed the advice provided by the computer and teachers discovered unsuspected lacks of knowledge.

1. INTRODUCTION

On account of curriculum differences between French baccalaureat forms, the population of students entering university is having a important disparity in level and quality of knowledge. The studies of mathematics and physics need a rather high level of knowledge, and teaching in Sciences and Structure of the Matter (SSM) actually only fits C baccalaureat curriculum [1]. Too many students still fail or give up.
In previous years, Paris 7 University and other universities developed remedial classes. But the students who needed help, were only oriented after a three months'work and that was actually too late to be really effective.
Some teachers thought it would be more efficient to select people needing help and to define what kind of specific help they need before the very beginning of usual courses. They decided to use computers to look systematically for the students'lack in basic knowledge.
The test is composed of two main parts. The mathematics part has been adapted from selected extracts of an existing test (1) described by G.Sol [2]. The second part has been conceived and carried out by the authors. It is composed of questions on physics. Moreover two questions on mathematics have been added.

2. GOALS

The product has to be produced in six months; it must
- test "fundamental knowledge" in mathematics and physics
- operate on personal computers with a session time less than two hours.
- yield specific pedagogical diagnosis to the student
- yield statistical profile of the student population for teachers.
Also the exploitation has to be rather cheap to fit the University budget.

2.1 The "fundamental knowledge"

Actually this expression means required background of a very intermediate level (but essential) and consists of basic calculus, proportionality notion, logic, analytical geometry, scalar product, derivation of function and trigonometry. The set of questions about physics is relative to the international system of basic units, vector calculus and mechanics: dynamics of accelerated motion and circular motion.

2.2 Computers and system

Paris 7 University has been equiped with IPT (2) materials pooled in one department.

* Unité de Formation et de Recherche
** Institut de Recherche pour l'Enseignement des Mathématiques

Therefore the computers are of two kinds Personna 1600 from Logabax and BM 30 from Bull company, with monochrome display, double drive, 256 ko of central memory. Financial reasons do not allow us to buy specific and expensive systems. Fortunately the Diane system was distributed in the IPT plan (Arlequin-Diane special University, an author language for CAL applications)

2.3 Pedagogical diagnosis

During registrations (July to September), students have been informed of the existence of a computer test in a self checking up way and of the notions to be known. After pedagogical enrolment, they came in groups to undergo the test. The main goal of the test was to convince the students needing help to follow specific classes in a freely accepted way. The test has to reveal to each student his actual level of knowledge and of ability to master fundamental notions after the baccalaureat and summer holidays.... The teachers of special remedial classes need to know the specific deficiencies of their students.

2.4 Pedagogical profile of population

Teachers should be informed of the statistical results of the test, frequencies of mistakes, correlation between typical errors and baccalaureat streams.

3. DEFINITION

The definition of the product is, in a large way, contained in the goals. The test has been designed and performed through a method derived from the methodology courses given at the CNEAO (3). The principle of this methodology has been described by F. DEMAIZIERE [3]. We also have been guided by J. FISZER's works [4]. In each case the definition of the product has to be accurately performed before any development.

3.1 Subject, target population and session conditions

.These specifications have been described in previous parts of the present paper. The nature of questions is based on the experience of the authors and confirmed by the use of a book of questions for a population similar to the target one.
The well-adapted representations of knowledge are obviously close to those used in the books of French secondary schools.
The presence of one teacher during the session was planned only in order to give technical help with respect to the use of computers.

3.2 Test structure and running time

The structure is practically sequential

however, randomness has been brought in at several points as shown on fig.1 and fig.2 .

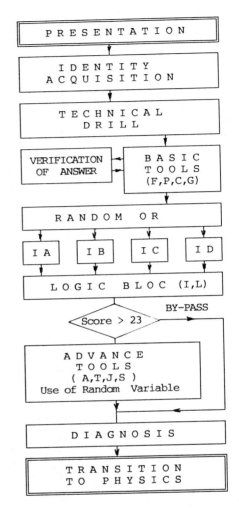

Structure of mathematics part

Figure 1

Taking into account the large population to be tested in a few day s' time, we must pay attention to the running time of a session.
However we were sure that the time was less important (significant) than the quality of the answer. Furthermore, statistical analysis needs information relative to different fields e.g. vector calculus is independent of one dimensional mechanics problems.
Therefore we decided to by-pass the last part of a set of questions when too many wrong answers were given.

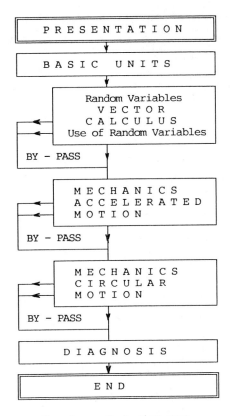

Structure of physics part

Figure 2

3.3 Standard screen

In order to keep unity throughout the whole test, we have taken care to define a typical screen as shown on fig.3. As often as possible, we used a column layout adapted to quick reading and giving, from our point of view, better aesthetics.
It has to be noted that comments and pedagogical help are physically separated from technical instructions.

4. CARRYING OUT

We first sought computer products and existing books of questions. Again we have to split in two parts:

4.1 Mathematics test

This part has been adapted from an existing computer test already mentioned [2]. Our contribution to the mathematical part of the test lies in selecting eighteen questions and adding two other ones. However we have also brought in randomness and by-passing in the structure.

Furthermore the unity of looking, described in 3.3, needed re-designing all the screens and implementing new traces and new marking produced changes in the flow chart.

4.2 Physics test

This part was performed through usual stages: after examining the existing tests (paper) we elaborated a set of questions and tried it on students in remedial groups. The results were used to select meaningful questions and to prepare answer analysis.
We carefully determined the order of questions in such a way that each question gives independent information. Then, the practice of any tool is checked before being used in a question.

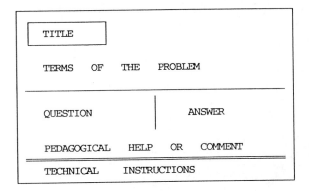

Standard screen

Figure 3

4.3 Informatical development

The different sets of questions have been elaborated independently of each other.
For a question, we have selected the form of presentation, taking into account the possibilities given by the chosen author language (Arlequin-Diane). For instance we first determined whether we needed graphics or not and tried to use "half-graphic" ASCII code as often as possible.
We have avoided the rather difficult way of formal analysis of answers in mathematics and preferred application in specific case.
However, in physics questions, we often get formal and numeric answers (with units indeed).
In these cases the formal answers (formulae) had to be given in the simplest form and only symbols used in the question were authorized. Commutative operations and inequal spacing are integrated in the answer model.

We have used the strategy of answer analysis developed by F.DEMAIZIERE [3] and successively looked for:
- empty answer or technical mistakes
- specific well-known mistakes
- lack of the fundamental part of right answer
- completeness and correct form of the respons.

4.4 Structures of traces

A run of tests produces data stored in a trace file made of identification, question traces and sum-up traces. Each question trace has the following form: question reference; error level; answer (if wrong); time; help counter. There is one sum up trace for one main part (mathematics, physics). It is made of the reference of questions that have induced a mistake and the mathematical sum up trace shows the total score, while the physical one is further composed of four error counters: vector calculus, mechanics, numerical calculus, units. After a run, a batch program copies individual traces to a general trace file on a pick up diskette. Afterwards this main general file is used to produce a data base file easy to consult.

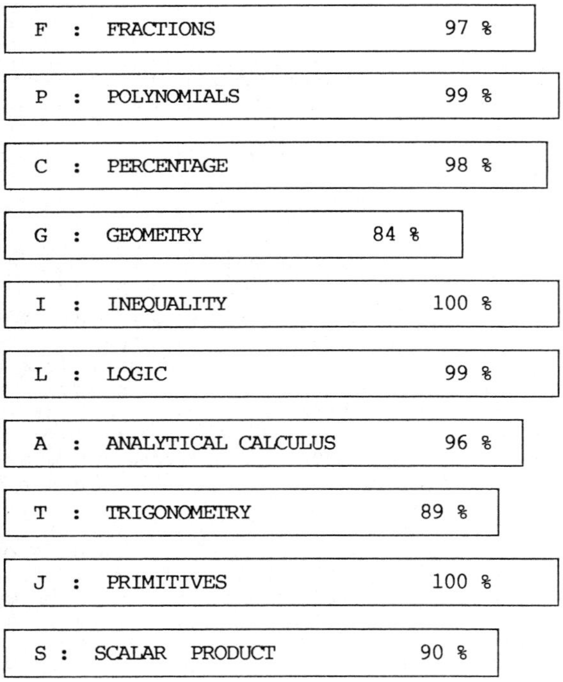

F :	FRACTIONS	97 %
P :	POLYNOMIALS	99 %
C :	PERCENTAGE	98 %
G :	GEOMETRY	84 %
I :	INEQUALITY	100 %
L :	LOGIC	99 %
A :	ANALYTICAL CALCULUS	96 %
T :	TRIGONOMETRY	89 %
J :	PRIMITIVES	100 %
S :	SCALAR PRODUCT	90 %

Answer rate versus question

Figure 4

5. OPERATION AND REACTIONS

One week before the beginning of the courses and after pedagogical registrations, the test was performed as expected.
Some technical advice was given on the board and orally by teachers in such a way that students needed no indication book.
The transition between the mathematics part and the physics part was done by the teachers in charge using a logical key. This operation gave rise to a dialogue relative to the relevance of "computer diagnosis". The same operation occurred at the end of the test, in order to comment the "computer advice" and the way to follow it.

5.1 Students' reactions

Students were very interested in the self-checking up aspect of the test; many of them have revised before coming to the test. The majority of them agreed with the diagnosis provided by the computer and some asked for a second run. Most of them stuck hard at computers and often spent more time than the foreseen two hours.
Furthermore, they carefullly noted the diagnosis and advice provided by the computer. They were convinced of the necessity of work to get a better practice of notions that seemed to them well-known before the test but actually were not.
It is possible to appreciate how much students accept this kind of test on fig.4. This scheme gives the rate of answer for each question or group of questions.
About the G question, relative to THALES and PYTHAGORAS theorems, it has to be noted that people sought for solution an average time of three minutes before going on. Then, we may say that they did not answer because they did not find and not because they refused to answer.

5.2 Teachers' reactions

Teachers were often surprised to find out some lack of "fundamental knowledge" or students who did not know what "literal answer" or "basic units" mean.
Some teachers also found out the interest of students for this kind of activity and now consider the use of computer in a different way than before... They are asking for new products.

5.3 Authors' feelings

The operation induced several critical observations .
The time of a run was rather longer than foreseen for students who had to complete the whole path. Two hours is closer to the mean time than the maximum one.
The differences between pre-test population

(students following remedial courses) and the target one (incoming students) induced some trouble with answer analysis, so that answers were sometimes wrong in a different way than foreseen and that the number of error patterns was greater than expected. We have to take it into account next year.

Authors have been impressed by the way the students have accepted the diagnosis of the machine as a fair and unquestionable judgment. However, the position of teachers towards students was quite different from the usual one: teacher and student were both human beings in front of the computer. This relation has nothing to do with the classical one, where the student is separated from the teacher by the corrected copy.

Furthermore, the immediate comment of results is much more pleasant for the student as well as for the teacher.

5.4 Analysis of results

At the present time (october 1987), traces are being exploited and results will soon be published. The immediate analysis of traces has given expected informations. Students needing help have been detected.

However, the acceleration process (by-passing) has introduced some difficulties in statistical analysis :

- in mathematics, the by-passing occured more often than expected because the logic questions seemed too difficult.
- in mechanics, questions relative to different kinds of motion used the same error counter. This introduced unwanted correlations (fig 5). This emphasizes the difficulty of time regulation in a by-passing way.

Correlations between the score in mathematics and the rate of success in a question ought to determine its discriminatory character.

Time analysis shows that people who give the right answers have needed time to do so.

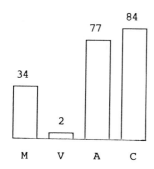

M : Mathematics, V : Vectors,
A : Accelerated motion,
C : Circular motion.

By - pass rate

figure 5

6 CONCLUSION

This kind of check-up operation turned out to be efficient in several ways.

Students seemed glad to have been individually welcome and accepted the test accordingly.

Revisions and quicker "taking off" in course work are induced.

Extra courses could be specifically organized for people needing help.

The actual level of incoming students is measured. However, at the present state of analysis, results are more interpreted in terms of mastery of practice than in terms of knowledge.

Time measurement introduced interesting but uneasy new analysis.

This experiment is going on: we expect to make correlation between the results of the test and the next examinations. We have to answer the question " Has the test any predictive efficiency ? ". Furthermore we have to build in a 1988 improved test.

NOTES

(1) Programme d'auto-évaluation (CREEM du CNAM et UER de Didactique des disciplines Université Paris 7)

(2) Plan national français " Informatique Pour Tous "

(3) Centre National d'Enseignement Assisté par Ordinateur, service commun inter universitaire PARIS 6 et PARIS 7

REFERENCES

[1] P. ARNAUD et al, "Description statistique du fonctionnement pédagogique d'un premier cycle universitaire DEUG A 1981-1985" Actes du colloque "Orientation et échecs dans l'enseignement supérieur" Paris - Dauphine May 1987 (French)

[2] Gilbert SOL, "Télématique et formation, cas particulier de l'enseignement des mathématiques", thèse d'Etat, Université Paris 7, UER de Didactique des Disciplines, September 1987, 147-158,(French)

[3] Françoise DEMAIZIERE, "Enseignement des langues Assisté par Ordinateur", thèse d'Etat, Université Paris 7, Département de Recherches Linguistiques, 1986, (French)

[4] Jacques FISZER, Methods of creating computer-based pedagogical products, Proceedings of the International Conference on Courseware Design and Evaluation, Ramat Gan, Israel, April 1986, 91-99.

COMPUTERS IN EDUCATION, F. Lovis and E.D. Tagg (eds.)
Elsevier Science Publishers B.V. (North-Holland)
© IFIP, 1988

AUTOMATED STUDENT PLANNING, EVALUATION & REVIEWING OF TRAINING ASPERT

Jean-Jacques DE CLERCQ

Polytechnic for Industrial Engineers IHR-BME

Schoonmeersstraat, 52

9000   GENT

Age of pupils : 18-20   Degree : Graduate in Data Processing

Under the actual constellation of High-Tech, one of the most crucial points in our informatics education is moving at the same pace with industry. At this moment, education is way behind, due to lack of funds, fear of having to bridge the knowledge gap and being withheld by the great educational inertia to adapt the programs. To this problem I see 4 solutions : - Play the sitting duck and let education be shot down by the High-Tech Industry, which will start a third training circuit on their own account. - Letting industry contribute with money and material to research projects, which will be accomplished completely within the school premises. This methodology is used in the States and there I see Universities like MIT specialized in software, U of California in hardware, Berkeley in Unix etc., avoiding all students who have no affinity towards their specialization. - Create software firms like they do in France, consisting nearly solely of students and headed by a very small professional administrative staff to run the company. This requires however a small change in the jurisdiction of the partnership. - However a less costly enterprise and the easiest to implement is assigning students to projects for and within industry. The student is free to select the project which best suits his capacities and field of interest. Industry pays all the costs during the student's stay at the firm. The student is well motivated, the firm gives full support, because it is a project they want to implement and even the teacher is taking advantage of the situation because he is exposed to the latest technologies. Because we have yearly about 150 graduating students in the field, doing job-training, we automated the follow-up by computer. A PC-version, written in DBASE-3 (trademark of Ashton- Tate), was developed specially for ECCE-88.   Not only the evaluation and the progress of systems-and program-development are being taken care of by the ASPERT system, but a forecast of time to be spent is also calculated with Function Point Analysis. Finally, it is not only this automated follow-up which is of importance, but especially how we managed to put students to work on industrial projects during their studies, with all the problems this causes.

INTRODUCTION :

The ASPERT system is used to follow-up student projects by computer, and give the necessary overview of the progress to the tutor. Before speaking about the system more closely it would be wise to give a picture of the full environment it is working in.

OBJECTIVES OF IN-THE-FIELD TRAINING OR WHY WE KEPT OUR AUTOMATION PROJECTS OUT OF THE SCHOOL ENVIRONMENT :

(1) Objectives for the student :

- to enable him to put the accumulated theory into practice

- to learn him to socialize with people and learn how a company works (hierarchy of responsibilities, organization chart, communication channels)

- to learn another computer, operating system, program ming languages and special software packages

- to learn and use software packages which a school would not be able to afford e.g. database, programming languages (professional cobol, artificial intelligence), analysis tools (James Martin Engineering Workshop), desktop publishing etc

- to enable him to work with very expensive material e.g. plotters, laser printers, CAD systems etc. Sometimes he receives a PC to develop the software at home

- to expose him to the industrial environment : if there is any thing wrong with his project he immediately gets an echo back from the users; he learns to work in a stress situation, he learns the shortcuts and the way analysis is really done in practice and he inherits a large amount of experience from the DP-cell working with him

Most of the students are enlisted after graduation by the company where they realized their project if they gave satisfaction to the company tutor.

(2) Objectives for the teachers :

- comes in touch with different computer environments and obtains a general knowledge of the different systems. Often firms come with their problems to the teacher because he has an overall view and knows in which firm they have met the same problems. He is also a candidate for industrial espionage. Care should be taken that he keeps the company secrets to himself. This is sometimes hard when another company comes up with problems an other has already solved and he knows how they managed to do it. Consulting can indeed be an indirect form of espionage.

- he will also have the same possibility as the student to participate in the company DP courses.

- we have experienced that our teachers involved in projects come close to the ideal mix I have always preached in the IFIP WG 3.4 : a teacher in the technical branch should be part-time in the school and part-time in industry (cfr. EDUCATION FOR SYSTEM DESIGNER/USER COOPERATION, IFIP 83, Training and retraining teachers for the future trends in DP, author JJ DE CLERCQ, p.76par.5.3.4). However our exposure to the industry is still too small (4 hours/week) and requires a lot of overtime work to become really effective. Those teachers, just like the students, spend most of their time increasing their company at tendance.

- teachers are sometimes able to borrow material and software from companies e.g. portable computers, video projectors, copies of licensed software just during the development period.

(3) Objectives for the school :

- free publicity for the school when some outstanding projects have been realized. This gives the school a good reputation among firms because nearly each year we end up in a magazine with one of our 100 projects.

- it is easier for the school to put his students into a job

- nearly all the hardware and especially the software we have are mainly gifts from computer companies because of our past realizations. We do have a large Siemens mainframe model 7530 with 32 videos, A Prime 250 with 24 videos, a Siemens Unix minicomputer with 6 videos, 15 IBM PC's and 6 AT-clones. This is still for us a low-end computerpark for about 1000 DP students and a totality of 1900 students out of the 3000 with hands on the computer. From Siemens only we received at least 200,000 dollars worth of free software. We only pay the maintenance contracts.

SCHOOL SCHEDULE :

Beginning of May (preceding the school year we are talking about) : the computer mailing for renewing the applications to the firms participating in the on-the-job-training for the former school year.

Beginning of June : reviewing of the firms who are willing to participate next school year and distributing the applications among the teachers in charge. There are two teachers for each class during the follow-up hours of the on-the-job-training to enable one of both teachers to have a look on the spot.

End of June : selection of the students who have succeeded in their exams and assigning them to the selected automation projects.

July-August : students start learning the systems software and try to write a couple of programs which have nothing to do with their automation project. We have experienced that the efficiency of the functional and application analysis is better if the student knows more about the singularities of the system on which he will realize his project. Also during the summer period there is a greater availability for workstations and computer resources which is an ideal environment to learn to use the machine. Some large firms give summer courses (CICS,DL1,IMS,IMAGE,ORACLE) for their programmers, which the students may also attend.

End of October : final agreement on the contents of the project between the tutors of the firm and the school. The tutor in the school is the teacher who will do the follow-up of that specific project. The students who have passed their exams of second session (September) have to start from scratch. During summer vacation teachers have been looking around for additional projects and have been following the first-session students in their summer work.

Beginning of November : all data of the projects and assigned students is inputted. The planning of the year will enable to fix all the due dates. Now the software contracts are printed with the computer. All kinds of listings will be generated : student and firm addresses, relation firm-project-students, due-date table, absentee table, year planning.

Beginning of January : the write-up of functional and technical analysis should be finished by now. During the Christmas vacation students have been able to write-out their thoughts and insert their different charts into the text. If the student makes use of word processing his thesis will already have a clean and readable look. Between now and the end of March the student will be scheduled by his tutor to give an oral explanation of how he conceived the system. He will be questioned thoroughly by his tutor about his conceptual scheme and IO-layouts.

End of March : the program manual should be finished by now with the exception of sourcelists and test results. During the month of March students have already started coding their programs.

Easter vacation : will mainly be used to key-in the programs, compile and run tests on them. This is the only time the student can work full days on the computer of the firm. Arrangements have been made between both tutors that during this period there is a workstation available for each student working on the project.

April-May : the programs should be running by now and a date for the demonstration will be fixed with the tutors. The system will be tested thoroughly on bugs by the tutors during the demo-session. If the student passes the test he is allowed to participate at the first term presentation.

May : students must turn in their papers consisting of analysis, program and user manuals.

June : final presentation of the project by the student before a jury consisting of the tutors and people from industry.

SPECIFICATIONS OF THE GRADUATING YEAR :

The student receives 4 hours a week to work on his project in the company. The preliminary exams for the theoretical courses is in February. Half of the month May is left for study. The final exams (written and oral) are during the month of June and are ended by the presentation of the thesis.

Marks : 3000 on the theoretical courses
        1000 for presentation
        200 for work during the schoolyear
        300 for presentation
        500 for the contents

PARTICIPANTS :

- **the contracting firm** : the company may as well be selling as using the software for his own needs. This is why tight contracts have to be made to avoid any problems of copyright and patenting. What if e.g. the student who realized the software package sells it to the competitor ?

- **the tutor of the firm** : it is the person in the company who is closely related to the project. Not necessarily somebody of the DP-team though, it could be as well the future user of the new system. Indeed, a large amount of firms make their first steps in DP with us.

- **the users of the new system** : these persons will give all the details of how the screens and printer layouts will look and pos sible exceptions and logic bottlenecks to look out for.

- **Tutor of the school** : is the teacher who is responsible for the choice and follow-up of the project. He will finally grade the student. He will also teach the student the necessary techniques and individual facts about the system he will be working on (e.g. Operating system, Job control language, editor, database and data dictionary). On an average each teacher will have between 15 and 25 projects to follow.

- **the Co-tutor**: is the second teacher who is not responsible for the project but who can eventually help the student while the tutor is in one of the 20 firms where he has projects running.

- **students working at a project** : if several students are working at the same project one of them will be chosen as project leader because of his leading capabilities. The project leader will be the go-between of the company and the school. He will also communicate the progress of the project to the tutor in the school.

THE PROJECT ENVIRONMENT :

(1) School environment :

Because we have too little hardware and software for the large amount of DP-students we do have no other choice than sending our students into alien computer environments. We have e.g. 14 day- and 9 nightclasses,with each a session of 2 hours a week. The two terminal rooms are scheduled daily from 8.10 in the morning until 20.30 at night all days of the week including Saturday. We only have 2 hours/week left for back-up and system maintenance left. This implies a very strict schedule for the student which doesn't give any flexibility for the company attendance. The 4 hours left in the schedule for company attendance are fixed and cannot be altered if it doesn't fit into the company schedule. A class which has e.g. its company attendance planned on Friday afternoon is out of luck. Most companies stop working at 3 o'clock in the afternoon leaving the

students with no support. Most of the company personnel take every two weeks off on Friday afternoon (38 hours/week schedules in Belgium). The school environment requires also a very strict attendance control of the student. For this purpose we have made tables which inform us on where the student may be found. The company has to fill in forms for every visit of the student and has to have it signed by the company tutor. The student has to give the school tutor an hourly evolution of his projects with a detailed explanation of how many hours he worked on every SDM-step. SDM or Systems Development Methodology divides a project into well defined steps identified by a SDM stepnumber. For every step the school tutor has to know the number of hours each student worked on it. The school insurance took us about 3 years to get it as we wanted it. Now the student is insured on his way to or from the firm and also during his attendance in the firm. Some difficult matters haven't been solved yet: the teacher is still not insured and what if the student destroys by accident company computer data or material. It hasn't happened yet but what if ... !

These are very important problems which still haven't been solved completely by the school management and which greatly worries the teachers.
Likewise only the displacements of the students and not of the teachers are compensated.

(2) Company environment :

On the first contact with the firm you get the impression the schedules are quite flexible. Nothing is further from the truth. It is one of our largest problems getting users interviewed on the hours the students may leave the school. At worst students have to skip regular courses to be able to meet the company personnel. Secondly a company never buys a workstation just as a standby. Nearly always the workstations are occupied between 8 and 5 all week long. Students have to sacrifice their evenings on the computer instead of studying for their theoretical courses. Sometimes their attendance in the company during weekends and evenings causes additional janitorial problems in entering and leaving the company enclosure. There is also the security problem. Therefore we have included in the softwarecontract a clause for professional secrecy.

The worst problem for getting projects is that the realization period of a project takes one full school year which is for most firms the worst obstacle. Sometimes we have to make a shortcut in the analysis and start programming nearly instantaneously to get the project into production within 3 months and doing an after-the-fact analysis to keep DP-management quiet. The stress environment and bad software support give the student a good idea of what is awaiting him in his later profession. Most firms are very suspicious about the capabilities of our students and are always afraid they are going to put more time into the students than they will get results from them. It is only after a very long period of sensitization that we succeed to convince them to start a project with our students. Once they have participated in a project with us they come back every schoolyear and become our steady "clients". Because the students population in DP is still in an upward movement we have to keep looking for additional companies. By experience it takes for the teacher 3 times more of his time,working with new firms. About 70% of the projects are in other cities which involves a loss of 1-2 hours in transportation per student visit. Similarly it is very hard for the teacher to visit the average of 20 firms continuously. At the most you can visit 2 firms on a half day. Starting January the students have to give an oral overview of the progress they have been making on their project. We call this the progress reporting. Because we can only take 2 projects/week for evaluation this keeps the teacher caught in the school be tween New-Year and Easter vacation. This means the teacher can only start-up and finish off the project. Transportation of the students is paid by the contracting firm. Teachers have to pay for their own transport. This requires a lot of idealism of the teachers because they not only have to spend most of their leisure time to those projects but also have to bear the overhead costs. They even have to pay for a special insurance because they leave the school premises.

In large companies the students are followed very closely and get an excellent software support. There the attendance and in dividual support of the student is minimized. If courses aren't provided in the company the teacher gives in the beginning of the schoolyear individual starter-courses for the different operating systems, programming languages and databases the students will be working with. This requires that the teacher has a very large experience in DP on different machines and that he keeps himself continuously up-to-date by following courses and doing self- study. DP teachers in my school must have at least 6 years experience in DP before they can be enrolled as regular teacher. Out of this group the best are selected on the basis of their realizations in and out the school. The relation of the teacher with the company must be one of mutual trust and often management come with their other DP problems to the teacher because he is neutral in his judgment and normally does not have any commercial ties. Management often expects this service because they con sider it as a part of the project. They take us for a software-bureau which will solve all their problems free !

THE SOFTWARE CONTRACT :

It is very surprising to find here a 3-partite contract, between parents (still responsible for the student), the school and the company.

Liabilities for the company :

(1) They will help the student and to the best they can give him the necessary computertime to realize his project without delays, taking the planned due dates of the student into account.

(2) The period the project will run, normally 1 schoolyear

(3) To provide a company tutor who is responsible to report to the tutor of the school and who will control the attendance of the student in the company.

(4) With exception of transportation fees there will be no financial commitment.

(5) The company receives the soft free of charge and may use it as it pleases. However it may not take any patents on the software without having the permission of the school. The reason for this is because we have met with a problem. Often teachers develop special systems and algorithms which are used by the stu dents in their projects. Before we included this clause a company patented one of our special algorithms. This meant we could not use our own developed algorithms next schoolyear because there was a patent on it.

Liabilities of the school :

(1) The thesis may be presented to the public and may be published. This means that the competition may eventually get to know the details of the project if they ask for it during the presentation. On the other hand the student and the school promise not to unveil the company secrets. This is sometimes hard to fulfill.

(2) The student stays under the jurisdiction of the school. There is no labor agreement between the student and the firm. Out of this results that :

    (a) the student is not paid

    (b) the student is not subject to social security rules

(c) for occupational or other diseases the health-service of the student is responsible. Accidents will be paid by the special insurance effected by the school for this purpose. The parents will renounce any claims for damage towards the firm.

(d) the civil liability of the student will also be covered by the school insurance. This takes care even for maltreatment of machines and dataloss. Indeed, what if the student e.g. working with a very complex operating system makes a mistake and erases very important data?

Liabilities of the student :

(1) the student accepts the company regulations during his stay there. In case of misbehavior the company is allowed to breach the contract but should do this in writing to school management.

(2) at the end of the project the student will deliver a write-up consisting of an analysis, program and user dossier in so far this corresponds with his realization. The company is allowed to keep one copy of manuals and floppies.

ATTENDANCE LIST :

Each time the student works in the firm the company tutor checks the list of hours worked and signs it. These are the only hours who are very hard to check. The students attendance in the school is no problem for the teacher. The whereabouts of the student are especially important for insurance purposes.

ACTIVITY LIST :

The student keeps an hour by hour list of his activities. Every activity in his project is identified by a SDM-stepnumber. The ASPERT system gives for each SDM-step the total hours worked up to now for each project and each student.

PROGRESS REPORTING :

The students of the project explain how they worked out their project up to now. The teacher will question the student(s) on different aspects of the analysis especially the conceptual scheme of the datamodel. The tutor of the school wants to evaluate the progress in the project and will try to correct any derailments in the project. Indeed the next step will be spitting out the programs and they had better translated the wishes of the users else the project would never get implemented. During the representation of the project they will be graded for the progress they have made up to now.

ASPERT SYSTEM :

(1) Students Screen :

The students are always identified by their enrolmentnumber (primary key) which is unique even if the student comes back to the school twenty years later. Not only the parents'address (for absentee reporting) but also the student's address during the school year is registered. If the tutor of the school wants to get urgently hold of the student he knows where to find him.

(2) Firm screen :

The address of the firm, the name of the company tutor and his phone number with extension. The company is identified by a sequence number.

(3) Relation Student-Project-firm screen :

By entering the enrolmentnumber of the student the parents address is picked out of the database; now the data of the project can be entered and afterwards be linked to the company by giving the company number.

(4) Project Description screen :

Every project receives a project key consisting of the schoolyear (f.ex.87-88), the student's class number and the sequence number of the project. The project description is entered into a separate dataset because the length of the text is undefined. It is also this description which will be printed out in the con tract.

COMPUTERS IN EDUCATION, F. Lovis and E.D. Tagg (eds.)
Elsevier Science Publishers B.V. (North-Holland)
© IFIP, 1988

NaviGroup :
Computer Network Based
Nondeterministic Educational Protocols

Jean-Luc Hardy
Brussels, Belgium

The use of computers in education allows the development of activities where facilitators are required to help the students in their learning projects. A NaviGroup protocol indicates to the facilitator how to NAVIGate in the GROUP of students. It tells which student should be helped next, after the current helping intervention. Each student requesting the facilitator's help is given a priority. This priority depends on the time that the facilitator has already spent with each student. The advantage of such a protocol is to share the facilitator's time equally between students and to encourage them to find solutions by themselves. This article describes several implementations of NaviGroup protocols. Computer networks are the most appropriate tools to support it.

1. INTRODUCTION

The last developments in the field of computerized education, especially the promising experiences done with LOGO, lead one to consider two important paradigms in education, as explained in [1] : one is deterministic and the other is nondeterministic. The former relies on the teacher's direction and the latter relies on the student's direction.

The word "facilitator", proposed in [2], is often used to designate the person who is responsible for an educational environment based on the students' projects. The tasks and the qualities of the facilitator are very different from those of the teacher. The teacher is a bit like a theater actor : he must be able to interest the students in the script he has prepared. The facilitator has personal relationships with the students, since he helps them to develop their *own* initiatives.

The teacher considers a pre-established set of educational objectives to be mastered by the students. The facilitator considers the students' projects. He will help them by providing the information they are requesting and by giving them some hints to stimulate more complex projects.

Likewise, classroom organizational characteristics and ergonomic features are different for both educational types. The classroom for deterministic education must be similar to an auditorium, since the teacher is explaining the same things at the same time to all students. The classroom for nondeterministic education is organized like a workshop, where each student is working on his own project.

2. CLASSROOM BEACONS

In deterministic education, the hand raising convention plays an important role. The students raise their hand to mean :

- either that they know the answer to the teacher's question;
- or that they do not understand what the teacher is explaining.

In nondeterministic education, this convention is inappropriate. The teacher will not see the student raising a hand when he is occupied with another student. Even when he has seen the raised hand, it not possible for him to abandon the student with which he is interacting.

As suggested in [3] and [4], "beacons" are used to establish a new convention that is suitable for nondeterministic education. A beacon is a simple device including a container and a peg , as shown in figure 1. The tips of the peg are painted green and red. When the green tip is visible, the student does not have problems. The student signals that he has a problem by inverting the peg. When the facilitator terminates his intervention, he puts the beacon in the green position.

The student inverses the beacon peg to mean
- either, that he needs information to continue his task;
- or that he does not understand the consequences of his action.

Figure 1. A simple classroom beacon

3. BEACON CIRCUIT RULE

The rest of this paper is concerned with the priority problems : what must the facilitator do when there are several simultaneous requests, i.e. when more than one beacon is red.

The simplest way to treat the priority problem is to establish a closed circuit that the facilitator follows in one direction. Each beacon is assigned a number that makes the circuit explicit. The facilitator visits the students requesting help according to the number on their beacon. Classroom beacons can be used not only for computer activities, but for many individualized activities as well.

From our daily experience, it appears that children appreciate the use of beacons. They consider the beacon system like a game. The rules of that game must be carefully explained to each student.

4. SENSITIVE BEACONS AND DEFERRED REGULATION

If the beacon is a switch and if all the beacons are connected to a computer, it is possible to produce a graph showing the distribution of the intervention requests for each student.

4.1 Synoptic view

The time is given in ordinate and the beacon numbers are given in abscissa. Each intervention request is represented by a vertical line whose length indicates a duration. Such a graph gives a synoptic view and indicates disproportions. The facilitator is notified that some children are requesting help much more often than others.

Usually, the facilitator inverts the beacon -- i.e. he puts it to green -- of the student requesting help when he terminates his intervention. Consequently, the intervention request times   include the time spent by the facilitator answering the student's request. On the graph, this time can be isolated if we can make two assumptions. First, the end of a facilitator's intervention coincides with the beginning of the next intervention. Second, after an interval of non-intervention (and non-request), the facilitator will help the first requesting student without delay.

Such a graph is presented in figure 2 which describes the following situation : the facilitator begins to help student 6, i.e. the student having the beacon number 6. After about one minute, student 11 inverts his beacon. After 2 more minutes, student 2 does the same. Three minutes later, the facilitator finishes helping student 6 and he goes on to help student 11, and so on.

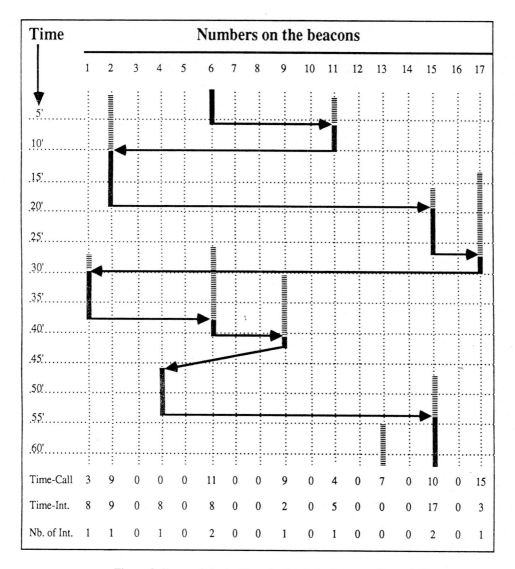

Figure 2. Trace of the facilitator's circuit during a one hour session.

Some additional remarks must be made about figure 2.

(a) At the 30th minute, the facilitator goes from student 17 to student 1. This happens because the beacon circuit is a closed circuit.

(b) The oblique line starting at the 43rd minute indicates that nobody is requesting help. Without additional information, it is not possible to say if the facilitator was simply taking a short rest or if he was helping a student who did not make a request.

(c) The facilitator starts again by helping student 4. Without additional information, it is not possible to determine if student 4 has requested help.

(d) Student 12 was requesting help when the session finished.

(e) The second row at the bottom indicates the total amount of time spent by the facilitator while helping each student. It appears that the student 15 received the most help. It is also directly visible that some students were not helped at all.

4.2 Additional rule

The drawbacks mentioned in section (b) and (c) call for a subsidiary rule concerning the use of beacons. We have to choose between two possible rules.
- The first is that only the student can invert the beacon peg from green to red. In that case, there is no doubt about the problem raised in section (c) : student 4 has definitely requested help. However doubt subsists about the problem mentioned in section (b) : was the facilitator resting or did he help a student who did not make a request ?
- The second possible rule is that the facilitator himself inverts the beacon taking initiative of helping a student. Given this second rule, the certainty and the doubt just described are reversed. Regarding section (c), we still do not know if student 4 has requested help. However, we are now sure about the problem raised in section (d) : the facilitator did take a short rest.

The second rule seems more advantageous than the first, at least for two reasons. First of all, the second rule allows for the facilitator's intervention time for each student. Secondly, it is more feasible inasmuch as students sometimes forget to invert their beacon when the facilitator is standing near them and available. In this case, the fact that the facilitator inverts the beacon underlines the necessity of using beacons.

To avoid the choice between one of the two rules, the beacon system could be enhanced with a button indicating the beginning of the facilitator's intervention. The use of this button allows for a unique interpretation of figure 2. The problem is how to stop the students from hitting the button, accidentally or by play. Since the beacon device must be controlled by software, the problem can be reformulated : how can the relevant actions of the button be selected ? How will irrelevant actions be filtered out ? The answer is easy when the facilitator is helping someone who has the beacon x, the end of his intervention will be notified by the inversion of the beacon x. In the meantime, the other buttons will not be operative.

4.3 Deferred regulation

The availability of a synoptic view after each session allows deferred regulation of the facilitator's work. Considering the foregoing section (d), it would be fair that student 12 be helped first at the beginning of the next session. Considering the section (e), the facilitator should propose his help to the students who never ask for it, to be sure that they are progressing well.

Deferred regulation allows large inequities in the time given by the facilitator to each of the students to be noticed. However, there is a drawback to such a system, since the regulation depends only on the facilitator himself. He must interpret the data and he must concentrate in order to decrease the discrepancies in the time offered to each student.

5. NAVIGROUP SYSTEM

The NaviGroup system is intended to help the facilitators in real time. This system is used in conjunction with a "gyroscope" used by the facilitator who is navigating among the group of the students. The gyroscope indicates which student must be helped next. The gyroscope is integrated in a computerized beacon system handled by a software package, called the "NaviGroup manager" and described below in section 6. The NaviGroup system can be either a special electronic system, called the "NaviGroup kit", or just a software system based on a computer network, called the "NaviGroup network".

5.1 The NaviGroup kit

The NaviGroup kit includes three parts : a set of special beacons, a gyroscope and a slave computer. The last links the two first parts with a computer, called the master computer, that handles the NaviGroup manager and includes the NaviGroup information files. Figure 3 represents a beacon and a gyroscope.
The beacons of the NaviGroup kit are sensitive and remotely controlled. Their principal parts are a button, a bulb and a plug. The bulb and button correspond to the peg of the simple beacon. When the student x needs help, he pushes the button. The request transits through the slave computer and reaches the master computer which commands the lighting of the beacon bulb. This light plays two roles : it informs the student x that his request has been accepted and it informs other students that the student x is requesting help.

The plug of the beacon is used by the facilitator to connect his gyroscope. The connection of the gyroscope on this plug plays two roles. First, it informs the NaviGroup manager that the facilitator is now helping the student number x, x being the beacon number. If the facilitator does not want to use the gyroscope, he can use a simple mooring that allows such updating of the NaviGroup manager database, but does not include a display to receive information from the manager. The second role of the plug is precisely to allow for the transmission of information from the manager to the gyroscope : since the beacons are permanently connected to the master computer, via the slave computer, information can transit through them.

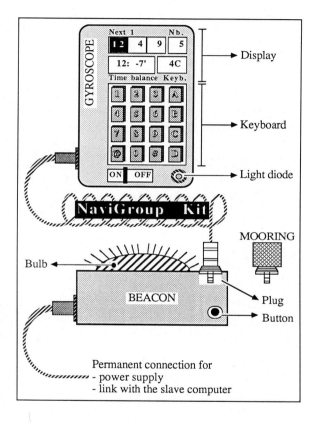

Figure 3. The NaviGroup Kit

The principal information of the gyroscope is the "Next 1" number displayed in the top-left corner. It is the number of the next student to be helped : number 12 in the example given in figure 3. The diode is the second important information : it lights up as soon as the NaviGroup manager decides that the facilitator had better go help another student. Other information is useful, but not indispensable. The second and the third students to be helped, respectively number 4 and number 9, are given on the right. The total number of students waiting for help is displayed on the right of the first line. The time balance display will be explained below. Finally the last window of the display is the keyboard display. The keyboard is used to control the NaviGroup manager.

5.2 The NaviGroup network

If a computer is available for every student and if a network links all the computers, the NaviGroup System should be integrated into this network. Each computer allows four selections to be performed, either by typing a function key or by choosing (with a mouse) an item from a permanent menu. We assume that desktop facilities are available for each computer of the network.

(a) The first selection is used by the student to signal that he needs help. As feedback, an additional (or reversed) word or icon is then displayed on the screen to acknowledge that the request has been accepted by the NaviGroup manager.

(b) The second selection is used by the facilitator to signal the beginning and end of his intervention. At the end of the intervention, the NaviGroup manager will inform the facilitator about the next student to be helped. During the intervention, the NaviGroup manager can send a message to facilitator to advise him to go help another student.

(c) The two last selections are less crucial. The third selection commands the display of a window presenting the status of all the classroom beacons. This window can be used either by the facilitator or by the students.

(d) Finally the fourth selection allows the facilitator to control the NaviGroup manager.

Here are the correspondences between the network features and the above mentioned kit features.

(a) The first selection corresponds to the beacon button of the kit. The feedback signal is equivalent to the lighting of the kit bulb.

(b) The second selection corresponds to the connection of the gyroscope wire on the beacon.

(c) Information from the third selection is similar to that provided by the overview of the beacon bulbs and by the gyroscope display.

(d) The fourth selection corresponds to the use of the kit gyroscope keyboard.

6. NAVIGROUP EDUCATIONAL PROTOCOLS

The NaviGroup manager is the software that has the responsibility for performing an educational protocol. This protocol decides which student must be helped next. There are several possible protocols. Let us consider three of them from the simplest to the more sophisticated.

(a) The beacon circuit rule described in section 3 can be a NaviGroup protocol : students are helped depending on their beacon number. It has the advantage of the simplicity. It can be easily understood, even by the young children. It does not require the real time capability of the previously described NaviGroup systems.

(b) The second protocol assigns the highest priority to the student who has been waiting for the longest time compared to the other students. It can be called the FIFO protocol, i.e. the first requesting student will be helped first. This protocol can not be handled by the facilitator alone, since the start of each request must be carefully recorded. The NaviGroup system is appropriate, the FIFO protocol being handled by the NaviGroup manager.

(c) The third protocol, called the time protocol, assigns the highest priority to the requesting student that has received the least help time from the facilitator.

7. MANAGEMENT OF THE TIME PROTOCOL

The time protocol requires two main roles from the NaviGroup manager :

(a) The first role of the NaviGroup manager is to designate the next student to be helped by the facilitator. For that purpose, all facilitator intervention times are summed for each student. The help priority is greater for students who have received less help from the facilitator, and vice versa. Each facilitator intervention changes only the priority of the student who is concerned with the intervention, and not the other students' priorities.

(b) The subsidiary role of the NaviGroup manager is to advise the facilitator to stop an intervention. For that purpose, the mean help time is calculated for the entire classroom and the differences between each student's time and the mean time are computed. The values are either positive if the student has received more help than the average or negative in the opposite case. These values, called "time balance", can be displayed on the facilitator's gyroscope (see figure 3). The manager decides that the facilitator should stop his intervention when two conditions are fulfilled :

- The time balance of the first requesting student is negative.
- The time balance of the student currently being helped is positive.

Since these conditions may change during one facilitator's intervention, the time balances should be computed in a cycle as frequently as possible.

REFERENCES

[1] Jean-Luc Hardy, Nondeterminitic education : a Theoretical Approach, in: *Proceedings of the 11th Western Educational Computing Conference* (November 1987) pp. 232-236.

[2] Gérard Bossuet, *L'ordinateur à l'école* (Presses Universitaires de France, Paris, 1982) p. 76.

[3] Jean-Luc Hardy and Marc Hardy, The use of beacons to improve the ergonomics of computerized classroom activities, in: *Proceedings of the 10th Western Educational Computing Conference* (November 1986) pp. 167-171.

[4] Jean-Luc Hardy and Marc Wathieu,
   - LOGO : Storms and Beacons, short strip presented at *EuroLog '87 Conference* (Dublin, September 1987, unpublished English version).
   - LOGO : Tempêtes et balises, *Magazine du Kids' Computer Club, 2* (August 1987, French version) pp. 3-7.

COMPUTERS IN EDUCATION, F. Lovis and E.D. Tagg (eds.)
Elsevier Science Publishers B.V. (North-Holland)
IFIP, 1988

TOWARDS A BETTER USE OF COMPUTERS IN COMPUTER SCIENCE TEACHING

Monique Grandbastien
Centre de Recherche en Informatique de Nancy
Campus Scientifique - BP 239
54506 VANDOEUVRE - LES - NANCY Cedex , FRANCE

Abstract: Computer science students use computers daily to run programs on them, but they do not often have the opportunity to use them as a help in learning new programming concepts. This paper first analyzes specific characters of computer science teaching, describes some interesting attempts and brings out special needs in this area.
The SAIDA system, an educational help to the implementation of abstract data structures in a data structure course, is then described as a possible prototype for new teaching tools in the software engineering area, using existing softwares and knowledge bases.
The paper concludes on the frames, methods and tools suitable for the development of such systems.

1. INTRODUCTION

Computer science teachers use few pieces of educational software [1] to teach computer science. This may seem surprising, but several reasons may account for such a situation ; however the need in this area is very important and many promising factors now allow one to build new pedagogical environments more easily. Existing attempts and special needs due to the original features of computer science teaching are analyzed in the first section.

SAIDA, a help to the efficient implementation of abstract data types in a data structure course, is then described as an example of a pedagogical environment to teach some concepts in computer science. It requires the students to write algorithms at the level of abstraction suitable for the given problem and for the modelling practice of the programmer; students have then to justify choices for implementations in terms of algorithm and environment characters such as memory size, and operators used... ; they are working in the ADA programming environment and use concepts such as program units and generic packages.

The pedagogical context and the system's aims are presented in section 3 ; the components and facilities offered to the users, teachers and students, are described in section 4. Section 5 deals with the design of such systems. There is not yet a general frame to build intelligent educational programming environments ; but expert system shells appeared after the design of lots of knowledge based systems, authoring systems proceeded from the design of a lot of educational software. We hope to contribute to the design of a more suitable tool in pointing out some main features for such systems and some difficulties encountered when building ours.

2. COMPUTER ASSISTED LEARNING FOR COMPUTER SCIENCE TEACHING

Computer science teaching may be characterized by several important features ; a detailed analysis of some of them has to be made before speaking of computer assisted learning for this subject. Contents are rapidly and continuously changing ; the computer is at the same time a teaching tool and something to be taught; students have to learn factual knowledge of course, but also skills enabling them to solve various problems ; lastly, computer science are used in vocational training as well as in general training. These features partly account for the relatively small amount of educational software in this area and the increasing number of new products; they point to some needs and directions for the coming years.

2.1. Some features of computer science teaching

2.1.1. Rapidly changing contents

Computer science was first introduced in curricula as a technique before setting up as a science. Many courses are still concerned with machines and software ; computer science teachers are not numerous enough to face all the demands; they spend a lot of time trying to understand technical manuals and building pedagogical presentations of the main concepts and commands they contain. When this pedagogical work is done, it would be possible to begin the design of some educational software on this subject. But as new tools become available, new investigations are made necessary and previous conclusions are partly cancelled. So, it is difficult to design and produce lasting software in this area.

2.1.2. The computer, as a tool for teaching and as an object to be taught

Computer science departments own numerous and various machines that students learn to use or even to build; their teachers are specialists in software design; machines and designers build a context which a priori seems better for computer science than for any other subject to develop educational software. This is partly true, and recent progress in programming environments allows the rapid realization of teaching tools.

But the duality, computer as a tool for teaching and as an object to be taught is a drawback too. Each use of the computer to introduce or illustrate some computer science concept, such as modelling data for a data base or programming by stepwise refinement, has side-effects; students are working with a machine and software which are merely tools today and which become objects of teaching the day after!

The educational software designer must not ignore these side-effects; on the contrary, he has to take them into account in his pedagogical project, to study possible interactions between the main subject for which the program is built and related topics. It is certainly an exciting challenge but not an easy task.

2.1.3. Factual knowledge and methods

Every computer science course includes some chapters on logical circuits, memories, keyboards, language syntax,.... For such topics, there are computer tutors that simulate the execution of a simple program, ask questions on it, control knowledge acquisition.

But the programmer must not only acquire knowledge about machines and languages, he must acquire skills to use this knowledge to solve problems in various areas. He must therefore use methods to overcome complexity and be able to communicate his work to others at every step of the development.

Everybody knows that it is easy to control syntax knowledge, compilers do that very well, but programming is better learnt through experience than through syntax teaching or even program construction teaching. Tutors cannot guide the programmer at each step of an application development. Software development methods such as Jackson's or SADT are intended to fill up this gap; but for educational purposes, we also need tutors to focus student's attention on particular development steps. MAIDAY [2] is an attempt in this way.

2.1.4. Vocational training and general education

For vocational training, it is necessary to use wide spread tools as often as possible. This requirement allows us to characterize most educational software in this field. With this software, students must learn to use widely spread tools to solve real problems; this means that teaching software must be built in reference to professional tools, even though some functions are hidden or some guidelines are added to them. These specific environments are needed for small groups of students, but they may be used for school purposes as well as for in service training purposes.

For general education, an objective may be to show how wide spread software such as DBASE, MULTIPLAN, a BASIC interpreter, are used and for that purpose, the same kinds of environments as for vocational training are required; only the pedagogical use of them will change. But the teacher's aim may be to illustrate a concept such as "text processor" or "programming language", and for that purpose, he may use specific teaching software, easier to understand than business tools. This software, especially software for computer science literacy, is needed for large groups of students.

2.2. Some interesting attempts

Our aim, of course, is not to present here an exhaustive study of educational software available in the field of computer science; an interesting synthesis on that topic is given in [3]. We only want to illustrate different kinds of software aids and to point out the directions in which much work has to be done.

2.2.1. Programming for beginners

Several systems were proposed to help the beginner in building small programs. Most of them, especially the oldest, are in fact "bug finders". LAURA [4] is given a skeleton of the expected program and looks at the student's FORTRAN program to decide if it is equivalent to the model. PROUST [5] works with a powerful knowledge base on program schemes and analyses the student's PASCAL program in such a way that it can find, for instance, a lack of index increment in a "for" loop. PROUST is not given any model of the problem solution, so it is perhaps one of the most interesting environments in this area; it is commercialized by a private software society. BIP includes an extended BASIC interpretor, a set of problem solving aids to give hints; it is intended to give a tutorial assistance without a thorough analysis of programs. About 100 problems with varying levels of difficulty are available; a student's model expressed in terms of the acquisition of fundamental skills enables individualized problem selection.

2.2.2. Programming in the large

Very little work has been done in this area, and we would like to draw special attention to an interesting attempt, IPHIGENIE [6], to model engineering activity in the field of large software engineering, allowing students to decompose their whole project into well identified steps and to make suitable choices at each step, their way of reasoning being helped by an expert system. Students are asked questions about all the problems they are confronted with and thus compelled to pay attention to facts that could have been considered as unimportant.

2.2.3. Educational environments

We have just seen in a previous section that educational environments built on existing software are certainly the best and the most needed educational tools for vocational training. Such software came out only recently; an interesting example is [7], sold by SOFTIA.

The aim of this product is to introduce the pupil to the frame of spread sheets and to have him discover and practise the main functions of the system; he has to solve problems in an exploratory and user-friendly environment. A pedagogical component is added to the system itself; this component works with a set of concepts listed as necessary to initiate beginners in such environments; it is also provided with a simple model of the learner, which allows it to propose graduated exercises.

An interesting feature is to bring the learner to look for missing information when he needs. One main difficulty in a course on such tools is to deal with a lot of concepts and commands, it is impossible to introduce them at the beginning, and it is impossible for the learner to memorize them.

LOGO was itself designed as an educational environment; PROLOG is sometimes used in the same way; POPLOG [8], SOLO [8] were created for the same purpose. These environments were enriched with various editing and tracing mechanisms, so that the student may easily understand how his program is running. But, once again, the emphasis is on mechanisms and not on methods to guide the student in modelling his problem universe in a functional style or in a relational style, and that would be at least as important as the understanding of interpretation mechanisms.

Future needs are in open programming environments, working with widely spread tools, providing methodological guides, founded on subject and pedagogical knowledge, using new techniques in software engineering and artificial intelligence. The next section describes a system which may be considered as a step in this direction.

3. THE SAIDA SYSTEM : CONTEXT AND TEACHING AIMS

3.1. The context

In computer science curricula, the field of study concerned with the use and implementation of data objects is usually called "Data Structures". Unfortunately, the data "types" available in most imperative programming languages are very "machine implementation dependent" and therefore far from the level of abstraction required by the increasing complexity of the problems.

To train students to deal with complex problems, we ask them to work at different levels of abstraction. The first draft of the algorithm they are designing to solve a problem must use objects belonging to the problem environment and operations usually performed on these objects. Then, the question is: How to represent these objects and these operations in terms of data types available in the chosen programming language; this second step may be partly automated or at least strongly guided if the first one leads to a precise and formal text.

What happens is that the first step is written on a paper with an "artificial formal language", whose syntax nobody respects because no compiler sends error messages! Students hope to save time in writing directly in the available programming language.

ADA offers an opportunity to change these practices. This language includes concepts such as program units and generic packages which allow the programmer to define and use abstract data types in writing his programs; he then has to describe the implementation of his abstract operators in another part of the code and to stick both parts together to build his whole program. The algorithm on abstract types is not an intermediate step, it becomes a part of the effective code.

When we chose ADA, there was a need for training students to use suitable levels of abstraction; there was an opportunity with the new ADA language providing the concepts of data types and data implementation; finally, there was a need to provide in-service training for programmers to the new programming language ADA, not only as a new syntax, but moreover as a new programming style using new programming concepts. This conjunction of needs was decisive in our choice.

3.2. Main purpose

Our aim is to focus students' attention on the following step of the programming process : how to make efficient choices of implementation for abstract data types. So they are first asked to write their algorithm in ADA, using a given

abstract environment including classical data structures such as lists, maps, sets, graphs, ... described as sets of objects on which a given set of operations is available. Let us illustrate this purpose by the following example:

Suppose we are given two words; the end of each word is marked by the special character"."; we want to write a program that counts the number of letters appearing in either word.

The problem universe deals with words and characters. How are we going to describe a word in terms of characters? We can think of a sequence, a list, a set. Suppose we choose to model words by sets and operations on words by operations on sets. Our student may consult the set abstract data type. The following operations are given (among others) :

init_set (E) : initializes E to the empty set,
is_empty (E): returns true if E is empty,
add_elem (E, X): adds the element X to the set E,
union (E1, E2, E3): returns in E3 the union of E1 and E2,
inter (E1, E2, E3): returns in E3 the intersection of E1 and E2,
belongs (E, X): returns true if the element X belongs to E,
card (E): returns the number of elements in E.

Our abstract algorithm on words described as sets consists of a procedure to fill the two sets representing the words with the corresponding characters, two calls of this procedure and the successive use of the given operations "**union**" and "**card**". This may be written in ADA :

```
procedure OUR_PROBLEM is
package MY_SET is new ???????? (character);
use MY_SET;
--   this is to create the type MY_SET of characters from
--   the given environment, the "?" will be replaced later;
WW,WORD1,WORD2 : SET;
--   declaration of three objects modelled as sets of
--   characters;
procedure READ_WORD (WORD : in out SET) is
C: character;
begin
get (C);
loop
exit when C = '.';
ADD_ELEM (WORD,C); get(C);
end loop;
end READ_WORD;
--   beginning of the algorithm itself;
begin
INIT_SET (WORD1); INIT_SET(WORD2);
READ_WORD(WORD1); READ_WORD(WORD2);
INIT_SET(WW);
UNION (WORD1,WORD2,WW); put(CARD(WW));
--   the required number of letters is displayed;
end OUR_PROBLEM;
```

To become an effective ADA procedure, the names of the packages used have to be added to the preceding text. Here we have only one abstract type, and two objects of this type on which we apply the same operators. We therefore have to bring in only one package. The choice of a package indicates a choice of data representation; there are a lot of implementations for sets; Appendix 1 shows an implementation as the list of the set elements and another one as a boolean array indexed on 'A'-'Z'.

Our example is too limited to illustrate here criteria to choose an efficient representation; the parameters to take into account are the size of the available memory, the length of execution time, the operators used.... For instance, if the most important operation is ADD_ELEM, if the number of set elements is not small, if there is no order on the elements, the best suited implementation is a linked list of the elements.

The system works with a knowledge base on criteria for efficient choices, depending on algorithm features and external constraints. An expert module asks the student various pieces of information so that it can fill in its own representation of the problem and can then explain its choices to the student.

3.3. Side-effects

This system was designed to compel the students to write abstract algorithms and to make systematic choices for efficient implementations of these types. As already noticed in section 1, it has several interesting side-effects.

First, the expert system, by the nature of the questions it asks, by the order in which the questions are asked, induces a method to analyze an algorithm and its external constraints, to abstract necessary information to make efficient representation choices. Then, it trains students to work with existing software components and provides a catalogue of reusable software. Finally, it offers examples of good programming style in ADA, it also enhances the development of object oriented programming, in which priority is given to the description of objects over the descriptions of processings.

So, it may be seen as an attempt to accustom our students to work on future programming environments that are moving from interactive ones to intelligent ones, as described in [9].

Let us now explain more precisely from what parts such a system is composed, how it works for the learner and for the teacher.

4. THE SAIDA SYSTEM COMPONENTS

4.1. The pedagogical documentation and the types library

Before or while working with the system and depending on the access rights given by his teacher, the student may consult formal definitions of available abstract types, the syntax and the semantics of operators. Examples of complete programs using the libraries are also given. Implementations of operators, that is package bodies in the type library, include lots of classical algorithms which may be studied for themselves. So the available documentation is partly textual and partly drawn from the ADA programs of the library.

A library of ADA packages for types such as lists, stacks, queues, sets, bags, maps, trees, graphs has been written. The user has to select, for a given type, a package corresponding to his implementation choice, to use it in the program and to link it to his files.

4.2. The rules base and the static algorithm analysis

For each data type, a set of rules has been written, summarizing main choice criteria to build efficient algorithms. Examples of rules about the set type were given in the previous section. To make these rules operational, the system must gather information about the algorithm and its environment from the student; if the information provided is false, the knowledge-based system will reason from false data! Some information must be given by the user, for instance, the relative length of time execution; some others may be found by the system itself after a static analysis of the algorithm.

The system uses a syntactic analyser, MENTOR-ADA, to get some of the needed information and to validate that provided by the student.

4.3. The teaching mode

The system's user enters his identity and the system identifies him as a teacher or as a learner. For a teacher, the following menu is displayed:

1 - information on the system purposes,
2 - components consultation,
3 - student work preparation,
4 - system modification,
5 - student mode.

Choice n°2 allows the teacher to read the texts of all the packages stored in the library and the rules of the knowledge base. Choice n°4 allows him to modify the library by adding new types, new operations on existing types or by changing algorithms implementing a given representation on an existing type. These changes are difficult when they concern the knowledge base and have to be done very carefully.

Choice n°3 allows the teacher to create the library he wants to give to his students, according to his own pedagogical aims. For instance, he may not want to give the set type, or he may not want to provide too many implementations for a given type. He may also set up different access rights according to the characteristics of the students: some are allowed to read all procedure texts; for others, the exercise consists in rebuilding the package bodies which are hidden to them. The teacher also has to decide which trace of his students' work he wants to store.

Finally, having configured his students' environment, the teacher may want to jump to the student experimental mode; this is possible with choice n°5.

The design of such a system needs a lot of work; so it seems very important to allow teachers to parametrize it according to their needs; if such an opportunity was not given, the system would not be used by enough people because there is agreement on some basic concepts for data structure courses, but there remains a large diversity in the types effectively used, in the order in which they are introduced and in the basic operations provided.

4.4. The learning mode

As we have seen in the teaching mode, each student is given by his teacher a set of access rights which determines the way he may use the system, (read and use or only use). When he is identified, the student is presented with the following menu:

1 - information on the system aims,
2 - libraries consultation,
3 - program creation,
4 - program execution.

With choice n°3, the student creates his ADA program using a text editor; a multi-windowing system allows him to look at type definitions or implementations at every stage. When the algorithm is created, he can call the expert system to receive help for data implementation choices, asking it to explain its questions and conclusions; but he can decide to make his choices alone; he then has to complete the algorithm text with implementation indications to build a complete main ADA procedure.

The ADA compiler and linker are available in the same environment, so the learner can compile and execute some code, come back to the assisted text building and change parts of the libraries he is using.

The student is guided on two points. First he is given a library of components, so he is compelled to express his algorithm at the level of abstraction suggested by the types included in the library. Secondly, he has to describe some features of his algorithm in a certain order and to deduce implementation choices from these data. On other points, he is free and may enter any kind of program and execute it on any set of data.

5 - TOWARDS FUTURE SYSTEMS

We want to train our computer science students in the latest developments in such fields as programming methodology, artificial intelligence and software engineering. We need to use these new developments when designing new educational software. In this section , we shall summarize some features of educational software for computer science and some qualities required for further building tools.

5.1. Features of educational software in computer science

This software must be open to the teacher and to the learner. Open to the teacher, that means at least a high degree of parametrization from several points of view (domain knowledge, pedagogical aid, ...) and a dialogue interface. Open to the student, especially to the computer science student, means possible access to other functions of the system and return to the learning environment, possible introduction of not previously registered exercises. This software must integrate subject knowledge and pedagogical knowledge; they must aim at developing problem solving skills and methods rather than control some special knowledge.

5.2. Building tools

The SAIDA environment is running on a SUN 3 MATRA DATA SYSTEME, using SUNTOOLS, an object oriented language, the VERDIX ADA compiler, the MENTOR-ADA environment and MORSE, an expert system shell written in LE LISP. The design of such an environment is a difficult programming task which requires high qualification to bring all these tools to work together. What we need is a further generation of authoring systems, allowing this kind of cooperation between different powerful software.

SAIDA is just a step, its knowledge base may be extended; tools are to be created for an easy and guided modification of this base; a student model may be added. It is not yet a tutor, but it allows the learner to work with real tools (ADA language, EMACS editor); we think it belongs to the new environments the learners are waiting for.

ACKNOWLEDGEMENTS

This project is partly funded by the French ministry of industry. I should like to thank Josette Morinet-Lambert for writing the programs and for providing helpful suggestions on the system.

REFERENCES

[1] P. FORCHERI, M.T. MOLFINO
An historical approach to educational computer based systems.
Revue d'Intelligence Artificielle, Vol.1, pp 53-70, Hermès, Paris, 1987.

[2] J. GUYARD, J.P. JACQUOT
MAIDAY: an environment for guided programming with a definitional language.
7° Software Engineering Conference, Orlando, USA, 1984.

[3] B. du BOULAY, C. SOTHCOTT
Computers teaching programming: an introductory survey on the field.
in Artificial Intelligence and Education, Vol.1, R.W.Lawler, M.Yasdani, eds.

[4] A. ADAM, J.P.LAURENT
LAURA: A system to debug student programs.
Artificial Intelligence, Vol.15, pp.75-122, 1980.

[5] W.L.JOHNSON, E.SOLOWAY
PROUST: Knowledge-based program understanding.
IEEE Transactions on Software Engineering, Vol. SE 11, n°3, 1985.

[6] B.COULETTE
Un didacticiel expert en méthodologie de développement de projets logiciels.
Congrès francophone EAO 87, Cap d'Agde, pp. 207-218, 1987 . (french)

[7] P.BROUAYE, E.BRUILLARD, E.FERRET, G.WEIDENFELD
APPAT: Un tuteur intelligent pour l'apprentissage des tableurs par la résolution de problèmes.
Congrès francophone EAO 87, Cap d'Agde, pp. 247-256, 1987. (french)

[8] T.O'SHEA, J.SELF
Learning and Teaching with the Computer, Artificial Intelligence in Education.
Harvester Press, Brighton, GB, 1983.

[9] D.R.BARSTOW, H.E.SHROBE, E.SANDEWALL (eds.)
Interactive programming environments.
Mc Graw Hill, New York, 1984.

APPENDIX 1 : ADA listings for the "word" program.

```
generic
type UNIVERSE is (<>);

package SET_MANAGER_LIS is
type SET is private;

procedure INIT_SET (E : in out SET);
function IS_EMPTY (E : in SET) return BOOLEAN;
procedure ADD_ELEM (E: in out SET; X: in UNIVERSE);
function BELONG (E: in SET; X: in UNIVERSE) return BOOLEAN;
procedure UNION (E1, E2: in SET; E3: in out SET);
function CARD (E: in SET) return INTEGER;


private
type UNIVERSE_SET;
type SET is access UNIVERSE_SET;
type UNIVERSE_SET is
        record   VAL: UNIVERSE;
                 NEXT: SET;
        end record;
end SET_MANAGER_LIS;


package body SET_MANAGER_LIS is

procedure INIT_SET (E : in out SET) is
begin   E := NULL;
end INIT_SET;

function IS_EMPTY (E : in SET) return BOOLEAN is
begin   return (E = NULL);
end IS_EMPTY;

function BELONG (E: in SET; X: in UNIVERSE) return BOOLEAN
is
begin   if E = NULL then return(FALSE);
        else P := E;
             loop exit when (P.NEXT=NULL) or (P.VAL=X);
                  P := P.NEXT;
             end loop;
             return (P.VAL = X);
        endif;
end BELONG;

procedure ADD_ELEM (E: in out SET; X: in UNIVERSE) is
P: SET;
begin   if (NOT BELONG(E, X)) then
             P := new UNIVERSE_SET'(X,E); E := P;
        endif;
end ADD_ELEM;

procedure COPY_SET (E1: in SET; E2: out SET) is
P1, P2: SET
begin   if (E1 = NULL) then E2 := NULL;
        elseP1 := E1;
             P2 := new UNIVERSE_SET'(P1.VAL, NULL);
             E2 := P2;
             loop exit when (P1.NEXT = NULL); P1 := P1.NEXT;
             P2.NEXT:=new UNIVERSE_SET'(P1.VAL, NULL);
             P2 := P2.NEXT;
             end loop;
        endif;
end COPY_SET;
```

```
procedure UNION (E1, E2: in SET; E3: in out SET) is
P1, P2: SET;
begin   if E1 = NULL then COPY_SET(E2,E3);
        else COPY_SET(E1,E3); P2 := E2;
             loop exit when P2 = NULL;
                  ADD_ELEM(E3, P2.VAL); P2 := P2.NEXT;
             end loop;
        endif;
end UNION;

function CARD (E: in SET) return INTEGER is
P: SET;
N: INTEGER;
begin   N := 0; P := E;
        loop exit when (P = NULL);
             N := N+1; P := P.NEXT;
        end loop;
        return (N);
end CARD;


end SET_MANAGER_LIS;

with text_io, SET_MANAGER_LIS;
use TEXT_IO;

procedure OUR_PROBLEM is
package IIO is new INTEGER_IO(integer); use IIO;
package MY_SET is new SET_MANAGER_LIS(character);
use MY_SET;

WW,WORD1,WORD2 : SET;

procedure READ_WORD (WORD :  in out SET) is
C: character;
begin   get (C);
        loop    exit when C = '.';
             ADD_ELEM (WORD,C); get(C);
        end loop;
end READ_WORD;

begin   INIT_SET (WORD1); INIT_SET(WORD2);
        READ_WORD(WORD1); READ_WORD(WORD2);
        INIT_SET(WORD3);
        UNION (WORD1,WORD2,WW); put(CARD(WW));

end OUR_PROBLEM;

generic
type UNIVERSE is (<>);

package SET_PAC_TABS is
type SET is private;

procedure INIT_SET (E : in out SET);
function IS_EMPTY (E : in SET) return BOOLEAN;
procedure ADD_ELEM (E: in out SET; X: in UNIVERSE);
function BELONG (E : in SET; X: in UNIVERSE)return BOOLEAN;
procedure UNION (E1, E2: in SET; E3: in out SET);
function CARD (E: in SET) return INTEGER;


private
type  SET is array(UNIVERSE) of BOOLEAN;

end SET_PAC_TABS;
```

COMPUTERS IN EDUCATION, F. Lovis and E.D. Tagg (eds.)
Elsevier Science Publishers B.V. (North-Holland)
© IFIP, 1988

THE USE OF A RELATIONAL DATABASE IN THE TEACHING OF COMPUTER SCIENCE.

by Jean-Claude KELLER, Teacher of computer science and physics
Gymnase du Bugnon, Place de l'Ours
Lausanne, Switzerland

Abstract
*Upper secondary schools, known as "Gymnase" in our education system,
refer to the three years period of education between compulsory school
attendance and university. It roughly covers the 16 through 19 years
old age group, and is a multidisciplinary education stage whose main
objective is to encourage students to think rather than to do . This
requires a method of teaching which concentrates on the stimulation of
the student's capacity for abstract thought; and includes in particular an analysis of the concepts of patterns and the "systemic approach". Computer science courses based on the carrying out of software projects and relying on the relational database system can undoubtedly contribute to the attainment of some of these objectives.
Such courses must be based on the study of the notion of pattern and
must emphasize the concepts of:*

- *structure, when organising in different modules and defining their
  properties and links,*
- *parameter definition, when identifying the specific variables of a
  system,*
- *and flow of information, with the essential communication of information taking place within the structure.*

*This paper highlights the principal features of this method of
teaching, proposes a course layout and illustrates these with several
examples of software projects (use of "4ème Dimension" Macintosh software package).*

1. INTRODUCTION.

1.1. At the "gymnase": learning to think rather than to do !

The "gymnase" is a school favouring the
development of general intellectual
skills, the emphasis being on the ability *to think rather than to do*. Placed
in a multidisciplinary environment, the
student exercises his wider intellectual
curiosity and learns to take a much
wider approach to the problems with
which he or she is faced. In this way
then, the student is for example encouraged to develop his ability to analyse
systems, to organize his work, and to
communicate information.

1.2. Computer science: integrated into other courses, or a separate course in itself?

Computer science deals with memory storage, with management and with processing of information, which is why it is
equally relevant to all the various
disciplines taught in the "gymnase".
Thus one can see it as *a melting pot of
interdisciplinarity* and thereby justify
its place in the "gymnase" curriculum.
The real problem is whether or not computer science ought merely to be placed
at the service of other disciplines, or
whether it deserves to be treated as an
autonomous discipline in its own right.
I will argue that it does in fact deserve to be considered as a separate
subject; and I will attempt to show that
from a *relational database*, computer
science projects can add an extra dimension to the educational process; precisely because this particular approach
encourages *thinking rather than doing*.

2. THE STUDY OF PATTERNS: THE MAIN THEME OF A COMPUTER SCIENCE COURSE.

The concept of *pattern* is essential to
the field of *abstraction*, and its study
can form the basis of a computer science
course in the "gymnase".

2.1. Aims: the understanding of notions of structure, of parametrisation, and of flow of information.

The reduction of a given situation to a representative pattern permits the development of the following notions:

- of *structure*, corresponding to the definition of different modules to be situated in order to describe a system,
- of *parametrisation*, corresponding to the description of a system as a series of dimensions or parameters,
- and of the *flux of information* corresponding to the definition of the flow of information in the structure under study.

The ability to grasp these notions, and to be able to organize them; these constitute the principal aims of this computer science course, and it is through *projects* such as those described below that these aims may be achieved. This type of approach has the advantage of providing an initiation in *doing* since the student has the opportunity to construct his pattern and to make it work. He is thus able to actually visualise these notions he has studied. The computer science environment acts as an aid to this sort of development and without doubt encourages *thinking* as opposed to *doing*.

2.2. Means: a relational database

Up until recently computer science teaching limited itself to the study of algorithms, and proceeded necessarily by way of learning a jargon of programming. Inevitably therefore it was aimed uniquely at students intending to follow scientific courses. The working environment was technically stifling and considerably restricted the spread of computer science projects.

Today we are faced with a completely new situation. Thanks to the evolution of micro-computing we have access to a whole *new technology of information* said to be *user-friendly* (available for example on the Macintosh). These new means are the word processor, relational database, software for desktop publishing, spreadsheets, the tools of management, programming workshop etc…; and this new working environment favours the carrying-out of computer science projects. The interface of communication between man and machine is easy to understand and use, making it accessible to all the students, whether they be scientifically oriented, students of literature, or of more general courses. The rich potential of these tools allows the output of conventional algorithmic applications (such as a sorting program) and the extension of the field of study so as to encompass problems of management, of filing, of accountancy, and of the drawing up of documents etc…

Among all these means, *relational databases* are, in my opinion, the tools best suited to the shaping of a computer science course whose aims coincide with the broader educational objectives of the "gymnase". Their use reveals a *structure*, its *parametrisation*, and the *flow of information* within it.

3. A SUGGESTED BASIS FOR A COMPUTER SCIENCE COURSE.

This course can be divided into 3 parts:

A) Getting to grips with the basics of the computer science environement.

This first part ought to be more or less advanced depending on the students' level of general computing knowledge, and on their subject streaming; it is a necessary first step, but does not constitute an end in itself, being principally concerned with explaining the notions of file, of record, of the link between fields, and of global and local variables.

B) Carrying out projects for individuals.

In this, the second part, the students carry out projects on their own which enable them to define the structure of a system (the threading of files), to describe its different component parts (the definition of fields and their contents), and to define the flow of information (the definition of the links between fields). Several examples of projects are given in the following chapter.

C) Carrying out group projects.

In the third part the students are offered sufficiently complex projects for a group to work on together. The point of this sort of project is that each individual must neccessarily organise his work according to the progress of the other group members. An example of a group project is given in the following chapter.

4. A LAYOUT OF SOME SUBJECTS FOR COMPUTER SCIENCE PROJECTS.

4.1. Projects for individuals.

- A study of the notion of file: the idea of an *inventory*.

This is a question of building a structure designed to index objects. So as to make it an easy project, it is decided that these objects have no links with other elements. Two different reports are provided by the system: firstly, a general frame for the management of these objects (fig.1), and secondly, another to appear in an annual report (fig.2). The file needed in order to accomplish this is shown as figure 3.

Inventaire du parc de micro-ordinateurs du Gymnase du Bugnon

salle 008

Disques durs

Modèle	Numéro	Date	Fournisseur	N° série	Remarques	Pannes
DataFrame	DD13	4/87	CSL	Q425660	-	-

Imprimantes à aiguilles

Modèle	Numéro	Date	Fournisseur	N° série	Remarques	Pannes
ImageWriter II	I1	22/12/86	CSL	7030880	avec introducteur feuille à feuille	-

Micro-ordinateurs

Modèle	Numéro	Date	Fournisseur	N° série	Remarques	Pannes
Mac SE	M14	22/06/87	CSL	C7202LVM	-	-

salle 200

Disques durs

Modèle	Numéro	Date	Fournisseur	N° série	Remarques	Pannes
Apple HD20	DD1	13/08/86	CSL	F6280BJM0135Z	-	-
Apple HD20	DD2	11/12/86	CSL	F60903SM0135Z	-	-

Figure 1

Inventaire du parc de micro-ordinateurs

Disques durs

Modèle	N° inventaire	Lieu	N° de série
Apple HD20	DD1	salle 200	F6280BJM0135Z
Apple HD20	DD2	salle 200	F60903SM0135Z
DataFrame 40XP (SC)	DD13	salle 008	Q425660
Promicro 20Mb (SC)	DD3	salle 200	BS001607
Promicro 20Mb (SC)	DD5	salle 200	BS004800

Imprimantes à aiguilles

Modèle	N° inventaire	Lieu	N° de série
ImageWriter II	I1	salle 008	7030880
ImageWriter II	I3	salle 200	7021659

Figure 2

Edition Mode Configuration
Structure de inventaire

INVENTAIRE	
Fournisseur	A
Date achat	D
No de série	A
Lieu	A
No de souris	A
No de clavier	A
Remarques	A
No auxiliaire	A

Figure 3

- A study of the notion of link: the idea of a *class list*.

This project consists of creating a structure which is capable of printing out a class list (fig.4). To accomplish this it is helpful to create 3 different modules: one "STUDENTS" file, one "CLASSES" file, and a "TEACHERS" file; and then to establish links between certain fields (fig.5). These links are vital to the free-flow of information within the structure.

Fichier Edition Mode Saisie Etats

Classe 1C1, conseiller: Jean-Claude KELLER

Titre	Nom	Prénom	Statut
*	BATAILLARD	FRANCOIS	
*	CANDIOTTO	FLAVIO	
	DANG	CHRISTINE	+
*	GAUDERON	ROMAIN	
. . .	. . .	. . .	. . .

Figure 4

Fichier Edition Mode Configuration
Structure de liste classe

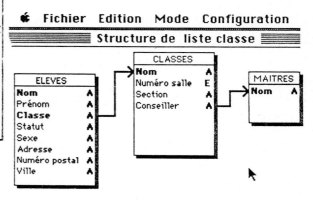

Figure 5

- A study of structures and of links:
the idea of a *directory*.

The aim of this project is to produce a
directory of the names of those teachers
who are able to teach several different
subjects in different schools. One seeks
to obtain 3 separate reports; one
listing of teachers according to their
schools, which also features the various
subjects taught by each teacher (fig.6);

Figure 8

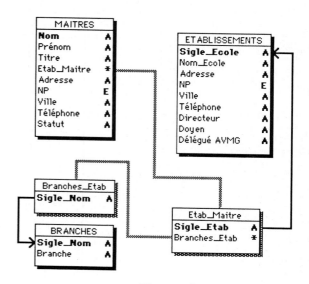

Figure 9

LISTE DES MAITRES PAR ETABLISSEMENT

		GYMNASE DU BUGNON	GBN
Place de l'Ours	1005 LAUSANNE	(021) 20 56 61/62	28 classes

Directeur: DUBOIS Michel   Délégués AVMG   JACCARD-Chilvers Monique
Doyens : BURNAND Pierre Marc   AMIGUET Jean-Daniel
         ZUBER Alain

Maîtres
AESCHLIMANN Denis (t)   philosophie   LAUSANNE (021) 32 65 36
AMIGUET Jean-Daniel (n)   histoire   PULLY   (021) 28 79 31
AMIGUET-Ripper Françoise (n) mathématiques   PULLY   (021) 28 07 30
ARNOLDI Bernard (n)   mathématiques   TARTEGNIN (021) 75 30 69
                                                        (825 30 69)

Figure 6

a second listing of teachers according
to their subjects, but also detailing
the schools in which a particular
subject is taught (fig.7); and a third
general listing giving the address and
telephone number of each person (fig.8).
The structure to be organized is
interesting because it introduces the
notion of "sub-file", and this on 2
levels. The field "SCHOOL_TEACHER",
belonging to the "TEACHER" file is in
fact a "sub-file", because the number of
schools may vary from one teacher to
another. Thus, there will be in this
structure a "sub-record" per school in

LISTE DES MAITRES PAR BRANCHE

			dactylographie
BUHLMANN Sylvette	CESSNOV	CARFAGNI Elmire	ESCL
CHALVERAT-Fleury Michelle	CESSEV	CHEVALLEY Marie-Claire	CESSNOV
CUENOUD Fabienne	ESCL	FASNACHT Gabrielle	ESCL
GIRARDET Françoise	ESCL	GUGGISBERG Marianne	ESCL
MERCIER-Badel Martine	CESSEV	NEUENSCHWANDER Pierrette	CESSEV
			dessin
DARBELLAY Anna-Hélène	GCI	FELIX Maurice	GBV,GM
FONTANNAZ Edouard	GBV	KELLER Pierre	GBN
MOUSSON Marc	CESSNOV	OTTH Marie-Jane	GCH,CESSEV
REYMOND Jean-François	GCI	SAVARY Karien	CESSNOV
WAGNON Aline	GCH		

Figure 7

Figure 10

Sigle_titre mo   Titre Monsieur
Nom KELLER   Prénom Jean-Claude
adresse_rue Av. du Temple 59   Téléphone (021) 33 30 90
NP 1012   Localité LAUSANNE
Sigle_statut t Statut temporaire   Fonction responsable
Sigles_établ GBN   informatique
Branches-ens. physique, informatique   AVMG membre

N°_établ E1   N°_branche B1
Sigle_ét. GBN   Branche physique
Branches_ét. physique,   Et._branche GBN
             informatique

Etablissement GYMNASE DU BUGNON
adresse_ét. Place de l'Ours
NP_ét. 1005   localité_ét. LAUSANNE
tél_ét. (021) 20 56 61/62   NB_classe 28
Directeur_ét. DUBOIS Michel   Doyens_ét. BURNAND Pierre
                                         Marc ZUBER Alain
Délégués AVMG JACCARD-Chilvers Monique
              AMIGUET Jean-Daniel
Délégué SVMS MAYOR Claude-Alain

Figure 10

which the teacher works. Similarly for the field "SUBJECTS", belonging to the "sub-file" "SCHOOL_TEACHER". In the same way it is easy to understand the drawing-up of the links which exist between certain fields from different files (fig.9).

On this theme it is possible to extend this idea and ask the students to create a structure composed of a single file which also provides the three reports described above (fig.10); it is then a case of showing that the information in it is badly managed, given the redundancy that this suggests (for example: if a teacher works in two schools, then he requires two records; and similarly if he teaches two subjects).

4.2. A group project: the theme of the school report.

The automatic processing of *school reports* (fig.11) is a project which lends itself well to group work. It can be easily divided into several elements: there is the management of classes, that of students, and finally that of the reports themselves (fig.12,13,14). It requires the drawing-up of several files, and of several links (fig.15). In order successfully to manage the different elements, certain procedures must be programmed, and therefore only advanced students may attempt this project. Figure 16 shows the dialogue which permits the dialling of a class, and figure 17 shows the procedure which is associated with it.

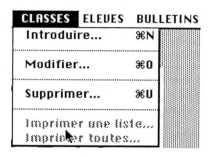

Figure 12

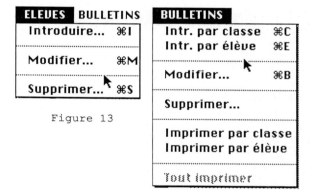

Figure 13

Figure 14

GYMNASE CANTONAL DU BUGNON   Lausanne, le 24.02.88

Tél. (021) 20 56 61
Place de l'Ours
Case postale
1000 LAUSANNE 4

Année scolaire 87-88

Demi-bulletin du premier semestre

Pierrot LALUNE, 1 D 1

Le directeur vous présente ses compliments distingués et vous communique ci-dessous les résultats obtenus au milieu du semestre en cours par l'élève cité en titre. Le conseiller de classe, les maîtres, les doyens et le directeur sont à votre disposition pour tous renseignements

	Coefficient	2	1	0
français		8,5		
allemand		7,2		
anglais		8,4		
italien		7,3		
histoire			6,8	
géographie			7,8	
mathématiques		7,8		
chimie			5,3	
musique				10,0
Totaux partiels:		39,2	19,9	
	2x⌐→		78,4	
Total général:			98,3 (seuil: 78)	

Moyenne: **7,561**

Ainsi, au vu des résultats actuels, Pierrot LALUNE réussit son semestre.

Observations:

Figure 11

---

5. THE SITUATION IN 1987.

Today in "gymnases" in the "canton de Vaud" (Switzerland), computer science teaching occupies only a small slot on the teaching timetable -In actual fact only two periods every fortnight, and for one year only. For the type of course set out above, this state of affairs is far from perfect; for a start, the time allocated is not enough to complete successfully an in-depth study of the structures, and moreover the frequency of these lessons is un-

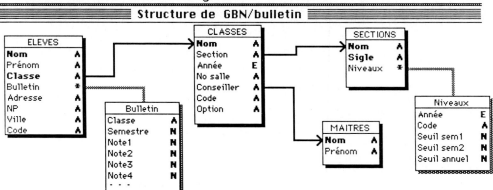

Figure 15

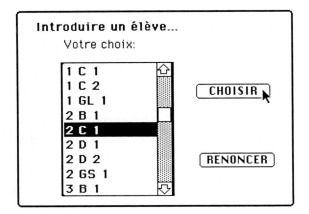

Figure 16

satisfactory. For the time being it has
proved impossible to increase the allocated hours, although it may prove
feasible to concentrate this course into
a single semester, which would be an
altogether better idea. However it still
remains difficult to follow the proposed
course in its entirety; we are forced
therefore to limit its objectives and
content ourselves with aiming at the
first two parts mentioned.

Unfortunately, it looks as though this
situation will persist unchanged for
some years to come; it simply is not
possible to give computer science a more
important place in the curriculum
without neccessitating a reassessment of
the whole school program.

```
` Auteur: J.C. Keller (oct. 87)
` Procédure associée au format Choix_classe
` Elle affiche les classes dans une zone de défilement
` Variables d'entrée:
` vTitre= message affiché dans la boîte de dialogue
` vChoix= type (ex: 2A,...), pour tous vChoix=""
` Variable de sortie: sClasse (nom de la classe)
` Après Choix_classe il faut tester la validité du choix:
` si (OK=1)  traitement... sinon pas de traitement
`
` Avant saisie: sélectionner les CLASSES
Si (Avant saisie)
 ` traitement avant l'affichage du format
 FICHIER DEFAUT([CLASSES])
 $NFICHES:=0
 LISTE0:=0
 Si (vChoix="")
  TOUT SELECTIONNER
 Sinon
  $Debut:=vChoix+" 1"
  $Fin:=vChoix+" 6"
  CHERCHE SUR CLE([CLASSES]Nom±$Debut;$Fin)
 Fin de si
 $NFICHES:=Fiches trouvees
 Si ($NFICHES=0)
  ALERTE("AUCUNE CLASSE DANS LE FICHIER!")
 Sinon
  ` s'il y a des fiches on les trie!
  TRIER SUR INDEX([CLASSES]Nom;<)
  $N:=$NFICHES
   ` initialise LISTE utile à l'affichage des classes
   ` dans la zone de défilement
  Tant que ($N>0)
   LISTE{$N}:=[CLASSES]Nom
   FICHE SUIVANTE
   $N:=$N-1
  Fin tant que

 etc...
```

Figure 17

COMPUTERS IN EDUCATION, F. Lovis and E.D. Tagg (eds.)
Elsevier Science Publishers B.V. (North-Holland)
IFIP, 1988

METHODOLOGY FOR TEACHING BASIC ALGORITHMICS

Jacques COURTIN and Irène KOWARSKI, University of GRENOBLE, FRANCE

Laboratoire de Génie Informatique
IMAG Campus
B.P. 53X, 38041 GRENOBLE CEDEX, FRANCE

We have felt the need to formalize the basis of algorithmics in order to obtain greater efficiency in teaching structured programming to beginners. The emphasis of the course is on construction of correct algorithms rather than on the elements of proof which we introduce at the same time. As well as the usual tools, such as top-down analysis, assertions, invariants, and specification of an algorithm by a precondition and a postcondition, we introduce a "recurrent reasoning", somewhat similar to the inductive reasoning of mathematics. This method has been widely tried out in the last two years, with several different types of audiences ; the results are encouraging.

1. INTRODUCTION

Having taught algorithmics for quite a long time, in particular to the students of the Département Informatique of the Institut Universitaire de Technologie in Grenoble, we have felt the need to formalize the basis of algorithmics in order to obtain greater rigour and efficiency.

Our main aim has therefore been to teach beginners how to program rigorously and correctly, and at the same time to bring them to assimilate correct elementary mechanisms. Once this step has been reached, repeating the same process for elaborating algorithms becomes useless, because we find that our students systematically program in a well structured manner. The emphasis of the course is on construction of correct algorithms rather than on the elements of proof which we introduce at the same time.

2. PROPOSED APPROACH

We use classical tools, many of which are already more or less familiar to our students :
- top-down analysis, which splits a problem into a certain number of sub-problems,
- "recurrent reasoning", somewhat similar to the inductive reasoning of mathematics,
- assertions concerning the state of variables at each step of the algorithm,
- the idea of invariant,
- specification of an algorithm by a precondition and a postcondition,
- a few elementary constructions borrowed from Pascal.

We have limited ourselves voluntarily, in the course and in the first exercises and programming assignments, to a very small number of Pascal constructions : "while" iterations and conditional instructions, procedures and functions, "integer", "character" and "string" elementary types.

We soon introduce the extension to structured types, during exercise and programming sessions, thus allowing the basic algorithms which have been developed in the course to be applied to different practical situations. The other constructions of Pascal : "repeat" and "for" iterations, the "case" selector, etc, are introduced progressively a little later. They are then used correctly without difficulty, giving more concise and elegant programs.

This approach is similar to teaching a foreign language to an adult : beginning with an elementary core, concerning both vocabulary and grammatical constructions, and giving an outline of the theoretical frame of the new grammatical system (declension cases, verbal modes and tenses...). The enrichment of vocabulary and grammatical constructions then follows quite naturally, on a solid basis.

3. ALGORITHM CONSTRUCTION METHOD

1) Analysis of the problem to be solved, definition of *preconditions* : assumptions which the input data must verify, and of *postconditions* : situations which must be verified after execution of the algorithm (values of output data, modifications of given data, sometimes printing of messages...)

2) Complex actions can often be expressed by calls to sub-programs (procedures or functions). At this stage, the sub-program need only be specified, by noting what it requires as input, with preconditions, and what it produces as output, with postconditions. It will be written in full later, according to the classical process of top-down analysis. Just as in mathematics a theorem is proved with the aid of tools which are already proven theorems, the construction of a complex program usually makes use of sub-programs whose structure is already well known. The aim of our course is mainly to give a method for building this "tool-box" which all programmers need.

3) The basic structure of an algorithm can be sequential, conditional, iterative or recursive. If the structure is to be iterative we use a "recurrent reasoning" as follows :

We suppose the problem partially solved, and that an assertion A is verified. This assertion therefore covers a part of the domain of definition of the algorithm (a certain data structure , an interval of integers...).

Then we examine all the possible situations. At least one possible situation is that the domain of definition has actually been entirely covered, or else that some test is now verified ("ending conditions"). The algorithm is then finished, and we can draw conclusions, that is, compute results. In the other possible situations, we execute one or several different actions in order to arrive in a state where the assertion A is again verified. If we begin with an initial state where A is verified, this assertion will therefore be an invariant of the reasoning. The ending conditions of the reasoning lead immediately to the formulation of an iterative instruction, of which A is an invariant.

The initialization which verifies the assertion must then be formulated; this is generally quite simple, it depends on the limits of the domain of the algorithm, and eventually the precondition.

4) Writing the algorithm itself then breaks down into the following steps :
- writing the iterative instruction, with the necessary ending conditions,
- formulating all necessary initializations
- checking, with the help of assertions, that the invariant is maintained,
- after the iteration, both the ending conditions of the iteration and the invariant can be asserted,
- we can then use logical calculus on the above assertions in order to draw conclusions; it is usually easier to use an "exit table" which summarizes all possible situations to arrive at the same conclusions.

We have applied this method to various different data structures : intervals of integers, sequential files, vectors (linear arrays), chained linear lists, *lifo* and *fifo* structures, etc. We have also extended the "recurrent reasoning" to recursive rather than iterative algorithms, first on the linear structures mentioned above, and then on arborescent structures where recursivity is the more natural approach. We also give some systematic methods for transforming recursive algorithms into iterative ones, using an explicit pile, in order to allow the use of programming languages which do not provide recursivity. The examples which follow will serve to illustrate the method.

4. EXAMPLES

4.1. Maximal value in a sequential file

For sequential files f, we use the following notations : f^- and f^+ respectively designate the part which has already been processed and the part which remains to be processed, so that the buffer variable $f^\wedge$ is the first element of f^+, and that the file f can be considered as the concatenation of f^- and f^+ : $f = f^- // f^+$. We use the predefined file opening procedures **reset** and **rewrite**, the input / output procedures **get** and **put**, which make use of $f^\wedge$, and the predicate **eof**. We adopt the following convention : $f^\wedge$ is undefined, and therefore must never be used, when eof(f) is true. The empty file is noted $< >$.

Let f be a non-empty file, with elements of type t. A total order relation noted $<$ can be defined on values of type t.

We want to find a value $\mathbf{m} \in \mathbf{f}$ and such that :
$\forall \mathbf{y} \in \mathbf{f}, \mathbf{m} \geq \mathbf{y}$ (in abbreviation : $\mathbf{m} \geq \mathbf{f}$).

We shall therefore write a function with the following heading :

function maxi (in f : file of t) : t ;

specification $\{ f \neq < > \} \Rightarrow \{ maxi \in f, maxi \geq f \}$

Recurrent reasoning
Suppose the first elements of the file (f^-) have been read, and that we have a variable max which verifies the following assertion :

$\quad$ max $\in f^-$, max $\geq f^-$.

There are then two possible cases :
. $f^+ = < >$
$\quad$ $f^- = f$, the algorithm is finished ($\mathbf{max} \in \mathbf{f}$, $\mathbf{max} \geq \mathbf{f}$).
. $f^+ \neq < >$
$\quad$ We compare the first element of f^+, or $f^\wedge$, to max.
$\quad$ Again there are two possible cases :
.. max $\geq f^\wedge$
$\quad$ Therefore max $\geq f^- // f^\wedge$. By executing **get (f)**, we again
$\quad$ verify the assertion : max $\in f^-$, max $\geq f^-$
.. max $< f^\wedge$
$\quad$ By executing : max := $f^\wedge$ we obtain max $\geq f^- // f^\wedge$.
$\quad$ And then by executing **get (f)** we again verify the
$\quad$ assertion : **max** $\in f^-$, **max** $\geq f^-$.

We shall thus obtain an iteration based on one condition only (end of file), in which we can "factorize" get (f).

Initialization : We suppose f is not empty; so we can initialize max with the first value in the file.
reset (f) ; $\{ f^- = < >, f^+ = < x_1, x_2.\dots > \}$
max := $f^\wedge$; $\{ f^- = < >, f^+ = < x_1, x_2.\dots >, max = x_1 \}$
get (f) ; $\{ f^- = < x_1 >, f^+ = < x_2.\dots >, max = x_1 \}$

$\quad$ **max** $\in f^-$, **max** $\geq f^-$ is then an invariant.

Hence the algorithm :
function maxi (in f : file of t) : t ;
specification $\{ f \neq < > \} \Rightarrow \{ maxi \in f, maxi \geq f \}$
var max : t ;
begin
$\quad$ **reset (f) ;** $\{ \neg eof (f) \}$
$\quad$ **max := $f^\wedge$;**
$\quad$ **get (f) ;** $\{ max \in f^-, max \geq f^- \}$
$\quad$ **while not eof (f) do**
$\quad$ **begin** $\quad \{ max \in f^-, max \geq f^- \}$
$\quad\quad$ **if max $< f^\wedge$ then max := $f^\wedge$;**
$\quad\quad$ **get (f)** $\{ max \in f^-, max \geq f^- \}$
$\quad$ **end ;** $\{ (eof (f), max \in f^-, max \geq f^-)$
$\quad\quad\quad\quad \Rightarrow (max \in f, max \geq f) \}$
$\quad$ **maxi := max** $\{ maxi \in f, maxi \geq f \}$
end ;

4.2. Finding an element in a sorted file

We want to write a predicate with the following heading :
function findsort (in f : file of t ; in val : t) : boolean ;

specification *{ f sorted }* $\Rightarrow$

$$\{(findsort , val \in f) \vee (\neg findsort , val \notin f) \}$$

We can always divide a sorted file f into two sorted subfiles f' and f" such that : $f = f' // f''$, $f' < val \leq f''$
N.B. if $f' = < >$ then $val \leq f$,
if $f'' = < >$ then $f < val$

We can therefore divide the algorithm into two parts : first obtaining $f' = f'$, then checking on equality between val and $f^\wedge$ (if $f'' \neq < >$).

First part : obtaining $f' = f'$
Recurrent reasoning
Suppose the first elements of the file (f^-) have been read, and that they are all smaller than val; the following assertion is verified : $f^- < val$
There are then two possible cases :
. $f^+ = < >$

The algorithm is finished, $f < val$ and $val \notin f$.
. $f^+ \neq < >$

By comparing val to $f^\wedge$ we again find two possible cases :
.. $val > f^\wedge$

By executing **get (f)** we again verify : $f^- < val$
.. $val \leq f^\wedge$

We must stop : we have found the first element of f".

We can now write an iteration with a double condition. In order to avoid "incoherence" at the end of the file, we use a boolean variable "lower". For the initialization, we note that $f^- < val$ is true when $f^- = < >$ (because $\forall x \in < >$, $x < val$).

The **invariant** is therefore $f^- < val$, and the beginning of the algorithm is :

```
reset (f) ;
lower := true ;
while not eof (f) and lower do
    if val > f^ then get (f) else lower := false ;
    { eof (f) v ( ¬ lower) , f⁻ < val }
```

Second part :
Analyzing the following table of conditions on exit of the "while" solves the problem :

eof(f)	¬ lower	result : findsort
true	true	*impossible*
true	false	false
false	true	val = f^
false	false	*impossible*

1st line : eof (f) , ¬ lower
Impossible because of if - else; lower cannot become *false* if eof (f) is *true*.

2nd line : eof (f) , lower
$val > f^-$, $f^+ = < >$, therefore val > f. All the elements of f are smaller than val. **findsort** must therefore be *false*.

3rd line : ¬ eof (f) , ¬ lower
$val \leq f^\wedge$, $f^+ \neq < >$. We can then test $f^\wedge$ in order to ascertain whether **val < f^** or **val = f^** : **findsort := val = f^**

4th line : ¬ eof (f) , lower $\Rightarrow$ (eof (f) v ¬ lower) is not an assertion.

function findsort (in f : file of t ; in val : t) : boolean ;

specification *{ f sorted }* $\Rightarrow$ $\{(findsort , val \in f)$
$$v (\neg findsort , val \notin f) \}$$

```
var lower : boolean ;
begin
    reset (f) ; lower := true ; { f⁻ < val }
    while not eof (f) and lower do
        if val > f^ then get (f) { f⁻ < val }
        else lower := false { val ≤ f^ }
    { f⁻ < val , ( lower , val > f^ ) v ( ¬ lower, val ≤ f^) };
    { eof (f) v ( ¬ lower) , f⁻ < val }
    if not eof (f) { ¬ lower } then findsort := val = f^
        { ( findsort , val ∈ f ) v ( ¬findsort , val ∉ f ) }
    else findsort := false { ( ¬findsort , val ∉ f ) } ;
    { ( findsort , val ∈ f ) v ( ¬findsort , val ∉ f )'}
end ;
```

4.3. Insertion of an element in a sorted vector

Let SV[1..n] be a sorted vector (linear array); we want to insert a new element, whose value is "val", so as to obtain a new sorted vector SV[1..n+1] which contains all the elements of SV[1..n], plus "val". We can go about it in two steps :
- find the position in which we shall insert val,
- then insert it.

procedure insertion (inout SV : vector ; inout n : integer ;
in val : t) ;

specification *{ n ≥ 0 , SV[1..n] sorted }* $\Rightarrow$
{insertion of val in SV , SV[1..n+1] sorted }
```
var place : integer ;
begin
    if n = 0 then
    begin
        SV[1] := val ; n := 1
    end
    else
    begin    { n > 0 }
        place := posit ( SV , n , val ) ;
    { SV[1..place-1] ≤ val < SV[place..n] ,place ∈ [1..n+1] }
        insertplace ( SV , n , val , place )
    end
end ;
```
where **posit** is a function which delivers the position in SV where "val" should be inserted, and **insertplace** a procedure which inserts val in the right place.

Finding the place where the element should be inserted

We want to find an index posit (posit ∈ [1..n+1]) which verifies :

(1) SV[1..posit-1] ≤ val < SV[posit..n]

N.B. For posit = 1, this relation reduces to :

val < SV[1..n] or **val < SV[1]**

and for posit = n+1 it reduces to :

SV[1..n] ≤ val or **SV[n] ≤ val.**

We shall use a dichotomy to find the value of posit : suppose part of the array has been eliminated, so that we have two indices **lo** and **hi** which verify assertion

A : SV[1..lo] ≤ val < SV[hi..n]

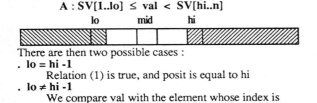

There are then two possible cases :

. **lo = hi -1**
> Relation (1) is true, and posit is equal to hi

. **lo ≠ hi -1**
> We compare val with the element whose index is **mid = (lo+hi)div2**. Then we set either lo or hi to mid, thus preserving assertion A.

Initialization : We first eliminate the border cases where posit is equal to 1 or n+1; then, knowing that

SV[1] ≤ val < SV[n] , we initialize assertion A by setting lo to 1 and hi to n. Assertion A is therefore an invariant.

function posit (in SV : vector ; in n : integer ; in val : t) : integer ;

specification *{ n > 0 , SV[1..n] sorted}* ⇒

{ posit ∈[1..n+1] , SV[1..posit-1] ≤val < SV[posit..n] }
var lo , hi , mid : integer ;
begin
   if SV[1] > val then posit := 1   *{ val < SV[1..n] }*
   else
      if SV[n] ≤ val then posit := n+1 *{SV[1..n] ≤val}*
      else
      begin
        lo:=1; hi := n ; *{ SV[1..lo] ≤val < SV[hi..n] }*
        while lo ≠ hi -1 do
        begin
           mid := (lo + hi) div 2 ;
           if SV[mid] ≤ val
             then lo := mid *{ SV[1..lo] ≤val }*
             else hi := mid *{ val < SV[hi..n]}*
           { SV[1..lo] ≤val < SV[hi..n] }
        end ;
        { (lo = hi-1 ,SV[1..lo] ≤val < SV[hi..n])
        ⇒ SV[1..hi-1] ≤val < SV[hi..n] }
        posit := hi
      { SV[1..posit-1] ≤val < SV [posit..n] ,posit ∈ [2..n] }
      end ;
   {(val < SV[1..n] , posit = 1)
   v (SV[1..n] ≤val , posit = n+1)
   v (SV[1..posit-1] ≤val <SV[posit..n] , posit∈ [2..n])
     ⇒ (SV[1..posit-1] ≤val < SV[posit..n] ,
     posit ∈ [1..n+1]) }
end ;

Insertion of the element

We now know the place where the element must be inserted. The new vector SV[1..n+1] is equal to
   SV[1..posit-1] // val // SV'[posit+1..n+1]
where   SV'[posit+1..n+1] = SV[posit..n]

We simply must shift all the elements of SV [posit..n] one position to the right, and then affect "val" to SV [posit] .

procedure insertplace (inout SV : vector ; inout n : integer ;
                 in val : t ; in place : integer) ;

specification *{ SV[1..n] sorted}* ⇒
{ insertion of "val" in SV[place] after shifting
             SV[place..n] one position to the right}
var i : integer ;
begin
   for i := n downto place do
      SV[i + 1] := SV[i] ;
   n := n+1 ;
   SV[place] := val
end ;

4.4. Sorting by segmentation, or Quicksort (Hoare)

Suppose we want to sort a vector V[lo..hi] (lo < hi) ; we shall begin by rearranging the elements of V in such a way that V is segmented into three sub-vectors : all the elements to the left of an index "place" (place ∈ [lo..hi]) will be smaller than or equal to V[place], while those to the right of "place" are greater than V[place].

lo	place	hi

≤ V[place]　　　　> V[place]

     V[lo ..place-1] ≤ V[place] < V[place+1..hi]
We now notice that :
1°) V[place] is correctly placed,
2°) V[lo..place-1] and V[place+1..hi] can now be sorted separately.

If we have a procedure called **segmentation (V, lo , hi , place)** which rearranges V in the manner described above, the sorting algorithm can then be written recursively :

procedure quicksort (inout V : vector ; in lo , hi : integer) ;
specification *{ }* ⇒ *{ V[lo..hi] sorted}*
var place : integer ;
begin
   if lo < hi then
   begin
      segmentation (V, lo , hi , place) ;
      quicksort (V, lo , place-1) ;
      quicksort (V, place+1 , hi)
   end
end ;

In order to sort a vector V[1..n] , this algorithm must be executed with lo and hi set respectively to 1 and n :
        quicksort (V, 1 , n).

Writing the segmentation procedure

We choose a "pivot" value **elem** which belongs to V[lo..hi]. Then we exchange elements in order to rearrange them in such a manner that :
$$V[lo..j\text{-}1] \leq elem < V[j\text{+}1..hi]$$

If no property of the elements of V is known, the pivot can be chosen arbitrarily. We decide to use V[lo] and to traverse V[lo..hi] from left to right.

Suppose we have already processed a certain number of elements, and that the following assertion is verified :
(1)   V [lo..i-1] ≤ elem < V [j+1..hi]

Nothing is known about V[i..j]. There are two possible cases :
. **i = j+1**
Assertion (1) becomes : **V[lo..j] ≤ elem < V[j+1..hi].** But elem =V[lo] , and by exchanging **V[lo]** and **V[j]** we obtain **V[lo..j-1] ≤ V[j] < V[j+1..hi].** The algorithm is finished.
. **i ≤ j**
Again we have two possible situations :
.. **V[i] ≤ elem**
Then V[lo..i] ≤ elem, and with **i := i+1** assertion (1) is again verified
.. **V[i] > elem**
by exchanging **V[i]** and **V[j]** we obtain V[j..hi] > elem, and with **j := j-1** assertion (1) is again verified

Initialization :

By setting **elem := V[lo] ; i := lo + 1 ; j := hi ;** we can write the **invariant** : V[lo..i-1] ≤ elem < V[j+1..hi].

```
procedure segmentation ( inout V : vector ;
                in lo , hi : integer ; out place : integer ) ;
specification { lo < hi }  ⇒ { place ∈ [lo..hi],
             V[lo..place-1] ≤ V[place] < V[place+1..hi] }
var   i , j : integer ;
      elem : t ;
begin
   elem := V[lo] ;
   i := lo+1 ;
   j := hi ;
   { V[lo..i-1] ≤ elem < V[j+1..hi] }
   while i ≤ j do
   begin
      if V[i] ≤  elem then
         i := i+1 { V[lo..i-1] ≤ elem }
      else
      begin { V[i] > elem }
         exchange ( V [i] , V[j] ) ; { V[j] > elem }
         j := j-1 { V[j+1..hi] > elem }
      end
      { V[lo..i-1] ≤ elem < V[j+1..hi] }
   end ;
   { ( i = j+1 , V[lo..i-1] ≤ elem < V[j+1..hi] )
        ⇒ V[lo..j] ≤ elem < V[j+1..hi] }
```

```
   exchange ( V[lo] , V[j] ) ;
   { V[lo..j-1] ≤ V[j] < V[j+1..hi] }
   place := j
end ;
```

It is fairly obvious that this algorithm entails some unnecessary permutations. It is quite possible to refine the reasoning in order to minimize the number of permutations.

4.5. Insertion of an element in an ordered binary tree (Example of reasoning leading to a recursive algorithm)

A node in a binary tree is defined by the following type declarations :
```
type  pointer  = ^node;
      node     = record
                    info : t ;
                    left , right : pointer
                 end;
```

A tree is designated by a pointer to its root ; the sequence of values at the nodes, in infixed order, is designated by root[+] . If this sequence is sorted, we say that the tree is ordered.

We want to insert an element in a non-empty ordered binary tree so that it remains ordered. As in all algorithms for insertion in a data structure, there are two steps :
. finding the place for insertion,
. inserting the element in that place.

```
procedure insertion ( in root : pointer ; in val : t ) ;

specification{root ≠ nil, root[+] ordered }  ⇒ { addition of
                           val in root[+] , root[+] ordered}
var address : pointer ;
begin
   address := place ( root , val ) ;
   insert ( val , address)
end ;
```

Finding the place for insertion :

We must find a node of the tree, which, after insertion, will be the "father" of the node containing the new element. This "father" node must verify :
  (father^.info ≤ val , father^.right = nil)
v (father^.info > val , father^.left = nil)
It is either a leaf, or a node with only one sub-tree. In order to find it, we shall carry out a search by dichotomy for the new element, and stop on the last obtainable node.

Noting that the tree is not empty, we reason as follows : there are two possible situations :
. **val < root^.info**
the place of val is therefore in the left sub-tree, there are again two possible cases :
.. **root^.left[+] is empty**
the algorithm is finished, we have found the node which is to become the father of a new node, on its left, containing val
.. **root^.left[+] is not empty**
we repeat the process with a recursive call to the same procedure, where the tree is replaced by its left sub-tree

. val $\geq$ root^.info
the place of val is therefore in the right sub-tree; the same reasoning as above applies to the right sub-tree.

function place (in root : pointer; in val : t) : pointer;

specification   { root $\neq$ nil, root^ ordonned } $\Rightarrow$
    {(val < place^.info , place^.left = nil)
v (val $\geq$ place^.info , place^.right= nil) }
begin   { root $\neq$ nil }
  if val < root^.info **then**
    if root^.left = nil **then**
        {val < root^.info , root^.left = nil}
      place := root
    else
      place := place (root^.left , val)
  else   { val $\geq$ root^.info }
    if root^.right = nil **then**
        {val $\geq$ root^.info , root^.right = nil}
      place := root
    else
      place := place (root^.right , val)
end ;

Insertion of the element in the tree :
We must create a leaf with **val** in the information field and then insert the leaf as a left or right descendant of the father node (the information concerning the side could of course have been passed down from the "place" procedure, but it is just as simple to find it again here).

procedure insert (in val : t ; in address : pointer) ;
var leaf : pointer ;
begin
  new (leaf) ; leaf^.info := val ;
  leaf^.left := nil ; leaf^.right := nil ;
  if address^.info $\leq$ val **then**
    address^.right := leaf
  else
    address^.left := leaf
end ;

5. CONCLUSION

The method for construction of algorithms which is presented in this paper has been widely tried out in the last two years, with several different types of audiences :
- subgraduate students in first year or "special year" (a more condensed course for students with some University experience) of the Département Informatique of the Institut Universitaire de Technologie in Grenoble,
- students of the same level, completing their education at evening classes,
- computer professionals, college graduates or not,
- university teachers : specialized in all branches of science, social sciences, literature, economy, ..., with or without any basic knowledge about computers,
- teachers in computer science at higher technical schools.

It is difficult to evaluate the results very precisely; nevertheless, we find them quite encouraging. Even when the "recurrent reasoning" is not formulated perfectly, the effort in analysis and reflection which it has entailed enables the student to write a well structured program, with results which are usually correct. The classical errors we used to find in so many programs have more or less disappeared : loops which are never entered or which never end, mistakes in initializations so that loops are executed the wrong number of times, recursive forms without a stop point, etc.

People already experienced in programming who have used our methods are often surprised by the quality of the algorithms they obtain and the ease with which the resulting programs are perfected.

REFERENCES

<1> A.V. AHO, J.E. HOPCROFT, J.D. ULLMANN. Data structures and algorithms. Addison Wesley 1983.
<2> J. ARSAC. Les bases de la programmation. Dunod, Paris 1983 (French)
<3> P. BERLIOUX, PH. BIZARD. Construction, preuve, et évaluation des programmes, Dunod, Paris 1983 (French)
<4> J. COURTIN, I. KOWARSKI, Initiation à l'Algorithmique et aux structures de données, Tome 1 : Programmation structurée et structures de données élémentaires, Tome 2 : Récursivité et structures de données avancées, Dunod, Paris 1987 (French)
<5> J. COURTIN, J. VOIRON. Introduction à l'algorithmique et aux structures de données. Cours polycopié, IUT B Grenoble 1974 (French)
<6> E. W. DIJKSTRA. A discipline of programming. Prentice Hall 1976.
<7> R. W. FLOYD. Assigning meaning to programs. Proc. AMS symposium in Applied Mathematics, vol 19 1967, pp 19-31.
<8> GREGOIRE. Cours d'informatique-Programmation. Tomes 1 et 2. C.N.A.M Cycle A. ESI 1984 (French)
<9> P. GROGONO. Programming in Pascal. Addison Wesley 1980.
<10> C.A.R. HOARE. An axiomatic basis for computer programming. Com. ACM, vol 12, oct 1969, pp 576-583.
<11> C.A.R. HOARE. Procedures and parameters : an axiomatic approach. Lecture notes in Mathematics 188. Springer Verlag 1971, pp 102-116.
<12> D.E. KNUTH. The art of computer programming. Vol 1 : Fundamental Algorithms. Addison Wesley 1969.
<13> D.E. KNUTH. The art of computer programming. Vol 3 : Sorting and searching. Addison Wesley 1973.
<14> N. WIRTH. Algorithms + data structures = programs. Prentice Hall 1976.
<15> N. WIRTH. Introduction à la programmation systématique. Masson, Paris 1977 (French)

COMPUTERS IN EDUCATION, F. Lovis and E.D. Tagg (eds.)
Elsevier Science Publishers B.V. (North-Holland)
IFIP, 1988

EUCLIDES 1: a program for geometry in CAI.

Albert Fàbrega

Programa d'Informàtica Educativa, Departament d'Ensenyament,
Generalitat de Catalunya, Jonqueres 2,3er.,3a.
08003 Barcelona, Spain

We present the program Euclides 1 for teaching computer assisted elementary plane geometry. The philosophy of the program is to create a tool which is easy to use in experimentation with geometric constructions done with a ruler and compass. It is an interactive program that obeys the commands given by the user. These commands are chosen from a well defined list. In the last few years the program has been tested with groups of students, and the results and opinions have been satisfactory. It is now being supplied to all the public schools which are administered by the Catalan autonomous government. We also provide the open line directions in which research on Euclides 1 is proceeding.

1. THE COMPUTER AND THE TEACHING OF GEOMETRY

The generally accepted point of view of the computer is that it is a tool. That is to say, an object that makes it easier or possible to perform tasks that otherwise are very difficult or impossible. In some cases learning how to use a tool is in itself a difficult task. The question is whether the effort dedicated to learning how to use this tool will allow an improvement of the results obtained with the old tools. In relation to this point, an obvious fact concerning teaching is that the tool must free us from the secondary aspects of the problem, and allow the user to concentrate on the relevant aspects.

In general it is characteristic of all tools that they require, to a greater or lesser extent, a level of manual ability. One requires training to obtain this ability, and this generally demands a great deal of attention, by the user, while he works on it. Many sheets of paper must be torn up before the child can use the compass with a certain amount of ease; and what's worse, even in that case he must pay special attention and be very careful each time he uses it. If he is making a construction with a ruler and compass this can distract him from the central aspects of the problem.

In this sense the computer is a tool which requires very little manual ability.

On the other hand, the way people make inferences and conjectures is a common problem found when teaching geometry and mathematics. One theorem and its demonstration cannot be questioned from the logical point of view, but how has that result been discovered? Geometry also has its experimental stage as Eves [1] indicates. A complete geometric exercise should have: experimentation, conjecture and theorem. In the first stages of teaching geometry this must be done with the geometric objects which are tangible for the child : shapes.

Suppose the geometry of a triangle is being studied, and that we propose that the student "discovers", by himself, that the three perpendicular bisectors of the sides of a triangle meet at one and the same point. Thus we must insist that the child repeat this exercise until he intuitively "sees" the conjecture that must be done: draw a triangle, determine the midpoints of the three sides, and draw the perpendiculars, to each side, that pass through the midpoints. To do this manually requires time and manual skills on the student's part. Most certainly, the time required depends on the ability of each student, but the student must have this ability in order to be able to draw the required lines passing through the same point. Randomness is also important if we wish to establish a general result, because it is clear that when humans have to draw triangles they tend to draw them equilateral because of reason of order, aesthetics, and symmetry. All these aspects can force the teacher to abandon the idea of having his students experiment, and that he or she decides to present the results in the traditional form: theorem and demonstration. Precisely what we are presenting here is a tool that will allow the teacher and the student to find it easy and desirable to confront the task of geometric experimentation.

2. THE PROGRAM EUCLIDES 1

The basic objects which the program Euclides 1 manipulates are points and segments. All the points have a label which is an alphabetic character and serves as a reference. The program is interactive, and it accepts a set of commands, given by the user, to which Euclides 1 responds with actions. In general the commands must start by indicating the function to be performed (the head of the command), and must end with the parameters which indicate on which objects it must be performed (the tail of the command). Certain commands randomly generate an object and don't have an tail.

For example, the experience about the perpendicular bisectors of a triangle, described in the previous section, can be done by Euclides 1 in the following manner:

Command	Action
triangle	A random triangle with its vertices labelled A,B,C, appears on the screen.
midpt(A,B)	On the screen appears a point labelled D that is the midpoint of side AB.
midpt (A,C)	On the screen appears a point labelled E that is the midpoint of side AC.
midpt(B,C)	On the screen appears a point labelled F that is the midpoint of side BC.
perp(AB,D)	A line that passes through D and is perpendicular to AB is drawn.
perp(AC,E)	A line that passes through E and is perpendicular to AC is drawn.
perp(BC,F)	A line that passes through F and is perpendicular to BC is drawn.

In reality the constructions which can be performed by this program are those that use a ruler and compass. In this sense of 30 possible commands, the three basic ones are:
Intll (line 1, line 2) which determines the intersection of line 1 with line 2. Line 1 and line 2 are strings of two characters each which correspond to two labels on the line.
Intlc (line, center, radius) which determines the intersection of a line with a circle. The first parameter consists of the labels of two points on the line. The second parameter is the label of the center of the circle, and the third one consists of the labels that determine the segment that is the radius of the circle.
Intcc (center 1, radius 1, center 2, radius 2) which determines the intersection of two circles. The significance of these parameters should be obvious.

The program maintains a file of all the commands that the user has typed, and of all the points which have been generated as a result of these commands. It also registers the graphics of the construction and allows for later editing.

We will now provide three examples of geometric constructions made with this program. The meaning and function of all the commands can be found in [2] and [3].

Circumcircle Construction

Commands	Points
triangle	A B C

midpt(A,C)	D
perp(AC,D)	E
midpt(B,C)	F
perp(BC,F)	G
midpt(A,B)	H
perp(AB,H)	I
intll(HI,FG)	J
circle(J,JA)	

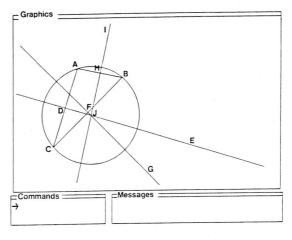

Fig. 1. Circumcenter of a triangle

Regular Pentagon Construction

Commands	Points	Values
sitpoint	A B	
line(A,B)		
circle(A,AB)		
perp(AB,A)	C	
intlc(AC,A,AB)	D	
midpt(A,C)	E	
intlc(AC,E,EB)	F G	
intlc(AB,A,AF)	H I	
cutseg(A,H)	J	2/1
circle(A,AJ)		
orto(AC,C)	K	
intlc(CK,A,AJ)	L M	
intcc(A,AJ,M,ML)	N	
intcc(A,AJ,N,ML)	O	
intcc(A,AJ,O,ML)	P	
segment(M,L)		
segment(M,N)		
segment(N,O)		
segment(O,P)		
segment(P,L)		

Construction of a moulding

Commands	Points	Values
sitpoint A B C D E F G H I J K L		
midpt(D,E)	M	
midpt(M,D)	N	
orto(MD,N)	O	
intll(AD,NO)	P	
midpt(M,E)	Q	
orto(DE,Q)	R	

```
intll(QR,PM)            S
pen                                 2
arc(P,PD,M,D)
arc(S,SM,M,E)
midpt(E,H)              T
arc(T,TE,E,H)
pen                                 1
orto(IJ,L)              U
intll(IJ,LU)            V
intlc(LU,V,VI)          W X
intcc(I,IV,W,IV)        Y
pen                                 2
arc(Y,YI,W,I)
segment(I,J)
segment(I,H)
segment(H,G)
segment(E,F)
segment(W,L)
segment(L,K)
segment(A,D)
segment(A,B)
segment(D,C)
segment(B,K)
```

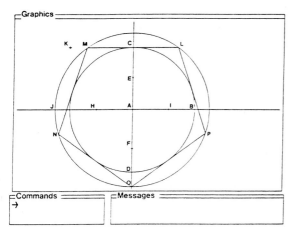

Fig. 2 Construction of a regular pentagon

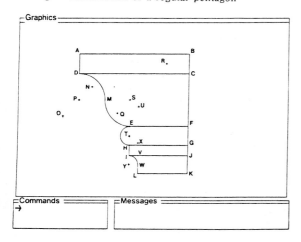

Fig. 3 Construction of a moulding

3. USE OF THE PROGRAM

In accordance with our findings we suggest the following work methods for the use of Euclides 1 in class.

1.- The problem suggested for study is, for example, to construct the three perpendicular bisectors of the sides of a triangle.

2.- The student must figure out the construction, and he must also figure out the sequence of orders for Euclides 1 that will produce the construction.

3.- If this is the case, the student must repeat the construction as often as necessary for him to think of a geometric property it has.

4.- In either case he must attempt to prove the geometric property he has thought of (if there is one), or try to demonstrate why the construction created is correct.

For example, it is clear that in the problem with the perpendicular bisectors there is a geometric property to be conjectured, and thus the student must rigorously attempt to prove this property in the last stage of his work. On the other hand, with the problem about the regular pentagon there is nothing to conjecture, the student only needs to effectively demonstrate why the construction is a regular one.

In the second stage of the previous procedure the student has available all of Euclides 1's commands. This introduces an undesirable problem which is that certain problems become trivial just as a pocket calculator makes multiplication trivial. In this sense, we consider it very convenient to propose problems that have as one of their conditions a limitation on the use of commands. For example, to draw a line passing through an exterior point and parallel to another line is trivial because Euclides 1 has a command that with the line and any point constructs the parallel asked for. Still we must give students this problem, but we should do it with restrictions such as, not using commands for perpendiculars and parallels, and only using commands for circles and lines. We might even give them more drastic limitations such as only using a fixed compass, this is to say, circles with one radius that is fixed beforehand.

The idea behind all this is to provoke "mental gymnastics" in the student, and to force him to solve problems utilizing different combinations of the available "tools". This is not new, everyone considers it important that people know how to multiply even if it is possible to do it by pressing the buttons on a calculator.

For the moment Euclides 1 has been used in some secondary schools with small groups of students learning euclidean geometry following the general directions indicated above. Generally, an increase in knowledge and motivation in applied geometry has been noticed among the pupils and now there are a lot of teachers that want to use it in their schools. The program is very versatile, so it can be integrated in a wide range of curricula going from primary to high school.

4. FURTHER DEVELOPMENTS

Euclides 1 is not designed for geometric
constructions which are "professional" or complex,
nor for any type of graphics design. It is an
essentially educational program. In practice this
makes it practically impossible to construct, using
this programme, curves as a geometric locus of points
(conics,conchoids,etc.). Also, some complex
constructions with a ruler and compass become so
complicated with Euclides 1 that what seemed to be
simple, and was supposed to liberate us from
secondary details, becomes a monster of details. To
cover this area more ambitiously, the author in
conjunction with A. Montes and A. Parra, has designed
a module of geometric functions which can be used
with languages of high level; such as, Pascal or
Modula-2, and permits us to attempt, with ease,
rather sophisticated geometric constructions. This
module is Euclides 2, and the present version of
Euclides 1 is only one of the many applications of
Euclides 2. With Euclides 2 we have constructed
conics using the properties they have and not
analytically. We have also constructed conchoids,
spirals, and a solution to Apollonius's problem which
is described in [4] and can be seen in fig. 4. The
complete description of Euclides 2 can be found in
[5]. Presently Euclides 2 is in its final debugging
stage,and the authors are developing applications for
CAI and the "professional" field.

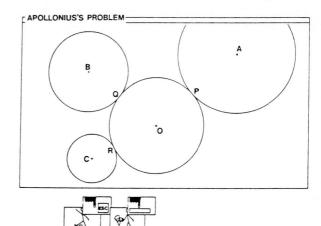

Fig. 4. Apollonius's problem

5. REFERENCES

[1] Eves,H., Great Moments in Mathematics (Before
    1650),The Dolciani Mathematical Expositions,
    No.5, The Mathematical Association of America,
    1980.
[2] Fàbrega,A., Euclides 1: Manual de referència,
    Barcelona, 1987. (Catalan)
[3] Fàbrega,A., Euclides i la Tortuga, Edicions UPC,
    Barcelona, 1987. (Catalan)
[4] Heath,T., A History of Greek Mathematics, Dover
    Publications Inc.,New York, 1981.
[5] Montes,A., Fàbrega,A., Parra,A., Euclides II:
    Manual de referència, FIB report 87/01,
    Universitat Politècnica de Catalunya, 1987.
    (Catalan)

COMPUTERS IN EDUCATION, F. Lovis and E.D. Tagg (eds.)
Elsevier Science Publishers B.V. (North-Holland)
© IFIP, 1988

INTELLIGENT COMPUTER AIDED MATHEMATICAL PROBLEM SOLVING IN A MODIFIED LOGO ENVIRONMENT

Andrew Jones and Michael Thorne,

Department of Computing Mathematics,
University College, Cardiff, Wales, UK.

ABSTRACT

In this paper we describe the development of an Intelligent Computer Assisted Learning environment using Smalltalk. We assess the general desirability of Smalltalk, and also its suitability for this type of application. In our environment, children use a programming language we have designed (called NOLOG) as a means of expressing solutions to number-theoretical problems. There is also an intelligent, expert-system based, help facility. We shall discuss some of the considerations necessary when developing such an expert system. Initial tests have given us good reason to hope that NOLOG is teachable and learnable, and may make a useful contribution to their mathematical development.

1. INTRODUCTION

We are interested in assisting children to develop their mathematical problem-solving capabilities. To this end, we have designed and implemented an Intelligent Computer Assisted Learning environment using Smalltalk [1] as an implementation vehicle. The basis of this environment is the programming language NOLOG. This enables children to produce a program which corresponds to a solution of a number-theoretical problem. However, our other desire is to make the programming environment 'intelligent' by helping them to produce these programs.

Research in ICAL often necessarily addresses a rather limited problem domain. We wanted to develop a system which would allow pupils to get help whilst working on as wide a set of problems as possible. In particular, we wished to find ways of representing the relatively small amount of programming knowledge we needed to impart efficiently and economically. We received inspiration from PROUST [2], which helps students write PASCAL programs. There, information concerning the way particular types of program could have been written is stored in the computer. When a program is submitted for compilation it is compared with the patterns which might be expected for a correct program. Then, if the comparison fails to find the fault an attempt is made to match the program with patterns for bugged versions of the program. Hence the patterns for a particular program need to be entered before help can be given for solving that problem. In our work we have tried to build on this idea so that it may no longer be necessary to have such prior knowledge.

2. NOLOG - A LOGO-LIKE ENVIRONMENT FOR NUMBER THEORY

2.1 Designing the system user interface

NOLOG retains from LOGO the idea of an object that moves under program control, except that in NOLOG we are moving aeroplanes ('planes') from one 'island' to another (this will be developed in sections 2.3 and 2.4). There is a NOLOG system window, which has two sub-windows. In one window the child types in the program, and in the other window the movement of the planes is observed. Another window allows access to the problem library where the child can browse among existing solved problems, and, if necessary, copy extracts from those solutions into the child's own solution for the problem on which he or she is working. Hence, a child can use building blocks from the library in order to solve a given problem. Figure 1 shows these two windows.

Text is entered by the pupil via an editor which is functionally very simple: a scroll bar can be moved using the mouse to view the required part of the program, and the mouse is used to place the 'caret' (text insertion point marker) wherever the child wishes to type. The only way that text can be deleted is by pressing the 'rubout' key in order to delete the character to the left of the caret.

As should be clear, a very important aspect of designing the NOLOG system was that we should provide far more than just a programming language. It was possible to attempt this because we had at our disposal a machine with the capability to run Smalltalk and, hence, a far cry from the dumb terminal on which some of us learned to program.

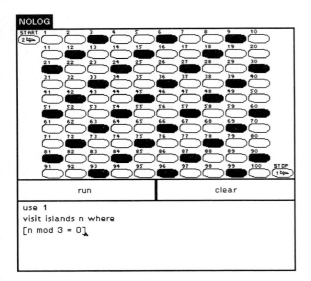

Figure 1

2.2 Reasons for restriction of problem domain

Initially we contemplated the possibility of producing some general kind of mathematical expert system. However, this is obviously a very difficult thing to achieve. There are books (e.g. [3]) which describe hints and techniques for problem solving, but they tend to be quite general, and the mapping onto a massive range of different kinds of problems is not easy to create. Even Burton's [4] relatively precise decomposition of problems into the techniques necessary to solve them is difficult to express in a form which can enable a program to offer sufficiently detailed advice about a given problem.

We also wanted to experiment with transformation of a problem statement by a process of text replacement, but found that when we took some problems at ran-

dom and tried to work out what transformations would be desirable, all the rules which we produced were much too specific to be of general use. In fact, they were not of much use for any problem other than the particular one for which they were invented. So we had a set of general rules which were difficult to apply specifically, and a set of specific rules which were difficult to generalize.

Consequently we felt that expert help for general mathematical problem-solving may not be impossible but it is difficult to see how to do this at present. As a result, we decided to restrict our problem domain in the hope that given the experience which we should gain through this project, we may be able to do something more general in the future.

Eventually we decided to invent a microworld [5] for number-theoretical problems, and use this as our problem domain. It had to be flexible enough to be interesting, and restricted enough so that our software could give the child user an intelligent response.

2.3 What is NOLOG?

A starting point was Papert's LOGO [6]. He conceived this as a 'microworld' for plane geometry. We have retained the concept of having some object whose movement can be controlled by writing a program. However, we have introduced some significant changes.

We provide a grid of islands numbered sequentially from 1 to 100. Planes fly from island to island under program control, and land on islands to create a pattern. The islands are initially outlined, and when a plane lands on one, it is filled in. The goal of a NOLOG problem is to write a program which produces the appropriate pattern of visited islands.

We can define a pattern of islands to be visited in two ways:

(i) By giving the child a picture of the pattern of islands to be produced, such as a triangle.

(ii) By specifying algebraically which islands are to be visited. For example, we could ask for a program to visit all odd-numbered islands or even all prime-numbered islands. In this case, we can arrange the problem so that the pattern produced is 'interesting'. A program to visit every odd-numbered island would result in a pattern of straight parallel lines of visited islands.

2.4 The Language

The major considerations initially were how we should design the programming language and how we should design the user interface. We wanted to ensure that the programming language was teachable, flexible, and not too complex. LOGO has been used successfully with children, and hence the decision to base our own language on the syntax of LOGO.

We commenced with what was essentially a subset of LOGO's capabilities, redefined to make sense in the plane-and-island world that we have created. Examples of commands which could actually be sent to the plane are: **take_off**, **land** and **fly** <no. of islands>. **fly** has as its argument an expression which determines the distance the plane is to move. It is relative to the current island, i.e. the number of steps the plane is to move. **take_off** is included, meaning that a landed plane must take off before flying anywhere, essentially so that we can tell a consistent story to the children (see example 1).

Problem

Write a program to cause 1 to visit islands 5, 10 and 16.

Solution

```
use 1
take_off fly 5 land
take_off fly 5 land
take_off fly 6 land
```

Example 1

Control structures were essentially those of LOGO, but we included the common extension that **repeat** could be followed by **forever**. This did not quite mean *forever* in fact, for we deemed that when a plane went off the end of the grid, it was considered to be no longer active. Then as soon as it was certain that there were no more active planes, and none were to become active due to another iteration of the repeat loop, the loop was exited (see example 2).

Problem

Write a program to cause plane 1 to visit every island that is a multiple of 2.

Solution

```
use 1
repeat forever [take_off fly 2 land]
```

Example 2

Hence we were able to write solutions to some simple problems, such as visiting every even-numbered island. Somehow we needed to allow variables if we were to enable the solution of a sufficiently large number of problems. Our first attempt was to make the use of variables explicit in some way. There was a 'flight recorder' which recorded the islands visited so far, and a 'base', which was a single variable holding one number (see example 3).

Problem

Write a flight plan to visit all islands which belong to the sequence: 1,1,2,3,5,8,13,21,.... (the Fibonacci numbers).

Solution

```
take_off fly 1 land
take_off fly 1 land
repeat forever
[read_recorder 2    (obtain number of last but
                     one island visited)
 take_off fly answer land]
```

Example 3

We were dissatisfied with this approach, since it did not give us easy ways to gain access to *sets* of 'interesting' numbers. For example, we may wish to visit each island which is a *function* of a prime number. This would not have been possible using the framework which we initially provided.

One possibility was to pursue the idea of programming by constraints. This has been done in Prolog-like languages [7]. Our version of this was to introduce 'bags' of numbers. Thus you may have a 'bag' of prime numbers or a 'bag' of multiples of 2. These bags may be used to define other bags and, eventually, bags exist from which the islands to be visited can be calculated. The basic idea is that one starts off with a bag full of all integers from 1 to 100 inclusive, and then specifies conditions which must all hold on these numbers (i.e. there is a *conjunction* of conditions). It is possible to specify a *negated* condition using **sift**, which 'sifts' out those numbers which satisfy the specified conditions.

These bags can then be used with the 'visit islands' construct, which is how a child specifies the islands to be visited in a constraint-based way. Example 4 will clarify this.

This allows us to deal with rather complicated types of patterns without too much difficulty. We have retained the old base and flight recorders so far, since we have not found a way of dealing with Fibonacci numbers, for example, using the constraint-based approach. The problem is, that we need to be able to define our set of numbers without resorting to an inductive (sequential) approach.

Problem

Write a NOLOG program to visit all islands whose
values are the sums of 2 primes.

Solution

```
define bag multiples(x)
bag contains n where
n mod x = 0
end

define bag primes
bag contains n where
sift [n in multiples(2)    n > 2]
sift [n in multiples(3)    n > 3]
sift [n in multiples(5)    n > 5]
sift [n in multiples(7)    n > 7]
sift [n = 1]
end
```

(Now follows the main program)

```
visit islands n where
[a in primes
 b in primes
 n is a+b]
```

Example 4

There are implementation difficulties and complica-
tions. We decided to reduce these by specifying that
at all times, a bag only contains numbers between 1
and 100 inclusive. The hope is that if the children are
clearly told that any bag will only ever contain numbers in this range, it should cause no difficulties, especially if we choose our problems so that any solution
would naturally assume such bags.

2.5 Results of pilot studies

We have been encouraged by the success of our pilot
studies. We have tried out our system with student
teachers, practising teachers, a local authority advisor
and in ordinary classroom situations.

They all seemed to grasp the main ideas of the programming language readily, and seemed to enjoy the
problems set them. The tests with children were particularly pleasing: they came up with the idea of writing
a NOLOG program to 'do prime numbers'. Better still,
one of the children *suggested* that they could base
such a program on his own program for sifting out
multiples of numbers. This encouraged us in our hope
that the NOLOG environment will also be regarded as
an environment for exploratory programming, as
LOGO tends to be. More recently we have been able
to test the constraint-based aspects of NOLOG. These
motivated some children to considerable experimentation with variations on the exercises which we set
them.

3. SMALLTALK AS A VEHICLE FOR IMPLE-MENTING NOLOG

Smalltalk is a somewhat unusual programming language. It is based around a very simple idea. *Everything* throughout the whole Smalltalk system is regarded as an **object** to which **messages** can be
sent, and from which a **reply** is received in response
to that message. This means that even things such as
strings and integers are regarded as objects. For
example, the expression:

3+4

is to be understood as meaning that we send the
message '+4' to the integer 3, which will reply with the
integer whose value is 7. This way of handling such
common data types seems odd at first, but one becomes used to it.

Unfortunately it takes a long time to become familiar
with the Smalltalk system. There are numerous different kinds ('classes') of objects in the system, and it is
necessary to have a general understanding of many of
them before any real programming can be done. In
our experience the ability to write Smalltalk programs
came very suddenly, as soon as we found that we had
enough knowledge and understanding of the Smalltalk system so that we could search the system for
more information.

However, a good feature of the Smalltalk system is
that when designing an application, one can often
model it naturally in terms of objects. For example, our
NOLOG environment uses many different classes of
objects including Planes, Islands, Flight Recorders
and Interpreters (an Interpreter interprets the NOLOG
language).

Smalltalk saves programming effort by providing
mechanisms for handling windows, the mouse, text
editing and many other program building blocks which
can be used as they are, or one may create 'sub-
classes' of these classes which behave slightly differently. For example, we created our own text editor
classes which were based on the system classes, but
which we thought were simpler for children to use.

One problem encountered was that there are some
'bugs' in the Smalltalk system (version T2.1.2a), and it
is somewhat undesirable to use a class with bugs in it
as a superclass of a new class. One particularly frustrating bug we encountered occurred when typing in
text: occasionally the text insertion point was moved
back by one character. This was bearable for us: we
knew the bug existed and simply typed accordingly.
But such a bug would be very unfortunate in an editor
for children. Our procedure here was to correct the
bug in the classes in which it occurred, which meant
that all editing then worked correctly. However, we
realised that it would have been safer not to modify the
system in this way.

Overall we were pleased with the Smalltalk system,
but some of the problems in the current versions of
Smalltalk are very frustrating. Perhaps the worst
problem for us is the fact that the number of objects

that can exist in the system is seriously limited. This is not true of all implementations, but of most, including that on the Tektronix 4404, which was used for this work.

4. THE PROGRAMMING ADVISOR

The programming advice section of the NOLOG environment is as object-oriented as we found possible, given the other constraints on the design of this part of the system. In more common expert systems terminology this corresponds somewhat to the idea of using 'frames'. Since this is the most recent part of the system to be implemented, our ideas are not fixed at the time of writing. But we suspect that rules may play a relatively minor part (perhaps no part at all). For the sort of knowledge we wish to store, and the operations we desire to perform on it, the 'frame' paradigm is probably sufficient.

Having said that, it may well be that we will wish to introduce 'rules' into our system, but perhaps not to have an inference engine that just keeps on firing rules and asserting facts (filling in slots of frames). This is the crux of the matter: we want to regard objects as more than just data structures with fields that can be filled in. We want them to be *real* objects, with the much greater flexibility possible. In fact, objects which already exist in the NOLOG environment performing non-expert tasks may get involved in our expert system.

5. CONCLUSIONS

The system is now virtually ready for a full-scale, formal, classroom based educational evaluation. If the response is positive enough to make it worthwhile, many kinds of feedback should be relatively easy to incorporate into the system, thanks to our use of Smalltalk.

ACKNOWLEDGEMENT

This work was undertaken whilst the first author was in receipt of a UK Science and Engineering Research Council Studentship.

REFERENCES

[1] Goldberg, A., Smalltalk-80: The Interactive Programming Environment (Addison-Wesley, Reading, Ma., 1984).

[2] Johnson, W. L. and Soloway, E., PROUST: An Automatic Debugger for Pascal Programs, in: Kearsley, G. (ed.), ICAL: Artificial Intelligence and Instruction: Applications and Methods (Addison Wesley, Reading, Ma., 1987) pp. 49-67.

[3] Polya, G., How To Solve It (Princeton University Press, Princeton, New Jersey, 1945).

[4] Burton, L., Thinking Things Through (Basil Blackwell, Oxford, 1984).

[5] Thompson, P. W., Mathematical Microworlds and Intelligent Computer-Assisted Learning, in: Kearsley, G. (ed.), ICAL: Artificial Intelligence and Instruction: Applications and Methods (Addison Wesley, Reading, Ma., 1987) pp. 83-109.

[6] Papert, S., Mindstorms: Children, Computers, and Powerful Ideas (Basic Books, New York, 1980).

[7] Jaffar, J., and Lassez, J. L., Constraint Logic Programming, in: Proceedings of the Conference on Principles of Programming Languages (Munich, 1987).

COMPUTERS IN EDUCATION, F. Lovis and E.D. Tagg (eds.)
Elsevier Science Publishers B.V. (North-Holland)
© IFIP, 1988

A MATHEMATICAL LABORATORY IN LOGO STYLE[*]

Bojidar Sendov, Darina Dicheva

Faculty of Mathematics and Informatics, Sofia University
5 A Ivanov bul, 1126 Sofia, Bulgaria

An approach of using the computer to enrich the mathematics learning environment - a Mathematical Laboratory is suggested. *A department* of the Mathematical Laboratory - the Plane Geometry System, has been considered. Its advantages have been discussed and have demonstrated   the basis of some problems.

1. INTRODUCTION

The experience of the Research Group on Education (at the Bulgarian Academy of Sciences and Ministry of Education) in teaching informatics with Logo as a programming language has confirmed our conviction that the *Logo style* should be the basic one when using computers in school. Recently our research has been devoted to the use of computers in the teaching of mathematics. The good possibilities provided by Logo in this direction are well known. It is often insisted even that *the turtle talks in a mathematical language*. Some researchers [1] note that the pupils are not always aware of that, though. Furthermore, the mathematical objects the pupils come   across in the high school become more and more complicated and the basic Logo possibilities - not quite adequate. Of course Logo still provides means for work in mathematics but *not on the surface* and thus hidden for the ordinary pupil (It is a different matter whether to reveal them wouldn't be a sufficient educational goal). In a sense Logo could be compared to *assembler for work in mathematics* - with great potential but all the same ... assembler.

We tend to continue using the computers in mathematical education in *Logo style* but to use a kind of Logo that would be still closer to mathematics. What we mean by *Logo style* is to create a research atmosphere on the base of tools enabling a direct manipulation with objects of interest. At the same time we tend to make use of the skills and abilities acquired when working with Logo. Bearing this in mind we came to the idea of creating a Mathematical Laboratory in Logo style.

2. THE MATHEMATICAL LABORATORY *(MATH LAB)*

What is actually meant by *laboratory*? The chemical, biological and the physical laboratories could serve as one well known example of this. Differently from their objects of research, the mathematical objects are not material but purely informational ones. Operations performed over them are information transformations. That is why *Math Lab* does not need flasks and scales but *a place enabling information to live*. Thus we came to the natural conclusion that the computer is the most appropriate place to build *Math Lab* in which mathematical objects could be created, manipulated with, observed and measured.

The way we envisioned *Math Lab* - as a place for research - determined our conception that it should be created in Logo style (which is hardly surprising, cf [2] [3]).

The first step in that direction was to develop a small laboratory by the name of *Plane Geometry System* [4]. This system has been developed as a *horizontal* extension of Logo. What is meant by this in this case is that when using Logo the pupils enter the turtle world, whereas when crossing *the threshold* of the system they leave the turtle world and enter *Flatland* - the world of plane-geometric objects. This means that one cannot control the turtle any more but can create geometric objects to be manipulated. All the other Logo tools are common - the commands for assignment, for cycle, for conditions, the procedures, input/output etc. alongside with some other facilities. One can see that the style and the potential of the system are quite different from the well known *Geometric Supposer* [5] .

---

[*]   This project has been supported financially by the Committee for Science at the Council of Ministers under Contract No 554.

The language of the system contains besides the usual Logo data types and operations, new data types with geometric interpretation (object types) and corresponding primitive operations. The basic object types are a point, a vector, a segment, a straight line, an arc and a circle. There is also a composite data type - a set of objects of basic types.

Functionally we divide the primitive operations into *constructors* by means of which we create new objects with predefined characteristics, and *selectors* which extract a characteristic of a given object. As a rule these functions have the name of the object they construct or extract. For instance,

POINT 10 40 creates a point with coordinates **(10,40)**,

CENTRE :K   returns the point which is the centre of circle **K**.

The operations **INTERSECT** (intersection) and **POINTON** (point on other object) can be used to define points as well. The operation **SET** creates a set of objects and can be used to define composite objects, e.g. a triangle (consisting of three points - vertices and three segments - sides), locus of points etc. The extraction of an element from a set of objects can be done using the operation **ELEMENT**.

When a value of geometric type is assigned to a variable it is also drawn on the screen and denoted by that name.

3. EXPERIMENTS IN *MATH LAB*

Let us try to feel more clearly some advantages of the use of *Math Lab*.

3.1. The Parallel Line Problem

There are two objects on the screen - a point X and a straight line L which are not incidental. Draw a straight line L₁ which passes through X, and is parallel to L.

X

L

In order to solve the problem the pupil can choose different ways:

Seeing that **L** is horizontal he may construct **L₁** as follows:

MAKE "L₁ LINE :X 0
(**LINE :X 0** constructs straight line through the point **X** forming an angle **0** with the axis **Ox**).

Such a solution should not be admired since the fact that the line looks like a horizontal one does not mean that this is the case.

It would be better if the pupil first had measured the angle between **L** and **Ox** using the selector **ANGLE :L**. If this angle equals **0** degree indeed, the construction made would be well argued. But this again is not the best solution. Why? The pupil has built a second line **L₁** which is horizontal (like the first one) and this implies that they are parallel. It would be better if the construction of the second line is described using a property which makes it explicitly parallel to the first

MAKE "L₁ LINE :X ANGLE :L,

or, even better,

MAKE "L₁ LINE :X VECTOR :L

(**VECTOR :L** returns a value which is the unit vector on **L**), i.e. the line **L₁** is described directly by the means of these elements of **L** which make the lines parallel. In this case **L₁** becomes dependent on **L** and therefore if **L** changes its position, the line **L₁** will automatically move too in order to preserve the constructive description. This example shows that when using the system the teacher could discuss indeed the essence of the relation between the mathematical objects on an elementary level.

3.2. The Cycloid Problem

By using *Math Lab* one can do many things in plane geometry without need of involving methods and means from other fields (e.g. algebra, trigonometry). As an example let us *construct a cycloid*. Its definition is a completely geometric one: *The curve traced by the motion of a point fixed on the circumference of a wheel, which is rotating without slipping on a horizontal line.*

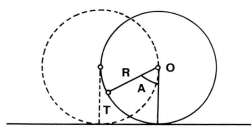

Let us describe the rotation of the fixed point after a turn of A degree:

The distance traced by the center from its initial locations is:

L = (*pi* *** R / 180) * A**

The coordinates of the given point **T** are:

y = R - R*cosA

x = L - R*sinA

This means that in order to find the coordinates of the consecutive points of the cycloid we use trigonometric expressions. The same is true if we would like to describe the cycloid as a turtle trajectory **[6]**.

When working with the *Plane Geometry* system the description and the construction of cycloid points can be done by using only plane geometry notions and operations. We shall use the fact that the point **T** is reached from the new location of **O** with a vector **V** of length **R** and heading **270 - A**. Then all the moving elements depend on **A** and can be constructed as follows:

MAKE "A 0
MAKE "DL PI * :R / 180
(where **PI** is a functon returning *pi*)
MAKE "O POINT :DL * :A :R
MAKE "K CIRCLE :O :R
MAKE "V VECTOR 270 - :A :R
MAKE "T POINT :O :V

Now we have the initial state. What is left to be done is to change **A** in order to get the corresponding state of the circle (with the point **T** fixed on it). In order to get twenty consecutive states of the circle while it makes a full turn the following command must be executed

REPEAT 20 [MAKE "A :A + 18]

Depending on our goals we could save the consecutive states of the different elements (the point **T**, the circle **K** etc.) in sets and use them afterwards. For instance we could join the points by a broken line thus giving a sufficiently good idea about the cycloid.

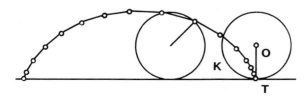

When constructing the cycloid we use some basic plane geometry notions and very elementary argu-

ments whereas the result is both attractive and achievable by most of the pupils. Furthermore the whole process is rich in content both concerning the plane geometry and the programming.

3.3. The Citadel Problem (Proposed by Ivan Tonov)

Finally we shall consider a problem difficult to investigate theoretically.

In a perfectly round citadel (C) with radius R an ancient cannon is put at the point P (different from the centre). Imagine that the cannon fires balls, which after rebounding off the citadel wall stop at a distance 2R from the shooting point. What will be the locus (of cannon-balls), if the cannon makes a full turn around its axis while shooting unceasingly.

In order to obtain the locus under consideration we shall project the cannon-ball's trajectory on the plane so that it depends entirely on the parameter **ALPHA** - the heading of the shooting. Assume that the citadel (circle) **C** and the cannon (point) **P** have already been constructed. We assign an initial value to **ALPHA**, e.g.

MAKE "ALPHA 0

Then we construct the line through **P** and the right point of intersection:

MAKE "L1 LINE :P :ALPHA
MAKE "X ELEMENT 1 INTERSECT :L1 :C

The function **INTERSECT** returns as a value the set of the two points of intersection, and **ELEMENT** takes that one pointed by its first input.

We draw the tangent at the point **X** where the cannon-ball bounces off:

MAKE "T LINE :X (HEADING LINE :O :X) + 90

Next we construct the point **P1** symmetrical to **P** about **T** and the reflected line trough **P1** and **X**:

MAKE "P₁ INTERSECT :T LINE :P (HEADING :T) + 90
MAKE "P1 POINT :P₁ VECTOR :P :P₁,

i.e. the point **P1** is reached by **P₁** with the vector determined by the points **P** and **P₁**. The reflected line is constructed by

MAKE "L2 LINE :P1 :X

and the point at which the cannon-ball stops is defined

as a point on the line **L2** at a distance equal to **2R** from its centre **P1**:

MAKE "B POINTON :L2 :R*2

If we want to clear away the unnecessary elements of the construction and to leave only the trajectory we must hide all the auxiliary lines and points. After that we shall construct the segments of which the trajectory consists:

(HIDE "L1 "L2 "T "X "P₁ "P1)
MAKE "a SEGMENT :P :X
MAKE "b SEGMENT :X :B

Thus we have obtained one point from the locus under consideration as a function of **ALPHA**. In order to see what happens when *turning* the cannon it is sufficient to execute the cycle:

REPEAT 18 [MAKE "ALPHA :ALPHA + 20]

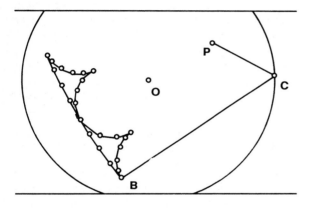

Thus we shall obtain 18 consecutive elements. If we save the different points in a set and then show them simultaneously on the screen, we shall get an idea about the locus which appears to be very unexpected and sophisticated. Many questions arise immediately, e.g.: *Whether the three curves are arcs of a circle?, Is the forth part of the locus a segment?* etc. All that could be checked easily by the use of the points having been already obtained.

That is how one terrible problem becomes an interesting object for research and reflection.

4. FACILITIES FOR EXPERIMENTAL WORK

A series of additional facilities have been implemented in the system which make it convenient for experiments:

–   The executed commands are consecutively added to the definition of a procedure. Thus the activity carried out is saved for further modifications and executions;

–   The procedures can be executed in a trace mode: before execution each command is shown on the screen and could be edited;

–   When changing a variable's value all the objects depending on it are redefined automatically in order to save the relations imposed and if they are shown on the screen they are redrawn as well. By request the object could be set free of this property;

–   The objects can be erased or *hidden*. The hidden objects are erased only from the screen and could be shown again;

–   When working one can change both the scale and the mutual position of the screen and the coordinate system;

–   The current nummerical value of a given variable could be made visible on a chosen place of the screen.

The system provides a convenient environment for carrying out experiments in the plane geometry since when using it one can:

–   watch the process of the geometric construction being performed;

–   easily modify the objects constructed;

–   extract with great accuracy the characteristics of the objects constructed (e.g. lengths, angles);

–   easily and quickly try different ways of continuing the work;

–   save the solutions for further analysis, comparison and refinements;

–   work with the objects of the field of investigation (if necessary the system uses methods from other fields of mathematics).

5. FINAL REMARKS

Our conviction is that the Plane geometry system can play an important role for developing a more productive environment for teaching mathematics and informatics. Let us list some of the advantages when using it:

- In order to create an object one must know exactly which are the elements determining it - characteristics, properties and relations between them. Thus the system contributes to better understanding and acquiring of the mathematical conceptions;

- When dealing directly with the objects one sees immediately the result of the operations having been performed, i.e. establishes facts emerging from a concrete activity. This could contribute to building a good intuition for some properties in the field;

- Mathematics classes are enriched by activities of a new type - setting and carrying out experiments. Thus one could find a certain property, to formulate it precisely afterwards and only then to try to prove it strictly. Such a way is much more natural for pupils;

- To discuss and analyse the solution becomes much more convenient. There are cases where the very process of looking for a solution coud be highly appreciated although the final result has not been obtained;

- Pupils are expected to find this kind of work more attractive;

- Programming methods are used quite naturally when solving mathematical problems.

We are going to extend further the system's possibilities. For example it seems quite natural to include all second-degree curves as objects. The goal is to enlarge the circle of problems to be treated and enable the comparing of different representations of mathematical objects or properties.

6. CONCLUSIONS

The first version of the system was developed at the end of 1986. Since then it has been popularised among teachers in mathematics and informatics. Since the autumn of 1987 it has been used in the regular mathematical classes in the RGE schools (7-9 degree). Besides it has been applied in different extra-classes activities in other schools as well. Our goal is to create a suitable methodology for its use. In addition we strongly rely on the experience, intuition and enthusiasm of the best teachers in mathematics whom we make every endeavour to involve in that activity.

REFERENCES

[1] Leron U., Some Problems in Children's Logo Learning, in: Proceedings of the Seventh International Conference for
the Psychology of Mathematics Education (Weizmann Institute of Science, Izrael, 1983).

[2] Jean-Claude A. et autres, GEOMETRICIEL - an outil pour la geometric au lycee ou au college (IREM de Grenoble, 1986).

[3] Marshman B., L.E.G.O. - An Interactive Computer graphics System for Teaching Geometry (WCCE, 1985).

[4] Sendov Boj, Filimonov R and Dicheva D, A System for Teaching Plane Geometry, in: Proceedings of the Second International Conference "Children in the Information Age" (Sofia, Bulgaria, 1987) pp. 215-226.

[5] Schwartz J. and Yerushalmy M., The Geometric Supposer (Educational Development Center, Inc., 1985).

[6] Leron U. and Armon U., How to Explain a Cycloid to a Turtle, in: Proceedings of the Second International Conference for Logo and Mathematics Education (University of London Institute of Education, London, 1986).

COMPUTERS IN EDUCATION, F. Lovis and E.D. Tagg (eds.)
Elsevier Science Publishers B.V. (North-Holland)
© IFIP, 1988

USE OF SPECIALIZED LANGUAGES IN EDUCATION.

Antonio MONTES

Facultat d'Informàtica de Barcelona.
Universitat Politècnica de Catalunya
C/Pau Gargallo, 5
08028 BARCELONA
SPAIN

ABSTRACT

Specialized languages are defined and their usefulness in education analyzed. By explaining the basic features of Euclid II module, a Geometrical language designed by us, and those of its predecessor Euclid I, the main characteristics of a kind of educational computer tools are shown. We see that Euclid language, whose objective is primarily the study of intrinsic Geometry in an experimental approach, becomes a natural way for introducing the students to programming. The language has been implemented as a Turbo-Pascal library, so students are required to learn programming in order to be capable of using the tool. But rather than an impediment, we conclude that this is perhaps a very natural way of learning structured programming. We also discuss how the language simulates the axioms of the theory, and how this encourages the research attitude of the students. Some light is given in order on the design of others specialized languages.

1. SPECIALIZED LANGUAGES.

The first question is to clarify what we mean by specialized languages. In some sense, they are similar to programming environments like Karel Robot [1], or some others, designed for working with robots or automats. The main difference is that their objectives, that is, the kind of problems that we can approach with them, must have a more universal character. Even if the object of the language continues to be specialized, and controlled by a small set of primitives, it must deal with a more "classic" kind of problem. By "classic" we mean something that is worthwhile studying in classroom.

The original idea arose from the computer program Euclid I, designed by A.Fabrega [2].[3] Even though this program is the subject of another communication to the Congress, we will outline here its basic features.

2. THE PROGRAM EUCLID I.

Euclid I is an interpreter of geometrical instructions. The instructions are direct orders given to the computer which are accepted and executed immediately. The instructions allow us to create points, segments and circles that will be plotted on the screen. They further allow us to make every geometrical construction with them, by just defining the relations between the data, using the appropriate primitives (segment determined by two points, intersection of two lines, or of line and circle, and so on).

This computer program, which is not very ambitious in principle, is in fact very interesting in education. What are the keys of its success?. First, its interest comes from the marvellous power, elegance and simplicity of intrinsic Euclidean Geometry: with a very little set of instructions it is possible to do a lot, or an infinite set, of interesting constructions, make evidence of theorems, and discover new and unexpected properties for the user. Secondly, it introduces the user to a specialized language allowing a rigorous and precise dialogue with the computer, that is also welcoming: the computer obeys the orders given by the user, and allows him to develop his own geometrical ideas.

The philosophy of Euclid I is in some way related to the use of LOGO in education, even though if it is less ambitious. It is not a programming language of general purpose. It does not allow the defining of procedures, nor building one upon another. Nevertheless it has also very positive features: because of its specialized character it is very well adapted to the scope for which it was designed: it allows, in a natural form, the randomness of the geometrical constructions, which is useful for making evident the invariant character of the intrinsic geometrical constructions.

3. POSITIVE FEATURES AND INSUFICIENCIES OF EUCLID I.

The educational interest of Euclid I suggested the design of Euclid II [4], and also the consideration of a more general point of view for manipulation with this kind of tool.

3.1. The success of Euclid I lies in

(i)   Allowing the study in depth of a particular kind of problems: in our case, the intrinsic Euclidean Geometry, which is at the same time universal enough to be of general interest.

(ii)   Giving the possibility of an algorithmic approach with a simple, precise and natural language.

(iii)   The beauty of the nature of the Geometry, and its fundamental importance for an adequate development of the scientific knowledge process of the students.

(iv)   Making proof of one of the basic characteristics of intrinsic Geometry: the invariance of constructions.

In order to clarify this last point, it has to be observed that, repeating the algorithm written for Euclid I, the answer of the computer will not be identical to the first one, but will be equivalent from a geometrical point of view.

3.2. The basic insufficiencies of Euclid I are

(i)   The inability of defining procedures that can be used in following constructions.

(ii)   The lack of control on the names of the new automatically created objects (points, segments, circles, and so on) which are created with the name given by the next following letter in the alphabet.

(iii)   The impossibility of programming the constructions, which obliges one to proceed with the construction, step by step directly on the computer, and resulting in less clarity of the corresponding algorithm and in a higher probability of introducing confusion in the whole procedure. Any way, we must say that Euclid I has the possibility of consulting the whole text of the instructions we have already given and the names of the objects created, so that the difficulties just noted are not so drastic.

(iv)   The incapacity to program the procedures is particularly serious when we try to construct a locus of points that verify some geometrical property.

4. EUCLID II.

In order to overcome these troubles, we considered another kind of tool. Instead of an interpreter, we designed a specialized language module which can be programmed in Pascal. Now we can talk about using a defined geometrical language with all the power that programming gives, rather than approaching geometrical problems with a computer tool which is easy to handle. Unfortunately, the increase of resources and power results in a loss of ease. The user-student has now to learn programming. But the great advantage is that he has the opportunity of learning programming in a natural form. We said that the programming language chosen is Pascal, concretely Borland's TURBO-PASCAL. And we do this for two reasons: First it is well adapted to the algorithmic reasoning which Geometry implies, allowing one to define words representing executable procedures (like LOGO). Secondly, it is a suitable form in which to learn programming in a structured form.

Possibly the reader will be affraid of this audacity! Requiring the students to learn Pascal programming in order to be able to use a geometrical tool! It seems too much. And if it were so, it would be effectively excessive. But we can turn over this argument. Programming in a specialized language with the objective of studying a subject, Geometry in our case, isn't a very good and natural method for introducing the students in programming? I think it is.

5. THE SECOND OBJECTIVE OF EUCLID II: LEARNING PROGRAMMING.

The language Euclid II, which is the object of discussion, allows and invites the design of algorithms in a precise and structured manner, in a language quite near to the usual one. The objective, the study of Geometry, invites one to create algorithms. And when we have designed one of them with a really simple syntax, we can incorporate it in a very simple form, in a Pascal program structure, and the program runs! The simplest Pascal structure supporting Euclid II is given in the same diskette and the user has only to incorporate his algorithm in it. Gradually, by designing increasingly complex geometrical algorithms, the user will begin to learn and to recognize the Pascal programming language. Like babies who learn to speak without previously learning the Grammar rules, the Euclid II user also learns Pascal programming without having first to learn its Grammar. Learning programming thus becomes the second objective of working with our tool.

6. FAST DESCRIPTION OF EUCLID II.

Euclid II basically uses two kinds of *Abstract Data Type* (A.D.T.), namely the type *point* and the type *segment*. These are the basic variable types which occur in the primitives of Euclid II. *Primitives*, that is, procedures and functions previously defined by Euclid II, have these kinds of variable as arguments and also return (in the case of functions) these kinds of variable. There are also some other kinds of auxiliary variables of Boolean type and label type, but these are unimportant for the comprehension of the philosophy of Euclid II. Basic variable types, point and segment, represent what, in the axiomatic theory, would be the "undefined terms".

We give now the set of all the primitives (functions and procedures) which are defined by the library of Euclid II. We classify them in four categories: Basic functions, Verification functions, Improper functions and Auxiliary procedures.

6.1. Basic function.

These are functions taking the role of the "axioms" or initial propositions of the geometrical theory, and allow us to construct geometrical objects, given the relations between them. All of them are functions which return a variable of basic type: *point* or *segment*. The list of these provided by the module is the following:

```
CreatePoint(lab:label;draw:Boolean):point;
CreateSegment(lab1,lab2:label;draw:Boolean):
        segment;
ConstructSegment(a,b:point;draw;Boolean):segment;
```

```
InvertSegment(s;segment):segment;
EndSegment(ori_end:two;s:segment):segment;
SplitSegment(s:segment;rate:real;lab:label):
        point;
BisectSegment(s:segment;lab:label):point;
Perpendicular(s:segment;p:point;lab:label;
        draw:Boolean):segment;
Parallel(s:segment;p:point;lab:label;draw:
        Boolean):segment;
CreatePointInLine(s;segment;lab:label):point;
CreatePointSegment(s:segment;lab:label):point;
IntersectionTwoLines(s,t:segment;lab:label):
        point;
IntersectionLineCircle(s:segment;centre:point;
        radius:segment;lab1,lab2:label;
        draw:Boolean):segment;
IntersectionTwoCircles(cen1:point;rad1:segment;
        cen2;point;rad2:segment;lab1,lab2:
        label;draw:Boolean):segment;
```

We can add three drawing procedures to this list which are not really basic because they do not define any geometrical object, but are, visually speaking, important enough to be included in this list. They are the following:

```
ExtendLine(s:segment);
Circle(centre:point;radius:segment);
Arc(centre:point;radius:segment;
        p1,p2:point;
```

6.2. Verification functions.

All these functions provided by Euclid II return a *Boolean* type variable. The interest lies in the possibility of verifying the conclusions or assertions of the construction, in a form not depending on the visual results and to have, in some way, more "axiomatic features". The functions are:

```
SamePoint(p,q;point):Boolean
SameSegment(s,t:segment):Boolean;
IsInLine(p:point;s:segment):Boolean;
IsInRay(p:point;s:segment):Boolean;
InsideSegment(p:point;s:segment):Boolean;
IsInLeftHalfPlane(p:point;s:segment):Boolean;
TwoLinesMeet(s,t:segment):Boolean;
LineCircleMeet(s:segment;centre:point;radius:
        segment):Boolean;
TwoCirclesMeet(cen1:point;rad1:segment;cen2:
        point;rad2:segment):Boolean;
LineCircleAreTangent(s:segment;centre:point;
        radius:segment):Boolean;
TwoCirclesAreTangent(cen1:point;rad1:segment;
        cen2:point;rad2:segment):Boolean;
```

6.3. Improper functions.

Euclid II also defines some improper functions, in the sense that they are not proper intrinsic. They must be used with care for didactical purposes or even not be used at all because they make the constructions not really intrinsic or geometrical equivalent. Nevertheless, they are included to provide the user with the possibility of better graphical results. The basic improper function is

SitPoint(x,y:real;draw:Boolean):point;

There are also three other improper functions which are not so dangerous. These are

Distance(p,q:point):real
PointLineDistance(p,point;s:segment):real;
LengthSegment(s:segment):real;

6.4. Auxiliary procedures.

There is a set of procedures that have to be used in order to initialize, define resolution, colours, write text, create windows and so on, which make the graphics more spectacular. They are not geometrical procedures. The list is the following:

Pause(time:integer):
Init;
ClearScreen;
Finish;
Palet;
LowRes;
HighRes;
BlackColor(color:integer);
TextColor(color:integer);
GraphColor(color:integer);
Writ(x,y:integer;text:alpha);
LabelPoint(var p:point;lab:
World(p1,p2:point;draw:Boolean);

We have a Boolean function which is also an auxiliary primitive. This is

IsInWorld(p:point):Boolean;

Even though their technical use requires a more detailed explanation of the primitives and the use of the module, which can be found in the Reference Manual [4], we see that they practically explain themselves.

7. EXAMPLE OF ALGORITHM WITH EUCLID II.

In order to understand the approach better, we give an example of a geometrical algorithm and the corresponding Euclid procedure. We want to obtain evidence of the fact that the three medians of a triangle meet in the circumcentre. The algorithm will consist of the following steps:

- Create three points.
- Join them by segments.
- Determine the middle points.

- Construct the perpendicular to the sides of the triangle at the middle points (medians).
- Determine the intersection point of two of the medians.
- (Optional) We can verify if the three medians meet at the same point.
- Draw the circle with centre at the intersection point and radius having its endpoint on a vertex of the triangle.
- (Optional) We can verify if all the vertices are on circle.

Looking at the picture, we shall verify the two optional points. But they can also be tested by querying with the primitives in a more "Axiomatic" form. In a first approach at the Euclid method with students, we shall not probably insist on this point. We give here the whole program.

The text of the algorithm in Euclid language will read like this;

```
Procedure Circumcentre
var   a,b,c,a1,b1,c1
      circenA,circenB,circenC:point;
      ab,bc,ca,ma,mb,mc,radiusA,radiusB;
      radius C: segment;
      proof:Boolean;
begin
      a:=CreatePoint('a',Draw);
      b:=CreatePoint('b',Draw);
      c:=CreatePoint('c',Draw);
      ab:=ConstructSegment(a,b,Draw);
      bc:=ConstructSegment(b,c,Draw);
      ca:=ConstructSegment(c,a,Draw);
      a1:=BisectSegment(bc,'a1');
      b1:=BisectSegment(ca,'b1');
      c1:=BisectSegment(ab,'c1');
      ma:=Perpendicular(bc,a1,'',Draw);
      mb:=Perpendicular(ab,c1,'',Draw);
      circenA:=IntersectionTwoLines(ab,ca,'o');
 {    circenB:=IntersectionTwoLines(bc,ab,'o');
      circenC:=IntersectionTwoLines(ca,bc,'o');
          Writeln('circenA=circenB ?',
          SamePoint(circenA,circenB));and so on }
      radiusA:=ConstructSegment(circenA,a,
          DontDraw);
          Circle(circenA,radiusA);
 {   proof:=(Distance(circenA,b)=LengthSegment
          (radiusA);
      Writeln('Is point b in circle?',proof);
                          and so on      }
end;
```

This procedure cannot be directly executed. Pascal obliges us to include it in a global program structure. This structure can be the following

```
Program Model;
{$I Euclid.eng}
var ch:char;
procedure Circumcentre; {to be included}
begin
     Init;HighRes;
     repeat
       Circumcentre;Writ(10,24,F'=quit');
       ch:='x';read(kbd,ch);ClearScreen;
     until(ch='F') or (ch='f');
     Finish;
end.
```

This elementary structure is always the same for other algorithms, and we have only to substitute the procedure we want to execute. The structure allows iteration of the procedure automatically, in order to observe regularities.

8. EUCLID II AND THE AXIOMATIC THEORY OF GEOMETRY.

We have seen how the Abstract Data Type (A.D.T.) of the computer model plays the role of the "not-defined terms" of the axiomatic theory, and the primitive functions (only those we denominate basic) that of the "axioms". A construction done using the language Euclid II can be interpreted as a "predicate", or a "non-demonstrated proposition" of the theory. It can be verified a lot of times without additional work, by asking the computational model with the aid of the verification's primitives, about the correctness of the proposition, theory. The simulation invites the user to understand the necessity of demonstration and aids him to induce whether a certain proposition is correct or not in the theory. In an elementary use of the language, this simulation is made only in visual form, by observing the screen.

Following the modelization of the axiomatic theory, we can restrict the number of primitives or axioms we allow to use. We can obtain, doing so, modelization of Affine Geometry. This kind of question will be discussed in a forthcoming paper.

9. CONCLUSIONS

Developing a specialized language whith the objective of approaching some "classical" domain of problems, leads us to design a programmable module in the form of a Pascal library, containing functions and procedures. This approach is not only useful for the domain of the considered problems, intrinsic geometry in our case, but seems also a natural way to introduce the students to structured programming.

(i)   The domain of problems to be modelled has to be of sufficient universal interest.

(ii) The programming language must be adapted to the nature of the problems which will be studied.

(iii) One has to be able to formalize the domain of the problems in question, in order to control them with a little set of primitives.

(iv) The Abstract Data Types (A.D.T.) of the computer model play the role of the "not-defined terms" of the axiomatic theory, and the primitives, that of the "axioms". The computer model simulates the axiomatic theory, and we can define the verification's primitives.

(v)   This kind of tool has a great didactical interest, because it is an open instrument and encourages the research attitude of the user. It seems also a natural way of learning programming.

REFERENCES

[1]   Pattis, R.E., Karel the Robot. A Gentle Introduction to the Art of Programming. John Wiley $ Sons. Inc. (English).

[1]   Pattis, R.E., Introducción Gradual a la Programación. El Robot Karel, Limusa, México, 1985, (Spanish)

[2]   Albert Fàbrega, Euclides I: Manual de Referència. Barcelona, 1987. (Catalan).

[3]   Albert Fàbrega, Euclides i la tortuga. ICE-UPC, Ed. Universitat Politècnica de Catalunya, Barcelona, 1987 (Catalan)

[4]   A. Montes, A. Fàbrega, A. Parra Euclides II: Manual de Referència FIB, report 87/04, Universitat Politècnica de Catalunya, Nov 1987 (Catalan).

3. New Technologies and their Educational Potential

COMPUTERS IN EDUCATION, F. Lovis and E.D. Tagg (eds.)
Elsevier Science Publishers B.V. (North-Holland)
© IFIP, 1988

ISSUES FOR INTELLIGENT TUTORING OF CONCURRENT PROGRAMMING*

Pentti Hietala

University of Tampere
Department of Computer Science, P.O.Box 607
SF-33101 Tampere, FINLAND

In this paper we consider issues for computer-aided instruction of concurrent programming: controlling devices capable of parallel processing - a skill of growing significance for the computer specialists of tomorrow. The main foundations of this instruction are described and intelligent, or knowledge-based, computer assistance is identified as one promising method of instruction. The first version of a prototype system aiming at this direction is under construction at the University of Tampere. It is being implemented using Prolog on a SUN-3 graphical workstation. The latter part of this paper comprises a description and discussion of this system.

1. INTRODUCTION

In this paper *concurrent programming*, i.e. those programming tools and techniques that deal with parallel processes, are discussed from the point of view of learning and teaching. It is interesting to note that in spite of a huge amount of research results in the area there seems to be very little textbook material (see e.g. [1,2,3]). A few chapters in an operating systems textbook (see e.g. [4]) seem to be sufficient to cover the matter; indeed, concurrency issues have traditionally been related to operating systems courses in the computer science curriculum. However, concurrent programming as such is gaining increasing popularity due to the recent advances in hardware and language design and therefore, we feel, deserves more attention also in university level teaching.

Our thesis is that in teaching concurrent programming the application of rigorous techniques will prove to be even more important than in teaching its sequential counterpart (see a discussion of the latter in [5]). In this paper most of our examples will focus on the question of *verifying concurrent programs* which has become one of the most prolific and interesting areas in today's verification technology, e.g. due to the intricate and intriguing problems of process synchronization and communication. We have argued elsewhere [6] that computer assistance is beneficial for the acquisition and learning of program verification techniques and demonstrated that by building a proof management system for sequential programs [7]. This system was also used in the classroom. Our conviction is that the assets of computer assistance will carry over to the teaching of concurrent programming.

Ultimate computer assistance would appear in the form of a machine tutor, i.e. having a computer to act as a private human tutor, being able to assist the learning in an individualized and knowledgeable way (this novel application of Artificial Intelligence techniques in education is often called *knowledge-based* or *intelligent tutoring* (see e.g. [8,9])). There exist several intelligent teaching assistants for sequential programming (see e.g. [10,11]).

We want to extend this approach so that we can assist the construction of programs with parallel processes; indeed, we envision as our long-term goal building a classroom computer tutor for concurrent programming. In this paper we consider the premises of this goal and outline a prototype system under construction at the University of Tampere. However, we start by examining issues central to teaching students how to construct programs dealing with concurrency. We also try to tie together computer tutoring and the domain of concurrent programming.

2. TEACHING CONCURRENT PROGRAMMING

In this section we first briefly give some definitions (for a more detailed discussion we refer e.g. to [12,13,14]) after which we try to identify what makes concurrent programming more difficult to learn than its sequential counterpart. A *sequential program* specifies sequential execution of a list of statements; its execution is called a *process*. A *concurrent program* specifies two or more sequential programs that may be executed concurrently as *parallel processes*. From the point of view of logical formalism, *distributed programs* are no different from any other kind of concurrent programs; however, they have additional constraints about process locations and process communication.

Besides a collection of processes a concurrent program consists of shared objects. The shared objects can be implemented in shared memory or might simply be a computer-communications network. Unexpected and/or unwanted modification of the shared objects may hinder or invalidate the progress of process execution in a subtle way bringing a new dimension to programming. In order to cooperate, concurrent processes must communicate and synchronize. *Communication* allows one process to influence execution of another and can be accomplished using *shared variables* (variables that can be referenced by more than one process) or *message passing* (where processes send and receive messages instead of reading and writing shared variables). *Synchronization* is often necessary when processes communicate; for example, the message receiving process must wait until the message has been properly sent from the other process.

* This work was supported by the Academy of Finland

2.1. Basic differences with sequential programming

While there is no logical difference between distributed and nondistributed concurrent programs, there is a fundamental difference between concurrent and sequential programs [13] which makes the introduction of concurrency concepts difficult to students who have prior familiarity with sequential programming. Namely, in sequential programs, one is concerned only with the relation between the starting and terminating state of program parts - the so-called input/output behavior. Thus, the input/output behavior of sequential statements , say

$$S1; S2$$

(the delimiter ";" meaning that statements $S1$ and $S2$ are executed in lexical order), depends only upon the input/output behavior of $S1$ and $S2$, not upon how this behavior is implemented. So one can say that *compositional reasoning* suffices for sequential programs.

On the contrary, input/output behavior is not sufficient for talking about concurrent programs. The input/output behavior of a concurrent construct like the **cobegin** statement

$$\textbf{cobegin } S1 \parallel S2 \textbf{ coend}$$

(which causes concurrent execution of statements $S1$ and $S2$ and terminates only when the execution of both $S1$ and $S2$ has terminated) is not determined by the input/output behavior of $S1$ and $S2$, since the two statements can "interfere" with one another. To handle concurrent programs, we must be able to talk about their complete behavior - what the program does throughout its execution - not just what is true before and after the execution. Lack of this "global" knowledge is often a reason for difficulties in concurrent programming. We might say that the analysis of concurrent programs calls for *global reasoning*. (However, we must admit that current research is very lively, e.g. in attacking the question of the modular proofs of concurrent programs, thus hoping to bring their manipulation nearer to that of sequential ones.)

The requirement of a global view is important with respect to teaching. In the sequential realm, it suffices mostly to stay in a closed and rather restricted area of program text and to base one's reasoning upon it. However, if we want to aid the understanding of concurrent programs we need to have a global view of the entire program. One has to have a look what is defined and postulated in other parts than that one currently examines. Plain text is not good in supporting global views, although some kind of condensed forms of the entire program - skeletons or compressed views - can be useful. Instead, *graphical representation*, i.e. pictures and diagrams come to play. It has long been known that harnessing parallelism will greatly benefit from visualization, in fact some approaches to parallelism (e.g. data flow and Petri net approaches) heavily depend on pictorial or graphical representation. Also, many of the tools implemented to assist the design of concurrent or distributed systems are based on these techniques (mostly on Petri Nets, see e.g. [15]).

We think visual tools and techniques will turn out to be indispensable to teaching in this area. A computer assistant capable of exploiting them would be an excellent aid in learning. Visualizations are not so often brought to bear in textbooks on concurrent programming, and not at all or very seldom in the context of verification (see [16,17,18]). In our opinion, for example those visualizations that some

environments for the CSP language [19,20] provide would be very useful in teaching. A more sophisticated form of visualization, *animation*, would of course be most advantageous in illuminating the execution of a program and, in fact, is often included in the support systems.

One trend that can be traced to the globality requirement is the fact that traditionally the (rather few) systems giving mechanical assistance for rigorous analysis of concurrent programs are more or less "batch-like". By this we mean that the program to be studied is first compiled in another representation, sometimes including generation of "all" the possible execution paths. Next, the user is able to ask the system some questions, e.g. whether a certain temporal logic formula can be satisfied with regard to the program (see e.g. CESAR [21] and EMC [22]). We would prefer more incremental interaction with the assisting system whenever it is possible. For example, from the learning point of view the possibility to obtain advice during the programming or verification process turns out often to be more valuable than advice afterwards.

2.2. Proneness to a new kind of errors

One issue making concurrent programming hard is that it introduces *new classes of possible programming errors* which seem to be inherent to it. These errors are often very subtle and different from typical errors made in the context of sequential programming. Knowledge from the sequential world does not always carry over to the world of concurrency.

The folklore of typical examples of concurrent constructs like semaphores, monitors and conditional critical regions contains lots of instances of common errors in concurrent programming. Also knowledge of more intricate errors, e.g. dealing with conspiring processes, is cumulating. One possibility would be to incorporate these error "schemas" into a knowledge-base as LeDoux [23] has done in her knowledge-based system for debugging distributed programs. She has enumerated errors associated with Ada tasking and built a knowledge-base which her knowledge-based debugging system YODA utilizes when dealing for example with deadness and non-serializability errors.

Reconstructing erroneous situations and showing ways to avoid them is an important part of teaching as well as acquiring a skill like programming. However, one has to bear in mind that there are correctness criteria of interest for parallel programs other than are usual with sequential programs; for example parallel programs may be designed for cyclic non-terminating behavior. This introduces new dimensions to the correctness concept and should be emphasized in teaching.

2.3. Absence of paradigms for concurrent programming

Another difficulty in concurrent programming lies in the *absence of applicable paradigms* [24]. Examples of paradigms for sequential programming include divide-and-conquer, dynamic programming, as well as use of stacks, queues and other data structures. Compared to a programmer who is about to construct a sequential program, a programmer building a concurrent program has a smaller collection available. One reason of course is that there is not yet enough experience to produce practical solutions to important and recurring problems in this rather new domain of programming. The task of the teacher, however, is to acquaint students as early as possible with those paradigms already available. According to Schneider and Lamport [24] these include the following: agreement and commitment, computing global state, state machine approach, and clock synchronization.

2.4. Possibilities for knowledge-based assistance

One possibility to alleviate teaching is to incorporate the knowledge of the above mentioned paradigms and error models into an assisting system, thus fulfilling one prerequisite of *knowledge-based assistance or tutoring*. By this we mean assistance based on a knowledge base, i.e. on a collection of information that is then used to guide the solution path, suggest possible strategies, and trace and explain actions to the user.

Concerning *knowledge of the concurrent programming domain*, it seems that the knowledge needed is cumulating (cf. above section on paradigms). Also, it is interesting to note that signs have recently emerged pointing out that knowledge-oriented techniques could be beneficial in programming itself [25,26]. For example, it has been suggested that a useful way to analyze distributed systems is in terms of knowledge and how communication changes the processes' state of knowledge. Reasoning about this knowledge can then be used to design and verify families of protocols [27].

Concerning *knowledge for teaching or tutoring* it is obvious that the more complicated the subject to be learned is the more the students would welcome systems capable of explaining or suggesting new strategies. We hope that it is possible to import the rather good results reported in the diagnosis and tutoring of sequential programming (see e.g. [10,11]) to the domain of concurrent programming. In the next section we describe our own initial attempts in this direction.

3. A PROTOTYPE SYSTEM

In our prototype system we have especially concentrated on illustrating the correctness aspects of programs, i.e. how well program text conforms with rigorous program specifications. The system we outline here is a continuation of an earlier system by Back and Hietala [7] intended for sequential programs. The theoretical basis of the system is described by Back in [28]. A central idea is to emphasize program correctness checking as a highly *interactive* process between the user and the assisting system where the *incremental* and *iterative* nature of proof process must be supported. The experiences from introducing the earlier system in the classroom [6,29] suggest the usefulness of such a tool in teaching.

The way we have chosen to approach parallelism is the "shared variable" approach and to prove safety properties with the extended Owicki-Gries method [30,14]. In this separate checks to guarantee "well-behaving" of the parallel processes are added to the axiomatic schema for dealing with sequential correctness. The verification of the parallel construct - the **cobegin** statement -

{P} cobegin S1 ‖ S2 coend   {Q}

takes place in four phases:

(1) check that the precondition P before the entire **cobegin** statement implies the preconditions of the individual processes S1 and S2,
(2) verify the processes S1 and S2 separately (sequential correctness),
(3) check that the conjunction of the postconditions of S1 and S2 implies the postcondition Q after the entire **cobegin** statement,
(4) check that the concurrent statements S1 and S2 do not *interfere* with each other, i.e. make sure for each statement in one process that the simultaneous execution of the other process does not invalidate this statement's use of shared variables.

One promising role here for an assistant system is to take care of the tedious calculations (for example to generate the checks needed above) as well as to keep track of the status of the remaining checks. In addition to this kind of support we outline below also more sophisticated assistance.

3.1. Interaction with the prototype system

Exploiting graphical workstations is considered (see e.g. [31]) to be one of the most promising paths to pursue in advancing program verification technology; moreover, workstations have proved very useful as educational environments. With this in mind we chose a workstation environment for our prototype - our earlier system was implemented on a mainframe and employed 24 x 80 glass display terminals on which we simulated the use of multiple windows. The new system is being implemented on a SUN-3 workstation in ASH-Prolog language [32] which is an extension of C-Prolog [33]. This language utilizes the lowest layer of BWE (Brown Workstation Environment) software [34] to combine graphical window management with logic programming.

Fig.1 depicts the basic screen layout of the system and illustrates how the user goes about in checking the correctness. The snapshot was taken in the midst of the phase 2 - separately establishing the sequential correctness of the two concurrent processes (see the above list of phases). The user has chosen (by pointing and clicking with the mouse) a statement in process p1 which he is interested to verify (each statement can be verified in isolation). Now the system displays information related to the verification of this particular statement. In our example program a bank account transfer takes place in one process while in the other the auditor is checking the cumulative sum of bank accounts for embezzlement [14] .

Interaction with the system is based on the use of *windows*. These can be invoked from the horizontal menu bar at the top of the screen (separate vertical menus will appear which will provide operations for dealing with each of the five specific types of windows - program, assumptions, lemmas, proof and proof status). These windows can be created and relocated at will.

In fig.1 the verification process is currently focusing on location 10 in the *program window* (see the boxed statement), the facts that are known to hold at that place can be seen in the *assumptions window*, the lemmas (verification conditions) that should be proved at that location are shown in the *lemma window* and the proof that should establish the lemmas from the assumptions can be given inside the *proof window* (a window at the right containing the Emacs editor). A mark after the location number on each program line in the program window (a space, a plus sign or an asterisk) indicates to the user the

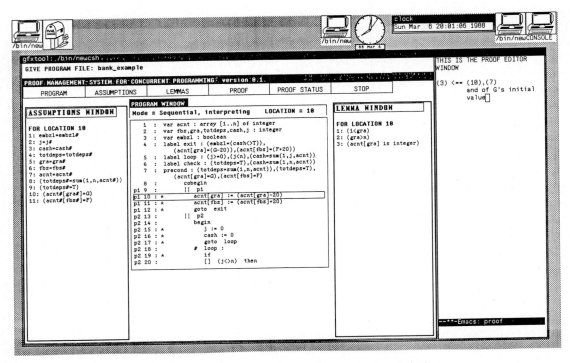

Fig. 1. Basic screen layout of our system on the Sun-3 display.

current proof status (i.e. whether this location is completely verified, partially verified, or does not yet have any proof). This information is intended to guide the user in his search for the next statement to prove. Besides inspecting this local proof status information it is also possible for the user to obtain a display of the proof status of the entire program (in a *proof status window)* where the program is represented as a tree (see fig.2).

At the moment the proofs for program locations are given as plain text, but we are exploring possibilities to use a theorem prover or a proof checker (either to build our own in Prolog or maybe to use an existing one, like the HOL system [35]). Note however that the underlying verification philosophy lies on the principle that the proof management and the actual proof can be separated [28], and in fact what we have here is a proof management system without the proof checker or theorem prover component. It was interesting to find out that already the availability of these modest supporting facilities turned out to be very useful in teaching the essentials of program verification (see [6]).

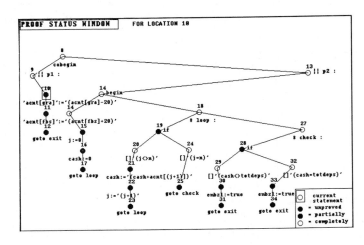

Fig. 2. Program proof status diagram

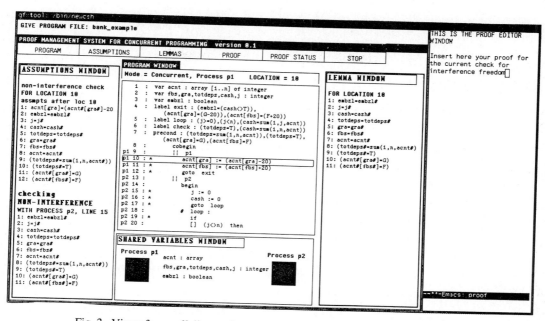

Fig. 3. Views for parallelism: shared variables (at the bottom of the screen) and interference checks (embedded into the assumptions and lemma windows)

A central new issue that the introduction of concurrency brings is the notion of *interference*, i.e. the non-deterministic manner in which the parallel processes can affect (interfere with) each other through operations issued for the shared variables. In dealing with this, several new views would be useful, e.g. a *shared variables window* - a graphical representation of the processes and their use of shared variables, and a window containing the *interference freedom checks* - these checks can be integrated into the assumptions and lemma windows (see fig.3). Also, a pictorial view of the status of interference freedom checks can be easily added to the above described proof status window. Moreover, a separate execution view with animation capabilities would be of great use in making the subject to be studied more concrete to the learner.

One further possibility would be to have the two separate ways to prove interference freedom juxtaposed: the original Owicki-Gries method [30] and the extended method by Schneider [14]. We think it might be educationally enlightening for the students to compare these two alternatives, first one which may be more intuitive, but tedious, while the other more concise, but also more demanding.

3.2. Knowledge-based assistance

What programmers know can naturally (see [25]) be divided into two parts: *programming knowledge* and *domain knowledge*. In the context of concurrent programming the first includes the paradigms outlined in Section 2, i.e. abstractions and plans to handle situations that occur in a variety of problems. For example, techniques of dealing with mutual exclusion belong to this category. The second category, domain knowledge, means knowledge specific to a particular concurrent application, for example to standard problems as readers-writers or dining philosophers.

The assistance given by our system will be based on a Prolog rule-base. Along the lines outlined above we envision this assistance to be organized into two classes of rules: exercise-independent and exercise-dependent. *Exercise-independent* rules will contain knowledge about general as well as derived rules of inference. These can be general rules of logic or related to concurrent programming knowledge. An exercise-independent rule might look like the following:

- rule: IF there-is-universally-quantified-goal
         THEN suggest-use-of-inf-rule: Univ-quantifier-elimination

On the other hand, we envision *exercise-dependent* rules to be available to the user by asking or when in a special working mode. They can be organized to form a hierarchy and be for example of the following type:

- rule: IF lemma-contains: predicate-philosopher **and** predicate-fork
         THEN provide-display-of:
              Fork-theorems-in-dining-philosophers-problem

A key function of a programming tutor is to examine a program written by a student programmer, find any errors in it and then explain the errors to the student in a way that will help the student learn [25]. Rules for common student misconceptions (e.g. in the manner of Anderson and Reiser [10]) with the system's reaction to them can be included into the above classes of rules.

The *timing of the assistance* can vary: it can either be given "on-the-fly", i.e. by all the time following the student and tutoring him, or by responding only when the student asks for guidance (coaching). In our first prototype we will concentrate on the latter approach and provide mostly exercise-dependent assistance.

The implementation of the knowledge-based part of our system will be carried out using the capabilities of Prolog (maybe using special techniques, such as the "blackboard" techniques, for this purpose). Logic programming in itself seems to provide an excellent framework for us. However, only extended use of the system in the classroom will validate and point out efficient forms of assistance.

4. CONCLUDING REMARKS

Computer programs teaching programming can be divided into tutors, bug finders and environments [36]. We think that all of these alternatives can be supported and will benefit from the knowledge-based approach. However, if compared to intelligent assistant systems for sequential programming, their concurrent counterparts must rely heavily on techniques capable of visual presentation and animation of the effects of parallelism.

When observing several processes acting parallel the cognitive complexity increases very rapidly. Any tool restricting this complexity and giving the learner a higher level, but at the same time concrete, model of the concurrent system seems profitable. We hope that our prototype presented in this paper is one step toward this direction in the domain of learning how to verify concurrent programs.

REFERENCES

[1] Ben-Ari, M., *Principles of concurrent programming*. Prentice-Hall, Englewood Cliffs, NJ, 1982.

[2] Holt, R.C., Graham, G.S., Lazowska, E.D., Scott, M.A., *Structured concurrent programming with operating systems applications*. Addison-Wesley, Reading, MA, 1978.

[3] Perrott, R.H., *Parallel programming*. Addison-Wesley, Reading, MA, 1987.

[4] Peterson, J.L., Silberschatz, A., *Operating systems concepts*. Second edition. Addison-Wesley, Reading, MA, 1985.

[5] Gries, D., Educating the programmer: notation, proofs and the development of programs. In Lavington, S.H., (ed.), *Information Processing 80*, North-Holland, New York, 1980, 935-944.

[6] Hietala, P., Teaching program verification with the help of an interactive support system. In Duncan, K., Harris, D., (eds.), *Computers in Education 85*, North-Holland, New York, 1985, 561-566.

[7] Back, R.J.R., Hietala, P., I3V: a program proof management system. Dept. of Math. Sciences, Univ. of Tampere, Report A136, December 1986.

[8] Sleeman, D., Brown, J.S., (eds.), *Intelligent Tutoring Systems*. Academic Press, New York, 1982.

[9] Yazdani, M., Intelligent tutoring systems: an overview. *Expert Systems* 3, 3, (July 1986), 154-163.

[10] Anderson, J.R., Reiser, B.J., The LISP Tutor. *Byte* 10, 4, (April 1985), 159-175.

[11] Johnson, W.L. , Soloway, E., PROUST: an automatic debugger for Pascal programs. *Byte* 10, 4, (April 1985), 179-190.

[12] Andrews, G.R., Schneider, F.B., Concepts and notations for concurrent programming. *ACM Computing Surveys* 15, 1, (March 1983), 3-43.

[13] Lamport, L., Basic concepts of distributed systems: logical foundation. In Paul, M., Siegert, H.J., (eds.), *Distributed Computing*. Lecture Notes in Computer Science 190, Springer-Verlag, Berlin, 1985, 19-30.

[14] Schneider, F.B., Andrews, G.A., Concepts for concurrent programming. In deBakker, J.W., deRoever, W.-P., Rozenberg, G., (eds.), *Current Trends in Concurrency*, Lecture Notes in Computer Science 224, Springer-Verlag, Berlin, 1986, 431-480.

[15] Dähler, J., Gerber, P., Gisiger, H-P., Kundig, A., A graphical tool for the design and prototyping of distributed programs.

ACM SIGSOFT Software Engineering Notes 13, 3, (July 1987), 25-36.

[16] Berg, H.K., Boebert, W.E., Franta, W.R., Moher, T.G., *Formal methods of program verification and specification.* Prentice-Hall, Englewood Cliffs, NJ, 1982.

[17] Hoare, C.A.R., *Communicating sequential processes.* Prentice-Hall, Englewood Cliffs, NJ, 1985.

[18] McGettrick, A.D., *Program verification using Ada.* Cambridge Computer Science Texts 13, Cambridge, 1982.

[19] Delisle, N., Schwartz, M., A programming environment for CSP. Proc. of the ACM SIGSOFT/SIGPLAN Software Engineering Symposium on Practical Software Development Environments, Palo Alto, CA, December 9-11, 1986. *ACM SIGPLAN Notices* 22,1, (January 1987), 34-41.

[20] Pong, M.C., A graphical language for concurrent programming. *IEEE Computer Society Workshop on Visual Languages,* June 25-27, 1986, Dallas, TX, 26-33.

[21] Queille, J.P., Sifakis, J., Specification and verification of concurrent systems in CESAR. *Proc. International Symposium on Programming.* Lecture Notes in Computer Science 137, Springer-Verlag, Berlin, 1982, 337-350.

[22] Clarke, E.M., Emerson, E.A., Sistla, A.P., Automatic verification of finite state concurrent systems using temporal logic specifications: a practical approach. CMU-CS-83-152, Carnegie-Mellon University, Department of Computer Science, September 1983.

[23] LeDoux, C.H., A knowledge-based system for debugging concurrent software. UCLA Computer Science Department, Technical Report CSD-860060, March 1986.

[24] Schneider, F.B., Lamport, L., Paradigms for distributed programs. In Paul, M., Siegert, H.J., (eds.), *Distributed Computing.* Lecture Notes in Computer Science 190, Springer-Verlag, Berlin, 1985, 669-716.

[25] Rich, C., Waters, R.C., Introduction. In Rich, C., Waters, R.C., (eds.), *Readings in Artificial Intelligence and Software Engineering.* Morgan Kaufmann Publishers, Inc., 1986, xi-xxi.

[26] Pettorossi, A., Skowron, A., Factual knowledge for developing concurrent programs. *Proc. AAAI-86, 5th National Conference on Artificial Intelligence,* Philadelphia, PA, August 11-15, 1986, 26-30.

[27] Halpern, J.Y., Zuck, L.D., A little knowledge goes a long way: simple knowledge-based derivations and correctness proofs for a family of protocols. *Proc. 6th ACM SIGACT-SIGOPS Symposium of Principles of Distributed Computing.* Vancouver, British Columbia, Canada, August 10-12, 1987.

[28] Back, R.J.R., Invariant based programs and their correctness. In Biermann, A., Guiho, G., Kodratoff, Y., (eds.), *Automatic Program Construction Techniques,* Macmillan, New York, N.Y., 1983, 223-242.

[29] Hietala, P., A course on program verification. Dept. of Math. Sciences, Univ. of Tampere, Report A137, December 1984.

[30] Owicki, S., Gries, D., An axiomatic proof technique for parallel programs. *Acta Informatica* 6, 1976, 319-340.

[31] Abdali, S.K., London, R., Exploiting workstations and displays in verification systems. In VERkshop III: Third Workshop on Formal Verification, *ACM SIGSOFT Software Engineering Notes* 10,4, (August 1985), 35-36.

[32] Michard, A., Monceyron, E., Le systeme graphique ASH-PROLOG et son utilisation pour le prototypage rapide d'interfaces homme-machine. INRIA-Centre de Sophia-Antipolis, Valbonne, 1986 (French).

[33] Pereira, F. (ed.), C-Prolog User's Manual, version 1.5. EdCAAD, Edinburgh Computer Aided Architectural Design, University of Edinburgh, 1986.

[34] Pato, J.N., Reiss, S.P., Brown, M.H., The Brown Workstation Environment: Programmer's Manual, version 2.0. Department of Computer Science, Brown University, Providence, RI, 1985.

[35] Gordon, M., HOL - a proof generating system for higher-order logic. In Birtwistle, G., Subrahmanyam, P.A., (eds.), *VLSI Specification, Verification and Synthesis,* Kluwer, 1987, 1-58.

[36] DuBoulay, B., Sothcott, C., Computers teaching programming: an introductory survey of the field. In Yazdani, M., Lawler, R., (eds.), *Artificial intelligence and Education,* Ablex, 1987, 345-372.

COMPUTERS IN EDUCATION, F. Lovis and E.D. Tagg (eds.)
Elsevier Science Publishers B.V. (North-Holland)
© IFIP, 1988

THE ABSTRACT MACHINE CONCEPT AS AN EDUCATIONAL OBJECTIVE IN COMPUTER SCIENCE

Dr. Diether Craemer and Rainer Mantz

Gesellschaft für Mathematik und Datenverarbeitung, Bereich Wissenstransfer
Schloß Birlinghoven, D-5205 Sankt Augustin, Federal Republic of Germany

This paper describes the work which introduces students in our computer science course to a broad concept of abstract machines which includes certain social scientific and philosophical aspects.

The paper consists of two parts. In the first part the development of the machine concept in modern western thought is outlined to provide the motivation for our educational objectives. The second part reflects our experience won in a teaching project where a complex task was solved by defining several abstract machines. Some specific advantages of the ELAN programming language and the EUMEL operating system, which the students used, are also discussed.

1. WHY TEACH "ABSTRACT MACHINES" ?

1.1 Introduction

That machines have played a fundamental role in every human civilization since the earliest beginnings of mankind, is an almost universally accepted statement in the contemporary scientific community*) , and taking this central theme as a starting point, we are going to analyze various aspects of the concept of "machine" on education.

Let us begin with a closer look at some common ideas about machines in general. Most people in our seminars, when asked what ideas come to their mind when the term "machine" is mentioned, would spontaneously describe some kind of mechanical machine made of steel or iron, probably noisy, and consisting of a multitude of moving parts which engage with one another. On second thoughts however, other concepts would be remembered as well, e.g. the machine-like aspect of bureaucracy, which once again is made up of a multitude of parts which engage with one other. There is an important difference, though; the parts of this second "machine" interact on a functional, not a mechanical level.

The use of the word "machine" in everyday language already supports the assumption that it is at least sometimes used to describe something that physically differs from a mechanical machine, but that is - not unlike say a loom - characterized by a complex pattern as to functionality and structure. Complexity, functionality and structure are the determining constituents of a concept which has been found basic to both natural and social sciences, i.e. the concept of system. (cf [9], p. 924, also [10])

The conclusion that there is a correlation between our understanding of machines and our insight into systems has in fact been drawn explicitly by at least two philosophers, who contributed to a theory of machines (see Baruzzi [2], p. 19, who in turn refers to [11]), and implicitly by Ashby in [1], pp.15 and 20. Ashby holds that Cybernetics provide a theory of machines *and* a scientific method to deal with complex systems. Rombach, one of the philosophers, ultimately looks at the machine as *the* model of a system.

The existence and importance of non-mechanical machines is also a central result of Mumford's work [8]. He undertook the challenging task of giving a comprehensive description of technology, its invention and development. One of his tenets (in [8], pp. 219 - 245), is that mankind invented very powerful machines, which he calls mega-machines, long before the modern mechanical machine appeared. This mega-machine consists entirely of human beings as "functional parts", its standard model is an army, and the most outstanding achievements accomplished by its use are the pyramids and other gigantic monuments of early civilizations.

Adopting Mumford's point of view it is easy to detect a fundamental identity behind two mega-machines of more recent origin - one almost non-mechanical, the other during its course of development becoming more and more mechanized: the French *manufacture* of the 18th century, and the factory of the 19th century. The development from one realization of this machine into the other is caused by the gradual replacement of human with mechanical functional parts, which work with a higher efficiency and productivity. The depletion in skill and creativity of the individual worker, however, has actually already taken place in the *manufacture*, although the social consequences of this depletion were felt more forcefully in the mechanized era of the 19th century. We may therefore see in the latest efforts towards CIM the logical outcome of a development which took up its course as early as 1700 and which still has an immense influence on our social structures. The few examples mentioned so far seem sufficient to show the explanatory power of the machine concept. But we shall see soon that there is even evidence for an almost universal presence of this concept in modern western thought.

---

*) Those writers who adopt a rather sceptical position towards the machine concept stress, by these critical efforts, the importance of this concept for modern western thought, cf. [8] and [4]. The mere existence of societies in history with an attitude towards machines different from the contemporary does therefore not affect the validity of our line of thought, because we attempt to reflect upon adequate educational means to help today's students to deal rationally with machines.

1.2 Machines, Language and Thought

Establishing the machine concept as a constituent part of western scientific thought seems largely to have been the work of Descartes (cf. [2], pp. 20 - 30). This French philosopher made a daring but highly influential attempt to systemize the act of thinking. In fact corroborating Rombach's point of view, we can find that Descartes already took machines as models for systems, as is stated for example in [8], p. 430, and in his *Discours de la Methode* the thinking process has all the characteristic features of a successful working machine.

Of course one might argue that with Descartes the use of the machine concept as a paradigm of scientific thought still has some aspects of a metaphor. But in the course of the development of modern science these metaphorical aspects were substituted more and more by reality. Baruzzi reminds us (in [2], p. 36) that even Galileo in his time had to "build" instruments to bridge the gap between nature and mind. Also Hobbes focuses on this creative act of building in philosophy - and we are on the safe side if we include science where philosophy is named - " ubi ergo generatio nulla .... ibi nulla philosophia intelligitur" .
(Thomas Hobbes, De Corpore, pI, Kap1, Sect 8, quoted after [2], p. 50)

Interpreting these ideas, Baruzzi summarizes that our reality of scientific experience is *produced* (our italics), as it were, somewhere in the middle between the reality of nature and the reality of mind, and that we have come to recognize this area in between as the area of instruments and machines. (cf. [2], pp. 40 - 41). In other words, we could oversimplify this by saying that scientists in the western tradition of Galileo, Descartes and Hobbes substitute (ever more complex) machines for nature, carefully analyze these machines and are repeatedly reassured that their approach is justified because they are always able to show that nature works basically like a machine.

Social sciences - at least during the last century or so - responded to this pattern of thought by trying to imitate it. Once having realized there is fundamental correlation between the concepts of machine and system, or to put it differently that there are non-mechanical machines , modern structuralism can be said to use non-mechanical or abstract machines to create models of reality. These models in turn create a reality of models, and it is for example in this second (man-made) reality where meanings are produced, (see [2], p. 174). To use a variation on a theme of the French structuralist Foucault in [5], "Les mots faient les choses".

To summarize: There is strong evidence that it is worthwile to deal adequately with machines in education because

- the machine concept is fundamental to western thought,
- there are non-mechanical, or abstract, machines,
- an abstract machine can be viewed as a canonical representation of a class of machines, which can be realized in different ways *), and
- the machine concept gains explanatory power by the inclusion of abstract machines.

---

*) cf. [1], p. 53 , where Ashby uses the slightly different term 'transformation', which we shall not introduce, so as to prevent terminology from becoming unwieldy.
cf.   also 1.1 of this paper on factories and their predecessors in history.

2. HOW TO TEACH "ABSTRACT MACHINES"

2.1 Which machines to choose

If we want students to grasp the machine concept by way of a variety of examples and by dealing actively with the subject, the digital computer - for economic reasons in most educational institutions the Personal Computer - lends itself as a means to realize abstract machines. For a more formal treatment of this representation see [6], pp. 166 - 167. We would like to note in passing that the choice of abstract machines realized on digital computers entails a further loss or abstraction i. e. the loss of motion, which is commonly associated with mechanical machines. There is hope, though, to win back motion further on the way via robotics.

While the place in the educational curriculum for our topic does not raise too many problems - at least in this paper, which refers to work in progress, we tacitly assume that computer science has to do the job - it is less easy to decide on an adequate representation of the abstract machines about which we are going to teach.

As a result of the proposed "hardware solution" we have to choose a suitable programming language for that purpose. This language ought to enable students to formulate functional modules and encourage a lucid and intelligible structural design.
[LISP or LOGO seem to be interesting candidates, but we have only used LISP in advanced AI courses, and lack experience with this language in more basic courses.]
Moreover ample use should be made of students' skills that already exist. These include almost certainly - regardless of scientific or mathematical talents - a linguistic component. Hence we suggest that the chosen programming language should support the choice of meaningful names in natural language for denoters, objects and functional modules. For the context of natural language and linguistic competence with adult learners in computer science we refer to [7].

A programming language that meets all requirements listed above is the ELAN language, embedded in the EUMEL operating system (not unlike C and UNIX).
[ELAN has been in use at the GMD, the Federal Republic of Germany's National Research Centre for Computer Science for educational purposes since 1980.]
As an important feature, ELAN provides the ability to describe the overall purpose of an abstract machine and successively of its functional parts in natural language. Syntactically one only needs to use the symbols "." and ":" to define meaningful names for programs or parts of programs.

For educational purposes this concept can hardly be overestimated. Students learn to define a program as an abstract machine simply by describing its functional parts in natural language. The corresponding functions of these parts are explained more precisely via refinements. Finally the level of ELAN keywords is reached at a stage where it is quite simple to code such a low-level refinement provided its function has been identified clearly.(see Koster [12])

With only 36 keywords the ELAN-language is easily learned and taught. Procedures, once tested and compiled error-free, can be integrated into the EUMEL Operating System via so-called packets. Hence an abstract machine can actually be realized on the user-interface level. As the EUMEL operating system is a multi-tasking, multi-user system, several different abstract machines can run concurrently on the same hardware, e.g. a machine for accounting transactions in one task, and a machine realizing simulation models programmed with the DYNAMO programming language in another.

2.2 A Teaching Project

We will describe an example taken from a half-year course at GMD, where people are trained to become application analyst-programmers. They started with a one week general introduction to basic notions in data processing, followed by a 3 week course on basic elements of programming (in ELAN), 3 weeks on data oriented design methods (exercises with the JACKSON method) and one week on file organization (sequential, direct, ISAM etc.).

By this time the 8 participants were tired of all the clear-cut small exercises and wanted to work on a *more realistic* program. Since three of them came from German Federal and State banks and the rest from public services departments (including the Federal Finance Ministry), a banking system was chosen as case study.
The highly motivated participants first defined the uppermost layer of user oriented operations (the *user machine*):

They made a distinction between three types of users and their corresponding operations

for the user at the office
   open account, change account, delete account,
   open standing order, change standing order, delete standing order,
for the cashier
   deposit, paying out, credit transfer,
for the user at the "back office"
   activate standing order, print balance sheet.

They used nets, JACKSON tree diagrams and verbal descriptions for a typical *top-down design*, an approach which they had learned earlier during the course. Although they sometimes used equations, their specification was far from being a formal specification of an accounting system, as defined in [3], pp. 83 - 90.

At a certain level of refinement they wanted a clear cut definition of the *base machine*. We used PCs with the operating system EUMEL (an extendable, multi-user operating system entirely written in ELAN - and in the meantime exported from Germany to Japan) and two layers above EUMEL: the first layer is an abstract machine to handle standard dialog situations with masks and menus, the second an abstract machine for files with direct access.

By now we introduced the concept of abstract machine and described the two lowest layers of the system in terms of *nets of types and operations*, see Figure 1.
As graphical notions we use:

(t)   for type t and   [o]   for operation o.

(t)→[o]   : objects of type t are input parameters to operation o,
   i.e. o *uses* objects of type t,

[o]→(t)   : objects of type t are output parameters to operation o,
   i.e. o *manipulates or creates* objects of type t.

Nets of types and operations (NTO) describe software on the level of abstract machines.

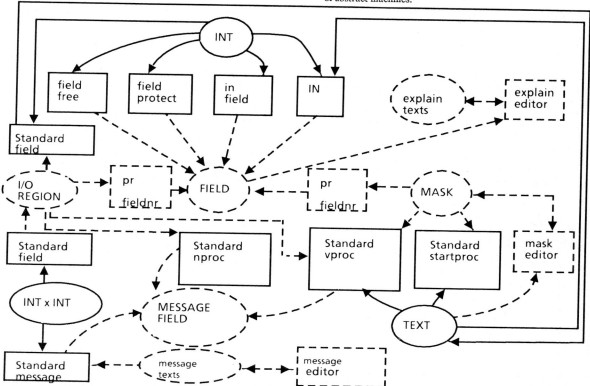

Figure 1: Abstract machine for standard-dialog situations with masks. Details which on this level of abstraction are hidden to the user of that machine, but which are needed for the explanation of the function, are represented with broken lines.

First layer
With the help of these visualisations of the "invisible machines" the participants were able to grasp the connections between the different operations quickly. Actually the abstract machine for the standard dialog consists of 10 operations only, the corresponding data-types of MASK, FIELD and I/O-REGION are hidden for the user of these operations.

We introduced them nevertheless within the NTO, the hidden parts represented by broken lines (Figure 1). Also the connection with the mask-editor, explain-editor and message-editor is shown, although those editors are not contained within that layer of abstraction.

It was necessary to show those hidden details, because we needed the notion of mask, field, message-field and input/output-region to explain the function of the operations:

standardstartproc	shows a mask with a name(TEXT) on the screen,
standardvproc	shows a mask and performs standardnproc,
standardnproc	shows the i/o-region within the mask and waits for input; the i/o-region is then filled and the message-field erased,
IN	is an operator which shows a TEXT-object within a field with fieldnumber(INT),
in field	moves the cursor in field with fieldnumber(INT),
field protect	protects field with fieldnumber (INT),
field free	releases protection of field with fieldnumber (INT),
standard message	shows message with message number (INT) on screen, eventually concatenated with a TEXT object as addition,
standard field	writes TEXT object in field with fieldnumber (INT) of the i/o-region,
standard field	yields the TEXT value of the field with fieldnumber (INT) of the i/o-region.

The two last operations have a generic name, and are distinguished by the types of their parameters. Actually the verbalisations of the standard-dialog operations are not very convincing; we used them as they exist (since the participants had to use the existing software).

To connect the hidden datatypes we introduced a hidden projection operation pr $_{fieldnr}$, which yields the field with the given fieldnr as projection from the mask or the i/o-region.

With the help of this operation a formal specification of the abstract datatypes involved can be given (but is ommitted here).

Second layer
The second layer of our base machine deals with direct access files.

Third layer
The next step within the project was to define a third layer (on top of the base machine) to realize the user machine.

The students defined their own datatypes CUSTOMER, TRANSACTION, STANDINGORDER, mainly with *conversion operations* to convert objects of those types into TEXT objects and vice-versa, as well as *assignment operators*.

The conversion operations are needed to store records as TEXT objects (although it would have been possible to store CUSTOMER, TRANSACTION and STANDINGORDER objects directly).

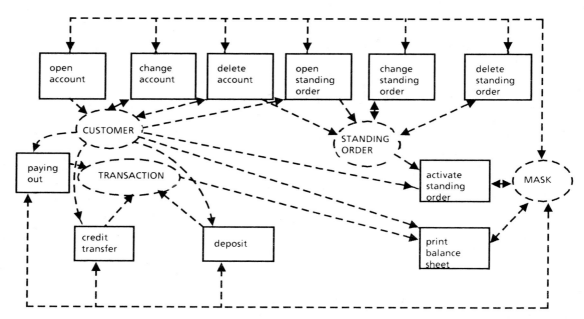

Figure 2: User machine of the account system, details hidden in lower layers represented with broken lines

The new types are structures (i.e. combinations of different types):

```
TYPE CUSTOMER =        STRUCT ( TEXT account number,
                                REAL balance,
                                TEXT family name,
                                TEXT christian name,
                                TEXT street,
                                TEXT nr,
                                TEXT postal code,
                                TEXT place);

TYPE TRANSACTION =     STRUCT ( TEXT account number,
                                TEXT date,
                                INT transaction type,
                                REAL amount);

TYPE STANDINGORDER =   STRUCT ( TEXT account number,
                                REAL amount,
                                TEXT transfer date,
                                INT transaction type,
                                TEXT target account number)
```

Since it is desirable at a certain level of abstraction to access the elements of these structures, it would have been necessary to define *access operations*. Our participants ommitted this; they used the dot-notation instead, i.e. for a CUSTOMER VAR person, the account number of that person is accessed by writing person.account number etc.

Now the *user machine* was formulated in terms of the newly created concept. It is shown in Figure 2, again with details which are hidden in the lower layers represented by dotted lines.

Using this design, the 8 participants produced a well functioning accounting system within 5 working days.

The final version of the program contained approximately 1050 lines written in ELAN.

We think, that such a result shows the productivity gained through the abstract machine approach in teaching. With this encouraging background we plan further courses focusing on the abstract machine concept.

REFERENCES

[1] W. Ross Ashby, Einführung in die Kybernetik (Frankfurt am Main, 1974)

[2] Arno Baruzzi, Mensch und Maschine (München, 1973)

[3] Alfs Berztiss, "Data abstraction in the specification of information systems", H. J. Kugler (ed.), Information Processing 86 (Amsterdam, 1986), pp. 83 - 90

[4] Hubert L. Dreyfus, Stuart E. Dreyfus, Mind over Machine (Reading, Mass., 1986)

[5] Michel Foucault, Les mots et les choses (Paris, 1966)

[6] John E. Hopcroft, Jeffrey D. Ullman, Introduction to Automata Theory, Language and Computation (Reading, Mass., 1979)

[7] Rainer Mantz, "Versprachlichung - ein für Erwachsene besonders geeigneter Zugang zum Erlernen des Programmierens", E. von Puttkammer (ed.), Informatik - Grundbildung in Schule und Beruf (Berlin, 1986), pp. 282 - 287

[8] Lewis Mumford, Mythos der Maschine (Frankfurt am Main, 1977)

[9] The Pocket Oxford Dictionary, ed. J. B. Sykes (Oxford, 1978)

[10] H. Rombach, Substanz, System, Struktur, 2 Volumes (Freiburg/München, 1965/1966)

[11] H. Rombach, Strukturontologie (Freiburg/München, 1971)

[12] C.H.A. Koster, Top-down programming with ELAN (Ellis Horwood Ltd., Chichester 1987)

COMPUTERS IN EDUCATION, F. Lovis and E.D. Tagg (eds.)
Elsevier Science Publishers B.V. (North-Holland)
IFIP, 1988

Development of Technologies for University Education in Computer Science: Progress Report of a "Modellversuch"[1]

Helfried E Broer
Udo Hafermann
Roland Vollmar

Technische Universität Braunschweig
Institute für Informatik
Bültenweg 74/75
D-3300 Braunschweig
West Germany

Summary

The pilot project 'Development of Technologies for University Education in Computer Science' has two main thrusts: First, the development of an entry-level course in computer science, based on the learning-by-doing principle. Second, the development and use of a certain 'education technology/methodology', in order to overcome the typical problems of students who take Computer Science merely as a minor subject. This report describes the motivations, objectives, and main activities of this project, namely the development of two Computer Science courses (in hardware and software), according to the proposed methodology.

1. Motivations and Objectives

The primary objective of the project 'Technologies for University Education in Computer Science' is the design and implementation of an 'Education Technology' for Computer Science at the Technical University of Braunschweig. The two main thrusts are: First, the development of an entry-level course in Computer Science, based on the learning-by-doing principle. Second, the development and use of a certain learning/teaching methodology, in order to overcome the typical problems of students who take Computer Science as a minor subject: These students have varying constraints imposed by their schedules, differ in respect to the total amount of time they can invest, have different backgrounds and therefore have widely varying needs. By an individually controlled study, there is no need for synchronization (among the students) and yet no loss with regard to the contents of the course.

Up to now, education technologies have only played a very minor role at universities. Neither the different forms of 'Programmed Instruction' (PI) nor the many variants of 'Computer Aided Instruction' (CAI) were able to conquer the universities. Considering the fact that there were attempts and concepts to 'automate' the education at the universities as early as in the mid-fifties, the question arises why there has been no break-through in this area, especially in the area of Computer Science where there is still a lack of education capacity.

In the literature we can find quite different explanations for this problem. Eyferth et al. (/1/) and Snyder and Palmer (/2/) name the following reasons: First, isolated learning (at the terminal) excludes social learning (in groups, mutual help etc.). Second, in spite of all advancements in teaching programs, the learning process is still a linear sequence of learning steps; quantum leaps, so-called 'aha-experiences', are not accounted for. Third, despite intensive research, the individual learning styles and strategies to which the learning sequences would need to be adapted are yet to be found. Fourth, the rules derived from behaviourism about subject presentation proved inadequate. Fifth, the constraints of practical programming reduce the number of possible paths through a learning sequence so much that there are only very few choices left for the presentation program. Sixth, the fundamental inability of the author of a learning sequence to foresee all possible answers, especially in a complex context, inevitably causes such a limitation of the processable inputs that the learning dialogue becomes rather

---

[1] The "Modellversuch" is a pilot project at the University of Braunschweig, jointly supported by the Federal Government (Ministerium für Bildung und Wissenschaft) and the State Government of Lower Saxony (Niedersächsisches Ministerium für Wissenschaft und Kunst).

restricted; in general, the students are 'allowed to choose' their answers from a small set of given possible answers.

According to many authors, the last two deficiencies especially are the main reason for the failing or the bad image of behaviouristically oriented education methods.

In response to this criticism, many so-called 'Intelligent Tutoring Systems' (ITS) were developed, which tried to elude those deficiencies by utilizing methods from the artificial intelligence research. In addition to the normal capabilities of tutoring systems, these programs are able to build and maintain a model of the knowledge of the student. This model is then used to control the explanations and the offered learning steps of the system (/3/). These intelligent tutoring systems employ so-called knowledge bases, which do not only contain the domain knowledge (what is to be taught), but also knowledge about the necessary communication and problem solving steps (/4/). 'Computers that teach should know what they teach.' This advertising slogan says that a teacher/tutor should have at least as much knowledge as he wants to teach in a session. 'Only when a teaching computer knows what he is talking about can he answer unexpected questions about the particular domain' (/5/, p. 95).

Even disregarding the fact that the prophecies about the capabilities of 'intelligent systems' have not nearly been fulfilled, there are other objections to be made against this statement.

First, we believe, in accordance with Nievergelt, Ventura and Hinterberger (/6/, pp. 25 and 27), that an artificial tutor should not pretend to be smarter than he really is. Otherwise the basis of trust which is necessary for learning can easily be destroyed. The dramatic performance decrease of these systems at the margins of the implemented knowledge area is especially critical. Up to now, neither the modelling nor the implementation of this non-domain specific general 'world knowledge' has been successful. Serious misjudgements by the artificial tutor are inevitable.

An even more serious problem, however, is that intelligent tutoring systems try to gain their power by hiding information from the user. With Nievergelt, Ventura and Hinterberger, again, we are convinced that the most fundamental problem of man-machine communication results from the fact that the user of the computer cannot directly see what is happening inside the machine. This problem especially arises in self-teaching applications. The following trivial example can illustrate this fact: Suppose a computer does not immediately respond to a given command. When the response of the computer takes longer than expected, an uncertain situation arises, especially for the

novice, which can be described by questions like: Did I give a wrong command? Did I mistype something? Did I maybe forget to press the return key? Or has the machine even crashed, maybe due to a hardware or software error? All these possibilities are in most cases indistinguishable from the outside. When one wants to save oneself from wasting time, one eventually has to react. Maybe the user decides to press the return key again, possibly even several times, just to make sure. Where will he eventually find himself, when the computer was actually just performing a large task and all these keystrokes were stored in the input-buffer for subsequent inputs?

This simple example, occurring every day in many variants, shows how important it is to have some 'insight' into what the computer is doing. Preventing this insight will almost inevitably cause these problems. Weizenbaum writes (in /8/, retranslated from p. 23 of the German edition): 'If his trust in such machines is to rely on something other than total hopelessness or blind faith, he must not only explain what these machines do, but also how they do it. This requires him to get a clear idea of their inner "realities".' But this especially is not supported in ITS, even rendered almost impossible: Which user of an ITS is, e.g., able to predict the responses of such a system? How should he know how to correct the model the system has made about him (e.g., about his knowledge)? Will not a novice especially be completely helpless in such a situation, which for the above mentioned reasons is almost inevitable? Will he not be disappointed and then turn away from the system?

For all of these reasons, we have decided to take an almost opposite approach to 'teaching systems'. We shall not incorporate methods of artificial intelligence in teaching systems, but rather deliberately wager on the human intelligence. Instead of leading the student by the nose through learning paths, we provide an experimenting environment. By means of prepared 'learning-' or 'playing worlds', in which the student has to achieve a certain task using some of the given tools, we attempt to give a comprehensive introduction to Computer Science. Using this 'education technology' we hope to be able to impart a realistic conception of the structure and operation of a computer, as well as a sound introduction to Computer Science in general.

2. The Software Course

With the course 'Introduction to Computer Science', we want to provide hands-on experience with the important concepts of Computer Science. The course consists of three parts. In all phases, the students work mainly at the computer/terminal, using a textbook. In addition, seminars are held where the students discuss special topics, ask questions etc. The forming of groups among the students is encouraged, but not a requirement.

In the introductory phase, the students are introduced to a simple 'programming world': the memory of a (virtual) processor consists of rectangular fields (arrays), whose elements can again be fields or elementary words, i.e. 'atoms' (at this point we already have nested data structures, which however are easily understandable). A simple programming language with a 'visible' stack (as in Forth) is provided. In this context, concepts like processor, memory, bit pattern, commands, data, program, data types, modelling, etc., will be introduced. The students are given the task of building a simple data base system. The available (nested) data structures of the programming language can show the student the many different possibilities in modelling, but also let him experience the easily arising complex interactions. At this point, we provide and stress the importance of appropriate visualization tools, using high resolution graphics.

As the first 'real' programming language to be learned in the second phase of the software course, we have chosen Modula-2. Modula-2 is a relatively 'small' language incorporating many elements considered state-of-the-art. The learning environment is an interpretive system specifically tailored to the requirements of a language designed for compilation. The students work with the system on two levels: with the language processor proper and with a so-called Ocular. This Ocular is like a window (an endoscope) through which the student can look into the inner structure and operation of the interpreter. Thereby he can watch the internal actions caused by his commands. At best, the Ocular is implemented using a second computer (or just a second high resolution screen). Alternatively, extra windows on the interpreter's screen can be used. The first approach, however, is preferred for at least the initial phase, to avoid confusion.

In the third phase, we want to show the student that many language processors and hence programming languages exist, which differ in non-trivial ways. Using the already introduced concepts, the student here should learn another 'real' language, e.g. APL, LISP, or PROLOG.

The visualizing systems used in all phases attempt from the start to provide the student with a workable, intuitive mental model of the systems he is working with. Similarities to good debugging systems are apparent, except that these assume that the user already has a working model of the language processor. Here, the main objective is to convey the first image of the underlying mechanisms to the student. When, later on, the Ocular providing this immediate introspection is no longer at hand, the student will hopefully be able to recall

the mental model as an aid in understanding the internal processes.

Currently, development of course software and course materials is well under way. Prototypes of the language processor for the introductory phase and for a visualizing APL-system for phase three, use APL as the implementation language. The Modula-2 system for phase two is being implemented in C, under Unix, and is being ported to IBM-PC and Atari-ST microcomputers.

In addition, systems using the 'visualization' or 'playing world' approach to teach other phenomena of Computer Science (e.g., automata theory), are being developed by graduate students.

3. The Hardware Laboratory

With the Hardware Lab, we want to give an introduction with hands-on experience to digital electronics, microprocessors, and process control, as well as to the related software issues (e.g., operating systems). For organizational reasons, the Hardware Lab is divided into several (sub-) labs with the same underlying structure.

Each laboratory consists of a 'core lab' and several 'appendices'. The core labs will teach a specific topic in a fairly complete way. The appendices then deal with special problems and/or alternative solutions. Both the core labs and the appendices consist of a tutorial describing the important concepts and their interactions, as well as a practical / experimental part where the students actually build something.

All labs strongly incorporate the learning-by-doing principle and are so set up that the students will be able to acquire the concepts and knowledge independently of one another. In their experimentally oriented work they will be guided by a textbook which contains sufficiently many hints and suggestions. In addition to the labs, there are discussion groups (seminars) where the students are introduced to scientific reasoning.

At present, the first and most important lab, the Digital Logic Lab, is completed. Starting with elementary circuits, this lab introduces basic digital electronics and then describes the concept of a micro-programmable von Neumann-computer. The basis of this lab is the 'LOGIBOX education system', which was developed in a number of student projects.

The LOGIBOX system consists of a plugboard and different boxes implementing logic functions of varying complexity. The boxes are designed in such a way that each box corresponds to a certain functional unit of block circuit dia-

grams at different levels (e.g., switch, register, memory, control unit, etc.). The boxes
are all designed for 8-bit parallel
'processing'; the connections were standardized with respect to mechanical, electrical and
logical characteristics. In this way, LOGIBOX
has become a universal construction system
where all boxes can be arbitrarily combined;
one only has to cater for the functional
dependencies (as in a block diagram design on
paper, where one does not yet bother about
timing and the like).

At the end of each lab section, the student
receives one box with the same functional
interface as the circuit he has just built out
of several boxes. Thereby, the number of boxes
necessary for each section can be kept about
constant, despite the rising circuit complexity. For electrical connections we use one-
wire (control-) lines but also 8-bit parallel
(data-) lines. This substantially increases
the clarity of the circuit on the plugboard and
makes the construction of non-trivial circuits
feasible.

Low-level electrical problems can almost be
ignored, i.e. from an electrical viewpoint the
boxes represent 'ideal circuits'. This was
achieved by the multi-stage master-slave behaviour of the boxes. A discussion of problems
like racing, hazards, unstable signal levels,
etc. is not needed for the experiments and can
be dealt with in one of the 'appendices'.

For the actual course operation with the LOGI-
BOX education system, a textbook is handed out
to the students at the beginning of the practical part of the course. Guided by this script,
the student is gradually introduced to the
LOGIBOX system and learns about, and experiments with, increasingly complex hardware
structures. The students are not required to
do a certain section/experiment within a certain time period. Instead, they can go through
the course as fast (or slowly) as they want or
can. The script attempts to be so comprehensive that individual assistance for the labs is
not necessary. Nevertheless, support is provided and contact with the instructors and with
fellow students is desirable and encouraged.

A second practical lab, the SOFTBOX Lab, is
under development. This lab is similar to the
(LOGIBOX) Hardware Lab described above, except
that here the designs and experiments are not
done on a plugboard but on the graphics screen
of a computer. The student selects boxes from
a library (or builds new ones), connects them
(using mouse and hi-res graphics) and then lets
the computer simulate the circuit.

4. Current Project Status

At present, the courses so far developed are
being evaluated and refined with a small group
of selected students. "Real" operation is to
be taken up in a following semester. Due to
restrictions imposed by the resources available
to the project, the number of participants will
be limited. Additional efforts are under way
to provide a help and documentation system to
accompany the course software and a communication network for the microcomputers.

5. Acknowledgement

We wish to thank Jürgen Heymann for his help in
preparing the English version of the paper and
our colleagues Gerhard Pogrzeba and Ulrich
Schwarz for valuable hints and suggestions.

6. References

/1/ K. Eyferth, K. Fischer, U. Kling, W.
Korte, J. Laubsch, H. Löthe, R. Schmidt,
R. Werkhofer: Computerunterstützter
Unterricht in der allgemeinbildenden
Schule. Inhalte des 2. BTZ-Symposions,
BTZ-Reihe Band 3, Bildungstechnologisches
Zentrum, Wiesbaden 1973.

/2/ T. Snyder, J. Palmer: In Search Of The
Most Amazing Thing. Children, Education,
& Computers. Addison Wesley Inc., 1986.

/3/ P. Häußler, V. Tremp, W. Ziebarth: Künstliche Intelligenz und Bildung in der Bundesrepublik: Eine Bestandsaufnahme.
Institut für Pädagogik der Naturwissenschaften an der Universität Kiel, Dezember
1986.

/4/ R. Gunzenhäuser, T. Knopik: Neuere Ent-
wicklungen des rechnerunterstützten Ler-
nens. In: 'Überblicke Informationsver-
arbeitung 1985', BI-Wissenschaftsverlag,
1985.

/5/ T. O'Shea, J. Self: Learning and Teaching
with Computers. Harvester Press Ltd.,
Brighton, 1983.

/6/ J. Nievergelt, A. Ventura, H. Hinterber-
ger: Interactive Computer Programs for
Education. Philosophy, Techniques, and
Examples. Addison Wesley Inc., 1986.

/7/ P. Schefe: Künstliche Intelligenz und
Bildung. Bestandsaufnahme und Folgenab-
schätzung. Gutachten im Auftrag des IPN
(included as appendix in /3/).

/8/ J. Weizenbaum: Computer Power and Human
Reason. From Judgement to Calculation.
W. H. Freeman & Company, 1976.

COMPUTERS IN EDUCATION, F. Lovis and E.D. Tagg (eds.)
Elsevier Science Publishers B.V. (North-Holland)
© IFIP, 1988

CONTINUED EDUCATION WITH ELECTRONIC COURSEWARE AND INTEGRATED LABORATORY

Dipl. Inform. Esther Berg
Prof. Dr. Gunter Schlageter
Dipl. Inform. Wolfgang Stern

University of Hagen (FernUniversität)
Praktische Informatik I
Postfach 940
D-5800 Hagen
West Germany*

Today almost everyone faces the continuous need to learn after leaving school. This results in an increasing demand for continued education. To effectively satisfy these requirements, learning by instruction and by doing should be combined. Traditionally, this combination has been offered in collective classroom teaching which cannot come up with an essential learning need of today: the individual decision where, when and what to learn. The computer as a teaching medium can individualize the learning process. An electronic tutor guides a student through both an instructional book and an experimental laboratory. How this architecture works in detail will be discussed within this paper.

1. INTRODUCTION

Traditional education is characterized by the following features:
- Students have to attend the teacher's lecture personally, i.e. they have to be present in a certain room during predefined lesson hours.
- Teaching subjects are chosen to transmit a framework of concepts which has to be filled during professional activity.

This first stage of education is not sufficient for a whole professional life. Almost everyone has to continue his studies to keep pace with an explosively increasing amount of knowledge in his field of profession. Companies themselves try to meet the problem of continued education by on-the-job-training. But in the long run this task will be beyond the resources of most companies. Obviously, continued education must also be provided by universities, with all types of industry-university cooperation. A most promising form of continued education there seems to be teaching by correspondence.

To be successful in continued education the characteristics stated above have to be broken up so that:
- Students can learn their lessons at their own pace wherever and whenever they like.
- Teaching subjects are presented with special regard to practical requirements.

From its foundation the university of Hagen has instructed its students by correspondence and is traditionally engaged in the field of continued education. Today a new concept is being implemented and tested within the department of practical computer science. Within this concept the computer itself is extensively used for the purpose of continued education. To

* This report is based on a project which is funded by the German "Bundesminister für Bildung und Wissenschaft" (Project No. M0538.00). The authors are responsible for the contents of this publication.

involve the computer into the teaching process is advantageous in several ways:
- The courses are open to everyone provided that a personal computer can be accessed. This is not a crucial restriction as PCs are widely spread nowadays.
- Students working on these courses do not have to attend lessons personally.
- An experimental environment called "laboratory" can be part of the course material within which students will be able to practise their newly acquired knowledge. An "electronic tutor" can keep track of the student's learning progress. And, finally the written material can be substituted by an "electronic book".

The following figure illustrates how laboratory, electronic book and electronic tutor are interconnected:

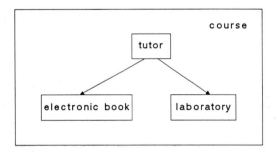

Figure 1: course architecture

The main task of the electronic tutor is not to monitor the learning progress but to individualize the student's walk through the learning material which consists of two separate parts: electronic book and laboratory. In the book part the student should acquire knowledge of a specific domain. In the laboratory part he should apply this knowledge to solve problems.
Acquiring and applying knowledge must be seen as two very different aspects of a learning process. In our opinion both aspects cannot effectively be taught by the same means. In a sole laboratory environment students may fail to discover essential features of the underlying knowledge domain which would have probably be pointed out in a book. If only a book is provided students may lack necessary experiences

in solving domain-specific problems which they would have probably acquired in a laboratory. As a book part seems as essential as a laboratory we have incorporated both in our course architecture.

Assuming general agreement on the necessity of book and laboratory, there still remains the question what special advantages can be achieved by embedding these components into a computer environment. Surely one can hardly imagine building a laboratory for topics in practical computer science without involving a computer. But as far as the book part is concerned doubts might arise. However, we shall point out some features of electronic books which clearly surpass properties of written books.
In printed books all information has to be presented statically and mainly monochromatically. Both restrictions are no longer valid in electronic books. Different colours can be used for several purposes like identifying or highlighting. Furthermore, animated cartoons can be composed to illustrate actions in progress.

Besides its role in the teaching process the computer has to offer valuable communication features. Communication forms a serious bottleneck in teaching by correspondence. Many students complain about the fact that it is much more difficult for them to get individual advice by the university staff or to contact their fellow students than in traditional universities. Even if an electronic tutor assists the student in learning it may fail to overcome the difficulties met, which have to be discussed with a human tutor. Therefore the student should have a cheap public network access at his disposal by which he can contact other persons.

So, from the student's point of view the main characteristics of our concept are:
- An electronic course is partitioned into book, laboratory and tutor. Within the book part the student acquires knowledge. Within the laboratory he applies the knowledge. Through both parts he is individually guided by the electronic tutor.
- Where the instructional potential of the electronic courses ends, the student can use a communication network to get human instruction.

We like to end this introductory chapter by shortly overviewing the main part of the article. In chapter 2 the system architecture is described more in detail. Not only components are identified which make up our system but also tools to develop them. Within the next chapter we deal with functionalities of course components offered by a fully elaborated system to illustrate the potential of this architecture. Chapter 4 contrasts our goal system to others in Intelligent Computer Assisted Instruction (ICAI) and reviews existing tools with respect to their usefulness in developing our system. In the book part some tools almost fit into our concept. In the laboratory part no appropriate tool base has been found. Problems which occur in designing such tools will be outlined. One of these problems will be worked out more in detail within chapter 5. The article ends with an outlook on our future work.

2. GENERAL ARCHITECTURE

To have a closer look on how the electronic book, laboratory, tutor and communication support work together, consider figure 2 on the next page.

In the figure the tutor is always split into two components, though it has been treated as a unit in the introduction. This functionality-driven separation is due to the fact that book tutors have to perform tasks totally different from those of laboratory tutors.

The computerized environment to develop courses is installed at "author stations". There, the author produces electronic books, elaborates sample solutions for laboratory tasks and predefines tutor's actions. He is assisted by the author system's editor and the laboratory definer. In administering courses the author is supported by his local course data base. This additional tool is especially useful when the author is working on different courses or different versions of course at the same time.

After the course is completed with respect to some university standards it is incorporated into the course data base of the university. Now the course is ready for distribution.

The computerized environment to work on courses is installed at the "learner station" which can be located at a student's home or at a university study center. The student walks through the material using features provided by book and laboratory. Within the book the student is allowed to highlight important passages, to add remarks etc, which amounts to changing contents of the book. Course individualisation is rendered possible by <u>local</u> access to courses. A private copy of each course to which a student has subscribed is stored into his local data base. The student's local activities on his course cannot be monitored centrally.

The communication network connects the learner with the central course data base and his human tutor. A student can load all the lectures into his local data base to which he has subscribed and he can distribute messages to fellow students and his human tutor. As the network is mainly accessed for loading purposes and not during work on courses, the student's network costs are kept low.

3. SOME FUNCTIONAL PROPOSITONS ON COURSE COMPONENTS

In this chapter we briefly discuss functionalities of book and laboratory tutors.

3.1. electronic books and their tutors

As electronic books resemble their printed cousins, they provide students with a familiar learning environment. The teaching medium computer, however, allows additional features to be incorporated which enhance functionalities of written books in an evolutionary way.

From a syntactical point of view electronic books are composed of texts differing in colour, type and size, and graphics. Sometimes sequences of graphics are combined as small motion pictures. This pure layout-information is arranged in small units called frames, a physical structure which hardly makes sense to the reader. He is

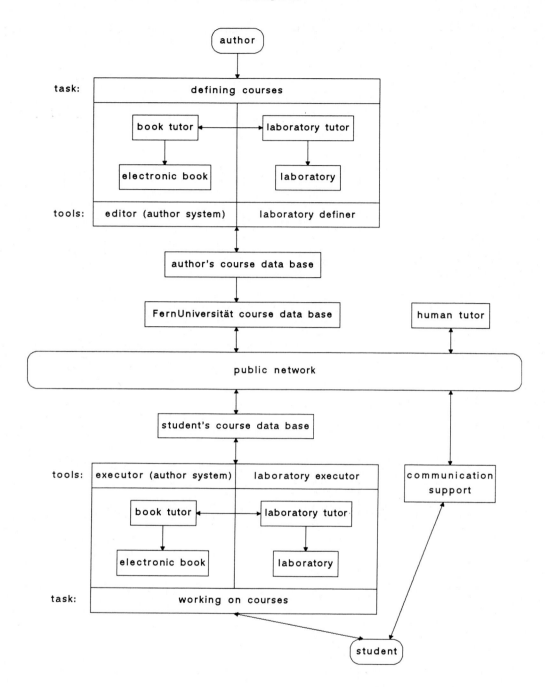

Figure 2: general architecture

much more interested in structures which reflect the meaning of what is presented to him. Therefore an ideal electronic book enables him to
- access the chapter hierarchy from every position within the book

- consult the subject index whenever he likes to
- continue with an example, a question or a laboratory task related to the topic he is just working on. This is especially useful if the student

doesn't feel sure that he has got the point
- recall the meaning of a subject which is presently used to define another one.

From this semantic point of view the student may also be interested in
- highlighting important passages
- writing down remarks in the book
- marking his present position in the book before he stops working on it.

The book tutor bases its actions on some knowledge about its students. The tutor's knowledge is comprised in a student's model. In this model the results of an introductory student's questionnaire (fields of interest, background knowledge,...) may be incorporated as well as a trace of former student's actions. With respect to its knowledge the tutor proposes actions to the student. The student can make use of the proposal but is free to choose every possible command. The chosen action is carried out by the tutor and its result is used to update the student's model.
We think that a friendly learning environment is more important than a comfortable author's support. Therefore we have neglected functionalities an author would require to build electronic books and their tutors. This aspect will be examined in other papers.

3.2. laboratories and their tutors

Laboratories provide the student with an almost instructionless learning environment. It allows the student to deepen his domain understanding by experimentation.
A minimal laboratory consists of real or simulated systems in computer science like
- development environments for different programming languages
- data bases
- expert systems etc

In this kernel configuration a student is totally free in experimenting. But if he gets lost in this instructionless environment, he needs some help to get on. Such critical situations are more likely to occur, if students are asked to solve special problems. To support students in solving problems the kernel can be encapsulated by a laboratory help component which hints at possible

actions to overcome difficulties. The help component forms the essential part of the laboratory tutor. It can be enhanced by an evaluation component which keeps track of the progress on laboratory tasks in the student's model so that both book tutor and laboratory help can base their propositions on a complete student's profile.

4. SAMPLE SYSTEMS AND DEVELOPMENT TOOLS

The question is whether there are any existing architectures which already cover the functionalities outlined in the introduction, and which development tools are available to build the outlined system. Firstly, let us have a look at existing systems.

4.1. some existing systems

The BALSA system [1], [2] focuses on visualizing the progress of algorithms in execution. A human instructor illustrates the algorithms' explanation by supervising the execution of predefined scripts on interconnected students' computers. The script-authors have specified which aspects of the algorithms are to be visualized by what presentation means. In an instructor independent session mode students can experiment with algorithms by supervising script execution of their own. A local-area network connects students' computers so that they can communicate with each other.
With respect to our goal architecture BALSA can be characterized as follows: A laboratory is provided which focuses on visualizing algorithms. But the student's possibilities to experiment with algorithms are limited. He can only take the instructor's place in supervising script execution but not the script-author's place in defining what and how to visualize. Communication between students is supported, but an electronic book and both tutors are missing.

The LISP-Tutor [3], [4] teaches basic LISP-programming skills. The electronic tutor's knowledge comprises an ideal model of how to solve given programming tasks as well as reactions on buggy programming attempts. The menu-driven tutor comprises a syntax-directed editor. So students mustn't pay attention to syntax-errors.

A LISP-programming laboratory including a good electronic tutor is provided. An electronic book and its tutor are completely missing. Only a written booklet gives a brief introduction. Communication support has totally been neglected.

The PROUST system [6], formerly known as MENO II [5], tries to debug faulty PASCAL-programs. The tutor isn't engaged in teaching programming but detecting semantic errors in PASCAL-programs which attempt to solve a very special programming task. It explains underlying misconceptions to the programmer and assists him in eliminating these faulty program constructs.
A PASCAL-programming laboratory including a specialized tutor is provided. The architecture lacks an electronic book and its tutor as well as a communication facility.

All these systems only make use of a special-purpose tailored subset of electronic book, electronic tutor, laboratory and communication network. Though they present valuable ideas, they do not offer all of the required functionalities.

4.2. development tools

Similarly, the existing development tools do not allow one to build the desired system components. Electronic books and their tutors are defined and executed by means of author systems. They have been examined in an EULE project-report [7]. The examination has been restricted to systems available on IBM PC and compatibles. The results can be summarized as follows:
Some systems fail to provide authors and students with normal book-functionalities. Authors cannot freely navigate through or reorganise their chapter hierarchy. Students cannot write down notes in the text, make use of a bookmark or consult tables of contents or subject indexes when they like to. Others neglect graphical animation or poorly support specification of the electronic book's tutor.

With respect to laboratories the situation is still worse. Of course, there are lots of data bases, expert systems and development environments for various programming languages in which a student can make experiments of his own. But only domain-dependent systems have been implemented which encapsulate these laboratory kernels by help and evaluation components. Only recently a first ICAI based attempt has been made to build a domain-independent laboratory environment [8]. But no efforts have been made to integrate an instructional and an experimental environment. Also the question hasn't been answered how deeply an author should be involved in defining laboratories.

As tools to develop electronic books are more sophisticated than tools for laboratories, we have decided to concentrate on the neglected area. One of the better authoring systems has been chosen as a base for defining and running books. The missing functionalities will be incorporated.

5. PROBLEMS IN INTEGRATING BOOK AND LABORATORY

In the following we shall concentrate on the question of how a unit can be composed of book and laboratory in an integrated way.

In a minimal laboratory configuration consisting of a sole kernel, a book tutor has to communicate directly with it. Their integration wouldn't be a serious task if both of them comprised interfaces to their outside world. Unfortunately, such features are, if at all, only implemented in book tutor and laboratory kernels in a rudimentary way. So it even causes trouble merely to switch between book and laboratory without any other functions.
The situation becomes even more complicated if switching is combined with contextual changes. If, for example, a laboratory task has been explained within the book part and the student chooses it, the laboratory has to be prepared with respect to the given problem. So the laboratory entry point has to be modified. If on the other hand a student wants to recapitulate a book passage which treats problem-relevant items, the appropriate book page has to be selected by the book tutor.
If the laboratory kernel is encapsulated by a help component the complexity still grows. As processes within laboratory kernels are hidden

from external observation the help component cannot treat students' help requests properly by monitoring their inputs and kernel outputs. The help component has to base its proposals on some knowledge about the kernel's interior. How this can be achieved is an open problem.

6. CONCLUSIONS AND FUTURE PERSPECTIVES

The architecture introduced in previous chapters forms an attractive learning environment for continued education. It is characterized by the following features:
- The learner can study almost independent of time and place.
- Learning by instruction (electronic book) is combined with learning by doing (laboratory).
- The learner can communicate to fellow students as well as to his human tutor.

Currently we concentrate our activities on
- improving the book tutor by the functionalites described in chapter 3
- developing a general laboratory concept
- integrating electronic books and laboratory kernels.

This base system will be evolutionarily extended to our goal architecture within the next few years.

Beside these activities we are also producing electronic courses. A basic set of them will be available from the beginning of 1988. The first courses will cover the area of artificial intelligence, UNIX and ADA.

REFERENCES

[1] Marc H. Brown, Robert Sedgewick, A System for Algorithm Animation, <u>Computer Graphics,</u> vol. 18, no. 3, July 1984, 177-186

[2] Marc H. Brown, Robert Sedgewick, Techniques for Algorithm Animation, <u>IEEE Software,</u> vol. 2, no. 1, January 1987, 28-39

[3] John R. Anderson, Brian J. Reiser, The Lisp Tutor, <u>Byte,</u> vol. 10, no. 4, April 1985, 159-175

[4] John R. Anderson, Edward Skwarecki, The Automated Tutoring of Introductory Computer Programming, <u>Communications of the ACM,</u> vol. 29, no. 9, September 1986, 842-849

[5] Elliot Soloway, Eric Rubin, Beverly Woolf, Jeffrey Bonar, Meno-II: An AI-Based Programming Tutor, <u>Journal of Computer-Based Instruction,</u> vol. 10, nos. 1 & 2, Summer 1983, 20-34

[6] W. Lewis Johnson, Elliot Soloway, PROUST: An Automatic Debugger for Pascal Programs, <u>Byte,</u> vol. 10, no. 4, April 1985, 179-190

[7] Kristine Fankhänel, Lehrsysteme für Personal Computer - Autoren- und Tutorsysteme -, EULE project-report, FernUniversität Hagen, December 1987

[8] Kazuhisa Kawai, Riichiro Mizoguchi, Osamu Kakusho, Jun'ichi Toyoda, A Framework for ICAI Systems Based on Inductive Inference and Logic Programming, <u>New Generation Computing,</u> vol. 5, no. 5, May 1987, 115-129

COMPUTERS IN EDUCATION, F. Lovis and E.D. Tagg (eds.)
Elsevier Science Publishers B.V. (North-Holland)
© IFIP, 1988

SATELLITES IN EDUCATION: A UK PERSPECTIVE

Judith CHRISTIAN-CARTER

Council for Educational Technology, 3 Devonshire Street, London W1N 2BA, England

Compared with other countries, in particular the USA, Australia, Japan, and India, the United Kingdom has been rather slow in utilizing the facilities offered by satellites for educational purposes. In the last four years there has been a steady UK increase in both interest and activity in the use of satellites in education. Much of this interest and activity is experimental and developmental in nature, allowing users to assess and evaluate the potential of satellites as an aid in the learning process. This paper explores recent activity and proposes that if the UK is to gain full educational benefit from satellites the primary need is a coordinated development strategy in all education and training sectors.

1.   INTRODUCTION

"One day a world-wide consortium of satellite universities may bring information and education to people wherever they need it. Those possibilities are getting closer, but there are still gaps in the satellite links. While some forms of communication, like news and telephone, have become common forms of satellite transmission, most of the global links are still being explored."
(E Silverman, 1986)

It is a commonly shared view that in Europe satellite technology is well ahead of its utilization, and that many applications are still in their embryonic stage. Such a view, however, is mixed with the belief that satellites are definitely part of the future educational scene and that this future is getting closer and closer. For education the significance of both the current and projected status of satellite technology cannot be ignored if the deployment of satellites is to be driven by educational needs and not those of technology.

2.   AN OVERVIEW OF THE UK SCENE

The successful launch of Ariane 3 in the early hours (GMT) of Wednesday 16 September 1987 with its payload of two satellites was greeted with relief in many quarters. However, 'one swallow doesn't a summer make' and a moment's reflection on the concern shown over the troubles which recently have beset both Arianespace and NASA serves to indicate that the successful deployment of satellites into orbit is fraught with uncertainties. This, coupled with a certain tendency not to become too enthusiastic about technological applications until it is critical to do so, may account for the apparent lack of UK educational application in the satellite arena.

A number of satellites is currently circling the earth in both geosynchronous (stationary) and polar orbits. These satellites carry out a number of functions and operate at different power levels of transmission. Whether satellites operate at different low, medium, or high power, they can transmit video, voice, graphics, and data. Some satellites receive signals via transponders from transmitting stations (uplinks) on the ground, process these signals and retransmit them back to receiving antennae (downlinks) on the ground. Other satellites have actual image, microwave, and infra red transmitters, or sensors, which can track the changes in weather, navigation, radiation, vegetation, etc. Therefore, satellite transmission, of whatever type, involves considerable investment in equipment on the ground, including terrestrial transmission and reception and the production of quality materials.

Educationalists in the UK are currently exploring four main areas of satellite use:

(i)   data transfer;

(ii)   television receive only broadcasting;

(iii)   direct broadcasting and teleconferencing; and,

(iv)   remote sensing.

Of those educational sites in the UK which are using satellites in some way, facilities vary from simple antennae to multiple Television Receive Only (TVROs). At the present time there are no official educational uplinks in the UK although some institutions do have up-link facilities. Of the educational applications currently employed in the UK, remote sensing seems to head the list although many educationalists are actively considering the use of data transfer, direct broadcasting by satellite (DBS), and teleconferencing for a variety of educational and training purposes.

One of the most influential stimuli to UK activity has come in the shape of European initiatives. Schemes such as the Programme of Advanced Continuing Education (PACE) and the Community Action Programme for Education and Training Technology (COMETT) have encouraged the development of Satellite User Groups in order to pool resources and to coordinate efforts for setting up various satellite programme projects. Another extremely potent development has been the free broadcast time being offered by the European Space Agency (ESA) on OLYMPUS-1 which, at the time of writing, is due to be launched in early 1989. This latter initiative has produced much UK activity, especially in the areas of further and higher education, adult and continuing education, and amongst those concerned with new training technologies.

It would be fair to assess the UK scene as one of informed interest and evolving enthusiasm. So informed is this interest that 'would-be' users already have identified areas of potential concern, such as tariff structures, technical standards, copyright laws, and funding restrictions. There would also appear to be a unanimous acceptance of the need for care to be exercised by those at the 'leading edge' to develop a sound satellite strategy, appropriate applications, and to ensure the cost-effective use of satellite technology. The Council for Educational Technology (CET), which has a remit to promote the application and development of educational technology and to provide a focal point for the collection and dissemination of information and advice, has responded to these various needs by undertaking a number of roles which brings it into close contact with most current and potential UK satellite users.

A more detailed discussion follows on the uses to which satellites are currently being put, along with some projected plans for future use.

3.   DATA TRANSFER

UK services in the area of information and data transfer are expanding at an ever-quickening pace. All sectors of education and training are now placing even greater store on the access to world-wide databases for retrieving and exchanging information and data. The means by which information is retrieved and exchanged is often via satellite whether employed in an overt or a covert sense. In an overt sense satellites are used by industrial and business communities for both internal and external data exchange although such a use has not met with considerable enthusiasm in the education community mainly because of the prohibitive costs involved. In five years' time the picture may be somewhat different as in a covert sense satellites are used to facilitate electronic data interchange (EDI) such as the European Academic and Research Network (EARN) which connects hundreds of computers together or where schools use electronic mail services to participate in exchanges with schools in other countries. In this way satellite costs are within the budgets of educational users and, once they are convinced of the potential, moves might be made by providers to reduce the costs involved in data transfer to a more practical level.

4.   TELEVISION RECEIVE ONLY BROADCASTING

The UK is just starting to realize that the latest development in entertainment technology will require new ways of thinking and reacting. For a country which took its time to adjust to the provision of a fourth television channel the advent of satellite broadcasting will either open the flood gates or take several years to be accepted. As with all new developments the education and training sector has been looking at potential spin-offs and the experiences gained by other countries.

The most immediate reactions were that TVRO could enrich curriculum opportunities for geographically dispersed groups or individuals, particularly in the more remote areas of England, Scotland, and Wales, provided that traditional TV broadcasts do not fulfill such a need. Perhaps more importantly, this means of delivery could improve foreign language study and lead to the development of skills which would enable English-speaking people to communicate better with people in other European countries. Additionally, such a development may also lead to a better understanding of other people's cultures through news broadcasts from other countries and could serve to show that because people communicate in different languages it does not necessarily mean that their cultures are totally different from one's own. Cultural programmes, programmes for expatriates and migrant workers, and religious programmes, have already made good use of this means of broadcasting.

It is easy to confuse TVRO with direct broadcasting satellites (DBS) and teleconferencing, and many people have fallen into this trap. In the UK educational broadcasting cannot be claimed to be a major success where a number of educational practitioners make very little, or no use of this medium. There is little reason to suppose that, given such a situation, TVRO will bring about a major revolution in educational broadcasting. Relative costs also mean that unless a large number of people are receiving a TVRO broadcast it is usually more economical to distribute the programme on video cassette via the postal system. This is particularly true when, because of the time the programme is broadcast, the majority of viewers will record the transmission for later viewing. One of the advantages given for TVROs over conventional broadcasting by cable is that it is much more flexible. Dishes, like TV antennae, are easily moved while cable is not. Whether, environmentally, one is content to see satellite dishes obliterating the sky-line in much the same way as UHF TV antennae do at present, is another debate altogether!

5.   DIRECT BROADCASTING AND TELECONFERENCING

As yet there are few DBS facilities available to education at a price it can afford due mainly to the lack of high-powered satellites in orbit. However, in the next few years this situation is likely to change dramatically as more DBS satellites are deployed, and through the use of OLYMPUS-1 the education and training world can start to prepare for the future.

The use of this type of satellite technology can help to make distance learning a reality for a large number of the population. It can assist in providing in-service training and staff development for academic and vocational teachers in remote areas. It can deliver training and retraining of adults, especially in rapidly changing high technology areas and where the amount of specialist/expert help available is sparse. It can deliver continuing education programmes for professional and vocational organizations by transmitting educational seminars, exchanges, and courses. It may also prove to be a cost-effective way of sharing research and resources, particularly in the higher education sector.

Apart from the high power of the transmission which allows for small receiving dishes (less than 1m in diameter), more transponder time, and, which perhaps, will lower the cost of transmission, DBS can be two-way, thus making programmes live and interactive. As yet, teleconferencing via present low-power satellites has not been used extensively in education due to the high costs involved. However, potential DBS applications include: meetings, information exchanges and training; research and course development between schools and universities; and seminars, case studies, and field support. A number of proposals for time on OLYMPUS-1 focus on some of these areas of use and, now these proposals have been accepted, it is important to identify existing pockets of experience into which OLYMPUS-1 users can tap. Experiments, e.g. the Satellites for Health and Rural Education (SHARE) project, have already taken place using INTELSAT, a low-power satellite, as a one-way video link up, along with terrestrial land lines, for two-way audio to encourage telecommunications development in rural and remote areas as a means of assisting in long-distance health care and education. The results from these experiments have been most encouraging and have served to show what can be done in a more limited way. With full two-way video and audio it is quite likely that the sky will be the limit for education!

6.   REMOTE SENSING

Remote sensing is the science of observation
at a distance. While remote sensing by
satellite is quite a different application of
satellite delivery from broadcasting and teleconferencing, its potential is gradually being
recognized by educationalists. The UK has a
well established reputation in this field and
through its National Remote Sensing Centre
(NRSC) undertakes much international work. The
NRSC is the UK Earthnet agent; Earthnet is the
ESA's network for disseminating remotely
sensed data.

Educational interest in remote sensing has been
generated by the ability to survey and monitor
the natural and cultural environment.
Geosynchronous meteorological satellites
provide data for weather observation as well as
vegetation changes, oil slicks, movements of
sea ice, desert locust breeding grounds and
sea temperatures. Polar orbiting satellites
provide more data per metre over both the sea
and the land, and, where satellites carry
instruments which penetrate cloud mass, information is obtained on both the earth's
atmosphere and its surface. All this data can
be enhanced by computer, far beyond the value
of an ordinary photographic image, and this
greater detail enables a far wider interpretation to be obtained. Equipment now exists
which enables students to obtain and process
their own weather images and the new generations of 16-bit and 32-bit computers have the
scope to process these and other images even
further.

The small-scale development initiatives so far
undertaken, mainly in UK secondary schools,
have shown that remote sensing rewards multidisciplinary work. Remote sensing can help
students to gain a better understanding of the
world because a global perspective has become
a visual reality; for example, the issue of
international cooperation can be raised quite
naturally. The use of data from satellites
encourages the interpretation, manipulation
and questioning of information. Spatial and
temporal data can be used in combination.
Science, technology, mathematics, and both
human and physical geography, can be readily
combined in order to engage students in diverse
activities which support the learning of key
concepts and skills.

The next generation of satellites for remote
sensing will be even more sophisticated than
the present ones. The ERS series, the first
of which is due to be launched by the ESA in
1990, will carry sensors which will enable
these satellites to work in all kinds of
weather and to produce their images regardless
of day or night. However, it has been pointed
out (Hunt & Fifield, 1987) that this increase
in data will bring with it a major challenge
for information technology in disseminating
the wealth of data that this will generate and
the provision of useful information and products. At the present time a number of
factors prevent people getting access to the
data currently available, such as the lack of
suitably processed data in a ready-to-use form,
the expense of obtaining such information, the
lack of suitable hardware and software for on-
site processing, and the lack of information
about what is available and how to use it.

7.   CONSIDERATIONS FOR THE FUTURE

It would appear that satellite technology
offers a number of benefits to education. The
delivery of learning by satellite means that:

(i)   information is carried quickly and
         uniformly;

(ii)   simultaneous communication can take
         place between widely dispersed
         audiences;

(iii)   there is a sense of immediacy and
         interaction for an isolated audience;

(iv)   specialists can present a single input
         rather than undertake multiple
         sessions;

(v)   educational opportunities not provided
         locally can be made available;

(vi)   students can be stimulated and moti-
         vated to use new technology;

(vii)   learning can be participative and
         interactive through video, voice, data,
         graphics, etc; and

(viii)   alternative methods are now available
         to meet a variety of educational needs.

Up to a point many of these benefits are of a
quasi-hypothetical nature. Not only does
further development work need to be undertaken
but also various areas of concern need to be
addressed not merely with words but with deeds.
For example:

(i)   monopolies and tariff structures govern
        most European communication systems and
        existing legislation often makes it
        difficult to move ahead in satellite
        usage;

(ii)   the cost of leasing land lines, up-
        links, downlinks, and transponder time,
        including technical back-up and
        support is out of range of most educa-
        tional budgets;

(iii)   the lack of technical standards and a
        common delivery system create a problem
        for pan-European satellite trans-
        missions although recent developments
        in this area are more encouraging,
        especially where equipment manu-
        facturers are concerned;

(iv)   some of the existing copyright legis-
        lation does not cover satellite trans-
        mission thus making it difficult to
        ascertain what may, or may not, be
        transmitted legally;

(v)   in order to ensure control over some
        broadcasts, in particular the security
        of proprietary information, some data
        and video signals will be encrypted
        which means that standards for encryp-
        tion will have to be established so
        that programmes can be coded and
        decoded as required; and,

(vi)   the need for education to find affluent
        partners in order to support this
        relatively new, and expensive, delivery
        medium for educational and training
        materials. This means that those
        contemplating the use of satellites for
        this end must consider the current and
        future funding of programmes and, in so
        doing, develop a strategy for long-term
        use. If this is not achieved then
        there is the strong likelihood of
        having a lot of unused hardware lying
        around in a few year's time. We need
        to give thought not only to what
        resources are required for present use

but also to our options in the future.

8.   SOME ASPECTS OF A DEVELOPMENT STRATEGY

Any system of learning is only as good as the
people who use it. One aspect of any development strategy, therefore, must be to address
a number of human factors in using satellites
for education and training. We will need to
know:

(i)   how people learn in distance learning
        environments where delivery of
        learning is by satellite;

(ii)   what styles of presentation are needed
        to teach via satellite;

(iii)   what types of interaction, reinforce-
        ment, and support materials are needed
        to get the most out of learning in a
        distance learning environment via
        satellite;

(iv)   the types of learner resistance and
        acceptance factors involved in this
        form of learning; and,

(v)   how students are motivated in distance
        learning environments via satellite.

In addition to information on human factors we
also need to explore satellite technology in
order to develop a strategy for its cost-
effective use. This means that evaluation has
to be a part of any developmental project; the
implications of which are that a methodology
and appropriate tools are generated by which
future evaluations can be carried out. Evaluation will also inform us of various modes of
educational use to which this technology can
be put. In this way we can all profit by the
success or failure of others and costly mistakes will be avoided by those that follow the
'pioneers' who are venturing into the medium
for the very first time.

For both the pioneers and future fellow
venturers the spawning of user groups and
interest groups will probably provide a much
sought after mutual support system. At the
time of writing user groups are only in their
pre-conceptual or embryonic stage but their
healthy birth is a matter of considerable
concern if a coordinated development strategy
is to become a reality. One topic for

discussion which should be on the agenda of any self-respecting satellite user group is the need to create a European educational channel. The creation of a specific channel on satellite for educational and training purposes is an important item for debate and, if agreed, would require an educational satellite users consortium to: coordinate and encourage the production of programmes; agree on a policy for priorities; and, provide guidelines for the use of such a channel.

9.   A PASSE AD ESSE

From a number of possibilities several realities have already dawned. CET recently undertook a major survey of the actual and potential use of satellites in education and, as a result, has initiated a variety of activities which are designed to meet some of the aspects previously identified.

A 'Satellite Forum' has been constituted, comprising those educationalists interested in using satellites for a variety of learning outcomes. The purpose of the Forum is to share information about satellite usage, to act as a pressure group on matters such as legislation, standards and strategy, and to provide a cohesive body for future developments. This group is already influencing both strategy and use, and will play an important role in future developments.

In relation to information exchange, CET proposes to establish a central clearing house for all those using, and interested in using, satellites in education. The information will be collated centrally and stored on CET's mini-computer for electronic and hard-copy distribution to interested parties. At this early stage of use and development the need for a central information source is vital if education is to move ahead in an informed and rational way. However, this is only one of a number of existing developments.

As far as schools are concerned two major developments have taken place. The Department of Education and Science (DES) and the British National Space Centre (BNSC) have set up a Remote Sensing in Schools Working Group. The group is responsible for originating and implementing a five year plan by which remote sensing will become a component of many subjects across the curriculum. With two major

national bodies backing such a venture it is action, and not merely words, which is the order of the day. Likewise, CET has responded to the growing interest in schools by producing an information pack for secondary (11-18 years) schools. The pack sets out to promote the use of satellites in the learning process, showing teachers the wide range of possibilities available and the means by which to achieve these in the classroom.

With the BNSC, CET is exploring the best way of developing the appropriate hardware for satellite reception in schools. A recent BNSC exploratory project to experiment with TVROs in ten secondary schools showed that current British hardware is not suitable in many respects. The need for appropriate hardware is, therefore, paramount if schools are to get the most out of satellites. Forthcoming proposals will make recommendations for a staged development of compatible hardware which is suitable for both current and future use.

Evaluation will be a feature of a number of UK initiatives. The Manpower Services Commission (MSC) is funding Plymouth Polytechnic to meet some of the demands created by adult and continuing education by using some of the free-time on OLYMPUS-1 to provide distance learning in a number of subject areas. CET has been asked by the MSC to evaluate this project which the former sees as an innovatory exploration of one-way video and two-way audio in this particular educational sector. In this respect and others the UK has, in more ways than one, started to tackle the problem of using satellites in education and training.

10.   CONCLUSION

However there still remains much to be done by all of us involved in, and concerned with, education and training.

"Satellites are not the panacea for unemployment, motivational problems, competition in the marketplace, or all educational needs. However, they are another option which must be addressed in the swiftly moving world in which we find ourselves, particularly as we approach the 21st century. The pace will continue to quicken. No one can afford to be left behind"
(CET, 1987)

REFERENCES

CET, ed, Satellites and Education: a report
on the current situ ation, Council for
Educational Technology for the United Kingdom,
London 1987, 48.

Garry Hunt and Richard Fifield, Remote sensing
and the whole world picture show, New Scientist
No 1574, August 1987, 46-51.

Eleanor L Silverman, Gaps in the global link-
up, Data Training, Vol 6, No 1, December 1986,
29-31.

COMPUTERS IN EDUCATION, F. Lovis and E.D. Tagg (eds.)
Elsevier Science Publishers B.V. (North-Holland)
© JFIP, 1988

Local Area Networks in Education: An Infrastructure Perspective

Robert S. McLean

Ontario Institute for Studies in Education
252 Bloor Street West
Toronto, Ontario, Canada   M5S 1V6

Local Area Networks (LANs) are not yet widely used in education, partly because they are "add-ons" to traditional microcomputer uses, usually just for economic reasons. However, when a local area network is designed into a widely used educational computing infrastructure, the LAN offers new opportunities. In Ontario, Canada, the Ministry of Education's specifications for computer systems for schools require a LAN system. An infrastructure of 20 000 LAN-based student stations is now in place. This paper reviews the Ontario experience, describes how the infrastructure approach influences microcomputer use and shows how educational materials take advantage of the LAN architecture.

1. INTRODUCTION

A significant educational computing infrastructure can be obtained by interconnecting student workstations with other computing resources in local area networks. A local area network (LAN) is a group of interconnected computer facilities within a restricted geographic area, such as a building or a campus.

Such interconnection is dramatically illustrated by projects at several post-secondary institutions.[1] There, LANs are being implemented with the intention of providing high powered and distributed computer systems, as generally available educational resources across their campuses. The network makes possible a qualitatively different and richer computing environment at each workstation than would be found at a stand-alone microcomputer.

Although LANs may also be found in elementary and secondary education, to date they have been implemented infrequently. The usual reason for using a LAN is to share peripheral devices among existing microcomputers, typically for convenience or economic reasons. The network and its use is grafted onto the normal use of microcomputers as self-contained units. Indeed, much of the debate of whether to network or not seems to be concerned with two things: cost savings and whether existing (stand-alone) programs can be run over the network (including whether it is legal to use the software in that way).

This paper examines the characteristics of LAN-based microcomputer systems in elementary and secondary education from the perspective of educational computing *infrastructure*. It reports on the first four years of such an infrastructure in Ontario, Canada, which now contains about 20 000 student stations, all organized into LANs.

2. THE *INFRASTRUCTURE* CONCEPT

In this paper, *infrastructure* means facilities which are deliberately planned and provided, usually by government, to serve a standardized purpose over a relatively long period of time. Such systems have stable characteristics which are publicly controlled and documented. These systems try to provide a complex set of services addressed to fulfill a diverse set of requirements. The characteristics are adaptable over time, but such evolution is controlled by the public authority rather than by the provider of the specific parts of the infrastructure.

These characteristics may be seen in many common infrastructures of modern life: public utilities, the telephone network, radio and television, rail and highway transportation networks, etc. Rarely have they been evident in the use of microcomputers in education, however. The province-wide implementation to be described here does have many of these characteristics.

2.1 The Ontario Example

In 1981, the Ontario Ministry of Education took the unusual step of trying to specify such an infrastructure for instructional computing in schools. The specifications [2,3] were issued early in 1983. Development of conforming microcomputer systems was encouraged by a system of grants to local school boards for the purchase of such microcomputer systems (to be known as "Grant Eligible Microcomputer Systems" or "G.E.M.S."). The result was the ICON* microcomputer system by CEMCORP,

---

* The following trademarks appear in this paper: Arcnet, CEMCORP, G.E.M.S., IBM EDNET, ICON, QNX, The Ambience, Unisys, UNIX.

marketed internationally by Unisys. In 1985, IBM created the EDNET microcomputer system which meets the G.E.M.S. specifications.

The Ontario process stands in contrast to the usual approach, where an educational jurisdiction selects a computer system from among existing products offered by vendors. The 1983 specifications govern the current G.E.M.S., and the first step of evolution of these specifications has now been taken. The result is a new set of specifications which simultaneously provide a common infrastructure for the Ministry's software and open the market to more system suppliers.[5]

Although the G.E.M.S. specifications appeared to focus on hardware, the Ministry of Education's concern was really educational materials -- educational software. An adequate educational computing infrastructure would provide well-defined characteristics of computers in the schools of the province, well suited to support the educational software -- lessonware -- which the Ministry planned to develop.

Since 1983, the Ministry has funded private development of over $18 million worth of educational software designed to be directly compatible with the curriculum guidelines issued by the Ministry. It distributes this software without cost to all schools in the Province, thus being able to create an infrastructure of educational software, parallel to that of the hardware.

This lessonware requires more powerful computer systems than are typically marketed to schools. Additionally, the infrastructure approach -- offering a standard set of capabilities that can be counted upon by software developers -- means that Ministry-funded software can be run at a large number of sites within its jurisdiction.

2.2 Educational Perspectives on LANs

The LAN is a central part of the Ontario educational microcomputer specifications. From the infrastructure perspective, the educational microcomputer system is viewed as a shared resource for creative use by students and teachers. Like other shared resources, such as the school library, it should be available on demand, have a wide range of materials appropriate to many learning activities, and facilitate the sharing of activities and accomplishments.

A LAN can be specified for many different reasons and it can be used for many different purposes. These will be influenced greatly by the prevailing model of computer use in education within the jurisdiction. Some of the prime motivations for adopting LAN-based systems are economic, managerial, and supportive.

The **economic factor** is perhaps the most frequently cited and also the most direct: the local area network allows many independent microcomputers to share expensive peripheral devices. Thus, each microcomputer need not have its own disk and printer, but can access these facilities over the network. They render "services" to all users of the network and are often called "servers". Thus, a user at any workstation can store files on the file server, print on the print server, communicate with distant computers over the communications server, etc. There is no requirement that the

workstations communicate with each other, as no particular functionality is assumed beyond that found in normal self-contained microcomputer systems. The economic factor is less important today than previously, since the cost of peripheral devices has fallen significantly. Still, there is a saving in larger networks.

The **managerial perspective** varies more widely with one's model of education. Certainly, central facilities on the network decrease the physical organization necessary to use multiple computers in a school setting. For instance, programs and data are resident on the fileserver, rather than requiring separate media (e.g., diskettes) for each computer. Going further, network software could take on some of the teacher's supervision duties; some equipment vendors envision large classrooms with one student per computer and the ability of the teacher to supervise the students' activities via the computer, in the style of language laboratories.

But the LAN can be seen from a **supportive perspective** as well. Here the LAN offers its economic benefits, but also supports a wider range of sharing of resources on the network to provide new capabilities and patterns of use not found in the stand-alone model of microcomputer use. A total, generalized interconnection of nodes and services of the network combines to facilitate the sharing of tools for educational exploration and the sharing of products of that educational process. The sharing concept can apply at all levels of the educational microcomputer system, from hardware and software to user behaviour.

Ontario has adopted the supportive perspective and we will cite example programs to illustrate a range of possibilities. The Ontario specifications specifically view education as a cooperative and shared experience, and suggest that experiences with computers should facilitate that view.

2.3 The Ontario Perspective

Philosophically, the Ministry of Education sees the microcomputer as a tool for "creative use" by children during their education. A policy issued in 1981, and still applicable today, expresses it thus: "There will be two fundamentally different ways to use computers in the process of teaching and learning. The more significant way will be the creative use of the computer by individuals: writing, composing, designing, analyzing, and other extensions of original thought. All students must be given opportunities to use computers in this way."[6]

In practice, this implies access to a wide range of programs which students can use in their learning activities. These include some fairly traditional tools and utilities, such as text editors and drawing programs. Each G.E.M.S. has as a standard component, an impressive array of programming languages: LOGO, BASIC, C, FORTRAN, COBOL, APL, Pascal -- some in multiple forms -- tailored to educational use. And, as described above, a growing library of educational materials targeted for use in specific areas of the curriculum is being developed by the Ministry of Education.

All of these programs must be available across the network

and, as described later, many take specific advantage of the opportunities provided by the network.

The remainder of this paper will first describe the computer facilities of the ICON microcomputer system. The ICON meets the Ministry specifications and has been the primary focus of its software development. The paper closes with a description of several innovative uses of the LAN which point to new paradigms for enriched computer applications in education.

3. THE ICON SYSTEM AND ITS LAN

The CEMCORP/Unisys ICON microcomputer system is a LAN, built around microcomputers, connected by a coaxial cable. The network is a token-passing architecture based on Arcnet. The LAN has a raw transmission speed of 2 megabits per second. All nodes have equal status, and each is a self-contained microcomputer in its own right. A typical network is illustrated in figure 1. Student stations have a display and keyboard. Each network has at least one file server (a "LEXICON") consisting of a hard disk, diskette drive, and communications interfaces for a printer and 2 serial ports.

The ICON runs the QNX operating system. It is "UNIX-like" but is smaller than UNIX and has extensions in the area of realtime operation. QNX is multi-tasking. That is, it is composed of several separate programs which co-exist in memory, each devoted to a particular portion of the computer's operations. User programs are also single or multiple tasks. When multiple tasks are used, they communicate by passing messages to each other. Message passing is not limited to one computer node, but may also occur over the network. For example, this is the means by which tasks on the individual student stations obtain files from the file server.

Multi-tasking also opens up a new opportunity to build application programs which are composed of several tasks, each operating on a different node of the LAN (and serving the student at that node) but communicating with each other directly (program to program) and in realtime.

The QNX file system on any particular fileserver is heirarchically organized, similar to that in UNIX. Such an organization is able to retain many separate users' files and programs, as well as files which are needed for system operation. Programs and data files can also be made accessible to groups or all users, so that the always-ready resource concept of the LAN is fulfilled.

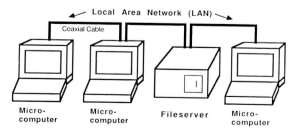

Figure 1. A typical small Local Area Network

4. LAN USES IN ONTARIO

Examples of LAN use in the Ontario experience can be grouped under several organizing ideas: 1) applications which exploit the concept of a network as a shared resource; 2) environments for direct communication between users in real time; 3) lessonware which implements program to program communication in large simulations; 4) special "server" applications where additional costly resources are shared among users; and 5) research into behaviour of students while using networked software.

5. THE LAN AS A SHARED RESOURCE

Three examples will be cited to show how both the concept of sharing and the technology of sharing can be implemented on a LAN. The first is a user interface which embodies these characteristics. The second is a school setting where the network concept is being extended very widely throughout a school. The third is a hypermedia-like community database built on the sharing concept.

5.1 The Ambience User Interface

Although the QNX operating system provides excellent support for many simultaneous users across the network and allows them to have access to a wide range of resources, it is -- like UNIX -- somewhat cryptic and requires a fair amount of computer familiarity and training for effective use. The Ministry of Education faces an environment in which they are creating lessonware intended for use by all teachers, not just the 5 to 10% who have computer skills. In addition, although the QNX file structure can support the concept of a shared resource, it does not impose any particular organization to accomplish those goals. The Ministry has created a user interface program, called The Ambience, to meet these requirements.

The Ambience serves as the organizing mechanism for the lessonware materials and their use. In a sense, it is similar to the resource librarian and card catalog of the school resource library. It organizes materials into "spaces". For example, Ministry lessonware is available in the Ontario Educational Software Service (OESS) space; each user has a "personal space" where they (or the lessonware) can store work in progress. Units of the school, such as classes, can also have common spaces, organized around two concepts: things to be done, in "task space" (i.e., assignments), and things which have been accomplished and are to be shared with others via the "display space" (analogous to the classroom bulletin board).

The Ambience thus imposes an educational organization (and hence, philosophy) on the more neutral QNX hierarchical file structure. It is based on sharing and open access to most of the materials held in the system. It maintains the many records necessary to support such sharing, but does not provide a computer-based instructional management (CMI) system. Rather, it relies on the teacher and traditional means of directing the educational process, in which the computer materials are just one resource among many.

From a technical point of view, the Ambience manages several residual problems of network use, e.g. the problems of multiple users trying to write the same file. It tries to insulate the user from many of the specifics of the underlying operating system, by being menu-driven rather than command-driven; using longer descriptions for files rather than short file names of the QNX directory; associating executable tasks with files so that most user products invoke the appropriate tools to work on them (editors, lessonware, etc.); and similar steps designed to be "user friendly".

Management of a LAN which serves as a resource for a large number of users can be a major problem. In the early trials of the ICON it quickly became apparent that someone must accept responsibility as "site administrator", requiring additional skills. Consequently, the Ambience provides assistance to the management of the LAN, by simplifying the installation and removal of lessonware resources, for example. This could otherwise be a major problem, since a typical Ministry-sponsored lessonware package is about 500 K of program and data. New technology, such as compact-disk read-only memory (CD-ROM) is being developed to address this requirement as well. Such a CD-ROM facility would also be an instance of a new kind of "server" being added to the network (see also below).

5.2 Large LAN experiments

The typical ICON network consists of one fileserver and 3 to 16 student stations. The student ICONs are either located in a laboratory setting (all in one room) or are distributed into several classrooms, with one or more in each. Often the resource centre or library has one or more stations as well. Only a fraction of the school's classrooms would have such computer access.

It is possible to extend the LAN so that it consists of many more nodes. Groups of ICONs can be associated in "clusters" and many clusters interconnected on the LAN. The effect is to create a very large computing resource which can potentially span an entire school, making the shared computer resources available at any node, in any room.

A few such networks were constructed in Ontario schools in 1987. For instance, one consists of about 70 workstations distributed throughout an elementary school. A typical classroom has 3 workstations and, through them, students can access materials stored on the fileservers anywhere in the school. This network experiment is being studied from many perspectives to determine the feasibility and usefulness of such a wide-ranging computing resource.

5.3 The LAN for a Community Database: CSILE

A LAN, with its fileserver(s), creates a shared file storage space which can be used for individual purposes or as a creation of the user community, working together. CSILE (for "Computer Supported Intentional Learning Environment", and pronounced "see-sill") is a research project which attempts to support a more "intentional" and cooperative approach to learning [7] through the use of a common database created by the students, themselves. The database entries are free-form text and graphics which chronicle the student's active exploration of knowledge and support it with various retrieval mechanisms.

The system is a form of "hypermedia", having similarities to Xerox's "Notecards"[8], with many interconnections between the various entries. The database consists of individual private entries and those which have been "published", thereby becoming a resource which all students are creating and which they can draw on -- as additional knowledge and as examples of peer accomplishments. The system has several more features, including graphics capabilities and the ability to annotate graphic materials, facilities for relating database items in time, and utilities for self-management of the learning process. The emphasis is on an integrated set of tools in the students' control, although there are teacher management utilities as well. CSILE is currently supporting two grade 6 classes and is being studied and developed within the theory of intentional learning.

The specific LAN contribution to CSILE is to provide (in this instance) 16 equally powerful and concurrent access points into the database which supports the class members' learning process. CSILE is a prototype which illustrates how generously available computer power could be integrated into the learning process to foster students' own initiative in learning.

6. PERSON TO PERSON COMMUNICATION

A fully generalized LAN, like the one in the ICON system, allows communication between all nodes in the network. More precisely, tasks (programs) running on different nodes can send messages to each other. One way to use this capability is to provide a utility program which allows the users to communicate with each other directly through their keyboards and screens.

6.1 CO-CO

One commercial program achieving popularity in Ontario is CO-CO[9], for "COnference-COordinator". It allows up to six users to communicate in a party-line fashion. Each user has a window which appears on the screen of each workstation which is participating in CO-CO. Each user is free to type at any time and what is typed appears in the corresponding window on all screens. Thus, all participating students can "talk at once", not having to wait until other students have had their turn. In many instances teachers have found that this encourages students who are otherwise reluctant to express themselves in face-to-face discussions.

CO-CO also has management and utility features. For example, a teacher may carry on a private "conversation" with a student over the network. Also, any user can review the transcript of the conversation using another option, during or after the "conference".

7. PROGRAM TO PROGRAM COMMUNICATION

The direct communication by a task running on one node to

a task running on another node can be harnessed to provide richer interactive environments for the system's users. The two or more communicating programs could create for their users a "shared space" on which to work, though they are at a distance from each other. As described several years ago by Gordon Thompson[10], shared space provides the same working environment for people working on separate computers; for instance, two or more users can work on exactly the same spreadsheet display, simultaneously. It is certainly possible for programs on different nodes to exchange information over a LAN so that their states and displays are identical, reflecting the joint contributions of all concurrent users.

7.1 Multi-node games

But the concept of shared space can be generalized to refer to a model with which students are interacting, for instance in a simulation, in the manner pioneered by Dwyer.[11] One OESS program is Math Race[12] which creates competition between two or more players on different nodes.

7.2 Larger simulations

A series of other programs implement larger simulation models, in which the student at each node has a specific role within the simulation. Thus, in Resort Development[13] the over-all simulation is about the interactions of the various interests in property development: developer, banker, and two levels of government. Each student interacts with a program which simulates the view of the development activity from the perspective of the specific role, and makes decisions appropriate to that role. The separate programs communicate with each other over the LAN, exchanging those decisions and advancing the over-all simulation.

8. EXTENDING THE "SERVER" CONCEPT

As previously stated, one function of a LAN is to share expensive or infrequently used peripheral devices among many workstations. Some discipline is provided so that tasks which need access to these resources can use them, on a shared or exclusive use basis. Common examples are file storage devices, printers and communications ports -- all provided in the ICON system.

8.1 A music server: M-Edit

The potential for other shared devices has been realized in at least one OESS program. A music editing program, M-Edit [14], is primarily designed to be used to manipulate notation on musical scores displayed on the screen. However, it is useful to be able to hear the music one has written. This is usually accomplished with a music synthesizer connected to a MIDI interface attached to the ICON workstation. However, it is not always feasible to have a MIDI interface and music synthesizer for each workstation. The M-Edit program has been implemented as a multi-tasking system in which the music performance task is separate from the editing task; they communicate by inter-task messages. It is a simple extension to have the tasks running on different nodes; the performance task, running on the node equipped with the MIDI interface and synthesizer, then becomes a "music server" for the other node(s).

8.2 Other servers

A similar arrangement is possible for other peripheral devices, though no other example is yet used in Ontario. There have been experiments with the ideas of process instrumentation and control, which could be of interest in the science laboratory, using a data acquisition server.

9. RESEARCH IN EDUCATIONAL USE OF LANS

Wilton [15] has provided a thorough description and analysis of student behaviour in a LAN-based group problem solving task. Her task was a game played at independent workstations, involving both a shared space game display and the ability to send textual messages via the keyboard and screen. The task required the work of all players to solve the game problem, that of locating hidden targets in a grid. Probes could be sent into the grid and the target locations could be inferred from the probe results.

She studied groups of two and four high school students, of same or mixed gender. While there was wide variation in the observed behaviour, the task seemed appropriate as a problem solving environment for high school students (and similar non-computer games are often used in instruction at that level). She verified the implicit communication through the shared space of the game board, and characterized the textual messages sent. Group structure and interaction seems to have evolved differently from what could be expected in face to face problem solving of this variety, as a function of the anonymity which a multi-station LAN environment may offer to the participants.

10. CONCLUSION

We have suggested that a local area network can be more than just a way to structure microcomputers and peripheral devices economically. If the LAN-based system is designed to permit node to node communication between programs in real time, new educational experiences are possible. If a standard LAN-based system is widely used throughout a large educational jurisdiction, it becomes a form of infrastructure, again increasing the range of its uses and influencing software development.

REFERENCES

[1] Cyert, R., Personal computing in education and research. *Science* 1983, 222(4624), 11.

[2] Ontario Ministry of Education. *Functional Requirements for Microcomputers for Educational Use in Ontario Schools -- Stage I.* Toronto: Ontario Ministry of Education, 1983.

[3] McLean, R. S., Ontario Ministry of Education Specifies its Microcomputer. *Fourth Canadian Symposium on Instructional Technology*, Winnipeg, 1983.

[4] McLean, R. S., Ontario Ministry of Education Specifies its Microcomputer, Part II: The Development Years. *Fifth Canadian Symposium on Instructional Technology*, Ottawa, 1986.

[5] Ontario Ministry of Education. *Functional Requirements for Microcomputers for Educational Use in Ontario Schools -- Stage II (Draft only)*. Toronto: Queen's Printer for Ontario, 1987.

[6] Ontario Ministry of Education. Memorandum 31, 1981-82.

[7] Scardamalia, M., Bereiter, C., McLean, R.S., Swallow, J., and Woodruff, E., Computer Supported Intentional Learning Environments. Unpublished manuscript, Ontario Institute for Studies in Education, Toronto, 1987.

[8] Halasz, F.G., Moran, T.P., & Trigg, R.H., Notecards in a Nutshell. Proceedings of ACM SIGCHI conference, Toronto, April 5-9, 1987, pp. 45-52.

[9] CO-CO program. Tando Corporation, 110-1555 Glenora Drive, London, Ont. N5X 1V7

[10] Thompson, G., *Memo from Mercury: Information technology is different*. Montreal: Institute for Research on Public Policy, 1979.

[11] Dwyer, T.A. & Critchfield, M., Multi-computer systems for the support of inventive learning. *Computers and Education*, 1982, 6, 7-12.

[12] Math Race program. Innovative Dimensions, 903 Bathurst St., Toronto M5R 3G4. (OESS Software)

[13] Resort Development program. Urbanprobe Associates Ltd., Box 12, Station G, Toronto M4T 2L7. (OESS Software)

[14] M-Edit program. Helicon Systems Inc., 142 Byng Ave., Willowdale, Ont. M2N 4K7 (OESS Software)

[15] Wilton, J.A., *User Behaviour in Synchronous Computer Networked Learning Environments*. Doctoral Dissertation, University of Toronto, 1987.

COMPUTERS IN EDUCATION, F. Lovis and E.D. Tagg (eds.)
Elsevier Science Publishers B.V. (North-Holland)
© IFIP, 1988

A design system for educational computer simulation programs for computers used in secondary education in the Netherlands.

P.G. van Schaick Zillesen & F.B.M. Min

University of Twente, Dept. of Education, Postbox 217, NL 7500 AE Enschede, The Netherlands

In this paper, we describe THESIS(MS-DOS version), our design system for educational computer simulation programs that can be executed on computers commonly used in everyday secondary education in the Netherlands. The system is used to create prototypes of applications for several subjects, such as biology, chemistry, mathematics and physics. The system is based on MacTHESIS [1], our design system for similar applications, which can be executed on Macintosh computers. We hypothesize that programs developed with THESIS(MS-DOS version) may prove to be very useful in everyday education, although the man-machine interface of the programs is less advanced than that of programs designed with MacTHESIS [1], because the last programs use superior hardware. However, most schools do not possess this hardware. The time required for the technical design of educational computer simulation programs (software design and coding) is greatly reduced by using a design system.

1. INTRODUCTION

Recently we developed MacTHESIS [1], a design system for educational computer simulation programs which can be executed on Macintosh, or slightly modified Atari ST computers. We used MacTHESIS to design applications for several subjects such as biology, chemistry, informatics, medicine, physics and economics. The applications support the use of the mouse as an input medium (the keyboard is completely redundant), multi-windowing techniques, on-line interventions and parallel animation and graphical registration of the results of the simulation (Fig. 1). Min et al [2] hypothesized that programs with these features enable the creation of an optimal learning environment.

However, most secondary schools in the Netherlands do not possess the hardware required to execute programs designed with MacTHESIS. Instead of Macintosh or Atari computers, many schools possess IBM, Philips or Tulip computers, placed by the so-called NIVO project (New Information Technologies in Secondary Education). These computers (In further text: the **NIVO-computers**) are provided with a MS-DOS 3.10 operating system and a educational software package. However, the NIVO-computers are not provided with a windowing package (such as MS-Windows or GEM) or with a user-friendly input device in addition to the keyboard (such as a mouse or a joystick). Moreover, compared with Macintosh or Atari computers, the NIVO-computers are slow and the creation of high quality graphical displays is hardly possible. Because of these features, a user-friendly man-machine interface such as that of programs created with MacTHESIS, requiring an additional input device and implying parallel animation and graphical registration, can not be implemented on a NIVO-computer.

However, educational computer simulation programs with a slightly less user-friendly man-machine interface may still be very useful in everyday education. We developed THESIS(MS-DOS version), a design system which enables the creation of such programs, in order to test this hypothesis. Programs designed with THESIS(MS-DOS version) can be executed on NIVO-computers, without any add-ons. We used THESIS(MS-DOS version) to gen-

erate six prototypes of educational computer simulation programs (AORTA, BOILER, FOOD-CHAIN, CHEMISTRY, LEMMING and FORMULA) for several subjects (biology, chemistry, mathematics, medicine and physics). In this paper, the process of program design with THESIS(MS-DOS version) is described.

2. THE STRUCTURE OF THESIS (MS-DOS version)

Designing an educational computer simulation program, implementing such a program within a curriculum and learning by means of such a program, each put different demands on the man-machine interface and on the technical knowledge of the user. For these reasons, we developed a separate working environment for each one of these three activities (just as we did with MacTHESIS). These environments are described below.

2.1. The students learning environment

The programs are usually provided on a turnkey floppy-disc. Because of this feature, students do not need to bother with the computers operating system in order to be able to use the program. After the insertion of the floppy-disc in the computer, the program can be started simply by switching on the apparatus.

When the program is started three or four windows appear usually one after another, each one containing a graph or a visualization of the conceptual model. The windows are like the pages of a book; all pages showing some dynamic aspects of the model. Students can always switch from one page to another using the menubar (see below), or by pressing the plus key (next page), or the minus key (last page).

In one of the windows, the conceptual model is visualized. Many systems of visualization can be used separately or in combination with each other, such as a diagram (Fig 2a and 2b), a formula, or a simple graphical display. Usually, the current values of the main variables are presented in this window by means of digits. The numbers of the function keys used to change the values of educationally rele-

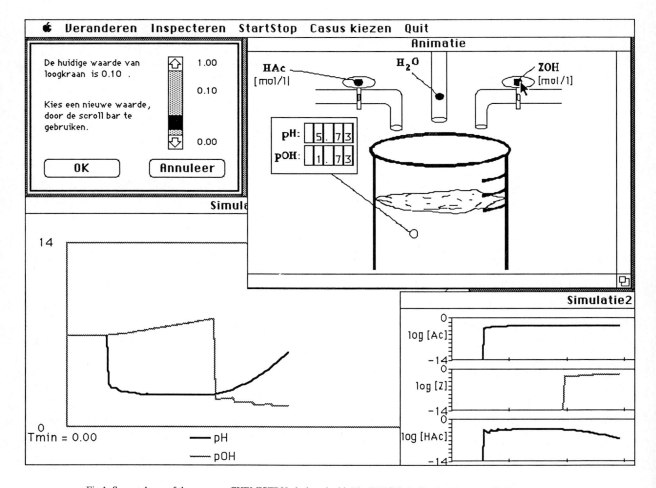

Fig 1. Screen dump of the program CHEMISTRY, designed with MacTHESIS. In the three largest windows, parallel animation and graphical time registration takes place. Students can intervene with the model, by clicking in a tap, using the mouse, at any time during the simulation.

vant parameters and variables are indicated as well (Fig 3). Besides this window, an unlimited number of windows can be present in which time registration of the main variables takes place (Fig 2c and 2d).

Students can control the program very easily by means of a menubar, which is always present on top of the screen. The menubar enables the students to select one of the following functions:

- starting the model (by selecting the option "Tijd" from the menubar shown in Figure 4)
- stopping it again (by selecting the option "Tijd")
- inspecting the values of the variables in the model (by selecting the option "Waarden")
- selecting a simulation case (by selecting the option "Toestand")
- asking for information about the program (by selecting the option "Uitleg")
- changing the values of the parameters of the model (by selecting the option "Verander")

- selecting another page (by selecting the option "Scherm")
- quitting the program (by selecting the option "Einde")

The menubar and the functions supported by it are controlled by means of the computers control keys and the RETURN (=ENTER) key.

The programs provided for are used in combination with a program manual. The only purpose of this manual is to explain the control of the program. Separate paper instructions with information, exercises and cases are used to guide the learning process.

2.2. The teachers environment

Many educational computer programs produce text in a language not known to the students, or use a terminology that differs from the terminology in the other educational materials (e.g. books) used by the students.

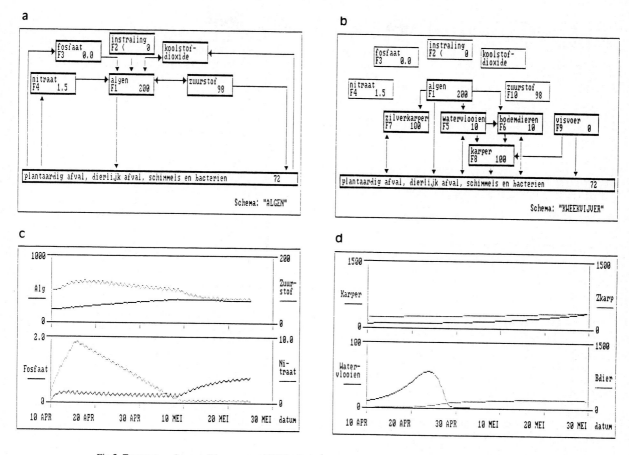

Fig 2. Four screen dumps of the program FOOD-CHAIN, designed with THESIS(MS-DOS version).
2a. A diagram of a simple food-chain.
2b. A diagram of a more complicated food-web.
2c. A graphical display showing time registration of the quantity of Algae, Oxygen, Phosphorus and Nitrogen.
2d. Time registration of the quantity of Carp, Silvercarp, Benthos and Zooplankton.

The teachers environment of the THESIS(MS-DOS version) system allows the teacher to adapt or translate all the text used by the executable programs. Furthermore, the static background of the graphs and the visualization of the conceptual model can be changed even after the compilation of the program. The adaptations are made using a window-editor (teachers version), provided on a separate floppy-disc.

The programs are meant to be used in combination with instructions provided on paper. By developing his own paper materials, or by selecting from existing materials and by using the window-editor, as described above, the teacher can create a students environment which conforms to his educational philosophy.

2.3. The designers environment

The following requirements are needed in order to develop an educational computer simulation program with THESIS(MS-DOS version):
- A NIVO-computer
- A floppy-disc containing TURBO-PASCAL, the THESIS library (MS-DOS version) and the THESIS(MS-DOS version) window-editor (extended version).
- A floppy-disc with MS-DOS 3.10 and a THESIS source-file (MS-DOS version) on it.

When the above requirements are met, a new educational computer simulation program can be developed as soon as a educationally interesting model is available. Four activities have to take place before the process of development is completed:

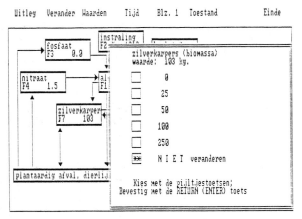

Fig 3. A screen dump of the program FOOD-CHAIN, designed with THESIS(MS-DOS version). In the diagram, the current values of the relevant variables and parameters are indicated. The values can be changed by pressing the function key related to the value (indicated in the diagram). After this, a small window appears, from which a new value can be selected, using the cursor keys and the RETURN key.

- First, the model has to be made "ready for implementation". This means coding the model equations in the Pascal language, making a list of parameters and variables, declaration of starting values for these parameters and variables, and development of relevant simulation cases. It also includes some decisions about the runtime of the model and the dimensions of the iteration process (usually Euler's method of integration is used).
- After this activity, the actual educational design of the program must be made. This includes the selection of relevant interventions, the graphical design of the static background of the graphs, the design of the visualization of the conceptual model and the composition of the text used by the program.
- When the educational design is completed, the technical development starts. This includes the adaptation of the THESIS source-file according to the results of the activities mentioned above, compiling this file and creating the so-called "window-files" (used by the executable program).
- After the completion of the technical development, the most time consuming phase of the process of development starts. This includes the design of the program documentation, program manual and description of the educational cases.

3. RESULTS

THESIS(MS-DOS version) is a design system, which can be used to design educational computer simulation programs for several subjects. Until now, THESIS(MS-DOS version) has been used to develop six prototypes of educational computer simulation programs. We use the programs for our research on techniques and methods for developing standardized educational computer simulations and animations. However, some of them may be very useful in everyday education. The following prototypes have been developed:

AORTA
This program allows students to study the basic hemodynamic relations between blood pressure, volume, flow, resistance and compliance. It allows simulation of the effects of hemodynamic disturbances on the pressure and flow in the major arteries. The program is meant to be used for medical education.

BOILER
This program simulates a system of solar heating. Students study the influence of changes of the properties of the system and changes in weather conditions on the performance of the system.

FOOD-CHAIN
This program (Fig 2,3 and 4) simulates the flow of materials within a fish breeding pond. Several food-chains and food-webs within the pond can be studied separately, or in combination with each other. With this model, students can learn about general ecological concepts like food-chains, food-webs and the influence of man upon ecosystems.

CHEMISTRY
This program (Fig 1) simulates titration experiments. Time registrations of the pH, the pOH and the concentrations of cation of base, anion of acid, not ionized base and not ionized acid are provided for. In a real laboratory, this complete information can only be achieved by means of expensive ionsensitive electrodes. The use of the program might be a useful exercise before the execution of real titration experiments.

LEMMING
This program simulates the population dynamics of a lemming and an arctic fox population on the arctic tundra.

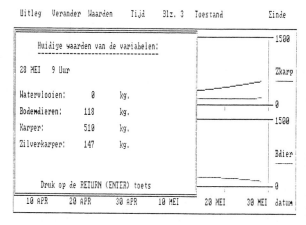

Fig. 4. A screen dump of the program FOOD-CHAIN, designed with THESIS(MS-DOS version). Students can control the program very easily by selecting one of the functions from the menubar, which is always present on top of the screen, using the cursor keys and the RETURN key. In this case, the function "Waarden" (= values) is selected. In consequence of this selection, a small window appears, in which the current values of the variables displayed in the time registration window are indicated.

Fluctuations in composition and biomass of the vegetation caused by grazing lemmings are simulated as well. With this model, students can learn general concepts like biological equilibrium, animal-plant relationships and predator-prey systems.

FORMULA

This programs allows students to approximate a sinus function or e-power function with a progression function. Students can make more or less accurate approximations by changing the number of terms in the progression function. The program my be useful in the practice of mathematical education.

4. DISCUSSION

The process of program development using THESIS(MS-DOS version) is similar to that when using MacTHESIS. For this reason, it is very easy to create a new application with THESIS(MS-DOS version) when an application created with MacTHESIS, based on the same mathematical model, is available. In the cases of the prototypes AORTA, BOILER, CHEMISTRY and LEMMING such an application was available. Nevertheless, some problems occurred when CHEMISTRY was developed with THESIS(MS-DOS version), which did not occur in the MacTHESIS version, caused by the less accurate calculations made in the THESIS(MS-DOS version) version (compared with the MacTHESIS version), combined with the great range of relevant values of some of the variables. The problems were overcome with a few adaptations in the model. In the development of the other prototypes (AORTA, BOILER, FOOD-CHAIN, LEMMING and FORMULA), no problems occurred.

MacTHESIS was designed in order to facilitate the development of educational computer simulation programs which enabled the creation of an optimal learning environment [2]. Latzina and Wedekind [3] and Daldrup [4] emphasized the importance of a man-machine interface such as that of the programs developed with MacTHESIS. However, THESIS(MS-DOS version) was designed with an aim which differs from that of MacTHESIS; it was designed to facilitate the development of educational computer simulation programs which are executable on a computer commonly used in everyday secondary education in the Netherlands (the so-called NIVO-computer). This more pragmatic aim implied some concessions with regard to the man-machine interface. The major differences between applications designed with MacTHESIS and applications designed with THESIS(MS-DOS version) are:

- In applications designed with THESIS(MS-DOS version) only serial presentation of graphical displays (e.g. figures, schemes and graphical time registration) is possible, while in applications designed with MacTHESIS, parallel presentation of graphical displays by means of partly overlapping windows is possible as well. The organization of the total display structure of the programs improves when partly overlapping windows are used [3]. On the other hand, the use of overlapping windows may lead to a great quantity of information being present on the screen at the same time. The results of a formative evaluation experiment suggest that this great quantity of information may confuse the students and that the students may find overlapping windows with graphical registration less easy to control than graphical registration presented in a serial way [5].
- Applications designed with MacTHESIS may use high quality graphical displays and vivid animations. When THESIS(MS-DOS version) is used, only simple graphical displays and animations are possible.
- Applications designed with MacTHESIS are controlled by means of a mouse, while applications designed with THESIS(MS-DOS version) are controlled by means of a keyboard. Compared with a keyboard a mouse is a more user-friendly input device. Nevertheless, in the practice of everyday education keyboard-controlled software might give better results, because nowadays most students are used to working with (user-unfriendly) keyboard-controlled software, while only a few of them have ever worked with mouse-controlled software.

Recently, formative evaluations of several prototypes developed with MacTHESIS (AORTA, BOILER) have been carried out. Students found these programs very attractive and easy to control, like video-games. We hypothesize that the same may be true for programs developed with THESIS(MS-DOS version), as the user-interface has similar characteristics. However, the prototypes look slightly less attractive, because of the lesser capacities of the NIVO-computer compared with a Macintosh. For this reason, further research will be carried out, in which the learning effects achieved by applications designed with THESIS(MS-DOS version) will be compared with those achieved by applications designed with MacTHESIS.

REFERENCES

[1] P.G. van Schaick Zillesen & F.B.M. Min, Mac-THESIS: a design system for educational computer simulation programs, Wheels for the Mind of Europe, no 2, 1987, 23 - 33

[2] F.B.M. Min, M. Renkema, B. Reimerink & P.G. van Schaick Zillesen, MacTHESIS: a design system for educational computer simulation programs. In: T. Moonen & T. Plomp, EURIT '86: Developments in Educational Software and Courseware, Pergamon Press, Oxford, 1986, 689 - 692

[3] M. Latzina & J. Wedekind, Simulationsprogramme: Systematische Beschreibumg und Bewertung, Log in, vol 6, no 5/6, 1986, 35 - 41 (German)

[4] U. Daldrup, Computersimulation im Unterricht: Neues lernen -neues Lernen? University of Oldenburg, Zentrum fuer paedagogische Berufspraxis, Oldenburg, 1987, 1 - 99. (German)

[5] P.G. van Schaick Zillesen & F.B.M. Min (in prep.), Een onderzoek naar computersimulatiemethoden en animatietechnieken ten behoeve van onderwijs en opleiding, Paper O.R.D. 1987, 1987/1988, Groningen (Dutch)

COMPUTERS IN EDUCATION, F. Lovis and E.D. Tagg (eds.)
Elsevier Science Publishers B.V. (North-Holland)
IFIP, 1988

OPPORTUNITIES FOR COMPUTER BASED MODELLING AND SIMULATION IN SECONDARY EDUCATION

Mary Webb and David Hassell

The Advisory Unit: Microtechnology for Education
Endymion Road, HATFIELD,
Hertfordshire. AL10 8AU

Computer based modelling offers a number of opportunities for the enhancement of learning. Children can construct, test and evaluate concrete representations of their own mental models. The active learning which is intrinsic to modelling facilitates the acquisition of a range of important cognitive and social skills.

An investigation of teachers' perceptions of modelling revealed that children do carry out a range of modelling activities at present and that there is scope for more, the main limitation being the lack of suitable media for building models. Teachers believe that modelling can be a valuable educational experience.

Software tools are required which allow children to build, adapt and explore a variety of model types.

1. INTRODUCTION

Models have been used in schools for many years and across a wide range of subjects. Concepts are frequently presented as models in order to communicate definitions and meanings to children. More recently a number of computer based simulations have been developed which allow children to explore models by changing their parameters. A vast majority of these models are inaccessible to the child and there has been little emphasis on children developing and adapting their own models. The computer can provide a medium where models are easy to manipulate, enabling children to express their own models of the real world and test and evaluate them. A joint project between the Advisory Unit and King's College, London, has investigated the software required for modelling with the intention of developing an integrated modelling package.

2. MENTAL MODELS AND ACTIVE LEARNING

When learning a new concept, the learner forms a model in his mind. The concept is assimilated into the learner's framework of knowledge by establishing links with other concepts. This theory of learning can be found in the writings of Kelly [1], Osborne and Gilbert [2] and Osborne and Wittrock [3]. The principal advantage of converting this internal model to an external one is that of giving concrete form to abstract ideas. The aim is to allow pupils to become active builders of their own intellectual structures. In the past teachers expected children to have their own mental models, but little attempt was made to develop them. Instead, the next stage, of hypothesis development and testing, was embarked on and the important step of model development was omitted. The process of modelling leads to better understanding by the following means:

a Raising the level of cognitive processes. Pupils are encouraged to think at a higher level and generalize about concepts and relationships.
b Encouraging pupils to define their ideas more precisely.
c Providing pupils with opportunities to test their own cognitive models and detect and correct inconsistencies.

According to Ginsburg [4] the fundamental requirement for learning is active engagement and commitment, particularly by manipulating thoughts as well as concrete objects. In modelling, the student is actively involved in thinking and understanding with the computer as a unique learning tool. The value of activity based and experiential learning is well established and is reflected in the importance of practical lessons and field work in schools. The need for process and skill based rather than content-oriented courses is also now recognised. Methods of learning which incorporate this change in emphasis are being encouraged and developed in schools and include guided-discovery and problem-solving approaches.

3.   TYPES OF MODELS

Models have been classified in many different ways e.g. discrete / continuous, dynamic / static, deterministic / stochastic, quantitative / qualitative. For the purpose of this research it was felt to be desirable to classify models on the basis of both the behaviour of the model and the methods of modelling. This classification could then be used as a basis for an investigation of the range of modelling activities and the possible scope for modelling in schools. Five families of models were identified:

1 Dynamic systems models
2 Spatial distribution models
3 Qualitative models of logical reasoning
4 Probabilistic event models
5 Data analysis models

These groupings are abstractions from a continuum and are not intended to represent discrete divisions. The tools required and the data used will certainly not be restricted to one or more modelling domains.

3.1.   Dynamic Systems Models

These have their roots in systems theory and are most easily described by relational diagrams. State variables represent accumulations within the system of, for example, weight, numbers of organisms or energy. Rate equations govern the change of levels with time.

Systems which can be modelled in this way include all those where the level of something changes over time. The systems dynamic method provides great flexibility and freedom from constraints and assumptions. It is particularly suitable for coping with non-linearity and feedback loops and models can be constructed to approximate as closely as possible to reality.

Several modelling packages are available for dynamic systems modelling on microcomputers including, DMS [8], STELLA [9] and Micromodeller [10]. STELLA is particularly promising for use by school children because models are constructed on the screen by building up relational diagrams.

3.2.   Spatial Distribution Models

This includes all those models in which the entities are positioned or moving in space. The models may be displayed as plan diagrams or maps and spatial patterns may be described by probability distributions.

Sophisticated spatial modelling tools are used in research which exploit the processing power of mainframe computers. Geobase [11] and QMAP [12], on microcomputers, both allow data to be displayed on maps but there are no packages for schools which allow any modelling to be performed on the data. Videoworks [13] on the Apple Macintosh allows animated sequences to be constructed.

3.3.   Probabilistic Event Models

In these models a series of discrete events takes place which depends on probabilities. The process of modelling in this domain involves determining the events and their order and then assigning a probability function to each event.

There are a number of specialised languages such as Simscript which are used in research and industry. However their complexity makes them unsuitable for use in schools. It is relatively easy to write these models in a programming language such as LOGO but a higher level language with more specialised facilities would be desirable for children to build models.

3.4.   Data Analysis Models

These models can be applied to data in order to identify patterns. They are most useful where the data contains many variables and in these cases multivariate models are used but a number of other simpler statistical techniques might be required. The latter may not strictly be described as models although they are facilities which are likely to be required in a modelling package.

There are a number of multivariate modelling techniques including principal component analysis, cluster analysis and reciprocal averaging. The large amount of processing required when dealing with many variables means that it can only be done effectively by a computer. A number of packages are available for use in research but none has been designed to be sufficiently easy for school children to use.

3.5.   Qualitative Models of Logical Reasoning

There are two main problems with quantitative models. First, the necessary data is often not available, particularly for environmental systems. Secondly, some situations are very difficult to model in this way. A method of model building is required which can incorporate qualitative information and knowledge based on experience. The construction of a knowledge base for an expert system requires this type of conceptual modelling.

4.   THE CURRENT PLACE OF MODELLING IN THE CLASSROOM

An investigation of teachers' perceptions of modelling (Webb [5] and Hassell [6]) revealed that children do carry out a number of modelling activities although teachers do not always recognise these as such. A wide variety of models were used from a broad range of topics. Table 1 provides a summary of these findings.

Table 1:   Present Modelling across the curriculum.

MODELLING DOMAIN	Maths	Science	Geography	History	RS	Econ	CDT	Home Ec.
Dynamic Systems	L	Y	Y	L		Y	Y	Y
Data Analysis	Y	Y	Y	Y		Y	Y	Y
Probabilistic	Y	Y	Y	Y		L	L	
Spatial	Y	Y	Y	Y		Y	Y	Y
Logical Reasoning	L	Y	Y	Y	Y	Y	Y	Y

Key: L = limited use   Y = considerable use

5.   TEACHERS PERCEPTIONS OF THE VALUE OF MODELLING

Of 45 Hertfordshire teachers who were interviewed, 41 stated that they felt that modelling is a valuable educational activity for children, 2 did not and the other 2 were unsure. As can be seen from the list in table 2, teachers have suggested a number of important educational processes which could be enhanced by modelling. The most commonly mentioned benefit of modelling was the aid to understanding. Modelling activities provide opportunities for learning a range of skills and should be integrated into a whole learning environment where the modelling process would be preceded by research and discussion. A science lesson, for example, might involve experiments followed by modelling of the results and a history or geography lesson might entail collection of field data prior to modelling.

6.   FUTURE SCOPE FOR MODELLING IN THE SCHOOL CURRICULUM

The teachers were able to propose many areas of the curriculum where modelling would be appropriate which suggests that there is a great deal of scope for modelling. The main limitation is apparently the availability of suitable media for building models. Due to the current lack of facilities teachers tend to concentrate on prebuilt models rather than asking the pupils to build models themselves, resulting in the underutilisation of modelling techniques.

The models suggested included examples from each of the five modelling domains. However these represent very broad categories of models and in order to identify the software tools which will be needed, it is desirable to subdivide the domains further.

7.   MODELLING DOMAINS AND TECHNIQUES

7.1.   Dynamic Systems Models

A large number of models used fall into this domain. This approach is suitable for any system which can be viewed as a number of compartments with inputs, outputs and flows between them. Many engineering, economic and environmental systems can be modelled in this way. STELLA, brings dynamic systems modelling within reach of more school pupils. This approach to building models by specifying values and relationships, via a graphical representation, without having to write

Table 2: The educational value of modelling

REASONS FOR MODELLING	NUMBER WHO SUGGESTED IT
Aids understanding.	15
Makes abstract concepts more concrete and hence clarifies thinking allowing children to deal with more abstract concepts.	15
Improves problem solving ability by modelling the problem or solution.	8
Trains children to think logically.	6
Helps in applying knowledge to new situations.	5
Allows greater testing and evaluation.	5
May save time by simulating experiments and allowing more output data to be generated more quickly.	5
Aids handling of information.	4
It is necessary to enable generalisation.	4
Helps improve pupils' ability to be selective.	4
Aids evaluation and analysing skills.	4
Encourages discussion and argument.	4
Aids decision making and balanced judgments.	4
Improves pupils' ability to assess outcomes, consequences and limitations of models.	3
Encourages active discovery learning because children can use the computer as a tool to discover for themselves independently of the teacher.	2
Needed for Nuffield A-level physics.	2
Enables realistic simplification.	2
Provides pupils with success and therefore motivation.	2
Increases empathy.	2
Promotes awareness of computer applications.	2
Helps to link theory with reality.	2
Required for CDT syllabus.	1
Could provide a richer classroom environment.	1
Highlights misconceptions.	1
May assist in dealing with data and fitting models to data.	1
May overcome problems which some children have with spelling or drawing.	1
Helps pupils to view problems from different angles.	1
Aids appreciation of design methodology.	1

algorithms to recalculate values over time, is very promising. STELLA obviously has limitations, the most significant of which, for an experienced modeller, is probably the inability to incorporate time lags in a model. Another feature, which would extend the scope of STELLA considerably, would be the incorporation of some qualitative modelling e.g. the value of a variable might be determined by inference using a rule base. Many dynamic systems models can be constructed using a spreadsheet which is a readily available tool for schools. An important accompaniment of a spreadsheet is good graphing facilities.

An important class of models described by science and CDT teachers was that of various types of circuits, including electronic, pneumatic and mechanical. The possibility that such systems could be modelled using a similar approach to the systems dynamic one was considered. However, there are several differences between these circuits and dynamic systems models. For these systems, it would be desirable to specify components and their behaviour. The main difference from the systems dynamic approach is that the input to a component is not necessarily a

quantity of material flowing into the compartment. In the case of an electronic circuit, the input could be several items, each in one of two states. Hydraulic and pneumatic systems do fit the flow metaphor more readily but again it would be desirable to be able to define specific components. A software tool is needed which allows components to be defined in terms of the type of inputs they require and how they process these to produce output. The components could then be linked together to model circuits. Each component would need to be represented graphically. An object oriented system in which new components could be defined which inherit characteristics of predefined components would be valuable.

7.2.   Spatial Distribution Models

This is a broad group of models and a variety of examples was provided by the teachers. The domain needs to be subdivided in order to identify suitable modelling techniques. The following represent groupings based on techniques which might be used to build the models.

> Static spatial models
> Animated-sequence models
> Dynamic spatial models
> Structural 3D models

(i) Static spatial models

Objects are positioned in space and their distributions can be shown on maps or diagrams. The objects may be distributed randomly, regularly, or clumped and different types of objects may be positively or negatively associated. The modeller attempts to fit a hypothesis or model to real data. This could be done by querying a database and displaying the results on a map or diagram e.g. testing the hypothesis that a certain plant species prefers acid soil by displaying areas where the plant is abundant on a map which also shows the soil pH. Alternatively a form of geographical information system where different data sets representing several maps can be interrogated, according to a user's model, to provide the best site/area for an activity. This might also be classified as data analysis modelling. Much environmental work involves collecting data and modelling in this way e.g. associations of animals and plants. There is no suitable software available for this at present apart from large scale GIS's on mainframe computers.

(ii) Animated-sequence models

Many physical and biological processes involve a sequence of events in which objects move in space. Video sequences have helped tremendously in aiding understanding of these phenomena but where the processes are at the molecular level and/or the sequence may be varied, it can be useful to construct models e.g. of crossing over during meiosis. Currently, such modelling is often done by drawing a series of sketches or using plasticine. A simple software package, such as VideoWorks [13], which allows animated sequences to be constructed would be very valuable. It would be even more useful if it were possible to program a number of possible events which could be controlled by rules or probabilities. Children could then build working models of their understanding of various processes. Teachers would also find such a tool invaluable for producing short film sequences to illustrate processes.

(iii) Dynamic spatial models

In these models the positions of objects in space change over time e.g. diffusion models. Another area is the investigation of the shape or form of a physical feature in geography e.g. a model of the deformation of a slope over time. If the movement is proportional to time it would be possible to write the model in a STELLA-like program or a spreadsheet and display the results on a map or diagram.

(iv) Structural 2 and 3D models

There are many structures in science and CDT e.g. crystals, molecules, cell organelles, bridges, of which scientists build concrete models. A software tool which aided the construction of such models and allowed for mathematical transformations, views from various angles, and sections would be valuable. However it would need a very sophisticated software tool to cope with the range of requirements. There are a number of CAD tools available which can be used in CDT. Research chemists build computer models of molecules and Molecular Editor [14] makes some of these facilities available on the Macintosh.

7.3. Data Analysis Models

Science, CDT and home economics involve a great deal of data analysis. This is not always regarded as modelling, especially where it is only necessary to apply simple statistical tests. However, when dealing with large quantities of data or many variables, the analysis involves searching for patterns in the data and setting up hypotheses to test. These hypotheses are actually models. A range of methods should be provided for univariate, bivariate and multivariate analysis.

Increasing computer power and software availability has extended the use of multivariate analysis in scientific research. The use of these techniques in schools could lead to a number of problems if such tests are used without full knowledge of their basis and limitations. Software tools are needed which not only provide a range of statistical techniques but also help users to select appropriate methods and interpret the results. A software package should be able to provide this sophisticated help facility.

A number of multivariate methods have been used in research and they have different advantages and limitations. The main reason for carrying out a computer based multivariate analysis in schools would be to search for patterns and this process may be facilitated by a graphical technique such as that described by Chernoff and reported in Everitt [7]. Chernoff devised a method in which each multidimensional observation is represented by the cartoon of a face, the features of which are governed by the values of a particular variable. Since people are used to studying and reacting to faces it is hoped that they will be able to detect significant differences and trends.

7.4. Probabilistic Models

It was useful to consider these models as a separate group because this made it possible to determine that a small but distinct group of models is found in this category. In addition a number of spatial and data analysis models make use of probability functions. The models which belong exclusively in the probabilistic domain are those which consist of a number of discrete events which depend on probabilities. The most important of these mentioned by the teachers were evolutionary models.

7.5. Qualitative Models of Logical Reasoning

A considerable proportion of the descriptions of possible future modelling tasks given by the teachers fell in this category. These models are based on heuristics rather than precise mathematical relationships and are concerned with relationships between concepts such as causality and dependence. Many teachers felt that it would be desirable to provide tools to aid pupils in structuring and ordering ideas and relationships. Recent developments in expert systems have created the role of a knowledge engineer who obtains the knowledge from a domain expert and structures it in a form which can be used by an expert system. Analogies can be drawn between this and the process which any learner undergoes when learning a new topic. Tools which aid the knowledge engineer should also help the learner. An interesting possibility is to place the learner in the role of both knowledge engineer and domain expert so that she has to understand the subject sufficiently well to "teach" a computer, which will then be able to solve problems in this domain. It is generally accepted that the process of teaching, clarifies a concept for the teacher as well as the learner.

Two types of qualitative models have been identified:

1 Expert systems which solve problems which may be concerned with planning, diagnosis, or advice, e.g. in R.E. building a knowledge base of the rules relating to the food different religious groups can eat.
2 Event based simulations where the events depend on decisions made by the user, rules, or probabilities. An example from history is a decision making simulation of exploration.

8. THE DESIGN OF NEW SOFTWARE TOOLS FOR MODELLING

It is now possible to identify a number of types of models and simulations which are used in schools or would be used if appropriate tools were available. Table 3 lists the types of models and the software tools needed for their construction.

Table 3: Types of models and software tools needed

Dynamic system

STELLA-like facility for building model via system diagram.
Graphs and charts.
Spreadsheet.

Static spatial

Database management system.
Facility to input maps/diagrams, by drawing, from coordinates, and from digitised data.
Facility to input and display data on maps and diagrams.

Animated sequence

Facility to input maps and diagrams by drawing, coordinates, and from digitised data.
Facility to build up sequences including the possibility of a branching simulation which allows the selection from several different sequences by rules or probability.

Dynamic spatial

STELLA-like facility for building model via system diagram.
Graphs and charts.
Facility to input and display data on maps and diagrams.
Facility to display the output of the model dynamically on a map or diagram.

Structural 3D

Facility to build 3D shapes on the screen, rotate, section, transform.
Facility to calculate areas, volumes and proportions.

Data Analysis

A range of statistical functions.
Graphical techniques for representing multivariate data e.g. "faces".
Graphs and charts.
Spreadsheet.
A sophisticated help facility for selecting methods and interpreting results.

Qualitative

Expert system shell.
Simulation builder.
"Hypertext" facility for providing explanations and textual information.
Diagrammatic representation of the simulation and rules to aid construction and debugging.

The design of software modelling tools for school children to construct models will draw on ideas from business and commercial software and will build on these tools wherever possible. In the case of the spreadsheet, in particular, it is hoped that an existing commercial product can be used.

A very important factor in the design of this modelling system for school children is the ease of using the package particularly in the introductory stage. Children and teachers cannot devote a great deal of time to learning how to operate the software. In addition, the other essential and perhaps conflicting requirement, is to allow the user a high degree of control.

9. IMPLICATIONS OF PRODUCING SOFTWARE FOR MODELLING AND SIMULATION.

The teachers who were interviewed had some reservations about modelling, particularly about the degree of difficulty and the time consuming nature of such activities. Teachers already feel pressurised by new developments such as G.C.S.E. and the proposed national curriculum, both in terms of demands on their own time for learning new skills and approaches and in terms of the teaching time available. It is certainly important that any package produced is supported by curriculum materials which take account of curriculum needs and varying classroom situations. Such materials need to be produced in close consultation with groups of teachers involved in curriculum development work. There will also be a substantial need for inservice training in order to assist teachers in exploring the capabilities of the software and to enable them to exploit the new opportunities which the software provides. It is envisaged that the provision of better facilities for modelling will influence the curriculum and offer new ways of learning a variety of skills. It is expected that, in future, modelling will be included as a process in a range of subject areas.

REFERENCES

[1]   Kelly, G.A., The Psychology of personal constructs (Norton, New York, 1955).

[2]   Osborne, R., and Gilbert, J., The Use of Models in Science Teaching (1982) School Science Review, No. 62.

[3]   Osborne, R. and Wittrock, M., The Generative Learning Model (1985) Studies in Science Education, No. 12, 59-87.

[4]   Ginsburg, H.P., Piaget and Education, in Entwhistle, N. (ed), New Directions in Educational Psychology (Falmer Press, 1985.)

[5]   WEBB, M., An investigation of the opportunities for and potential benefits of computer based modelling in secondary school science. Dissertation for Associateship in education, Kings College, London. Unpublished. 1987.

[6]   HASSELL, D., The role of modelling activities in the humanities curriculum, with special reference to geography: an investigative study. Dissertation for Associateship in education, Kings College, London. Unpublished. 1987.

[7]   Everitt, B.S., Graphical Techniques for Multivariate Data, (Heinemann, 87-94, 1978).

SOFTWARE

[8]   DMS - Dynamic Modelling System, Nuffield Chelsea Curriculum Trust, (Longman Micro Software, 1985).

[9]   STELLA, High Performance Systems Inc, (Dartmouth, USA, 1985).

[10]   MICROMODELLER, (IRL Press, Oxford, 1986).

[11]   GEOBASE, (Longman Microsoftware, York, 1986).

[12]   QMAP, (The Advisory Unit: Microtechnology in Education, Hatfield, 1984).

[13]   VideoWorks, (Macromind Inc., USA, 1986).

[14]   Molecular Editor, (Kinko's Academic Courseware Exchange, Santa Barbara, USA, 1985).

COMPUTERS IN EDUCATION, F. Lovis and E.D. Tagg (eds.)
Elsevier Science Publishers B.V. (North-Holland)
© IFIP, 1988

NERO IS DEAD: ENHANCING A CLASSROOM SIMULATION THROUGH COMPUTER SUPPORT

Allan MARTIN

School of Education
University of Leeds
Leeds LS2 9JT
UK

Nero is Dead, a simulation exercise focused upon power struggles in the first-century Roman Empire, was originally evolved as a board-based game for use in secondary school history and Classical Studies classrooms. However, the development of a computer-supported version, currently under way, offers major enhancements in the actuality and effectiveness of the simulation exercise. This is a situation therefore where the adoption of new technology is of genuine value. A number of possibilities exist for computer support of the simulation, involving generic (content-free) software packages as well as software specifically designed for the exercise.

1. COMPUTERS AND SIMULATION

Providing support for a simulation exercise is one way in which information technologies may be effectively utilised in the school classroom. The simulation may be relevant to any particular curricular area; its use may involve the development of a variety of skills and concepts; and the teacher's time and attention is freed from low-level clerical activities so that he is enabled to concentrate upon more centrally educational aspects of his role.

In referring to simulation exercises, the distinction should be underlined between simulations of the "in-screen" and "out-screen" type. In the former, the representation of the object system simulated is restricted to the computer; observers "outside" the screen set parameters, supply data, and note the outcomes of simulation runs. In the latter, however, the simulation exercise extends beyond the machinery and involves an element of human role-playing participation. Whilst the in-screen simulation can be seen as a logical or mathematical process, the out-screen simulation is a social process.

The computer's role in supporting an out-screen simulation may be relatively simple: it may function as a message-editor, number-cruncher, or record-keeper. Or it may be more complex, taking for example the form of an in-screen simulation generating outcomes for decisions entered. Often, however, it will be a combination of several functional elements. Simulation exercises of the out-screen type, whether supported by computer or not, have gained wide acceptance in fields of education and training, particularly in the human and social sciences. It is this type of simulation exercise with which this paper is concerned (the distinction between in-screen and out-screen simulations

is further explored in (1)).

2. SIMULATIONS IN THE HISTORY CLASSROOM

The use of simulation excercises figured as one of the techniques introduced to teachers of History in the early 1970's as part of the approach to History-teaching known in the UK as the "New History". This approach focused upon enabling school students to investigate and to experience history, in so far as this could be made possible, rather than committing to memory or to paper lists of facts or accounts of "key events". Role-playing exercises would, it was hoped, permit students to empathise with the participants of historical situations; there would also be a beneficial spin-off in terms of social and decision-making skills. (2, 3)

However, the use of role-playing simulations was perhaps slower to take off in history classrooms than some of the other methods of the New History, such as the study of evidence. This may have been partly because of the unfamiliarity of teachers with a technique which, to many, must have seemed very different from the history teaching to which they had been accustomed. But there were also organisational reasons. A packed curriculum, to be accomplished in small packets of time, does not easily permit the setting up and running of role-playing exercises.

The arrival of the microcomputer provides a means which can lead to these problems being overcome. Some of the time-consuming organisational effort, of setting up the initial situation, monitoring the state of play, providing appropriate responses to decisions made by participants, can be handed over to the machine. And, through a software facility for saving the current state of play at the end of any session, the exercise can be run over a series of short

meetings. To anyone who has faced the problem
of saving the current state of a board-based
simulation in a classroom "until next week",
this is a major advantage.

Simulations can offer the secondary school
history teacher a means of effectively using
limited resources of computer technology and
time. An appropriately designed simulation
program can enable a single computer to be used
effectively by a whole class over the course of
a limited number of short time-periods. It
should not be surprising then that simulations
are commonly used software items in those UK
history classrooms in which information technology is being employed, or that many simulation programs should be available for History
teachers. A recent survey of available history
software lists 58 simulation programs, 23 rev-
ision/teaching aids, and 12 data retrieval programs. (4) Clearly the simulations in use in
schools involve a wide variety of types, from
which those which are little more than animated
diagrams to those which involve a complex array
of activities and experiences.

3. NERO IS DEAD: THE BOARD GAME

NERO IS DEAD was conceived in 1977. It was
originally designed as a board-based simulation
game involving up to five players; and this
game was extensively tested inside and outside
the classroom with participants aged from ten
to forty. In the classroom, it has been used
with Integrated Humanities, History and Classical Studies classes aged from eleven to eighteen.

The model represented is that of a political
system in which power, military strategy and
economic resources are interdependent. Details
are:

a) extent of territory controlled depends on the
ability of a leadership to move armed forces
into a particular area as necessary to ensure
control and defend its frontiers.

b) raising and maintenance of armed forces
requires constant expenditure of resources;
extent of forces maintained will depend upon the
resources allocated to them.

c) extent of resources available to a leadership
depends on extent and wealth of territories
controlled; more can be extracted from rich
provinces than poor ones.

d) military strategy involves movement of armed
forces by a leadership and neutralisation of
armed forces of other leaderships.

e) quality of all armed forces is held as equal;
victory in armed encounters is solely dependent
upon numerical superiority to a ratio of 2:1.

f) natural disasters, activities of powers outside theatres of conflict, and other incidental
events are represented in the model as chance
elements.

The historical situation in the context of which
the simulation is presented is that of the first-
century Roman Empire. The period between the
death of Nero in July of AD 68 and the assumption by Vespasian of the imperial insignia in
December 69 was one in which, in a situation of
central power vacuum, commanders of major military blocs were presented with the opportunity
to intervene directly in the political structure.
This situation is reproduced in the simulation.
However, the activities and ambitions of provincial governors and key political figures in
the imperial capital, who were not commanders
of major military blocs, are not represented.
It is not intended that the simulation should
replicate precisely the events which took place
in AD 68-70.

Players assume the roles of commanders of major
legionary blocs (of at least three legions).
The game board, shown in Appendix 1, is based
on provincial boundaries as of July AD 68; the
starting position is based on major military
dispositions of the same time. Expansion of
territory controlled is achieved by the movement of game blocks representing military units
(legions). Military forces, however, must be
maintained by payments by commanders, resources
for which are drawn from taxes raised upon
provinces controlled. Taxation rates of provinces, expressed in talents of silver, are based
upon the relative wealth of the provinces
controlled; these are marked on the game board.
Payment of forces and collection of taxes takes
place once a year; each round (ie cycle in
which each player makes a move in turn) in the
simulation is held to represent three months.
Taxes raised are received in paper notes from
a bank, payment of legions is made to the bank.
Unpredictable events are represented by Event
Cards drawn at intervals during play. A time
chart on the game board shows whether taxation
of provinces, payment of legions, or the drawing of an event card occur at the beginning of
any particular round. The exercise terminates
either when one player achieves total supremacy
or by mutual agreement between the players.

Events in a round are indicated in figure 1.

The major educational objectives of NERO IS
DEAD in its board version are as follows:

i.   Development of an awareness of the relationship between political power and economic
resources.

ii. Opportunity for empathetic involvement
in political and economic conflict in the
Classical period.

iii. Development of familiarity with various aspects of the Roman Empire.

iv. Stimulation of interest in the Classical world.

v. Development of problem-solving and planning skills through strategic thinking.

In its board game version NERO IS DEAD has been enjoyably played by secondary school pupils, professional archaeologists and ordinary families. Families and lower school pupils played the game largely as a form of strategy game (like RISK or chess), though an interest in the period was stimulated. Older pupils appreciated more fully the military-political-economic connections, and were keen to know "what really happened" when Nero was dead. The archaeologists developed a high degree of involvement with their role figures, and became obsessively enthusiastic about the game.

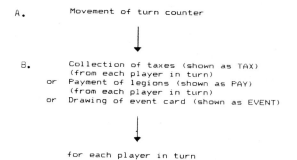

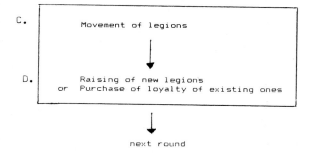

Figure 1. Phases in a round of NERO IS DEAD

4. PROBLEMS WITH THE BOARD GAME

For the teacher wishing to use it in the classroom, the board version of NERO IS DEAD suffers from three major problems:

a) The average length of a game is between

two and two and a half hours. Stopping play with the intention of restarting later is an inconvenient process, either time-consuming (if positions are recorded in writing), or prone to accidental loss of data (if the board with pieces on it is placed in a "safe" place, such as on the top of a cupboard). This places severe constraints on use in educational settings since it is only convenient to play at the end of term, when normal timetable may be suspended or examinations are over, or with sixth form classes who may have double or treble periods, long patches of self-study time, or a combination of both which can give a full morning or afternoon.

b) The board version is most convenient played by individuals or pairs, due to problems of crowding with larger numbers. It can only b practically be employed with a full class if several games are played simultaneously, or if those not involved in the game are set another activity.

c) Each player can observe the full state of the board. This is not a reflection of most situations of political struggle, where knowledge available to each participant is partial and to some extent unreliable.

5. THE COMPUTER-SUPPORTED VERSION

A computer-based version of the game is therefore currently being developed. This would overcome the difficulties raised in connection with the board game.

a) Storage of the current position is easily achieved. Thus the game may be played over several short periods rather than one long one. The current position may be stored on disk at the end of one session to be reloaded instantly at the start of the next; a printout can be provided at restart to inform players of their assets and positions.

b) As the computer monitors the progress of the exercise, grouping of players round the board is not necessary. Use of the game by a full class divided into groups in separate areas in the classroom, or even in different rooms is thus made possible.

c) Each group, representing a power-base, can be presented by the computer with a less-than-complete picture of the current situation, with the amount and reliability of information declining with distance from one's frontier. This enhances the realism of the situation.

Being able to present a selective picture of the situation allows the following objectives to be added:

vi. Assesment of evidence from a variety of sources.

vii. Experience in making decisions without full information available.

Running this exercise with groups rather than individuals allows a further item to be added to the list of educational objectives:

viii. Practice in group discussion and decision making.

In facilitating these advances, the computer is enhancing the realism and educational potential of this exercise. It can therefore be judged a genuinely useful application of the computer to the learning situation.

In its simplest form, the computer version of NERO IS DEAD may be played by a class divided into groups. The computer, discreetly situated on the fringe of the classroom, will be supervised by a secretariat. One member of each team will in turn be called to the computer to enter moves; a printout of the consequences will be provided to take back to the group workspace. Each group will have a board and pieces representing legions, in order to visualise as much as they know of the situation. The learning activities thus continue to take place where the players are, and will not be transferred to the location of the computer.

A further stage in the development of the game will be the employment of networking facilities to allow it to be played by groups in different rooms, or in different locations altogether. A computer at the disposal of each group could permit the use of a spreadsheet to store details of current situations and to supply answers to some kinds of "what if" questions. Electronic mail could make it possible for this exercise to be run with teams in different schools, cities or even countries.

The simulation exercise is intended to be embedded in a wider unit of work, say on the first-century Roman Empire, or on Power as a historical theme. Thus work on the simulation will be carried out in conjunction with other classroom activities related by the structure of the unit of work. These activities also may be supported by computerised facilities, as for instance a database on provinces of the Roman Empire, or on personalities of the first century, or a simulation of the archaeological uncovering of Roman remains. NERO IS DEAD, as well as the other elements in the unit of work will also, it is assumed, be supported with other resources which can be made available, such as books, slides, videos, visits, and so on. Making use of a computer should not reduce the demand for such resources.

Implicit in the description of the use of NERO IS DEAD and the objectives suggested for it are significant pedagogical implications. It is not intended for a classroom where a whole class is presented with pieces of information

(cast as "facts") by the teacher, along with the promise of imminent testing of their retention. It is intended for the classroom where the understanding of history is held to be a more profound concept than the retention of selected items of information, involving ideas such as causality, the analysis of evidence, empathy, and the critical study of the historians' accounts of events. It is also intended for the classroom where individual and group work on learning activities is at least as normal as whole class work.

The teacher's role, as manager of the simulation exercise, is very different from his role as purveyor of information. Computer-based simulations offer the teacher a powerful and flexible facility, permitting development of a wide range of skills. In employing such materials, the teacher can focus less on knowledge-purveying, more on skills-development and management of the learning situation. This does not mean less work for the teacher, but it should mean more interesting and fulfilling work. The computer-based nature of the material does not do away with the need for expert teacher input: the teacher in fact becomes more necessary in the computer-supported classroom, for his expertise as thinker, stimulator, and manager become more important than his facility as a repository of knowledge. His role as expert and critical assessor of materials must also be retained, since computers can support both good and bad material.

7. CONCLUSION

It is, or should be, one of the lessons of history that every situation is dynamic, trailing behind it the roots of its present, and thrusting out ahead of it potential futures. The use of the computer in the history classroom possesses visibly such a dynamic aspect. NERO IS DEAD is intended to help realise some of its potential futures.

REFERENCES

(1) Martin, Allan, Out of the Screen: Computers and Simulation, in: Simulation/Games for Learning, Vol. 18, No. 2, 1988
(2) Birt, David and Nichol, Jon, Games and Simulations in History (Longman, London, 1975)
(3) Tansey, P.J. and Unwin, Derick, Simulation and Gaming in Education (Methuen, London, 1969)
(4) Blow, Frances and Dickinson, Alaric, New History and New Technology: Present into Future, (Historical Association, London, 1986, 68-71)

Appendix 1.

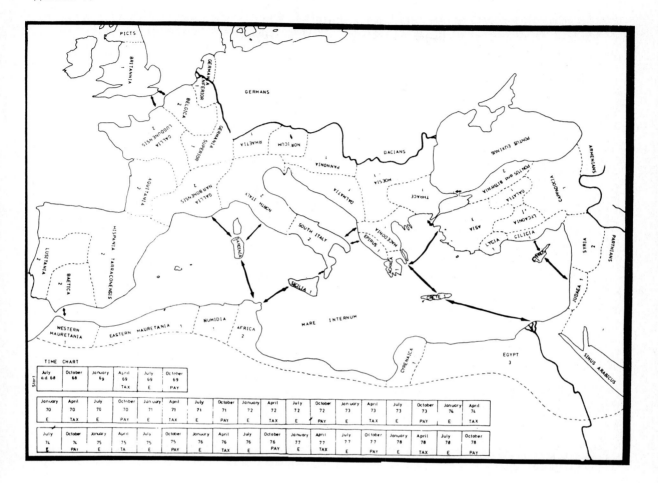

COMPUTERS IN EDUCATION, F. Lovis and E.D. Tagg (eds.)
Elsevier Science Publishers B.V. (North-Holland)
© IFIP, 1988

DIMENSIONAL DESIGN: A NOTATION FOR STRUCTURED THINKING

Michael J. COLEMAN

School of Information Science,
Portsmouth Polytechnic
Hampshire Terrace
Portsmouth PO1 2EG, United Kingdom

Current pedagogical approaches in computer-based education - such as flowcharting, discovery learning through LOGO and the teaching of the programming language BASIC - encourage poor and unstructured thinking. Dimensional Design is introduced as the type of design notation that should replace flowcharting and be used as an essential support tool in programming language instruction.

1. INTRODUCTION

Today's children are tomorrow's designers. The next generation of designs - cars, office blocks, aeroplanes, robots, computer programs - will be the product of their thinking. How, then, are youngsters being trained to think? Is it in a way that supports the business of design?

Design is an activity that requires a notation. One might go further and say that a design notation actually influences the design process. Teaching by means of a poor notation, then, encourages a poor mentality for tackling the task of design. An examination of three prevailing notations and their associated mentalities illustrates the point.

2. THREE MENTALITIES OF UNSTRUCTURED THINKING

2.1 The Flowchart Mentality

The flowchart mentality encourages thinking which says that problems are seen, and solved, in their entirety. Moreover, it suggests that a solution is always viewed as a sequence of actions, some of which are a response to yes/no questions. It approaches problems at the micro level, promoting a design philosophy which is one-dimensional: this, then this, then this ..

Figure 1 (adapted from [5]) is an example of how this thinking is promoted. In this flowchart the overall (and no doubt attractive) problem of How To Frighten Mum is submerged in the detail of an unstructured solution.

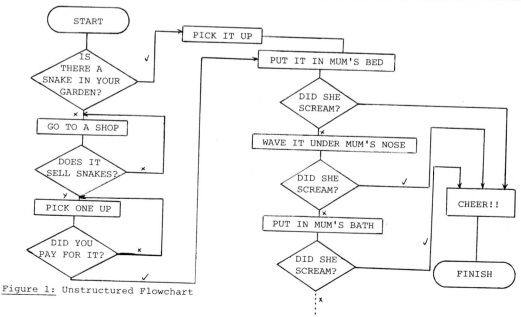

Figure 1: Unstructured Flowchart

The impossibility of tackling a larger and more complex problem in this way means that repetitive design cycles are compounded. Taking the case of computer program design, design errors only manifest themselves at the testing stage. There is then an overwhelming temptation to get the program working before returning to the flowchart. Design after the event becomes a way of life.

2.2 The LOGO Mentality

Proponents of using LOGO in the classroom stress the way in which the language (meaning, often, the 'turtle graphics' capability) promotes learning by discovery. Piaget and Papert are quoted ad nauseam and LOGO mentalities abound.

But a LOGO mentality looks upon design of the final product as being reached after a voyage of discovery - a voyage that was for the most part unplanned, uncharted and, without doubt, unstructured. To put it in words that have a less academic ring about them, what we see is a process of trial and error. Figure 2, and its associated pieces of LOGO [4], give an example of this in practice. Discovery it may be, but design it certainly is not.

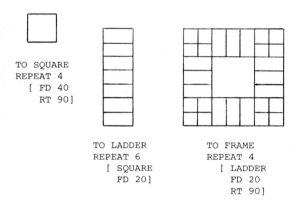

```
TO SQUARE
REPEAT 4
  [ FD 40
    RT 90]


TO LADDER          TO FRAME
REPEAT 6           REPEAT 4
  [ SQUARE           [ LADDER
    FD 20]             FD 20
                       RT 90]
```

Figure 2: The 'Discovery' Approach of LOGO

Discovering learning, by definition, does not encourage the sort of structured thinking that is required in good design. Would you have confidence in an architect who designed by discovery?

2.3 The BASIC Mentality

The attraction of teaching computer programming is that the subject enables a student, in a wonderfully compact manner, to experience the whole design and development life-cycle. It should therefore be used as a vehicle for the inculcation of good design practice; an academic discipline in the fullest sense of the term.

So what happens? Pupils are taught to program in BASIC, and cultivate a BASIC mentality. A BASIC mentality combines the worst of all worlds. Because the language is interactive it encourages design in front of the computer, a particularly pernicious combination of discovery learning and the LOGO mentality. Even if this does not happen, the language itself, with its line numbers and GOTO statements, virtually guarantees the development of a flowchart mentality to some degree or another. Figure 3 is a very simple, but unfortunately typical, product of the approach.

```
10 IF A=1 THEN 60
20 X=1
30 IF C[]3 THEN 80
40 Y=1
50 GOTO 90
60 W=1
70 IF B[]2 THEN 90
80 Z=1
90
```

Figure 3: Unstructured BASIC

3. THE COMPONENTS OF STRUCTURED THINKING

A structured design can only be the product of structured thinking; to deny this is to believe that a chimpanzee could have painted the Mona Lisa given enough time. Structured thinking involves a systematic approach to problem solving. This approach, the author contends [1], involves a process of stepwise refinement - the gradual decomposition of a problem into smaller and smaller subproblems. Automatically the emergent, structured, design will exhibit two major characteristics:

* it will be hierarchical in nature, with clearly-defined component parts; such parts will themselves be hierarchically structured.

* the whole structure will be based on a known, finite, and probably small, number of elemental structures.

Moreover, the actual process of structured thinking will better equip the designer for the crucial task of explaining the resultant design. (How many programming teachers have been faced with a pupil claiming: "Don't ask me how it works, it just does!"?). Ideally, then, a further characteristic might be added to the structured design so produced:

* it will contain explanatory detail showing how the design evolved the way it did, and why.

A structured design can only be represented in a suitable notation; the process of structured design - structured thinking - only promoted by means of a suitable notation.

But what is suitable? 'Flowchart notation' submerges structure. 'LOGO notation' is able to produce a structured design, but is normally used to do so as a by-product rather than a goal. (Some might argue that this is bottom-up design - to which the author would respond by saying that the term is a contradiction. Design determines where the bottom is!). At best, the same can be said for some versions of the 'BASIC notation'; others versions are little less than entropy generators.

With these tools to help their thinking, is it any wonder that some pupils are unable to organise arguments, write essays or spell long words?

Structured thinking must have a structured notation in which to express itself.

4. DIMENSIONAL DESIGN NOTATION

Dimensional Design [2,3,6 and the Appendix to this paper] is such a notation. As an illustration consider Figure 4, equivalent to the 'snake flowchart' of Figure 1.

Dimensional Design notation operates in three dimensions. <u>Sequential</u> elements of the algorithm appear in the Y-dimension. In the X-dimension appear <u>conditional</u> elements, and thereby the different steps of the algorithm associated with them. Arguably, the Z-dimension is the most important of all. This dimension is used to detail <u>refinements</u>, the step-by-step design process through which the whole problem is gradually broken down into smaller and smaller sub-problems.

Dimensional Design notation is easy to learn. It contains few symbols and has no special graphical requirements such as peculiarly-shaped boxes. Most of the elements are introduced in Figure 4, but the full list is given in the Appendix to this paper.

Figure 4, then, is a structured design in a way that the equivalent flowchart is not. It is hierarchical. Moreover, its use of the X and Y dimensions enables the conditional parts of an algorithm to be separated, rather than rolled with the sequential steps into one spaghetti jumble. Dimensional Design facilitates the representation of elemental constructs - such

```
How To Frighten Mum
 \
  Get a snake
  |   \
  |    |________________________________
  |    |                                |
  |   ( Snake in garden               ( ELSE
  |    |                                |
  |    Pick up snake                    Buy a snake
  |    |                                |  \
  |    -                                |   REPEAT
  |                                     |   |   \
  |                                     |   |    Call into shop
  |                                     |   |    |
  |                                     |   |   ( UNTIL find one that
  |                                     |   |    |      sells snakes
  |                                     |   |    *
  |                                     |   |
  |                                     |   Pay for snake
  |                                     |   |  \ ..
  |                                     |   -
  |                                     |
  |                                     Pick up snake
  |                                     |
  Do something with it                  -
  | \
  |  CHOOSE
  |  |  \
  |  |   |______________________________________________________ _ _ _ _
  |  |   |                                  |                  |
  |  |  ( Put it in                        ( Wave it under    ( Put it in
  |  |   | Mum's bed                        |  Mum's nose      |  Mum's bath
  |  |   -                                  -                  -
  |  |
  |  IF
  |  |  \
  |  |   |____________________________
  |  |   |                            |
  |  |  ( Mum Screams               ( ELSE
  |  |   |                            |
  |  |   Cheer!                       -
  |  |   |
  -  -   -
```

<u>Figure 4</u>: Dimensional Design for 'How to Frighten Mum'

as IF and REPEAT. Finally, through the
refinement dimension it has self-evident levels
of design detail which effectively 'explain'
how the design has evolved.

   The design process is thus encouraged to
begin at a high 'abstract' level and refine
down to detailed lower levels. In the case of
computer program design the lowest design level
amounts to program code. Languages such as
LOGO facilitate structure although the LOGO
mentality approaches it from the wrong
direction. By constructing a dimensional design
before moving to the computer, attention is
focussed on the language's structured features
automatically. Figure 5, for instance, is a
dimensional design for the program of Figure 2;
this could be generated by a pupil before s(he)
heads for the computer to see how the LOGO
program runs.

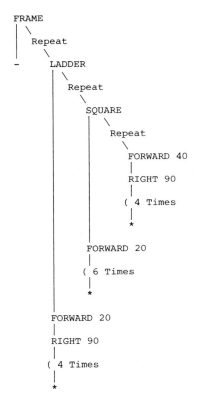

Figure 5: LOGO Program Dimensional Design

   Finally, the notation promotes the use of
elemental structures in a design. For a computer program, therefore, this means that at
least the dimensional design solution has
structure even if - as with the more awful
versions of BASIC, for instance - the final
program does not. Figure 6 is a design which
might still refine down to the code given in
Figure 3, but at least it is the product of
thinking which is structured.

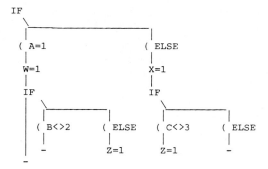

Figure 6: Structuring Unstructured BASIC

6. CONCLUSIONS

   A new approach needs to be taken so as to
encourage structured thinking. If this is to
take place a simple notation needs to be
adopted which can be used in the classroom to
represent the products of such thought. A
notation such as Dimensional Design satisfies
the criteria of representing in one diagram the
requirements of hierarchical structuring,
elemental design structures and 'what-to-how'
design explanation.

REFERENCES

[1] Coleman, M.J. and Pratt, S.J., Software
    Engineering for Students (Chartwell-Bratt,
    Bromley U.K., 1986), pp. 92-94.

[2] Coleman, M.J. and Pratt, S.J., Software-
    Taming with Dimensional Design (Chartwell-
    Bratt, Bromley U.K., 1987).

[3] Jonsson, A. and Patel, M., An Interactive
    Flowcharting Technique for Communicating
    and Realizing Algorithms, Thesis No. 28,
    Dept. of Computer and Information Science,
    Linkoping University, Sweden (1984).

[4] Laridon, P., LOGO and the Intelligence,
    WCCE 85: Proceedings of the 4th World
    Conference on Computers in Education,
    (1985) pp. 605-10.

[5] Larsen, S.G., Computers for Kids,
    (Creative Computing Press, Morristown, NJ,
    1981) p. 5.

[6] Witty, R.W., Dimensional Flowcharting,
    Software: Practice and Experience, Vol. 7,
    (1977) pp. 553-584.

APPENDIX: DIMENSIONAL DESIGN NOTATION

Dimensional Design notation is characterised by its simplicity. The basic elements and their meanings are as follows:

text - a text string, of any length, is used to represent a subsystem. It can thus range from a totally abstract element of a high-level design description through to a specific statement in a programming language. In a design structure most subsystems will be both part of a refinement from a higher level and the source of a refinement down to the next level.

        connects together two subsystems in sequence.

        connects together two subsystems in parallel.

\   connects together two subsystems in hierarchy; that is, the second sub-system is the initial element in a refinement of the first subsystem.

\ ..   hidden refinement subtree.

[]   refinement subtree (i.e. subsystem) defined elsewhere.

[*]   subsystem called recursively.

-       terminates a non-iterative sequence of subsystems.

*   terminates an iterative sequence of subsystems.

(selection (conditional) indicator.

[..]   parametric information. Used to follow either subsystem text or termination symbols with entry/exit values.

COMPUTERS IN EDUCATION, F. Lovis and E.D. Tagg (eds.)
Elsevier Science Publishers B.V. (North-Holland)
© IFIP, 1988

Didactic and Software-Ergonomic Aspects of Dynamic Modelling and Simulation Systems

Peter Gorny

Universität Oldenburg, Fachbereich Informatik
Abteilung Computer Graphics und Software Ergonomie
P.O.Box 2503, D-2900 Oldenburg

Simulation systems and dynamic modelling systems for educational purposes are mainly found in those categories of computer-enhanced learning environments that support 'open learning' and 'guided discovery learning'. From the point of view of didactics, the paper shows the importance of the 'open learning method' for both simulation systems and dynamic modelling systems in order to allow the formation of an adequate mental model. These demands are transferred to requirements for the design of the user interfaces for the computer enhanced learning environments. They result in such program construction techniques as direct manipulation, iconic (semi-concrete) representation of data and results, possibilities to intervene into (but not to break off) the calculation process of the running model and a visual representation of the model.

1. Introduction

Software systems for educational applications are dominantly developed by amateur programmers, mostly teachers, who base their design decisions on their own classroom experiences. Some of the resulting products impress by their intuitive ingenuity, but most of them show the lack of systematic design methods as known from software engineering and especially - in regard to the human-computer interface - from software ergonomics, this only twenty year old field where cognitive science and informatics meet.

Also the normal rules of didactic evaluation of new teaching methods or materials are widely neglected, when schools or companies apply information technology for learning and teaching. So we can state that educational technology for learning and teaching is still in the replication period and the empirecal period of the *BRETAM* model of technological progress (*B*reakthrough: creative advance made; *R*eplication period: experience gained by mimicking breakthrough; *E*mpirical period: design rules formulated from experience; *T*heoretical period: underlying theories formulated and tested; *A*utomation period: theories predict experience & generate rules; *M*aturity: theories become assimilated and used routinely [Gaines87]).

It is the aim of this article to further the progress towards Maturity by offering some theoretical aspects derived from the empirical introduction of software in schools, from the professional software development, software engineering, and - last not least - from learning theories.

Though many different kinds of educational software could be presented here, we concentrate on the modelling and simulation systems, which are widely used in the training of engineers and in science teaching. These systems represent the full didactic spectrum from "learner-oriented" open learning support to "teacher-oriented" guided instruction (see Table 1). In our context *simulation* is the manipulation of a dynamic model of real or hypothetical components (of a physical, chemical, biological, social or economic system) in order to reproduce its operation on a set of data as it moves through time. For further definitions, also for the terms "model" and "system" we refer to the broad literature on this field [e.g. Lehman77].

2. Modelling and simulation for open learning and guided discovery

Dynamic modelling systems (Table 1-1a) allow the user to construct models of systems, while simulation systems (Table 1-2a) contain complete unchangeable models, where the (non-programming) user is restricted to manipulating the model by changing the data.

Examples of *dynamic modelling systems* are STELLA [HighPerform87], DYNAMIS [Häuslein86] and DYSIS [Bossel86]. STELLA and DYNAMIS are integrated systems, which allow the user to construct the model (with a visual language supplemented by some mathematical equations) and operate it with different sets of data. In DYSIS, the model construction process is done with paper and pencil in a visual language, but the user has to accomplish the transformation to a computer model on his own, by translating the visual description into BASIC statements by a well described method which thereafter are inserted into a frame program.

There are many examples of *simulation systems*, which normally contain only one model. Sometimes the models can be "loaded" into a frame program, a method which is also practiced in DYSIS. The main characteristic of these systems is that the user has to be competent in a given programming language and the operating system at hand, in order to change the model, or to construct a new one. In German literature we find, as one example, the simulation programs

```
(1)  Open learning support:
     (a)  problem solving tools ("Tools for thinking with"):      Learner-oriented
          •  programming systems such as LOGO, PROLOG,
                                       BOXER, GARDEN...,
          •  dynamic modelling systems such as STELLA, DYNAMIS, ..,
     (b)  tools for structuring knowledge by organizing data:
          •  textprocessing and document preparation,
          •  drafting and design,
          •  data bases
          •  spreadsheets.

(2)  Guided discovery learning:
     (a)  simulation systems,
     (b)  computer-assisted (educational) games,
     (c)  process and robot control.

(3)  Resources for teaching and learning:
     (a)  electronic blackboard etc.,
     (b)  communication systems,                                  Teacher-oriented
     (c)  information retrieval,
     (d)  tutorials,
     (e)  drill & practice.
```

Table 1: Didactical Categories of educational Software applications   [ATEE86, GORNY86]

of [Koschwitz85]. A system with a thoroughly developed frame program is SIMSEL [GMD86], allowing the teacher to program new models in a special educational programming language (ELAN, under the operating system EUMEL). A Dutch example of a frame system is MacTHESIS [Min87], which contains at least two very important achievements: the authors make full use of the possibilities of the software ergonomic research results (see chapter 4) and they include the feature of interventions (in to the running model).

The simulations included under the term *"drill & Practice"* (Table 1-3e) are dynamic models of technical systems, where the educational objective is to train the learner in operating the model and to reinforce certain skills while he operates it (e.g. a flight or a driving simulator). We shall not discuss these systems here.

Nor shall we consider industrial simulation systems, for non- educational purposes often based on expert systems and implemented on high level workstation computers (e.g., LISP-machines), though these systems often have an exemplary user surface (e.g., SIMKIT [IntelliCorp85]).

3. Pedagogical Objectives for modelling and simulation

From the point of view of didactics, we have to point out that the pedagogical objectives are very different for modelling systems and simulation systems.

In a rather eclectic approach to learning theory and learning styles, we can divide *learning* into associative learning (learning of emotions), instrumental learning (learning of habitual behavior) and cognitive learning (learning of knowledge structures) [Edelmann79]. Cognitive learning, resulting in the acquisition of structured knowledge, can be described as occurring within three layers (following Bruner and Klafki [Klafki85]), beginning with the lowest layer:

- in the direct exploration and proving of attributes and possibilities of the "real world", in the direct verbal communication and in experiencing and discovering emotional-social relations (*action layer* - enactive representation of knowledge);

- in the medium of pictures, schemas and visual displays (*schema layer* - iconic representation of knowledge);

- in the medium of abstract notion ("symbols") , only mentally executed operations and theoretical argumentations (*abstract-symbolic* layer - symbolic representation of knowledge).

It is necessary to learn on the action layer first, before learning can be successful on the schema layer, and before the abstract-symbolic layer can be reached. It has, though, to be stressed, that this learning process is not linear, but moves up and down between the layers of acquiring knowledge.

It is, therefore, very important that a learner can gain practical experience (action layer) with a physical, chemical or biological problem, before he is presented with an iconic representation in a readymade simulation system (schema layer). It is also necessary that he understands the abstraction that reality has undergone, the mathematical model beneath the simulation system surface (abstract-symbolic layer). A sound cognitive structure can only be acquired by learning to construct and/or change the model itself.

Donna Berlin [Berlin87] distinguishes between the categories of movement (static, animated or manipulatable representation of the model) and of representational level (concrete, semiconcrete or abstract). In her "instructional model", the simulation sytems are semiconcrete animated resources; the possibility of interventions (MacTHESIS) points to semiconcrete manipulatable resources, while dynamic modelling systems can be categorized as abstract manipulatable resources (Figure 1).

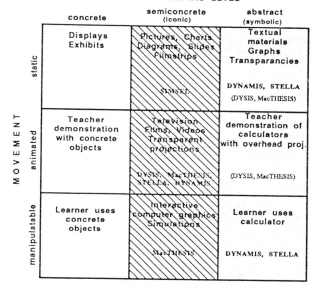

Figure 1: The "instructional model" [Berlin87] applied to simulations (striped area) and dynamic modelling (dotted area). [Names of program systems and areas added by the author]

Transferring the briefly outlined categories and hypotheses from the theory of learning to learning objectives, a simulation system can only be used for the lower Bloom categories (knowledge, understanding, application), while modelling systems will also help to reach the higher categories - analysis, synthesis and evaluation.

4. Software Ergonomic Aspects

Software-ergonomics in regard to computer simulations in the teaching of science, is mainly concerned with the problem of transferring the interhuman communication to a human- computer interaction, in which the user communicates with the programmer(s) of the system via technical media, and all possible variations of the communication process have to be split up in advance into isolated dialog steps by the system designer(s).

The state of the art of human factors research has not yet yielded recipes for the programmer, on how to design a "user-friendly" human-computer interface. There are, though, several catalogs of design requirements (for details, see [Viereck87], [Balzert87] and [Schönpflug87]), most of them basing on the IFIP model, which in Germany has led to the draft standard DIN 66234 (dialog design) [DIN84].

The transfer of the three layers of learning from the learning theory (section 3) to the design of the "user-surface" of dynamic modelling and simulation systems, leads directly to the requirement that the learner user should have the opportunity to manipulate data and model in the most direct way possible [Daldrup87]. The design principles for user surfaces "direct manipulation" and "iconic representation" (on systems with the "desk top metaphor" and "windowing systems" on high resolution graphic raster displays, e.g. XEROX Star and Apple Macintosh), give the best foundation for application systems which do not distract a non-expert user from the topic to be learned, even if a simulation system can only support the "lower" Bloom categories, or the two lower levels of learning (action layer and schema layer):

- The use of direct manipulation in simulation systems allows, for instance, the graphical input of data (In MacTHESIS and SIMKIT the "scroll bar" is an analogy for linear potentiometers). (Figures 2 and 3)

- The direct output of the running model as a function graph is an animation of symbolic-abstract data. This is realised in STELLA, DYNAMIS, DYSIS and in the "traditional" programs of [Koschwitz85], but, for example, not in SIMSEL, where the results are stored on disk before they can be displayed either as table or graphs.

- The intervention, i.e. a change of variable values at any time while the model is running, gives the learner an immediate impression of the consequences of his decisions. (Figure 4)

The "abstract symbolic" learning layer is directly supported in dynamic modelling systems, in which the learner can develop the model, not only in the form of a textual representation in a programming language, but in a visual representation ("visual programming" [Gorny87]) and - without changing the medium - can run the model:

- The model is represented in a graphical (iconic) form as a net, which is a more efficient way than only in verbal (textual/numeric) representation, as shown by [Vent85]. The user can construct this net as he would construct a circuit layout, by adding and deleting elements to change the model. (Implementations of STELLA and DYNAMIS on Macintosh).

- The layout of the net can be changed by moving the node icons and connections to modify the visual representation (STELLA and DYNAMIS). (Figure 5)

Thus the system produces a continuous direct feedback and allows an "objective" observation of the manipulation of the model and the model data, and, in terms of learning theories

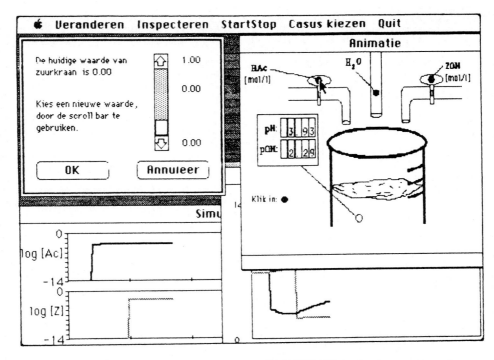

Figure 2: Output from the MacTHESIS model "CHEMISTRY" (a nitration experiment).
By clicking the black dot (arrow) the valve can be opened to control the flow of a
liquid. The value is input by moving up and down the "scroll bar" in the input
window at the upper left.

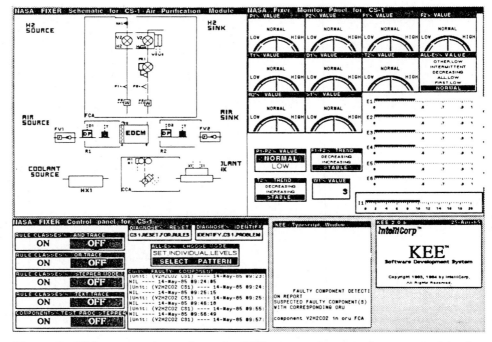

Figure 3: This screen picture from the KEE system shows analog outputs (circular
"instruments" - upper right corner) and analog input devices (linear "potentiometers"
- right edge/center)

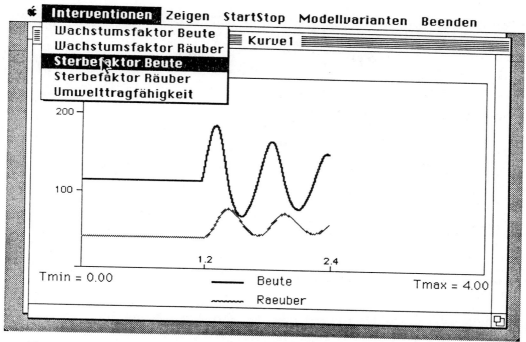

Figure 4: MacTHESIS (German version by author) allows the user to intervene in the running simulation and change any of the model variables. Here the Lokta-Volterra model is stopped to increase the value of the prey birth rate ratio (1st intervention at t=1.2) and to change the death rate ratio (2nd intervention at t=2.4). The way to choose the new value is shown in fig.2 (scroll bar in the window at the upper left corner)

and current artificial intelligence research, it offers the experimental testing of one's own cognitive structures in concrete models.

The possibility of direct manipulation of objects in the visual representation of models as semantic nets, with the aid of an interactive net editor, is also realised in the general purpose visual programming systems BOXER and GARDEN (A.diSessa resp. S.P.Reiss in [Gorny87]).

5. Conclusions

Well known theories from cognitive science, pedagogics and informatics have to be applied when designing educational software systems. This has been exemplified with dynamic modelling and simulation systems. The theories result in a set of design requirements:
- the system should allow a graphical representation of the mathematical model as close as possible to pictorial representation;
- the system should allow a direct manipulation of the model;

- the system should allow access to different representations of data, i.e. numerical, textual or different graphical representations;
- the system should allow direct manipulation of the data;
- the system should allow intervention into the model, i.e. the variation of variables while the model is running;
- the results of running model should be presented in animated pictorial form (and not only as animated graphs and/or as tables);

Thus the learner has the possibility to move up and down between the different layers of learning - from the more concrete to the more abstract - at his/her own initiative and speed.

The operationalization of these requirements is possible on the background of a professional approach to educational software design and evaluation.

In this article we have refrained from discussing the general problems of educational software design especially in regard to the integration of programs into a computer enhanced learning environment [Gorny86] and the requirements for a HELP-module, which has to be divided into (active) monitoring functions and (passive) consulting functions [Balzert87].

References

ATEE86: ATEE: A Model Syllabus for Literacy in Information Technology for All Teachers. Part 1: Tom van Weert (Ed.): Teaching about IT. ATEE Brussels, 1984. Part2: Rhys Gwyn(Ed.): Teaching and Learning with the New Technologies. ATEE Brussels 1986.

Balzert87 H. Balzert: Software-Ergonomie und Software Engineering. 1987 (In preparation)

Berlin87 D. F. Berlin: A model for the design of the learning environment: integration of technology into the classroom. In: Preprints 2nd Int'l. Conf. Children in the Information Age: Opportunities for Creativity, Innovation and New Activities. Sofia May 1987. Vol 1, 66-83.

Bossel85 H. Bossel u.a.: Dynamik des Waldsterbens. Berlin u.a.: Springer 1985.

Daldrup87 U. Daldrup: Computersimulationen im Unterriocht: Neues Lernen - neues Lernen? Schriftenreihe des Zentrum für pädagogische Berufspraxis der Universität Oldenburg. Oldenburg 1987.

DIN84 Deutsches Institut for Normung: DIN 66234. Bildschirmarbeitsplätze. Grundsätze der Dialoggestaltung. Entwurf 1984.

Edelmann79 W. Edelmann, Einführung in die Lernpsychologie. Bd 2.: Kognitive Lerntheorien und schulisches Lernen. München 1979.

Gaines87 B.R. Gaines: A Methodological Framework for the Design and Evaluation of Software in Systems Involving Complex Human-Computer Interaction. In: W. Schönpflug (Hg.): Software-Ergonomie '87. Proc. of the German Chapter of the Association for Computing Machinery Conference Berlin 1987. (Berichte des German Chapter of the ACM Band 29). Stuttgart 1987.

GMD86 Gesellschaft für Mathematik und Datenverarbeitung: schulis - Simulationssystem SIMSEL, D-5205 St. Augustin 1, 1986.

Gorny86 P. Gorny: Software Development for Educational Applications. In: Proc. Int'l. Seminar Information Technology and Education Sofia October 1986. (In preparation)

Gorny87 P. Gorny & M.Tauber (Eds.): Visualization in Programming. Proc. of the 5th int'l. workshop on Informatics and Psychology at Schärding, Austria, 1986. (Lecture Notes in Computer Science). Berlin, Heidelberg.., 1987.

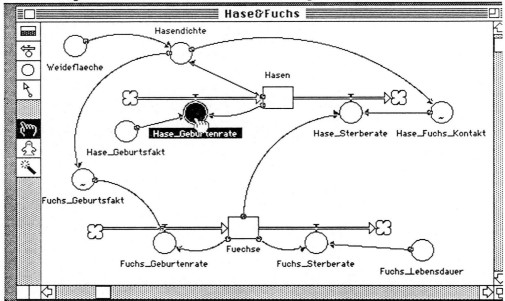

Figure 5: The system diagram window of STELLA (German version by author) allows the editing of a network. The network is the graphical representation of the model. By pointing and clicking once at one network element this can be deleted or moved; by clicking twice it is "opened" (Then numerical or algebraic specifications of the model can be defined).

Häuslein86   A. Häuslein & B. Page: DYNAMIS: Ein Modellbildungs- und Simulationssystem mit objekt-orientierter Benutzeroberfläche. In: G. Hommel u. S. Schindler: Gesellschaft für Informatik: Proc. 16. GI-Jahrestagung. Informatik-Anwendungen - Trends und Perspektiven: Berlin Oktober 1986. (Informatik-Fachberichte: 126). Berlin u.a., 1986, Band 1, 329-343.

HighPerform87   High Performance Systems: STELLA. High Performance Systems, Inc., Lyme, New Hampshire 03768. 1987.

IntelliCorp85   SIMKIT - Knowledge-based simulation in KEE. IntelliCorp, 1975 El Camino Real West, Mountain View, California 094040

Klafki85   W. Klafki: Neue Studien zur Bildungstheorie und Didaktik. Weinheim, Basel 1985.

Koschwitz85   H. Koschwitz u. J. Wedekind: BASIC-Biologie-programme. Stuttgart 1985.

Lehman77   R. Lehman: Computer Simulation and Modelling: An Introduction. New York 1977.

Min87   F.B.M. Min & P.G. van Schaick Zillesen: MacTHESIS: a design system for educational computer simulation programs. Enschede 1987 (In preparation for Computers and Education).

Schönpflug87:   W. Schönpflug (Hg.): Software-Ergonomie '87. Proc. of the German Chapter of the Association for Computing Machinery Conference Berlin 1987. (Berichte des German Chapter of the ACM Band 29). Stuttgart 1987.

Vent85   U. Vent: Der Einfluß einer ganzheitlicher Denkstrategie auf die Lösung von komplexen Problemen. Institut für Pädagogik der Naturwissenschaften an der Universität Kiel. Arbeitsbericht Nr. 61, Kiel 1985.

Viereck87   A. Viereck: Klassifiakationen, Konzepte und Modelle für den Mensch-Rechner-Dialog. Doctoral dissertation. Berichte aus dem Fachbereich Informatik der Universität Oldenburg Nr. 1/87.

COMPUTERS IN EDUCATION, F. Lovis and E.D. Tagg (eds.)
Elsevier Science Publishers B.V. (North-Holland)
© IFIP, 1988

STELLA AND ITS IMPACT ON THE TEACHING OF MATHEMATICAL MODELLING

A. H. WHITFIELD

ICL (UK) Limited, Computer House, 127 Hagley Road,
Birmingham B16 8LD, United Kingdom

Despite its central rôle in the prediction and subsequent control of system behaviour, mathematical modelling of dynamic processes has traditionally played little or no part in many undergraduate courses. The paper suggests reasons for this absence, gives an overview of STELLA, a software product for the Macintosh range of computers, and outlines its integration into a course on mathematical modelling. Particular emphasis is placed on its ease of use, conceptually simple terminology and the consequent lack of mathematical expertise needed to develop meaningful models of a wide variety of systems in both engineering and non-engineering disciplines.

1. INTRODUCTION

A significant proportion of modern engineering design relies on the availability of a suitable mathematical model to describe the system at hand. The complexity of such models is as wide ranging as is the field of engineering itself, encompassing static descriptions of deterministic surfaces at one extreme and the prediction of the dynamic time evolution of a potentially stochastic system at the other. Systems which have spatial as well as temporal distribution are classed as "distributed parameter" and are typically described by one or more partial differential equations with associated boundary conditions. Systems in which spatial variation is negligible are called "lumped parameter" and, when continuous in time, are typically described by one or more ordinary differential equations and their appropriate initial conditions. This paper is concerned with the derivation of mathematical models for continuous lumped parameter systems. Two very different approaches can be adopted to provide a solution to this problem. One is the approach of system identification [1], [2] where inputs to the system and consequent outputs from the system are recorded and passed to an identification algorithm which produces a model describing the input/output behaviour of the system. The advantage of this approach is that it is black-box and requires relatively little effort or thought. Its major disadvantage is that it is black-box (!) since it yields little or no insight into the interrelationship of entities within the system from which the observed input/output behaviour has arisen. The alternative approach to producing a set of equations to adequately describe the behaviour of a system is that of mathematical modelling. Here we consider the component parts of the system and deduce an overall system model by considering the interaction of the parts and their individual mathematical models; such individual models are often available as a result of previous experimentation and derivation. This approach demands considerable thought but promotes an understanding of the overall system behaviour via a detailed understanding of its component parts and their interaction.

From an educational standpoint we seek to engender fundamental understanding and hence mathematical modelling might be expected to play a prominent role in engineering courses; unfortunately this is seldom the case and one can only postulate the reasons for its absence. Perhaps the most important reason is the problem of predicting the behaviour of the model and thereby gauging its accuracy as a representation of the real world system. Such behaviour can generally be sought from three potential routes. Firstly the analytical approach in which, by any one of several mathematical techniques, one seeks the analytical solution of the governing equations. This approach is usually extremely time consuming, demands a reasonable level of mathematical skill and is limited to systems which are primarily linear and are governed by a low order ordinary differential equation. A second approach is afforded by analogue simulation of the model equations. This is generally performed on an electronic analogue computer and is often tedious to implement, requires some mathematical knowledge to provide appropriate scaling of variables and is most easily applied to linear systems. Additionally, analogue computers are dedicated pieces of equipment which can be expensive. However, a major advantage of analogue computers is that parameter values can, within reason, be readily modified and the subsequent model behaviour can be immediately observed qualitatively on an oscilloscope. The third route to evaluating the performance of a mathematical model is digital simulation. This is most easily achieved through a continuous system simulation language (CSSL), e.g. DYNAMO [3], ACSL [4], ESL [5], which can handle non-linear systems as easily as linear ones. The problem here is that the modeller requires some degree of proficiency in digital computation since some knowledge of the computer operating system and a text editor is demanded. Further, any CSSL is, by definition, a high level language in its own right and its attendant conventions are most easily grasped by those who are already familiar with other general purpose high level computing languages. Simulation via a CSSL is often a distinctly non-interactive activity requiring off-line model formulation and a loop consisting of text editing, language compilation, model simulation and graphics post-processing. Such a large loop, which entails significant computer contact time, does not naturally lend itself to model perturbation, experimentation and development. We therefore summarise that a major problem in all three approaches to mathematical model verification is the level of expertise and time taken to simulate any hypothesized model.

A further problem in mathematical model development is the nature of the thought processes required to create a model. This problem was addressed by Forrester [6] who created the formalism of 'system dynamics' within which mathematical models of lumped parameter systems could be evolved and described pictorially prior to digital simulation. System dynamics gives a natural thinking environment for the development of mathematical models but we have, until recently, still been faced with the problem of model simulation.

STELLA (Structural Thinking, Experiential Learning Laboratory with Animation) [7] is a software product for the Apple Macintosh range of computers which combines the thinking environment and symbology of system dynamics with immediate simulation facilities and a user-friendly windows environment to provide an exceptionally powerful interactive tool for the development of mathematical models. Using STELLA the necessity for subsidiary skills, such as mathematical manipulation and computational knowledge, is minimised and a proper emphasis can be placed on the creation of mathematical models rather than on their subsequent manipulation which is, after all, relatively meaningless if the student cannot produce a viable model in the first instance. In this paper we shall outline the nature of STELLA and how it has been used in an undergraduate course on control engineering. However we will hopefully also convey the fact that STELLA should significantly broaden the rôle of mathematical modelling in other disciplines such as business management and the social sciences and should also allow some elements of modelling to be introduced to students at high school level.

2. AN OVERVIEW OF STELLA

STELLA requires a 512K Macintosh computer and utilises the windows environment and the concept of object orientation to the full. Thus only a minimum knowledge of any windows environment is required to become immediately productive in creating mathematical models. STELLA utilises four basic windows: a *diagram* window in which to create the model (and to provide qualitative simulation post-processing), a *graph pad* window to provide more meaningful graphical post-processing, a *table* window to provide numerical post-processing and an *equation* window which displays the equations which underpin the model that the user has created in the diagram window. A traditional Macintosh menu bar at the top of the screen gives access to a set of pull down menus which offer a variety of facilities for constructing, manipulating, simulating, printing and saving mathematical models. In the following sections we shall

briefly outline many of the facilities offered by STELLA and shall note several features which make its practical use extremely easy and flexible and therefore amenable to both the inexperienced and the expert modeller alike. To convey the extent of STELLA to experienced modellers some mathematical notation is included in the discussion; this would be avoided when introducing STELLA to students.

2.1. The diagram window

The initial empty diagram window is shown in fig.1 with four basic *building blocks* and three associated *tools*.

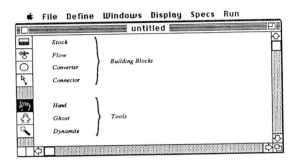

Fig. 1. An annotated initial STELLA diagram window.

(i) *The stock* ▦ , *flow* ☞ , *converter* ○ *and connector* ↖
icons
The *stock* and *flow* icons embody the essence of the technique for model construction and have evolved directly from comparable icons used by Forrester in the system dynamics modelling methodology. Both icons represent components in a fluid flow analogy where fluid (the stock) is contained in a tank. One or more inflows can be attached to the tank as can one or more outflows, the flow rates being dictated in the appropriate flow icons. The stock then behaves as would an incompressible fluid in a tank of unit uniform cross-sectional area: its (rate of change of volume) = its (rate of change of level) = (total volume inflow rate) − (total volume outflow rate). Thus the STELLA model shown in fig.2

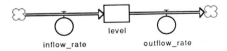

Fig. 2. A stock with inflow and outflow.

is represented mathematically by the equation

$$\frac{d}{dt}(\text{level}) = \text{inflow\_rate} - \text{outflow\_rate}$$

with an associated initial condition level (at time t=0), or by the integral statement

$$\text{level (at time } t) = \text{level (at time t=0)} + \int_0^t \{\text{ inflow\_rate}(\tau) - \text{outflow\_rate}(\tau)\}\ d\tau$$

Thus any accumulation process that can be represented by a first order ordinary differential equation may be shown diagrammatically via a stock and its associated inflows and outflows and higher order systems can be developed by connecting such first order processes together. The clouds at the start of the inflow and the end of the outflow represent an infinite source and an infinite sink of the flow respectively. The precise manipulation of the mouse to place an icon in a given location on the diagram and connect it to another icon are trivial and once practised are never forgotten; they will not be described here.

The *converter* icon is used to introduce intermediate variables and functions into the model. *Connectors* are used to dictate that one variable in the model depends on one or more other variables in the model. Thus in fig.3 outflow_rate is dependent on velocity which is itself dependent on both gravity_accel and level.

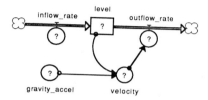

Fig. 3. Converters, connectors, a stock and flows.

(ii) *The hand* 🖑 , *ghost* 👻 *and dynamite* 🧨 *icons*
When icons are placed on the diagram only functional dependency is indicated, thus the initial value of any stock is undefined (indicated by a ?, as in fig.3) as is the definition of any flow rate or converter function (also indicated by a ?). The *hand* icon is used to point at any stock, flow or converter whereupon double-clicking on the mouse then enters a dialogue box which allows definition or redefinition of the variable concerned. Fig.4 illustrates a typical dialogue box when defining the velocity variable in fig.3. A single-click on the mouse with the hand icon pointing at a stock, flow or converter allows the user to change the default name (noname1, noname2 etc.) of, or rename, the target stock, flow or converter by simply typing a meaningful model parameter name at the keyboard.

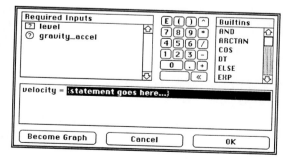

Fig. 4. Defining a converter.

A single-input/single-output flow or converter can be defined either algebraically or graphically while a multi-input/single-output flow or converter can only be defined algebraically. In either instance definition is simplicity itself with all the available *built-in* STELLA functions (table 1) being displayed in and accessed from the **Builtins** scrollable list (see fig.4) and all variables which were dictated as inputs to the flow or converter by connectors being similarly displayed and accessible from the **Required Inputs** list. The diagram window contains the precise structural definition of the model and STELLA exercises a useful interactive check on all flow/converter definitions by demanding that all, and only those, inputs to a flow/converter, as specified by connectors in the diagram, appear in the flow/converter definition; it prohibits acceptance until this is obeyed. An interactive check is also made on the arguments to built-in functions as supplied by the user. If incorrectly specified, STELLA prompts the user with the correct number and rôle of the arguments for the built-in function which the user has requested; this obviates the need to memorize such details and is extremely useful in practice. Graphical definition of a flow or converter (via **Become Graph**, as in fig.4) utilizes eleven input/output pair nodal values with intermediate piecewise linear interpolation and linear extrapolation beyond the lower and upper bounds. Nodal values are input numerically from the keyboard or by vertical manipulation of a node via the mouse. Thus imprecise non-linear input/output characteristics are rapidly defined with a minimum of effort.

AND	Logical	OR	Logical
ARCTAN	Trigonometric	PCT	Mathematical
COS	Trigonometric	PI	Mathematical
DT	Special	PMT	Financial
ELSE	Logical	PULSE	Test Input
EXP	Mathematical	PV	Financial
FORCST	Special	RAMP	Test Input
FV	Financial	RANDOM	Mathematical
IF	Logical	SIN	Trigonometric
INIT	Special	SMTH1	Special
INT	Mathematical	SMTH3	Special
LOG10	Mathematical	SQRT	Mathematical
LOGN	Mathematical	STEP	Test Input
MAX	Mathematical	TAN	Mathematical
MIN	Mathematical	THEN	Logical
NORMAL	Mathematical	TIME	Special
NOT	Logical	TREND	Special

Table 1. Built-in STELLA functions.

In larger models one variable may have an influence on several others and hence several connectors may emanate from one source and, when the appropriate connections are made, the diagram can become spaghetti like. The ghost icon is used to create ghosted (duplicate) images of stocks, flows or converters which can then act as points from which a connector can emanate. Ghosts are therefore used to clean up a potentially messy diagram. The final tool is the stick of dynamite which has the obvious property of blowing away any undesired item of the diagram.

Further functions offered within the diagram window include the ability to visually zoom into and out from parts of the model and the facility to animate the levels of the stocks and the flow rates so as to gain a rough qualitative feel for the behaviour of the model.

2.2. The graph pad window

This window allows the rapid graphical post-processing from a simulation of the model contained in the diagram window. The minimum and maximum values for plotting any of the model variables may be prescribed via the **Scale...** option of the **Run** menu. A single page of the graph pad can illustrate the behaviour of up to four variables plotted as time series or two variables plotted one against the other as a scatter diagram. An extremely useful feature of this window is the facility to turn the pages of the graph pad, backwards or forwards, while the simulation proceeds. Fig.5 illustrates typical contents from one page of the graph pad.

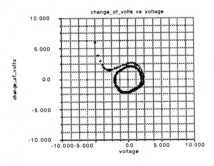

Fig. 5. A phase plane plot.

2.3. The table window

In certain instances more precise information than can be provided graphically is required for model verification and subsequent design analysis. The table window allows the user to track the precise numerical values of one or more model variables over a period of time in either fixed or floating point form. An interesting feature of this window is the facility to scroll back through numeric data which has previously scrolled past the top of the window.

2.4. The equations window

As soon as the stocks and flows have been plumbed together and all initial stock levels, flows and converters have been defined, the system of equations which underpins the diagram window is well defined. These equations can be viewed, though not modified, at any time in the equations window.

2.5. The STELLA menu bar

(i) File

This menu is used to open, close, save and selectively print STELLA documents. Additionally both the model diagram and any page of the graph pad can be saved in either MacDraw or MacPaint format thereby allowing the user to add further annotation for subsequent report generation.

(ii) Define

Amongst other features this menu provides facilities to define those variables to be plotted on various pages of the graph pad and enumerated in the window. In either case a scrollable list of all model variables is available and a variable is selected for presentation by simply clicking on it.

(iii) Windows

This menu allows the user to define the foremost window as either the diagram, graph pad, table or equations window; it is worth noting that the contents of all the windows are updated during the course of a simulation and a user may bring anyone of the windows to the foreground at any stage.

(iv) Display

This menu presents a range of options to manipulate the various STELLA window displays. Thus the contents of the diagram window can be enlarged or reduced (a necessity when viewing the interconnections in a large model), a grid can be added to or suppressed from the pages of the graph pad etc.

(v) Specs

STELLA employs three integration algorithms: Euler's method, 2nd order Runge-Kutta and 4th order Runge-Kutta. The computation method is selected via this menu as is the start time, the stop time and the step size for the chosen algorithm. A **Numeric Format...** option allows definition of the numeric format of the tabulated data as either fixed or floating point with a specified number of significant digits within each format. **Animate What...** allows the user to dictate which elements of the diagram are to be animated.

(vi) Run

Offers control over the running of a simulation via **Start/Restart**, **Pause/Resume** and **Stop**. The **Scale...** option applies a linear scale to each plotted variable. Within this option an **AutoScale** facility runs the simulation in the background to ascertain the minimum and maximum values attained by each variable. These are relayed to the user who can use them directly or give more convenient plotting limits.

3. USING STELLA TO TEACH MATHEMATICAL MODELLING

3.1. Engineering systems

Standard modelling courses [8] classify the elements of engineering systems into five categories: mechanical translational, mechanical rotational, electrical, fluidic and thermal. The similarity between the governing equations of ideal elements in each category then leads to a characterization of component variables as either *through-variables* (e.g. force, torque, current, fluid flow rate, heat flow rate) which have the same value at each end of the element, or *across-variables* (e.g. translational velocity, rotational velocity, voltage, pressure, temperature) which are specified as relative values or differences between the end values. Ideal mechanical, electrical, fluidic and thermal elements can then be classified into three generalized types in each case having a known equation: an A- or capacitance-type element, a T- or inductance-type element and a D- or resistance-type element. A description of the dynamic behaviour of the system is then derived from the flow of energy within the system via the interconnections of the elements and the overriding *compatibility* conditions applied to across-variables (e.g. Kirchoff's voltage law) and *continuity* conditions applied to through-variables (e.g. the conservation of force in a mechanical network). A- and T-type elements act as energy storers and their governing equations can be written as single time domain integrals and hence as stocks and flows in STELLA while D-type elements act as energy dissipators whose governing equations can be written in simple algebraic form and hence as converters in STELLA. The basis for a systematic approach to modelling a wide variety of engineering systems is therefore already established and can be conveyed in a concrete manner to students.

However, as with most aspects of mathematics, mathematical modelling skills are only fully developed by significant student participation. To this end, practice in model building is given by a series of increasingly complicated tutorial questions which are given to the student in written form. The student is also supplied with a disc which holds a STELLA document pertinent to each question. Each such document contains a template with two sets of information. Firstly the laws governing idealizations of the system A-, T- and D-type elements are supplied in the form of a disconnected STELLA diagram; in early tutorial questions all the required laws can be presented, though such information can be reduced in subsequent questions to reinforce the learning of elemental equations. The second set of template information takes the form of a series of graph pad pages which contain graphs of one or more inputs and corresponding transients resulting from a simulation of a model which the tutor has prescribed as sufficiently accurate for the problem at hand. In the absence of actual plant data, these transients form the basis for validation of the student's model. To create and retain such transient graphs the tutor builds an accurate model of the plant within STELLA and plots any desired transients on one or more pages of the graph pad. Each graph pad page is *locked* by

means of a visual lock and key and the model diagram is then deleted from the diagram window. As previously suggested, appropriate componental laws can be placed in the diagram window and the whole STELLA document is then saved, typically under a filename corresponding to the written question number. When answering a question, the student opens the attendant STELLA document, interactively builds a model using the given elemental laws and simulates the system for one or more inputs and initial conditions. The transients from these simulations are plotted on pages of the graph pad and the model is verified by comparison with the transients on the locked pages.

3.2. Modelling in other disciplines

Developing a suitable mathematical model for an engineering process is usually a prerequisite to understanding the process and forms the basis for subsequent design and control considerations. Identical and crucial questions relating to system performance prediction and control are also raised in several other disciplines including economics, business management, biomedicine and psychology. In many instances the appropriate model will be ideal for development in STELLA i.e. lumped, continuous parameter subject to either deterministic or random inputs, and it is perhaps in these other disciplines that STELLA may make the biggest impact.

Students in such disciplines may be less familiar with digital computers and standard CSSL's may well prove too demanding. Additionally, the lack of immediate interaction with mini/mainframe based CSSL's prohibits discussion of and experimentation with componental laws which are generally less well defined than in the engineering sphere. STELLA, however, provides immediate feedback on the performance of a hypothesized model, uses conceptually easy and precise terminology to build a model and minimizes knowledge of background mathematics (little or no knowledge of the various integration schemes is required provided some simple rules regarding the selection and reduction of step-size are followed). Thus mathematical modelling of dynamic systems and processes may be expected to play an increasing rôle in non-engineering disciplines and can also be introduced into various curricula at a much earlier stage, perhaps even at high school level.

3.3. Report generation

From the time it is first conceived, a mathematical model is subject to development and amendment as new data becomes available and new factors come into play. Such amendment means that either one or a number of persons must return to a model time and again to provide adequate updating. For this process to be performed accurately and efficiently it is essential that the model and its underlying hypotheses and assumptions are well documented. It is therefore important that students become familiar with, and adept at, producing high quality documentation, preferably with a minimum of effort.

Frijda [9] has previously commented on the inadequacy of many published reports on simulation. In the past a stream of flowcharts, program listings, annotated input and output and background material were required to document a model and its digital simulation. However documenting models developed in STELLA is far less tedious. Firstly, a STELLA model and associated simulations are entirely self contained with both the model itself (the contents of the diagram and equations windows) and any transients (the contents of the graph pad and table windows) being held in one document. Secondly the Macintosh and its large range of desktop publishing software offers an almost ideal environment for the development of formal written reports. Thus powerful WYSIWYG wordprocessors such as WriteNow, Word and MacAuthor are able to incorporate both text and graphics in a single document and produce extremely high quality printed output via Apple's LaserWriter or other Postscript devices. STELLA is fully integrated into the Macintosh environment and has a range of facilities to export its internal graphic images to such applications. Thus whole screens can be dumped to a MacPaint file via the usual Command Shift 3 key press combination, while the contents of the diagram window or any page of the graph pad can be saved as either a MacPaint document or, for more precise subsequent manipulation and annotation, as a MacDraw document. Additionally, mathematical formulae processors such as MacΣqn and Formulator can be used in those reports which seek to elaborate the mathematical background of the model.

4. CONCLUSIONS

STELLA provides an excellent workbench for an introduction to the mathematical modelling of continuous dynamic systems. Its user friendly interfaces, speed of interaction, conceptually simple basis and background mathematical solution routines have allowed much greater emphasis to be placed on the production of mathematical models rather than on their subsequent manipulation. It does not replace the thought processes from which a model is evolved but certainly minimizes the need for subsidiary skills to validate hypothesized models. Since model development productivity is typically increased by at least an order of magnitude, students may tackle a far more extensive set of modelling exercises than has been possible to date and their skill in mathematical modelling is correspondingly enhanced.

STELLA has been used to great effect on a course in mathematical modelling for engineering systems where many elemental governing equations are well developed and the modelling problem is really one of providing the appropriate interconnections. However its appeal is far more widespread and its potential as a modelling tool in study of business, biological, ecological and other diverse systems is clear. Mathematical modelling can also now be integrated into curricula at a much earlier stage with a consequent consolidation of students' awareness and understanding of interconnected system behaviour.

Several features of STELLA, its integration within the Macintosh environment and the availability of powerful wordprocessing and desktop publishing software further combine to significantly enhance the production of high quality, accurate and informative model documentation, a process which is vital in practical modelling situations.

ACKNOWLEDGEMENTS

This paper is published by permission of ICL (UK) Limited whose support the author gratefully acknowledges.

REFERENCES

[1] Eykhoff, P., System Identification (John Wiley and Sons, London, 1974).

[2] Young, P. C., Parameter estimation for continuous time models - a survey, Automatica, vol. 17, no. 1, 1981, pp. 23-29.

[3] Pugh III, A. L., DYNAMO II User's Manual (MIT Press, Cambridge, Mass., 1976).

[4] Mitchell & Gauthier Associates, ACSL User Guide /Reference Manual, 1981.

[5] Hay, J. Σ., ESL - Advanced simulation language implementation, Proc. UKSC 84 Conference on Computer Simulation, University of Bath, September 1984, pp. 1-10.

[6] Forrester, J. W., Principles of Systems (MIT Press, Cambridge, Mass., 1968).

[7] High Performance Systems Inc., STELLA for Business, Lyme, New Hampshire, 1987.

[8] Shearer, J. L., Murphy, A. T., and Richardson, H. H., Introduction to System Dynamics (Addison-Wesley, Reading, Mass., 1971).

[9] Frijda, N. H., The problems of computer simulation, Behavioural Science, vol. 12, 1967, pp. 59-67.

COMPUTERS IN EDUCATION, F. Lovis and E.D. Tagg (eds.)
Elsevier Science Publishers B.V. (North-Holland)
© IFIP, 1988

A CASE STUDY IN REJUVENATING AN EXISTING LEARNING PROGRAM THROUGH COMPUTER TECHNOLOGY

Curt Shreiner

Educational Technologist
1105 Spruce Street
Philadelphia, PA 19107 USA

This study documented the process by which an existing learning program was redesigned to optimize new technology. Based upon criteria for good program design, an exemplary program was selected. An interview with the original program designer established parameters for the redesign. Attributes of the new delivery system were then correlated to nine computer-based instructional strategies for specification of the computer's contribution in each strategy.

One selected learning unit was analyzed according to the criteria established by the designer and the capabilities offered by the CBI strategies. Unit learning activities were redesigned using an IBM graphics program. Formative testing and thorough assessment by the original program design team have indicated that new technology can indeed foster rejuvenation of programs.

INTRODUCTION

The literature abounds with methodologies and models for guiding the developer of instructional materials. While Gustafson [5] has reported that virtually hundreds of these models are available, the accelerated rise of computer technology has noticeably outstripped the ability of practitioners and theoreticians to create a sound methodology for optimizing this newcomer to the field of instructional delivery. Can the potential of new technology be optimized without a well-considered methodology?

Nevertheless, new educational materials and courseware are being developed, and at a swift pace. Models have surfaced to guide courseware developers in utilizing this new, complex technology for instructional delivery. Control Data's Courseware Development Process [4] is one example.

While resources come to bear upon issues of new courseware development, attention lacks elsewhere - specifically, the wealth of programs developed prior to the emergence of contemporary delivery systems. What potential does computer technology hold for programs that have already been developed and are effectively being used in print format, for example?

To date, little research has been published that examines the redesigning of successful learning programs so that the unique educational capabilities of the computer may be apparent. Consequently, limited research has hampered the development of a clear methodology by which to rejuvenate existing programs and materials.

A quality program should have, built within it, the pedagogical constructs to transcend time and technology. However, educators and developers, enamored by the state-of-the-art, may brush aside that which appears dated, even though the materials may reflect the highest of quality and the finest of pedagogical treatment. Herein lies the problem. There needs to be a means of retooling these materials by capitalizing upon the technology. Redesign implies rejuvenation, as opposed to reinvention. The rejuvenation approach may provide a remarkable opportunity for the developer, but also poses some questions.

How does the existing program change when delivered by a new technology?

What decisions need to be made in order to capitalize upon the attributes of the new, yet retain the vitality and effectiveness of the old?

This study has explored the process of transferring already-proven content and planned educational processes to an inherently different vehicle for presentation.

DESIGN OF THE STUDY

Clearly, a need exists to exploit the potential embodied in computer technology. I propose that an experienced developer can specify the processes by which learning programs can be redesigned to optimize new technology. By carefully documenting each decision in the development process, both the product and the recorded procedures may shed light upon a previously unexplored problem.

RESEARCH QUESTIONS

A series of questions have been addressed, and have constructively shaped the direction of this study:

1. How can the computer optimize the pedagogical strengths already inherent in the learning experiences?
   a. Can the power of learning be improved by using the special properties of the computer?
   b. How will the redesigned learning experiences compare with those found in the original program?
   c. Do new possibilities arise that weren't possible before?

2. What are the implications for delivery of the program?
   a. Will this be a substitutive function, delivering printed text on screen, or is it more involved?
   b. Will the use of the computer be less cumbersome?
   c. What are the cost implications for the learner and the organizations using the program?
   d. Will fear of technology impede users of the system?

3. Decision-making procedure
   a. How detailed?
   b. What mechanism is best used to record the decisions?
   c. How will the factors influencing the decisions best be articulated?

d. Will this cumulative record of decisions truly reflect the redesign process?

PROCEDURE

Virtually any existing learning program could be selected for study. However, less-than- quality materials in such a developmental study may inject subversive variables that would detract from the desirably tight focus. Consequently, I have selected a well-designed and developed multimedia intervention, so that attention can be appropriately placed on the issues of design and technological optimization.

CRITERIA OF GOOD PROGRAM DESIGN

A considerable amount of literature addresses the topic of effective program design. From this wealth, the criteria of good program design might best be represented by the Instructional Development Institute Model from the National Special Media Institute [6]. A majority of the other program design models reflect a variation on the IDI's stages of: a) Definition; b) Development; and c) Evaluation. However, layers of detailed substages differentiate the IDI model by virtue of its attention to thoroughness.

To begin, the Definition Stage identifies the problem. This requires conducting a thorough needs assessment, establishing priorities among the needs, and stating one or more problems to be addressed. Step Two further specifies additional data to be collected regarding learner characteristics, conditions under which development must occur, constraints on any given solution to the identified problem, and availability of relevant materials and resources for both developing and delivering the solution. The Definition Stage concludes with organization of the development team.

The IDI Model's Development Stage, starting with the identification of objectives, is similar to most other models in that it requires behaviorally stated objectives. Unlike other models, these objectives are specified <u>only</u> after considerable data has been collected regarding the needs of the learners and the problem to be addressed. Consequently, a tighter correlation can be drawn between the learners' needs and the desired outcomes of the program. Following this step is the speci- fication of the methods, pedagogical strategies, and media appropriate for delivery of the program.

In the Evaluation Stage, prototypes of all components of the program are constructed, given the decisions made in previous steps. Formative evaluation with the population of learners follows the development of these testable materials. The criteria is specified for analyzing results of learner achievement, effectiveness and practicability of the methods of instruction, and appropriateness of the evaluation techniques. The final step in the IDI Model is to "recycle", if a deficiency exists, or to implement the solution if proven effective. Recycling implies a return to the original problem and re-analyze needs.

THE PROGRAM SELECTED FOR STUDY

As a program that exemplifies such design criteria, THE ADKINS LIFE SKILL PROGRAM: CAREER DEVELOPMENT SERIES has been selected. This multimedia intervention, having already served an estimated 750,000 learners, meets the criteria specified in the IDI Model, and goes beyond. For example, Adkins' Reconnaissance method [1] of assessing needs, and sequencing those needs into a taxonomy for selection of problems to address, is an assessment methodology more rigorous than any recommended by the IDI Model.

Behind THE CAREER DEVELOPMENT SERIES is The Adkins Life Skills Approach. This methodology concentrates on the direct training of learners through carefully developed, sequential learning experiences and multimedia materials that are delivered by counselors in a small group format.

The Life Skills System [1] consists of the Four-Stage Structured Inquiry Learning Model, a program development system, a staff training program, and the processes that enable efficient installation, organizational development, and dissemination of training. THE CAREER DEVELOPMENT SERIES is an embodiment of this system.

The ten-unit CAREER DEVELOPMENT SERIES is based on the tasks of vocational development and vocational maturity, as reported by Super et al. [7]. The individual unit titles, learning objectives, and activities reflect Adkins' [1] refinement and specification of these vocational tasks. The program's learning activities and materials have been fashioned for the reading level and learning styles of disadvantaged adults and youth.

THE CHALLENGE

Simply put, how can the computer be used to redesign learning experiences found in THE CAREER DEVELOPMENT SERIES? This group-oriented counseling/learning system already incorporates over 265 video, print, and audio components. The potential does exist, however, to further enhance the effectiveness of certain career development activities through this technology.

Upon initial examination, it seemed most likely that the learning experiences replaced or supplemented by the computer would be those exercises found in the printed textbook. Perhaps these print materials could be made more responsive and interactive for the learner. Using the greater flexibility of the computer medium, the potential of improved interactivity will be explored. It remained to be seen if a medium, such as the computer, could optimize the pedagogical strengths already inherent in the program without losing the vitality that it currently enjoys. Therein lies the challenge.

DEVELOPMENTAL TASKS

The tasks involved in documenting the redesign process were as follows:

TASK 1. Describe THE ADKINS LIFE SKILL PROGRAM: CAREER DEVELOPMENT SERIES regarding: a) Learner characteristics; b) Pedagogical design of the current learning experiences; and c) Attributes of the current delivery systems.

TASK 2. Identify the parameters for redesign, as established by the designer.

TASK 3. Identify the specific attributes of the computer medium, in order to assess those

characteristics that may prove
favorable for utilization.

TASK 4. Describe characteristics of 9
computer-based instructional
strategies that may be utilized in
the redesign of the learning
experiences.

TASK 5. Select one unit from THE
CAREER DEVELOPMENT SERIES. Describe
possible treatments of the learning
experiences, based upon: a) the
parameters established by the
designer; b) capabilities of
the computer.

TASK 6. Using a graphics tool program
for generating screen representations,
design the prototypical computer-
based materials. Carefully document
the decision-making procedure.

TASK 7. Since the development tool is
limited in its interactivity, devise
formative testing based upon
comprehension of interface factors.

TASK 8. In consultation with the
original program designer and his
team, assess the potential utilization
of materials. Decide whether to invest
in actual programming of the
prototypical materials.

TASK 9. Quantify the decision-making
procedure used in the study and
convert to graphic representation.

TASK 10. Articulate conclusions
derived from the redesigned program,
and from the redesign process.

PROCEDURE

The first four tasks in the study
required the gathering and
organization of information crucial to
the decisions involved.

THE CAREER DEVELOPMENT SERIES has been
briefly described earlier. This a
group-oriented counseling/learning
system, geared for the needs of the
disadvantaged learner, already
incorporates over 265 video, print,
and audio components. An interview
with the originator of the program,
Dr. Winthrop R. Adkins [2], proved
most beneficial for identifying
parameters in shaping the redesign.
Adkins requested these considerations:

1. Use the group format as the primary
learning mode, for reasons of
economics and efficiency of

dissemination. Adkins believed in the
implicit value of group dynamics. This
also maintained the social context for
dealing with emotional issues.

2. The program must be self-contained
and staff must be trained using the
Life Skills training program.

3. The program must be intrinsically
exciting and motivationally rewarding.

4. The quality of the program must
justify purchase of necessary
equipment by potential users.

5. Incorporate individualization that
will encourage, not diminish, group
participation.

6. The redesign must be economical;
the cost should go down, usability
increased, tailorable for subgroups,
learning power should increase, time
on task improved, and incorporation
into the current program be possible.

7. The learner should be able to
easily translate the material into
usable, competent behavior.

Following Adkins' wishes to keep the
group as the primary learning mode,
the place where the computer seemed
most likely to enhance the program was
the third stage of the program's Four
Stage Learning Sequence, the stage
which allows for pursuit of individual
study. Coincidently, most of the
program's print materials are brought
into the learning experience here.

After describing the program and
identifying parameters set by the
original designer, specific attributes
of the computer were articulated and
useful characteristics were pinpointed. The list of over 40 attributes were categorized according to:

1) Individualization Capabilities; 2)
Psychosocial Factors; 3) Diagnosis and
Evaluation; 4) Feedback and
Reinforcement; 5) Recordkeeping and
Management; 6) Data Storage; and
7) Enhancements (such as color, sound
and use of peripherals).

The attributes were then correlated to
nine commonly used strategies that
might exemplify current computer-
based instruction, as identified by
Alessi and Trollip [3]. This cross-
referencing served to clearly
differentiate each strategy, and to
note specific attributes that
contribute to each particular method

of instruction. Computer-based learning strategies described for possible use in this study included: 1) Tutorial; 2) Drill and Practice; 3) Educational Game; 4) Simulation; 5) Problem Solving; 6) Data Base Management; 7) Diagnostic Testing; 8) Tool Application; and 9) Inventory for Identification of Personality Traits.

At this point, criteria for the study was in position. The first unit of THE CAREER DEVELOPMENT SERIES was then analyzed, and possible treatments of the learning experiences were described, based upon: a) the parameters established by the designer; b) capabilities of the computer, based upon the atributes described by each CBI strategy.

Using THE DAN BRICKLIN DEMO PROGRAM, a graphics program for the IBM that generates still screen representations, prototypical computer-based materials were designed. Throughout the six months of designing, decisions were carefully documented. I found the process to be one of collating each learning experience with the most appropriate CBI strategy, then employing adept screen design to bring vitality and elegance to the flow of the materials.

Upon completion of the prototyping, formative testing began with a population of disadvantaged learners. Due to limited interactivity of the materials, testing was based upon the effectiveness of such interface factors as screen design, ease of use, comprehension of text, and visual comprehension.

At the time of this writing, Adkins and the original design team are evaluating the redesigned program's potential in courseware format. Decisions warranting the investment in actual programming of the prototypical materials are forthcoming.

CONCLUSIONS

New technology can optimize the pedagogical strengths already inherent in an existing learning program. The resulting computer-based materials actually displayed depth and intrinsic value far beyond a mere substitutive function of delivering the printed text on screen. It was noted that careful treatment of these learning experiences revealed an overall pedagogical enhancement through the rejuvenating process.

The preliminary assembly of criteria, specifically, establishing redesign parameters, identifying unique attributes of the technology, and correlating the attributes to CBI strategies, proved to be quite laborious. However, with the appropriate criteria in position, the decision-making process became one of collating each learning experience with the most appropriate CBI strategy, then employing adept screen design to bring vitality and elegance to the materials.

A strong design sense and the ability to employ concepts of visual literacy has proven beneficial in optimizing these interactive technologies. Adeptness in the use of graphics, and the ability to weave continuity, consistency, and user control into the overall design of the interface warrants considerable attention. Once mastered, however, the new technologies have the potential to provide fresh opportunities for existing programs.

REFERENCES

[1]   Adkins, W.R. (1984). Life skills education: a video-based counseling/learning delivery system. In D. Larson (Ed.), Teaching psychological skills: models for giving counseling away. Monterey, CA: Brooks/Cole.

[2]   Adkins, W.R. (September, 1986). Interview with W.R. Adkins, developer of The Adkins Life Development Series.

[3]   Alessi, S.M., & Trollip, S.R. (1985). Computer-based instruction: methods and development. Englewood Cliffs,NJ.

[4]   Courseware Development Process (1979). Minneapolis, MN: Control Data Corporation.

[5]   Gustafson, K.L. (1981). Survey of instructional development models. Syracuse, NY: ERIC Clwaringhouse on Information Resources.

[6]   National Special Media Institute (1971). What is an IDI? East Lansing, MI: Michigan State Univ

[7]   Super, D.E., Crites, J.O., Hummel, R.C., Moser, H.P., Overstreet, P.L., and Warnath, C.F. (1957). Vocational development: a framework for research. New York.

COMPUTERS IN EDUCATION, F. Lovis and E.D. Tagg (eds.)
Elsevier Science Publishers B.V. (North-Holland)
© IFIP, 1988

THE ROLE OF "MACHINE LEARNING" IN COMPUTER COURSES FOR GENERAL EDUCATION

H.Goorhuis, Inst. für Informatik, ETH Zürich, Switzerland

We describe four main problems in today's computer courses in secondary education and we present one way to overcome them. It is a difficult task to give students a good education in understanding complexity, in understanding expert systems and artificial intelligence and to give them a correct impression of programming now and in future. Nonetheless it is essential to do this in a modern computer course.
We present the topic "machine learning" as a tool which gives an appropriate and fascinating impression of new developments in the computer field and allows a lot of practical work. To do this, we developed a simulation of a neural network for computer courses, allowing the quick building of pattern recognition systems by way of a learning mechanism.
We present two case studies, that show how working with this simulation gives an opportunity to teach complexity, artificial intelligence, and modern programming.

1. FOUR PROBLEMS IN TODAY'S COMPUTER COURSES

1.1 Teaching Complexity

One of the important problems of computer applications today is complexity. Programs of more than 100,000 lines of code exhibit strange and unaccountable behaviour. The coexistence of several faults often leads to synergic effects, making it almost impossible to find the faults. A well known example is the MVS System of IBM mainframes, where faults which become apparent are no longer corrected but only documented. The problem was recognized at the first software engineering conference in '68 but is still not solved. Much effort is put in the development of well-structured and strong-typed programming languages [1]. Large-scale networks and parallel distributed processes also show specific behaviour that cannot be explained with a realistic effort. The same kind of problems occur.

An intensive discussion on these effects came up with the "Strategic Defense Initiative" (SDI) with an estimated 100 million lines of code. The famous software engineer David Parnas refused to work for SDI for this kind of reason [2].

The view of someone who took a computer course is very different. Students who have created several pages of programs have other notions of large and complex systems; they do not see problems of complexity. An inquiry in West Germany showed that most students with little programming experience think that SDI is a realistic software project. They do not understand the discussion about it because they do not understand complexity [3].

One of the tasks of computer courses should at least be to give an impression of what complexity is and where the problems with complex computer programs set in. Because there is no time to look at large-scale programs, we propose to look at machine learning (ML) phenomena to study the effects mentioned.

1.2 Teaching Expert Systems (ES) and Artificial Intelligence (AI)

Teaching AI is a trend in computer courses even in general education [4]. Students are very interested in this topic, but teaching it poses some problems. First of all, languages like LISP and Prolog are not easy to learn. Secondly, interesting programs in AI are large and complicated to write as well as to understand. Showing some existing software packages in the field can be interesting but does not give much possibility of practical work for the student. And last but not least, observing a running ES is tedious and does not show the complex mechanisms that lead to decisions. All you do is answer some questions and then you get an answer - a frustrating experience for students. Building one's own ES is too time-consuming and difficult.

Even in this field, we propose to work with trainable software: You can quickly build interesting software, you can create your own ES, and you can analyse learning mechanisms.

1.3 Differing Interests of Students

As several authors mention, the interests of students in the computer field differ extremely: some are fascinated with computer technology and are willing to invest a lot of time in practical work with computers, others have a critical point of view and do not like working at the machine [5].

An enquiry based on 400 students aged 15 to 18 showed an extremely biased distribution. The students had to articulate their interest in different topics involving computers. One of the most distinguishing factors is sex, and in their eight favourite topics, girls agree with the boys in only two, as can be seen in the following table.

An enquiry based on 400 secondary school students in Switzerland on the question: [6]

"Please indicate your degree of interest (0-3) in the following topics involving computers."

The favourite topics were:

	girls	boys
1.	computers and future	applications
2.	applications	simulations
3.	computers and psychology	problem-solving
4.	what computers cannot do	programming languages
5.	computers and society	computers and future
6.	privacy of data	software packages
7.	what can a computer do better than I can?	practical experience
8.	difference between man and machine	how does a computer work?

and the least favourite were:

22.	production of computers	history of computers
23.	electronics	can machines think?

We do not want to analyse the issue why sex is an important distinguishing factor. For the purpose of this paper, we take it as a factor that shows very clearly how interests differ. It could just as well be some other factor. But we are convinced that computer courses to date mainly cover the boys' profile of interest. The girls' profile of interest is much less technical and requires a broader view of computer courses.

One direction is to include questions about how computers affect society. This is very difficult for most computer course teachers because they are not used talking about non-technical subjects.

Another solution is to include more philosophical questions of the kind:

-Can machines think?
-Can machines learn?
-What is knowledge?
-What is the difference between man and machine?
            and so on

A lot of literature exists on these questions [7] [8] [9] and we think it is a challenge to include these topics in computer courses. Our experience shows that within these kind of questions, the difference between interests disappears immediately. And what is more, these topics allow fascinating discussions between the girls' and the boys' profiles of interest. The only requirement is a specific starting point and again, we propose the topic of ML, where questions like "Can machines learn?" cannot only be discussed theoretically, but can

be accompanied by practical work and practical observations.

1.4 Teaching the Right View on Programming

What importance does programming have in today's computer courses? Weizenbaum stipulates that programming has no importance at all for general education [10]. Michie predicts a "programming by example" revolution: "We have only seen the beginning of the 'programming by examples' revolution. When we have seen the end of it, programming as we know it today will have taken its place in history's museum of antiquities." [11]

At MIT, Lieberman developed an example-based environment for beginning programmers, called Tinker, in which a programmer presents examples to the machine, distinguishing accidental and essential aspects of the examples. The programmer demonstrates how to handle the specific examples, and the machine formulates a procedure for handling the general case [12].

This all leads to the question: what level of man-machine communication is important to teach in general education computer courses?

We propose human learning mechanisms as a model to understand the levels of man-machine communication and programming. Traditional programming corresponds to "learning by instruction" in the human model. Functional and declarative programming styles tend towards the human "learning by heart" as "programming by example" corresponds to the "inductive learning" of the human being.

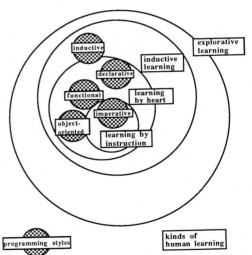

2. TEACHING ABOUT MACHINE LEARNING

2.1 Theses on ML

We propose two theses:

• Within the next few years, AI will become one of the main topics in computer courses in general education. AI software products will force teachers to discuss the following questions:

    -what is intelligence?
    -can computers be intelligent?
    -what are the concepts behind AI
     software?
    -what is knowledge and how is it
     represented?

• In this AI field, ML will be the central point of interest. Talking about and working with ML software allows students to work independently in the field of AI and get a good impression of AI methods, AI possibilities and AI problems.

2.1 History and state of the art in ML

ML is a hot topic in computer science. We would like to give a brief impression of the history of ML. Instead of summing up the main research results, however, we present two practical examples that can be used at school and represent the main steps of development in the field.

Tree Extension

A famous example of a learning mechanism at school is the tree-extension mechanism, mostly seen in LOGO courses. It is important that the student themselves are given the opportunity to play with this program. The computer tries to guess an animal by asking some questions. On a wrong guess, a learning cycle is triggered and the new animal is inserted in the knowledge tree together with a quality that distinguishes it from the others.

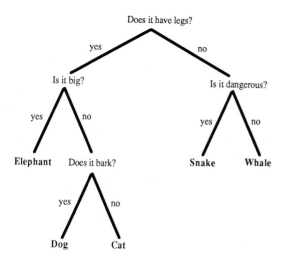

What are the qualities of this kind of knowledge representation? The students can discuss what kind of information this knowledge tree can produce.
Examples:
What is the difference between dogs and cats?
    Dogs bark.
What is the difference between dogs and whales?
    Dogs have legs.
What do you know about cats?
    They don't bark, they are smaller than elephants and they have legs.

The disadvantages of this type of knowledge representation can easily be discussed:

What kind of questions cannot be answered?
    E.g.: Do snakes bark?

Can the tree be extended in a way that this kind of questions can be answered?
    No, because of the hierarchical structure. Every subtree would have to contain all the information of all other subtrees.
Another disadvantage is the accidental priority of the primary questions. The tree can become extremely biased, depending on the user's choice of questions.

Tree Creation

One of the first algorithms that was really called a learning mechanism was Quinlan's ID3 algorithm [13]. A good environment to investigate the qualities of this "learning by example" mechanism is the "Super Expert" package of ITL Glasgow, created by D.Michie [14]. It is an inductive expert system shell that generates rules from examples. The result is also a decision tree like the above example. But the bias problem is solved by generating the most unbiased tree possible.
We could take the same topic as above and create a non-biased decision tree. But students have more imagination in using this software package. I once saw a student creating a decision support system to tell him whether he had to get up in the morning or not. He presented examples like:

-slept 6 hours, am alone, it's 9 o'clock, am sick, it's sunday, no holiday --> stay in bed
-slept 10 hours, am alone, it's 8 o'clock, am healthy, monday, school --> get up

The system generates:
slept less than 8 hours --> stay in bed
                    else --> get up

With another example:

-slept 11 hours, nice girl, do not care about the time, healthy, monday, school --> stay in bed the system generates:

```
slept less than 8 hours  --> stay in bed
         else alone  --> get up
              nice girl  --> stay in bed
```

The more examples are presented, the better the decision tree reflects the real situation. In our experience, this is a fascinating and suitable tool to discuss human and machine learning and to analyse the qualities of such a system. There is a lot more to tell about the practical work of students with systems of this kind but the main conclusion should be that a hierarchical knowledge structure does not reflect the human decision making system. For example, the system cannot decide if one factor is not known. Therefore, we have to look to network structured systems that have associative qualities.

2.2 A Simulation of a Neural Network

For this purpose, we create a simulation of a multi-processor network machine like the connection machine [15]. The simulation runs on a Macintosh II and shows the possibilities of machine learning in networks. It is designed in such a way that students can use it without much knowledge about parallel processing. All the knowledge acquisition is done in learning cycles. The system is based on the work of Rumelhart et.al. as presented in various papers and books [16] [17].

The system simulates 50 highly parallel processors, i.e. each processor is connected to all others. In general, this leads to $n(n-1)/2$ connections, in our case to 1225 connections. The simulation is designed according to the principles shown in [18].

Using the system is easy and takes place in three steps:

- first the user determines how many processors are concerned with input and how many with output concepts. The remaining processors represent inner layers. The user can name all concepts. For pattern recognition, a specific input concept is used.

- secondly, examples for input-output-behaviour are presented to the machine. Every example triggers a learning cycle.

- thirdly, the general behaviour of the system is analysed by watching the output of a given input.

A snapshot of all processor states and connection weights can be observed at any time. The encircled points are activated processors, the other points are non-activated ones. Line thickness represents the weight of the connections.

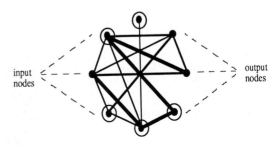

A more detailed description of the system can be found in [19].

2.3 Case Study: Pattern Recognition

One application is the creation of a pattern recognition system as described in [20]. In a field of 6 by 6 squares, various patterns are presented to the machine together with their meaning. One possibility is to present letter patterns and to create concepts of letters on the output side.

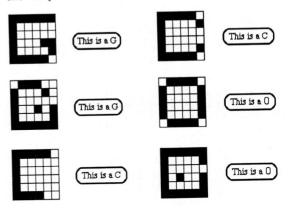

These are six learning cycles for three different letters. After these learning cycles, the system can be asked about the meaning of new patterns. It will answer with one of the letters learned, depending on its similarity to one of the patterns learned. It is a fascinating experience to examine the behaviour of the pattern recognition mechanism.

The next step is recognition on word level. Letters are more easy to recognize when taking into account the context. On word level, four 6 by 6 squares are the input and word concepts the output. The number of processors is increased to 200. They are no longer all connected, because otherwise, the system would become too slow.

A more detailed description of this case study will be found in [21].

2.4 Case Study: Animal Identification

Another example is similar to the first example of hierarchical knowledge structure: The identification of animals depending on some qualities. We present examples like:

- barks --> dog
- big, grey, trunk --> elephant
- white, eats grass --> sheep
- like a sheep, but horns --> ram
- like an elephant, but no trunk --> rhinoceros

The system builds a network with these facts. We can ask the system something like: What animal is grey and has horns? Processors representing the elephant and the ram will be slightly activated until we give more information. Students can do a lot of practical work in observing the associative capabilities of a multi-processor network. They can compare ML with their own learning processes in experiments like the following: Give both the computer and the student information which is new to them and compare their behaviour after the learning process.
A more detailed description of this case study will be found in [22].

3. BACK TO THE MENTIONED PROBLEMS

3.1 Complexity and ML

Practical exercise with the neural network gives the student a good impression of what complexity means. After two or three learning cycles, the input-output behaviour can be analysed by calculating the effects of the weight of the connections. But after further learning cycles, analysing gets far too complex, just like in large software systems: factors influence one another and exhibit remarkable synergic effects. The only way to analyse a network system or a large software system is testing, meaning that one never knows what happens exactly in all cases not tested. Theoretically, both are calculable, but practically, their complexity is far too high.

3.2 AI and ML

Showing small AI programs often leads to the disappointment that AI is also exact software running on a deterministic foundation. Where is the intelligence, where is the magic? This superficial opinion does not reflect the situation very well. It is again the fact that small programs cannot show what complex programs can. In other words, there is more to AI than a few rules in Prolog or a small LOGO program generating poems. But how do we show this to students in a short amount of time? Let them play with the neural network. They will get an impression of what ML, representing one of the most important fields in AI, can be.

3.3 Interests and ML

Sherry Turkle [23] describes several situations where people who are more or less interested in computers suddenly become rather concerned as soon as the discussion touches AI, or in other words the difference between man and machine. This is easy to understand, since AI is the only topic in the field of computer science where computers exhibit human-like behaviour.
We have experienced more than once that people with the girls' profile of interest show a high interest in AI topics, especially in ML. In one class, there were two girls who refused to sit at the computer until we presented the ML example of animal learning. It was then that they got interested, and they worked a lot with it, analysing its qualities.
We also found that a discussion between the two groups of interest profiles is nearly impossible, except when they discuss the difference between man and machine. This works even better than discussions on the impacts of computer development in society. The latter is often chosen for the purpose of encouraging communication.

3.4 Programming and ML

How important is programming in general education? Working with a system like the connection machine reflects the importance of the traditional programming style. A course in programming does not give the right impression of what programming on different levels can be now and in the future. One should at least complete the course with some ML experience.

4. OUTLOOK

Computer courses in general education are gradually covering more philosophical and sociological questions, at least in European countries. More and more, they are becoming courses on technological developments and their consequences in general. Topics like future possibilities, dangers, responsibility are slowly being included in the curriculum. But it's not easy to talk about these subjects in an understandable way. In the world of students, complex systems do not play an important role. ML gives a chance to introduce these topics into the course in a solid way.

Literature:

[1]   Rechenberg P., Schauer H., Schoitsch E.:
      "Software-Engineering". München:
      Oldenbourg, 1983
[2]   Parnas D.L.: "Software Wars". Washington:
      DOD, 1983
[3]   Markowski K.: "Wozu dient der
      Informatikunterricht an Schulen?" in Löwe
      M., Schmidt G., Wilhelm R.: "Umdenken in
      der Informatik". Berlin: VAS, 1987
[4]   Hugelshofer R.: "Informatik". Aarau:
      Sauerländer, 1988
[5]   Pfluger, Schurz: "Der maschinelle
      Charakter". Opladen: Westdeutscher Verlag,
      1987
[6]   Schnebeli A.: "Informatik an den
      Gymnasien. Schülerumfrage". Liestal:
      Erziehungsdirektion des Kantons Baselland,
      1987
[7]   Dreyfus H., Dreyfus S.: "Mind over
      Machine". New York: Free Press, 1986
[8]   Schank R.: "The Cognitive Computer".
      Addison Wesley, 1984.
      Ritchie D.: "The Binary Brain". Boston:
      Little, 1984
[9]   Sand S.: "Künstliche Intelligenz".
      München: Heyne, 1986
[10] Interview with Weizenbaum J. in LOGIN 7.87
      p. 34-38,München: Oldenbourg, 1987
[11] Michie D.: "Expert Systems in the
      Microelectronic Age". Edinburgh:
      University Press, 1984
[12] Lieberman H.: "An Example Based
      Environment for Beginning Programmers" in
      Instructional Science 14 (1986) p.277-292.
      Amsterdam: Elseviers Publishers, 1986.
[13] I.Quinlan,J.Ross "Learning Efficient
      Classification Procedures" in "Machine
      Learning: An Artificial Intelligence
      Approach" Michalski et. al., Palo Alto,
      Tioga Publishing Co. 1983
[14] Michie D.: "SuperExpert". Glasgow: Turing
      Institute, 1984
[15] Hills D.: "The Connection Machine".
      Cambridge MA.: MIT Press, 1985
[16] Michalski R.et. al.: "Machine Learning".
      New York: Springer,1984
[17] Rumelhart D. et. al.: "Parallel
      Distributed Processing". Cambridge MA.:
      MIT Press, 1986.
[18] Goorhuis H.: "Principles of the
      NESSY-System". Zürich: ETHZ, Institut für
      Informatik, 1988, to be published
[19] Goorhuis H.: "Technical report of the
      NESSY-System". Zürich: ETHZ, Institut für
      Informatik, 1988, to be published

[20] Minsky M.: "Perceptrons". Cambridge MA.:
      MIT Press, 1969.
[21] Goorhuis H.: "Case study: pattern
      recognition with the NESSY-System".
      Zürich: ETHZ, Institut für Informatik,
      1988, to be published
[22] Goorhuis H.: "Case study: animal
      identification with the NESSY-System".
      Zürich: ETHZ, Institut für Informatik,
      1988, to be published
[23] Turkle S.: "The second Self". New York:
      Simon and Schuster, 1984

COMPUTERS IN EDUCATION, F. Lovis and E.D. Tagg (eds.)
Elsevier Science Publishers B.V. (North-Holland)
© IFIP, 1988

PROLOG AS A MEDIUM FOR LEARNING IN THE CLASSROOM: ASSESSING A BROAD RANGE OF COMPUTER-BASED ACTIVITIES

Geoff Cumming and Elizabeth Abbott

Department of Psychology, La Trobe University
Victoria, Australia 3083

Ten to sixteen year olds used the logic programming language Prolog in the classroom. They worked, usually two to a computer, at activities ranging across and beyond the curriculum; their work was at first guided by structured worksheets then became more project-like. Performance, attitudes, and generalisation to higher cognitive abilities were assessed. We found that acceptance and attitudes were positive, and that children of both sexes and across the full ability range were well served. A top-down curriculum approach was best, and there is some evidence of general cognitive gains. Prolog is a useful educational medium; enhanced interfaces will increase its value further.

We give a brief report of more than three years of using Prolog as a medium for learning in the classroom. Some 317 children in Grades 5 and 6 (aged 10 to 12 years) and 117 children in Grade 10 (aged 15 to 16) have had 28 to 64 hours of Prolog experience over periods ranging from half a year to two school years.

Our work has had two main aims: to develop procedures, activities and materials that are effective in normal classrooms; and to identify the cognitive, affective and social outcomes. The assumptions underlying our work are:

1. The logic programming language Prolog has distinctive properties that make it worth exploring as a medium for learning. It is good for expressing, exploring and transforming information, and for reasoning about that information; Prolog has potential because these are all activities at the heart of education.

2. The aim is to present activities across and beyond the curriculum, with an emphasis on expressing, exploring and thinking about information. Children will acquire some computer programming skills, but computer awareness and computer science issues are secondary.

3. The surface syntax and user interface must be excellent, so that maximum attention is available for the substance of the activities.

4. It is important to work with unselected students and teachers, in normal classrooms. Children across the full range of ability, and of both sexes, must be well served.

5. The main outcomes being sought are general cognitive abilities. In addition the activities should promote a positive attitude towards computers, and positive and cooperative interactions among children.

For almost four school years we have worked at a Roman Catholic primary school in an industrial suburb: in 65% of homes a language other than English is used to some extent. We have worked for one year in a Catholic secondary school in the same area. In each case we have used a network of 64K CP/M Microbee computers, and micro-Prolog 3.1 from Logic Programming Associates, London.

Classes have used Prolog for two or three periods each week in the computer room, children usually working two to a computer. Children had had little or no previous computer experience. In Grades 5 and 6 the regular class teachers, who were also new to computing, took the classes with the support of the curriculum designer, the second author. At the Grade 10 level the curriculum designer was the sole teacher.

Assessment of the whole program is based on observation, classroom experience and a variety of paper and pencil measures. This paper describes the approach taken and results obtained in the areas of interface design, curriculum approach, cognitive outcomes, student diversity, social and attitudinal effects, and amount of Prolog skill acquired. Knowledge representation and artificial intelligence (AI) aspects will also be mentioned.

1. SURFACE SYNTAX AND USER INTERFACE

Micro-Prolog 3.1 has a Lisp-style syntax replete with multiple parentheses. It was chosen by de Saram [7], but Ennals [9] and most other early applications in schools used the front end SIMPLE. SIMPLE lives on, appearing recently in [12], but most current educational use is based on MITSI [2]. In [1, 5, 6] we describe the shortcomings of SIMPLE, the advantages of MITSI, and our developments to form EMITSI.

A Prolog program is a set of facts and rules; Prolog uses backward chaining inference to find answers to queries posed by the user. In EMITSI (and MITSI) facts and rules are stated in a way that can be read as being close to English (any word starting with **some** is a variable):

> **Josie likes eating**
> **Bill has cake-recipe**
> **Josie has cake-recipe**
> **someone makes cakes if someone**
has cake-recipe and someone likes eating

Queries use a similar format:

> **Josie makes something?**

EMITSI uses only the binary infix format, although lists may be used. A statement is added to the program by typing it, followed by a full stop. Commands are followed by !. Typing **why?** after a query has been answered gives an explanation by showing the steps in the Prolog chain of inference.

To assist the user explore a program we implemented the **seek** command, which gives information about any specified object or relation name appearing in the program. There is also an ask-the-user facility that allows the program to ask the user for further facts that may be needed to answer a query; this is especially useful in programs designed to offer advice in some knowledge area.

We trapped error conditions very early so that error messages could identify the type of problem and prompt what should be done next. Improved error messages can have an immediate and marked effect on the children's ability to recover from problems by themselves.

EMITSI is neat, consistent, powerful and easy to use; it works well in the classroom. The essential features of EMITSI have been included in the revised MITSI recently prepared by Briggs [3].

2. CURRICULUM APPROACH

Any practical educational evaluation is never of a computer language alone, but must be of a complete treatment, including curriculum approach, materials, classroom practices, and teacher and student characteristics. We identified two dimensions along which curricula of computer-based activities vary. The first refers to whether activities are structured and specified in detail, e.g. via worksheets, or are left to the interest and initiative of individual children. The second distinguishes a top-down

approach, in which children start by exploring and using pre-written programs, and a bottom-up strategy in which children first learn the syntax and construct their own programs.

In [4, 5] we discuss how recognition of these dimensions influenced our design for the Prolog-based activities. Considering the first dimension, we used worksheets that were initially highly structured but which later encouraged students to take more initiative and develop their own projects. The reasons for our initial use of worksheets included: practical considerations in classes of 30 or more, our concern that even low ability children should be well served, and our interpretation (despite [11]) of the literature describing the educational use of Logo.

We adopted the top-down or bottom-up issue as our first empirical question. One grade 5 class and one grade 6 class saw a bottom-up approach for two periods a week for six months; other grade 5 and grade 6 classes saw a top-down program of work. The children used Prolog in a wide variety of subject contexts, the emphasis being on information handling activities and program content rather than on the Prolog language. Activities included mapping, games and puzzles, mysteries and databases. Despite this emphasis, the main measures used to compare top-down and bottom-up were of a range of Prolog skills.

The results showed that top-down and bottom-up children had, not surprisingly, a different profile of Prolog skills, but that overall the top-down approach had been more successful. Top-down children outperformed bottom-up learners by an average of about half a standard deviation. If it is confirmed that top-down experience does lead to better learning even of syntactic details of a language, possibly by fostering integration with a richer mental model of the system and making early activities more meaningful, then the current predominantly bottom-up approach to introducing artificial intelligence languages to children will have to be questioned.

Keeping the two approaches separate became difficult and artificial: each has its educational value. Our recommendation is that both should be included, but that a strong initial top-down emphasis is best.

3. GENERALISATION TO HIGHER COGNITIVE ABILITIES

The strongest advocacy for wide use of Logo and Prolog in education [11, 10] is based on claims of generalisation from some computing experience to higher cognitive abilities. Demonstrating such gains arising from the use of Logo - the language most studied - has been problematic. Relevant issues are the curriculum and teaching approach used, the limited duration of experimental trials, individual differences among children, and the difficulty of defining appropriate control treatments.

We have taken a variety of approaches to identifying possible cognitive generalisations from our Prolog-based activities. Most have shown only equivocal and small differences favouring Prolog over control conditions. The clearest finding came from an experiment in which a Grade 5 class used Prolog-based activities for three periods a week for half a school year; a matched control class spent equivalent time on non-Prolog computing activities. The Prolog children out-scored controls strongly and most clearly (ES=.88, p=.00; ES is the effect size i.e. the difference expressed in standard deviation units, and the p value is a one-tail probability) on a written worksheet test similar in format to the Prolog activities but not using a computer language; they were also better on tests of reasoning (ES=.56, p=.00) and text comprehension (ES=.32, p=.04). This pattern of differences suggests a gradient of generalisation, the largest effect being on the measure most similar to the Prolog treatment (the worksheet test) and the smallest on comprehension, an ability much less closely related to the treatment.

Such findings are encouraging, especially since they come from a realistic classroom setting, but must be considered with caution: possible teacher differences cannot be ruled out and Prolog children had somewhat more adult attention than did the controls; in addition the treatment under test is the whole curriculum, and not just the Prolog language.

4. STUDENT DIVERSITY; SOCIAL AND ATTITUDINAL EFFECTS

Children's self-concept, assessed by paper-and-pencil tests, in relation to the Prolog computing work is positive and generally higher than that in relation to other school subjects and, most importantly, holds up well for children of low general ability. Correlations between measures of Prolog ability and measures of more general ability such as non-verbal IQ (Ravens), reasoning and comprehension range from 0.3 to 0.6, indicating a quite reasonable moderate positive relationship. These results confirm classroom experience that children of the full range of ability are being well served, although lower ability children do need extra help at first. We have studied pairs formed of mixed ability children and homogeneous pairs, and found no marked differences on learning or attitudes between the two.

Sex differences in Prolog ability and computing self-concept are generally small, but in both cases any difference usually favours girls slightly. The language-based nature of most of the activities may be a factor here, but the main reason that girls feel as positive as boys about computing is probably that there is sufficient hardware, and so no competition with boys for computer access, and also that

computer use is a regular, time-tabled part of normal class routine, taken by the class teacher.

Detailed time-sampling observations of the behaviour of Grade 5 and 6 children established that, when working in pairs on Prolog activities, 81% of time was spent on task, and 47% of time in task-related interactions with others. More recently extra hardware was installed and Grade 5 and 6 children each had their own computer; in this case 91% of time was spent on task, including 19% of time in task-related interactions with others. Such measures are highly dependent on teacher style, but here the averages were over 3 or 4 different classes and teachers. These are very high time-on-task values for a regular whole-class activity months after any novelty had worn off. The proportion of time spent in interactions suggests that, even in the extreme case of a computer for each child, much cooperation can occur and there is little danger of such computing leading to social isolation.

The observational data also show that the time on task values do not vary across general ability, and so confirm the conclusion that children of all abilities are well served.

5. AMOUNT OF PROLOG SKILL ACQUIRED

Although gains in curriculum area understanding and in higher cognitive abilities are the main aim, the amount of Prolog skill acquired should be assessed. Performance of children of all abilities should be described, not only of those especially able or keen. Analysis of completed worksheets and of Prolog tests suggests that at Grade 5 and 6 level even most low ability children knew the basics: they understood and used the binary infix format securely, could formulate simple queries and use variables in queries. They could interpret the output from using **seek** and **why**, and so explore a simple pre-written program to some extent. Supportive context was, however, vital, and was necessary if they were to formulate and add facts to a program. They had little understanding of rules.

The more able children were less reliant on supportive context and could explore programs confidently and with initiative. At Grade 6 level they could understand and use rules reasonably well, but still had only a very limited ability to generate rules.

Grade 10 students moved much more quickly from needing the direction of structured worksheets to being able to undertake projects. Handling the syntax was less of a problem, but even at this older age less able students needed guidance and context. Most Grade 10 students could explore a program and comprehend explanations, including rule use, quite well. They, like the younger children, were much less competent at designing programs and expressing information in good Prolog form. Many needed support to formulate useful rules, even in English, and only a minority could formulate good rules and express them accurately in Prolog, although carefully designed Prolog activities did lead to clear progress being made in these difficult areas.

We saw great advances in children's ability to work independently as we moved from SIMPLE to MITSI and then the improved EMITSI, but even so lower ability children still spent much time and effort coping with the computing system and the syntax, and thus had reduced capacity for thinking about the activities. Highly desirable developments include: a syntax-based screen editor; windows allowing simultaneous views of user interaction, the program and an inference chain; and a well-designed graphical representation of inference. A simplified form of AORTA diagram [8] may meet the latter need. Error messages giving advice that is even more detailed and specific would be valuable, again especially for lower ability children. The more powerful hardware now becoming available should be able to support such enhancements easily.

The text-based nature of Prolog means that typing is important; children with some keyboard skills make better progress at the Prolog activities.

Maintaining facility with the system and syntax, and continuity on an activity from session to session are both vital, so frequency of Prolog sessions is important: 3 or, better, 4 each week lead to much better progress than 2 per week. Total amount of time spent is also, not surprisingly, important: Grade 6 children about to leave the school after some 40 to 64 hours of Prolog work show proficiency that is supporting worthwhile activities in curriculum areas. It is unfortunate if they cannot exploit this proficiency further.

6. KNOWLEDGE REPRESENTATION

The current emphasis in educational computing on generative - bottom-up, in our terms - activities has led to Prolog being advocated because it allows learners to express information in the form of a program. If the program includes rules it could even be termed an expert system, albeit a toy, and so the learner could be said to be engaged in rudimentary knowledge engineering. We have designed and used many such activities and find them valuable, but offer two qualifications. First, our preference for a wide spread of types of activities, and our finding that a top-down approach outperforms a bottom-up curriculum, suggest that such program construction activities should be only a proportion of a balanced curriculum, and at first should be outnumbered by top-down activities in which learners use, explore and extend pre-written programs.

Our second qualification is that only quite restricted forms of knowledge representation are provided by the simple rule-based, backward chaining facilities of micro-Prolog. Examples of expert systems and knowledge engineering activities put forward by advocates of student program building cover in fact only a limited range: usually little beyond natural taxonomies, systems of rules or regulations, fault diagnosis, treasure-hunt style mysteries, and some limited forms of advisor. It can be extremely difficult, given an arbitrarily chosen subject area, to go much beyond a database and build a program incorporating a useful and non-trivial set of Prolog rules. We are rediscovering the artificial intelligence conclusion that it is vital to have available a rich variety of forms of knowledge representation; good educational use will be able to be made of AI developments in this area.

7. COMPUTER SCIENCE AND AI

Using Prolog across and beyond the curriculum fits easily with typical class organisation in primary school. In secondary school broad use has just as much potential, but, with specialist teachers, an initial approach via one subject is in practice more likely. This need not be computer studies, but if it is there is ample scope to use the capabilities of Prolog to introduce many important concepts. It is especially tempting to work with small versions of expert systems and other basic types of AI programs. We have used EMITSI for this purpose at secondary level and also with psychology undergraduates.

8. CONCLUDING COMMENTS

Being able to express information and rules, and to reason about the information can be very valuable. The educational benefits of using these basic Prolog facilities will be increased by enhancements to the interface that will be possible on more powerful hardware. Even so, the current EMITSI facilities can support activities across and beyond the curriculum that are educationally worthwhile; it can do this in unselected mixed-ability classes with unselected although willing teachers. Careful design of activities, teacher involvement, and sufficiently frequent sessions are important.

Top-down, bottom-up and mixed activities can all have value. Despite the current vogue for advocacy of construction of programs by learners, we stress the value of top-down activities, especially at first. A vital part of the value of working with a language, rather than a shell or other application software, is that the same syntax supports a wide variety of types of activities. Also, it can be used by students first for exploring a pre-written program in a top-down way, then for extending and modifying that program, and finally for building their own programs.

Structured worksheets offer a viable approach in full-size, mixed-ability classes, although low ability learners still require help at first. Detailed support can be reduced as children move more to project work, although for many children constructing worthwhile programs continues to require considerable guidance. The development of the 'personal advisor', or 'smart worksheet' program, in which the feedback of error messages and guidance of a worksheet are combined with even rudimentary sensitivity to the individual learner's progress is an attractive prospect. It would be important to give maximum control to the learner and to encourage progress towards the independence and initiative of project work.

Prolog-based activities, initially closely guided, can serve well across the full ability range. Attitudes towards computing and the activities are good, and girls do at least as well as boys and feel just as positive about what they are doing. Having adequate computer access and integrating computer work with other normal class activities are important.

Gains in higher cognitive abilities have proved hard to demonstrate unequivocally, but our results so far, classroom experience and teacher reports lead us to conclude they can occur. Careful design of activities and clear recognition of goals by the teacher are important; the teacher should encourage reflection on strategy choice and other metacognitive aspects.

ACKNOWLEDGEMENTS

This work was made possible by the generous cooperation and support of the Principals, staffs and students of St Clare's Primary School, Thomastown, and St Monica's College, Epping.

The work was supported by the Australian Research Grants Scheme.

REFERENCES

[1] Abbott, E., & Cumming, G. (1987) Making front-ends friendly: The case of Prolog <u>Australian Educational Computing</u>, <u>2</u> (1), 26-32.
[2] Briggs, J. (1984) <u>micro-Prolog Rules!</u> London: Logic Programming Associates.
[3] Briggs, J. (1988) <u>Revised MITSI</u>, London: Kingston Polytechnic. (In preparation)
[4] Cumming, G., & Abbott, E. (1986) It's the educational strategy that matters, even if the language is Prolog. <u>Australian Educational Computing</u>, <u>1</u>(1), 34-39.
[5] Cumming, G., & Abbott, E. (1987a) Prolog and Expert Systems for Children's Learning. Paper given at Frascati Conference, May 1987, IFIP TC3 "AI Tools & Education"
[6] Cumming, G., & Abbott, E. (1987b) Making front-ends friendly: Designing Prolog to fit children's minds. In Nichol, J., Briggs, J., & Dean, J. <u>Fifth generation computing in education 1: Prolog, children and students</u>. London: Kogan Page.
[7] de Saram, H. (1985) <u>Programming in micro-Prolog</u>. Chichester: Ellis Horwood and Halsted Press.
[8] Eisenstadt, M., & Brayshaw, M. (1987) <u>An integrated textbook, video, and software environment for novice and expert Prolog programmers</u>. Paper presented at Annual Conference of the Prolog Educational Group, Exeter, July.
[9] Ennals, J. R. (1983) <u>Beginning micro-Prolog</u>. Chichester: Ellis Horwood and Heinemann.
[10] Kowalski, R. (1983) Foreword. In Ennals, J. R. <u>Beginning micro-Prolog</u>. Chichester: Ellis Horwood and Heinemann, p.9.
[11] Papert, S. (1980) <u>Mindstorms: Children, computers and powerful ideas</u> Brighton, Sussex: Harvester.
[12] Prigmore, C. (1987) <u>A Prolog primer</u>, London: Arnold.

COMPUTERS IN EDUCATION, F. Lovis and E.D. Tagg (eds.)
Elsevier Science Publishers B.V. (North-Holland)
© IFIP, 1988

LEARNING EXPERT SYSTEMS CONCEPTS: AN EXPERIMENT.

Albert HERREMANS

Education Technology Program Manager
IBM International Education Center
La Hulpe - Belgium

Institut d'Administration et de Gestion
University of Louvain
Louvain-la-Neuve - Belgium

ABSTRACT.

Developing an application when being an "end-user", supposed, up to now, the learning of a programming language, or the use of an existing software (spreadsheet, text processing, ..).
When this is not possible, for some reasons, what does one do? It seemed to us that the availability of Expert Systems shells to be used on PCs could be an interesting approach, at least to acquire a better understanding of what Expert Systems are, their possibilities and limits, to understand the underlying concepts, etc...
Nowadays, indeed, no one can read a recent book or a magazine, without being exposed to discussions, opinions, trends, etc.. about Expert Systems! But not too much is said about practice and experiments; and the literature leaves open a certain number of questions.
What is exactly an Expert System? How does one build and use one? What does it allow us to do, and even more important where does it not apply? Can an expert possibly write a system himself, without having to go through a time consuming process of discussions with "knowledge engineers"? Do we need to use big computers, and large software, even just to test the idea, to build prototypes?
We decided to experiment all this, despite the limited resources we had at our disposal in terms of time, computer hardware and software, knowledge of Expert Systems.
The paper describes the experiment framework, the choice of the Expert Systems shell, how students were brought to the necessary level to develop a limited Expert Systems prototype in a very short time, which applications they choose to develop, and the learning process they went through. It also discusses performances of an Expert System on different PCs.

1. EXPERIMENT FRAMEWORK.

Adults, having a University degree (in Engineering, Law, Physics, etc...) attend a 2-year evening post-graduate programme at the Business School of the University of Louvain (Belgium), to get a degree in Business Management.

The "Diplome en Management" programme is made of eight 45-hour courses, one of which is the Data Processing for Business Management, that includes theory and some practice (on microcomputers).

The student population is very heterogeneous: very few are Data Processing professionals; another few are "passive" users, working on terminals or PCs with application programs developed by others; the majority never used a terminal or a PC, but feels it important to be able to do so for their day-to-day work, be it as employees or as independent workers.

The course used to be rather technical, oriented towards Data Processing professionals; the emphasis was progressively changed and put on users' problems and viewpoint. As part of this, we introduced more practice on PCs, teaching the fundamentals of BASIC and using spreadsheets, to develop limited applications.

Then it was decided, by all professors and assistants involved in Data Processing courses, that one should not teach programming languages any more on PCs, leaving this for work on minicomputers and mainframes; and we looked at another means of getting students develop a small application, using other tools. The availability of a certain number of Expert Systems shells to be used on PCs looked very attractive to us!

Some said it would be impossible to get a valuable result in such a short time (out of 45 hours, 9 are normally available for practice, starting from scratch: most of the students have to learn how to start a PC, MS-DOS commands, etc...). We decided to take a chance! Even more when we knew that the number of students attending the course would be lower than for the previous courses, which would allow us to devote more time to each one in order to get him there!

2. CHOICE OF THE EXPERT SYSTEMS SHELL TO BE USED.

University budgets are what they are; and we did not want to use too big or complex (and therefore expensive) an Expert Systems shell, just to develop small Expert Systems prototypes. So we looked at different Expert Systems shells, and more particularly at:

- ESP/Advisor from Expert Systems International is interesting, but too close to the PROLOG language and reasoning, and too close to programming as such; we could not go that far with our students in the available time span, and it was definitely not in line with the above mentioned strategy of not teaching programming languages any more.

- Expert-Ease from Expert Software International (ESI) is easy to learn and to use; data representation is limited to table form, as a spreadsheet, already used with the students; we wanted to introduce the concept of production rules!

- M1 from Framentec, a subsidiary of Teknowledge (USA) and Framatome (France) is a very good shell, and has an interesting feature for education: the windows (PANEL ON command) give the user the possibility to follow the steps of the inference engine reasoning: in one window appears the rule presently evaluated, in another the temporary conclusions already reached and in a third one the goal which is pursued; unfortunately, M1 is rather expensive for an educational activity, even more when it has to be bought in quantity.

- Insight1 from Level Five Research (USA) looks like an easy and rather cheap entry point; it comes with a PRL Tutor (production

rule language) which is a very good self-study tool; but basic functions (like OR) are not included, and any way, a new version of the product is already available!

- Insight2+, also from Level Five Research (USA), does not offer the didactical facility of M1, but is very well documented and offers enough possibilities for the type of Expert Systems we wanted to build; its price is much lower than that of M1, and this would have been a good reason to buy it! Unfortunately (and this made us think about the Murphy's Law...) the time taken to decide, added to the delivery time to get the product in Europe, was too long to get it at the course start time! On top of that, the PC laboratory used at the Business School is now organized in a network, and the disk drive A: is made unavailable to the user; it would not have been obvious to install the Expert Systems shell on the network server (for different reasons), and not easier to use the 3 diskettes (of which one with examples files) of the product on a single disk drive (B:)

- we finally decided to use GREX (Graphical Expert System), a shell written by Martin Klein, from IBM Austria, who allowed us to use it, and furthermore agreed to improve his package, based on our suggestions made while developing our applications; this gave us an exciting opportunity both to use a tool and participate in its ultimate development!

3. THE EXPERIMENT.

The teacher had first to learn to master the Expert Systems shell, and to prepare a progressive approach for the students to acquire rapidly the knowledge needed about Expert Systems in general, and about the particular inference engine of GREX.

Students were, in parallel with that activity, brought to the appropriate level of PC knowledge, in a 3-hour session, each PC being used by one or two students: how to start the PC, how to format a diskette, MS-DOS commands, use of a text editor to enter ASCII characters in a file (necessary to prepare the rules file), save and print files; this was made easier by the utilization of a users' manual prepared by an assistant, and the availability of the needed software on the network to which all PCs and printers are attached.

The exercise we developed progressively was a PC software advisor:

- as a first step, the users are offered a suggestion to buy PC software, depending on what they want to do: program themselves OR buy applications packages; in either case, they are allowed to choose one or 2 programming languages, corresponding to 2 different types of programs, or one or 2 applications packages, corresponding to 2 different types of applications

- the system was then modified, so that the users could choose either programming or applications packages, or both simultaneously (the MULTIvalued attribute concept)

- the 3rd step consisted in adding prices, including a total price for the suggested combination of programming languages and/or applications packages; also, some by-products were added: e.g. if the BASIC language is suggested, the package "Learn BASIC" (a CBT) is also proposed; and some specific hardware is also suggested in particular cases: e.g. when scientific programs are going to be written, users are advised to buy a high resolution color display and a plotter, of which prices are also given.

- the next step was to increase the number of program types (and so the offering of programming languages), and the number of applications types (and so the number of applications packages)

- cleaning followed: we introduced our own prompts, we avoided letting unnecessary attributes appear in the menus and in the conclusions, etc..

- we also improved the system performance by eliminating some double counting: unnecessary rules, or lines in some rules

- finally, the last step consisted in introducing for some program types and for some applications types, different software offered for the same program or application type, depending on different criteria, such as required level of complexity, file size, etc...

We stopped the exercise there, although we could have continued and added a complete hardware suggestion, the facility to express all prices in different currencies, etc...

On top of this, a 3-hour presentation was made on Expert Systems basics, and 3 times 1-hour on the used Expert Systems syntax, associated with the progressive example; this in the classroom, not in the PC laboratory.

Students were asked to choose a prototype project, either alone or in groups of 2; a list of suggestions was given, but it was said that the preference would go to prototypes corresponding to real live problems (in students' firms or institutions), or to problems in relation with the other 7 courses of the "Diplome en Management" programme.

Here is the list of suggestions given to the students as a guide for their thinking:

- portfolio advisor
- PC configurator
- risk analysis for a mortgage loan
- risk analysis for an insurance contract
- urgent security actions in case of emergency
- advisory machine operator in case of failure, anomaly
- help desk: orienting questions to the right specialist
- orienting a person for his education programme
- choosing the appropriate PC software for graphics, text processing,..
- bank services advisor
- insurance services advisor
- selecting the best forecasting method and/or software
- advising on the use of a micro-, mini- or mainframe computer for a specific application
- Local Area Network structure advisor
- buy/rent/lease decision advisor
- advising on in-house programming, getting programmed outside, or buy an existing software
- wine advisor
- determining the exact flower, plant, mushroom found in a garden or in the forest

After having understood and played with the different phases of our progressive exercise, students looked at possible Expert Systems prototypes to be developed, either as a tool in their day-to-day work or as an illustration of another course from the "Diplome en Management" programme. After an unexpectedly long thought, they came out with the following prototype projects:

- computer network control (detect anomalies, suggest corrections)

- choice of the best process for the production of a chemical product

- priority grid for the booking of sport facilities in a club

- choice of a heating system for a private house

- determination of the company department that will have to process an order, when different divisions are equipped to do it

- process monitoring in the steel industry: interpretation of physical measurements and alarm system

- choice of the adequate steam-boiler according to the requested utilization

- selection of elementary drawings to illustrate gymnastics books

- classification and information retrieval about ISDN documentation

- retirement plan advisor

- selection of the best wine to get with meals

All these topics, but the last one, are in direct relation with the student's professional activities; so, this was a test of the "expert" developing his/her own system; the last subject was interesting for another reason: it was a test of how easy it is to collect the data from an outside expert in order to build a system.

4. THE LEARNING PROCESS.

We first tried to understand the difference between any of the small Expert Systems prototypes we intended to develop, and the same application developed in conventional programming. We arrived at the following conclusions:

- the Expert Systems shell simplifies and shortens to a great extent the time spent to analyze the problem and to write the application program; less people are involved, and the expert does a great deal of the work himself

- it offers a much clearer "program" to look at (even by those who did not develop it) and/or to change; rules are easy to read and understand; it is as easy to add or delete some, or change their content (have a look at a BASIC or Pascal or APL program written by somebody else, just to see how easy it is to figure out what the program does!)

- the Expert Systems shell offers a range of "utilities" like the WHY? and WHAT? functions that would have to be programmed in a conventional approach; automatic prompts also exist

- it offers the possibility to control the application development, step by step, by using the facility of looking at the steps already gone through in the reasoning process, analyzing the Context (the Expert System "memory" in which one can see the sequential list of the knowledge already acquired during the session) at any point in time

We then started to develop very simple subsets of our selected applications, in order to acquire the Expert Systems approach and reasoning

in a way that we had totally under control: it is important to gain confidence by being able to run a session and get the expected results. Some of us made the mistake of starting immediately with a bigger example, closer to reality; but the debugging was made more difficult, and finally everybody was happy to come back to simpler examples.

This already showed us the extreme importance and advantage of the WHY? and WHAT? (called KNOWN in our Expert Systems shell) functions when developing a prototype (as well as when running it later).

Then we added functions like the MULTI that allows attributes to take multiple values, and therefore the expert to develop more complex applications, closer to the real live problems. Here also, it took us some time to really master that kind of reasoning.

After that, we polished a bit our prototypes: cleaning the menus and conclusions by not letting appear those attribute values that do not help the user and may be hidden; we also introduced our own prompts text, instead of using the default queries provided by the Expert Systems shell.

Then, we introduced more complex inferences, not just linear ones (e.g. if the user wishes to use different application types, it might be interesting to suggest integrated software instead of several packages), numeric values and logic operators, etc...

Those who already had a little experience with PCs went even further: they used the graphics function of GREX (the power to call graphics prepared with various packages, either to make a question clearer, or to illustrate the conclusion); some also used the possibility of calling from GREX external programs (e.g. BASIC, Pascal, ..).

While going through these steps (in 3 labs of 3 hours each), students went from a real fright (are we going to be able to make it? in such a short time? starting from very little knowledge?), to a limited confidence (first little example successfully run) and progressively to real confidence, creativity and proudness of achieved prototypes....

Some students discovered after a while that their prototype was going to be shown as too simple (and would prove nothing!) and they either changed their mind, or imbedded more realistic data to make it closer to real life! Others discovered that, despite what had been shown and suggested, they started too fast, trying to build the complete prototype at once, instead of building it progressively; they quickly lost control of the system, and had to go back to a more methodical development methodology.

The author of GREX was of great help, all the experiment long! He daily answered our questions about the optimal use of GREX, modified some coding to include suggested additions to his system, and sent us new releases during the experiment. Not only did we use electronic mail for our contacts, but we even ended the course by a 1-hour video conference between the students and the author of GREX (in Vienna), during which a very interesting exchange of ideas took place.

The final list of prototypes submitted looks as this:

- diagnostic of an alarm system

- process monitoring in steel industry (moulding)

- fire insurance advisor

- choice of the right heating system for a building

- therapeutic decision strategy

- selection of the right steam-boiler

- selection of the most effective production unit in a multinational corporation

- suggestion of the most appropriate readings about ISDN

- selection of an activity at the Club Mediterannee

- wine selector

5. PERFORMANCE.

We carried out some tests on the performance of our systems, testing them on different PCs; here are the conditions and the results of a test made with one of the final prototypes:

- the GREX shell may be used in 2 ways, once the production rules have been entered with any editor, in an ASCII file:

  1. either it reads and checks the syntax of every rule at each run (interpretation mode)
  2. or it compiles the production rules, and checks their syntax only once

- we used the same prototype, giving the same answers to the same queries, for every run, on the following PCs:

  1. PC/G 512K, diskette drive (360Kb)
  2. PC/AT 640K, diskette drive (360Kb)
  3. PC/AT 640K, diskette drive (1.2Mb)
  4. PC/AT 640K, hard disk (20 Mb)
  5. PS/2 mod 80, 2 Mb, diskette drive (750Kb)
  6. PS/2 mod 80, 2 Mb, hard disk (71 Mb)

- the size of the prototype was as follows: 47 rules and 223 lines in the file (including comments, attributes specifications, prompts, etc... on top of the rules themselves

- the run test included 8 answers from the user to different queries; it should be noted that this does not go faster on a PS/2 mod 80 than on a PC/G, and may explain some of the apparent contradictions of the following table, that shows the results of the test

	Not compiled		Compilation time	Compiled	
	load time	run time		load time	run time
PC/G diskette 360K	1'20"	1'58"	0'33"	0'43"	1'47"
PC/AT diskette 360K	0'50"	0'40"	0'26"	0'26"	0'40"
PC/AT diskette 1.2M	0'49"	0'43"	0'27"	0'24"	0'40"
PC/AT hard disk 20Mb	0'30"	0'41"	0'08"	0'05"	0'40"
PS/2-80 diskette 750K	0'16"	0'21"	0'32"	0'30"	0'17"
PS/2-80 hard disk 71Mb	0'12"	0'18"	0'04"	0'04"	0'17"

Comments:

- it is worth compiling an expert system once it is considered good enough; the loading time is much shorter, but the running time is not considerably improved; at least for the small prototype we tested, compilation time is short, so after modifications of the source file, another compilation will not hurt

- moving from a PC/G to an AT and then to a PS/2 model 80 represents a considerable improvement, both for compiled and not compiled versions, as well as for compilation itself

- on an AT, the type of diskette used (360K or 1.2Mb) is irrelevant; only the use of a hard disk brings an improvement

6. CONCLUDING OBSERVATIONS.

Few people will apply Artificial Intelligence in industry by using Artificial Intelligence languages (PROLOG, LISP,...); big existing Expert Systems software require the intervention of Knowledge Engineers, Data Processing specialists, on top of the expert of the subject matter; therefore, we believe that using PC shells, despite their limitations, helps to put the fingers into Artificial Intelligence, understand the concepts, have a good idea of its possibilities and limits, and of its applicability in our day-to-day life

Surprisingly enough, the choice of a subject for a prototype was much more difficult, and so longer, than expected; despite the numerous examples and ideas suggested during the class, most of the students had a hard time finding a prototype subject in their day-to-day life! Some came out with a first candidate that was really not appropriate, or much too complex for beginners, taking into consideration the limited available time!

Those who already programmed in a conventional programming environment had more difficulty to catch the Expert Systems way of working; the others found much more easily how to think in order to formulate the rules in an effective way. It is not obvious at all just to tell the system WHAT to do, letting it decide upon HOW to do it, when one is used to program both the WHAT and the HOW...

We also understood the necessity to learn to walk before trying to run: develop a prototype slowly, progressively, keeping everything under control, is essential to get confidence in the system (and in oneself!). Those who tried to go too fast, to involve too many attributes and/or rules immediately, had to step back and start more systematically.

When the number of rules gets bigger, the response time increases very quickly: using the same model on a normal PC, then on an AT, and finally on a PS/2 (Mod 80) showed how important the machine capacity and speed are; this makes very clear the need for parallel processing for Artificial Intelligence programs when developing real live applications, with their complexity and size.

All in all, a very good experiment; most of the students have decided to pursue their effort after the course, and to suggest that their company   seriously think about the development of real Expert Systems where appropriate.

Here are some of the final written comments made by the students

- I had to start from zero, to learn the PC, DOS, an editor, the concepts of Expert Systems, and GREX! I never thought it would work. It worked! Now, I have bought a PC, convinced my manager to do so, and we decided to investigate further the potential of Expert Systems for us... (this comment is not unique; others are similar, although expressed in other words)

- Expert Systems are easy to use, easy to explain to non specialists

- Expert Systems are easy to update

- they allow one to suppress many encumbering documents (this refers to a discussion about the possibility to replace thick technical manuals by an expert system)

- the Expert Systems language is ours!

- the interaction is very useful, attractive

- while writing his own system, the expert learns more about his domain, because of the rigour of the Expert System shell logic! it shows you holes, fussiness, inconsistencies in your own thinking process and/or knowledge, which you are forced to clarify first...

4. Social and Psychological Aspects

COMPUTERS IN EDUCATION, F. Lovis and E.D. Tagg (eds.)
Elsevier Science Publishers B.V. (North-Holland)
© IFIP, 1988

SYMBOLIC COMPUTATION — A NEW CHANCE FOR EDUCATION

Klaus ASPETSBERGER, Bernhard KUTZLER

Research Institute for Symbolic Computation (RISC-LINZ)
Johannes Kepler University
A-4040 Linz, Austria

Symbolic computation is a research field covering all aspects of algorithmic solutions of problems dealing with symbolic (i.e. non-numeric) objects. This paper suggests methods to make use of symbolic computation software systems for reaching certain teaching goals. Our emphasis lies on high school education, but the methods can be adapted to university education also. Concrete examples are presented, which are all solved using existing software systems. For each example, we discuss the possible effects by listing the mathematical skills that are improved and the insights that are gained.

1 What is Symbolic Computation?

Traditionally, computers are used to solve *numeric problems*, i.e. problems dealing with floating point numbers. For this purpose, they have become a well established tool in all branches of engineering and have also found their way into all levels of higher education.

In the last two decades, a lot of effort has been undertaken to apply computers to solving *symbolic problems*. The research field of symbolic computation, as defined for example in [1], consists of four subfields, each covering all aspects of algorithmic solutions of problems dealing with a certain type of symbolic objects:

computer algebra — algebraic objects; typical topics are symbolic integration and differentiation, symbolic solution of (differential) equations, term simplification, arithmetic in algebraic domains, polynomial factorization.

computational geometry — geometric objects; typical topics are representation of geometric objects, geometric modelling, computer aided construction (design), geometry theorem proving, robotics.

automatic reasoning — logic objects; typical topics are (universal) automated theorem proving, unification, automated proof checking.

automatic programming — (assertions about) programs; typical topics are automatic program verification, automatic program synthesis, symbolic execution of programs.

In all of these areas, a main interest lies in the design of software systems solving the above mentioned problems. In computer algebra, there are already many powerful systems available, which cover the whole range of problem types and which can perform tasks which go far beyond the capabilities of human experts (in complexity, speed and accuracy). Most of the systems have also found their way to commercialization. Currently, much emphasis is put on good man-machine interfaces, which are necessary for a broad acceptance. For computer aided design, highly developed commercial systems are available. For the other branches of computational geometry only prototypes exist. Currently, a new effort on synthetical computational geometry is undertaken which aims at making extensive use of an existing computer algebra system. In automatic reasoning, many prototypes for special problem types are available at research institutions, but in general, the systems can not reach the capabilities of human experts. One aspect of automatic programming is the programming language PROLOG, for which many commercial interpreters and compilers are available. Other tasks in automatic programming are closely connected with automatic reasoning. Many problems in this field can be reduced to mere proof problems, hence sophisticated theorem provers would be required.

The automatization of symbolic computation will certainly have a great impact on science and engineering. The effects will be much more significant than was the case with the automatization of numerical computation (cf. the introduction of pocket calculators). It will as well play a crucial role in all levels of higher education, both for supporting traditional subjects like algebra, calculus, and analytic geometry and for teaching new subjects, as described later. In the following sections, each of which is dedicated to one of the four sub areas of symbolic computation, we describe how one can make use of such software systems in high school education and what effects can be achieved. (The ideas can easily be adapted for university education also.) The collection covers a broad range of possible applications but can only be exemplary in its character. For each item, we give a concrete example, list the mathematical skills that are trained, and discuss the insights that will be gained.

Beside the (educational) effects which are specific to each sub area and which are discussed in the following sections, there are a few ones that apply to all four areas:

- By making use of symbolic software systems as "symbolic calculators", one can *automatize tedious tasks* (like computing derivatives and integrals, simplifying expressions, applying inference rules, constructing geometric objects, etc.) and hence *concentrate on the creative parts* of the problem solving process (finding the mathematical formulation of a specific problem, developing a strategy for solving a specific problem, etc.).

- By utilizing symbolic software systems for sophisticated computer-aided instruction, one can *improve the individual training*. Such a system can serve as a tutor for students who perform badly and as a stimulus for good students.

- By studying concrete algorithms ("How does the computer solve a specific problem?"), one can *motivate systematic (algorithmic) problem solving*.

- By studying rewrite rules and their applicability (transformation rules, inference rules, etc.), one can *improve the capability of abstraction*.

2 COMPUTER ALGEBRA IN EDUCATION

One of the starting points for using computer algebra systems in education was a paper by D.R. Stoutemyer ([2]). A first systematic discussion on this topic was held at a special session during the International Conference on Mathematical Education 1984 (see [3]). At the University of Waterloo, the computer algebra system MAPLE is extensively used in undergraduate mathematics classes ([4]). At the University of Hawaii, experiments with muMATH (a computer algebra system for PC's) in calculus classes have been made ([5]). We have concentrated our interest on high school education. Based on our former experiences which are described in [6], we have started an effort to use computer algebra systems for reaching certain teaching goals. A course, which is currently held at the Stiftsgymnasium Wilhering (Austria) is described in detail in [7]. The following examples are solved in muMATH ([8]), which we found a good means for educational purposes. In order to improve legibility, the syntax has been slightly modified.

2.1 Task: Solving complex mathematical problems

Example: (An optimization problem)

"Find the rectangle with largest area that can be constructed within a isosceles triangle, such that one side of the rectangle lies on the basis of the triangle. The triangle is given by its base length a and height h".

The student now has to "understand" the problem (e.g. by

drawing the following picture) and to find the mathematical formulation, i.e. the goal function to be optimized and the side conditions:

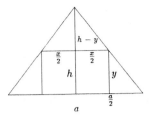

```
gf:= x.y;        sc:= a/2 : h = x/2 : (h - y);
```

The computer can be used to express explicitly y from `sc` and substitute the resulting expression in `gf`:

```
ye:= SOLVE(sc,y);      gf:= SUBSTITUTE(gf,y,ye);
```

yielding the new goal function

$$x\frac{h}{a}(a - x).$$

Then the first derivative of this expression w.r.t. x is computed by

```
gf1:= DIFFERENTIATE(gf,x);
```

giving

$$\frac{h}{a}(a - 2x).$$

Finally, the zero of this expression, regarded as an equation in x, is computed and the result is substituted in ye

```
xsol:= SOLVE(gf1=0,x);
ysol:= SUBSTITUTE(ye,x,xsol);
```

resulting in the final answer

$$\text{xsol} = \frac{a}{2}, \qquad \text{ysol} = \frac{h}{2}.$$

Furthermore, one could also let the system compute the second derivative of `gf`, evaluated at the solution point for reasoning about its sign and hence the type of the optimum.

The students learn

- to solve a problem by dividing it into subproblems (here: explicitly expressing y from `sc`, substituting the expression found for y in `gf`, computing the first derivative of `gf`, etc.),

- to concentrate on the creative parts of the problem (the students will understand what the crucial points of an example are and learn to separate them from tedious tasks that can be done automatically),

- to delegate the solution of such tedious tasks to a computer,

- to carefully distinguish the different roles of the variables (here: a, h are parameters, x, y are indeterminates).

Insights gained:

- Mathematical problems consist of creative parts (here: find the goal function and the side conditions, subdivide the problem into smaller problems, combine the solutions found for the subproblems, which have to be solved by humans, and of non-creative parts (here: solving equations, computing derivatives, substituting), which can be solved even by a computer.

- There are only a few basic problem types in mathematics. (The problem type "solving equations" appears twice in the above example: for explicitly expressing y from the side condition and for computing the zeros of the first derivative of the goal function.) Even in university mathematics, the number of problem types is fairly limited, see [9] for a systematic study.

2.2 Task: "Simplify" expressions

In muMATH, the application of transformation rules is controlled via assignments to certain variables. In our opinion, this method is not adequate for educational purposes, because the applications are automatically iterated. In the following example, an imaginary function TRANSFORM is assumed, which allows the performing of a single transformation step by specifying the rule and how to match the rule to the expression.

Example: (The distributive rules)

"Given a set of transformation rules

$$(\text{r1})\ a \cdot (b + c) \leftrightarrow a \cdot b + a \cdot c, \quad (\text{r3})\ \frac{b+c}{a} \leftrightarrow \frac{b}{a} + \frac{c}{a},$$

$$(\text{r2})\ \frac{1}{a} \cdot \frac{1}{b+c} \leftrightarrow \frac{1}{a \cdot b + a \cdot c}, \quad (\text{r4})\ \frac{a}{b+c} \leftrightarrow \frac{1}{\frac{b}{a} + \frac{c}{a}},$$

transform the expression $\frac{3+x}{3x}$ into the goal expression $\frac{1}{3} + \frac{1}{x}$."

Assuming the first expression to have been assigned to t1, the suitable rule r3 (left-to-right reading) can be applied to it by

t2:= TRANSFORM(t1,r3,forw,($b \leftarrow 3, c \leftarrow x, a \leftarrow 3x$)).
The expression $\frac{x}{3x} + \frac{3}{3x}$, which is obtained by a mere syntactical application of r3, is automatically simplified to $\frac{1}{3} + \frac{1}{x}$, which is already the desired result. (If the specified rule is not applicable to the expression using the given substitution, an appropriate error message is displayed.)

The students learn

- to recognize patterns in expressions (which is necessary for the applicability of transformation rules),
- to recognize the structure of an expression (which is, for example, necessary for solving equations, since one has to recognize the outermost function symbol in order to apply the correct equivalence transformation).

Insights gained:

- The notion of "simplicity" heavily relies on how to process the expression further. (For computing the zero, $\frac{3+x}{3x}$ is much more convenient than $\frac{1}{3} + \frac{1}{x}$, whereas the latter is preferable for computing the limit for x going to infinity.)
- (For teachers:) Never ask a student to "simplify" a given expression, without specifying "simple". (Or give them also the solution and ask for a correct sequence of transformation rule applications.)

2.3 Miscellaneous applications

Above, we have applied a computer algebra system to improve the mathematical skills of the students. Such a system can also be used as a general instrument for teaching mathematics and science, e.g.

- for preparing assignments and tests,
- for illustrating new mathematical contents,
- for solving problems which lie beyond the capability of the students (and which arise as subproblems in some larger problems, e.g. solving higher order equations, computing integrals which require trigonometric substitutions),
- for applying methods which have not yet been taught. (In physics it is the lack of knowledge how to solve differential equations that hinders the attack on many problems, although it is often quite easy even for high school students to formulate the corresponding differential equations.)

3 COMPUTATIONAL GEOMETRY IN EDUCATION

Geometry has always been a subject which plays an important role in education, because it is very illustrative. For construction and proof problems, two main approaches for an automatization have been investigated so far. By an *axiomatization*, the problem is expressed in terms of a first order theory. An *algebraization* leads to a corresponding algebraic problem. In the following example, the use of a construction system is demonstrated ([10]); for the input we follow the syntax used in the proof system [11].

3.1 Task: Specify geometric objects

Example: (Construct a square)

"Construct a square, whose lower left corner lies in the origin, whose lower right corner lies on the x-axis, and whose side has length 1."

Typically, one could start by fixing the points
A(0/0),   B(1/0)
and demanding the following properties (is-perpendicular-to, length-of, etc. are primitives, which are understood by the system):

    (h1) AB is-perpendicular-to BC,
    (h2) length-of AB = length-of BC,
    (h3) BC is-perpendicular-to CD,
    (h4) length-of BC = length-of CD.

A software system for automatic construction will find the following solutions (if an insufficient number of points has been fixed, the system returns an appropriate error message)

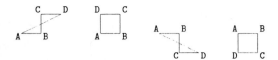

which is not quite what was desired. Adding

    (h5) AD is-perpendicular-to AB

makes the specification less ambiguous, but still gives rise to two solutions:

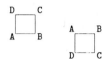

Fixing an orientation by

    (h6) A,B,C,D are-ordered-counterclockwise

one finally arives at the intended object:

(Competition: Who requires the fewest tries? Another interesting task is to let the students define new predicates and functions in terms of the existing primitives.)

<u>The students learn</u>

- to consider all possibilities in advance and hence to specify carefully,
- to distinguish between independent and dependent objects (independent points can be chosen arbitrarily, dependent points meet certain conditions w.r.t. the other points).

<u>Insights gained</u>:

- A satisfying (intended) solution for a problem can only be obtained if the problem has been carefully and unambiguously specified. (Discuss the corresponding situation of specifying the input/output behaviour of a program (see section 5).)

- A correct identification of independent parameters is also part of the specification (too few: infinitely many solutions; too many: no solution).

4   AUTOMATIC REASONING IN EDUCATION

In the former sections traditional mathematical subjects were treated. The following two sections require the teaching of the method of mathematics, which is quite unusual for today's high school mathematics. But in times when mathematical knowledge is exponentially growing and the demands for a well-founded and application-oriented education are also increasing, one can master the situation only by concentrating on "How to do mathematics", rather than overloading the curriculum with many variants of "What to

do in mathematics". Students who have learned the method of mathematics can easily acquire any kind of mathematical knowledge. For university education, [12] was one of the first textbooks following this approach.

A central interest lies in considering the whole problem solving process, which mainly consists of three steps: *modelling* the real situation using mathematical notions (i.e. specifying a corresponding mathematical problem), *solving* the mathematical problem (i.e. collecting knowledge about the considered domain, proving new knowledge, etc.), and *applying* the model solution to reality, thus receiving the real solution. (Although not taught today, this whole process is required for many examples which are treated in today's high school mathematics, cf. the optimization example presented in section 2.)

Finding an appropriate model for a "real" problem is very essential. The effort necessary for solving the problem depends heavily on this choice. (A bad model can even hinder the solving of the problem.) Modelling requires a lot of creativity, which, in our opinion, will never be achieved by a computer.

One of the most essential parts of solving mathematical problems is the finding and the proving of new knowledge. Whereas the finding mainly depends on creativity, the proving can be automated in large parts. The following example uses PROOF-PAD, a system for interactively generating proofs ([13]). This system automates the tedious tasks of theorem proving (e.g. applying inference rules); the creative parts, such as the decision of which inference rule can be applied, which substitution should be made, etc., have still to be done by the students. The notation of rules follows Gentzen.

4.1   Task: Interactive Theorem Proving

<u>Example</u>: (Theorem on bounded functions)

"Prove the following theorem:
    Let F and G be real functions:
    If F and G are bounded, then $F \oplus G$ is bounded."

Throughout the whole dialogue, all user input lines start with the prompt symbol "?", whereas the output of PROOF-PAD is marked by "$\star$".

First, the student has to specify the proof problem by defining the syntax, entering the axioms and definitions, e.g.

    ? DEFINTION: bounded(F) : $\longleftrightarrow$
                     $(\exists x)(\forall y)(\text{abs}(\text{apply}(F, y)) \leq x)$ (DEF1),
and finally formulating the goal

    ? GOAL: $(\forall F, G)$ bounded(F)$\wedge$ bounded(G) $\longrightarrow$
                          bounded($F \oplus G$) .

The interactive generation of the proof can be started by eliminating the universal quantifier, which appears as outermost symbols in the goal formula. This can be achieved by applying the A-introduction rule, which automatically introduces two new constants and generates a subgoal:

? RULE: A-introduction (GOAL,(F,G))
* CONSTANTS: f,g: realfunction
* SUBGOAL: bounded(f)$\land$ bounded(g) $\longrightarrow$
$$\text{bounded}(f \oplus g) \quad \text{(G1)} \ .$$

The logical structure of the subgoal is an implication, which is split into an assumption and a new subgoal by

? RULE: IF-introduction (G1)
* ASSUMPTION: bounded(f)$\land$ bounded(g) (A1)
* SUBGOAL: bounded($f \oplus g$) (G2) .

This can further be attacked by applying the definition of bounded:

? RULE: definition (G2,DEF1)
* SUBGOAL: $(\exists x)(\forall y)(\text{abs}(\text{apply}(f \oplus g, y)) \leq x)$ (G3) .

The new subgoal is an existentially quantified formula; hence a solving expression for the existentially quantified variable would be required. Therefore, mere routine stops here. Now the assumptions are further processed by splitting the conjunction (A1) into two single assumptions and applying the definition:

? RULE: AND-elimination (A1)
* ASSUMPTION: bounded(f) (A2)
* ASSUMPTION: bounded(g) (A3)
? RULE: definition (A2,DEF1)
* ASSUMPTION: $(\exists x)(\forall y)(\text{abs}(\text{apply}(f, y)) \leq x)$ (A4) .

An existential quantifier in an assumption can be eliminated by introducing a new constant:

? RULE: E-elimination (A4,(x))
* CONSTANTS: a: real
* ASSUMPTION: $(\forall y)(\text{abs}(\text{apply}(f, y) \leq a)$ (A5) .

Similarly, (A3) is processed, producing a new constant named b. Now, a solving expression for (G3) can be constructed, using a and b.

? RULE: E-introduction (G3,$((x, a+b))$)
* SUBGOAL: $(\forall y)(\text{abs}(\text{apply}(f \oplus g, y)) \leq a + b)$ (G4)

This was the only crucial point in the proof. The remainder is pure routine work and can be found in [13].

The students learn

- to distinguish clearly between what is given and what has to be shown,

- to analyse proof situations carefully,

- to apply inference rules correctly,

- to work systematically. (The students are forced by the system to take care of all details, without having to carry actually out all the tedious rule applications by hand.)

Insights gained:

- Most theorems are only valid w.r.t. a given set of axioms and definitions.

- There are some essential parts in a proof which require an idea (e.g. the elimination of an existential quantifier in a goal statement.) Nevertheless, an actual proof consists also of all the details shown above.

5   AUTOMATIC PROGRAMMING IN EDUCATION

The basic idea in automatic programming is that it suffices to give a specification of a program, rather than writing the program itself. This can be achieved either by using a software system, that automatically transforms a specification into a (Pascal-)program, or by using a high-level language whose syntax accepts specifications as programs. The latter is realized in PROLOG (= PROgramming in LOGic) which allows Horn clause formulae as programs. A nicely written introduction is [14], which refers to micro-PROLOG, a logic programming language for PC's.

5.1   Task: Programming by specifying

Example: (Sorting a list)

"Write a program that sorts a list of arbitrary length."

A customary specification of an appropriate binary predicate is-a-sorted-version-of, which can be found in most textbooks, is

```
x is-a-sorted-version-of y if
                x is-a-permutation-of y and
                x is-ordered.
```

(micro-PROLOG allows infix notation for the binary predicates, which makes the programs easy to read. We use a flexible notation also for the other predicates.) This specification is already a (micro-PROLOG-) program for sorting a list, assuming that the predicates used (is-ordered, is-a-permutation-of) are also properly specified, e.g.

```
() is-ordered
(x‖x1) is-ordered if
        x is-the-minimal-element-of (x‖x1) and
        x1 is-ordered.
```

Here, () denotes the empty list and ‖ is a binary function that takes an element e and a list l as arguments and returns a list with e as its first element and l as its rest list. Furthermore, this definition is recursive in its nature, which is quite common for logic programs.

Another solution of the above problem is the following alternative specification

```
() is-a-sorted-version-of ()
(x‖x1) is-a-sorted-version-of y if
        x is-the-minimal-element-of y      and
        z is-obtaind-by-deleting x from y and
        x1 is-a-sorted-version-of z
```

Testing both programs by computing concrete examples, the second version turns out to be much faster.

The students learn

- to specify programs (using recursion),

- to solve problems by splitting them into subproblems.

Insights gained:

- Satisfactory solutions (programs) require a careful specification (cf. also section 3).

- The higher the level of the programming language, the easier is the programming. (It is often a hard task to develop a Pascal program from a mere first order logic specification.)

- The greater amount of mathematical knowledge used, the more efficient is the program. (The second version of is-sorted-version-of contains some algorithmically useful knowledge about iteratively bringing the smallest element to the left, whereas the first version involves only a systematic verification of all permutations of the input list, which is the reason for its bad performance.)

6 CONCLUSION

Using symbolic computation software systems allows concentration on tasks that do not get enough attention in today's education. By this, we do not mean the inclusion of new mathematical contents but concentration on the essential parts of the problem solving process. Learning "how to solve problems" should definitely be one of the central goals in education. We are aware that this makes mathematics much more demanding for students, since routine work is replaced by tasks which require creativity. Therefore, one has to plan carefully how to integrate these systems into education, such that education can profit from symbolic computation software systems.

ACKNOWLEDGEMENT

This work has partially been supported by the European Community (project COST 13).

REFERENCES

[1] B. Buchberger et al, Symbolic computation (an editorial), *Journal of Symbolic Computation*, vol. 1, no. 1, 1985, 1–6.

[2] D.R. Stoutemyer, Computer Symbolic Math & Education: A Radical Proposal, *SIGSAM Bulletin*, vol. 13, no. 3, 8–24.

[3] B. Buchberger, D.R. Stoutemyer eds., Papers from the Special Session on Symbolic Mathematical Systems and Their Effects on the Curriculum at the International Congress on Mathematical Education (Adelaide, Australia, August 24–30, 1984), *SIGSAM Bulletin*, vol. 18, no. 4.

[4] B.W. Char, K.O. Geddes, G.H. Gonnet, B.J. Marshman, P.J. Ponzo, Computer Algebra in the Undergraduate Mathematics Classroom, *Proc. SYMSAC'86*, Waterloo, Canada, July 21–23, 1986, 135–140.

[5] R. Freese, P. Lounesto, D.A. Stegenga, The Use of muMATH in the Calculus Classroom, *J. of Computers in Mathematics and Science Teaching*, vol. 6, 1986, 52–55.

[6] K. Aspetsberger, G. Funk, Experiments with muMATH in Austrian High Schools, *SIGSAM Bulletin*, vol. 18, no. 4, 4–7.

[7] K. Aspetsberger, B. Kutzler, Using a Computer Algebra System in an Austrian High School, *RISC-LINZ Tech. Rep. 88-5.0*, U. Linz (Austria), 1988.

[8] The muMATH-83 Symbolic Mathematics System — Reference Manual, Softwarehouse Inc., Honolulu, USA.

[9] B. Buchberger, Mathematik für Informatiker II (Problemlösestrategien und Algorithmentypen), Lecture Notes, U. Linz (Austria), 1984.

[10] T. Baumgärtler, PROLOG for Geometric Construction, Diploma Thesis, U. Linz (Austria), 1986.

[11] K. Kusche, B. Kutzler, H. Mayr, Implementation of a Geometry Theorem Proving Package in SCRATCHPAD II, *Proc. EUROCAL'87*, Leipzig, GDR, June 2–5, 1987, Lecture Notes in Computer Science, Springer.

[12] B. Buchberger, F. Lichtenberger, Mathematik für Informatiker I (Die Methode der Mathematik), Springer Verlag, 1980, 1981.

[13] T.A. Henzinger, H. Hofbauer, PROOF-PAD — An Interactive Proof Generating System using Natural Deduction, *Proc. Österr. Artificial Intelligence Tagung*, Wien, Austria, Sept. 24–27, 1985, Informatik Fachberichte vol. 106 (Subreihe Künstliche Intelligenz), Springer Verlag, 173–184.

[14] T. Conlon, Start Problem-Solving with PROLOG, Addison-Wesley Publishers, 1985.

COMPUTERS IN EDUCATION, F. Lovis and E.D. Tagg (eds.)
Elsevier Science Publishers B.V. (North-Holland)
© IFIP, 1988

THE ROLE OF DYNAMIC GRAPHICS WHEN LEARNING PROGRAMMING -
implications for cognition.

JANNI NIELSEN

The Royal Danish School of Educational Studies
Emdrupvej lol
2400 Copenhagen NV
Denmark
telph. 1 69 66 33

ABSTRACT.

Programming is emphasized as enhancing formal operational thinking.
However, research has shown a strong tendency among pupils to prefer
graphics.
Research on the role of picture/text is discussed, introducing empirical data; the ambiguous role of dynamic graphics is investigated, -
showing that it
- may lead to fixation
- may enhance learning.

It is suggested that
- visual perception and its integration with language must be considered,
- the development of visual operational thinking may be an essential
link between concrete operational and formal operational thinking.

INTRODUCTION.

The LOGO program, making such good use
of the visual graphic has especially
been emphasized as enhancing procedural
or formal operational thinking. Programming and the necessity of debugging
have been ascribed importance for this
acquisition.
However, Perkins (1) concluded when
evaluating a number of investigations,
that one cannot speak of a "fingertip
effect". On the contrary, to learn programming is a very time consuming process. It requires thought and hard
work, and as pointed out by Noss(2) it
cannot be learned without a teacher.
These conclusions find support in the
empirical investigations of Pea and
Kurland (3)(4). They conclude that programming and debugging demand qualifi-

graphics as opposed to programming,
suggesting an investigation of the role
of pictorial information in the learning process.

PICTURE AND TEXT.

It is often stated, that younger children rely more on picture material,
compared with older. Otte(7) found,
that 4th graders could mention significantly more similarities between
objects presented in pictures, than
objects presented in verbal form. However, Nelson(8) concluded, investigating psychology students, that "Pictures are typically easier to remember
than words". Thus pictures are more
easy perceived. But the results also -
suggest that although the age distinction is important, other factors play a
role too.
Pezdek and Stevens(9) investigated 5
year-old children's relation to verbal
and visual information, respectively.

One investigation presented the children with a video from Sesame Street, with an arbitrary sound track from another sequence. The results showed that without correlation between the visual information and the verbal, the visual perception rules. In another investigation they tried with sound track alone, compared with video and correct sound track. The results showed no difference, visual and verbal information were equally important.
Reid, Briggs and Beveridge (10) found, investigating the influence of pictures on reading of school science topics among 14 year olds, that "when pictures were presented, the topic was more easily remembered", concluding that "pictures enhance the memory of words and phrases".

However, the interesting part of this investigation is another conclusion, "pictures had little effect upon pupils' ability to COMPREHEND the topic ". This points to the central aspect: Learning and thinking are not just to recognize and remember, but to understand, become cognizant of, and able to make use of what is learned.
Salomon (11) pointed to this conclusion, when investigating children's perception of television and printed text, "Children perceived it (TV) as more realistic and easy. Print was reported to demand more effort, but led to better inference making". This conclusion raises the question of the cognitive qualities in the visual dynamic images. Thus Singer (12) argued that visual dynamic images leave a holistic recognition, but hinder "deep processing".

COMPUTER GRAPHIC AND LEARNING.

Hammond (13) made use of computer - graphics when communicating new information to medical students and found that it enhanced learning. Also Baltz (14), Caputo (15) and Reif (16) found that graphic representation enhanced acquisition of basic knowledge.
However neither Edyborn (17) nor Smith (18) found any significant difference in the performance among students exposed to computer graphics, as opposed to non-computer graphics. Nielsen (19) in an analysis of 15 year old pupils' programming work, concluded that the tendency was "when something was drawn on the screen, the problem was considered solved".Thus graphics led to a

fixation on the product. However, Nielsen (20), investigating 30 pupils' programming work points out that though the tendency was to rely on the dynamic graphics, the actual workprocess, and the outcome would differ. She emphasizes that the graphical representation serves as an essential basis for pupils approach to computers, suggesting that the role of dynamic graphic/text in the learning process be investigated.

THE DIFFERENT ROLES OF COMPUTER GRAPHICS.

In the following, three cases are presented. They differ in terms of actual work process, and in outcome, though they all have one thing in common: All the pupils prefer graphics to text. The cases are drawn from videotapes of 14-15-year old pupils working with a Danish variation of Logo (approximately 12 hours experience) in which text/dynamic graphics are integrated(20), allowing for both a symbolic and/or a graphic dynamic approach.

ON THE SAFE SIDE.

Beth and Kathrine (20,p. 66-75) rely heavily on graphics, either by drawing or by having programs executed, which they painstakingly copy from the exercise book. Though Beth and Kathrine express happiness when a figure is completed, being captured by the graphics, they are neither fascinated nor enthusiastic.
When copying programs, they create no mental images of what they execute. "I just want to see what it is" says Beth, and comments on the figure being executed, "It is that, isn't it?" checking in the book.
They skip exercises if they do not understand the instructions,which they read with hesitant voices. Unless there is a program to copy, they will look for illustrations which they will attempt to reconstruct by drawing. This work is done mainly by trial and error, leading on to homing-in(6) irrespective of any degree of the angles.
The girls have to write a program which will execute the following illustration from the book, (figure no.1).

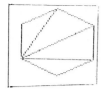

no. 1

Though they clearly perceive the task
as difficult (they sigh heavily) the
figure captures their attention. Beth
works out the reckoning from the illustration and dictates, Kathrine starts
drawing. They guess at every turn, try
it out, and if they do not, with their
eyes, judge the turn as correct, they
clear the screen and start all over
again. At the sixth attempt they are
lucky, "It must be 50 to 60, more or
less" states Beth, Kathrine types 60.
But the correct turn has no effect on
their understanding. Because during the
subsequent moves, the approach is trial
and error, eventually homing-in.The
result is considered acceptable, though
"We did not get it to fit in the
angles".
To the girls there seems to be no relationship between the program text and
the figure. They have very little, maybe no, knowledge of angles. They start
with trial and error, rely on their
visual perception, move on to homing-
in, and depending on the outcome, continue to draw or clear the screen.

GRAPHIC FIXATION.

Jane and Susan (20. 51-66) also prefer
graphics, but they are fascinated by
the figures.
They also tend to copy programs without
discussion of outcome. Just as their
attention may be captured by an illustration. The following program instructions and an illustration (figure
no. 2) are shown.

no. 2

The girls skip the instructions, head
straight for the program,and copy
:TURN, REPEAT(6), TRIANGLE, RIGHT
TURN(10), TO HERE, END. When the program is executed, smiles gradually grow
on their faces. They laugh happily, and
surprised, " Did we do that?"
Then variables are introduced. Again
the girls head straight for the copying
of the program. But they do not include
a value when they ask to have it executed, and the cursor just turns noisily
around on the spot. However Jane and
Susan stare fascinated and break out
laughing. With intent expressions and
with their eyes glued to the screen,
they repeat the execution. Again they
bend over screaming with laughter.

In a subsequent exercise, they have to
exchange TRIANGLE for SQUARE. They read
the instruction, and exchange TRIANGLE
for SQUARE: TURNA, REPEAT(31), SQUARE,
RIGHT TURN(10), TO HERE, END. But the
girls have no SQUARE program, thus the
cursor just turns noisily around. Something is wrong, and Jane speculates
that, "It is just because we have forgotten to write that it must go forward, it is bloody well not enough to
write that is must turn".
In the second attempt FORWARD(50) is
included. In the third attempt RIGHT
TURN is changed to 90. In the fourth
they remove FORWARD and change RIGHT
TURN to 95. Every time a program is
executed, the girls smile expectantly -
though they do not know what to expect.
Except surprises maybe, and they scream
with laughter every time. However, they
have a clear understanding of not understanding, "I don't understand a damn
thing, quite honestly".
By the fifth attempt the program looks
like this:TURNA, REPEAT(31), SQUARE,
FORWARD(50), TO HERE, END. When it
is executed, the girls breathlessly
stare at the screen. They are lucky,
because a figure gradually unfolds.
"Finally it worked ".(figure no.3)

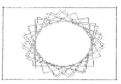

no. 3

It is the dynamic graphics which faci-
nates and captures the girls - as the
figure gradually unfolds, so their smiles grow gradually, eventually resulting in happy laughter. Even when the

cursor only turns noisily, they are
fascinated.
The visual perception rules their
approach to the world, and it is not
the programming, but the figures which
are incredible. "How cute " they happily comment on the above figure, not
checking the program. When there is a
product, the problem is considered
solved.

READING DYNAMIC GRAPHICS.

The domineering workstyle of Tina and
Cecily (20, p.81-90) is to skip instructions, copy programs mechanically,
and have them executed. With excited
faces, they follow the movement of the
cursor, expressing enthusiasm when new
unexpected results appear. Unexpected,
because they do not, from the program
create mental images. This can be seen
when programs with "strange" names are
copied, "I wonder what it does?" And
when it executes known figures, the
reaction is, "How exciting", but Tina's
voice is in contradiction of her verbal
statement.
But halfway into the videotaped process, a change occurred. The girls had
just copied a program executing a
SPIRAL. The figure excited them and
they managed, in the next exercise, to
change the RIGHT TURN angle from 90 to
88.
By now they were so captured by the
graphics - one may speak of them as
being seduced - that they went on to
the next
illustration(figure no.4). The instruction asks them to write a program which
will turn a triangle around, at the
same time making it bigger and bigger.

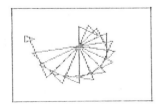

no.4

An analytical approach would be to
break down the problem posed to entities, e.g. 1) a triangle program 2) a
variable, 3) a turning order, and 4)
finally the program has to call itself
with an increment to the variable. But
Cecily and Tina's primary way of relating to the world is through the body

and especially the senses. The dynamic
figures, which gradually unfold fasci-
nate them, and the immediate visual
perception rules. But they are not totally fixated to the appearance. They
try to step behind it, and make the
direct appearance indirect.
Completely lost, Cecily then happens to
notice the SPIRAL program. Hesitantly,
but intuitively, she takes point of departure here. "Then we just have to do
it with a TRIANGLE, don't we?" Interrupted by long breaks of thoughtful-
ness, loud speculations, and doubts,
during which Tina establishes "we are
just guessing, .. ", the girls reach
this suggestion: TT, FORWARD(A), RIGHT
TURN (120), SPIRAL(A+2),END. Hypnotized
they stare at the screen, and comment
on the stepwise movement of the cursor
and the subroutine drawing SPIRALS,
"Yes, but then it has to go FORWARD and
TURN, FORWARD and TURN". Thus naming
the necessary steps in the triangle.
Little by little, by "reading" the
figure gradually unfolding, they reach
the conclusion, that a program for a
triangle has to be written. They succeed with this using trial and error,
and by browsing through the book. But
they maintain the subprocedure -
SPIRAL(A+2). As Cecily exclaimed in
despair " Why does it keep drawing
squares?"
At the fourth attempt the girls, with
their eyes glued to the dynamic
graphics when each program is being
executed, reached this: TT(A),
REPEAT(3), FORWARD(A),RIGHT
TURN(120),TO HERE, SPIRAL(A+2),END. A
teacher helps and during the discussion
which unfolds it becomes clear that the
problem is the subroutine. Cecily has
contextualized to the visual dyamic
movement, and SPIRAL(A+2) =TURN/GET
BIGGER.
Thus it is the graphics the girls rely
on, it is the figures they debug
through the iconic reading of the dynamic information. It is not the programs
and the temporal logic they follow.

DISCUSSION.

In all three cases, it is the dynamic
graphics which capture the girls attention. This is the source of their motivation. Programs are copied mechanically, but the text, the temporal logic
and the relations between text and
graphics do not seem to enter into their
perception. However, there are differences.

In the case of **Beth and Kathrine** they simply stay with the graphic. The function of an order is immediately visible - a direct relation between the verbal input and the visible output, - and they rely on their visual perception. But even drawing figures is not perceived as easy - they sigh - because trial and error, gradually leading on to the stepwise process of homing-in characterizes their work process. Perception rules but **the dynamic images do not enhance memory, neither comprehension nor learning.**
Several interconnected explanations may be suggested. Despite Beth and Kathrine's age, due to which the girls, in principle, should have reached a higher cognitive level than the younger children mentioned earlier, they prefer the drawing mode. It does have to do with this new domain, as this is rather unknown, and as it is the visual perception through which we first and directly encounter the world, they stay on the graphics. But one also has to look at the programming language. Many of the functions of the programming orders take place within the machine, and can be neither seen, nor felt or heard. They are - apart from FORWARD and TURN - abstract and decontextualized symbols, and besides the relationship between them is defined by an apriori temporal logic. Beth and Kathrine have no understanding of this logic. The programming text is incomprehensible, therefore they cannot perceive the relationship between text and graphics. The girls simply do not understand what it is they have to understand - though they do have a very clear comprehension of not understanding.
This may also be seen when they read instructions - with very hesitant voices. This problem leads to focusing on the girls' **relation to language.** It seems that to Beth and Kathrine **language is not a tool for understanding.** This seems to be their most severe problem, and one may wonder if these girls will, at all, benefit from working with computers at the present stage.
Beth and Kathrine deal with what is more familiar - drawings - but this demands all their attention. The movements forwards and backwards result in lack of interrelationship, and as a consequence the girls' knowledge becomes fragmentary; hence no meaning can be derived. Thus the possible cognitive quality in pictorial information does not come into play. I would suggest that the girls are experiencing psychological overload. Thus one **cannot** speak of pictures enhancing, either memory,

or understanding or learning, though pictures are certainly perceived as easier than text.

With **Susan** and **Jane** it is different. They are deeply fascinated and they work without stopping, letting themselves be seduced by the graphics. Not even the many mistakes and problems can cool their enthusiasm. No matter what, the computer, like Merlin, "can take on a thousand forms" (22). Any mistake just seems to act as yet another incentive to wander further into the magical world.
The direct visual perception governs their approach, and what the eyes see becomes the determining factor in their work process. This may be seen when they copy programs. It is not the program but the expectant pictorial outcome, the graphics and the dynamic movements which fascinates. This may be why, despite lack of familiarity with computers, they seem much more at ease, than Beth and Kathrine. If they were not enchanted, they would not keep on - thus **the dynamics and the graphics may enhance motivation.**
Also here, FORWARD and TURN are readily understood. But Susan and Jane have also understood, and are able to make use of their acquired knowledge of turns of 90 and 120 degrees. As it is the graphics, not the programs, and the visual perception which characterizes their approach to the world - one may speak of the **visual images as enhancing the memory** of angles.
At the same time, however, it is exactly the enchantment, which also causes them problems. They seem to have very little understanding of the text/-graphics relation. This may be seen when they mechanically copy programs which results in surprises. "Did we do that". Or when a program through arbitrary corrections eventually produces a figure and they conclude that they succeeded. Their fascination leads to a **fixation** on graphics and prevent them from moving on. Thus **visual images may enchant, but in this case one cannot speak of them as enhancing learning.**
This may be explained from the girls perception of programs, graphics and movement. Thus they do not seem to perceive a written program as a whole, that is with the relationship between the orders. Instead they seem to perceive each order almost as an autonomous entity. As if they draw their conclusions directly from their experiences with the visualized stepwise movements each order causes when they draw. Similar to the way movies were perceived in the beginning, when people

were unable to connect mentally one
sequence with the next. As a consequence, the new image was perceived as a
totally new story.

Not being able to make the connection
mentally, Susan and Jane cannot perceive the dynamic interrelatedness in
the text either. Thus orders may be
changes, added or excluded arbitrarily,
without a view of the whole. In this
sense dynamic graphics do not enhance,
but rather prevent them from becoming
cognizant. and images do not lead to
holistic recognition. On the other
hand, dynamic graphics may help, e.g.
when the cursor just moves noisily
around on the spot. Here they immediately conclude that a FORWARD order must
be introduced. Thus this **special dynamic information may lead to some kind
of inference.**

Again one has to look at the girls'
perception of language, e.g. when a
subroutine is introduced. A program
which calls another program was explained thus by Susan, "The machine
then gives it the name of the new program". The concept and the function of
the subroutine is abstract, without
meaning. But the girls attempt to make
it understandable by contextualizing it
directly in everyday life. Thus their
relation to language is very concrete.
Language as a tool for the intellect,
to deal with the world on an abstracted
level, is not yet part of their qualification.

However, it is important to maintain
the role of the visual images. Despite
the lack of text/dynamic graphics interrelatedness, the latter allows for a
certain comprehension and inference,
however small.

  Tina and **Cecily** are also fascinated by
the beautiful figures. They too start
out with mechanically copying programs,
creating no mental images on the basis
of the text, and skip instructions if
they do not understand immediately. But
half way into the process, they move
from **fixation** where visual perception
rules, to beginning **analysis**. What has
to be noted here is, however, that it
is the dynamic movements which the
girls read. Thus it is not the program
they debug - but the figure, and the
girls are able to make this visual
graphic information operational. Thus
it is dynamic graphics which play a
crucial role in their thinking processes. Despite the fact that the girls
are very hesitant, and hold rather
little understanding of the programming
order, with respect to the logic, they
get fairly far, by relying on graphic
information, their intuition and by tacit inference. In the example with Tina

and Cecily the force of the visual way
of relating to the world is seen. At
the same time also the limits of it are
demonstrated, because the girls could
not achieve the final steps.

Again one must look at their relation
to language. Thus the subroutine is
contextualized directly - not in everyday life - but as dynamic visual information. Language is not yet a tool
for the intellect, to the extent of
being able to deal with the subroutine
at an abstract level. However, the
girls would never have got so far, if
they had not relied on their visual
perception.

In this case then, one may speak of
**dynamic visual information as enhancing
motivation, memory and
comprehension.**Despite the very little
correlation perceived between figure
and text - thus perception rules - the
girls are able to reach some kind of "
deep processing ". What is seen is a
beginning of realization of a **dissonance** between the visual information and
the abstract text. This dissonance may
point towards formal operational
thinking, but it is the dynamic visual
information, which makes up the essential base. Thus one cannot speak of
formal operational thinking, but rather
of a thinking which may be termed
visual operational thinking. I will
suggest that it is not programming, but
the stepwise unfolding of the dynamic
graphics, **which enhances procedural
thinking.**

Concluding remarks.

The pupils relation to language, - as a
tool, and its extent of concreteness/
abstractness is important when learning
programming. Thus the learner's way of
relating to the world, and her cognitive level must be taken into account.
However, also the role of visual perception and its interaction with language
must be considered. Thus it is of the
utmost importance, when introducing
pupils to Logo, that more attention be
paid to the integration of text and
dynamic graphics. Dynamic graphics may
lead to a fixation on the product -
visual perception rules. On the other
hand it may enhance learning - and the
development of the visual operational
thinking may be the essential connecting link when moving from concrete
operational to formal operational
thinking.

Acknowledgment: This work has been made possible through a grant from The Danish Research Council for the Humanities.

References.

(14)Baltz, B.L.(1977), Computer graphics as an aid to teaching mathematics. Unpublished doctoral dissertation. Ohio State University.

(15)Caputo, D.J.(1981), An analysis of the relative effectiveness of a graphic enhanced microcomputer-based remedial system in a university basis mathematical skill deficiency removal plan. Unpublished doctoral dissertation. Univ. of Pittsburg.

(17)Edyborn, D.L.(1982), The effects of two levels of micro-computer graphics on reading comprehension. Normal, Illinois, Illinois State University, ERIC reproduction service, No. ED 218 593

(13)Hammond, . (1971),Computer graphics as an aid to learning, Science, 172, p. 903-908.

(8)Nelson D.L. and D. Castano(1984), Mental representation and words: Same or different? American Journal of Psychology, Spring, vol. 97, no. 1, p. 1-15.

(18)Nielsen, Janni(1986a), NOT THE COMPUTER BUT HUMAN INTERACTION is the basis for cognitive development and education, Education and Computing, vol, 2,p. 53-63.

(21)Nielsen, Janni(1986b), 15 kommenterede procesbeskrivelser af nogle 14-15 }rige drenges og pigers introducerende arbejde med datamater.(15 commentated process descriptions of 14-15 year old boys'and girls'introductory work to computers). The Royal Danish School of educational Studies, Copenhagen.

(20)Nielsen, Janni(1987a), DATAMATER OG ERKENDELSESPROCESSER - en teoretisk analyse af erkendelsesparadiger, set i relation til nogle 8. klasse elevers arbejde med datamater. (COMPUTERS AND COGNITIVE PROCESSES . a theoretical analysis of cognitive paradigms, seen in relation to 15 year old pupils'work with computers) The Royal Danish School of Educational Studies, Copenhagen.

(6)Nielsen, Janni and Lisbet Roepstorff(1985) Girls and computers - worlds apart? Revised edition of paper presented at the THIRD GASAT conference, London.

(5)Noss, Richard(1985), Creating a Mathematical Environment through programming: A study of young children learning Logo. University of London, doctoral dissertation.

(2)Noss, Richard(1987) Synthesizing mathematical conceptions and their formalization through the construction of a Logo-based School mathematics curriculum.International journal of Mathematics Education in Science and Technology, in print.

(7)Otte,W.(1962),The differential Effects of verbal and pictorial representation of stimuli upon responses evoked. Journal of Verbal Learning and Verbal Behavior, 1,p. 192-196.

(22) Papert, Seymour(1980) Mindstorms, Children, Computers and powerful ideas. Basic books inc. New York.

(3)Pea R. and M. Kurland (1983a) On the cognitive prerequisite of Learning computer Programming. Bank Street College, New York.

(4)Pea R. and M. Kurland (1983b) On the cognitive effects of learning computer programming. Bank Street College, New York.

(1)Perkins D.N.(1985) The Fingertip Effect: How Information Processing Technology Shapes Thinking. Educational Research, vol. 14, 7, aug./sept. p. 11-17.

(9)Pezdek K. and E. Stevens (1984), Childrens' memory of auditory and Visual Information on Television. Developmental Psychology, vol. 20, no. 2, p. 212-218.

(10)Reid D.J. Briggs N. and M. Beveridge (1983) The Effect of Picture upon the readability of a school science topic. British Journal of Educational Psychology, 53, p. 327-335.

(16)Reif, F.(1986) Scientific approaches to science education. Physics Today, nov. p. 48-54.

(11)Salomon Gavril (1984), Television is " Easy " and Print is " Tough ": The Differential investment of Mental Effort in Learning as a Function of Perceptions and Attributions. Journal of Educational Psychology, vol. 76, no. 4, p. 647-58.

(12)Singer, J.L.(1980), The power and limitations of television. A cognitive-affective analysis. Tannenbaum P.H. and R. Abeles (eds) The Entertainement functions of television. Hillsdale N.J. Erlbaum.

(19)Smith, C.L.(1985) Analysis of student performance in punctuation using graphic versus non graphic microcomputer instruction. Delta Phi Epsilon Journal, 28, p. 105-116.

COMPUTERS IN EDUCATION, F. Lovis and E.D. Tagg (eds.)
Elsevier Science Publishers B.V. (North-Holland)
© IFIP, 1988

THE ROLE OF SOFTWARE SPECIFICATION IN THE TEACHING OF PROGRAMMING

Peter G. Thomas and Hugh M. Robinson

Faculty of Mathematics, The Open University
Walton Hall, Milton Keynes
MK7 6AA, United Kingdom

Software specification using formal methods plays an important part in software development, primarily for the benefits it brings to program verification and maintenance. Coupled with high level languages which support encapsulation, formal specification can have a profound effect on programming methodology. This paper argues the case for teaching formal methods at an early stage in the teaching of programming, since many of the concepts to be learned by programmers occur in specification, but without the hindrance of the details of a specific programming language. A good specification can be transformed into a correct program with minimum effort. This paper describes a formal specification technique that has been used in the teaching of programming and illustrates how, with a few simple rules, a student can quickly turn a specification into a working program.

1. INTRODUCTION

Formal software specification plays an important role in improving program correctness and in reducing software maintenance costs. The authors have come to realise that formal specification, provided it is easy to apply, can also be of tremendous help in the teaching of programming. Much has been said over the years about the use of "pseudo-code" in program development, particularly about the need for a language which is so devoid of intrusive detail that beginning programmers can get to grips with the skills of problem solving without having to become involved with the details of programming language syntax. Typically, procedural programming is taught through piecewise refinement tempered with a lot of good advice about well structured programs. Piecewise refinement is of limited application since it is primarily suited to the evolution of complex algorithms. This methodology does not help directly with modularisation, except, perhaps, on the grossest of scales.

The new developments in object oriented programming (OOP), see [3] for example, are of particular interest because they seem to offer some solutions to the above problems. Unfortunately, even with the OOP approach, the programmer is once again often unduly influenced by the programming language, particularly when choosing objects and their attributes. What is required are methodologies for program design that overcome this tendency. At the present time such methodologies are only just emerging. In this paper we want to illustrate a methodology for teaching programming based on formal specification. It turns out that objects are closely related to abstract data types on which our chosen specification technique is based.

We shall demonstrate how specification techniques (which,

by definition, are programming language independent) can lead to well structured, correct and easily maintained programs. We shall show that the kind of programming language used for implementation is of secondary importance and can as easily be a conventional procedural language (like Ada) or an object oriented language (such as Smalltalk), although we prefer those languages which support encapsulation since their use greatly reduces the burden of implementation [2]. We claim that formal specification techniques are of such importance that they should be part of a student's first training rather than left until later as currently tends to happen.

2. THE SOFTWARE LIFE-CYCLE

To illustrate the relationship between specification and implementation it is useful to examine the software life-cycle. The remainder of this section is adapted from [10].

The design and construction process for software is decomposed into subtasks, and there is general agreement that the stages shown in Fig 1 provide an appropriate subdivision. Output from one stage of the software life-cycle, often in the form of a written document, forms the input to the next stage. The process is iterative: the documents which form the interface between stages can be incomplete, ambiguous, or even erroneous so that one stage cannot be completed without reference back to one or more of the earlier stages. The whole process is cyclic since software ages and becomes obsolete and, because the reasons for which the original software were written are no longer valid, the software must be redesigned. This means that the requirements must be re-evaluated and the cycle repeated. Further details can be found in [8].

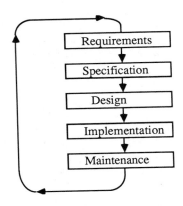

Fig. 1. The software life-cycle

The specification stage is concerned with describing *what* has to be produced. Contrast this with the design stage which determines *how* a program will produce the required results. Specifications are usually written in a mathematical way in order to take advantage of well established fields of knowledge which enable us to reason and argue about the specifications in a way that gives us confidence in their correctness. As a simple illustrative example suppose that you have the problem of rearranging a large set of names into alphabetical order. The specification of the program can be expressed in the following terms:

a program is required which will take as its input a set of names and will produce as its output the same names but in alphabetical order.

Notice that the specification says nothing about how the re-ordering is to take place. There is no mention of the sorting method, nor how the data is to be represented in the program. As far as the specification is concerned, provided the output from the program is an ordered list of the input names the method of producing the output is immaterial. The advantage of removing the details of how the program produces its results (the implementation details) into the design stage is that the implementation can be altered at will: the design can be changed without altering the specification. As long as the design faithfully matches the specification then we can have confidence that the design is "correct" in the sense that the design and the specification carry out the same task: they have the same functionality. There is also an intellectual advantage to separating out the "what" from the "how". It reduces the complexity of the problem by removing unnecessary details and, as a result, we often describe this process as one of abstraction.

3. SPECIFICATION

The remainder of this paper illustrates the approach to programming through an example, beginning with a written description of the problem. The description is deliberately informal and incomplete.

A company has decided to keep an up-to-date internal telephone directory on a computer. It is assumed that the problem has been analysed and that a list of requirements

has been drawn up. The requirements are given as a set of operations that must be supported by the system:
(i) add an employee's name and telephone number to the directory;
(ii) remove an employee's name and telephone number from the directory;
(iii) retrieve an employee's telephone number given the employee's name;
(iv) display, on a terminal, the whole directory in alphabetical order;

Thus, part of such a directory could be as follows:

Name	Number
Baker	2060
Grey	2431
Smith	2117

The next step is to encourage students to criticise the list of requirements in order to determine where the requirements are deficient (they may be inconsistent, ambiguous or incomplete). For example:

add: takes an employee name, a telephone number and a directory as source data, and returns a directory with the employee data inserted. If the employee name already exists in the directory, a suitable message is returned.

remove: takes an employee name and a directory as source data and, if that employee name exists in the directory, removes the name and the associated telephone number from the directory and returns the modified directory as its result. If the employee name is not in the directory a suitable message is given.

retrieve: takes an employee name and a directory as source data and, if that employee name exists in the directory, returns the associated telephone number. If the employee name is not in the directory a suitable message is returned.

display: takes a directory as its source data and causes a listing (in alphabetical order of employee name) to be printed at a specific terminal device. (In any real life specification the type of device would be defined, thereby acting as a constraint on the implementation.)

createdirectory: takes no source data and returns a new, empty directory as its result.

isindirectory: takes an employee name and a directory as source data and returns the value true if the employee name exists in the directory, and the value false otherwise.

The important feature of these descriptions is that they emphasize to students what the operations are and not how they are to be carried out. From these descriptions a more formal specification can be drawn up. We usually study both axiomatic (algebraic) and constructive specification, and have found both to be equally easily understood by students. Here we shall demonstrate an axiomatic specification since it is usually considered the more difficult approach. Further details can be found in [5, 6].

NAME
directory(employee)

SETS	SYNTAX
D set of all directories	**createdirectory:** $\rightarrow$ D
N set of employee names	**isindirectory:** $N \times D \rightarrow B$
T set of telephone numbers	**retrieve:** $N \times D \rightarrow T \cup M$
B {*true, false* }	**add:** $N \times T \times D \rightarrow D \cup M$
TL set of terminal listings	**remove:** $N \times D \rightarrow D \cup M$
M {*employee not in directory,*	**display:** $D \rightarrow TL.$
employee already in directory}	

The notation of the syntax is approached as follows. The **directory** ADT is specified by six operations, the syntax of which defines their source data and their results. For example, the operation **isindirectory** takes two items of source data, an employee name (in the set N) and a directory (in the set D) and returns, as its result, a member from the set B (the set of Boolean values, *true* and *false*). The cross ($\times$) indicates the Cartesian product of two sets but is here simply interpreted by the student to mean "and" in the sense of "an element of the set N and an element of the set D". The operations **retrieve, add** and **remove** each return a single result which can be either a message (from the set M) or a telephone number (in the case of **retrieve**) or a new directory (in the case of **add** and **remove**). The symbol $\cup$ represents set union which, in this particular specification can be interpreted as "or" as in "an element from the set T or an element from the set M (but not both)". The arrow ($\rightarrow$) simply separates the source data from the result(s). Thus, the *SYNTAX* component defines the sets which are associated with each operation and shows the student the mapping from source data to results.

The final but significant component of the formal specification is the *SEMANTICS* in which the meaning of each operation is defined in a way that is independent of any computing device or programming language. Here we shall exhibit an axiomatic approach which illustrates well the ability to provide independent specifications.

Axioms are viewed as a set of relations between the operations, and to generate a set we begin by identifying *constructor operations*. In this case, the operation **createdirectory** is one constructor (it constructs new, empty directories). A second constructor, one that creates a new, *non*-empty directory from an existing directory, is needed. It is an operator that takes an existing directory (from D) and adds a new item (consisting of a name and a telephone number) to produce a new directory. It is named **makedirectory**, with syntax given by:

$$\textbf{makedirectory:}\ N \times T \times D \rightarrow D$$

Makedirectory is similar to **add** except that it does not yield a message when an attempt is made to add an item that is already present in the source directory. This is not a

problem since **makedirectory** is a *hidden* operator (used in the specification alone, not by any application); we shall never use it in a situation where an item is already in the directory. A formal specification for the semantics of **makedirectory** should be given but, in the interest of economy of space, we shall avoid doing it here.

One further decision must be made before the semantics are written down. Should a directory maintain its items in order? For illustrative purposes we shall assume that the items are ordered but this does not significantly affect what we do in the remainder of the paper. If $e \in N$, i.e. an employee name, then the axioms for **isindirectory** are:

$$\text{isindirectory (e, \textbf{createdirectory})} = \textit{false} \qquad (1)$$

isindirectory (e, **makedirectory**(n, t, d)) =
(e = n : *true* {the name is in the directory}
| e < n : *false* {the name is not in the directory}
| e > n : isindirectory(e, d) {check sub-directory d} (2)

Axiom (1) simply says that if the directory is empty then asking the question whether the item e is in the directory must yield the answer *false*. The notation used in axiom (2) is intended to convey the fact that, because the directory is ordered there are three cases to consider: (i) when the item e is the same as the first item in the directory (n), (ii) when e comes before n, and (iii) when e comes after n. The student is shown that the use of the operation **makedirectory** as a parameter to **isindirectory** is as a "deconstructor" which allows us to examine the items in a non-empty directory one by one. That is, a directory should be viewed as a first item (containing the two pieces of data n and t), at the front of a sub-directory d. Of course, the sub-directory d could be empty in which case axiom (1) applies.

It is made quite clear that such axioms are recursive and to reinforce what this means many exercises are given. The student is given examples of directories described in terms of the constructor operations as in

makedirectory (smith,2, **makedirectory** (jones, 8,
createdirectory))

that is, in canonical or reduced form [7], and is asked to apply the axioms to determine the value of such constructs as:

isindirectory (roberts).

A more difficult situation is faced in the specification of the operation **add**. Once again two axioms are required to define the operation ($p \in T$):

add(e, p, **createdirectory**) =
makedirectory(e, p, **createdirectory**) (3)

add(e, p, **makedirectory** (n, t, d)) =
  (e = n : employee name already in directory
  | e < n : **makedirectory** (e, p, **makedirectory** (n, t, d))
  | e > n : **makedirectory** (n, t, **add**(e, p, d)))   (4)

The explanation of these axioms to students is along the following lines. Axiom (3) simply states that when adding an item to an empty directory it must end up being the first item and that, of course, is precisely what **makedirectory** does! Axiom (4) is a little more complicated. The case when the item to be added has the same employee name as the item at the front of the (sub)directory is straightforward: the message *employee name already in directory* is returned, to avoid adding duplicate employee names. When the name to be added, *e*, comes before the name at the front of the current subdirectory, *e < n*, the new name has to be added to the front of the subdirectory. The final case, *e > n*, means that the new name should be placed in the directory somewhere after the first item, (*n, t*), so it must be added to the subdirectory *d*.

The emphasis at all times is on specifying the semantics of the operations without once talking about a programming language or computer. Our aim is to capture all the necessary information at the specification stage.

4. THE REPRESENTATION

We shall represent a directory as a linked sequence (list) of records. This representation includes a dummy item so that an empty sequence can be treated in the same way as any other sequence. For example:

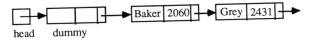

head   dummy

Fig. 2. A representation of the directory

The empty directory looks like this:

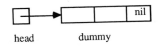

head   dummy

Fig. 3. A representation of the empty directory

It is important to realise that, once again, no programming language has been involved in the discussion.

5. THE IMPLEMENTATION

To implement the directory abstract data type we use the information contained within the specification together with the details of the representation. Here we shall show how an implementation in MODULA-2 [11] using modules and the principles of information hiding is developed [9]. To begin with we write a definition module. In essence, all that is required is a list of the headings of the procedures which implement the abstract data type operations. Our

first guideline is:

there should be one procedure (or function) for each ADT operation.

A second guideline is:

implement each operation as a function wherever possible.

For many languages, including Pascal, there are restrictions on what a function may return and we have to resort to procedures. The reason for this guideline is to reinforce the idea of a mathematical function and to make the conversion from specification to implementation as simple as possible.

To create a suitable definition module we need only the information in the *SYNTAX* of operations. The *SETS* are mapped directly into types. The implementation (and indeed the representation) is to be keep hidden from any user of the procedures so we define the type Directory to be an opaque type (it will be defined in the corresponding implementation module).

```
DEFINITION MODULE DirectoryOps;
TYPE
    Directory;
    EmpName = ARRAY[1 .. 20] OF CHAR;
    PhoneNo = CARDINAL;
PROCEDURE CreateDirectory ( ): Directory;
PROCEDURE IsInDirectory (N: EmpName; D: Directory):
                                            BOOLEAN;
PROCEDURE Add(N: EmpName; T: PhoneNo; D:
                                    Directory): Directory;
PROCEDURE Remove (N: EmpName; D: Directory):
                                            Directory;
PROCEDURE Retrieve (N: EmpName; D: Directory):
                                            PhoneNo;
PROCEDURE Display (D: Directory);
END DirectoryOps.
```

The guideline for the construction of the definition module is, therefore:

the parameters of the functions are the source data and results of the operations; the types of the parameters correspond to the sets of the specification.

The information about the types of the items in the directory is essential to users and so must be defined in the definition module. Hence, our next guideline is:

keep the implementation details of the ADT type hidden, and ensure that the parameters of the procedures have types which do not reveal their implementation.

A well designed definition module should not reveal any information about the implementation or representation of the abstract data type.

The corresponding implementation module will use the information provided by the *SEMANTICS* of the operations interpreted in terms of the chosen implementation. First we deal with the representation of the ADT itself.

```
TYPE
    Directory = POINTER TO NodeRecord;
    NodeRecord = RECORD
                    EmployeeName: EmpName;
                    TelephoneNo: PhoneNo;
                    Next: Directory;
                 END RECORD;
```

Each item in the directory is represented by a record with three fields, the last of which is a pointer to the next record. This is in keeping with the notion that a directory, like a list, is either empty or consists of a first item together with a (sub)directory. The procedure CreateDirectory must create the situation shown in Fig.3.

```
PROCEDURE CreateDirectory ( ): Directory;
VAR
    D: Directory;
BEGIN
    Allocate (D, SIZE (NodeRecord ));
    With D↑ DO
        EmployeeName := " ";
        TelephoneNo := 0;
        Next := NIL;
    END;
    RETURN D;
END CreateDirectory;
```

We shall not show all the bodies of the procedures here; instead we shall indicate how the implementation proceeds by looking at an example. Axioms (1) and (2) specify IsInDirectory. Our aim here is to write a correct procedure which conforms exactly to the axioms. The axioms are written recursively so we expect to produce recursive procedures. The axioms distinguish between an empty and a non-empty source directory. Therefore, the procedure will start by testing the source directory, using a hidden procedure named IsEmptyDirectory. A hidden procedure is one that is used in the implementation but which is not made available to the eventual users of the module.

```
IF IsEmptyDirectory(D)
THEN RETURN FALSE
ELSE
    (* code for axiom 2 *)
END
```

Axiom (2) has three cases to be considered and this implies a nested IF construct similar to:

```
IF E = N
THEN RETURN  TRUE
ELSE  IF E < N
        THEN RETURN  FALSE
        ELSE  RETURN  IsInDirectory (E, d)
      END
END
```

where d is the subdirectory obtained by removing the first item from the source directory D. To extract the subdirectory d we assume the existence of a suitable function. In fact it is beneficial to write a set of functions which return the values which are obtained by decomposing the (non-empty) directory D into its first item and the subdirectory:

```
PROCEDURE  SubDirectory (D: Directory): Directory;
PROCEDURE  FirstName (D: Directory): EmpName;
PROCEDURE  FirstNumber (D: Directory): PhoneNo;
```

Another important issue concerns the relational operators <, =, and > which, in general, will not be available for all types. In Ada we can overload these operators, in MODULA-2 it means writing suitable functions. Here is the completed procedure; students are encouraged to appreciate how closely it mirrors the axioms, and how recursion is handled by the programming language. Our experience is that placing emphasis on recursion at the specification level reduces subsequent difficulty in implementation of the concept.

```
PROCEDURE IsInDirectory (E: EmpName; D: Directory):
BOOLEAN;
VAR
    d: Directory;
    N: EmpName;
BEGIN
    IF IsEmptyDirectory (D)
    THEN RETURN FALSE
    ELSE  d := SubDirectory (D);
          N := FirstName (D);
          IF Equal (E, N)
          THEN RETURN  TRUE
          ELSE
              IF Before (E, N)
              THEN RETURN FALSE
              ELSE  RETURN  IsInDirectory (E, d)
              END
          END
    END
END IsInDirectory;
```

Probably the most important teaching point to be made at this stage is the way in which the constructor operations (**createdirectory** and **makedirectory**) are used on the left hand side of the axioms. This implicit use of the constructors in the axioms must be replaced by explicit deconstructors (SubDirectory, FirstName and FirstNumber) in the implementation.

This method of implementation, keeping close to the axioms, may not be efficient but has the advantage of producing correct code very quickly. However, it has deferred the implementation of the composition operator **makedirectory**, the decomposition operators SubDirectory and FirstName, and the relational operators Equal and Before. These procedures act directly on the representation (as does CreateDirectory), but are quite easy to implement. It is useful to point out that with our methodology only the constructors and deconstructors act directly on the representation; the remaining operations have been implemented in a way that is independent of representation, further helping with maintenance (students appreciate this more when asked to change an implementation).

We have proposed a "two-level" implementation methodology in order to clarify the roles of the axioms and the representation. The result is a set of "higher level" procedures which implement the axioms and a set of "lower level" procedures acting on the chosen representation. To change the representation is now very straightforward and easy to achieve.

At present, we do not attempt to teach program proving, but we believe that this would be an easy development with our methodology, as discussed in [1], as a direct result of the close correspondence between specification and implementation.

6. THE APPLICATION

Students are expected to design and implement a "real" application based on the ADT directory. Such an application would be a menu and option system allowing the user easy access to the information held in the directory. Applications consist almost entirely of calls to the procedures which implement the directory and therefore illustrate how the original operations are used and how the application program is independent of the implementation of the abstract data type.

7. CONCLUSIONS

A methodology for teaching programming has been proposed in which a student is exposed to:

(i) Formal specification methods (discussed in an earlier paper);

(ii) The difference between implementation of abstract data types and applications which use the ADT;

(iii) The importance of information hiding and high level languages which support encapsulation;

(iv) How abstract data types help with program modularisation;

(v) A two level implementation method in which the code that implements the abstract data type operations corresponds very closely to the axioms of the specification, and in which only the implementation of the composition and decomposition operations depends on the representation.

Experience has shown that students have little difficulty with the formal aspects of the specification and find that implementation is very straight-forward.

ACKNOWLEDGEMENTS

Thanks are due to the students of the Open University, UK, and The University of Denver, USA who put our ideas into practice.

REFERENCES

[1] Backhouse, R.C., Program construction and verification, (Prentice-Hall, Englewood Cliffs, 1986).

[2] Bishop, J., Data abstraction in programming languages, (Addison-Wesley, Wokingham, 1986).

[3] Cox, B.J., Object oriented programming, (Addison-Wesley, Wokingham, 1986).

[4] Emms, J.M., Robinson, H.M. and Thomas, P.G., Aspects of teaching software engineering at a distance, Education and Computing, in print.

[5] Horowitz, E. and Sahni, S., Fundamentals of data structures, (Pitman, London, 1976).

[6] Jones, C.B., Systematic Software development using VDM, (Prentice-Hall, London, 1986).

[7] Martin, J.M., Data types and data structures, (Prentice-Hall, London, 1986).

[8] Sommerville, I., Software Engineering, (second edition), (Addison-Wesley, Wokingham, 1985).

[9] Stone, R.G. and Cooke, D.J., Program construction, (Cambridge University Press, Cambridge, 1987).

[10] Thomas, P.G., Robinson, H.M. and Emms, J.M., Abstract data types, (Oxford University Press, Oxford, 1988).

[11] Wirth, N., Programming in MODULA-2, (third edition), (Springer-Verlag, Berlin, 1985).

COMPUTERS IN EDUCATION, F. Lovis and E.D. Tagg (eds.)
Elsevier Science Publishers B.V. (North-Holland)
© IFIP, 1988

USING EXPERT SYSTEM TECHNIQUES FOR CASE STUDY TEACHING

P.R. Gamble & J. Hearn

Department of Management Studies for Tourism and Hotel Industries
University of Surrey
England

By representing a case environment on a computer, tutors are able to create case study problems more rapidly, to monitor student learning stratagems and to provide further tutorial guidance with small, limited domain expert systems. Students are able to manipulate the case material more effectively using business applications on microcomputers and to control the pace of their own learning. Work at the University of Surrey has shown that using expert system techniques for management teaching is generally well received by students. However, development costs are high and a great deal of commitment is needed to achieve integration between subjects.

1. TEACHING AND LEARNING FOR VOCATIONAL MANAGEMENT STUDENTS

There is no single academic discipline upon which a hotel or restaurant manager might draw in order to do his or her job. On the contrary, as situations arise which bring new problems, the manager must be able to select the technique appropriate to that particular circumstance. Thus the range of disciplines needed for vocational first degrees in management such as those in Hotel and Catering Management at the University of Surrey, is extensive.

The Multidisciplinary Framework of Decision Making
in the Hospitality Industry

Philosophy Logic				Economics Marketing
	Values Ethics		Utility Satisfactions	
Psychology	Individual behaviour	DECISION MAKING PROCESS	Group behaviour	Sociology Social Psychology
	Models Plans Budgets	Production processes	Environments	
Mathematics Statistics Operations Research Finance	Natural sciences Nutrition			Law Politics Engineering Architecture

Figure 1

Figure 1, proposed by Gamble [1], illustrates some of the potential difficulties for both teaching and learning in such a multidisciplinary subject area. A very diverse faculty is needed to cover all the domains, often requiring academics who have both a specialist and applied expertise which is not always easy to find. An expert in law or economics may have had little actual experience as a hospitality manager. Thus there is a strong need both to demonstrate applications and to integrate one subject area with another, so as to offer a coherent teaching framework.

From a learning viewpoint, difficulties are equally apparent. When Copernicus and Galileo were alive, it would not have been unreasonable for either of these great men to say that he was fully familiar with the entire body of scientific knowledge existing at that time. Even as late as the nineteenth century it might have been possible for a scientist to possess a full grasp of every branch of his field. Today, no one person could even attempt to keep abreast of all but an aspect of his or her scientific discipline. How then can a hospitality manager claim an understanding of several disciplines?

In terms of curriculum development therefore, a design is followed which offers a formal transfer of knowledge, exercises where appropriate and opportunities to synthesise theoretical knowledge in the context of the industry. Part of this application takes place in industry itself when students are seconded for training and part takes place in classroom situations. A useful device for synthesising application skills is the case study.

2. TEACHING WITH CASE STUDIES - SOME ISSUES

Case studies provide a forum in which techniques previously taught in the context of a directed exercise can be integrated to classify, evaluate and organise data at the discretion of the learner. The student becomes involved in judgments concerning the appropriateness of a technique or concept and in evaluating the relevance of data. Case studies offer a method of representing management problems that might be obscured by other kinds of formal teaching. Take, for example, the problem of teaching financial management. In an exercise, all the data necessary to perform calculations has to be offered. Whereas in practice the difficulty of the task may actually reside in identifying and collecting the basic data.

Case studies are therefore attractive because they expose students to the open-ended, conflicting situations of greater relevance to vocational training in business and management. Resolving these issues benefits students in several ways. Not only are they able to cultivate applied problem solving and decision making skills but important social skills development also occurs. Case studies can provide a foretaste of the need for management even in student work, encourage creativity, and even foster self analysis through group criticism.

For reasons of this sort, management courses often include case studies in different forms. However, these benefits are not without cost. Some students find the transition from traditional teaching difficult since the learning task is generally more complex. In a substantial study the student has to understand and retain the artificial world of the case while seeking to apply a principle or technique learned in another context [2]. The very strength of group based learning may be lessened as the varying motivations, abilities and even availabilities of participants make themselves felt [3].

The debate surrounding the validity of using case studies in management education is reviewed by Smith [4]. In particular, Smith highlights two factors which may affect the transference of skills learnt from case study work to on-the-job problem solving. First it is difficult to devise a case situation which accurately represents the complexities and inconsistencies of the real world. Any case scenario, however well conceived and implemented, is bound to be a simplification of an actual business problem and may not demand the full range of reactive and proactive decision making skills required by the practising manager. This naturally weakens the value of the teaching method.

Second, the success of the case study method is highly dependent upon the skill of the tutor as the facilitator of the case study. Learning under these conditions should be student-centred with minimum reliance on the tutor. Yet the tutor can powerfully control the direction of learning and promote or inhibit skill acquisition. Overall, there may be a residual uncertainty about the "rightness" of any chosen answer: a sneaking feeling that the tutor does have one correct solution in mind but is being typically obdurate in refusing to make his secret objective explicit. Tutors who develop case material are often torn, to cite extremes, between developing something comprehensively large or something simplistically small. As a result of these problems the influence of the case study method on learning and skill acquisition needs to be understood.

3. AIMS OF THE EXMAN (EXPERT MANAGER) PROJECT

Recognising these features of case study teaching, the Department of Management Studies for Tourism and Hotel Industries at the University of Surrey set out in 1985 to develop a computerised case environment. The primary aim of the project, known as EXMAN (EXpert MANager), was to allow controlled, dynamic management decision making within the context of a case study. There were four initial aims. First, to investigate barriers which inhibit the efficient application of computer based procedures by potential managers. Second, to evaluate commercially available techniques designed to reduce those barriers; for example, windowing and mouse driven systems. Third, to develop and test interactive teaching packages and intelligent front ends which would foster the skills associated with systems analysis, selection and implementation. Fourth, to develop "expert" packages which would simplify the use of computer based techniques for both students and managers by providing advice on decision making.

In addition to giving students better, self-paced tuition, the project aimed to provide a mechanism for applying theoretical knowledge in a realistic and appropriate context. Intelligent assistance from the computer was intended not only to have learning benefits but, coincidentally, to improve students' understanding of computers as a management tool. The mechanism chosen for this development was that of expert systems.

The idea of a case study 'world' linked in well with the technical requirements of expert system design. Expert systems operate best within restricted worlds or domains. The approach chosen was to build an expert system related to the case study material, which could be interrogated by the student to provide advice. This line of development was seen as favourable because, in theory, it allowed boundaries or limits to be set for the expert system knowledge base.

3.1 The Application of Expert System Techniques to Management Decision Making

Expert systems seek to capture enough of a human expert's knowledge to ensure that, given an identical problem, the human expert and the computer will reach the same conclusion [5]. They have scored notable successes, particularly when applied to problems that involve some sort of diagnosis. Examples include medical diagnosis, geological exploration, computer fault diagnosis, telephone cable maintenance and configuring computer systems [6]. Commercially they are becoming very important, so that business, industry and government are investing millions in expert systems development [7]. Successful examples of expert systems usually relate to a well defined body of knowledge which is generally deterministic and stable in character. This is somewhat atypical of management decision making situations.

Managers have to cope with implicit as well as explicit changes in the problem environment and with apparent contradictions. Both problem recognition and the applicability of chosen outcomes are ambiguous. A manager is rarely certain that the absolute best decision has been made. The transaction rate (the number and frequency of decisions) on such systems is also higher. Taken with a more complex form of uncertainty, the scope of management expert systems is probably narrower than that of their technical counterparts. The environment of a case study allows some of these potential problems to be offset, since an element of control is available to the case writer(s).

3.2 Long Term and Short Term Structure of the EXMAN Project

In the long term, EXMAN will support a number of roles. For the student or manager it will offer at one level, personal tutoring in the use of management techniques, such as forecasting, spreadsheet usage or linear programming. At another level, it will support complex gaming and simulation, either in competition with other groups or individuals, or against the computer [8]. Games may be played in either open or closed mode in which the game model is more or less explicit to the user. In open mode, the computer will forecast the likely outcome(s) of possible decisions for the student.

To cope with the help and guidance needed by users, EXMAN comprises a number of modules. These will include a database and report generator, a number of small expert systems in problem specific areas, such as how to conduct a feasibility study, or how to analyse a set of financial statements, and a reasoning and inference mechanism to facilitate development and gaming rules. The latter will allow tutors and trainers to parameterise case situations in a way that is both simpler and more complete than a hand written case.

The EXMAN project therefore intends to support case teaching in several ways. On the one hand, an expert system will simplify the generation of case material. On the other, it will support and guide the learning process. A student will be able to explore the world of the case through the computer and will thus need to expend less effort on constructing and retaining it. The direction and pace of exploration will be determined by the student, thereby giving him maximum control over learning strategy and the manipulation of content [9]. The student will also be able to call on the computer for guidance about problem solving methods and the use of techniques. The nature of the guidance obtained in this way will provide useful feedback to tutors concerning the efficacy of the teaching and learning environment.

It is intended that the expert system will be usable at many different levels. In the short term, initial development concentrated on writing and testing a new case study conventionally and then extending and re-testing the case on a limited problem, set using a computer. These two phases are now complete. The third stage, commencing in March 1988, requires rewriting the case study in an object-orientated language such as Smalltalk [10] and increasing the rule base of the expert guidance module.

4. PROTOTYPING THE EXPERT SYSTEM WITH A SHELL

To recognize the importance of the multi-disciplinary base of management studies and the value of case study learning, a new case study was developed to form the core of part of final year undergraduate teaching. The case was designed and written by specialist academics who acted as domain experts. In order to limit its initial scope, the case was concerned with the prospective takeover by a French company of a run-down hotel in the docklands area of East London. Such a situation allowed for problems in a range of disciplines, including hotel and catering management, financial management, marketing, management science and tourism.

Developing the case itself represented the preliminary stage of knowledge elicitation and involved close liaison with domain experts. Several interviews and informal discussions were held with various experts (subject lecturers) to establish key principles and obtain the knowledge required to complete the exercise.

In order to speed the development process it was decided to prototype the expert system using a commercial shell [11], Expert Edge, from Helix Systems. In the first phase test in the Autumn of 1986, this shell was used to assist students in formulating business strategies. The shell helped to emphasise the need to formalise knowledge during the process of knowledge elicitation. It also provided some useful initial evaluations of knowledge representation schemas and control strategies. Furthermore, student experiences of using the shell based expert system could be analysed, using personal interviews and self-completion questionnaires.

The shell therefore made a useful contribution to rapid prototyping, which is a particularly valuable phase in early development [12]. In areas of expertise where knowledge was amenable to a rule based structure, the shell could be fed with the facts and produce a turn round, mini system :allowed the knowledge engineer to test the validity of any rules and to maintain the interest of the domain expert.

However, it became evident from both the knowledge elicitation process and the student evaluations that a commercial shell was unlikely to offer a long term development environment. There were too many difficulties in representing conflicting data, there were problems of representing uncertainties and there was a loss of control over the user interface. In short, a shell seemed likely to prove too inflexible. In January 1987 therefore, it was determined to continue the development with a custom based system.

5. THE HARDWARE AND SOFTWARE ENVIRONMENT OF EXMAN

5.1 The Development Environment

The main development environment took the form of a Sun 3/75 artificial intelligence work station with 4 Mbytes of main memory, a 19" monochrome screen, a 71 Mbyte disk drive and an ethernet interface. The Sun 3 is really ideally suited for Computer Assisted Design but this very capability means that it is equipped with excellent facilities for multi-tasking, using a windowing environment.

In terms of software, the operating system which supported this environment was Unix version V and a proprietary window management system known as Sun Tools. It was initially decided to use Prolog as the main logic programming language and Quintus Prolog was chosen. Pascal was selected as the main procedural language for phase II and this was also purchased for the Sun.

5.2 The Delivery Environment

Since the target users of the system were potential managers, it was important to implement EXMAN on a computer system typically representative of that likely to be encountered in industry. Accordingly, the IBM PC ATs were chosen as the target machines. These were configured in a network of 8 machines, linked by PC NET, plus 4 free standing machines.

The operating system used for the IBMs was PC-DOS 3.1. To counterpoint the Suns, both Turbo-Prolog and Turbo-Pascal were purchased, as was a Microsoft Assembler, to be used for a program to monitor actual key sequences used by students. In addition, business applications software such as Supercalc 4, Word Perfect, Reflex (a database manager), Pertmaster Advance (a critical path network program) and Superkey (a keyboard macro generator) were utilized in the project.

5.3 Problems of Compatibility

The Sun and IBM computers chosen are driven by different microprocessors. The Sun by a Motorola 68000 and the IBMs by an Intel 80286. This incompatibility of hardware architectures was offset to a great extent by the use of Prolog to do most of the development work on the Sun. Prolog allows rapid prototyping of software and the use of this language facilitated the transfer of modules from one system to the other. However, the initial development versions of what became known as the guidance system were actually run on the Sun 3.

6. THE STRUCTURE OF THE EXMAN SYSTEM

Figure 2 illustrates the design approach used.

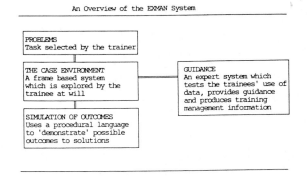

An Overview of the EXMAN System

Figure 2

The Management Expert System, EXMAN, essentially comprises 4 modules:

(i)   A knowledge base editor to incorporate and relate case study material.

(ii)   A retrieval system for exploring the case environment and for explaining how to conduct case study work. This system produces data for tutors about how students have explored the case information, such as which frames have been examined, the order in which information was obtained and the amount of time spent on each frame.

(iii)   An expert system which explores how the information has been used and guides students in formulating conclusions.

iv)   A simulation which models the effect of the students' chosen solution. This module is to be developed in 1988.

The first module, the Interactive Frame Editor (IFE), manages the relationship of knowledge frames based on a tree structure.

The second element consists of an Information Retrieval System (IRS). The IRS consists of a large number of frames and some mechanism by which students can move between them. Certain frames contain many pages of text while others are spreadsheet or database files. Thus the IRS effectively becomes the case environment which the students can explore. As can be seen from the sample screen shown in figure 3, the frames are divided into information about: a company, the environment, the unit, the location, the market and case studies. Like the IFE, this is written in Turbo-Pascal for an IBM PC AT.

An Overview Map of the Information Retrieval System

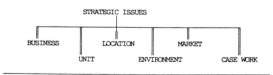

Figure 3

The third element is the questioning/guidance element developed in Quintus Prolog on the Sun 3. Given information about a student's use of the IRS, passed by the IRS via a file, this system asks a series of questions designed to test how well the student has understood and used the information in the case. Based on the answers, it provides guidance about how to

explore the data more fully or, at a certain level of knowledge, guidance on conclusions that might be drawn from the data which drew on the experimental work carried out with the expert system shell in phase I of the project. The general structure of the EXMAN system therefore follows the Roberts and Park model [13] of an intelligent instructional system with the three components:

(i)   expertise module (the content to be taught);

(ii)   student module (a mechanism for understanding the progress of student learning);

(iii)   tutoring module (the inherent teaching strategy)

This approach aims to provide individualised instruction to student learners whether using the system alone, or as a member of a case study group [14].

6.1 The user interface

The way in which the learner, whether a student or a practising manager, may wish to use the computer for expert guidance varies according to the experience and needs of the individual. The design of the user interface is crucial to the acceptance and consequently the success of the system. Expert systems must be good consultants as well as good problem solvers [15]. Conscious of this, the EXMAN interface is designed for simplicity. The student can maintain complete control of the case by merely using the keys on the computer's numeric pad.

6.2 The General Context of EXMAN Phase II

Phase II of the project was implemented in the Autumn of 1987. As in Phase I, a group of about 75 final year hotel management undergraduates were involved in the case. For this purpose, the students were divided into groups of 4 or 5 people in the previous (Summer) term. During small group sessions they then prepared a (computer analysed) critical path network for the management of their projects in the Autumn.

During the Autumn term, they were introduced to the case and were set a number of problems to solve, spread over three principal subject areas, hotel and catering management, marketing and tourism. Using the computer to explore the case, they investigated each respective issue and prepared both a written report and a verbal presentation, as required in each subject. This involved a total of 4 subject tutors, plus the research team. A fifth tutor provided extra support to deal with technical aspects of applied financial management.

7. DEVELOPMENT COSTS

The total development cost of the project so far has been in the order of £60,000. This represents the cost of the Sun hardware, the salary of one full time research officer and a proportion of the salaries of the two academic staff who constituted the balance of the development team. A small budget was also set aside to conduct a third party evaluation of the project, by the University of Surrey's Director of Computer Assisted Learning. This was designed to ensure an impartial and objective assessment to pre-empt a possible tendency to confuse sophistry with sophistication, hopefully minimising the tendency to use technology for its own sake.

8. EVALUATION

8.1 The Development Process

The Expert Manager or EXMAN project has undergone a long development period since it was commissioned in September 1985. Difficulties which have hindered the project included limited resources, difficulties in recruiting and retaining staff and problems of project management.

Against all this, when work began in earnest in February 1986, there were long periods of uncertainty, whilst objectives were defined, refined, discussed, tested and evaluated. This is characteristic of many research and development projects, particularly in CAL.

The project has formulated and tested a completely new case study as the basis of integrated management teaching in a vocational area. This material has now been formalised into a computing environment which provides expert guidance for students and management information for tutors. The case is integrally linked with standard business applications software, such as spreadsheets, database managers and word processors.

In the Autumn of 1987, this material was used as integrating course material in the final year of a vocational management degree and formally evaluated. Informal discussions with other institutions so far indicate a considerable level of potential interest in the work.

The original aims of the development were ambitious. However, all its aims have been met to some extent. In addition, the work so far has enabled the Management Studies project team to be more confident that the parameters of the problem environment are better understood. The present limitation of the project is that it currently addresses problems only in one context, that of a prospective business takeover.

Phase III of the project, now in hand, involves re-developing the case environment in an object orientated language, Smalltalk, so as to support a true frame based system. This will increase the range of problems that can be addressed and facilitate case development by trainers. The expert guidance system is also being extended in the form of several small expert systems, each capable of offering specialist advice on limited aspects of marketing, profit planning, corporate strategy, human resource management and other areas relevant to the case. Finally, a simulation program is being written in a procedural language, which will model the effect of certain decisions.

8.2 Student Views

Preliminary evaluations on phases I and II resulted in varied student opinions on the value of the expert system. There appear to be few difficulties associated with presenting the case in a computer based medium, though some still prefer a more transparent approach to both obtaining information and generating solutions. The system appears to be most useful for students who have done little preparatory work. They seem to find that EXMAN both stimulates and directs the work of the group in a positive manner. Others already well committed to an approach seemed to judge it less rewarding. However, the balance of opinion indicates that the method is viewed favourably and students welcome the opportunity to assess at first hand the potential role of expert system techniques in managerial work.

References

[1] Gamble P.R., Small Computers and Hospitality Management, Hutchinson, London, 1984.

[2] Miles W.G., Biggs W.D. & Schubert J.M., Student Perception of Skill Acquisition through Cases and General Management Simulation, Simulation and Games, vol.17, no. 1, March 1986, 7 - 24

[3] Papaloizos A. & Stiefel R., The Effectiveness of Management Teaching Methods, Management Decision, Vol 9, Summer, pp 111-121.

[4] Smith, G., The Use and Effectiveness of the Case Study Method in Management Education - A Critical Review, Management Education and Development, vol 18, part 1, Spring 1987, 51 - 61.

[5] Michie D. & Johnston R., The Creative Computer: Machine Intelligence and Human Knowledge, Pelican, Harmondsworth, 1985.

[6] Alty J.L. & Coombs M.J., Expert Systems: Concepts and Examples, NCC Publications, Manchester, 1984.

[7] Harmon P. & King D., Expert Systems: Artificial Intelligence in Business, Wiley, New York, 1985.

[8] Findley C.A., Gaming Simulation in Management Education: State of the Art, Educational Technology, January 1986, 47 - 50.

[9] Laurillard D., Computers and the Emancipation of Students: Giving Control to the Learner, Instructional Science, vol 16, 1987, 3 - 18.

[10] Goldberg A. & Robson D., Smalltalk-80: The Language and Its Implementation, Addison-Wesley, Reading Ma., 1983.

[11] Wilson B.G. & Welsh J.R., Small Knowledge Based Systems: Something New Under the Sun, Educational Technology, November 1986, 7 - 13.

[12] Dear B.L., Artificial Intelligence Techniques: Applications for Courseware Development, Educational Technology, July 1986, 7 - 15.

[13] Roberts F.C. & Park O., Intelligent Computer-Assisted Instruction: An Explanation and Overview, Educational Technology, vol 23, no. 12, 7 - 12.

[14] Yang J-S., Individualizing Instruction through Intelligent Computer Assisted Instruction: A Perspective, Educational Technology, March 1987, 7 - 15.

[15] Berry D.C. & Broadbent D.E., Expert Systems & The Man-Machine Interface. Part Two: The User Interface, Expert Systems, vol 4, no. 7, February 1987, 18 - 27.

COMPUTERS IN EDUCATION, F. Lovis and E.D. Tagg (eds.)
Elsevier Science Publishers B.V. (North-Holland)
© IFIP, 1988

Confronting Science Misconceptions: A Computer-Based Methodology

Paul Brna

Department of Artificial Intelligence
University of Edinburgh
Scotland

The starting place is the assumption that students have beliefs about the real world that conflict with the 'received' version. As these beliefs have been found to be hard to change, a methodology has been developed to confront students with inconsistencies entailed by these beliefs.

This methodology is also founded on the assumption that students need to build their own explicit models of events and situations —and that this is often best done using computer-based modelling facilities.

The approach is illustrated with reference to two physics subdomains of distinctly different character. Finally, both the advantages and disadvantages are briefly assessed.

1 STUDENTS' BELIEFS AND CONFRONTATION

During the last ten years or so there has been an increased interest in examining the belief systems that students (of all ages) bring to the investigation and learning of science topics.

There has been a move away from the domain driven approach. Early attempts to construct a teaching sequence started with the assumption that, provided the student already knew the necessary prerequisite knowledge, the task was simply to add some new skill/fact. Yet students almost always have some beliefs about a new skill or domain before it is actually taught. Again and again it has been shown that students have a fairly stable set of beliefs about the real world which are extremely difficult to uproot by teaching or through the interpretation of observations.

In the context of secondary level science education, there is an increasing number of workers who advocate a constructivist approach to students learning science <1,2,3>. There have been a large number of studies about 'misconceptions'. For example, studies have been made in the areas of heat <4>, the nature of the planet Earth <5>, the concept of Plant <6>, floating and sinking <7>, light <8>, energy <9>, gravity <10> and so on.

In this paper the term *misconception* should be understood as referring to a conception embedded in a complex net of conceptions which may not be consistent and is potentially in disagreement with scientist's science or curriculum science. Driver, <1>, is strongly associated with expounding the implications of such structures which are given the name *alternative frameworks* while the distinction between *children's science*, *scientist's science* and *curricular science* is made by Osborne *et al.* <3>.

The problem that is addressed here is how, starting from the the student's own understanding, to provide a means of encouraging students to reflect on their own assumptions and beliefs so as to promote the revision of beliefs found to be inadequate or faulty.

2 THE CONSTRUCTION OF BELIEFS

We advocate a methodology linking a confrontationist approach with a constructive one. The means to extract the constructions of the students is best encouraged through explicit model building for which computer environments have many advantages.

2.1 The Fundamental Aim

The problem is to encourage students to develop robust and explicit concepts in the scientific domain. We aim at the development of *robust* concepts in order to combat the strength of the beliefs derived from experience that students bring to their science work. We choose to encourage the development of *explicit* concepts as a necessary aspect of the route from naiveté to a reasonable level of competence for schoolchildren in the age group 14–17.

The means chosen to encourage the construction of explicit concepts is that of a reactive learning environment. The environment most suited to this approach emphasises modelling rather than the exploration of a simulation. Consequently, the agenda for a thorough discussion should include these aspects:

- The provision of simple modelling languages
- The importance of students' misconceptions
- Educational issues re: management, learning physics and modelling overheads

The first of these items is illustrated but not discussed in detail. The main interest in this paper is on the last two items.

The environment in which learning is supposed to take place includes the student (or students), the computational environment and the teacher. We also accept that both students and teachers need a variety of forms of assistance in such situations. Simple modelling environments can be strengthened by the provision of a set of integrated tools which are under the control of the student. The nature of the tools that would prove useful is of considerable interest but depends crucially on an analysis of the needs of the students.

2.2 The Motivation of the Basic Approach

The approach taken is inspired by work done within the

field of Artificial Intelligence (AI). The "Learning Mathematics through Programming" project at the Department of Artificial Intelligence, Edinburgh University was derived from the idea of students constructing a representation of their mathematical knowledge using LOGO <11,12>.

The particular areas chosen to illustrate the methodology are taken from the domain of physics. We briefly illustrate the methodology in two specific physics subdomains that can be seen as representative of different approaches to understanding. The *dynamics* domain —see section 3— stresses an understanding of process: how things are made to happen. We want students to have various models of how things change. A similar understanding is also desirable in the *electrical circuit* domain -see section 4. Yet the more common approach to circuit analysis involves the solution of a set of constraints. Students have a problem with knowing which facts are relevant and making suitable deductions. As a first approximation, this difference can be regarded as that between procedural and declarative knowledge.

2.3   The Methodology

Students should produce models which embody their beliefs about various physics concepts in an explicit way. We also mentioned our interest in helping students to develop robust models. Given that research has indicated how deeply various beliefs, and belief systems, are held, we also accept the need to *confront* students with the consequences of their beliefs. This confrontationist approach is supported by a growing number of workers (see, for example, <13>). This still leaves a number of questions unanswered —such as which of several possible confrontations should be selected and how the confrontation should be engineered.

The Misconception Test   Research results are used to derive a set of physical situations which are known to be critical. Various possible beliefs might be associated with these situations. Each situation requires a problem (or problems) to be solved. The solution of each problem is intended to be within the grasp of each student in principle, i.e., at the very least, the student has formally covered the ground in physics classes. The important point is that the solution of each problem is associated with at least one potential misconception. This ensures that students are placed in predicaments where, if they have a misconception, they might well produce an incorrect answer.

The Construction Phase   After producing a detailed response to the various problems in the *misconception test*, the student is now required to construct models of the various situations. This requires knowledge of the modelling system, the modelling process, the concept of hypothesis testing, experimental design and, finally, the requisite physics.

This is complex, so in order to reduce the difficulties, the modelling system has to be conceptually easy to use and time is needed to teach the fundamental ideas. Given that the student can adapt to the modelling environment and that suitable tools are provided, we can follow the development of crises within the modelling activity. Some of these crises are the desired confrontations with the student's

firmly held beliefs. Not every such crisis will be resolved but we hope that, even in the situations where no revolution takes place, there are possibilities that can be used to advantage.

2.4   Some Comments

It is worth noting a few points about the methodology in connection with *misconception tests*:

- They are designed in close conjunction with the modelling systems. The design of both the test and the modelling environment are intimately connected.
- These 'tests' provide opportunities to extract as much information as possible about the beliefs of the students. They are not designed to discriminate between expert and inexpert students or to provide some idea of the mastery of a topic.
- They are designed to focus on situations that are known to be associated with at least one potential misconception. Hence they should be validated in terms of how well they *confront* students' range of conceptions about some situation.
- A well designed test should encourage the students to be explicit about their comprehension of the problem and their beliefs about the situation.

The results of applying such a test provide a control on the progress of the students through the *construction phase*. This phase is designed to take the student through a construction of each of the situations found in the *misconception test*. In constructing each situation the students may echo the beliefs that surfaced in the test. It is also possible to observe the emergence of other misconceptions which had not previously appeared. A major aim is to force the student to reflect on the processes at work through the activity of modelling.

It is believed that this methodology is novel and that it can be exploited in a range of domains. It also offers an interesting approach to the use of computers in the classroom.

3   THE DYNAMICS DOMAIN

The methodology is now illustrated for the the domain of dynamics. A simple **DYN**amics **LAB**oratory called DYN-LAB was built and then used with a group of ten 15 to 16 year old students from a local boys school. All the boys had recently taken their Physics 'O' grade examination.

The methodology was applied in three distinct phases: the *misconception test*, the *introductory phase* in which the students are introduced to the features of the system and the *construction phase*:

The Misconception Test: The students were all given forty minutes to answer ten questions selected from the research literature on students' misconceptions in dynamics. The main criterion for selection was that the situation described by the question could be modelled reasonably successfully using DYNLAB. The questions were rephrased where necessary and put in a somewhat arbitrary order. The function of the test was to provide a crude assessment of the students' own models of a number of situations. This was vital in that it provided a basis for observations made in the *construction phase*.

The Construction Phase: A period of two hours was available for the next phase. During this period, the students were permitted to take as long as necessary for them to model one or more of the situations selected from the *misconception test*.

3.1 Misconception Test Results

An example problem is shown in figure 1. The design of this was prompted by a suspicion that students are not good at distinguishing distance-time graphs from displacement-time graphs. Some research indicates that younger children can confuse the actual path of the object with the graph itself <14>.

Summarising the test results: eight produced a correct response for the first part with the other two giving variations on a distance-time graph. For the second part, six were correct, two produced graphs of the magnitude of velocity against time and one produced what appeared to be a displacement-time graph having produced a distance-time graph for the first part. Only one person actually produced a graph with time *flowing backwards*.

A ball moves from A along a smooth table and hits a vertical wall at B.

The ball bounces back along the way it came.

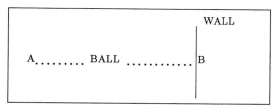

Sketch
a) The displacement-time graph
b) The velocity-time graph

Figure 1: An Example Dynamics Problem

3.2 The Construction Phase

Programming DYNLAB involves a number of stages. The problems that students encountered can be divided into three types:

- Trouble with the Diagram
- Trouble Defining the Object
- Trouble Impelling the Object

Here, we look at the first solution of 'student G' who was one of the weaker students. Some further details can be found elsewhere <15>.

Such diagrams tend to fall into three categories: standard, simplified and incorrect. A popular decision was to simplify the picture by removing any representation for the WALL. Student G used this simplification —see figure 2 for his first attempted solution in the form of a program. In defining the object, Student G failed to say anything about the mass of the ball. This leads to some difficulty with the next stage because he now has no idea of the momentum of the ball as it approaches the wall.

MAP

DISPLACEMENT (from) A (to) B
    (of) 10m (in direction) 90

JOURNEY BALL

START (at) A
VELOCITY (at) A
    (of) 1m/s (in direction) 90

FORCE BOUNCE

FORCE (name) THERE
    (of) 1N (in direction) 90
    (until magnitude of)
    DISPLACEMENT (is) 10m
ACTS (on) BALL
KICK (name) BACK (at) B
    (of) 5Ns (in direction) 270

Figure 2: Student G's First Attempt at EIGHT

In defining how the ball is impelled, Student G added a force that accelerated the ball but only until it reached the wall. He took some time to realise that the kick he gave had slowed up the object kicked but he was surprised when it was suggested that this object had been accelerating. To solve the problem he did not remove the accelerating force —just increased the KICK.

The graphs were interpreted satisfactorily despite his inability to correctly generate either of the required graphs during the test.

4 THE ELECTRICAL CIRCUIT DOMAIN

Next, we illustrate the methodology for the domain of simple electrical circuits. A simple electrical circuit modelling environment called ELAB was built and used with two groups from the same local boys' school as before —one group of four 15 to 16 year old students and the other of four students in the school year above.

The same basic methodology was applied. This time, however, each student's work was split into four parts —the extra part being a *project phase* during which the students completed six very simple projects. Also, during the *construction phase*, students were to model all the circuits used in the *misconception test* —in whatever order they chose. We concentrate here, as before, on the *misconception test* and the *construction phase*.

4.1   Misconception Test Results

Here, we focus on the single question illustrated in figure 3 which was selected from a paper by Johnstone and Mughol <16>.

This would seem to be a very straightforward factual recall question. Nevertheless only four students out of eight produced a completely correct response, i.e., selected option c) as correct and stated that the other three were incorrect.

The clue to the popularity of this option may well lie in a context trigger —the word *parallel*. Students may associate the concept of *equality of potential differences* with the trigger word *parallel*.

The most popular misconception seemed to be that the functional requirement for the Iron and Toaster was that they should have identical currents. This suggests the belief that the objects are wired in series. Although the students should have realised that the objects were wired in parallel, the diagram does not indicate a clear *prototypical* instance of two objects wired in parallel. It is easy enough to interpret the diagram so that the toaster and iron are wired in series.

An alternative account of why some students opted for choice a) is that they may believe that devices require certain currents to flow and that if a device needs a current then

---

The two appliances are wired to the mains parallel with each other so that they may have the same

    a) Current in them
    b) Operating temperature
    c) Voltage across them
    d) Power supplied to them

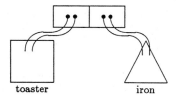

Figure 3: An Example Electrical Circuit Problem

---

it draws it. This might be given the name *wants-current—gets-current*. Such a misconception is an instantiation of a class of misconceptions along the lines that "if a device wants or needs a certain amount of X to work properly then it gets that amount of X".

Of the options proffered, b) proved unpopular and, although offering a plausible function for electricity in the

case of the objects (iron and toaster), the students seemed to realise that the argument did not generalise.

Option d) would seem to be more plausible. Certainly Johnstone and Mughol claim that this option is the most 'powerful' distractor. Students are often informed that electrical energy can be converted to other forms —including mechanical energy. Here, we may have an instance of the misconception *wants-power—gets-power*.

4.2   The Construction Phase

The remaining set of errors can be categorised as connected with methodological problems and with beliefs about various electrical concepts. The categories connected with methodological problems include: lack of realism, too much realism, failure to confirm the effects of changes, failure to control variables properly and failure to interpret data correctly.

We can also examine the beliefs connected with electrical concepts in relation to: the circuit, electrical relationships and 'basic' concepts. Here, we briefly look at some problems connected with the basic circuit definition.

During the discussion of the example question in section 4.1, it was suggested that some students might have believed that the iron and toaster were wired in series despite the clear statement that they were wired in parallel. Two students had opted for the two objects having the same current —student B and student E. In the *construction phase*, student B made two separate attempts to model the situation and both times he constructed a series circuit. Student E had other problems in connection with controlling the variables in his circuit.

Student A initially put the iron and toaster in series. He, realising his error, decided not to rewire. He chose to represent one object by two resistors and proceeded to add two more resistors on a parallel arm. Such a move is difficult to follow but can be detected provided the onlooker is prepared to try mapping the student's circuit on to the one required.

5   DISCUSSION

In short, experience in using both DYNLAB and ELAB suggests that it is practical to require students to build and run models. Various misconceptions reported in the literature were re-examined in connection with the use of both DYNLAB and ELAB and their widespread occurrence further confirmed. These systems proved to have a number of specific benefits in detecting certain classes of problems.

Apart from the specific ways in which the particular systems proved to be of use there are four aspects of more general interest: the underlying physics, the modelling phase, experimental methodology and interpretation of data. We do not pursue further, deeper analysis here. It is worth noting, however, that there are classes of problems that manifest themselves in the explicit model built by the student —an example of a faulty model was presented in section 3.2. There are also classes of problems that can be spotted by the vigilant teacher (of which some could be handled by more intelligent systems) —methodological problems often fall into this category. Finally, there are some problems for which the application of the methodology proved to be inadequate —the obvious example are problems connected with beliefs about current behaviour which could not easily be detected using ELAB.

5.1 The Place of Modelling in Education

Modelling environments specialised for specific domains can be used in a way that fits in with the current physics curricula. There are, however, a number of advantages in the use of such environments that do not fit in at all well: the exploration of inadequate or 'incorrect' models and the transition from one model to a new one. The problem lies in recognising a curriculum need —that a less than ideal model is still a subject for explicit, possibly qualitative, exploration.

The curriculum implications are summarised in relation to the wider implications only:

- Redundant physics principles may be a way of saving time in the coverage of the curriculum material but do not promote a robust understanding of principles. A good example is the rule for obtaining no current in a typical Wheatstone bridge problem.

- The exploration of 'bad' models needs a place in the curriculum. The curriculum process might, however, tend to 'freeze' the description of what inadequate, or incorrect, models should be explored. The provision of a modelling environment gives greater scope for flexible curriculum development.

- The design of misconception 'tests' and practical work based on them is feasible and needs further exploration to assess the effectiveness and suitability for building such work into the standard curriculum.

In the classroom, modelling environments can be used successfully in traditional ways: setting up demonstrations, testing students' experimental methodology, and so on. On the other hand, modelling environments have several other functions:

- Enabling the exploration of the implications of incomplete or incorrect models

- Aiding the construction and performance of critical experiments

- Exposing underlying misconceptions

- Allowing for the construction of new models from old

Each of these aspects requires the teacher to possess special skills. In order, for example, to encourage the exploration of a given model the teacher will need to be aware of the class(es) of models that can be constructed. Sometimes the teacher will not know the implications of a model built by the student. Sometimes the student might know more about the current model than the teacher. This means that the teacher may have to adopt an unaccustomed rôle —she or he must be prepared to help the student design a research program to explore the model. To do this, the teacher must be willing to accept the student's model for what it is and think carefully about whether, or when, woeful inadequacies

should be pointed out.

The student is confronted with a requirement to learn a complex system. The underlying vocabulary of modelling any system has to be learned. The student needs to participate in modelling all aspects of the situation —both the structure and the behaviour of models. In order for this to work, students are needed who are mature enough to handle the concept of alternative physical theories.

5.2 Weaknesses of the Historical Approach

In the educational research literature there is frequent comment about the similarity between student's misconceptions and previous scientific theories. For example, Osborne and Freyberg quote a nineteenth century explanation by Ampère of the behaviour of electricity in a simple circuit that matches well with their own *clashing currents* model <17>. Similar statements have been made by a variety of workers about the nature of misconceptions about simple dynamics <18,19,20,21>.

Parallels of this kind are often suggested to justify a particular approach to *scientific epistemology*, i.e., students' scientific understanding recapitulates the development of scientific ideas through recent history.

If a commitment is now added to teaching through confrontation, a possible teaching program is defined: identify the current theory held by the student, determine its weaknesses, devise experiments for which the student's theory predicts observations in conflict with those of the 'correct' theory and require that the student explore and explain these differences in some way.

There is, however, a major difficulty with identifying the 'current theory'. In order to simplify teaching practice it is necessary to provide a fixed, small set of possible theories. The teacher has to make the decision as to which theory is owned by which student. There are several practical difficulties:

- The teacher may be forced to design learning experiences and/or course material for the 'best' alternative theory for the class. The best may be the median alternative theory, in which case the teacher has to know the current beliefs for the whole class. In practice, teachers may be guided by statistical evidence of the form provided by Osborne and Freyberg regarding the age distribution of certain theories <17>.

- In order to provide individualised learning experiences, the teacher may have to make many assessments of the current theory held by each student —it may well be difficult to keep in touch with the student's development.

- Even if it is possible to identify which of the possible alternative theories the student possesses, it will then prove difficult to find the variations of the basic theory actually held by the student.

6 CONCLUSION

The methodology described in this paper is potentially more flexible than that described in section 5 as the *historical* approach. Students are provided with modelling facilities which enable the construction of a high level description of their current beliefs. The system has to convert the high level description into a runnable program which can perform the required simulation. A mechanism is then needed that can compare the student's high level description with some standard description of the 'correct' theorem.

From the set of differences it might be desirable for the system to construct a set of experiments that will yield differences in observations between the two theories. If the system is able to suggest problems that the student might wish to solve, the student can be confronted with evidence contradictory to the student's beliefs.

The advantages that such a modelling approach brings include:

- The model built by the student can, as a first approximation, be regarded as the current theory that the student holds.
- The system can handle changes in the student's model.

We have sought to provide: a methodology for confronting science misconceptions, further evidence for the widespread nature of fundamental misconceptions and a demonstration that modelling provides some (partial) solutions. In addition, we have considered the context of the educational process and it has been argued that the modelling approach provides advantages that cannot as easily be provided by the classroom teacher.

ACKNOWLEDGEMENT

The work described here is based on an unpublished PhD thesis <22> and was supported in part by a studentship from the ESRC. My thanks are due to Professor Jim Howe and Dr Peter Ross for their supervision.

REFERENCES

<1> R. Driver. Pupil's alternative frameworks in science. *European Journal of Science Education*, vol. 3, no. 1, 1981, 93–101.

<2> R. Driver. *The Pupil as Scientist?* Open University Press, 1983.

<3> R.J. Osborne, B.F. Bell, and J.K. Gilbert. Science teaching and children's views of the world. *European Journal of Science Education*, vol. 5, no. 1, 1983, 1–14.

<4> G. Erickson. Children's conception of heat and temperature. *Science Education*, vol. 63, no. 2, 1979, 221–230.

<5> J. Nussbaum and J. Novak. An assessment of children's concepts of the earth utilising structured interviews. *Science Education*, vol. 60, no. 4, 1976, 535–550.

<6> B.F. Bell. What is a plant? some children's ideas. *New Zealand Science Teacher*, vol. 31, 1981, 10–14.

<7> J.A. Rowell and C.J. Dawson. Teaching about floating and sinking: an attempt to link cognitive psychology with classroom practice. *Science Education*, vol. 61, no. 2, 1977, 245–253.

<8> D.M. Watts. Student conceptions of light: a case study. *Physics Education*, vol. 20, no. 4, 1985, 183–187.

<9> J. Soloman. Learning about energy: how pupils think in two domains. *European Journal of Science Education*, vol. 5, no. 1, 1983, 49–59.

<10> S. Ruggiero, A. Cartelli, F. Duprè, and M. Vicentini-Missoni. Weight, gravity and air pressure: mental representations by Italian middle school pupils. *European Journal of Science Education*, vol. 7, no. 2, 1985, 181–194.

<11> J.A.M. Howe and B. du Boulay. *Teaching Mathematics through LOGO Programming: An Evaluation Study.* Research Paper 115, Department of Artificial Intelligence, Edinburgh, 1979.

<12> J.A.M. Howe, P.M. Ross, K.R. Johnson, F. Plane, and R. Inglis. Teaching mathematics through programming in the classroom. *Computers in Education*, vol. 6, 1982, 85–91.

<13> A.I. Zeitman and P.W. Hewson. Effect of instruction using microcomputer simulations and conceptual change strategies on science learning. *Journal of Research in Science Teaching*, vol. 23, no. 1, 1986, 27–39.

<14> S.E. Avons, M.C. Beveridge, A.T. Hickman, and G.J. Hitch. *Effects of Spatial Correspondence and An Experimental Study. Degree of Interaction.* Technical Report, Department of Education and Department of Psychology, Manchester University, 1981.

<15> P. Brna. *Confronting Dynamics Misconceptions.* Research Paper 356, Department of Artificial Intelligence, University of Edinburgh, 1987.

<16> A.H. Johnstone and A.R. Mughol. The concept of electrical resistance. *Physics Education*, vol. 13, no. 1, 1978, 46–49,.

<17> R.J. Osborne and P. Freyberg. *Learning in Science: The Implications of Children's Science.* Heinemann, 1985.

<18> A. diSessa. Unlearning Aristotelian physics: a study of knowledge based learning. *Cognitive Science*, vol. 6, no. 2, 1982, 37–75.

<19> J. Clement. A conceptual model discussed by Galileo and used intuitively by physics students. In D. Gentner and A. Stevens, editors, *Mental Models*, Lawrence Erlbaum Press, 1983.

<20> M. McCloskey. Naive theories of motion. In D. Gentner and A. Stevens, editors, *Mental Models*, Lawrence Erlbaum Press, 1983.

<21> L. Viennot. Analysing students' reasoning in science: a pragmatic view of theoretical problems. *European Journal of Science Education*, vol. 7, no. 2, 1985, 151–162.

<22> P. Brna. *Confronting Science Misconceptions with the Help of a Computer.* PhD thesis, Department of Artificial Intelligence, University of Edinburgh, 1987.

COMPUTERS IN EDUCATION, F. Lovis and E.D. Tagg (eds.)
Elsevier Science Publishers B.V. (North-Holland)
© IFIP, 1988

COMPUTER IN DEVELOPMENT STIMULATION

M.A. Balaban* and T.Gergely** and L.Kálmán ***

*Computation Center of Moscow State University,Lenin Hills, Moscow, USSR
**Computing Applications and Service Co.,P.O.Box 146, Budapest 1502, HUNGARY
***Foreign Trade College, Chair of English,Budapest ,HUNGARY

Ardent computerizers do not take into account some inherent limitations, predetermined by the Rationalist origin of modern "form-lesson-subject" (FLS) educational mechanism, functioning as a regular semi-automaton, designed to be served by a non-professional operator (teacher). Invented in the XVII.c. by Y. Comenius for mass-teaching literacy, the FLS-automaton is used (like its prototype - the flourmill) - for simultaneously *processing* a homogenous group of pupils (Form) during a fixed period (Lesson) with special instrument texts on a (Subject), in order to get the product, automatically determined by the examination sieve. Hypertrophy of formal "knowledge" in FLS-automaton for semiotic processing human beings is circularly connected with the explosive growth of its semantic and pragmatic periphery - science and industry. Its further computerizing will only increase the detrimental effect of "processing humans". And the way out of this vicious circle is in the opposite direction - to break the monopoly of the FLS-automaton in education by an alternative and much less bureaucratic educative automaton that would provide its user with adequate intellectual "food" direct experience for natural, but rapid, development of needed skills. Our experiments have shown that specially designed "trophic educational games" might do the job.

1. ORIGINS OF MODERN EDUCATIONAL MECHANISM AND ORGANISM

H. G. Wells was not the first (and by far - not the last) to warn us that "human history becomes more and more a race between education and catastrophe". As many other progressists, Wells believed in the *eternal* value of Enlightenment, although the fundamental ideology of modern mass education, based on Form-Lesson-Subject (FLS) technology of schooling, was elaborated by Y.A. Comenius only about three centuries ago. Up to now his "Magna Didactica" remains the principal operational basis for investigations in this field, in spite of the fact that there is nothing more in it than a kind of *operator's instruction* for a FLS teacher.

So, it may well happen that the ultimate cause of the impending doom is skilfully concealed by the more "positive" notion of FLS- education. It is universally regarded as one of the most beneficial features of our civilization. But as this beneficial FLS - school automatically promotes scientism, we are all inevitably fostered in it. Thus, irrespective of our moral beliefs and spiritual preferences, practically everybody regards propagation of "knowledge" the principal aim of any education, while really it is only a recent invention closely connected with FLS-school.

Nobody knows what this "objective knowledge" is, but we all manage to teach it to our pupils and students in an interim form of a *text*, in which it somehow resides. The texts are said to contain (more or less terminologically codified) information.

In most cases this "information" (about the "objective world") is formulated as a sort of calculus - nomenclature of items and a number of rules, according to which one can easily manipulate those items in a computational way. These computational procedures with elements of different calculi (representing different school-subjects) are supposed to model, in FLS-schooling, the activity of human mind, reason, intelligence, etc.

Numerous proponents of such a computational model of human mind, beginning with Plato, Cartesius, Hobbs, Leibnitz and ending with K.Popper [10], and S.Papert [11], have never clamed that it is a complete operational description of human intellectual activity. But, evidently following the example of the anecdotal drunkard (who looked for his lost key under the lamp post, only because "it was lighter" there), this mechanistic *metaphor is widely used as an operational model of learning.* Together with a few controversial admonitions concerning pupils' souls and emotions, this model constitutes a kind of *theoretical foundation,* not only for current pedagogical and psychological studies, but also for analysis of perspectives in education, especially those connected with its computerizing. This utterly inconsistent approach explains the impotence of cognitive science, doomed to inefficient dabbling with its notorious subject-matter that is constantly "rising in complexity". We think that such a situation is a symptom of "culturally-induced" fallacy, that has been and still is engendered by the FLS-school.

2. FLS-SCHOOL- A SEMI-AUTOMATON DESIGNED FOR NON-PROFESSIONAL USERS

Being a miller`s son, Y.Comenius might be completely unaware that he had skilfully adapted the flourmill technological scheme, while creating such a reliable system of primary school that could meet the requirements of the religious Reformation. Having abolished the corpus of professional spiritual leaders (the priests of Catholic (church) the Reformation had to solve a rather controversial problem. It was necessary to provide every member of the congregation with the ability of "direct access to the data" in the Holy Scripture, i.e. to teach them literacy, but without creating a new caste of spiritual professionals. The problem was brilliantly solved by Comenius, who proposed a very cheap and simple social mechanism that can be quite an effective instrument in the hands of a non-professional user. Any literate person, possessing neither theoretical information, nor experience in education, could successfully teach literacy (and now - practically any other school-subject), following several simple instructions.

It is interesting to note that nowadays a similar set of technical problems connected with "computer- literacy" and "direct access" for the unprofessional computer-user is supposed to be solved by means of the "dialogue in a natural language". In Luther`s time the Protestants also hoped to solve all such problems by translating the Bible into the vernacular.

In spite of its apparent simplicity, the FLS-automaton has some latent fundamental features that can be revealed only by a sort of genetic analysis. For example, the structure of the school-group (form) of pupils seems to be an independent variable, because any configuration of subgroups is practically possible, although, as a rule, they do not work, due to a very rigid structure of the form. But this property is easily realized, only if we recall that the structure ot its prototype - the grain portion processed by the mill-stones - is rigidly horizontal as predetermined by the grinder. In this context the class of pupils looks much more uniform in its absolutely "horizontal" structure, formed by the mere presence of the grinder-teacher and enforced by all the teaching procedures.

The mechanical nature of FLS-school is disguised by the fact that the mechanism is used for processing human beings without evident violence or bloodshedding. So the pupil, being actually used as raw-material from which the end product (or by-product) should be produced, is often wrongly considered to be the "user" of the school mechanism. This widely spread fallacy (about the pupil coming to school by his own free will to obtain some "useful knowledge") is evidently connected with the image of ante-Comenian school - medieval European university. But being constantly preached to the utterly subjected students of compulsory FLS-schools of all academic ranks, it finally becomes a major hindrance for realistic analysis of educational systems. No amendment in the curriculum ot methods of teaching can change the subjected status of the student in the FLS-system of education.

No significant change in such original state can be produced by introducing the ability of " freechoice" of the subjects to study, as is done in British grammar schools or some colleges in the USA. Equally futile are all the hopes that some sort of intricate audio-visual technical aid or a computerized course will drastically increase the efficiency of FLS-schooling. You cannot seriously increase the productivity of an automaton by painting anew the push-buttons or by accompanying its work with the recording of the best symphonic orchestra.

Like many other semi-automatic (i.e. requiring a human operator) devices, the FLS-school secures its mass production by *uniformly processing a homogenized group of* pupils (the school-form). Every micro-, macro- or mega-round of processing (every lesson, term, schoolyear, etc.) is followed by a kind of *group-test* on the appropriate examination sieve. It should be done for constantly homogenizing the interim product, arranged (for the convenience of its processing" on various subjects" by different grinder-teachers) in absolutely horizontal structures of school-forms.

An experienced technician can easily predict that in such an arrangement, there must be a kind of "primary" subject, whose regime of processing would predetermine the methods and constants of all the other "secondary" or "tertiary" academic subjects in an FLS-school. Any deviation from primary technology should be mercilessly stamped out as an obstacle for efficient mass-production, thus securing not only stability, but a kind of sacredness of the original construction described in "Magna Didactica"

3. TOWARDS THE NEW SYNTHESIS IN EDUCATION

Formulating a consistent set of the alternative (to "evident" Platonian conventions) operational principles for a more natural kind of education is a hard task. It proved to be as cumbersome as an attempt to produces something like a "new synthesis" in the cognitive science. We are forced to reshuffle a lot of "petrified severances" that have long ago become a sort of *absolute scientific values*. It happens mainly due to almost universal "verbal (terminological) commitment" of modern science to neoplatonian ideology (cf.Kayre' [7]). The classical way to avoid making havoc of conflicting (but consistent) models is the presentation of one of them as an extreme variation of another. The metaphor of "petrified severances" is just based on the assumption of this kind: all the fundamental scientific notions are but consecutively arranged personal views on the organization of this world. They stand for "objective laws of nature" only conventionally, being universally accepted by the scientific society.

Plato's objective idealism, quite beneficial for studying "inert nature" by modern science, has led to a mechanistically perverse reduction of all the s*ubjective* features of human knowledge.

Accordingly, the subjective idealism of Aristotle might be equally beneficial for adequate study of the "subjective world", where all the problems of education belong. (Gaines-Show [3], Marchetti [8]). Our attempt to create a modern version of the Aristotelean cognitive theory (Balaban [1]), was based on that often neglected fundamental assumption of the subjective idealism. The Stagirite's closed and completely preorganized Cosmos should be regarded as an extreme in the development of the utterly *subjective image* of the world, into which one is born. So, one's personal experience may be represented as gradual, hierarchic *articulation* (severance) of this world (Gaines-Show [3]), which is much less articulate (organized) at the beginning of one's life than at the end.

In this "organic" perspective of multi-dimensional articulation of one's personal closed, but infinite Cosmos, the FLS-schooling occupies a specific position. It stimulates the development of either a genuine skill to produce "linear articulation" of the non-linear world, or (with the majority of those who cannot assume it properly) - some practical skills for formal imitation of "learning". Genuine rationalism, that FLS-educationalists are forced to profess, is not detrimental, unless it is obtruded upon the whole generation by means of compulsory education in FLS-schools, the term of which now already exceeds 10 years. Serious investigations have confirmed the opinion maintained by many humanitarians [6], that so extensive a FLS-schooling may be harmful for the personality of the pupil: not more than 2% of the population can stand this lasting processing without considerable moral or intellectual losses   So, in this respect, the FLS-system is not idling at all.

But if this detrimental effect of FLS-education can really be explained by its inherent trend improperly to generalize a specific form of "world articulation", there is an obvious way out. It seems to be effective, although neither immediate nor direct. As any other powerful bureaucratic system of cultural administration (that always degenerates, but never shrinks), the FLS-school can be neither amended, nor abolished, as they have tried to do during the "cultural revolution" in China. European cultures are still more dependent on this FLS-narcotic: even mass production of the elementary "3 Rs+" (reading, writing and arithmetic + a lot of hypocritical conformity in perception) can now be adequately provided only within the frame of the FLS-mechanism, without which its generators are helpless. We can rely only on gradual inner shifts of the system ,that can be induced by proper simulation.

There are some reasons to expect, that being adequately simulated, the FLS-system of education has a chance to regenerate into a more benefical social organism, if it loses its absolute monopoly and begins to compete. But it may happen, if there is an alternative educative force that would be able to rehabilitate such more natural cultural values as nonverbal skills, etc. This "New Synthesis" in education may come true, if the stimulating force is:

(1) organically (i.e.- mainly genetically) pedagogical by nature;

(2) much *more efficient* in teaching than any form of normal practice in the skill;

(3) sufficiently *automatic* to secure "mass production" of skills, that might stand competition with the formal knowledge of FLS-schools.

4.   A TROPHIC PERSPECTIVE OF COMPUTERIZED EDUCATION

Theoretic analysis, as well as several machine-experiments, has provided ample evidence that technologically the COMPUTER GAMES are fit for the task. If they were supplied with adequate abilities for simulation (Goncalvess-Mendes [4], Hall-Layman [5]), and oral production of speech commentary (Nakatam et al [9]), computer games could meet all the requirements for a proper automatic instrumental system, that might constitute the core of the alternative pedagogy for the post-industrial society.

Playing games seems incompatible with the hard work of learning that is constantly preached by the proponents of FLS-education. But the harder this work becomes, the poorer are its results, because, originally ,schooling had nothing to do with the severely restricted and painful activities that the notion of "work" implies. The true original meaning of the Greek "skhole" is LEISURE, understood even in those times as the situation of maximum freedom. Giving this name to an educational establishment, they stressed the fact, that the actual development of a personality may take place only in the conditions of non-restricted ability for self-expression.

Only a game, modelling a real situation, and not competing (officially) with formal instruction, can afford to supply the learner with normal "food" for his harmonious (intellectual, perceptual and even physical) development. FLS-food is rather harmful for normal trophic processes of the human mind. It contains mainly pre-digested ingredients, such as departmentalized (by scientific calculi and terminology and rather randomly organized) descriptions of separate objects, events and phenomena.

Only in an intelligent and quite fair game may an individual afford a really "risky" action. In a good educational computer game one will be not only allowed, but even prompted and encouraged to such normal trophic "risky" procedures of producing his own, quite *original severance*, perceptual articulation of the world. Such natural risk is as beneficial for intellectual maturation as any other kind of actual and natural trophic diet. If one's risky action in a computer game is inconsistent with the situation (i.e.- with life and nature, which it models), the pupil-player will loose a round, a game, etc. but neither his face nor his self-esteem, as happens at a school-lesson.

Just that feeling of "safe risk" contributes to creating the well-known state of "open mind" - very favourable for the assimilation of intellectual food. Thus, a computer game, that provides ample opportunities for such safe risk, is a mighty impetus for efficient learning ,which is an aspect of natural adaptive development. The naturality of this trophic procedure is clearly manifested not only by rapid development of the skills, but also by their stability: they cannot be "forgotten", because they have never been memorized. Our experiments have convincingly demonstrated a very high efficiency of such "trophic" learning procedures. Whenever a learner was given a chance and properly encouraged "to risk in safety", the learning efficiency was multiplied. This effect was much less noticeable when the object of learning was some kind of normal "knowledge" (explicitly formulated rules, formulae, texts, etc.) and not a kind of more or less natural skill (Balaban[1]).

This very important limitation predetermines the strategy of mainly extra curricular circulation of the courseware for such Trophic Educational Games (TEG). Thus, avoiding any direct confrontation with either "contents" of FLS-learning or its methods, TEG can gain its own specific position in modern education. In order to survive and develop, TEG-learning should not trespass upon the realm of the FLS-system of academic" knowledge. Otherwise, it will be quite automatically (i.e. without any evil will) stamped out, as has been done with all the efficient competitors of the FLS-system. Just one example: about 200 years ago, Bell and Lancaster proposed a very efficient system of schooling, which broke the "horizontal" structure of the school-form. Pupils gained their "knowledge" (or rather - adequate experience) by means of adequate real practice - imparting it to the "younger ones". The impeachment of all such attempts was consistent only with the notions of FLS-fallacy, but up to now it reads:"they try to replace one good (?) teacher by several bad ones".

Keeping all that in mind, we have decided to create the first generation of TEG-courses for teaching a subject of very low academic rank - the foreign language (FL), which is much more of a natural skill than the calculus (of vocabulary and grammar) taught at FLS-school. TEG-ideology automatically excludes any confrontation: TEG-course in FL provides a proper FL-skill by means of *gaining experience* in FL-intercourse, which can be organized without taking into account the previous formal "knowledge" of the FL to be taught (Balaban-Gergely-Kálmán [2]).

5. SOME POSSIBLE CONSEQUENCES OF TEG-EDUCATION

It is evident that in the middle of the XVII.c nobody expected that the success of the humble, simple and cheap Comenian FLS-school might result in a major change in the culture of our civilization. We hope that neither will anybody (influential in education) suspect that TEG-automata might bring a significant change in social mentality. But the professional analysis of possible consequence (if our hypothesis on the role of the mass-school is correct) provides a lot of serious evidence in favour of this. Some significant and positive modifications in the material and spiritual culture of the society will inevitably occur under the influence of indirect competition of the FLS-school with the TEG-education.

The major cultural effect of the Comenian school was connected with the "democratic" nature of the FLS-automaton in two respects: practically anyone (who is literate) could serve as a FLS-teacher- operator, as well as anyone, who is a "normal human being" (i.e. without any outstanding abilities), could stand the FLS-processing, thus getting the appropriate "education". Only now has it become evident that such a combination of "accessibility merits" in one social mechanism must inevitably lead to a "circle of degradation", reflected, in particular, by the effects of "mass culture", environment pollution, consumer society, etc.

TEG-automaton will have to break that vicious circle because of the mere fact that nobody would ever use it if the factual, logical or figurative contents of the computer game are still expressed in the verbal or graphical forms of the boring

scientistic *"codificate"* used in the textbooks. To be a success, the educational computer game is doomed to be "artistic", i.e. its contents should be expressed in verbal, graphical or any other form of *"phenomenated"* characteristic for the works of art. Including the professionals of communication (artists, writers, actors, etc.) in the active pedagogical force, we diminish the demerits of excessive circular "democracy" in education.

A really good courseware, such as a prominent work of art, like an outstanding film, novel, etc.) will not only multiply the effectivity of learning, it will cure the post-industrial society of a number of its intellectual deficiencies. We have already observed a marked psychotherapeutic effect of many trophic procedures that will be simulated by TEGP-automata. And just this aspect of TEGP-learning warns us against hasty administrative measures of "rapid development and introduction" that might only compromise the TEGP-approach, we are advocating for.

But, on the other hand, no masterpiece in the field of TEGP-courseware will ever be created in the absence of developed hardware which has already been extensively used for just this purpose of TEGP-education. This consideration predetermines our plan of developing and perfectioning hardware and software for TEGP-automata in the course of exploiting the most primitive types of it in the practice of learning the foreign languages. In this branch of schooling,there is a good tradition of trophic learning (referred to as the natural or intuitive method). On the other hand, there are no preconcieved ideas as to the *contents* of the texts to be   ideal in FL-learning, while in all the other respectable branches of knowledge there is a traditional assortment of such texts, that are considered to contain the FUNDAMENTAL, essential elements of the science.

Thus, having created even a primitive version of TP-automaton for trophic instruction in foreign languages (TIFL-automaton) we shall obtain a powerful instrumental complex enabling us to investigate didactic, computational, linguistic and engineering problems of the trophic computerization of education. As every possible kind of multi-language precedential data-base is substantially convertible, TIFL-automata, even of the most primitive sort (a computer-game with coordinated tape-recorder one of oral commentary in a couple of languages) must be a commercial success due to its convertibility. It will be useful for those millions of its potential consumers who have in vain wasted a lot of time at school, "studying" a modern language or even two of them. It is most important that quite a modest aim of receiving "painless and even joyful practice" in the language that one presumably KNOWS (but "has forgotten" due to lack of practice) will help to overcome one of the greatest psychological obstacles in the way of TP-education. That is the almost physical necessity to have somewhere (in the memory?) "the objective knowledge", i.e. something quite palpable, like words, rules, texts, etc. Just in this respect, K.R. Popper [11], reflects something quite real in our culture. This objectivized notion of human knowledge, created by Vertical processing-schooling, not only makes us undervalue all sorts of non-verbalized (and noverbalizable) knowledge, but really lowers quite markedly one's ability to learn, when it is impossible to see discrete substantial object-like entities (codes), to be retained by the memory. TEGP-learning (in which the phenomena stand for the codificate of Verbal processing-pseudolearning), seems a kind of a mystical trick for a modern primitive realist. So he does not *believe* in all that "stuff", and like any disbeliever, becomes in this respect really deaf and dumb. TIFL-automata, on the contrary, will have an army of *believing* and that's why- successful users.

REFERENCES

[1] Balaban, M.A.,Linguistic Data in Automatized Systems. (Moscow University Press, Moscow,1985).

[2] Balaban, M.A., Gergely ,T., and Kálmán, L., Development stimulation in computer based foreign language teaching, in: Moonen, J. and Plomp,T.(eds.) Development in Educational Software and Courseware, (Pergamon Press, Oxford, 1987) pp.75-80.

[3] Gaines, B.R. and Show, M.L., A learning model for forecasting the future of information technology, Future Computing Systems, vol. (1986) No.1. pp.31-69.

[4] Goncalves,M.E. and Mendes T., Teaching simulation, in: Moonen,J. and Plomp, T(eds.), Developments in Educational Software and Courseware, (Pergamon Press, Oxford, (1987) pp.143-147.

[5] Hall, W. and Layman, J. Implementing problem solving in the curriculum using computer simulation. in: Moonen, J. and Plomp, T.(eds.),Developments in Educational Software and Courseware. (Pergamon Press, Oxford, 1987) pp.361-367.

[6] Illych, I., Deschooling Society. (Penguin, London, 1974).

[7] Koyré, A., Études d'historie de la pensée philosophique (Armand Colin, Paris, 1961).

[8] Marchetti, L., Society as a Learning System, Report RR-79-13.

[9] Nakatani, L.H., Egan,D., Ruedisueli, L.,Hawley,P. and Lewart, D., TNT: an automated 'N' trainer using synthetic speech and mastery learning pedagogy, in: Monnen,J. and Plomp, T.(eds.), Developments in Educational Software and Courseware (Pergamon Press, Oxford, 1987) pp.163-169.

[10] Papert, S., Mindstorms: Children, Computers and Powerful Ideas (Basic Books, New York,1980).

[11] Popper, K.R., Objective Knowledge (Oxford,University Press, Oxford, 1975).

COMPUTERS IN EDUCATION, F. Lovis and E.D. Tagg (eds.)
Elsevier Science Publishers B.V. (North-Holland)
© IFIP, 1988

COMPUTER ORIENTED ATTITUDES AS A FUNCTION OF AGE IN AN ISRAELI ELEMENTARY SCHOOL SAMPLE

Yaacov J. Katz and Baruch Offir

School of Education, Bar-Ilan University, Ramat Gan, Israel

This study examined the relationship between students' age and computer oriented attitudes, namely, computer motivation, computer effectiveness and computer transfer as perceived by elementary school students. Additionally, the connection between extra-curricular computer programming undertaken by students and computer oriented attitudes was investigated.

Students' responses to the research questionnaire yielded two significant factors, namely computer motivation and computer effectiveness. An analysis of the data obtained in the study indicates that there is a definite hierarchical relationship between a student's age and computer motivation and effectiveness. Also, extra-curricular computer programming lessons were found to have a significantly positive effect on students' perception of the computer as an instrument that can be successfully used in many fields of educational endeavour.

1. INTRODUCTION

Learning theories indicate that it is most important for the learner actively to confront the subject matter on his own so as to facilitate the establishment of a schema of the subject matter as well as to remember the material [1]. The fact that the computer is considered an instrument which may be used to analyze learning achievement and has the capacity to produce speedy feedback to the learner [2], is the basis for the popular thesis that the computer can and must be utilized in the instructional process as well as in individualized learning [3-4].

Research studies have indicated that the student develops thought processes, problem solving ability and learning proficiency as more years are spent within the school framework. The increments in these fields correlate positively with an increase in the student's self-study ability and negatively with a need for assistance from a teacher. The teacher adds experience, interpersonal expertise and balanced decision-making to the learning process for the benefit of the student, but as the student develops, dependency on the teacher diminishes [5]. Therefore it may be inferred that with the passage of time the student refines self-learning ability and dependence on teachers for facts and information diminishes. Any system, such as the school computer, which provides a stimulating alternative to the teacher may be perceived as a worthwhile and satisfactory substitute.

However the expectation that the computer would become an especially effective instrument integrated into the teaching process, has thus far not been satisfactorily fulfilled [4,6-8]. The reasons for the failure to integrate the computer successfully in the instructional process are not as yet clear. There are a number of suggestions as to why the computer has not yet been fully utilized in schools. There is no uniformity in the use of educational software. Neither is there any uniformity in the use of hardware [9]. As a result it has become increasingly difficult to arrive at an acceptable theory that can provide answers regarding ways to integrate the computer in teacher based instruction as well as how students can optimally utilize the computer in the learning process [10].

Schools do not appear to have the ability to absorb the rapid ongoing developments in technology oriented teaching aids. Many schools have adopted computer assisted instruction as a direct result of pressure brought to bear by parents, inspectors and the educational authorities without really being able to utilize these computers satisfactorily. The decision making process in schools is highly subjective and as a result it is most difficult to implement some of these decisions, especially those dealing with modern technology, a field far removed from the expertise of the majority of school administrators [11-12].

The educational establishment, now more than ever, needs to concentrate on applied research regarding those variables relating the computer with instructional and learning processes. Once these processes are better understood, hypotheses regarding instruction, learning and their inter-relationship with computers may be advanced and tested for the benefit of teachers and students alike [9,13-34]. The computer will then be utilized only in those areas where empirical evidence suggests that it is a suitable teaching or learning aid. Teachers will more fully understand their roles in relation to the computer, thus streamlining the educational process.

2. GENERAL AIM OF THE STUDY

The aim of the present study is to attempt to answer the following questions:
a. Does the computer positively motivate students involved in the learning process?
b. Is the computer perceived by students to be an efficient aid in the learning process?
c. Do students feel that the use of the computer in the learning process is confined to those subjects taught by CAI?

3. METHOD

3.1. Sample

The research sample comprised 158 elementary school students aged 8 through 14 who were assigned to a state elementary school in Israel's northern district. All students studied arithmetic by computer assisted instruction in two hourly sessions every week. In addition, 58 of them participated in one weekly voluntary computer programming lession as part of their extra-curricular activities. The remaining 100 students had no additional computer experience other than the two weekly hours of CAI in arithmetic.

3.2. Apparatus

A research questionnaire geared to investigate computer-oriented attitudes of elementary school students was especially compiled for the purpose of the present study. At the outset, the questionnaire consisted of 50 items which were presented to three computer experts for fact and content validity evaluation. Twenty-four items met the validity criteria used by the evaluators and were included in the questionnaire administered to the research sample. After administration the responses of the students were factor analyzed in a principal components analysis. Thirteen items met the criterion of statistical significance (.30), and so were used for data analysis. The 13 items were distributed in 3 factors each of which had a latent root of unity and explained at least 10% of the variance. These factors were labelled "computer motivation" (the will to use the computer in the course of the learning process), "computer effectiveness" (the belief that a computer is an effective and useful instrument that facilitates the learning process) and "computer transfer" (the belief that one can utilize computers in a variety of learning situations and not only in those specifically initiated by the school authorities). The reliability coefficient of the final 13 item questionnaire, estab-

lished by the Cronbach Alpha Method, was .64.

3.3. Procedure

The questionnaire was administered to the subjects in their usual school classrooms. The general goals of the research were explained and final instructions relating to the administration of the questionnaire were given. Thereafter the subjects were asked to answer all items and to hand in the questionnaires as soon as they were completed.

4. RESULTS

Results of a multivariate ANOVA indicate a definite and significant relationship between computer motivation and students' age ($F=2.95$, D.F.$=5$, $P<0.02$) as well as computer effectiveness and student's age ($F=3.48$, D.F.$=5$, $P<0.01$). The relationship between computer transfer and student's age was not statistically significant. Post-hoc Duncan tests indicated that for both computer motivation and computer effectiveness, 14 year-old, 13 year-old and 12 year-old students had significantly more positive attitudes than 8 year-olds. In addition, although no significant differences were found between the other age groups, a definite hierarchical pattern emerged with 14 year-olds having the most positive computer oriented attitudes followed by 13 year-olds, 12 year-olds, 11 year-olds, 10 year-olds, 9 year-olds and 8 year-old students in descending order.

Three t-tests were conducted in order to ascertain possible differences on the three research factors between students who participated in extra-curricular computer classes and those who did not. Results of the t-test computed for the computer transfer factor ($t=2.14$, D.F.$=156$, $P<0.05$) indicate that students who participated in computer programming lessons were significantly more positive about computer transfer than their counterparts who did not participate in these extra-curricular activities. No significant differences were found between those who participated in computer programming lessons and those who did not in the t-tests conducted for computer motivation and computer effectiveness.

5. DISCUSSION

From the results of this study it may be postulated that as prepuberty, puberty and adolescence set in, the traditional teacher-student relationship undergoes significant changes. It appears that the 8 year-old student remains dependent on the teacher-student relationship for successful learning experiences and the computer is not perceived by him as an essential element in the learning process. However as time passes and the student demonstrates greater independence, the computer plays an increasingly more important role in the learning process, resulting in the adoption of positive computer oriented attitudes which demonstrate that at adolescence, the 14 year-old is able increasingly to fulfill his self-learning needs through CAI.

It may be further hypothesized in the light of the t-test results achieved in this study, that students who participate in computer programming lessons are more open to familiarisation with the computer's potential and are able to see the implications of computer use in a variety of learning situations. These students can appreciate the principles of computer aided learning and understand that these are not confined to any specific area. However, students who did not participate in programming lessons and have no computer experience other than the particular CAI that they undergo in the course of their formal schooling, find it significantly more difficult to appreciate the potential the computer has in additional fields of learning endeavour.

In the light of the findings of the present research, it is possible to hypothesize that superior utilization of the computer in educational frameworks conceivably takes place in the upper classes of the elementary school where students have reached the age of adolescence. Stress should be placed on this aspect of computer usage and perhaps time, effort and large financial outlays can be avoided if the target population of CAI is narrowed down to that which can obtain maximum benefit from CAI. It is therefore suggested that further investigations be carried out in order to confirm and pinpoint a suitable student age range that best facilitates the use of computers in the learning process.

REFERENCES

[1] Shuell, J.T., Review of Educational Research 56, 4 (1986) 411.
[2] Meyer, A.L., Elementary School Journal 87, 2, (1986) 227.
[3] Brodeur, D.R., Educational Technology 25, 5 (1985) 42.
[4] Moore, P., Journal of Curriculum Studies 19, 2 (1987) 187.
[5] Siegler, R.S. and Glaser, R., Encoding and Development of Problem Solving (Lawrence Erlbaum Associates, Hillsdale, 1985).
[6] Finch, R.J. and Crankilton, R.J., Curriculum Development in Vocational and Technical Education: Planning Content and Implementation (Allya & Bacon, Boston, 1948).
[7] Cohen, V.C., Educational Technology (1985) 33.
[8] Salomon, G., Journal of Educational Psychology 20, 4, 207.
[9] Becker, H.J., Educational Computing 2 (1987) 149.
[10] Offir, B., Educational Technology 27, 4, (1987) 47.
[11] Rockman, S., Educational Technology 25, 1 (1985) 48.
[12] Heywood, G., Research in Education 33, (1986) 41.
[13] Goodwin, L.D., Goodwin, W.L., Mansel, A., Melm, C.P., American Educational Research Journal 23, 3 (1986) 348.
[14] Griffin, B.L., Gillis, M.K., and Brown, M., Elementary School Guidance and Counseling 20, 4 (1986) 246.

COMPUTERS IN EDUCATION, F. Lovis and E.D. Tagg (eds.)
Elsevier Science Publishers B.V. (North-Holland)
© IFIP, 1988

Experimental Introduction of Computers into Education of Lower-Form Pupils

A.A. Duvanov, L.V. Mel'nikova, Yu.A. Pervin
Pereslavl-Zalessky, USSR

Abstract

In a country with a centralized system of education, the introduction of a school computerization program should be preceded by pedagogical experiments. In the town of Pareslavl-Zalessky, in schools providing general education, a set of experiments is being carried out on early education in informatics. The aims and environment of the experiment are described along with its organization. An example of experimental educational program is presented.

In the last year in Pereslavl-Zalessky, a small Russian town 130 kilometres to the North-East of Moscow, an Institute of Program Systems has been founded under the USSR Academy of Sciences that comprises a Laboratory of School Informatics. The efforts of the laboratory are directed mostly to development of a concept of teaching informatics to lower-form children. Due to the Institute's activity, computerization of all the municipal secondary schools has become possible; and since it is planned to reduce the age level of the pupils studying informatics, a wide experimental verification of the software and methodological support for teaching the fundamentals of informatics in lower forms has become topical in Pereslavl.

Different variants of Logo and propaedeutic system Robotland, which is built around a set of executors that develop in lower-form pupils certain experience in operational thinking, have been used as software tools in the experiments. The need of the Robotland system was due to the authors' conviction that the experience of lower-form pupils must be constructively formed in particular, specific situations, rather than to any doubts in the high methodological advantages of Logo that were repeatedly confirmed by practice.

To this end, a set of executors - program models of robots - has been designed, some of which will be described below.

The Painter executor colours closed figures in black-and-white contour pictures. The pupil uses the computer's set of colours.

The Ant executor can crawl along the checked field and push lettered blocks. The letters of the desired word are "scattered" over the field checks, and the task is to construct the word by compiling a program from the executor's instruction set. The pupil operates with a coordinate grid over plane.

The Organ-Grinder executor enables one to compile simple melodies on the lines and perform them.

The Cockroach executor is Ant's extension : some of the blocks are turned upside down and the Cockroach can check the characters on them and make decisions depending on the results of the check.

The Erudite executor proposes to insert into a line of the form of "a?b?c?=d" the signs of appropriate arithmetic operations, so as to provide equality. Complexity of the generated examples is controllable. The pupils quickly gain experience in oral counting.

The Engine-Driver executor controls a shunting locomotive that sorts out cars and makes up trains at goods station, thus developing logical thinking of the pupils.

The Metal-Cutter and Turner executor (screen model of the turning machine) give the pupils experience required by the polytechnization program. To the same end, are addressed the inclusion in the experimental curriculum laboratory, of classes on hardwired implementations of training robots and devices having built-in microprocessors that are connected to personal computers.

The Corrector executor operates with infinite tape like the Turing machine. By means of this executor the pupils consider the sort and search problems, as well as those concerned with the development of logical thinking.

The voyage over the Robotland is completed by more advanced robots, such as Arithmosha (stack calculator for computational problems), musical robot Musician, robot-decorator Artist, and robot Mathematician extending the possibility of the Arithmosha.

Although each executive has its own instruction set, the system has a single linguistic interface. The Robotland language is simple, and its syntax is described by several definitions only :

```
<program>::= PROC
<identifier><procedure body> END
<procedure body>::=
<structure>|<procedure
body><structure>
<structure>::=<procedure
call>|<branching>|<cycle>
<procedure
call>::=<identifier>[<parameter list>]
<parameter list>::=
<parameter>|<parameter list>
<parameter>
<branching>::=IF <condition> THEN
<procedure call>
[ ELSE <procedure call> ]
<cycle>::=LOOP <integer><procedure
call>
```

On the whole, the Robotland system precedes methodical study of educational high-level languages such as Logo.

It was important to verify the hypothesis on the propaedeutic role of the Robotland system in teaching informatics to the lower-form pupils. This question can be finally answered only by a pedagogical experiment. Therefore, parallel education of several groups of children has been started in Pereslavl using different methodologies : one imbeds the pupils directly into Logo; in the other, a rather detailed acquaintance with the Robotland executors precedes the study of educational linguistic programming systems.

Hand in hand with the comparative analysis of two educational programming systems, it was necessary to compare other elements of educational process support. For example, the Logo system has different lexical versions. True the present writers are staunch supporters of national educational lexical systems, especially at the initial phase of teaching informatics, but since the English version, as a traditional international tool of education, is supported by a wide informatics community, it has been decided to carry out another parallel inside the experimental groups using Russian and English versions of Logo. In essence, a system of comparative experiments has been suggested whose parameters are the level of teacher's training, types of personal computers used, software systems, their lexical contents, age of the beginners and experiment length. The experiment which started in Pereslavl-Zalessky is angled at working out substantiated recommendations to the USSR Ministry of Public Education for teaching the fundamentals of informatics at earlier age (currently in this country, informatics is taught in two upper classes of the secondary school).

Among the experiment goals are also :

- verification of the hypothesis about the effectiveness of forming operational thinking of lower-form pupils through studying algorithms and ways to their construction and realization on computers;

- experimental verification of program and methodological facilities for teaching informatics in secondary schools of a small town within agricultural milieu;

- determination of the age limit for early education in the fundamentals of informatics;

- comparison of original and traditional educational programming systems;

- verification of the influence of early teaching of informatics on the nature of inter-subject relations and determination of directions for their remaking; and

- verification of the hypothesis about the effectiveness of teaching informatics in lower forms with national vocabulary.

The experiment involved typical schools without any screening or selection of children. To carry out the experiment, it was necessary to change the standard curriculum by adding two hours a week for each of the experimental forms.

In the 1987-1988 school-year, the experiment was started in two third (9 year of children) and two fifth (11 year old children) forms, of which one third and one fifth form are using experimental educational programs conventionally referred to as Robotland-3 and Robotland-5, and the two other (third and fifth) forms are studying the programs called Logo-3 and Logo-5. Below, in the appendix, the Robotland-3 program is presented by way of example. Like other experimental programs, it includes, along with lessons on programming and fundamentals of informatics, topics on different computer applications, ranging from teaching the street traffic rules, through fairy-tale editing, to formation of personal contact culture.

The next school-year adds to the experiment two more third forms that work in school classes of informatics with soviet computers and Russian vocabulary-based programming system.

The lessons in the experimental forms dre given to groups equal to a half-form each. The experiment envisages education in informatics up to the end of secondary school, but the program for the experiment in upper forms is compiled as a draft and is liable to corrections.

In the experimental forms, teaching is done by both the staff of the School Informatics Laboratory and school teachers who had taken a year course of weekly seminars on informatics and an intensive summer seminar just before the experiment.

Appendix

Educational plan of the Robotland-3 experiment

3rd form (2 hours a week, 64 hours per annum)

1.	Computer games	2 h.
2.	Laboratory classes : control of programmable cybernetic devices, planet research vehicle	3 h.
3.	Notion of executor : the Painter executor	2 h.
4.	Editor of contours for colouring	4 h.
5.	Computer education : street traffic rules	4 h.
6.	The Ant executor	3 h.
7.	Computer education : rules of behaviour	3 h.
8.	Musical ABC; the Organ-Grinder executor	6 h.
9.	Keyboard simulator	2 h.
10.	Fairy-tale editor	2 h.
11.	Computers in manufacturing; the Metal-Cutter executor	4 h.
12.	Test work (operation with test program)	1 h.
13.	Initial education in programming through the Cockroach executor	27 h.
	13.1 Acquaintance with the executor and its computer model; working in the executor's operating environment; control of the executor in the direct instruction execution mode	4 h.
	13.2 Operation with program editor; procedures	6 h.
	13.3 Branches in programs	6 h.
	13.4 Cycles	6 h.
	13.5 Infinite recursion	2 h.
	13.6 Finite recursion	3 h.
	13.7 Test work	1 h.

4th form (2 hours a week, 64 hours per annum)

1.	Operation with game constructor	4 h.
2.	The Erudite executor	3 h.
3.	Computer education : operation with town and locality plans; route planning and travelling along it	4 h.
4.	Operation with graphic editor	4 h.
5.	The Machine-Driver executor	3 h.
6.	Operation with text editor	4 h.
7.	Programming of the Machine-Driver executor	5 h.
8.	Computers in manufacturing : model of program-controlled machine tool	5 h.
9.	Laboratory classes : control of programmable cybernetic device	2 h.
10.	Test work	1 h.
11.	Programming of Corrector executor	28 h.
	11.1 Acquaintance ith the executor; control of the executor in the direct instruction execution mode	4 h.
	11.2 Structural design	4 h.
	11.3 Recursion	4 h.
	11.4 Arithmetics of numbers and sticks	4 h.
	11.5 Search problems	4 h.
	11.6 Text processing problems	4 h.
	11.7 Elements counting problems	2 h.
	11.8 Problems on cyphers and ordering	2 h.
12.	Test work	1 h.

5th form (2 hours a week, 64 hours per annum)

1.	Operation with game constructor	4 h.
2.	The Arithmosha executor, propaedeutic of the notion of function	4 h.
3.	Computer education : rules of behaviour	2 h.
4.	Operation with a simplest information system	4 h.
5.	Programming of the Musician executor	6 h.
6.	Checking work	1 h.
7.	Computers in manufacture	8 h.
8.	Laboratory classes : control of programmable cybernetic devices	4 h.
9.	Programming of the Artist executor	4 h.
10.	Programming of means of computers : computer newspapers, computer conferences	8 h.
11.	Programming of the Mathematician executor	14 h.
12.	Editor of animated cartoons	4 h.
13.	Test work	1 h.

6th and 7th forms : Computers at home. Computer in professional activity. Computer education. Computer communication. Advanced study of programming on the basis of the Lego language.

8th and 9th forms : Computers and society. data resources and their access. Bases of knowledge. Algorithmic language as a universal tool for writing algorithms. Programming in the Rapira language.

10th form : Continuation of the "Computers and society' topic. Modern computers. Modern software. Continuation of the study in algorithms and methods for their construction. Realization of algorithms in Rapira. Overview of the modern programming languages.

COMPUTERS IN EDUCATION, F. Lovis and E.D. Tagg (eds.)
Elsevier Science Publishers B.V. (North-Holland)
© IFIP, 1988

379

PRESCHOOLERS' INTERACTIVE BEHAVIOURS WHILE PARTICIPATING IN
COMPUTER BASED LEARNING ACTIVITIES: SOME PRELIMINARY FINDINGS.

Alison ELLIOTT

School of Policy and Technology Studies in Education,
The University of Wollongong, P.O. Box 1144,
Wollongong, 2500, New South Wales, Australia.

This paper reports on some of the preliminary findings of an Australian study of four
year old children's interactive behaviours as they participated in computer based
learning activities in preschool classrooms. Results indicate that developmentally
appropriate computer activities can create an environment in which children's
interactive behaviours flourish.

1. INTRODUCTION

That computers and related information technologies will have an instrumental role in the educational, social and occupational futures of today's young children is widely recognised; deciding exactly how these technologies can be used and which applications are most appropriate in early childhood education pose questions of increasing importance and concern to the early childhood field, especially at the preschool level. (In this context "preschool" is the term used to cover the year of formal learning undertaken by many Australian children before they commence primary school at five years of age).

Emerging from this concern are demands for research which will help educators determine parameters for the implementation of computer based learning experiences that enhance learning opportunities for young children within the framework of contemporary policies and curricula. Of special interest in the Australian context is the role of computer based learning activities in supporting well established goals relating to the enhancement of aspects of a child's affective development, particularly prosocial behaviours.

A major fear of both educators and parents is that the widespread introduction of computers will create a situation in which children lack opportunities to develop the social behaviours necessary for successful participation in the wider society, and, more immediately, in the first years of primary school. The expectation of preschool experience largely as one that will provide the foundations for child's social adjustment is reinforced by the primary school where teachers value the ability to adapt to the existing routines and organisational patterns, and interact amiably with other children.

At this stage there are very few computers in Australian preschools. In fact, Australian early childhood teachers are reluctant to introduce computer based learning experience to their classrooms. Many are still uncertain about the role of computers in society and education in general, let alone in the early childhood classroom. Few have any experience with computers in educational or any other contexts. Some are suspicious of anything that challenges traditional curriculum heritage, regardless of its potential to enrich learning opportunities for children. Others simply haven't the money available to spend on computer technology [1].

This paper reports on some of the preliminary findings of a study of four year old children's interactive behaviours as they participated in computer based learning activities. It provides descriptive data on the nature of children's interaction in the computer area with the aim of reassuring early childhood teachers that the use of computers in the classroom need not lead to a highly impersonalised and isolating educational experience. The results reported in this paper represent only a small part of the findings of a comprehensive study of children's behaviours in computer active preschool classrooms.

2. FACILITATING COMMUNICATIVE BEHAVIOURS

Widespread recognition amongst early childhood educators of the importance of developing appropriate interpersonal skills and behaviours is reflected in the orientation of preschool curricula in Australia. Indeed, perhaps the major goal of contemporary Australian preschool curricula is to help children develop social competencies by promoting opportunities for social interaction in a variety of play settings. Given the emphasis on this aspect of children's development it is important that learning experiences in the preschool provide opportunities for children to develop appropriate social skills. If computer based learning experiences are to be considered appropriate for preschool children they must provide opportunities for learning which support and complement the goals of the preschool program.

The few studies which have explored the role of computer based learning experiences in supporting aspects of young children's social development suggest that participation in computer based activities seems to foster interactive behaviours. Borgh and Dickson [2] after working with 20 preschoolers suggest that "given appropriate software and a classroom policy emphasising sharing, the microcomputer can be used to increase the amount of cooperative, collaborative interaction in preschool classrooms". In fact, they believe that the social interactions that take place between children using a computer may be of greater educational significance than the interactions that take place between children and the computer itself. A number of other authors also report that computer based activities seem to encourage social interactions between young children. One problem with most of these studies is that sample size was very small [3-10].

3. METHOD

The typical Australian preschool program tends to have a "free play" session in which learning centres, with appropriate materials, are set up and children choose their activities from those available. In this study a "computer corner" was added to the range of learning centres already in existence in four preschool classrooms and children chose to work in the "computer corner" just as they would choose to work in any other "learning centre" or activity area. Observations of children's behaviours were made in a naturalistic setting amidst the day to day activities of the preschools.

3.1 Subjects

Subjects of the study were 90 children (42 males and 48 females) with a mean age of 4 years, 4 months. The children were enrolled in four Sydney preschool classes and were from middle to upper middle class, mostly Anglo-Australian, family backgrounds.

3.2 Procedure

After a period of familiarity with the computer (and popular commercial software) children's behaviours in the computer corner were observed as they used two problem solving activities: a drawing program which acted as a pre Logo activity, and a single key stroke version of Logo used with a floor turtle. As both activities are of the type which promote open ended exploration of microworlds they were in keeping with the overall play orientation of the preschools' curricula.

Children's interactive behaviours in the computer corner were observed during each of two free play sessions over a six week period. Frequency and duration of children's play in the computer area was also recorded.

Episodes of interactive behaviours were coded in the following categories:

A. Showing/explaining
B. Describing/commenting
C. Hypothesising/predicting
D. Laughing
E. Sharing
F. Silence
G. Fantasy
H. Questioning
I. Mumbling
J. Teacher talk
K. Arguing
L. Responding to questions
M. Active listening
N. General conversation

This categorisation of behaviours had its origins in Elliott and Hall's [6] and Klinzing's [7] studies of computer active preschool classrooms and was tested and refined in a pilot study in 1986. Categories that are not self explanatory are described under the relevant headings in sections 4.2.1-4.2.13.

4. RESULTS AND DISCUSSION

4.1 Frequency and Duration

During the period of the study most children (93%) were observed in the "computer corner" at least once or twice. The average total amount of time spent in the computer corner by all children was 88.5 minutes. Boys spent more time in the computer corner than did girls (p. < .01). They were recorded as being in the computer corner for an average of 106.8 minutes over the observation period. Girls spent a total of 72.6 minutes in the computer corner. Boys also used the computer more often than did girls. It was also noted that children preferred to work in the computer corner in pairs or groups, usually with other children of the same sex.

4.2 Interactive Episodes

There were 4,729 interactive episodes included in the preliminary data analysis. The number of interactive episodes in each category are shown as percentages of the total number of interactive episodes in **Figure 1.** No observations were recorded for the six children, five girls and one boy, who did not venture into the computer corner during the observation periods.

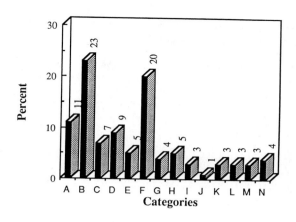

Figure 1
Interactive episodes in each category as a percentage of the total number of interactive episodes (to the nearest whole number).

Findings in each category are described in more detail in the following sections.

4.2.1 Showing and Explaining (A)

Episodes categorised as **Showing and Explaining** accounted for 11 % of the total number of interactive episodes. Boys were more likely than girls to be involved in episodes of **Showing and Explaining** behaviours (p < .01). This may be because boys tended to spend more time in the computer area than did girls, and were more confident in their use of the equipment. These episodes provided clear examples of prosocial behaviours such as helping, demonstrating and cooperating. Frequent and experienced computer users often acted in a peer tutoring role with less confident or inexperienced users. One child who experienced a speech impairment, and rarely talked with other children, became the "computer expert" in his class and spent considerable amounts of time helping other children become familiar with the computer and various aspects of each program. The following conversation typifies the sort of exchanges that were included in this category.

Elizabeth:	Press. That's too much...Too many. Turn...Now turn again...Do another one.
Georgina:	This time you do this and I'll do this. (Pointing) Too many times, too many times. Press, this one... Too many times. Oh! It's going to crash.
Elizabeth:	Not it's not.
Georgina:	You press that and that... Not too many times...

4.2.2   Describing and Commenting (B)

This category accounted for 23% of the total episodes of interactive behaviours. Again there were significant gender related differences in the scores, with boys more likely than girls to be recorded as engaging in episodes of **Describing and Commenting** behaviours ($p < .01$). Language classified in this category was typically that in which children described or commented upon what was happening on screen, or on the floor, in the case of the turtle. Their talk was usually related to the activity at hand, such as identifying colours, shapes, keys, positional relationships, and counting. Sometimes the talk was directed at other children or adults. At other times it was non social in nature, although there may have been other children in the computer corner. In many of these instances children seemed to be talking to the computer. In the following exchange children are focusing on selection and identification of colour as they used the drawing program.

Ruth:	There's purple! I like purple. That's a lovely purple. Now green... I like green. That's quite a funny sort of darky colour.
Catherine:	Green! There's green.
Ruth:	I'm changing (colour) again. (Presses two colours at the same time). I've done that before and it's funny when you do two together.
Catherine:	It's pink.

Even when children worked alone in the computer corner they often talked, either to themselves, or to the computer, or the turtle. Some children maintained a running commentary on every move they made: a sort of thinking aloud process. The following excerpt is from the transcript of a child's interactions as he worked alone at the computer.

Nicholas:	I'm pressing F. When I press F it goes. When I press S it stops... I'm making a city. Now yellow. F... I'm going this way. Oh, the end. Now I'm going to green.

4.2.3   Hypothesising and Predicting (C)

The computer based activities used in this study were of the sort that invited children to use divergent problem solving strategies. They had to make predictions and generate and test hypotheses as they searched for solutions to the various problems posed in each situation. The interactive nature of the computer meant that they were provided with immediate feedback and observable consequences that gave them the information needed to make further decisions. Some 7% of all communication was classified in this category and boys were more likely than were girls to be observed "hypothesising and predicting" ($p. < .01$).

4.2.4   Laughing and Exclaiming (D)

Children seemed to derive a great deal of satisfaction and enjoyment from being in the computer corner and their enthusiasm was often reflected in their giggles, laughter, exclamations and general "high spirits". Some 9% of interactive episodes were identified as being of this nature. Occasionally, like in any other play area, this sort of behaviour got out of hand and a child had to be cautioned by an adult.

4.2.5   Sharing/Turn Taking (E)

As is the case in most activities in which children have to share materials some of their verbal interactions (5%) related to turn taking, usually in respect of negotiating who would press the keys.

Borgh and Dickson [2] in a study of children's initial experiences with computer based activities report that some 12% of interactions were related to turn taking. Some early childhood teachers feel that turn taking should be regulated by a queuing system. Such a practice was not found to be necessary in this study. It was felt that children were capable of organising turns at the computer, just as they were capable of sharing materials in other play areas. There was little need for adult intervention in process and very little arguing amongst the children. The following example is typical of the exchanges in this category.

Georgina: My turn to press (the keys) Elizabeth.

Elizabeth: No it's Emily's. Your go Emily.

Emily: Yes, my turn now. My turn. It's not your turn Georgina. You've had lots of goes.

A comparison of sharing and turn taking episodes on the basis of sex revealed significant differences (p. < .01), with girls being more likely than boys to negotiate about sharing and turn taking.

4.2.6   Silence (F)

Times when children were silent were also recorded during these observations. Episodes of silence, which accounted for 20% of the total observations, tended to occur when children were watching the activity, but not obviously participating or interacting with other children. Parton's categorisation of playstyle termed this "onlooking" behaviour [11]. Klinzing, [7] found that children were silent for 37.5% of the time when engaged in non computer based activities and for 30% of the time while using the computer.

In this study girls were more likely than boys to be silent in the computer corner (p. < .01). This seems to be related to the finding that girls spent more time than boys in an "onlooking" capacity. Anecdotal evidence suggests that this seemed especially true if a group of boys happened to be using the computer. In these cases girls appeared to be reluctant to break into the existing group.

4.2.7   Active Listening (M)

The 3% of interactive episodes included in this category were those instances in which it was clear that a child was actively listening to another person. A teacher may, for example, have been giving a child specific directions. In other cases a child may have been concentrating on listening to instructions or explanations given by another child. In each case though, it had to be clear to the observer that a child was listening "actively". An important characteristic of behaviour categorised as active listening was eye contact between speaker and listener. It is possible that some episodes of "silence' would have been more accurately classified under this heading.

4.2.8   Fantasy (G)

Episodes of fantasy play accounted for only a small proportion (4%) of all interactions. For the purpose of this study fantasy play was said to occur when play themes involved children in creating fantasy, pretend or imaginary situations. When fantasy play was observed it often focused on action themes involving war, space, robots and cars.

Significant sex differences (p. < .01) occurred in respect of fantasy play and, given the typical nature of the play themes, it is not surprising to find that manifestations of fantasy play were greater for boys than for girls. In the following example David, Max and Rory have turned the computer screen into a battle field.

David: Look, let's get it.
         Up the stairs. It's going to blow up.
         I'm not going to play anymore (leaves).

Rory: Make it as long as I was. Crash it. Oh! (Makes explosion noise)... Now down to there.

Max: OK. I'll get it now. As long as yours.

Rory: Wow! It's tall.

Max: It's going on the track. See there's a little track. Don't let it crash. It's going to crash. Look the plane's crashing.

According to Connelly and Doyle [12], Garvey [13] and Smilansky [14], an important function of fantasy play is its role in helping children develop a repertoire of competent social behaviours. It was evident from observing these sorts of play episodes that considerable collaboration amongst children occurred as they pursued fantasy play themes.

4.2.9 Questioning (H) and Responding to Questions (L)

Interactions of the type in which children asked a question or responded to a specific question asked by another child or an adult accounted for 8% of all interactions. Questions and answers were often concerned with operation of the keyboard and program characteristics. Girls were more likely to ask questions than were boys (p. < .01), perhaps because they were less familiar with the computer due to the shorter amounts of time spent in the computer corner.

4.2.10 Teacher Talk (J)

The small amount of teacher talk (1%) observed in the computer corner is not unexpected. In this study children were quite familiar with the computer before the commencement of the observations and minimal teacher intervention was required to facilitate effective use of the technology. The small amount of teacher talk also reflects the dominant approach to curriculum in Australian preschool settings. Emphasis is on the "enrichment" model of self-directed learning and activity through play, with the teacher responding to the child's needs as required, rather than imposing direct guidance of instruction. The frequency of instances of peer tutoring also meant that teacher intervention was not as important as it might otherwise have been in this context. It's possible too, that teachers were reluctant to interfere with what they perceived as "a special research project"

4.2.11 Arguing and Aggression (K)

The few episodes recorded in this category (3%) tended to occur as children argued over establishing turns and rights to items needed to enhance the quality of the play. For example on one occasion two children disputed the "ownership" of some blocks which were being used to make roads, tunnels and bridges for the turtle robot. Instances of aggressive behaviours were confined to one girl who experienced a whole range of behavioural problems in the classroom. While she was an enthusiastic and competent computer user she was inclined to sabotage other children's work and sometimes hit, pinch or push another child.

4.2.12 General Conversation (N)

The results of this study indicate that the computer corner offered plenty of opportunity for children to use language. Language classified as general conversation was that which was not specifically related to what was happening on the screen, or with the floor turtle. For example, conversations about weekend outings, parents, siblings, new clothes, visiting friends, and birthday parties were recorded in this category. However, the small amount of behaviour classified as "conversation" reflects Beard's [15] claim that because of the engaging and interactive nature of many computer activities most talk will focus on the task at hand. Indeed, only 3% of verbal interaction was coded in the category general conversation.

4.2.13 Mumbling (I)

When children's utterances were unintelligible, for whatever reason, they were scored in the category **"Mumbling"**. A total of 3% of communicative episodes were not able to be understood in the recording and transcribing process and were included in this category.

5. CONCLUSION

Children's talk is an important element in the establishment and maintenance of social interactions. An environment that promotes the sharing of ideas, goals and processes, whether it be computer or non computer based, is likely to provide a setting for fostering children's use of language. If computer based activities are to provide a vehicle for social exchanges then they must be of the sort that lend themselves to the involvement of more than one child in a situation that invites complex patterns of social interaction. The open ended nature of Logo type activities would seem to provide this sort of environment. Using the drawing program and the floor turtle required children to formulate their own problems so determining the structure and direction of the learning.

The findings emerging from this study support Borgh and Dickson's [2] assertion that rich social and verbal interactions can occur in the computer corner. In fact, this study suggests that the computer corner was a "hive" of communicative activity and that children engaged in a variety of interactive exchanges. Of interest to teachers concerned with facilitating the development of children's social skills is the considerable evidence of cooperative encounters between children, with frequent occurrences of behaviours such as sharing mutual goals, making joint decisions, sharing ideas and materials, negotiating and bargaining, coordinating actions to accomplish goals, and evaluating progress. The many examples of peer teaching in the category **Showing and Explaining** are particularly encouraging.

Equally encouraging is evidence of episodes of fantasy play, as this type of play is regarded as being very important in the development of social competence. Preschool teachers strive to provide a variety of classroom situations that serve to stimulate such play. Easy access to materials such as blocks, cardboard boxes, Lego pieces and other toys seemed to facilitate imaginative play in the computer corner. The question of the value of superhero and war play is however debatable.

For preschool teachers the finding that computer based learning activities can act as catalyst for the generation of problem solving behaviours is also important. Listening to children's talk as they work through a problem is particularly interesting as it provides an insight into the sorts of thinking processes used to arrive at an answer. Their talk also illustrates some of the concepts being explored. Importantly too, as Goffin and Tull [16] stress, engagement in challenging open ended problem solving tasks in which children can see the impact of their actions enhances their sense of competence and helps gain a feeling of mastery over their environment.

The findings reported in this paper suggest that the computer was a "hive" of social activity in which a range of communicative behaviours flourished. Such findings are encouraging as they should serve to reassure teachers that computer based activities, if developmentally appropriate, can create new settings in which children can develop both social and cognitive competencies. As such they serve to complement more traditional classroom learning experiences.

If, as it appears, these sorts of computer based activities do provide valuable learning opportunities then they must be equally afforded to all children. Findings in this study which show significant sex differences in participation in the computer corner and on a number of dimensions of communicative behaviours warrant further investigation as early childhood educators are concerned about issues relating to gender and equity. There is an urgent need for researchers to address this issue and to endeavour to structure the learning environment in such a way as to encourage all children to gain the maximum benefit from participating in educational valid computer activities. The issue of sex differences in children's computer play is currently being explored in more detailed analyses of these and other data collected in the course of this study.

REFERENCES

[1]   A. Elliott, Computers in early childhood education: An Australian perspective. Paper presented at the Annual Conference of the National Association for the Education of Young Children, Chicago, November, 1987.

[2]   K. Borgh and W.P. Dickson, Two preschoolers sharing one microcomputer: Creating prosocial behaviour with hardware and software, in P.Campbell and G.Fein, (eds) *Young children and microcomputers,* Prentice-Hall. Englewood Cliffs, NJ., 1986, 37-46.

[3]   S. Blemmings, Microcomputers in Queensland preschools: an investigation, in J. Hancock (ed.), *Tomorrow's technology today.* Proceedings of the Australian Computers in Education Conference. CEGSA, Adelaide, 1987, 83-86.

[4]   K. Swigger and B. Swigger, Social patterns and computer use among preschool children. *AEDS Journal,* 17 (3), 1984, 35-41.

[5]   R. A. Williams, Preschoolers and the computer, *Arithmetic Teacher,* 31(8), 1984, 39-42.

[6]   A. Elliott and N. Hall, Microcomputers: enhancing curriculum goals in the preschool, in proceedings of the 17th triennial Australian Early Childhood Conference, *Early childhood: Ideals and realities,* Vol 2, Brisbane, September, 1985, 372-386.

[7]   D. Klinzing, A study of the behaviour of children in a preschool equipped with computers. Paper presented to the Annual Meeting of the AERA, Chicago, March, 1985.

[8]   A. Muller and M. Perlmutter, Preschool children's problem solving interactions at computers and jigsaws. *Journal of Applied Developmental Psychology,* 6, 1985, 173-186.

[9]   J. A. Kull, Learning and Logo, in P.Campbell and G.Fein (eds.), op. cit., 103-130.

[10]   J.L.Wright and A.S. Samaras, Playworlds and microworlds in P.Campbell and G.Fein, (eds.), op.cit., 73-86.

[11]   M.Parton, Social participation among preschool children, *Journal of Abnormal Psychology,* 27, 1932, 243-269.

[12]   J.A. Connolly and A. Doyle, Relation of fantasy play to social competence in preschoolers, *Developmental Psychology,* 20(5), 1984, 797-806.

[13]   C. Garvey, *Play,* Harvard University Press, Cambridge, M.A., 1977.

[14]   S. Smilansky, *The effects of sociodramatic play on disadvantaged preschool children,* Wiley, NY, 1968.

[15]   R. Beard, Children's language and literacy and the microcomputer, in *MEP, Infant and first schools:* The role of the microcomputer, MEP, UK, 1985.

[16]   S. Goffin and C.Q. Tull, Problem solving: Encouraging active listening, *Young Children,* 40(3), 1985, 28-32.

COMPUTERS IN EDUCATION, F. Lovis and E.D. Tagg (eds.)
Elsevier Science Publishers B.V. (North-Holland)
© IFIP, 1988

LEVEL OF SITUATIONAL COMPUTER ANXIETY IN FIRST-GRADE PUPILS

Violeta TZONEVA, Lydia MITEVA

Violeta TZONEVA, People's Republic of Bulgaria, Research Institute in
Education - Sofia (address for correspondence: Violeta TZONEVA, Research
Institute in Education, bul.Lenin 125, block 5, 1113 Sofia, BULGARIA)
Lydia MITEVA, People's Republic of Bulgaria, Central Laboratory in
Psychology by the Bulgarian Academy of Science - Sofia

A method for determination of situational computer anxiety in first-grade pupils (6-7 years old) is worked up and tested. The subjects were 57 pupils (28 boys and 29 girls), tested after 16 microcomputer-based lessons in the Bulgarian language and in mathematics. The method is of a projective-evaluative character. The level of situational computer anxiety (individual/general) is determined on the basis of the number of negative emotional appraisals and the total sum of positive and negative appraisals, referring to 9 learning situations. These situations are presented on pictures, where pupils are using microcomputer. Experimental results show that the level of situational computer anxiety in first-grade pupils depends mainly on the individual success in working with microcomputer and on the conditions for education (appropriate partner, reliable hardware, proper organization of education).

1. INTRODUCTION

The implementation of microcomputers in education changes the learning conditions in class, sets new demands for pupils and teacher. In order to follow the effectiveness in pupil's using microcomputers, systematic pedagogical and psychological studies have to be carried out.
One of the main aspects of the process of microcomputer's implementation as a teaching-learning means is the motivation to work with it. When appropriate motivation, positive attitude and cognitive interest toward the learning process in general and the work with microcomputer in particular do not exist, a specific state of anxiety arises, which is experienced as negative emotion by the pupils.
We assume the statement that situational anxiety (or state of anxiety) is the initial emotional-situational reaction to different stressors. That is

why it is inseparable part of emotional experiences of the participants in a given significant activity [1]. Different states of anxiety, according to Spielberger [2,p.247] are characterized as consciously perceived subjective feelings of threat and strain, accompanied by activation of the nervous system. As anxiety is highly dependent on the situation, then an assumption can be made about the manner it occurs in education. It is logical to presume the existence of relation between this behavioral characteristic of pupil and the specific learning situations.
According to a study of pupils' attitudes towards computer-based professions, conducted by J.L.Moore [3] , a detectable effect on the level of pupils' computer anxiety (even when the pupils have been taking a school course of computer studies for over a year), has their home-use of the micro. This relation has to be taken into consideration but it does not influence the results of our study, because the microcomputer is not widely spread in Bulgarian homes at the present moment.
In our study the level of situational anxiety in first-grade pupils is being determined, without considering personal anxiety (as a constant trait of personality).
Our method is a modification of the method constructed by the Soviet psychologists N.V.Imedadse and A.A.Alhasyshvily [4]. They applied a method for determining the level of anxiety in elementary schoolchildren. The authors studied the psychological state of the pupils in different situations by means of 12 pictures, representing patterns of pupil's behavior in class-examination and in preparing homework.

2. EXPERIMENTAL CONFIGURATION

Our method includes a series of 9 coloured pictures, which show the process of working with microcomputers in

class. Their contents includes typical
teaching-learning situations based on
computer use. A pupil (one or two) and
a microcomputer are present at each of
them, and only at some of them is the
teacher present as well. The situations
are as follows:
1.Two pupils, sitting in front of the
computer, not working (with hands on
their knees). The boy - raising his
hand. The teacher - facing them.
2.Two pupils, sitting in front of the
computer. The boy - working with hands
on the keyboard. The girl does not
work.
3.One pupil, working with computer.
4.One pupil in front of the computer,
not working.
5.Two pupils, working with the computer.
6.Two pupils, sitting in front of the
computer, not working.
7.Two pupils, not working with the computer. The teacher is between them,
working with the computer.
8.Two pupils, not working with the computer. The girl - raising her hand.The
teacher - facing them.
Pictures of situation 3 and 4 have two
variants - for boys (a boy, working
with the computer) and for girls (a
girl, working with the computer).
Pupils' heads are presented in contour. Four portraits are drawn separately - of two girls and of two boys.
One boy and one girl have smiling faces,
happy expression. The other two (a boy
and a girl) are frowning, with sad expressions.
The experimental study's procedure is
as follows:
Four portraits are suggested to each
pupil individually for the identification of the happy and sad faces. After
that the pictures are offered one by
one. For each of them the pupil has to
choose and put on the contour those expressions, which he considers as most
suitable for the given situation. The
pupil has to explain his choice (of sad
or happy expression). The pupil's choice for each situation and his explanations are fixed by the experimentist.
The method described is of a projective
character. It is expected that pupils
will identify themselves with boys and
girls (respectively) presented at the
pictures. We assume, that the contents
of the situations will make pupils reveal their emotions (positive or negative), which they have experienced during lessons based on computer use.
The level of situational anxiety we determine as a ratio between the number
of sad faces chosen for the situation
(situations), i.e. of negative appraisals, and the sum of sad and happy fa-

ces (positive and negative appraisals
of the situation). In other words, we
use the formulae:

Level of situational anxiety =
$$= \frac{number\ of\ sad\ faces}{number\ of\ sad\ \&\ happy\ faces}\ 100[\%].$$

For example, if a pupil chooses only
happy faces and no sad face, then his
level of situational anxiety equals zero. When half of the faces chosen are
with happy countenance, and the other
half - with sad faces, the level of situational anxiety equals 50.
In February and March 1987, 57 first-
grade pupils from secondary school N104
in Sofia were tested after having completed 16 computer based lessons in
spelling instruction and in mathematics
[5]. The principle pedagogical objectives of the educational process that
preceded our test concerned the use of
microcomputer as a means of acquiring:
-skills for phonic analysis of words in
the Bulgarian language;
-skills for self-control in the process
of learning;
-concepts related to certain basic geometrical figures (circle, triangle,
square, rectangle);
-skills for operational-technical interaction with a computer's keyboard.
Pupils had no initial experience in
working with a microcomputer. They used
it at lessons in the Bulgarian language
and mathematics at the very beginning
of schoolyear. Pupils worked with a
microcomputer in pairs. Different types
of pairs were formed on the basis of
different rapidity of work.

3. RESULTS AND DISCUSSION

All pupils identify correctly happy and
sad faces, and give explanations of
their choice for each situation.
The data received determined the following forms of situational computer anxiety:
1.Individual level of situational anxiety for all of the situations.
2.General level of situational anxiety
(for all of the situations).
2.1. For girls.
2.2. For boys.
2.3. For each class.
2.4. For all pupils tested.
3.Individual and general level of situational anxiety for each situation, i.e.
determining the situation/situations,
which most strongly causes pupils' state of anxiety.
Results show that the individual level
of situational anxiety varies from its
absence in three of the pupils to 69.

Half of the pupils have an individual level of situational anxiety from 35 to 50.

Table 1: General level of situational anxiety for girls

Class	Number of negative choices	Number of positive choices
I^C	53	73
I^D	42	93
Total	95	166

$$\frac{95}{95 + 166} \cdot 100 = 36 \ [\%].$$

The general level of situational anxiety (for all situations) for girls is 36. It was determined on the basis of the results, shown in table 1, where the absolute values of negative and positive choices for girls for all 9 situations are presented.

Table 2: General level of situational anxiety for boys

Class	Number of negative choices	Number of positive choices
I^C	75	78
I^D	57	42
Total	132	120

The general level of situational anxiety for boys for all situations is determined on the basis of data, shown in table 2. The absolute values of negative and positive emotional choices for all 9 situations are presented there.

The general level of computer anxiety observed in boys is 52.3 [%].

On the basis of data presented in table 1 and table 2, the general level of computer anxiety in each class is determined. Its values are presented in table 3.

Table 3: General level of computer anxiety in each class

Class	Value of general computer anxiety
I^C	46
I^D	42

The general level of computer anxiety in all pupils tested is 44 [%].
Boys show a comparatively higher level of anxiety than girls, while the general level of anxiety is nearly the same in both classes.
Further, the level of computer anxiety referred to different situations, was determined on the basis of the number of negative and positive choices made by each pupil for each situation. The results are shown in table 4.

Table 4: General level of computer anxiety in each situation

Situation N	Girls	Boys	Total
1	27.5	25	26.3
2	17.8	51.7	35
3	32	6.9	19.2
4	85.7	65.5	75.4
5	25	3.4	14
6	82.1	82.7	82.4
7	71.4	55.1	63.1
8	71.4	24.1	47.3
9	60.7	10.3	35

Determination of the level of computer anxiety for the situations shows, that each situation, represented at a picture, is causing anxiety to a different degree. In our case, it turned out that situation 6 causes the highest level of anxiety both in girls and in boys - 82.1 and 82.7 respectively. Another critical situation concerning anxiety is the fourth one. The lowest level of anxiety projected is for situation 5 - 3.4 for the girls and 25 for the boys. Comparatively low are the values for situation 3.

In table 4 one finds the obvious absence of significant differences between level of anxiety for girls and for boys in situation 1 and situation 6. At the same time differences between levels of anxiety for girls and for boys are very strongly expressed in situations 2,3,4,5,7,8 and 9.

It is obvious, that the highest level of anxiety is being provoked for those learning situations, where pupils are in front of the computer, not working with it.

Statistical reliability of the differences between levels of anxiety for girls and for boys was determined applying criteria x^2 [6] for situations 2,3,4,5,7,8 and 9 separately. The zero hypothesis states: the distributions for girls and for boys are equal, i.e., the number of the positive/negative choices for girls and for boys has one and the same probability. The alternative hypothesis states: the distributions for girls and for boys differ. As an example we shall show verification of the initial hypothesis, concerning one of the situations (for instance, situation 2).

The values of observed and expected frequences of positive and negative choices for girls and for boys are presented in table 5.

Table 5: Observed (f_1) and expected (f_2) frequences of positive and negative choices for girls and for boys in situation 2 (absolute values)

	Girls		Boys		Total
	f_1	f_2	f_1	f_2	
Number of positive choices	14	18.8	23	18.2	37
Number of negative choices	15	10.1	5	9.8	20
Total	29		28		57

Using the discrete distribution of the checking quantity

$$\sum \frac{(f_1 - f_2)^2}{f_2}$$ the continuous distribution x^2 is being determined.

Thus

$$\sum \frac{(f_1 - f_2)}{f_2} = \frac{(23 - 18.2)^2}{18.2} + \frac{(5 - 9.8)^2}{9.8} + \frac{(14 - 18.8)^2}{18.8} + \frac{(15 - 10.1)^2}{10.1} = 7.2$$

For probability of error $p \leqslant 0.05$ % and degree of freedom 1, using a table [6], we determine the critical value of x^2, i.e., $x^2 = 3.84$. As 7.2>3.84, the zero hypothesis is being rejected and the alternative – accepted. For the next situations the values of x^2 are as follows:

for situation 3: $x^2 = 10.72$; $x^2_{critical} = 6.64$ at $p \leqslant 0.01$:
for situation 4: $x^2 = 9.63$; $x^2_{critical} = 6.64$ at $p \leqslant 0.01$;
for situation 7: $x^2 = 10.68$; $x^2_{critical} = 6.64$ at $p \leqslant 0.01$;
for situation 8: $x^2 = 12.72$; $x^2_{critical} = 10.8$ at $p \leqslant 0.001$;
for situation 8: $x^2 = 15.9$; $x^2_{critical} = 10.8$ at $p \leqslant 0.001$.

The values of x^2 give us the grounds to reject the zero hypothesis for situations 3,4,7,8 and 9 and to accept the alternative one. The distribution x^2 cannot be applied to situation 5, as one of the restricting initial conditions for its usage is not fulfilled, i.e., the frequences expected for negative choice of girls and of boys are not higher than 5 (4.07 and 3.94 respectively). Besides the quantitative analysis of the level of computer anxiety, the qualitative aspects of the problem under investigation are of a special importance. Contents of the emotionally negative choices were presented in several groups. On their side they can be considered as general factors of pupils' situational computer anxiety:
= distress (or discontent) at microcomputer's work;
= dissatisfaction with partner's actions (classmate's or teacher's);
= dissatisfaction with microcomputer-based activity in education;
= discovery of one's own failure;
= discovery of failure in partner's actions;
= expectation of failure;
= actions for overcoming failure.

The discontent at the microcomputer's defects at work most often are expressed by the phrases: "They are sad, because the computer does not work","The computer is out of order". Pupils express dissatisfaction with their partner in the next way: "They have quarrelled", "The boy does not let the girl to the keyboard","Only the teacher is working, they don't work", "Children are pouting, because they don't play. The teacher plays herself", "The boy is sad, because the teacher has told them to leave the computer hall and go to the classroom". First-grade pupils' dissatisfaction with the work with microcomputer is caused by the self-critical mind towards the results of their activity: "He is sad, because doesn't like what he has done"; as well by the fact of being alone: "The girl is sad, because she had been put to work alone with the computer", "Sad, because he is alone and there is nobody to help him". The discovery of one's own failure is connected with pupil's becoming conscious of one's lack of knowledge: "He cannot work", "Does not know how to go on", "They have made a mistake". In some cases the one's own discovery of failure is being accompanied by discovery of partner's failure: "The boy is sad, because he sees that the girl is pressing the button incorrectly. The girl is sad, because she has made a mistake (girl's answer, who has worked in pair with a boy, situation 5). First-grade pupils usually connect teacher's actions with their expectation of failure: "The boy thinks the teacher will fail in repairing the computer" as well with actions necessary for overcoming one's ignorance: "They call the teacher to help them".

The qualitative analysis of the level of computer anxiety manifests the following aspects. The situational anxiety is observed mainly in connection with pupil's failure - 40% of the cases of emotional dissatisfaction among boys are due to personal failure, among girls the percentage of such cases is 30. Dissatisfaction with the defects of the hardware's functioning and with partner's actions is observed in identical degree, but its values for girls are considerably higher (21.6%) than for boys (14.6%). Most rarely are observed expectation of failure from work with the microcomputer and accomplishment of actions to overcome failure.

Following the objective of checking the suitability of the method applied in respect to its reliability, 10 of the pupils were tested for a second time a month later. It turned out that the level of computer anxiety for 8 of them was the same, and for the other 2 it was slightly higher or lower (with about 10%). The identical results in first and in second test prove that pupils' replies in both cases are not an accident and manifest indeed the level of computer anxiety.

The entire results are indicative of the fact that the level of computer anxiety (or satisfaction) depends both on a pupil's success in his work with the microcomputer and on the conditions of education as well (reliable hardware suitable partner, proper organization of education, etc.).

The casual relationship between subjective pupil's evaluation of his failure

and the conditions for computer-based education is of special interest. Anxiety conceived as a result of dissatisfaction [7] with one's own learning actions could be treated in our opinion as an emotional product, on one side, from the low degree of learning abilities, and, on another side - from educational conditions, inadequate for pupil's actual needs.Knowing the factors of a pupil's situational computer anxiety opens the possibility of exerting influence on the pupil's emotional-motivational sphere through intentional change.

The type of situational anxiety treated here refers to the negative aspects of computer-based education, which arise, according to our empirical study, "from the new dimensions which the computer gives to old problems, rather than from inherent merits or defects which the computer itself possesses" [8] .

REFERENCES

[1] Ханин, Ю.Л., Вопросы психологии (1979), №6, 95.

[2] Хекхаузен, Х., Мотивация и деятельность (Педагогика, Москва, 1984, том I).

[3] Moore, J.L., Computer Education (1987) 13.

[4] Амонашвили, Ш.А., Воспитательная и образовательная функция оценки учения школьников (Педагогика, Москва, 1984).

[5] Tzoneva, V., Pavlov, D., Miteva,L., Karabsky, B.A Study of the Utilization of the Microcomputer in the Instruction of First-Grade Pupils, in: Second International Conference "Children in the Information Age: Opportunities for Creativity, Innovation and New Activities (Sofia, 19-23 May 1987) pp.286-300.

[6] Клаус,Г., Ебнер,Х., Основи на статистиката за психолози, педагози и социолози (Наука и изкуство, София, 1971).

[7] Паспаланов,И., Шетински,Д., Психология (1979), №1, 1.

[8] McCulloch, D.W., Educational Technology (1980) 12.

COMPUTERS IN EDUCATION, F. Lovis and E.D. Tagg (eds.)
Elsevier Science Publishers B.V. (North-Holland)
IFIP, 1988

393

ROBOT PROGRAMMING AND THE DEVELOPMENT OF PREOPERATIVE INTELLIGENCE

NEW TECHNOLOGIES AND THEIR EDUCATIONAL POTENTIAL

by Chantal GAUTIER, Claude Bernard University, CREFIP Lyon, France

ABSTRACT

Presented with a programmable, mobile robot, a group of five to six-year-old children works out a realistic objective (devising a path), writes the corresponding program, runs and corrects it. For them it is the occasion, in an active and autonomous way, of elaborating representations of states and movements, breaking up the representation of a global transformation into concrete and infralogical operations (in Piaget's sense), symbolising this sequence of concrete operations through a one-to-one correspondence between an action and its symbol, putting to use measuring skills.

Our purpose is to show all the interest of this pedagogical situation as regards the development of preoperative intelligence.

The use of computer-using teaching devices is spreading through pre-school, primary and secondary teaching.   Two problems arise:

- what is the real interest of the device?
- what objectives and strategy are to be used?

Our purpose is to try and bring a precise answer to the first question by using a specific tool, but it can also be seen as a suggestion of teaching objectives and thus as an initial element in the answer to the second question.

1.   THE EXPERIMENTAL SITUATION

We are dealing here with an actual teaching situation in which a group of six five and six-year-old children program a robot called a tortoise.   It is able to perform rotative and translatory movements and, by using a central pen, it can leave the mark of its displacement on the floor.   The children can use four punched cards (Forward (FW) - Back (BK) Turn right 90° (TR) - Turn Left 90° (TL), which command the corresponding movements of the robot.   They are supposed to:

- suggest an objective: here placing on the floor one or two skittles which the tortoise has to knock over.

- write the program which will perform this task, using symbols which they have previously defined themselves.

- run this program and correct the mistakes they have seen.

The teacher accompanies the group's research by structuring it but without intervening in the task itself.

1.1 Situation A:

objective   Path A

Program: 1.   TL FW - 2. TR FW - 3. TL FW
           2.   TR FW - 5. TL FW - 6. TR FW - 7 FW

Fig. 1: Situation A

dotted line: the course as planned by the
              children
continuous line: the course as executed and
                  drawn on the floor by the tortoise

This course required seven successive programs. For each one, the teacher asked the children if the tortoise would knock the skittle over; if the answer was positive, the program was run.   When the shortcoming was noted, the program was amended, and so on until the aim was reached.

1.2 Situation B:

Objective   Path B1   Path B2

Fig. 2: Situation B

Programs: B1 : FW FW FW TL FW
            B2: BK TR FW TL 6FW

            Fig. 2: Situation B

The children did not try to reach the first
skittle in the direct way.   Their plan required
the teacher's intervention so that the tortoise
might be pointed correctly (the punched card
corresponding to the required rotation was
not available for the children).

According to the children, program B1 could
knock over both skittles: actually, the
tortoise did not even reach the first one.

Program B2 corrects and completes program B1.
It was made with the help of cardboard arrows
which have the same length as the tortoise's
step.

Note: There was a week's interval between
situations A and B, during which the children
had three sessions with the tortoise.

2.   REPRESENTATION OF THE TRANSFORMATIONS - MENTAL IMAGES

This experimental situation especially
enables us to analyse the child's representations of space and of the movements of the mobile as well as their respective evolutions.

We will deal with these representations for
each situation: first, under its operative
aspects, that is to say concerning the
transformations and everything which modifies
the object, second, under their figurative
aspects, that is to say everything concerning
the configurations, the states and their
static representations.

2.1 Situation A: pre-operative representations:

(i) operative aspects:

The way the "ideal vector" is drawn on
the floor by the children with their fingers
and the way it is sought out through the
successive anticipations (the untested programs),
is a slightly curved diagonal; it is the
course the child would follow, if he or she
were placed in the situation of the moving
object.   So the anticipations are simple:
a rotation to "look at the tortoise", followed
by a translation.   The representation of the
displacement which first emerges is therefore
that of the sensorimotor schema of the displacement itself.

In fact this representation will not be
modified by failure and the successive
anticipations will all try to carry it out,
to no avail.   Moreover, these anticipations
are of a repetitive nature.   This points to
an activity which is more assimilative than
accommodating.   The problem is solved by the
repetition of the schema with an automatic
regulation (TL-FW and TR-FW alternate

regularly) through a simple compensatory
correction.

If there is accommodation it is to the situation and not to the object: the laws which
govern its displacement (the 90° rotation and
length of the translation) are not taken into
account.

One may notice the children's attempts to
stop the rotation while it is under way or
their expression of disappointment when the
expected orientation is exceeded, but there is
no search for another strategy as regards the
displacement; this tends to show that the
succession TL FW - TR FW, or vice-versa, is
not meant to come back to the starting
position but rather constitutes the search
for an intermediate direction.   What is at
stake here is not the reversibility of the
rotation, and the angle itself is not represented as the invariant of the transformation.

So the representation of the displacement is
really of a pre-operative type: it is
linked to familiar situations, does not
take into account the internal coordinations
of the mobile, and its invariants (measure of
the angle and position of the mobile for the
rotation, direction and length for the translation) are not apprehended as such.

(ii) figurative aspects:

The problem which mobilises the children's
research is the direction of the displacement.
The aim of the successive rotations is to
obtain that "the turtle watches the skittle":
this configuration symbolises the familiar
displacement.   The anticipations thus worked
out take into account the position of the
goal compared with that of the mobile: it
is situated on its right or its left and the
space is divided into two parts on either side
of the axis of symmetry of the mobile.
Furthermore, the distance which is to be
covered never holds the children's attention
and no measuring behaviour can be noted; the
representation of the course is a continuous
line.

Thus the represented space is a topological
space in which certain relations are
favoured (way and direction), others are
ignored (distance), and in which the bearings
are those of the mobile and not those of a
"containing" space in which the mobile and the
goal are situated.

Solving the problem required a representation
of the course to be followed in a space which
belongs to a projective type, coupled with
coordination in an orthonormal space:

Fig. 3   Solving situation A

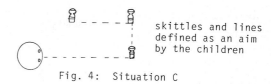

skittles and lines
defined as an aim
by the children

Fig. 4: Situation C

The representation of the displacement operates
indirectly by dissociating the translation on
the x-axis from the translation on the y-axis:
in order to built this representation, the child
must move the mobile away from the goal, then
bring it back nearer, which corresponds to
another sensorimotor schema. If this type of
representation does not correspond to the one
of the displacement itself, it is nevertheless
familiar to the pre-school child who is used
to square pattern exercises. This is probably
why one may note that, very rapidly, the
representation of the course to be followed by
the mobile will be situated in an orthonormal
projective space.

2.2 Situation B: from pre-operative
representations to concrete operations.

(i) Operative aspects:

The first task, carried out by two
children, is to place on the floor the two
skittles that the tortoise will have to knock
over.

Watching the children, one sees their hesitations, which reveal a problem solving behaviour:
placing the skittles so that they can be knocked
over by the tortoise. This activity requires
a representation of the possible movement:
two elements lead one to think that the
children do not only take into account the
figurative aspects of the displacement, that
is to say the representation of a "path" (as
it was more especially the case in situation A):

- the hesitations with placing one skittle in
relation to the other (changing the place of
one skittle entails a related change for the
other) and the eye motions to and from the
tortoise to the skittles.

- the "planned course" which reveals taking
into account, at least partially, the "laws
of tortoise movements": the coordinations
differ from those of the movement itself.

One particular element of the situation is not
taken into account in an adequate way: the
direction of the tortoise. On the other hand
it will be taken into account in situation C,
which is similar as far as orders are concerned
and which directly followed situation B.

This evolution toward a definition of aims which
take into account the internal coordinations
of the moving object (in particular, the 90°
rotation) will be largely borne out in the
following sessions. The figurative aspects
of the representation of the movement going in
a similar way toward a growing precision and
adaptation (see 2.2 (ii)).

Thus the displacement taken as an objective
by the children is no longer, as it was in
situation A, a representation (based on a
mostly assimilative activity) of the sensorimotor schema of the movement itself. Here
one may observe the development of a schema
more adapted to the internal coordinations of
the moving object. It is probably also an
accommodation of schemata which were experimented with in activities involving courses with
obstacles, psychomotor activities (working
on space bearings), practising square patterns
etc. This accommodating activity can be
seen in particular through imitation play:
"walking like the tortoise", a game which
particularly contributes to elaborating representations of the displacement.

Here a first level of adaptation is carried out.
Eventually a very active exploration of the
schema will be observed through the creation
of drawings which will be well adapted to the
moving object.

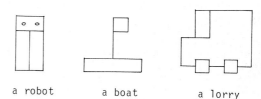

a robot   a boat   a lorry

Fig. 5   drawings created by the
         children to be made by the
         tortoise

However, in situation B, on the operative
level, the important element is the articulation
between anticipations B1 and B2: the children
do not continue with program B1 by using a
regulation (here TR FW) but they make the
moving object go the reverse way: BK TR reverse
of TL FW, bringing it to the position it held
when the mistake was made.

We have here the representation of a reversible action or concrete operation.   It coordinates two transformations which are themselves reversible and which both contain invariants: the angle measure and the position of the moving object on the floor as regards the rotation, the direction and length as regards the translation.   The existence of these invariants for the children will be clearly brought to the fore eventually, on the occasion of devising more complex paths, when the teacher asks the children: "after FW (or BK), in which direction will the tortoise point?", "after TR (or TL) where will the tortoise be?"

Unlike what was observed in situation A, in which the succession of TR FW - TL FW did not correspond to the wish of going back to the starting direction, we have here the constitution of two pairs of opposite movements: TR - TL and FW - BK.   We will also note the trial-and-error experimentation of other pairs which allow going back to the starting situation:

    TR - TR TR TR

    FW - TR TR FW TR TR

These will be quickly discarded to take advantage of inverted pairs, which are more "economical".

The construction of simple operative processes can first be seen in the situations which involve correcting mistakes.   There these processes will constitute basic procedures for conception and realisation.   Indeed the coordination of these two pairs of inverted transformations TL - TR and FW - BK will quickly enable the children to plan, then program very complex drawings.

The narrow range of available actions which the children have to coordinate probably facilitates the development of simple operative processes.   The gradual availability of extra cards (several lengths of translation, several complementary angles of rotation) will allow the exploration of concrete equivalent pairs (TR 90 = TR 45 + TR 45, etc.) as well as far more complex coordinations, the relations between translations being mastered before those between rotations.

Furthermore, programming the planned drawing, then correcting programming efforts, places the children in a situation in which they have to coordinate the representations of transformations.   The teacher's questions invite them to justify these representations.   Thus, the teaching strategy adopted here tries to develop the representation of transformations and the operative abilities of the thinking.

(ii) Figurative aspects:

- In situations B and C, when the skittles are placed and the path devised, or during the imitation game ("walking like the tortoise"), the representation of the 90° angle is fairly precise.   So is the representation of the axis of symmetry of the moving object.   The axis determines in particular the direction of the translation.   In any case, it is precise enough, considering the dimensions of the object which allow the children to achieve the aim, in the situations described, despite a certain amount of error in the representation of the rotations and straight lines.

- Apparently, the representation of the "path" to be followed is now built gradually, according to successive systems of orthogonal marks.   One of the axes is the axis of symmetry of the moving object and the other is the direction of the orthogonal projection of the aim on this axis.

For example:

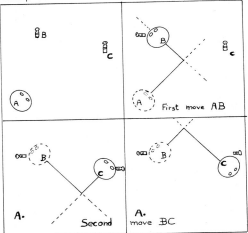

Fig. 6: construction of the displacement
         representations

The drawings in fig. 5 constitute a simplication made by the children.   All the displacements are achieved according to a single system of axes (at first, the axis of symmetry of the mobile and its perpendicular) which the tortoise carries "on its back" so to speak.   This makes it possible to organise space step-by-step.   Paradoxically, the mobile is the fixed part (i.e. the origin of the axes) while the system of axes is mobile.

- In addition, situation B allows the children to be faced with measure problems as regards translations.   Anticipation B1 (3 FW TL FW) is partially based on the fact that the representation of a "long path" is assimilated to that of a previous activity (drawing a square whose side precisely equalled 3 FW).   But the evaluation activity remains approximate and incomplete since the second part of the path, the more remote in time, is not evaluated.

With the execution of program B1, the necessity of measuring the distances to be covered is asserted by some of the children who select a cardboard stick of the same length as a "tortoise step". Measuring the lengths will be carried out through iteration of this measure unit on the plan drawn on the floor.

In situation C, this measuring skill will be brought up to the level of the definition of the aim itself: the position of the skittles on the floor is taken into account again during the programming so that the aim may actually be reached at the end of the translation.

The introduction of a punched card allowing a displacement equal to half the first one will eventually allow the construction of equivalent relations:

2 AV10 = AV20

3 AV10 = AV20 AV10

and experimenting on commutative relations:

AV10 AV20 = AV20 AV10

Furthermore, the gradual change from the actual plan, drawn on the floor, to the reduced plan, through an evolution of the aims (drawing stairs or a truck), gives the children opportunities of experimenting with proportional relations, reduction and enlarging.

3. SYMBOLISATION OF THE TRANSFORMATIONS

3.1 The symbols:

The construction of the program in the experimental situation is based on some initial work consisting in exploring the cards and the symbolisation of the movements made by the moving object. This is worth explaining in detail.

The children are provided with blank punched cards, they will test them and find a means of identifying them reliably, all the more so as, since the children operate in several successive groups, the symbols retained by some will have to be identifiable by the others. This is a situation in which a system of social symbols is created, which furthermore expresses concrete logical relations: relations of similarity (two translations in the same direction, two rotations of the same angle) and inverted relations (two translations along the same line but in opposite directions, two rotations of the same angle but in opposite directions).

The symbols retained by the children vary according to their level of development, more especially in the field of the semiotic function and their ability to find marks in space:

- from a fairly close image of the moving object and its movements

(the rotations are never represented as retaining the position, thus they are dissociated from a translation).

- to the symbol, more detached from its concrete content:

(here the direction of reading and writing is used as a reference for FW).

- to the sign : FW RE TL TR

(signs written on the cards by the maker, presenting a maximum potential for socialization and a minimum amount of specific representation).

For writing the programs, the various systems will be used, sometimes successively. Images and symbols, being for a long time a precious help as regards space marks (right-left), can be kept for identifying cards therefore movements, whereas the signs are used for writing the program.

3.2 The programs:

Writing the programs leads the children to breaking up a global and continuous representation (of transformations and/or configurations) into an ordered succession of representations (of transformations and/or configurations), therefore leading toward an algorithmic approach. Correcting the program will also be an opportunity of gradually elaborating a working method (as well as a method for group work with some sharing of the tasks: suggestions, verifications, writing).

The program establishes a one-to-one correspondence between two series: the transformations series and the symbols series. Verifying a program, searching for a mistake (a programming or writing mistake?) requires <u>finding one's way around in these two heterogeneous series</u> (the drawing of a path and a succession of symbols). This difficulty is particularly visible in the early forms of program writing which are often doubly representative:

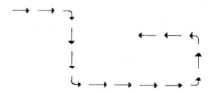

the transition to linear program writing (which) can be observed about the age of six), like the transition from symbols to signs, reveals a gradual detachment between the signifier (symbols, programs) and the signified (simple transformation, path).

The writing of the program also demands time coordinations: FW - TL symbolise a displacement which differs from TL - FW; the relation of their succession in time is not commutative, and the ordered relation contained in the program is fundamental, considering the type of transformation which is experimented upon.

4. CONCLUSIONS

This analysis was meant to show that the teaching situation of robot programming concretely offers a very rich field of experiments to children who become the builders of their own knowledge:

- by developing the representations of configurations in space, with a topological dominant characteristic which, however, becomes gradually organized into partial, orthonormal, spaces of a projective type.

- by developing the representations of transformations in which simple operative processes are set up, implying reversibility and coordinating the operations into a system.

- by building a system of socially shared symbols.

- by concretely exploring relations of equivalence, of correspondence between series, of commutativity, of associativity, of proportionality, on the three levels of their actions, their representations through mental images, their written symbols.

A pedagogical characteristic of the above situation is to allow children, who act autonomously (choosing the aim and procedures, manipulating the computer), to verify how adapted their anticipations are when compared with their plan, through action and the mediation of a machine which they soon regard as reliable. Operating on concrete objects and actions, this situation is an incentive to making plans, to projecting in space and time by the means of mental representations in which the development of concrete, infralogical, logical-mathematical operations is the necessary condition for achieving increasingly ambitious projects, elaborated by the children.

BIBLIOGRAPHY

(1) A.MATTRO, "Dictionnaire d'épistémologie génétique", Presses Universitaires de France, Paris, 1966 (French).

(2) M. BODEN, "Piaget", Harvester Press, London, 1979.

(3) D. COHEN, "Faut-il brûler Piaget?" Retz, Paris, 1981, (French).

(4) J.M. DOLLE, "Pour comprendre Jean Piaget", Privat Toûlouse, 1974 (French).

(5) R. DROZ, M. RAHMY, "Lire Paget", Mardaga, Bruxelles, 1978, (French)

(6) H.E. GRUBER, J.J. VONECHE, "The Essential Piaget": An Interpretive Reference and Guide" Basic Books, New York, 1977.

(7) J. PIAGET, "Six études de psychologie", Gonthier, Genève, 1964 (French)

(8) J. PIAGET, "La psychologie de l'enfant" Presses Universitiares de France, Paris, 1966 (French)

(9) J. PIAGET, "Psychologie et Pédagogie" Denoël, Paris 1966, (French)

(10) J. PIAGET, "Réussir et Comprendre" Presses Universitaires de France, Paris 1974 (French)

(11) S. PAPERT, "Mindstorms, Children, Computers, and Powerful Ideas", Basic books, New York, 1980.

COMPUTERS IN EDUCATION, F. Lovis and E.D. Tagg (eds.)
Elsevier Science Publishers B.V. (North-Holland)
© IFIP, 1988

An Approach to Computer Control in the Primary and Secondary School.

H.B.Fielding and J.Taylor

Birmingham Educational Computing Centre, The Bordesley Centre,
Camp Hill, Stratford Road, Birmingham B11 1AR.
West Midlands. United Kingdom.

The terms "Microprocessor Control", "Computer Control", "Control Systems" often fill the recipient with pains of anxiety which in turn lead to a complete withdrawal from any further participation with the concept. Computer control need not be a difficult concept to comprehend provided that the major obstacle "I need to understand electronics to do this" is eliminated at the start by the use of purpose built equipment. This paper outlines the steps undertaken by the authors to create a complete package, allowing computer control to become a part of project work and problem solving throughout all phases of education.

1.Introduction

The computer should be seen as a resource for use in the classroom and not as a specialised piece of equipment for occasional use. General purpose computers are finding increasing use in many if not most UK Primary and Secondary schools. The uses range from wordprocessing to interrogation of remote data bases via the telephone system. One area that is in the early stages of development is the use of a computer to enhance and extend projects involving control of real devices. An electric motor built into a model of a fairground roundabout would be an example of a "real device". This is where the problem begins, most computers have means of connecting external devices such as printers, modems and the like, but where do I plug in my electric motor? Of course motors and other devices have been connected to and have been controlled by computers. To do this has demanded a knowledge and expertise in electronics posessed by relativly few teachers. There is a need for a system that could bring together the use of computers and existing project work.

Birmingham is a large Education Authority of over 450 Primary and Secondary Institutions. All of these have some computing provision ranging from single stand alone computers to multiple station network systems. Standardisation of equipment has meant that Primary schools have used Research Machines 480Z systems, the secondary area used Research Machines 380Z and 480Z systems. Recently Research Machines Nimbus systems, either stand alone or networked have been introduced into both areas.

The curriculum areas involving computer control are:

CDT Craft Design Technology.
There is an increasing awareness of the use of a computer as a controller in design projects.

Computer Studies.
In most examination courses there is a section on the use of a computer in a control situation.

Science.
There is a frequent need for data logging equipment to record values in practical experiments and demonstrations.

Information Technology.
Demonstrating the real applications of computers in control situations.

Primary project work.
This should be seen as an extra facet or dimension to add, when relevant, to existing project work.

The authors, working at the Birmingham Educational Computing Centre, were asked to give help and advice in the role and implementation of computers into those curriculum areas.

The problems faced were:
A range of equipment throughout the age range, further complicated by the fact that the City's CDT area used BBC B machines.

A range of ages and abilities.

A wide variety of uses to which the computer was to be put.

It was decided to adopt a common range of hardware and software for the City. This would have advantages in purchasing, distribution, staff training and support. The advantage to the pupil would be a common system that would help provide some continuity between the primary and secondary phases.

There was nothing on the market that would meet the wide range of needs and so a set of hardware modules were designed by the authors.

2.Solution

2.1 Hardware.

The core of the system is an interface unit that can plug into any of the computers currently supported by the Authority. At present this includes Research machines 380Z / 480Z / Nimbus, BBC B machines together with a number of IBM PC's in Primary schools involved in the IBM Schools Project. The unit, called the ABI , (Adaptable BECC Interface), buffers all the 8 input and 8 output lines and together with 2 sets of LED's provides a visual indication of the state of these lines. Each of the input and output lines has a standard DIN socket to allow external devices to be connected as shown in figure 1.

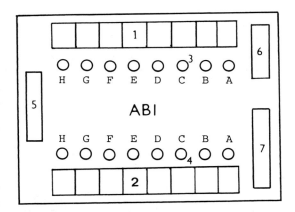

1 One of eight output sockets.
2 One of eight input sockets.
3 One of eight output indicators.
4 One of eight input indicators.
5 Connection to computer.
6 10 way output connector.
7 26 way input/output connector.

Figure 1. The interface unit, ABI.

As it stands, the interface unit cannot supply enough power to drive any motors or external lamp units. A relay switch unit, ABR, (Adaptable BECC Relay), can be plugged into any output socket. This relay unit will switch power to a device. The power supply is matched to the device. This method has several advantages, one of which is that there is no restriction on the type of motor used, (other than the current limit of the relay and Health and Safety requirements).

There are good reasons for using this arrangement, it brings out the ideas of signal paths and power supply paths as shown in figure 2.

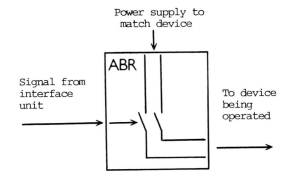

Figure 2. The relay unit, ABR.

Relay units can be plugged into any or all of the output sockets if and when required. As a further provision, the relay units have a switch that allows the unit to operate as either a power ON/OFF switch or as a power reversing switch. By using two relay units, one as a power ON/OFF switch and the other as a power reversing switch, a motor can be controlled and reversed. Two sets of relays, (4 relays using 4 signal lines), can control two motors on a model "buggy" to allow it to be moved and steered. The control of the motors is limmited to on or off. When finer control is required the relay units can be replaced by a dual motor control unit, the ABM, (Adaptable BECC Motor unit). This is a pulse width driver unit that allows each motor to be set to one of 7 motor speeds in either direction. Once the unit has been given the speed and direction values for each motor a memory stores the values and allows the unit to function without constant control by the computer.

A range of sensors, ABS, (Adaptable BECC Sensors), was developed to plug into the input sockets. At present in the range are mechanical switches, optical switches and magnetic switches. All are based on a common sized circuit board to house a minimal number of comonents. In practice this allows pupils to quickly replace a sensor with an alternative to investigate practical advantages and disadvantages of a range of sensor types. Many of the sensors are purely switches, others require a low voltage power supply and this is taken from the input socket on the ABI.

All the input sensors are used to provide digital signal, when analogue values are needed, for instance, temperature values in a science experiment, an analogue to digital converter is needed. The ABA, (Adaptable BECC Analogue unit), is a four channel, three range unit. This enables the output from say a temperature probe to be linked to a computer via the ABA and ABI. The signals to and from the converter can be seen, helping in any explanation to the pupils of how it operates.

In use, the equipment should be seen as a means of building and evaluating a total system. Parts can be quickly plugged together during a lesson and just as quickly dismantled when required by other pupils.

All the units are built on printed circuit boards with all components in view. The larger units have a transparent plastic cover that carries a legend. This is deliberate, we want pupils to see the component used and stimulate interest that may have links in other areas. For instance, many of the sensor units are based on a resistive chain, one fixed, the other variable. The principles involved in resistor chains form part of all physics courses and could provide a useful cross-curricular link.

2.2 Software.

However simple and convenient the hardware system, it demands an easy to use computer program to be effective. A suite of programs collectivly called BEACONS, (Birmingham Educational Adaptable CONtrol Software), was written as an integral part of the system. The main programs in the suite are the Creator / Editor and the Program Converter.

The Creator / Editor program is a LOGO style language based on ARROW written by Oxfordshire originally for the Research Machines 380Z / 480Z range of computers. The syntax and structure remains common to ARROW, the Turtle graphics commands being replaced by commands relevant to control.

The display screen shows a mimic of an ABI as shown in figure 3. The lower part of the screen displays the commands or instructions as they are typed in from the keyboard.

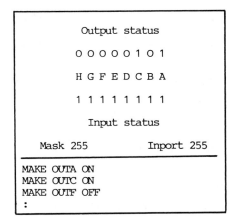

```
        Output status

        O O O O O 1 O 1

        H G F E D C B A

        1 1 1 1 1 1 1 1

         Input status

  Mask 255          Inport 255

 MAKE OUTA ON
 MAKE OUTC ON
 MAKE OUTF OFF
 :
```

Figure 3. Screen display.

As an example, to switch on the lowest significant bit of the output port of the computer.

MAKE OUTA ON

The output line A on the ABI goes on and the computer screen also shows this change.
The lines, (bits), of the computer port are referred to by a letter rather than a number. There are two reasons for this, one, that we did not want to equate using the program with mathematics and two, to remove any ambiguity, the 8 lines can be referred to as lines 1 to 8 or lines 0 to 7. The two possible states are referred to as ON or OFF although the alternative of 1 or 0 can be used if desired.
Altering one of the 8 lines does not affect the remaining ones. There is an alternative command when and if more than one line needs to be changed at once.

MAKE OUTPORT 255

will turn on all the output lines regardless of their previous state.

As an example, a program to turn a lamp on and off at a set rate could be written thus

MAKE OUTA ON   Turns line A on

```
WAIT 20            Does nothing for 2 seconds

MAKE OUTA OFF      Turns line A off

WAIT 20            Does nothing for 2 seconds
```

The WAIT instruction is a time delay with increments of 1 tenth of a second. It was thought that an increment of 1 hundredth of a second would be difficult to appreciate by younger pupils and a full second increment was too coarse.

The program supports procedures that may be written by the pupils or, in the early stages, by the teacher. Procedures can call on other procedures in building a control program.

After the control program has been written, it can be tested and proved by running it at a much reduced speed. This enables the pupil to see what is happening and what should be happening. The lower part of the computer screen displays the current instruction or command, whilst the upper part displays the mimic panel of the interface unit. Once the program has been proved, it can now be converted to a form that will run in BASIC on the host computer. The speed of operation is now much faster and should prove satisfactory for most control applications in school.

At this point it becomes obvious that the host computer is mostly redundant. The control program uses the ABI interface as the sole input / output path. There is no need for a keyboard / monitor / disk drive etc. What is now needed is a small computer controller that could run the developed control program. Realising this, we designed a small single board computer controller to fit this need, this became the ABC, (Adaptable BECC Controller), It is based around the Zilog Z8 controller chip. This has a built in BASIC and among many features a serial port for data transfer. The minimum system has 2K of program memory and a single input / output port, (8 lines in, 8 lines out). The memory can be expanded by 2K and then 8K to form a maximum of 12K. A second I/O port can be added to give a total of 16 input and 16 output lines.

In use the ABC is loaded with a program through the serial port. This program is in Z8 BASIC that has been converted from an original LOGO style control program. Once the program is in memory, it can be started simply by altering the memory mode switch from RAM to ROM and then pressing the Reset button. The memory chips can be replaced by battery backed versions and so programs can be retained even when power to the board is removed. The use of RAM memory means that fresh programs can be run simply by reloading with another program.

The great advantage of the ABC in this situation is that it releases the host computer for other tasks and is a much more cost effective solution than buying extra computers.

3. Example.

As an example of how computer control can be added to a primary school project the following is taken from part of a major staff In-Service course put on by BECC in the spring of 1987.

The course for primary school teachers involved "computer control" as one of the four main areas of study. The theme of an exercise was to discover how computer control could be added to existing project work and not be seen as a new area. The teachers were set a task to build a model lighthouse and to develop a means of producing a flashing light that would operate automatically at night. Furthermore, the flashing light was to be unique, so that it could be identified. Each team contained two teachers. The object was to start from a base that the teachers would feel experienced and confident and then to extend this by adding the computer control. A wide variety of lighthouse designs were produced but all had lamps switched on and off under computer control. To sense light and dark, a light sensor was incorporated into many of the designs. The control software was developed on the host computer, tested out and then converted to run under BASIC. Several points emerged from the group, they found it very easy to change the flash rate if they found another group with an identical sequence. If the lighthouse operated in the day time but not night time, it was easy to alter a small part of the control program to the correct operation. An example of one such control program is shown below.

```
IF INA = ON THEN STAY

MAKE OUTA ON

WAIT 20

MAKE OUTA OFF

WAIT 40
```

The first line tests for daylight. The sensor produces a 1 or ON value in daylight. If it is daylight then the program remains on that line and continues to test over and over until the value of INA is not ON and then it continues down the remaining operations. The lamp is switched on for 2 seconds and then off for 4 seconds. The program then goes back to the first line. To introduce the idea of computer control to younger pupils, the teacher could have first produced two procedures

DARK

this would check for darkness, if light then stay at this point in the program.

FLASH ON,OFF

this controls the time the light is on, and the time the light is off.

eg. FLASH 2,4

would carry out the times 20 units ON and 40 units OFF. The times would then be in seconds for the pupils'use.

Once the lighthouses are operating this could provide a starting point for other studies and activities. Each lighthouse can be controlled by its own ABC. These now automatic model lighthouses can be spread around the school playing area. If the pupils are given the flash identifications and a "map" of their positions then they could do some practical navigational work on bearings and position.

The figure 4 outlines the stages in the development of such a project.

4.Conclusion

The system developed at BECC provides a cost effective solution where practical computer control is involved.

There is little redundancy in the equipment. Systems can be built up from the range of units. There can be a progression in the design process because of the wide range of units.

The system has been enthusiastically received by all phases within the City of Birmingham, so much so that all the units are now available commercially from a major educational electronics manufacturer.

The system has been in operation in projects from Primary school pupils of 9 and 10 years old to Secondary school and 6th Form students.

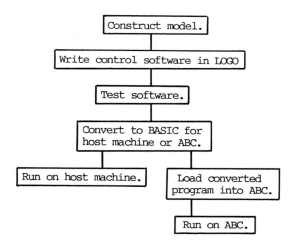

Figure 4. Development stages.

COMPUTERS IN EDUCATION, F. Lovis and E.D. Tagg (eds.)
Elsevier Science Publishers B.V. (North-Holland)
© IFIP, 1988

LEGO with COMAL
An interactive process control- and learning environment

Leo Højsholt-Poulsen

Aarhus Amts Informatikcenter and Silkeborg Amtsgymnasium
Graham Bells Vej 1 A, DK-8200 Aarhus N, Denmark

This paper describes one of our greatest successes with the integration of computers in the education of 16 to 19 year old students in the Danish gymnasium: A small washing machine model built from Lego bricks is controlled from an inexpensive microcomputer. The programming language is Comal whose kernel of keywords has conveniently been extended to include a programme package containing the basic instructions for the washing machine. This combination of a small washing machine that tangibly illustrates the effect of the students` instructions and a friendly programming environment that allows interaction between student, computer and process, enables the students to approach many vital subjects during only two hours of exercises.

1. INTRODUCTION

1.1 The purpose

When the students are working with the computer, it is useful for them to see a direct result of their efforts e.g. a graphics picture or as described in this paper, a machine responding to instructions received from the computer. It is possible to use these alternatives successfully to teach the students computer science by means of mathematical or statistical subjects. In this way the students learn about subjects related to engineering such as process control, signals in/out, timers, counters, light sensitive diodes and motors, as well as subjects related to computer science such as procedures and functions, variables, expressions, conditional branching and loops.

1.2 The background

During the last ten years we at the Silkeborg Amtsgymnasium (Silkeborg Community College) have been working with the integration of computers in the teaching, specially in physics, described in English in [1, 2]. The students now experiment routinely with the collection of data from measurements and the control of arrangements through computer signals. Development (also in society) has made it natural to follow up with "the automated process", in which the microprocessor controls almost the entire sequence of operations. There may be different lines of approach to this. Naturally, the most appropriate thing to do, is to let the students work with a **real process**. As this most often is impossible or rather expensive, a solution is to let the students work with a **model**.

1.3 The programming environment

Along with the testing and developing of the laboratory equipment, we have experimented with the programming environments from where the equipment is controlled. As regards fast measurings it is necessary to use programmes partly written directly in assembly language. We have also experimented with the programming lan-

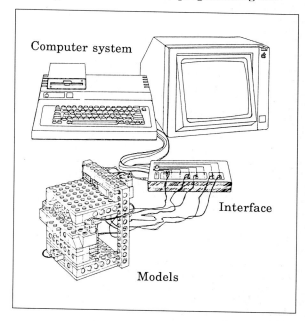

Figure 1: Student setup; microcomputer, interface box and washing mashine model built from Lego bricks.

guages Basic, Logo and Pascal. In cases where the students take an active part in the programme development phase, we have decided to use Comal [3]. Comal is structured, powerful and available for almost any microcomputer in Northern Europe. Furthermore, it is the preferred programming language in Danish computer science teaching.

2. THE HARDWARE

It is of importance to the students that they are familiar with the environment. Among the many possibilities of automated processes with the Lego models, we chose a washing machine. Almost every student in Denmark has tried washing with an automatic washing machine (anyway, we thought so). In concert with the Tønder College of Teacher Education [4] and the company Lego A/S [5] a student set-up was constructed, shown in figure 1, in which a washing machine built from Lego bricks is controlled and monitored from an inexpensive Commodore 64 microcomputer. The signals to and from the computer pass through an interface that partly protects the computer against destructive current intensities and partly amplifies the computer signals to the washing machine. The interface shown in figure 2 is fit for two computer inputs and six computer outputs. The washing machine model has two signal lamps, a motor and a photo sensor to control that the door on the washing machine is closed (figure 3).

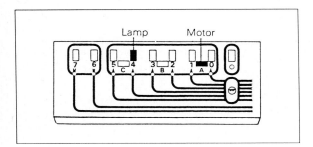

Figure 2: *The interface between microcomputer and model is fit for two computer inputs and six computer outputs.*

3. THE SOFTWARE

For the control of the experimental set-up it is necessary to use instructions the computer recognizes. Furthermore, some of the instructions must be translated into signals for the controlled machine. One of Comal's many advantages is its well defined kernel of keywords. The user may extend this kernel with her or his own modules containing custom-built procedures and functions exactly tailored for a determined purpose. In this case,

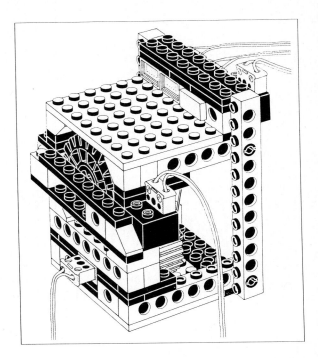

Figure 3: *Lego washing mashine with signal lamps, motor and photo sensor to sense whether the door is closed.*

the UniComal Comal [6] was used on a Commodore 64/128, a computer that is common in many Danish physics laboratories. In addition Comal is well suited because all instructions are syntax analyzed instantly, which means that the students are guided with information of errors or of further coding.

It is also important that a language is structured. A procedure or a function may be independently tested immediately after coding. In the following, Comal's keywords will be written in UPPER case. In table 1 one finds the special procedures and functions that transmit signals to and receive signals from the arrangement. These instructions are contained in a Comal package located on a disk, developed by [4]. When the procedures of the packages are read from the disk, these too will be recognized by the system. Thus a programme that has to control a process may consist in a combination of specific signal procedures and Comal keywords.

4. THE EXPERIMENT

4.1 Initial arrangement

The students start with the construction of the washing machine, if this has not been done already. Then computer, interface and washing machine are connected. The equipment is turned on,

```
biton(out_no)
bitoff(out_no)
getbit(in_no)
settimer(clock_no,clock_time)
gettimer(clock_no)
setlevel(out_no,power)
getlevel(out_no)
motor(out_id,state,power)
setcounter(in_no,state)
getcounter(in_no)
wait(sec_10th)
alarm // beep
water_on // white noise on
water_off // white noise off
cut
stopbox
```

Table 1:   Comal package control procedures and functions

and the package with signal routines is loaded from disk. Then control is carried out to prove that the interface is active and correctly connected.

The students now learn step by step to control the machine. At first the inputs and outputs must be identified:

4.2 Control of outputs

One of the lamps on the washing machine is connected with output 1. When the command **biton(1)** is entered on the computer, the lamp on the washing machine is lit. It can also be verified that the signal lamp 1 on the interface is lit. **bitoff(1)** will switch off the lamp. Thus the students learn to control if there should be voltage to an output by typing **biton(out_no)** and **bitoff(out_no)**.

The motor in the washing machine is connected with output (4-5) - across. **biton(4)** then activates the motor to work in one direction. **biton(5)** activates the motor to run in the other direction. The students try out the instructions and learn the importance of stopping the motor from time to time with **bitoff!**

The motor's speed of rotation is regulated as follows:

```
biton(4)          // the motor rotates
setlevel(4,2)     // the speed of rotation is reduced
bitoff(4)         // the motor is turned off
```

Then the students experiment with the direction and the speed of rotation of the motor. They make use of the possibility to control the intensity of the voltage. **setlevel(4,8)** is maximum speed. **setlevel(4,0)** turns off motor 4.

4.3 Reading of inputs

The photo sensor placed at the door on the washing machine is connected with input 6. On the interface the lamp at input 6 may be observed when opening and closing the door. The signal on/off = closed/open is transmitted to the computer where it is read in, using the function **getbit**. By use of the command **PRINT getbit(6)** the computer writes 1 or 0 depending on whether the door is open or closed. Again this time the students advance by experimenting. Thus by using the function **getbit(in_no)** it is possible to receive signals from input 6 or 7.

In this way, the students in the beginning learn how the basic procedures and functions of the Comal package can be used to control and monitor a process: A procedure can be used to carry an action into effect; a function to measure and read a value which it returns to the system. Therefore, you may, for example require to have the value of a function printed (e.g. PRINT getbit(6)). The instructions are carried out instantly when the <Return>-key is pressed.

After this the students proceed by themselves to extend the possibilities of controlling their own procedures and functions that may include one or more basic control instructions: First the procedure has to be programmed and made recognizable to the system; then it is activated by calling it by name. In the typical Danish way we began with encapsulating the English operating instructions in national names, e.g.:

```
PROC tænd(no)              (tænd = English: turn on)
    biton(no)
ENDPROC tænd
```

When this user defined procedure has been SCANned, it is known to the system. Lamp 1 may then be activated using the command **tænd(1)**.

A user defined procedure may consist of several different statements:

```
PROC quickwash(no)
    biton(no)
    wait(50)
    bitoff(no)
ENDPROC quickwash
```

The students experiment with this procedure using a previously defined washing time, e.g. for **quickwash(4)**, the motor will rotate in 50/10 seconds. The procedure may be changed and extended with new programming sentences just by listing it on the screen (**LIST quickwash**) and overwriting the existing statements with new ones or adding supplementary lines:

```
PROC quickwash(no,duration)
    biton(no)
    wait(duration)
    bitoff(no)
ENDPROC quickwash
```

This procedure may be tested, using the command: **quickwash(5,30)**.

The students have now already learned uncommon subjects such as <u>variables</u>, <u>structured programming</u>, <u>procedures</u> and <u>transfer of parameters</u>. When programming "a dumb machine", it is very important to follow the instructions to the letter and not believe that the computer will guess what is "missing". Even though the Comal system often helps the programmer, e.g. in case a line is not typed in correctly, it is necessary to maintain a reasonable programming discipline.

By continuing to experiment, some of the students may end up with the following procedure, in which the speed of the motor is regulated and the green lamp is lit, when the motor is working:

```
PROC quickwash(no,duration,speed)
    biton(1)
    setlevel(no,speed)
    biton(no)
    wait(duration)
    bitoff(no)
    bitoff(1)
ENDPROC quickwash
```

4.4 Measurements of time periods

To continue the students now have to learn about timing. Time measurements can be accomplished by five different clocks. The clocks can be set independently using the procedure **settimer(*clock_no,c_time*)**. A time indication from a clock can be obtained using the function **gettimer(*clock_no*)**. The application of clocks is necessary throughout the complete cycle of the washing machine as an instrument to control the entire correct washing time. A test may be carried out in the following way:

```
settimer(1,0)          // reset clock 1
PRINT gettimer(1)      // read time on clock 1
```

The students then set several clocks and read the time on each of them. As the clocks work independently of each other, the students have been introduced in an elementary way to the subject <u>parallel processes</u>.

4.5 Control structures

Until this moment the students have directed all the processes. Now they proceed to monitoring by the use of <u>control structures</u>.

The washing machine is going to wash for some time, but to stop if the door is opened. This can be done using the following programme section, where the students for the first time are going to make a user defined function:

```
FUNC door_open          // This function reports
    RETURN getbit(6)    // if the door is open
ENDFUNC door_open

PROC wash(no,dur)
    setlevel(no,2)                 // set moderate speed
    biton(no)                      // start motor no
    settimer(1,0)                  // reset time
    REPEAT                         // REPEAT
        IF door_open THEN          // IF the door opens THEN:
            alarm                  // start alarm
            settimer(1,dur)        // set time to out of time
        ENDIF                      // END of IF
    UNTIL gettimer(1)>=dur         // UNTIL time is concluded
    bitoff(no)                     // turn off motor no.
ENDPROC wash
```

The function is tested independently. While the door is open and closed, respectively, the command: **PRINT door_open** is entered. Then follows the most difficult task up to now, namely testing and understanding the effect of a command such as **wash(4,100)** (the washing machine starts working in one direction and will run for 10 seconds, if the door is not opened. If the door is opened, the alarm starts, and the washing machine stops).

The students now have learned about <u>control structures</u>, <u>conditional execution</u> and <u>repetition</u> and <u>loops</u>. By seeing the washing machine work, the programme execution becomes evident to the students. The typical course of the experiment is that the students lack comprehension of the procedure when this is typed in. But when it is executed and the washing process is compared to what is written on the screen, they understand what happens and why.

From here, further procedures must be added, so that the washing process continues after a possible opened door has been closed again. Furthermore, a washing machine changes direction of rotation many times during a washing process:

```
PROC laundry(wash_time)
    settimer(2,0)
    REPEAT
        wash(4,20)
        IF door_open THEN pause
        wash(5,20)
        IF door_open THEN pause
    UNTIL gettimer(2)>wash_time
ENDPROC laundry
```

```
PROC pause
    remtime:=gettimer(2)
    REPEAT UNTIL NOT door_open
    settimer(2,remtime)
ENDPROC pause
```

The complete washing programme can be started using the command: **laundry(300)**. For the sound effect the students always choose to add some programming lines that "let water into the washing machine": **water_on**. Most frequently this results in a febrile typing of the command **water_off** or a fast lowering of the monitor's sound intensity.

5. CHALLENGES

The one third of the students who during the two hours of practice went beyond the obligatory process previously lined up, were challenged to continue working on their own with for example programming a spin drier. However, at this point we had to face an unexpected problem. We were very surprised, when we realized that a considerable number of students did not know what a spin drier is, or how it works. Some of the boys answered: "We asked an expert - a girl." Only a few got as far as to the last item in the instructions for the exercise - to make a complete, possibly menu operated, washing programme. The task could be extended in accordance with the students' wishes, but were at least to consist of the following:

start machine	(lamp is lit)
enter water	(possibly add soap)
rinse	(repeat several times)
spin-dry	(possibly observe door)
let water out	
turn machine off	(light off)

6. CONCLUSION

Until this year, in the Danish gymnasium we have tried, with varying degrees of success, to integrate computer science in the existing curriculum. Therefore we have found it vital to introduce the students to the computer in a way that made it possible for all the students to benefit from the teaching, even though they possess very different qualifications. One of the problems in connection with the whole integration model is precisely the large differences in the students' knowledge (and the teachers') about computers and how to work with programming and programme execution.

The students' evaluation of this experiment has without any exception been extraordinarily positive. The exercise has been carried out in groups of 2-3 students. No student has felt it silly to work with the Lego bricks although some were content to start with a ready made washing machine, where it had been constructed previously. What all the evaluations had in common was that the students would have liked to be able to spend much more time on the experiment, and many were surprised that "all the difficult things with computers and so on" could turn out to be so exciting. Especially many of the girls with technophobia became very enthusiastic (the washing machine effect?). We also noticed another effect on the "computer freaks" in the class - he who knows everything about computers or at least thinks he does; in this experiment the students have been given free hands. There has been no limit. Some of these students worked several days after school on the subject: the perfect washing machine. Who knows, maybe several students gave a helping hand next time their family's clothes went into the washing machine.

REFERENCES

[1] Frank Bason and Leo Højsholt-Poulsen, Computer Use in Undergraduate Physics Teaching, <u>Proceedings of WCCE 81</u>, Lausanne, Switzerland, North-Holland Publishing Company, IFIP 1981, part 1, 81-88.

[2] Leo Højsholt-Poulsen, Frank Bason and Aage Andersen, Inexpensive Microcomputer Interfacing for use with Undergraduate Physics Teaching, <u>Proceedings from working conference of Involving Micros in Education</u>, University of Lancaster, England, North-Holland Publishing Company, IFIP 1982.

[3] Frank Bason, COMAL: A Procedural Language Learning Environment, <u>Proceedings from conference of Information Technology and Education: The Development Perspective</u>, Sofia, Bulgaria 1986.

[4] Børge Christensen, Tønder Statsseminarium, Tønder, Denmark.

[5] Lego A/S, Billund, Denmark.

[6] UniComal A/S, Tværmarksvej, Søborg, Denmark.

5. Local, Regional National and International Projects

COMPUTERS IN EDUCATION, F. Lovis and E.D. Tagg (eds.)
Elsevier Science Publishers B.V. (North-Holland)
© IFIP, 1988

CONSIDERATIONS ABOUT THE LOGISTIC
INFRASTRUCTURE FOR FULL INTEGRATION OF COMPUTERS IN EDUCATION

Ben - Zion Barta

Daniel Millin, Asher Youval, Ahuva Feinmesser

Ministry of Education and Culture
JERUSALEM, 91911, ISRAEL

As the integration of computers into the schooling process reaches the scale of whole educational systems, educational authorities have to provide the logistic infrastructure necessary to ensure their efficient and effective use. From the applications point of view 3 subsystems are considered:#1-Computer Aided Learning; #2-Learning of Computer Science and Applications; #3-Educational and General Management. These three form an integrated system needing common infrastructure. The main goals of this infrastructure and its centres of activity are described; human resources development, standardization and licensing of hardware, software, courseware and configurations are other aspects referred to. Finally, the organization and operation of Support and Advice Centres for Educational Computing, one of the main components of the logistic infrastructure, are described.

1. INTRODUCTION

To keep a computer installation operational, there is an obvious physical infrastructure necessary - adequate equipment, housing and related installations, a digital communications network, etc. The physical infrastructure is a necessary condition, but it is not sufficient for having the system operational and efficient.

To ensure smooth and efficient operation, good logistic infrastructure has to be provided, in order to supply all the needs of system operation. It should cover the development of the human resources with related advice and support; planning and selection of applications and organization of their operation; maintenance, repair and immediate solution to technical problems; continuous updating on new applications, new capabilities and new equipment; exchange of information between users, suppliers, developers; and some more...

Any country faced with large scale use of computers in its educational system should take care to provide this infrastructure, as it cares for its all other aspects.

This paper describes the approach that is recently developed in Israel. Section 2 describes the structure of the supported system, emphasizing three related subsystems, each one of them dealing with a specific range of computer applications in education. Following, section 3 presents the main components of the logistic infrastructure, as we see them.

2. STRUCTURE OF THE SUPPORTED SYSTEM.

The system we are referring to is the whole educational system of Israel on its way to make full use of the range of computer based activities, as they can be foreseen now. At present about 60% of the existing 1300 primary schools and about 90% of the existing 600 secondary ones are equipped with computers, most of them making 10-40 workstations available to their pupils.

The rather high rate of computer usage in the primary schools is at present almost unique to our country <1>, the general trend being to have most schools equipped within a few years with one workstation for perhaps every 15-20 pupils.

Concerning secondary education, the situation is quite similar to that in many developed countries. The main trend of development in secondary education is the widening of the range of computer uses. This trend increases the number of workstations, the number of people involved and the variety of applications.

Schools are gradually increasing their usage of computers for administrative purposes, the trend being to use available computer communication facilities for operating an administrative network connecting the schools to the local, regional and central authorities.

One important conclusion from the consideration of these trends concerns the logistic infrastructure needed to support the system in an effective way.

At present and in the near future, schools may get equipment without being adequately prepared to use it or to maintain it. They may not have their manpower trained for successfully and fully exploiting the educational, pedagogical and administrative capabilities of the new tool. The inadequate preparation of the schools results from two facts. On one hand, the systems – hardware, operating systems, networks, courseware, software – get more advanced and sophisticated and, on the other hand the rate of training personnel lags behind the rate of installing new systems.

This rather undesirable situation requires the involvement of the educational authorities to prevent the difficulties (or to cure the problems) which may undermine a potentially radical and far reaching improvement of the present educational system.

Following, we now shortly describe the main components of the educational computing system, and the main agencies involved with its operation.

2.1 Subsystem #1 : Computer Aided Learning

This subsystem is the most important one, from the point of view of the potential to improve the teaching and learning processes and their basic organization. It covers the whole range of methods and approaches for integrating computer - usage in teaching and education, as described in many places in the past 2 - 3 decades, < e.g. 2 - 6 >.

This subsystem usually uses a small subset taken from a myriad of courseware.

software, data bases, etc. prepared by various persons, publishing houses, teachers and pupils, for different machines, in various programming languages or authoring-delivery systems in some cases without fully reliable professional background, only partly documented, not completely debugged...

The persons operating this subsystem are members of the usual teaching staff, in many cases with rather limited knowledge of computers and of the methodology of their educational applications. They have to operate their computers under the pressure of their pupils who are usually eager to get more and more, even after the class period is over... In such conditions, even professional computer personnel and experienced teachers may get confused.

The incomplete preparation of the schools for operating the equipment they purchase is obviously undesirable. Despite the awareness about it, this situation still occurs in many countries, and while making due efforts to prevent it, it has to be also cured by adequate training and support to each school according to its actual difficulties.

This support is needed not only because of the temporary lack of trained manpower. A wide range of current issues will need on-going support, for a long time, time, maybe as a permanent service, that will change its nature according to to the development of the state of the art.

The most outstanding aspects of the infrastructure needed for CAL are:
a. On-going updating about goals, methodology, contents, materials as they become available for the various subject matters and for educational or other formative or instructive activities.
b. Setting up and updating standard requirements for courseware of all types, for system software and software tools, and for hardware and hardware configurations for educational uses. These requirements include communication facilities for educational purposes, like access to data bases, down-loading, etc.
c. Testing and evaluating the products offered to schools, for authorizing their distribution and providing objective and reliable information to the educational community about them.
d. Providing continuous guidance and advice to schools and teachers concerning problems related to planning, purchasing and performing the daily

activities. These should cover general issues, as well as specific subject-matter oriented ones. These actions should include a telephonic hot-line service, to help solving urgent problems, mostly technical difficulties.

e. Setting requirements for the training necessary to all members of the school staff, and providing the means for carrying out this training, pre-service and in-service.

f. Evaluating the whole process and providing feedback to all the agencies concerned.

2.2 Subsystem #2 : Teaching of Computer Science and Computer Applications.

This subsystem includes all activities related to the direct teaching of computer science and applications, at any level, from the beginners' introduction to computers and data handling up to advanced high-school teaching of Computer Science as well as vocational training of computer professionals and computer end users.

While the problems related to the operation of this subsystem are not as hard as those of computer aided learning, still there are some important issues to be taken care of:

a. Providing adequate curricula, materials and methodology.

b. Providing an examination and certification system for students completing their studies.

c. Defining the requirements for the qualification of teachers and providing a framework for licensing teachers.

d. Providing scientific, didactic and technical updating to the licensed teachers.

e. Standardization, testing and evaluation of products - similar to points b. and c. in section 2.1.

f. Providing guidance and advice - point d. in section 2.1.

g. Providing evaluation and feedback.

2.3 Subsystem #3 : Educational and General Management.

Many schools, especially the bigger ones, are already using computers for their general management; some of these have also computerized many of the educational management elements.

The management of learning achievements, presently mostly based on the overall achievement data provided by the

teachers, will develop to provide testing and diagnostic facilities to help teachers and pupils to plan and carry out the teaching-learning process.

Other aspects of management, perhaps mixed educational and administrative in nature, should be part of the system, e.g. the management of human resources and their development, school scheduling, follow-up of the final examinations of the pupils, attendance, library and bibliographic services, medical and social follow-up.

Finally, the more general aspects of administrative applications may provide many useful facilities to the teaching staff as well: electronic mail and announcement-board, word processing and publishing services, data bases, electronic spread sheets, etc.

A computer communication network connecting the schools to the different agencies with which they are cooperating and to which they are reporting, is expected to cause a far reaching change in the way that most of their paper work is organized and performed. In fact, we have to be ready to replace most of the paper work by computer-aided generation, transfer and analysis of the relevant information, followed by computer-aided decision and management systems.

Concerning logistic infrastructure, the requirements of this subsystem are not much different from those mentioned in 2.1 and 2.2. However, there are some specific points of interest:

a. Aspects of communication facilities, protocols, and system compatibility.

b. Data security and protection (also important for CAL systems that keep track of pupils' learning history).

c. Human resources development programmes for the clerical staff, for the management and teachers.

d. The hot-line help desk is of most importance for this subsystem.

e. The uniformity of the operation procedures for all users.

2.4 Basic and Applied Research and Development.

Research and development are not directly involved with the operation of the system we are dealing with, but they are strongly related to it. Most applications operating within the three mentioned subsystems, are the outcome of research and development. Nevertheless, the outcome of the supervision and of the evaluation,

which are part of the logistic
infrastructure, provide important input
to the development processes and even
to the ideas of the basic research.

2.5   Involved Institutions and Agencies

The operation of a nation wide system
must rely on coordination among
interested institutions and agencies
and their cooperation, even if
sometimes their points of view and
direct interests may be different and
even opposing.

The range and diversity of these are very
dependent upon the specific country.
In our case, the following list has
been compiled:
* At school level: the school itself;
  the local parents organization.
* At regional level: the regional
  offices of the Ministry of Education;
  the Municipalities, each one with
  its education department; schools
  of education; educational research
  & development institutes.
* At national level: the central offices
  of the Ministry of Education; the
  coordinating office of the Municipalities; the national parents association;
  school-ownership institutes; public
  financing institutes.

2.6   The Integrated System.

As a summary of the system as described
by the previous paragraphs, fig. 1
provides a pictorial representation
of its parts and their inter-
relations.

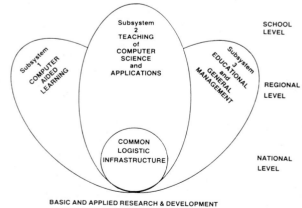

Fig. 1 :   Schematic representation of
          the Educational Computing
          System.

The main issue pointed out in this
figure is the coexistence of the 3
subsystems, each one having its own
goals, means and methods, but all 3
relying on a common base of logistic
infrastructure.

3. OVERVIEW OF THE REQUIRED INFRASTRUCTURE.

3.1   Main Goals of the Infrastructure.

In a very concise way, one may state that
the main goal of the logistic
infrastructure is to ensure the smooth,
efficient and effective operation
of the educational computing system.

Having this goal in mind, it has to cover:
a. The planning of the educational
   computing activity of the
   individual school, according to
   its structure, its needs and its
   possibilities.
b. Planning the configuration – hardware,
   software, applications–, planning
   the purchase, selecting brands and
   suppliers, budgeting.
c. Planning of human-resources and providing adequate staff-training.
d. Actual purchase, installation, testing
   of the system and putting it in full
   operation.
e. On-going maintenance, upgrading,
   training, advice, to keep the
   system operational and to provide
   services to all the users.

The criteria for efficient operation of
the system include the type of the
services provided, their quality and
outcomes, the number of the pupils
that used computers, the access time
of each one, the total time that the
system has been operational and in
actual use.

3.2   Centres of Activity

i. The School.

Our main concern is the activity carried
out at the school level. Many parts
of it are specific school activities,
rather independent of any external
relations. Others, such as the
communication-base administration, are
strongly dependent on external relations.

Except for the very big and advanced ones,
schools are not geared, and do not
have the means to care for all aspects
of the logistic infrastructure.

A minimal local capability is a necessary condition for any school operating a computer. The local staff has to be able to schedule and organize the educational uses and to integrate them into the other teaching activities of the school. It has to be able to plan the performance of the administrative tasks and to coordinate the people performing them. It has to be able to operate the system and to overcome simple technical difficulties, to be able to call for the right help when needed and to follow telephonic advice. It has to care for information exchange and cooperation with the support centres and with other schools.

The school management itself has to have enough knowledge to be able to provide leadership and to supervise the whole computer based activity, as an integral part of the entire school activity.

ii. Hot-line help desk

A service, quite new for the educational community, is the hot-line telephonic help desk. Its main goal is to provide "first aid" to operational problems as they may occur during the daily school activities. It may also help to solve pedagogic and organizational problems, but the nature of those is usually not so urgent as to need immediate answers.

The telephonic help desk is active during most of school operating hours. It is not planned to provide actual maintenance. It has to provide help for performing necessary tests and actions, before calling the maintenance. Then to take care to call the right people, to follow up the execution of the repairs and to manage a permanent record of the problems that occurred and the way to their solution. One of the main difficulties in providing this service is the variety of hardware, software and courseware operating in schools. It is hard to find a person to deal with this variety, but it can be accomplished by team work and it gets easier as more experience is accumulated.

It should be mentioned that the help desk is not only providing real help. It also provides a feeling of security that is important to unexperienced persons who otherwise might even not try to use the technology.

iii. The support and advice centres

Among the new agencies needed to provide the logistic infrastructure we include Support and Advice Centres for Educational Computing. Such a centre is a regional one - providing support to several tens of schools grouped on a regional basis. It has to be small enough to enable the personal contact between the advisers of the centre and the staff of the advised schools.

The regional centres have qualified staff able to support all computer applications that a school may implement. This support covers basic information about available materials and related methodology, detailed pedagogic and organizational guidance, providing solutions to problems related to the operation of these applications. The centre provides its services by offering contact hours after the normal time of school operation; by organizing courses covering various issues of interest; by visits to schools, to learn the local problems and to provide on-the-spot advice; by the possibility of telephone calls to the advisers during scheduled hours.

At the regional centres, one may find a library of periodicals, books, software, courseware, information on training possibilities and other subjects of interest to those involved in Computers in Education. It also provides a place where interested teachers may find the possibility to try out their ideas and to develop their initiatives.

The typical organization of a Regional Support and Advice Centre for Computers in Education - RESAC - and its relations with other agencies is described in fig. 2.

An actual RESAC will usually provide only part of the function appearing in fig. 2, according to local needs and possibilities.

The help-desk (3.2.ii) may be part of the center, but not every center has to keep a help-desk. If a help-desk exists, it gets help from all of the teams of the centre.

The National Support Centre for Computers in Education, manages and coordinates the professional activity of the regional ones. It provides guidelines for their operation, collects and distributes information and materials, maintains a data base of the schools and of the RESACs and their activities, a data base of computer based educational materials, etc.

The up-dating and in-service training of the professional staff of all RESACs is another role of the central one.

The actual activities of the RESACs are the result of the guidelines from the national centre, adapted to the specific needs of each district as required by its superintendent.

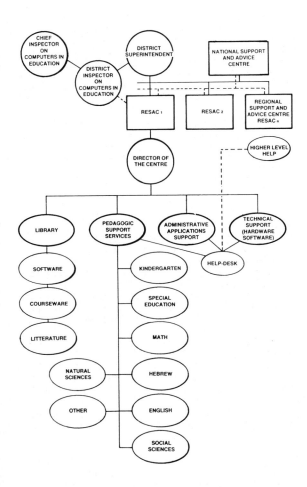

Fig. 2 : The organization of a regional support and advice centre.

The director of the RESAC reports to the district superintendent (mainly on general educational and administrative matters) and to the director of the national centre (mainly on professional matters). The district inspector on

computers in education acts separately from, but coordinated with the regional centres. In some cases, he may act towards the centres as the representative of the district superintendent.

iv. The suppliers

Naturally, the main goal of the suppliers is to supply their goods and to have good business. However, any supplier understands that this cannot happen without a keen effort on his part to have his clients satisfied.

It is our role to help the suppliers know what are the needs of the schools, to define clear requirements about the minimal services they have to provide, and to make sure that these services are really provided in an effective way.

The most basic requirement from the suppliers is that they should rigorously care to provide schools only with approved products fitted to the needs of the purchasers. This is considered to be within the responsibility of the supplier, because in many cases he has better knowledge than the schools buying the products.

Maintenance and repair services in many cases, are provided by the supplier. The time to repair and its reliability have to be clearly defined and their execution closely controlled.

The suppliers are also involved in training activities and demonstrations of their products. They have to be guided, so that the training provided is adequate to the school staff and to the educational goals and so that their demonstrations provide accurate and relevant information.

Ensuring the cooperation of the suppliers to provide honestly their services, enables the better operation of the schools. Suppliers who may consider these requirements as a burden at first, later realize that they fit well into their legitimate commercial interests.

3.3   Human Resources Development.

It is well known that even the best technical system cannot execute better than its operators are able to achieve. For educational computing, the operators are mostly members of the school teaching and managing staff, the supervising staff and many members of the administrative staff of the Ministry of Education, local authorities and other related agencies. Accordingly, as an integral part of the logistic infrastructure, we have to deal with the development of human resources. This development has to be done pre-service, in-service and as an ongoing continuous activity < 7,8,9 >. It has to cover over-all training of most of the staff and specialized training of those actually involved with the use of the system. Human resources development is also related to the definition of new functions and provision of adequate training. The whole range of aspects of human resources development is far out of the scope of this paper. We preferred not to treat it partially; just to point out its paramount importance.

3.4   Standardization and Licensing of Physical Resources.

i. The rationale for standardization, testing and licensing.

From the system's point of view, there are not many advantages for having several different types of computer facilities. Such diversity may give some local, limited advantages. On a wider scale, the problems of compatibility of software and courseware, the coordination of maintenance, advice and training are much easier to solve if the diversity is kept to a minimum. At the other extreme, having only one type of computers is impractical, from several points of view. Our intuitive, practical solution is to be limited to some three different types and to withstand fast changes of models which do not provide far reaching improvements.

Such decisions can be taken only by the central authorities and they must be based on clear standardization of requirements for the educational computer systems, followed by thorough testing and comparison of the different alternatives, finally licensing the selected types for purchase by schools.

Such a procedure selects not only the equipment but also the suppliers, and allows to define their commitments. Further on, it provides some means to supervise their activities within the schools.

ii. Hardware and system software

The selection of the hardware, system software and the adequate configurations, are in fact the selection of the technology to be installed within the schools and of the diversity to be allowed. The range of possible configurations is wide: several applications will require stand alone workstations, perhaps with a limited facility to share common peripherals; others may require a network with configuration, having some 10 - 40 workstations concentrated in one room; a school-wide network having workstations partly spread-out into the class rooms and others concentrated in one or two rooms is the most advanced configuration that a school may need.

Among the shared devices, the availability of outlets to wide-area-networks, is not to be disregarded. The connection to these networks is a clear requirement of the administrative subsystem and may be useful for the Computer Aided Learning Subsystem.

The system software should support the usual programming languages and the related facilities, Logo included, as well as basic off-the-shelf application software packages. The availability of authoring and delivery systems is an important requirement for an educational computer configuration.

iii. Courseware

The evaluation and selection of courseware is a lengthy process to be executed by well qualified personnel. The need for agencies authorized to test and license courseware for school usage is justified, by the expertise needed and by the difficulty of individual school to perform this task for itself.

In our approach the Ministry takes responsibility for such an agency, which provides its services (remunerated) < 10 > to the producers of courseware. The recommendations of this agency are the main factor considered by the Ministry for licensing courseware.

3.5   Supervision, Evaluation and Feedback

Operating all aspects related to the infrastructure has to be accompanied by adequate supervision and evaluation. This is a legitimate component of any organization, but it seems to be very important in our case, as new approaches and ideas are put in operation. Feedback based on evaluation, provides the necessary information to change approaches and adapt them to new requirements.

4.   IMPLEMENTATION.

Planning of the framework described in this paper started in March 1987 (parts of it have been functional for a long time and they fit into the general framework). Its partial implementation, as an experimental phase, started with the 87/88 school year, having in mind that 88/89 will be the first year of real, sound operation of the framework.

5. REFERENCES

[1]   Cohen, D. , Survey of computers in the Israeli school system. 1988. Szold Institute, Jerusalem. (in Hebrew).

[2]   Bork, A. , Personal Computers for Education, Harper and Row Publishers, New-York, 1985.

[3]   Bork, A. , Learning with Computers, Digital Press, Bedford, Mass., 1981.

[4]   WCCE85, Proceedings of World Conference on Computers in Education, Elsevier Publishers, Amsterdam, 1985.

[5]   Hopkins, J., The Learning Center Classroom; Computing Teacher V 13(4) Dec-Jan. 1985, pp. 8-12.

[6]   Moskowitz, J., Birman, H., Beatrice, F.; Computers in the Schools - Implications of Change; Educational Technology, 25(1) Jan 1988 pp. 7-13.

[7]   Millin, D.; Barta, B. , In-service and and Pre-service Training of Primary School Teachers in Informatics and Computer Applications in Education, Informatics and Teacher Training, Lovis,Tagg (eds), North Holland, Amsterdam, 1984.

[8]   Barta, B., Impact of the Penetration of Informatics into the Education on the Training of Educational Personnel - The Israeli Scene - to be published by UNESCO, 1988.

[9]   Barta, B., Training of Teachers and Educational Staff for the Information Technology Age, PROSPECTS, Spring, 1988.

[10] Levyn, T. Evaluation and Licensing of Courseware, Report prepared for publication, University of Tel-Aviv, School of Education, 1988. (in Hebrew).

COMPUTERS IN EDUCATION, F. Lovis and E.D. Tagg (eds.)
Elsevier Science Publishers B.V. (North-Holland)
© IFIP, 1988

A NATIONAL CURRICULUM INFORMATICS FOR LOWER SECONDARY EDUCATION

IJ. H. van Weering

National Institute for Curriculum Development (SLO)
P.O.Box 2041, 7500 CA Enschede,
The Netherlands

Abstract:
In 1985 the National Institute for Curriculum Development (SLO) published a
national curriculum informatics (or computer education) for lower secondary
education, as the result of a two year curriculum development project.
The curriculum was accepted nationwide and is now being implemented in
schools in The Netherlands.
This article describes the content of the national curriculum for informatics
and the process of implementation in the traditional schoolcurriculum.

1. THE NATIONAL CURRICULUM INFORMATICS FOR
    LOWER SECONDARY EDUCATION

At the end of 1982 the Advisory Committee for
Education and Information- technology (AOI)
advised the Ministry of Education to add to
the existing school curriculum a new school
subject called informatics for all pupils, to
be introduced in lower secondary education.
This new school subject should deal with
learning about automatic data processing and
all its applications.

In 1983, the National Institute for
Curriculum Development launched a curriculum
development project with 100 schools all over
the country to determine the content of the
new school subject. The Ministry of Education
raised the funds for this project and for
microcomputers, teacher training and other
support as well. As a result of this project
a national curriculum for informatics for
lower secondary education was published and
examples of teaching materials, including
software, were produced.

The general goal of the national curriculum:

Education in computer and information
literacy should enable pupils to react
intelligently to situations in which the use
of data processing systems is possible or
necessary.
Moreover, it should enable pupils to use data
processing systems, and judge critically the
social significance of the use of such
systems.

As sub-goals were defined:

A. The education should enable pupils to
    gain insight into the applications, the
    possibilities and the limitations of
    automatic data processing systems.
B. Moreover the education should enable
    pupils to process data and extract the
    desired information from a selected
    amount of data.
C. The aim of the education is for pupils to
    be able to operate data processing
    systems and to use them on the principle
    of a functional model.
D. The education should make pupils aware of
    the significance of information
    technology for the individual and for
    society, and enable them to express an
    opinion on this.

Elements of education are divided into four
categories derived from the four
distinguished sub-goals. The categories are:

A. Applications of information technology.
B. Information and data processing.
C. Data processing systems.
D. Social significance of information
technology.

In category A (applications of information
technology) elements are enumerated giving
pupils insight into the kinds of
applications, possibilities and limitations
suitable for their level.
Category B (information and data processing)
centres on elements related to data and
information, and how information can be
obtained, processed and made available by
pupils.

Without knowledge of category C (data processing systems) and without operational skills based on the principle of a functional model of such systems, pupils cannot hold their own in the information society. For this reason a number of elements has been formulated.

The last category D (social significance of information technology) needs a more extensive explanation. The reader is referred to the relevant elements and the explanation given there.

A. Applications of information technology

1. The pupil can gain access to existing data bases, also using telephone lines.
2. Pupils have knowledge of various search strategies which can be used to obtain information from data bases, such as catchwords, alphabetic sequence, page number, category.
3. Pupils know which kind of data are stored in a wide variety of data bases in all areas of society, such as catalogues, the telephone directory, viewdata, civil registration, school administration.
4. Pupils are acquainted with methods of protecting data bases, both at machine level (locking the keyboard; limited access to computer centre) and at user level (password) and at data base level (access code).
5. Pupils know advantages and disadvantages of the use of automatic data bases in comparison to other forms of data storage.
6. Pupils can use a word processor for writing short and simple texts on paper, applying insert, search and replace, adjustment of margins and displacement of text blocks.
7. Pupils know various possibilities of word processing, such as correction of spelling, standard correspondence (mail-merge), and they know various limitations, such as loss of information as compared with handwritten text.
8. Pupils can manage simple administrative applications, such as stock- keeping, money transfer systems, financial administration, and they know that the correctness of the administration depends on the proper input.
9. Pupils have knowledge of pros and cons of administration by means of a computer; pros such as speed, accuracy, verifiability; cons such as loss of flexibility.
10. Pupils are able to work with computer simulations, such as games, probability experiments, growth phenomena, whether biological, physical or economic.
11. Pupils have knowledge of the purposes of computer simulations, such as predicting the behaviour of a system, education and training; they know various stages in the development of a simulation model (among which, comparing the model with reality),

and they are informed of the pros and cons of computer simulations.
12. Pupils can solve practical problems involving process control situations using components such as sensors and actuators; for instance, by assembling a robot arm taking away bricks of a certain size from a conveyer-belt or by making a computer-controlled thermostat.

In category A (applications of information technology) the emphasis is on elements by which pupils learn principles, possibilities and limitations of applications via simple examples. Which applications teachers are to choose will depend on the computers available in their school.

Moreover their choice is strongly dependent on the developments in information technology. It is suspected that applications based on graphical possibilities and expert systems will become increasingly popular in the future.

B. Information and data processing

13. Pupils have knowledge of various principles for organizing data, such as alphabetical, numerical, chronological, and schematic systems including tree structures, and they are familiar with accepted systems of coding, such as morse, braille, barcode, catchwords.
14. Pupils know various means of recording data, such as paper, magnetic, electronic and optical memory, and they can use these data bearers.
15. Pupils gain some experience in formulating algorithms, for instance with block or structural diagrams, and in addition they learn to use elementary concepts such as check, sequence, choice and repetition.
16. Pupils gain some experience in the implementation of an elaborated algorithm in a data processing system, without getting involved in the details of a programming language.
17. Pupils form an idea of characteristics of programming languages, such as commands, syntax rules, variables.
18. Pupils understand a number of concepts necessary for handling data, such as source, communication, sender, message, receiver, noise, data bearer, and they are able to distinguish between the various forms of information and its content, knowing that the form in which the data are presented may influence their informative value.

The elements in category B (information and data processing) are not included to teach the pupils to program, but to make them aware of the steps necessary to make data ready for automatic data processing.
Mostly the data will have to be arranged and algorithms must be formulated, before the

problem in question can be solved with the aid of a programming language and a computer specialist. It was never our intention to have pupils translate complicated problems with the aid of programming languages into computer programs. There is no harm in introducing pupils to some peculiarities and properties of a programming language, it may be even right to demystify a computer by making a simple computer programme and concluding that the computer simply does what it has been instructed to do.

C. Data processing systems

19. Pupils have a working knowledge of data processing systems, particularly with computers, including peripherals, software and user guides designed for pupils.
20. Pupils can form a functional idea of data processing systems because they encounter various manifestations of data processing systems, such as micro, mini and mainframe computers, networks, robots, and they learn the functions of the parts which computers and peripherals are built of, such as the memory chip, the processor, input and output devices.
21. Pupils are acquainted with basic functions of data processing systems, such as measuring, counting, calculating, reading, writing, storing, selecting, visualizing, representing, ordering, selecting, sorting, combining.
22. Pupils have knowledge of the advantages of data processing systems, such as speed, repetition, accuracy, storage of a large amount of data, efficiency, verifiability, and of disadvantages, such as loss of flexibility, and they realize that only certain aspects of reality can be quantified and subsequently processed by data processing systems.
23. Pupils are acquainted with aspects of ergonomics and user-friendliness of data processing systems.

In category C (data processing systems) the object of the elements is not to go deeply into the construction of data processing systems. Electronics and Boolean algebra, for instance, are to be left out. Our guideline is the general goal which states that pupils must be able to react intelligently to situations in which the use of data processing systems is possible or necessary.

D. Social significance of information technology

24. Pupils have knowledge of the changes being brought about by all kinds of applications of information technology in various sectors in society, particularly important applications such as data base, word processor, administration, process control, telecommunication, simulation, calculation.
25. Pupils have knowledge of the influence of information technology on (the kind, amount and quality of) labour, communication between people, privacy, environment.

The elements of category D (social significance of information technology) need some further explanation. It is impossible and unnecessary to consider the influence of information technology on all possible sectors in society. It is preferable to make a choice from:
- office, business and shops
- industry, production and trade
- agriculture and fishery
- public health
- transport, traffic and telecommunication
- recreation
- space and air travel
- defence
- education
- household
- banking
- politics and government.

It is important to realize that pupils in lower secondary education are too young to go deeply into social issues like privacy. It is better to offer this to pupils who have concrete experience with certain aspects of privacy. This can be achieved by having pupils put their personal data in a data base and showing them how others can manipulate their data. Such an experience lays a base for the treatment of the principle later on.

2.   THE PROCESS OF IMPLEMENTATION

In 1985 the National Institute for Curriculum Development (SLO) advised the Ministry of Education to add to the existing obligatory timetable in schools a new school subject, informatics, for 80 lessons and to suggest to the schools that they investigate the integration of parts of the informatics curriculum into other school subjects as a beginning of the complete integration of informatics into the existing school curriculum.

The Ministry of Education decided not to go quite as far as the advice. Two hundred schools were allowed to introduce the new school subject into their timetable for 40 lessons at the most, and were asked to try to integrate parts of the informatics curriculum into other school subjects.

In 1986 the National Institute for Curriculum Development was asked to develop examples of teaching materials for informatics as a part of the curriculums of the subjects Dutch, science and social studies.

A survey in the same year showed that schools did not succeed by themselves in integrating parts of the informatics curriculum into other school subjects. Informatics was mostly dealt with as a separate subject, and was put on the timetable for 20 or 40 hours. Many schools spent more lessons on informatics, even a total of 160 was mentioned, but in all cases informatics was taught as a autonomous subject within the lessons for mathematics, Dutch, social studies, science and other school subjects.

The process of implementation in schools turned out to be very difficult due to the lack of sufficient support, so The Advisory Boards for Primary and Secondary Education published a report in which they proposed to include a maximum of 20 hours for informatics on the timetable, more or less as an introduction to the use of information technology.

The Boards "urged" schools to try putting more emphasis on the use of computers as a tool in other school subjects.

By that time the Academic Board for Governmental Policy (WRR) issued a proposal for a common core curriculum for lower secondary education with informatics as a part of that curriculum, the aims of which corresponded to the aims of the national curriculum for informatics, published in 1985. The WRR also proposed a uniform timetable for all schools in which 80% of the lessons should be prescribed, 20 lessons of which were to be devoted to informatics. The proposal of the WRR is to be discussed by the Government during 1987 and 1988.

The outcome is expected to be that schools should spend at least 20 lessons on informatics. In practice schools will spend more lessons on informatics depending on the existence of good examples of teaching materials, including software for use within lessons in different school subjects.

The situation in The Netherlands is quite favourable, thanks to the announcement in 1986 of the NIVO-project, a joint venture between the Ministry of Education, the computer industry and the teachers' organisations. This NIVO-project (New Information Technology for Education) provides micro-computers (MS-DOS), teacher training and courseware for all schools. The teacher training and the delivery of computers started during 1987.

The production of courseware is concentrated in a 4-year project which started at the end of 1987 (POCO).

In this favourable climate the National Institue for Curriculum Development (SLO) has the opportunity to develop examples of informatics with teaching materials and software.

The following teaching materials have been developed:

*   <u>Introduction to the computer</u> (5 to 10 lessons)
    10 simple examples of the variety of applications for which computers can be used.
    (sorting, writing, calculating, designing, combining, playing, etc.)
    with SLO-software: 10 simple programs

*   <u>Information handling and data bases</u> (10 to 15 lessons)
    - what is information?
    - what to do with information?
    - how is information processed?
    - using data bases
    with SLO-software: a data base for food nutrients

*   <u>Wordprocessing</u> (10 to 15 lessons)
    - what is word processing?
    - how to use a word processor
    - applications of word processing
    with SLO-software: a word processor with all essential components of a professional word processor, including mailmerge, and easy to use for pupils of all ages.

*   <u>Informatics with LOGO, a basic course</u> (ready in 1988): (20 to 25 lessons)
    SLO software: . turtle graphics
                  . a data base
                  . a statistical package
    originally developed in IBMLOGO but now written in LCNLOGO, a Dutch version of LOGO.

*   <u>The computer is everywhere</u> (2 lessons)
    with videotape

*   <u>Information processing in the hospital</u> (6 lessons)

Teaching materials produced for integrating parts of informatics in other subjects are:

*   <u>Information and information processing in writing and literature</u> (ready in 1988): (10 lessons, Dutch) for use with word processor and data base

*   <u>Computers and privacy</u> (10 lessons, social studies)
    with SLO-software: data base with search language

*   <u>Technology and work</u> (completed in 1988): (10 lessons, social studies)
    with SLO-videotape

*   <u>Simulations</u> (available in 1988): (10 lessons, science)
    with several SLO-simulations including sunboiler, ecosystems

* <u>Informatics</u> (10 lessons, to be taught in an informatics course or to be integrated in other subjects):
  . Data bases
  . Word and picture processing
  . Administration and registration
  . Simulation
  . Process control and robotics
  . Technology in the future

6 school television programs, developed together with Dutch School Television (NOT) and Dutch Broadcasting Company (NOS) including a booklet with teaching materials.

An interim assessment of the lesson series "Information handling and databases", "Word processing and Information" and "Information processing in writing and literature" has been supplied by the National Testing Institute (CITO). The results are encouraging.

By the end of 1988 the national curriculum for informatics for lower secondary education will have been translated into many examples of teaching materials for a separate subject informatics for as many as 80 lessons and in several lesson series of at least 50 lessons integrated in other school subjects.

<u>Bibliography</u>:

Hartsuijker, A.P. en IJ.H. van Weering. Curriculum Aspects of the Development of Educational Software in the National Project for Computer and Information Literacy. In: <u>Eurit '86. Developments in educational software and courseware. Proceedings of the first european conference on education and information technology. (Jef Moonen en T. Plomp ed.) Oxford etc. 1986</u>

COMPUTERS IN EDUCATION, F. Lovis and E.D. Tagg (eds.)
Elsevier Science Publishers B.V. (North-Holland)
© IFIP, 1988

WHAT TO TEACH IN INFORMATICS AND HOW - A BULGARIAN EXPERIMENT[*]

Rumen Nikolov, Evgenia Sendova and Darina Dicheva

Research Group on Education, Bulgarian Academy of Sciences
Bd Vitosha 5, 1000 Sofia, Bulgaria

This paper describes a five-year experience of teaching informatics in 5-7 grades in the framework of the Research Group on Education (RGE), affiliated to the Bulgarian Academy of Sciences and the Ministry of Education. The principles of teaching informatics are related to some more general educational principles in school. The belief that the principle of integration of different school-subjects could be best realized by the means and methods of informatics has been confirmed by the experience of the RGE.

1. INTRODUCTION

One of the major problems education faces nowadays is: *What to teach and how to teach now that we have computers at school?* The answer is neither simple nor unique, but we shall try to propose one on the base of five years experience of teaching informatics in the Research Group on Education (RGE). This group was set up in 1979 and is supported by the Bulgarian Academy of Sciences and the Ministry of Education. One of the fundamental principles guiding the activity of the RGE is the integration of school subjects being almost totally applied to the primary school [10,11]. Special attention is paid to the active forms of education as well.

At the RGE schools (now 27) informatics appears implicitly as a part of the encyclopaedic education for the first four grades. Children become familiar with some basic notions of informatics - graphs, algorithms, coding, decoding etc. A more systematic teaching of informatics begins at the fifth grade (pupils 11 years old) with Logo as a programming language.

2. TEACHING INFORMATICS FOR 5-7 GRADES - A FIVE-YEAR EXPERIENCE

At the beginning of 1983 our country had no microcomputer production. This has determined our basic tools for teaching informatics - the microcomputer Apple II and the original version of Logo (Terrapin Logo). Informatics textbooks and complementary educational software have been developed. On the basis of a two years experience as well as of the remarks and recommendations of teachers, pupils and researchers, a Bulgarian version of Logo for the Bul-

garian microcomputer Pravetz 8, new editions of the textbooks and educational software have been worked out. Useful educational experience in school has been accumulated.

2.1 Basic goals

The initial teaching of informatics in grades 5-7 (of the junior high school) aims at qualifying pupils:

a) to obtain basic skills and habits of using computers and other products of the new technologies;
b) to obtain ideas of some basic (both present and future) applications of computers;
c) to acquire skills and habits of applying software tools in various fields;
d) to determine what problems can be solved (in a reasonable way) with the help of a computer;
e) to acquire and use some basic notions of informatics;
f) to use Logo in a good programming style when solving problems in various fields: mathematics, languages, physics, music etc.;
g) to become familiar with some basic information structures in order to apply them effectively when solving problems;

Pupils' knowledge in informatics could be extended in the form of extra-classes activities. Though we do not expect all pupils to become good programmers, everybody should be given the chance. At the same time all the pupils should become good users of computers.

2.2 Informatics textbooks and educational software

The informatics textbooks for the fifth and sixth grades

---

[*] This project has been supported financially by the Committee for Science at the Council of Ministers under Contract No 554.

(in two editions) [3,6,8,9] are the main tools of realizing the basic goals of teaching informatics. The principle of the *anticipating demonstration* and that of knowledge representation in the form of a spiral have been adopted.

As was said above one of the goals of teaching informatics is to qualify pupils so that they should become familiar with some reasonable applications of computers. This goal is achieved mainly in practical cources, where the pupils solve different problems [4,7]:

a) drawing geometric objects and experimenting with them;
b) equations with one unknown, extraction of roots, finding the greatest common divisor and the least common multiple, drawing graphs of functions, finding the sum of an arithmetic progression, transforming numbers in different positional systems;
c) physics problems related to distance, velocity and time; force, mass and acceleration; work and energy; illustration of some natural laws and phenomena graphically or by simple animation;
d) language problems: extending the vocabulary of the turtle with new words in several languages, illustrating the sense of sentences by simple animation, writing letters with the help of a text editor , taking part in linguistic games, an algorithmic description of basic grammar rules etc.;
e) developing programs using Logo extensions for music and animation; using graphic and music editors;
f) using educational computer games which allow for experimentation in physics and mathematics;
g) using programs realizing well known algorithms in the field of AI, e.g simplified versions of *Eliza* and *Animals*;

The variety of problems and activities contributes to the implementation of the major RGE principle - that of integrated learning. Furthermore such a variety enables every single pupil to choose a problem according to his interests and thus - to find his own way to informatics. Different talents can join forces for more ambitious projects.

Pupils are acquainted with new notions, principles and methods of informatics by using such examples that are close to their experience [7]. Textbooks demonstrate some advantages of top-down programming together with the requirements of the structured programming. Pupils can experience the natural process of developing a program passing through the stages of analysis, designing, coding, debugging and refinement. They are not saved from possible mistakes either. An approach to teaching mathematics in accord with Papert's ideas to create *Mathland* as well as with the RGE idea about integrating languages and mathematics has been adopted.

The software is supposed to pursue a concrete educational goal, be attractive, convenient and reliable to use. In addition, programs should be *transparent*, i.e. readable, relatively short and such that their execution would have a visual effect [5]. The transparent programs represent a suitable extension of the learning materials and enable the realization of the principle of the *anticipating demonstration*. The idea of the conceptual machine [1] has been realized when designing the programming tools. The operation of a given program system is described in terms of the corresponding conceptual machine by the means of suitable metaphors and analogies. There are programming tools visualizing the way the machine *works*. Thus the unnecessary details remain hidden from the pupils and stress is put on those program system components which are of primary significance for the achievement of the educational goals. A typical example in this direction is the description of the way the program *Animals* works.

2.3. Results and Conclusions

One of the main RGE concepts is to carry out a large experimental research activity related to the educational tools and the methodology of their use. For instance the development of textbooks undergoes three stages: a first edition which is tried out in three classes (a *narrow* experiment); a second edition in which the results of the narrow experiment are taken into consideration (a *large* experiment - carried out in 27 schools); a third edition, reflecting the opinion of all the RGE teachers and other specialists.

The annual RGE conferences play an important role for the evaluation of the experiment's results. Both the informatics textbooks and the educational software are in the stage of the large experiment. Here are some of the more important conclusions derived from our now five years experience:

a) most of the pupils do not find it difficult to work with the textbooks and the assisting software. Some of the difficulties are due to gaps in the learning some of school-subjects where the methods of informatics are applied;
b) the use of the original version of Logo could contribute to the learning of English provided that the teachers in informatics work in cooperation with the teachers in English. Otherwise the results could be even negative. This version of Logo is more appropriate for schools with increased teaching of English. At the same time a Bulgarian version is acquired better both by the pupils and the teachers since it contributes to a more natural contact with the computer [15];
c) informatics can truly play a fundamental role

towards an integrated approach to educatiion: a number of concepts in mathematics, physics and the theory of music can be illustrated and interpreted in a new way, which makes their understanding easier **[15]**;

d) the pupils like to work with a computer. Every program developed by a pupil is a kind of *snapshot* of his possibilities to solve problems, thus providing a valuable information for the teacher.

e) the pupils can use the computer as a laboratory where they manipulate with some mathematical objects conveniently and become familiar with their properties and relations **[13,14]**. The skills of generalizing, comparing, selecting the most rational strategy are developed

f) it is possible to combine individual work and work in groups. Some of the teachers report that group work is welcomed because it favours the exchange of experience and results, creates the right atmosphere for true discussions; the less proficient pupils can learn from the style of work of their brighter classmates **[15]**. Others in turn, point out that often the group-leaders deprive the rest of the chance to make progress. Their recommendation is that the groups should be formed (if necessary) of pupils whose abilities are approximately equal;

g) the children are trained into aesthetic tastes and certain moral virtues - persistence, patience, self-control and high personal standards, collective spirit.

3. EXTENSIONS OF THE EXPERIMENT

Teaching informatics from fifth to seventh grade is based on the integral approach not only to match the basic principle of the RGE but to give an idea of various applications of the computer. Further on the goal is to represent the basic notions of informatics on a higher level. It seems to us that the most natural way to achieve this is to integrate informatics with mathematics.

3.1 The experimental eight grade textbook "Mathematics and informatics"

The idea for such an integration was basic to the xperiment extension for the eight grade - on one hand we wanted to introduce elements of informatics by using the mathematical subject matter and, on the other, to use them for illustration of that matter. The latter principle assures an *openess* of the experiment, i.e. to enable the pupils from other schools to join the RGE school system. Besides, the Ministry of Education assigned to the RGE the task of writing one of the textbooks in mathematics and informatics for the school of general education. (Let us explain that the Bulgarian educational system is strongly centralized

and all the schools of the same kind have the same curriculum. Furthermore, till recently, there existed only one textbook for each school-subject. It was for the first time last year when the Ministry of Education decided to engage two teams as authors of textbooks in mathematics and informatics and to let the teachers choose one of them.)

The requirement for an openness turned out to be difficult to satisfy since the RGE pupils have been studying Logo for three years whereas the rest have not studied informatics at all. That is why we decided to begin teaching informatics (again by introducing Logo) without the assumption that the pupils have studied anything. The basic notions and conceptions of the language though are introduced more concisely and at a higher level. On the other hand the development of additional learning material is envisaged to be used by the advanced pupils.

"Mathematics and informatics" **[12]** represents an attempt to integrate the two subjects. For instance the first turtle commands as well as the notion of procedure have been introduced in order to draw geometric objects and their images in symmetry, rotation and translation. The notion of variable in Logo is related to the variables well known from algebra. The coordinate graphics commands have been introduced to draw graphs of functions.

One of the basic goals when writing the textbook has been not to mix mechanically the elements of mathematics and informatics but to integrate them as far as possible. Thus mathematics motivates the introduction of elements of informatics and uses them later for clarifying some mathematical conceptions, e.g. the operations have been introduced by using the notion of function and the relation between mathematical induction and recursion has been considered.

This line is also maintained in the project for textbooks for the next two grades. However an enrichment of the learning environment in the mathematical classes is envisaged by using a computer *mathematical laboratory* **[13]**. A first example of such a laboratory is the *Plane geometry system* **[14]**. The ideology of this system represents an extension of the Logo ideology. Since the system has the basic plane-geometry objects as elementary objects (data types) together with the basic operations over them, it represents a powerful tool for illustration, experiments, forming hypotheses etc. On the other hand some informatics concepts as, for example, different programming methods and techniques could be introduced quite reasonably by using the system. This system is a part of a unified software environment developed by the means of a specially created L-system **[17]**. The L-system will serve as a base of some other specialized systems, e.g. in the field of algebra.

Other topics to be considered are the introduction of the notions *information, information activities processes, data, data structures, data bases, expert systems* etc.

The possibilities for using Prolog in the teaching of informatics are to be investigated and discussed.

A project for development of pupils' literacy by means of computers (as an extra-classes activity) has been worked out. The goal is to stimulate the creative abilities of the childrens, to teach them to compose, to edit and publish (using textprocessing systems) texts of different styles - journalistic, administrative etc. The first issue of a bulletin - written, designed and published entirely by pupils of an RGE school has already appeared.

3.2 Teaching informatics in the first three grades

Some attempts have been made to extend the teaching of informatics to the primary school as well. This has been done in three directions:

– to check to what extent and how the textbooks of informatics for fifth and sixth grade can be adapted for the second and third grade pupils of the primary school;

– to design and experiment educational programs assisting the teaching of mathematics and Bulgarian language;

– to organize sort of children's *software house* as an extra-class activity - where the seventh grade pupils develop educational programs in order to contribute to the teaching of the first-second grade pupils.

The two years experience in the first direction has shown that some topics of the textbooks [8,9] can be used with second grade pupils provided that the tasks of the exercises are well tuned to the character and abilities of the age group [15]. This makes it indispensable to derive new tasks and problems, graded in their degree of difficulty; to give some additional information - measuring angles, size of the angle in degrees, adjacent angles (which properly is fourth-year material) and by aid of good examples and problem solving make it digestible. Alongside with the new knowledge, the extra classes in informatics enable the pupils to assimilate their standard material by naturally integrating some topics considered in the textbooks with that of the other subjects taught in RGE schools as for example *I read, I write, I calculate; I draw and design; I sing and I play*.

Experiments in the second direction have been performed in one of the RGE schools during the last year [2]. The goals have been to give the children an idea of what the computer can do; to teach them to work with the keyboard and floppy-discs, to react to the motion of figures on the screen and to help them practise the knowledge acquired in the subject *I read, I write, I calculate*. The first results show that the number of both double and single mistakes has been reduced approximately twice in two consecutive lessons. The most typical mistakes have been discussed with the primary teachers thus providing useful information about the topics that should be taught additionally. Some new programs are to be experimented with in the following two years: mazes - preparing the children for Logo, and simulation games. When using these programs the children are expected to get an idea about algorithms and game winning strategies.

Educational programs of the kind described as a third direction have been developed for the lessons in Russian, Bulgarian, mathematics, in music classes, and when studying chess. The young programmers entered the role of teachers and were eager not only to check the knowledge of the first-graders but also to teach them. When seeng the effect of their work with the youngsters, the seventh grade pupils got even more involved in learning informatics. According to the teachers the use of educational software in the first grade will reduce the gap between the pupils who work with computers as an extra activity and those who do not. This small experiment within the big one shows that the principle of integration could be achieved not only by integrating the subjects but also by a cooperation among the teachers in different subjects and, which is not very common, - by cooperation among pupils of different grades.

The way to better results in the teaching of informatics depends largely on the choice of methods, approaches and means of training [16]. All these can provide for the intellectual development of pupils and their creative skills on different levels in accord with their individual character which in fact is the final goal of the RGE project.

4. CONCLUSION

Beyond doubt, there are problems accompanying the realization of each project (it is not by chance that the name RGE is translated in Bulgarian as *Problem Group on Education*). The first impressions though are that informatics (if taught appropriately) can help each child to show his or her worth. No wonder in a composition under the title *My greatest wish* an RGE pupil has matched the non-informatics teachers (in couples) and sent them for a four-year honeymoon in order to have informatics classes at leisure during all that time.

REFERENCES

[1] duBoulay, B., O'Shea, T. and Monk, J., The Black Box Inside the Glass Box: Presenting Computing Concepts to Novices, Int. Journal of Man-Machine Studies (V.14, N.3, April, 1981) pp 237-249.

[2] Nenova, M., Computer Games and Mathematics for First Grade Schoolchildren, Proceedings of the Second International Conference "Children in an Information Age (Sofia, 1987) pp 109-124.

[3] Nikolov, R., Logo. An Experimental Textbook for the 5-th Grade (RGE, Sofia, 1983) (in Bulgarian).

[4] Nikolov, R., Teacher Training in Logo, in: Lovis, F. and Tagg, D., Informatics and Teacher Training, Proceedings of the IFIP WG 3.1 Working Conference (North-Holland, Amsterdam, 1984) pp 59-68.

[5] Nikolov, R., A Learning Environment in Informatics, Ph.D. Thesis (Sofia University, 1987) (in Bulgarian).

[6] Nikolov, R. and Sendova, E., Language and Mathematics. Logo for the 6-th Grade (RGE, Sofia, 1984) (in Bulgarian).

[7] Nikolov, R. and Sendova E., Informatics textbooks for Beginners, in: Proceedings of the First International Conference "Children in an Information Age" (Varna, Bulgaria, 1985) pp 621-629.

[8] Nikolov, R. and Sendova, E., Informatics-1. Logo (RGE, Sofia, 1985) (in Bulgarian, Russion and Spanish).

[9] Nikolov, R. and Sendova, E., Informatics-2. Logo (RGE, Sofia, 1987) (in Bulgarian)

[10] Penkov, B. and Sendov, Bl., The Bulgarian Academy of Sciences Research Group on Education Project (BARGEP), Int. Conference in Math Education (UCSMP, Chicago, 28-30 March, 1985).

[11] Sendov, Bl., To the Heart of the Matter (RGE, Sofia, 1986) (in Bulgarian).

[12] Sendov, Bl. at al, Mathematics and Informatics, A Textbook for Eighth Grade (Narodna Prosveta, Sofia - in press) (in Bulgarian)

[13] Sendov, Boj. and Dicheva, D., A Mathematical Laboratory in Logo Style, this volume.

[14] Sendov, Boj., Fillimonov, R. and Dicheva, D., A System for Teaching Plane Geometry, Proceedings of the Second International Conference "Children in an Information Age" (Sofia, Bulgaria, 1987) pp 215-225.

[15] Sendova, E., ed., Creative Teaching Informatics. Papers Delivered by Teachers at the RGE Conference (RGE, Sofia, May, 1986).

[16] Sendova, E. and Nikolov, R., Teachers Have Been Growing up, this volume.

[17] Fillimonov, R., Diploma Work (Sofia, 1987).

COMPUTERS IN EDUCATION, F. Lovis and E.D. Tagg (eds.)
Elsevier Science Publishers B.V. (North-Holland)
© IFIP, 1988

THE IEA STUDY 'COMPUTERS IN EDUCATION': A MULTI NATIONAL LONGITUDINAL ASSESSMENT

Willem. J. Pelgrum, Tjeerd Plomp

Department of Education, University of Twente
Enschede, The Netherlands

The introduction of new technologies leads to innovations in society and as a consequence also in education. The introduction of computers in education is probably the first major educational innovation which can be studied systematically almost from its earliest state of development. The IEA (International Association for the Evaluation of Educational Achievement) has started an international study in which data will be collected regarding the content and outcomes of this innovation in more than 20 different educational systems. The study focuses on national and school policies and practices, the type of use of computers by teachers and students and the consequences of computer use on achievement and attitudes of students with respect to computers as well as the traditional subjects. The design of the study provides opportunities to investigate the change in these aspects over time. The data collection for the first stage of the study is planned for the end of 1988 and the beginning of 1989.
In this paper the design and planning of the study will be described.

INTRODUCTION

One of the primary goals of education is to prepare children to be able to function adequately as citizens and professional workers. Educational systems are usually supposed to be set up in such a way that this goal is realized as best as possible. Throughout the world different mechanisms are used to ensure that the cultural and technological inheritance of a nation is transferred to a new generation with the best of the available means. If major innovations occur in a society educational goals have to change accordingly and ways need to be found to realize these goals as best as possible. The study which is presented in this paper deals with one of the most recent innovations in society and education, i.e. the introduction of computers, or more generally, new information technologies.

Authorities have to control and direct the functioning of an educational system and its subsystems. In case of shortcomings it is necessary to determine which measures for improvement have to be taken. This may be done by monitoring the outcomes of the educational system. Monitoring is a broad term referring to the collection of information which is relevant to evaluating the system output in terms of goals to be achieved. For directing innovations and implementation, monitoring is important in order to check empirically whether, and to which extent, changes occur in the desired directions . In order to evaluate the information with respect to current and past developments, reference information is of crucial importance.

One of the many possible ways to collect this reference information is through conducting international comparative research. Especially with respect to the use of computers in education, a study of multi-national nature, covering a large range of countries that are in various stages of development with regard to the introduction of computers

in education, should be invaluable for any country in which developments in this field are taking place. Information may be produced about the various approaches which are used to integrate new technologies into the curriculum of traditional school subjects, while at the same time, various policies and practices with respect to introducing computer education as new subject matter can be compared.

Different perspectives are possible to study the contents and effects of new information technologies. The current study may be broadly characterized as a multinational large scale assessment with a longitudinal component.

In order to determine which information needs to be collected in this study, it is necessary to develop a framework which identifies the key factors the study is aimed at. For the elaboration of this framework we will use ideas from system theory, curriculum theory and theories about educational change.

The educational system, curriculum and change

The framework for the study consists of concepts derived from system theory, curriculum theory and theories with respect to educational change.

A system may be characterized by its system space, input, throughput and output. The educational system is a complex system which consists of different subsystems. Coleman [1] refers to the concept of pluralistic educational decision making, which means that the functioning of the educational system depends on decisions taken by several interacting persons and agencies. Usually a distinction is made between different *levels of educational decision making*, such as the macro-, meso- and micro level. On each of these levels different *actors* are influencing educational decisions, i.e. respectively higher order administrators (e.g the ministry of education), school administrators, the staff of subject departments within schools, individual teachers and students. External influences may be exerted e.g. by industries and parents. The different levels in an educational system may be conceived as subsystems which can be characterized by their own system space, input, throughput and output. These different subsystems may be characterized in terms of their input and output by *concepts* which are developed in *curriculum theory*. Conceptually a distinction can be made between the intended, implemented and attained curriculum. The intended curriculum refers to what Goodlad [2] called the ideal and formal curriculum, i.e. the curriculum plans, which may be laid down in official documents or which may exist as shared conceptions of what the important curriculum content is. The implemented curriculum consists of the content, time allocations, instructional strategies, etc. which the teacher is actually realizing and practicing in his/her lessons. In this meaning the implemented curriculum is the contraction of Goodlad's perceived and operational curriculum. The attained curriculum is defined as the cognitive skills and attitudes of students as a result of teaching and learning (Goodlad's experiential curriculum).

In conceptualizing this study, we recognize that the domain "Computers in Education" is in a constant state of flux. There are many pressures for the acceptance and incorporation of computers acting at all levels of education. These pressures are as stated earlier derived from a variety of sources, including parents, teachers, administrators, industry etc. and have a continuous influence upon what happens in schools. Therefore, any longitudinal study of computer use is inevitably a study of *educational change* in action. In recognizing this fact, we must take into account what is already known about the conditions under which change is brought about both in education and in other settings.

The system model stresses the "gatekeeping" function which actors may exert at the interfaces between successive system levels. The literature of educational change suggests that the extent to which this function is exercised tends to depend on a relatively small number of critical factors, which recur throughout the system, though at different levels of generalization.

These factors include [3]: objectives, resource provision, support & leadership, capacity to deliver, communication, evaluation and feedback

Although in the first stage of this study the main focus is on the degree of implementation of computer use, attention is also paid (but less extensively) to situations where implementation is not yet started and where schools may be in a stage of orientation or adoption.

This study incorporates the three different perspectives which are described above. The global conceptual framework for the study, in which the three perspectives are related to each other, is depicted in figure 1.

The framework in figure 1 identifies the actors which operate at different levels in an educational system. The model assumes that the different educational system levels influence each other via the curricular products which can be identified at each level. The curricular outputs at the macro and meso level can be conceived as mechanisms for directing the outcomes at student level. Different processes (indicated as influencing factors), derived from the literature on educational change, mediate and determine these characteristics of the curricular products at several levels. The picture illustrates that different subsystems interact (sometimes mediated via other subsystems) and that the "behavior" of a certain subsystem can only be understood if context information about "neighboring" subsystems is available. Certain factors in the framework may exert an effect as primary variables and as context variables at the same time. So the implemented curriculum may be important in itself when studied from an implementation perspective, but at the same time it may be conceived as context information when one is interested in studying student outcomes.

We have characterized the educational system in terms of levels of decision-making and capacity to affect changes. The model we are proposing reflects the hierarchical structure of most educational systems, but acknowledges that decisions which promote or inhibit the implementation of computer-related curricula are made at all levels. This may cause discrepancies between the different curricular definitions. An identification of these discrepancies may in itself be an important starting point for improvements in education.

In order to get a full definition of the different components of the model, we will in the next sections describe the domain of Computers in Education and elaborate the factors which are important in affecting the different curricular outcomes in more detailed operationalizations.

THE DOMAIN OF STUDY

In this study we distinguish between a new computer education curriculum and the application of computers in curricula of already existing subjects. It needs to be specified which characteristic skills are assumed as being essential to be taught in school as part of computer education. Just like in research with respect to traditional curricula (such as mathematics and science), we also need for this study a taxonomy of content and behavioral objectives in order to describe the intended, implemented and attained curriculum.

In defining the domain of computer education we will not emphasize a distinction between computer literacy and computer science as at this moment the differentiation between these subdomains is still highly controversial. Instead a taxonomy will be developed which in principle can cover computer education and it will be considered an empirical question to determine (by analyzing intended and implemented curricula) which parts of the taxonomy belong to either subdomain.

VARIABLES TO INCLUDE IN THE STUDY

Factors which were identified in the previous sections have been explicitly considered in designing instruments for different levels of decision-making which have been identified in this study. We have described above a number of variables to be taken into account at each level, and these have formed the basis for the development of instruments targeted at teachers, subject departments, and school administrators.

Key features of these questionnaires operationalize aspects of the critical factors relative to the specific levels of decision-making identified in the systems model, from the individual teacher through higher orders of administration.

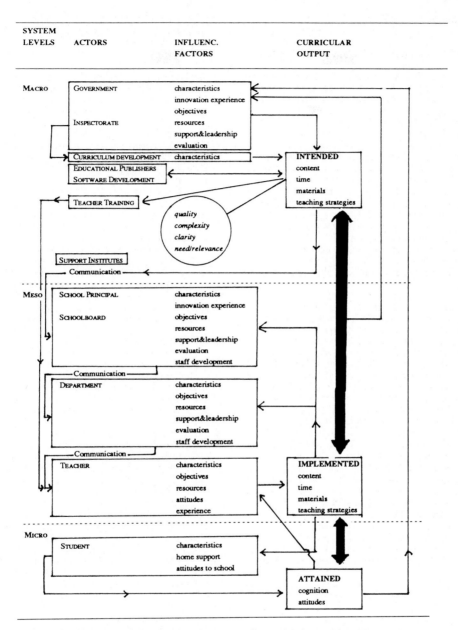

SYSTEM
LEVELS   ACTORS   INFLUENC.   CURRICULAR
                          FACTORS   OUTPUT

MACRO   GOVERNMENT   characteristics
                          innovation experience
                          objectives
          INSPECTORATE   resources
                          support&leadership
                          evaluation
          CURRICULUM DEVELOPMENT characteristics   INTENDED
          EDUCATIONAL PUBLISHERS   content
          SOFTWARE DEVELOPMENT   time
                                                        materials
          TEACHER TRAINING   teaching strategies

                          quality
                          complexity
                          clarity
                          need/relevance

          SUPPORT INSTITUTES
          Communication

MESO   SCHOOL PRINCIPAL characteristics
                            innovation experience
          SCHOOLBOARD   objectives
                            resources
                            support&leadership
                            evaluation
                            staff development
          Communication

          DEPARTMENT   characteristics
                            objectives
                            resources
                            support&leadership
                            evaluation
                            staff development
          Communication

          TEACHER   characteristics   IMPLEMENTED
                            objectives   content
                            resources   time
                            attitudes   materials
                            experience   teaching strategies

MICRO   STUDENT   characteristics
                            home support
                            attitudes to school
                                                        ATTAINED
                                                        cognition
                                                        attitudes

Figure 1: global model of the study, showing relations between components and
information channels)

STRUCTURE OF THE STUDY

The present study is conceived as a two stage investigation. The first stage, approximately three years in duration, is aimed at gathering information from a representative sample of schools at the primary, lower secondary and upper secondary levels in the participating countries with regard to the current state of computers in education. It is primarily descriptive in nature, focusing on how computers are currently being used, the extent and availability of computers in schools, the nature of instruction about computers, and estimates of the effects that computers are having on students, the curriculum and the school as an institution, as well as other factors influencing the use of computers in schools. The information obtained from this stage will be of considerable value to policy makers, educators, and curriculum and software developers as well as computers manufacturers since it will provide a panorama of experience with computers in education. The results of this stage will be vital for the detailed planning of the second stage of the study. In the next paragraph we will discuss in more detail the main activities of stage I of this study.

Stage II of the study is planned to start in 1990. As we will not present the aims and design of stage II in this paper we give a very short description here.
Stage II will consist of two parts. The first part will be a follow-up study of those schools surveyed in Stage I. In this part, data collection will center on a school questionnaire, that will be closely related to the school questionnaire used in Stage I. In this way, it will be possible to determine the rate of development of computers in education over a period of roughly three years.
The major purpose of Part 2 of Stage II is to study the relationships between policy, practice and outcomes with respect to computers in education. Specifically, the study aims to relate policy variables to school, teacher, and classrooms practice and to student variables such as general level of computer literacy, specific knowledge about and experiences with computers and attitudes towards computers and its uses. The study will be survey in nature and will collect data at three levels: school, teacher and student.
The target populations for part 2 of stage II will be the same as for Stage I and part 1 of Stage II, viz. primary, lower secondary and upper secondary level of education.

Instruments for stage I

There will be three instruments in Stage I of the study. Also one instrument as an international option will be developed.
Each participating country will be asked to prepare a *national case study* to provide background information such as the existing national policy with regard to computers in education, the provision of pre- and in-service teacher training, the degree of centralization in administration, the soft- and hardware infrastructure and the prescribed curriculum. Further, additional information will be sought to supplement the information gathered from schools for facilitating an interpretation of the data collected from schools within its own national context.
To get a comprehensive understanding of the current situation with respect to the degree and ways of the use of

computers in education, a *school questionnaire and a subject matter questionnaire* are being developed to collect information from all levels of schools, namely, primary/elementary, lower secondary and upper secondary schools. The *School Questionnaire* consists of two parts. The *first part* is intended for all schools (users as well as non-users). Filter-questions in the beginning of the questionnaire point the respondent to answer certain questions, depending on whether the school is user or non-user. The non-user part contains questions about the reasons for not-using computers and questions to determine whether learning about computers is part of the school curriculum despite the fact that computers are not present.
The part for using schools, addresses issues related to the history of computer use in the school, the distribution of use across subjects, numbers of teachers and students involved, the policies of the school with respect to computer-use, the training of teachers, the available support and the problems the school experiences, when introducing computers. A separate section is included to register the characteristics of the school with respect to size, location and student(background) characteristics.
The *second part* of the school questionnaire is meant for schools which use computers (see earlier definitions), and consists of questions related to technical matters. This part of the questionnaire should be answered by a knowledgeable person (preferably the computer co-ordinator), who has information available or easy access to the information which is addressed in the questions. The questions relate to the equipment available in the school, available software, production and evaluation of software, organization of computer use, computer co-ordinator tasks and problems with respect to the use of computers.
The *Subject Matter Questionnaire* is intended to collect information about teaching and learning activities in existing subjects for the grade range as specified by the sampling and population decisions. It is an *informant* approach intended to elicit answers which generalize across teachers in a subject in a certain school, in contrast with the *respondent* approach for e.g. the Teacher questionnaire where teachers provide only information about themselves. The meeting agreed on some general guidelines for constructing this questionnaire (see summary 3) and left the further operationalizations to the International Co-ordinating Center.
A problem with administering this questionnaire may arise in those countries or school situations where teachers in a certain subject are rather loosely coupled within a school (no common strategies, meetings, information exchange, decision making, etc.). For these countries a single informant approach may not be appropriate and probably the answering of questions should be done by the teachers of a certain subject together (as has been the case with opportunity to learn ratings in earlier IEA studies).
As an international option, a *teacher questionnaire* for selected teachers may be administered. It will attempt to collect information on teaching practices with computers, teachers' knowledge and attitudes or views about computers in education. Countries are encouraged to use his instrument, along with the school- and subject matter questionnaire mentioned above, in the Stage I.

Data Analysis

Since Stage I is mainly descriptive in nature, the data

analysis will consist mainly of descriptive statistics, means, standard deviations, proportions, percentage, frequency distributions, crosstabulations and correlations. The intention at this stage is to represent the extent and nature of computers in education at each of the target population levels.

Data Reporting

An international report of Stage I, which is descriptive in nature, will be prepared. In addition, countries participating in this study will be encouraged to publish the outcomes of their findings as national reports.

GENERAL ORGANIZATION AND PLANNING

In the organization and planning of the study, activities at the national level may be distinguished from activities at the international level.

Table 2: list of participating systems (as of March 1988)

Belgium (Flemish)	Ireland
Belgium (French)	Israel
Canada (British Columbia)	Italy
Canada(Ontario)	Japan
England	Luxembourg
France	Netherlands
Federal Republic Germany	New Zealand
Greece	Poland
HongKong	Portugal
Hungary	Switzerland
India	USA

Participating systems

As in some countries more than one educational system is operating IEA prefers to use the word 'system'. Table 1 lists the systems which are participating in the study. Besides the systems listed in table 2, other systems from Asian and East European countries are still considering their possibilities for participation.

Organization

The project is embedded in the IEA organization which consists of a General Assembly of representatives from national centers of countries which are member of IEA.. Different committees exist to monitor the progress of the study and to give technical advice. Major decisions about the content of the study are made by the General Assembly, consisting of representatives from systems which participate in a certain study. Within a system a Research Coordinator is responsible for conducting the study. A Steering Committee of specialists within a system acts as a discussion platform for reviewing the design of the study and the applicability of the study within the system. Each system can make proposals and provide suggestions for

the international design of the study. The activities within and communication between the different systems are coordinated by an international co-ordinating unit assisted by an international steering committee. The international co-ordination for this study is located at the Department of Education of the University of Twente in Enschede, the Netherlands. The project director is Dr. Tj. Plomp and the international co-ordinator is Drs. W.J. Pelgrum.

TIME SCHEDULE

The time schedule for the study is summarized in table 2:

Activity	Start	End
Stage I		
Instrumentation	3-1987	11-1988
Data collection	2-1989	7-1989
Data processing	7-1989	6-1990
Reports	1-1990	12-1990
Stage II		
Instrumentation	12-1989	10-1991
Data collection	11-1991	12-1992
Data processing	2-1992	12-1993
Reports	10-1992	12-1994

CONCLUDING REMARKS

In the previous sections we have described very briefly the design and planning of an international study regarding the use of computers in education. The official start of the study was in April 1987 after preparatory work of several years. The data collection for stage I of the study will take place from December 1988 until March 1989 and the first descriptive reports can be expected in 1990. Important features of the study are the longitudinal character and the possibility to add national options to the international design of the study (like case studies in selected schools, additional instruments, special additional samples, etc.).
More information about this project (e.g. full project proposal) can be requested by writing to the International Co-ordinator of the study:

Drs. W.J. Pelgrum
Department of Education
University of Twente
P.O. Box 217
7500 AE Enschede
The Netherlands.
(Or via BITNET/EARN:TOPELGRM at HENTHT5

REFERENCES

[1]Coleman, J.S., Issues in the institutionalization of social policy, in: Husen, T., Kogan, M.,(Eds), Educational research and policy: how do they relate? (Pergamon, Oxford, 1984).
[2]Goodlad, J. et al. , Curriculum inquiry, the study of curriculum practice. (McGraw Hill, New York, 1979).
[3]Fullan, M., The Meaning of Educational Change. (OISE Press, Toronto, 1982).

COMPUTERS IN EDUCATION, F. Lovis and E.D. Tagg (eds.)
Elsevier Science Publishers B.V. (North-Holland)
© IFIP, 1988

COMPARATIVE REMARKS ON SOCIAL AND ECONOMIC DIMENSIONS OF NATIONAL STRATEGIES IN SCHOOL COMPUTING

Mihály CSAKO

Sociologist
Dohány u. 16—18.
Budapest, Hungary *

A cross-national study of broad socio-cultural, economic, and institutional context of computer use in schools was carried out to support the elaboration of a conceptual framework for a research project on "New technology and schools" in Hungary. The main dimensions of comparison were defined as answering a series of "what does it depend on?" type questions. Four large sets of factors influencing computer use in schools were   identified: (1) national computer industry, application, and culture, (2) organization and financing of the educational system, (3) pedagogical traditions, and (4) aims, methods, and organization of national school computer programmes.
Countries were selected for comparison in order to gather a great variety of experience in each dimension allowing the exploration also of cross-dimensional interaction of factors. Analysis was extended to nine countries.
Relationship between industry and education as a market, dominant ideologies and the perception of the role of computers in education, the political system and school computer programmes, the pedagogical tradition and the number of computers in schools could be stated in conclusion. Besides the four dimensions, the paper presents five main results of the comparison.

1.   INTRODUCTORY REMARKS

This paper is based on a comparative study aimed at forging conceptual tools for a research project on social, economic, and cultural factors in the computerization of Hungarian schools.

Hungary launched an ambitious national school computer programme in 1983. A new school computer (resembling one of the TI models) was developed, following the specifications determined by the Institute of Informatics of the Ministry of Culture. The main goal of the programme was to give one or two school computers to every secondary school. Schools willing to enter the programme had to employ at least two "computer-literate" teachers. Familiarizing courses of 2—4 days were organized at several centres of higher education and the pedagogical research to give teachers the opportunity to get the training required. Two years later, the programme was extended to the primary schools.

In this context there was no need either to fill every gap in the information available at first hand, or to standardize data series by year or other aspects.

The empirical variety of computer use in schools was chosen as a starting point and a series of „what does it depend on?" questions formulated that led us through a very limited number of steps to *four large sets of factors* influencing computer use in schools.

These sets are the following:

(1)   Development of national computer industry and application, as well as the level of computer culture in the population.

(2)   The system of decision and of financing of national education (from the highest level to schools).

(3)   Teachers' knowledge and skills and pedagogical tradition in the country.

(4)   Aims, methods, and organization of the National School Computer Programme, if there is one.

The last point could be subsumed under the second one and its separation is motivated simply by the fact that a national school computer programme is a special type of institutionalized action essentially aimed to organize activities we are interested in.

Countries were selected for comparison by several criteria — such as the amount of experience in school computing, centralized/decentralized system of public education, type of pedagogical tradition, specialities of national school computer programmes — in order to have a large variety of all the four sets of factors taken separately and in interaction. This goal was not hard to achieve and leaves a large margin to chance in the availability of information.

* The research project on "New technology and school in Hungary" was sponsored by OMFB (National Office for Technological Development) and co-ordinated by the Institute of Social Science, Budapest, Hungary. For further information write directly to the author.

Eight papers resulted from this work, summarizing the experience of Bulgaria, Canada, France, Great Britain, Japan, Sweden, the United States, and West Germany. Hungarian experience has been integrated, as explored in the research project.

Neither national features nor comparative results can be reported here in detail. A cross-national overview of the four sets of factors and the most important statements resulting from the comparative analysis will be given in this paper.

2.   FOUR SETS OF FACTORS IN CROSS–NATIONAL PERSPECTIVE

2.1 Computer industry, application, culture

All the countries compared, with the exception only of Bulgaria and Hungary, belong to the world developed in computer industry and application. Nevertheless the U.S. and Japan are the most advanced and are followed by European nations at the distance of a few years. Differences in the second group are insignificant.

The position of a country in this respect can be seen in different ways and there are observable differences in perception. France felt the glory of the nation in danger by the backlog of the national computer industry so they thought it was a duty of the state to intervene. A similar perception is followed in Bulgaria and Hungary, only the ideological motivation is not nationalism but competition with capitalism.

Although only sporadic information about national computer cultures was gathered and analysed, it suggests the trivial statement that the more developed a nation's computer industry, so the applications are the more widespread and sophisticated computer culture is in the society.

2.2. Educational system

The system of public education is highly decentralized in Canada, Great Britain, the U.S., and West Germany, and centralized in Bulgaria, France, Hungary, Japan, and Sweden. Financing is generally decentralized, even in centralized systems, but in Bulgaria and Hungary local funds are set at governmental level. (That means that the municipality decides the investments in local schools but the greatest part of the municipal budget comes from the national one.)

2.3. Teachers and pedagogy

Teachers — employees of an essentially conservative system of institutions — resist innovation everywhere in the world especially because they remember some recent experience of failure (e.g. programmed learning, teaching machines, overhead projectors, etc.).

Two pedagogical traditions can be distinguished. A more rigid one, different versions of which dominate most part of continental Europe: in Germany and Hungary we know it as the tradition of Herbart. Another liberal tradition prevails in America and Great Britain and its followers often reclaim the heritage of Piaget. Labels have no importance in our perspective.

In fact, the first tradition allows less autonomy for both teachers and children: the whole class tends to be more important for teachers than children as individuals. The liberal (or pragmatic, or child-oriented) tradition reverses these relations.

2.4. National school computer programmes

The compared countries started national school computer programmes, apart from the U.S., Canada and Japan. [1, 2, 3]

In the U.S., some programmes function at a state level, nevertheless tax incentives mainly play the same role in spreading computers in schools as national school computer programmes in other countries. In Canada, provinces have their particular educational systems and several of them launched a school computer programme (e.g. Ontario, Quebec). Japan introduced computer education into professional schools in the seventies and integrated only optional courses into general education.

The first governmental programme directly equipping schools with computers, though involving only a limited number of institutions, seems to have been the French programme called "58 lycées", launched in 1971. At the same time, the Swedish government began a long-term research project to explore the possibilities of computer use in schools .

The national school computer programmes we know today — based on microcomputers and extended practically to every secondary and often also to primary schools in the country — started mainly in the eighties, as shown in Table 1.

Table 1.

START OF SOME NATIONAL SCHOOL
COMPUTER PROGRAMMES IN EUROPE

Year	Country
1978	France (*)
1979	Great Britain (**)
1983	Hungary
1984	Sweden (***)
1985	Bulgaria
	West Germany

(*) This "10.000 micros" programme was extended to "100.000 micros" in 1983.

(**) Governmental decision was taken, but the programme (MEP) started only in 1981.

(***) Riksdag voted the programme "Education for the Computer age" in that year, but the programme started practically in 1985.

3. SOME RESULTS OF COMPARATIVE ANALYSIS

Relationship between national computer industry and education depends on the strength of the former and the volume of the latter as a market. There are three possibilities:

(1) Strong computer industry in search of new markets pushes schools to use computers (or government to computerize schools).

(2) Computer manufacturers agree to produce school computers specified by the educational government if the national or educational budget subsidizes this effort.

(3) Uncompetitive national computer industry cannot satisfy the needs of the education: schools purchase a wide variety of imported hardware.

The only example of the first way is the U.S. with an educational market large enough (adding Canada) to attract industry. Even in this case tax incentives played an important role in orienting manufacturers towards schools.[4, 5]

Most European countries follow the second way, as their educational market is too small to raise economic interest.

As an example of the third way, Hungary's computer industry could compete with imported models only if subsidized. In fact, it could not get adequate state support at the moment when the government tried to revitalize the national economy in crisis, by minimizing interventionist policy and replacing it with market mechanisms.

The other socialist country in the analysis, Bulgaria, not so much engaged in a new market economy, decided to support national school computer production — following the second way. [6] (The Bulgarian Pravets series is an Apple II-like construction capable of using the huge collection of educational software available for Apple II.)

Even a rapid growth of computer industry and application does not need computer literacy of the population.

Most developed countries have a constant manifest demand for, even a shortage in, computer professionals, but no need for general computer culture has been expressed on an economic basis. In this respect, the "Japan miracle" is very instructive: the spectacular growth of Japan's computer industry was achieved with no computer literacy pumped by schools into the population. [7]

The only exception is again the U.S., where economic need for computer literacy was formulated in the seventies by Arthur Luehrmann and refuted in 1984 by Joseph Weizenbaum:

"Why doesn't the Random House publishing company invest in teaching people to read? Because people might well go out and read Scribner's and Doubleday books. And so reading is taught in schools. For the same reason, computer use must be taught in schools". [8]

Luehrmann's *argumentatio per analogiam* keeps its validity only if computer culture is needed in the same way as reading. Weizenbaum doubts it and proposes another analogy:

"There are undoubtedly many more electric motors in the United States than there are people, and almost everybody owns a lot of electric motors without thinking about it. They are everywhere, in automobiles, food mixers, vacuum cleaners, even watches and pencil sharpeners. Yet it doesn't require any sort of electric-motor literacy to get on with the world, or, importantly, to be able to use these gadgets." [9]

All the other experience, and especially that of Japan, proves that while the integration of computer education into professional schools and universities is a top priority for modern economy, computer literacy programmes are promoted generally *post festam* (if at all) and rather with social or cultural motivation (e.g. in Sweden [10]).

Hungary's stressing the economic motives finds its explanation in the next point.

In highly centralized political systems national school computer programmes tend to be inserted into the range of the policies of "overtaking" the more developed countries.

Bulgaria and Hungary give the best examples of this situation (although in Hungarian documents a survival value of computer literacy is also stressed).

It is interseting to see that this motivation could be first observed in France, in the early seventies. Since the French government could not purchase the large mainframe systems needed in nuclear research, development of a national computer industry was recognized as a vital need of the nation and educational background as a necessary infrastructure to satisfy this need.

This tendency for continuous comparison with more developed countries is probably the result of the combined impact of a dominant ideology — communism or nationalism — and state control.

Centralized educational systems seem to be more successful in diffusing hardware and face more problems in integrating it into curricula and school activities in general. Where local initiatives prevail, the heterogeneity of hardware can be a major obstacle to educational software development, especially if the market is not large enough.

Decentralized systems have the advantage of autonomous teachers, who may not be too willing to learn and use new technology, but those who agree to do so have the professional imagination and skills necessary to succeed in any innovation.

In this respect, France can be considered the golden mean developing and distributing hardware and software tools supported by a national school computer programme budget on the one hand, and assuring great autonomy to teachers in their application on the other.

Unfortunately, Hungary succeeded in gathering all the inconveniences of centralized and decentralized systems, being willing to move from the first type to the second. In the Hungarian National School Computer Programme hardware and formal quantitative criteria prevailed, no good support materials for application being given, instead the teachers' autonomy was stressed. Yet teachers' autonomy in computer use is illusory while teachers have no autonomy in other fields. While centralized hardware distribution was troubled by shortages and importation problems, software development was passed to groups in market economy, without having either a real software market or an educational market.

At the source of all this trouble, we find the political effort of liberalizing the national economy and institutions trying to change a barrel of tar with honey, drop by drop.

Bulgaria's school computer programme has more chance of success, because in a politically homogeneous atmosphere, an equally centralized production and distribution of hardware and software, teacher training, and curricula planning can be more easily realized.

An important relationship can be stated between pedagogical tradition, computer use, and the number of computers in the schools.

A recent survey in Hertfordshire, England, established that primary schools had 1.5 computers on average (for about 250 children) and they used mainly drill and practice and "open-ended" programs. [11]

Surveying three counties in Hungary in 1986—1987, not a single teacher was found using a computer regularly for other goal than teaching elementary programming in Basic.

Hungarian teachers seem to have adopted the quantitative criteria of the National School Computer Programme saying: one machine is no machine, we need one computer for every two children. (The same argument was accepted in France as a basis for the development of the *nanoréseau*.) Today, as schools obtain hardware in the required quantity, teachers demand that machines be tied up into local networks, so as to be able to use them in teaching.

This quantitative approach has a solid support in Hungary's long pedagogical tradition, dominated by the so-called "frontal" method of teaching, i.e. when a teacher deals with the whole class together. Sticking to this methodology one cannot use one computer in the classroom, except as a demonstration tool (not too visible from the back rows, at that).

In another pedagogical tradition, a more liberal one, teachers can take advantage of using even a single machine, as the British (and many another) example shows.

REFERENCES

[1] Anderson, W. S., The techology race: how America could lose, *Computers and People,* January—February 1983, 7—11, 26.

[2] Sullivan, E. V. et al. *The development of policy and research projections for computers in education: a comparative ethnography:* Social Science in Humanities Research Council of Canada, project number: 499—83—0017, December 1986.

[3] Osamu Sekiguchi, Data processing education at the high school level, *Jipdec Report,* no. 53, 1983, 29—37.

[4] Stark, F. H. (Pete), The best way to put computers into schools today, *Communications of the ACM,* vol. 27, no. 3, March 1984, 186—189.

[5] Berghel, H., Tax incentives for computer donors is a bad idea, *Communications of the ACM,* vol. 27, no.3, March 1984, 188—192.

[6] Panova, R. and Prof Pisarev, Computers in Bulgaria's educational system, in: Nick Rushby and Anne Howe (eds.), *Educational, training and information technologies — economics and other realities,* Kogan Page, London/Nichols Publishing Company, New York, 1986, 61—67.

[7] Mikio Kakei, Computer education in technical schools, *Jipdec Report,* no. 53, 1983, 54—61.

[8] In: Taylor, R. (ed.), *The computer in the school: tutor, tool, tutee,* Teachers College Press, New York — London 1980, 127.

[9] Weizenbaum, J., Another view from MIT, *Byte,* vol. 9, no. 6. June 1984, 225.

[10] *Policy and points of departure,* Swedish National Board of Education, Stockholm, 1985.

[11] Jackson, A., Fletcher, B., Messer, D. J., A survey of microcomputer use and provision in primary schools, *Journal of Computer Assisted Learning,* 1986, 2, 45—55

COMPUTERS IN EDUCATION, F. Lovis and E.D. Tagg (eds.)
Elsevier Science Publishers B.V. (North-Holland)
© IFIP, 1988

PROSPECTS & PROBLEMS: A PAN-EUROPEAN PERSPECTIVE ON TECHNOLOGICAL INNOVATION AND EDUCATIONAL PRACTICE

M H Aston and R Templeton

The Advisory Unit: Microtechnology In Education
Endymion Road, HATFIELD,
Hertfordshire   AL10 8AU

The authors' participation in the Commission of the European Communities' FAST (Tecnet) Project over the past two years has afforded them a unique insight into the diversity, and at the same time, the commonality of the experiences of different European countries in the introduction of Information Technology in schools.

This paper highlights the importance of a number of universal pragmatic problems and obstacles, such as the logistics of In-Service training, hardware and software provision and anti-technology sentiment among educational practitioners, together with the more positive aspects inherent in the exciting developments that are taking place in schools throughout the continent of Europe.

1.   INTRODUCTION

There is no doubt that a wind of change is blowing through the classrooms of Europe. The microcomputer and associated technology provide a catalyst, but it is not easy to judge the effect. The Commission of the European Communities (EEC) through Directorate General XII (DG12) has developed a programme known as the FAST (Forecasting and Assessment in Science and Technology) which, through its Tecnet network, looks at issues concerning the attitudes of teachers to new information technologies and attempts to assess the nature of educational change. The constituent countries of Scandinavia meet together with similar aims under the Nordic Council of Ministers concerned with cultural co-operation. The State Committee for Science and Technical Progress in Sofia, Bulgaria has hosted two major conferences focussing on Children and Learning in which all the countries of Eastern Europe have had the opportunity of joining in the dialogue about the impact of information technology <1>. Few countries in Europe have yet to engage in a national initiative.

2.   NATIONAL STRATEGIES

2.1   Educational Philosophy

It is interesting to compare the adopted models for initiating change through the use of new information technologies. The accepted educational philosophy of a nation cannot be changed overnight and it is against this national backcloth that an I.T. evolution has to take place. Nevertheless, there is evidence that I.T. can provide a catalyst for curricular change and may well speed up the process by virtue of its unique capacity for subverting traditional methods. England, Wales and Northern Ireland, where the devolution of power permeates every level of the system from teacher to the Secretary of State for Education, have already experienced a number of schemes attempting to give equal opportunities to every school in the country. In contrast, Spain has concentrated its resources on clusters of schools in different provinces, centred on the older age group of pupils. Every country in Europe is noted as making a conscious decision to introduce computing into the curriculum of secondary pupils (age 11-12) first. Often, the primary pupils below the age of 11 continue to be ignored. We record that only a limited number of countries have specific plans to support this fruitful phase of education.

2.2   Political Will

It is also the case that resources to implement a national strategy are released on political decisions which focus on the longer term provision of a 'computerate' work force or the development of an information technology industry. Politicians are not so often concerned with improving the quality of teaching and learning and this is understandable when one looks for hard evidence on the basis of current research. Figure i personifies the problem we all face in education, that of being technology led.

Fig. i
From Computer in Unsere Schule?
(c) IPN (University of Kiel)   Acknowledged with thanks.

2.3   Teachers and the younger generation

Education systems were devised to resist change and to provide a series of anchorages for children to use as stepping stones to adulthood. Rapid advances in the technology are providing special problems for teachers that are not necessarily mirrored in the activities of their pupils. The microcomputer is as much part of the younger generation's gadgetry as the video recorder or the bicycle. It is worth bearing in mind that to a child, for whom all technology is new technology, the ramifications of powerful database software may present no more conceptual problems than changing channels on a television set. It is already part of their culture and may well be taken for granted.

3.   HARDWARE CANNOT BE IGNORED

3.1   The Manufacturers

In some countries, the penetration of the computer manufacturers has been extremely significant in determining strategy: for example Apple in the Republic of Ireland, IBM/Philips in the Netherlands and Thomson in France. In many cases, the companies have made offers of subsidized hardware that Ministries of Education have found hard to refuse in the light of overstretched budgets. In the case of IBM, some of the American philosophy of education is associated with the offer and this is reflected in the design of the educational software, which is not necessarily in tune with the European country's thinking.

3.2   National Standards

In spite of efforts by multi-national microcomputer manufacturers to have their particular models adopted in a country's classrooms, the indigenous machine has also made considerable impact. In the U.K., the government offered subsidies on machines as long as they were British. Today its classrooms are reasonably well stocked with BBC Acorns, Research Machine Nimbus and a scattering of Sinclair's low priced models. Financial incentives were not necessary for Denmark to adopt widespread use of the Piccolo and Norway, the Tiki. In Bulgaria and Romania we see locally manufactured Apple lookalikes. There is no doubt that the rapidity of technological change continues to take everyone by surprise in the world of education and there are no signs that we will have an opportunity to become complacent.

4.   PAN-EUROPEAN INITIATIVES

The importance of I.T. in learning is recognized by the EEC in the DELTA Project. DELTA stands for Development of European Learning through Technological Advance, an ideal that could cost between £55 - £60 million and take seven years to develop <2>. Individual nations have also given names to their projects, such as NIVO in the Netherlands <3>, ATANEA in Spain <4> and MINERVA in Portugal. Some adopt a top down approach, perhaps led by the universities, e.g. in Belgium, others allow the curriculum to develop from the grass roots, which is, perhaps, the British way. Both have their merits, and of course, a good mix of both can provide a good opportunity for combining research with development.

5. SOFTWARE - A SUITABLE CASE FOR GROWTH

It is encouraging to note that the powers of content free software exchanges (or software tools) are being recognised in the context of learning. Throughout Europe, we hear words like 'spreadsheet', 'paintbox', 'database', 'wordprocessing' and 'videotex' being used to describe learning environments. This is encouraging, particularly as this kind of software more easily transcends national boundaries, cultures and even mother tongues.

The FAST (Tecnet) Network has recently gathered over 100 case studies from a number of widely different countries in the EEC and we offer some comment on commonality and individuality of approach <5>, <6>.

6. COMMON GROUND

It is in many ways surprising, though also certainly encouraging, that it is not difficult to find common preoccupations and common initiatives throughout Europe in the field of educational development of Information Technology. A cursory scan of the contents pages of the collected case studies compiled under the FAST (Tecnet) Network reveals considerable common ground, although it is refreshing to note a healthy diversity of philosophy and approach.

6.1 Special Needs

One important area is where the technology has been identified and harnessed as a vital liberating factor for learners and other individuals, with special needs. FAST case studies include:

- the use of interactive video for teaching sign language in Belgium;
- applied computer technology for the blind (Braille output, synthesised speech, etc.) in Germany;
- a comprehensive view of the work of a special unit for the deaf in Northern Ireland;
- a hardware solution to some of the problems of an Orthopoid child in England;
- a study of technical aids to promote the independence of disabled people in Italy;
- work with pupils with learning difficulties at the College Chantaco in France.

6.2 Women and technology

This demonstrates an encouraging concern in all countries to use the technology for the enhancement of the lives of every citizen. Further evidence of this is the work in Germany (at the Institut Frau Gesellschaft - the Institute of Women And Society) and in the United Kingdom (the WISE - Women In Science And Technology - Project) which is looking at the relationship between women and new technology, reflecting the concern in many schools that girls are often less eager than boys to adopt information technology.

6.3 Logo

It is not, however, solely in work in areas of special educational needs that there is common ground. It is interesting, for instance, to see the extent to which the Logo language has been adopted in many countries. Again, the FAST (Tecnet) report reveals work in Spain, Belgium and Scotland - and we know also of important developments in the Netherlands, Finland, Romania and Poland. Logo is a particularly interesting case in point; with its emphasis on initial simplicity and its development of more complex microworlds, it is an ideal medium for adoption in many different cultural contexts, where the simple entry can be common, but the development can be more culture-specific. What's more, versions of Logo in different mother tongues, such as the Dutch MSX-LOGO, have helped to promote further the use of this powerful educational environment.

6.4 Language learning

Another major common area is that - appropriately enough - of language learning, from simple drill and practice software, through powerful exploratory language environments, to major computer-managed systems. To cite some anecdotal evidence, the authors of this paper, when presenting a week-long course in Information Technology Across the Curriculum in Helsinki, were particularly impressed by the number of modern language teachers who were eager to harness the power of the new technology for their own purposes. It was also interesting to note how British software packages which were written (in English) to support learning in subjects as diverse as History, Geography and Economics, were enthusiastically taken up by Finnish educationalists as resources for the teaching of the English language.

7.   DIVERSITY

If taking a pan-European view enables us to see the common ground among the various countries, it also has to be said that it enables us to see the diversity as well. It is interesting to note, in particular, the philosophical differences that distinguish those countries with a primarily didactic approach to learning, and those which favour a more heuristic approach. Although the power of computers seems especially suited to offering a more exploratory educational environment, it is true that old pedagogical practices die hard, and it will require more than a change in educational media to effect such a fundamental shift in certain countries. Having said that, as we have already suggested, the universal adoption of content-free packages, such as spreadsheets, databases, word-processors etc., is certain to promote a more autonomous mode of learning, whether national governments like it or not.

7.1   Microelectronics for all?

It would appear to be only in the United Kingdom that there has been any attempt to implement a programme of comprehensive technical microelectronics education, through the unique Microelectronics For All project, which has produced a pack including hardware, software, curriculum materials, worksheets, etc., and the philosophy of which is that all children should learn the rudiments and principles of microelectronics. It should, of course, be emphasised that this scheme has not met with anything like universal approval, even in the UK. However, it is perhaps significant that in the FAST (Tecnet) report, the only case study from any country other than the United Kingdom that was specifically electronics-based, was a single one from Germany.

8.   CONCLUSIONS

Our work with the FAST programme, our continuing contact with educational I.T. units overseas, including our experience of visiting and co-operating with colleagues in many other countries, has enabled us to make some interesting observations, and to draw a number of important conclusions about the ways in which I.T. education has developed in the continent of Europe.

One general observation concerns the way in which, in virtually every country of which we have knowledge, I.T. related educational innovation is still in the hands of a vanguard comprising a comparatively small number of teachers. This is true even in those countries where the most progress has been made. This is not to say that there are not many other interested teachers, simply that the permeation of I.T. throughout the educational process - or the development of whole-school policies in this area - still has a very long way to go, before it could be said to be properly institutionalised. Furthermore, it is also true to say that some of the more exciting developments in the field are happening at grass-roots level, rather than at a higher level (governmental or academic) - whether the initiative of an enthusiastic individual teacher, or of a locally-based institution.

No country, as yet, seems to have satisfactorily solved the many dissemination problems which are inherent in such radical educational innovation - teachers from every European state will tell similar stories of lack of information, of insufficient practical advice, of problems of evaluation, of lack of curriculum guidance, and so on. Perhaps some of these issues will become less of a problem as I.T. education is properly integrated into all pre-service training programmes. Again, there is a long way to go before that will be achieved in any country, although there is some evidence that the situation is beginning to change, in the UK at least (cf. the papers by Gardner and Tapsfield on the training of secondary and primary teachers, respectively, in the FAST (Tecnet) report).

Another problem that has yet to be satisfactorily resolved in many countries is that of defining what resources are actually going to be allocated to the development of I.T., given a general context of educational cutbacks and retrenchment. Something has to give; in some countries, perhaps, the decline in time allocated to Religious Instruction, or to the classical subjects, like Latin and Greek, has freed some resources for the purpose, but the genuine integration of I.T. as an educational medium will surely require some concessions from every direction.

The teaching of computer studies is no longer the issue that once it was, although misguided parental pressure still has a tendency to try and fight that particular battle. It is worth noting that commerce and industry recognise the importance of the I.T. education in other spheres - such as the development of collaborative and problem-solving skills, rather than specific technical knowledge. Some countries may be still looking to develop a national I.T. syllabus, but rapid technological change is likely to prove an insuperable barrier to the production of any workable national standard in this field.

Finally, while Europe in general, and the UK in particular, have probably led the world in the assimilation of microcomputers in the home, there is no real evidence, as yet, of any resultant educational spin-off. On the contrary, the home computer is still very much a solution in search of a problem, used, more than anything else, for playing games that are probably more educationally stultifying than edifying.

9. RECOMMENDATIONS

It is somewhat unusual for a conference paper to conclude with suggestions for possible future activity, but we felt that, in this case, the opportunity should not be missed. The field of I.T. in education is fast moving and conventional wisdom may not be the ideal way to cope.

A number of positive steps seems to us to be of value to the whole European community:

9.1 Software

A European standard for operating systems and programming languages is unlikely to be attained [7]. More important, though, is the necessity of having data interchange standards that allow data sets to be exchanged between nations and between different software tools,for example spreadsheets, database systems etc. A published set of guidelines would be helpful.

9.2 Curriculum development

The authors note the alarming increase in the number of 'whistle stop' tours by educationalists to I.T. Centres in Europe. We question the value of the 4-hour visit to both the visitor and the visited. The rarity of longer term exchanges between centres is observed by all concerned.

We should like to see resources being made available to fund a series of extended (i.e. 3 - 4 months) exchanges between development centres throughout Europe.

9.3 Information

Keeping teachers and educational decisions makers informed has to be the most difficult task of all. In the midst of an Information Technology explosion, we fail miserably in using I.T. to help ourselves.

There is an urgent need to identify a number of information centres throughout Europe and to widen their remit to cover a number of specific international responsibilities, such as:

Major curriculum development projects
On-line database for I.T. resources in education
Register of teacher training centres and courses
Special educational needs, curriculum datasets, etc.

REFERENCES

[1] Blagovest Sendov and Dr Ivan Stanchev, Children in an Information Age, Pergamon, Oxford, 1986.

[2] BIS Mackintosh, DELTA Workplan Development: Executive Summary, Commission of the European Communities DGXIII, Bruxelles, 1986.

[3] PSOI, Computers in Education: A Future Oriented Analysis, Ministry of Education and Science, Den Haag, 1986.

[4] Obdulio M Bernal, Cuadernos de Educacion y Nuevas Tecnologias de la Informacion, Fundesco, Ministerio de Educacion y Ciencia, Madrid, 1986.

[5] M Aston and R Templeton (eds), Information Technology in Education and Learning - 101 European Case Studies, The Advisory Unit, Hatfield, 1987.

[6] E Barchechath (ed), Pour une Renaissance de l'Education en Europe, CESTA, Paris, 1987.

[7] M H Aston and J Rantenen, Towards a Set of European Standards for the Development of Educational Software Tools for 16/32-bit Microcomputers, Proceedings of Eurit 86, Pergamon, Oxford, 1987, 257-265.

COMPUTERS IN EDUCATION, F. Lovis and E.D. Tagg (eds.)
Elsevier Science Publishers B.V. (North-Holland)
IFIP, 1988

IMPACTS OF NEW LEARNING TECHNOLOGIES ON AN ACADEMIC INSTITUTION AND ITS ENVIRONMENT

A.C. DERYCKE, J. LOSFELD

Centre Université Economie d'Education Permanente
Laboratoire TRIGONE
Université de LILLE I
59655 VILLENEUVE D'ASCQ CEDEX - FRANCE

Our Institute is devoted to the further education of adults and basic researches in education sciences. Eight years ago, we introduced new learning technologies in three steps : the pioneer stage, when hardware was first available ; the stage of generalization and education of our educators ; and the capitalization phase, bringing reinforcement of our methodologies.

The impact was great, not only on our Institute but also on our environment : our proposed solutions were selected for the French national plan "Informatique Pour Tous" or "Illiteracy Battle" plan.

1. INTRODUCTION

Since the late (19)70's, we have introduced new learning technologies (N.L.T.) in our academic institution "Centre Université Economie d'Education Permanente" (C.U.E.E.P.). We have had the opportunity to observe the impact of this new technology not only on our institute, but also on our environment, both regionally and nationally. Effectively, our progress during the last few years and the critical dimension we have grown to, have given us the opportunity to influence or to direct the major changes which are brought about by new policies for the introduction of these N.L.T. on a large scale in France.

We have introduced some innovative methodology and practices which have greatly modified our evolution and the behaviour of our instructors. This evolution has taken place in several steps, which will be described after a general presentation of the C.U.E.E.P.

2. THE C.U.E.E.P. : AN ACADEMIC INSTITUTE FOR FURTHER EDUCATION

The C.U.E.E.P. is an institute of the University of LILLE I in northern France. It has specialised in the field of adult education since 1968, with two interrelated missions : to continue the education of these adults and to carry out research in the different fields of this education.

A few statistics can give an approximation of our activities :

- We have more than 13 000 people enrolled each year for curricula of varying duration, ranging from sixty hours to nine hundred hours. The social origins of these people are very varied : from engineers to managerial staff, from big entreprises to workers of traditional industries like textile, steel..., unemployed people who make up nearly 10 % of the potential workforce in our region, and also people who are not involved in economic activity (mothers at home, members of social associations...).

This makes more than one million people hours of courses which are taught by more than half of the 180 permanent members of the institute and roughly 800 part-time instructors. It is interesting to note that these instructors, also, have broad social origins : besides professional teachers involved in the initial education of children or students, this is also a whole range of people as diverse as retired professionals and trades-union leaders...

- We have more than ten different locations throughout the Nord/Pas-de-Calais region, in order to ensure that people can find a welcome, advice and a large choice of courses, not too far from their home.

We have two characteristics which give our institute special status in comparison to other University Institutes of further education :

. firstly, courses are given at all levels from illiteracy remedials to engineer degree standard ;

. secondly, most of our activities concern the basic disciplines : mathematics, written expression, languages, acquisition of scientific concepts, introduction to modern information technology.

As a scientific research centre, we conduct basic research in the field of educational sciences : cognitive sciences, social aspects of continuing adult education, pedagogy and didactics of disciplines, psychological aspects of new learning technologies and design of tools: computer hardware and software, courseware, tutoring systems, complex systems based on computer networks and "telematics".

The TRIGONE laboratory ("Education, New technologies, and Development") is located in the institute C.U.E.E.P. and it offers courses in educational sciences for Master and PhD degree levels.

There is a strong reciprocal relationship between research and activities in the classroom. We believe that it is not possible to conduct major research into education if we are not the main protagonist of the processes : curricula definition, creation of the specific actions, education of the instructors, design of pedagogical tools and methods, evaluation, delivery of certification, overall observation...

3. THE FIRST STAGE : THE SEARCH FOR TECHNICAL SOLUTIONS, AND THE PIONEERS (1979 to 1983)

In the late (19)70's, we introduced the first microcomputers to the institute. They were used primarily in the computer curriculum : introduction to computer sciences, BASIC programming.

It rapidly became clear that these computers could be used as pedagogical tools by means of Computer Assisted Instruction . Our first experiments were conducted in two fields :

- in the field of computer sciences [1] , because teachers had knowledge of the computers and they could programme the contents of the courseware themselves.

- in the field of mathematics, mathematics teachers were rapidly able to use the new pedagogical tools, owing to their scientific primary education and their ability to use abstraction.

Spontaneous working teams then emerged, joined also by teachers from other disciplines. A core of about ten people became the pioneers of the C.A.I. in the institute. It was decided to purchase computer hardware for the creation of C.A.I. laboratories dedicated exclusively to the basic disciplines. The biggest problem was the cost of such computers for an institute of our kind (i.e. one involved in the social promotion of adults). So we chose low level, cheap home computers with restricted resources (tape recorder, small memories, Basic interpretor...).

These tools were not designed for educational purposes at this time. This led us to design

our proprietary tools : a computer classroom network and various authoring language systems and environment.

This was the time of anarchical development of courseware : each team or instructor began to design courseware for any level and without any general imposed directions.

In the perspective of the IX national plan, we worked closely with the Regional Council to promote an ambitious plan for the introduction of information technology in schools, high schools, and institutions like the homes for youth and culture in major cities...

In 1983, the first equipment plan was in operation and a Summer University was organized in order to introduce these new pedagogical tools : mastering the computer hardware and software, introduction of C.A.I. in instruction, use of LOGO, etc. [2] .

4. THE GENERALISATION STAGE (84-85)

Following stage 1, it was decided to adopt a general policy for the introduction and use of new learning technologies in the Institute.

Firstly, we decided to promote a comprehensive training of our instructors, be they permanent employees of the Institute or part-time ones. 50 % of the funds for this ambitious plan came as an award from the Social European Fund (C.E.E.). The other half came from the Institute. More than one hundred people were educated in two stages of 300 hours each :

- an introduction to the computer system, use and evaluation of the courseware library.

- and some instruction in computer programming, in order to be able to change some parts of the available courseware.

Some of our instructors received more advanced courses in computer science. In each team, there was often a technical designer of C.A.I. modules, who gave assistance to the least advanced instructors.

In parallel with this program, we decided to industrialize the classroom computer network of our design with the help of a local firm. This gave us the possibility to standardise the system for all our locations (today we have more than 150 workstations in operation every day).

The process of design, experimentation, and refinement of the system is original and has given a well-suited, widely accepted solution. [3] [4] [5] .

At the beginning of 1985, the Prime Minister launched an ambitious plan called "Informatique

Pour Tous". After evaluation, our system "Nanoreseau" was selected and several computer firms were linked in order to assemble and distribute the systems. In one year, more than 15 000 "Nanoreseau" were installed, in conjunction with 100 000 workstations located in primary schools and high schools.

In fact, the small computer, which was selected, had had no large user base. Consequently, we did not have a lot of software to back it up. In order to remedy this problem, we promoted a regional plan for software and organized a "task force" with our various partners.

Our internal methodology for the design of courseware was made widely available. It consisted of several phases : prototype design or research into existing prototypes, experimentation and evaluation, and for the most interesting pieces of courseware, there is some technical work to ensure reliability and redaction of manuals. In approximately five months, we were able to produce more than three hundred pieces of courseware and distribute roughly 20 000 packages !

Our contribution to the regional effort was the diffusion of approximatively one hundred programs, designed in our institute.

This huge task was possible because the general policy of education of teachers in our region was ambitious : by means of Summer Universities or permanent academic education centres, we trained either advanced users or courseware designers.

This was also possible because the State put some young people, with a scientist's degree, or equivalent in computer science, into various educational institutions for the duration of their national service.

5. THE CONSOLIDATORY AND METHODOLOGICAL PHASE (1986)

5.1 A more coherent production of courseware

Following the phase of generalization of new learning technologies in our educational practices, we observed two important evolutions :

(i) Firstly, our production of courseware or pedagogical tools was, by then, more co-ordinated. We applied our production process (prototype, experimentation, validation, industrialization and transfer) to the design of packages related to a complete set of instruction modules. The most interesting example is LUCIL, which is a package designed to reduce illiteracy in adults. LUCIL was developed by a team of researchers and instructors with the technical help of a

software company. The production of such a package was subsidised by the "Ministry of Employment and Professional Education" within the context of a plan called "Battle Against Illiteracy" (see the LUCIL-box). It is important to note that our teachers are the main proponents of teacher training apparatus.

(ii) Secondly, it was clear that setting up separate teams according to discipline (e.g. Mathematics, Written expression...) was not an adequate solution, especially for a low level of education. We have developed a broader perspective and approach to our actions at these levels. Figure (1) shows how a necessary disciplinary coherence interacts with an equally necessary interdisciplinary coherence, based on the people involved in the action in question.

An example of this approach is the "MAC 6" package for mathematics "à la carte" level 6, where a team of educators from the mathematics department, but also from the written expression or "illiteracy" department, have designed a module which contains courseware, computer software, open tools, booklet... In the same way, other packages were designed - such as EQUIPELEC for the scientific and technological concepts, or "Nanoburotic", which is a special package of integrated tools similar to those found in integrated business software (calc, data-base, word processor...). But these features and the human-interfaces are specially designed for the development of people's capabilities in the domains of mathematical abstractions, logical thought development, analysis of the terms of a problem.

5.2 The development of "self learning workshop" and resource centres

The introduction of new learning technology, particularly computer-based, allowed us to put more emphasis on the individual self-paced learning of each person.

This was made possible by the creation of self-learning workshops where, under the help of an instructor, each person can learn at his speed a particular part of a curriculum. A larger approach consists of resource centres where people have access to, and can use books, courseware, videotapes.

Interest in this approach has grown in our environment. For example, big major firms in the Mail-order-selling business have installed such resource centres, operated by our teachers, for the instruction of their employees.

5.3. A greater integration of research and education

As mentioned above, we also have a research function as part of a University. We specialise in the field of education and our work is guided by the principle of action/research. The introduction of New Learning Technology has forced us to adopt a more critical view of our research processes.

In fact, any important actions, in terms of hours or numbers of people, must be close to the model given in figure (2). There is a high level of interaction between four domains : accreditation and validation of prerequisites, research, education of groups of people and teacher training.

6. THE FUTURE : THE BEGINNING OF LARGE PROJECTS

As we have acquired some experience and made a certain impact upon our environment, we are now able to launch some large projects.

First, is a project of Open learning and teletutoring. Using computers at home and computer networks ("telematics"), we have found funds for the production of 300 hours of self-learning in the field of data processing, computer science, economics and business. We are now in charge of a team of four regional Universities for the creation of an Open University, which will use advanced information and telecommunication technology, as specified in the DELTA project of the C.E.E. [6] .

We also conduct research into and design of pedagogical tools for the new generation of microcomputers (e.g. 052 DOS on PC/AT model), especially in the field of application of Object Oriented Programming languages, like Smalltalk, to the human-interface, and of the uses of CD/ROM.

7. CONCLUSION

We have introduced New Learning Technology on most of our adult courses, especially at low level instruction. This introduction has been a success, not only for our internal use, but also for our environment. We believe that this success is due to two decisions :

- The first was to integrate basic research and educative actions to a high degree.

- The second was to have bet on the human factor with an ambitious policy of teacher training which has intensified their motivation. Collectively, they have had the opportunity to acquire skills in the use of these tools, either for an intelligent classroom purpose or in order to design new pedagogical tools themselves. Despite the cost

of this, in comparison with the cost of the hardware and software that we have bought, it has proved to be the most important and productive investment of all.

REFERENCES

[1] A.C. Derycke, J-M. Thibaut, The use of the personal computer for assisted instruction of the architecture of computer, WCCE 81, Ed. R. Lewis, E. Tagg, North Holland, Amsterdam, 1981, 858-859

[2] J. Losfeld, A.C. Derycke, Formation aux technologies nouvelles et technologies nouvelles dans la formation dans le Nord/Pas-de-Calais, proceeding of ANTEM II, C.E.S.T.A., Paris, March 84 (French).

[3] A.C. Derycke, P. Loosfelt, G. Cornilliet, Cheap local computer network : an ultimate solution for the classroom ? , EURIT 86, Ed. J. Moonen, T. Plomp, Pergamon Press, 207-210.

[4] A.C. Derycke, P. Loosfelt, Les leçons de la réalisation du Nanoréseau et de l'utilisation grandissante de la normalisation, Actes du Cinquième symposium sur la technologie pédagogique, Conseil National Recherche Canada, Ottawa, 589-594, (French).

[5] A.C. Derycke, P. Loosfelt, C. Vieville, Toward a pedagogy in networks, Proceeding of the international conference on Computer Assisted Learning in post-secondary education, University of Calgary, Alberta, Canada, 93-98.

[6] J. Whiting, D.A. Bell, Tutoring and monitoring facilities for european open learning, North Holland, Amsterdam, 1987.

LUCIL
(Campaign Against Illiteracy)

In response to a call from the Ministry of Employment and Professional Training, and the Nord/Pas-de-Calais Regional Council, two bodies - VENDOME FORMATION and the C.U.E.E.P. (University of Sciences and Technology, Lille, France) - have drawn up and implemented a training programme aimed at illiterate people.

This programme, called "Programme LUCIL" (Campaign Against Illiteracy), caters for the needs of illiterate people or, more specifically, anybody with little or no grasp of writing, who has difficulty when faced with situations involving comprehension and written expression.

LUCIL sets out to give these people an active and intelligent understanding of writing.

LUCIL uses a comprehensive set of teaching methods intended for independent use by trainers, who need not be specialists in this field. The programme amounts to 150 hours of training.

The complete package includes :
- *training of trainers and a teaching guide;*
- *90 hours worth of various activities run in conjunction with teaching aids in the form of dossiers ;*
- *a series of exercises in a Computer Assisted Instruction format, lasting 40 hours and accompanied by a C.A.I. guide.*

LUCIL's originality resides in its use of traditional teaching methods alongside Computer Assisted Learning. Throughout the period of instruction, LUCIL provides the teaching staff with guidelines for the course, together with traditional teaching dossiers and educational computer programmes.

Computer Assisted Learning constitutes the basic framework of the LUCIL programme. The whole programme is presented in the form of a series of themes based on role-playing situations taken from everyday life, so as to allow study of realistic written texts : identity checks, handling money, getting from place to place, asking the way, looking for accommodation, classified advertisements...

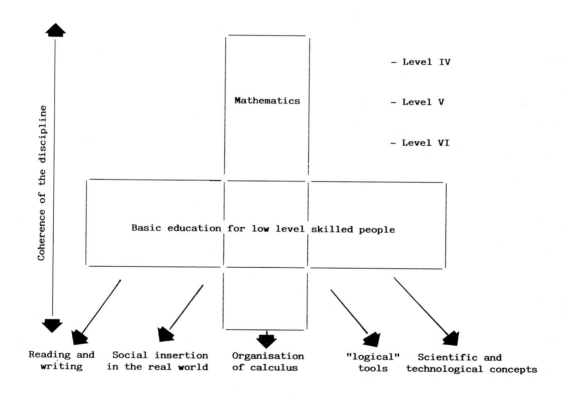

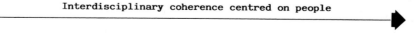

Figure 1 : The pluridisciplinary horizontal organisation is supported by transverse methodological capabilities.

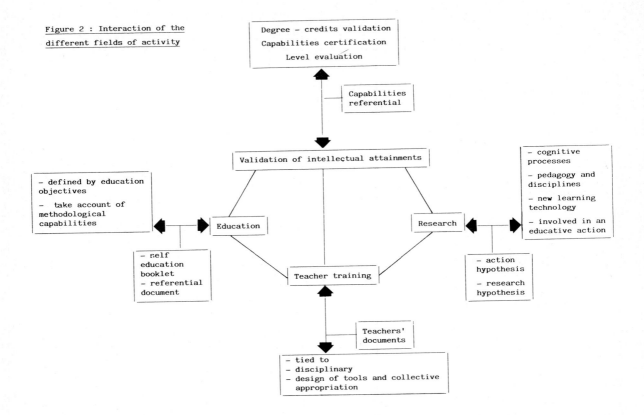

Figure 2 : Interaction of the different fields of activity

COMPUTERS IN EDUCATION, F. Lovis and E.D. Tagg (eds.)
Elsevier Science Publishers B.V. (North-Holland)
IFIP, 1988

PACE : A EUROPEAN PROGRAMME FOR ADVANCED CONTINUING EDUCATION

Norman LONGWORTH

External Education Programmes Manager
IBM International Education Center
135, Chaussee de Bruxelles
1310 La Hulpe - Belgium

Programme for Advanced Continuing Education
Universite of Paris Dauphine
75016 PARIS - France

ABSTRACT

The Continuing Education of European Engineers and Scientists at an advanced level is crucial
to the competitiveness and technical vitality of European Industry. This paper describes a
satellite education delivery facility with terrestrial computer conferencing feedback to provide
advanced education from European Centres of Expertise, usually based in Universities, to
engineers in industry at their own workplace.

1. AN INTRODUCTION TO PACE

1.1 Why PACE ?

It is estimated that USA Industry spends more than 40 billion
dollars per year on Continuing Education, comparable to all
the funds available to public and private universities together. And in a fast- changing technology-oriented world it
is easy to guess why. Continuing Education of a nation's
engineers, scientists and managers is the only way to
maintain their technical vitality and hence the competitive
edge which both companies and nations need to survive in
that world.

But Continuing Education is expensive, at an advanced level
it is in short supply and both the need and the demand for
education are growing rapidly. Individual companies do not
have the resource to meet the growing need, which is anyway often difficult to find; in Europe, even individual nations
have difficulty in supporting education, research and development in *all* the rapidly advancing technologies.

PACE, as a European facility, aims to communicate advanced level courses for engineers and scientists via satellite and to instal an advanced computer conferencing
network to establish feedback and interactivity. This has several advantages

- it shares the cost of Continuing Education to be shared

- it gives access to the best European centres of expertise

- it enables education to be taken in the workplace, flexibly

- it provides motivation for scientists, engineers and
managers to update themselves

1.2 The origins of PACE ?

PACE derives its origins from the first Europe/USA Forum
on Continuing Education in September 1986, when a group
of 50 key European industrialists and academics went to the
USA to explore several aspects of the Continuing Education
scene there. The use of satellite to deliver Interactive Television (ITV) from University Centres of Excellence to Industry
was a particularly attractive feature and the idea of establishing a similar facility in Europe was born.

Five major companies in Europe - Thomson, British
Telecom, IBM, Philips and Hewlett-Packard - got together in
a cooperative venture to provide the necessary cash, resource and impetus and established a series of Action
Groups to give life and direction to the new body. These
have since been joined by five more sponsors - DEC Europe,
Danish Enterprise/University Systems, IRI, a Portuguese
Consortium and Bull. Thus representatives from companies
in Belgium, Holland, France, UK, Italy, Denmark, Portugal
and Switzerland have given an initial commitment to help
launch this unique and much-needed programme.

The PACE Steering Committee, chaired by Hubert Curien,
former French Minister of Research and Technology, also
contains representatives of the Standing Conference of
Rectors, Presidents and Vice-Chancellors of European Universities (CRE), The European Society of Engineering Education (SEFI); observers from COMETT, the European
Programme to encourage Continuing Education and
Industry/Education cooperation, and DELTA, the European
Educational Technology Programme, regularly attend Steering Group meetings.

2. THE MANY FACES OF PACE ?

2.1 PACE has to be seen in three ways.

- firstly, as a *delivery system* which establishes the *technical infrastructure* to enable educational supply meet
educational demand through satellite and terrestrial
networks.

- secondly, as an *educational infrastructure* which selects
advanced educational topics, identifies European
centres of excellence, and uses or commissions
courses in those topics from those centres.

- thirdly, as a *financial and promotional organisation*
which redistributes payment from course receivers to
course suppliers, negotiates with Industry, Education
and Government for resources to maintain itself and
informs and publicises its activities to existing and potential clients and users.

2.2 Who benefits ?

In performing all these functions it is creating and nurturing a **European Continuing Education culture** which other advanced industrial countries in the world have built up over many years. The benefits of this will extend to

- *industry,* in the form of better-educated employees and a sharper competitive edge

- *education,* in the wider markets higher education can obtain for its courses, and the challenge of new ideas and methods

- *government,* in the greater wealth produced by industry and better-informed research departments and

- *individuals,* in the better quality and quantity of education available to them.

3. THE PACE CONCEPT

PACE aims to establish a system to deliver education by satellite from European Centres of Competence to European Industry. Centres of Competence will most often be found in Universities, though PACE also intends to provide seminars and offer courses from other centres of excellence eg industry. Universities themselves can also act as course receivers in the PACE structure.

Many PACE courses will be delivered live. Some will be taped and then distributed slightly later. Most will be lectures which would have been given in the normal course of events to a regular audience of students, researchers and/or scientists.

Feedback will probably take place in four ways

- In live broadcasts, by direct voice contact to the lecturer, thus offering the student immediate response to questions

- For all courses, the lecturer will be asked to set aside defined periods of time when he/she can be contacted by telephone, thus offering the opportunity to discuss in more detail.

- In most PACE courses, an advanced computer conferencing facility will eventually exist for student to teacher, and student to student, interaction.

- In addition, course providers will be expected to devise a series of follow-up materials for individual study and assessment. These will be delivered both by post and by electronic mail through the conferencing system.

Special Events, comprising such occasions as research seminars and conferences, state-of-the-art surveys, and technical press conferences, are also planned.

4. PACE'S ORGANISATIONAL STRUCTURE

Figure 1 illustrates how PACE will operate organisationally.

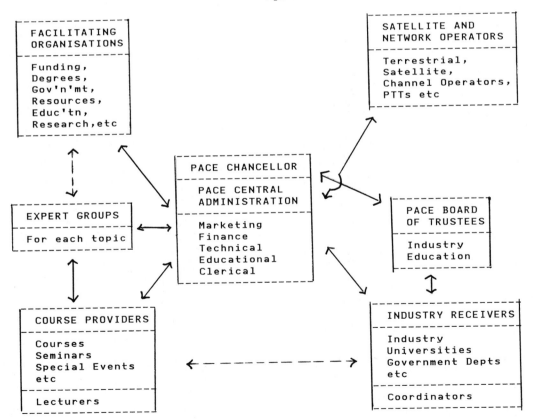

Figure 1. PACE Organisational Structure

PACE will be a non-profit organisation administered by a *Board of Trustees*. This Board will comprise executives from those companies which are prepared to guarantee for three years payment of the full sponsor membership fee, plus representatives of major European educational organisations. It will contain a maximum of 20 people and, after a period of four years during the settling-in period of PACE, a plan to encourage new members to serve on the Board will be implemented.

In addition, the Board's educational function will be enhanced by *Programme Advisory Groups* which contain experts from both industry and education to supervise content, curriculum and educational matters in each of the subject areas and recommend the best course providers.

PACE Administration, including the Director, Secretariat and Faculty members, will be responsible for negotiating with the many organisations with which PACE must negotiate.

5. THE PHASES OF PACE

The process of setting up PACE has already begun. After the highly successful Second Europe/USA Forum in Paris, June 1987, the following were agreed to be the major implementation phases.

- *PREPARATION (July to December 1987)* - Some full-time and seconded staff will be recruited, a Director-designate found and a secretariat established. Negotiations will begin with education suppliers and other groups through the newly set up Programme Advisory Groups, potential sponsor companies will be approached and the non-profit making company established.

- *LIMITED PILOT (January to August 1988)* - some courses and special events for a limited experimental audience will be provided in some of the chosen topics.

- *FULL PILOT (September 1988 - August 1989)* Courses will commence in all the selected topic areas and industry will be invited to register students for these. There will be a build-up of experience both in delivering and receiving courses at distance.

- *YEAR ONE...(from September 1989)* - Full courses will be delivered by major European Centres of Competence. Many of these will probably be offered for European accreditation.

6. MEMBERSHIP OF PACE

There are three categories of membership of PACE

- *Full Sponsor* - which gives the right to sit on the Board of Trustees. The present recommendation for this category of membership is 90,000 ECUs per year. PACE Full Sponsors have the right to influence the direction and curriculum of PACE through membership of all Programme Advisory Groups and will pay reduced site and student rates for PACE courses.

- *PACE Subscriber* - which gives the right to appoint members on to a maximum of three Programme Advisory Groups, to elect one member to represent subscribers on the Board of Trustees and to reduced site/student fees.

- *PACE Client* - a company or university which uses PACE services and pays a fee based on the number of sites and students.

7. THE LANGUAGE QUESTION

The multiplicity of European languages is an acknowledged problem. In deciding a language policy three considerations have to be taken into account.

- *Firstly*, it would be extremely costly to provide a large range of languages.

- *Secondly*, the language which course providers feel most comfortable with is their own.

- *Thirdly*, a large majority of European engineers and scientists accept English as a lingua franca for communication and many research papers are written in that language.

Thus, PACE will, by and large, adopt a policy which takes into account these considerations and reaches the majority of engineers and scientists at reasonable cost. Where translation is necessary, simultaneous interpretation, 'voice-over' and 'two-version' techniques may be used as appropriate. It is intended to use the 'limited pilot' phase to experiment with translation methods and to modify the language policy in the light of the information obtained during that phase.

8. PACE COURSES

8.1 Topics

There are, of course, many fields of advanced research which PACE could deliver. However, it would be wrong in the early days to become too ambitious in both topic and audience. Consideration has been given to the fact that PACE sponsors are mainly from the information technology industries or have a high information technology component to their operations. Thus the fields chosen and outlined below reflect this bias.

PACE FIELDS

MICROELECTRONICS

EXPERT SYSTEMS

SOFTWARE ENGINEERING

TELECOMMUNICATIONS

TECHNOLOGY MANAGEMENT

ADVANCED MANUFACTURING TECHNOLOGY

Figure 2. PACE Fields

Special themes from these fields will be delivered as both short and longer courses, and also as special events. In addition special events might deal with such additional fields as **Superconductivity** and other important technological breakthroughs with immediate interest. The lectures will be given by the most up to date experts, with supporting materials and systems.

8.2 Selection of course providers

Programme Advisory Groups will contain experts representing European organisations which have knowledge about the Centres of Competence able to deliver PACE level courses. Above all, they will take into account the reputation of the centre in its own field and its willingness to back up courses with good materials. Subsidiary parameters may include the availability of technical facilities for delivering courses, the translation opportunities existing in the organisation, experience in providing Continuing Education for industry and geographical equity.

8.3 A typical PACE course

A typical PACE Course consists of

- *Video Delivery* of lessons from the Centre of Excellence. These may be either live or taped for slightly later delivery.

- *Voice Feedback*, by telephone. This may be either immediate or at a slightly later time, or both.

- *Follow-up Materials*, which take the form of lesson notes, assignments and assessments.

- *Computer Conferencing Link* for student to teacher interaction, and for delivery of materials.

The length of course will vary according to topic and need, but it is expected to average about 30 hours, of which about 10-15 hours would be teacher to student face to face delivery.

PACE recommends, if possible, an in-company tutoring facility for courses with large numbers of students at the same site, or the use of a local university for follow-up assistance.

9. WHERE WILL PACE FIT INTO A COMPANY'S EDUCATION STRUCTURE ?

PACE is not aimed at the general or basic education market. It is an advanced level Continuing Education facility to keep a company's engineers, scientists and managers at the forefront of technological change in key areas. It will probably not satisfy more than five per cent of a company's educational need, but participation in PACE will be a powerful investment in the ability of European industry to compete in future marketplaces and an opportunity to gain access to an extremely scarce educational resource.

10. ASSESSMENT AND ACCREDITATION

Assessment of PACE courses will be carried out by the providing institution. This can be done by a system of feed-back exercises distributed by post or by electronic mail. The receiving organisation will need to supervise this process and to monitor procedures.

It is expected that, in the longer term, such examinations will lead to the award of a credit. The collection of appropriately similar credits will lead to the award of a PACE degree. The exact details of a degree-awarding scheme have yet to be worked out, and it is possible that the European Commission ERASMUS programme, recently adopted, will provide a focus for work in this area.

11. PACE FINANCE

PACE will receive income from two main sources

- From *Sponsoring Companies* in the form of subscriptions and site fees

- From *Students* in the form of course fees. These will usually be paid by the employer.

In addition, it is hoped that the *European Commission* within the framework of COMETT and possibly other educational programmes, will support PACE, especially in the early phases and to assist those countries and organisations less able to find their own resources.

Additional potential sources of income are national government subsidies, foundations and other European Programmes, though these are not taken into account in the present financial planning cycle.

Ultimately, it is expected that PACE will be self-supporting by its third year of operation.

COMPUTERS IN EDUCATION, F. Lovis and E.D. Tagg (eds.)
Elsevier Science Publishers B.V. (North-Holland)
© IFIP, 1988

TRADE UNION EDUCATION ON NEW INFORMATION TECHNOLOGY
AN ITALIAN EXPERIENCE

by Sandro Bianchi * and Piercarlo Maggiolini**

* Fiom-Cgil National Education Commission, ** Politecnico di Milano

The paper presents motivations, story and content of the complex and articulate education activity of Fiom-Cgil (Union of metalworkers) in the field of new information technology.

Fiom in 1984 proposed that a group of experts with different backgrounds (computer scientists and technologists, experts in industrial automation, in organization and management, an historian, a sociologist, a psychologist) should experiment with a new educational union project at national scale on the aspects and effects of new information technology in industry. The course, called "Workers inside technological innovation", was actually designed by these experts (who would play the role of teachers) together with Fiom unionists of the National Education Commission. From November 1984 to July 1985, the educational experience was developed, involving (during seven editions of the course at regional and inter-regional levels) three hundred unionists and shop stewards, active members of Fiom. After this test, didactic materials were published in January 1986 (seven workbooks). In 1987, in order to serve an increased pool of course trainees, nine videos were made in cooperation with the "Archivio audiovisivo del movimento operaio" (Video Archive of the labour movement), and a project of tutor training started.

1. CONTEXT

Since a long time, the union movement, in different countries in Europe, has realized the necessity to negotiate a fair distribution of the economic and social costs and benefits of new technology and has performed some initiatives, in this respect, aiming at some national and local agreements, and achieving a series of supporting labour laws.

The union action, starting from Norway, and in general from the Scandinavian countries in the early 70's, in order to control and negotiate the development and the application of information technology, has already spread over many countries of the Western Europe, from England, where there are more than hundred local agreements on new technology, to France, where - on the pressure mainly of Cfdt - the left government introduced in 1982 some amendments to the labour Code, allowing broader rights to get information, negotiation and the use of specialists on the corporate committee, regading the introduction of new technology. To say nothing of the FRG, where codetermination laws (as from 1972) offer large opportunities and rights to workers, to be used, and actually used, in the field of new technology too.

Also in Italy, the demands concerning technological agreements exist (without mentioning informal practices of affected codetermination, also existing).

The most relevant reference agreement is the IRI (1) - Trade Unions one of the 1984, which attemps to establish a "model" of industrial relations for the co-determination, in a certain on technical and organizational change (2). As far as private companies are concerned, some of the first agreements covering information rights and preventive consultation on change plans were achieved in 1985 at Zanussi (controlled by Swedish Group Electrolux (3)) and at Sasib, metal entreprise in Bologna which belongs to the holding CIR (linked, in its equity, with the Olivetti Group) (4).

Furthermore, there are some negotiation and law tools which could be used in this field.

Above all, we can mention the first part of craft national agreements (including those of 1976 and the last ones (signed in 1987) in particular the metalworkers national agreement, where the information right is recognised, a preventive information in certain circumstances, on technological changes and on their effects on employment and working conditions (5).

And so we can also mention "Workers Statute", 1970, and above all, the article n.4, forbidding a distant control over the labour activity through visual devices, which have been sometimes used (and could be more broadly used) to negotiate or to object to some aspects of computer-based information systems.

What is particularly meaningful, new and of great significance in the European and Italian experience, is the demand (6) - accepted in some cases - for procedures of negotiation or, at least, of consultation on new technology, beginning from the phase of systems design, the so called "ex ante negotiation", considered the most effective to influence in due time corporate policy and, consequently, the pertaining effects on the workforce.

It is necessary to underline that the agreements (and laws) ruling the negotiation on new technologies, which are mere tools in workers' hands, fix the preliminary conditions but are not, absolutely, enough to enable unions to control and to act in the field of technological change and technical-organizational innovations, resources and conditions which sensible and open-minded employers have accepted to allow, in exchange, substantially, for consent to the innovation and technological-organizational restructuring, which has existed more and more radically and deeply in the last few years.

Here and there a new model of industrial relations is flourishing, in accord with which unions can not only react, be antagonist, but also propose and even take steps and particularly stimulate, just the innovation, in order to be protagonist.

How can unions influence the innovation process, how can they actually play a positive role, take initiatives and not only react or defend, which are the tools that enable unions to do that "ex ante" bargaining of change, about which we speak a lot?

Should unions achieve the right to be preventively consulted, (or really to negotiate) on technological and technological-organizational change, the issue of turning this right into a practice will remain a problem.

Fundamentally, what did unions try to do? They have tried to limit the damage of innovation and sometimes to negotiate the sharing of the benefits which, more or less, concerning also profit, innovation produces.

But there is no doubt that this is a defensive role and that the active one is a prerogative of employers.

And consequently, in order to act in advance, what do we need to do? We need an autonomous union strategy on innovation. In other words, we shall be able to take advantage of negotiation rights and tools, won or demanded, if we have an autonomous strategy related to technological change.

This autonomy can but be a result from a cultural autonomy in the field of new technologies.

An absolutely essential condition of this strategy is the chance, the skill to win information rights (preventive and consultative) and make them applied. This skill is linked, in turn, to the capability to observe and understand phenomena of change with its relative preconditions and implications, both at micro and macro levels.

In order to build this this autonomous strategy, we need a cultural autonomy, which can but come from research activity, training, socialization of experiences done.

In this context we can evaluate the complex and articulated activity of Fiom-Cgil (7) in the cultural field, started in 1984, which we are going to illustrate.

2. MOTIVATIONS

The matter consists, first of all, in giving reasons why Fiom-Cgil, as well as unions in general, entered the way of a comprehensive project of education as regards new technologies and explaining the essential features of the choices which characterise this effort.

In the 70's, the strength and effectiveness of union bargaining, opened a crisis in the fordist model of work organization. Meanwhile, during the same period, the change in the size and nature of markets corroded traditional assumptions and corporate structure based on rigid hierarchy. In order to cope with this first break, the corporate system attempted to react, also relying on the intermediation of unions.

It is symptomatic that, in the second half of the 70's, companies defended themselves from the fordism crisis by a managerial style that accompanied general agreements with unions (we can refer to the unique point of escalator agreement) with a sort of "organizational reformism", always in the terms of given technology, by job enlargement and enrichment).

These attempts are integrated also with experiments of radical technological changes (we refer to assembly aisles, LAM or Digitron introduction at FIAT) still tending to overcome particular forms of social conflict and bottlenecks in production process.

But, at the end of the 70's, a turning-point occurred, from this defensive phase, which launched once more entreprise, its political-cultural and socio-economic centrality, via technological means.

The break in the 35 day strike at FIAT in 1980 is emblematic: it is the jump from the "human face fordism" towards a policy of heavy restructuring, with the unilateral decisions of dismissal of thousands of workers, by a flexible robotization of motor assembly at Termoli (in South Italy), by "quality groups" and with the attempt to sweep away the same union intermediation.

Moreover, almost in all industrialized countries, the new technological phase coincided with a disruptive initiative of employers, which broke the consolidated equilibrium of industrial relations, by mass dismissals, with a new managerial style, characterized by an aggressive attitude against unions, and aiming at building a consent on a new corporate basis. This directly political use, together with the feared social effets of the technological revolution, have mobilised the European Union Movement in an intense effort aiming at a cultural review, and great educational commitment to cope with technological challenge.

But at this stage, totally new for a whole European Union generation (and not only in Italy) the old model of training, that enabled union officers to act on the base of practical and organizational information to do "the job of unionist", appeared obsolete.

At the same time, global theories revealed themselves non-existent as a means of offering a valid key for understanding reality in movement. On the contrary, these theories also stopped acting as an ideological compensation to support a militancy in a critical phase.

From the failing of these two models of union education, although opposite each to the other, a new signal arises; most European unions seem to need to go back to reality. However, the urgent demand to gain again the full control of the scientifical and technical subject, sometimes risks compromising the delicate equilibrium between the systematic exploration of the new technological environment and the strains in the empirical consciousness of workers.

The link between the knowledge of the corporate restructuring mechanism and technical change and the perception of the new dislocations and new forms of social contradiction, runs the risk of breaking suddenly.

In order to sharpen our sight and to improve our analysis of machine systems we risk seeing no human being.

These processes introduce relevant changes - i.e. a cultural leap characterized by an authentically "epochal" passage - in consciousness, culture and power relationship. They require, consequently, completely new tools of control and action.

The factory is changed and goes on changing. A discontinuity, a deep break has been produced with previous taylorist and fordist experience. We witness the interruption of a continuity, a sort of conceptual curve of learning for both workers and unions.

For this reason unions need to improve their capacity in analysing, interpreting and intervening.

The tasks of union education consist in sharing the necessary quality jump, achieving and organizing pieces of knowledge and understanding tools to elaborate a renewed bargaining power of both workers and unions on new technological and organizational models.

But to be able to act, we need first to rebuild the capacity to observe and understand. The question is to form or rebuild a new and autonomous point of viex. Through a critical approach, determined by the support of different disciplines, a course was built coping with the subject of technological change in order to take a cultural jump in the understanding of processes and therefore become capable to intervene "ex ante", when the new technical systems are introduced.

For this reason, the general lines of the course can not be similar to an "ABC union course", i.e. a conventional union training, and, substantially, an adjustment of the human language to the language of the machine in the human language.

3. STORY

Fiom proposed to a group of experts with different backgrounds and disciplines to experiment with a new educational union project on the issues and effects of new technologies, particularly on the application of computers in industry.

In order to cope with the technological challenge, the Fiom standpoint is the conviction that the task of union educational work consists in sharing the necessary cultural efforts, through a reflexion on this phenomenon, seen from different scientifical and disciplinary point of view. In fact, considerations from different points of view - from the computer expert, to the psychologist, from the historian to the technologist, from the information systems expert to the sociologist - can indicate rational paths reaching a possible, common and synthetic outlook on processes in progress.

Having started from this demand, the educational course "Workers inside technological change - man, machines, society" (*I lavoratori dentro le innovazioni technologiche - uomini, macchine, società),* was designed by some experts (who would play the role of lecturers) together with Fiom unionist of the National Education Commission.

This joint work enabled us to build, step by step, an educational "curriculum" and specific teaching methodologies to be adopted (see tab. 1).

From November 1984 throughout July 1985, the educational experience was developed involving (during seven editions accomplished at regional and inter-regional level) three hundred trainees, amongst full-time trade unionists and shopstewards, members of Fiom.

In its concrete story, the course, meeting with different cultural contexts, diversified subjective and collective attitudes, has been step by step changed and focused.

This running in, necessary for every educational project, was the result of a rich interaction between lecturers' knowledge, disciplinary tools, didactic experience and trainees' "lived" experience, points of view, capabilities to propose.

On the whole, the experience was very positive and on that basis the didactic materials have been written and published.

The materials, published before a concrete verification with users, should be unavoidably different.

On the contrary, feedback evaluations of the trainees (who filled in "feedback scales" and expressed written considerations on all course stages), discussions in work groups and assembly debates, offered very stimulating elements.

In each edition of the course, a different specific case of corporate computerization was presented. Contemporarily, every lecturer could usefully compare himself with other lecturers' point of view, enriching his knowledge and experiences.

4. THE COURSE REPRODUCTION ON VIDEO CASSETTES

In the Spring of 1986, an increase in the pool of course users was stressed: from hundred of full time trade unionist to various thousands of shop stewards and workers. A jump that, as is easy to understand, presented not only a quantity problem, but a quality issue. If, on the one hand, in fact, it was not even unimaginable to satisfy a demand of such a width utilizing the same lecturers, on the other hand, the problem of their replacement presented many risks for the course's quality.

In short, it was necessary to find a way to satisfy a wide request for knowledge on new technologies, without the possibility of engaging different disciplinary experts, but just utilizing their competence. The idea to make some videocassettes, or to be more precise, some visual lessons, came up as follows. The operation - which was developed in co-operation with the "Archivio audiovisivo del movimento operaio" (Video Archive of the labour movement) - was shown to be much more binding than we had imagined at the beginning, in order to get some effective visual lessons. Of course, we took the opportunity of redesign the whole course, now based on nine lessons, partially re-elaborated and adjusted in comparison with the original ones and with the publication of didactic materials, partly inserted "ex novo", satisfying requirements and needs presented during the different editions of the course itself (Tab.2).

The lecturer's absence during the course causes, however, new problem: the video can be stopped on a particular image and can be seen again, but not questioned. On the other hand, it being absolutely excluded that the tutors can replace the different disciplinary experts, the trainee could imagine coping with a technological barrier: all knowledge behind the screen. How to change therefore this situation of clear impotence into an opportunity of learning and education? In order to achieve this target, it is necessary to activate a particular dynamic: just the lecturer's absence "compels" the workers, who cannot speak to T.V., to do it by themselves, trying to put again some fragments of knowledge and experience together, comparing them with the information and lecturers' opinion received through video.

But this way, this learning dynamic, is not easy and natural at all. It must recover the different individual subjectivities, trying to give some instruments through which these can become a collective subjectiveness, i.e. a work group, a learning group.

In order to get this result, it is necessary to provide people with a space (a topic, a schedule, a physical space) where they can meet, listen to, compare themselves with a task (learning), without causing some pre-constitued hierarchies and making a true exchange among people with different working, professional and trade union backgrounds.

It can so determine a collective mental space, by common language recovery, by knowledge and experience interlacing, by discovering the bricks to build a new collective knowledge.

Fiom, therefore, thought of integrating viedocassettes by an educational methodology, assigning a basic learning role to the group. About forty Fiom tutors attended more specific courses in order to learn how to coordinate some learning groups on the basis of project -"Progetto Ulisse" (Ulysses Project) - examined together with a psychologist, who assured his supervision and two experts in group dynamics.

The new course, based on video use and work groups of Progetto Ulisse was already partly experimented with (videos were not ready yet) in Lazio, Emilia-Romagna and Piemonte.

The complete experimentation started from the Autumn of 1987, through different regional experiences (Campania, Toscana, Emilia-Romagna and Lazio) all carried out at the same time.

----

(1) IRI - Istituto per la Ricostruzione Industriale (Institute for Industrial Reconstruction), the main Italian state-owned holding.

(2) IRI-Trade Unions Agreement provides for a set of information and consultation procedures aiming at the Unions' participation in every phase of the executive planning, implementation and monitoring of employment, economic and industrial policy of the IRI and its companies. To this aim, a series of consultative joint committees was established. They act after the formal approval of the initial project and before settlement of the final project and its feasibility plan.

The tasks of these Committees are as follows: examination and preventive investigation of the strategical options in the industrial and economic policy, relevant operational project of restructuring and development, significant aspects of labour policy; assessment and formal opinion, which is compulsory but not binding, in respect of these issues, as well as suggestions of possible options and alternative programmes; verification and control of implementation phases of guide-line programme; elaboration of proposals concerning work organization, industrial relations and labour market.

(3) "Taking into consideration the quantity and quality size of technological investments, Zanussi will provide Trade Unions with preventive information at plant or division levels, in the frame of a technical place, without however any obligation to negotiate, as regards organisational change, skill lowering and the relative needs of vocational training" (From Zanussi Agreement, May 1985).

(4) "The firm will provide preventive information on technological and organisational changes of particular significance (as Cad, Cam systems, FMS, Office Automation and in general relevant mechanization and computerization processes) concerning employment, professional skills, working conditions. The content of information will have to allow workers' representatives an adequate evaluation" (from Sasib Agreement of May 23, 1985)

(5) The article n.3 (information at company level), first paragraph ("Technological, organizational and production changes) of the 1987 Metalworkers Collective Agreement, states that "management of plants, which employ more than 200 workers, will inform local Union representatives and through the competent association of industry employers, the Provincial Union, about major changes in the productive system, involving, in a determinated manner, technologies so far used and work organization in the whole, or the kind of the existing production and influencing employment on the whole.

(6) From negotiation platform of the Fiom-Fim-Uilm Ialian Metalworkers Agreements, approved in 1986: "As to firms, which employ more than 150 workers, a preventive examination on technological changes, on work organization and on the product is requested. An investigation phase will be provided in binding and fixed dates. A written opinion, expressed by the parties concerned, will conclude this investigation. The investigation phase will be accomplished by a joint company/union commission, with the possibility for

the union and Works Council to appoint, respecting the confidentiality , also, also external experts.

---

tab. 1

The program of the Fiom-Cgil course
"WORKERS INSIDE TECHNOLOGICAL CHANGE"

Time schedule
First day

9.15-9.30 a.m.	presentation of goals and methodological characteristics of the course
9.30-10.30 a.m.	*" An Introduction to Informatics"* by P. Mussio
11.00-12.00 a.m.	work groups (usually 3)
12.00 a.m.-1.00 p.m	discussion in plenary assembly
3.00-4.00 p.m.	*The Components of Information Technology"* by F.Graziani
4.30-5.30 p.m.	work groups (usually 3)
5.30-6.30 p.m.	discussion in plenary assembly

Second day

9.00-11.00 a.m.	practical approach to computer (2 groups): examples and analysis of typical problems
11.30 a.m.-1.00 p.m.	discussion in plenary assembly with the lecturers of the first day
3.00-4.30 p.m.	a case study of computerization
5.00-6.30 p.m.	discussion

Third day

9.00-9.30 a.m.	introduction to the third day lessons
9.30-10.30 a.m.	*"Factory Automation and Work Organization"* by A. Dina
11.00-12.00 a.m.	work groups (usually 3)
12.00 a.m.-1.00 p.m.	discussion in plenary assembly
3.00-4.00 p.m.	*" Automation, Technocracy Ideology and the Workers' Movement in the 50's"* by A. Lombardo
4.30-6.30 p.m.	discussion in plenary assembly

Fourth day

9.15-9.30 a.m.	introduction to the fourth and fifth day lessons
9.30-10.30 a.m.	*"Technological Challenge and Social Change: Economic Systems, Life Environment and Work Conditions"* by P.Ferraris
11.00-12.00 a.m.	work groups (usually 3)
12.00 a.m.-1.00 p.m.	discussion in plenary assembly
3.00-4.00 p.m.	*"New Technology Negotiation in Europe"* by P.Maggiolini
4.30-6.30 p.m.	discussion in plenary assembly

Fifth day

9.00-10.00 a.m.	*"The Individual in Front of Technological Change"* by E.Rebecchi
10.00-12.00 a.m.	work groups (usually 3)
12.00 a.m.-1.00 p.m.	discussion in plenary assembly
3.00-6.30 p.m.	final discussion between participant and lecturers

Tab..2

The nine video lessons of the new version of·the Fiom course

First lesson
"An Introduction to Informatics" by P.Mussio (47'05")
a) Culture, not only technique for informatics (14'08")
b) We can influence the development of informatics (14'15")
c) Let us learn to influence informatics (18'42")

Second lesson
"The Components of Information Technology" by F.Graziani (42'13")
a) Computer functions (11')
b) How computer really works (15'53")
c) How computer use is changing (15'10")

Third lesson
"Factory Automation and Work Organization" by A.Dina (56'25")
a) From rigid to flexible automation (20'40")
b) Flexibility and integration (16'08")
c) Man in a flexible and integrated system (19'38")

Fourth lesson
"Information Technology as Organization Technology" by P.Maggiolini (50'10")
a) Information technology as work tool in the office (13'54")
b) Information technology as coordination technology (17'20")
c) Information technology as exchange technology - The information technology evolution in the firm (18'46")

Fifth lesson
"Production an Market" by P.Bianchi (51'20")
a) Production organization (18'50")
b) Markets transformation (13'28")
c) Innovations and strategies (19'02")

Sixth lesson
"Technological Challenge and Social Change" by P.Ferraris (55'46")
a) Electronics within product (16'32")
b) Telematics and electronics within production equipment (16')
c) Skill, power and control in new working conditions (10'15")
d) Employment, time strategies, education (12'49")

Seventh lesson
"The Individual in Front of Technological Change" by E.Rebecchi (45'45")
a) Computer paints the town red (17'24")
b) Phantoms, losses (15')
c) Against robotization of mind (13'21"

Eithth lesson
"New Technology Negotiation in Europe" by ADina (49'26")
a) Some European experiences (18'47")
b) Model of entrepreneur answer (11'34")
c) Italian experiences (19'05")

Ninth lesson
"Hypothesis for Negotiation: When, How, What" by A. Dina (5&'35")
a) Why to negotiate ex ante (13'07")
b) Tools, procedures, conditions (16'43")
c) What we can negotiate (2&"45")

Lecturers
P.Mussio, professor of Systems Theory at University of Milan
F.Graziani, consultant of informatics in Milan
A.Dina, director of the Observatory on New Technologies of Fiom-Cgil
P.Maggiolini, professor of Management Information Systems at Politecnico di Milano
P.Bianchi, professor of Industrial Economics at University of Bologna
P.Ferraris, professor of Political Sociology at University of Camerino
E.Rebecchi, Professor of Social Psychiatry at University of Bologna
A.Lombardo, professor of Contempory History at University of Siena

COMPUTERS IN EDUCATION, F. Lovis and E.D. Tagg (eds.)
Elsevier Science Publishers B.V. (North-Holland)
© IFIP, 1988

FROM GAME PLAYING TO COMPUTER PROGRAMMING DURING "HOLIDAYS WITH A COMPUTER"

Adam Czerwiński

Pedagogical University of Opole
Oleska 48
45-951 Opole, Poland

The following paper is the presentation of the results of research
dealing with teaching the fundamentals of programming to schoolchildren
between the ages 8 and 15. The focus has been laid on examining the
practical application of the elaborated teaching concept of such classes.
The experiment took place during "Holidays with a Computer", i.e. during
the summer camp in which the programming classes were being held.

1. INTRODUCTION

Polish schoolchildren in the age group
between 8 and 15 /i.e. Primary School
students/ are not so far being prepared
at school for the "computer revolution"
- as we normally call the role, range
and speed of the changes connected with
the popularization of the means and
methods of computer science in technology, economy and culture. However,
some intensive research has recently
been carried out, having as its aim the
popularization of computer science education, and aiming, at the same time,
to introduce it into Primary Schools
curricula. The experiment described in
the following paper is connected with
the search for the most favourable solutions for teaching purposes to be used
at schools. It referred to the teaching of programming fundamentals at the
Polish Primary School level. The aim of
the experiment was to verify in practice
an original teaching concept for computer science classes. Undertaking this
research, it was assumed that nowadays
it is not possible, at least temporarily, to make use of computers in computer assisted teaching in Polish Primary Schools. Such a situation results
from a common lack of a satisfactory
teaching software [1]. However, at present computer science teaching as a
preparatory stage for the mass utilization of microcomputers in education
is possible. Thus, teaching the elements
of programming as a part of computer
science teaching constitutes a solid
preparation of the youth and the teachers for the changes in the whole
educational system awaiting them.

The experiment was carried out during
"Holidays with a Computer", which was
the name of the summer camp for Primary

School children. It took place in July
and August, 1987, in a little castle
in Dąbrowa Niemodlińska, near Opole.
During the two camp sessions a total
of 140 schoolchildren of different
backgrounds, coming from different
towns of Northen Poland, took part.
Each of these two sessions lasted three
weeks. Apart from camp activities, such
as sports, games, excursions, disco-
theques, etc., microcomputer classes were
also held. These classes were arranged
in such a way as to enable each of the
participants to have an average of 1
hour-long contact with a microcomputer
per day, which, in the long run, made
16 hours during the whole stay. The children were divided into four age groups:
8-9, 10-11, 12-13, 14-15. The children
from the same age group took part in classes under the rule that not more than
two children were to work on one computer.
It should be emphasized that the children were in no way selected or chosen
to participate in the camp beforehand.
What is more, for a overwhelming majority of them, it was the first contact
with a microcomputer in their lives.

At the class instructor's disposal
there were eight UNIPOLBRIT 2086 computers, compatible with ZX SPECTRUM,
one memory station on 3 inch floppy
discs and a SEIKOSHA GP 500 printer.
During classes, the Polish version of
the LOGO language interpreter and a typical set of skill-preparatory and simulation games were used.

2. CLASSES TEACHING CONCEPT AND ITS REALIZATION

In this part of the paper, the classes

teaching concept, including the adopted
methodology, aims and contents, will
be described. In the presentation of
aims and contents of teaching, we concentrated mainly on the enumeration of
the topics dealt with during classes,
together with the range of skills and
knowledge a participant should possess.
For a full characterization of a teaching situation, we also each time provided an assumption to be fulfilled
before the accomplishment of each of
the successive stages.

In principle, however, the whole assumed
contents of teaching may be realized in
teaching elements of the LOGO language.
The fact that in the inculcation of a
correct programming style and characterization of its very essence, this
language has been chosen needs no further comment [2]. In this particular situation, the Polish version of the LOGO
language was employed since it guaranteed a full reliability of the tasks to
be accomplished and a possibility for
application of the letters with diacritical marks characteristic of the Polish
language /e.g. ą,ę,ś,ć, etc./. To heigh-
ten the level of the classes attractiveness /there were holidays after all!/
it was decided to make use of computer
games as well. One should bear in mind,
however, that within the proposed
scheme of a teaching concept, computer
games were helpful only in instruction
of how to operate a microcomputer.
Now, let us proceed to a detailed description of particular stages of
instruction.

Stage I
Topic:
Functioning of a microcomputer keyboard.
Assumption:
The students cannot operate the keyboard;
the contact they have had so far with
a microcomputer is limited only to computer games.
The realization of this stage was
initiated by suggesting to the children
to write letters to their parents with
the help of a computer. It created a
very convenient opportunity to use small
and capital letters, correct punctuation
and the letters with diacritical marks.
For the sake of convenience, this task
was realized under the LOGO editor.
While writing letters, the students were
being instructed and introduced to different sorts of keyboard's modes, together with the simplest editorial possibilities, i.e. with the deletion and
insertion of signs into a text.
Acquired skills and knowledge:
ability to operate the editor and mastery of the microcomputer keyboard's modes.

Stage II
Topic:
A Dialogue with a Microcomputer
Assumption:
The students have had a certain contact
with the microcomputer's reaction to the
insertion of unintentional commands.
The realization of this stage was not
initiated until the students were fully
aware of a need to communicate with a
computer in a language so far unknown
to them.
The students, while trying to make use
of their experience with letter-writing,
came across the LOGO interpreter's answers: "I do not know how to do ...".
This evoked in them an urge to get to
know the words that could be correctly
interpreted and then well performed.
Such a positive motivation made it
easier for them to acquire some knowledge of the "Turtle Graphics" [3].
The possibility of an immediate observation of the results of the given
commands, i.e. the very fact of leading
a dialogue with a microcomputer stimulated a similar positive motivation.
Acquired skills and knowledge:
ability of correct formulation and
command editing and mastery of some
basic commands within the range of the
"turtle graphics".

Stage III
Topic:
Constructing simple drawings on the
microcomputer screen.
Assumption:
The students have acquired some knowledge enabling them to construct simple
drawings.
The realization of this stage was initiated by suggesting to the students that
they should make simple drawings on the
screen. The students' invention was not
in any way restricted. Nonetheless, the
most frequent drawings were: a house
/Figure 1/ and a flower /Figure 2/.

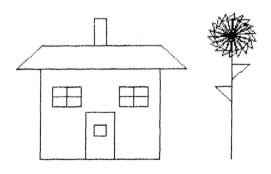

Figure 1   Figure 2

The most characteristic thing, however,
was an unconscious application of the
"attempt and error" method in, for instance, finding a given point on the
screen. The elder children were at an
advantage, for they were able to operate
within the Descartes system of XOY
co-ordinates.
Acquired skills and knowledge:
ability to encode drawings in a shape
of sequence of commands in the LOGO
language and mastery of the ways of
transcribing drawings on to the printer
or in the computer's external memory.

Stage IV

Topic:
Correct programming style.
Assumption:
The students are able to draw simple
drawings on the screen.
The realization of this stage was initiated by suggesting that students make
some drawings of decidedly complex
structure. Similarly, as in the previous
stage, the students' invention was not
restricted; however, they were encouraged to create certain compositions on
the screen. Thus, such drawings were
made as:
- a mountainous landscape /Figure 3/,
- a train /Figure 4/,
- a castle /Figure 5/.

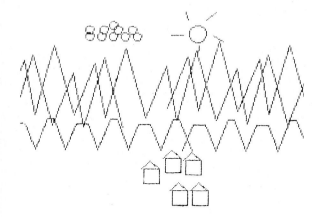

Figure 3

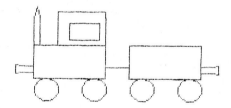

Figure 4

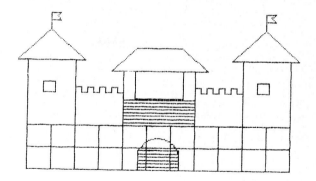

Figure 5

The students did discover quite soon,
however, that the ad hoc approach proved ineffective in that particular
case, which completely discouraged some
of them from drawing. During the discussion on the causes of difficulties,
the students were gradually becoming
aware of the fact that while drawing
on the paper, they were naturally decomposing a picture into some less complex
fragments and, what is more, that the
same idea could be applied during their
work with a computer. In order to
divide a picture into several parts,
one needs some new tools of a programming language. In LOGO, these are the
procedures and mechanism of their composition. Therefore, acquiring some
knowledge in this field by the students
is fully justified. From the very beginning of instruction in programming,
some features of a good programming
style were being inculcated as well,
e.g. programming by the top-down method,
with the aid of the hierarchical structure of modules. A good illustration
of this thesis is the procedures used
for drawing the composition shown
in figures 3, 4, 5. For instance, in
order to draw a mountainous landscape,
the student applied the procedures drawing mountain tops, hills, cottages,
clouds and the sun. Then, to draw the
sun, he applied the following procedures: the circle and the rays, etc.
Acquired skills and knowledge:
ability to divide the complex tasks
into the simpler ones and ability to
edit procedures, mastery of the ways to
define procedures and of the analytical
way of designing a drawing on the screen.

Stage V

Topic:
The essence of programming - discovering
rules, generating algorithms and their
coding.
Assumption:

The students have been satisfactorily
acquainted with the "Turtle Graphics".
The realization of stage V was initiated by bringing forward a problem,
the solution to which was unknown to
the students. The kind of graphic problems which have a simple and effective
solution in LOGO is generated by fractal structures drawing. Hilbert curves
and "snow-flakes" were taken as examples. Drawing basic curves, i.e. second
order curves /Figure 6 and Figure
7/ was not difficult for the students.

Figure 6   Figure 7

On the other hand, however, it was more
difficult for them to define the rules
that allow the construction of curves
of any order /they were shown fourth
order curves, for example - see
Figure 8 and Figure 9/.

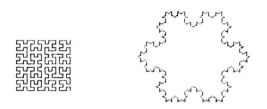

Figure 8   Figure 9

No sooner was the systematic transcription of the procedures drawing the
successive curves introduced, than the
students were able to generalize them
into the procedures drawing curves of
any order. There followed a discussion
of this issue, making referance to the
essence of programming. It enabled the
students to characterize programming
as the activity consisting of   generating algorithms and their coding.
Acquired skills and knowledge:
ability for logical conclusion and generalizing observations, mastery in
procedure modification and systematic
approach to problem solving.

3. CONCLUSIONS

On the basis of the experiment,
    one may arrive at the following
conclusions:
A.
The classes proved the fact that thanks
to the suggested teaching concept, it is
possible for beginners to acquire the
fundamentals of   correct programming
during several hours spent on working
with a computer.
B.
In the youngest age group /8-9 year-
olds/ we consciously limited ourselves
to the realization of only a part of the
concept, i.e. to the first three stages.
Several years' experience in teaching
"Turtle Geometry" to such young children
indicates the difficulties arising in
teaching the mechanisms dealing with
procedures and the mathematical concepts
such as invariances under rotation and
transformation [4]. These were the elements which constituted, among others,
the contents of our considerations of
the stage IV classes. Therefore, after
giving them up, we concentrated on inculcation of the length and angle measure
concept. It was observed, then, that
using a turtle "as an object to think
with" in constructing simple drawings,
makes the children's understanding of
angle measure considerably easier,
cf. [5].
C.
Initiation of the particular stages of
instruction only after the realization
of previously specified assumptions and
with an active participation of the
students influences favourably their
motivation and heightens the attractiveness of the classes.
D.
The parallel application of computer
games in teaching the elements of programming may have a motivational significance, as well. Having encountered
some difficulties in acquiring new
contents:
- firstly, thanks to the games, the
  children were not completely discouraged from working with a microcomputer,
- secondly, the games were often a sort
  of relaxation time, after which it was
  possible to come back to discussion of
  the reasons for the difficulties which
  arose.
E.
The cause of errors committed by the beginners during the "Turtle Graphics" learning is a lack of immediate realization
of graphic commands in procedure defining.
One may avoid the strenuous following up
of erroneous graphic procedures after
defining them. It is enough to introduce

a window in which a suitable picture
will show up during procedure defining.

REFERENCES

[1] Madey J. and Rogowski Z., Kształce-
nie informatyczne młodzieży szkół
średnich - propozycje i zamierze-
nia, in: Materiały Konferencji nt.
MIKROKOMPUTERY W KSZTAŁCENIU
/Poznań, 1986/ pp. 17-28.
[2] Harvey B., Computer Science LOGO
Style /M.I.T. Press, 1985/.
[3] Abelson H. and di Sessa A., Turtle-
Geometry /M.I.T. Press, 1981/.
[4] Hillel J., Understanding of Procedures by Young Children Using Turtle-
Geometry, in: Proceedings of II International Conference: CHILDREN IN
THE INFORMATION AGE, vol.1 /Sofia,
May 1987/ pp. 265-281.
[5] Loethe H., Geometrical Problems for
a Turtle with Direction and Distance
Finder, in: Proceedings of the LOGO
and Mathematics Educational Conference /University of London Institute of Education, 1985/.

COMPUTERS IN EDUCATION, F. Lovis and E.D. Tagg (eds.)
Elsevier Science Publishers B.V. (North-Holland)
© IFIP, 1988

A NATIONAL PROJECT ON COMPUTER INTRODUCTION INTO SECONDARY SCHOOLS IN BULGARIA AND AN APPROACH TO ITS IMPLEMENTATION

DONCHO DONCHEV, MIHAIL DRAGANOV

Prof. Doncho Donchev, Ministry of National Education;
Mihail Draganov, Ph. D., Ministry of National Education
Ministry of National Education
18 A. Stamboliiski Blvd.
Sofia 1000
Bulgaria

The paper offers a general description of Bulgaria's national project for introducing computers in secondary schools, and discusses an approach to its implementation.

The project's major goal is formulated taking into account both the students' point of view, and societal considerations. The major tasks to be accomplished in pursuing this goal fall into two groups: content-oriented and organizational. The former covers computers and the methods of their application. The organizational tasks are related to equipping schools with computers and providing teachers with the respective qualifications. The content of the project is presented regarding computers both as a subject of study and a teaching tool. The approach adopted in implementing the project has been described as well as the organizational structures and mechanisms needed. Special attention has been paid to employing computers as a teaching tool. The results obtained have been cited, together with their evaluation.

1. INTRODUCTION

Of late computers have been increasingly used in education in numerous countries. Bulgaria started using them in secondary education in 1981, when the first 200 Bulgarian personal microcomputers were produced and supplied to schools. Over the period 1982–1984 a large number of micros was introduced into schools to be employed in the initial stage of providing teachers and school children with a computer awareness, for experimental teaching and amassing experience in the educational uses of computers.

Since late 1984, the mass introduction of a large number of computers into Bulgarian secondary schools has begun. This was the time when the first comprehensive programme for education and work with computers was adopted [1]. This programme is being regularly updated, and the tasks it contains are being elaborated in further detail and implemented on a planned basis. Gradually, an overall project on computer applications in secondary schools evolved, together with an approach to its implementation.

2. PROJECT GOALS AND TASKS

2.1. Major Goal

The project's major goal may be regarded in two aspects, depending on the viewpoint. From the point of view of the individual personality, the goal is to train young people for working and living in the context of the mass advent of computers in all fields of human activity: industry, transport, management, business, everyday life. From the point of view of society, the goal is to provide trained staff and specialists for computer production and usage as well as high quality training for specialists in various subjects by employing computers as teaching tools.

2.2. Major Tasks

In terms of content the tasks in achieving the project's main goal fall into two groups: content-oriented and organizational.

(i) Content-oriented Tasks

The first two of these treat computers and their uses as a subject of study:
— to train skilled personnel with secondary education for programming tasks, computer usage, maintenance and production (professional aspect);
— to enable young people to study the fundamentals of informatics and computer science, acquire mass computer literacy and an insight into the computers' functions in industry, everyday life and management, and their role in society in general, to provide young people with basic skills and experience in using computers (educational and cultural aspect).

The third content-oriented task appertains to computers as a teaching tool and is formulated as follows:
- to bring about, using computers as teaching tools, an appreciable rise in the quality and efficiency of the students' training and to raise also the general intellectual and cultural standards of students.

(ii) Organizational Tasks

The organizational tasks appertain to the technical and personnel back-up of the project:
— training teachers to employ computers in instruction;
— fitting computer classrooms in schools.
The training of teachers depends on the goal:
— training for a teaching qualification in informatics and computer science;

— training teachers in different subjects to use computers in class.

The project does not envisage upgrading the teachers' qualification for a vocational training of secondary school specialists in programming, computer maintenance, exploitation and production, since such teachers should have a preliminary highly specialized training.

A detailed programme for the period up to 1990 has been elaborated for teacher training and qualification upgrading, together with the respective curricula and syllabuses. The programme is under way at present. The qualification courses envisaged are of a duration of one week, one month, three months or a year.

A detailed plan and schedule have also been elaborated for fitting schools with computers, covering the period up to 1990. Schools are equipped mainly with the Bulgarian-made Apple-II compatible 8-bit 'Pravetz 8' machine. At present each Bulgarian school has at its disposal an average of some 15 micros. There are small schools with only five or ten machines, and also large ones possessing over 100 computers. In 1987 the introduction began of another Bulgarian-made 16-bit computer — 'Pravetz 16', IBM PC/XT — compatible. These are to be used mainly in vocational training.

The above division of the tasks into organizational and content-oriented is rather general and formal. Thus in order to solve any of the content-oriented tasks a host of organizational ones have to be tackled.

3. PROJECT CONTENT

3.1. Computers as a Subject of Study

Numerous programme tasks have been formulated, related to the goals and major tasks of the project.

With regard to specialists with secondary education to be employed in computer production and utilization, an analysis has been made of the professions in this field of vocational training, and their qualification characteristics have been updated, together with the syllabuses and curricula. The needs of such personnel have been estimated and the network of the respective secondary vocational schools has been established.

With a view to ensuring mass computer literacy, a compulsory subject has been introduced in secondary schools with the following syllabus:

— Fundamentals of mathematics. Nature, essence and major characteristics of information. Information processes and activities.
— Introduction to computers. Nature and principles of operation. Introduction to the school machines.
— Algorithms and programming.
— Programming in BASIC.
— The module principle in programming. Subprograms.
— Data arrays. Main data structures and data processing algorithms.
— Operational systems.
— Computer-aided problem solving.
— Computer applications.
— Most common applied programs and systems and their usage.

The whole course is supplemented by numerous practical laboratory sessions.

3.2. Computers as a Teaching Tool

(i) Determining Factors

In terms of content, the task of using computers as a teaching tool for a significant rise in the quality and efficiency of learning is the most difficult one, for it depends on a number of factors.

— the system of instruction (class sessions or individual learning);
— computer availability in schools;
— amount and quality of the machines used;
— level of teacher training;
— availability of adequate textbooks and educational software; and many more.

(ii) Basic Principles

In drawing up the project, some basic principles were formulated, stemming from the country's specific conditions and the goals to be attained.

— to preserve the class sessions system of teaching;
— to retain the role of the teaching as the guiding element in the process of learning;
— to leave the computer merely the function of a tool to be used both by teacher and students;
— to ensure highly efficient use of the computer classrooms available;
— to achieve a mass-scale, unified approach to using computers in schools throughout the country;
— to determine the role and place of computer in class according to the type of the lesson;
— to introduce computers in schools in stages;
— to determine a priority ranking of school subjects in terms of CAL, etc.

(iii) Main Directions of Computer Uses

In drawing up the project, the most efficient (as we see them), directions of computer uses in secondary schools, were set out:

— in the field of theoretical and applied study of the fundamentals of informatics and programming and their applications;
— as a universal computing device for the natural sciences and the technical subjects;
— for mathematical modelling and illustration in studying the nature of processes and phenomena;
— for numerical methods and optimization procedure software;
— as an application of CAD systems;
— as word processing and text editor systems;
— for the development and use of educational tool and environs;
— for furnishing specialized classrooms and laboratories for the natural sciences and the technical subjects;
- in vocational training - for simulation models of industrial units, machines and systems, lines and productions;
— in vocational training — for developing digital program control software and technological process control packages.

4. AN APPROACH TO THE PROJECT'S IMPLEMENTATION

4.1. Content-oriented Approach

The content-oriented uses of computers as a subject of study follow logically from the content of the project itself. Its vocational aspect is specific for each individual subject. The general-educational and cultural aspect of the project, aimed at providing general computer literacy, appertains to the place and contents of the compulsory subject 'Fundamentals of Informatics and Computer Science' and falls within the range of interest of the respective experts. Special attention is paid in our project to the uses of the computer as a teaching tool.

The approach adopted in implementing that part of the project which is related to employing computers as a teaching tool in secondary schools, will be illustrated by an example concerning a single subject in a single grade. A similar approach is adopted in this respect both for the same subject in the rest of the grades and for all other subjects.

It boils down to:

The existence is assumed of a textbook, or at least a detailed syllabus, in the respective subject for the respective grade. A working team is composed of University lecturers, experienced secondary-school teachers, textbook writers and others, including CAL experts and software developers. The team is then asked to make a detailed analysis of the subject-matter, taking into account the project's general principles and major aspects of computer usage. As a result, the subject-matter should be divided into methodological teaching units. The possibility and advisability, the place and manner of using the computer in learning should be determined for each unit individually. The analysis of the subject-matter should be most exhaustive and detailed, so as to be directly used for developing the educational software, setting clearly the goals of the respective courseware. Besides developing educational software, additional hardware development projects are envisaged to broaden the capabilities of the universally used machines, as well as for simulation devices and other specialized computer-based devices and systems.

After the subject-matter has been analyzed and the tasks (designs) for the educational software formulated, an expert assessment is made of the results. If the tasks and designs for educational soft- and hardware are judged positive, the projects for their development are then effected. Dividing the process of development of educational software into two phases — designing and programming, allows software to be judged even at the designing phase. Should the designed software not fit the goals, or should it fail to meet the basic principles and orientations of computer implementation, as outlined by the National Project, no programming action is undertaken.

4.2. Organizational Structures and Mechanisms

The general manual on the introduction of computers into each subject in education should find methodological guidance from the national problem-and-methodology experts' commission on the respective subject. The overall manual on the introduction of computers into education should find methodological guidance from the national council of experts on the introduction of computers into education.

The functions of these problem-and-methodology commissions should include an evaluation of the analyses of cur-

ricula and the existing educational software. The materialization of the adopted approach amounts, in practical terms, to the writing of textbooks of a new type, an integral part of which would be the diskettes with the respective software and user manuals for both teachers and students. Good educational software, for the time-being, may be said to be scarce. Publishing houses are still not capable of distributing diskettes. Our project envisages that the development of educational software will be state-financed, and that the final products will then be distributed free-of-charge. To this end, a network of one national and other regional software libraries is being established, to provide schools with the software they need. A system of regional educational software-developing bodies is being set up, too. The teachers to take part in writing the software are selected through regional and national competitions. The best products are bought and then distributed free-of-charge throughout the schools.

5. RESULTS AND EVALUATION

The results obtained so far may also be considered in terms of the three basic components of our project. While the vocational and the general educational, cultural, aspects of computer uses in Bulgarian secondary schools may be said to have been brought to a certain stage of completion and to have obtained definite results, the computer has just begun to be used as a teaching tool. In our opinion, it will take four or five years for definite positive results to be obtained in this respect. This holds true, however, of the mass-scale introduction of computers into secondary schools throughout the country, for even now there are individual schools keeping in close contact with research institutes and educational software developing teams and conducting experiments in this area, where definite positive results have already been obtained. What has been accomplished in fitting computer classrooms in schools, and as regards teacher training, is on a par with the progress of the project as regards its contents. Our plans also envisage all secondary school teachers to have passed, by the end of 1989, a seven-day qualification course on employing computers in education.

6. CONCLUDING REMARKS

The project on introducing computers in Bulgarian secondary schools is a strategic goal of our educational system. We have every reason to believe it will be carried to a successful end, the project being state sponsored and all prerequisites for its implementation provided. The organizational structure for its implementation has been elaborated, and we regard the objectives and set tasks to be correct, essential, realistic and feasible.

REFERENCES

[1] Министерство на народната просвета, Комплексна програма за създаване на комплексни условия за обучение и работа на младежта с електронно-изчислителна техника (София, 1985, in Bulgarian).

COMPUTERS IN EDUCATION, F. Lovis and E.D. Tagg (eds.)
Elsevier Science Publishers B.V. (North-Holland)
© IFIP, 1988

COMPUTERIZED DIDACTIC SYSTEM OF THE CZECH TECHNICAL UNIVERSITY IN PRAGUE

Jan FANTA, Petr MAJER, Jaroslav JÄGER

CZECH TECHNICAL UNIVERSITY
Zikova 4, 166 35 Prague 6, Czechoslovakia

The computerized didactic system of the Czech Technical University includes, beside the usual data processing facilities, a direct connection to a closed television subsystem permitting use of graphic terminals in combination with video recordings. This expands the scope of teachers´ and students´ work by audio and video facilities, including the use of standard equipment such as projector cameras, video recorders, etc.
The computer´s terminal is fitted with a synchronizing unit for transmitting the television signal to the terminal screen as well as to the closed television circuit, thereby providing the option of combining digital and analogue signals for further processing in the classroom. The software of the classroom system takes these facilities into account and helps rid the teacher of tedious routine work.

This computerized didactic system is a complex of computer hardware and software designed for modern teaching methods supported and/or controlled by a computer. The comprehensive approach to problem solving requires that students be able to work with data processing technology and formulate problems so as to render them solvable by means of this technology. For many problems, the interactive mode of computer operation is important. It is essential that the students involved come into active contact with data-processing technology during their studies.

The design of this complex for the needs of all departments of the Czech Technical University is based on the present-day demands placed on didactic methods in terms of intensity, clarity and efficiency of the teaching process.

The computerized didactic system comprises three mutually related subsystems:
- data processing technology subsystem
- television technology subsystem
- conventional teaching aids subsystem.

The system is built around a minicomputer with a network of colour graphic terminals.

In order to interconnect effectively all the subsystems, individual terminals are fitted with PAL digital signal coders. The outputs from these coders are connected to the television subsystem of the complex, see Fig. 1.

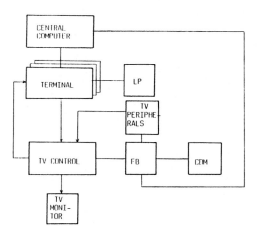

Fig. 1 Computerized didactic system

The television subsystem is based on a central television exchange which permits the selection of individual television inputs, such as the terminals, a video recorder, a text reader and other television signal sources, and to allocate them to the respective outputs. These television signals are displayed on the terminal screens which then serve as colour monitors. The colour graphic terminals are thus used for displaying alphanumerical, graphic and other types of information needed in the teaching process, and are shared by the computer and television subsystems. All input television signals can be fitted with that of an electronic pointer used by the teacher.

The computerized didactic system makes it possible for the students to interact with the control computer and utilize all of its capabilities for the solving of their assignments. This mode of work allows for personalized speed of each of the students´ operation. On his control monitor, the teacher can supervise the students´ work and flexibly interfere with it, using at the same time the classroom television subsystem. By way of combining the various didactic media, the teacher is able to affect significantly the quality of the teaching process.

For a better elucidation of certain phenomena, computer animation and television-signal digitization can be employed. In this way very complicated situations, kinetic structures, three-dimensional solutions, etc. can be explained to the students. At key points of a complex problem solution, previous procedures or information stored in the system´s data base can be hinted at, or referred to.

Complicated verbal formulations are considerably simplified with the help of the graphics; moreover, any programming language can be used and the correct answer can be indicated in a diagram, a part of the picture, text, etc. The use of colour graphics is versatile and it is on the teacher´s creative inventiveness how he employs it in the teaching process.

Lectures on specialized subjects can be brightened by demonstrating phenomena or behaviour of systems simulated on program models. This didactic means helps improve the clarity and efficiency of computer science and programming classes; the same applies to the demonstration of the user´s approach to computers, for instance, utilization of data processing services and information stored in data banks, work with expert systems and similar uses. This interactive facility helps enrich the teaching process and allows data processing technology to be demonstrated in the practical aspect of every specialized subject.

Team work appears most frequently in the terminal classroom. This includes testing the students´ knowledge, assigning individual homework and its supervision.

The principal benefit of a computer in collective teaching is that it allows a personalized approach to the students: each one of them can work at his own rate on differing formulations of a problem. The computer evaluates the work done by each student and controls its further course.

Individual work proceeds in the adjacent study with eight terminals. The operating system enables each user to work with a different program, including some special teaching programs.

The automation of a portion of the teaching process releases the teacher for creative activity, and the teacher may then devote more time to education itself. Teachers´ work is partially transferred into the sphere of preparation for classes, when they store their pedagogical and expert skills in scenarios of didactic programs and the "production" of the class.

The diagnostic capabilities of the teaching programs are wide ranging. Errors can be detected and identified, and students led to correct solutions. The computer is able to generate problems, create tests, process and evaluate answers, etc. Question banks can be stored on disk memories. The teaching programs take into account the students´ individual speeds and the history of their learning, and allow them access to information data banks. Small-sized data banks are stored directly in external memory media, while access to large-scale data banks can be ensured by hooking the control computer to the mainframe computer in which these data banks are operated and maintained.

The third subsystem is composed of conventional teaching aids; it is very flexible and allows for a wideranging utilization of data processing and didactic technologies in the process of teaching. All the controls of the computerized didactic system are located on the teacher´s workstation. The teacher controls the data processing subsystem via a terminal, and the television and didactic subsystems from his control panel.

The synchronous displaying of digital and analogue pictures on a single screen is secured by the terminal´s synchronizing unit. Beside this internal TV circuit, the teacher also has access to the external TV circuit which serves as a "blackboard" for completing lectures, if need be.

The microcomputer system contains a logic unit, a parallel communication interface, the IRPS and V 24 serial communication interfaces, a CCIR-PAL coder, a synchronizing unit and a television input for analogue CCIR-PAL, CCIR-K and SECAM television signals. In this version, it permits not only alphanumeric and graphic modes of terminals but also the displaying of analogue television signals issued by the text reader, video recorders and other sources, see Fig. 2.

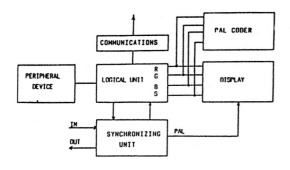

Fig. 2 Block diagram of workstation

The interconnection between the logic processor, the synchronizing unit and the PAL coder is ensured by the terminal's television control unit.

This unit makes it possible to display digital alphanumerical, graphic or colour graphic information, analogue television signals, and simultaneous analogue and digital television signals on the terminal's CRT. The terminal's television control unit is fitted with a television input and output for connecting into the television subsystem.

The normally used terminals do not permit the processing of analogue television signals or the simultaneous displaying of analogue and digital signals; nor is it usually possible to connect terminals into television circuits.

Our design is based on the following principle: the terminal's logic unit, which generates alphanumeric, graphic or colour graphic information, is completed with a synchronization unit,

which secures the synchronization of the input analogue television signal with the digital signal generated by the terminal's logic unit. The signals outputed by the logic and synchronizing units, and the input analogue television signal are transmitted to the block of analogue and digital television signal processing, one output of which is linked to the input of the display, while the other is connected to the television circuit. Thus the simultaneous displaying of the analogue input television signal is ensured together with the digital television signal generated by the terminal's logic unit on the VDU's screen, with the option of an independent visualization of each of the signals and with the possibility of connecting the output television signal to the television circuits.

The advantages of the terminal's television control unit include its capability to combine digital and analogue television signals and display them on the terminal screen, and the option of using the output television signal for subsequent processing.

The classroom television subsystem features a highly efficient feedback - an aspect in which the conventional terminal classrooms are completely lacking.

Via the classroom television circuits, various other didactic media can be introduced; for instance, video recordings, static pictures and texts.

A large-sized screen of television subsystems is installed for every three students' terminal stations, serving as the teacher's television-circuit workstation.

The television circuit makes it possible to transmit a picture from any of the students' displays to the teacher's terminal, thereby allowing him to oversee the work of each of the students. The content of terminal screens can be displayed by the classroom external TV circuit, which helps the teacher point out errors made by the students and/or show the correct solution.

With all its capabilities, the closed television circuit will greatly enrich synchronized teaching.

The same purpose is served by the conventional teaching aids installed in the terminal classroom. An overhead, a 16-mm and a slide projector are controlled from the teacher's station. The classroom is large enough to accommodate high-quality audio equipment as well.

All teaching programs are designed so
that users unfamiliar with programming
can employ them. In fact, the motivation underlying the use of the terminal
classroom is to enable teachers having
the minimum knowledge of programming
and none of the operating system, to
prepare their own teaching programs.
The same applies to students. Even without knowing the operating system, and
acquainted only with the mere basics of
programming, a student must learn how to
make use of all of the computer's capabilities for the solving of his problems
and assignments. ·

The system's software has been developed
in several basic directions:
a. testing and examination programs;
b. programs permitting personalized assignment and supervision of problems;
c. sets of standard subroutines for the
   most important sections covered in
   class;
d. consultancy and teaching programs for
   research into difficult subjects,
   using literature and computer;
e. programming by individual students.

The testing and examination programs
created for the computer generate extensive sets of questions and process them
automatically, in keeping with the teacher's intentions, into tests of varying lengths and at different levels of
challenge. They provide for individual
formulations and on-line and final control, with printout of each student's
results.

The programs developed for use during
class allow individual formulations for
each of the students on the basis of a
generally solved problem, and evaluation of their work and results.

The system helps rid the teacher of routine tasks, i.e. assignment of problems,
their differentiation for each indivi-
al, checking of results, etc. It enables
the teacher to become completely involved in specialized problems and in work
with students in the form of consultations on the difficult points they encounter. It also permits each student to
maintain his own tempo and evaluates his
results objectively. The work of each
student and the whole class is logged in
detail throughout the semester, including records of the number of incorrect
answers, the time spent on a problem,
etc. Improvement of this section of the
software is the most important task in
our future endeavours.

The standard subroutines for the solving of basic and frequently repeated
problems are used for the processing of
extensive and more complex projects, in
which the emphasis is on developing independent thinking of the students
without overburdening them by tedious
numerical calculations, which, however,
must be performed during the solution
procedures. The subroutines cover, for
instance, basic calculations involved
in operational analysis, testing of
sets, mathematical and economic statistics (basic characteristics of statistical sets), extensive sets of linear
or differential equations and other
problems.

With the help of consultation programs
for studying difficult parts of the
subject matter, the learning process
based on research of literature is controlled and supervised by computer. In
the form of questions and tests, the
computer checks the studied text has
been grasped by the student, evaluates
the level and accuracy of his answers,
informs him about it, and responds to
errors and shortcomings.

The programs developed by the students
themselves mostly concern their independent scientific and specialized projects, term assignments, diploma theses
and similar tasks. These programs,
which may also be of a more general
character, are archived for possible
future utilization.

By way of summarizing, we can say that
this specific application of up-to-date
teaching facilities has fully proved
its worth and, in spite of initial difficulties of a predominantly organizational nature, is being developed successfully; it represents a new quality
in the education of specialists in
technical fields. At the same time, it
should be noted that the "production"
of classes and software is time-inten-
sive with great demands on the teachers'
specialized skills, and that any improvement in the quality of the teaching
process is preconditioned precisely by
the teachers' greater efforts invested
into the preparatory work. These new
forms also call for novel organizational attitudes and the establishing of
work teams composed of experts in the
computer, as well as other sciences
and professions.

COMPUTERS IN EDUCATION, F. Lovis and E.D. Tagg (eds.)
Elsevier Science Publishers B.V. (North-Holland)
© IFIP, 1988

Some Psychological Aspects of Computerisation of Education

E. Ya. Karpovsky (USSR), N.N.N. Nsowah-Nuamah (Ghana)

Odessa Institute of   University of Ghana
National Economy

Abstract

The role of Computer in education is over-estimated nowadays. The concept of individualisation of learning by computer has come to stay, creating social and psychological problems for users - naivety, formalism and fanaticism. We argue strongly against maintaining a high level of computerisation of education, suggesting an approach whereby the individual learns to acquire the skill of learning by computer within a group, studying conditions and norms and developing interpersonal relations. This will increase the learning speed of the individual and raise the level of professional knowledge of learners and users.

1. Introduction

In one of the USSR youth magazines "SMENA" (No. 4, 1987), among reflections about the problem of loneliness in modern world, was a letter by one A. Sergeiv which raises the question of whether to love a computer. The author writes that he finds "... more interest in a computer than in people. In designing programs for a computer, I feel creative. I can create a companion who speaks in "my language" and is pleasant in all relations. But it is very difficult to associate oneself with people, and with a lot of them if is simply boring : trivial words, dreams".

In our opinion, this quoted letter is a serious warning about the bad side of computerisation of learning : excessive individualization and inability to associate oneself with a social collective body. In our opinion, reality turns into a situation of fantasy which a well known American Scientist and Science-fiction author, Isaac Azimov, wrote about, when a robot read a person's thought and always answered his questions so as to please him (according to Azimov's first law of robot engineering).

It is traditionally considered that the computer, as a means of learning, may be used for :
- demonstrating laws and phenomena of nature;
- modelling processes and objects of knowledge;
- training with the aim of acquiring art and skill, and ability;
- working with users' programs, processing text and mathematical expressions, data files, results of laboratory and practical works etc;
- controlling knowledge, art and skill, ability;
- processing results of larning so as to determine psychological peculiarities and individual degree of preparation of the learner;
- planning of the individual's learning strategies;
- strictly individual learning.

Individualisation of learning by using computer has, for some time, been appraised as a positive factor, helping to shorten the length of learning period and raising the quality of knowledge. In addition, in an adaptive learning system, there is a possibility for every learner to find the only rational sequence of understanding the concepts and operations under them, and this brings maximum learning effect for the given individual.

Adaptation system of learning by computer is based on the results of solving two dimensional problems of individual learning ;
- psycho-subject diagnostics on the basis of determining psychological peculiarities and the individual degree of preparation of the learner, bearing in mind specific features of understanding learning material;

-   optimization of the process of individual learning by computer on the basis of psycho-subject profiles; that is, the degree of expressionness of some -tuple of psychological peculiarities in the individual, realised by learning a given subject area.

A similar approach to individualisation of learning by computer has two distinguished features :

(1) it is postulated that the learning level of a professional group of people is formed by summing up knowledge, art and skill, and ability of separate group members;

(2) it does not take into account the appearance of a new system effect (positive or negative) from pooling the individuals into a group.

Therefore, individualisation of learning by computer, as a general rule, does not implant in the individual an art and skill of group professional activities; among other things, group decision making.

In this present paper, we suggest a combined approach to computerisation of learning, linking individual's aquisition of knowledge, art and skill, and ability with group exercises, providing the study of group conditions and norms and the development of interpersonal, emotional and information relations, bearing in mind the form and character of activities.

In analogy with Kendall's classification of the queuing theory we introduce notations of variants of building systems of learning by computer, as shown in fig. 1.

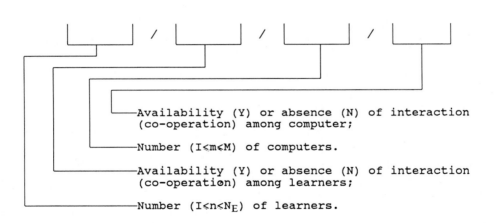

Availability (Y) or absence (N) of interaction (co-operation) among computer;

Number ($I \leqslant m \leqslant M$) of computers.

Availability (Y) or absence (N) of interaction (co-operation) among learners;

Number ($I \leqslant n \leqslant N_E$) of learners.

Fig. 1 : Notation of learning System by Computer

Then from the point of view of the socio-psychological aspect of group learning we shall be interested in the following variants:

1. Group learning with one computer, that is n/Y/1/N.

2. Groupe learning with m computers linked/not linked with a local computer network, that is n/Y/m/N; n/Y/m/Y; n/N/m/Y.

With the aim of gradually making the results under discussion more complex, we shall first consider the variant 2/Y/1/N the 3/Y/1/N and later move on to variants n/Y/m/N and n/Y/m/Y. The variant n/N/m/Y should more or less interest the specialist on artificial intellect (AI), with the view of studying then "psychology" of inter-machine interactions in local computer networks, and so it is not discussed in this paper.

2. Learning System 2/Y/1/N

In studying the psychological aspect of interpersonal interaction between two learners by using one computer, computer modification of the non-zero sum game of the type "Prisoner's Dilemma" <1> is used.

The substance of the game consists of the following. Two prisoners are waiting for a trial on one and the same case and are in different cells. The Public Prosecutor, not having enough evidence, informs each prisoner (for example, Mr. A. and Mr. B) of the conditions of the trial process, as shown in fig. 2.

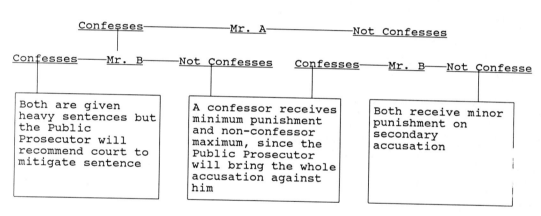

Fig. 2 : Conditions of trial process of Mr. A and Mr. B

In executing the experiments, the personal computer "Robotron-1715" was used, which in interactive mode informed the participants of the rules of the game and the payoff matrix, and then ensured operation in the mode "no contact" and "contact". In mode "no contact", each of the participants of the game had the right to make one move only and choose a strategy, independently and secret from the other participant. In mode "contact", players, with the help of C R T terminal (display), could convey to each other the necessary information. In "non-simultaneous choice" of decision the first player's move appeared on C R T terminal display for the information of the second player until the time when the latter made his choice of move. The condition of

"reverse" decision means that after the choices of move had been made and had appeared on the C R T terminal display, any one of the players could change his move without any preliminary ennounce-ment. Three set-ups were used :

y1. To collaborate with opponent, bearing the latter's interest in mind.

y2. To consider only his own interest.

y3. To strive for the improvement of his position, and at the same time that of his opponent.

From the result of the analysis of large empirical material (more than 600 groups) using the principal components method, the major components determining psychological compatibility were marked; degree of preparation of both members of the group to collaborate, readiness to collaborate for compromise, positive set-ups on the game exercise with computer and on each other, purposefulness of emotional manifestations.

In a controlled experiment, the role of the second player was performed by a personal computer. As compared to the controlled group (50 persons), it turned out that in system 2/Y/1/N both players agreed on collaboration. On the average, collaboration between them was chosen up to 92% of the players, but only 37 out of the 50 persons preferred to collaborate with computer. Set-up y1 brought an increase in the number of collaboration of both players, and for set-up y3, players turned to a strategy, corresponding to set-up y2. Under conditions of "non-simultaneous choice" in set-ups y2 and y3, it turned out that there were very few collaborated pairs for system 2/Y/1/N (up to 12%), and only 6 players chose collaboration with personal computer in a controlled group.

The possibility of contact turned to be greatest influence in set-up y2, when the number of players who chose collaboration increased to 84%, and only 26 people preferred to collaborate with computer. A large percentage of collaboration in set-up y2 was not attained even under conditions of "reversibility", when players could withdraw their proposition about collaboration if they did not meet mutuality from their pair. This psychological peculiarity of inter-personal contact in this given experiment was once again distinctly manifested under conditions of "non-simultaneous choice" of decision in set-up y2.

The use of the suggested experiment for system 2/Y/1/N permits us to observe various co-operative types of inter-personal interactions and makes it possible to move on to considering psychological compatibility in a group learning by computer with positions "CONGRUITY-COMPLEMENTARITY". In systems of group learning by computer, two types of psychological compatibility are distinguished, in which emotio-dynamic indicators of compatibility

combine with stability of autocratic structure (leader-subordinate) or with flexibility of structure of inter-personal control, suggesting free exchange of ideas among members of the group (complementary type).

The two distinguished types of psychological compatibility were used as a basis for forming pairs to learn the algorithmic language "BASIC", using computer. One group of the pairs was made up of a "leader" - a good student and a "subordinate" - a weak student. The second group of pairs as formed from approximately equal students (complementary type structure).

For estimating knowledge the following formulae were used :

$$e = \sum_{i=1}^{n} w_i \, x_i \qquad (1)$$

$$E = e \, / \, n \qquad (2)$$

$$R = \begin{cases} 2, \text{ if } A \le C_2 \\ 3, \text{ if } C_2 < A \le C_3 \\ 4, \text{ if } C_3 < A \le C_4 \\ 5, \text{ if } C_4 < A \end{cases} \qquad (3)$$

In eq. (1) - (3), e is the number of points obtained by the learner for answering n questions; x_i is the marks (in points) obtained for answering i-th question; n - the number of controlled questions; $W = \{w_i\}$ - the vector of weighted coefficients of question; w_i W - weighted coefficient of i-th question; E - mean point; $C = \{C_1, C_2, C_3, C_4\}$ - the vector of boundary values; $A = (E_1, E_2, d, r, t,)$ - mean point for weighting marks, which depends on the mean point of the first learner (E_1), the mean point of the second learner (E_2), the number of mutual consultation in studying (d), the number of mutual consultation in controlling knowledge (r), the length of learning (t).

The results of comparing estimates of knowledge showed statistically reliable (1- =0.95) difference of average value R for groups "leader-subordinate" (R=3.92) and groups with complementary type structure (R = 4.46). With a degree of freedom equal to 48 and standard error $S_d=0.23$, value of t statistic t=2.35, we can draw a conclusion that the account of psychological compatibility raises effectiveness of learning by computer in a group, and what is more, for groups of two learners, the more effective turned out to be the complementary type structure. We note that in traditional learning without the use of computers preference is normally given to the study group with a leader. It seems in the case 2/Y/1/N, the role of a leader is carried out by computer used in learning. We shall consider whether the correctness of the given conclusion holds with three learners in a group, when it is possible to reduce the role of computer in learning.

3. Learning system 3/Y/1/N

We shall consider the experimental research results of psychological peculiarities of interpersonal inter-action of learning group members :

(1) who have the same or different levels of knowledge in a given subject of a field.

(2) who are studying different places in a structure of formal relations in a group;

(3) who are in a defined interpersonal relation;

(4) who are performing the role of "leader" in a group or serial member of the group.

For the formation of groups, the results of the analysis of system 2/Y/1/N were used. A problem involving a test on concentration and distribution of attention was placed before participants in the experiment. Each of the three members of the group should have recognized a given geometric figure in the picture shown on the C R T terminal assigned to a given participant of the experiment. The time and accuracy of each observer's work were fixed.

In the second stage of the experiment, the group was informed that the total result of their abswers did not tally with a given value, exceeding a feasible level of error. This information was, as a matter of fact, false. Observers, without the knowledge of each other, or, observing the conditions of type y1, y2 and y3, expressed their opinions about the fault of each of the participants or computer in its mutual mistakes. As a result of processing observer's opinions with the help of computer the "culprit" was determined, and it was suggested to him to repeat the performance of his task.

If the "culprit" was declared by computer, then on the C R T terminal display, a new picture appeared and the experiment was fully repeated.

Depending on the results and distribution of roles and opinions, the whole procedure may be repeated; among other things, each observer (as if) checks the work of his colleague in the group. A consideration was taken of the possibility of controlling experiment, observing the ethical norm on the basis of changes about each other, aimed at diagnosing participants' interpersonal relations among those chosen to carry out concrete tasks in the experiment. As a result of experimental researches, carried out with 62 groups of 3 persons, primary data were obtained. After processing, with the help of the principal component method, such basic components as the following were selected : mutual confidence (F_1 ; 32% of general variation), confidence in computer (F_2 ; 27% of general variation), mutual appraisal (F_3; 18% of general variation), communicative-ness (F_4; 11% of general variation), mutual understanding (F_5; 7.9% of general variation).

Substantial increase of complexity of interpersonal interactions model in a group of 3 persons (as compared to system 2/Y/1/N) and extrapolation of a rise in psychological complexity, as the number of persons in a group increase, brought about the necessity of posing and solving a process control problem of group learning by computer.

4. Control of group learning by computer

To control group learning by computer (cases n/Y/m/N and n/Y/m/Y) we suggest using a model which determines conditional quantity of new study information, necessary for presenting a given group V in an immediate i-th learning step;

$$I = \frac{1}{(V-1)n} \sum_{i=1}^{V-1} \frac{\overline{R}_i^{(0)}}{t_i^{(0)}} \sum_{j=1}^{n} \frac{t_{ij}}{r_{ij}} + \sum_{j=1}^{n} \frac{\tau_{ij}}{R_{ij}}$$

(4)

In eq. (4) $R_i^{(0)}$ is the normative value of mean group marks for i-th learning step (i-th studying task), $t_i^{(0)}$ - the normative time of understanding i-th studying task; n - the current quantity of group members who have completed studying i-th studying task; t_{ij} - the time spent by a j-th group member on individual studying of i-th studying task; r_{ij} - the marks for j-th group member on i-th task carried out individually ; τ_{ij} -the time spent by j-th group member ; R_{ij} - the marks obtained by a group member for carrying out i-th group task.

Since studying concepts includes the composition of each studying task, together with semantic completion, then the general quantity of studying concepts in i-th studying task could be determined with the help of the expression

$$\Psi =] \Psi^{(0)}/I [$$

(5)

In eq. (5)].[is the operation of calculating the integer part of numbers; $\Psi^{(0)}$ - the quantity of studying concepts which may be assimilated by one (statistically) average learner in individual learning in one studying task.

From the experimental research results of the psychology of interpersonal interactions in system 3/Y/1/N, we can conclude that the calculated quantity Ψ from eq. (5) is only necessary for including i-th studying task in a group and not ensuring condition of sufficiency. Satisfying condition of sufficiency, linked with psychological aspect of interpersonal contact in a group, helps us inthe process control of group learning by computer, to include in i-th studying task the number of concepts more than Ψ. Then the quantity of studying concepts necessary and sufficient for presenting a concrete group of a learner in i-th task in account of interpersonal interaction may be defined as

$$\Psi^* = \frac{1}{n} \sum_{j=1}^{n} \Psi k \exp(\frac{\overline{R}}{R_{ig}})$$

(6)

In eq. (6) 0<K<1 is the coefficient, reflecting the structure of studying group (K=1 in complementary type of structure and K=0 in autocratic type of structure); R - the mean total estimate of knowledge of group members in the previous study task; R_{jg} - the estimate of initial level of knowledge of j-th group member in a given subject area.

For obtaining the value R_{jg}, the Bayesian procedure of testing is used <2>.

5. Conclusion

To achieve raising the degree of preparation of learners towards joint activities in a group process of decision making, in a series of cases, it is useful to apply group learning by computer.

An account of psychological aspects of interpersonal interaction in groups permits us, in a corresponding building of group structure, to increase learning speed and to raise the level of professional knowledge, as compared to individual learning by computer.

Finally, we shall note that modelling psychological aspects of group learning by computer is useful in building automated multicomputerised learning system. We believe that with all the insufficient theoretical examination of the problem under discussion in this paper, the obtained results are sufficiently useful now for practical application and will stimulate further researches in this area.

<1> Thomas B. Sheridan and William R. Ferrell, Man-machine System: Information, Control and Decision Models of Human Performance, the MIT Press, Cambridge, Massachussetts and London, 1978, pp. 376-385.

<2> E. Ya. Karpovsky, N,N,N, Nsowah-Nuamah, Bayesian Decision Making About Software Reliability, Computer and Information Sciences, No. 3, Vol. 35.

6. Educational Aims, Policies and Curriculum

COMPUTERS IN EDUCATION, F. Lovis and E.D. Tagg (eds.)
Elsevier Science Publishers B.V. (North-Holland)
IFIP, 1988

NEW INFORMATION TECHNOLOGY -

A SURVEY OF THE SITUATION IN THE FEDERAL REPUBLIC OF GERMANY

Dr. Ulrich Bosler
IPN - Institute for Science Education
Olshausenstr. 62
D - 2330 Kiel 1

This article provides an up-to-date survey of various aspects of New
Information Technology (NIT) in general education and may be seen as a
continuation of the World Conference publication of 1985 (cf. [1]).
Major changes are taking place in lower secondary education. Much is being
done to develop syllabi and to produce teaching units for computer literacy
valid for all pupils at the age of 13. But there is still a disparity
between recommendations and realization in appropriate teaching units.
The reasons for the small amount of NIT in elementary education (age 6 to
10) are indicated, as well as those for the slow but continuous introduction
of courseware in various subjects.

FEDERALLY STRUCTURED SCHOOL SYSTEM

The Federal Republic including West Berlin has
a total population of approximately 62
million. The "Land" (state) of North Rhine-
Westphalia, with 17 million, has the highest
number of inhabitants, while Bremen, with
750 000, has the lowest.

The authority for the school system lies with
the 10 "Länder" and West Berlin. Authoritative
control includes regulations regarding the
curriculum, time schedules, professional
requirements and recruitment of teachers,
school buildings and equipment. The system
helps to ensure that irregularities in
facilities and teaching personnel are avoided
to a large extent.

The educational system in the FRG is primarily
chararacterized by its 4-year elementary
school ("Grundschule", age 6 to 10), followed
by the tripartite system of secondary education, with "Hauptschule" (up to age 15),
"Realschule" (up to age 16) and "Gymnasium"
(up to age 19). In upper secondary education
at the Gymnasium (age 16 to 19), a system of
courses providing for various optional subjects has been introduced.
A minority of Länder, most private schools and
the several dozen comprehensive schools spread
throughout the FRG, either postpone the decision as to which type of school a pupil should
attend, or use a setting system.

Judging from various reports, I should estimate that approximately 60 % of general
schools - especially in upper secondary education and excluding the Hauptschule and the
primary sector - are well equipped with microcomputers of different makes, or have access
to a large computer.

INFORMATICS IN OPTIONAL COURSES

Projects for the introduction of informatics
in the Federal Republic of Germany were first
focused on pupils aged 16 to 19, where informatics developed into an independent subject.
The application-oriented content of this
subject, together with the projects currently
in progress, bear witness to a high level of
informatics (for more details see [1]).
Due to this concentration of work in the
highest grades only, however, computer literacy as a general school discipline developed
more slowly than in other countries.
Nevertheless, informatics content in various
forms has in recent years become a feature of
work for pupils aged 13 to 16, although usually still only for a proportion.

NEW INFORMATION TECHNOLOGY FOR ALL PUPILS

From 1983 onwards, educationalists increasingly discussed the issue of microcomputers
and school. As in many other countries, a

variety of views have been expressed on this subject, which need not to be repeated here (cf. [2]).

A new aspect which has entered the discussion is the demand for computer literacy for all pupils at lower secondary level. Between autumn 1984 and spring 1985, recommendations were published: the most important was made by the joint (federal/"Länder") commission for education planning and research promotion. This framework for new information technology for all pupils stressed the applications and effects of data processing (cf. [3]). The German Society for Informatics published a proposal which emphasized problem solving with algorithmic methods (cf. [4]).

The major recommendations were for the development of a computer literacy syllabus, valid for all pupils at lower secondary level, to be introduced into schools as soon as possible.

IPN CURRICULUM COMPUTER LITERACY

The Institute for Science Education (IPN), which operates at national level, took the initiative to put this recommendation into practice. It drew particularly on work carried out in Holland and by the Association for Teacher Education in Europe (ATEE) (cf. [5]). The special tool of the curriculum conference was then used to develop proposals for computer literacy for all pupils at the age of 13.

The major decisions were as follows:
The curriculum for all 13-year-old pupils should encompass approximately 60 periods. It should be realized as an integral concept and not be treated as an independent subject spread over several years.
Perhaps the most important idea in the IPN curriculum was to aim at a clear delineation of the tasks of basic work and of further instruction. During basic education, the pupil should play the role of a "conscious user", changing to the role of a programming expert during further instruction.
The principle of the "conscious user" should be implemented as consistently as possible. Instruction projects were proposed, based on the "real-life" experience of 13-year-old pupils.
The "conscious user" principle also involves the use of "protecting" software tools, such as suitable database systems (for example, a "protecting" version of dBASE) used for the implementation of algorithms rather than programming languages like BASIC or PASCAL.

For informatics as a subject option and at upper secondary level, suitable programming languages are to be used. Software tools can, however, replace previously used programming languages for the application of microcomputers in a number of subjects.

The following areas are to be dealt with as an integrated whole:

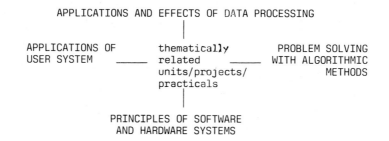

APPLICATIONS AND EFFECTS OF DATA PROCESSING

APPLICATIONS OF USER SYSTEM ———— thematically related units/projects/practicals ———— PROBLEM SOLVING WITH ALGORITHMIC METHODS

PRINCIPLES OF SOFTWARE AND HARDWARE SYSTEMS

The core of the 60-period curriculum is thus to be projectoriented. The pupils begin, for example, by dealing with their own leisure activities. They compile relevant lists and try to classify the various items. They produce a suitable program and feed in the data. During this process, the pupils deal with the principles of the construction of software and hardware systems. As the work progresses, the pupils see the stored and evaluated data about themselves. This can lead to treatment of issues such as data protection, as well as the application and outcomes of data processing.

IMPLEMENTATION IN PILOT EXPERIMENTS

Several "Länder", e.g. Bavaria, Berlin (West), Hesse, Rhineland Palatinate and Schleswig-Holstein have drafted teaching material in large pilot experiments.
In Lower Saxony, an integrative concept in the existing subjects and in different grades is being developed. This "integrative approach" proceeds from the assumption that all subjects can be involved (cf. [6]). 16 mainly subject-related commissions were set up. The work can be compared to the composition of a mosaic, each piece contributing to the whole.
My impression is that such an approach would at present be extremely difficult to implement in the FRG, but that this pilot experiment could yield a range of ideas for the use of computers and NIT in various subjects.

A strategy which promises to be realistic for the FRG is being tested in North Rhine-Westphalia, the "Land" which houses about 1/3 of the West German population. Teachers of Mathematics, Physics or Technology, and of German as a first language, teach the 60-period curriculum mainly to 13 year-old pupils. The approach is to a great extent project-oriented.
Teaching materials and a concept for In-Service Teacher Training (INSET) are being developed in a 4-year pilot experiment ("Modellversuch") scheduled to finish in 1989 (cf. [7]).
One of the central considerations is how to reflect the changes NIT has brought to our work and leisure activities in the three learning areas (1) "robotics", (2) "word processing and databases" and (3) "simulation". Several teaching proposals were developed for each learning area. The assumption is that basic instruction will consist of one unit chosen from each of the three categories.
About 10 teaching units were developed e.g. "controlling robots", "data processing using the example of pupils own leisure activities", "(school) newsletters" and "a lake goes out of balance".

This pilot experiment is now at the stage of being gradually introduced to all pupils. Hardware was provided: about 80% of the schools in the pilot experiment were supplied with MS-DOS-computers. Software tools were improved, e.g. easyBase was developed, the dBASE-software tool with an additional shell for pupils.

TEACHING NIT IN ELEMENTARY EDUCATION

In most Länder in the FRG, the elementary school, attended by every child, comprises only four years - in contrast to many other countries (e.g. folkeskole in Denmark). The "Länder" spend quite a lot of money establishing computer literacy in about grade 8 and want first to stabilize that area.
The situation has not changed since the Norfolk conference in 1985: The educationalists still have great reservations about the extensive introduction of "informatics" in these first four years.

As reported in Norfolk 1985, the reasons, in my opinion, are as follows:

- The FRG has a well established curriculum of good quality, highly interactive in its social, physical and emotive dimensions (cf. also [8] and further literature recommended there);

- It is based on the assumption that direct experience with people, nature and technology provides the fundamentals of child development, including cognition;

- The historical experience with the "book school" fosters the apprehension that informatics at too early an age may reduce direct experience, leading to "verbalism" void of under-standing;

- International research has barely touched on the question of personality change and child development through extensive computer use. Projects such as PAPERT´s have concentrated on cognition within highly favourable environments uncommon in the normal school setting.

COMPUTER ASSISTED LEARNING

This area has changed greatly in the last two years. In the FRG, Computer Assisted Learning (CAL) is still used less than, for example, in the United Kingdom. Between 1971 and 1975, a large amount of financial support was given to the promotion of CAL (cf. [9]), with remarkable research results. However, these remained simply the products of research groups and were not disseminated further. One of the reasons for this is that expectations with regard to CAL had been much too high, with the result that supporters were greatly disappointed when the expected success failed to come. CAL using large computers was also too expensive and the dissemination into the schools was missing.

The disappointment at this lack of success lead to a careful production of high quality courseware. A first step was the documentation and assessment of courseware (cf. [10] and [11]). Some Länder (e.g. Bavaria, Berlin (West), Lower Saxony and North Rhine-Westphalia) and institutes (e.g. IPN in Kiel and DIFF in Tübingen) offer an information service.

All the Länder and all the institutes dealing with courseware established a common computer-grid to document and evaluate courseware. This pool is filled on a voluntary basis (cf.[12]). Some publishers like Klett, Westermann and COMET are producing courseware, sometimes adaptions of foreign courseware.

I anticipate that in about 5 years computer literacy will have been introduced to quite a lot of pupils. This will probably lead to a different attitude on the part of teachers. I assume that a lot of them will then use good courseware in their subject, beyond computer literacy courses as such.

FURTHER INFORMATION

The situation reports in Peschke et al. [13] and Bosler [14] provide a detailed survey of the current level of informatics and computer literacy in the various "Länder".

A comprehensive bibliography and references to various institutions are contained in an introductory leaflet for new teachers and parents ([15]), which also provides hints on textbooks.

The specialist publication "LOG IN - Informatik in Schule und Ausbildung" provides a regular view of the situation in the FRG.

REFERENCES

[1] Bosler, U.: Teaching Informatics at Various Levels in General Education, in Duncan, K. and Harris, D. (eds.): Proceedings of the 4th World Conference on computers in education (North Holland, Amsterdam, 1985) pp. 959-966.

[2] Bosler, U., Hampe, W., Wanke, I., van Weert, T.: Grundbildung Informatik (J.B.Metzler, Stuttgart, 1985).

[3] Bund-Länder-Kommission für Bildungsplanung und Forschungsförderung (Hrsg.): Rahmenkonzept für die informationstechnische Bildung in Schule und Ausbildung (B-L-K, Bonn, 1984), Polyskript.

[4] Gesellschaft für Informatik (Hrsg.): Entwurf einer Rahmenempfehlung für die Informatik im Unterricht der Sekundarstufe I, in: Arlt, Haefner (Hrsg.): Informatik als Herausforderung an Schule und Ausbildung. GI-Fachtagung Berlin, 8.-10. Oktober 1984 (Springer, Berlin, 1984).

[5] van Weert, T. J. (ed.): A model syllabus on literacy in information technology for all teachers (ATEE, B-1050 Brussels, 51, rue de la Concorde). Deutsche Fassung in LOG IN 4 1984) issue 4.

[6] Niedersächsisches Kultusministerium (Hrsg.): Neue Technologien und Schule, in: Schulverwaltungsblatt 8/85, pp. 227-229.

[7] Landesinstitut für Schule und Weiterbildung (Hrsg.): Informations- und kommunikationstechnische Grundbildung. Übersicht und Entwürfe der Unterrichtseinheiten (Soest, 1986) Polyskript. Available: LSW, Paradieser Weg 64, D-4770 Soest.

[8] Frey, K., Lauterbach, R.: Primary Science Education in the Federal Republic of Germany. Italien-USA-Seminar on Primary Science Education (IPN, Kiel, 1983) Polyskript.

[9] Bundesminister für Bildung und Wissenschaft (Hrsg): Zweites Datenverarbeitungsprogramm der Bundesregierung (BMBW, Bonn, 1971).

[10] Lauterbach, R.: Bewertung pädagogischer Software, LOG IN 6 (1986) issue 5/6.

[11] Biehler, R., Rach, W., Winkelmann, B.: Dokumentation und Bewertung von Software für den Mathematikunterricht (available by Landesinstitut für Schule und Weiterbildung, D-4770 Soest, 1987).

[12] LOG IN issue 5/6 of 1986 with the topic "courseware".

[13] Peschke, R., Hullen, G., Diemer, W. (Hrsg.): Anforderungen an neue Lerninhalte. Band 1: Ergebnisse der Fachtagung "Mikroelektronik und Schule III"; Band 2: Sachstandsbericht zum Informatikunterricht in der Bundesrepublik Deutschland, Schule und Datenverarbeitung in Hessen (HIBS, Bodenstedtstr. 7, D-6200 Wiesbaden, issue 20).

[14] Bosler, U.: Informationstechnische Grundbildung - Übersicht über die Arbeiten in den Bundesländern, LOG IN 6 (1986) issue 5/6.

[15] Bosler, U., Kapune, Th. (Hrsg.): Computer in unsere Schule? (Beltz, Weinheim, 1985).

COMPUTERS IN EDUCATION, F. Lovis and E.D. Tagg (eds.)
Elsevier Science Publishers B.V. (North-Holland)
© IFIP, 1988

COMPUTER BASED LEARNING IN AUSTRALIAN SCHOOLS

Neil Hall

School of Policy and Technology Studies in Education
The University of Wollongong
PO Box 1144
Wollongong   NSW   2500,   Australia

This paper describes and analyses computer based learning in Australian schools.

The paper begins with a brief description of computer applications in Australian schools over the past twenty or so years. The paper then turns to a consideration of what is presently happening in Australian schools in terms of the educational applications of computers. Reference is made to computer education conferences held in recent years, and to the first large scale data gathering research activities in Australia to find out exactly how teachers are using computers in their classroooms.

The author argues that computers are not being used to their fullest educational potential, and that there may be some lack of foresight in the use of computers in schools. Finally, the author seeks to bring to the attention of educational policy makers the need to consider the effective educational use of computers more seriously.

1. INTRODUCTION

Australian education is characterised by centralised and bureacratic administration and management. Thus a common mode of change in Australian schools is to have an innovation thrust from above [1-5]. A notable exception to this situation, and one may argue a unique exception, has been the introduction of computers into Australian schools. The growth of computers in Australian schools was very much a grass-roots development. At first, teachers interested in computers introduced them into schools. This was followed closely by parental and employer pressure to make students computer literate, supported strongly by commercial interests who saw a new and large market opening before them.

2. COMPUTERS IN AUSTRALIAN SCHOOLS UP TO 1980

The first computer uses in Australian schools were through a batch card system. This development began in the late 1960s and grew in popularity during the 1970s. The early 1970s saw the introduction of programmable calculators into some mathematics classrooms, providing a resource for programming and for the development of mathematical concepts. At this time too on-line terminals began to appear in small numbers in some schools, generally so as to allow senior school students to learn programming.

From 1977 small numbers of microcomputers appeared in schools. Of course, there was the major difficulty of a lack of educational software.

This resulted in programming being taught, since there was little alternative if the computer was to be used by students, and besides, often this was the main reason the teacher wanted to purchase the computer in the first place. Another result was that some teachers, who saw that the computer had greater potential as a teaching aid than as a machine to be programmed, wrote their own programs - and so a large quantity of public domain software made its appearance.

The picture of computers in Australian schools at the end of the 1970s was one of some states making a commitment to computers in schools, but the majority of states ignoring the issue. There were few computers in schools, and the great majority of school students were unlikely to have any access at all to computers. Where there were computers in schools, they were mainly used for programming activities. There was almost no teacher professional development available in this area, and professionally orientated computer education groups were rare.

3.   COMPUTERS IN AUSTRALIAN SCHOOLS IN THE EARLY 1980s

In the first years of the 1980s state departments of education began to fund teacher development activities in the area of computer applications in schools. These courses were heavily reliant on those teachers who had been using computers in schools, and were exemplified by learning through sharing.

The early 1980s emphasis was on more and more teachers wanting to learn about computers. Computer education groups were formed in a number of states, providing a focus for teacher professional development, organising annual conferences and lobbying government bodies. At this time there was a general feeling that one had to learn a good deal about the technology before it was possible to consider its educational potential. Conference Proceedings of the computer education conferences of the early 1980s reflect this view [6,7]. It needs to be stressed though that the percentage of teachers showing this kind of interest was extremely small in comparison to the total number of teachers in any particular state, and that in the classroom most teachers were undecided as

to how to use computers except for programming. Papers delivered at the 1983 Australian Computer Education Conference [8] indicated the movement away from the technology for its own sake, to beginning investigations about the computer as a teaching aid, as a mode of delivery: a movement from learning about the computer, to learning with and through the computer. State and National conferences in 1984 and 1985 provided many papers on the educational applications of Logo, word processing and the use of data bases [9-12]. The movement of computers across the curriculum, away from programming, and away from drill and practice activities was well under way. The movement was not universal across all schools, but was particularly evident with those teachers who had been using computers for a year or more, and with teachers beginning to use computers who saw the potential to connect process writing or problem solving with computer based activities.

The various pressure groups lobbying for computers to be introduced to schools had a number of successes during the period 1982-6. Parents wanted their children to know about computers to increase their likelihood of gaining employment after leaving school; employer groups wanted their new recruits to be computer literate; and computer sales groups wanted to expand their potential market. A downturn in the economy, an increasing rate of unemployment and a need for a better educated workforce were themes common in the press at the time - computers in schools were seen as part of the solution to these ills. The publicity given to a number of pressure groups created the political will to act. State governments wrote what was for the majority of them, their first policy statement on computer applications in schools, and the federal government funded a three year computer education project from 1984-86.

And so we arrive at the mid-80s. The quality of educational software now available commercially means that teachers are able to use the limited computer resources in their schools in a wide range of educationally valuable learning activities. Papers presented at the 1986 and 1987 Australian Computer Education conferences [13,14] show that such conferences now almost never consider the technology for its own sake, and that we have moved beyond the kind of unsystematic observation so often presented in papers in the past. There is now the beginnings of a broad educational research base on the use, role and potential of the educational applications of computers in Australian schools.

The first systematic study of how computers were actually being used by teachers in Australian classrooms was carried out in 1985 by Fitzgerald et al. [15]. This research group sought to provide information on the use of computers in Australian classrooms which could assist in the development of policy.

Included in the group's findings were the following points:

- 55% of elementary schools had computers (average 3);
- 98% of high schools had computers (average 14);
- two to three teachers per school acted as computer resource persons;
- 69% of computer resource persons had no qualification or training in computers or in computer applications in education;
- more than 50% of secondary schools reported using their computers for programming, word processing, computer awareness activities, data bases, simulation and gaming, maths/science, drill and practice and in specialised Year 11 & 12 courses;
- more than 50% of primary schools reported using their computers for drill and practice, word processing and simulation and gaming;
- almost 50 % of primary schools reported using their computersfor Logo, maths/science and computer awareness.

4. CONTEMPORARY APPLICATIONS

A more recent report for the Australian Commonwealth Schools Commission provided a very detailed account of the use of computers in Australian rural schools [16]. This report provided information about how school computers were financed, how teachers developed and expected to continue to develop skills for using computers in their classrooms, what software is used in schools and the extent to which schools react to local

political and economic considerations. The report supported a number of findings in the earlier Fitzgerald report, provided more detailed data in some instances, and considered a range of issues important to policy makers that were not considered by the earlier researchers.

This report [16] found that with the exception of word processing, there was no computer application used by the majority of primary schools on a daily basis. More than half of the primary schools engaging in drill and practice, computer awareness, and computer applications in maths and science did so at least weekly. All other possible applications explored in the survey are used occasionally, if at all, in the primary schools in the sample. That is, most rural primary schools rarely or never use computers for data base activities, in simulations, in problem solving, in communication with other schools or remote data bases, or in other creative educational applications of computers.

The researchers found the pattern for secondary schools somewhat different. Word processing is a daily feature of secondary schools' activities for more than half of the schools surveyed, together with computer awareness and school administration. Activities engaged in on a weekly basis included spreadsheets, using existing data bases and computer programming. It appears to be unusual for rural secondary schools to use computers for electronic communication or for technical, humanities and social science subjects.

5. LACK OF FORESIGHT IN EDUCATIONAL COMPUTER APPLICATIONS

Is it the case then that schools are not making the most use of their computer facilities? On the one hand this may be true of some schools, but one has to acknowledge that the amount of computer equipment per school is quite small. It would be unrealistic to expect any one school to pursue a wide range of computer activities on a frequent basis if there is little computer equipment available. Further, schools may well involve students in a range of activities over a longer period, but within a short time span, say a day or a week, the number of activities may be few. All the same, there is some evidence to suggest that computers are not being used in schools in as educationally beneficial a manner as would seem possible.

In at least some schools it is certain that computers are used for mundane purposes, for purposes that may be educationally questionable, and certainly in activities that are a long way from making use of the computers' full range of capabilities.

One would reasonably anticipate that there are many factors operating here, and indeed there is no data available about these specific aspects of computer applications. All the same, given our general knowledge of teachers and computers in schools, it is extremely likely that many teachers are happy with their present teaching methodologies and classroom management techniques. It must be stressed that in many classrooms with access to only one or two computers, teachers appear to make excellent use of this aid, providing challenging activities for their students. There's no reason why one computer cannot be used with a whole class of students, either by rotating students through small group activities or by using the computer as an electronic blackboard. Teachers suggesting that such innovation is not possible may find themselves embarrassed by their colleagues in other schools already pursuing these kinds of activities quite effectively.

And so the saving grace of what may be a disappointing picture is in the quality of much of the work being carried out with computers and computer related technologies, particularly in the quality of good classroom practice reported in many recent conference papers and other publications. There are many of these in the literature, one need only glance through recent journals and conference proceedings. While such excellence is possible it is not the typical picture of present classroom practice in the area of computer applications. There is cause for concern here. And there is the greater concern of what this picture will become in the future. There is little in the present picture suggesting that imminent change is likely. So we are left with the vexed question of how 'average' teachers will react to the technological changes that will undoubtedly continue to come about in the future.

6.   IMPLICATIONS FOR POLICY MAKERS AND DECISION TAKERS

Today Australia is confronted by a balance of payments problem, with a significantly large foreign debt, and facing a situation where the servicing of that foreign debt poses a major economic development stumbling block. Politicians are once again seeing the education system at fault. As a consequence of the economic situation and politicians' reactions to it, the current trends in Australian education may be viewed as ones involving financial constraint (do more with less), pragmatism (follow government initiatives) and short term planning (limited to the next budget).

Introducing efficient widespread use of computers and computer based technologies into schools will not solve these economic problems, nor will any single or series of changes to the schools system. But changes involving a significant introduction of computer technology into schools and restructuring of components of the school curriculum and organisation are likely to be necessary prerequisites to the solutions.

Policy makers and decisions takers in Australia have for too long put off the day of making 'hard' decisions, those that are electorally unpopular. For too long Australia has depended on agricultural and mineral resources for its wealth, with the result that the balance of trade has been in decline for decades. Part of the solution to this reality lies in a better educated populace. A better educated workforce as a whole, particularly one that is more technologically skilled and adaptable, will certainly be strongly advantageous to the country's future, and the place to begin this technological awareness is in the early years of schooling.

Future generations of Australians will not thank today's policy makers for continuing with their procrastination. A valuable starting point for the long term restructuring of the economy is in schools. And since technology will inevitably play a major role in future developments world wide, the issue of technology in schools needs to be faced. Our children need to learn about technologies, and to use computers and computer based technologies in the learning process. This paper has suggested that excellence already exists in the use of computers in schools, but it has also suggested that presently this is the exception rather than the rule. Policy makers need to adopt as a goal the widespread and appropriate use of computer technology in schools. Australia will benefit greatly from such a policy, its implementation ought not to be delayed.

REFERENCES

1   L.E. Foster, Australian Education: a Sociological Perspective, Sydney, Prentice-Hall, 1981.

2   A.G. Maclaine, Australian Education: Progress, Problems and Prospects, Sydney, Novak, nd (late 1970's).

3   C.J. Marsh, Curriculum: an Analytic Approach, Sydney, Novak, 1986.

4   C.J. Marsh and K. Stafford, Curriculum: Australian Practices and Issues, Sydney, McGraw-Hill, 1984.

5   W.G. Walker, The governance of education in Australia: centralisation and politics', The Journal of Educational Administration, VI(1), 1970, p17-40.

6   CEGV (Computer Education Group of Victoria), Proceedings of the Fourth Annual Conference, Melbourne, CEGV, 1982.

7   I. Webster, (ed.), Computers in Education: Working Conference, NSWCEG Notes 2, Sydney, NSW CEG, 1982.

8   A.D. Salvas, (ed.), Could You Use a Computer, Proceedings of the 1983 Australian Computer Education Conference, Melbourne, CEGV, 1983.

9   J. Hughes, (ed.), Computers and Education: Dreams and Realities, Proceedings of the Second Australian Computer Education Conference, Sydney, CEG NSW, 1984.

10   A.D. Salvas, (ed.), Computing and Education - 1984 and Beyond, Proceedings of the Sixth Annual Conference of the Computer Education Group of Victoria, Melbourne, CEGV, 1984.

11   A.D. Salvas, (ed.), Communication and Change, Proceedings of the Seventh Annual Conference of the Computer Education Group of Victoria. Melbourne, CEGV, 1985.

12   B. Rasmussen, (ed.), The Information Edge: the Future for Educational Computing, Proceedings of the Third Australian Computer Education Conference, Brisbane, CEGQ, 1985.

13   A.D. Salvas, and C. Dowling (ed.s), Computers in Education: on the Crest of a Wave?, Proceedings of the 1986 Australian Computer Education Conference, Melbourne, CEGV, 1986.

14   J. Hancock, (ed.), Tomorrow's Technology Today, Proceedings of the Fifth Australian Computers in Education Conference, Adelaide, CEG SA, 1987.

15   D. Fitzgerald, J. Hattie and P. Hughes, Computer Applications in Australian Schools, Canberra, AGPS, 1986.

16   C. Fasano, N. Hall and J. Cook, Schooling in Rural Australia: Information Technology and the Provision of Educational Services in Rural Areas, Interim Report to the Australian Commonwealth Schools Commission, 1987.

COMPUTERS IN EDUCATION, F. Lovis and E.D. Tagg (eds.)
Elsevier Science Publishers B.V. (North-Holland)
© IFIP, 1988

CURRICULAR CHANGES AS A CONSEQUENCE OF COMPUTER USE.

Tjeerd Plomp, Anke H.M. Steerneman, Willem J. Pelgrum

University of Twente, Department of Education
Enschede, The Netherlands

Many claims are formulated about what might be accomplished in the actual teaching practice when computers are used in a proper and intensive way. From survey studies we may expect a limited degree of integration of computers in the curriculum. It is therefore worthwhile to analyze what changes are taking place in the curricula of existing school subjects as a consequence of the integration of the computer. In this study three schools in the sector of lower general secondary education are analyzed in this aspect. The results are showing that the schools who can be seen as fore-runners have hardly passed the stage of grassroot developments.

1. INTRODUCTION.

Nowadays, computers are widespread in schools in West-ern-Europe and Northern America. Becker [1], e.g., reports that computers are used for instruction in more than 90% of US-high schools. In the Netherlands in 1986, 69.3% of the schools in lower secondary education were using computers for instruction [2], while a national scheme will result in 100% of the schools doing so by the end of 1988 [3]. Similar developments are taking place in other countries.

Next to the 'old' problems related to the introduction of computers in education, i.e. teacher (inservice) training, educational software development and hardware provision, these developments are resulting in a growing attention to the curricular and implementation aspects of the introduction of computers in education [4].

With respect to the curricular aspects, many claims are formulated about what might be accomplished in the actual teaching practice, when computers are used in a proper and intensive way. Some of these claims are:
-educational goals and objectives may change in the direction of more productive skills (as opposite to reproductive skills) like problem solving, information handling, inquiry skills, etc. ([5], [6], [7]);
-the content of the curriculum may change, due to the special features of computers, with a consequence that students will have the opportunity to work on more real-life problems ([8], [9]);
-the teaching strategies (and as a consequence the role of teachers) may change,
-students will work more in small groups, or individually at the computer ([1], [10]), in different locations and for different periods of time;
-the assessment of students'achievement may change [11].
With respect to the implementation aspects, we suspect that an important part of the disappointments when introducing computers in schools [12] is due to insufficiently taking into account factors which play a crucial role in educational changes (see e.g. [13], [14]). There are hardly any reported empirical data about whether and how schools and teachers are integrating computers in their daily practice and what factors are determining successes and failures.

Surveys like those of Becker ([1], [10]) and the Dutch Inspectorate [2] give rise to the expectation that in many schools we may expect some degree of integration of the computer in the curriculum. It is therefore worthwhile studing the changes which took place in these schools, to trace the factors which were determining these changes and to investigate what further developments might be expected.

2. RESEARCH QUESTIONS.

The central question in this study is *what changes are taking place in the curricula of existing school subjects as a consequence of the integration of computers in these curricula?*.

First we shall indicate what we understand by the concepts of curriculum and integration.

Following others (e.g. [15]), we distinguish the following parts of the curriculum: goals and objectives, content, instructional strategies, grouping patterns, materials, student evaluation, time and space. The integration of computers in school curricula may affect any of these.

With respect to the concept of integration, we distinguish several aspects. At school level, the integration of computer use refers to a number of variables: the number of subjects, grades, classes per grade, teachers per subject and all or a special group of students. Within subjects, it refers to the frequency of use per student per year, the time spent on the computer each time it is used, the lesson phases in which the computer is used (e.g. presentation of new subject matter, practising, testing, feedback), and finally the 'level' of application, which may vary from drill & practice to sophisticated CAI-applications, such as computer coaching. Without trying to construct a measure for the integration of the computer in the curriculum, we shall, after investigating the use of computers in a school, give a qualitative indication of the degree of integration.

3. METHOD.

The lack of empirical data about what might be expected as answers to our research question, indicates the exploratory character of the study, for which, therefore, a case study methodology [16] is appropriate. The study can be characterised as an embedded multiple case design [16].

To enlarge the chance to observe changes in the curriculum in schools as consequences of computer use, it was decided that the 'case study schools' should be schools which can be considered as 'fore-runners' with respect to computer use. From the survey and interviews of the Dutch Inspectorate, we asked the Inspectorate to indicate three schools in the sector of lower secondary education. The selected schools were willing to cooperate in the case study. It is important to remark that a weak point of this selection procedure is that no objective criteria were used to determine whether a school is a fore-runner or not, but that the interpretation of the survey and interview data by the Inspectorate was the main determinant for calling a school a fore-runner.

The following *procedure* was planned for each of the three schools. The principal and the computer co-ordinator of the school should be interviewed to acquire context information, e.g., the history, policy and the degree of computer use at school level, the available facilities, and information about the factors which (according to e.g. Fullan [13]) influence the implementation of an in-novation. The computer co-ordinator was asked to point out the three subjects in which the computer is being used the most, and then for each subject, a teacher who used the computer, as well as a teacher who did not use the computer, was interviewed. The 'using' teachers gave information about how they were using computers, what changes had taken place in their curriculum as a consequence of this use, and what factors influenced their use. The 'non-using' teachers gave their arguments for (still) being a non-user. Besides, for each selected subject, some lessons in which the computer was used were observed, as well as some other lessons. Furthermore, documents on the school's policy about computer use, the curricular materials (including educational software) used in lessons in which computers are being used, as well as materials from the lessons in which the computer was not used, was analysed. We sometimes had to deviate from this procedure, due to the circumstances in the schools; for example, in one of the schools the computer was only used in two subjects.

As *instruments*, several questionnaires were developed to serve as a checklist during the interviews. Furthermore, checklists were constructed, to describe software and other materials which were used in the classroom, as well as for the observation of the lessons, so that changes in the level of curriculum-materials and in the operational level could be established.

To take care of the validity of the study, several sources and methods were used to acquire the same information and the draft case-studies were checked for completeness and correctness by the interviewed persons. The procedure for data collection, the checklists for the interviews, and a database for the collected data [16] contribute to the reliability of the study.

4. RESULTS.

In this section some background data of the participating schools will first be presented, which may serve as an interpretation context for the remaining results. Next, results on school level (in 4.2) and on subject matter level (in 4.3) will be given and discussed in the context of important implementation factors. Finally, in 4.4, changes in the curriculum will be analysed on the curricular variables, as mentioned in section 2.

4.1. Some background data.

Since 1984 in the Netherlands a national informatics stimulation plan, a five year program, is under execution. The educational part, directed at general secondary education, is a cooperation of the government and some computer manufacturers. The goals are to provide each lower secondary school with 9 MS/DOS microcomputers in a Local Area Network (LAN) and two other machines, to train three teachers per school in the use of computers in education (familiarization course) and to provide a national infrastructure for software development. The provision of all schools with the same type of hardware will self-evidently lead in the near future to a certain standardization of hardware.

The three schools in the case study are in the sector of general secondary education; two of them, viz. A and B, are already provided with hardware and have three teachers trained in the context of the national scheme. It should be noted that all schools (private as well as public ones) in the Netherlands are paid for by the government; schools may also raise funds by themselves, e.g. via an extra contribution by the parents.

Some background data of the schools are:

School A: private, part of an organization with 49 schools in several cities; contains pre-university and higher general secondary education; grade range 1-6, age range 12-18; 67 teachers; 1180 students.

School B: public; contains pre-university education, higher and middle general secondary education; grade range 1-6, age range 12-18; 100 teachers; 1700 students.

School C: private, part of an organization with three schools in one city; contains middle general secondary education only; grade range 1-4, age range 12-16; 21 teachers; 274 students.

Although two of the schools have a grade range of 1-6, the case studies were restricted to the lower secondary education grades, i.e. grades 1-3. It is important to point that school A is part of a large private association which governs many schools.

4.2. Computer use on school level.

Before discussing the use of computers, we first present an overview of the available facilities:

School A: 13 Commodore-64 and 13 IBM-MS/DOS computers. 8 Commodores are placed in a LAN as well as 8 IBM's, both LAN's are placed in the computer laboratory for students. Most of the other computers are placed in the computer laboratory for teachers.

School B: 8 New Brain computers and 28 Phillips-MS/DOS computers. Of the Phillips computers, 22 are placed in a computer laboratory and 9 of those in a LAN.

School C: 9 TANDY computers, of which 8 in a LAN in the computer laboratory.

As a consequence of the grassroots developments, which

started before the execution of the national informatics stimulation plan, different computer types are present in the schools. Schools A and B acquired their MS/DOS machines not only as part of the national scheme, but also as part of other projects in which they participated. The organization of the computers in school B allows for using computers with a full class (1 or 2 students per machine) which is more optimal as compared to schools A and C (three students per machine). It should be noted that school A does possess the hardware to create a more optimal situation in terms of computer:student ratio. Schools A and C are 'early' users, they started using computers in 1974 and 1975 respectively, while school B got involved in a special project in 1983.

In table 1, some data are summarized on personnel resources, available software and degree of integration of computer use in existing subjects at schoollevel, grades 1-3.

From this table, we see that school A is active with computers in many more subjects than the other two schools; also a relatively higher number of teachers is involved. It should be marked that there are great differences between the schools in the choice of subjects and grades in which computers are being used; this confirms that there is clearly no centralizing tendency in the Dutch national policy which is directing schools.

Almost all the software used is developed within the school, which points to an overall lack of software in the public domain.

All schools do have a computer co-ordinator, but only in school A does this person have less than the normal number of teaching periods in order to be able to spend part of his 'paid' time for co-ordinating computer activities. The number of periods for other teachers to spend on computer-related activities, is also the largest in this school.

The teachers in school C received only an internal programming course when they started their developments. The other schools organized internal introductory courses on how to use computers, while as part of the national

scheme, three teachers per school were allowed to take part in an external course. No teachers participated in other external courses, although they were available.

From table 1, it can be concluded that in school A computer use in french, mathematics and mother tongue is especially for lower ability students; in this school, it was decided to restrict the use of computers mainly to remedial teaching *outside* the normal classes.

In summary, we may conclude that only in school A can one speak of a certain degree of integration of computers in the school; in the other 'fore-runner' schools, the developments -even when they have lasted for several years as in school C- are very modest. In these schools, one cannot speak of any real integration of computers in the school curriculum.

The question may be asked which factors are determining this rather disappointing picture of schools who are considered by the Inspectorate as fore-runners. Summarizing the literature on the implementation of innovations, Fullan [14] concludes: "It is known that change in practice occurs when certain elements occur in combination: attention to the development of clear and validated materials; active administrative support and leadership at the district and especially the school level; focused, ongoing inservice or staff development activities; the development of collegiality and other interaction-based conditions at the school level; and the selective use of external resources (both people and materials)."

We collected data in the three schools on many of these elements, which are summarized in table 2. Some conclusions can be drawn from these data. First, none of the schools has a clear educational vision of what they would like to achieve with the new technologies; the statements are vague, there is no written policy presenting 'leading ideas' which may structure activities on school level. Given Fullan's elements, we can say that
-there is a need for materials, also for time;

Table 1. Personnel resources, available software, degree of integration of computer use at schoollevel

Personnel resources	subjects	degree of integration[1]				
		1	2	3	4	5
School A:						
- 1 computer co-ordinator with 13 special periods	english	5	5/13	2,3	13/13	all
- 14 special periods for other teachers	french	75	5/5	1-3	19/19	l.a.
- 52% teachers trained by internal introductory course	geography	2	3/3	1	7/7	all
- 4% teachers trained by national scheme	mathematics	20-30	4/4	1,2	13/13	all,l.a.
	mother tongue	15	4/6	1-3	5/13	l.a.
	physics	20-30	3/3	2,3	13/13	all
	95% of software selfmade, 5% acquired					
School B:						
- 1 computer co-ordinator without special periods	mother tongue	12	2/12	3	2/16	all
- 4 special periods for other teachers	physics	1	3/5	2	16/16	all
- 30 % teachers trained by internal introductory course						
- 3% teachers trained by national scheme						
	100% of software selfmade						
School C:						
- 1 computer co-ordinator with 1 special period	french	4	1/1	1,2	6/6	all
- 1 special period for other teachers	mathematics	4	3/4	1,2	5/6	all
- 80% teachers followed internal programming course	music	1	1/1	1-3	9/9	all
	89% of software selfmade, 11% acquired					

[1] Legend:
1: number of programs
2: number of using teachers out of total using teachers
   (e.g. 5/13: 5 out of 13 teachers)
3: grades in which computers are used

4: number of classes in which computers are used
   out of total number of classes
5: type of students who are using computers,: all
   students or lower ability (l.a.)

TABLE 2. Some implementation factors (partly reported by (vice)principals and computer coordinators)

Schools: Factors:	A[1]	B	C
Reason to start	Possibilities to implement new teaching strategies	Use of computers by schools became usual (rivalry) Possibilities to implement new teaching strategies	Possibilities to use the computer in school Chance for school to become a forerunner
Policy	No written or informal long-term policy informal decision for reteaching	No written or informal long-term policy	No written or informal long-term policy
Facilities	Lack of hardware, memory capacity, software and time	Lack of software, time and finances	Lack of hardware, software and and time, slow network
Organization		Problems with scheduling the use of computer laboratory	Problems with scheduling teachers for computer education Problems with location of computers
External training	3 Teachers attended	3 Teachers attended	
Internal training	No follow-up on introductory course	No follow-up on introductory course	No follow-up on BASIC-course
Internal support	Teachers and coordinator report school administration fulfills necessary conditions only More teachers working with computers	Teachers and coordinator report that administration is stimulative More teachers working with computers	Teachers and coordinator report that administration is stimulative More teachers working with computers
External support	Government supplies hardware and training Board of school supplies hardware, software, time information, expertise	Government supplies hardware and training Board of school supplied hardware COI[2] supplies hardware and expertise Software from SLO[3]	

[1] The administration of school A reported no problems, source of problems: the computer coordinator.

[2] COI: Center for education and information technology
[3] SLO: National Institute for curriculum development

-there is administrative support on school level, but the administration is merely stimulating that something should be undertaken and not 'what, why and how' (schools B and C reported also organizational problems on how to use the computers); it is illustrative that in one of the schools the administration reported no problems, while the computer co-ordinator mentioned the lack of policy at school-level as one;

-we concluded earlier that the national scheme is imposing some conditions on school level, but it is not inducing directions for the developments on school level; this was also manifest from the interviews;

-staff development is not ongoing;

-there is limited use of external resources, e.g., almost all software is selfmade and training is mainly internal.

Although our design does not allow for causality, it is clear that most of the conditions mentioned by Fullan are not fulfilled in the fore-runner schools. Because this conclusion at school level does not exclude that the computer is integrated in some subject matter domains, we shall analyze developments in three subjects per school in the next section.

4.3. Computer use in some subjects.

For each school, three subjects were selected in which the computer is used relatively intensively. Table 3 contains data about computer use in these subjects. We see that computers are not frequently used and that the use is often of the drill & practice type. Furthermore, in school A in french, mathematics and mother tongue, the computer is not used during class periods, but only outside the class for remedial activities with weaker students. No other conclusion can be drawn than that we cannot as yet speak of a real integration of the computer in existing courses.

Looking for possible explanations for this lack of integration, nine teachers (one teacher for each selected subject in each school) were asked which problems they encountered in using computers, by checking from a list of 12 possible problems those which are most important for them.

Teachers who actively use computers, most frequently mention as their problems a lack of software, curricular materials, hardware, and time, and organizational constraints. It is interesting that all these problems are in the domain of the conditions for using computers. Plomp & Carleer [17], found the same type of problems in a study of problems during the implementation of information literacy, the Dutch variant of computer literacy.

Only for the subject of physics, in school B, was a perceived need mentioned for which the computer might offer an instrumental solution, viz. with the help of the computer, the teacher will be able to follow the progress of students when they work in groups. The other teachers give more general reasons for using the computer like: to improve students' achievement, to use new teaching methods, to motivate students or to meet needs of the society.

4.4. Changes in the curriculum.

As computers are not yet integrated in fore-runner schools, or in specific subjects in these schools, we cannot expect to find much change in the curricula. So in this section,

TABLE 3. Degree of integration of computer use at subject level

Subject	Lesson phase [1]				type of use			freq [2]	length [3]
	presentation	practice	testing	r.t. [4]	d&p [5]	simulatie	tool		
School A:									
french				x	x			5	50
mathematics		x		x	x		x	3	45
mother tongue				x	x			4-6	50
School B:									
mother tongue	x	x					x	12	50
physics		x				x		1	50
School C:									
french		x			x			3	25
mathematics 1st grade		x			x			4-5	25
mathematics 2nd grade		x			x			2-3	25
music	x	x					x	13	-

1) Lesson phase in which computers are used.
2) Freq: Frequentie, number of times the computer is used per year; in the subjects where the computer is used for reteaching, this number stands for the average time the computer is used per student, per year.
3) Length: average length of time spent behind the computer by students.
4) r.t.: remedial teaching
5) d&p: drill and practice

we can only indicate very tentatively which changes occurred as a result of the limited degree of integration and experience of teachers.

We asked teachers about changes in the curricular aspects, as mentioned in section 2. The results are summarized in table 4. In this table, the curricular aspect of material is not included, as this can be seen as the independent variable, as a consequence of which changes in the other aspects might occur. Teachers reported that students were evaluated in the same way as before the use of computers, so the aspect of student evaluation in table 4 refers to the degree of direct feedback the students receive.

We can conclude from table 4 that teachers reported hardly any changes, except for changes which are directly related to the use of this medium, e.g., changes in the grouping patterns, in the degree of feedback and in the rooms which are used.

Indications for changes are reported by several teachers. In school A, in french, more attention is paid to speech practice, as the computer can take over the practising with grammar. In school B, for both subjects, a change in content is reported. For the subject of mother tongue word-processing is added to the curriculum, replacing some drill exercises, and for physics, the computer adds the possibility of testing connections. In school C, the changes reported for french and mathematics are due to spending more time on the topics which are taught with the computer.

In school B, there are relatively more changes, which is probably due to the more sophisticated uses of the computer, such as, word-processing and simulation.

A general trend seems to be the use of the less sophisticated possibilities of the computer, which is probably due to the fact that most software is teacher made and does not take advantage of the full possibilities of the computer as an educational medium. So the degree of implementation on which most claims about possible effects are based, is still not realized.

5. DISCUSSION

From this study it appears that the fore-runners schools have not yet fully integrated the use of computers, neither at school- nor at subject-level. Although the survey results suggest a lot of activities with respect to computers in education, we see that fore-runner schools have hardly passed the stage of grassroot developments. Given this situation, it is hardly surprising that we did not find much change in existing subjects as a result of the use of computers. It would be interesting to repeat this study in the same schools after a few years, to see whether the schools take the chance to integrate the use of computers in their curriculum more fully.

Due to these grassroot developments, there is a variety in what schools are doing with computers, and how. It is not clear yet whether the national scheme will result in more convergence of these activities at school level.

Another effect of grassroot developments is what might be called the disadvantage of early starters. We observed, for instance, at school C, that due to their fore-runner position, the delivery of sophisticated hardware is postponed until late starters had received their hardware. This situation may slow down the development of computer use in such schools.

The innovation plans at national, as well as at school level, are merely directed at the fulfilling of some necessary conditions, such as hardware, a few trained teachers and a starter's package of software. A shortcoming of these plans is that there has been little attention to the implementation factors which are known to influence an innovation and to the development of a 'leading idea'. The idea which is currently dominating at school is to avoid change in the existing organisation and curricula.

Furthermore, different educational actors seem to be waiting for each other. Schools wait for teachers to start activities, teachers, however, wait for a policy at school level. Both schools and teachers are waiting for a policy at national level.

So it appears that to solve the problem of the lack of integration of computer use, clear plans at national and school level and well organized support for the schools is needed.

TABLE 4. Changes as reported by teachers.

School:	A			B		C		
Subject:	french	math1)	mt2)	mt	physics	french	math	music
Parts of curriculum:								
change in goals . productive skills	no3) less4)	no less	no less	yes less	yes equal	no less	no less	no - 5)
change in content . real life content	no less	no less	no less	yes less	yes less	no less	no less	- -
discovery oriented strategy	less	equal	?	less/equal	less	equal	less	equal
working individual or in groups	more	more	more	more	more	more	more	equal
student evaluation	more	more	equal	equal	more	more	more 1st grade equal 2nd grade	-
more than 1 room used during class	n.a.	n.a.	n.a.	no	no	yes	yes	no
change in time spent on certain topics during class	yes	no	no	no/yes	no	yes	yes	no

1) math: mathematics

2) mt: mother tongue

3) yes or no: the change did or did not occur as a consequence of computer use.

4) more/equal/less: more/equal less in computer lessons as opposed to normal lessons.

5) -: hard to specify

REFERENCES

[1] Becker, H.J., School uses of microcomputers, issue 1-6 (The John Hopkins University, Centre for the social organization of schools, Baltimore, MD, 1983).

[2] Ministerie van Onderwijs en Wetenschappen, Onderwijs en informatietechnologie. Een beschrijving van de stand van zaken in het schooljaar 1985/1986. Inspectierapport 7, deel 1 en 2 (Inspectie voor Speciale Diensten, s'Hertogenbosch, 1986).

[3] Deursen, K. van, The introduction of information technology in the Dutch educational system, in: Plomp, Tj. et al. (eds.), CAL for Europe: Computer-assisted learning for Europe: proceedings (North-Holland, Amsterdam, 1986).

[4] Plomp, Tj. & van den Akker, J.J.H., Curricular and implementation aspects of the introduction of information technology in education, in: Moonen, J. & Plomp, Tj. (eds.), Eurit 86, Developments in educational software and courseware (Pergamon Press, Oxford, 1987).

[5] Anderson, J.S.A., Implementing information technology across the curriculum - what does it mean?, in: Moonen, J. & Plomp, Tj. (eds.), Eurit 86, Developments in educational software and courseware (Pergamon Press, Oxford, 1987).

[6] Simon, H.A., Designing organisations for an information rich world, in: Greenberger, M. (ed.), Computers, communications and the public interest (John Hopkins Press, Baltimore, 1971).

[7] Geest, Th. van der, De computer in het schrijfonderwijs, Perspectief voor een procesbenadering, (Universiteit Twente, Toegepaste Onderwijskunde Enschede, 1986).

[8] Moonen, J.C.M.M., Toepassingen van computersystemen in het onderwijs (Staatsuitgeverij, Den Haag, 1986).

[9] Bergers, A.H. & Achterberg A.M., The micrcomputer in teaching school science and mathematics, Report of an international workshop (Universiteit Twente en VALO, Enschede, 1986).

[10] Becker, H.J., Instructional uses of microcomputers, reports from the 1985 national survey, issue no.1 (The John Hopkins University, Centre ‐ for the social organiza-tion of schools, Baltimore, MD, 1986).

[11] Linden, W. J. van der, Computerondersteund toetsen: technische ontwikkelingen en nieuwe toepassingsmogelijkheden in: Heene, J. & PLomp, Tj., Onderwijs en informatietechnologie. Verslag van een SVO/CDO symposium (SVO, 's Gravenhage, 1985).

[12] Cory, S., A 4-stage model of development for full implementation of computers for instruction in a school system, The Computing Teacher, 11, 4, (1983).

[13] Fullan, M., The meaning of educational change (Teachers College Press, Columbia University, New York, 1982).

[14] Fullan, M., Curriculum implementation, in: Husen T. & Postlewaithe, N., The international encyclopedia of ed-ucation (Pergamon Press, Oxford, 1985).

[15] Gerlach, V.S., & Ely D.P., Teaching and media. A systematic approach (Prentice Hall, Englewood Cliffs, 1980).

[16] Yin, R.K., Case study research. Design and methods, (SAGE, Beverley Hills, 1984).

[17] Plomp, Tj. & Carleer, G., Towards a strategy for the introduction of information and computer literacy courses (ICL), Computers and Education, 11, 1, (1987).

7. Courseware Development

COMPUTERS IN EDUCATION, F. Lovis and E.D. Tagg (eds.)
Elsevier Science Publishers B.V. (North-Holland)
© IFIP, 1988

511

THE ET PROJECT:
ARTIFICIAL INTELLIGENCE IN SECOND LANGUAGE
TEACHING

Danilo Fum(*), Paolo Giangrandi (˜), Carlo Tasso (˜)

(˜) Laboratorio di Intelligenza Artificiale
Dipartimento di Matematica e Informatica
Università di Udine, Italy
(*) Dipartimento dell'Educazione
Università di Trieste, Italy.

ET is an intelligent tutor working in the domain of second language teaching which is devoted to help students in learning the English verb system. ET exploits a blackboard-based architecture in order to obtain the cooperation among its modules and is grounded on a temporal model of situations and events which allows inferring the relations that should be taken into account in determining verb tenses. The paper is focused on the problem of tense determination and on the issue of adaptive modelling, i.e., the capability of keeping track of the student knowledge by using different techniques according to the difficulty of the modelling task. An example of system operation is also given.

1. INTELLIGENT TUTORING SYSTEMS AS AN AID FOR SECOND LANGUAGE TEACHING

In the course of its evolution, English has developed a verb system which allows expressing very subtle meaning distinctions through a highly sophisticated use of tenses. Learning how to use English verbs, however, is extremely difficult for non-native speakers and causes lots of troubles to people who study English as a foreign language. In order to overcome the difficulties which can be found in this and in several other grammatical areas, various attempts have been made to utilize Artificial Intelligence techniques for developing very sophisticated tutors, called Intelligent Tutoring Systems, in the specific domain of foreign language teaching (Barchan, Woodmansee, and Yazdani, 1985; Schuster and Finin, 1986; Weischedel, Voge, and James, 1978; Zoch, Sabah, and Alviset, 1986).

An *Intelligent Tutoring System* (ITS for short) is a program capable of providing students with tutorial guidance in a given subject (for a review, see: Lawler and Yazdani, 1987; Sleeman and Brown, 1982). A full-fledged ITS: (a) has specific domain expertise; (b) is capable of modelling the student knowledge in order to discover the reason(s) of his/her mistakes, and (c) is able to make teaching more effective by applying different tutorial strategies. ITS technology seems particularly promising in fields, like language teaching, where a solid core of facts is actually surrounded by a more nebulous area in which subtle discriminations, personal points of view, and pragmatic factors are involved (Close, 1981). While traditional teaching methods based on the explicit study and application of grammatical rules have been shown to be insufficient, this does not mean that knowledge of the grammar is unnecessary. Grammar, on the contrary, can provide initially a form of declarative knowledge which, through exercise and practice, should later be 'compiled' to be effectively used (Anderson, 1983). ITS can be helpful in mastering grammatical knowledge by monitoring the learner progress and by furnishing an exploratory environment for language manipulation.

In this paper we present some of the results obtained within a

research project, jointly carried out at the Computer Science Department of th University of Udine and the Department of Education of the University of Trieste, aimed at developing *ET (English Tutor)*, an ITS which helps students to learn English verb usage. In this paper we concentrate on the two most important modules of the system, the Domain Expert, which includes most of the system linguistic competence, and the Student Modeller, which is devoted to create and successively update a model of the student competence. The following section illustrates the general philosophy, specifications and architecture of ET. Section three deals with the problem of tense determination in second language teaching and presents the Domain Expert module which is devoted to generate, in a cognitively transparent way, the right tense for the verb(s) appearing in the exercises presented to the student. Section four discusses how ET tries to infer from the student behavior what he really knows and presents the requirements, organization and mode of operation of the Student Modelling module. In section five an example of the behaviour of which ET is capable is given. Section six presents the conclusions of the paper.

2. THE ENGLISH TUTOR

ET is an intelligent tutor working in the domain of second language teaching which is devoted to help Italian students in learning the English verb system. The general philosophy on which the system is grounded is that of coaching (Goldstein and Carr, 1977), i.e. in the educational setting the system plays the role of a trainer who monitors and looks after students' progress. ET proposes adequate exercises, analyses the students' responses, hypothesises the reasons underlying the students' mistakes and makes them aware of their misconceptions. The system monitors the level of the student knowledge by means of an explicit 'student model'. The system is addressed to people that have just learned the 'rules' of the grammar and must therefore practice and refine their knowledge by putting into use what they have learned.

Tutoring is accomplished in ET by generating appropriate

sequences of exercises which take into account the story of the system-student interactions and the student model. The exercises proposed are essentially of the fill-in kind. The student must conjugate a given verb in the right tense according to the context determined by the rest of the sentence. The system has no predefined list of correct answers but generates the solution by itself. In doing this, it keeps track of the pieces of knowledge it has utilized and tries to determine if the student shows the possession of the same knowledge.

The overall architecture of ET is illustrated in Figure 1 and is organized around the three basic modules of an ITS (Sleeman and Brown, 1982), namely: the *Tutor,* devoted to manage the teaching activity and the interaction with the student, the *Domain Expert.* which is an articulated expert in the analysis and generation of English sentences, with specific reference to tense, and the *Student Modeller,* which is able to evaluate and possibly diagnose the student competence in the specific domain.

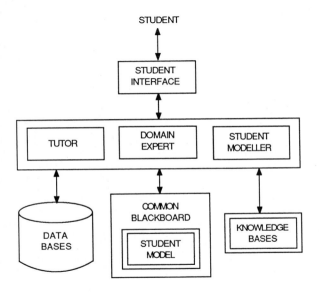

Figure 1. Overall architecture of ET

At the beginning of each session, the Tutor starts the interaction with the student by presenting a first exercise on a given topic. The same exercise is then given to the Domain Expert which will produce both the correct solution and a detailed account of the reasoning and knowledge employed for producing it. At this point, the Student Modeller analyses the answer provided by the student and compares it with that of the expert in order to identify the kind of errors, if any, and to formulate hypotheses about their causes. On the basis of these hypotheses, the Tutor will select the next exercise, which will test the student on the critical aspects pointed out so far, and will allow the Modeller to gather further information useful for refining the hypotheses previously drawn. Eventually, when some misconceptions have been identified, the refined and validated hypotheses will be used in order to explain the errors to the student and to suggest possible remediations. When a topic has been thoroughly analysed, the Tutor will possibly switch to other topics. Beside the above mentioned modules, which constitute the kernel of the ET system, a *Student Interface* manages the interaction with the student. The cooperation among the four modules, aimed at obtaining the overall

behaviour of the tutoring system, has been based on a blackboard architecture with a shared memory, called *Common Blackboard,* which is utilized for storing all the information needed to deal with a specific session. The Common Blackboard represents both the working memory of each module and the communication medium among them. More specifically, the Common Blackboard contains the *Student Model,* that explicitly describes the student currently interacting with the system, and various other information concerning the overall control of system operation. This is managed by a *Task Scheduler* (a module not shown in Figure 1) and is organized around a basic 'schedule-assign' cycle. At each cycle, the Task Scheduler inspects the Common Blackboard and identifies the most promising module to which control should next be assigned. When the chosen module terminates its current operations, it returns control back to the Task Scheduler and another cycle will start.

All the modules of ET are supported in their operations by some knowledge and data bases. The knowledge bases are structured into the following three parts:

• the *Control Knowledge Base,* which contains knowledge about the overall operation strategies utilized by the Task Scheduler for managing the task of assigning control to the appropriate module at each 'schedule-assign' cycle.
• the *Domain Expert Knowledge Base,* which includes both procedural and declarative knowledge concerning conjugation and use of English tenses.
• the *Student Modelling Knowledge Base,* which encompasses different kinds of knowledge concerning the modelling process and which is utilized in order to analyse the student answers and to evaluate the level of the student knowledge.

The data bases utilized by ET are:

• the *Syllabus,* which contains a structured list of the topics, which the system is competent about;
• the *Exercise Data Base,* which includes all the exercises organized according to the topics appearing in the Syllabus; and
• the *Dictionary,* which contains lexical, syntactic, and semantic information on all the verbs known by the system.

3. TENSE DETERMINATION IN ET

An important part of sentence meaning is constituted by temporal information. The tense of the verb indicates the relation between the situation described in the sentence and the moment in which the sentence is uttered *(deictic temporal relation)* and may also indicate more subtle relations between the main situation and other situation described in, or implied by, the same sentence *(anaphoric temporal relations).* Other information can be derived from the mood and aspect of the verb, from the lexical category which the verb is a member of and, more generally, from several kinds of temporal expressions that may appear in the sentence. Very complex relationships exist among all these features which are automatically taken into account by native speakers in understanding a sentence or in generating an appropriate tense combination for a given sentence.

The problem of the choice of the correct verb tense in order to convey the exact meaning a sentence is intended to express has aroused the interest of linguists, philosophers, logicians, and people interested in computational accounts of language usage (see, for example, Ehrich, 1987; Fuenmayor, 1987;

Matthiessen, 1984). However, there is no agreement on, and no theoretical account of, the factors that play a role in tense determination. The different proposals which exist in the literature greatly vary according to the different features that are actually identified as being critical and to their level of explicitness, i.e. which features are directly given to the tense selector in an explicit form, and which, on the contrary, must be inferred through some form of reasoning.

Our interest in this area is essentially pragmatic and is aimed at developing a Domain Expert for tense selection capable of covering most of the cases which can be found in practice, and usable in teaching English as a second language. An important criterion, followed in designing the expert, is that not only the final result (i.e. the tense which is generated), but also the knowledge and reasoning used in producing it should mirror those utilized by a human expert in the field, in our case by a competent native speaker. The Domain Expert must be therefore an 'articulated' or 'glass box' expert. Among other things, this means that the features which are taken into account in selecting the right tense are not necessarily spelled out completely to the system but their explicitness has been reduced and maintained at a level which allows to emulate some of the reasoning that takes place in experts when they face the problem of tense choice.

The main task of the Domain Expert is that of generating the right answers for the exercises proposed to the student. Usually, exercises are constituted by a few English sentences in which some of the verbs *(open items)* are given in infinitive form and have to be conjugated into an appropriate tense. Sometimes, in order to avoid ambiguities, additional information describing the correct interpretation of the sentence (as far as the temporal point of view is concerned) is given. Consequently, the Domain Expert must be able:

i) to select the grammatical tense to employ for each open item of the exercise in order to correctly describe the status of the world the sentence is intended to represent, and

ii) to appropriately conjugate the verb according to the chosen tense.

Beside these basic functionalities, the tutoring environment in which the Domain Expert operates imposes a further requirement, i.e. the expert must be able

iii) to explain to the student how the solution has been found, which kind of knowledge has been utilized, and why.

While the sentences that are presented to the student are in natural language form, the expert receives in input a schematic description of the sentence. Every clause of the sentence is represented inside the system through a series of attribute-value pairs (called *exercise descriptors)* that highlight useful information for the tense selection process. The Domain Expert, when solving an open item, infers from the exercise descriptors all the remaining information needed to make the final choice of the appropriate tense. This information is constituted by several *tense features,* each one describing some facet of the situation that is necessary to consider.

The choice of which tense features are to be taken into account in the tense selection process represents a fundamental step in the design of the verb generator. This problem has no generally agreed upon solution, and it constitutes by no means the most critical part of any theory of tense generation. The main features considered by the ET verb expert are listed below. Some of them are directly included in the exercise descriptors (1 to 4), whereas others have to be explicitly inferred at run-time (5 to 8).

1. *Category,* which identifies the kind of situation described by the clause (e.g., event, state, action, activity etc.).
2. *Aspect,* which concerns the different perspectives that can be utilized for describing a situation.
3. *Intentionality,* which refers to whether the situation describes a course of action that has been premeditated or not.
4. *Context,* which concerns the type of discourse in which the clause or sentence appears.
5. *Duration,* which refers to the time span (long, short, instantaneous, etc.) occupied by the situation.
6. *Perspective,* which refers to the position along the temporal axis of the situation or to its relation with the present time.
7. *Temporal Relations,* which refer to the temporal relations (simultaneity, contiguity, precedence, etc.) that occur between the situation dealt with by the current clause and the situations described in other clauses.
8. *Adverbial Information,* which is related to the meaning of possible temporal adverbials specified in the same clause.

System operation is performed mainly through a partitioned set of production rules which express in a transparent and cognitively consistent way what is necessary to do in order to generate a verb tense. The Domain Expert activity is mostly concerned with the derivation of the tense features strictly related to temporal reasoning. The exercise descriptors include for this purpose only basic information related to the specific temporal adverbials or conjunctions which appear in the exercise. This information is utilized to build a temporal model of the situations described in the exercise. Initially, the model is only partially known and is then augmented through the application of a set of temporal relation rules. This rule constitutes a set of axioms of a temporal logic - similar to that utilized by Allen (1984) - which has been specifically developed for: (a) representing the basic temporal knowledge about the situations described in the exercise; (b) reasoning about these knowledge in order to compute tense features not explicitly present in the schematic description of the exercises.

More specifically, the expert module derives from the exercise descriptors the first version of the temporal model; then, by means of the temporal axioms, it completes the model with all the possible temporal relations among the situations described in the sentence. At this point, for every clause of the exercise, it identifies the so called *reference time,* i.e., the moment of time which the situation described in the clause refers to. In order to determine the reference time of every clause, the expert utilizes a set of *reference time identification rules.* Later, the expert only looks for the clauses with open items: for each of them it computes, (through the temporal axioms) three temporal relations (Ehrich, 1977): deictic (between reference time and speaking time), intrinsic (between event time and reference time) and ordering (between event time and speaking time). When these relations are computed, all the needed tense features are known, and the final tense selection can be performed. Again, a set of rules *(selection rules)* takes care of this activity. Once the tense to be used has been identified, the verb is conjugated utilizing an appropriate set of *conjugation rules.*

4. STUDENT MODELLING IN ET

In contrast with traditional CAI approaches, which were based on the assumption that any mistake possibly made by the student had to be anticipated in advance, ITS are provided with the knowledge necessary to enable diagnostic skills and are able not only to recognize that a mistake has been made, but also to discover its causes and motivations in order to adapt the teaching process to the characteristics of each student. The task of inferring from the students' behaviour what they really know is made really difficult by the fact that the students' actions sometimes do not actually reflect their conceptions *(noise);* by the fact that an error can be induced by multiple causes *(apportionment of blame)* or, vice versa, by the fact that a correct answer may be given for completely different reasons.

The specific choices made in designing the ET *Student Modeller* are the result of a preliminary analysis performed on protocols collected by asking a group of students to solve a sample of typical exercises taken from English textbooks and grammars (Thompson and Martinet, 1984; Graver, 1986). The results of this analysis can be summarized as follows:
- the issues which students have to master in learning English verb usage range from simple concepts to quite complex decision rules to be utilized in reasoning;
- some aspects of the problem, such as the ability to perform verb conjugation, can be analyzed simply by looking at the single answers given by the students; moreover, the frequency of occurrence of many conjugation errors allows to compile a list of typical mistakes; finally, a single answer may often contain multiple conjugation errors;
- the choice of the tense is much more difficult to analyse, since the problem is characterized by several factors, and the consideration of a single wrong answer is not sufficient to capture the deep reasons of the mistake but allows only drawing some partial hypotheses. It is therefore necessary to monitor the student behaviour during a longer period of time (at least a few answers to well selected and meaningful exercises), in order to isolate student misconceptions. Moreover, these are usually constituted by slight perturbations of expert knowledge (e.g., generalization of a rule by relaxing some condition or specialization of a rule by adding further conditions) and do not appear according to systematic patterns;
- noise occurs especially in the choice of tense: in order to reduce as much as possible its influence, it is appropriate to analyse more than a single answer;
- the student behaviour is frequently influenced by the knowledge of the mother tongue.

These results have been taken as requirements in the design of the Student Modeller. According to them, the modelling process has been organized around a *Student Model,* devoted to store all the knowledge necessary to describe the status of the student knowledge about the domain under consideration, four *modelling processors* (namely, the *Morphological Analyser,* the *Differential Analyser,* the *Diagnoser,* and the *Bug Generator)* in charge of the different activities needed for generating and maintaining the Student Model, and a *Student Modelling Knowledge Base,* partitioned according to the competences of the four modelling processors. The modelling process is incremental, i.e. the model is possibly refined each time the student gives answers to exercises, and basically data-driven, since at each refinement only some of the four modelling processors intervene, depending on the kind of information gathered from the student answer. The modelling strategy devised has been called *adaptive modelling,* since it is constituted by three basic strategies (overlay, bug collection, and bug construction) appropriately combined and utilized in accordance to specific situations.

The structure of the Student Model reflects the strategy adopted in ET for adaptive modelling. It comprises:

- the *Conceptual Model,* which constitutes the overlay com-

ponent of the model and includes information about the level of familiarity of the student with the knowledge involved in the domain;
- the *Bug Catalogue,* which is the bug collection component of the model, being constituted by stereotyped malrules about the conjugation of English verbs;
- the *Inferred Malrules Base,* that includes rules generated by the system for modelling unknown erroneous behaviours in tense selection and is the bug construction component of the model;
- the *Session History,* i.e. a log of all student answers to preceding exercises, results of all the analyses performed by the modeller, hypotheses on student misconceptions, etc.

The modelling process is organized into four phases, each one performed by one of the four processors. The first phase, called *Morphological Analysis,* processes the verb contained in the student answer in order to extract its morphological features (voice, tense, number, mood, etc.). It tries to recognize which conjugation rules have been utilized by the student and the conjugation errors contained in the answer, if any. In doing this, the Morphological Analyser is supported by a specific partition of the Student Modelling Knowledge Base, which specifically contains production rules for conjugation and for stereotyped errors, and by a dictionary, utilized also by other ET modules.

The following phase consists in the so called *Differential Analysis,* devoted to compare the results of the preceding analysis with what has been found by the Domain Expert. This allows an evaluation of the correctness of the student answer and, consequently, an update of the model. More specifically, the Conceptual Model is updated in order to take into account the good, wrong, or missed use of knowledge shown by the student in solving the last exercise. This overlay model is implemented through standard counters. In a similar way, values of the counters contained in the Bug Catalogue are increased to reflect the usage of malrules. The activity carried out in this phase actually implements two of the three strategies adopted in ET for modelling, namely, overlay and bug collection, which are adequate for evaluating the general knowledge of the domain and for very trivial or persistent a-priori known conjugation errors.

The first level of modelling performed during Differential Analysis is the base on which the bug construction component of the Student Modeller can operate. This is aimed at identifying persistent, a-priori unknown errors on the usage of English verb tenses, and is performed during the Diagnosis and the Bug Generation phase.

Diagnosis is devoted to guess possible causes of the erroneous answers. More specifically, by inspection of the current content of the Student Model, it is able to assess (by means of a rule-based process) the level of knowledge shown by the student. For what concerns the selection of the right tenses, the assessment just mentioned allows the Modeller to propose some hypotheses on the likely nature of the errors. It is important to stress that, during this phase, the Modeller considers all information accumulated so far about the students, and not only the last answer.

Bug Generation is activated when some of the hypotheses refer specifically to a perturbation of the expert knowledge about the selection of tenses or when the evaluation of the student answer gave useful results for refining some new bug rule already under construction. The strategy followed by the Bug Generator in this phase is the following: a persistent error in the selection of a tense, e.g. tense T1 in place of tense T2, causes the modeller to guess that both the rules for the use of T1 and the use of T2 are perturbed in the student knowledge, and therefore have to be modified in order to reflect what is happening in student mind. There are two kinds of modifications performed on expert rules during Bug Generation. This process is continued until the new malrules are considered sufficiently validated from successive observations of student answers.

5. AN EXAMPLE OF INTERACTION WITH ET

This section is devoted to illustrate a sample of student-system interaction, with emphasis on the activity performed by the Student Modeller for diagnosing the student observed behaviour. We will consider a session in which ET examines the student knowledge about past tenses.

ET > EXERCISE-1: "He always (carry) an umbrella when he was in England"
Student > **was carrying**

The system analyses the answer and, by comparing it with that produced by the Expert, realizes that the student mistakingly used the past continuous instead of the simple past. The modeller tries to discover the cause(s) of the error, and to this purpose makes the following three hypotheses:

- the student does not know the rules for the application of both the simple past tense (which should have been utilized, but was not) and the past continuous (which was used incorrectly);
- the student does not know the simple past, and uses systematically the past continuous;
- the answer is wrong due to 'noise'.

The first hypothesis triggers the Bug Generator, which starts to work on building new malrules which account for the student erroneous behaviour. The Tutor assigns then another exercise:

ET > EXERCISE-2: "I (share) a flat with him when we were students."
Student > **shared**

The answer is correct: the second hypothesis is therefore discarded, and ET proposes another exercise:

ET > EXERCISE-3: "I (make) a cake when the light went out."
Student > **made**

The student is again wrong about the differences between simple past and past continuous, and the third hypothesis concerning noise is also discarded. The system tries then to refine the new malrules, and assigns two other exercises similar to the preceding ones:

ET > EXERCISE-4: "I lit the fire at 6.00 and it (burn) brightly when Tom came in."
Student > **burned**
ET > EXERCISE-5: "Last winter on holiday her mother often (tell) her that she (spend) too much money ."
Student > **was telling**
Student > **was spending**

The information gathered so far allows ET to interpret the student behaviour and to furnish the following diagnosis:

ET > Answers to exercise 1, 3, 4, and 5 are wrong. Your knowledge about the use of the simple past and the past continuous seem to be the following:

* You utilized the simple past according to the rule:
"When a clause describes a single action or a state that take place in the past, then use the simple past "

This rule does not take into account the further condition that:
"When the action or the state takes place simultaneously to the reference time of the clause, then the tense to be used is the past continuous"

* You utilized the past continuous according to the rule:
" When a clause describes a habitual action in the past, then use the past continuous"

This rule does not take into account that:
"When the clause describes a habitual action in the past, the past continuous is utilized only if the action is frequently repeated and probably, annoys the speaker or seems unreasonable to him".
An example of such a sentence is:
"He was an awful boy: he was always getting in trouble".

* The solution to Exercise-1 is:
Tense: simple past
Conjugated verb: carried,

because:
the action takes place in the past
the action is habitual
....

ET continues with the solutions to the other exercises and with new exercises on other aspects of the past tenses.

6. CONCLUSIONS

In this paper we have presented the main results of an ongoing research project aimed at developing a tutoring system capable of helping Italian students to master the core and the fine nuances of English verb usage. In the course of the project a prototype English Tutor (ET) has been designed and implemented. ET shows some interesting and original features concerning both the general issue of ITS and the more specific application of second language teaching. From a general point of view, ET is focused on what we call adaptive modelling, i.e. the capability of keeping track of the student knowledge by using different techniques according to the difficulty of the modelling task. We utilized a blackboard architecture in order to obtain the desired interaction and cooperation among the different modules of the system. Considered from the point of view of language teaching, ET expert module embodies the knowledge underlying tense determination which tries to capture the competence of a native speaker and which should be mastered by the student. This knowledge is represented through a set of production rules expressing not only grammatical knowledge, but also some subtleties and idiosyncrasies of language use.

The prototype is implemented in MRS on a SUN workstation under UNIX. A reimplementation in PROLOG is currently under development. The Domain Expert Knowledge Base and the Student Modelling Knowledge Base are constituted by 140 and 110 rules, respectively. There are about 60 exercises, all concerning the indicative mood.

Future research directions include the extension of the Syllabus and the Exercise Data Base to the rest of the verb system, the development of tutoring capabilities beyond diagnosis, and a systematic field testing of the prototype.

REFERENCES

Allen, J.F. (1984) Towards a General Theory of Action and Time. *Artificial Intelligence,* 23, 123-154.

Anderson, J.R. (1983) *The Architecture of Cognition.* Cambridge, MA: Harvard Univ. Press.

Barchan, J., Woodmansee, B.J. and Yazdani, M. (1985) A Prolog-Based Tool for French Grammar Analyzers. *Instructional Science,* 14.

Close, R.A. (1981) *English as a Foreign Language* London: Allen & Unwin.

Ehrich, V. (1987) The Generation of tense. In: G. Kempen (Ed.), *Natural Language Generation* Dordrecht, The Netherlands: M. Nijhoff, 423-44.

Fuenmayor, M. E. (1987) *Tense Usage Characterization and Recognition for Machine Translation* IBM Los Angeles Scientific Centre Report 1987 - 2796, Los Angeles, CA.

Goldstein, I. and Carr, B. (1977) The Computer as Coach: An athletic paradigm for intellectual education. *Proceed. of AAAI-84,* 227-233.

Graver, B.D. (1986) *Advanced English Practice* Oxford: Oxford University Press.

Lawler, R.W. and Yazdani, M. (Eds.) (1987) *Artificial Intelligence and Education.* Norwood, NJ: Ablex.

Matthiessen, C. (1984) *Choosing Tense in English* Research Report 84-143. University of Southern California.

Schuster, E. and Finin, T. (1986) VP2: The role of user modelling in correcting errors in second language learning. In: A. G. Cohn and J.R. Thomas (Eds.) *Artificial Intelligence and Its Applications.* New York, NY: Wiley.

Sleeman, D.H. and Brown, J.S. (eds.) (1982) *Intelligent Tutoring Systems.* London: Academic Press.

Thompson, A.J. and Martinet, A.V. (1984) *A Practical English Grammar* Oxford: Oxford University Press.

Weischedel, R.M., Voge, W.M. and James, M. (1978) An Artificial Intelligence Approach to Language Instruction. *Artificial Intelligence,* 10, 225-240.

Zoch, M., Sabah, G. and Alviset, C. (1986) From Structure to Process: Computer assisted teaching of various strategies of generating pronoun construction in French. *Proceed. of COLING-86,* Bonn, FRG.

COMPUTERS IN EDUCATION, F. Lovis and E.D. Tagg (eds.)
Elsevier Science Publishers B.V. (North-Holland)
© IFIP, 1988

TIME EXPENDITURE IN COMPUTER ASSISTED VOCABULARY LEARNING

P.J.M. Uffing, F.J.J. van Bussel, A. Schouten

Tilburg University, Instructional Psychology Department
P.O. Box 90153
5000 LE Tilburg, The Netherlands

This study reports on an experiment in foreign language vocabulary learning. Two computer implemented conditions are compared. In the first condition only three main options-learning, games, and list- were available to the student. In the other condition six options were available. Twenty-eight students (20 girls and 8 boys), aged about 13, at a normal secondary school participated in the study. Results are reported on learning gains and special attention is given to the relations between the options available to the student, the time spent in the options, the amount of learning and some measured student characteristics. No significant differences between conditions in amount of learning were found. The role of games in computer aided instruction and differential results between girls and boys are discussed.

1. INTRODUCTION

In this paper we will present results of a pilot study on computer assisted learning (CAL). The study concerned the learning of vocabulary in a foreign language. The main subject of interest of the study to be presented was to investigate the relations between the options available to the student, some measured student characteristics and the amount of learning. After some remarks on the properties of Computer Assisted Learning systems (CAL) (section 2) we will focus on ideas about vocabulary learning (section 3). The CAL system ELLA that is used in the study is described in section 4 and in section 5 the research questions and the description of the experiment are presented. In the next section the results of the study are presented (section 6), followed by a final discussion in section 7.

2. COMPUTER ASSISTED LEARNING (CAL)

It is widely acknowledged that the development of CAL software, also known as courseware, has been less successful than was expected a few years ago. It is not the quantity of courseware that is lacking, as we see a large number of courseware packages on the market. Recently Bork [1] stated that almost all commercially available computer-based learning material for school use at the present time is poor and that much of this material is trivial. This state of affairs is caused by an apparent lack of proven guidelines for the development of courseware. Given the fact that according to Bork [1] within twenty years the computer will be the major delivery system for education at all levels and that the computer in practically all subject areas will replace books and lectures, it will be necessary to obtain scientific knowledge about how computer-based learning material should be developed. Our research project, in which the reported pilot study was done, aims at the development of a design methodology which is based on tested instruction strategies and feasible models of student characteristics, subject matter, and student - system interaction. Computer assisted learning (CAL) is being developed to assist students in performing specific learning tasks. Usually learning tasks vary in a number of ways. In some tasks, for instance, rote learning is the key element, whereas in other tasks the acquisition of insight in a complex problem is the main goal. Still other tasks require the learner to have or to develop an overview over certain subject matter. Because different task elements can address different levels of knowledge and require different levels of expertise, it will be clear that there will be no such thing as a single CAL system to fit all needs. Moreover, not only tasks may differ, learners too are different. Students will have different initial levels of required knowledge and skills. And personality trait differences will affect the effectiveness of student-system communication. Stated otherwise a CAL system has to be an adaptive teaching instrument. Adaptive teaching is defined by Corno and Snow [2] as:

"teaching that arranges environmental conditions to fit learner individual differences. As learners gain in aptitude through experience with respect to the instructional goals at hand, such teaching adapts by becoming less intrusive. Less intrusion, less teacher or instructional mediation, increases the learner's information processing and/or behavioral burdens, and with this the need for more learner self-regulation. ... As the learner adapts, so also must the teacher [or the CAL system, p.u.]."

By this definition a CAL system should both adapt to the learner and should allow the learner to adapt to the instruction. The system-learning transaction is viewed as a dynamic one and should be tuned to aptitude complexes in the learner that encompass intellectual abilities, personality motivation characteristics and cognitive styles. One of the goals of our research project is to study these aspects of this system-learning transaction in order to formulate specific CAL development rules.

3. VOCABULARY LEARNING

The ultimate goal in foreign language learning is to acquire a sufficiently deep knowledge to be able to read, write, speak, and understand the language. Learning an adequate vocabulary is a phase of foreign language acquisition that has been, and will be, one of the major problems of any practical foreign language program.

There are probably more varied methods for teaching vocabulary than for any other aspect of language teaching. To be able to understand a language well one must passively understand the meaning of about 6000 words. In addition to this, in (Dutch) secondary schools students are supposed to learn a set of about 2000 words (actively) in order to be able to speak a language. The slow reading pace of students who have studied a foreign language for several hundred hours, and their continual flight to dictionary or end-vocabulary, give evidence of something very deficient in their ability to extract meaning from sentences consisting of unknown words in the foreign language.

In nowadays methods for vocabulary learning, much emphasis is put on 'the meaning of a word in a specific context' [3], [4]. The context serves as a help in 'guessing' the meaning of a particular word and, in case there are several meanings, restricts the number of correct meanings to the one(s) applicable to the given situation. Even if someone is able to understand and/or read a foreign language, often a specific text will contain unknown words. Therefore guessing abilities have to be strengthened in vocabulary learning. Furthermore, research [5] indicates that words guessed correctly from the context are better memorized than words that are looked up in a dictionary and/or for which a translation is given.

Schouten [3] proposed several conditions for the optimization of the process of contextual guessing in vocabulary learning:
- The first time a word appears in text, it should appear in a significant (or pregnant) context.
- Often one context will not be enough to elicit a sufficiently definite comprehension, so it will be necessary to offer some consecutive contexts (e.g. by means of a context vocabulary).
- In the target context not too many new words should be presented in order to avoid slow reading and too much 'puzzling' by the students.
- The new words must be important to understand the text in order to stimulate the student to search for the meaning of these words.
- The native-language translation can be given in a unobtrusive way for unfamiliar words, not belonging to the target set but necessary for the composition of good, meaningful texts.
- The difficulty level of the target words must be

taken into account. Important factors are: frequency of the words, length, concreteness vs. abstractness, kind of words (noun, verb, adverb, adjective), 'false friends' or incompatible words.

4. ELLA SYSTEM

In its present form the ELLA system is a combination of subroutines written in the programming language Pascal. It can be used on each personal computer working with the MS-DOS operating system. ELLA was developed in cooperation with the Institute for Perception Research (IPO) [8]. One of the aims of the project is to improve ELLA on the basis of experience with the system in a school setting. The user communicates with ELLA by means of the keyboard or a 'mouse' (a device used to 'point' to a screen position). Whenever possible pointing is preferred to typing because of the expected low typing skills of the users (students of about 13 years old). So, except for test-situations and in certain games, answers can be given by pointing to specific positions on the screen.

ELLA provides the student with a number of options, each of those presenting a different way to 'work' with the material. Options are presented in menus. If options are not available, they are not present in the menu. The system also has a general help-function. The help file contains information about the contents of the options and about the way they should be used.

The corpus of the ELLA system consists of words, descriptions of meanings and context sentences selected from a standard English idiom textbook. The words-to-be-learned can be presented by the system in six different ways ('options'). The simplest option is *list* . If this option is chosen the student merely sees a list of the (English) target words used in the specific session. In two other options the words are presented one by one. In the *browse* option each word is accompanied by its translation(s). In the *repetition* option this translation is initially not present, but can be requested using the mouse. In both options the student can get more information about each word. If the student asks for this information, the relevant context sentence(s) and description(s) of meaning are listed.

There are also two pairs of options in which a sentence is presented. In one of the *learning* options the target word is left out, but a description of its meaning is also on the screen. In this case the student is asked whether he knows which word should fit. If the answer is 'yes' the system responds either by asking ' is this "......." the word you had in mind ? ' or by asking the student to type the word on the keyboard. Depending on the student's response the system reacts with a sign of approval or with full information about the target word. In the other *learning* option the full sentence is presented and the student is asked to give the correct translation of the target word in the sentence. The system's responses to the student's answers resemble those described for the first *learning* option. The other pair of options in which a sentence is presented on the screen is called *test* . In both *test* options the target word is left out of a context sentence presented on the screen. In the first option a description of the meaning of the word is also given and the student is asked to type in the target word. In the other *test* option a target word is suggested. The student is asked to decide whether 'yes or no' the target word fits in the sentence. In either case the system reacts on student's response as in the *learning* option. The last set of options in the present form of the ELLA system is called *games* . Three games are available: Word Scramble, Master Word and Spy Code. All three games are more or less based on letter juggling and word recognition. Only words from the set of target words were used.

5. EXPERIMENT

The main research question for the pilot study was: "Does ELLA work ?" or "Do students learn using ELLA ?". In this paper special attention is given to the relations between the options available to the student, the time spent in the options, some measured student characteristics and the amount of learning.

The experiment was carried out at a normal secondary school. Twenty-eight students (20 girls and 8 boys), aged about 13, all of them member of the same school-class, participated in the study. Two experimental conditions were used. In one, called L-, only three options were available: *learning* , *games* , and *list* . In the other, the L+ condition, students could choose among all six options described above. There was an equal number of students in each condition (4 boys and 10 girls). The two groups of 14 students were comparable with regard to prior knowledge of English, as measured with a pretest, and field independence. Seven Olivetti M19 computers were available. So seven students participated at a time, each student working at his or her 'own' computer. There were two try-out sessions, and five learning sessions, each lasting about 45 minutes. An ELLA session started with a pretest. Next came a period during which the student studied the English words using the available options. At the end of the session, a post-test (similar to the pretest) was administered to measure learning gain. Tests were so called "Clozetests", consisting of ten items. A sentence was presented on the screen with the target word left out. A description of the meaning of the target word was also given. The student's task was to answer the question: "Which word fits in this sentence?". The student answered this question by means of the keyboard. Then the system responded with the qualification: "right" or "wrong". After that, the next sentence appeared on the screen.

With respect to the task, i.e. vocabulary learning with the ELLA system, the following learner characteristics were judged to be relevant:

- Intelligence: it can be expected that amount of learning as well as learning speed are related to aspects of intelligence. In this pilot study students' latest report-marks for English, and averaged report-marks for English, German, French and Dutch, as well as for Mathematics and Physics were used as global indicators of intelligence level.

- Field-independence: studies concerned with self-guided learning showed that field-independence or structuring tendency is a relevant factor in this process. As students are working individually in the ELLA experiment it can be expected that field independence plays a role in this study too. Especially in the L+ condition the student must find his own way through the options and make decisions about which option fits him best. Field-independence was measured by a Dutch version of the Group Embedded Figures Test.[6]

- Interest in English and computers: learners generally will show better results when they are interested in the subject. So two questionnaires were filled out by the participants in the study to establish their interest in both the English language and the use of computers.

Learning outcome was measured in several ways. For each session the gain was computed by taking the difference between post- and pretest scores. After the sessions were completed, the average amount of learning for each computer session was computed. Before the first session two paper and pencil pretests were given. One of the tests resembled the "Clozetest", the other consisted of a list of English words which had to be translated in Dutch. The items in these tests were randomly sampled from the items implemented in the ELLA system. After the five learning sessions, students were given two post-tests similar to the the pretests. Again the items were randomly chosen from the ELLA corpus.

6. RESULTS

Three variables were constructed to indicate the amount of learning. The first variable, *session*, represents the average amount of learning per computer session. Scores on the second variable, *cloze* , were computed as the difference of pre- and post-test scores on paper-and-pencil clozetests.

	Both Cond.		Cond. L-		Cond.L +	
	M.	S.D.	M.	S.D.	M.	S.D.
session	3.43	1.35	3.26	1.17	3.61	1.53
cloze	4.20	4.38	5.11	3.77	3.29	4.88
words	4.94*	3.21	4.00**	2.64	5.82	3.53

(* n=27 ** n=13)

Table 1: Gain scores on *session, cloze* and translation (*words*) tests. (each condition: n=14)

The third variable represented the amount of learning derived from the words translation pre- and post-test. This variable is called *words* . Means and standard deviations of the three variables representing amount of learning are presented in table 1. Measures are given for the whole group as well as for the separate conditions (L- and L+).

	session	cloze	words
Both cond.			
session	1.00		
cloze	.31	1.00	
words	-.01	.06	1.00
Condition L-			
session	1.00		
cloze	.15	1.00	
words	.24	.59*	1.00
Condition L+			
session	1.00		
cloze	.46*	1.00	
words	-.19	-.10	1.00

* p <.05   ** p< .01   *** p< .001

Table 2:   Correlations between gain scores
          (each condition: n = 14)

Table 1 shows that learning gain is positive in both conditions, but the standard deviations of all variables are substantial. The means of the overall measures *cloze* and
words in the L- condition differ from those in the L+ condition, *cloze* being larger in the L- condition and *words*
being larger in the L+ condition. However none of these
differences is statistically significant.

Table 2 shows that *cloze* and *words* are positively correlated in the L- condition, but not in the L+ condition. A
comparable difference in relationships is found for *session*
and *cloze* . In this case a significant positive correlation
exists in condition L+, but no such correlation is found in
the L- condition. Correlations for the group as a whole are
not significant.

In table 3, the variable *English* represents the report-
marks for English, the variable *language* represents the
average score on Dutch, English, German and French and
the variable *science* represents the average score on mathematics and physics. These variables show a positive correlation with the amount of learning per session, *session* .

Scores on the Embedded Figures Test are called *Geft* and
scores on interest in English and computers are called *interest English* and *interest computers* respectively. As shown,
these interest scores are positively correlated with *cloze* .
For each session the percentage of time spent on each
available option was calculated. Afterwards the percentages were averaged over the 5 experimental sessions.

Table 4 shows means and standard deviations of these averaged time expenditure variables. In this table, *choice* represents the percentage of time spent in choosing between
options. Large differences exist between students' time expenditure during the main ('learning') part of a session. In
figures 1 and 2 the percentage distribution of the options is
given for each session separately, respectively for condition
L- and L+.

In condition L- a clear relation exists between *session* and
the time spent in the *learning* option (r = .67, p<.01). In the
L+ condition no such clear relation was found, neither for
learning nor for *test* . As can be seen in figures 1 and 2 the
'dominant' option in L- is *learning* while in L+ this is the
test option. In this last condition there is a shift from the
learning option towards the *test* option towards the end of
the five computer sessions. In condition L+ students did
spend significantly more time in the test option in lesson 4
and 5 as compared to lesson 3 (respectively t = 2.62,
p< .05 and t = 3.44, p< .01). For the time spent in the
learning option the situation is reversed, i.e. in lesson 5 significantly less time is spent in this option than in lesson 3 (t
= 2.79, p < .05). It seems likely that students in this condition began to choose this Test option more often in favour
of Learning because this option resembled the post-test of
each computer session.

It appeared that there were differences between boys and
girls in time expenditure in both conditions. In condition
L+ there is a significant difference between boys and girls
in the time spent in the *Learning* option (girls 22% vs. boys
6%, t = 2.39, p< .05). In condition L- there also were significant differences in *Learning*, and given the limited number of options in this condition, as a matter of course in
Games. (*Learning:* girls 73% vs. boys 39%, t = 2.51, p< .05;
Games: girls 21% vs. boys 54%, t = 2.35, p< .10).

	session	cloze	words
english	.42*	-.18	.18
language	.44**	-.09	.07
science	.34*	-.25	.04
geft	.21	-.12	.23
inter.Engl.	.03	.38*	-.03
inter.comp.	-.13	.45**	-.13

* p< .05   ** p< .01   *** p< .001

Table 3:   Correlations between student characteristics
          and gain scores (both conditions: n=28)

	Cond.L-		Cond.L+	
	M.	S.D.	M.	S.D.
learning	63.04	30.41	17.79	18.36
browse	n.a	n.a	9.90	10.75
repetition	n.a	n.a	8.41	10.61
test	n.a	n.a	45.21	19.05
games	30.62	27.39	10.82	10.83
choice	4.87	3.42	6.83	2.12
list	1.49	1.28	1.05	.81

Table 4: Time expenditure during sessions
         (each condition: n = 14; n.a: not available)

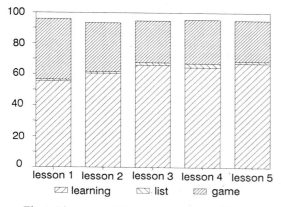

Fig. 1: Time expenditure per session, condition L-

7. DISCUSSION

A general conclusion from this experiment is that the students indeed showed a significant learning gain. No significant differences however were found between the experimental conditions of Ella. Especially the mean amount of learning per session seems to be determined by learner characteristics, i.e. mean report-marks for English, the other foreign languages and mathematics and physics.

The *games* option contributes little to learning gain and seems to be used (especially in the L- condition) as an 'escape' from the learning task. The L+ condition shows that this option can be omitted entirely if alternative ways of learning, i.e. self-testing, are available. This finding is especially important because the games used in the learning system were aimed at and embedded in the learning task, contrary to much courseware where games are in no way related to the task.

Students who reported interest in computers did not learn better than those who did not. This contrasts with results of an unreported study [7] of some years ago where interest in computers correlated positively with learning gain. Our hypothesis is that this contrast is due to the introduction of computers at Dutch secondary schools in the past few years, which caused an increased familiarity with computers.

An interesting observation was made by the experimenters with respect to the games activities. In the experiment several students expressed verbally after two or three lessons that they would switch from playing (games) to learning. Apparently the feedback given in earlier lessons gave them the insight that games were not effective in learning vocabulary with ELLA.

Measured differences between girls and boys in 'explorative' behavior are attributed to a possible difference in learning style [2].

Interestingly only on the *session* score in condition L+ , girls significantly performed better than boys (girls m = 4.11, boys m = 2.33, p< .05). In relation to this difference between boys and girls in time expenditure it should be noted that boys are significantly more interested in English **and** in computers. Further analysis showed that in the condition L- 'good' students (with high scores on *English* , *language* , and *science*) spent a relatively long time in the *learning* option and less in *games* . In the L+ condition 'good' students spent relatively little time in the option *repetition* . In this condition *interest English* and *interest computers* are related to *learn* and *test* : the higher the interest in English and computers, the more Testing activity and the less Learning activity. Students with a high interest in computers and English are probably more explorative. Explorative behaviour, however, only pays off in the long run, and apparently five lessons are not enough to show the possible effectiveness of this kind of behaviour.

REFERENCES

[1] A. Bork, Learning with personal computers, Harper & Row, New York, 1987.

[2] L. Corno, R.E. Snow, Adapting teaching to individual differences among learners. In: Wittrock, M.C. (ed.), Handbook of research on teaching. New York, 1986.

[3] C. Schouten - Van Parreren, Woorden leren in het vreemde talen-onderwijs, Amsterdam, 1985 (Dutch).

[4] F. Twadell, Vocabulary Expansion in the TESOL classroom. In: Croft, K., Readings on English as a Second Language, Cambridge, 1980.

[5] S.A. Stahl and M.M. Fairbanks, The effects of Vocabulary Instruction: A Model-Based Meta-Analysis, Review of Educational Research, 1986, 56, 1, 72-110.

[6] H.A. Witkin, P.K. Oltman, E. Raskin & S.A. Karp, Manual for the Embedded Figures Test. Palo Alto, 1971.

[7] Don Bouwhuis, I.P.O. Eindhoven, personal communication

[8] H.A.A. Otten, Het ELLA-systeem: documentatie van de ontwikkelde software. IPO rapport, no 499, 1985.

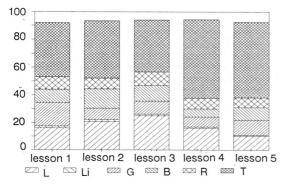

Fig. 2: Time expenditure per session, condition L+.
(L=Learning, Li=List, G=Games, B=Browse, R=Repetition, T=Test)

COMPUTERS IN EDUCATION, F. Lovis and E.D. Tagg (eds.)
Elsevier Science Publishers B.V. (North-Holland)
© IFIP, 1988

Lexivisual Tools Design for Language Learning

Rolf Ferm, Mikael Kindborg, Anita Kollerbaur
CLEA Computer-Based LEArning Environments Laboratory
Department of Computer and Systems Sciences
University of Stockholm
S-106 91 Stockholm
Sweden

Abstract

The design of a computer-based tool for language learning is described in this paper. The objective is to suggest a new approach to language learning through the use of a new medium. Prototyping and user involvement are the main characteristics of our systems development method. Ideas also derive from professional experience in the communication field and from research on human-computer interaction. Examples are given of hypotheses proposed for the design prior to testing, as well as results from test evaluation. The overall conclusion is that the the design process has proved successful. It points to an innovative method for language learning through the use of a functioning tool for creating lexivisual word lists.

1. Design Considerations

The methods and tools applied for systems development naturally influence results. Prototyping, suggested recently by MacKenzie (1987) and Steed (1987), includes students as important actors in educational program development.

Various CLEA projects since 1973 (Kollerbaur et.al 1983; Ferm et.al 1987) have involved users in prototype development. In an iterative process, prototypes are continuously tested and revised. The testing is done in the laboratory and in field tests. Interface design can cause misunderstandings (Frye 1987) both in the operational and instructional aspects of a program. With prototyping such problems are revealed during the development stages.

A team developing innovative uses of interactive systems for education, should be interdisciplinary and - in addition to students and teachers - consist of subject specialists, designers with advanced knowledge of computer potentials and the use of media, and implementation experts.

Our concept of tools for learning was developed in the PRINCESS project (Kollerbaur 1975; Kollerbaur 1983). It is based on the cognitive perspective on learning, first introduced by Piaget (1973) and Bruner: As learners we construct knowledge actively, rather than discover ready-made knowledge passively. We build individual models and theories, based on our own experiences and our own perception of reality. A computer-based learning environment should stimulate the user to explore new concepts and ideas.Therefore an approach where the system guides and assesses the learner is less likely to be successful. It is important that the user should be the controlling party. Our system has the flavour of a tool box or a laboratory.

Experiences from human-computer interaction research should be utilized for the design of computer-based learning tools. We also believe it is important for the designer explicitly to refer to design issues from such research.

Besides being a kind of engineering, design is also an art (Heckel 1984, Kindborg & Kollerbaur 1987). Design can only in part be described with formalisms. That is why it is so important to document considerations given and ideas abandoned during program design. Examples of bad design might be as useful as examples of good design.

One can easily be misguided by conventions and established solutions. We were for instance heavily influenced by the Smalltalk-80 system (Goldberg 1983) in the beginning of our work on the lexicon program. Later we found better designs for some parts of the program.

2. On Communicative Interactive Systems

A major problem of human-computer interaction is how to communicate the model or the metaphor of the system to the user in a clear, unambiguous way. Bad communication is responsible for misinterpreted information, incorrect assumptions about current context, ambiguity about what is happening, etc. Good communication can lead to a clearer understanding of the system, reduce the number of mistakes, and stimulate the exploration of system potential.

Communication in interactive systems is mainly based on visuals, i.e text and pictures. Information from the system and visual feedback from user actions are presented on the screen. Therefore the design of the screen presentations is of particular importance.

CLEA studies show how a lexivisual presentation technique (Lidman 1972) enhances human computer communication. It is essential that the presentation has visual totality and that text and picture interact to clarify the information.We know from research that a picture without text can cause communication problems, as it has no single interpretation (Pettersson 1986).

The use of good metaphors increases the user's understanding of a system, and improves communication. A good metaphor communicates differences, if any, between the computerized model and the real model. Otherwise the advantages of metaphors will be impaired. (Heckel 1984).

3. On Communicative Language Learning

Communicative language learning syllabuses, first appearing on the scene some 15 years ago, (Wilkins 1974), make great demands on teacher and learner readiness to explore new methods to meet new challenges. A lot of importance is attached to the interactive aspect of language. The emphasis in the language teaching situation is on the <u>use</u> of the language rather than on the study of language. A learning-by-doing philosophy has evolved from this with a demand for task-oriented environments (Phillips 1986). A task should as far as possible be genuine, one for which authentic language has to be dealt with rather than a task set to deal with a linguistic problem.

Even before the advent of communicative syllabuses it was a commonly known trick of the trade that authentic reading texts, still so fresh from the print that no expert word lists were supplied, have highly motivating effects (Grellet 1981). It is their not being dated and not experienced as part of a language learning materials package that gives such texts an attractive flavour of authenticity.

But such authentic texts were never written with the language learner in mind. This inevitably presents the learner with comprehension problems, which, if not solved, will result in the learner avoiding texts just because they are felt to be too 'difficult'. The learner may thus miss the opportunity to raise the motivation level by getting access to interesting, enjoyable texts.

To meet this particular challenge a variety of pre-computer methods have been tried, some with disproportionately high teacher-learner time and energy tolls to be paid, others with reasonable input-output ratio: the reactivation and further development of mother tongue reading skills, instant teacher vocabulary aid, individual learner dictionary work etc. (Nuttall 1982)

The pre-computer 'shoebox' solution to the problem is based on the reasonable assumption that the heavy workload of looking up dictionaries has to be rationalized, by several members of a group sharing the job. With the 'shoebox' approach, students write definitions of words and phrases, usually in their own handwriting, on cards which they sort alphabetically or otherwise into a box.

In theory the contents of this box are supposed to be easily accessible to all members of the group. In practice a lot of queuing is unavoidable. This is mainly due to the fact that
- one box has to serve several users simultaneously
- multiple categorization is usually not available
- handwriting may be difficult to read.

Although there is enough evidence, in spite of these and other drawbacks, to show that this approach can be made to work, it is evident, too, that its unwieldiness and inflexibility has prevented it from being universally introduced.

This is where the idea of a 'computerized shoebox' came in. The basic idea is that student-designed computer-based lexivisual word lists will serve the double purpose of providing each student with
- an easily accessible mini-dictionary
- an environment suited to exploration for creative writing

4. The Lexicon Program

The lexicon program is in a way a computerized shoebox. It is a tool for describing words by means of text and pictures with a lexivisual approach. It has been implemented in MS-Windows on a PC-AT computer with a colour screen that has a resolution of 640*480 pixels.

General requirements for the lexicon tool are that
- the facilities for editing text and pictures and the database tool should be integrated in the same environment
- the different facilities should be simultaneously available
- the number of functions should be perceived as appropriate for the users and the lexicon problem area
- the database should be accessible in a local area network

One solution could have been to use existing software tools, for instance MacWrite and MacPaint or HyperCard, developed for the Macintosh system. In our view these tools are too sophisticated for the present problem area, at the same time as they do not include important functions. It is important that the tool does not require too much effort to learn and to operate. This is especially true of a learning situation, where the subject area as such has to be in focus.

4.1 Metaphors

The basic concepts (metaphors) in our lexicon program are
- a stack of cards
- a card with a description
- text and picture boxes (inspired by comics)
- a collage model for editing text and picture boxes
- categorization facilities like headings and indexes in a book

The crucial information is contained in cards, lists of headings and lists of words. A number of questions occurred during design. Should there for instance be one or several cards on the same screen? Should the contents of a card card be presented at the same time as the Headings and Words lists?

After some early attempts we decided on the design shown in **figure 1** for the first prototype to be tested with students.

A design with tiled windows was chosen, research having shown that it is easier to use systems with non-overlapping windows (Bly & Rosenberg 1986). This may seem contradictory to our card stack metaphor, and it is in the sense that we cannot look at the contents of several cards at the same time.

4.2 Editing functions

A minimum number of editing functions for text and pictures was chosen to reduce the time for learning and increase efficiency in handling the tool.

The metaphor used, with a card as the limiting factor, excluded functions for page handling. We also decided that functions for handling margins and blocks were not necessary, since the box model provides the necessary flexibility. When a student wants to have a more sophisticated layout, separate text boxes with different sizes can be used.

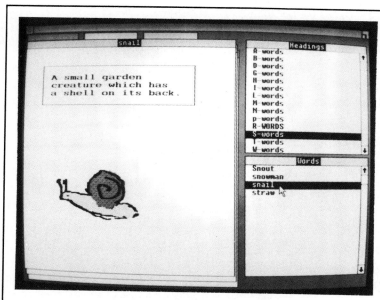

Lexivisual totality: *Important contextual information is shown. Users can see what words are presented and under what heading to find them. The presentation is close to reality by means of a card stack metaphor. The descriptions within a card were designed in a lexivisual fashion with text and picture boxes. The boxes can be arranged as a collage model. The model includes pieces of paper that can be freely positioned and repositioned on a sheet of paper. There are disadvantages with the collage model, too. A box can for instance obscure another box, a presentation can be cluttered etc.*

This as well as the following pictures were created by twelve-year-old children in primary school.

Figure 1. *The appearance of the Lexicon Program.*

Within a text box, functions are available enabling the student to
- move the box within the card
- change the size of a box
- make a copy of the box
- change the font size
- change the frame type (bubbles or squares or none)

The text editor works with word wrap for more efficient use, and in insert mode. Erasing can be done backwards character by character with the delete key and more extensively with the middle button on the mouse. Within a box it is only possible to have one font size. The text is adjusted to the border of the frame with the distance of the font height.

It has been a problem to decide how to handle the text when the user wants a change in box or font size. In order not to frustrate the user with text disappearing, we decided always to present the text written (Smith 1987). This implies an automatic change of the size of the text, so that it will fit into the box. When changing the text size, the box size is adjusted accordingly.

In accordance with our general philosophy of keeping the number of functions down to include the most important painting functions only, we settled for two: colour and the shape and size of the painting tool.

We have tried to avoid strictly predefined single functions. To begin with, we did not pursue this intention for the choice of colours. In our first design the number of colours was fixed, which would have been a severe limitation in a system to be used by children.

In our current design, students can mix colours of their own, based on three primary colours: red, green and blue (see **figure 2**).

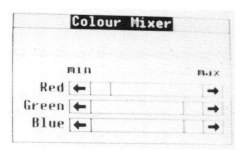

Figure 2. *The Colour Mixer.*

A picture is created within a box, as is the text. A picture box can be moved, reshaped, copied, erased and used as a paintbrush, thus allowing a large number of custom brushes to be created.

4.3 Menus

Commands are given to the system by menu selection. In modern systems two types of menus are used, pull-down menus and pop-up menus both invoked by pressing a mouse button. A pop-up menu is shown at the position where I ask for it, whereas I have to move the mouse to a specific heading in a menu bar in order to bring forth a pull-down menu. An example of a pop-up menu is shown in **figure 3** at the top of the next page.

Figure 3. *An example of a pop-up menu.*

We have chosen pop-up menus because
- they give more flexibility in design, so that. if new menus are to be added, this can easily be done.
- only the alternatives relevant for a decision at a certain moment are shown. The user does not have to bother about which menu to choose. This is in keeping with the idea of lexivisuals.
- it minimizes the number of steps necessary, to fulfill a certain task.
- the screen becomes less cluttered, since menus are visible when used only.
- extensive mouse movement is avoided.

There are also negative aspects of pop-up menus. Users do not see what menus are available. They must either have learned about the menus, or they will have to try to see if there is a menu at a certain point. We assume that this problem can be solved by visualizing where pop-up menus exist, and by good documentation.

4.4 The mouse

When designing the system we have studied how many buttons the mouse should be equipped with. The Macintosh family has a one-button mouse and argue that this is the best. For the Star system, a two-button mouse was chosen, based on research presented in Smith (1982). In our system we chose a three-button mouse, where the left button is used for selection and working with what is seen on the screen, the right button for activating pop-up menus and the middle button for erasing. Our argument for the three-button mouse is that it is necessary in order to establish a consistent use of buttons and a rational way of working. So, for instance, the number of menu levels can be decreased with a three-button mouse.

Our previous experience with children has shown that it may be difficult to distinguish between mouse buttons. Therefore we painted the mouse buttons. We chose yellow (left), orange (middle), and red (right), based on advice given by an expert on the use of colours in graphical design.

4.5 The browser

Searching is accomplished by browsing through the Headings and Words lists. These lists can be characterized as scrollable menus. By pointing at a word in a list, the corresponding card is shown on the top of the card stack. The design of the browser was inspired by Smalltalk-80 (Goldberg 1983). Word and phrases entered can be deleted, changed and sorted. A word or a phrase under Words must relate to at least one heading, but can appear under several headings, allowing non-hierarchal structures. We chose to have two levels in the browser, because one level was not believed to be sufficient for structuring information. More than two levels was considered to be too difficult for children. A more advanced structure is probably necessary for adults.

A possible alternative design of the browser is a network of related nodes, as in NoteCards (Halasz 1987). However, we considered the word list approach more natural in a dictionary. A common task, like looking up alphabetically, is for instance easily accomplished with the current design.

It is also possible to browse through the stack of cards by pointing at a corner of a card in the stack.

The browsing style is motivated by ease of use (as opposed to query languages) and for pedagogical reasons. While browsing through the card stack for example, one might come across information otherwise not found.

Lexical entries can also be looked up by pointing at a word in a text box, like embedded menus (Shneiderman 1986). This is a simplified version of the functionality found in hypertext systems (Conklin 1986).

5. Testing the Computer Aid Design

The lexicon prototype here described is still at the development stage, where more knowledge about users' perception of it and about its functional usability needs to be gained from more extensive tests.

So far a laboratory test and the initial phase of a field study have been conducted. These represent two phases in the prototype development. In the laboratory tests a number of students aged 8-12 and some teachers were under observation while working with the prototype. Development team members observed their work and discussed the computer aid prototype with them. Particular attention was being paid to the design aspects described above but also to other critical incidents (Flanagan 1954), positive and negative.

In order to communicate the model of the system to the user a well-planned introduction and good documentation is needed. Our previous research has shown that there is a definite correlation between the way a computer aid is introduced and described, and the effects and success of its use in educational situations.

So it is that our tests start with an explanatory introduction to the computer aid. A short presentation is made of the basic metaphors used, by referring to their application in reality. The tasks to be performed are normally to be chosen by the users; in some cases we presented users with authentic text material.

This method of not controlling the more detailed tasks was chosen, since in addition to testing different functions it also provides information on the relevance of the functions and the possible need for added functions.

6. Laboratory Tests

6.1 Pedagogical conclusions

Observing users working with a prototype does not only give designers verification or deverification of their design. Preliminary pedagogical conclusions can be drawn from the tests. The users enjoyed working with the program. The role of visualization seemed to be important and will have to be further investigated. Further observations have to be made of user exploitation of the visualization facility to shed light on its effects in a number of cases:

Clarity of definitions: It seems pretty obvious that a picture helps in making the lexical definition of a concrete but unknown object clearer. If the user of a dictionary is no wiser from reading the wordy definition of say a 'scroll' or a 'gargoyle', a picture may be a necessary complement to put the idea across.

Users' frequent, groping attempts to use pictures to define abstract concepts too, seem to indicate that the need for visualization must not be underrated. Concepts of time and space may stand out clearer in the dictionary user's mind, when attempts are made to visualize concepts like 'ago', 'for' and 'before' used of time, or 'within', 'inside' used of space.

Mnemonics: It seems like an extremely reasonable hypothesis that seeing a picture as part of a definition will help the dictionary user not only to understand words and phrases but also to memorize them more easily. What needs to be observed is, however, whether there is a critical point, beyond which the sheer number of pictures creates an overload that hampers the memorization process.

Learning-by-doing: A new type of learning-by-doing activity in language learning may accrue from exploiting computer potentials. The making of lexivisual presentations is in itself a language act. We want to find out what effects, if any, such an act may have on the language learning process.

Also it is part of our present test series to evaluate possible effects on learning of the facility of juxtapositioning these presentations in our prototype and the exploration of new combinations as the basis for creative language work.

6.2 Conclusions related to prototype design

All the users understood and could use the system. No such observations were made as might reveal problems related to the proposed metaphors. The teachers ran up against more problems over details than the children.

The following is a list of examples of some detailed observations:
- It was a surprise to us that no user had any problems over structuring the information at the two levels. It also appeared that the two-level structure of word lists is sufficient.
- Another finding worth noticing was that the collage metaphor was so easily understood.
- The number of functions in the text editor was felt to be sufficient. A fill-in function was asked for in the painting tool.
- Some users made very positive remarks about the painting tool. We had anticipated some problems over using the colour mixer, but none occurred.
- No major problems were experienced over the boxes and the frames. But some observations led us to believe that layout efficiency may improve, if boxes are somewhat bigger when they first appear. On the other hand the users handled the enlargement-diminishment function of boxes without any difficulties.
- The users wanted a more flexible order for the creation of new cards. Options should include the possibility of starting with the Words instead of with the Headings. A case was also made for the alternative route of going straight into the lexivisual area to create definitions.
- Using the browsers and the three-button mouse caused no problems.
- The users did not have any problem to locate the pop-up menus or to choose in menus. A certain confusion appeared when editing a picture box, as some users did not understand which of the menus to use.
- A few functions and possibilities were not utilized. No one used the possibility to create individual brushes.

7. Initial Field Studies

Prior to the field study teachers were given a course on computers and their use for learning. Some of the teachers involved in the studies have also contributed to the design of the lexicon system.

At the time of writing this paper, the system has been used by one class of twelve-year-olds in primary school for four lessons. The class had used a manual 'shoebox' in the classroom before they used the computers. They were given one sheet which described the basic concepts of the lexicon program before the first lesson with the computers. The lessons have taken place in a computer room with eight computers.

During these first lessons the students have entered words from a dictionary. The choice of which words to enter have been their own. They have also looked at each other's words. The next step will be to enter additional words and short descriptions of various concepts.

We have made both structured as well as more unstructured observations during the lessons.

The following are preliminary results from the initial field studies:
- The students had hardly any problems learning how to use the program. Their earlier experience of the 'shoebox' model may have contributed to this.
- The short documentation of the system which was given to the students, was hardly used at all.
- No major problems with the three-button mouse occurred. The colour coding seems to work well.

One disadvantage with colour coding is that users have to look at the mouse in order to identify a button. It is possible that some kind of sensory stimulus should be employed in addition to colour.
- There was no evidence of difficulties in understanding the concept of a hidden menu that pops up, when a button is pressed.
- A lot of time was spent on making pictures. All the students created pictures with almost every word they entered in the dictionary. In some cases there was greater emphasis on picture drawing than on writing text.
- Mixing colours was another time consuming activity. Some colours (e.g brown) are difficult to obtain. Colour mixing is regarded as fun.
- The simple painting tool available - a brush that can vary in size - is sufficient for making reasonably sophisticated pictures. But there were large individual differences.
- The network approach has been successful so far. The students found it stimulating and enjoyable to look at each other's work. This seems to have a positive learning effect.
- The approach which freely allows students to choose what words to enter seems to have a very positive learning effect. In some cases rather 'advanced' words were chosen.
- Technical problems and bugs seem to be far more serious than problems related to the design of the system.
- Students complained about long initial starting-up time (2 - 3 minutes).

8. Conclusions

So far, our approach has been successful. We believe that by employing a design philosophy with subject specialists, professional designers, interface designers etc working together, the number of iterations in the design process has been reduced. Student and teacher participation has been of vital importance.

The more extended field studies will show whether our preliminary results are still valid. First and foremost, these tests are hoped to add to our knowledge of the language learning effects of a lexivisual tool such as ours.

We think the issues of visual presentation and interface design are of vital importance in the design of computer-based learning environments. An additional reason for our initial success is that we have based our design on research results from these domains.

Acknowledgements

This research has been funded by The Swedish National Board for Technical Development (STU),
The Swedish National Board of Education (SÖ) and
The Ministry of Education Computer Programs Committee (DPG).

References

- Bly S. and Rosenberg J. *A Comparison of Tiled and Overlapping Windows*. In Proceedings from CHI'86, Boston, 1986.
- Conklin J. *A Survey of Hypertext*. MCC Tech. report STP-356-86. 1986.
- Ferm R., Kindborg M. and Kollerbaur A. *A Flexible Negotiable Interactive Learning Environment* In Proceedings from HCI'87, Exeter, England, 1987.
- Flanagan J. C. *The Critical incident technique*. Psycol. Bull. 51, pp 327-358, 1954.
- Frye D. and Soloway E. *Interface Design: A Neglected Issue in Educational Software*. In Proceedings from CHI'87, Toronto, 1987.
- Goldberg A. and Robson D. *Smalltalk-80. The Language and its Implementation*. Addison Wesley, 1983.
- Grellet F. *Developing Reading Skills*. Cambridge University Press, Cambridge, 1981.
- Halasz F. et.al. *NoteCards in a Nutshell*. Proceedings from CHI'87, Toronto, 1987.
- Heckel P.*The Elements of Friendly Software Design*. Warner Books, 1984.
- Kindborg M. and Kollerbaur A. *Visual Languages and Human-Computer Interaction*. In Proceedings from HCI'87, Exeter, England, 1987.
- Kollerbaur A. *Status report from the PRINCESS-project*. CLEA 1975. (Swedish text).
- Kollerbaur A. et.al. *Final report from the PRINCESS-project*. CLEA 1983. (Swedish text).
- Lidman S. *Tell with Pictures*. Bonniers 1972. (Swedish text).
- MacKenzie D. *Instructional Prototyping: A CBT Development Strategy*. Proceedings from Learning in Future Education, Calgary 1987.
- Nuttall C. *Teaching Reading Skills in a Foreign Language*. Heinemann, London, 1982.
- Petterson R. *Image-Word-Image*. Presentation at the 18th annual conference of the International Visual Literacy Association. Madison, Wisconsin, Oct.30 - Nov.2 1986.
- Phillips M. *Communicative Language Learning and the Microcomputer*. The British Council, London, 1986.
- Piaget J. *To Understand is to invent*. The Future of Education. New York, Grossman Publishers, 1973.
- Shneiderman B. *Direct Manipulation: A Step Beyond Programming Languages*. IEEE Computer, August 1983.
- Smith D., Irby C., Kimball R., Verplank B. *Designing the Star User Interface*. Byte, April 1982.
- Smith R.B. *Experiences with the Alternate Reality Kit*. In Proceedings from CHI'87, Toronto, 1987.
- Steed M. *Educational Software Evaluation State of the ART*. Proceedings from Learning in Future Education, Calgary, 1987.
- Wilkins D. *Notional Syllabus Design*. Longman, London 1974.

COMPUTERS IN EDUCATION, F. Lovis and E.D. Tagg (eds.)
Elsevier Science Publishers B.V. (North-Holland)
© IFIP, 1988

KNOWLEDGE ENGINEERING FOR CAL

Philip Barker

Interactive Systems Research Group, School of Information Engineering,
Teesside Polytechnic, County Cleveland, United Kingdom.

Computer-based interactive learning systems can provide many novel and effective ways
of implementing a variety of pedagogic processes. The successful realisation of such
systems depends critically upon the utilisation of appropriate knowledge engineering
techniques for the creation of sophisticated knowledge-based structures to support the
operation of adaptable instructional software units. This paper discusses some
approaches to the fabrication of a linguistic interface to support the creation of
such structures.

1. INTRODUCTION

Over the last decade or so the use of the computer
for the implementation of teaching and learning
processes has grown substantially. This growth
has taken place both within academic establishments
and in commercial/industrial environments [1].
Within the United Kingdom developments in the
academic utilisation of computers for learning
have taken place at all levels of the curriculum:
in primary schools [2]; in secondary education [3];
and at the tertiary level – within colleges and
universities [4,5]. This growth of application
within the UK has been paralled by similar developments in other European countries [6,7] and, of
course, in the USA [8], Canada [9,10] and Japan[11].
In this paper the term 'CAL' is used to refer to
any pedagogic application of a computer; CAL is an
abbreviation for 'Computer Assisted Learning'.

Fundamental to the successful utilisation of
computers for teaching is the preliminary process
of instructional design [12,13,14]. Primarily,
this design activity is concerned with the specification of pedagogic processes that achieve particular teaching and learning objectives. The
design process commences with an initial needs
analysis and a formal requirements specification.
These are then used to guide the formulation of
instructional blueprints (or plans) that can be
used to realise the pedagogic objectives that are
embedded within the formal requirements specification. The instructional design process involves
a number of different phases. Three of the more
important of these are: (1) the specification and
organisation of the content of the various learning
units that compose a course of instruction; (2) the
selection of appropriate presentation/delivery
strategies for the different learning units; and
(3) the creation of suitable assessment metrics
that will allow (a) the learner's current states
of knowledge to be assessed and (b) the extent and
effectiveness of skill/knowledge transfer to be
gauged. This paper is primarily concerned with
items (1) and (2) although some aspects of item (3)
are also discussed in the context of deriving
student models.

Sometimes, a special name is given to the second
of the instructional design phases listed above;
it is often called 'media selection'. In a
multi-media learning environment many different
types of resource are likely to be used. Many of
the advantages, disadvantages, merits and limitations of conventional media (such as books,
lectures, instructional television, and so on)
are well known and have been extensively documented in the literature. One of the major
criticisms of most of the 'mass' knowledge
dissemination techniques based upon the use of
conventional media is their inability to cater
for the individual needs of particular learners
or learning situations. Earlier in this section
considerable emphasis was given to the important
fact that there is a growing utilisation of the
computer as an instructional resource. One of
the major reasons why computer-based interactive
learning systems are becoming so popular is the
potential that they offer for overcoming many of
the limitations inherent in the use of conventional
media. This is particularly true in the context
of the individualisation of instruction. A second
major reason for the growing popularity of computer
based study is the active nature of the learning/
training methodologies that CAL techniques are
able to provide.

The pedagogic success of an interactive learning
facility is critically dependent upon the way in
which it is designed and used. A successful
design will undoubtedly require the development
of instructional software (courseware) that is
adaptable to the needs of individual users. In
addition, through the appropriate use of multiple
media [15], this courseware must also be stimulating and pedagogically effective. In this paper
we discuss the importance of knowledge engineering
techniques in the context of the design of courseware for the support of highly interactive CAL
activity.

2. KNOWLEDGE-BASED CAL

Knowledge may be conveniently regarded as the collective total of human experience. This important commodity exists in many different forms. Some examples of the more common and well-known of these are: factual, procedural, conceptual, instinctive, experiential and documented. Because of the wide variety and significant volume of knowledge that exists taxonomies and schemata are often needed [16]. These may be used to structure and organise knowledge into more manageable sub-divisions. From the point of view of knowledge-based CAL an extremely useful way of sub-dividing knowledge is into knowledge domains [17,18]. A domain is simply a segment of some larger knowledge unit (called a universe of discourse) that has been identified and isolated for some particular purpose. Implicit in this statement is our definition of a universe of discourse as an aggregation of knowledge domains according to some unifying theme. Within a domain smaller epistemological units can be introduced. Two important ones are concepts and topics. As we shall discuss below, concepts and topics may be aggregated and inter-linked in various ways in order to produce different views of a learning domain.

that any given learning domain is likely to consist of a number of student views [1..P]. These views will reflect the different backgrounds and current knowledge states of the various categories of learner for which the system caters. Each view is likely to consist of a sequence of learning units [1..N]. Each unit, in turn, has concepts [1..M] that are expressed in terms of component topics and levels at which these topics may be taught.

The types of representational structure involved in our implementation of knowledge-based CAL are illustrated schematically in figure 2. This shows how some particular universe of discourse may be organised into an appropriate set of domains (denoted by squares), concepts (denoted by circles), and topics (denoted by triangles). Inter-relationships between these various epistemological units are represented by directed arcs that connect together adjacent related items. A contiguous sequence of directed arcs that form a common relationship is referred to as a thread. Threads link together concepts and topics within any given learning unit. A thread is often used to represent a learning pathway for a particular student. Different threads may thus be used to represent different learning pathways and, to some extent, different views of a learning domain.

The various levels at which topics and concepts may be taught are represented by the system's repertoire of plans and scripts that cater

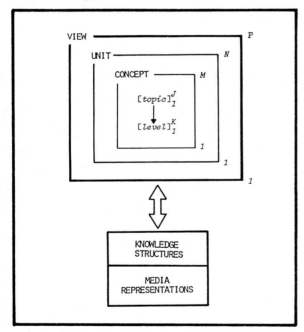

Figure 1 Views of a learning domain.

Our basic approach to knowledge-based CAL is summarised in figure 1. This diagram depicts how knowledge structures and media representations must be made to support multiple views of learning units that are composed of various concepts and topics that may be taught at a variety of different levels. The pictorial notation used in the upper part of figure 1 is intended to express the fact

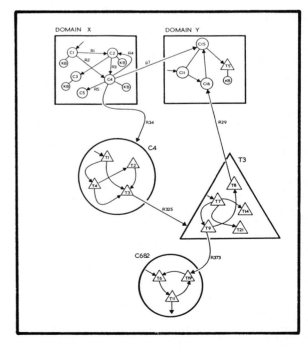

Figure 2 A knowledge-based structure.

for different categories of user. These relationships are indicated below in terms of generic Prolog knowledge structures:

```
concept(...........,<script>).
topic(.............,<script>).
usertype(<category>,<script>).
user (<identity>,<category>).
```

A user's category may change dynamically thereby forcing a change in script level. The system is therefore able to adapt and thus exhibit some sensitivity to the individual needs of particular user types. Currently, plans and scripts are manually produced. However, in principle, it should be possible to facilitate the dynamic generation of each of these types of item through the use of heuristics that are developed as a result of machine learning activity [19].

Structures of the type shown in figure 2 form the underlying basis for our approach to knowledge-based CAL. Obviously, our implementation is heavily dependent upon the development and application of appropriate knowledge engineering techniques. Within this current project there are two areas where these techniques are being employed. First, for the development of an authoring facility that enables structures of the type shown in figure 2 to be created. Second, to represent the organisation of the knowledge embedded within the instructional resources that are used to support teaching and learning operation. Each of these aspects of our work is discussed in turn in the remaining sections of this paper.

3. AUTHORING FOR KNOWLEDGE-BASED CAL

Several authors have commented on the severe limitations of the currently available methods of generating courseware material [4,8,20]. In the light of these comments we have been investigating ways in which artificial intelligence methodologies might be used to improve both the authoring process and the student's interface to the learning materials that are embedded within sophisticated knowledge-based structures similar to that illustrated in figure 2. This section of our paper therefore presents an overview of the work we have been undertaking towards the realisation of a linguistic interface that is capable of allowing courseware authors to create and manipulate these types of structure.

When designing an authoring facility for use with an interactive CAL system two levels of design need to be considered. First, there is the conceptual level in which the functionality of the author's interface is specified. Then comes the level of design that is needed to support the implementation phase. This latter phase is concerned with using the available interface technology and fabrication tools in order to realise the functions specified in the initial design stage. Each of the above aspects of our work is described in the remaining parts of this section.

3.1 Conceptual Design

The conceptual command set which we propose should form the basis for a courseware author's interface to our system is presented in figure 3. At present the commands fall into three basic categories that fulfil the higher level functional requirements of structure creation, navigation, and display, respectively. Each of these command subsets is briefly described below.

The creation commands enable domains, concepts and topics to be created and inter-linked in various ways. The command subset listed on the left-hand side of figure 3 therefore provides the courseware author with a set of tools with which to generate knowledge-based structures of the type previously illustrated in figure 2. As we discuss later (under the title of media representation), a further set of commands is now needed in order to create knowledge bases (KBs) for different concepts and topics and also enable instructional material to be introduced into the system. We are currently working on the design of an appropriate subset of commands to achieve this.

Navigation commands enable users of the system to move around their knowledge-based structures and explore the representational frameworks that they have created using the creation commands that were described above. Currently, the navigation command set contains only seven primitive operations. The Move-to command allows any node within the currently active domain to be made the user's present node of interest. A domain (within its parent universe of discourse) is made active by means of the Select command. In contrast, the Enter command makes the logically initial node (marked with an arrow in figure 2) the commencing point for system exploration. The Next and Prior commands allow node-at-a-time traversal of the framework. Similarly, the Follow-Thread facility allows an organised series of nodes to be accessed in a pre-defined order. The Exit command deactivates the currently active domain making a prior domain (if one exists) the active one.

In order to provide a facility that enables courseware authors to examine (in a global fashion) the logical structure of the frameworks that they create, a system browser facility is available. This presents views of the knowledge based structures in ways that are easily assimilated by their users. The browser is controlled by a logical command set that is channelled on to the physically available control primitives of the target hardware. The browser maps the actual knowledge-based structure on to a 'graphics window' that is controlled by the subset of primitive commands listed on the right-hand side of figure 3. These commands allow the complete structure to be displayed or sections of it to be isolated and viewed in greater detail. Provided colour graphics hardware is available the command set enables the author to display concepts, topics, links and threads in colours that are most meaningful to his/her particular authoring activity. One important feature that we have not yet considered and which must be investigated is the control of the view that particular authors have of the system. Controlled viewing is likely to be implemented by means of a Block command that prevents certain authors looking at certain types of object or segments of a shared knowledge-based structure.

3.2 Interface Implementation

In order to implement the linguistic interface described in the previous section we have been using a version of Prolog that runs on a Prime 9755 minicomputer system [21]. Our reasons for choosing Prolog for the initial implementation of the interface were: (1) its highly interactive nature; (2) its rapid software prototyping capability; (3) the ease with which it allows the creation of data bases; (4) the potential extensibility of data base relations and clauses; and (5) the facilities it offers for the manipulation of list structures. This latter reason is particularly important since lists are extensively employed to represent most of the aspects of the knowledge structures of the kind shown in figure 2.

Essentially, the interface system consists of four major components: a data base; a data dictionary; a command interpreter; and a snapshot facility. Within the data base each epistemological entity class used within our system is represented by an equivalent Prolog relation. As new instances of any of the allowed entity classes are generated new clauses are inserted into the data base thereby extending the number of entries within its parent relation. These relations are listed in table 1 in order to illustrate the nature of their arguments.

For each of the relations listed in table 1 the first argument is used to provide a naming facility; subsequent arguments are then usually list structures that specify ownership and interconnection details. The data dictionary (which is also implemented as a Prolog relation) is used in a global way to keep track of each object's name, its entity type and its ownership details.

The command interpreter provides the author's operational interface to the authoring system. Its purpose is to analyse the text strings typed by the user, check that these represent valid commands and, if so, implement them. Each command offered by the interface is implemented as a series of Prolog goals. Obviously, textual command driven systems have severe limitations and so one important future development that we will need to undertake is an investigation of pictorial

Creation Commands	Navigation Commands	System Browsers
Make-Domain[X]	Select Domain [Y]	Show All
Make-Concept[C1] in Domain[X]	Enter	Move [Up/Down/Left/Right/In/Out]
Link[X→Y] in Domain [P] called [R1]	Move-to [T23]	Show Concept(s) [Q,...] in Domain [Z]
Link [X] in Domain [Z] to [Y] in Domain [G] called [R7]	Follow-Thread [T2]	Show Topic(s) [R,...] in Concept [J]
Make-thread [T1] from [R1,R2,R3] called [J]	Next [Concept/Topic]	Show Link(s) [P,Q,...] in Domain [T]
Make-KB for concept [Q]	Prior [Concept/Topic]	Show Thread(s) [S,T,V,...]
Make-Topic [T23] within Concept [C2]	Exit	Show Concept(s)... Colour [W]
Make-Topic [X32] within Topic [T23]		Make Topic(s)... Colour [J]
Delete [T34]		Make Link(s) ..... Colour [M]
		Make Thread(s) ...... Colour [S]

Figure 3 Conceptual command set to support knowledge-based CAL.

Table 1 Prolog Relations for the Linguistic Interface

```
domain(<name>,<contents-list>,<linkage-lists>).
concept(<name>,<contents-list>,<linkage-lists>).
topic(<name>,<contents-list>,<linkage-lists>).
link(<name>,<to-object>,<from-object>).
thread(<name>,<contents-list>).
datadic(<name>,<entity-class>,<owner-list>).
```

dialogue methods that might be usefully employed to facilitate authoring. Some initial design for such a facility (based upon the use of a mouse, icons, windows and pull-down menus) has already been undertaken [12,18]. However, significantly more development effort needs to be conducted before this type of authoring interface can be made operationally available to courseware developers.

The snapshot facility is responsible for generating pictorial representations of the current status of a knowledge-based structure. Unfortunately, this facility could not be implemented easily within the current version of Prolog that we are using - primarily due to the absence of any graphics primitives. Consequently, this function had to be provided by a post-processing facility programmed in Fortran. Although inconvenient, the mechanism by which this graphics processor operates is fairly straightforward. When this authoring option is selected (perhaps via the Show All command listed in figure 3) the command interpreter simply places a copy of the current status of the system data base into a text file. This is then used by the graphics processor to create pictorial views of the knowledge-based structure. It is hoped that future implementations of our system will be undertaken using a microcomputer version of Prolog that embeds appropriate graphics primitives [22] - thereby eliminating the need to adopt the approach we are currently using.

4. MEDIA REPRESENTATION

Through the knowledge-based structures that have been described in the previous section we are able to provide courseware authors with an instructional design environment that enables the basic framework of a learning domain to be mapped out. The knowledge structures that are generated interactively at the designer's workbench [12] allow relationships between learning elements to be specified. However, the detailed pedagogic nature of those learning elements is not necessarily specified at the time the structures are produced. As we suggested at the end of section 2, this aspect of courseware production is dealt with in a subsequent phase of the instructional design process - media selection.

As we have described in detail elsewhere [1,4,15, 23], wherever possible we advocate the use of the multi-media approach to the implementation of

learning and training processes. When selecting appropriate media it is important to consider how the available alternatives can be used to best advantage. Where several candidate media present themselves for consideration, a variety of other factors may also need to be taken into account before a final choice is made. For example, cost effectiveness, communication bandwidth, ease of use, interactivity, and ease of sharing may all play a part in determining the optimum media mix to be used in any given situation. Of course, media selection will also be strongly influenced by the nature of the pedagogic processes to be implemented and the characteristics of the learning/training processes to be supported.

Obviously, the most useful media will probably be those that are able to support knowledge and skill transfer using textual display, graphic/pictorial forms, and sound. Naturally, an authoring facility must provide mechanisms whereby each of these modes of knowledge transfer can be efficiently utilised by the courseware author and, the results of his/her labour then appropriately embedded within the host media that have been selected to support the instructional processes that are to be undertaken. Unfortunately, there are few (if any) really adequate tools available to support this aspect of the courseware production process. In view of this we have been giving considerable thought to the design of an instructional designer's workbench and the nature of the software tools that such a workbench should make available [12].

One important tool that we feel should be available is one that provides a facility to enable authors to create and maintain a 'concept dictionary'. This concept dictionary must allow its users to keep track of the concepts (and/or topics) that they introduce and the media upon which these concepts are represented. It must also provide facilities for the instantiation of concepts - allowing for the fact that these instantiations may be retrieved from any of the media supported by the workbench. Because of its potential importance as a workbench component we have been modelling and exploring the properties of a prototype concept dictionary generator using Prolog as the implementation language.

The generic knowledge structure used to build a simple concept dictionary and a segment of a Prolog representation of such a dictionary are each illustrated in figure 4A. Given that a

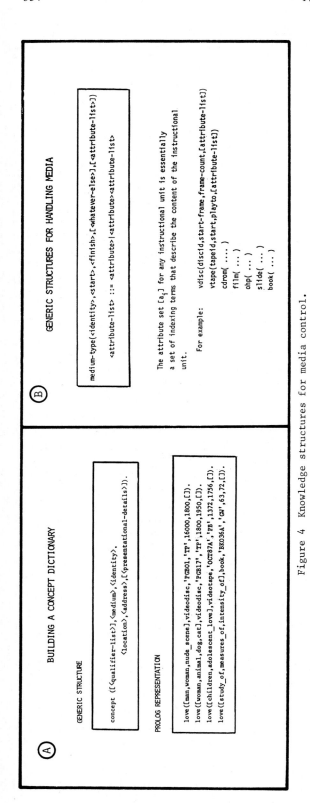

Figure 4   Knowledge structures for media control.

concept dictionary can be created it becomes possible to use this dictionary to answer questions of the form:

```
Where can I find
        - a piece of text,
        - a picture,
        - a picture sequence,
        - a sound effect.
        - a narration,
        - a reference,
        - a piece of equipment,
        - an algorithm,
        - a learning strategy,
            etc,
            relating to concept X?
```

Answering such questions depends critically upon our ability to develop search algorithms that will access the Prolog data base and retrieve the details that are required. We are currently involved in specifying and implementing these algorithms.

An important type of imperative command that the workbench must support is one which requests the display of particular types of material at the workbench itself. For example, an author might make a request of the following form:

```
Show me the video disc
        representation(s) of concept X.
```

In order to support requests of this type two major problems have to be overcome. First, a number of generic structures are needed for handling media representations of instructional material. Second, facilities must be developed to enable the control of external storage media from within Prolog. The types of structures that we are currently exploring from the point of view of media representation are listed in figure 4B. Because of the powerful facilities that it offers we have been particularly interested in the use of video disc as a storage medium for multi-media instructional resources. This medium is also attractive from the point of view of the ease with which images (and image sequences) can be retrieved. Consequently, we have been actively involved in developing Prolog software to enable the control of a number of video discs that are attached to the author's workbench. Again, using Prolog, we are developing appropriate algorithms (in terms of goals such as findall(X,Y) and findany(X,Y) where X is a concept and Y is a medium) that are able to search structures of the type shown in figure 4 and extract the information needed to retrieve pictorial knowledge from the video discs and display it to their user. Although we are some way from final implementations of these facilities the results that we have achieved to date are extremely encouraging.

5. CONCLUSION

Computer assisted learning methods are having a significant impact upon knowledge transfer for instructional purposes both in academic instit-utions and in commercial organisations. Too often, however, the very laudable aims of CAL are thwarted by inadequate and inappropriate courseware. Consequently, this paper has emphasised the need for instructional software that is effective, efficient and adaptable to the needs of individual learners. One of our funda-mental tenets is that CAL can meet these needs provided appropriate knowledge engineering methodologies are developed and are rigorously applied to the courseware development process. Unfortunately, implementing knowledge-based CAL is a complex process due to: (1) the many different types of user likely to interact with the instructional system; (2) the wide range of dialogue levels needed to support effective communication; and (3) the difficulties associat-ed with providing multiple views of shared knowledge domains. In this paper we have described the approach that we have been adopting in order to generate a framework within which to investigate some of these problems. As soon as it becomes easily possible to create and maintain the types of knowledge-based structure that we have described in this paper an attempt can be made to utilise them to support the generation of adaptive and flexible courseware for CAL applic-ations.

REFERENCES

[1] Barker, P.G. and Yeates, H., Introducing Computer Assisted Learning, Prentice-Hall, Hemel Hempstead, 1985.

[2] Russell, T., Computers in the Primary School, Macdonald and Evans, Plymouth, 1985.

[3] Watson, D., Developing CAL: Computers in the Curriculum, Harper and Row, London, 1987.

[4] Barker, P.G., Author Languages for CAL, Macmillan Press, Basingstoke, 1987.

[5] Courseware Directory, FEU Courseware Unit, London, 1987.

[6] Leiblum, M.D., Derks, K. and Hermans, D., A Decade of CAL at a Dutch University, Computers and Education, 10(1), 229-244, 1986.

[7] Whiting, J. and Bell, D., (eds), Tutoring and Monitoring Facilities for European Open Learning, Elsevier/North-Holland, Amsterdam, 1987.

[8] Bork, A., Learning with Personal Computers, Harper and Row, New York, 1987.

[9] Gillies, D.J., CAL in Canada: Innovations and their Sources in Teaching and Learning, Computers and Education, 10(1), 221-228, 1986.

[10] Proceedings of the 5th Canadian Symposium on Instructional Technology, Ottawa, 5-7 May, 1987.

[11] Terada, F., Hirose, K. and Handa, T., Towards Self-paced Learning Support System, 39-44 in Proceedings of the IFIP 5th World Conference on Computers in Education, Norfolk, Virginia, USA, July 29 - August 2, edited by K. Duncan and D. Harris, North-Holland, Amsterdam, 1985.

[12] Barker, P.G., Towards an Instructional Designers Intelligent Assistant, paper presented at ETIC 87, University of Southampton, 1987.

[13] Romiszowski, A.J., A New Look at Instruct-ional Design. Part I. Learning: Restructuring One's Concepts, British Journal of Educational Technology, 12(1), 19-48, 1981.

[14] Romiszowski, A.J., A New Look at Instruct-ional Design. Part II. Instruction: Integ-rating One's Approach, British Journal of Educational Technology, 13(1), 15-55, 1982.

[15] Barker, P.G., A Practical Introduction to Authoring for Computer Assisted Instruction. Part 8: Multi-media CAL, British Journal of Educational Technology, 18(1), 25-40, 1987.

[16] Christiansen, D., Artificial Expertise, IEEE Spectrum, 24(1), 25, 1987.

[17] Barker, P.G., Knowledge Based CAL, 137-143 in Proceedings of the 5th Canadian Symposium on Instructional Technology, Ottawa, Canada, May 5-7, 1986.

[18] Barker, P.G. and Proud, A., A Practical Introduction to Authoring for Computer Assisted Instruction. Part 10: Knowledge-based CAL, British Journal of Educational Technology, 18(2), 140-160, 1987.

[19] Self, J.A., The Application of Machine Learning to Student Modelling, Instructional Science, 14, 327-338, 1986.

[20] Whiting, J., Conceptual Design of Advanced Authoring and Tutoring Systems, paper submitted to 'Creating Adult Learning - International Conference on Educational Design', Middelburg, The Netherlands, 1987.

[21] The University of Salford LISP/Prolog Reference Manual, Second Edition, University of Salford, 1984.

[22] Borland International Inc., Turbo Prolog Owner's Handbook, Borland International, Scotts Valley, CA, 1986.

[23] Barker, P.G., Multi-media CAL, chapter 13 in Tutoring and Monitoring Facilities for European Open Learning, edited by J. Whiting and D. Bell, Elsevier/North-Holland, Amsterdam, 1987.

COMPUTERS IN EDUCATION, F. Lovis and E.D. Tagg (eds.)
Elsevier Science Publishers B.V. (North-Holland)
© IFIP, 1988

A SOFTWARE TOOLKIT FOR HUMAN-COMPUTER DIALOGUE DESIGN AND DEVELOPMENT

NOEL WILSON, ARNOLD McALPIN, IAN McCHESNEY

University of Ulster, Shore Road, Newtownabbey, Co Antrim, Northern
Ireland, BT37 0QB

This Paper describes a Dialogue Design Toolkit (DDT) which has been created
to assist with interface prototyping and generation of the human-computer
interaction component of educational software. The current implementation
of DDT is associated with menu-based interfaces; a review of the underlying
design principles for menu design, upon which the DDT facilities are based,
is included. An extensive qualitative evaluation of the system is
provided.

1. INTRODUCTION

A basic requirement in the design of the Toolkit
was to incorporate features which were consistent
with the notion of "good dialogue design".
Research in this area is extensive but, in
general, does not specifically relate to
educational software design. In order to meet the
particular needs of the educational software
designer [1,2] it has been necessary to examine
the various issues arising in research and assess
their relevance to an audience consisting of a
typical undergraduate course-year group in the
subject specialism associated with the software.
(The issues described throughout the paper relate
to courseware design in an undergraduate
environment). It is therefore appropriate to
consider dialogue aspects associated with the
naive user, presentation and content of error
messages, integrated help features and error
correction mechanisms for erroneous input.

The relationship between good dialogue design
criterion and the ability to realise these on a
specific item of hardware; that is, the student's
computer terminal, is also a necessary design
consideration.

The following sections of this paper discuss the
design philosophy associated with the Toolkit; its
application to interface design and current work
associated with its developments.

2. REVIEW OF EXISTING DIALOGUE DESIGN SOFTWARE TOOLS

There are already several dialogue design tools in
the marketplace. In a number of instances these
tools are a direct consequence of research work,
particularly when the tool has been developed in
an academic setting. It is also interesting to
note the variety of methodologies associated with
the dialogue design process, for example, state
transition diagrams [3,4], dialogue programming
rules [5] and graph theory and path algebra [6].

The SYNICS2 system produced at Leicester Polytechnic, by Edmonds and Guest [4], consists of two
modules; one to specify the dialogue logic and the
other for the specification and transformation of
input strings. This system is based on state
transition diagrams. BASYS, [7] developed by
Gaines and Facey is an implementation of the
dialogue programming rules concept and illustrates the programming technique necessary for the
implementation of a number of useful dialogue
concepts, for example "reset" and "backtrack".
Alty used the notion of path algebra theory and
state transition diagrams in the development of a
system called CONNECT [6], which is an implementation of an adaptive interface facility.

Commercial software is also available, where many
packages tend to concentrate on prototyping
facilities; for example, to permit the dialogue
designer to "paint" screen/form designs and these
before potential customers. MANTIS, marketed by
Cincom Systems Ltd, is a typical example of this
type of system. This package commences with a
blank screen onto which the designer constructs a
set of screen layouts, in an interactive manner.

Work which preceded the design of DDT, investigated the use of a dialogue schema [8] in the
specification of a human-computer dialogue, where
the schema comprised a set of inter-related nodes,
each node possessing a series of attributes consistent with "typical" educational software dialogue characteristics. A prototype of this
concept was devised which also illustrated the
ability to implement a multi-facet interface, for
example offering both a menu and command driven
interface to the same item of software.

3. FUNCTIONAL REQUIREMENTS FOR THE TOOLKIT

A study of the research literature associated with
man-machine interaction (MMI) has been a necessary
prerequisite to the establishment of the
functional requirements of the Toolkit. Considering the need to facilitate a spectrum of

ability levels, within an educational environment, the idea of a multi-level adaptable interface is perhaps most appropriate [9]. However, a difficulty in establishing this form of interface relates to the need to encourage active academic staff participation in the creation of the dialogue text: the volume of information associated with multi-level interfaces being much greater than a single-level alternative.

In terms of the three most frequently used and most widely accepted forms of dialogue, Schneiderman [10] lists menu, prompt and response and keyword driven interfaces. The design of DDT facilitates the inclusion of these three dialogue formats within any educational package, although the present implementation only includes generation facilities for the menu option. Several guidelines are already available which are specific to menu-based interfaces; for example, conciseness of menu item text, ordering and identification of menu items, spacing of information and titling.

Choice of hardware both for the implementation of the Toolkit and the interface designed through its use, is dictated by availability within the University. The majority of terminal devices support the Digital Equipment Company VT100 protocol, which provides sufficient video features in order to realise the facilities required for "attention getting", "highlighting", "cursor positioning" and "screen fragmentation". Unfortunately colour is an unsupported facility.

The "dialogue node" representation [6] was chosen as the most appropriate technique for the design of the dialogue framework.

The final consideration in the Toolkit design refers to the method of assembly of dialogue information relating to a specific educational program. In order to design and develop a Toolkit offering maximum flexibility, it was considered appropriate to assign external Dialogue Information Files (DIFs) to each style of dialogue created for a program; it would therefore be feasible to offer DIFs for a variety of menu, command based and prompt-and-response type interfaces. In this way it is possible to achieve a multi-lever user-interface for any parent application, as illustrated in Figure 1.

In order to achieve this form of interface (via DIFs) it is necessary to devise a Toolkit consisting of essentially two main components:

... Tools to create the DIF - the Dialogue Generator (DG)

... Tools to manage the interaction between a DIF and parent program - the Dialogue Manager (DM).

The conceptual model of the Toolkit is illustrated in Figure 2.

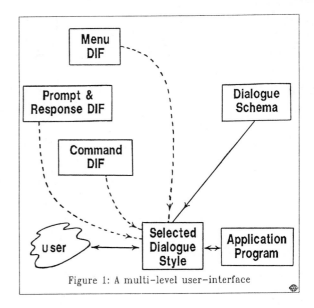

Figure 1: A multi-level user-interface

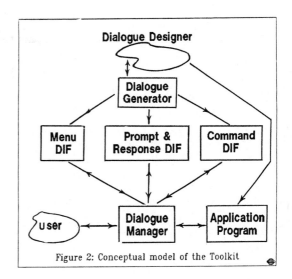

Figure 2: Conceptual model of the Toolkit

4.   TOOLKIT DEVELOPMENT

4.1   Design of Dialogue Information File (DIF)

The DIF structure must facilitate both the textual content of the dialogue and the organisational detail necessary for its display. Implementation of the node attributes associated with the dialogue schema [6] requires careful choice of constraints, for example, to implement a menu-style interface each menu must be presentable within the maximum number of lines available on the display. The limits chosen are as presented in Table 1. To facilitate fast and efficient access to attribute records, the DIF has been designed as a random access file with relative addressing. Information for each node is held sequentially and each respective node is also sequential. However because a particular dialogue schema could involve many branches, node accessing via relative addressing was considered to offer optimal DIF access. A 'pointer algorithm' has been devised to evaluate the offset, from a 'node base', for each specific node attribute. This pointer is an important feature of the Dialogue Development Toolkit, common to both the Dialogue Generator and Dialogue Manager.

TABLE 1: Node attributes for a menu style dialogue

	Attribute	Maximum Number of lines (80 chars/line)
1	Menu subtitle	1
2	Question text	2
3	Menu list	8
4	Instructional text	1
5	Input validation mask	1
6	Help	5
7	Error text	2
8	Node (O/P buffer) management	1

There is also a requirement to provide detail on the hardware characteristics to be associated with each node attribute. In accordance with the concept of "uniformity and consistency" [3] it is only necessary to elicit this information from the designer once and apply it uniformly across each node within the DIF. The detail is stored as a vector of "dialogue parameters" within a "header" created at "the top" of the DIF. Typical information includes the video attributes associated with the menu title and text (for example; bold, reverse video, blinking), character sizes associated with various menu entities and features for help and error diagnostics.

4.2. The Dialogue Generator

The function of the Dialogue Generator is essentially one of obtaining node information from the dialogue designer and compiling the DIF, for the parent application. This function is illustrated in Figure 3. The interface associated with the generator comprises two distinct styles:

... menu selection for set-up of dialogue parameters;

and

... prompt and response for specifying node attribute detail.

Table 2 illustrates the bank of dialogue parameters and associated video features available to the designer of a menu-style dialogue.

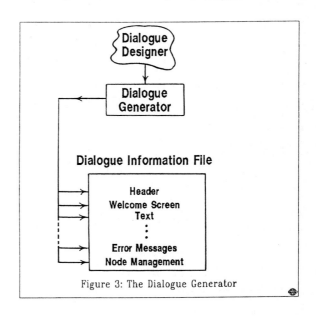

Figure 3: The Dialogue Generator

TABLE 2: Dialogue Parameters for a menu style dialogue

		Field in Header Record
1	Subtitle video features	F2
2	Main title character size	F3
3	Menu item video features	F4
4	Item label type	F5
5	Selection field video features	F6
6	Menu item selection technique	F7
7	Question text video features	F8
8	Instructional text video features	F9
9	Help text video features	F10
10	Error text video features	F11

Note: video features are:

1 Normal; 2 Blinking; 3 Bold;
4 Reverse Video; 5 Underline

The detail associated with each node attribute is prompted for in a sequential manner, and the dialogue designer has a facility whereby the entire node information may be loaded to the DIF as either a single operation or as a sequence of phases. The dialogue generator also provides primitive editing features which enable the correction of node data or the addition/deletion of nodes from within an established dialogue schema, and hence DIF.

One particular node attribute which involves more than merely loading textual data, is the validation mask. The "top level" of input validation refers to the type of input item; that is integer, real or character type variable. The designer must specify the data type associated with each input node, and for numeric data a "second level" of validation must be specified. Specification of "second level" validation must be of the format:

... * > X;   ... * < X;   ... X < * < Y

where * denotes the input item (type integer or real) and X, Y specify limits. Validation of X and Y are an integral feature of the dialogue generator. For character type input, the designer may specify a mask which passes:

. any alphanumeric character(s)

. selected, and specified, keywords

. characters within a stipulated range; x < ch < y

A maximum of 10 keywords, each consisting of a maximum of 7 significant characters, is permitted for the keyword mask.

The dialogue generator also facilitates the specification of additional 'parent program data,' essentially of an administrative nature, for example, program name and title.

4.3   The Dialogue Manager (DM)

The primary function of this component of the Toolkit is the "management" of the run-time dialogue between student user and educational program. The activity schedule of the manager is illustrated in Figure 4. In the present implementation of the manager, DIF attachment to parent application is established using program name and usercode identifiers. University of Ulster undergraduate computer users are designated usernames derived from their course-year group; this coding system provides a convenient, yet simplistic, method of choosing a DIF whose style best matches the user's experience and level of computing expertise. For example, it is assumed that students associated with Humanities and Education courses will be more naive than those within Science and Technological-based disciplines; furthermore a final year student is assumed to possess a higher ability level than a fresher. Having passed both username and program name

(parameters passed to the manager from the operating system) it is possible to generate the DIF filename and attach it to the parent application. Subsequent to this task, the manager extracts the "header information" and establishes the video attributes to be used for the menu layout on the associated hardware device.

Upon initiation of a dialogue between student and parent application, the dialogue manager is passed the identifier of each dialogue node as it is activated. Using the node identifier, the manager can interrogate the DIF to extract the textual information to be displayed within the dialogue framework, or menu template. In response to user input, the manager passes control to the input parser where the user's input stream is matched against the node validation mask; acceptable input is forwarded directly to the parent whilst erroneous data is rejected, the appropriate error message displayed and the dialogue status returned to "await re-input of data".

During input string validation the manager allocates priority to checking for special dialogue features, typically "help", "backtrack" and "reset" operators. Upon receipt of one of the directives, the manager either retrieves additional information from the DIF or establishes the new active node identifier, using the internal representation of the dialogue schema. The "pointer facility", referred to earlier, is the key feature within the dialogue manager and is especially relevant to the operation of "backtrack" and "reset" facilities.

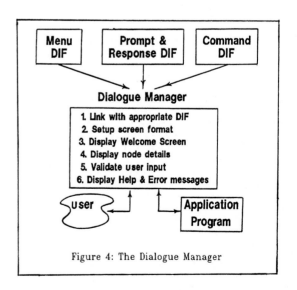

Figure 4: The Dialogue Manager

Implementation of the dialogue manager is currently undertaken as an integral component of the parent application; that is, the manager is realised as a controlling procedure. It is also feasible to detach the dialogue manager from the parent application and implement it in a "loosely coupled" fashion. In this latter approach the manager would be realised as a stand-alone program with parameter passing, to the parent, being established via a parameter file mechanism or "process mailbox" (an operating system facility for interprocess communication).

5.   EVALUATION

A qualitative evaluation of the present implementation of the Toolkit has been conducted. The approach adopted was to elicit views from both practising dialogue designers and end-users of educational systems. In advance of the evaluation interviews each evaluator was presented with an overview of the Toolkit facilities; this approach was considered appropriate, so that information of specific relevance to the Toolkit facilities and objectives could be obtained.

During the evaluation interview each evaluator was invited to construct a trivial Dialogue Information File (DIF) using the Dialogue Generator (DG), and incorporate their implementation of the DIF with a previously established parent application package. Each evaluator was also invited to use an already created DIF associated with a prototyped system and comment on its features. The results of the evaluation sessions may be classified as those relating to:

... Choice of certain "good dialogue design principles"

... Dialogue Manager (DM) features

... Dialogue Generator (DG) features

5.1   Comments On Design Principles

The main comment received related to the general applicability of the "backtrack" feature. Instances were cited in which evaluators felt that it was not always feasible to "undo" certain actions, for example "file deletion". The basic problem with this dialogue feature is the need to implement partial backtracking and identify phases of a dialogue schema within which backtrack would not be applicable, or should be inoperative.

A further comment related to the desire to provide comprehensive validation masks as a mechanism for exclusion of input parameters, which could cause the application program to "terminate unexpectedly". The observation made was that "syntactic validation" did not necessarily ensure a combination of "acceptable" input parameters defining a realistic, or practical, model. This problem could often arise in simulation or modelling programs whenever a user prescribes a set of parameters inconsistent with a realistic model. Whilst no further dialogue features are available to eliminate this type of problem it was recognised that validation masks were a provider of "partial protection" to the parent program, and not "total protection".

5.2   Dialogue Manager Features

The main observation on this aspect of the toolkit related to the implementation of the in-built help facility. Whilst the interface to the Dialogue Manager (DM) was also designed to conform to good design principles, a number of evaluators felt there was a need to "reduce confusion" by removing all other information from the screen whilst displaying help text.

A further series of comments related to the implementation of "backtrack" and "reset" facilities. The choice of symbols for both operations were termed "cryptic" and considered to be "badly located" on the particular keyboard used. These points were accepted by the designer of the Toolkit. However the problems were really those of hardware ergonomics and not strict dialogue design. An alternative realisation of the features using keywords, as oppposed to keysymbols, was suggested as a realistic solution.

A further observation also related to the "backtrack" feature: it was the opinion of several evaluators that previously input data items should be displayed as the backtrack mechanism moved the pointer to each preceding dialogue node. In a similar manner, the need to clear erroneous input fields upon the initiation of data editing was also suggested. In the light of experience in the use of the facility both points are considered valid.

Overall, evaluators highlighted the robustness of the Dialogue Manager, and the effectiveness and clarity of its screen design.

5.3   Dialogue Generator Features

The main comment associated with this component related to inadequate editing features. For example, the process of including, or deleting, a node is cumbersome, even though the ability to undertake this task is highly desirable. Some further comments related to style of delimeters and validation mask operators; these issues are really of an ascetic nature and not directly associated with MMI principles.

6.   IMPLEMENTATION

The current version of DDT has been developed using Digital Equipment Corporation's (DEC) implementation of FORTRAN '77 on a DEC VAX 11/780 system. A number of DEC-specific language features have been used, and DEC Run Time Library routines associated with Screen Management (SMG) are used for screen and cursor addressing. The choice of implementation tools, whilst not portable to other manufacturer's systems, have provided an optimum development environment and are consistent with the environment used within the University for the development of an educational software library service to the undergraduate community.

7.   CONCLUSION

The dialogue development toolkit which has been described provides facilities for creating menu-based interfaces, independent of the parent educational software. The features of the Toolkit facilitate easy modification and maintenance of the interface, a desirable attribute particularly whenever educational systems are in frequent use by a large audience.

Experimental use of the facilities have been encouraging; the concept of prototyping being invaluable in reducing preliminary design developing time, and the ability to separate the overall software design and development task into two components; interface and processing modules, being particularly significant.

Current developments should enable a full system to be produced around the initial concept of the dialogue schema. Once this work has been completed a full user evaluation will be necessary before proceeding with "live usage" of the tool. However, qualitative feedback from both educational software developers and end-users is encouraging and sufficient to reinforce the potential of the project.

Further work is in progress to expand the facility to include "form design" features and examine ways in which multi-media interfaces may be incorporated.

8.   ACKNOWLEDGEMENT

The authors would like to express their gratitude for the help and financial assistance received from the Institute of Informatics at the University of Ulster.

REFERENCES

1. HEINES, J., Screen design strategies for Computer Assisted Instruction (Digital Press, 1984).

2. LANDA, R.K., Creating Courseware - A Beginner's Guide (Harper and Row, New York, 1984).

3. GUEST, S.P., The use of software tools for dialogue design. Int. J. Man-Machine Studies. (1982) Vol. 16. pp163, ff.

4. EDMONDS, E., and GUEST, S.P., The SYNICS2 user interface manager, in: Human-Computer Interaction - INTERACT '84 Proceedings, (1984) pp375-378.

5. GAINES, B.R., The technology of interaction - dialogue programming rules. Int. J. Man-Machine Studies. Vol. 14, pp133 ff.

6. ALTY, J.L., The use of path algebras in an interactive adaptive dialogue system, in: Human-Computer Interaction - Interact '84 Proceedings, (1984) pp351-354.

7. GAINES, B.R., and FACEY, P.V., BASYS - a language for programming interaction, in: Computer Systems and Technology Conference proceedings, (1977) pp251-262.

8. WILSON, R.N., Designing user interfaces for educational software, in: Moonen, J., and Plomp, T., (eds.) EURIT '86 - Developments in Educational Software and Courseware, (Pergamon Press, London 1987).

9. ROBINSON, J., and BURNS, A., The use of multi-level adaptive user-interfaces in improving human-computer interaction, in: Symposium on Empirical Foundations of Information Software Science, (Atlanta Plenum 1984).

10. SCHNEIDERMAN, B., Software Psychology pp238-241, 247-266. (Winthrop Publishers Inc., Cambridge, Massachusetts 1980).

COMPUTERS IN EDUCATION, F. Lovis and E.D. Tagg (eds.)
Elsevier Science Publishers B.V. (North-Holland)
© IFIP, 1988

ADAPTABLE INTERACTIVE CBL DESIGN TOOLS FOR EDUCATION

PETER CHANDRA

Computer Assisted Learning Group, Computing Unit,
University of Surrey, Guildford, Surrey, GU2 5XH, England.

The design team approach to the development of Computer Based Learning (CBL) courseware relies heavily on the effective communication between different members of the team, including up-to-date paperwork and documentation. This is important for the accurate and efficient overall coordination of the courseware design, and for future maintenance of the courseware developed. These require a greater investment in time and finance, resources that the field of education can hardly afford. General purpose application packages (or content-free software) could be adapted so as to provide interactive tools for CBL design, particularly in the areas of design specification and storyboarding, flowcharts, user documentation, and initial courseware evaluation analysis. This is especially helpful for the CBL designer/author who does not know, or want to be involved in the detailed programming, or who does not have access to development tool kits or powerful workstations. In this paper, some specific examples are given using readily-available general purpose software packages developed for microcomputers, especially for the Macintosh microcomputer.

1. INTRODUCTION

One of the approaches in developing good Computer Based Learning/Training courseware is the Design Team Approach [1,2,3]. Such a model is shown in Figure 1 which depicts the different expertise provided by the team members for the various design stages [4]. The design team approach, however, has been hampered by the lack of suitable authors who have the technical appreciation of how their ideas and teaching strategies can be implemented on a computer. In the development of Computer Based Learning (CBL) courseware, it would be useful if design tools were provided for the author/designer to be able to place his ideas in computer form so as to obtain an immediate visual feedback. This is particularly helpful if the author does not want to be involved in the programming of the courseware, but wants to ensure that the final outcome meets his requirements without the need for very detailed specifications or reliance on the programmer's interpretation of an author's brief specification - hence, one of the reasons for the increasing popularity of authoring systems or development tool kits. However, most authoring systems and tool kits still require a certain amount of programming skills which most subject authors do not possess [5,6]. In addition, most subject experts in the primary and secondary education level have access only to microcomputers (if any at all) and not minicomputers or workstations, and so are not in possession of powerful development systems or tool kits on which to formulate their ideas directly on to

the computer screen. There is also the problem of making sure that any design documentation is kept up-to-date with both the designers and programmers keeping well informed of the latest changes made.

Adapting existing content-free software can be advantageous to designing CBL materials, especially when the designer or his educational establishment does not have the resources or finance to develop appropriate design tools to meet the designer's specific needs. The advent of system software that provides concurrent running of software in an environment where data can be transferred between software packages has further stimulated such ideas. This paper provides some suggestions of how generally available application software can be adapted or used as interactive design tools for programming-shy designers, following the design model shown in Figure 1. Although the examples given are based on software designed for the Macintosh microcomputer, the principles, ideas and suggestions written here could be implemented on software for any microcomputer. In this paper, the word "author" will refer to the writer of this paper, and the word "designer" to the author and/or designer of an intended CBL courseware.

2. DESIGN SPECIFICATIONS AND STORYBOARDS

It would be helpful to the designer at the initial design stage (Stage 1 in Figure 1) to be able to implement different ideas directly on the computer, so as to see and "get a feel" of the effect of his ideas on the computer screen - what the author calls "interactive design". It is a level in-between paper-based design and rapid-prototyping. This is where the designer would be able to formulate his ideas directly on to the computer and, with the aid of some software application programs, provide an immediate visual feedback of his ideas. In addition, any instruction that was needed to be communicated to the computer programmer could be made on-screen, with additional notes to himself or other evaluators.

As an example, this author uses two general software packages - a graphics editor (MacPaint) and a sequencer (Slide Show Magician) to accomplish such an effect. Figure 2 shows the Design Specification Sheet (DSS) layout that was designed to provide the template for this interactive design storyboard. It is, in effect, a graphics file, i.e. a

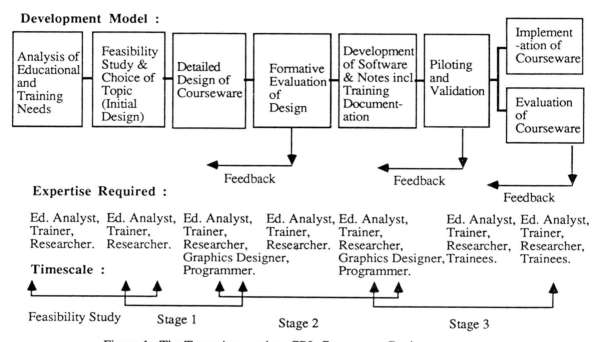

Figure 1. The Team Approach to CBL Courseware Design

MacPaint document. A box is provided to demarcate the screen design, with two boxes provided for instructions to the programmer and for the designer's notes. The designer first draws out the intended screens (with the graphics editor) and saves it as separate files. These become his design specification sheets (Figure 3 provides an example). He then uses the sequencer (Slide Show Magician) to link in the separate graphic files according to the sequence in which he thinks he would like the program he is designing to be presented. Added facilities of interaction and routing are provided by this sequencer. For example, the designer is able to control the time delay between each screen/design specification sheet display, and to route it according to screen location pointers. With the sequencer, the designer is thus able to obtain an immediate "feel" of how the intended courseware should be presented.

Using a third program, which acts at the system level, to provide the running of programs concurrently or to have different programs co-resident (in this case, the Macintosh program is called Switcher), the designer is able to toggle between the graphics program and the sequencer program. The designer is thus able to make any changes he sees necessary on the design specification sheet, and by toggling on to the sequencer program, he is able to "run his program" and obtain immediate feedback on the flow and execution of his program. In this way, the designer can interactively design his specification sheets. Once satisfied, a print-out can be obtained providing the necessary design documentation for the programmer to implement on a computer, a list of the intended sequence, and further notes for the designer. Interactive and automated design specification sheets are thus achieved.

3. STRUCTURE/FLOWCHART GENERATOR

An important documentation needed by designers and programmers at the initial and detailed design stages of the development process (Stages 1 and 2 in Figure 1), is the flowchart or structure chart. For educational or training courseware, where the level of routing required is basic and straightforward, the possession of an outline program (outliner) that has the facility of producing tree diagrams could be adapted to provide an elementary structure chart generator. For example, an outline program called MORE (the Macintosh version of ThinkTank 512 for the IBM pc) has the ability, at a keystroke, to produce tree diagrams from the headings assigned in the outliner program (what they term as "tree charts"). So, for example, Figure 4 shows the headings, including different sub-levels of headings, that have been assigned as outlines within MORE. These, for our purposes, are the "procedures" for the intended software.

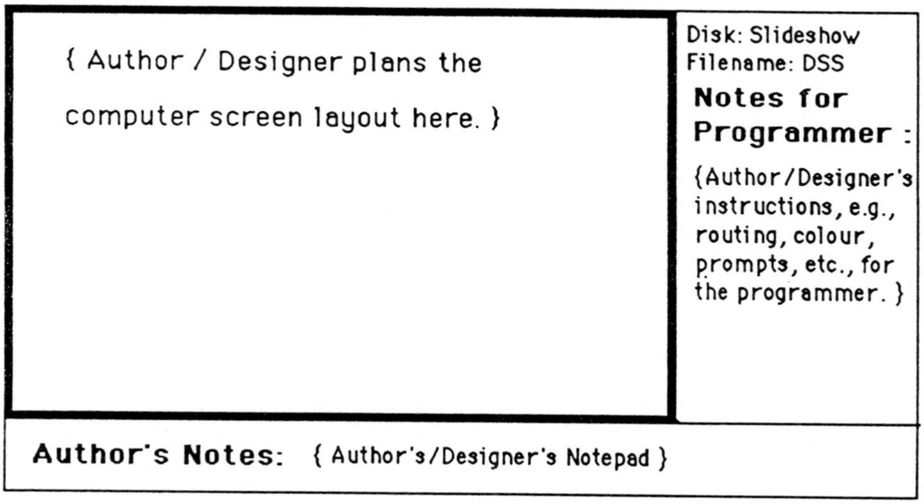

```
{ Author / Designer plans the

computer screen layout here. }
```

Disk: Slideshow
Filename: DSS
Notes for Programmer :

{Author/Designer's instructions, e.g., routing, colour, prompts, etc., for the programmer. }

Author's Notes: { Author's/Designer's Notepad }

Figure 2. Example of a Design Specification Sheet, DSS (a MacPaint Document)

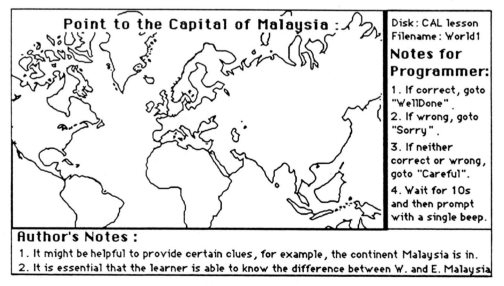

Point to the Capital of Malaysia :

Disk: CAL lesson
Filename: World1
Notes for Programmer:
1. If correct, goto "WellDone".
2. If wrong, goto "Sorry".
3. If neither correct or wrong, goto "Careful".
4. Wait for 10s and then prompt with a single beep.

Author's Notes :
1. It might be helpful to provide certain clues, for example, the continent Malaysia is in.
2. It is essential that the learner is able to know the difference between W. and E. Malaysia

Figure 3. Example of a DSS with author's instructions and notes

```
Intro. to Commonwealth Countries
1.Looking at countries by Continents(*)
    1.1.  Introducing .... Asia (*)
        1.1.1.  Basic Information : Position, History
        Malaysia (*)
            Population (o)
                Repeat until Done
            Climate (o)
                Repeat until Done
            The Capital (o)
                Repeat until Done
            Question/Test (o)
                Q1: Population Profile
                Q2: Relief of country
                Q3: Main towns
                Q4: Profile of capital
                Q5: Simil./Diffs. of E/W Malaysia
                Repeat until 4/5 questions correct
        Thailand (*)
            Population (o)
                Repeat until Done
            Climate (o)
                Repeat until Done
            The Capital (o)
                Repeat until Done
            Question/Test (o)
                Q 1-5
                Repeat until 4/5 correct
        Look through any country again (*)
    1.2.  Introducing ...Europe (*)
    2.   According to Language (*)
    2.1.  Chinese
        2.1.1.  Origins
        2.1.2.  Type of script
    2.2.  English
        2.2.1.  Origins
        2.2.2.  Type of script
```

Figure 4. Headings and sub-headings in MORE

At the stroke of a control key, this set of headings and sub-headings can be made to become a tree chart, which in essence is the makings of a structure diagram. Changes can be made to the outlines and a different tree diagram generated immediately. The use of such an outliner, with its sophisticated wordprocessing facilities and the added facility of a tree diagram generator, can thus provide a very handy interactive tool for the design of simple flow/structured charts.

4.   INTERACTIVE USER DOCUMENTATION

Poor user documentation has led to a number of good software packages being under-utilised. In CBL courseware, it is important to distinguish further whether the "user" is the trainee/pupil or the trainer/teacher (Stage 3 in Figure 1). Appropriate, and thus different "user" documentation, should be written for the different user types (between trainee and trainer, and even between different trainees) if proper implementation and integration of the CBL courseware is to take place [7].

Increasingly, a greater number of user documentation is now being produced on wordprocessors before being printed out. The author's rationale is that if such documentation is on a wordprocessor, why not use a general purpose hypertext program to generate an interactive user documentation? "Hypertext" was a term coined in the early 1960s to describe a non-linear body of information with "links" between documents or different parts of a document, that guides the reader from one to another [8]. At present, such a program (called GUIDE) exists for the Macintosh microcomputer which also provides all the facilities of a powerful wordprocessor.

The skills needed to write hypertext media, however, are not exactly the same as compared to those needed for wordprocessing. More thought has to be given in considering the amount of text to be revealed or hidden, but readily available. In this way, help prompts could be easily embedded to guide the user along the way, only when it is either necessary or called upon. Time will also have to be spent on what and how the writer would want his document to "open-out" and flow. The full power of graphic images and drawings of the Macintosh are also available. This is beneficial where graphic illustrations are crucial to explain better or describe a particular concept or procedure. Other facilities provided by such hypertext programs include the provision of "pop-up" text which could be used as calls for definitions of words, glossary/index, etc. (see Figure 5).

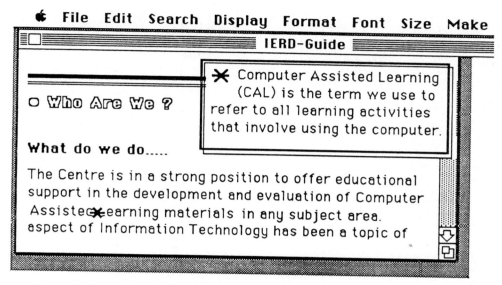

Figure 5. Example of a Hypertext document with "pop-up" window

This "interactive documentation" could be taken one step further to include animated sequences to elaborate powerfully a difficult procedure. For example, using an animated simulation to show a naive user how a computer program is loaded into a microcomputer. The use of such a software application package, as for example, "Videoworks", would be suitable for this type of need. Videoworks is a package which allows different objects/drawings to be assigned as "actors". Such "actors" could be made to "play out" the sequence to illustrate the action required. Taking the above example, a sequence is animated to show the precise way in which the user needs to put a disc into the disc drive and enter the appropriate commands to load in the computer program.

This animation could be activated at the appropriate part of the interactive user documentation by using another general purpose program that generates "macros" (similar to that used in spreadsheets). An example of such a program for the Macintosh computer is called TEMPO. In this way, a specific user action could be suggested by the interactive documentation which involves the pressing of a specific key. This calls up a "macro", which then calls up the animated program and appropriate animated sequence, via the program Switcher. Once the dynamic illustration is over, another appropriate key stroke would bring the user back to the user documentation where he had left off.

It would not be difficult to see that such a combination of general application programs could

also be used as an interactive and dynamic storyboard, where the implementation of the program would be on other types of computers. It could also be possible that these set of programs could be used for the actual delivery of courseware on the particular computer itself. This concept is an adjunct of hypertext, called "hypermedia". Hypermedia is the logical extension of hypertext, encompassing graphics, animation, video, sound, etc. Blocks, or pieces of documents can thus be linked to form multi-webs of information which could be presented to the learner/student in an open-ended but dynamic way [8].

5. AUTOMATED EVALUATION ANALYSIS

It is essential that any CBL development project should have time built in to conduct an initial evaluation of the courseware being produced (end of Stage 3 in Figure 1). This phase of a project has a tendency to be excluded, especially when there is a pressure of deadlines to be met. The analysis of the evaluation might consist of a questionnaire which would provide simple indicators (involving simple frequency counts) of the performance of the courseware, plus a bank of relevant, but short, comments made. This would be sufficient to provide valuable, initial feedback. An automation of this stage would be useful.

One of the ways of achieving this is to provide the questionnaire directly on computer. It is suggested in this paper that this questionnaire is actually a template of a spreadsheet - the questions are the rows of the spreadsheet, and the answers are those to be placed in the columns (normally a rating scale of 1-5). The spreadsheet itself is part of an integrated package with database, chart generating and wordprocessing programs. The questionnaire is completed by the courseware evaluator directly on the computer. Once a number of questionnaires have been completed in this way, the results of each questionnaire (found in the columns of each spreadsheet file) can then be copied on to the columns of a master spreadsheet (with the use of suitable macros). As a questionnaire comes in, the master spreadsheet could be updated. The value of using an integrated package (for example, Framework II on the IBM pc, or Jazz on the Macintosh) is that the values of these columns could be mathematically manipulated with simple statistical functions provided, and the questionnaire results automatically displayed in the form of suitable charts or graphs.

A further idea would be to provide the questions for the questionnaire as records of a file in a database. A library of questions could thus be compiled. Combinations of questions could be found by the use of keywords assigned to specific questions in the database. With the use of specific macros in an integrated package, these questions could be automatically selected from a database and copied on to a spreadsheet which then becomes the template for your interactive questionnaire. In this way, customised questionnaires could be designed, depending on the type of courseware being evaluated and the target audience. For example, the questions directed for a teacher/trainer would be different to the questions needed for a pupil/trainee; while a CAL software could be evaluated and distinguished from a CAD program by using different questions.

6. CONCLUSION

The suggestions discussed in this paper can provide design tools which facilitate up-to-date and immediate feedback. Using general purpose software packages to provide immediate reflection of any changes made in the design, affords an interactive form of designing courseware. Furthermore, using design tools on a computer which generates the "paperwork" can be advantageous as it provides a rapid form of updating of documents. In this way, better record keeping of existing documents and a more efficient form of housekeeping can be established. These interactive design and user documents could be mailed electronically to other design team members, an option particularly helpful if the team is widely spread out geographically. Any printouts obtained

would also be legible, an added advantage when it comes to different handwriting amongst team members !

It is tempting for the designer to seek for design tools that could generate actual software code to be implemented on different computers, i.e. design tools which provide machine-independent code which could be translated automatically for different computers. Maybe the day will come soon when this could be achieved at a price that educational establishments can afford. However, the value of the suggestions provided here in this paper is that these programs are available now for the educational market, and that by using pieces of existing general purpose software, designing CBL courseware could be easier and more enjoyable.

REFERENCES

[1] Beech, G. (1983) Computer Based Learning, Sigma.

[2] Crossfield, L.P. & Hinton, T. (1984) "A Methodology for the Design and Development of CAL Courseware". Paper presented at the Micros in Education Conference, Loughborough, April.

[3] Dean, C. and Whitlock, Q. (1983) A Handbook of CBT. Kogan Page, London.

[4] Chandra, P.; Black, T. and Hinton, T. (1986) "The Design of Interactive Video Training Courseware for Water and Sanitation Engineers in Peru - Some Initial Considerations". Proceedings of the Int. Conf. on Courseware Design and Evaluation, L. F. Lewis and B. Feinstein (eds), Israel, April 8-13, pp 393-398.

[5] Black, T. (1987) "Prototyping CAL Courseware: A Role for Computer-Shy Subject Experts" Paper presented at the Ed. Tech. Int. Conf. (ETIC-87), Univ. of Southampton, 13-15 April.

[6] Hinton, T. (1984) " Authoring Systems in CBT" Paper presented at the conference on CBT organised by the Danish Postgraduate Engineering Society, Denmark, 3 May.

[7] Laubli, M., Pope, M. and Hinton, T. (1985) "Implications for the Cross-Cultural Transfer of Computer Based Education Courseware - A Case Study". PLET 22(3), pp224-229.

[8] Osgood, D. (1987) "The Difference in Higher Education" in BYTE, Feb., pp165-178.

COMPUTERS IN EDUCATION, F. Lovis and E.D. Tagg (eds.)
Elsevier Science Publishers B.V. (North-Holland)
© IFIP, 1988

USING DATABASE SYSTEMS FOR PRODUCING COURSEWARE

Roumen K. Radev

Department of Software Engineering, Institute of Mathematics,
"Acad. G. Bounchev" Str., bl. 8, 1113 Sofia, Bulgaria

This paper consists of two parts. In the first part the role of database systems in courseware production is investigated. Possible links between authoring languages and authoring systems on the one hand, and database management systems (DBMS) on the other, are indicated. In the second part a new authoring tool is proposed - a system for building teaching materials, called SPOM. The structure of SPOM and its authoring language AULA are discussed. It is shown how an authoring language can be "opened" to DBMS and the advantages of this connection are considered.

1. WHAT IS THE SITUATION ?

Computers may be applied in education in many different ways. The preparation of teaching programs or teaching courses, i.e. courseware and then running them on computers is such a way. But the way from the idea to the computer programs is long and the teacher has to pass through several activities, which may be divided into two groups. The first group contains specific (pedagogical) activities and the second is connected with using computers and specialized software tools such as authoring languages or authoring systems. We will consider, in turn, the relation between teachers' activities on one hand and database systems on the other.

1.1. Teachers' activities- do the teachers need database systems?

These activities include (according to [1]):
- collecting information - textbooks, lessons, exercises, notes, courseware available, statistical data about the students, etc.;
- planning the goals to be achieved and how to do it;
- reviewing and revision of the materials together with colleagues and experts;
- describing materials at conceptual level;
- producing materials- getting texts, pictures, tests, etc. into the computer, creating teaching programs and so on;
- translation or making teaching programs comprehensible to the computer;
- testing and correcting by the teachers (authors);
- trial use and discussing the results.

Database systems can help in providing support and preservation for all data needed to prepare courseware and they also can function as an information system for the "courseware building" materials. Database systems allow a uniform method of organization and access (catalogues, files, libraries, etc.).

1.2. Relations between authoring languages and database systems

Authoring languages are authors' tools for development courseware. Some specialists state that there are more than 75 authoring languages, excluding high-level programming languages [4]. A good authoring language must provide facilities for [10]:
- displaying information, usually on the screen. Information may be retrieved from a database system;
- accepting user (student) input (and storing it into a database system for further analysis);
- processing user input. The corresponding algorithms must have at their disposal sample answers, rules for estimating, messages to the users and all these may be stored in a database system;
- identifying locations in program or database (interface to database systems);
- sequence execution;
- recording and manipulating data for the learning process or for later use. In this case, database systems are, perhaps, the best solution;
- user tools available within the context of interactive processor;
- coding convenience, e.g. a variety of alphabets as in PILOT;
- help and utility functions.

The connection authoring language - database systems may give the authors more information and more facility with less effort.

1.3. Authoring systems - can DBMS be a part of them ?

The authoring systems are complex (more or less sophisticated) software systems which enable the authors to create courseware with little or no knowledge of programming. They have two unique functions in contrast to authoring languages [5].

- Course management. It comprises the capability to define or select a particular instructional strategy (e.g. drill, quiz, tutorial, etc.), the specification of response data to be collected, the capability to try out a lesson just created, the control options available to the students, the capability to document lessons and courses.
- Authors' environment. It means that the authoring systems have to adapt to the authors' requirements and to produce different types of interaction for different authors.

These functions may be easier realized when an interface to the DBMS is built into the authoring systems. Having DBMS as storage and retrieval apparatus, authoring systems become more flexible, user- and machine-independent and may provide richer possibilities for the authors. Database systems may play the role of an information - retrieval system which automate routine actions thus permitting the authors to concentrate on subject-matter and lesson design.

1.4. A look at the reality

All considerations up to now are theoretical. Of course, database systems are used in real systems but mostly for storing data about the students' learning or for administrative purposes. Moreover, they are not general purpose database systems (GPDB) but their own subsystems included in an authoring system. The applications of a database system for creating courseware proves to be a most difficult problem. After two years of research work, we have found only a few systems in which authors have been supported in any way by GPDB. These are:
- an authoring system for teaching elementary algebra which uses DBMS GUERY/3000 and runs on Hewlett-Packard [6];
- the system STUDIO for teaching medicine using DBMS DMSII for B1700 [7];
- the system "EKSTERN", implemented at Moscow State University [3]. It uses its own DBMS for both preparing courseware and teaching.

Why are GPDB not preferred? Because the designers of authoring systems have always believed that their own DBMS are better than GPDB; because the GPDB are not sufficiently open to link with other components of authoring systems; because the mastering of new DBMS requires too much time.

These opinions seemed to be true in the mid 70-ies. But now the situation has changed. Newer and newer DBMS are offered on the market for all kinds of computers (mainframe, mini, micro). They support various data structures and possess "friendly", user-oriented languages facilitating development of application products. They may be utilized in a stand-alone way and may be embedded into the programming languages as well. Such GPDB reduce time and efforts needed for development courseware.

Another approach can be seen in such authoring systems like GALTS [8], MUMEDALA [11], BOOK [12, 13]. They offer a collection of software tools which allow the teachers to write different teaching modules or to link a number of such modules together (GALTS, BOOK), to create or update libraries of teaching modules (BOOK), and to use the advantages of new information media (MUMEDALA).

Shortly, we claim that it is worth considering the construction of an integrated courseware development system which enables teachers to construct courseware according to their own capabilities and practical needs. It would be reasonable to involve GPDB as an important part of such a system. They may support the preparation and preservation of teaching materials as well as storing data about the learning process.

2. AN INTEGRATED SYSTEM FOR PRODUCING COURSEWARE

Our ideas about linking GPDB with authoring systems are implemented in an authoring system called SPOM. A "top-down" approach has been chosen in designing SPOM, i.e. we offer a nucleus of software tools and means for its modifying and expanding. By using appropriate tools, end-users can produce various applications.

2.1. A formal model

Let us have a collection of software products (we will call them shortly packages) L1,L2, ...,Ln, n > 1. Each package is destined to carry out one or more data processing functions. Then we define SPOM as a set {L1,L2,...Lk}, k > 1, of packages. These packages can be general purpose high-level programming languages, authoring languages or purpose-built authoring systems, editors (for text, graphics, sound, characters, etc.), database systems, packages for calculations, modelling, and statistical analysis, means for planning and designing teaching programs and courses, word processing packages, facilities for program testing and documentation, expert systems or other artificial intelligence tools, and so on.

We assume, as a rule, that the packages have been developed by experienced programmers and there are no links between them. Nevertheless, it does not mean that SPOM is simply lumping together all the software available. The following four main principles which are a conceptual base for building SPOM have to be applied in each package.

A/ SPOM is an open and dynamically changing environment. There exist compulsory rules for including, excluding and updating of packages, for organizing of joint action of packages, for data management and for interacting with users. These rules are necessary for all packages.

B/ All packages use equal means for entering, updating, storing and spreading of needed information. This information is organized and managed by means of GPDB and a corresponding DBMS.

C/ End-users choose any package in a dialogue mode.

D/ All packages perform their functions, as far as possible, in a dialogue mode.

The first principle necessitates the presence of a special package supervisor to control the whole work of SPOM. Let us denote this package by M.

Adherence to the second principle requires the existence of a separate package for accessing databases. This package consists of two parts: one for accepting and responding to requests from packages and the other for interacting with underlying DBMS. We denote this package by I.

The main role of SPOM is to enable the users less experienced in programming to construct courseware. For that reason there must be at least an authoring language in SPOM. A new authoring language called AULA has been devised in our institute and a package for programming in AULA is offered as a part of SPOM. Let us denote this package by A.

The packages M, I, A form the nucleus of SPOM. Hence, we can consider SPOM as a set $\{M, I, A, L1, L2, ..., Lk\}$, $k > 1$. The packages are developed independently, in accordance with the four above mentioned principles. Each package has to be presented in the form <P, R, H, O>, where the elements have the following meaning.

P means a set of modules which realize package functions. (These are modules which can be run on the computer.)

R denotes a set of rules describing relations between modules in P.

H contains instructional (help) information about the package. This set can be used for organizing (automatically by the package M) a concise teaching course for those who wish to try out the SPOM package capabilities.

O contains description of possible outputs of the package: text, pictures, programs, etc., where the output is stored and how it can be used in further work.

The supervisor package M works as an interpreter of rules describing packages, their relations and the interaction with users.

2.2. The authoring system SPOM

We try to sustain our ideas by practical realization. The result is the above mentioned system SPOM.

The availability of GPDB (and DBMS) is the corner stone of our design. In order to fulfill the second main principle of SPOM we have developed a special language called TABELA (borrowing some ideas from [9]). It can be used in three ways: independently, as a part of our authoring language AULA and from other packages of SPOM. It is important here that the users have at their disposal the same language constructions and may obtain the same results in all three cases. Since the end-users are usually not experienced in programming, the database structure has to be transparent to them. In our case the information is presented to the users as a set of tables. Each table consists of columns and they denote the attributes of the table. Each table has also a unique name (for reference) and (not necessarily) a list of names of other tables being related to this. The advantages of this approach for naive users are well known [2]. Therefore, TABELA is a table manipulating language and the package I is that one which accepts queries expressed in TABELA and retrieves the necessary information from the database. It provides independence of the DBMS employed because it lies between the user interface and the data manipulation language of the concrete DBMS.

In the second place, we have developed a new authoring language, the above mentioned language AULA. By means of AULA the teachers can determine the contents of teaching modules and present them to the students. Students' answers can be accepted and analysed using five embedded procedures. Moreover, the teachers can develop their own procedures for answer analysis. Facilities for arithmetic and symbolic data manipulations have been provided. AULA distinguishes itself by the following features: independence with respect to the subject-matter, expandability, capability for generating parts of teaching modules, separate description of contents and of control structures. The main merit of AULA is that the language TABELA is embedded in AULA. In such a way direct connection between the end-users and the database has been established. This substantially assists teachers in producing courseware, giving them an on-line access to the database. Such a capability is very rare occurrence in today's authoring languages.

The connection authoring language - database is of a great interest in team courseware production. By using SPOM packages, individually or in combination, the experienced teachers can produce different small units or modules of teaching material, which can be regarded as samples for given subject-matter. Furthermore, other users of SPOM may integrate such modules into a complete purpose-built teaching program or course, in accordance with their own needs and understanding. Thus, step by step, a variety of teaching materials can be accumulated and the system capabilities enhanced.

We hope that producing courseware by means of SPOM decreases the need of programming skills, facilitates the teamwork, overcomes some problems of courseware portability, and (perhaps) makes the users' life easier.

Full description of AULA and TABELA can be found in [14]. SPOM has been implemented on CM-4 computers (PDP 11/45 compatible) and currently is being elaborated for IBM PC/XT/AT.

REFERENCES

[1] Dean, Chr. and Whitlock, Q., A handbook of Computer Based Training (Kogan Page, London, 1983).

[2] Ullman, J., Principles of Database Systems (Stanford University Computer Science Press, Stanford, 1980).

[3] Pashin, E.N. and Mitin, A.I., Avtomatizirovannaia sistema obuchenia EKSTERN (Mir, Moscow, 1985, in Russian).

[4] Voyce, St., A Functional Analysis of Courseware Authoring Languages, AEDS Journal, SPRING (1982), pp. 107-125.

[5] Kearsley, G., Authoring Systems in Computer Based Education, Comm. of the ACM, vol. 25 (1982), no 7, pp. 429-437.

[6] Detmer, R.C. and Smullen III, C.W., Course Management Using a Database Structure, Computers & Education, vol. 3 (1979), no 3, pp. 213-218.

[7] Grahne, G., Adaptive Features of a CAL System Based on Information Retrieval, Computers & Education, vol. 6 (1982), no 1, 1982, pp. 99-104

[8] Tait, K., The Building of a Computer-based Teaching System, Computers & Education, vol. 8 (1984), no 1, 1984, pp. 15-19.

[9] Vandijck, E., Towards a More Familiar Relational Retrieval Language. Information Systems, vol. 2 (1977), no. 2, pp. 159-169.

[10] Zinn, K., Requirements for Effective Authoring Systems and Assistance, International Journal of Man-Machine Studies, vol. 6 (1974), no 4, pp. 403-413.

[11] Barker, Ph., MUMEDALA - an Approach to Multimedia Authoring, in: Duncan, K., Lovis, F. (eds.), Proceedings of the 4th WCCE (North-Holland, Amsterdam, 1985) pp. 165-172.

[12] Otsuki, S. and Takeuchi, A., A Unified C.A.L. System for Authoring, Learning and Managing Aids, in: Lovis, F., Tagg, D. (eds.), Proceedings of the 3rd WCCE (North-Holland, Amsterdam, 1981) pp. 249-256.

[13] Otsuki, S. and Takeuchi, A., Intelligent CAL System Based on Teaching Strategy and Learner Model, in: Duncan, K., Lovis, F. (eds.), Proceedings of the 4th WCCE (North-Holland, Amsterdam, 1985) pp. 463-468.

[14] Radev, R., Ekspertnost i informativnost v avtomatiziranite sistemi za obuchenie (Dissertation, Sofia, 1987 in Bulgarian).

COMPUTERS IN EDUCATION, F. Lovis and E.D. Tagg (eds.)
Elsevier Science Publishers B.V. (North-Holland)
© IFIP, 1988

COURSEWARE FOR LSP (LANGUAGES FOR SPECIAL PURPOSES) :

Creating units at will in a selection system.

J. Colpaert
W. Decoo
E. Van Elsen

University of Antwerp (U.I.A.)
Departement Didactiek en Kritiek.

1. Two examples

Marianne Lebon, a French law student, has received a graduate grant to do specialized studies for one year at the University of Bologna in Italy. She has four months to update and expand her mastery of Italian, which she has learnt at an elementary level. The objectives are clear: reactivation and development of basic vocabulary and communicative structures, in order to be able to function on a threshold level in all daily situations; huge expansion of receptive skills, in order to understand lectures and publications on specialized legal subjects.

Joop van den Bossche, a Dutch engineer in dike construction, receives an assignment to go for three weeks to Valdivia in Chile to check the development of a local project. He has one month to learn some specific Spanish which he needs to communicate with his peers. The objectives are clear: limited communicative structures in terms of making acquaintance, greeting, apologizing for his low language level; a series of specific questioning structures which are part of the checking assignment; a large amount of specialized terminology to fill these structures.

Both Marianne and Joop could profit from computer-assisted language training, provided the courseware matches the objectives precisely. The challenge to make specific courseware for these cases and myriads of other divergent cases, seems staggering. With a selection system, however, it becomes possible to generate the exact learning units needed, in a matter of seconds.

2. A selection system with databases

In language courseware production, one of the most crucial capabilities of the computer is the power of immediate selection and combination from databases. Indeed, for a large part of linguistic material, the computer is able to select and to combine at will precise elements from a wider corpus, so that this selection matches precisely the initial situation of particular students.

The traditional distinction which is often made between "open courseware" and "closed courseware" is not valid for a selection system. "Open courseware" is understood as authoring systems and authoring languages, which offer frames allowing the input of any material. It gives freedom to the producer of courseware to make the learning units he wants, but it requires a lot of work and the final result is a fixed unit that cannot be changed easily, except by more similar work.

"Closed courseware" is viewed as already tailored material, immediately available as such on the market. The lessons do not require any work in setting up, but they have a compelling content. A major problem of such courseware is the inadequate correlation with specific needs, like those Marianne and Joop have.

What we present, however, is a different system, combining the advantages of both the open and the closed courseware. The user still has the freedom to determine his own content, but it requires from him less than one minute of easy work. If the databases on the disk are well organized, using high quality procedures and index sequential organization, the program can generate thousands of different units, matching the most varied lessons.

The principle of a selection system is simple: a maximal learning content is stored in a database within the program. Simple menus allow the teacher (or the student, if so desired) to select precisely the elements that are to be studied and practiced, according to a specific learning situation. Any elements that are not to appear in this situation can thus be discarded. The selected elements are automatically placed in the didactic frame of the courseware, which itself can be manipulated in various ways: display mode, practice forms, help functions, testing, scoring, selective randomization, etc.

The menus are easy to work with, so that the user need not program or type any words. Only the cursor control keys and the "enter"-key are necessary.

3. Contents

3.1. Standardization of the files

This entails complex research and preparation, whereby some subjective decisions cannot be avoided. The following four files constitute a normal base, although other files are not excluded:

i. Fundamental lexicon
Here we use the common fundamental vocabulary lists, usually based on frequency and disponibility. As such, our Vocapucesfile for French, which contains approximately 5 000 items, draws from several sources: the older "le Français Fondamental" by Gougenheim, which is based on frequency, the "Niveau-Seuil" of the Council of Europe, which we use for general and specific notions, and "Eventail", a specific method containing also highly modern words. All the items have been placed in short semantic contexts which sustain their meanings.

ii. Basic communicative structures
The work done by the researchers around the "Niveau-Seuil" or "Threshold Level" of the Council of Europe provides us with a large taxonomy of language

functions that is extensive enough to cover almost all linguistic intentions. The file can, of course, be adapted at any moment.

iii. Specialized terminology
This remains the richest and most difficult part of the endeavour. Our team has developed automated instruments to analyse source material and draw up frequency lists which can be compared with other lists, according to all possible variables. It is necessary to work in close collaboration with representatives of each field involved and draw heavily on work already done in terminology databases. At the same time, definitions, polysemic remarks, updates, etc., must be given.

iv. Specialized communicative structures
It is clear that, parallel to the specialized terminology file, we need a file that covers the language functions specific for a given register. Within the language of a sales-representative, the communicative skill of demonstrating/explaining will be more elaborate than the one of turn allocation, which is more likely to be crucial in the speech of a manager.

3.2. Database organization

The aim of the courseware is to train specific units, matching precisely specific needs. To make our point clear, let us start from the situation of a German heart surgeon who is appointed for some training sessions at the English speaking University of Lagos in Nigeria. His linguistic needs can be pinpointed quite accurately and the computer program can select and combine the training units needed. As such, he will have to learn to say a sentence like "I advise you not to tear up the external pericardion".

To reach this level of precision, each item in any file is defined according to a number of criteria, of which the following are the most important, because they are immediately available to the user:

i. Frequency selection
We start from the principle that frequent items are normally learned first and that the decrease in frequency may dictate the order of presentation. Each item is so coded that

constant selections are made possible on the basis of these "degrees of difficulty". For the learner, it means that the program can be used in a 'chronological' order. A beginner, who still has to learn most of the language, would enter on a low level and define small pieces to work with. An advanced student could try higher levels and/or work with larger entities.

When a user goes through the program in this chronological order, the context presenting each item will contain only words studied previously. This strategy sustains the semantization and integration of the new material. It is part of the larger didactic framework in which the programs are developed.

ii. Speech acts selection

The taxonomy of speech acts itself gives the codes to be attached to each communicative structure. Thus, an expression like "I advise you not to..." has the code I.8.5, meaning: I = Order / I.8 = Propose to someone to do himself / I.8.5 = Dissuade.

iii. Notional selection

The largest files are the lexical files, containing on the one hand the fundamental lexicon, and on the other hand the specialized terminology. All items are coded according to their respective taxonomies.

The fundamental lexicon follows the repartition of the Niveau-Seuil, adapted to our needs into 193 semantic fields and subfields. Thus "to tear up" bears the code C.9.3.2, meaning: C = Specific notions / C.9 = Physical aspects / C.9.3 = Movement of the body + object / C.9.3.2 = Act upon the object.

The specialized terminology follows the taxonomy developed for the particular field. All items have to be coded according to a structure of logical entities. For our example from medicine, the term "external pericardion" would carry the code II.2.1, meaning: II = internal medicine / II.2 = circulatory system / II.2.1 = parts of the heart.

iv. Grammatical selection

Finally, the user could also concentrate on certain parts of speech, or a combination of these. He may notice problems with adverbs of time, or prepositions to express a location, or adjectives to define quality. To that effect, a code to identify the word class is added to each item: noun, adjective, pronoun, verb, adverb, preposition, or conjunction. To these we also add expressions.

3.3. Combinability of all selections

In a matter of seconds, the user can determine a unit chronologically, meaning any level or combination of levels, combined with any speech act or series of speech acts, combined with any notional field or series of fields, combined or not with any limitation in parts of speech. Thousands of combinations are possible. For instance:
- Chronological approach combined with a notional limitation:
    - All the items, from the beginning until level 3, about "food".
    - All the speech acts where "food" is relevant.
- Notional approach combined with a grammatical limitation (concentration on specific lexical needs or problems):
    - The adverbs of time
    - The prepositions of place
    - The adjectives expressing a colour

4. The menus

4.1. The basic menu: "A la carte" or "Plat du jour"

The program can be approached in two basic ways. The first menu on the screen allows the user to make this choice.
- "A la carte" opens all menus for the user, who can himself adjust contents and strategies at will. He can do so by going through a series of convenient menus which appear in overlapping frames on the computer screen. In this way he can choose particular levels, and/or particular speech acts, and/or particular notional fields, and/or particular parts of speech (cf. 4.2). Next, he selects the required strategy by using similar menus: presentation, practice or test (cf. 4.3).
- "Plat du jour" is meant for users who need more external guidance, or who must work according to a very precise learning scheme. "Plat du jour" offers the user a precise content, which was defined in advance by a particular teacher, for a particular

class, for a particular lesson (cf.
4.4).
- When the user has gone through the
basic menu (usually less than one
minute of work for "A la carte"; 5
seconds work for "Plat du jour"), the
system will select in a split second
the chosen items from the data banks
and the user can begin to work with
the various strategies.

4.2. A la carte

In "à la carte" the user makes the
selections himself. This is appropriate
for advanced students who want to work
on particular areas, which they define
themselves at the onset. Any combination is possible. The first "à la
carte" menu presents the following
choices:

Which level?
Which items?
Which strategies?
Which options?

A simple touch of the cursor control
keys allows the opening of each possibility. Secondary menus superpose each
other logically, allowing further
selections quickly.
- "Which level" allows for selections
  within the chronological dimension,
  corresponding to a growing degree of
  difficulty.
- "Which items" opens the following
  menu:
  All items
  By speech acts
  By notions
  By word class
  Each of these choices opens a wide
  array of further menus, allowing more
  detailed specifications.
- "Which strategies" will be discussed
  under 4.3.
- "Which options" will be discussed
  under 4.5.

4.3. Strategies

The first menu gives:
  - See selection
  - Presentation
  - Practice
  - Test

i. See selection
"See selection" gives immediately a
full overview, in the target language,
of all the items within the defined
unit. A number indicates how many are
included and one can survey the selection with the cursor control keys. With
"page up" and "page down" it is possible to change a full screen at once.

ii. Presentation
"Presentation" presents the items
selected in alphabetical order, with
translation in the source-language and
with a context for unilingual study and
revision. Another useful application of
"presentation" is the selection of
items for other objectives. A teacher
can call for series of items according
to parts of speech, to make grammatical
exercises or tests, or he can get a
precise list of items belonging to a
particular field to make a situational
exercise. Students also can use the
system to make their own texts or
prepare conversations. Immediately,
"presentation" will offer them all
items of a particular subject matter,
within precise boundaries of levels and
parts of speech.

iii. Practice
"Practice" opens a couple of overlaying
menus, allowing various didactic
strategies. The sequence of presentation in the menus corresponds with a
growing degree of difficulty, but is
not compelling. Gap exercises, with or
without hint and translation exercises,
can be combined with multiple choice,
oral or written practice. Such exercises and other are generated automatically according to randomization
criteria. The user will always be asked
how many items he wants to do (all
items selected, or in series of 10).
"Help" is available in exercises:
translation, first letter, first and
second letter, solution. With multiple
choice (indicating the answer) and
written exercises (typing in the
answer) there is always immediate
feedback: acceptance or rejection of
the answer, corrective help for minor
spelling errors. An immediate error
analysis in multiple choice and in
written exercises, allows the program
to generate remedial material automatically, precisely geared to the specific problems of the student. This is
presented in "digestif", which appears
in the main menu.

iv. Test
"Test" can be entered at any moment.
This allows the student to switch to
testing as soon as he feels confident

enough. No "help" is available in
testing and no reaction is provided
when a wrong answer is entered. At the
end of the test, the result is provided, together with an overview of the
items missed, showing the correct
answers. The user can at each item also
ask for his original answer, to make a
comparison between the correct answer
and the error.
An immediate error analysis in testing
allows automatic generation of specific
remedial material, geared to the
problems of the student. This is
presented in "digestif", which appears
in the main menu.

4.4. Plat du jour

"Plat du jour" allows the definition
and storage of particular units for
later use, so that these units remain
immediately available. This avoids for
the student the need to make himself
any selections in "A la carte". Indeed,
in school situations students will have
to work on items in direct relation to
the material a teacher wants them to
learn or to review. The student will
simply select "Plat du jour" and he
will receive an overview of the lessons
available, organized according to the
teachers using the program and the
various classes of each teacher, and
also according to the specific lessons
planned for each class.

As soon as the student has selected his
unit, it is composed from the database
in a fraction of a second, exactly as
the teacher has predefined it, by using
the separate teacher's entry.

4.5. Supplementary options

The user can change a number of standard options, also by a simple menu-
system:
- corrective help or not for minor
  spelling errors
- timing or not in testing, and which
  timing
- sound or not, and which sound
- monochrome or colour
- indication or not of interruption
  during the work
- number of lines per screen
- indication or not of score

5. Didactic justification

5.1. The need for didactic decisions

When working with data-based courseware, the most evident power lies in
the storing of maximal content, because
this subject matter can be selected at
will. When the content becomes more
complex and contextual, didactic
criteria will have more influence on
the selection and organization of the
subject matter, such as the chronological definition of the corpora, the
criteria for contextualization, the
place of translation. Still, the
program offers quite a large number of
different implementations, through its
large array of strategies and of
supplementary options.

5.2. Systematizing the acquisition of
communicative structures and
terminology

Current courses in foreign languages
lead many students prematurely into a
maze of authentic texts and conversations. They tend to follow the "produc-
tive-communicative approaches", which
originate from intensive language
teaching to adults. These methods
usually deal with structures and
vocabulary in an inaccurate way and
presuppose that the student will
"receptively" find his way through the
lexical wilderness. Many students will
lose their grip on the subject matter,
leading to careless language learning
and to discouragement. We prefer the
didactic concept of careful and explicit systematization.

5.3. Maximal versatility and accuracy

The contextualized items supply complete syntactic and semantic entities.
This way the user receives a stream of
natural language awareness. Therefore,
working with the contexts is to be
recommended, rather than working with
the translation of separate items. It
turns out to be more effective if the
foreign language is at first acquired
as perfectly as possible at the so-called 'recurrent level' (the student only
has to repeat correct items) or at the
'operating level' (the student is asked
to supply items that he can handle

flawlessly). As such, the student is not asked to produce language too quickly at a 'creative level', where he would hesitate and make mistakes. Therefore, the strategies are presented in a recommended order, going from a recurrent to a complex operating level.

5.4. Towards real interaction

Courseware is not a goal. It is a step helping towards the application of subject matter outside the domain of the computer. Especially in language learning, it is important that the experience leads to a natural, communicative use of the language.

A transitional stage is possible by working two by two in front of the screen. This provides the users with the opportunity to train contextual reply forms directly in a question-answer game. One participant asks the question, the other answers. This is possible both at the "presentation"-level, and in the several strategies with gap exercises.
But the final stage is away from the computer.

6. Some other characteristics

6.1. Ergonomics of the user-interface

The program uses the most advanced techniques in software production with a view to ergonomics which should increase the didactic and educational-psychological value of the program. Some striking aspects are:
- Speed: the index-sequential structure of the data banks provides a very high working speed, so that the user never has to wait; also, the menu-ramification, the scoring, the error-analysis and the generation of remedial material are realized in fractions of seconds.

- Layout: menu-system with overlay-windows; reserved zones for indications, for dialogue-boxes, for messages and for operating keys; functional use of the display-screen; centring of the cursor; extreme simplification of the display-screen.
- Constant input-control: the erroneous use of keys is not possible.
- Start up- and End procedure: maximally user-friendly. The system is started up autonomously and can be left at each moment.
- Availability of help

6.2. Programming efficiency

- Turbo Pascal
- index sequential organization of databases
- recursive procedures
- compacting procedures

7. Conclusion

The selection system is especially suitable for any learning content that works with clearly defined elements and expands these elements constantly, over a long period of time. Vocabulary, conjugations, declensions, and the use of prepositions are examples of excellent material that can be built into a selection system. As we saw, even contextualized items can be placed in databases, working with the same principles.

It is more difficult to apply when the material becomes broadly contextual, such as practising reading and writing skills in full texts. But even here, it is possible to generate practice forms, based on databanks identifying the nature of content. Our Textapuces, developed within the Dutch NIVO-project by OMO in Tilburg, is a typical example of the broader applications of a selection system.

COMPUTERS IN EDUCATION, F. Lovis and E.D. Tagg (eds.)
Elsevier Science Publishers B.V. (North-Holland)
© IFIP, 1988

COURSEWARE DEVELOPMENT IN THE NETHERLANDS

Leon Henkens and Koos van Deursen

Projectstaff for Education and Information
Technology

Ministry of Education and Sciences
PO Box 25000
2700 LZ ZOETERMEER
The Netherlands

ABSTRACT

The availability of courseware is a
bottleneck for introducing computers in
education. In The Netherlands the production
of educational appliances, and thus of
courseware, is in general the ground of commercial publishers. At this stage
publishers are reluctant to invest in
courseware development. So the Dutch
government has stimulated courseware
production. The approach of the NIVO-project
is discussed. Recently two large scale
courseware production projects have been set
up.

Both projects aim at a fully commercial
production after the stimulation period. They
have, however, quite a different approach.
The project concerning secondary education
aims at creating favourable conditions for
commercial publishers. The project for higher
vocational education stimulates the founding
of a new company.

1.   Introduction

In January 1984 the Dutch government
presented a policy document called "The
Information Technology Stimulation Plan"
(INSP). It's a multi-purpose plan to
stimulate the business world, the academic
world, education and government and semi-
government to attune quicker to the
applications of micro-electronics and
information technology. This five year plan
(1984-1988) is coordinated by the Minister of
Education and Sciences. It has a total budget
of 1.7 billion Dutch guilders, of which 270
million guilders have been allocated to
education.

Education plays an important role in
preparing people for the changes taking place
in society. Since information technology is
extremely pervasive in society, education has
to incorporate information technology.
Information technology has become a necessary
part of the curriculum. Moreover, information
technology not only improves the quality of
education, but also the productivity and
efficiency of education.

With this in mind, various activities in the
INSP have been designed. Some activities are
designed to create appropriate conditions for
the introduction of IT in Dutch education as
a whole, others relate to a particular type
of school.

The former are for example setting up an
infrastructure for courseware development,
in-service training, promotion of expertise
and knowledge of teachers, supportive
research for education.

Of the various school sectors priority has
been given primarily to vocational education
and secondly to general secondary education.
Concerning applications the ranking is the
following:
1. Teaching about information technology.
   In general secondary education all schools
   will present a computer literacy course
   dealing mainly with applications of IT. In
   vocational education all relevant
   curricula are being changed as education
   should match the needs of the labour
   market both by producing more computer
   specialists and by adapting to the
   knowledge required for every job with
   respect to the IT developments.

2. Computer assisted learning.

3. Computer managed instruction.
   This type of applications, i.e. the
   computer as an instrument for the teacher
   as manager of the learning process, is
   increasing in importance.

The INSP is approaching its end. In general
it has been a success. Schools have been
provided with hardware. Many teachers have
attended in-service training courses. More
and more it is, however, becoming manifest
that the development of educational software
of courseware is the central nerve of the
introduction of IT in education. It is a
vulnerable nerve. Things can go wrong easily,
because of:
- the high costs of development,
- the difficult technical aspects of the
   development process,
- the conceptual relation to curricula.

The Dutch Ministry of Education and Sciences
has taken several measures to stimulate
courseware production. Some large scale
initiatives will be outlined. In section 2
the NIVO-project will be described. In
section 3 and section 4 two courseware
development projects are presented.

For a good understanding of the measures, it
is essential to know that the production and
distribution of learning materials in The
Netherlands is the domain of commercial
publishers. The influence of the government
on the day to day curricula is limited mainly
to fixing the number of lessons and the
examination demands. Within these conditions
it is up to the individual schools to
organize their education. This freedom of the
individual schools and teachers is highly
valued in the Dutch system. This freedom is
guaranteed in the constitution. The
stimulation actions of the government will
aim at promoting or at least not hindering
the commercial activities of the publishers
and the freedom of choice by the schools.

2. NIVO-project

In 1985 three computer firms - IBM, Philips
and Tulip Computers - presented a plan to the
Ministry of Education and Sciences. This plan
intended a quick and large-scale introduction
of IT into general secondary education.
In-service training, software development and
hardware supply were key elements of the
plan. As a result these computer companies,
the Minister of Education and Sciences and
the four national educational organizations
signed the NIVO-agreement on 15 October 1985.

The costs of the NIVO-project amount to about
130 million Dutch guilders. The government
provides 47 million guilders for in-service
training and courseware development. The
remaining 83 million guilders for equipment
will be contributed by industry. IBM, Philips
and Tulip donated 33 million Dutch guilders,
the rest has to come from other industries
through sponsoring.

All of the 2 000 participating schools get a
computer laboratory of nine 16-bits MS-DOS
computers in a network and two stand-alone
computers. For the equipment delivered at
cost-price, the three companies guarantee
full compatibility. Schools will only receive
equipment if three teachers attend specially
designed in-service training courses. This
involves about 6 000 teachers.

With respect to courseware development in
this project several initiatives have been
taken:
- All schools get a free software package of
   about ten general purpose programs. A lot
   of learning materials have been developed
   for these software programs.
- Computer literacy courses are being
   developed by commercial publishers. Nearly
   all schools give such courses in the first
   or second grade.
- For various disciplines CAL-projects are
   underway.
- All schools get a free software voucher to
   be spent on listed products of educational
   publishers or other commercial companies.
   The voucher has two goals, i.e. to
   stimulate the efforts of the private
   sector in developing educational software
   and thus increase the number of software
   packages schools can buy, and to get the
   schools used to the idea that software
   products have to be paid for by the
   schools.

The NIVO-project is well received by the schools. More and more teachers are willing to use computers in their subject courses. There is however a lack of good and sufficient courseware. Because commercial perspectives are not promising, commercial firms are reluctant to produce courseware on a larger scale. A courseware shortage may cause a loss of momentum in the process of implementing computers as an educational tool. That is why the Minister of Education and Sciences has launched a large-scale courseware project in 1987: the POCO-project.

3.   POCO-project

This project is focussing on producing learning materials that can be used by teachers in a meaningful way in their regular teaching activities and that can be used with such frequency that they become common (tools) to the teachers. These stimulation actions that are temporary, should in no way disturb the development of a future commercial market for courseware. The government hopes that through and after the four-year POCO-project courseware will be produced by the private sector without special governmental support.

The POCO-project concerns courseware that can be directly used in existing curricula. The courseware should also be useful for initial and in-service training of teachers. In order to steer these production efforts a strong project management concentrated in one location is needed. This task has been assigned to the Educational Computing Consortium (ECC), the former Centre for Education and Information Technology (COI).

The POCO-project has an annual budget of 6.5 million Dutch guilders. It produces courseware for primary, general secondary and (lower and middle) vocational education.

Four stages are scheduled for the process of the courseware production:
(I)   choosing priorities,
(II)   formulating product descriptions
(III)   technical production,
(IV)   courseware distribution.

(I) Choosing priorities:
Within the constraints of the available budget priorities will be set according to the most pressing needs of the educational sector and the most promising application areas for IT. It is a premise of the POCO-project to produce courseware packages that relate to concentrated areas of the curriculum or to aspects of the teaching/learning process in which frequent use of these packages can be expected. It is assumed that this is a necessary condition for the computer becoming a common tool for the teacher.

In consultation with the educational sectors involved ECC will give advice about the priorities. After consultation with some advisory bodies the Minister of Education and Sciences will decide which areas and subjects will be handled.

(II) Formulating product descriptions:
Following the selection of priorities, ECC will be responsible for the development of product descriptions and specifications of the software and accompanying learning materials. These descriptions and specifications will be the basis for the subsequent technical production of the courseware. This phase will be carried out by hiring specialists from universities, teacher training institutes, educational support institutes, schools, etc.

(III) Technical production:
Via a tender procedure, open to all parties interested (software houses, commercial publishers, etc), contracts will be given for the production of specific courseware

packages on the basis of the product descriptions mentioned. Production contracts can also be given for modifying existing products so that they better reflect the standards of the POCO-project and the needs of the Dutch educational situation. POCO will set standards for the production process as well as standards for the software itself; both of which will contribute to the "user-friendliness" of the software.

(IV) Courseware distribution:
The end products will be distributed at a reasonable price for the customers (schools) through commercial publishers.

The POCO-project has a time limit of four years, in which several production cycles will be performed. The first phase, including a complete production cycle, will expire at 31st December 1988. During 1988 an interim evaluation of the project will take place so that about January 1989 the Minister of Education and Sciences can decide whether the second phase will continue.

The POCO-project has an extremely tight time schedule. ECC presented its priority advice at 1st December 1987. At the 15th January 1988 the Minister confirmed the priorities. Product descriptions have to be ready by the 1st May 1988. Technical production, including field tests and subsequent changes, have to be performed not later than the 1st December 1988. The products of this production cycle will be available for the schools about January 1989.

At this moment it is still too early to say whether the approach of the POCO-project will be a success. In general, however, the reception of the POCO-project by the educational institutes, commercial publishers and politics has been positive.

4. Courseware development in higher vocational education

The position of commercial publishers is quite different in Dutch higher vocational education. The number of pupils/students is

much smaller and there are many specialisms. Teachers often use own materials and foreign books. Moreover, the learning process is more individualized than in secondary education.

In 1986 in the framework of the INSP a feasibility study was undertaken to investigate the possibilities of the use of CAL on a larger scale in the higher vocational schools. The study was done by a private courseware firm. It showed that 5 to 10% of the curriculum could be covered by CAL and, moreover, that such production could take place on a commercial basis.

As a consequence the Ministers of Education and Sciences and of Economic Affairs decided to launch such a courseware project. A tender procedure was set up. Combinations of commercial firms and higher vocational institutes were invited to subscribe. The target would be to produce in the period up to the 1st January 1990 1 000 - 1 200 hours of courseware for higher vocational education. As an input two main sources would be available. First, through a special scheme about 90 teachers could be recruited by secondments at the expense of the Ministry of Education and Sciences. These teachers should be trained to become professional all-round courseware developers.
Secondly, the Ministry of Economic Affairs would dispose a grant of 6 million Dutch guilders. From 1990 on the project should be self-supporting on a commercial basis.

Six proposals were received from firms and schools willing to undertake the project. After selection the project was assigned to Courseware Europe, a well-known Dutch coursewarehouse, and the Hogeschool Midden Nederland, located at Utrecht. They founded a firm Courseware Midden Nederland (CMN), in which they both invested own (venture) capital.

CMN started in May 1987. By August 1987 about 90 teachers had been selected. Two full-time training courses of one year have been started in September and December 1987. These training courses are specially designed. Several expertisecentres (universities,

softwarehouses, etc.) are being contracted by CMN to take care of part of the training.

The financing of the government is conditional. Two evaluation moments have been fixed. The goals set have to be reached by CMN in order to get funds for the next phase. The interference of government with the whole enterprise is minimal. The project has been set up and will be run like a commercial firm. The Ministers check the targets and the accounts at two evaluation dates.

At the end of 1988 the following targets have to be reached:
- At least 60 teachers should have finished their training with good results and should still be involved in the project.
- A systematic production process should be well underway.
- 100 hours of courseware should be ready (for sale).
- About 400 hours of courseware are in the stage of development.

A final evaluation is planned on the 1st November 1989. Targets are:
- 60 courseware specialists have agreed to work as employees of the commercial firm CMN from 1st January 1990 on.
- About 1 000 hours of courseware are ready.
- Revenues should be realised in the amount of at least 2 500 000 guilders in the years '88 and '89.
- There is a real perspective of a turn-over of 5 000 000 in 1990.

From 1990 on CMN will be a fully commercial company without special government support. The higher vocational education sector will be an important market, but also other markets have to be developed by CMN.

The CMN project has shown a good start. However, it is still too early to say whether the targets will be met. On behalf of the Ministers involved the acceptability of the CMN project by higher vocational education will be monitored in 1988. The results will be of importance for the decisions at the time of the first evaluation.

5.   Conclusions

Courseware products are educational
appliances. In the Dutch context this implies
that courseware has to be produced by the
private sector, particularly by the
educational publishers. The schools and the
teachers are free to choose which educational
appliances, and so which courseware they want
to use. Dutch politics and Dutch education
esteem both factors highly.

Yet the production of courseware is - at
least at this stage of development -
different from the production of books.
Whereas there is a pupil market for books,
the courseware market is a school market.

This means that the number of products sold
is orders of magnitude smaller. The
development of courseware requires expertise
from outside the traditional educational
sector and is expensive. These are the main
reasons why commercial perspectives for
courseware are not rosy and why publishers
are reluctant to invest in courseware.

Yet the availability of courseware is a
necessary condition for getting the
introduction of IT, particularly of CAL, well
off the ground. That is why the Dutch
Ministry of Education took the initiative to
start two large scale courseware production
projects. Although both projects have only
just started, their start has been
auspicious.

COMPUTERS IN EDUCATION, F. Lovis and E.D. Tagg (eds.)
Elsevier Science Publishers B.V. (North-Holland)
© IFIP, 1988

Computer Based Learning for Accounting
using A.I. and video-disc technology

Comtesse Xavier

University of Geneva
Computer Science Department
Switzerland

We have developed CBL material to teach the principles of general accounting: as a base for the lessons, we formalized a model of the subject domain. The model is divided into five levels of knowledge:
1) A low level, representing the traditional sequencing in learning accounting, starting from the inventory, the initial balance sheet, the opening of the different accounts, going through the entries to the closing of accounts, the exploitation account, the result and the final balance sheet.
2) A declarative level, including an accounting expert system.
3) A visual level, including a videodisc.
4) A corpus level, providing definitions and explanations for most usual technical terms.
5) A strategy level, where the lessons are tailored to the specific needs of the learner.
The paper focuses on the description of this model; however, the run-time environment, the pedagogical choices and the visual environment of apprenticeship will also be described.
This CBL material is characterized by its ability to integrate new rules, new pedagogical choices, new accounts, wordings, (etc...) since the data, the rules and the code are totaly separate from each other, thus allowing some adaptability for its use in school (academic) situations.

I. Introduction

The aim in Computer Based Learning is to build programs presenting a subject in the form of interactive lessons. Well engineered programs containing some knowledge of the subject being taught are to be the result of a collaboration between specialists of the subject (teachers) and computer scientists. Quite often, the knowledge is imbedded in the code, making it difficult to distinguish between the pedagogical aspects and the information processing.

The goal of this paper is to show how the author builds up a solution to this problem. The use of expert system techniques has two advantages: making the knowledge (i.e. rules) of the subject domain explicit, and also making the underlying pedagogical rules of the learning process explicit [1][6].

II. The structure of the model

Within the context of developing CBL material, we have been brought to formalize a model that allows the learner to define his own strategy of learning and to change it at any moment when a conceptual difficulty becomes a problem.

The learner has therefore five levels at which he can work to acquire the knowledge of the studied domain. These five levels can be summarized in the following way:

1) procedural form: The sequential ordering of the apprenticeship follows the accounting logic, i.e. from the first day of the year with the inventory and the initial balance sheet, to the opening of the accounts and the entries all along the year, until the closure and the final balance sheet at the end of the year.

2) The declaratory form: Here, there is no more sequencing. Instead, a set of rules handled by an inference engine allows one to find the accounting rule applicable to the problem to be solved.

3) Visual form: one resorts to sequences of video images, a kind of videoclip, on the basic accounting notions, thus allowing the learner to be faced to an accounting process in a concrete situation.

4) The corpus form: to define clearly the accounting concepts and their contextual usage.

5) Strategic form: the learner is allowed to ask for some orientation advice. He can, by this mean, find out the progress of his work as well as his semantical and syntactical errors.

In its structure, the model reflects (fig. 1) these levels of interaction and allows, within a teaching by discovery, to elaborate individualized strategies to eliminate the pedagogical difficulties which, in this case, deal with the global accounting of a firm [3][4].

III. The data processing program

Designed in a modular way, the CBL material is made out of different programs, partly written in Turbo-Pascal (for the main flow of control), in Turbo-Prolog (for the expert system) and in assembler (for the interrupt handler and the videodisc driver).

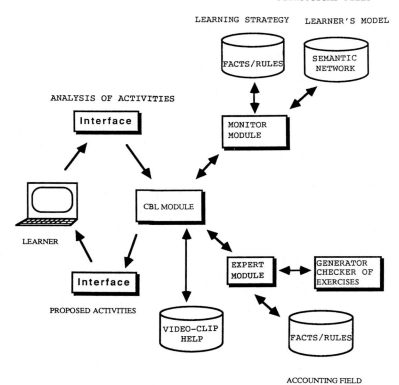

Fig. 1 : Overall structure.

All these programs are either chained or reside in memory in order to be activated at any moment. We can distinguish the following modules:

1) The configuration module is composed of the program allowing one to enter new accounts, new rules about accounting entries (used also for the expert system) and also to generate exercises.

2) The monitoring module handles an account book and a state graph representing simultaneously, in a semantic network, the knowledge about the domain and the progress of the learner. This monitoring is also used as a teaching guidance, by suggesting appropriate exercises to the learner. It is also used to control the validity of the learner's answers.

3) The expert module is a resident program allowing the learner to define the accounting rule to apply in a given situation and determined by certain facts.

4) The video module is also a resident program, allowing the viewing of a video sequence, organized as clips, about the basic notions of accounting. The shots have been taken in a real firm in activity.

5) The CBL module is the heart of the system. The other programs are either chained to it or accessible from it. We'll give further explanations on the choice of such a mode of apprenticeship<8><9>.

IV. The CBL Module

The module is composed of three distinct parts corresponding to three phases in the accounting of a company. These three phases are the "picture" of the company at the beginning of the exercise (usually on the first of january), the "film" of the flow of operations and the "picture" at the end of the exercise. This corresponds to the following accounting activities:

1 - Inventory
   - Initial balance sheet
   - Opening of accounts

2 - The accounting entries along the exercise

3 - The closure of accounts
   - The exploitation account
   - The result
   - The final balance sheet

The sequencing of these events is done in practice on a day by day basis<5>. The software simulates this very well. Thus, the learner is placed in a situation where he has to do the accounting corresponding to what he can see in the videodisc sequences.

The balance sheets, the book and the journal are shown to the learner in a form very close to the actual

ones. The learner's assignment is to give the accounting entries. A set of function keys allow him to access:
- the monitoring for some guidance or for a validation,
- the expert system to search an accounting rule,
- the videodisc to make the connection with the reality of the firm and its accounting,
- the corpus for an explanation of a common term
- the balance sheet and the inventory to find back some information.

This whole set provides a kind of control panel that allows the learner to achieve his work with full knowledge of all the facts. This original approach allows, in fact, to get in an interresting way the desired information without leaving one's screen. This is the basis for a teaching by discovery, since the learner's difficulties can only be found out through the learner's activities.

V. The expert module

The basic principle of this model is to make explicit, in the form of rules, accounting laws corresponding to the domain being taught. This way of proceeding has, from the teaching point of view, a number of advantages such as:

- the learner is forced to specify the accounting situation he has to deal with. In other words, he has to state correctly the initial facts leading to the problem.

- the learner can get from the system the rule(s) that he can use. It's however up to him to map it to the actual initial situation<7>.

For the implementation of this module, accountants were interviewed and the semantic tree and the cognitive rules were built out of their knowledge. To make things clearer, here are three examples:

VI. The monitoring module

This module offers guidance inside the current program, on the basis of the rules used by the teacher. These rules express the choice of apprenticehip strategy. They are of the following type:

IF model of the learner in state X THEN suggest activity Y

In the most general case, it is the program that takes the initiative of starting activities. The learner can however, at any moment, change the orientation according to how his apprenticeship evolves.

The second important activity of the module is to verify the validity of the new accounting entries. In fact, the learner can also ask for this validity check at any moment he wishes. The module will point out his mistakes, telling the error and the corresponding entry number as a compiler would do.

VII. The videoclips on videodisc

Making things look realistic has always been a problem in teaching. It is easy to speak about Brazil, the atomic bomb or accounting. It is much more difficult to understand what Brazil, the atomic bomb or accounting is, if one has never been to Brazil, seen the effects of the atomic bomb or seen a firm in its activities.

Thanks to the use of a videodisc, the learner can be placed by the software in a situation where he can explore the reality of the firm of which he is doing the accounting. This mixture of reality and simulation in the exercises eliminates a number of teaching difficulties.

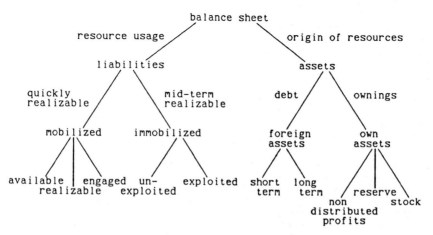

Fig. 2: semantic tree for the balance sheet.

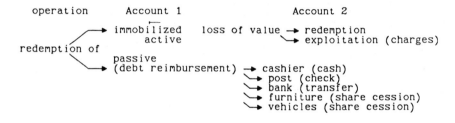

Fig. 3: accounting operation for redemption.

initial_balance_sheet_rule_2 :

if initial_balance_sheet and if passive_account then right_entry;

Fig. 4: balance sheet creation rule.

The software has been designed in such a way that, at any moment, one can invoke an image and a videodisc sequence to get complementary explanations or to view the activity of the company concerned.

The contribution of images is capital, for it offers a palette of familiar schemes specific to the determination of a new learning strategy: the discovery by the practice. This notion is dominant in the elaboration of this software, and will subsequently permit the elaboration of a general methodology.

The video is therefore not only present to grab the reality, but also as a learning strategy.

VIII. The corpus

In order to balance the video, the software includes a textual approach to the help in getting informations.

From the algorithmic point of view, this help is organised in a tree structure, allowing the learner to find the meaning of a specific concept or accounting operation.

There is nothing special to say about this traditional approach, except that it is necessary to include it, not because it is pedagogically better, but rather because people are used to it and it is useful to have links relating usual practice to new educational approaches.

IX. The apprenticeship environment

The term "environment" encompasses two aspects:

1) The computer environment, consisting in a micro-computer, a keyboard, a mouse, a videodisc player and a "bi-standard" colour screen capable of switching between different video sources.

2) The educational environment, where the learner's behaviour is taken into account. This matter of educational environment is crucial in our software. In fact, the situation of apprenticeship must reflect as close as possible the actual conditions in which accounting is done.

This is why the apprenticeship is built around the notion of a main screen, a kind of working area that one leaves only to gather other information (i.e. initial balance sheet, inventory, expert, dictionary, calculator...).

The main screen is therefore composed of the account book and of excerpts from the journal, both of which are fundamental accounting documents for the posting of entries, as shown in the following figure.

One can notice that from this main screen, we can have access to all the functions of the system, including those concerning the videodisc and the expert system.

The strong point of this CBL material comes from the integration of different functions, starting from a main screen that constitutes the working area, as for example, with a word processor or a spreadsheet. The CBL material then becomes an instrument at the orders of the learner<2>.

X. Conclusion

Concerning the choices we made during the development of this material on accounting, we had in mind the following :

1) The learner must have available a visual educational environment that is clear and that integrates all his activities.

2) The learner must get by himself all the information he needs.

3) The learner must be able to find familiar schemes (as defined by Jean Piaget) that eliminate the educational difficulties that can lead to problems<10>.

4) The learner must establish his own apprenticeship strategy.

In order to satisfy all these requirements, it is necessary to make at least the following three choices :

1) use video sequences to introduce a visual dimension to knowledge.

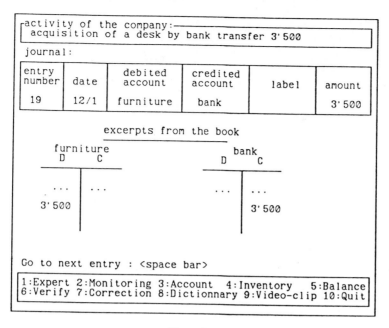

Fig. 5: Screen layout.

2) use an expert system to represent the knowledge being taught.

3) have some monitoring (a kind of guiding program) that allow a more intelligent teaching process.

As a conclusion, we can say that this software fulfils the programming requirements we have stated. We have now to evaluate it systematically in educational situations.

Bibliographical references:

<1> A. Bonnet, L'intelligence artificielle, promesses et réalités, Inter Editions, Paris, 1984

<2> G. Cellerier, Structures and function, Genetic Artificial Intelligence and Epistemics Laboratory, University of Geneva, Memo no.3, 1986

<3> X. Comtesse, B. Ibrahim, B. Levrat, A cognitive model of representation applied to CAL, Proceeding of IASTED / Expert System 87, Geneva, 1987

<4> X. Comtesse, A. Boder, Un modèle d'acquisition des connaissances basé sur le rôle organisateur des schèmes, Proceedings of IASTED / Expert System 87, Geneva, 1987

<5> A. Cottier, Traité de comptabilite générale, Georg éditeur, Genève, 1985

<6> J.P. Laurent, (Texte réuni par) Journées nationales sur l'intelligence artificielle, CEPADUES Editions, Toulouse, 1986

<7> R. Lelouche, Apports de l'EIAO à l'EAO, Actes du Congrés EAO 87, 1987, pp. 173-181

<8> R.S. Michalski, J.C. Carbonell, T.M. Mitchell, Machine learning, Vol I & II, Morgan Kaufman Publishers Inc., New York, 1986

<9> M. Minsky, The society of Mind, Simon and Schuster Books, New York, 1986

<10> J. Piaget, Connaissance de l'intelligence chez l'enfant, Delachaux et Nestlé, Neuchatel, 1936

<11> Ph. Vignard, Représentation de connaissance, mécanisme d'exploitation et d'apprentissage, INRIA, Rocquencourt, 1985.

COMPUTERS IN EDUCATION, F. Lovis and E.D. Tagg (eds.)
Elsevier Science Publishers B.V. (North-Holland)
© IFIP, 1988

THE DISCATEXT PROGRAMME. IN AID OF TEXT-COMPREHENSION LESSONS IN SECONDARY EDUCATION

Prof. dr. W. Decoo, the University of Antwerpen, Universiteitsplein 1, B-2160 Wilrijk
Belgium
drs. A.M. Cartigny, Ons Middelbaar Onderwijs Apennijnenweg 11, 5022 DT Tilburg,
the Netherlands

1. DESCRIPTION OF DISCATEXT FRENCH

1.1. Brief characterization

The Discatext programme has been developed as
an aid for the text comprehension lessons as
they are given in the higher forms of the Dutch
"Algemeen Vormend Onderwijs" (Comprehensive
school). The student is enabled to go through a
text with the help of a computer and ask for
help when he encounters problems. These problems
fall into 4 categories: problems on word, sentence, paragraph and text-levels. After the
student has finished studying the text he may
ask for an exercise with the words he has
called up. Lastly a final test is available
through which the student may check whether he
has thoroughly understood the text at hand.
In the first instance there is a choice of 20
texts on three levels of difficulty.

1.2. Aim of Discatext

Discatext offers the student a learning environment in which he can tackle problems he
encounters when working his way through the
text with regard to linguistic problems and
problems as regards contents. In this way it is
possible to create an efficient learning strategy for individual pupils so that more time
will be available in class-instruction for
transferring information about more specific
elements of the French language and French culture.
Students who are not able to study a text on
the basis of questions they formulate themselves are offered a possibility by the programme
systematically to call up that information
which he needs in order to understand the text
and in order to answer the questions correctly.

1.3. Application

In the first instance the programs have been
developed to function within a reteaching context. That is to say, for a relatively small
group of pupils who cannot really keep with the
instruction given in class because they have
had too little training in dealing with texts.
Because of the fact that at this moment the
number of computers at schools is only small a
more extensive use of these programs is not yet
feasible.
At a later stage - when at school and at home
more computers will be available - it will be
possible to use these programs as teaching programs, i.e. that students may study texts independently at home or during lessons reserved
for study at their own specific levels. Texts
may then later be discussed in class on the
basis of results achieved and problems encountered.

1.4. Interaction

The programme supplies students with information
at 4 levels:
Word-level
The programme differentiates between words
which are backed up by information and those
which are not. Only those words which are at a
specific advanced learner's level or those
which are specific for the text under consideration have no back-up. When a student calls up
a word, there are two possibilities: either he
gets the meaning of the word and a semantic
response sentence (to support word understanding
and fixing it in his memory), or, if the word
is specific for the text, only its translation
will appear.
Sentence-level
At sentence-level syntactic difficulties and
difficulties as regards the contents of the
sentence are explained. Our team have taken
those difficulties which always cause problems
in class-situations.
Explanations at sentence-level are given without
using meta language as much as possible. The
typical possibilities that are offered by the
computer and the computer screen are used in
this process (e.g. moving parts of sentences
and highlighting by means of colours).
Paragraph-level
At paragraph-level the student may test himself
by means of multiple choice questions whether
he has understood the contents of the paragraph
correctly. He can also ask for a presentation
of the contents. These are presented through
a paraphrase or a basic sentence.
Paraphrase and basic sentence are rendered in
words from the French Fundamental or advanced
level words used in higher form instruction.
Text-level
At text-level the student may call up help in
three ways:
a. The student may call up the overall structure
   of the text. This structure is then presented. Alternatively, the student may test
   himself to see whether he has understood

the overall structure. In that case the main
elements of the text together with appropriate conjunctions appear on the screen.
The student must then show, by putting the
conjunctions given in their proper positions,
that he has acquired insight into the
overall structure of the text.
b. The student may call up a summary of the
text. This summary is presented with the
help of basic sentences per paragraph. The
student may also want to test himself whether
he has understood the text. In that case
the basic sentences appear in random order
on the screen and the student is given the
assignment to put them in the correct order.
c. Finally the student may ask for the theme
of the text. He may also test himself by
means of a multiple choice questions to
find out whether he has grasped the theme
of the text.
After going through the text the student has
the option of practising the words he has
called up:
1. Through a presentation of semantic response
sentences in which he has to fill in blanks
orally or in writing.
2. Through typing in the missing words in
blanks in parts of the original text.
Lastly the pupil may choose to do a test which
is comparable to the exam tests that are taken
at the final exams.

1.5. Contents of the programs

Texts have been chosen by the teachers on the
basis of 2 criteria: learning contents and
appeal to youngsters.
Help at word-level, sentence-level, paragraph-
level and text-level has been formulated by
the teachers on the basis of their experience
with higher form students.

1.6. Route

The programme may be used in various ways by
the students depending on the instructions that
are given to the student by the teacher. It
is possible that the student chooses his own
route all by himself, possibly led by the test
questions he may call up. In this way a
situation is created analogous to that of the
final exam, at which the student carefully
studies the text and simultaneously tries to
answer the exam questions on the basis of his
reading. This procedure, which will probably be
followed in the highest forms, will only be
efficient if the student has been trained beforehand in the use of information presented
in this way.
This way means that teachers in the lower forms
will prescribe to their students which routes
they should follow when going through the programs. There are many possible variations
between an open and a closed route through the
programme.
After the testing stage it will be considered
whether it will be necessary to enable teachers,

via a "menu" of options, to structure the student's route.

1.7. Justification

Two clear reasons may be put forward to account
for the development of Discatext. Firstly text-
comprehension lessons in secondary education
constitute a problem. In view of the weight that
is carried by text-comprehension at the final
written exam much time is spent in class on
text-comprehension training. It is very difficult to make these lessons interesting to students.

Since texts are tackled in a class-situation
much time is spent on specific linguistic problems. There is hardly any time left for vocabulary training. Thus it is possible that students in higher forms have a more limited active command of words and idioms than students
in lower forms.
Furthermore the computer is a highly suitable
medium to support quickly the various problems
the student may have when studying a text.
Speed and quantity of good linguistic information are important in language teaching.
In building up the text-comprehension programme
as a "wandelmodel" (i.e. where the student may
wander freely among sources of information in
order to come to a correct understanding of
the text) and certainly in the build up of the
"oefenmodel" programme (i.e. where students
may practise with words, idioms, constructions
etc. occurring in a text) two notions have been
of utmost importance:
a. The "monitor" as the ability of the human
being to learn the principles of language
through his intellectual understanding.
b. The "organizer" as the ability of the human
being through which he uses language and
accordingly employs the principles of
language.
Research had indicated that the organizer does
not exclusively operate on intellectually understood language principles. The organizer has
its own operating principles which are developed
by actually dealing with language.
From these principles the following must be
concluded:
1. The feeding of the monitor, for example with
grammatical rules, thereby omitting to feed
the organizer, does not lead to a better
command of the language.
2. The transfer of language principles, mastered
through the monitor, to other linguistic
situations is very limited. Transfer will be
natural and quick if command of the language
has been accomplished through the organizer.
3. Language teaching should not emphasize feeding the monitor, but it should supply input
for the organizer so that students experience
language as a phenomenon which is very much
alive.
4. The so-called "input hypothesis" is of importance, i.e. in teaching, the emphasis
should be on supplying the organizer with
the largest possible input, taking into

consideration that this input should supplement the principles that are mastered through the monitor.

The computer is able to help the student to be engaged in actual language experience and it may thus be a good supplement to teaching practice as it is known in secondary education.

1.8. Discussion

In test situations it will be checked to what extent the student will be able to establish the lack of information he has got and thus ask questions on the various levels. His ability to solve exam questions will in many cases be representative of his accomplishments. It should be investigated whether, through teaching students a systematic approach to texts, they are being helped to deal with a text more from the point of view of text-comprehension than from a necessity to answer questions put by others.

A second issue is how to deal with a surplus of information. In the class situation the teacher will limit the information given. In the computer programme the student may call up information about almost *any* word and *any* sentence. Using information efficiently in a select and moderate way has to be learned.

1.9. Production strategy

Workability and applicability of educational software in schools by teachers are central concepts in software production by O.M.O. Involvement of a large group of teachers is essential in project work in order to make certain that knowledge of the learning child and the school world are the basis of the product to be developed. Within the production process the following stages may be distinguished:

Selection of texts
The 18 teachers of the test-group and development-group have gathered 70 texts which they considered suitable for text-comprehension lessons. Collecting these texts was undertaken on the basis of a number of criteria regarding length, themes to be covered, various levels of difficulty, etc.

Evaluation of texts collected
In this second stage the teachers have evaluated the texts collected in foursomes. If 3 or 4 teachers were of the opinion that texts were suitable to be incorporated into the programme, they were so chosen. In this way 20 texts have been selected.

Developing a prototype
In this third stage one text has been completely analysed and supplied with help at three levels. This has been done by the development-group. The development-group consists of 4 teachers, Professor W. Decoo of the UiA, J. Roovers MA, lecturer at the HKLT (the former Moller Institute) and two educational experts of O.M.O.

Implementing the framework programme
The fourth stage is being worked out by the test-teachers. Each of them has tackled one text. This entails the analysis of student problems and the development of supporting material. They have scenarios at their disposal so that their output will fit into the framework programme that has been developed.

1.10. Market

In developing the programme the makers have had the concept of a market in mind. That is to say that a student, according to the nature of his questions, may turn to the various stalls and get what he needs. The aim was to provide solutions for all types of questions a student might have. In the testing phase it must be checked whether the students are not being confused by the large variety of possibilities open to them. A learning route will have to be indicated. In terms of a market one will have to try and find out whether it is wise to display all information possible in those stalls and whether it is wise to let the younger students wander freely among the stalls. Through a "menu" of options it will be possible - certainly in the beginning - to force students to go through lower level information first and only then proceed to higher levels of information. Through the "menu" also the time at which test-questions will be made available to the student may be fixed.

A possibility is under consideration of differentiating between the last stage of final exam training and the first stage of getting acquainted with texts that have to be studied. In the case of exam training the test-questions might be a means in itself to study the text. In the first text-comprehesion lessons a guideline should be given to the student who is undertaking to understand a text.

2. SCHOOL BASED SOFTWARE DEVELOPMENT

The 20 programmes of O.M.O. Discatext French have been developed and tested within the framework of an educational development project which was set up by 50 VWO/HAVO/MAVO schools in Noord-Brabant and the rest of the Netherlands. These schools reside under one authority and have established a joint service which has been assigned to back up educational innovations and changes at those 50 schools. The basis of this programme development is a decision of the managements of those 50 schools that information technology should be incorporated into the curriculum. The schools should get acquainted with information technology on an experimental basis and gradually integrate it. The school managements have supported this decision and have promised to cooperate

2.1. Production criteria

Since production of educational software is partly financed by the schools themselves, a number of criteria have been carefully formulated. Programs and programme-production should meet these criteria, so that schools may benefit directly from the output.

Criteria for contents

Software should be relevant to a considerable amount of subjects of tuition.

These subjects of tuition in their present shape should give rise to difficulties so that there is a genuine need for computer programs to support regular teaching.

Anchoring the programs in school should be possible because the programs' didactic methods fit in with the teaching methods that are used and also with the philosophy on which lessons are based. It should also be clear at which places in the curriculum the computer programs should have a function.

The programs must be suitable for incorporation into the teachers's organisation of his lessons. Preparing lessons should not take up too much time and there should not be the danger that during lessons the group process is disturbed and the follow-up of lessons should not require too much time. Computer supported lessons may be a variation within class teaching but it must not break the rhythm of this form of teaching. Class structure may be very much recognised in the set up of schools. Educational software then must be able to function within a school with an overall class organisation within a schedule of 50 minutes per period. Furthermore, for the time being, only 10 computers are available for every 700 pupils in secondary education.

Criteria development organisation

In view of experiences in the period preceding the project, in which software development was more or less amateurishly worked on, the following requirements were formulated:

a. There should be separate systems of development: an educational system and a technical system and a test system.

b. In the educational system experts in teaching practice (i.e. teachers) should be involved, along with experts in the specific fields of knowledge, as well as teaching methodology experts and COO-experts.

c. In the educational system of the development of programs that should support the learning process of students, experts in teaching practice should constitute the majority.

d. All co-workers in the educational system should be rewarded in some way, in order to ensure their lasting commitment.

e. In the programming system professional programmers should be used, who can choose tools that are best suited for the educational specifications (not teacher-programmers).

f. There should be a very close link between the educational and technical programming systems.

g. All programs should be tested in schools in many different situations, not only by the teachers who are involved in the development, but also by a larger number of teachers who are not part of the development group. This

test should be carefully set up, both in the field of organisation of lessons and the school organisation.

Criteria regarding distribution

In view of the fact that software development was organized by an institute that considers rendering direct services to the 50 schools as its chief aim, it is expected in the development work that the teachers of all schools should be involved in the choice of topics that are suitable for educational software. In the process of development teachers must get the opportunity to be informed about the results of the work and the insights that were gained into the consequences for the use of the product.

After the development stage has been completed there should be an guarantee that all teachers and teaching departments of all 50 schools will be enabled to follow courses in the use of the programs that have been developed.

2.2. Course of development work

Preparatory phase

The starting points of the development work were the brush-up seminars that were organized by the O.M.O.-schools for their foreign language teachers. Professor Decoo of the University of Antwerp roughly outlined the potentialities of the computer in support of text-comprehension lessons. An inquiry among the 250 foreign language teachers showed that one was aware of the usefulness of this application of the computer and that one was willing to use software, once it had been developed.

Starting phase

In the inquiry names had come up of teachers and schools that were willing to cooperate in the development of software.

Staff members of the Education Bureau, together with Professor Decoo, set up a project plan which was submitted to the management of the Dutch NIVO-project for financing. Subsidies were granted in the form of non-teaching periods for teachers and financial means for education experts, programmers and an advisory relationship with the University Institutions of Antwerp (UiA)

Phase of prototype development

The actual development started on August 1 1986. A development group, consisting of 4 teachers, two teaching methodology experts and Professor Decoo of the UiA, devised proposals for help at word, sentence, paragraph and text levels. These proposals were developed on the basis of one text, namely "L'argent plus que la gloire". A group of 12 test teachers analysed texts of their own after a scenario set up by the development group. As a result, in September 1987 a prototype for some 15 texts had been finished and their contents had been worked out, ready for programming.

In May/June of 1987 all teachers of the 50

O.M.O. schools were invited at 2 seminars to get acquainted with the principles behind the text-comprehension programme as it had been developed. Also the first parts of the prototype were shown and discussed. The testing of the programs which had been developed started in November 1987 and continued (sic!) until August 1988. The teaching methodology experts of the "Hogeschool Katholieke Leergangen Tilburg" are well acquainted with the programming because of their involvement with the development effort.

After the various programs have been finished they will create opportunities for teachers of O.M.O. schools to be able to use the programs at their schools by means of special courses and training.

2.3. Evaluation of the work

Development work as described above demands a complex organisation. Teachers of 15 schools are involved as well as staff members of 3 institutes. A number of guarantees have been built into the development work:

a. Programs are being developed on the basis of experience with the daily teaching routine.
b. Programs are being developed in such a way as to be usable as reteaching programs within the school organisation and with the schools' equipment, i.e. programs that are very useful for small groups of students.
c. Programs are being developed under the responsibility of the joint school managements, so that the project management may expect support from the schools. The test teachers, too, may expect help from the school managements.

2.4. Characterization of the working process

Because of the fact that, under shared responsibility and in close cooperation, schools undertake the software development, 3 stages overlap: the production process of software, a training process of teachers and a process of change in schools. This method does not necessarily lead to a perfect product, but a number of aspects have certainly been given attention to:

1. Immediate applicability in class.
2. A good preparation for the distribution to more schools.
3. An efficient production process, because schools have been able to control the product directly, in order to ensure that the schools' money, which has been invested next to subsidiary funds, is being used in a responsible manner.
4. A relatively cheap production process, because teachers, schools, school boards, training institutes seemed willing to co-invest since participation in such a development process appears to be fruitful as regards enlarging teachers' expertise and creating a better insight into the possibilities of information technology in schools; a further step towards the use of information technology for management purposes.

2.5. Discovery

The development work connected with 7 packages of educational programs, has shown that developing costs are so disproportionate as regards the possibilities of distribution of educational software, that it is unthinkable that educational publishers will make profits in this area of the educational appliances market.

The fact that every four years information technology creates new possibilities may give risen to the expectation that publishers, who have been profitably producing educational appliances thanks to the conservatism of the educational system, will not be able to keep up with these new developments. Perhaps a development method in which teachers, schools, training institutes, school boards, the authorities and maybe hardware manufacturers co-invest, possibly in cooperation with publishers in their role of distributors, is the only feasible method in the production of teaching appliances in the field of information technology. It might be an instrument with which educational institutes themselves may take their own responsibilities in order to ensure that education may proceed beyond the use of textbooks and thus will fulfil its task of preparing young people for a society which is increasingly concerned with information technology.

COMPUTERS IN EDUCATION, F. Lovis and E.D. Tagg (eds.)
Elsevier Science Publishers B.V. (North-Holland)
© IFIP, 1988

READING WITH COMPUTERS:
A MODEL FOR ENHANCING METACOGNITION AND COGNITION

Tamar Feuerstein and Miriam Schcolnik

Abstract

A model for enhancing reading comprehension in a foreign language through the use of computers was developed, based on the assumption that reading courseware can provide learners with a rich learning environment in which first language reading skills and strategies are brought into awareness for transfer to a second language. The model is based on schema theory which identifies three components in the comprehension process: pragmatic, linguistic and discourse knowledge. The first two are part of an optionally accessible computerized information bank which prevents unnecessary interference in the reading process. The cognitive strategies taught aim at the development of global discourse comprehension and metacognitive awareness.

1. SCHEMA THEORY, METACOGNITION AND READING COMPREHENSION

According to schema theory, reading is a process in which the reader constantly guesses or makes hypotheses. These are subsequently tested, verified or rejected. Readers bring to the text a pragmatic or world knowledge, as well as a linguistic and discourse knowledge. Pragmatic knowledge determines the readers' expectations from the text allowing the use of high-order cognitive processes such as making hypotheses, deducing, predicting, inferring or implying. Linguistic knowledge includes a knowledge of morphology, syntax and lexis (vocabulary) and is usually associated with the decoding of the text by employing lower-order skills. Discourse knowledge includes familiarity with different text-types, their organizational structure and genres. The three levels of analysis interact with each other in order to attain comprehension.

Current literature dealing with reading comprehension theory emphasizes the cognitive skills and strategies employed by readers during the process of reading [1, 5, 12, 13, 15, 16]. These theories assume that readers develop certain mental abilities that allow them to process texts. Therefore, the ultimate goal in teaching reading comprehension is the internalization of the strategies to ensure their transfer from one reading text to another.

Of the multitude of cognitive strategies available, different strategies are consciously or unconsciously selected by readers. The selection may be effective and result in comprehension of the text or it may prove faulty, resulting in its misinterpretation. Research done with reading in one's first language seems to support the notion that metacognitive awareness of the selection and use of these skills and strategies enhances comprehension.

These findings are particularly valid for second and foreign language acquisition. The reading strategies may have already existed in the learner's first language reading competence and have not been transferred to foreign language reading or they may have never been activated for a particular reader. In either case, their activation is beneficial in that it allows metacognitive awareness of skills previously acquired in the first language, and the internalization of new skills and strategies.

The term metacognition was introduced by developmental psychologists to refer to the deliberate conscious control of one's own cognitive actions, i.e., to the awareness of one's own mind and the degree of one's own understanding. Metacognition in reading refers to at least two separate components: to the awareness of what skills, strategies and resources are needed to perform the reading task effectively, and to the ability to use self-regulatory mechanisms to ensure the successful completion of the task [4, p. 22].

---

* School of Education, Tel Aviv University

These self-regulatory or comprehension-monitoring mechanisms are cognitive activities in reading whose goal is successful comprehension. They include clarifying the purpose of reading, focusing attention on major content rather than trivia, keeping track of and evaluating the success with which one's comprehension is proceeding, planning ahead, testing and revising one's strategies to ensure that the process continues smoothly, and taking remedial action if necessary [3, 4, 6, 7].

Metacognitive awareness can be taught by directing the reader's attention to the mental processes he employs to comprehend a passage. The methods or techniques that can be used to instill metacognitive awareness in the reading process are problematic: Reading is by its very nature a private and individual undertaking as well as a continuous process. Therefore, any intervention in it will, by definition, interfere with comprehension in one way or another. The acuteness of this problem can be seen in the literature dealing with metacognitive research, where the methods themselves are criticized for being "disruptive of the normal reading process" [4, p. 23].

2. TEACHING READING COMPREHENSION: CLASSROOM PRACTICES AND COMPUTER COURSEWARE

A variety of solutions have been attempted in the language classroom. These include direct and indirect teacher intervention; teachers frequently stop students in the process of reading to pose retroactive questions requiring the reader to refer to the material just read, or proactive questions, requiring the reader to read ahead in order to search out an answer or confirm prediction. Textbook or task intervention include inserted questions, directive tasks, and marginal commentaries -- these are regarded as inducers of metacognitive skills. A more recent solution consists of introspective and retrospective techniques which allow learners to review and think back about the processes they employ. The techniques are considered facilitators of reading comprehension since they help externalize the metacognitive strategies involved in the process of reading.

In second or foreign language reading, another problem manifests itself - that of over-burdening cognition. The reader may already be over-burdened with difficult vocabulary, with syntactic structures that have not been fully mastered, with text structure, and possibly with cultural variables. Any additional element of instruction, such as the induction of metacognitive awareness will possibly interfere with the flow of reading. This aspect is generally overlooked in the literature dealing with the topic.

There are a number of purposes for reading which result in different ways of reading. These distinctions are to be taken into account in any discussion of reading instruction regardless of the approach adopted. One such distinction is that between extensive and intensive tasks. Extensive reading is usually undertaken for enjoyment. In this respect, any attempt at metacognition will be futile. Intensive reading, on the other hand, involves reading for a utilitarian purpose, either for textual analysis or for extracting information and knowledge from the text, often constituting part of a learning experience. Academic reading is an example of such intensive reading.

It is mostly in academic reading, at the initiation of academic studies or in reading for special purposes in professional or technical colleges that problems manifest themselves. Reading tasks become ineffective when faulty strategies are applied. At this stage, reading habits are already deeply rooted and at best one can only attempt remediation. Preventive measures should be taken at a much earlier stage, i.e., if the reader acquires effective skills and strategies at an early age, he will be equipped to deal with the required intensive reading tasks later.

Taking into consideration the problems mentioned and the existing solutions, a different procedure was attempted in which the computer is a teaching - learning tool. The basic assumption behind the techniques developed is that although teaching reading with the aid of a computer constitutes intervention, it is of a different kind. By allowing readers access to linguistic and background information on an optional basis, the element of interference is minimized. Thus, intervention is not negative interference but positive guidance towards the achievement of a specific goal.

Therefore, the main endeavour of the computer reading course is to fulfill the above needs by dealing with appropriate skills and strategies in the reading process, providing readers with metacognitive awareness of the processes - without interfering in the reading process or over-burdening cognition, and beginning at an early stage of reading in the second or foreign language learning process.

Two arguments are made to justify the use of computers to reinforce reading skills: a. the psychological advantage of immediate feedback, and b. the individual and private characteristics of computer work. Psychologically, the delay in giving the student feedback about the level of his performance on a reading comprehension exercise is a great weakness. Meticulous correction of errors may be wasted if the student has forgotten most of what was read and why he chose the answers he did [8]. Computers can overcome that problem by providing immediate and relevant feedback. Reading is one of the areas of the curriculum where Computer Assisted Learning holds the greatest promise. By its very nature, reading is an individual and idiosyncratic process. The reading class demands an individualized, student-centered approach [17].

To these arguments we may add the advantages of introducing and possibly diagnozing which skills and strategies have already been acquired and which need to be dealt with or reinforced. Moreover, the computer may be used for providing readers with metacognitive awareness of the skills and strategies used in a non-judgemental environment.

Typical reading comprehension educational software includes tasks concerned with sight vocabulary (drill and practice of isolated words or contextualized vocabulary), word identification (usage and identification of syntactic, semantic and structural cues), language skills (grammar and sentence manipulation), critical thinking (usually associated with simulation software -- problem-solving activities), and study skills (learning techniques for studying, researching and reporting) [14].

Since reading educators as well as researchers emphasize the active and the interactive nature of reading, and the reconstructive nature of the task, in which the information is assimilated with that already stored in the reader's mind, prior knowledge is one of the most significant factors in determining reading comprehension. Prior knowledge was found important for comprehending,

remembering and interpreting textual information, for the recall of the information in the text and especially in answering inferential questions [2, 9, 11]. A number of techniques were suggested for the assessment of prior knowledge: free recall, word association, structured questions, recognition of multiple-choice answers and unstructured discussion [10].

3. THE COMPUTER AS A TUTOR FOR COGNITIVE SKILLS AND STRATEGIES IN READING

In the reading courseware produced by the authors [18] prior knowledge is not only assessed but also systematically taught. Pre-reading activities are used to foreground or provide readers with the necessary background knowledge. This is accomplished through activities that have set induction at their basis. They include, inter-alia, prediction activities -- from the title, the opening sentence, the structure or lay- out of the text and/or a prediction of genre. Skimming the passage for the gist is used to allow readers to develop realistic expectations as to the actual content of the passage. Exploring the "universe of the text", i.e. focusing attention on extra-textual information (such as headlines, titles and discourse markers, place and year of publication, charts, pictures) is used to bring both topic and genre into awareness. To activate previous knowledge, intriguing questions as well as simulation activities and brainstorming techniques are used, demanding selection and classification of information.

The most salient features of the text have been identified and analysed to provide the basis for while-reading activities. This analysis provided the features that need to be reinforced or brought into awareness: An array of reading skills and strategies were identified and activities designed for training sessions. e.g. procedural texts suggested activities for sequencing, cause-effect relationships and classification of information, while narratives such as legends suggested prediction of information, sequencing of events and evaluation of connotations.

The while-reading activities focus on a multitude of reading skills and attack strategies including:

* Classification into meaningful units, by associations, discrimination and comparison of ideas and words that have something in common.

* Locating main ideas by focusing attention on the most relevant information and distinguishing it from the supporting material.
* Recognizing examples and increasing awareness of their nature and function in the text, stressing that they aid understanding by illustrating and supporting concepts.
* Reading for factual information, focusing on certain types of reading materials such as tourist guides, cook books, and instructions.
* Recognizing classifications: divisions and organizational devices within the text, both explicit (i.e. using rhetorical markers) and implicit.
* Identification and comprehension of comparisons and contrasts by focusing attention on similarities and differences and their rhetorical markers.
* Inferences and recognition of implicit information; this is achieved by raising awareness of readers as to their abilities to make intelligent and relevant inferences about and through implicit information.
* Highlighting of cohesive devices and procedures meant to increase awareness of cohesive signals, redundancies and other markers of consistency such as anaphoric relations and chronological and logical sequencing.
* Understanding of logical relations among propositions such as cause and effect relationships.

Post-reading activities commonly include test-type recall questions. This procedure is contrary to the approach taken here. At its best form, the procedure tests memory, at its worse it discourages readers -- in neither case does it facilitate comprehension. Therefore, at this stage in the reading process, the courseware deals with summaries and a number of evaluation processes. These are skills that go beyond the text, use the readers' extra-textual knowledge and provide tools suitable for critical reading. Post-reading activities therefore include:

* Summarizing by condensing or reducing the information in a text through the selection of the main ideas, a skill which no doubt requires a thorough understanding of the material read.
* Evaluating texts - which is a high order process- by reading critically to recognize the writer's stand (subjective or objective) and by differentiating between material approved of by the author and material which the author tries to refute. The

readers' awareness of bias is also enhanced by bringing their attention to connotative word meaning.

Throughout the series, skills and strategies are re-entered and re-activated in a variety of text types and genres. The underlying assumption is that skills activated in one text are not always automatically transferred to another.

4. THE COMPUTER AS A TUTOR FOR META-COGNITIVE AWARENESS

In the interactive reading process there are at least four intervening factors between the reader and the text:

READER ---> a. background ---> b. syntax ---> c. lexis ---> d. suitable text-attack strategies---> TEXT

Let us analyze the difference between common reading instruction practices in the English as a Foreign or Second Language classroom and computerized reading instruction according to our model. In a regular reading lesson, the background knowledge required to cope with a specific reading text is usually imparted before the text is read, sometimes elicited from those students who possess it so as to be absorbed by those who do not. The instructor frequently takes care of presenting difficult syntactic structures and lexical items so students can cope with the text in question. Both students who need this pre-preparation and those who in fact do not, undergo the same treatment. Components a, b and c thus constitute a required part of the classroom reading lesson, whether needed by the individual student or not. In foreign language instruction these components tend to be perceived as main sources of difficulty by both students and instructors, and are therefore highlighted. Component d, the instruction and acquisition of effective attack-strategies, takes a secondary position although research has shown that without it, comprehension may fail.

Considering that components b and c are discrete and do not bridge over to the text as a whole, we believe instruction focusing on them to constitute a source of interference in the reading process. That is not to say that classroom lessons cannot be organized in a different manner, allowing for self-access to information sources in case of authentic need and for a more direct path leading to comprehension.

The computer, on the other hand, due to its unique characteristics for information storage and individualization of instruction can ideally serve as a tool for enhancing rather than interfering with reading comprehension. One must however admit that a lot of the existing "reading comprehension" software is in fact a replica of the regular classroom pattern.

In our computer model (cf. fig. 1), components a, b and c are part of an information bank accessible on request. This prevents the difficulty mentioned before, that of compulsory instruction of secondary components instead of voluntary access to them. Component d, the reading strategies, can deal with both micro and macro elements in the text, but proper emphasis and sequencing can ensure the development of global discourse comprehension and therefore constitute a lesser source of interference. Moreover, our model allows for an escape option which does not usually exist in a regular classroom lesson. This ensures that instruction of the skills can be "turned off" when the student considers he understands the text.

Another argument for the importance of emphasizing component d is the fact that the reading strategies seem to be transferable to other texts, whereas that is not necessarily true about the other levels (a, b and c). The model allows for emphasis on the main component in the reading comprehension lesson rather than on the secondary components whose place is in the language or in the subject area lessons.

COMPUTERIZED READING COMPREHENSION LESSON MODEL

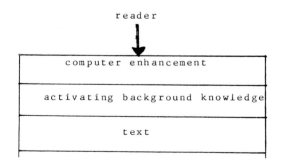

self-access options:

glossary
(access to unknown vocabulary)
grammar
(access to unknown structures)
information bank
(access to unknown facts)

focus: building up strategies for transfer to other texts

salient discourse features:

metacognitive awareness
tasks and activities
remediation if needed

helpful text-attack strategies:

metacognitive awareness
tasks and activities
remediation if needed

self-assessment

escape possibility

↓

comprehension of text

Fig. 1

The traditional classroom approach to reading comprehension emphasizes product. The learner is expected to understand and remember factual information, answer questions related to the readings, manipulate various aspects of the text (mostly structures), or relate to its organization, vocabulary or grammatical structures. Tasks that go beyond the text usually deal with the message of the passage and its implications.

Our approach emphasizes the cognitive processes employed by the reader during

reading. The underlying assumption is that reading courseware supplies the learner with a rich learning environment in which previously acquired reading skills and strategies are activated and others brought to awareness. Our courseware focuses on the most salient and relevant strategies required for the comprehension of a certain text. By a series of interactive tasks and techniques it attempts to instill in the learner reading habits that will eventually be transferred to other texts. Explanatory feedback including clues is given to the learner, with the aim of remediating incorrect answers or reinforcing the correct answer and the cognitive processes that led to it. The goal is thus to attain the internalization of the processes and their application in subsequent reading experiences.

REFERENCES

[1] Adams, M.J., and Collins, A. 1979. A schema-theoretic view of reading. In R.O. Freedle (ed.). New directions in discourse processing (pp.1-22). Norwood, N.J.: Ablex.

[2] Anderson, Richard C., Rand J. Spiro, and M.C. Anderson. Schemata as Scaffolding for the Representation of Information in Connected Discourse. American Educational Research Journal, vol.15 (Summer, 1978), pp.433-40.

[3] Baker, L. Do I understand or do I not understand? That is the question. Champaign: University of Illinois, Center for the Study of Reading, Reading Education Report No. 10, July, 1979.

[4] Baker, Linda and Ann Brown. Cognitive Monitoring in Reading. In J. Flood (ed.), Understanding Reading Comprehension: Cognition, Language, and the Structure of Prose, International Reading Association, Newark, Delaware, 1984, 21-44.

[5] Baten, L. and A.M. Cornu. Reading strategies for LSP texts: a theoretical outline on the basis of text function, with practical application. In Pugh, A.K. and Ulijn, J.M. (eds.) 1984. 190-201 . Reading for Professional Purposes. London: Heineman.

[6] Collins, A., J.S. Brown, and K.M. Larkin. Inference in text understanding. In R. Spiro, B. Bruce, and W. Brewer (eds.), Theoretical issues in reading comprehension. Hillsdale, New Jersey: Erlbaum, 1980.

[7] Flavell, J.H. Metacognitive Aspects of Problem Solving. In L.B. Resnick (ed.), The Nature of Intelligence. Hillside, N.J. Lawrence Erlbaum, 1976

[8] Harrison, C. & T. Dolan. Reading Comprehension - A Psychological Viewpoint. In Mackay, R., B. Barkman, & R.R. Jordan (eds.) Reading in a Second Language. Newbury House Publishers Inc., 1979.

[9] Holmes, Betty C. The Effect of Prior Knowledge on the Question Answering of Good and Poor Readers. Journal of Reading Behavior, vol. 15, no.1 (1983), pp. 73-84.

[10] Holmes, Betty C. and Nancy L. Roser. Five ways to assess readers' prior knowledge. The Reading Teacher, vol. 40, no. 7. March, 1987

[11] Johnston, Peter. "Prior Knowledge and Reading Comprehension Test Bias." Reading Research Quarterly, vol. 19 (Winter, 1984), pp. 219-39.

[12] Rumelhart, David E. and A. Orton. 1977. The Representation of Knowledge in Memory. In Anderson, Spiro, and Montague (eds.) Schooling and the Acquisition of Knowledge. Hillsdale, N.J. : Lawrence Erlbaum. pp.99-135.

[13] Rumelhart, David E. 1984. Understanding Understanding. In Flood, James (ed.) Understanding Reading Comprehension. Newark, Del.: International Reading Association.

[14] Scott, Diana and Jeanne Baker. Guidelines for selecting and evaluating reading software: Improving the decision making process. The Reading Teacher, May, 1987.

[15] Smith, F. 1982. Understanding Reading. N.Y. CBS College Pub.

[16] Stanovich, Keith E. Toward an interactive-compensatory model of individual differences in the development of reading fluency. Reading Research Quarterly, XVI, No.1, 1980.

[17] Wyatt, David H. Computers and ESL. A publication of CAL prepared by ERIC. Harcourt Brace Jovanovich, Inc., 1984.

[18] Turn On To Reading. Ramot, Tel Aviv University Publishers, 1986.

COMPUTERS IN EDUCATION, F. Lovis and E.D. Tagg (eds.)
Elsevier Science Publishers B.V. (North-Holland)
© IFIP, 1988

TOWARDS A KNOWLEDGE-BASED TOOL FOR CORRECTING FRENCH TEXT*

Louisette Emirkanian+ and Lorne H. Bouchard§

Université du Québec à Montréal
C.P. 8888, Succursale "A"
Montréal (Québec)
CANADA H3C 3P8

We present a morpho-syntactic analyzer for French which is capable of automatically detecting and of correcting (automatically or with user help) spelling mistakes, agreement errors and certain syntactic errors which are frequently encountered in children's texts. Emphasizing the specific language knowledge that is used, we describe the major sub-tasks of this analyzer: word categorization by dictionary lookup and spelling correction, contruction of a parse tree or of a forest of parse trees, correction of syntactic and morphological errors by processing the parse tree.

1.   INTRODUCTION

There seems to be general agreement concerning the fact that word processing is a tool which helps in the learning of writing. The act of writing is a complex act which according to Smith [1] can be subdivided into three major sub-tasks: prewriting, writing and rewriting. The positive effects of the use of word processing in these three areas have been identified and evaluated by Bradley [2], Daiute [3], Schwartz [4] and Schwartz [5]. In general, it is observed that children write more and more often. Little is said, however, about the positive effects on text content. Word processing encourages children to revise and correct, but offers little help in these areas. More recently, some word processors offer a spelling correction option. In all cases, however, word processors limit themselves to the words in the text. On the other hand, a number of tools for English text analysis have been developed. The Writer's Workbench [6] is a collection of tools developed at AT&T's Bell Laboratories. The two most important tools address proof reading and style analysis. The EPISTLE project [7], still in the experimental stage, is a vast project undertaken at IBM's Thomas J. Watson research laboratory. The long term goal of this research is a system which not only supports writing, but also text understanding. WANDAH [8] is a system that was developed in UCSD Pascal at UCLA. The system comprises three sub-systems: a word processor designed to support interactive composition, tools to assist composition and tools to help in the editing and the revising phases. These systems are difficult to adapt to French, since they are based on knowledge which is specific to English. Furthermore, in these systems the knowledge is rarely represented explicitly: indeed, the knowledge has most often been "compiled" for reasons of efficiency. Thus, these systems cannot easily reason about the knowledge they have. Finally, these systems are not usable as they exist, in the primary or secondary education environment.

2.   TOWARDS A ROBUST AND EFFICIENT MORPHO-SYNTACTIC ANALYSER

As a modest attempt to fill this gap for French, we have undertaken a research project the goal of which is to construct a morpho-syntactic analyzer for French capable of automatically detecting and of correcting (automatically or with help from the user) spelling mistakes, agreement errors and the most important syntax errors. This tool could be used to analyze word processor output.
This research project aims to develop an expert system in the area of French orthography, morphology and syntax. The novel feature of the system is that it is based on an integration at different levels of the knowledge of French. This knowledge is represented explicitly in the system and the system keeps track of the decisions it has made, which allows it not only to justify its decisions but also to reason about its reasoning.
The main problem is in the integration of knowledge of the language, knowledge which is at different levels: knowledge of orthography [9], of traditional grammar [10-11], of syntax [11-13] and also of the most frequently

---

*   This research is funded by the Social Sciences Research Council of Canada (SSRCC grant #410-85-1360).

+   Département de linguistique

§   Département de mathématiques et d'informatique

encountered errors [14-16]. In order to be able to use such knowledge, it must on the one hand be made operational and it must on the other hand be orchestrated.

In our system, these sources of knowledge are used as follows. Each sentence of the text is split up into words. Each word is categorized by dictionary look-up; knowledge of French orthography is represented as a collection of correction rules. An efficient parser, driven by a context-free grammar, builds a parse tree or a forest of parse trees in the case of ambiguity. This parser is deterministic in the sense that it blocks as soon as an error is detected. The parser can recall the spelling corrector. Then, knowledge of the sub-categorization of French verbs allows the system to eliminate automatically certain ambiguities and to detect and correct many errors. Finally, the user is consulted whenever the system cannot intervene.

Before presenting the system in depth, we must emphasize that the system we have designed is intended to assist at the knowledge level and not at the competence level. It is not designed as a tool to improve written communication skills.

The main sub-tasks of the analyser are as follows:
- word categorization by dictionary look-up and spelling correction,
- construction of a parse tree or of a forest of parse trees in cases of ambiguity,
- correction of syntax errors, detection and correction of morphological errors by processing the parse tree.

We shall now examine these three phases.

3.   WORD CATEGORIZATION AND SPELLING CORRECTION

3.1.   Classification of spelling mistakes

We have adopted Catach's classification [14], from where we also borrow the examples. She distinguishes phonetic errors (*puplier* instead of *publier*), from phonogrammic errors (the child knows the sound without knowing the transcription), some of which can modify the phonic value of a word (*gérir* instead of *guérir*, *oisis* instead of *oasis*) whilst others do not change the phonic value (*pharmatie* instead of *pharmacie*). In addition to these two types of errors, morphogrammic errors (caused by faulty knowledge of non-phonetic orthography) in grammatical elements (number agreement, for example) or in lexical elements (*enterremant* instead of *enterrement*, *abrit* instead of *abri*, for example), confusion of lexical homophones (*vain / vin*) or grammatical homophones (*on / ont*), problems with ideograms (punctuation, for example) and finally problems with non-functional letters which are derived , for example, from the Greek origin of a word (*téatre* instead of *théatre*).

We have excluded from our area of investigation all phonetic errors - errors which can be caused by faulty pronunciation.

On the other hand, our system can handle all the phonogrammic errors. Morphogrammic errors in grammatical elements are detected during the later morphological analysis phase. Errors in lexical morphemes are corrected during this phase, as well as errors which are due to the existence of non-functional letters. As for problems with homophones, grammatical homophones are detected during the parsing or the syntax analysis phases, but only some lexical homophones are detected during these phases: we can correct *vain / vin* but not *chant / champ*, since these elements, in addition to being homophones, belong to the same lexical category. The semantic knowledge available in our system is not sufficient to resolve this ambiguity.

Regarding spelling mistakes, phonogrammic errors (i.e., those due to the transcription of sounds) are the most frequent in French, mainly because of the problems caused by the phonic/graphic correspondence. For example, the sound *[o]* can be written in many ways: *au, aud* (at the end of a word), *eau*, etc. This is not the case in English, where the main spelling mistakes are due to random insertions or suppressions of letters, substitution of a letter for another, or transposition of two letters. We prefer to refer to these types of errors as typographical errors. Peterson, in a survey paper [17], summarizes the techniques used for detecting typographical errors in English text, and in a monograph [18], he describes in depth the design and implementation in Pascal of a typographical error detector. In a recent paper [19], Peterson presents statistics on the frequency of typographical errors in English.

Lahens, in his thesis [20], describes the Vortex system which shares some of the objectives of our system. However, Vortex uses a probabilistic approach. Furthermore, the endings of words are not singled out for special treatment in that system.

3.2.   The dictionary

Our system is based on two dictionaries, a dictionary of stems and a dictionary of endings. Associated with a stem, in the stem dictionary, a pointer is stored to a list of one or more endings which are stored in the endings dictionary. In this way, our system can handle all inflected forms efficiently, whilst also dealing efficiently with the numerous exceptions. Based on a suggestion by Knuth [21], a *trie* data structure is used to index the stem dictionary. Diacritical signs are removed from the letters when the *trie* is constructed and also when the a word is looked up in the *trie*. Indeed, the letters modified by the diacritical signs are only stored in the leaves of the *trie*. This allows our system to handle accent errors, a common spelling mistake, very efficiently.

Instead of entering "chameau", "chameaux", "chamelle" and "chamelles" in the dictionary, we store the common form "cham-" in the stem dictionary, together with its lexical category. We also store there, as pointers to the endings dictionary, the corresponding rules for constructing the number and gender endings and any additional syntactic or semantic information, as required. Note that we have defined the stem of a word to be the longest invariable part of the word.

For verbs, morphological, syntactical and semantical information is stored. The semantical information is not intended to exclude a sentence such *la table dort*, but rather to help resolve certain cases of structural ambiguity.

3.3. The look-up algorithm

The word to be looked up is scanned from left to right: each letter, stripped of its diacritical sign if need be, controls the walking of the stem *trie* until a leaf is reached. Associated with the leaf, we find the lexical category and the ending rules for the stem. Remaining letters of the word are looked up in the list of endings associated with the stem: the entry corresponding to an ending records, for example, the number and gender of nouns and adjectives, or the person, time and mood of the verbs which have this ending (the endings lists contain all possible endings of the verbs [10]). The most important ending errors are also recorded in the endings lists. Using this information, the system can already detect and correct ending errors at this level: for example, *chevals* instead of *chevaux*, *cloux* instead of *clous*.

A block during *trie* traversal signals the detection of a spelling mistake. The context of the letter responsible for the block is used to index a large set of rewrite rules, called correction rule, which are derived mainly from the phonic/graphic transcription rules of French [9]. These rules characterize the knowledge of French orthography which is used to correct the spelling error.

3.4. The correction algorithm

Although the set of correction rules is mostly based on the phonic/graphic transcription rules of French, certain rules are not based on such a strict correspondence at all, since the programs can also, for example, correct *enui* to *ennui* and *gérir* to *guérir*.

When a leaf is finally reached, the rule or rules which were applied to unblock the walk in the *trie* are used to correct the misspelt word.

In addition to substitution rules, we have a set of rules which are used only on the ending of a word. These rules are applied after the substitution rules and before moving back the blocking point. For example, for the word *tros*, the system proposes *trot*, *trots* and *trop* and for *blan* it proposes *blanc*.

If the user is not satisfied with the proposed correction, the system can propose another in some cases. For example, in response to the word *ventte* the system proposes *vente* (the noun and the verb) and if the user requests another correction, it then proposes *vante*.

In many cases, however, when the error is located before the blocking point, the correction algorithm must move the blocking point back and thus perform a systematic search of the dictionary, backtracking upon failure. Indeed, for the word *entente* spelt *antente*, the first blocking point is just after the second *n*, since *antenais* and *antenne* are in our dictionary [22].

The size of the dictionary and of the set of correction rules is large. The system uses simple metrics as heuristics [23], in order to filter the set of correction rules and reduce the search space. The selected rules are analyzed and those that do not increase *trie* penetration depth, or those that do not allow the system to move forward in a word (simple metrics of progress towards the goal of accounting for all the letters in a word) are rejected. Note that the expectations of the dictionary, represented as a *trie*, also effectively constrain the search space.

3.5. Word categorization

At this point, a word can have been assigned a single lexical category, as for example *cahier*: N [F-, etc.]. The word can also be assigned a wrong category, as for example in *il *pin*:: N [F-,etc.] which was written instead of *il peint*.. Finally, a word can be assigned many categories (case of lexical ambiguity), as for example *il vente*: N [F+,etc.] / V [present 1st /3rd person of indicative / subjunctive / imperative, etc.].

4. CONSTRUCTION OF A PARSE TREE OR OF A FOREST

We have compiled an empirical grammar of written French which is described by a context-free grammar. Our parser is based on the work of Tomita [24-25]. In a Tomita parser, a general purpose parsing procedure is driven by a parsing table which is generated mechanically from the context-free grammar of the language to be parsed. Tomita's main contribution has been to propose the use of a graph-structured stack which allows the parser to handle multiple structural ambiguities efficiently. We use YACC [26], a LALR(1) parsing table generator available in UNIX, to generate automatically the parsing table which drives the general parsing procedure. When generating the parsing tables, YACC detects and signals cases of structural ambiguity.

Many cases can arise in parsing French. Consider first the case when a word has been assigned multiple categories. Some of the ambiguities can be resolved by considering the expectations of the grammar. Consider the word *court*, which can be an adjective, an adverb, a noun, or a verb. If *court* is found in the context *il*: [ProCl] *court*:Adj / Adv / N / V [3rd person singular, etc.], the grammar accepts only the verb at this point. Similarly, the word *une* which can be a determinant, a noun, or a pronoun can automatically be reduced to noun in the context *il a lu la une du journal*.

Consider now the case when the parser cannot derive a parse tree: based on the hypothesis that there may be a spelling error which caused an erroneous category to be assigned, the parser calls the spelling corrector to revise the spelling of a word and hence the category assigned to it. In the case of the previous example *il *pin*, of the spelling alternatives for *pin*, only *peint*, the verb, is retained since *pain* is no more possible in this context than *pin*. Indeed, in our grammar of the sentence, only a verb or another clitic pronoun may appear after a clitic pronoun. Similarly, in the sentence *ils *on apporté le livre*, *on* will be corrected to *ont* . The parser efficiently constructs a parse tree, or a forest of parse trees which account for the sentence. In a Tomita parser, the forest of parse trees is represented efficiently by the use of a data structure analogous to a *chart* [27], which suppports "local ambiguity packing".

5. ANALYSIS OF THE PARSE TREE OR FOREST

A forest of parse trees can be produced in cases of structural ambiguity, such as in *il a rapporté des porcelaines de Chine*. It can also be caused by cases of lexical ambiguity such as *il veut le boucher*. In many cases, only some of the trees in the forest need be retained, since the system can automatically clear the forest. For example, although two parse trees are constructed for the sentence *Jean n'a pas effectué de lancer* (*lancer* being an infinitive verb or a noun), only the tree with *lancer* categorized as a noun is retained. At this level, the sub-categorization of the verb is a great help: this information is also stored in the dictionary, of course. For example, *effectuer* does not allow an infinitive phrase as a complement. Similarly, in the sentence *il a remarqué Marie arrivant à toute allure*, *Marie arrivant à toute allure* could be an adverbial phrase, *Marie* could be the object of *remarquer* and *arrivant à toute allure* could be an adverbial phrase, finally *Marie arrivant à toute allure* could be the object of *remarquer*. The first hypothesis (tree) is rejected since *remarquer* is sub-categorized as requiring a direct complement. Verb sub-categorization also allows the system to correct spelling mistakes at this stage. For example, the sentence **il panse que Marie viendra* will be corrected to *il pense que Marie viendra*, since *panser* does not accept a completive.

Similarly, in *il va *ou il veut* , **ou* is corrected to *où*. At this level we also correct, using information stored in the dictionary, an error of the type **quoique tu dises, je partirai* to *quoi que tu dises, je partirai*, since the sub-categorization of *dire* is not satisfied in the first case. Verb sub-categorization information also allows us to correct certain trees and improve others.

Consider the case of correcting a tree. For the sentence, *il punit qui ment*, initially *qui ment* is labelled as a sentence connected to the verb *punir*; but since *punir* cannot be sub-categorized by a completive sentence, the sentence *qui ment* is relabelled noun phrase.

Consider now the case where the sub-categorization allows us to improve a tree. In the sentence *Pierre mourra cette nuit*, *cette nuit*, initially labelled noun phrase, will be relabelled adverbial phrase, since *lire* cannot be sub-categorized by two noun phrases, as *nommer* can be, for example. The problem, however, is that the sentence *Pierre lit la nuit le journal* will be treated similarly! This is due to the lack of semantic information in our system. The formalization of the semantics of natural language is a major research problem [28]. We have had the opportunity to investigate this problem [29-30] and we believe that it would be presumptuous to hope to solve it in this project. In any case, these ambiguities do not have any bearing on the problem of agreement. On the other hand, in the last example, if the noun phrase *la nuit* had been enclosed inside commas, this noun phrase would have been labelled automatically as an adverbial phrase. Unfortunately, in children's texts [31], we observe that only the full stop is mastered at the end of primary school; thus we cannot rely on punctuation to help parsing very much.

6. CORRECTING SYNTAX ERRORS

A study of the syntax of primary school students [32-33] has shown that syntax errors in students' texts are rare. Out of 6580 communication units, only 79 (1.2%) were found to be ungrammatical. The unit of communication is equivalent to what the traditional grammar calls the sentence; that is, the root sentence and any embedded sentences [34]. We observed [16] that the most frequent problem is in the use of subordination (53% of the errors), in particular, the use of complex relative clauses (24 cases out of 42). Children also have problems with multiple embeddings: in general, when they connect an embedded sentence to another, the resulting sentence is ungrammatical, the main sentence being absent or incomplete. The other problems are related to coordination, to constituent mobility and to the use of clitic pronouns, where we observed a strong influence from the oral.

As for relative clauses, we counted non-standard clauses as ungrammatical, though they follow rules as much as the standard relative clauses. *La fille que je te parle* et *la fille que je parle avec* are examples of non-standard relative clauses, whilst the sentence **la fille dont que je te parle* is ungrammatical.

We have chosen for now to focus our attention on two of these problems: complex relative clauses and sequences of clitics. As part of a previous research project, we developed algorithms for handling complex relative clauses [30] and sequences of clitics [35]. For the sentence *la fille que je te parle*, the syntax correction algorithm proposes *la fille de qui/dont/de laquelle/avec qui/à qui/ à laquelle je parle*. On the other hand, in response to the sentence *la fille que je te parle*, the algorithm proposes *dont*, *de qui* and *de laquelle*, as possible choices. Again, it is the sub-categorization of the verb which gives us a handle on the problems of sequences of clitic pronouns. The program corrects ** je lui aide* to *je l'aide*, for example. However, in most cases, only an error is reported, the system being unable to correct the error, since it cannot identify precisely the referent of the clitic. **J'y donne* and **je lui donne* are examples of ungrammatical sentences; the system cannot propose with certainty the missing clitics: it will propose *la lui*, *le lui*, etc..., in the first case and *le lui*, *la lui*, *lui en*, etc..., in the second case.

7. CORRECTING AGREEMENT ERRORS

During morphological analysis, based on the information gleaned from the dictionary, the information collected in the parse tree and the agreement rules of French, the system isolates the noun phrases and checks to see if the agreement rules for number and gender have been applied. It then checks for agreement between the subject and the verb. Note that, for example, in the case of **les belles chameaux*, the system proposes both *les beaux chameaux* and *les belles chamelles*. In response to the sentence **le professeur explique la leçon aux élève de la classes*, the system proposes *le professeur explique la leçon aux élèves de la classe* and also *le professeur explique la leçon à l'élève des classes*, even if, based on our knowledge of the world, we know that only the first answer is possible. The agreement rules which we have formalized, some of which are recorded in the dictionary, allow our system to correct the errors most frequently found in student texts [36-37]. These errors are due, in particular for number agreement, to semantic interferences or to the proximity of other elements: for example, * *il veut être très riches* instead of *il veut être très riche*, *je les voient* instead of *je les vois* and * *Michel nous donnent des bonbons* instead of *Michel nous donne des bonbons*.

Finally, certain lexical ambiguities (there are relatively few remaining at this stage) could be resolved here: for example, this is the case for *le chouette anglais*, but *la chouette anglaise* still remains ambiguous.

8.   CONCLUSION

The automatic correction of French text is a major project. Knowledge at many different levels must be integrated and coordinated in the system. Only the construction of a prototype can attest to the success of such an integration. We have developed a prototype of the correction program in LISP, on a MacIntosh Plus. The behaviour of the final system will be refined by weighting the rules according to their utility. Statistics gathered from many different users will help us tune the general behaviour of the system, whilst statistics gathered for a given user will allow us to tune the behaviour of the system to the problems specific to that user.

ACKNOWLEDGEMENTS

We thank research assistants who are involved in the project, most of all, Sylvie Ratté, graduate student in Mathematics and Computer Science, who has been actively involved in the project since the beginning. We also thank Yves Bonnier (Mathematics and Computer Science undergraduate), Jacinthe Dupuis (graduate student in Linguistics), Denis Mousseau (Linguistics undergraduate) and Astrid Vercaingne (graduate student in Linguistics).

REFERENCES

[1]   Smith, F., Writing and the Writer (Holt, Rinehart and Winston, New-York, 1982).

[2]   Bradley, V., Improving Students' Writing with Microcomputers, Language Arts, 59, n°7 (1982) pp. 732-743.

[3]   Daiute, C. A., The Computer as Stylus and Audience, College Composition, 34, (1983) pp. 134-145.

[4]   Schwartz, M., Computers and the Teaching of Writing, Educational Technology, 22, n°11 (1982) pp. 27-29.

[5]   Schwartz, L., Teaching writing in the age of the word processor and personal computers, Educational Technology, 23, n°6 (1983) pp. 33-35.

[6]   Frase, L.T., The Unix Writer's Workbench Software: Rationale and Design, BSTJ (1983) pp. 1891-1908.

[7]   Miller, L. A., Heindorn, G. E. and Jensen, K., Text-Critiquing with the EPISTLE System: an author's aid to better syntax, in: AFIPS Conference Proceedings (1981) pp. 649-655.

[8]   Friedman, M., WANDAH: Writing-aid and Author's Helper, Prospectus, UCLA (1984) 26p.

[9]   Catach, N., L'orthographe française (Nathan, Paris, 1980) 334p. (French).

[10]   Le nouveau Bescherelle, I-L'art de conjuguer. Dictionnaire de 12000 verbes (Hurtubise HMH, Montréal,1980) 158p. (French).

[11]   Grevisse, M., Le bon usage, 9e édition (Duculot, Gembloux, 1969) 1228p. (French).

[12]   Gross, M., Méthodes en syntaxe (Hermann, Paris, 1975) 414p. (French).

[13]   Boons, J. P., Guillet, A. and Leclère, Ch., La structure des phrases simples en français (Droz, Genève, 1976) 377p. (French).

[14]   Catach, N., Duprez, D. and Legris, M., L'enseignement de l'orthographe (Nathan, Paris, 1980) 96p. (French).

[15]   Clas, A., and Horguelin, J. P., Le français, langue des affaires (McGraw-Hill, Montréal, 2e édition, 1979) 391p. (French).

[16]   Lafontaine, L., Dubuisson, C. and Emirkanian, L., "Fot s'avoir écrire": les phrases mal construites dans les textes d'enfants du primaire, Revue de l'association Québécoise de Linguistique, vol.2, n°2 (1982) pp. 81-90 (French).

[17]   Peterson, J. L., Computer Programs for Detecting and Correcting Spelling Errors, Communications of the ACM, vol.23 (1980) pp. 676-687.

[18]   Peterson, J. L., Computer Programs for Spelling Correction: An Experiment in Program Design (Springer-Verlag, Berlin, 1980) 213p.

[19]   Peterson, J. L., A Note on Undetected Typing Errors, Communications of the ACM, vol.29 (1986) pp. 633-637.

[20]   Lahens, F., Un modèle stochastique pour la vérification et la correction automatique de textes: le système Vortex, Thèse de docteur-ingénieur (Université Paul Sabatier, Toulouse, 1987) 166p. (French).

[21]   Knuth, D. E., The Art of Computer Programming: volume 3/Sorting and Searching (Addison-Wesley, Reading MA, 1973) 722p.

[22]   Robert, P., Dictionnaire (Le Robert, Paris, 1967) 1970p. (French).

[23]   Romanycia, M. H., and Pelletier, J. F., What is a heuristic? Computational Intelligence, vol.1 (1985) pp. 47-58.

[24]   Tomita, M., Efficient Parsing for Natural Language (Kluwer, Boston, 1986) 201p.

[25]   Tomita, M., An Efficient Augmented-Context-Free Parsing Algorithm, Computational Linguistics, vol.13, n°1-2 (1987) pp. 31-46.

[26]   Johnson, S. C., YACC: Yet Another Compiler-Compiler, in: Unix Programmer's Manual, vol.2 (Holt, Rinehart and Winston, New-York, 1983) pp. 353-387.

[27]   Winograd, T., Language as a Cognitive Process, Volume I: Syntax, (Addison-Wesley, Reading MA, 1983) 640p.

[28] Jackendoff, R., Semantics and Cognition (The MIT Press, Cambridge MA, 1983) 283p.

[29] Emirkanian, L. and Bouchard, L. H., Exploitation des connaissances de la langue dans la création d'un didacticiel, in: Actes du Congrès francophone sur l'enseignement assisté par ordinateur (Agence de l'informatique, Paris, 1987) pp. 197-205 (French).

[30] Emirkanian, L. and Bouchard, L. H., Conception et réalisation de logiciels: vers une plus grande intégration des connaissances de la langue,Revue Québécoise de linguistique, vol. 16, n°2 (1987) pp. 189-221 (French).

[31] Emirkanian, L., Dubuisson, C. and Poulin, M., La ponctuation au primaire: un point d'interrogation, in: Recherches Linguistiques à Montréal, vol.19 (1983) pp. 73-82 (French).

[32] Dubuisson, C. and Emirkanian, L., Complexification syntaxique de l'écrit au primaire, Revue de L'association Québécoise de Linguistique, vol.1, n°1-2, (1981-1982) pp. 61-73 (French).

[33] Dubuisson, C. and Emirkanian, L., Acquisition des relatives et implications pédagogiques, in : Lefebvre Cl. (ed.), La syntaxe comparée du français standard et populaire: approches formelle et fonctionnelle (Gouvernement du Québec, Office de la langue française, 1982) pp. 367-397 (French).

[34] Loban, W., Language development: kindergarten through grade twelve, NCTE Research report n°18, (Urbana IL, 1976).

[35] Emirkanian, L. and Bouchard, L. H., Conception et réalisation d'un didacticiel sur les pronoms personnels, Bulletin de l'APOP, vol.III, n°3 (1985) pp. 10-13 (French).

[36] Lebrun, M., Le phénomène d'accord et les interférences sémantiques, in: Recherches sur l'acquisition de l'orthographe (Gouvernement du Québec, 1980) pp. 31-81.

[37] Pelchat, R., Un cas particulier d'accord par proximité, in: Recherches sur l'acquisition de l'orthographe (Gouvernement du Québec, 1980) pp. 99-114.

COMPUTERS IN EDUCATION, F. Lovis and E.D. Tagg (eds.)
Elsevier Science Publishers B.V. (North-Holland)
© IFIP, 1988

COMPUTER ASSISTED LEARNING IN BIOLOGY: STUDENTS' ACHIEVEMENT BY GENDER AND COGNITIVE
OPERATIONAL LEVELS

Dr Reuven Lazarowitz
Department of Education in Technology and Science
IIT Technion, Haifa 32000. ISRAEL

Dr Jehuda Huppert
School of Education of the Kibbutz Movement
Haifa University, Oranim, Tivon 36910. ISRAEL

ABSTRACT

A computer assisted learning unit in biology, "The Growth Curve of Micro-organisms", was implemented
in 10th grade in a kibbutz comprehensive school. The unit included classroom instruction, laboratory work, and simulated experiments on the microcomputer. In the simulated experiments, students
had to investigate the impact of three variables: temperature, nutrient concentration, and the
initial number of individuals, separately and simultaneously, upon the growth curve of micro-
organisms population.

The sample consisted of 58 students (34 boys and 24 girls) and lasted four weeks, including the
testing procedure. Students' achievement was assessed by a multiple choice questionnaire, and their
cognitive operational level by a video-taped group test procedure. Data was treated by two-way
analysis of variance. The results indicated that girls received higher scores than boys, but the
differences were not significant. Significant differences in achievement were found among the three
groups of students categorized by cognitive operational level. No interaction was found between
gender and cognitive operational level.

The problem of the appropriateness of a CAL unit in biology with simulated experiments, to be used
with high school students of different reasoning levels, is discussed.

1. INTRODUCTION

Using the microcomputer for content instruction
is known as computer assisted instruction (CAI)
in the USA, or computer assisted learning (CAL)
in England and other countries. In this study,
the term CAL will be used. The CAL is used in
different forms, such as test reading, games,
tutorial, drill and practice and simulations.
In science teaching, CAL can play an important
role, either in classroom or in laboratory
instruction, not as a substitution but as an
additional tool. This tool can be used in
simulating real objects of events when there is
a shortage of time or equipment, or where there
is an opportunity to raise the level of instruction to a higher cognitive level. The microcomputer enables students to deal with one or
more variables simultaneously in simulated
experiments, following real ones in which each
variable was treated separately.

In this study, a CAL unit "The Growth Curve of
Micro-organisms" was implemented in the 10th
grade biology classes, in a kibbutz high
school, in order to find out possible relations
between academic achievement and students'
gender and cognitive operational levels.

The use of the microcomputer gives the opportunity of involving the learner actively in the
learning process, due to the fact that it can
be used either in small groups of two or three,
or on an individual basis. The microcomputer
can allow students to progress at their own
pace, thus having an important implication for
the gifted learner as well as for the slow one.
The advantages and disadvantages of CAL were
described in [1]. Long term experiments which
require expensive equipment and materials can
be simulated; the use of microcomputers enables
remedial education, and may help students develop creative abilities; as a result changes are
to be expected in students' cognitive and
affective domains. As for the disadvantages of
using CAL, to mention some of them: teachers
and teacher trainers need to adapt to new
methods of instruction; they may not have the
necessary expertise in using the microcomputer,
a fact which may arouse fears and antipathy;
the cost of the equipment; the available software which often is not adequate, according to
the content and the methodology used. Several
factors which characterize poor software are:
a) the inadequate use of the interactive and

individualizing capabilities of the micro-computer, b) use of multiple choice items as weak interactive forms, c) text presentation, and d) use of pictures and materials of little educational objective purpose [2]. Two kinds of software were identified in [3]: 1) Software which is prepared by experts in the subject matter area, who are able to design instructional software and to program it as well. There are very few of these. 2) Software developed by a team-effort, an approach which is called top-down programming technique.

In [4] it was specified that while the microcomputer may be used in an existing curriculum in order to improve problem solving and logical thinking, the computer is, unfortunately, mostly used for mastery of facts by drill and practice type software. Following the above assumptions and based on the approach described in [5], we developed a software program, "The Growth Curve of Micro-organisms", which was integrated into a modular course of an existing curriculum for 10th grade, called "The Micro-organisms and Man" developed by [6]. See Flow Chart 1.

While the learning unit software will be described later on, we shall refer here only to the fact that the most important part of the software includes simulations of experiments, in which students have to deal with three variables, separately or simultaneously: 1) the initial number of cells in a population; 2) the range of the temperature; 3) the nutrient factor. Students were asked to perform simulated experiments in which they had to find out the impact of those three factors, as well as their interaction in the growth curve of a micro-organism population.

The role of a simulation is not to replace the experiments performed in the laboratory, but to give students an opportunity to receive supplemental contact with the variables tested in the real experiment. Students should be active during the simulation experiment, by writing down their hypothesis, collecting data, plotting this data again in the computer and using it for gathering new results, or graphs, tables, etc. Thus, students will have active interactions with the microcomputer instead of being passive learners [7-8-9-10-11].

FLOW CHART 1

A MODULAR COURSE "MICRO-ORGANISMS AND MAN"

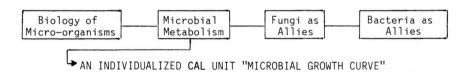

AN INDIVIDUALIZED **CAL** UNIT "MICROBIAL GROWTH CURVE"

ACTIVITIES FLOW CHART

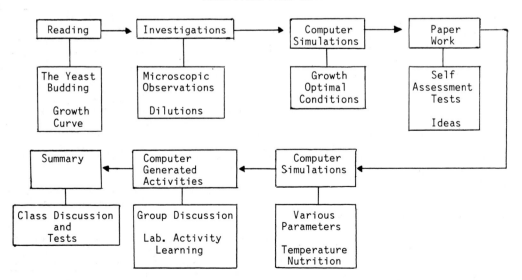

1.1 Literature Survey

In the literature there are indications that learning to program computers may require the use of logical thinking skills [12-13]. Those skills are characterized by formal operational levels according to [14]. In a meta-analysis study, [15], was found an effect size of +.82 (under one standard deviation), on students' performance when microcomputers were used in instruction. The use of computer-assisted instruction improved the academic learning by below-average and average students at the middle school level [16].

Improvement in achievement while CAL was implemented was reported in [17] and [18]. Higher achievement obtained by students taught by microcomputer simulations, laboratory activities, and a combination of these two strategies vs. conventional classroom instruction, was described in [19], in which differences in achievement were found among students with different levels of logical reasoning ability. Those findings may raise the question of the appropriateness of the CAL mode of instruction to all kinds of middle school students.

It will be of interest to mention that in [20] it was reported that computer simulated experiments were found to be as effective as hands-on laboratory experiments, and that no significant differences in performance were found between females and males in learning the volume displacement concept, and that males' retention was even better than the females.

Computer simulations were found also to enhance students' active involvement in the learning process, to make possible the applying of principles which otherwise would be practised less often, and to help students to meet the learning unit objectives [21].

Interesting too are the findings reported in [22] that "high school females performed better than males in some specific areas of programming, such as analysis and algorithmic application, where the problems were expressed verbally rather than mathematically".

All of the above findings, as well as the importance of the graphs in science learning discussed in [23] supported our selection of the independent variables to be investigated in this study: 1) Gender differences in achievement learning while a CAL unit is used along with hands-on laboratory work; and 2) the use of graphs as a way of applying students' results from the simulated experiments.

Our research model followed the recommendations found in [15], in which the authors suggested that instead of conducting studies in which CAL is compared with other methods of instruction, it would be more worthwhile to investigate by what is called a "direct instruction" approach, which has a strong association with high achievement. By direct instruction, one may refer to clear objectives, appropriate practice, frequent assessment and objectives-oriented feedback. The opinion expressed in [15] is that "microcomputers can be used to provide all of these features" and to have a positive impact on instruction. These facts support the call for studies which may investigate the "most effective ways to achieve certain instructional goals by using microcomputers".

While they may not have general applicability, evaluational studies upon hypotheses testing may be preferred; they can even be primarily for local utility [15]. So, studies which investigate "the impact of particular pieces of computer-based simulation, would be of higher priority than testing more general hypotheses about the use of computers in classrooms" [15].

Following these suggestions, we chose the use of a CAL simulation integrated in an existing curriculum taught in regular classroom-laboratory settings, in order to investigate the impact of the CAL unit the "Growth Curve of Micro-organisms", [6], on the academic achievement of 10th grade students, in relation to their gender and cognitive operational level. This subject is important not only from the biological point of view, but also for its possible relation to the requirement of higher cognitive levels of thinking.

Learning the factors which influence the growth curve of micro-organisms population and using them separately or simultaneously in simulated experiments through the microcomputer, can save not only time and equipment, but also permit students to perform experiments not done before in the high school laboratory. Thus, those simulated experiments may enhance students' ability to apply the skills learned to any other subject in which the growth of different populations is considered. While application and transfer skills were not investigated in this study in particular, we do ask if microcomputer simulated experiments in the subject of the growth curve of micro-organisms may offer an equal opportunity in achievements to girls and boys, and to students characterized as concrete, transitional and formal operational reasoners.

2. RESEARCH DESIGN

2.1 The sample

The sample consisted of 58 students (34 boys and 24 girls) from three 10th grade classes from a comprehensive kibbutz high school. They study biology as an elective course for four periods per week (each period 50 minutes), using in their regular classroom-laboratory instruction the Biological Science Curriculum Studies (BSCS), Yellow Version, [24]. While studying the chapter which deals with micro-organisms, the CAL unit "Growth Curve of Micro-organisms" was introduced to them, thus adding to their laboratory periods the microcomputer, Apple IIe. Since in this school most of the students have learned how to use a micro-computer, which is widely used in different subject matter instruction, no one was con-fronted with this mode of learning for the first time. The three classes were taught in their classrooms two periods per week and in the laboratory the other two periods. Each class was taught by a different high school biology teacher. All three of them had a B.Sc. in biology and a Certificate of Teaching in high school, and participated in a workshop in which they learned how to use microcomputers, as well as how to integrate them in an existing curriculum. So for both the students and the teachers, the microcomputer integration in the learning process was a common well-known tool.

3.   A DESCRIPTION OF THE SOFTWARE "THE GROWTH CURVE OF THE MICRO-ORGANISMS"

3.1   A simulation

The biology of Micro-organisms is one of the important subjects taught at the junior college and high school level. While the cell struc-tures and physiology of micro-organisms can be studied in the regular course sites of the classroom and laboratory work, some other aspects cannot always be taught, for different reasons. One of the aspects neglected is the issue of the "Growth Curve", since its study requires several long term laboratory sessions, and materials and equipment which are not always available. The study of this topic is important, since it enables students to inves-tigate the nature of the growth process of micro-organisms and to study the impact of various environmental factors, such as tempera-ture, nutrient concentration, and the initial number of individuals, on the population growth.

Our goal was to use the microcomputer for experiment simulations as a tool for overcoming the shortage of time, material and equipment, and to use it at the same time for high cogni-tive level activities in the instructional process. Simulating experiments requires students to exhibit specific skills such as decision making and problem solving.

The modular course included classroom instruc-tion, in which students learned the character-istics of the micro-organisms, such as their structure, the life processes and other related facts. The students became acquainted with the definition of population, generation time, lag phase and exponential phase of the growth of micro-organisms.

In laboratory work students examined yeast cells under a light microscope, studying their reproduction and budding process and learned how to count cells with a haemocytometer. Students learned also how to dilute yeast cell culture and how to calculate the actual cell numbers in the sample.

The simulation program made it possible to perform many "experiments" in a short time and to follow the influence of various factors such as temperature, nutrient conditions, etc., on the growth curve in a very quick way. The microcomputer simulation was integrated into the sequence of the learning activities in the classroom and laboratory, which were performed at the students' own pace.

4.   THE LEARNING PROCESS AND PROCEDURE

The following steps were studied in the computer simulations:

a)   students were required to feed data into the computer related to the initial conditions of the yeast cells' growth. The data included different temperatures, different nutrient concentrations and different initial numbers of cells of the culture.

b)   students counted the number of cells as they were exposed on the screen in a frame of a simulated haemocytometer under various growth conditions, as mentioned above, and recorded the obtained data in their notebooks.

c)   students were asked to plot the results of the population growth, in order to form a graph of a growth curve on the screen, and were required to analyze the results obtained in the simulation program by using a worksheet. The concepts of a population growth curve, such as the lag, log stationary phase, were explained in the worksheet and helped students to inter-pret the graph results.

In the following stage students were required to count the initial yeast cells sample again, which was kept at a constant temperature. The students had to define (with the use of the graph obtained earlier) the growth phase of the original yeast culture.

Computer Generated Assignments – Within this frame, students were required to apply the growth curve pattern to other populations and to hypothesize the impact of external factors on a population growth curve. Then the hypo-theses suggested in the above step served for classroom discussion.

The CAL unit included a self-assessment test with twelve multiple-choice questions. The following procedures were sequenced in the test. When the students chose a wrong answer they were not able to try for another answer or to pursue a new question. Instead, they were given remedial instruction for the particular knowledge regarding the question. Following this reiteration, the program allowed them to continue and to try to answer again. If after this second attempt they succeeded in selecting the correct answer, the program allowed them to pursue the next question. In case of a mistake at the second attempt, the student was asked to consult the teacher. This self-assessment test helped students to prepare themselves for the achievement test given at the end of the CAL unit.

4.1 The Implementation Process of the CAL Program in the Classroom

Three factors should be considered in relation with the implementation process:

1) <u>The classroom setting</u>: The laboratory classroom setting was made suitable for individualized or small group learning. The computers were situated in different corners of the laboratory and so was the necessary equipment. No special lessons were used to work on the simulation program and therefore it was studied in a regular biology lesson held in the laboratory classroom.

2) <u>The student</u>: The program "Growth Curve" was used as part of a modular course "Micro-organisms and Man". This course was based on self-paced student progress. The students worked on different assignments at the same time, progressing at their own pace. The simulation program "Growth Curve" was integrated into the learning process of the module as one of the various assignments. Three Apple IIe microcomputers were available in the laboratory and the students worked independently (or in small groups) on the simulation program. The self-paced progress enabled the efficient use of the computer time. In Flow Chart 2, students' self-paced activities are presented.

3) <u>The teacher</u>: The self-paced study of the simulation program urged certain changes in the teacher's role in the classroom. The teacher was now expected to be able to manage a more complicated learning structure and to be able to manage successfully the use of a microcomputer. The teacher was acting more as an advisor than as a source of knowledge. During the classroom discussions held as a summary of the simulation program, the teacher was acting as a motivator to help the students gain an overall picture of the programs' concept – "The population growth curve".

FLOW CHART 2

THE CLASSROOM MANAGEMENT

OF AN INDIVIDUALIZED CAL UNIT IN BIOLOGY

The Self-Paced Progress Enables an Efficient Use of the Computer Time

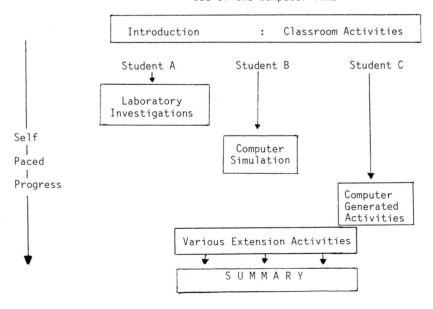

5. INSTRUMENTS

5.1 Achievement test on the Growth Curve subject

This test was administered at the end of the CAL unit. The test included 15 multiple choice questions, taken from the BSCS [25], and 5 open questions. The questions' content were related to: micro-organisms' size, reproduction and multiplication, population growth, growth phase regulation, and mutual relations among populations. The test has content validity assessed by 5 high school biology teachers who reached an inter-judge agreement of 90% regarding: 1) test questions' adequacy to the content taught; 2) the appropriateness for 10th grade students; 3) the language used; and 4) the correct choice out of four items.

The reliability of the test was calculated, based on students' answers, and a —Cronbach value of .85 was obtained.

5.2 Instrument for assessing students' cognitive level of operation

Students' cognitive operational levels were assessed by a Video-Taped Group Test (VTGT), [26]. The VTGT is a 12 tasks test, which asks for the following formal reasoning patterns: conservation of weight and volume, control of variables, proportional, probabilistic, combinatorial and correlational reasoning. The VTGT has an internal reliability of .82 with 10th grade students and its inter-judge percentage of scoring procedure agreement was found to be 91%. The VTGT was content validated by a group of 5 science educators as appropriate for a study with high school students. Testees can score 0 to 2 points for each task and 0 to 24 points for the complete test. Although the VTGT total score can be considered as a continuous variable, students were classified by their VTGT scores in the following way: 0 to 8 points as concrete reasoners; 9 to 16 points as transitional reasoners; and 17 to 24 points as formal reasoners. This classification is based on the analysis of tasks' level of difficulty described in [26]. While the tasks were shown to students in a Video-Taped presentation, students answered the tasks through a paper and pencil procedure.

6. RESEARCH PROCEDURE

The CAL unit was taught during three weeks in the classroom and laboratory, as explained above. At the end of the CAL unit, students were given the two instruments in each classroom, one period for the administration of the VTGT and one period for the achievement test on the Growth Curve. Each period lasted for 60 minutes.

Thus the independent variables in this study were: 1. gender; 2. students' cognitive operational level; and 3. the mode of instruction. The dependent variable was students' score on the CAL learning unit, the Growth Curve of Micro-organisms. The following research questions were investigated:

Are there differences in achievement mean scores attributed to students' gender and cognitive operational level?

Is there any interaction between gender and cognitive operational level in the mean scores obtained by students?

Data collected by the VTGT instrument served for categorizing students by their cognitive operational level, according to their gender. Then the mean scores on the Growth Curve CAL unit were analyzed and compared for statistical purposes. Data was treated by a two way analysis of variance, using the GLM model from the SAS program.

RESULTS

The mean scores of the groups by gender and cognitive levels and their standard deviation error of the least means (STD ERR LS MEANS is an estimate of what the standard deviation of that distribution would be), are presented in Table 1.

From the table, one can see that: 1) there are differences in means between boys and girls; 2) there are differences between the three students' cognitive levels; 3) the differences in students' cognitive levels are consistent by the gender, too. In all cases, girls achieved higher than boys.

Are these differences significantly higher? To answer this question, a two-way analysis of variance was performed and the results are presented in Table 2.

The results show that the differences among students' cognitive levels are significant; boys and girls did not differ significantly, and no interaction was found between students' cognitive operational levels and gender.

8. DISCUSSION

The CAL Growth Curve of Micro-organisms while making it possible for students to study at their own rate, asked for a learning process in which students were interactive with the micro-computer. This interaction called students to use simultaneously three variables which influence the growth curve of the micro-organisms' population. While students learned about each variable separately in the classroom and laboratory work, in the microcomputer simulation they were asked to perform several simu-

Table 1

Mean scores and standard deviation errors of the means of students' achievement on the growth curve by gender and cognitive operational levels

Groups	Gender	N	Growth curve X	STD ERR LS MEAN		P
1	Boys	34	80.02	2.21	Groups	
2	Girls	24	81.70	2.63	1-2	NS

Cognitive Level					Scheffe-Test*	
1	Concrete	3	59.25	7.21	1-3	0.5
2	Transitional	32	78.79	2.08	2-3	NS
3	Formal	23	86.78	2.66	3-1	0.5

Cognitive Level By Gender						
1 Boys	Concrete	1	50.00	11.78		
2 Girls		2	68.50	8.33	1-2	NS
3 Boys	Transitional	17	77.52	2.85		
4 Girls		15	80.06	3.04	3-4	NS
5 Boys	Formal	16	84.56	2.94		
6 Girls		7	89.00	4.45	5-6	NS

STD ERR LS MEAN = Standard deviations error of the least means
NS = non-significant
* Scheffe-test between groups

Table 2

Two-way analysis of variance on the mean scores on growth curve by gender and cognitive operational levels.

Source	df	ss	ms	F-value	P
Groups	5	2137.98	427.59	3.08	.01
Error	52	7219.60	138.83		
Corrected total	57	9357.58			
Cognitive levels	2	2062.57		7.43	.001
Gender	1	354.46		2.55	.116
Cognitive levels x gender	2	158.14		0.57	.569

lated experiments with different combinations of the three variables. According to students' decisions, they were asked to monitor the results and then to construct a growth curve based on their results. Then they were asked to apply their former knowledge to a new situation by combining three variables at a time. Students had to plot the results in a graph.

then to analyze the graph and to find out the impact of the three variables on the growth curve. This analysis asked students also for an interpretation of the results regarding the growth curve of any other population.

While girls obtained higher grades than the boys, the differences were not statistically significant (see Table 1). The results show that girls did as well as the boys on the CAL biology learning unit in all the unit requirements. These results can be explained by the fact that the CAL enabled students to learn at their own pace and probably the individualized mode used (students learned individually or in groups of two) offered an opportunity for the girls to achieve as well as the boys. These results are similar to [27-28] findings, in which it was shown that when an individualized mode of instruction or small group approach was used in high school learning, girls can achieve equally to boys and even a little better. These simulated experiments in a CAL setting probably freed the girls in the classroom from both the competitive learning environment climate in the frontal classroom approach and from the students' and teachers' social expectations that girls are expected to do less in science. This freedom, maybe, made possible that girls who are free from fears and social expectations can use their academic potential and achieve higher. Thus, can we add the CAL approach to the individualized and small group modes of instruction, as suggested strategies in which girls can achieve in science learning as well as the boys, or even higher? More research with larger samples is needed in order to answer this question.

As to the significant differences found regarding students' cognitive operational level, these results are similar with [12], who found a relationship between learning to program and logical thinking skills. In our case, while least square means analysis among the three cognitive operational level groups yielded significant differences between groups 1:2, 1:3; and 2:3, a more rigid analysis, the Scheffe technique, located the significant difference at .05 point level between the concrete and formal groups, but not between transitional and formal ones (see Table 1). So, since in our sample only 3 concrete reasoners were found and no significant differences were found between transitional and formal ones, we do not have grounds for deciding whether or not the CAL unit was adequate for all operational level students. But we can say that even those students who were found to be in a transitional level between the concrete and formal achieved as well as the formal students, the difference being 7 points only. At least we have a partial answer to the question of the appropriateness of a CAL simulation unit to different operational high school students' levels.

The simulated experiments in the microcomputer required students to manipulate three variables at a time, to investigate their impact on the growth curve and to apply the knowledge acquired in the classroom instruction and laboratory work to the new situations to which they were exposed in the microcomputer. They had to choose which range of temperature they would like to experiment with. They had to decide with what nutrient concentration to work and with what initial number of individuals to start each simulated experiment. Thus, they were asked to use skills such as decision making, application, growth curve construction and interpretation. In all these skills, the transitional students did as well as the formal ones. More research with a greater sample, together with a careful analysis of the learning skills required by CAL simulation, is needed in order to answer the question of the fitness of the CAL simulations to different students' operational levels.

REFERENCES

[1]   A.J. Chambers and W.J. Sprecher, Computer Assisted Instruction: "Current Trends and Critical Issues", Communications of the ACM, The Association for Computing Machinery, June 1980.

[2]   A. Bork, Education and Computers: "The Situation today and some Possible Futures", T.H.E. Journal, 1984, 92-97.

[3]   D.J. Spain, Why isn't there more good instructional software?. The American Biology Teachers, vol.47, no.6, 1985, 378-380.

[4]   J. Graef, Teaching Science with Computers, The Physics Teacher, October 1984, 430-436.

[5]   M. Daley and D. Hillier, Computer simulation of the population growth (Schizosaccharomyces pombe) experiment, Journal of Biological Education, vol.15, no.4, 1981, 266-268.

[6]   J. Huppert, The Micro-organisims and Man, A Modular course in Microbiology, Ph.D. Dissertation, University of Bath, England, 1982.

[7]   J. Dennis, The Illinois series on educational applications of computers, Urbana, Illinois: College of Education, 1979.

[8]   V. Lunneta and A. Hofstein, Simulation in science education, Science Education, vol.65, no.3, 1981, 243-252.

[9]   G. Marks, Computer simulations in science teaching: An introduction, Journal of Computers in Mathematics and Science

Teaching, vol.1, no.4, 1982, 18-20.

[10] N. Roberts, D. Anderson, R. Dean, M. Garet, and W. Shaffer, Introduction to computer simulations, Addison-Wesley, Reading, Massachusetts, 1983.

[11] E.L. Shaw, M.L. Waugh, and J.R. Okey, Using Computer Simulations in Classrooms, Paper presented at the Annual Meeting of the National Association for Research in Science Teaching, Dallas, Texas, April 1983.

[12] K. Padilla, J.R. Okey, and G. Dillashaw, The relationship between science process skill and formal thinking abilities, Journal of Research in Science Teaching, vol.20, 1983, 239-246.

[13] F.G. Dillashaw and S.R. Bell, Learning outcomes of computer programming instruction for middle-grades students: A pilot study, Paper presented at the Annual Meeting of the National Association for Research in Science Teaching, French Lick Springs, Indiana, April 15-18, 1985.

[14] B. Inhelder and J. Piaget, The growth of logical thinking from childhood to adolescence, Basic Books, New York, 1958.

[15] K.C. Wise and J.R. Okey, The impact of microcomputer-based instruction on student achievement, Paper presented at the Annual Meeting of the National Association for Research in Science Teaching, Dallas, Texas, April 1983.

[16] H.J. Becker, Instructional uses of computers, Reports from the 1985 National Survey, Center for Social Organization of Schools, The John Hopkins University, Nov. 1983, 3.

[17] H.J. Hallworth and A. Brehner, Computer assisted instruction in schools: Achievement, present development, and projections for the future, Calgary University, Calgary, Canada, ERIC Document Reproduction Service no. ED 200188, 1980.

[18] P.K. Burns and W.C. Bozeman, Computer-assisted instruction and mathematics achievement: Is there a relationship?, Educational Technology, vol.20, no.11, 1980, 32-39.

[19] E.D. Shaw and J.R. Okey, Effects of microcomputer simulations on achievement and attitudes of middle school students, Paper presented at the Annual Meeting of the National Association for Research in Science Teaching, French Lick Springs, Indiana, April 15-18, 1985.

[20] B. Soon Choi and E. Gennaro, The effectiveness of using computer simulated experiments on Junior High students' understanding of the volume displacement concept, Journal of Research in Science Teaching, vol.24, no.6, 1987, 539-552.

[21] R.H. Rivers and E. Vockell, Computers simulations to stimulate scientific problem solving, Journal of Research in Science Teaching, vol.24, no.5, 1987, 403-415.

[22] R.E. Anderson, Females surpass males in computer problems solving: Findings from the Minnesota Computer Literacy Assessment, Journal of Educational Computing Research, vol.3, no.1, 1987, 39-51.

[23] R. Nachmias and M.C. Linn, Evaluations of science laboratory data: The role of computer presented information, Journal of Research in Science Teaching, vol.24, no.5, 1987, 491-506.

[24] BSCS, Biological Science Curriculum Studies Yellow Version. The Israeli Centre for Science Teaching, The Hebrew University of Jerusalem, Jerusalem, Israel, 1975.

[25] BSCS, Biological Science Curriculum Studies, Resource book of test items for biological science. An inquiry into life, Education Improvement Corporation, Boulder, Colorado, 1968.

[26] M. Shemesh and R. Lazarowitz, The development of a video-taped group test for assessing formal operational level, International Conference on Education in the 90's: Equality, Equity, and Excellence in Education, Tel-Aviv University, Israel, December 18, 1984.

[27] R. Lazarowitz and J. Huppert, The development of individualized audio-visual learning units in junior High School biology and the students' achievement, European Journal of Science Education, vol.3, no.2, 1981, 195-204.

[28] R. Lazarowitz, J.H. Baird, R. Hertz-Lazarowitz and J. Jenkins, The effects of modified Jigsaw on achievement, classroom social climate, and self-esteem in high school science classes, In R. Slavin, et al. (eds.), Learning to Cooperate, Cooperate to Learn, Chapter 9, Plenum Press Publishing Corp., New York, USA, 1985, 231-253.

COMPUTERS IN EDUCATION, F. Lovis and E.D. Tagg (eds.)
Elsevier Science Publishers B.V. (North-Holland)
© IFIP, 1988

RESEARCH ON THE CONTENTS OF A BIOLOGY COMPUTER-BASED LEARNING PRODUCT AND PEDAGOGICAL ACHIEVEMENTS GIVING ACCESS TO THE STUDY OF DIFFERENT THEMES THROUGH A MULTIPLE-ENTRY PROCEDURE

Colette FAVARD-SERENO,   Michel LAUTHIER,
Jacques FISZER and Nicole BERNARD-DAUGERAS

Université Paris 6 et Université Paris 7, France *

Mailing address: J. Fiszer, Université Paris 7, OPE-Biologie,
2 place Jussieu, 75251 PARIS Cedex 05, France

The pedagogical procedure here described offers any student the possibility to select, in the subject matter covered by a previously achieved Biology computer-based learning unit, the definite topic he is concerned with at a given moment. With this design, and on the basis of the contents of the whole unit, we defined several themes of study. For each theme, a computer-based dialogue is built up, utilizing some of the constituent materials of the unit, but with a new type of organization. In addition, we worked out further materials specifically related to the theme. A choice of entries, shown on a menu, is given to the student. Each entry gives access to a definite theme. This new procedure allows each learner to manipulate Biology concepts in different contexts and, thereby, to get to the mastery of the studied area.

1. INTRODUCTION

In previous papers (10-11) were described the main features of our recent pedagogical research and of our Molecular Embryology computer-based learning materials, dealing with Biology of Reproduction and Development, in conjunction with Molecular Biology, the general goal being to attain the most appropriate integration of three different aspects: descriptive, experimental, molecular.

The purpose of this paper is to report further didactic developments which are being applied to previously achieved computer-based learning materials, and to explain the design of a new pedagogical procedure which allows the students to manipulate the different Biology facts and concepts in many and varied contexts. Such a procedure should improve the understanding of different aspects of a given subject, in order to reach the mastery of the studied area.

2. BIOLOGY COMPUTER-BASED LEARNING MATERIALS

Like all former OPE-BIOLOGY dialogues (2-3-4-6), our current pedagogical products are meant for University students, more particularly for first and second year medical and biology students. Before practising these computer-based pedagogical materials, the students must already be acquainted with the subject matter - whatever their regular courses and handbooks may be.

The major pedagogical purposes of our Biology courseware include among others: training in logical reasoning (deductive as well as inductive reasoning) and training in experimental methodology (2).

2.1. Main outlines

The whole set of Molecular Embryology computer-based learning materials is to be built up in a great number of "units", which are autonomous or semi-autonomous, and which can be interlinked in a variety of ways, under proper conditions (10-11).

These pedagogical materials cover important aspects of gametogenesis (which is the process of production of sexual cells or gametes) in terms of Molecular Biology, and their consequences on embryonic development (7-9-12).

A first group of three units deals with chromosomes as they can be observed du-

* C. Favard-Séréno: Université Paris 6 et Institut de Recherche en Biologie moléculaire,
      Tour 43, 2 place Jussieu, 75251 PARIS Cedex 05, France.

   M. Lauthier: Université Paris 6, Laboratoire de Biologie du Développement,
      Bâtiment C, 4 place Jussieu, 75230 PARIS Cedex 05, France.

   N. Bernard-Daugéras: Université Paris 6 et Muséum d'Histoire Naturelle,
      7 rue Cuvier, 75005 PARIS, France.

ring some time in the course of gameto-genesis. These chromosomes, owing to their very particular aspect during that time, closely related to the way they are functioning, are currently referred to as "lampbrush chromosomes" (1-5-8).

These three units are respectively dealing with :
- characterization,
- chemical constitution,
- biosynthetic activity, of lamp-brush chromosomes.

This third unit constitutes the mate-rial for the present research.

2.2. Contents and objectives

The "biosynthetic activity unit" covers: identification, localization and precise nature of synthetic activity in lampbrush chromosomes. The key objectives which we assigned to this unit are specified in a previous paper (11).

While building up the scientific content and the pedagogical procedure of this unit, we had to define and organize the different constituent elements of the sub-ject which is to be studied. These consti-tuent elements correspond to the succes-sive stages or levels characterizing the typical pedagogical progression within the entire unit. We finally determined a sequence of 22 "didactic levels", which are displayed in Table 1.

Each one of these didactic levels in-volves a definite class of facts, concepts, methods, and it may embody a multiplicity of information, data, illustrations, questions, experimental situations, comments, reme-dial materials, representing a ramified part of the flowchart of the whole unit (Fig. 1 shows, as an example, one part of the flowchart, corresponding to level 10).

Each level or group of related levels is assigned to a definite pedagogical objective.

3. THE THEMATIC APPROACH PROCEDURE

Any student may practise the above men-tioned unit taken as a whole and, thereby, should get a better knowledge as well as a synthetic view of the subject.

3.1. A new procedure, for what?

Owing to its subject, the biosynthetic activity unit covers numerous and rather complex Biology facts, concepts and me-chanisms. In addition, in conventional teaching, the molecular mechanisms which are involved are usually taught in sepa-rate chapters, or even in different courses. So that a proper integration of the studied concepts turns out to be a very arduous job for most students.

Moreover, since we are involved in conventional teaching, we know from ex-perience that for a given subject, appro-priate knowledge and mastery can be attain-ed by different students through quite different ways and means.

Therefore, we developed a pedagogical procedure which allows each individual learner to study the same given facts and concepts from various angles and in va-rious contexts, to consider the different aspects and the different implications of the subject. And this is our thematic approach procedure.

3.2. Specifications

In order to work out this procedure, we defined different possible approaches of the contents of the biosynthetic acti-vity unit. Each approach covers a dis-tinct theme, which is built up on the ground of different constituent materials of the whole unit, but with a new type of organization.

Basically, these constituent materials correspond to the different didactic levels, mentioned in section 2.2., and forming the whole unit (see list of the didactic levels in Table 1).

Once we defined the different themes, we worked out the respective dialogues on the ground of the following guiding rules.

Thus, for each theme :
- the relevant didactic levels, among those which are the constituent materials of the whole unit, are utilized,
- and additional materials of several sorts are designed.

The materials of the didactic levels are kept intact and unmodified, but the didac-tic levels may have to be arranged into a different order whenever it appears logi-cally necessary, so as to achieve the pe-dagogical progression appropriate to the theme. And each didactic level keeps the relevant path indicators and counters, which are continually taking a record of the learner's performance, so that, by testing their value in due time, the pe-dagogical progression is being adapted to the student.

As for the additional materials, they consist of connecting texts establishing a link between some materials originally not in a consecutive sequence, as well as conclusions specifically relating to the studied theme. Also, prerequisite condi-tions are defined for each theme, so as to establish a preliminary test. Further-more, along the different pathways of the dialogue on a given theme, new codified marks, path indicators, counters, in ad-dition to those which are normally in ope-ration within the whole unit, are posi-tioned. These additional indicators and counters are to be tested only at the end of the dialogue. Considering the data thus recorded, and taking into account some

TABLE 1: Didactic levels of the biosynthetic activity unit

L 1 : Macromolecules which are synthesized by any chromosome in general.

L 2 : Period of time during which lampbrush chromosomes can be observed.

L 3 : Macromolecules which are being synthesized and macromolecules which are not being synthesized by lampbrush chromosomes.

L 4 : Methodological approaches which are to be used for the study of a biosynthetic process.

L 5 : Observation of lampbrush chromosomes activity with the use of a light microscope.

L 6 : Localization of biosynthetic activity in lampbrush chromosomes with the use of an electron microscope.

L 7 : Definite structural elements of a lampbrush chromosome which are the revealing outcomes of biosynthetic activity.

L 8 : Effects of short-time applications of some specific inhibiting substance.

L 9 : Effects of long-lasting application of the same inihibiting substance.

L 10 : Uncoiled parts of the chromosomal strand and biosynthetic activity in lampbrush chromosomes.

L 11 : Uncoiled chromosomal strands and biosynthetic activity inside any cell nucleus, during a definite period of a regular cell cycle.

L 12 : Limited synthetic activity of the uncoiled chromosomal strands during any common cell cycle.

L 13 : Identification of the enzyme which is involved in the studied biosynthetic process.

L 14 : Direction of the enzyme-controlled biosynthetic process alongside the chromosomal strand in lampbrush chromosomes.

L 15 : Direction of biosynthetic process alongside the chromosomal strand within any regular cell nucleus.

L 16 : Comparative estimation of gene activity intensity in lampbrush chromosomes and inside any ordinary cell nucleus.

L 17 : Origin of the proteins which combine with the macromolecules being synthesized.

L 18 : Mode of association between proteins and macromolecules which are being synthesized.

L 19 : Release of the newly synthesized products and of the enzyme as they reach the terminal point of the gene.

L 20 : Ceasing of biosynthetic activity and coiling up of the chromosomal strands.

L 21 : What is to happen next inside the cell to the newly manufactured macromolecules.

L 22 : Programme of ulterior utilization of newly manufactured macromolecules.

General conclusion of the unit: main significance and implications of gene activity in lampbrush chromosomes, with respect to ensuing fertilization and embryonic development.

significant correlations between them, further materials are so designed as to draw the student's attention to the difficulties he met and the mistakes he made. And additional materials can be elaborated in order to cope with, and properly process, every possible situation. For instance, a new statement can be made about the defective points; or, according to the case, a few new questions or/and exercises can be supplied; and so on.

3.3. The different themes

In Table 2, eleven entries are displayed, relating to the eleven themes which we elaborated, as well as the didactic levels which are successively involved within the respective themes. The students are not informed of these didactic levels.

The student is shown a menu where the list of entries is simply arranged in alphabetic order (according to their respective French denomination), so as to prevent any notion of hierarchy between them.

4. AN EXAMPLE : THEME 3

By selecting entry number 3 in the menu, the learner chooses to study the theme devoted to a comparison between biosynthetic activity in lampbrush chromosomes and in any regular chromosomes.

4.1. Specific features

(i) Objectives

Among the key objectives of the biosynthetic activity unit, one objective is defined in (11) as follows: the student will be able to "find out which configuration of the chromosomal strand is necessarily correlated to biosynthetic activity". And this is the major objective of the dialogue on theme 3. But this dialogue involves further related objectives, namely:

- state that the configuration condition applies to both lampbrush chromosomes and regular chromosomes, but with some definite differences;

- estimate the intensity of biosynthetic activity;

- draw a parallel between modes and conditions of biosynthetic activity in lampbrush chromosomes and in regular chromosomes, and point out the essential similitudes and differences.

These objectives are to be reached by the student in an active manner, by means of observation, comparison, analysis of experimental results, and logical reasoning.

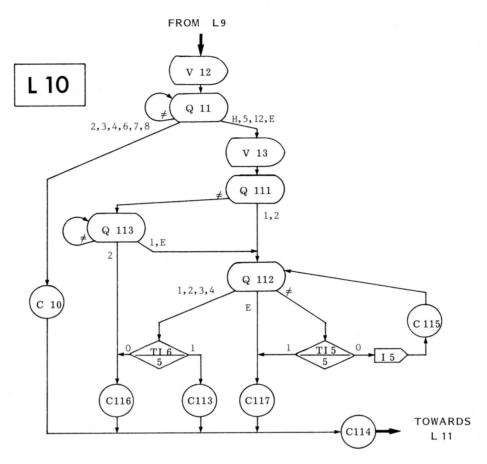

FIGURE 1 :   Simplified   flowchart   of   L 10   (didactic   level   no.   10)

. V12 :   Automatic projection of slide no. 12.

. Q11 :   Question no. 11.

. 2,3,...,5,12 : Each one of these numbers refers to an expected type of
         answer. Each type of answer may have been formulated by the stu-
         dent in various manners. A specific comment is associated to each
         type of answer. Different types of answers are grouped at
         different branch points, each branch point corresponding to a distinct
         way of processing.

. ≠ : Code referring to expected answers not explicitly mentioned on
       this flowchart, as well as to unexpected answers (in this defi-
       nite case, the corresponding branching is a loop, back to the
       same question, Q11).

. E : Code referring to the case where the number of loops adds
       up to a definite limit (in order to prevent the student staying
       endlessly at the same point of the programme).

. H : Code referring to a student's request for help or for
       further information.

. C10, C116,... : Specific treatments, comments, and so on.

. I 5 : Binary path indicator no. 5.

. TI 6 : Test of path indicator no. 5. If the value of this indicator
          is 0, the student is given C116, then C114; if it is 1, the
          student is given C113, then C114.

TABLE 2 : List of entries and the related themes

Number of the entry	Theme of study and didactic levels
1	Biosynthetic activity and configuration of the chromosomal strand: **6 – 10 – 20.**
2	Analysis of biosynthetic activity: **7 – 8 – 13 – 14 – 16 – 17 – 18 – 19.**
3	Comparison with biosynthetic activity of chromosomes during any regular cell cycle: **1 – 5 – 6 – 11 – 2 – 20 – 12 – 16 – 3.**
4	The future of newly manufactured macromolecules: **21 – 22.**
5	Specific inhibition of the biosynthetic process: **7 – 8 – 9 – 20.**
6	Methods for the study of biosynthetic activity: **4 – 7 – 8.**
7	Modes and conditions of gene expression: **13 – 14 – 15 – 16 – 17 – 18 – 19.**
8	Period during which lampbrush chromosomes can be observed in the course of gametogenesis: **2.**
9	Regions of a lampbrush chromosome which are the sites of biosynthetic activity: **5 – 6.**
10	Relationship between biosynthetic activity and morphological aspect of lampbrush chromosomes: **5 – 6 – 7 – 10 – 20.**
11	Type of biosynthetic activity performed by lampbrush chromosomes: **3 – 5.**

(ii) Content

In theme number 3 (see Table 2), nine out of the 22 didactic levels of the biosynthetic activity unit are used. As visualized in Figure 2, these nine levels are arranged in the following sequence: L 1; L 5; L 6; L 11; L 2; L 20; L 12; L 16; L 3.

Among these didactic levels:

- L 1, L 11 and L 12 deal with configuration and synthetic activity of any regular chromosome;

- L 5, L 6, L 2, L 20 and L 3 are devoted to synthetic activity of lampbrush chromosomes in connection with their configuration;

- L 16 concerns one definite aspect of the synthetic activity of both lampbrush and regular chromosomes.

The way these didactic levels are, so to speak, interlaced all along the courseware, is so designed as to have the student's attention focused alternately on the two chromosomal aspects which are to be compared, from a morphological as well as from a physiological point of view.

It must be emphasized that such a comparative study of these two aspects of chromosomes is rather unusual in regular Biology courses and textbooks. And from this comparative study can be brought out different concepts and conclusions, which are of great importance in many respects.

4.2. The running dialogue

Once he has selected entry number 3 in the menu, the student is informed that before actually entering the theme, he should pass a preliminary test relating to the kind of cells which display lampbrush chromosomes. When facing this prerequisite condition, the student may choose either to return to the menu, or to try the test.

This preliminary test consists of three successive questions. A correct answer is required to each one of these questions, failing which no entry is allowed into the dialogue on theme 3, and the student is then sent back to the menu, where he may select some other entry. Depending upon the precise step where he had made a mistake (or where he could not give any answer), the student may be informed that he could possibly find a benefit in practising some other definite theme, or some other unit, before trying again to enter the theme number 3.

The student who satisfactorily passes the preliminary test is admitted into the dialogue on theme 3, and he then proceeds through the constituent materials, i.e. the nine didactic levels mentioned in the described sequence (Fig. 2).

When the last didactic level, namely L 3, is completed, and before the conclusions specifically relating to theme 3, the student can be told, if appropriate, that

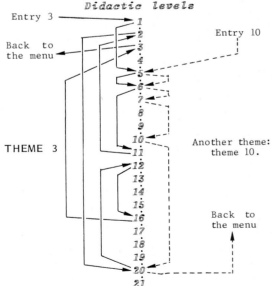

FIGURE 2: Sequence of the didactic levels which are utilized in theme 3.

As a further example, the organization of a different theme is shown (theme 10).

he had met some difficulties and that he had made some definite mistakes, so that he is going to receive a re-statement about the corresponding points. This can be done through testing the additional path indicators and counters, specifically set up for theme 3, which were in operation throughout the dialogue. By the end of the dialogue, these path indicators and counters are tested, taking into account, for each student, definite correlations which might exist between his difficulties and/or errors. The series of tests is organized in such a way that the needed re-statements are arranged into a logical sequence.

Having received the re-statements specifically relating to his personal work through the courseware, the learner is finally given the conclusion of the studied theme. Then he may go back to the menu in order to select some other entry, or some other unit, according to his wishes.

5. CONCLUSION

This multiple-entry procedure utilizes different parts of the original computer-based pedagogical product, like building-blocks for the construction of different dialogues, dealing with different themes. As such, it provides the students with a versatile learning material, which can be used either after the practice of the whole unit (which covers the subject matter in an extensive way), or without any prior practice of this unit.

The student can use this pedagogical tool in order to reinforce his knowledge in some definite areas. But the practice of this kind of courseware can also help to a better structuring of the student's knowledge in different contexts, and to deeper comprehension and mastery of Biology concepts. This approach should turn out to be an efficient pedagogical procedure, which may have to be applied in the future to different kinds of courseware.

This pedagogical research is supported by a grant from the French Ministry of Universities: contract No. 6-15-01 (Research for pedagogical innovation in Higher Education).

REFERENCES

[1] Alberts, B., Bray, D., Lewis, J., Raff, M., Roberts, K. and Watson, J.D., *Molecular Biology of the Cell* (Garland, New York, 1983). In French: *Biologie moléculaire de la cellule* (Flammarion Médecine-Sciences, Paris).

[2] Anxolabéhère, D., Daugéras, N., Favard-Séréno, C., Fiszer, J., Lauthier, M. and Périquet, G., Entraînement au raisonnement logique et à une méthodologie expérimentale par l'emploi de l'ordinateur dans l'enseignement des Sciences biologiques, in: Lecarme, O. and Lewis, R. (eds.), *Computers in Education* (North-Holland, Amsterdam, 1975), 643-647.

[3] Anxolabéhère, D., Bernard-Daugéras, N., Favard-Séréno, C., Fiszer, J., Lauthier, M. and Périquet, G., A contribution of the computer to Biology education at the University, *European Journal of Science Education, vol. 2, No. 4* (1980), 377-394.

[4] Anxolabéhère, D., Bernard-Daugéras, N., Favard-Séréno, C., Fiszer, J., Lauthier, M. and Périquet, G., The OPE Biology education project: current trends and new developments, *European Journal of Science Education, vol. 6, No. 4* (1984), 349-360.

[5] Berkaloff, A., Bourguet, J., Favard, P. and N. and Lacroix, J.C., *Biologie et Physiologie cellulaires, vol. IV: Chromosomes* (Hermann, Paris, 1981).

[6] Bernard-Daugéras, Utilisation de l'ordinateur comme outil pédagogique dans l'enseignement de la Biologie du Développement, Congrès de la Société Française de Biologie du Développement, Forum Enseignement (Marseille, 1985).

[7] Brachet, J., *Introduction to Molecular Embryology* (Springer Verlag, Heidelberg/New York, 1974). In French: *Introduction à l'Embryologie moléculaire* (Masson, Paris, 1974).

[8] Callan, H.G., *Lampbrush Chromosomes* (Springer Verlag, Berlin/New York/Tokyo, 1986).

[9] Denis, H., *Précis d'Embryologie moléculaire* (Presses Universitaires de France, Paris, 1974).

[10] Fiszer, J., Bernard-Daugéras, N., Favard-Séréno, C. and Lauthier, M., Une autre conception du didacticiel en Biologie: unités interconnectables, *Enseignement Public et Informatique, No. 35* (1984), 75-84.

[11] Fiszer, J., Bernard-Daugéras, N., Favard-Séréno, C. and Lauthier, M., A first step in computer-based learning of Molecular Embryology at the university and first achievements, in: Duncan, K. and Harris, D. (eds.), *Computers in Education* (North-Holland, Amsterdam, 1985), 199-206.

[12] Malacinski, G.M. and Klein, W.H. (eds.), *Molecular aspects of early Development* (Plenum Press, New York, 1983).

COMPUTERS IN EDUCATION, F. Lovis and E.D. Tagg (eds.)
Elsevier Science Publishers B.V. (North-Holland)
© IFIP, 1988

THREE DIMENSIONAL ANALYSIS OF BIOLOGICAL DATA: ISSUES RELATING TO EDUCATIONAL SOFTWARE DESIGN IN WINDOWS

Sophie McCormick & David Squires

Educational Computing Unit, King's College, University of London, 552 Kings Road, London SW10 0UA.

This paper describes the design and implementation in the Microsoft WINDOWS operating system of a data analysis program for biological and ecological field studies data. The program enables the analysis of data in terms of three related variables by using a three dimensional pictorial representation of a database. This development is used as an example to base a discussion of the educational issues relating to the use of WINDOWS in educational software development; highlighting some of the advantages and disadvantages of the system.

1.   INTRODUCTION

The introduction into schools of more powerful microcomputers has opened up the possibility of using more sophisticated software within an educational context. One such example is the possibility of using the Microsoft WINDOWS operating system as a development tool. Such a system offers a combination of technical advantages, notably portability and compatibility with other software, and a user interface incorporating modern and flexible screen management. Applications design work in this area is new and necessarily exploratory and there are no clear guidelines and experience on which to draw.

The authors have been responsible for the development of a program concerned with the analysis of biological data using WINDOWS. This development has taken place in conjunction with a group of teachers and biologists working with teachers in schools and ecology field study centres, who were initially unfamiliar with software such as WINDOWS, but who recognised their needs for more adaptable and powerful data analysis software.

This work has shown that WINDOWS can offer a very powerful and flexible development environment with some clear advantages. It has also become apparent that there are educational disadvantages associated with using WINDOWS in this context. This experience may provide a useful contribution to the formulation of guidelines for the use of WINDOWS in educational software development.

2.   DATA ANALYSIS IN BIOLOGY

Scientific investigations in schools often follow classic methodology: change one variable at a time and keep all others constant. Results are usually taken in a measured range of some varying condition and others are kept (or more generally assumed) to remain unchanged. In the physical sciences such assumptions are generally where experimental work is usually undertaken in the laboratory under controlled conditions. In the biological sciences such assumptions can rarely be made so easily.

Plants and animals exist within dynamic and complex ecosystems in states of continual flux. The interrelationships between living things and with the physical world are extensive and the significant factors at any one time are not always easy to identify. Results taken at any one time or place only provide part of the total picture. Where that part lies in the whole pattern of trends can only be appreciated by comparing sets of results. Most school biological investigations, which are inevitably based on simplified methods, monitor too little and make many assumptions. An example is in the collection of field data. Pupils are taught methods of sampling, counting and recording species in specific locations at particular times. The experience gained and the results collected only provide an impression of the environment and can only quantify what existed in the specific conditions current when the observations were made. In fact, these conditions are often unknown. Such results, however, are used by teachers to illustrate complex long term concepts and principles; biological phenomena, such as zonation on a sea shore or succession on a sand dune. In reality it is impossible to distinguish a relatively static zonation from a changing succession, except over a period of time when one can identify regular patterns of change and simple fluctuations. The need to consider such a time factor as an additional variable in school biological investigations has been described by Crowther and Lucas (1982).

Biology teachers are not unaware of such limitations in current experimental work. It is not the difficulty of collecting useful data that

presents a problem, but rather the difficulty
of handling and analysing large quantities of
data after it has been collected. A half day's
excursion with a single class may take hours to
follow through with collation and analysis.

Graham (1987) has shown that the use of datasheets and spreadsheets has been of value not
only in ecological studies but also in physiological investigations. However, the standard
format of commercial spreadsheets or related
applications, such as Ecosoft (1984), allows
the manipulation of only two variables at a time;
for example, the abundance of various species at
various locations, or the rate of activity of an
enzyme at various substrate concentrations at
various temperatures. Although the graphical
and statistical facilities provided by some of
these packages are very helpful in analysing
the relationship between the two variables to
establish trends and/or find out more about
controlling factors, most biological investigations really need to consider more than two
variables at a time.

BIOVIEW introduces the concept of a three
dimensional datasheet providing some of the
facilities of the traditional approach with the
ability to manipulate three variables at the
same time. As described in ecological studies,
this third variable is often time. How does the
abundance of any one species change over a
period of time? What is happening at any one
location over a period of time? Only two variables are considered together - species and
location; species and time; location and time -
but what is inherent in the design is the ability
to switch readily between any of the three variables to look for patterns and trends.

3.   THE DESIGN OF BIOVIEW

The original idea for this program grew out of
discussions between a group of biology educators
and biology teachers during 1984. They were
particularly concerned with the collection and
analysis of field study data by pupils. Preliminary discussions focussed on the representation
of field studies data in a two dimensional grid,
typically containing abundance values for the
occurrence of various species at different
sampling station positions. The structure of
such a grid is shown in Figure 1.

Abundance values for a particular species are
entered in a row with each column corresponding
to a station. Thus the abundance value for a
particular species and station is given by the
intersection of the appropriate row and column.

It was planned to provide simple graphical and
statistical functions associated with rows and
columns. By selecting a row (or column) it was
intended that pie charts, histograms and line
graphs could be selected, showing the variation
of abundance for a species for all the stations

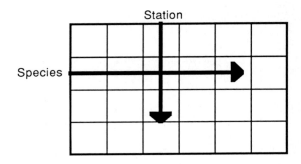

Figure 1   A simple two dimensional grid for
            species and sampling station

(or at a station for all the species). In a
similar way, totals, means and standard
deviations could be selected.

Some original exploratory work was conducted
using the BBC microcomputer. During this phase
of the development it became apparent that in
practice pupils would often want to complete a
datasheet at different data sampling times.
This is represented in Figure 2 for four datasheets.

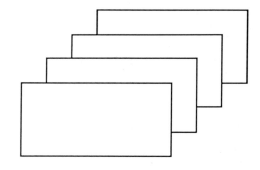

Figure 2   Four datasheets recorded at
            different times

This use of multiple datasheets in effect
introduced a third variable (time) to the data
structure, in addition to species and station.

If the multiple datasheets are viewed from the
point of view of fixed station positions
(rather than fixed points in time), then they
can be considered as a set of species against
time datasheets, as shown in Figure 3.

If the datasheets are viewed from the point of
view of a fixed species, they can be considered
as a set of datasheets, showing how abundance
values at the various stations vary with time.
This is shown in Figure 4.

Hence three different sets of datasheets, based

representing a three variable database as a cuboid emerged. This is shown in Figure 5.

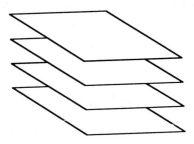

Figure 3   Multiple datasheets for particular stations

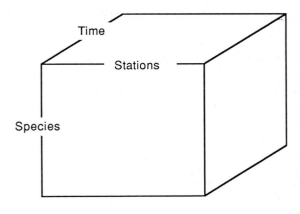

Figure 5   Cuboid representation of the database

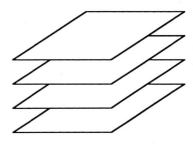

Figure 4   Multiple datasheets showing data for particular species

The cuboid could be 'cut' in three commonly orthogonal directions to give three different sets of datasheets. In the quoted example, these would be:

Chosen time values : species/station datasheets
Chosen stations   : species/time datasheets
Chosen species   : stations/time datasheets

It was obvious that this form of representation could be generalised to include any three variable set. For example, in photosynthesis the three variables could be pH, temperature and carbon dioxide concentration.

Following this original exploratory work, it was decided to attempt an implementation which would use the visual representation of a cuboid. It was considered essential to represent the direction of the cuts on the screen and to relate this to the resulting choice of a datasheet. It was also thought necessary to relate the graphical and statistical output to the row or column involved. The software attempts to satisfy these criteria by regarding the screen as a set of functional windows.

on three intersecting orthogonal planes, were envisaged – all with access to the simple graphical and statistical methods of analysis outlined previously.

The first version of this program (developed on a BBC microcomputer with 6502 second processor and a mouse pointing device) attempted to implement the use of multiple datasheets. The choice of which datasheets were to be viewed was made by a dialogue sequence expressed completely in text which provided no overall concept of the database as a whole. Although it was possible to choose a set of datasheets, the effective moving between datasheets and hence around the database, depended on the pupil having a clear mental model of the relationship between the three variables involved – a relationship that is perhaps better expressed in pictorial terms. Pupils are not usually encouraged to think in such terms, possibly due to the lack of an appropriate medium in which to present and use pictorial representations. In this case it was decided to use a pictorial representation to provide a link between the structure of the database and its analysis.

By thinking in pictorial terms, the idea of

The four most commonly used windows are the cuboid window, the datasheet window, the graphical results window and the statistical results window. It is possible to use other windows, but these four provide all the basic functions. Each window is described below:

1   The cuboid window represents the database as a cube with labelled axes. By selecting the appropriate face of the cube, the required set of data sheets can be chosen. Once a set is selected, it is then possible to move through the datasheets in the set. An

example of a cuboid window is shown in Figure 6.

2 The datasheet window shows all or part of a datasheet. The datasheet displayed in this window corresponds to the current position (datasheet) chosen in the cuboid window. As the datasheet is moved through a set of data-sheets, or the orientation of the chosen set is changed, the datasheet display will change. This window allows databases to be loaded and analysed, or data to be entered to create a new database. An example of a datasheet window is shown in Figure 6.

Thus two essential guidelines were identified:

1 The three variable nature of the database was represented in a pictorial way which would allow the dynamic selection of any one of the three sets of datasheets and the selection of specific sheets within a given set.

2 The major functions of the program – pictor-ial representation and selection; datasheet presentation; graphical output; and statist-ical output – were to be represented in related windows on the screen.

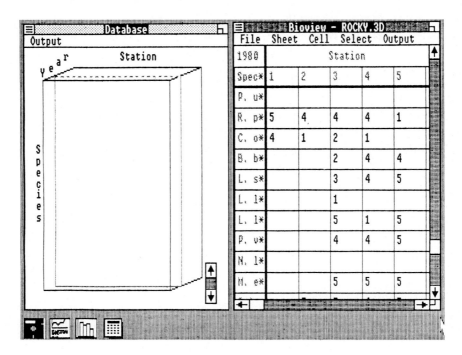

Figure 6   Two windows: cuboid and datasheet windows

3 The graphical results window enables histo-grams, pie charts and line graphs of a chosen row or column to be displayed. It is possible to compare displays of the same type for two different rows or two different columns from the same datasheet. It is also possible to compare the same row or the same column from different datasheets in a set. As the selection of a row, a column or a datasheet is changed in the datasheet window, the graphical display in this window will change. An example of a graphical results window in shown in Figure 7.

4 The statistical results window enables totals, means and standard deviations to be selected. This window is linked to the cuboid and datasheet window in a similar way as the graphical results window.

4   THE IMPLEMENTATION OF BIOVIEW

The software has been implemented in the C programming language in a 16 bit microcomputer environment (RM Nimbus and IBM PC). The original 8 bit development system using BASIC did not provide adequate memory or processing power. In addition, the Microsoft WINDOWS operating system has been used to provide a basis for the software design; providing a powerful and flexible medium in which to explore ideas. This operating system provides a multi-tasking screen management system, based on the partition of the screen into windows which may be 'tiled' or 'pop-up' as in this example. The operation of the windows is controlled by pull-down menus in each window. The screen may be partitioned by the pupil, choosing the size and screen position of any of

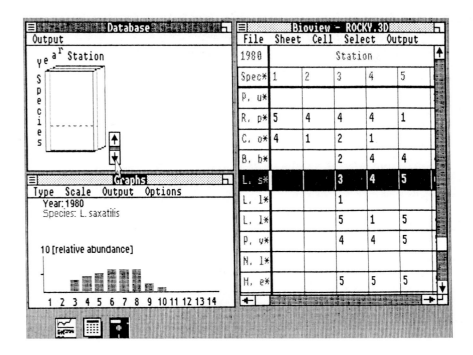

Figure 7   Three windows: cuboid, datasheet and graphics results window

the windows. Windows may be 'removed' from the main screen and placed in a small reserved area at the bottom of the screen where they are represented by icons. Figures 6 and 7 provide an example of the flexibility inherent in the system. The screen shown in Figure 6 has only two windows on the main screen, with the remaining windows represented by icons in the bottom of the screen. In the screen shown in Figure 7, the main screen shows three windows, since the icon representing the graphics representation window has been moved from the bottom of the screen to establish a window in the main screen area.

5.   WINDOWS AND EDUCATIONAL SOFTWARE

The use of WINDOWS raises some interesting issues concerned with the use of software by pupils.

Norman (1983) has proposed that software can be viewed from three perspectives: the user's model; the designer's model and the designer's model of the user's model. The third perspective has often dictated the design of educational software, tending to emphasise the designer's control of the learning experience through their perception of how pupils and teachers will use the software. WINDOWS changes this. The event driven nature of WINDOWS, with users being responsible for the path they take through a program, puts more control in the hands of the pupil, resulting in them using the software in a far less predictable fashion. This marked transfer of control had radical implications for design. In the ideal learning environment it can be regarded as an advantage (Wong 1987), but in practice this increased control carries with it marked overheads for the user.

Most open-ended styles of software, although allowing greater flexibility, are bound by a learning framework imposed on the user through the design of the user interface. In this sense, the software is 'navigable' in an educational sense. Although WINDOWS offers a clearly articulated user interface, the design is based on operational features associated with screen management; in this sense, the design of a WINDOWS based user interface does not convey the educational aims of the software.

The development of BIOVIEW provides examples of this issue. One example relates to the use of the pictorial representation of the database, i.e. the cuboid. 'Traditional' design would typically have ensured that this representation was always visible, thus ensuring that the designer's model was always presented to the user - imposing the designer's conception on the user. In BIOVIEW, the user is able to remove the cuboid representation from the main screen. This can be advantageous for the experienced user, but can pose problems for the inexperienced user. Additionally, it is easy to create very complex screen displays which

are effectively unusable. These are examples
of the problems encountered when pupils are
placed in situations where they only have a
partly formulated mental model of the data
structure in question, within a software
environment with few constraints and hence no
clear choice of pathways. Experience suggests
that limitations and restrictions imposed on
the system are just as important as the flexibility retained.

6.   CONCLUSION

In conclusion it is felt that WINDOWS clearly
offers a powerful and important educational
design environment. However, there are disadvantages associated with its use in schools.
Notably, we are concerned that consideration
should be given to managing complexity through
a clear realisation of a subject focus, which
may result in a design which concentrates only
on certain aspects of WINDOWS. This design
process should involve designer, teacher and
student during the development process. Although
this leads towards more discipline orientated
educational software, the very fact that
WINDOWS is used makes customisation much easier.

REFERENCES

Crowthers, O.H. and Lucas, A.M., Putting
students out to grass; the Nettlecombe experiment after thirteen years. Journal of Biological Education 16 (2) 108-114.

Graham, I., The application of spreadsheets to
data analysis in biology. (1987) Journal of
Biological Education 21 (1) 51-56.

Norman, D., Some observations on mental models,
in: Getner, D., and Stevens, A., (eds.) Mental
Models, Lawrence Erlbaum Assoc. Inc Hillsdale,
NJ, (1983) 7-14.

Strack, G., ECOSOFT, Advisory Unit, Hatfield
Hertfordshire. (1984).

Wong, D., Teaching A level physics through
microcomputer dynamic modelling. Journal of
Computer Assisted Learning. 3 (2), (1987)
105-116.

COMPUTERS IN EDUCATION, F. Lovis and E.D. Tagg (eds.)
Elsevier Science Publishers B.V. (North-Holland)
© IFIP, 1988

ON HOW TO CONCEIVE SOFTWARES FOR TEACHING MATHEMATICS

P. LAURENT-GENGOUX[*], H. LEHNING[*] and D. TRYSTRAM[+]

ATELIER LOGICIEL de l'ECOLE CENTRALE
Grande Voie des Vignes
92 295 Châtenay Malabry Cédex

In France, Computer Science has recently entered the teaching area. Namely, Universities and Preparatory Classes for French Engineering Schools have been provided with micro computers. In that respect, little software has been or will be developed as courseware for traditional scientific matters, without overburdening the students. However, the role of computers remains to be precisely defined.
This paper aims at presenting the approach followed by the "Software Workshop of the Ecole Centrale" for developing original software tools.

1. INTRODUCTION

1.1. Computer Science:
An Improvement in the Way of Teaching

Day after day, Computer Science becomes more present in teaching. Each student will soon dispose (or already disposes) of large computing power and will manipulate huge data. Therefore, the teaching of scientific matters does change.
On the one hand, the computer widens the student's scope, but on the other hand it requires new qualities of strictness and precision.

1.2. What kind of software to conceive ?

First, it is important to define precisely the place of computers in teaching Mathematics. Put aside traditional Computer Aided in Teaching which proves to be tedious. The student needs to remain active with the computer, which should not inhibit him, but provide him with easy and powerful computing.
The computer permits one to visualise abstract items and to perform the most complex operations we meet in Mathematics. As we shall see further, the experimental attitude regains value in the field of Mathematics.
The required strictness can help students to understand the need for some formalism, which could have seemed useless. In that it favours an algorithmic approach, it leads the mathematical reasoning towards a more concrete way of thinking. An ordered presentation of mathematical proofs becomes more natural. As the students cannot devote much time to the computer, one should limit time consuming works that postpone essential activities.

One can find in [Cr] a description of the national project, and the basic tools for using micro computers (involving MSDOS® and Turbo-Pascal®, and a brief description of existing software used as courseware in Mathematics and Physics).

2 PRESENTATION OF THE SOFTWARE WORKSHOP

The Software Workshop of the Ecole Centrale (SWEC in short) was created two years ago by the authors for the introduction of Computer Science in preparatory classes of French Engineering Schools. There are equipped with Personal Computers, the official computation language is a basic kernel of Turbo-Pascal (developed by Borland®). The SWEC joins teachers of Scientific Universities and Preparatory Classes and students of the Ecole Centrale.

The aims are to develop software which will be able to help the people while studying traditional scientific matters. We can distinguish software of two main levels:
- First, the students can use opened modular library for developing their own programs. Such components are joined together in the national project *Modulog* [Mo]. It contains for instance Input/Output basic routines and some of the frame calculation routines. The students have only to include these modules in their programs, in order to limit the specific problems due to the computer.
- The second level consists of using ready made software as a complement of their usual lectures. Their use is very quick, we dispose for instance of sophisticated inputs which permit the manipulation of expressions and formulae in the usual form in Mathematics. The goal of this software is to allow the students to do experiments or simulations very easily. We use them to:

illustrate lectures with attractive pictures
confirm the results of a problem which has been studied traditionally
help in the resolution of a problem, the power of the computer suggests a conjecture that the students will try to demonstrate
simulate the behaviour of systems which cannot be studied at the usual mathematical level of the students.

The complete list of existing software (study of numerical sequences and series, linear algebra, physics ..) can be obtained directly from the editor [Fil].

---

[*] ECP, Grande Voie des Vignes, 92 295 Châtenay Malabry Cedex (France)
[+] Laboratoire TIM3, 46 rue F. Viallet, 38 031 Grenoble Cedex (France)

This software is created so as not to overburden the students. The main rules we have followed in developing it are [Sp]:
It requires short little times for conversing with the users. The codes used are very close to normal language and the vocabulary is very simple (but not simplistic). The exchange uses clear hierarchical menus.

3. SOME APPLICATIONS

3.1. Graphics

We shall present here some applications of some basic softwares [GL]. It can be used only for drawing curves or to illustrate the essential notions of Analysis [JL]. The aims are on one hand to plot common plane curves in geometry and on the other hand to show sequences of functions of a real variable.
It allows many useful applications like defining functions with parameters (and then, a class of functions), representing curves with cartesian or polar coordinates, changing scales. The functions are input in the usual form we find in Mathematics (one can for instance expect the multiplication symbol or some brackets ..). It is also possible to represent the integral of a function and many other facilities: the sum, product and iteration are basic operations.

The series $\Sigma \cos(3^i\pi x)/2^i$ for $-1<x<+1$, defines a function which is nowhere differentiable. This property can be explained by the following pictures : they show a visualisation of the Weierstrass function and a zoom neighbourhood of any point of the curve. This second picture reproduces with a lower scale the same oscillations as the global picture (with a sum restricted to the first 30 terms). This fractal aspect of the curve is the key idea of the local behaviour of the function.

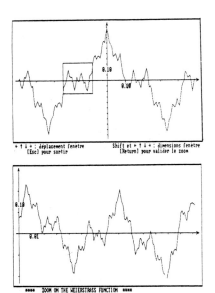

figure 1 and 2: Weierstrass function

3.2. Mathematical Analysis

The second example we have chosen to present, deals with the convergence of an indefinite integral. Let us consider the function:

$$f(n,x) = [(x^2-1/n)\exp(-x^2)]/(x^2-1/n)^2.$$

The pointwise convergence of the sequence towards $\exp(-x^2)/x^2$ leads most of the students to conclude the divergence of the associated integral. And even if the convergence is known, the proof of this convergence is not obvious because of the strange behaviour of the sequence. However, we can draw the graph of the function f between -1 and 1 (for n=5, 6, 7, 8, 9 and 10. See figure 3), and plot the integral of $f(n,.)$ between -1 and 1 (depicted in figure 4). The software allows to verify that the integral remains finite (contrarily to the appearances) and point out that it is due to a balance between the positive and negative parts near x=0.

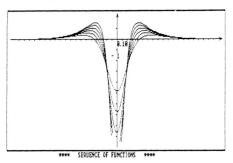

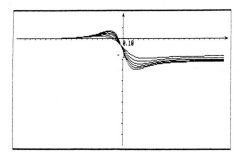

figure 3 and 4: convergence of an integral

3.3. A more specific software

Let us consider other software developed by the SWEC, which concerns linear algebra. It allows one to define easily any matrices (with facilities for special structured matrices like tridiagonal or Toeplitz) and any algebraic operations. Various visualizations of the matrices are available: a usual numerical representation or a tridimensional one to point out the relative moduli of the entries. Moreover, one can perform quickly the usual matricial operations (like the ones used in Gaussian elimination for instance: inner product, permutation of rows or columns, column cancelling). It also allows to make the mathematical abstractions to be made more concrete. The third example we give deals with the well-known gradient method [GV]. This method permits a linear system Ax=b to be solved while building a sequence of vectors which minimizes the function:

$$f(x) = 1/2\ x^t.Ax - x^t.b$$

The software allows one to compute easily the solution step by step by defining another function:

$$g(x) = x - \rho(Ax-b)$$

whose iterates $x^{k+1} = g(x^k)$ perform the terms of the sequence. A visualisation of the vectors at different steps illustrates the global decreasing of the function and its rate of change.

The following example is concerned with the convergence of the well-known QR method for determining the whole eigenvalue set of a linear operator [GV]. The method builds a sequence of matrices A_k which converges towards a diagonal matrix equivalent to A. Here, we define a function whose iterates provide the sequence A_k.

$$A_{k+1} = R_k Q_k \text{ where } A_k = Q_k R_k \text{ with } A_0 = A.$$

A visualisation of a few steps of the algorithm points out the key properties of the convergence: the different speeds of the decreasing of the subdiagonal elements of the matrix A_k and at the same time, ordering the eigenvalues (in the general case) in the final matrix.

These two basic properties are easy to remember here and allow a deep understanding of the method. Moreover, it is easy for the professor to introduce the shift technique to accelerate the algorithm, and to compare step by step with the basic method.

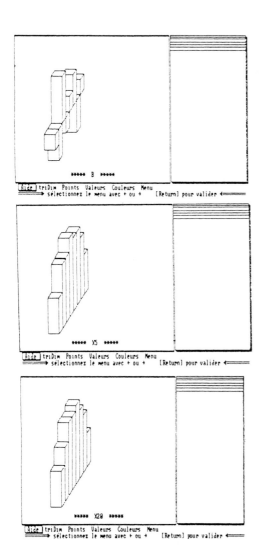

figure 5, 6, and 7
Gradient iterations for a 8 by 8 matrix

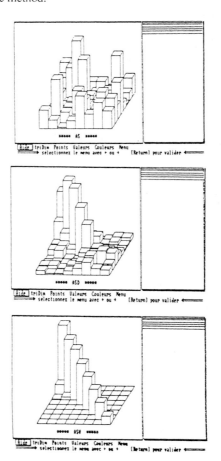

Figure 8, 9 and 10
Representation of some steps of the QR method

4. PERSPECTIVES

We have described in this paper the approach of the WGEC for conceiving software. Some applications are already available, and some new areas are now being studied (like developing software for teaching Finite Element Method and Formal Computations). Some experiments of this software show great interest to use them as a complement of the mathematical courses.

REFERENCES

[Cr]   A. CREDI, Approche de la programmation avec Turbo-Pascal, (BELIN, Paris, 1987)

[Fil]   FIL, Catalogue des logiciels pédagogiques sur PC, (Tour Gallieni 2, 93175 Bagnolet Cedex 1987)

[GV]   G. GOLUB and C. VAN LOAN, Matrix Computation, (Johns Hopkins Univ. Press, 1984)

[GL]   B. GRABENSTATTER, P. LAURENT, H. LEHNING and D. TRYSTRAM, Etudes Graphiques, (FIL, Paris, 1987)

[JL]   D. JAKUBOWICZ and H. LEHNING, Mathématiques pour l'informatique individuelle, (MASSON, Paris, 1982)

[Mo]   Modulog, reference manual, (IREM Marseille, 1987)

[Sp]   J.C. SPERANDIO, l'Ergonomie du travail mental, (MASSON, Paris, 1983)

COMPUTERS IN EDUCATION, F. Lovis and E.D. Tagg (eds.)
Elsevier Science Publishers B.V. (North-Holland)
© IFIP, 1988

MATHEMATICS OF TOMORROW

Hervé LEHNING

chairman of ALE Sup
13 rue Letellier 75015 Paris France

A number of teachers and researchers has been studying for a long time the contribution of computers to the teaching and the learning of mathematics. But too often, they are satisfied with doing the same mathematics as in the past, even with the use of a computer.In this paper, I hope to show that in fact the use of computers transforms the mathematics to be taught by its methods of calculation or ways of intuition, as well as in the notion of result, or proof itself. I shall therefore be led to propositions for a new curriculum.

1. INTRODUCTION.

To say that : "Placing computers - those powerful tools of calculation - at everybody's disposal will modify the teaching and the learning of mathematics" has been commonplace for a long time. Nevertheless, we find few modifications in the curricula ; as a matter of fact, they still seem to be the ones which Cauchy defined in his time. The first reason for this may be the essential question which is too seldom asked : "What are the aims of the teaching of mathematics ?". If we first answer this question, we shall be able to analyse the impact of computers on mathematics more easily, and thus the changes to foresee in the teaching and in the syllabi.

2. AIMS OF THE TEACHING OF MATHEMATICS.

2.1. Formative aspects.

To the question : "Why is mathematics taught ?", many mathematics teachers answer : "Mathematics is very formative" or "Mathematics is a school of consistency", etc., and this is true. But is it sufficient to justify teaching it for so many hours ? In fact, mathematics is not the only subject to answer those criteria and if this were its essential aim, chess-game professionals, for example, could legitimately claim a compulsory and heavy teaching of their subject. For the same reason, cultural motivations cannot prevail, since our compulsory teaching does not include important parts of our heritage.

2.2. Training mathematicians.

The neophyte could also answer that we have to train mathematicians. But then we can wonder why everybody should be trained, since industry uses very few mathematicians as such. Of course, it is not the right answer and this aim is not the main one.

2.3 Mathematics : a service subject.

In fact, we have to wonder : "What is the use of mathematics ?", answer that question and we shall know why it must be taught. If we ask that question, we have nearly answered it : mathematics was created, has been created and will always be created to solve problems.
These problems may be asked :
- by land-surveyors and elementary geometry was created,
- by merchants, and elementary arithmetic was created,
- by physicists, and we have to solve differential equations,
- by meteorologists or rocket makers, and all these problems are far from being solved.
In all instances, the mathematician solves a problem which is set by others. Of course, this solution itself may lead to some problems and the mathematician becomes a problem creator; nevertheless, mathematics is mainly a service subject. At this level, the aims of the teaching of mathematics become clear : essentially, the matter is to train students to solve problems set by other subjects (see [4] too).

3. NATURE OF THE IMPACT OF COMPUTERS.

In this way, we easily understand the importance of mathematics in the syllabi. We also understand the nature of the impact of computers : the question is not to use computers in order to do the same mathematics as before, but to rethink the mathematics to be taught.

3.1. Changes in the methods of calculation.

As a matter of fact, the use of one calculation tool rather than another changes the way of solving a problem.

(i) arithmetical calculations.

In the examples in paragraph 2.3, we can see that the quoted professionals proceed in a way that depends on the time they are living in. The accounts of a commercial firm are not held in the same way as in the Middle-ages : it is still - and perhaps more - essential to understand the meaning of the elementary operations, but it is less useful to know how to achieve the old algorithms which were used for that purpose (see [10]). This way of thinking - scandalous according to some people - will be clearer if we put it in the historical context of mathematics. Nowadays, few people know how to achieve the usual calculations in the way that the ancient Egyptians did : the way of writing numbers and algorithms has changed, ours is simpler and easier to use. Nobody finds it scandalous that those methods should not be emphasized in our teaching. So, nobody should find it scandalous that the teaching of the "manual" practice of some algorithms should be reduced. The most important thing is to train students to solve varied problems : this is the real aim of mathematics teaching, even if some people forget it too often.

(ii) discrete representations of continuous problems.

Another domain in which calculation methods have changed, leads to more important problems. The effective solution of differential equations requires more and more - for quantitative questions - approximating methods. Then generally, we transform a continuous problem - the differential equation - into a discrete problem obtained through an approximating method, this kind of problem being easy to solve numerically, thanks to computers. Now, it is to be noticed that the continuous problem has often been obtained in the original subject by transforming a discrete phenomenon so that it can be adapted to a known mathematical tool : the dynamic models in biology are no doubt a good example, since the figures of populations are real numbers. In fact, the choice of a mathematical model depends on the existing mathematics, a fact that is overlooked by some people who really think that the real number - essential for the continuous - has a genuine reality, whereas it is just a model. Thus, there is no doubt that the evolution of mathematics will induce some users to change their mathematical models and then give a new value to discrete mathematics, even if continuous mathematics still remains better for qualitative results.

(iii) simulation.

In the same way, nowadays, the power of calculation of computers gives a great importance to the simulation of real experience for the resolution of some problems. It is particularly the case in the theory of probability. To be more precise, let us give a small example : "A chocolate maker puts the picture of a member of the soccer team of Lausanne in each of his bars. On average, how many chocolate bars must a consumer buy, in order to own pictures of the whole team ?" The theoretical resolution of this small problem is interesting, but the use of a simulation is quicker, more directly understandable and also closer to the reality we were looking for. The same kind of method can be used to solve problems of loci or of kinematics (see [5]) as, for example, the research of curves of pursuit. Here, we can also wonder if a change in the mathematics we teach is not necessary.

(iv) geometry.

The old methods of visualization are mainly descriptive geometry and calculus (the sketching of parametrical curves). The new ways of visualization do not use the same methods; for example, knowing the techniques of descriptive geometry is now useless in the sketching of curves, particularly the intersections of surfaces, even if one wants to create a visualization software (see in [3]).

3.2 Changes in the notion of result.

On the other hand, this change of methods of calculation changes the notion of result. Then the final result of a mathematical problem can be : the solution is provided by this software. Let us take an example : it is classical to face problems like this : "Find the curves satisfying this differential condition" (for example : research of tractrix, tautochrone, geodesics, etc). Generally, we find as solutions - except for a transformation - the solution curve of a differential equation with an initial or endpoint condition. In the old days, we arranged to tackle problems with a solution by quadratures, a solution which the student was supposed to achieve. In our days, obtaining this equation with the use of software for integration should be sufficient for the quantitative part. The qualitative part of the question rarely requires the resolution of the equation by quadratures and has become easier through the quantitative study. As a matter of fact, if we see that the solution has some qualitative property, is periodic, or a circle, for example, it will be more easily demonstrated (see [5] and [8] for completely developed examples).

3.3 Changes in the ways of intuition.

In the above example, we saw that the quantitative resolution of a problem may allow us to conjecture the qualitative properties of the solution. Here, we are approaching one of the fundamental aspects of the contribution of the use of computers in mathematics: the possibility to check the well-founded truth of conjectures quickly. Of course, this type of attitude is not new; for example, the asymptotic formula of the repartition of primes was conjectured by this kind of method during the 19-th century, before being demonstrated. At that time, the calculations were enormous, nowadays they can be achieved by a student, which allows a less artificial and especially more formative presentation of this formula (see [3] for the complete development of this example). To follow this line, computers can be very useful assistants in solving problems that have so far been considered as purely theoretical; for example, the study of the convergence of series (see [7] and [9]) : computers are problem solving assistants.

To give an example at a very elementary level, giving students an intuition of the notion of variable can be supported by geometry - which is excellent and allows a good illustration of many formulae such as the one which gives the square of a + b - but equally well by the use of computers. A function, that can, on the one hand, be visualized geometrically, which remains fundamental, can also be realized through software, which is more correct for intuition than the constructions of tables, which are inevitably discrete. Thus, continuity takes different intuitive meanings through geometric visualization and through informatic realization (a line which we can sketch without lifting a pen or the connection between a real value and another, such that a "small variation" on the first value involves a "small variation" on the other); those two meanings are equally important in order to obtain a correct intuition of continuity and, moreover, are both more important for intuition than the rigorous definition of Cauchy. (see [5] for more examples, particularly concerning the notion of differential, using a curve sketcher with zoom possibility). This aid to intuition must not make one forget the importance of the notion of proof in mathematics, an importance especially revealed by some mistakes at the end of the 18-th century and which explains Cauchy's definitions.

3.4 Changes in the notion of proof.

When we approach the notion of proof, we also approach the foundations of mathematics; moreover, the adjective "mathematical" means "indisputably established", for the man in the street. Nevertheless, at any time, the meaning of the word "rigorous proof" in mathematics is the result of a consensus between the mathematicians of the time. Regarding the use of computers in a proof, this consensus is yet to occur. It may appear of very little importance, since the theorems which have been initially demonstrated with the help of computers do not belong to the basic curriculum. In fact, the question lies at the level of teaching, because such a proof can be found in a student's work, especially in arithmetic. This is the kind of possible reasoning (see [8] for more details) : let be an equation in integers ($x^4 + 2 y^2 = 11210386$, for example), at first we classically prove that the solutions are bounded by a number, which we find : then, with the help of a computer, we test all possible solutions.

Faced with this kind of proof, what criteria must the teacher have ? Even if we exclude the problem of the possibility of an error of the computer (which cannot be absolutely reliable), we have to prove the program we have used. Therefore, it is necessary to obtain a consensus on the level of required proofs : it seems that it would be good to require just one proof of the loops which are used.

4. THE PLACE OF COMPUTERS IN A DIDACTICAL DIAGRAM.

Here, a fourth partner (computers) steps into the usual didactical triangle (subject, teaching, students) and it acts upon the other three. Moreover, it takes part in a more general framework (activities, mathematical models) in which computers also step in (mathematical models may change with calculation tools) and this fact must not be forgotten. Figure 1 shows this didactical diagram, now including the impact of computers (we shall only mention what concerns this matter).

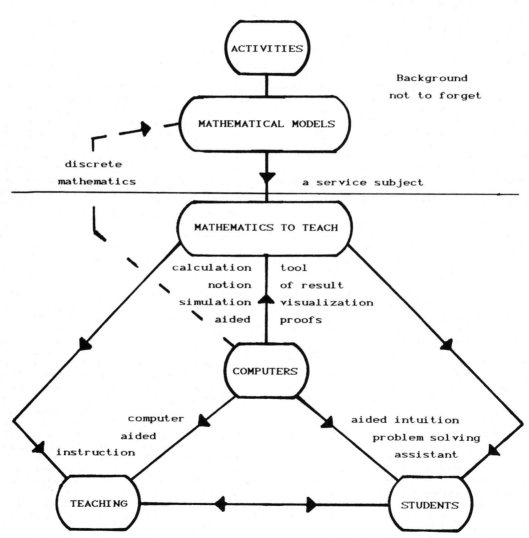

Figure 1
A new didactical diagram.

5. ABOUT A NEW CURRICULUM.

Through the examples in section 3, we see that the use of computers in mathematics cannot simply be added to the old curricula, but must transform them deeply. The aims remain the same but the means are changing. Essentially, at all levels, we must provide the mathematics which it is necessary to understand - and if possible - use mathematical models of varied activities. In what follows, we do not presume to describe new curricula in detail, but with an example - the scientific undergraduate one - and without aspiring to exhaustion, provide major principles for some desirable modifications in current curricula (so we shall not quote what does not seem to need any change).

(i) calculus.

The curriculum should insist on the discrete expression of continuous functions, which is moreover one of the big fields of application of matrix algebra (discrete functions). A parallel should be stressed between continuous functions and discrete functions : derivation and finite differences, integration and summation, searching of extrema. This discrete process can be compared with the opposite process. In the treatment of differential equations, the quantitative and qualitative questions should be better defined. The present emphasis on the resolution by quadratures should be reduced. In the same way, a greater importance should be given to questions on the calculation algorithms of functions, then the notions of transcendental or special functions- and particularly of results written with them - should be limited. On the contrary, the purely technical questions concerning the calculation of primitives, the sketching of curves (by hand) should be reduced.

(ii) linear algebra.

As pointed out above, the links between algebra and calculus should be better stressed. We should insist more on algorithmical aspects and distinguish better between an existential and a constructive result. Then, the calculation of determinants does not seem essential, as compared with the approximate solving of linear systems.

(iii) general algebra.

The general study of structures should be reduced, to introduce combinatorial mathematics (brief notions on graphs and paths, trees). The notions of the complexity and proof of algorithms should be tackled (but just in a limited way), as well as the questions of errors of calculation.

(iv) topology.

The topology of spaces of finite dimension should be better studied, because it is the framework which is essential to understand numerical methods, even the most elementary ones of linear algebra.

(v) geometry.

Conventional geometry should be better studied than in the past because it is a foundation for intuition, which is essential to understand a lot of physical and mathematical phenomena. Nowadays, its study has the benefit of the possibilities of the visualization of computers (see [3]), which allows reduction in the practical questions of sketching curves; the study of descriptive geometry should be left to mathematics historians.

(vi) probabilities.

Concerning probabilities, one should insist on the methods of simulation and their justification.

REFERENCES

[1] ICMI Study Series, The influence of computers and informatics on Mathematics and its teaching, Cambridge University Press, 1986.
[2] Jean Dhombres, Nombre, mesure et continu, Cedic, Paris, 1978.
[3] Hervé Lehning and Daniel Jakubowicz, Mathématiques par l'informatique individuelle, Masson Paris, 1981. La matemica e il personal computer (Italian). Matematicás para la informática personal (Spanish).
[4] Gérard Vergnaud, Réflexion sur les finalités de l'enseignement des mathématiques, Gazette des mathématiciens, vol. 32, 1987.
[5] Hervé Lehning, Mathématiques supérieures et spéciales, Masson, Paris, 1985.
[6] R.P. Driver, Why Math ?, Springer Verlag, New York,1984.

[7] Hervé Lehning, Computers as mathematical problem solving assistants, A computer for each student, IFIP, 1987, North Holland.

[8] Hervé Lehning, Mathematics in computer age, Computers for teaching university course, ECM 87, North Holland.

[9] Atelier Logiciel de l'Ecole Centrale, Etude des suites et séries numériques, FIL, 1987.

[10] Georges Ifrah, Histoire universelle des chiffres, Seghers, Paris, 1982.

COMPUTERS IN EDUCATION, F. Lovis and E.D. Tagg (eds.)
Elsevier Science Publishers B.V. (North-Holland)
© IFIP, 1988

COMPUTER DATA GENERATED BY GEOMETRY STUDENTS:
CRITERIA FOR AN APPROPRIATE INFORMATION.

Michal Yerushalmy

The University of Haifa
School of Education
Mount Carmel, Haifa, 31999
Israel

The use of computers in the learning of geometry introduced a phase that
had not been a traditional part of high school learning: learning with
the aid of empirical information. In this article we will try to clarify
which properties of information, students are most likely to pay attention
to while working with software and how they use the information they
generate. The data for this analysis was collected during the last five
years while working with students using the Geometric Supposer: computer
software which provides information of various kinds without
interpretations. As a result of long term observations, we classify
students' expectations of empirical data in geometry and suggest factors
that could stimulate better use of this information.

1. NUMERICAL AND PICTORIAL INFORMATION IN GEOMETRY

The role and the types of information relevant
to the learning of geometry is not usually
discussed. In the following sections I will
define pictorial and numerical information in
geometry and will state a few criteria for
measuring the quality of these types of
information in terms of their contribution to
the learning process.

1.1. Types of information in geometry

The rationale for teaching geometry as part of
the standard secondary school curriculum is that
students can be taught deductive reasoning by
exposure to the classical Euclidean geometry;
the archetypal deductive system. We believe that
geometry instruction would be more effective if,
rather than teaching definitions and theorems as
given and concentrating on proofs, it were to
give students an opportunity to experiment with
the entire domain of geometric elements and move
back and forth between the particular experience
and the general theorems. The question is:

What are the types of information we would
like students to manipulate and experience?

Throughout the traditional geometry curriculum,
two types of information are introduced: visual
information, such as pictures, constructions and
drawings, and numerical information that
presents geometric relations. Using the computer
as an environment for geometric experiments
introduces new aspects of the same two types of
data, and I will briefly explore the traditional
and the modified uses.

(i) Visual information.

The use of visual information in geometry is
traditionally limited to the presentation of a
diagram: a drawing that acts as a model, not as
a specific entity. It has a reference field
larger than itself. However, it is not possible
to produce a universally valid picture that
represents its reference field exactly. There is
always the risk that a certain facet of the
infinitely numerous characteristics of the
picture will be identified by the viewer as a
property of the reference field.
Thus, in traditional geometry courses, most
diagrams are illustrations that attempt to
represent a general model. Using the computer,
it is possible to help users examine a picture
in geometry as a special case within many other
special cases which are easy to obtain and view.
In this process, visual information evolves into
data about the **process of pictorial changes**
rather than information from **a static picture.**

(ii) Numerical information: Measurements and
Relations.

Measurements produce numerical data that
represent special properties of a concrete shape
or object.
Relative numerical information, on the other
hand, consists of geometrical results in the
form of numbers. For example: the numerical
property which represents the intersecting point
of medians in any triangles is the ratio 1:2.

Why do we introduce measurements as a
component of learning Euclidean geometry?

It is difficult to convince those who believe
that a formal geometry course should not involve
measurements, that numerical data are important.
Those who hold such a view tend to argue that
the ability of the computer to provide large
amounts of measurements of different kinds (such
as lengths, areas and angles), is likely to

cause students to rely more on data than on deductive proof. Polya <1> argued that the mathematician, especially while investigating geometrical conjectures, follows a similar process to that of a physicist, who obtains his data from experiments and makes a conjecture. Even before proving it, he derives various consequences from the conjecture. He seeks tests to try the consequences of his conjecture and he experiments within the limitations of the physical world. Lakatos <2>, from the philosophical point of view, argued that facts alone do not supply conjectures and suggested that the manipulation of a large quantity of data without the knowledge of heuristics patterns is a waste of time.

From our experience, students attain the essential ability to identify numerical patterns and 'relative numerical information' as a result of their exposure to measurements <3,4>. We therefore argue that the manipulation of measurements, which is sometimes considered as a procedure closer in spirit to the "informal" geometry curriculum, plays an essential part in the development of the reasoning skills necessary for the deductive system.

Using these types of data for geometry, I will now state the criteria for evaluating the quality of such information.

1.2. Evaluating empirical information in mathematics

Suggestive and Conclusive information.

Traditionally, the major role of computers was in handling numerical manipulations such as analysis and the presentation of computation results. The computer, in this case, was conceived of as a provider of **conclusive information.** The use of the computer as an environment for experimenting in geometry should stimulate a different perception of information; information which is more similar to that gathered in the chemistry lab, than to the computation results from the computer. This information should be perceived as suggestive in nature <5>; and may lead to a new conjecture or help to relate to an already known theory or phenomenon. Unlike conclusive information, for which quick and accurate production is expected, the quality of suggestive data are difficult to define. The following is an attempt at framing an evaluation.

(i) Can we evaluate the effectiveness of data in geometry?

I will borrow Tufte's <6> definition for the excellence of graphic display, to evaluate the quality of suggestive data in geometry. Tufte's main concern about the display of information (with or without computers) is its effect on the creation of ideas; Tufte's definition of excellence is:

> Graphical excellence is that which gives to the viewer the greatest number of ideas in the shortest time with the least ink in the smallest space.

By the same token, suggestive information can be considered as excellent information if it can

most efficiently help to stimulate mathematical ideas.

(ii) Can we measure the reliability of data in geometry?

While looking for excellence in information display, we often find that the will to transfer, or suggest, a certain message using the data, causes distortion in its representation. Tufte suggests a way of preventing possible distortion; and in so doing he forms an evaluation of the "integrity of information". Tufte argues that:

> (1) Visual representation has to be consistent with other parallel representations; (2) The method of representation of information has to be context dependent; and (3) Information should not be quoted out of context.

In our context, Euclidean geometry, the integrity of the information is presented by constantly interrelating the three multiple representations: the geometric language, the numerical information and the pictorial representation.

Having defined the types of data, and the possible criteria relevant to information in geometry, I will now briefly describe the properties of the Geometric Supposer and the learning environment in which this tool is being used.

2. THE GEOMETRIC SUPPOSER: TOOL AND PEDAGOGY.

The Geometric Supposer <7> is a computer program that allows the user to make any construction that he or she wishes on a random or self-constructed shape such as a triangle or quadrilateral. The program allows any construction that can be done with straight edge and compass, and it records the construction as a procedure. The program can then repeat procedure on any other example of the shape. The program has supporting procedures such as the measurement of any element, rescaling, and the option of returning to previous shapes with the same or different constructions. The program was designed to provide a domain that would turn the student into a conjecture maker within Euclidean geometry.

Using the Supposer, it is immediately possible for the user to explore the validity of discovered relationships in a large number of equivalent cases. It also allows one to ruffle through a large number of equivalent exemplars in the hope of inferring some regularity that belongs to the class of images.

During the years 1983 to 1987 we have studied geometry classes that were working with the Geometric Supposer <3,4,8>. All but one of the observed classes consisted of high school students of different levels, teachers, school systems and countries. Each study had its specific purpose and design, but in all cases we recorded qualitative and quantitative data about the students' interest in accepting information from the computer. Using this data, I formulated a framework for evaluating the **students' identification** of critical components in computer generated information; as described in the following section.

3. COMPONENTS OF COMPUTER GENERATED INFORMATION AS IDENTIFIED BY STUDENTS.

As a rule, students at the beginning of their work with the Supposer considered the properties of accuracy, large quantity and the accessibility of information as the major criteria for the quality of the data. Pilot observations of various learning groups, which used the Supposer, indicated that this approach was taken even by those who had prior training in Euclidean geometry, and prior learning of the principles of the deductive system. This finding suggests that no matter how knowledgeable in mathematics the user was, the introduction of this computerized tool stimulated the formation of certain requirements and expectations from the information. A question then arose:

Does the intensive use of computer, as a major component of the learning, perpetuate students' expectations or change their standards for the use of computer information?

Here are a few examples of students' criteria for the quality of data, at the beginning of their learning and during the learning process. Examples are grouped according to the following three considerations: the accuracy of data, the amount of data and the objectivity of the data.

3.1. Accuracy of information

The first and strongest expectation from the Supposer was that it would perform accurate measurements and computations. We should recall before proceeding that Supposer measurements are accurate only to about two decimal places (somewhat better than typical geometry measurements, however), so that errors can accumulate, and roundoff errors are sometimes observable. The frustration and inconvenience of working with suggestive data which are rounded to the second decimal place was expressed by most new users of the Supposer. The users' previous experience in geometry, their age and ability did not make any difference in this respect. Frustration appeared in three phases:

(i) The data contradicted trivial geometrical fact or conjecture.

For example, the area of a shape was computed in two different ways, producing two results differing by .01: can there be two different areas?
or the following dilemma: If the angles in an isosceles are measured to be 69° and 68.9^o, is this a contradiction to the theorem? By the same token, if they are both 69°, is this a demonstration of the theorem's truth?
Such difficulties arose mainly when the geometrical activity with the Supposer was to check trivial known results. In such episodes the Supposer failed to meet the requirements of the users.

(ii) The data were accepted as 'the rule' without being supported by an idea.

Some teachers claimed that as a result of the Supposer's inaccuracy, students arrived at false conjectures. These teachers ignored the real difficulty of their students: their tendency to generalize a phenomenon from one measurement, and without paying attention to its geometric meaning.

(iii) Calculator computations of Supposer data resulted inaccuracies.

We urged students to use calculators for any computations that were not easy to carry out with the Supposer. Here is a quotation from one student's work:

"(U)sing a calculator I computed three ratios of 6 measurements from the Supposer and got: 1.6903225, 1.6893939 and 1.6863421. Is that close enough to assume that they all equal?"

While this question demonstrates a certain level of sensitivity to the accuracy issue, it also presents the difficulty in differentiating between relating to the results of computations as **The final product**, and the suggestive role of comparing these three numbers in order to **evaluate geometric properties**.

The episodes described above present criteria for accuracy which appeared in the early stages of learning with the Supposer; criteria which were absent in the advanced stages of this course. Students started to provide different interpretations of the numerical and pictorial information <3>. Students learned to appreciate numerical information in geometry in the analysis phase but they also learned not to use the data as evidence or in lieu of a proof.

3.2. Large amounts of information: an advantage or a disadvantage?

How much geometric data is suitable to collect using the Supposer? Students had an especially hard time answering this question because learning geometry in an inquiry environment with the Supposer contradicted each of the following expectations:

(1) In most mathematics classes, the amount of work required of the students, in order to complete a certain task, is clearly specified. Since, in our pedagogical approach, we defined the amount of information needed as a function of the plausibility of the data, the amount collected became more of a personal decision than a standard.
(2) Tools and technology are usually connected to the automization of processes and to the easy production of large quantities of any kind.
Such expectation from the technology may cause the criterion for the amount of information to be related to the capacity of the tool, instead of to the excellence of the data.
(3) Traditional learning of geometry does

not make use of large quantities of information: **a single** diagram is often considered sufficient.

It is therefore especially interesting to observe students' needs, reactions and independent evaluation of large amounts of information. From such observations I will present two main considerations:

(i) How to manipulate a large quantity of visual information?

The Supposer provides options for comparing both numerical and visual information. However, while computations allowed students to condense the amount of numerical data by replacing it with formulae, there is no comparable method of condensing pictures. Students developed techniques to collect large quantities of pictures. They first prefered to record enormous amount of drawings but later on had learned to classify important visual information. Lengthy work with numerous pictures certainly left its impression on students as one of them expressed it:

"In geometry pictures help a lot. You just draw them out. This could be it and this could be it or even this could be. You have a bunch of ideas...just kind of brainstorm" <4>

(ii) How do the needs for different amounts of information vary?

A process of change in the need for many examples was observed and documented in a long-term follow up <3>. The main stages of the observed process are:

(1) Insufficient number of examples:
The examples were related to a narrow subset of the data, while the conclusion related to the full range of the set.

(2) Amount of data as a function of the Supposer's menus:
When students already understood that a certain amount of data was required as a minimum, they started to use a fixed quantity in a fixed order to address any problem. The order was sometimes one that a friend or the teacher had recommended as a useful method. At other times it was the order of the appearance of elements in the Supposer menu (right triangle, acute, obtuse, etc.). For a month, students always provided **three examples to confirm** true conjectures as well as to **contradict false conjectures!**

(3) Data replaced by a strategy and an idea:
At the stage which I consider to represent the most intellectual use of data in geometry, students chose to shift the emphasis from the amount of data, to the conjecture resulting from the data. They made their intention explicit when they dramatically reduced the amount of data presented in their written reports and paid more attention to ideas and arguments. Here are two examples: A group of experienced students wrote: "The data was collected and discussed in

our group" and attached to this statement they offered a diagram and conjectures that presented the general idea derived from the data, but no record of the data itself. However, records from observations in the lab revealed that these students had collected the data before deciding not to report on it in detail.
In an interview at the end of the course another student expressed her disappointment of the impotence of large amounts of information: "Giving us a lot of information that is irrelevant and has no use to us." <4>

3.3. Should random data be considered as good data?

Do students accept information just because it is generated by the computer? or maybe as Davis and Hersh <9> proposed, they behave like mathematicians who reject information just because it was produced by the computer?
Part of the rationale behind the creation of the Supposer is to teach the difference between a special case and a well-defined class of shapes. For example: in terms of geometric properties the **class** of equilateral triangles is identical to **an** equilateral triangle. But a class of acute triangles consists of geometrically different triangles. In order to teach these different concepts, the Supposer asks the user to define a class of shapes and it then produces a random member of that class. However, learning with examples always creates the need to check a well-defined special case which cannot be defined by the specification of a general class (for example: a triangle with sides whose lengths are represented by three consecutive numbers).

Our first hypothesis was that, at the beginning of the work, students would prefer the option of obtaining a random member of a class (since it saves the time needed to define the exact construction of the shape), and only after learning the centrality of convincing arguments in geometry, such as observing extreme cases, would they use the other option. The findings present a different picture:
Students were interested in checking the information provided by the computer. Most **beginners' checks were geometrically irrelevant**, while skilled students presented **a strategy of choosing their check points.**
High school students, as well as six graders who were working with the Supposer for their first time and had never been introduced to the "do it yourself" option, tried to explore their own specific triangles and did not trust the computer's random creation. Since at this stage they did not have formal knowledge of methods of argumentation in geometry, I tend to explain their behavior as simply seeking control over the information, since the 'random' members of the class did not meet the image they had in mind.
One of the several examples to back up this assumption is as follows: A pair of 10th graders who could not believe the result produced by the automatic Repeat option, since the construction result looked very different from their expectations (three altitudes met at point external to the triangle), chose to reconstruct using a step by step, manually driven procedure.

They were then finally convinced that the data provided by the 'uncontrolled' option was correct.

In a further stage of the course, students usually 'trust' the data from the Supposer and use the 'Your Own' option to construct shapes with certain properties (such as a rectangle whose sides have the ratio 1:10) to confirm or refute a conjecture.

The conclusion is that exposure to the data created by the computer 'semi-automatically' did not lead to uncritical acceptance of occurrences as 'the truth'. On the contrary, the use of self-made shapes was more frequent than expected.

At the same time, contradictory though it may seem, students were aware of the unique property of the computer which provides 'uncontrolled' information (at least from that point of view they appeared computer literate). Below are quotations from an interview with a couple of students using the Supposer <4>.

Usually, in the computer laboratory, students work in pairs while using the Supposer. They find this cooperative work productive, and it meets our pedagogical goal of motivating students to talk and share data and arguments with their classmates. While interviewing students (at an advanced stage of the course) about their work with the Supposer, we realized that they found different ways of using the tool:

Interviewer: Are you saying that you guys work on two separate computers, sitting side by side?
J: Yes. On the project we're doing right now you have to do three medians and a triangle
A: And three bisectors and altitudes.
..When we are doing an angle bisector or something like that and she'll have something that makes sense and I don't, I'll look at hers ...I'll do it again and find out that either she was right or she was wrong.

It became clear from their explanation that they chose to work this way not only because of the larger amount of information attainable in a shorter time, but they also appreciated the increased chance of producing unexpected shapes that would widen their range of examples. They assumed that they were doubling the capacity of the tool!

This issue, the amount of control students wield within a mathematically driven environment that generates unexpected instances, appears to be an interesting major domain that needs further research.

4. AN AFTERWORD: QUALITY OF DATA AND SOFTWARE DESIGN.

An analysis of the data gathered from our observations and briefly presented above revealed a shift in the attitude towards information in geometry. While studying various aspects of geometry learning with the Supposer, we identified a few factors that could assist students in understanding the role of information in geometry and that could speed up the formation of a better evaluation of computerized data in geometry. To mention only three: the effect of experience in an inquiry environment <3>; the effect of different written material that directed students in their learning with the Supposer <10>; and the effect of certain teaching strategies and approaches <4,8>. However, the question that is still under investigation is:

How **improvements** in the software could possibly direct students to form better criteria more rapidly for the acceptance of data in geometry?

In the search for such improvements at least three questions should be considered:

(i) Would narrowing down the amount and the type of information lead to faster mathematical analysis of the information?
A limited facet of this question was addressed in a study carried out by Chazan <8>.

(ii) Would the introduction of built-in analytical tools, which would be created specifically for the presentation of mathematical content, encourage better analysis? At present, our main developmental efforts focus on building such tools, in addition to those available in the first version of the Suopposer. Some are already the subject of field experiments, and others will soon be completed.

(iii) Would the availability of general purpose tools, such as drawing packages and numerical analysis utilities, encourage better analysis of the information?
A more appropriate framework for reacting to this question is within another discussion about the nature of the work motivated by mathematical driven environment, as opposed to tools that operate under technical interactions. We have not take any steps towards integrating such environments into the Supposer.

REFERENCES

<1> George Polya, Induction and Analogy in Mathematics. Princeton University Press, 1954.

<2> Imre Lakatos, Proofs and Refutations. Cambridge University Press, Cambridge, 1976, 73.

<3> Michal Yerushalmy, Induction and Generalization: An Experiment in Teaching and Learning High school Geometry, A doctoral thesis, Harvard University, 1986.

<4> Michal Yerushalmy, Dan Chazan and Myles Gordon, Guided Inquiry and Technology: A year study of children and teachers using the Geometric Supposer. Technical Report for the Education Technology Center, Harvard Graduate School of Education, MA, November 1987.

<5> James J. Kaput, Information Technology and Mathematics: Opening new representational windows. Education Technology Center, Harvard

Graduate School of Education, MA, 1986.

<6> Edward R. Tufte, The Visual Display of Quantitative Information. Graphics Press, Cheshire, Connecticut, 1980, 51.

<7> Judah L.Schwartz and Michal Yerushalmy, The Geometric Supposer (computer software) Sunburst Communications, Pleasantville, NY, 1985

<8> Daniel Chazan, Similarity: Exploring and Understanding of a Geometric Concept. Education Technology Center, Harvard Graduate School of Education, MA, 1987.

<9> Philip J. Davis and Reuven Hersh, The Mathematical Experience, Houghton and Mifflin Company, Boston MA, 1982.

<10> Michal Yerushalmy, Dan Chazan and Myles Gordon, Effective Problem Posing in an Inquiry environment: A case study using the Geometric Supposer, in preparation.

8. Long Term Educational Research and Evaluation

COMPUTERS IN EDUCATION, F. Lovis and E.D. Tagg (eds.)
Elsevier Science Publishers B.V. (North-Holland)
© IFIP, 1988

A USER PERSPECTIVE ON INFORMATICS EDUCATION

PATRICK RAYMONT

Manager of Corporate Affairs
The National Computing Centre Ltd
Manchester
United Kingdom

This paper is written from the view-point of a former educator now addressing the problems of informatics skill shortages from a user perspective.

It is argued that users can participate in curriculum development at the Macro-level. Specific user education requirements discussed include:-

- the teaching of the principles of administration

- the development of team working skills

- the need for evaluation of student systems by typical end-users

- the application of coaching techniques to improve informatics skills

Some specific ways in which users can become involved with an educational organisation are also outlined.

1. INTRODUCTION

1.1 The genesis of this paper

The author has recently been involved in a number of activities concerned with education and training, but as a representative of the computer user rather than as a provider of education and training. These activities include discussions of skill shortages by the UK National Computer Users Forum (of which the author is Secretary-General), debates in a user panel of the education and training aspects of IT'86, the UK information technology research programme which is planned to succeed the current Alvey programme, and an involvement as an industrial associate with the Information Technology Institute of the University of Salford in devising a new approach to informatics education at the first degree level<1>

As a former educator/trainer and as a member (and former Chairman) of IFIP WG 3.4 on Vocational Education and Training, the author has found this change of perspective rather enlightening. The objective in writing this paper is to share this experience with a wide audience of educators and trainers.

1.2 Categories of computer users

There is a tendency to discuss the needs of computer users as if users were a homogeneous group having broadly similar requirements. The author has argued elsewhere that this is not the case <2>. Here it is enough to point out the very different needs of users in the following sectors

- the high technology engineering sector (including the electronics industry itself)

- the administrative use of informatics

- the use of robotics in engineering production

- the use of informatics in the design function

The concentration of this paper is on the needs of users in the administrative function, whether in private or public enterprises and covering such applications as payroll/accounts inventory control, office automation, computer integrated manufacturing, decision support systems etc. This concentration arises as a result of the rather narrow experience of the author rather than as a result of any analysis of the importance of the field. Nevertheless in employment terms, it is a very important field. In the UK about 45% of professionally skilled informatics staff work in it <3>.

1.3 Categories of education and training

This paper also concentrates on one area of education/training, namely that which produces informaticians at a level roughly approximating to first degree studies or a little below. This is because, from the point of view of the user sector identified in section 1.2 above, it is this level of qualification which is mostly sought. Typical of the qualifications involved, apart from first degrees themselves would be HNC/HND in the UK, HIO/BIO in the Netherlands, DATANOM in Denmark or Informatics Assistant in the Federal Republic of Germany: these qualifications are described at least as they then were, at an IFIP WG 3.4 conference in Amsterdam in 1979<4>.

It is worth noting that the secondary level is ignored in this paper. This reflects a mainly negative attitude to the teaching of informatics in schools, at least in the UK, on the part of the computer users. The main reason for this is that, with a few honourable exceptions, teachers at this level do not have (and cannot be expected to have) an up to date knowledge of the administrative use of informatics.

Those who do have such knowledge are too readily lured away from secondary level teaching by higher salaries in either the tertiary education sector or industry and commerce itself. This situation may not arise in other countries especially if some form of state direction in employment is practised.

2. PRINCIPLES OF CURRICULUM DEVELOPMENT

2.1 The user role in curriculum development

Educators often express dissatisfaction with attempts by users to formulate views on the educational requirements for people aiming to make a career in the administrative use of informatics.

However, in the opinion of the author, this is only to be expected. Users are busy people and furthermore, have no experience of the complexities of curriculum development. It is important to be clear as to what can be expected from users, and what cannot.

Certainly users can (and do!) express views on the existing curricula. They are clearly in a very strong position to determine the relevance of current curricula to actual industrial/ commercial practice, and also to note omissions from the curricula.

On the other hand, they cannot be expected to work out alternative curricula. Too many factors are involved of which they are unaware, some of which are noted in what follows.

The main role envisaged for users in this paper is the enunciation of 'Macro-level Statements of Educational Requirements" (MLSER) which can serve as inputs to the process of curriculum design to be carried out by the educators. Several examples are given below.

2.2 Fundamentals and current practice

The gulf which exists between educational offerings and user requirements is often stated in terms of the dichotomy between fundamentals and current practice. Educators argue that users are only interested in current practice, and want people who have exactly the skills needed to become immediately operational in the users specific environment; and if this environment is somewhat conven-tional (unstructured methods, COBOL etc) then this is all that is required. But from the user point of view, a knowledge of fundamentals is of value only in so far as it is related to current practice (eg. how do COBOL and structured programming relate?). On the other hand educators see their role as primarily concerned with imparting fundamental knowledge and basic principles.

To the author, much of this discussion is vitiated by a lack of clarity on what is fundamental and what is current practice in the field of informatics. In such a fast moving field what appears at the time to be fundamental is seen a few years later to have been merely a matter of current practice and vice-versa (eg consider the transformation of the field of computer graphics brought about by the PC revolution).

In the view of the author, the teaching of fundamentals ought to be tied closely to current practice, the one reinforcing the other and each enlarging the understanding of the other.

The fundamentals of programming languages, for example, are best understood if related to currently used languages of as wide a range as possible; and certainly the most commonly used language (in the sector with which this paper is concerned), COBOL, should not be neglected (why is it so much used when theoretically "better" languages are largely ignored?)

Thus one of the macro-level statements of requirements to be made by users might be

MLSER 1

Discussions of fundamental principles should always be related to current practice: the reasons why current practice is as it is, ought to be studied.

3. INFORMATICS EDUCATION FOR ADMINISTRATIVE APPLICATIONS

3.1 Technology and administration

Let us reiterate that in the context of this paper "administration" refers to all forms of record keeping and processing in commercial, industrial and government enterprises.

It is clear, at least to users, that to work effectively in this field as an "analyst/programmer", the most typical early employment of qualified staff in this field, a knowledge of administration is clearly of similar importance to a knowledge of the technology.

Just what should be taught under the heading of "administration" is, however less clear. Any particular administrative function may or may not be relevant in future employment situations. For example, a study of inventory control would be of little relevance to someone working in the banking sector. However, what a user might expect (and often fails to get), is an understanding of the basic principles governing administrative applications; principles of control (to ensure, for example, the input data is complete), principles concerned with the monitoring of systems performance (eg, to monitor input error rates and take appropriate action if these are too high) and principles concerned with the relationship of information to business objectives, so that, for example, information systems are geared to helping an organisation to achieve its critical success factors rather than being, as is so often the case, aimed merely at administrative cost reduction. These principles should clearly be taught in the context of specific examples, and require a background knowledge of administrative terminology and procedures. The role of office automation is also of obvious relevance.

Hence

MLSER 2

Curricula should include material on the general principles of administrative information systems, illustrated by case examples.

3.2 Information systems development as a team activity

A frequent complaint by users is that the graduates of educational courses do not fit easily into their development teams. This should not be too surprising, given the ethos of educational establishments where

individual achievement is the overriding criterion of success. Team
activity, in such an environment,
savours of cheating!

Yet, in the real-life context,
team working is essential to achievement. The skills necessary for
effective team working can, moreover,
be taught; for example techniques
such as structured walk-throughs can
be taught and practised. The absence
of such team work from educational
programmes is also responsible for
another aspect of informatics
education which users find unsatisfactory, namely the lack of
experience of realistically sized
programs.

In educational programmes, students
often write programs of less than a
hundred lines of code; rarely if ever,
do they write more than a few hundred
lines of code. This is indeed stret-
ching the capability of the lone
worker. Yet real-life programs have
lengths measured in kilo-lines-of-
code (KLOCs) and are, perforce,
developed in a team environment. The
problems of managing and participating
in such a development are very
different from those of the typical
short student program. Academics
will argue that team working makes
individual assessment difficult; but
users are faced with this very problem
all the time and deal with it in at
least a tolerably satisfactory manner.
Are they so much more skilled than
their academic counterparts?

Relevant here is the approach being
experimented with at the Salford Infor-
.mation Technology Institute. Here
realistic problems are being used,
provided by industrial associates.
Student teams, housed in purpose
designed "team-rooms" are being
organised in which first-year students
do much of the hack work, second-year
students do some of the more difficult
work and third-year students are
responsible for the project management
and for co-ordinating the work of
their juniors. Hopefully the
industrial partners will also stay
involved in a monitoring and
evaluation role. The Institute is only
two years old so we cannot yet
evaluate this approach, but it seems
promising. It is, at least, a step

in the right direction.

Hence another macro statement

MLSER 3

Team activities should be included in
the curriculum, enabling students to
gain experience working on realistically large systems.

3.3 Developing systems for end-users

A third common complaint by users is
that graduates from educational
establishments have no idea how to
make systems usable by non-specialists
the so called "end-users" who interact
with the system in the normal course
of their job.

Again, this is hardly surprising in
an environment where students usually
do all their own system definition,
program writing, testing documentation
and where, if the concept of operational use occurs at all, it will be
fellow students who use the system
bringing to it all their special
knowledge and experience.

Users would argue that developing
effective end-user dialogues, for
example, and testing these with real
end-users should be an essential
discipline for students to learn.
There are usually plenty of potential
end-users around. Systems intended
for the naive end-user can be tested
by any non-specialist students.

Systems intended for accountants can be
tested with accountancy students, for
managers by business studies students
etc. Of course, it requires some
cross-departmental links to be
established if this is to be possible.
But properly arranged, the experience
can also be a valuable ingredient
of the education of the other students
involved (in learning how to interact
with informatics specialists etc).

We conclude that:

MLSER 4

Curricula should include work
requiring systems developed by
students to be tested and evaluated
by persons typical of the intended
end-user population.

3.4 Coaching in informatics skills

The typical educational institution carries out its teaching activity on the lecture/tutorial model originating from the practices of the early classical and mediaeval institutions which were their fore-runners.

It has to be questioned whether this is still relevant in the informatics age. One respect in which it is not and in which users have a great interest, is in the development of skill as opposed to the acquisition of knowledge.

It is arguable that the development of skills should be carried out using the model of "coaching" as, for example, in the development of sporting skills. This requires skills to be practised under the watchful eye of a coach, who will use various techniques to build on the skills already possessed by those being coached to create ever higher levels of skill.

Such an approach can be applied widely in informatics courses to cover such skills as

- report writing

- presentation techniques

- end-user interview methods

- programmer team methods

- dialogue design

- developing training material

- writing instructional manuals.

MLSER 5

Curricula should contain elements devoted to improving skills using a "coaching method".

4. IMPLEMENTING USER ORIENTED COURSES

4.1 The selection of students

In the UK it is a frequently cited objection to proposals to increase the provision of informatics degree course places, that the pool of students with the necessary entry qualification in mathematics/physics etc, is proving a bottleneck. This reveals a fundamental misunderstanding of the basis of the sort of course being considered in this paper. Naturally, there will be informatics courses with a leaning towards hardware systems, software etc, where a good background in mathematics/physics is necessary.

But for the courses here proposed, with a main emphasis on the use of informatics in administration (as defined above), such a background is by no means necessary. Indeed, a major expansion of the provision of such courses would prevent the mismatch between current user needs and educational supply, which has often been remarked in eg, the UK <5> and the USA <6>.

It is worth considering the inclusion in the entry requirements for such courses some vocational testing element to supplement the more usual academic requirements. Of course properly validated testing batteries should be used in such cases.

This leads us to a final MLSER

MLSER 6

Curricula for user oriented courses should be devised to emphasise the administrative aspects of informatics at the expense of the mathematics/ physics aspects to enable students to be drawn from a much wider pool.

4.2 Involving the user

The Salford IT Institute offers some interesting ideas on how to involve users in both devising and running a course.

The so-called "associates" mainly industrial and commercial organisations, participate in a variety of ways, including

- sitting on a "Programme Advisory Committee" which advises the Institute on the academic content of its courses

- contributing hardware, software teaching materials, case studies etc

- teaching short intensive courses (this is easier to arrange than a contribution spread over a longer time)

- contributing to seminars on specific topics

- advising on the Institute's research programme and being involved in specific research projects where appropriate, either as partners in the research or as "uncles", keeping a friendly eye on the research to help ensure its relevance to the real-world informatics.

- seconding staff to the Institute; it should be mentioned here that such staff are much more effective in a tutorial role than in a conventional lecturing role; for example, they may make a major contribution in project team work

- offering work placements eg, in the summer vacations.

4.3 Curriculum and Staff

Experience of curriculum development (eg in the early days of planning the Salford courses), has led me to the conclusion that there is a vicious circle of staff expertise and curriculum content which needs to be broken .

Many innovations in curriculum content are stifled at birth by the simple remark "that's a very interesting idea - but we don't have anyone who can teach it".

Similarly, when an outline curriculum is devised which is quite radical,by the time this is translated into specific teaching programmes (by the institution's teaching staff), these programmes tend to look much more like the traditional stuff of informatics degree courses!

To break this circle, whereby the structure and content of informatics courses is preserved from generation to generation, it is essential to seek an external contribution (for example, as described in the previous section of this paper). This external contribution must be supported and encouraged from the top level if it is to be able to be effective.

5. CONCLUSION

This paper has argued that computer users can contribute to curriculum development at a macro level and has exemplified this in terms of;

- relating fundamental principles to current practice

- defining the principles of administrative information systems

- involving students in team activities

- making systems usable by end-users

- using a "coaching" approach to informatics skills acquisition

- creating opportunities for those not qualified in mathematics/physics

The paper has also suggested ways of involving users at this level. Only by increasingly adopting such practices can we hope to develop the people we need to make our commercial manufacturing and governmental administrative systems effective in sufficient numbers and with the skills which match user needs.

6. ACKNOWLEDGEMENT

The author is grateful for the support of the UK National Computing Centre and especially for the encouragement of its Director, Mr J B B Aris, which has sustained him in doing work outside his specific remit, resulting in this paper. It is clear that the views here expressed are the personal views of the author, and not necessarily those of the Centre.

7. REFERENCES

<1> An introduction to the IT institute at the University of Salford a report issued by the Institute.

Also see J J Turnbull, One Work-Station per Student, in Lewis and Tagg (eds), A computer for each student, North Holland 1987.

<2> P G Raymont, Skills shortages and the User, Computer Bulletin Vol 2 part 1 March 1986.

<3>   Helen Connor and Richard Pearson
Information Technology Manpower into
the 1990's, Institute of Manpower
Studies 1986.

<4>   HLW Jackson, G Wiechers (eds)
Post-secondary and Vocational
education in data processing, North
Holland 1979.

<5>   Education and training for IT
skills,a report of the UK National
Computer Users Forum 1986.

<6>   W W Cotterman, Post-secondary
education for the systems analyst/
system designer (in <4> above).

COMPUTERS IN EDUCATION, F. Lovis and E.D. Tagg (eds.)
Elsevier Science Publishers B.V. (North-Holland)
© IFIP, 1988

AN AGENT OF CHANGE - THE COMPUTER AND THE USE OF KNOWLEDGE BASED SYSTEMS IN TEACHER EDUCATION

Martyn Wild

Exeter University School of Education and
The Advisory Unit: Microtechnology for Education
Endymion Road, HATFIELD,
Hertfordshire. AL10 8AU, UK

This paper explores the potential that Knowledge Based Systems (KBS) provide for (i) developing the use of the computer in education and (ii) turning the computer into a vehicle for positive educational change. There exist a series of identifiable barriers to the successful spread of the computers in education. One way of breaching these barriers may be to place within the hands of teachers powerful software tools that recognise the teacher as a developer of the curriculum and which, in turn, provide the means for those teachers to reflect upon and develop their pedagogic practice.

1.   INTRODUCTION

This paper reflects in part, results of a research programme seeking to evaluate various models of in-service education for teachers (INSET) and initial teacher education (ITE) in educational computing [1]. This research originally extended over 1986-7 and was based upon a number of ITTE (Information Technology in Teacher Education) courses. Essentially, the objective was to evaluate these courses in terms of the changes that may or may not have been experienced by the teacher/student teacher as a course participant.

Results emerging from the research programme have since provided the basis for this paper. The thesis presented here is that the use of Knowledge Based Systems (KBS) can provide a powerful medium for not only developing the use of the computer but for facilitating meaningful educational changes through that use.

But what is meant by educational change?

2.   CHANGE   -   A   MEASURE   OF EFFECTIVENESS

Change in this sense is taken to be fundamental change in the teaching/learning experience of both teachers and children. To clarify the nature of such change we can isolate a series of variables in the teaching/learning experience that are susceptible to change:

(i)   teacher behaviour (in the classroom);
(ii)   teacher characteristics (attitudes, values, expectations, etc.);
(iii) quality of student learning experiences;
(iv)   student outcomes (that is, pupil knowledge, abilities, etc.);
(v)   curriculum.

It would appear feasible to measure change for each of these categories and thereby offer a causal evaluation of each ITTE course being considered. For example, it should be possible to measure the degree of success of a particular course by the change it may or may not engender in terms of the teacher's behaviour, her characteristics, the quality of pupil learning experiences, etc. However, in practice to measure change in these ways is extremely problematic. The pupil related variables are especially difficult to evaluate and indeed, most research into teacher education eschews pupil learning as an outcome [2]. The reasons, apart from the usual difficulties of measuring change, agreeing on criteria and finding standardised measures of achievement, are simple: teachers do not have exclusive access to students and therefore are only partially influential on their learning.

We have seen over the last 15 years or so movements in education that have described desirable changes in the curriculum (e.g. Nuffield Science; Schools History 13-16 Project; Schools Maths Project). These descriptions have been in terms of the content of the curriculum as well as the processes of learning. Such desires for change have in general, found concrete expression in both curriculum statements and practice, in the new examination movements at 16+ as well as in various policy documents issued from time to time, for example, by the Department of Education and Science (DES) [3].

However, whilst it may be relatively easy to prescribe or describe a change in the content of any curriculum and the attendant methods of evaluating it, it is far more difficult to effect change in terms of teachers' characteristics (such as attitudes and expectations; teaching style; the role assumed in the classroom). Yet it is precisely this type of change that is necessary before **successful** curricular changes can follow. (That is, it is possible to direct changes in the curriculum without addressing either the teacher or the pupil and therefore change **what is taught** but not **how it is taught** or **how it is learnt** - this is barren change, indeed).

3. THE PREMISE

The computer may be seen as an agent of educational change - in this sense, fundamental change on behalf of the teacher and her perception of the learner, the learning process and her own role in that process. One way of fostering such change is by the use of certain 'software tools, tools which incorporate facilities that in themselves may promote a pedagogical approach that is based on understanding children's thinking and on the role of the teacher as facilitator rather than director of the learning process. Items of KBS software, developed in Prolog, are used in this paper as examples of such tools; this software is referred to as Prolog 'shells' [4]. Details of these software shells and how they might be used are given below (see 4.1)

4. THE CONTEXT FOR CHANGE

A number of assumptions are implicit in this paper: (i) that the use of the Prolog shells presents new learning and teaching opportunities; (ii) that teachers need these opportunities; (iii) that we do not already have an enlightened network of computer literate teachers expanding educational horizons with the use of new technology. It is important to examine these further.

4.1 The use of Prolog - some characteristics

The claims for the use of Prolog in education are well documented [5]. These claims range from the consideration of Prolog as a means of improving logical thinking, to Prolog being seen as

a panacea for all education ills. Certainly it is clear from many studies that Prolog as a language has inherent features that might justifiably commend its use in the field of teaching and learning. Such features include:

(i)   the support it lends to both declarative and procedural thinking;

(ii)   its logic (rule) basis;

(iii the fact that it is easily extensible (so that new predicates can be created by the user to enhance an application of the language);

(iv) the fact that its close proximity to natural language and its pattern-matching facility make Prolog applicable to language based problem-solving activities;

(v)   relatively simple notation;

(vii) the support it provides for learning of a reflective kind where one is engaged in the construction of mental models of the world, of oneself and of the learning process. These models are developed through intellectual exploration - in other words, activities of metacognition;

(vii) its semantic representation of knowledge.

However, Prolog in its raw form is notoriously 'unfriendly'; to realise its full potential in education it is necessary to protect the naive user from being exposed to the internal syntax of the Prolog language. It is possible to 'package' certain facilities of Prolog, creating 'application shells' that provide a programming environment in which teachers and children can explore domain specific processes, ideas and knowledge by designing and writing 'programs' [6].

There are three Prolog shells referred to in this paper, each providing knowledge-based environments of various sorts. **Detect** is a shell which enables the building of investigative-style micro-worlds, where interaction consists of asking questions of people in that world, searching people as well as places, reading letters and other documents, all with the purpose of solving a problem described in terms of the micro-world, by a teacher and/or children. **Linx** is a shell which allows the building of an event-driven environment where a teacher and/or children are able to describe and interact with, a micro-world structured in the form of events and their consequences. Any one such micro-world may include people, places, time and complex, consequential relationships. **Adex Advisor** is an expert system shell which enables teachers and children to build and interact with representations of their own or someone else's expertise. This expertise is produced in the form of knowledge statements and rules. Useful features of this shell include an explanation facility which makes explicit the reasoning (i.e. the inference mechanism) of the expert system [7].

These software shells have been used in various ways. For example, **Detect** has been used by one teacher to create the framework of a medieval village. By asking questions of its inhabitants, children may explore this village, building up a picture of its structure. Children are also able to add to the elements within the village, expanding upon the variety of people, their roles in medieval society, the structures of families, etc. With **Linx**, another teacher has simulated various events involved in the construction of a motorway. Children may explore these events, challenging causal links between events and consequently altering the simulation to accommodate their own ideas. With **Adex Advisor** children have used a computer expert, created by a teacher, to find the necessary information to combat plague. From this children have gone on to teach the computer about cholera and typhoid, including various means of treating such infections.

In all these activities the children and teachers concerned are approaching and using knowledge in new ways. In particular, teachers are able to use the shells flexibly to support and experiment with a range of pedagogic approaches, from teacher-centred to child-centred practice. It is not being suggested here that by simply providing the teacher with such software tools will we witness positive educational change. What is evident, however, is that the processes of designing and writing programs within these shells can help to involve teachers in developing changed perceptions of their own classroom role, the nature of the learning process and their relationship with the learner [8].

4.2 The need for new opportunities

A BBC/MEP survey revealed, in 1984, that only a small proportion of teachers were using computers to support and extend their teaching [9], whilst the results of a DES survey, in 1985, concluded that only a minority of children made use of the micro outside of Computer Studies or Information Technology classes [10]. We might legitimately expect there to be an increasing take-up of the use of micros to support learning across the curriculum as years pass, although recent studies have suggested that this expectation is perhaps fundamentally mistaken [11].

However, simply using the micro in the classroom does not automatically lead to good educational practice. For example, Anita Jackson's survey of Hertfordshire Primary schools revealed that even when it was possible to identify applications of the computer in the classroom, they were ones which, in a majority of cases, reinforced very limited learning experiences [12].

There are, perhaps, three principle reasons why good computer related learning is generally not more evident in our classrooms. The first concerns the irrelevance and poor quality of software available [13]; the second relates to the barriers teachers face in the application of computers to their subject areas, barriers which range from the nature and structure of the school system itself through to the conservative forces of both fellow teachers and students [14]; the third reason concerns the lack of training and support in the use of computer technology available to teachers [15].

Arguably the most significant of these reasons is concerned with software. In the first instance, a piece of software often precludes concern for the teacher as curriculum developer. All software to a greater or lesser extent, incorporates a certain philosophy of practice (involving ideas about pedagogy and learning), a philosophy which under-pins the way in which the designers expect the software to be used. This philosophy in a large number of cases, is fixed and may not be negotiated by the individual teacher using the software. In the second instance, software does not always offer anything that is perceived to be either significant or new to the learning process. Why should an effective, yet hard-pressed teacher learn how to use a micro and the piece of software concerned if the software is inflexible and the results are perceived to be dubious?

There is evidence to suggest that software that allows teachers to develop the use of the computer in ways which complement individual classroom practice and allows teachers to reflect on that practice has implications for (i) increased take-up of the use of computer technology in the classroom; (ii) changed teacher attitudes to pedagogy and learning.

5. THE PLACE OF PROLOG IN ITTE

For most teachers the educational application of the computer is an innovation. A number of reports have maintained that the successful implementation of an educational innovation such as the enlightened use of the micro depends on the active involvement of the teachers as decision-makers [16].

At various levels the use of Prolog shells puts teachers in a position which requires action as decision-makers. The Prolog shells are context free and as such to use them in the classroom forces a teacher to consider the learner in terms of such pertinent issues as:

- what perceptions of learners and their involvement in the learning process may be supported by the Prolog shells?

-   what opportunities for the development of the learner are included in the use of the Prolog shells?
-   what is the focus of the activity : the class, the individual or the group?
-   what learning styles are anticipated by the use of Prolog shells?

Indeed, different answers to these questions could lead to different courses of action in the classroom. It may be that teachers will see that the use of Prolog shells provides opportunities for developing cognitive abilities such as deductive reasoning. On the other hand, they may perceive that their use provides opportunities for affective involvement of learners, such as promotion of feelings of empathy.

Equally, learners may be perceived as passive acquirers of knowledge whose role is to absorb and retain information. Conversely, learners may be viewed as active and autonomous participants, who seek answers to their questions in ways they devise themselves. By working within the environment provided by the shells it is perhaps possible for teachers to reject the first orientation, although it may be prevailing in the curriculum, and be able to create new learning experiences.

In these ways the use of the Prolog shells involves teachers in the process of curriculum development and as such enhances the teacher's position as an autonomous individual, fostering the reflective stance that is important for participation in learning innovations and reform.

6.   SOME FINDINGS

The ideas expressed in this paper spring in part from the findings of a research programme conducted to assess different models of INSET and ITE courses. The programme evaluated eight different forms of courses with a total of some 100 participants; data was collected by pre- and post-testing of course participants, a follow-up questionnaire and interviews. Two principle themes extrapolated from the original data and relevant here are highlighted below. The first concerns how teachers use the Prolog shells progressively, to develop their classroom practice; the second provides an insight into how the use of this software can become a basis for cross-curricular initiatives.

6.1   A model for development (1)

When such tools are placed in the hands of teachers a pattern in how they are used may be identified. **The first stage** (Teacher-centred

framework, figure 1) concerns the teacher using a particular tool to create her own linear (and limited) micro-world. This would be provided to the children in the class and they, in turn, might be expected to undertake specific and pre-planned forms of interaction with it. This would usually be limited to exploring a number of paths in the micro-world, making decisions along the way and thereby learning 'pre-packaged knowledge'.

The second stage (Learner-centred framework, figure 2) is reached when children are expected to construct a micro-world of their own, perhaps using external resources to do so. This stage usually involves children using a sub-set of the facilities provided by the tools to create an impoverished environment, partly with the purpose of learning how to operate the facilities of the tools themselves.

The third stage (Teacher-facilitated framework, figure 3) concerns the teacher providing a micro-world with which the children are expected to interact fully; this involves not only exploring the micro-world but challenging certain of the

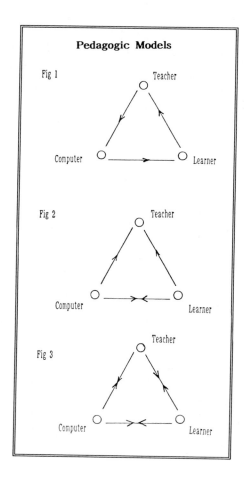

principles upon which it has been built. As such, children would change elements of this world, add to it and generally develop it in line with their own understanding of the concepts within the micro-world. The learning situation at this stage enables children to express their understanding freely but in relation to the structures provided by the teacher. The teacher provides a context and framework for learning, the child may explore and then extend that framework whilst the feedback (in the form of the changing micro-world itself), needed by both the teacher (to assess the level at which the child is learning) and the child (to evaluate what is being learnt) is immediate.

The processes described above are progressive and are a function of the software used. In this sense the Prolog shells operate successfully in the classroom since they serve to develop the role of the teacher as well as that of the learner. Not only do they provide for new and, importantly, meaningful activities but make the teacher responsible for the software in terms of the model of learning it promotes. In two case studies teachers have commented that the application of the Prolog shells 'encourages you to take chances with your teaching practice'; that 'it changes the emphasis of teaching ... by taking the onus away from the teacher'; 'it allows me to change my position in the classroom ... and I am able to intervene more readily to help the children'; 'the computer is entirely organic to classroom practice'.

6.2   A model for development (2)

The implication   **of** the role this software has in promoting cross-curricular links is significant. For example, there is a distinct pattern in how the Prolog shells were taken up and used outside the initial curriculum areas in which they were first established and supported.   Figure 4 represents the progressive use of the software to support teachers of other curriculum areas.

6.3   Other findings

In particular, the data collected from the research programme supports a number of specific points. These are listed below:

1.   The Prolog shells provide the means by which children can represent and store their knowledge within the computer and by doing so give the teacher the opportunity for examining children's thought processes. In this sense, the use of the shells encourages positive interventionist strategies on the part of the teacher, where, for example, the teacher is able to clarify

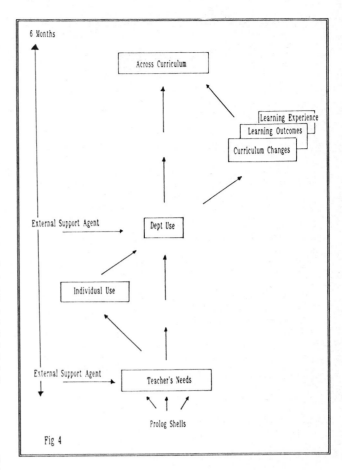

Fig 4

students' values and attitudes by reflecting them back to the learner.

2.   The use of the shells in different areas of the Humanities curriculum allows new learning activities to take place.

3.   The software provides an authoring environment for both teachers and children to create working computer programs to their own design. In this way the shells support a number of different teaching/learning models. For example, the teacher is able to create learning resources in response to the needs and desires of specific children; in another example a child is in control and is able to identify and solve his/her own problems.

4. The nature and flexibility of the Prolog shells potentially allows the computer to assume a central rather than peripheral and occasional role in the classroom. That is, the number of possibilities for supporting and extending the curriculum is increased by the use of the shells. It is pertinent to suggest that in this sense, the computer is able to provide a central rather than peripheral answer to the needs of children.

5. As a neutral and impartial medium the use of Prolog shells enables children to take risks with their learning and teachers to take risks with the learning process. In particular, the shells offer a supportive and non-evaluative learning environment thereby reducing external threats and facilitating learning.

6. The Prolog shells provide the focus for changed classroom relationships where communication, co-operation, deliberation and reasoning all assume new importance in children's learning. The teacher is also confronted with increased autonomy on the part of the learner.

7. The shells provide the context to explore and monitor specific areas of learning activity, such as modelling, simulation and re-creation.

7.   CONCLUSION

The ideas packaged in this paper describe significant implications for the use of Prolog shells (as KBS) in teaching. Such software may encourage (i) the increased use of micro's as a central rather than peripheral classroom resource and, (ii) the creation and support of positive learning experiences. Importantly, the use of Prolog shells can facilitate educational change - change in terms of a teacher's perceptions and practice and, from this, changes in the curriculum and in the quality of learning experiences.

The characteristics ascribed to the Prolog shells are not unique and they may be found in other software items. It is not the software that is significant here, but rather the potential it represents to teachers and to teacher-development.

REFERENCES

[1] Wild, M., Models of Effective In-Service and Initial Teacher Education, MPhil thesis, University of Exeter, in print.

[2] Wragg, E. C., A Review of Research in Teacher Education (NFER-Nelson, 1982) pp 50 ff.

[3] See, for example, Department of Education and Science, The National Curriculum - A Consultation Document (DES, London, 1987).

[4] Nichol, J., Dean, J., and Briggs, J., (eds), Prolog Across the Curriculum, Prolog Children and Students (Kogan Page, 1988); Briggs, J., Why Teach Prolog? The Uses of Prolog in Education, in: Nichol, J., and Briggs, J., (eds), Proceedings of the Prolog Education Group Conference Vol 1, (PEG Exeter, 1986), pp 148-155.

[5] Briggs, J., Why Teach Prolog? The Uses of Prolog in Education, in: Nichol, J., and Briggs, J., (eds), Proceedings of the Prolog Education Group Conference Vol 1, (PEG Exeter, 1986), pp 148-155; Briggs, J., and Ennals, R., Fifth Generation Computing : Introducing Microcomputers into the Curriculum, in: Journal of Educational Computing Research, Vol 1 No 1, (1984).

[6] Briggs, J., Why Teach Prolog? The Uses of Prolog in Education, in: Nichol, J., and Briggs, J., (eds), Proceedings of the Prolog Education Group Conference Vol 1, (PEG Exeter, 1986), pp 148-155.

[7] Nichol, J., Dean, J., and Briggs, J., Teachers Encounter Prolog, in: Lewis, R., (ed), Journal of Computer Aided Learning, Vol 2 No 2, (Blackwell Scientific, 1986) pp 74-82; Briggs, J., Expert Systems in Further Education - A Starter Pack, (Further Education Unit, 1987).

[8] Wild, M., Models of Effective In-Service and Initial Teacher Education, MPhil thesis, University of Exeter, in print.

[9] British Broadcasting Corporation, Microcomputers in Secondary Schools : a Survey of England, Wales and Northern Ireland Secondary Schools, (BBC, 1984).

[10] Department of Education and Science, Statistical Bulletin, 18/86 : Results of the Survey of Microcomputers in Schools, (DES, London, 1986).

[11] Heywood, G., and Norman, P., Problems of Educational Innovation : the Primary Teacher's Response to using the Microcomputer, in: Lewis, R., (ed), Journal of Computer Assisted Learning, Vol 4, No 1, (Blackwell Scientific, 1988), pp 34-43; Wellington, J. J., Computer Education in Secondary Schools, in: Lewis, R., (ed), Journal of Computer Assisted Learning, Vol 4, No 1, (Blackwell Scientific, 1988), pp 22-33.

[12]   Jackson, A., Fletcher, B., and Messer, D. J., A Survey of Microcomputer Use and Provision in Primary Schools, in: Lewis, R., (ed), Journal of Computer Aided Learning, Vol 2 No 1, (Blackwell Scientific, 1986), pp 45-55.

[13]   Self, J., Microcomputers in Education - A Critical Appraisal of Education Software, (Harvester Press, 1983). As Self suggests, 'the case for computer assisted learning using present software seems very weak' (p 167).

[14]   Hart, R. and Wild, M., Barriers to Innovation, in print.

[15]   Griffen, J., Who Uses Micros?, in: The Times Educational Supplement, 23/10/87, (Times Newspapers 1987); Gardner. J. and Megarity, M., IT and In-service Teacher Education, Economic and Social Research Council Information Technology Programme, Report No 21/87, (ESRC, 1987).

[16]   Fullan, M., The Meaning of Educational Change, Teachers Press, (Columbia University, 1982); Wright, A., The Process of Microtechnological Innovation in Two Primary Schools - a case study of teachers' thinking, in: Educational Review, Vol 39, No 2, (1987); Johnston, V. M., Attitudes Towards Microcomputers in Learning (2), in: Educational Research, Vol 29, No 2, (June 1987), pp 137 ff.

COMPUTERS IN EDUCATION, F. Lovis and E.D. Tagg (eds.)
Elsevier Science Publishers B.V. (North-Holland)
© IFIP, 1988

COMPUTERS AND CURRICULUM IN 1999

Mr. Tim Crawford

Simcoe County Board of Education   Home Address
421 Grove Street East   R. R. #1
Barrie, ON Canada   Oro Station ON
L4M 2R8   Canada L0L 2E0

ABSTRACT

This paper considers the current state of educational software. It
touches on some current research, especially brain research and on
theories of multiple intelligences. The work of Piaget, Bloom and
Gardner provide a basis for speculation about the function of the next
generation of courseware. Learning could be accelerated and perhaps
the very nature of how students learn may be altered. Artificial
intelligence software could tailor learning to help each student
achieve his/her potential in a number of intellectual realms, at
various stages of intellectual maturation.

1.0 INTRODUCTION

1.1 Setting the Stage

Children born this year could have a significantly different early childhood education than current school-age children.
By the time they reach the middle grades
their schooling could be radically
different. Observations based on brain
research, child psychology, and experimental forms of education may direct
the evolution of computer hardware and
software resulting in some dramatic
implications for educators.

It is the intent of this paper to
identify trends in education and educational software, hypothesize as to their
implications, and extrapolate to predict
future educational issues. Educators
could nurture trends leading to those
forecasts which are desirable, assuring
their fruition, and terminate trends
leading to undesirable forecasts before
damage is done.

2.0 TRENDS IN CLASSROOM USE OF COMPUTERS

2.1 A Faltering Beginning

Drill and practice was the first form of
educational software to be used by
children. It has very limited application. **Tutorials**, particularly those
which take the form of interactive games
are considered to be more appropriate.
There is some discussion that well-
designed tutorials and certain types of
simulations create very special and
unique learning experiences. In fact

there is a notion that these experiences
may stimulate thought processes which
never before occurred in a human brain.
There are too few curriculum units of
this type of software.

There was a time when educators were
excited about the potential of **electronic
data bases** and **spread sheets.** After
experimenting with their use, too many
educators abandoned them (except those
teaching courses in computer applications). Setting up and using such
utilities frequently was not educationally productive. The software seemed to be
too isolated from other activities in the
class and from curriculum. The educational experience was too artificial or
trivial. For some teachers the era of
disillusionment arrived.

2.2 Software With Potential

Another class of software is flourishing.
Word processing or language processing
has become an exciting tool. If students
learn to keyboard at say 24 words per
minute, they will be producing **twice** the
output than by handwriting--36 w.p.m.
would produce 3 times the output. In
theory, twice the amount of writing
should accelerate improvement in composition. In addition, the spelling checker
and parsing software will be a personal
and constant tutor, the like of which has
not been possible in the past!

Art processors are being used effectively
by leading teachers to enable students to
use a myriad of colours, textures,
designs and other images in a way not
possible in any other medium. In

addition, animation enables students of
all ages to explore an art form previously reserved for the cinematographers.
Related software such as LOGO and CADD
will ultimately be integrated into art
processing software, putting awesome
power under the control of creative
minds.

Music processors will free students from
the drudgery of learning and applying
harmonic rules, enabling them to focus on
the aesthetics of composition and
harmonization. The multiplicity of
voices available on computers linked with
synthesizers will enable young Mozarts to
output fully orchestrated compositions
with a minimum of theory and a maximum of
creativity.

There are some excellent examples of
thematic software. The **Voyage of the
Mimi's** beautiful books, the well played
out drama on video tape, the worksheets,
and the computer software all create a
range of cohesive, dynamic, interactive,
educational experiences.

Well-designed thematic software can
create an almost infinite combination of
learning experiences. Such software
could be integrated with relevant educational utilities such as a word processor, remote data access, and video clips
of drama--real life, scientific drama or
staged drama.

The use of the computer as a monitoring
and diagnosing tool is in its infancy. In
the next decade such an application could
create a specific example of future shock
for educators.

2.3 A Software Continuum

Educational software could be considered
to fall along a continuum. At one end
would be the **receptive** software which
provides information to be received by
the student. Examples include drill and
practice (drill and kill as some educators call it), one-way tutorials (electronic page-turners) and (passive) data
bases.

The other end of the continuum would
represent software which would foster or
promote creativity. This type of
software could be called **expressive,
generative,** or **creative.** Word, art and
music processors are examples of such
software. See figure 1.

2.4 **Proving the Benefits**

One of the problems faced by educators is
the dearth of proof that the computer
does in fact work in the classroom--that
it is not just a novelty. Some hard data
is becoming available but the research
needs to be replicated. Once replicated
it needs to be shouted out, if not from
the proverbial roof tops, at least by
those who have influence in developing
educational policies and priorities.

One example that software is effective
comes from an unpublished study which
describes one class of grade 4 students
in a Toronto school which had unlimited
access to word processors with a spelling
checker. The students had an average
increase on a standardized language
assessment instrument of one full grade
(one year) during only four months of
use. In ten months the students had
achieved results indicating 2.4 years of
language growth. Another unpublished
study in Ottawa suggested that special
software enabled students who were three
years behind in mathematics to catch up
in only three months.

Another study described students alter-
nating daily between writing with a word
processor and pen. The handwritten
stories were keyed into the word processor by typists. The assessment by
independent evaluators of the output was
that there were **two different groups,** one
producing more and better quality work.
More significantly, the evaluators
thought that the **very nature** of the work
of the superior group was different from
the other group. This observation is
fascinating. It would appear as if
Seymour Papert's (1980) electronic pencil
might alter the very nature of the
writing style of students.

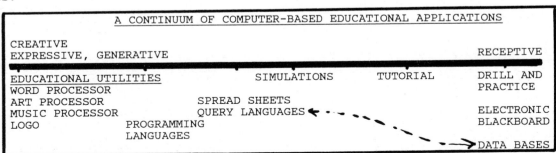

Figure 1

Educators must set as a high priority the documentation of such benefits and use the results to influence administrators and other teachers indifferent or hostile toward computer use. According to Dr. Ken Brumbaugh of the Minnesota Educational Computing Consortium, 80% of the classroom teachers are indifferent to the use of computers, and are therefore denying their students the benefits which could accrue by using them.

3.0 BRAIN RESEARCH

3.1 **Physiology of the Brain**

Current research on the brain is providing new information for curriculum designers. The specialization of brain hemispheres has been widely discussed in the literature by Durden-Smith and DeSimone (1983), Levy (1978), Springer and Deutsch (1985). The integration of the brain, both top down (the neo cortex to the limbic), and laterally, between the right and left hemispheres has implications for educators.

Children's brain mass grows in cycles of spurts-and-plateaus which repeat about every four years. After each growth spurt there seems to be corresponding period of 'new capability'. Such findings are not inconsistent with the observations of Piaget.

Still controversial but now generally accepted are the findings that, in general, the brain of the female is physiologically and functionally different from the male. Durden -Smith and DeSimone (1983) and others have documented that on average the size of the left hemisphere of girls is larger than boys of the same age and the **corpus callosum** joining the two hemispheres is much thicker in girls than in boys. Sucl differences are noted in young children as well as in adults.

The growth spurts in girls occur at different times than in boys. For example, Epstein (1978), points out that on average, at the latter half of the age 10-to-12 spurt, girls experience a two- to three-fold advantage in brain growth over boys. (The boys catch up later.) Clearly educators must address these differences.

3.2 **Functions of Components of the Brain**

The right hemisphere tends to deal with thought-related spatial representation, Gestalt, and the intuitive. The left tends to deal with logic, mathematics and language. The typical male brain is dominated by the left hemisphere and has less integration of the two hemispheres than the left dominant and more integrated brain of the typical female.

The question for those interested in education software is: to what degree will educational software designers use the knowledge of brain growth, and the differences between the male and female brain, to optimize learning?

4.0 INTELLIGENCES AND GIFTEDNESS

4.1 **The Ignored Students**

Clark (1983), suggested that educators are now busy establishing criteria to label giftedness as it relates to academic ability. Part of the assessment is the administration of I.Q. tests which tend to assess language capability, and ability to reason logically. Students who averaged above 132 on a number of I.Q. tests are serious contenders for gifted programs. Other observations by teachers, psychometricians and parents complete the overall assessment.

Once gifted students are identified the more difficult task exists of establishing suitable programs for them (curriculum sequences, not computer programs). This programming is difficult, for the students tend to absorb quite quickly material which may have taken the educator/coach many hours to develop. Clearly the use of the computer may enable more effective learning experiences for the gifted. They would be able to progress at their own (speedy) rate, explore topics quickly to whatever depth they needed, and would be challenged.

4.2 **The Theory of Multiple Intelligences**

As suggested earlier, I.Q. tests which purport to measure a person's intelligence seem to measure mainly two facets of brain activity. If there are two facets might there be three or more? Howard Gardner (1983) suggests that there are at least 7 realms of intelligences: "I believe that human beings are capable of developing capacities of an exquisitely high order in at least seven semi-autonomous intellectual realms...(including):
  1. Language
  2. Music
  3. Logic and Mathematics
  4. Visual-spatial Conceptualizations
  5. Bodily-kinesthetic Skills
  6. Knowledge of Other Persons and Things
  7. Knowledge of Ourselves."

It is useful to consider to what degree these realms could be applied to brain research and ultimately to the development and use of the next generation of educational software. In what way may computer software serve, foster and promote the development of each of the realms of intelligences suggested by Gardner, in girls and in boys?

4.3 Bloom, Piaget and Gardner

Bloom suggested that the brain is capable of a hierarchy of thinking; from memorizing (facts), translation, interpretation, analysis, synthesis up to evaluation. Piaget found that young children went through a series of stages. It would be an interesting study to correlate Piaget's stages with students' ability to think at various levels of Bloom's hierarchy.

It would be a more interesting task for a researcher to prepare a matrix which would take into account current brain research, particularly as it applies to females and males, Piaget's observations, Gardner's multiple intelligences and Bloom's taxonomy. Figure 2 provides a rough outline of such matrix.

Perhaps with the aid of computer, educators could watch for a youngster to develop a new capacity to learn in one or a combination of Gardner's realms at stages described by Piaget. As the child matures, researchers aided by sophisticated software would be able to provide a guide as to what levels of thinking, according to Bloom, might be experienced in a particular realm. It is tantalizing to consider that a child at about nine years of age, if given the opportunity, might be able to think at the highest level in one particular realm but at a very primitive level in another.

5.0   TRENDS IN COMPUTER SOFTWARE

5.1   Preschool Computer Uses

In about two years an 18-month-old child will open a Christmas present. It will be a doll. When switched on, the doll will say: "Hello, what is your name?" The child will respond, and the doll will ask the child to give it a name. This doll will be full of sophisticated software designed by educators who are specialists in child psychology and early childhood development and education. It will have voice recognition and response modules. It will have considerable memory and will begin to accumulate information about the child.

Daily the doll makes suggestions about what to do. Each suggestion would be fun but would also involve a learning experience. Of course the doll would be programmed to be funny, friendly and congenial. (Compare this role model with that of mother or dad who are not always funny, friendly nor congenial! This aspect certainly has some implications for software designers.) Periodically the doll could be linked to the psychometrician's computer so that the information about the child which has been accumulated by the software could be analysed, and perhaps certain software modules down loaded to bring about some desired objective.

One day the doll is turned on and says: "Bonjour", and introduces the child to another language. When ready, the child would become immersed in 'Frenchland', as Seymour Papert (1980) would call such an environment. Perhaps within three months the child is functionally bilingual. One day the doll is turned on and says: "Bonjourno!" Three months later, trilingual. Then, "Buenos dias"-- quadilingual.

In the meantime the child has developed skills in music, art, language, as well as interpersonal skills, an appreciation of society, a great self-image and good self-esteem. All this and the child has not yet started formal schooling!

5.2   Educational Utilities

The focus of future software will be to nurture creativity. Regarding the use of computers in education the Ontario

BRAIN GROWTH CYCLES FEMALE/MALE		PIAGET	GARDNER'S REALMS							BLOOM'S TAXONOMY
			1	2	3	4	5	6	7	
16+	16+	Abstract	.	.	.	.	.	.	.	Evaluation
.	.	Symbolic								Synthesis
.	.	Concrete	.	.	.	.	.	.	.	Analysis
.	.	Operational	.	.	.	.	.	.	.	Interpretation
.			.	.	.	.	.	.	.	Translation
0-2	0-2	Pre-operational								Learn Facts

Figure 2

Ministry of Education, in policy Memorandum No. 47 states: "...the more significant way will be the creative use...for writing, composing, designing, analysing, and **other extensions of original thought**" (emphasis added). Word, art and music processing software clearly has the potential to meet these needs.

Data base software combined with simple to use artificial intelligence software will enable students to combine and select out information, discover new relationships, draw inferences and develop new methods of problem-solving. Software would exist to do life skill arithmetic as well as operations required up to and including first year university mathematics. (MathCad and CalculusCad is here now.)

There will be a multiplicity of very low cost but cleverly designed special purpose computers which could be used for unique learning experiences. If appropriate they could be plugged into the child's personal computer to affect greater specialization for the child.

5.3 **Thematic Software**

Educational software designers will ultimately develop a shell or authoring structure for facilitating the development of thematic units. The gifted teacher, perhaps computer illiterate, would be able to use the shell to create a simulation which would be the main focus of the unit. The unit would be designed so that students would access relevant data bases, likely on read-write compact disks, and view a collection of documents, illustrations, graphs and video clips. **Immediate information** may be acquired from satellite transmission, such as weather, current events and topography data.

Ancillary capabilities would enable the student to take notes using the word processor, make sketches electronically, capture a quote or illustration, and develop in the computer a personalized **mind map** spread sheet which would provide an external representation of the internal structure of the way the information about the topic is being assimilated in the student's brain.

Artificial intelligence background tasking software, using A.I. principles, would monitor student progress, and direct outcomes, at least to some degree. Such outcomes may include a formal written essay or producing a documentary.

5.4 **The Computer as a High Technology Diagnostic Tool**

One could imagine each student having a personal computer that changed in form from the doll to some other perhaps non-intrusive form, as the student matured. The software would monitor personal health and report certain types of anomalies directly to a medical team. It could monitor mental health and provide appropriate activity to enhance deteriorating self-esteem. It could identify brain growth spurts and provide activities which would take advantage of a new potential due to a spurt. Teachers and psychologists would be advised of any special needs of the child.

5.5 **Implications for Teacher Training**

The teacher has been the deliverer of knowledge, tutor, assessor, muse and educational coach. The role of the teacher will change. No longer will the teacher be working at the bottom end of the hierarchy of educational experiences. These will be taken over by the computer. The teacher will need new skills to interact with the student at the upper end of the hierarchy, where human skill and judgement are most important. As Dr. Wallace Judd suggests in an unpublished paper: "teachers will teach values and analogies only...they will only need to help the student transfer the acquired knowledge and skill (likely acquired from the computer) into real life situations, and will show the student how to do so, with the ethics and values of a truly human society". See figure 3.

5.6 **Implications for Curriculum**

Ultimately curriculum will change. New curriculum will be developed to take advantage of the computer's capability. Researchers might discover that the use of spcial software produces new brain functions which have never previously occurred in the human brain. This will stimulate the development of software capable of probing deeper, and developing further the potential of the brain.

Gifted and talented students will not be held back. It may be possible that some six-year-old protégés may have accelerated through Piaget's ages and stages and have insights in such things as high level mathematics (using MathCad as a tool), perhaps at the university level. The talented student will be stimulated and the talent developed. Girls will progress and excel like never before, with few negative blocks from stereotyping. The various realms of intelligences

THE TEACHER, THE COMPUTER AND THE LEARNING PROCESS			
HIERARCHY OF EXPERIENCES	TEACHER TIME PRE-COMPUTER	COMPUTER APPLICATIONS	TEACHER TIME POST-COMPUTER
PHILOSOPHICAL SPIRITUAL COMPLEX HUMAN RELATIONSHIPS VALUES AESTHETICS CREATIVITY MOTIVATION NON-HUMAN RELATIONSHIPS CONCEPTS FACTS		CREATIVE TOOLS PAPERT'S ENVIRONMENT CREATOR SIMULATIONS TUTORIAL DRILL AND PR.	

Figure 3

will be **probed,** as Marshall McLuhan would say, to help create, then capitalize on teachable moments.

Traditional curriculum might give way to such curriculum areas as:
- ** personal health and body monitorization
- ** information sources, selection, validation and synthesis
- ** image processing (planning the impact, creating the image)
- ** entertainment strategies and modes
- ** aural creativity (sound, including music)
- ** ethics, morality and law
- ** language
  - i) as a (blunt) form of communication
  - ii) as an art
- ** people and their environment
- ** earth sciences as they relate to the individual.

Other courses such as accounting, music theory, and mathematics beyond the basic fundamentals will be optional for those few students with a special interest and aptitude.

6.0   SUMMARY

Although the science of education is in its infancy, new information related to education, combined in a unique way, may provide revolutionary insight into educational processes. Such insights could foster spectacular educational software which will provide all students with new opportunities and a new freedom to progress at their own rate in realms not previously fully explored, motivated and encouraged by a patient, perceptive electronic partner, and coached by one or more wise humans.

BIBLIOGRAPHY

Clark, Barbara. Growing Up Gifted. 2nd. Edition. Columbus: Charles E. Merrill, 1983.

Durden-Smith, Joe, and Desimone, Diane. Sex and the Brain. New York: Arbor House, 1983.

Epstein, H. T. "Growth Spurts During Brain Development: Implications for Educational Policy". In J. S. Chall and A. F. Mirsky (eds.) Education and the Brain, Seventy-seventh Yearbook of the National Society for the study of education, 2, Chicago: University of Chicago Press, 1978.

Gardner, Howard. Art, Mind and Brain: A Cognitive Approach to Creativity. New York: Basic Books, 1982.

Lee, Ken. "Brain Scan". Forum. Toronto: Ontario Secondary School Teachers' Federation, Vol. 12, No. 1, February/March 1986.

Papert, Seymour. Mindstorms: Children, Computers and Powerful Ideas. Basic Books, Inc. New York: 1980.

Springer, Sally P., and Deutsch, George. Left Brain, Right Brain. W. H. Freeman. New York: 1985.

Toepfer, Contrad. "Brain Growth Periodization: Implications for Middle Grades Education". Schools in the Middle. NASSP, April, 1981.

COMPUTERS IN EDUCATION, F. Lovis and E.D. Tagg (eds.)
Elsevier Science Publishers B.V. (North-Holland)
© IFIP, 1988

MATHEMATICAL ASSESSMENT OF COURSEWARE EFFICIENCY

I. O. KERNER

German Democratic Republic, Paedagogische Hochschule Dresden
Sektion Mathematik, Wigardstr. 17
Dresden, DDR-8060

ABSTRACT:

The work of a teacher can hardly be compared with the work of a courseware program. But with some mathematical assumptions, it is possible to compare two or more courseware programs. Every courseware program has a structure of branching points. The author must make an estimation about the partitions of the set of students which are going into the different branches. This estimation depends on the difficulty of the question relative to any branching point and on the density of abilities of the student manifold. then a standard set of users is passed through the program, going from branching point to branching point at any step. The expected value of necessary steps, the total amount of steps until the whole set has passed, and the didactical resistance with respect to the didactical conductivity or the holding back capacity of the program structure, are computed and can be used for comparing or characterizing purposes. Furthermore, a theorem concerning these characteristic values is formulated.

1. INTRODUCTION

No courseware program is used for one student only. In any case, a set of users exists. Therefore, we have to look at this set if we are trying to assess the efficiency of such a program or to compare some of them.

In courseware every teaching or learning program can be described by a numbered directed graph. The numbers represent an evaluation at the edges and give the percentage of the output at this edge for the input (100) of any node. Therefore, only the branching points of the graph are important for this consideration.

This means in the example of Figure 1 that for a set of students reaching the node N and answering a question, 30% will reach node R, 40% node S, and 30% node T, according to their answers. A manifold of students has a density function D(c) of their knowledge, their ability and skill. There will be a minority of very good students, another minority of very bad ones, and a majority near the mean. Other densities are possible, of course. of course. An example is shown in Figure 2.

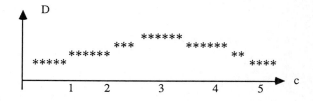

Figure 2. Density function

In general, we assume a scale of one to five credits. Giving a task or a question at a branching node in a courseware graph, the author has to estimate the partitions of the input set coming to the output branches according to the function D(c) and the difficulty of the task of the question. Of course, this estimation is in

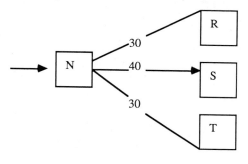

Figure.1 Valuation of the edges from a
branching point

some sense subjective and a factor of uncertainty in this method. But for comparing two or more course-ware programs for the same content to be taught, an estimation by the same teacher (pedagogue, psychologist) would eliminate this uncertainty to a great extent. (Another attempt would be the use of a standard density, in the most simple way the uniform density.)

		A	B	to C	D	F
from	A	q	p	O	O	O
	B	q	O	p	O	O
	C	q	O	O	p	O
	D	q	O	O	O	p

with p = 0.5 and q = (1 - p) = 0.5 .

Further, a courseware program with respect to its graph G has a starting node and a final node (the aim or goal). It is a network. A student reaching the final node has reached the aim of the program. In any program there is an optimal (shortest) path with m steps from the starting to the final node. But not all students of a given set with a given density would give the optimal answers at all branching points. Therefore, the number k of steps for a particular subset with the portion O<d(k)<1 reaching the final node is greater than m. For the assessment of a courseware program the average or the expected value of the number of steps for a given set of students is therefore important.

At the start or step 0, all students are at mode A and nobody is at B, C, D, or F. The first step will result with 0.5 at A, because of the feedback, 0.5 at B, because of the transition, and 0 at C, D, F.

The program for the computation of a sequence of transitions is very simple. In general, one will have n nodes and two vectors for their values, V0 before the step and V1 after the step.

2. STATIC TRANSITION

$$V1[k] := \sum_{i=1}^{n-1} M[i,k] * V0[i] \quad \text{for } k = 1(1)$$

n-1

A much more important objection to this fixed or static valuation of the edges is that the splitting of the set of students at the branching nodes, the feedback and the union of different subsets of the students, would not change the density function for the input set of a node. The proposed valuation does not take into consideration the dynamic learning or working history of the students. Only the fact that the density function does not change mirrors the learning or teaching effect: students from the bad side of the density function who are forced to feedback have then a part at the better side of the density function.

but for the last node - the goal node- where the successful part of the set is assembled

$$V0[n] := V0[n] + \sum_{i=1}^{n-1} M[i,n] * V0[i]$$

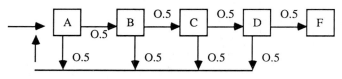

Figure 3 An example for a courseware program graph

For the courseware program - the graph is shown in Figure 3 - the matrix M with the transition probabilities is

or $V0[n] := V0[n] + d(s)$

where d(s) is the successful subset during step s.

Start with V0[1] := 1, and V0[i] : = 0 for i = 2(1)n.

or if $\quad 1 - \sum_{k=0}^{k} d(k) < 0.0001$

Stop with 1 - V0[n] < 0.005 or with d E(s) < 0.001.

After 4 steps, the best students (1/16 of the set) reach the final node (cf. table 1). After 10 steps, a quarter of the set, after 22 the half, and after 400 steps nearly all have reached the goal.

This means almost all students have reached the final node. In the example of Figure 3 the expected value of steps is 30 (cf. table 1).

The computation of the expected value follows the formula

A courseware program P1 is better than another P2, written as

if $\qquad$ P1 { P2

$\qquad$ E(S1) $\quad$ < E(S2)

$$E(s) = \sum_{k=0}^{\infty} k * d(k)$$

in which k is the number of steps with which a portion of students have reached the final node (F in the example of Figure 3). In practice, the summation will be stopped (not with infinity) but

if $\quad$ d(k) < 0.0001

Table 1 Passing the set through the graph of Figure 3 (p=q=0.5)

S	A	B	C	D	F	E
0	1					
1	0 5	0.5			-	
2	0.5	0.25	0.25			
3	0.5	0.25	0.125	0.125		-
4	0.5	0.125	0.125	0.062	0.062	0.25
5	0.469	0.25 .	0.125	0.062	0.094	0.406
6	0.453	0.234	0.125	0.062	0.125	0.504
7	0.437	0.227	0.117	0.062	0.156	0.812
8	0.422	0.219	0.113	0.059	0.187	1.062
9	0.406	0.211	0.109	0.057	0.217	1.326
10	0.392	0.203	0.105	0.055	0.245	1.609
20	0.271	0.140	0.073	0.038	0.478	5.149
30	0.187	0.097	0.050	0.026	0.693	9.206
40	0.129	0.067	0.035	0.018	0.750	13.125
50	0.090	0.046	0.024	0.013	0.827	16.606
60	0.062	0.032	0.017	0.009	0.881	19.545
70	0.043	0.022	0.012	0.006	0.917	21.945
80	0.030	0.015	0.008	0.004	0.943	23.859
90	0.020	0.011	0.006	0.003	0.961	25.359
100	0.014	0.007	0.004	0.002	0.973	26.518
200	<0.001	<0.001	<0.001	<0.001	0.999	29.845
300	0	0	0	0	1	29.994
400	0	0	0	0	1	30

Table 2 passing the set through the graph of Figure 3 with p = 0.8 and q = 0.2

S	A	B	C	D	F	E
0	1					- -
1	0.2	0.8				- -
2	0.2	0.16	0.64			- -
3	0.2	0.16	0.128	0.512		- -
4	0.2	0.16	0.128	0.102	0.410	1.638
5	0.118	0.16	0.128	0.102	0.492	2.048
10	0.043	0.042	0.044	0.044	0.827	4.620
20	0.005	0.005	0.005	0.005	0.982	6.746
30	<0.001	<0.001	<0.001	<0.001	<0.998	7.197
50	0	0	0	0	1	7.206
60	0				1	7.207

To show the influence of a better transition probability matrix M, look at Tab.2 with the same graph as in Figure 3, but with p = 0.8 and q = 0.2.

This courseware program has a better efficiency. The expected value of necessary steps is 7.21 - smaller than 30 - and the convergence for reaching this value during the computation is with 40 or 50 steps - better than 400. This is the expression of the fact that bad students will reach the goal faster.

3. STATIONARY ASSESSMENT

Another consideration for the mathematical assessment of courseware programs is based on the assumption that during every learning step a new set or manifold of students will enter the program at the starting point. After some steps the state of the program or the graph will come to a stationary situation. The *state* means the contents of the nodes or the subsets of students which are working at the different nodes. This consideration is named *stationary assessment* and it has some dynamic content.

Of course, at the stationary state the (constant) output of the program is equal to the (constant) input, namely 1. Furthermore, at the stationary state a constant subset of students will work, in every point or node of the graph. These amounts are characteristic for the underlying courseware program. The program possesses a resistance to the learning process. The author can look at points with an unexpected high number of working students holding back and can change the structure of the program. The sum of these amounts is named *didactical resistance* of the courseware program and is in some sense a further characteristic number like the expected value of necessary steps.

The program with the graph of Figure 3 and with the case p = q = 0.5, is used for a computation as an example in table 3.

The sum of the holding back amounts or the didactical resistance in the example of table 3 is obviously 30 and this can be seen very easily because of the simple structure of the program. Taking the transition probabilities p = 0.8 and q = 0.2 with the same program structure or the same graph, the holding back amounts are not so easily seen:

$$A = 2.441$$
$$B = 1.953$$
$$C = 1.562$$
$$D = 1.25$$

with the sum of 7.206, better than in the first case.

Table 3 Stationary assessment for the program at
Figure 3 and with p = q = 0.5

S	INPUT	A	B	C	D	OUTPUT
0	1					
1	1	1				
2	1	1.5	0.5			
3.	1	2	0.75	0.25		
4	1	2.5	1	0.375	0.125	
5	1	3	1.25	0.5	0.187	0.062
10	1	5.187	2.391	1.090	0.490	0.217
20	1	8.523	4.121	1.988	0.956	0.458
40	1	12.425	6.145	3.038	1.501	0.741
60	1	14.291	7.113	3.540	1.761	0.876
80	1	15.609	7.576	3.760	1.886	0.941
100	1	15.609	7.797	3.895	1.945	0.972
200	1	15.990	7.995	3.997	1.999	0.999
300	1	< 16	< 8	< 4	< 2	<1
400	1	16	8	4	2	1

With these two examples , the theorem:

The expected value E(s) of necessary steps of a courseware program is equal to the didactical resistance of this program

can be seen. A courseware program P1 is better than another P2, written as

$$P1 \{ P2$$

if the *didactical resistance* R(P) or the *didactical conductivity* C(P)

$$C(P) = 1/R(P)$$

$$R(P) = \sum_{k=1}^{n-1} V0[k] \text{ at the stationary state}$$

holds

$$R(P1) < R(P2) \text{ or } C(P1) > C(P2).$$

4. DYNAMIC TRANSITION

The students fed back during their work with the courseware program have learned something. Their knowledge density function is shifted to better credits. This can be simulated by changing the valuation of the graph according to the step number. By this method, the matrix of the transition probabilities becomes a function of the steps.

For example, the function

$$f(s,p1,p2) = (p2 - p1) * \exp (c * \exp (s-s0)) + p1$$

is used for decreasing transition probability from p2 to p1 (with p1 < p2) , and

$$g(s,p1,p2) = (p1 + p2) - f(s,p1,p2)$$

for increasing transition probability from p1 to p2 . Of course, it is

$$c < 0$$

and c=-0.002 would be a quite acceptable value.

The parameters c and s0 belong to the branching nodes of the graph. For instance, the transition matrix of the example of Figure 3 becomes, with p1=0.5 and p2=0 for f and p1=0.5 and p2=1 for g:

S	A	B	C	D	F
A	0.5exp (c (s-1))	1-0.5exp (c(s-1)) 0		0	0
B	0.5exp (c (s-2))	0 1-0.5exp c(s-2))		0	0
C	0.5exp (c (s-3))	0	0	1-0.5exp (c (s-3))	0
D	0.5exp (c (s-4))	0		0 1-0.5 exp (c (s-4))	

At every step the sum of a row of the matrix must be equal to 1.

The effect of this modelling method is shown in table 4.

Table 4 Dynamic transition with the starting transition probability 0.5 for all branches, feedback decreasing to 0 and forward increasing to 1.

S	A	B	C	D	F	E
0	1					-
1	0.5	0.5				-
2	0.488	0.262	0.25			-
3	0.470	0.267	0.137	0.125		-
4	0.451	0.268	0.146	0.072	0.063	0.25
5	0.400	0.266	0.153	0.080	0.100	0.439
6	0.367	0.245	0.157	0.087	0.144	0.702
7	0.333	0.231	0.149	0.093	0.194	1.049
8	0.299	0.216	0.145	0.091	0.249	1.488
9	0.266	0.199	0.140	0.092	0.304	1.989
10	0.234	0.181	0.132	0.090	0.362	2.566
20	0.038	0.039	0.038	0.036	0.849	9.866
30	0.002	0.002	0.003	0.004	0.989	13.219
40	>0	>0	>0	>0	<1	13.571
50	>0	0	0	0	1	13.579

5. EXPERIENCES

Some real courseware programs were checked with this method. they have had between 20 and 40 branching points with a number of branches between 2 and 5. For the modelling of the different working times between the branching points, different numbers of simple transition points with single output edge (value 1) were incorporated. The results were compared with assessments subjectively given by pedagogical experts. In some cases, the correspondence was very good. In some others, the difference could be eliminated after a discussion concerning the estimation of the valuation of the edges (the transition probabilities). Only a few programs had different assessments by the mathematical method and the pedagogues. Then the programs were checked with real students and there was the same situation. Some programs have had a good agreement and others not. With the latter cases, something remains to be learnt for the starting estimation of the transition probabilities.

COMPUTERS IN EDUCATION, F. Lovis and E.D. Tagg (eds.)
Elsevier Science Publishers B.V. (North-Holland)
IFIP, 1988

657

QUALITY ASSESSMENT POINTS IN A METHODOLOGY FOR THE DEVELOPMENT OF COURSEWARE
based on practical experience in the Regional Education Authority district of Lyon, France

by René JAFFARD, Chantal GAUTIER, Paulette PETRI[+], Claude Bernard University, Lyon.

ABSTRACT   At the "Centre de Recherche, d'Etudes et de Formation à l'Informatique Pédagogique" (C.R.E.F.I.P.)[++] at Claude Bernard University, Lyon, France, we have formulated a methodology for the development of courseware. We have also defined certain "quality assessment points" for the evaluation of programs in the development stage with reference to appropriate criteria, viz:
(i) suitability and originality
(ii) accuracy, topicality and impartiality of content
(iii) pedagogical effectiveness
(iv) program feasibility and cost effectiveness.
Our objective is to explain at what point in the development of courseware, assessments should be made, and thus to demonstrate the relationship between development, experimentation and assessment.

I. METHODOLOGY FOR THE DEVELOPMENT OF COURSEWARE: THE BACKGROUND

1.1 Introduction

The French government-sponsored "Informatique pour tous" (computer literacy for all) plan came into effect early in 1985. The objective to be attained by the end of the year was to train 100 000 teachers in computer science, to install 120 000 micro computers in schools throughout the country (107 800 home computers and 16 900 PC compatible machines). Schools received a standard software package, and could select programs from a catalogue of 687 titles available. The aim was to make this generation of school children "the best-trained ever" (1).

Then, in July 1985, M. Martin, Dean of the School Inspectorate, criticized "the mediocrity of pedagogical applications, which were frequently dull and repetitive" (2) and raised the question of the quality of the software available.

1.2 In the Lyon Regional Education Authority District

The aim of the C.R.E.F.I.P. is to provide assistance for teachers who produce courseware, either in teams or individually, however modest their efforts may be. It is essential that their "initial enthusiasm" (2) should not be dampened. On the one hand, we have to avoid a personal commitment which may sometimes be out of all proportion to the result obtained, but at the same time we do need to ensure that the end-product is of satisfactory quality. We also evaluate commercially available courseware. We have therefore developed:
(i) a methodology for the production of a paper model of a courseware program, including tools to assist in the process of program development.

(ii) a structure for assessment comprising a Scientific Committee which follows the development of the program throughout the drafting process (see appendix I). It also evaluates commercially available courseware.

Our aim is to assess each aspect of the factors which will determine the quality of a program at the appropriate time during the development process. This has led us:
(i) to define quality criteria
(ii) to define QUALITY ASSESSMENT POINTS, i.e. appropriate points in time for the assessment of a program with reference to these criteria.
(iii) to develop appropriate tools for assessment at each quality assessment point.

This approach is the result of both theoretical research and also our own experience in dealing with teams of authors and in evaluating commercially available courseware.

We present below the quality criteria that we use and the specifics of each quality assessment point. The complex relationship between successive steps in the methodology, successive phases in the development of a program and the quality assessment points is described in detail in Section 3 below.

The work presented in this paper has been performed by the Working Group for the Development, Experimentation and Assessment of Courseware (R.E.E.L.E.) within the C.R.E.F.I.P.

2. THE QUALITY CRITERIA

2.1 Important note

Courseware may be prepared with one or more of several objectives in view, for example, to impart new knowledge to learners, to enable them to practise acquired knowledge, to check the

---

[+] all of the R.E.E.L.E. Group, C.R.E.F.I.P. 9me avenue, La Duchère, 69009, Lyon France
[++] Centre for Research, Study and Training in Information Technology in Teaching

amount of knowledge acquired, to develop certain aptitudes, etc.   Consquently, courseware is produced in a wide range of different forms in order to meet different requirements.

The development which follows is of necessity limited to general principles, and will therefore cover the three main types of educational software that we identify, viz:
(i) programs which admit a limited extent of teacher intervention (e.g. instructional or drill-based programs)
(ii) programs which encourage pedagogical intervention, adapted by the teacher for a specific application (e.g. graphics-based learning programs)
(iii) programs which are tools for the visual display of problems or "activity tools" (e.g. word processing programs, simulation programs, laboratory or workshop assistance programs).

It follows that certain sub-headings in the quality criteria may not be applicable in all cases.

2.2 Suitability and originality

Here we are attempting to respond to a demand on the part of the teacher:
(i) by solving an actual "pedagogical problem" in accordance with the school syllabus as regards content and objectives.
(ii) by using a pedagogical approach based on the specific features of the micro computer and, where appropriate, other media (from paper documents to video discs).
(iii) by avoiding duplication with other programs either already on the market or in course of development.

2.3 Accuracy, topicality and impartiality of content

(i)   In the context of the school syllabus and the learners involved, there can be no concession in respect of accuracy.   The following points must be made clear from the very beginning of the program development process, as well as in any accompanying literature:
(a)   the underlying theories and/or models employed
(b) spelling and numerical tolerances.

(ii) It is essential to check all verbal and numerical displays and all graphics for:
(a)   accuracy of content
(b) correctness of the French language and of any scientific notation employed.
(c) use of the S.I. system of units
(d) impartiality of the message, i.e. in particular, absence of sexually or racially discriminatory elements, absence of violence, etc.

(iii) Where a program uses data which may vary over a period of time, provision must be made for updating such data.

Where a program can use data which is adaptable to the level of the learner, this possibility must be taken into account.

2.4 Pedagogical effectiveness

Courseware should provide an effective answer from the teaching point of view through:
(i) the use of the specific features of the microcomputer and, where applicable, of other media.
(ii) a globally descending pedagogical analysis, taking into account:
(a) the difficulties experienced by both learners and teachers in the learning/teaching situation, and
(b) the most appropriate learning activities.
(iii) the possibility of differentiated paths in function of the learner's responses.
(iv) student/machine interactivity, which should be both appropriate and adapted to the learners concerned through:
(a) analyses of learner responses, commentaries and pedagogical assistance,
(b) ergonomic qualities of the program
(c) where appropriate, evaluation of the learner's work (formative and/or summative).
(v) flexibility in teaching use: ability to handle input/output, to cope with interruptions in the course of the work session, facilities for up-dating and/or adaptation, etc.
(vi) ease of use of the program, both by the teacher and by the learner, in particular through accompanying literature of good quality both from the pedagogical point of view and as regards technical/computer aspects.

2.5 Program feasibility and cost effectiveness

(i) Program feasibility

Throughout the draft program development stage, it is necessary to check that the paper description is capable of translation into a computer program.   Where modifications are required to make this possible, care should be taken to check that they do not affect other aspects of program quality.   Program feasibility concerns mainly:
(a) graphics, animations, simulations, data banks,
(b) micro computer response time
(c) the ability to handle:
- pedagogical aids and/or techniques
- evaluation of learner's work (where applicable)
- input/output, and interruptions in the course of the work session
- adaptations and/or updating (where applicable)
- batteries of exercises chosen at random but graduated
- screen displays and screen clearing, and learner operation (keys made inoperative)
(d) maximum ease of setting-up and using the program , both for the teacher and for the student,
(e) ensuring that the program does not "crash" during operation.
It is worth checking that information on these

points in the accompanying literature is clear
and adequate.

(ii) Cost effectiveness

Throughout the draft program development
stage, it is necessary to estimate the final
cost of the prototype program. Whenever a
significant increase in the estimated final
cost appears, an attempt should be made to
modify the program so as to minimize the cost
increase, without affecting other aspects of
the quality of the program.

3. QUALITY ASSESSMENT POINTS IN DEVELOPING
COURSEWARE

3.1 Methodological stages

Five distinct stages occur in the methodology of developing courseware:

- stage 1: opportunity study
- stage 2: pedagogical design
- stage 3: pedagogical development, comprising
two levels:
. links between modules and between pedagogical
  scenes in each module, together with any
  testing of branches required.
. detailed descriptions of learning activities
  and (where applicable) methods for evaluating
  the learner's work, together with screen-
  pages and their external environment (what
  is visible on the screen) and internal
  environment (micro computer software)
- stage 4: programming: generally effected
by a team of programmers in close contact with
the team of authors.
- stage 5: prototype program tests, both in
the laboratory ("in vitro") and in the classroom ("in situ") in accordance with a precise
test schedule. These tests are carried out in
liaison with the team of authors but not
actually by them.

3.2 Quality Assessment Points

(i) Introduction

Our experience in following the development
of educational software has demonstrated that
we need to define phases in the development
process and to provide tools so that the work
of the teams of authors and evaluators may be
simplified and correlated.

These phases in the development process, five
in all, do not coincide with the five methodological stages previously described.   The
phases are as follows:

- phase 1: general presentation of the project
- phase 2: presentation of the pedagogical
scenario
- phase 3: presentation of a significant
module or partial model on paper and in
computer format,
- phase 4: presentation of the complete model
of the program on paper, together with
accompanying literature,
- phase 5: presentation of the prototype
program in computer format, together with
accompanying literature.

One quality assessment point corresponds to
each of the above phases, and each provides the
appropriate material for its evaluation. The
project is subjected to overall evaluation at
each quality assessment point, on the basis
of one or two dominant criteria.   At the same
time, a follow-up check is effected of the
dominant criteria of the preceding phase of
development.

(ii) General presentation of the process

- Quality assessment point n° 1

The authors present their draft program in
the form of a completed questionnaire, which
also constitutes a preliminary approach to
the opportunity study.

This presentation allows an evaluation of the
opportunity and originality of the project,
and a preliminary estimate of its computer
feasibility and its likely cost.   The project
is subsequently either accepted or refused.

We must admit here that considerable difficulty
is encountered in avoiding duplication of
courseware which is being developed or already
on the market, for in France no exhaustive
catalogue exists on the subject.

- Quality assessment point n° 2

The authors supply the "pedagogical scenario"
of the draft program, i.e. a detailed presentation of each of the following points:
. method of structure of the content
. analysis of objectives, in descending order
. identification of likely areas of difficulty
  for learners
. didactic and pedagogical features
. learning activities used in each pedagogical
  scene and each module
. types of evaluation of the learner's work,
  follow up (where necessary) and ultimate
  objectives
. possible links between the modules and any
  branching tests
. possible links between the pedagogical
  scenes of a given module and any branching
  tests, and possible recourse to assistance
  modules (computer or pedagogical).

Thus a basic evaluation of the pedagogical
effectiveness of the draft program is achieved,
notably by an overall analysis of objectives
in descending order.   The accuracy of the
content to be written in is also checked
(underlying theories and/or models used, and
tolerance thresholds) together with suitability
for the learners concerned.

- Quality assessment point n° 3

The authors supply a paper model of a significant module and the programmers supply a computer model of the same module.   We consider
it essential not to request the formulation of
the paper model of the complete draft program
until the quality of the paper model (and, if
possible, also the computer model) of a
SIGNIFICANT module of the project has first
been evaluated.   The computer model,

partially programmed as in stage 4 of the
methodology, serves to appreciate, among other
features, computer feasibility and also certain
aspects of pedagogical effectiveness. Experience demonstrates that there is risk of error
in evaluating on the basis of the paper model
alone.

We also consider it very important to have the
partial model tested "in vitro" (i.e. in the
laboratory) by a small team of teachers and a
small team of learners from among the target
public, so as to enable a concrete evaluation
of the pedagogical effectiveness of the module
to be made.

It is thus possible to suggest corrections and
improvements to the significant module while
there is still time, together with any other
recommendations on the overall project.

- Quality assessment point n° 4

   The authors supply the paper model of the
complete program, together with a preliminary
version of the accompanying literature. In
the first place, we check whether the recommendations regarding the significant module
have been taken properly into account.

Each of the other program modules is then
evaluated, as at point 3, on the basis of the
paper model only.

The pedagogical effectiveness, computer
feasibility and likely cost of the complete
program are evaluated at this point.

Particular attention is paid to the accompanying
literature and especially to its pedagogical
content, which in our view, should contain
examples of pedagogical applications. The
preliminary version is evaluated at this quality
point.

- Quality assessment point n° 5

   Working in close cooperation with the team of
authors, the programmers supply the prototype
software and the authors produce a second
version of the accompanying literature, taking
into account both technical and computer aspects
as well as pedagogical aspects.

The prototype software and accompanying literature
are then tested "in vitro" in order to evaluate
the following criteria:

- accuracy, topicality, and impartiality of
content,
- pedagogical effectiveness (this is perhaps
the most important point),
- cost effectiveness.

Then follow "in situ" tests with learners.
They are carried out in various different places
in order to achieve a representative selection
of the target public. We consider it

indispensable to require both teachers and
learners to complete an evaluation form drawn
up according to a precise test format.

This enables both pedagogical effectiveness and
the accompanying literature to be evaluated in
a real life situation. Frequently it is also
an opportunity to improve the literature so as
to make it more suitable for use with learners.

The courseware and accompanying literature is
then ready for production and distribution:
we like to think that by then it can be justly
called "QUALITY courseware".

4. CONCLUSION

Our research into the methodology of formulating
courseware and our experience with authors have
convinced us of the usefulness of evaluating
a project on the basis of the most appropriate
quality assessment points and pertinent criteria,
during the actual program development process.

Definition of the quality assessment points and
appropriate evaluation tools lead us simultaneously to:

- specify the quality criteria and their
indicators, so enhancing methodological
assistance to authors

- require authors to produce successive versions
which are adapted to evaluation, thus enabling
separate phases of development to be distinguished at each stage of the methodology

- define the place, objectives and testing
methods of the prototype program in a real
teaching situation: a kind of "final verdict"
on the draft which will provide a wealth of
information on two levels:

. the draft program itself
. the development methodology (quality
   criteria in particular)

The relationship between the three activities,
Development, Evaluation and Testing, becomes
clear at this point. If quality courseware
can be achieved through the quality of the
development methodology, then in return the
evaluation and testing of the courseware makes
it possible to achieve a development methodology
of equally high quality.

Thus it is demonstrably preferable that the
three functions should not be performed
separately, but rather combined so that
authors, evaluators and testers can compare
their respective objectives and methodologies.

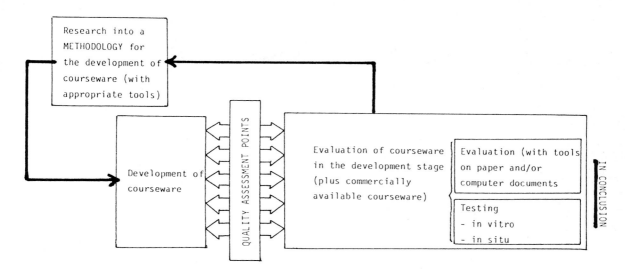

ACKNOWLEDGEMENTS

Mr Jacques Gautier, Director of Studies of the
C.R.E.F.I.P., besides his personal contribution
to the R.E.E.L.E. group, has given us unending
assistance and advice, in particular for contacts
with research teams outside Claude Bernard
University, and in providing material help with
the project.   Our sincere thanks are due to
him.

REFERENCES

(1) Jean-Pierre Chevènement, speech at Palais
de la Découverte, Paris, 25 January 1986 (French)

(2) Rapport de l'Inspection générale sur les
applications pédagogiques de l'information dans
l'enseignement secondaire, Le Monde de
l'Education, 1985 (French)

APPENDIX I

PARTICIPANTS IN THE EVALUATION PROCESS:

1.   Project leaders
2.   The Scientific committee
3.   Teachers and learners who test the
courseware.

1.   PROJECT LEADERS
     Project leaders take part in the working
group for the development, experimentation and
evaluation of courseware: their role is to

. follow the overall process
. formulate and adjust the methodology and
tools.

They may also:

. use courseware with learners
. train teachers in the use of the computer
   for teaching purposes
. teach computer science or related subjects

Each courseware project is followed by a project
leader who

. coordinates evaluation at each stage
. communicates the results of evaluation to
   the authors and determines objectives for
   amendments with them.

2.   THE SCIENTIFIC COMMITTEE comprises
(a) specialists in the subjects covered by
the courseware which is being developed or
evaluated.   They may be consulted on the
scientific quality of the product.
(b) specialists in teaching the subjects
concerned.   They may be consulted on the
pedagogical quality of the courseware.
(c) Teachers who have specific knowledge of
existing conventional and/or computer-aided
methods.   They may be consulted on the
pedagogical interest of the courseware.
(d) computer specialists. They may be consulted
on project feasibility.
(e) ergonomists.

N.B. Points (b) and (c) are generally covered
by the same person.

The members of the Scientific Committee may be
consulted at various stages of the development
of the courseware, according to their respective
speciality.   The project leader is responsible
for coordinating this consultation and
communicating the results to the authors.

Direct communication between any member of the
Scientific Committee and the person in charge

of a project can be arranged for specific problems.

- **or** from teachers who are familiar with the courseware and teaching applications, notably those who have taken a C.R.E.F.I.P. course (quality assessment point n° 5)

3. TEACHERS AND LEARNERS WHO TEST THE COURSEWARE

Teachers are selected on the basis of evaluation objectives:

- either from teachers who are already using courseware without any special training in computer-aided teaching methods (quality assessment point n° 3)

APPENDIX II

SELECTED EXTRACTS FROM EVALUATION FORMS

1. Extract from an evaluation form employed at quality assessment point n° 2

Evaluation by PROJECT LEADER

OVERALL EVALUATION

		Ø	5Ø	1ØØ
*	(1) conformity of "opportunity study"			
*	(2) accuracy of pedagogical scenario			
*	(3) coherence of file			
—	(4) degree of attainment of objectives			
—	(5) areas of difficulty			

2. Extract from an evaluation form employed at quality assessment point n° 3

— (4.2) Numerical displays:

   - accuracy
   - pertinence
   - suitability for target learners

— (4.3) Graphics

   - accuracy
   - pertinence
   - suitability for target learners

— (5) quality of displayed messages

COMPUTERS IN EDUCATION, F. Lovis and E.D. Tagg (eds.)
Elsevier Science Publishers B.V. (North-Holland)
IFIP, 1988

663

CORRECTING EXAMINATIONS BY COMPUTERS

Françoise MADAULE

Laboratoire MASI, Université Pierre et Marie Curie
4 Place Jussieu 75252, PARIS CEDEX 05 FRANCE

In this paper we discuss the problem of marking students by appropriate test-intended software. We first examine the required features of such systems, concerning safeness, reliability, ease of use, and we show why existing tutoring systems do not fulfill these requirements. In the second part of this paper, we describe ACCORD, a software which has been used in our university for about five years. ACCORD enables students to take interactive examinations, and teachers to collect the results, or to get easily corrected written examinations. As a conclusion, we point out how this examination form is perceived by students and teachers.

It is almost a philosophical point among people dealing with CAL, that computers should not be used to give marks to the students, and we heard many times that such a grading would stress students...

As a matter of fact, existing authoring systems generally do not offer automatic marking abilities [1]. Authors are free of programming any kind of numerical evaluation they may want, but it may be tedious to do so, and this is not recommended by the user's manual of the system.

In this paper, we first expose the reasons that we see for this state of fact, and deduce some features of test intended computer softwares. We then present ACCORD software which has been used at the "Université Pierre et Marie Curie" for now five years, and examine the teachers' and students' reactions.

1. WHY ARE NOT COMPUTERS USED IN EXAMS ?

1.1. CAL is mainly intended to help students, not teachers.

The first enthusiasm (as soon as the sixties!) [2] about computer aided learning -or even training- has dwindled when people became aware of how difficult it is to make good courseware [3]. This is particularly true in France, where programs have been launched as "Projet National pour l'E.A.O.", "DIANE" [4], and, more recently, "Informatique pour tous" [5]. Elementary and high schools, colleges and universities, even libraries received microcomputers : at present time most educational institutions are equipped with microcomputers, but good educational software and courseware are scarce, so that we are afraid that most of these machines remain in cupboards...

Meanwhile, attention focused on means to help students to understand things, and great hopes were put into artificial intelligence techniques : experimental prototypes appeared, for instance GUIDON [6] , PROUST [7], or G system [8]. But we are still very far from the general, adaptive, efficient and convivial courseware which is dreamt up for the purpose of intelligent computer aided learning. Computer based training systems are not so well considered : however, they are easy to make, and helpful for the teacher, who is discharged from the less interesting part of teaching. As a matter of fact, a large amount of the teacher's uninteresting work is to correct exams and tests, which are rather numerous in French secondary and universitary curricula. In some important national competitive exams, such as medical "internat", or admission into "Grandes Ecoles", involving thousands of candidates, multiple choice questions or questions with short answers are used, and correction is made with automatic (although manual) techniques, such as transparent correction grids. But students are not directly in touch with computers.

1.2. Test-intended computer systems must be different from tutoring systems.

With tutoring systems, courseware gives explanations, asks questions and directs the student to the next unit according to his answer : answer analysis is needed for orientation purposes, so that some inconsistency in the answers may be ignored, or solved by re-asking the question. Generally many possible paths exist, following the level of understanding of each student. On the other hand, it may be tolerable (although certainly not advisable!) that the system reacts badly to a completely erratic student answer.

In a test-intended system, all students have to follow the same path, in case of questions depending on each other, or must answer a number of independent questions, in any order. Dialogue units are the same for all students. Answer analysis must be uncontestable, since it determines the marks given to the student : the teacher may appreciate the answer as good, bad, or possibly "half good" (or "nearly good, but...") and this must be taken in account by the system. Of course, the specialized software may not fail, and recovering procedures must palliate operating system crashes. At last the system must offer as much security as the traditional exams, with a written paper.

1. 3. Stand alone micro-computers are not well-suited for testing groups of students

Testing software is more efficient using a shared computer system - either a large processor with numerous terminals, or a net of microcomputers. A lot of manual work is necessary to gather and classify results, and this is typically computerizable. If the test is undergone by groups of students using individual microcomputers, the teacher need handle a lot of diskettes for this purpose!

2. FEATURES OF A COMPUTER AIDED TESTING SOFTWARE SYSTEM

We identified some properties of such a system : safeness, reliability, ease of use. Furthermore, it must be different from tutoring systems.

2. 1. Safeness

Students tests must be achieved as safely as by traditional ways, i. e. written exercises or oral interviews. This means that in no case could the test be taken in a self-service modality : actual human supervision is required, exactly as usual.

The teacher may or may not define a maximum time for the test.

Students can neither undergo the examination more than once, nor modify their answers after finishing the test. Software access rights must be carefully controlled, particularly when the host computer may be accessed from remote terminals.

After the results are published, students may be allowed to see their answers once again, and to compare them with the expected answers; this point is important, as a program may fail to acknowledge some sorts of formulations, and human opinion is sometimes necessary to soften rough computer judgments...

2. 2. Reliability

Obviously, all software should be fully reliable! Here, this demand is still more important, as it is nearly inconceivable that the testing program should crash in the middle of the test, for instance because the student has typed letters instead of digits! Of course, it is easy to prevent such software misconduct (although this kind of problem arises in some educational software available in France...), but everybody knows how subtle bugs may introduce themselves in programs! So, a test intended system has to be carefully checked and verified again and again, to be reasonably sure of its correctness before it comes into real use.

On the other hand, the software must afford protection against inopportune shutdowns of the host system, by the way of well-defined recovery procedures. These procedures must allow a student to reenter an interrupted test, (but not to reenter a terminated test), without loss of his previous work, nor reckoning the time elapsed during the interruption.

2.3. Ease of use

(i) - for the student
He must be in at least the same conditions as for usual examinations : he must be able to re-read and modify his answers, and to choose in which order he will treat the independent items. To be tested by a computer can be somewhat stressing, so we must try to give him as much intellectual comfort as possible. We have previously written that he will be allowed to access a correct version of the answers, after the examination is ended.

(ii) - for the teacher
First of all, the system must be a simple authoring system, i.e. the teacher need not have programming abilities : it is hard enough to prepare an examination in that way, because he must define the questions, the expected answers, and the corresponding marks, avoiding any ambiguity, and then verify everything in the same context as the students. After all the students have completed the test the teacher has to gather results, reordering them according to students' names, to obtain usual lists of results; other features may be useful such as statistics about a test (general average, bar diagrams, and so on...), or grouping results of different tests for the same students. The software system must include these facilities, as the work before the examination -which is conception work- is certainly increased by using computers, but the work after the exam - which is the tedious task of correcting numerous papers- must be made as automatic as possible.

2. 4. Differences from tutoring systems

We have already pointed out that there are no students' individual paths through the courseware. Even if they run it in different order, all students will see the same questions, whatever their previous answers. Accordingly, the author does not deal with successors when treating answers. As for answer recognition, it must be completly unambiguous, therefore natural language is excluded. The author has not to know all the subtleties of smart answer analysis, as they are implemented in tutoring systems such as ARLEQUIN [9] or PLATO [10] for instance, but he needs very reliable modalities to distinguish between "good", "false", or even "nearly good" or "not so bad" answers, which may be textual or numerical.

In this perspective, obviously multiple choice questions are completely safe - at least when the texts for the question and for the displayed answers are clear, but this concerns the author and not the software. Open questions implying short answers (a few words, not a sentence, or a numerical expression, not a formula) may also be accepted : the system must offer a simple but staunch answer analysis, according to teacher specifications, which depend generally on the subject taught.

Concerning the questions themselves - and, more generally, the displayed data - they need not to be as attractive as in a complete courseware where the aim is to get the student to learn something without pain. Here the student stands in a "captive" and rather uncomfortable situation : displayed data have to reassure him, and to give him accurate indications to formulate his answers, not to please him ! So graphical and full-page editors may not be as necessary as in other authoring systems.

3. THE ACCORD SYSTEM

3. 1. Context for this system

UPMC ("Université Pierre et Marie Curie") is a big scientific university with about thirty thousand students. Several thousand of them take courses in computer science. Classical written examinations occur three times a year, with numbers of students as large as three hundred for the same test. The university is chronically lacking in sufficient room, so that examinations are taken in unadapted amphitheaters, where copying is very easy, and is too often practised. In these conditions, it is nearly impossible to give exams that can be rapidly corrected, such as multiple choice questions, and corrections give a lot of work to teachers. Furthermore, the author of this paper is responsible for selecting about two hundred students each year, and has to deal with several computer science and mathematics tests in three weeks only .

At the beginning of the eighties, UPMC (with other universities) was equipped with Multics, a large time-shared computer system. We decided about 1982 to use computer facilities, first to test our own classes of students, then, more generally, as an aid in testing students. Thus came ACCORD (in French "Aide au Contrôle des Connaissances par ORDinateur", that means "Computer Aided Testing").

3. 2. Main characteristics of ACCORD

ACCORD is an authoring system which presents the features detailed above, and, due to specific conditions at UPMC, enables to introduce certain degrees of variability inside the tests. Thus we hoped that students would lose their nasty habits of copying during exams.

Another feature due to our context is that we use different terminals connected to the Multics system : each kind of display needs different controls to manage the full page screen, and few are really graphical; we deliberately chose to use the screen in scrolling mode, which of course is always available.

Three kinds of users are involved by ACCORD : the student, the teacher, author of the test, and the teacher, responsible for a group of tests (often the same person).

3. 3. Student modes

Three student modes are available in ACCORD :
- in <u>normal mode,</u> all the safety switches are "on", and both the actual shape of the questions and the student answers are kept in a Multics file; this file is updated at each question, and is the basis for recovery procedures, and for gathering the results; after the normal end of the test, the file is put out of reach of the student.
- in <u>correction mode,</u> the student sees once more questions, with his answers, the correct answers, and possibly brief comments.
- in <u>training mode,</u> the test is presented to the student exactly as in normal mode, immediately followed by correction mode, but no trace is kept of his answers after he has finished the test. He may do the test again as many times as he wants to. Due to randomization abilities of ACCORD, questions may be slightly different each time.

To enter one of these modes, the student types one of the commands : "ec interro", "ec corrige", or "ec exercice", followed by the test subject file name, and the name of the teacher responsible. At times defined by this teacher, these commands are available only to the students concerned. The ACCORD part dealing with files availability and safety switches is made with Multics executable commands, whereas the test interpreter itself is a PASCAL program.

General features such as title, optional time limit, questions (and their possible variants), answers models, links between questions, and marking points, are stored in a file called "subject file". The PASCAL interpreter manages questions display, answer analysis, marking, time control, and, in correction mode, correct answers and comments display.

Figure 1 shows an example of screen viewed by a student : here ACCORD messages are, of course, in French, whereas English texts come from the subject file.

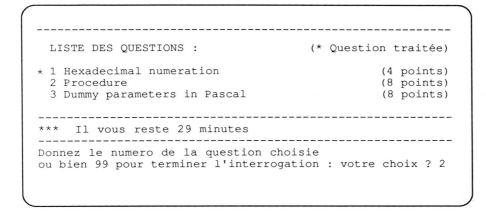

Figure 1

3. 4. Author mode

The author builds the subject file from several text files, each containing either a self-consistent question or a subquestion, several subquestions making a problem. We name each of these text files a "unit". Units are created with a text editor available, use of which is the only computer-related skill required of the author. Reference [11] contains a complete description of ACCORD abilities.

(i) Units
A unit is made of lines. Some lines are particularized by their first characters, chosen among a few *key characters* which are summarized in table 1. The title line indicates the type of the unit (multiple choice question or open question with short answer).

Table 1 : Key characters for lines

Q	Multiple choice question (in title line)	
L	Open question with short answer (in title line)	
F	Line always displayed	
Vn	Line displayed for variant number n	
Rn	Model for good answer to variant n	
An	Model for "half good" answer to variant n	
En	Comment upon variant number n	
%i	Numerical variable definition	
$$i$	Textual variable definition	

Answer treatments are defined by a few other characters given by table 2; one of those characters necessarily follows Rn (or An) in L-type units. The author may give as many response models as he wants. Unit texts are validated by a program which checks them for consistency and shows them in student mode.

Table 2 : Answer treatment characters

I	Identity between student's answer and model	
B	Identity is checked after blanks removal	
M	Letters case is not taken in account	
Z	Same as "B" + "M"	
C	Radicals research in student's answer (possibly exclusion)	
D	Same as "C", neglecting letters case	
&	Numerical answer (value or expression) possibly within a given interval	

(ii) Subject file
It is built by the author, using units to define simple or compound questions. Here the software guides the author through a series of menus. Figure 2 shows two of these menus. In addition to units, and if he has the ability, the author may insert in the text questions programmed as PASCAL procedures. Thus ACCORD is a fully open system.

(iii) Test randomization
As we designed ACCORD, we wanted to prevent student copying as for as possible. Therefore, we introduced several levels of randomization for a given subject file, in order more or less to change the form of a test, from one run to the other.

First, for multiple choice question, numbering of displayed answers is always randomly defined. Other features are optional for the author :
. questions may be numbered randomly.
. he may define "equivalent" questions : according to the time of day when a student is sitting the examination, the used unit is chosen among those he proposes.

```
Dans le contexte actuel, vous pouvez :

    t - Modifier le Titre
    c - modifier la CLASSE et (ou) la limite de temps
    a - AJOUTER une question
    s - SUPPRIMER une question
    f - FINIR

Que choisissez-vous ?
(Répondez "t","c","a","s","f")? a

LA QUESTION EST LA QUESTION NUMERO 2

Dans le contexte actuel, vous pouvez :

    a - définir un AIGUILLAGE (question à options)
    p - définir une question PROCEDURE
    u - définir une question UNITAIRE
    e - définir des questions EQUIVALENTES
    s - définir une SERIE de questions enchaînées

Type choisi ?
(Répondez "a","p","u","e","s") ? u
```

Figure 2

. "variant" lines in the unit texts allow up to nine different forms (and consequently different good responses) for a given unit.

. the values of textual or numerical variables are defined, at run time, by random drawing according to author's initial choices.

(iv) Test checking :
Of course, the author may check the test in student-like mode, that is he can see how the questions are displayed and how the answers are recognized.

3.5. Responsible teacher mode

After the author has finished preparing and checking the test, the responsible teacher uses ACCORD pre-defined Multics commands to open the examination for students. After the examination, he has at his disposal various ACCORD modules to obtain lists of results conveniently.

3.6. Other ACCORD abilities

It is not always possible for students to get access to computer terminals, and regulations for graduating examinations are rather strict, so that generalization of interactive computer testing is more or less limited. Therefore the problem of easily correcting examination papers remained unsolved at UPMC. We added to ACCORD a module which uses a subject file, as defined above, to produce printable files. One file contains a lot of distinct examination forms, ready to be filled in by students. These forms are numbered, and are made by systematic combinations of questions and/or variants, instead of drawing them randomly as in interactive mode. Variable values remain randomly defined. A second file is a summary of the correct answers for all the numbered forms. After using this module, the teacher need do nothing other than print as many copies of the first file as necessary. From our experience, about ten different texts appear as a good setting for amphitheaters filled with 150 to 200 students. With the aid of the second printed output file, correction is made very quick : for an examination lasting two or three hours, correction time falls from about ten minutes by test paper to less than three minutes...

4.EXPERIMENT WITH ACCORD AT UPMC

4. 1. Conditions for use

In September 1982, we used a first version of ACCORD, including only multiple choice questions, for computer science and mathematics tests with our own students. We were then responsible for both, but we entirely defined the computer science tests, whereas the mathematics tests were designed by a non computer specialist colleague. Since then, this experiment has been renewed every year, and ACCORD has evolved according to students' - and, to a lesser extent, teachers'- reactions .We consider that it has now practically reached its final version.

The ACCORD module for examination papers production has been extensively used for computer science examinations of second year students. We also use for some of these students the ACCORD interactive program as a partial substitute to oral interwiews. After the session with the computer, the student looks at the correct version and is allowed to discuss his marks with the teacher; if he wants, he may ask for a normal interview.

4. 2. Teachers' reactions

Teacher reactions are largely positive : they must take more time in preparing the tests, but they gain a lot of correction time. Moreover, text files for questions used in a test are stored in a proper data base and may be re-used for further tests, under the same form or after small changes. Thus preparation time is diminishing year after year. The teachers involved, once they have made the (small) effort of learning to build test files, use the system easily.

4. 3. Students' reactions

Students' reactions depend , of course, on the importance of the test in their curriculum... For second year students, who underwent their final examination by the way of computer-prepared papers, we never received protests about this kind of copying prevention. Honest students - who happily are the most numerous! - were rather glad to have this method.

As for computer science students, who knew that their results to the tests would be used to decide their admittance to UPMC, they were very anxious when examined in interactive mode. We had often to comfort them, and we concluded from their attitude that it is absolutely necessary that the computer judgment might be changed by a possible appeal to human opinion. Systems such as ACCORD must help teachers, not replace them. We had understood the lesson when we set up the use of ACCORD instead of oral interviews, and it was well accepted because of the human simultaneous attendance. Nevertheless, this method divided by three (at least) the time spent in these interviews.

5. CONCLUSION

Our experience shows that it is quite possible to be aided by computer software in the time consuming and repetitive task of giving examinations to large numbers of students. One may pay attention to this use, giving a certain psychological preparation to the students, and maintaining in any case a human recourse. The software system must be completely reliable, and its properties are not the same as tutoring or even intelligent educational software.

REFERENCES

[1] F. Madaule, Barril, B. de La Passardière, F. Le Calvez, M.M. Poc and M. Urtasun, <u>Techniques et Science Informatiques,</u> Vol 6, n° 1, (1987), pp 5-20. (French)

[2] S. Papert, Mindstorms : Children, computers and powerful Ideas,(Harvester Press, New-York, 1980).

[3] J.Arsac, Les Machines à penser, (Seuil, Paris, 1987) (French)

[4] Rapport EAO : specifications du projet Diane, (Agence de l'Informatique, Paris, 1981). (French)

[5] Mission aux Technologies Nouvelles, Informatique pour tous, (CNDP, Paris, 1985). (French)

[6] W.J. Clancey, <u>J. of computer-based Instruction,</u> Vol 10, (1983) pp 8-15.

[7] W. L. Johnson and E. Soloway, Intention-based diagnosis of programming errors, in : Proc. of Nat. Conf. on Artificial Intelligence, (Austin, Txs, Vol 1, 1984), pp 162-168.

[8] M.W.F. Meurrens, An "intelligent" approach of Computer Aided Learning : G, in : Proc. of 5th Canadian Symposium on Instructional Technology, (Ottawa, 1986), pp 121-124.

[9] N. Rodriguez and D. Valentin, Lire ARLEQUIN, (Cedic Nathan, Paris, 1985). (French)

[10]C.A. Hawkins, <u>Computer and Education,</u> Vol 3, (1979), pp 273-280.

[11 F. Madaule, MASI report n° RT5, (Université P. et M. Curie, Paris, 1986). (French)

Panel Sessions

Panel Session 2.4: Computer Assistance to the Academic Staff

Chairperson: N Longworth (GB)

Whether it takes place in an Industrial Training, a Higher Education or a Schools Environment, effective administration of the educational process is becoming a key issue. Partly, this is a response to the increasing demand for education at all levels and a need to exercise some control, however loosely it is applied, across the range of educational opportunities. More pertinently, it is because the software and the understanding now exist to help those involved with the delivery of education use technology more effectively.

The existence of new, improved administrative systems software obviously helps, but the key to its effective use remains, and always will remain, the willingness of people to use the technology available, and the extent to which individuals have access to, and control over, educational decisions made on their behalf.

This series of talks - to be followed by general discussion - describes projects to use technology to improve the administration of education and training in a variety of environments. In some the control is in the hands of the administrator, in others it lies with the individual. In all, the computer is a key element to more effective education.

Panel Session 3.4: Priorities for Research

Chairperson: R Lewis (UK)

Many of the applications of new technologies in support of learning have had a pragmatic basis up to now. The experience gained, however, now allows us to identify issues which are researchable. The outcomes of such research should enable us to make better use of the opportunities to enhance learning which we are offered by the information technologies

The identification of researchable topics and their organisation into a research agenda with priorities is urgently needed. The creation of such an agenda requires us to be clear about the ways in which the outcomes of the research are assimilated into practice. Which research outcomes are likely to have most impact on practice and policy making? Which research outcomes can inform the design of new curricula and learning materials?

Certain research areas are dominated by technological development. The application of new software tools and environments provides the opportunities to experiment with advanced authoring environments for intelligent or 'clever' computer assisted learning software and more appropriate forms of learning-machine interaction.

Research in the field of artificial intelligence may provide insights into cognitive development as models of the learner or machine learning are explored. At the social psychology end of the spectrum, we need to identify factors which allow learners of all ages to make use of the opportunities provided by advanced, low cost communications technology for distance and open learning.

But many of the items on a research agenda are likely to be those which are important in the absence of the new technologies. Management and organisation of classrooms, the role of the teacher, teacher education, including continuing support for innovatory teachers, learner-learner interaction, are all significant factors, influential in the support of learning in their own right. The presence of technological resources, however, appears to bring them into sharper focus.

Contributions to a discussion on research agenda items and priorities will take place. The variation in views which results naturally from diverse socio-political structures in different countries is expected to lead to lively debate.

Panel Session: Impact of New Man-Machine Interfaces on Training

Chairperson: P G Raymont (UK)

User Interface Management Systems give facilities to enable users to interact more effectively with computers. As examples, the use of windows, icons, mice and pointers (WIMPS) and the improvements to dialogues which can result from the use of artifical intelligence (AI) techniques can be cited.

What training is needed by the designers of educational software to enable them to exploit these possibilities? Clearly, ergonomic factors concerned with screen layout, colour, etc, will be important. But we need to reach beyond such simple considerations to achieve interactions which are stimulating, varied, matched to users' capabilities, etc, rather than (as so often is the case now) boring, routine and off-putting.

We need to integrate the work of ergonomists, psychologists and computer scientists. How can this be done? What is the target audience and what are the educational objectives for courses in this area? How much time is needed? What numbers are we talking about? Are the resources to mount such courses available?

Another aspect of the problem is the impact on users of the availability of such improved interfaces. On the one hand, the result might simply be that less training is needed to enable users to cope with systems of current complexity.

On the other hand, it may be that users will find themselves able to utilise systems of far greater complexity with little or no additional training. This latter possibility raises the additional question of how far the user needs to understand the workings of the system he is using. This is already a key question in some AI systems, where facilities may be provided to explain to the user how the machine had reached its conclusions. Again, an interdisciplinary approach is needed.

How do we assess the nature and extent to which users need to understand the system they are working with? Finally, how do we feed this back into the training for designers?

Panel Session:

WG 3.5:   Informatics and Elementary Education

Chairperson: Frank Lovis   (GB)

Above all other spheres of informatics education, the elementary level (up to 12/13 years of age) is certainly the problematical one.   Its first difficulty lies in the remarkably different stances which the various member countries of IFIP have taken towards it.   Some are totally and irrevocably committed to developing the use of computers in elementary schools as quickly and as widely as possible. Others have turned their faces resolutely against any such development. Psychologists, as might be expected, argue both ways at once.   Many teachers are keen to employ computers: others see them as producing nothing but extra work and problems.   All in all, WG 3.5 has a veritable "devil's garden" to pick its way through.

There is no doubting the commitment and enthusiasm of the members of WG 3.5.   Moreover, their collective experience is growing fast and offers a valuable commodity which could assist all teachers who are looking to start or extend their own work in this area.

Yet our plans are currently hamstrung by two problems: the lack of a lingua franca and the niggardly financial provision which is available to elementary teachers.   It would be helpful if we could come to be recognised as the special case which we undoubtedly are, but, to date, such organisations as IFIP and UNESCO seem to look upon us as just one branch of the family of education, without seeing that we are a valuable, but extremely poor relation.

This panel session will start with a quick résumé of the Working Group's activities since its formation in 1984 and then get down to the vital, discussion - in which the audience must become fully involved - of what we should do in the coming few years and how the serious problems described above can best be overcome.

Panel Session 3.6: Distance Learning

Chairperson: Gordon Davies (UK)

WG 3.6 is the most recently established Working Group pf TC3. It was formed in response to the growing realisation by people in many countries that Distance Learning has become one of the most successful and economic forms of education. While the advent of computers has had an impact on education generally, in the field of Distance Learning the use of computers will have an even greater impact; the computer has a vital role to play in the future development of Distance Learning.

We can consider first the effect on the teaching of Computing or Informatics. The advent of cheap personal computers makes it possible for us to teach these subjects in the home much more effectively than has hitherto been the case. Students can now purchase their own machine on which to carry out the practical work and can plan their acivities independently of any host institution. Furthermore, the use of telecommunication systems and computer networks enables students to interact both with fellow students and their tutors. Conferencing facilities and electronic mail are now being used by both students and tutors, and this again is being done in their own homes.

Another important facet of the computer in both these situations is that the computer can also be used as a tool for teaching other subjects, in addition to the teaching of Computing. Computer Assisted Learning is now being used at both ends of the computing spectrum as an important part of the teaching process. From the small personal computer to the large powerful work station, the written text and the computer are being combined to provide an integrated teaching medium.

The Aims and Scope of the new Working Group reflect this variety of interests and technological innovation. There are many exciting developments in the area of Distance Learning and it is intended that the Working Group will be a forum for members to share their experiences and to discuss these exciting developments.

The Panel will consist of academics who are actively involved in using the computer in the Distance Learning environment.

Panel: The Pedagogics of Networking

Chairperson: R Gwyn (UK)

There is a growing realisation in educational circles that the micro-computer should not be looked at solely as a stand-alone device. It is recognised that the connectivity made possible by both Local Area and Wide Area Networks brings a considerable value-added element to the educational potential of the micro, and this recognition is reflected in mani-festations as diverse as, for example, EARN (European Academic Research Network) at Higher Education level, The Times Network for Schools at Secondary and Primary levels, and the utilisation of various LANs at the school level. In each such case, the capacities of the stand-alone micro are very considerably enhanced by the fact of being linked to a wider range of facilities.

The LAN concept is in itself very interesting as a model for the development of school facilities, and already there are trail-blazing examples of how LANs can enhance a total school resource (a prime example from the UK: Felsted School, Essex). The focus of this Panel Discussion, however, is on the less-researched end of the spectrum, namely the educ-ational potential of Wide Area Networks.

The key concept is that of convergence: the convergence, that is, of different technologies in such a way as to increase exponentially the capacity of any technology viewed in isolation. In respect of WANs, the critical convergence is that of the microcomputer with the telephone, a convergence which in principle makes immediately possible the global electronic village.

The identification of connecting on this scale raises a number of critical questions for its utilisation in education; these include, for example, questions of access to remote resources and - perhaps most interestingly of all - questions of possible collaborative activity between classes geog-raphically remote from each other.

Thus, to address the issue of the pedagogy of networking is to raise at least two major issues, which are;

a)   What do teachers need to know about the technicalities of networking to enable them to become effective network users?

b)   What new perspectives on teaching and learning do teachers need to acquire if they are fully to exploit the potential offered by Wide Area Networks?

The Panel Discussion will address these issues with particular reference to the PLUTO European network for teacher education.

Concluding Presentations

COMPUTERS IN EDUCATION, F. Lovis and E.D. Tagg (eds.)
Elsevier Science Publishers B.V. (North-Holland)
© IFIP, 1988

THE IMPACT OF MASSIVE COMPUTING POWER ON THE UNIVERSITY ENVIRONMENT

Bernard Levrat

Chairman of ECCE88 Programme Committee
University of Geneva
24, rue General Dufour
1211 Genève 4, Switzerland

I. Perspective

The computing power at the disposal of the average university user has grown in the last ten years in proportions that are difficult to realize. I should like to consider the University of Geneva as a rather typical example of European institutions of higher education : it has a body of 11 400 students (8 500 in 1978), 435 (380) professors, 1070 (893) teaching staff and 1028 (902) technical and administrative personnel.

In 1978, it had a computing centre with a time-sharing machine sporting 1 Mbyte of central memory - actually 256K words of 36 bits - and slightly over one Mips of computing power. Two dozen interactive terminals were attached to it, either locally or through 1200 baud modems. About the same number of key punch machines fed the local card reader, or remote job entry stations built around mini-computers. The administration worked in COBOL, balking at the effort of using CODASYL DBMS, while scientists used FORTRAN along with some packages like SPSS for statistics.

Departmental mini-computers were found in science departments, doing little more than data acquisition and process control, while large amounts of data were stored on magnetic tapes, waiting to be processed on some central facility. All big on-line experiments, especially at CERN, were computer hungry and looked outside for extra computing power. Some could be found on large machines, in Geneva, at the "Hôpital cantonal" and, at the EPFL in Lausanne; physicists, astronomers, econometrists, ... had to bargain a lot and to travel even more.

Changes were in the making, with text processing becoming commercially affordable, PASCAL and relational data bases getting out of computer science departments and micro-processors being mass produced, soon to become the basis of the micro-computer revolution.

Dramatic advances in networking were also taking place. Arpanet was linking together most of the research centres in computing in the United States, providing an example of a national wide area network. Ethernet had been defined in 1976 and was adopted soon afterwards by DEC, INTEL and XEROX, as the basis for Local Area Networking.

II. Planned evolution

The shortage of adequate resources made stop gap measures unavoidable. Over one hundred new terminals were bought and connected to interactive mini-computers, either directly or through telephone lines. Different text processing systems started appearing on secretary desks, not to mention the flurry of micro-computers bought on individual research budgets.

In view of the ever increasing demand, it was decided not simply to replace the central computing facility, but to build an infrastructure that would last until the 21st century. A network interconnecting distributed resources was carefully designed to link most of the eighty-six buildings in which parts of the University are located throughout the city : Ethernet cables were installed by the Department of Public Works inside the buildings and the Swiss PTTs provided optical fibre links between them. Interestingly, the financing followed the same procedure as for a new building.

With information transfer proceeding at 10 Mbits/sec, it was a simple matter to allow all existing terminals to connect to new computing facilities, (including an IBM 3090/180 for number crunching, file serving and administrative data processing, several VAX computers, our old 780's and new 8700 and 8300), for interactive use, either under VMS or under UNIX, those in turn giving access to a worldwide electronic mail service (EARN), public telecommunication facilities (Telepac), or to the CRAY-1s installed in Lausanne.

Connecting PCs to Ethernet requires special hardware and software which, originally, could only be found for IBM PC compatibles. Close to 800 of them are connected, locally sharing resources like printers or disk files and being able to emulate DEC or IBM terminals and to access any of the machines. It is now possible to connect MacIntoshes as well, but without full support for all functions.

According to the plan, introducing new machines does not require extra expense beyond an Ethernet coupler. Departments have already bought CONVEX and ALLIANT vector-computers which have been easily integrated. Foreseeable bottlenecks can be alleviated by adding the necessary servers at the appropriate place, at the computing centre if they require operators, otherwise closest to the demand, in order not to load the network unnecessarily.

It was postulated from the beginning that the full use of such an environment can be made only through workstations : single user machines with a large screen, which can support multi-window and multi-process operations, thus sharing many resources available from the network in a uniform way. A call for tenders was issued, which showed that workstations with all the desired characteristics existed at affordable prices. About one hundred of them are being installed, mostly SUNs, but also APPOLLO, DEC, HP and MAC II, when users request them. All SUNs come with desktop publishing software and there are over twenty laser printers, accepting Postscript for output.

III. Levels of acceptance

The scene is set : for someone who really wants to use it, there is available today an almost unlimited - at least to accomplish traditional tasks - computing power, access to large storage capacities and unprecedented communication facilities. Will the university community

make use of it, will it become part of the research and teaching process in all disciplines, or will it remain the sole domain of researchers who are able to master the complexities of programming ?

Ten years is a very short time for a University and the distances to cross from a traditional approach to one's discipline to a computer supported environment differ according to each person's background and tastes. Some people feel uncomfortable with computers and will keep on refusing to use them, which is their right. Others will suffer from different degrees of computer addiction, spending most of their time "hacking" complicated solutions to simple problems, such as setting up and maintaining small databases, using graphics and various approximations to desktop publishing.

The "Services Informatiques" are striving to offer a computing environment that will minimize the time and effort an individual should invest to make use of it. Although it is not yet as fully integrated, or as user friendly as we would like it to be, the following observations can be made.

Office automation is very much appreciated after an initial period of learning the basics of MS-DOS, word processing and associated packages. The worst problem is the loss of precious documents because of mistakes or troubles with the hard disk on a PC. A pilot project using the network allows archiving of any PC file or directory on the IBM mainframe.

Communicating through electronic mail is exciting at first, fantastic for researchers working on the same project from different locations, but lacks too many organizational functions for the support staff in research groups to feel comfortable. An improved mail system, which is planned for the near future, based on X.400 protocols, will have to be installed without interrupting current services : a real challenge !

Doing research work with the help of a workstation comes naturally to someone who has used computers previously. Physicists, chemists, statisticians have no difficulty importing programs which previously ran on a mainframe. The integrated environment offered on a workstation includes a transparent multi-window system, GKS for graphics and a document preparation system. Moving stuff from any window into the printable document is easy. We are still looking for a true WYSIWYG to enter complicated formulae.

New applications stem from much improved computer graphics and there is a high level of interest in image processing, ranging from medical sciences to geography, where new approaches based on teledetection (satellite pictures) are being explored, in addition to the more traditional work with maps.

Image synthesis remains the privileged field of chemists and crystallographers for drawing atomic and molecular structures, of medical people showing various views of the inside of the human body, but there is also a strong demand from many disciplines to produce realistic renderings of objects and even animation, which will justify further increases of desktop computing power.

In fields where the use of computers is relatively new, or has only been pioneered by a few scholars in special settings, the lack of adequate tools may hinder progress for some time. For example, users in the humanities want to be able to handle all sorts of fonts in Ancient Greek, Hebrew or Russian, with full string manipulation capabilities. Although the problem has been elegantly solved in particular systems, it is not yet as generally available as FORTRAN subroutines. In this respect, I should like to mention the Thesaurus Linguae Graecae data bank, compiled by T. F. Brunner from the University of California at Irvine, with a substantial help from the Packard Foundation. It contains all the known Greek texts prior to A.D. 600, amounting to 60 million words. They are available on tape or on a specialized system called IBYCUS. Making this resource generally available through our environment raises many questions from character representation on screen and printers to copyright.

One can see from the examples above that computers are used by all disciplines for office automation and electronic mail. They are becoming an indispensable partner for researchers in an increasing number of disciplines. In others, pioneering work is done sporadically, but integrated tools are not yet available. A major concerted effort should be made in this direction.

IV. The present situation for students

Except in computer science, where the Swiss central government has supplemented local efforts in appropriating money to buy workstations specifically for their use, students access the network resources from terminals, or can use PCs in strictly controlled circumstances. It must be added that a large number of students have PCs at home.

What students receive most generally on these machines is an introduction to computing, either through computer based learning, or through programming courses with exercises that show various degrees of automation. Quite often, exams are administered by computers and one can wonder if the sense of user friendliness and partnership is adequately conveyed under these circumstances.

Many experimental CBL materials have been tried, with varying degrees of success. They usually address elementary concepts, far from the currently hot research topics. For economic reasons, students, with very few exceptions, are not permitted really to use the resources available to other members of the academic community.

V. Computing power, research and teaching in universities.

It is usually stated that in order to provide teaching at a high level, universities must also be excellent in research. New knowledge must flow rapidly from teachers, who are deeply involved in research projects, to students, who struggle to get a degree.

Up until now, this has been done through the sharing of written documents and the delivering of lectures, which is supposed to enhance the understanding of the subject matter by the student, owing to a direct (visual) link with the professor. Will the advent of massive computing power change the situation in other ways than producing better documents and much improved visual aids for the lectures ?

There is a number of conditions to be met for communication on a similar level through the computer to be seen as a vehicle for information storage and transfer. User friendliness must be emphasized in order that the human relationship between student and teacher will not be impoverished. It also implies the development of improved communication facilities, where the willingness to open channels can remain compatible with a reasonable amount of control over one's own time and a way to keep abusers out of the system. But above all, ways are needed of easily scaling down applications.

Most research programs like to make use of all the facilities available and do not accept restrictions. Standards must be flexible enough to give them all the services that they need, since otherwise there is no way of forcing researchers to accept the standards. But if they do, there should be easy migration paths, including scaling down of performance, towards the machines commonly available to the students. Projects at Brown, at MIT and at Carnegie Mellon University seemed to be going in this direction and some of the software, such as X-Windows, is already quite valuable. Standards are evolving. The exercise must be constantly pursued, in spite of its lack of market value in terms of immediate returns, because it is worthwhile from the point of view of the global human resource management of a university.

VI Influence on society

The students of today are the teachers of tomorrow. It is predictable that they will try to reproduce in their teaching environment the conditions they experienced while they were students. If they can integrate the computer environment in their studies, there is no doubt that they will consider it a partner in the future.

This has to be opposed to the view that teachers must accept supplementary material developed on the computer, which they feel is competing with them for the students' attention. It will take years, but I am sure that computers with reasonably uniform, user friendly interfaces, will be used to communicate knowledge across educational networks from human being to human being.

It will be exciting, challenging and the rate of scientific discoveries will continue to accelerate. There will be more and more things to learn and one can wonder if learning as we know it will still be necessary.

With so much knowledge stored on computers and readily available, it will be sufficient to know which keyboard keys to press or which keywords to speak. Memorizing facts may become a thing of the past, in the way pocket calculators made human computing abilities obsolete. Nobody feels sorry about that ! I have faith that human curiosity will find many new alleys to explore and that there is a lot of work in front of us to make it happen. Let's meet again in a few years to see where we stand.

Acknowledgment: The author is extremely grateful to the Editor in Chief of the Proceedings, Frank Lovis, who improved both form and contents of this paper.

COMPUTERS IN EDUCATION, F. Lovis and E.D. Tagg (eds.)
Elsevier Science Publishers B.V. (North-Holland)
 IFIP, 1988

COMPUTERS AND THE FUTURE OF EDUCATION*

Tom STONIER

Professor, Science and Society, University of Bradford
Bradford, Yorkshire BD7 1DP, England

Invited Address to E C C E 88
European Conference on Computers in Education
Lausanne, Switzerland
24-29 July, 1988

1. INTRODUCTION

1.1. The Economic Value of Education

Information has displaced land, labour and capital as the most important input into modern productive systems. For example, when land becomes expensive, as it does in the centre of a city, we build skyscrapers. The information to accomplish such a feat did not exist until about a century ago. Similarly, every time a robot displaces a worker, we have a classic example of knowledge displacing labour. The computer industry itself represents the best example of how information, in the form of technical and organisational know-how, has reduced the requirements for inputs of capital, energy, and raw materials: Chris Evans [1979] in his book The Mighty Micro pointed out a decade ago that had the automobile industry made as much progress in thirty years as did the computer industry, it would have (by the end of the 1970s) produced Rolls Royces for £1.35; cars would be able to drive 3 million miles on a gallon of petrol, and their reduction in size and weight would allow one to park six of them on a pinhead. By the late 1980s, four decades of development meant that the price of computers had fallen by a factor of a million, the size had decreased from requiring a small hall to house, to becoming the size of a plastic credit card or a wrist watch, while the energy inputs declined from a million watts to a few ten- millionth watts. It is these examples which illustrate the axiom that **the most important input into modern productive systems is information** -- more important than land, labour, capital, raw materials and energy.

When information is coupled to people, we find that educated and skilled labour tends to be more productive. Hence, there is a continuous selective pressure favouring the educated and skilled, while the uninformed and unskilled are discriminated against. As a category, the worker with a shovel is displaced by the bulldozer driver; the filing clerk is displaced by the computer programmer.

Human capital is the most valuable asset a company (or a country) possesses. Physical assets, though helpful, are no guarantee of a company's future. In a rapidly changing environment, a series of wrong decisions can cause a company which relies only on its physical assets, to end up in oblivion. There was nothing more powerful a hundred years ago than American railways. Fifty years ago it was steel -- twenty years ago, automobiles -- ten years ago, oil. It is the quality of its human capital, the skills and education of its workforce, in particular its managerial workforce, which determines the long-term success of a company. By continuously upgrading its personnel through education and training, the human capital of a company can appreciate with time. Physical assets tend to depreciate; the opposite holds true for properly managed human capital. In an uncertain world, the best single investment any organisation can make is in upgrading its own intellectual infrastructure.

The same may be said for a country. Because education adds value to human capital, and because, in an information economy, human capital is a country's most valuable resource, education will evolve to become the number one industry in all advanced countries. Education, early in the next century, will absorb a larger share of the GNP of Western countries, than any other single economic activity. Furthermore, the education system will become the largest single employer. The matter has been discussed in greater detail previously [Stonier 1983,1988].

1.2 The New Objectives in Education

Because we live in a rapidly changing world, education becomes crucial to providing people with the intellectual tools required for survival. If we are moving into a society in which most physical work is going to be done by robots - a society in which a mere fraction of the workforce can produce all our material wants and goods, then education for employment, although still a part, would become only one of the several objectives of the new education order. At least as important will be 'education for life', 'education for the world', 'education for self-development', and 'education for pleasure'.

Education for employment. It is clear that society is going to need an increasingly versatile labour force, able to respond to the needs of a rapidly changing economy, and a rapidly changing society. Students of today are likely to undergo two or three careers in their lifetime. Some of the most important things we can teach are certain categories of organisational skills which allow individuals to develop entrepreneurial self-reliance to hunt skilfully for new areas of employment, or even start up their own business. A great part of education for employment will involve training, both for specialised skills, and for the five sets of basic skills needed for manoeuvreing in an advanced information economy (to be discussed below).

Education for Life. The primary emphasis of the new educational order must involve a shift in objective from making a living to learning how to live. There are two major aspects of learning how to face life in the twenty-first (or any other) century. The first involves understanding the world, the second involves understanding oneself.

Education for the world. It is not possible to understand the world if we do not understand the impact science and technology have on all aspects of society. Government, commerce and industry can no longer be run by technological illiterates. At the same time, we need to avoid training scientists, engineers and other specialists who do not understand the impact their efforts are making on the social system. That is, we can also no longer afford a society whose progress depends on technologists who are humanistic illiterates.

Understanding the world requires not only exposure to traditional disciplines -- ranging from the natural sciences to the social sciences and the arts -- which allow students to understand the natural and social world in which they live, but what is also needed, is a more global focus. We are all members of the human race living on an isolated planet, floating in a hostile space. We need education for environmental responsibility and, what is even more crucial now, education for developing harmonious relationships within and between societies. This means a playing down of ethnocentric and nationalistic values and an expansion of a more humanistic, anthropological approach. Young people must learn to enjoy and accept cultural diversity.

Apart from improving relationships within the immediate community, the major problem confronting this generation is to close the gap between the rich and poor nations of the world. If that cannot be accomplished within a reasonable period, it must presage international conflict. Improvement in third-world productivity will come, partly through the transfer of capital, but largely as a result of the transfer of education and information, leading to productive technology. Our students, as well as the educational establishment as a whole, must become increasingly involved. We need to expand the exchange of students and academic experts to provide practical solutions to problems confroning those parts of the world desperately struggling against poverty -- a poverty not of their own making.

At the more individual level, we need to teach a whole series of skills on how to survive in this world. Most of these are either not taught at all or relegated to a minor position in the curriculum: how to deal with government bureaucrats, how to get the most out of interviews with physicians, how to be successful teenagers, how to be good lovers, how to be effective parents, how to grow old gracefully, how to face death. Most of the really important decisions in life are not based on information acquired during formal education. Why not?

Education for self-development. It has always been the dream of educators to develop critical faculties so that students are able to understand concepts and develop them on their own. This should be expanded, however, not only to foster more creative imagination, but also artistic, physical and social skills. Particularly important among the latter are communicative and organisational skills. It is one of the sad features of the present education system that it gives the students very little chance to organise things themselves or to prepare for real-life situations. In the real world it is not only what you know that counts, but also how fast you can find out new things. Furthermore, the major activities of the real world involve interacting with people. Social development (in contrast to intellectual development) has always been part of the hidden curriculum. Such skills need to be fostered in a more conscious and systematic fashion.

Education for pleasure. First, we must educate
for the constructive use of leisure time.
Since the early nineteenth century the work
week has been cut by half, and this trend will
accelerate. Second, education itself must
become a pleasurable activity. There has long
been a hidden puritanical tradition in much of
the curriculum which can be summed up by the
attitude that 'it doesn't matter what you teach
them so long as they don't like it'. The new
attitude recognises that students are going to
live in an information explosion and that they
themselves must pick out of that mushrooming
growth of new information what they consider
interesting and enjoyable. Otherwise, the
richness of the new information environment
could lead to a sort of neurological
indigestion -- possibly leading to serious
psychological disturbances.

There is another more vital aspect: in the
future, obtaining and organising information
will become the dominant life activity for most
people. What one enjoys learning most, one
learns best. Enjoyment contributes
substantially to the cost-effectiveness of time
spent learning.

1.3 Education and Training

Education has many aspects and dimensions.
Educators should concentrate on these
dimensions. Conversely, the education system
should not have to worry about job
specifications! From here on, the function of
education should not be to provide industrial
fodder, nor for that matter, advanced
information technology specialists. **The
function of education should be to produce well
educated people.**

**Training should provide the link between the
world of education and the world of work.**
A properly educated workforce becomes easy to
train: It should become possible to train
welders in a matter of a few weeks, computer
programmers in a matter of a few months, and
doctors within a year. In addition, training
should foster five basic skills which ought to
be embedded in the general education programme.
No youngster can be considered well educated if
he or she lack a reasonable proficiency in
these skills. They are:

1. Literacy and communication skills
2. Numeracy and quantitative analysis skills
3. Information technology and data management
   skills
4. Wroughting and mechanical manipulation
   skills
5. Driving and associated safety and navigation
   skills

All of the above can be greatly aided by using
computers -- even driving skills can be
improved by means of simulation -- the way

pilots are taught. In addition, the education
system must become a cradle-to-grave system.
Much of mid-life educational activity will
centre on upgrading existing skills, or
acquiring new ones for professional purposes.
Adult, and Further Education are a
prerequisite for operating a complex
technological economy. They are even more
important for maintaining a sane citizenry.

The above have been discussed in greater
detail elsewhere [Stonier 1979,1985,1988].
The author's feelings about the shift in
education from an industrial to an information
society have been summarised in the Prologue
to The Three Cs: Children, Computers and
Communication [Stonier & Conlin, 1985], which
is reprinted here:

Sometime,
during the second half of the 20th century,
     Western Society evolved from an industrial
          to a post-industrial, or to be precise,
an Information Society.

Education for an industrial society
               centred on teaching the Three Rs:
"Reading, 'Riting, and 'Rithmetic."
Its aim was to produce
   a disciplined workforce --
      punctual, conformist, specialised --
         to operate
the brute machinery of the nation-state.

Education for an information society
               will centre on the Three Cs:
"Children, Computers, and Communication."
Its aim will be to produce
   a creative workforce --
      adaptable, entrepreneurial,
                         interdisciplinary--
         to help solve
the problems of this planet.

2.   THE NEW METHODS OF EDUCATION

2.1 Computer-based Education (CBE)

Not only must we expand the objectives of
education and extend education to a
cradle-to-grave system, we must also alter the
methods.

Over the next few decades, traditional
institution-based education will give way to
computer-based education (CBE). CBE will
result in a pronounced shift of educational
activity back into the home as the primary
seat of learning -- a shift away from the
current institutional settings such as
schools, colleges or universities.

Actually, in many technologically advanced
countries television is a more important
educator than the traditional education

institutions. In such countries, one could argue that there has already been a return to the home-based education which prevailed prior to the advent of universal education in schools. That is, "mass education" is already taking place in the home. Most educators, however, downgrade this informal education system even though by far more images and knowledge about the world is derived from TV than from teachers and textbooks.

What advances in computer pegagogy will achieve, is a return to the home of formal learning systems. At the moment, however, there exist at least three kinds of impediments which prevent the current experiments in computer-assisted learning (CAL), computer-based training (CBT), and other related activities described at this conference from blossoming into full-fledged CBE systems: (1) Hardware prices, (2) software production, and (3) the lack of involvement of a sufficient number of able educators.

(1) Hardware prices in most countries for most people are still too high to be cost effective. The lower price range of computers lack the memory power and other facilities (eg, communication cards) to suffice; "good" machines are still far too expensive for the average householder. For CBE to become practical there must exist not only extensive computer facilities at all education institutions, but all homes must possess at least one high quality micro. At home, micros must become as commonplace as TVs, probably closer to radios. Furthermore, TV sets must have a video disc facility to permit interactive video systems to be utilised.

Having said all that, compare the micros of the early 1980s with those of the late 1980s. By the turn of the century, it appears likely that the hardware requirements for CBE will have been met.

(2) Software is still too expensive to produce. However, just as over the past half decade there has been an enormous improvement in hardware capability, so have there been great strides forward in authoring systems. Particularly praiseworthy at the time of this writing has been the development of Apple's Hypercard/Mac-2 system. Further simplification in animation and other visual inputs, auditory and text inputs, coupled to laser printing will allow able educators to produce multi-media learnign packages with ease by the turn of the century. At Bradford University we are currently trying to establish a prototype "electroning learning-package factory" (ELF) system with a view to reducing the time spent by an author by a factor of ten. One of the main functions of the ELF system will be to allow a teacher to modify existing software to suit the requirements of the course, or the needs of the learner.

(3) Because of the limitations of existing hardware and software, working with computers is simply not cost effective for most educators. Furthermore, educators are both conservative in their methodology, and beleaguered by the rapidity of the changes occurring around them. This does not favour experimenting with a still rapidly evolving technology. Educators need to be inspired -- they need to be given a vision of the advantages and possibilities of the new technology. Once they have acquired such a vision, they then need to be taught how to use such technology effectively.

Here too, changes will be exponential: The more educators become involved, the easier it becomes to involve still more educators. And more educators will become involved because of pressures from enthusiastic peers, sophisticated students, and enlightened administrators. This pressure will increase each year as the technology continues to evolve.

It is probably true to say that at this point in time (1988), it is the education and training of the educators, rather than the hardware and software limitations which place the greatest restraint on the progressive evolution of educational methods from sporadic exercises in CAL, CBT, etc., to full-fledged computer-based education systems.

2.2   CBE

What will the CBE system of the future look like? Much of this has been described elsewhere [Stonier & Conlin, 1985] but it might be useful to summarise the broad features:

All children will have a microcomputer system at home. This system includes devices which allow children to network to their own school, the local education system, and data bases around the world. In addition, the electronic learning packages will use compact disks to allow for interactive audio, and visual material. Electronic mail facilities will allow interaction between student and teacher and very important -- student and student. International "electronic penpals", will be an automatic requirement for language studies. Student homework will be presented in both electronic form and as print-outs.

Schools will have more extensive (compatible) computer, printing and communications facilities, and more elaborate means of involving students in group activities such as the use of robot turtles for LOGO and other specialised equipment such as CAD/CAM facilities. Pupils will be introduced to concepts and learn skills in the primary and secondary schools which at the moment, are taught at university and post-university level.

The results of these developments will be that the traditional skills such as reading, writing and arithmetic will be learned at home. Introducing subjects such as biology, history, economics, etc, will also be done at home.

As these systems come in place early in the next century, young children working with computers will learn to read and write about as fast as they learn to talk. With further advances in hardware -- voice chips, cheap printers, voice-to-print, voice-to-voice, cheap interactive compact disks, optical fibre links to intelligent data bases, etc. -- almost all twelve-year-olds will understand calculus and will have reached comparable levels of understanding in science, engineering, geography, history, and anything else that the emotional maturity of a young teenager can handle.

Children will go to school because they need to play with each other, to acquire social skills, engage in sports, go on field trips, fiddle with machinery, perform experiments, dance, put on plays, etc. In short, home will become the place to go to learn -- school, where you go to play.

Older people are one of the great under-utilised resources of Western society. We should create a new kind of teacher -- grandmothers (and grandfathers). The old are natural for working with computers. Computers require neither strength nor physical agility. They can, however, be a source of enormous stimulation and entertainment. The old also have a natural affinity for the young. Thus retired people would supplement their income by working as surrogate grandparents for ten to fifteen hours a week with one, or a pair of local children. The grandparent would provide psychological support, and a view of the past and the local community. The computer would provide educational stimulation, and a view of the future and the world. The education system of enlightened countries would assure that all children, in their own home, would have a CBE system -- and a grandmother. The CBE system will have built in a human touch. In a sense, education technology would have come full circle: From grandmothers to computers, and back again.

3. CONCLUDING OBSERVATIONS AND REMARKS

The computer will invade the home and the education system in a way unparalleled in previous education history. This leads to a number of questions, both practical and social. Among the practical questions, we need to know what are the most appropriate reward systems for motivating children to learn with the help of computers. Do all audio or visual rewards reinforce the learning experience, or do they distract? Are such rewards merely frivolous? Might computer-based learning systems hinder certain kinds of learning? Might they inhibit genuine curiosity? Might they undermine long term interests in a topic?

At the social level we should ask: What will be the impact on society? What will be the impact on children? The hypnotic effect of computers is well-known. Young boys (and older ones) love the violence expressed in certain computer games. Will such games reinforce violent behaviour? Will the anthropormorphisation of computers and, in due course, robot toys, cause children to behave like robots themselves? Alternatively, if the computer or robot is the perfect slave to be turned on and off at will, will children confuse accepted behaviour with robot toys with how they ought to behave with real people? What about the incredible amounts of information which will comprise the environment of children of the future, will it cause information overload? What are the symptoms and pathologies of information overload? Lastly, a very real problem is shaping up in the technologically advanced countries where middle-class families will avail themselves of this new technology to give their children maximum educational advantages. Will this lead to a new polarisation in Western societies between the information haves and the information have-nots?

To what extent will this process exacerbate a global society structured along potentially divisive lines?

On the positive side, boys playing football, girls jumping rope (or vice versa) -- games, parties and discos -- these are all fun. We have overlooked the enormous educational value of these activities in teaching both physical and social skills. In contrast, our Victorian puritanism has made learning intellectual skills, most of the time, into an onerous task. The computer will reintroduce fun into that process of learning.

Children having an early experience with computers, will develop a technical expertise as second nature. In the early 1980s, one of the sources of amazement to teachers and parents watching young children working computers, was the rapidity with which they learned how to load a program, run a tape recorder, and carry out all the procedures necessary for making a computer work. In part, this astonishment reflected our own cultural experience: We overlooked the fact that early in the nineteeth century, five-year-old children used to work machinery in the industrial mills of Northern England, and that in Third World countries, five-year-olds still have significant responsibilities -- the girls in bringing up younger siblings, the boys in taking care of the family cattle, or in other ways helping out. A helpless childhood is a Western construct.

Perhaps the most important impact computers will have, is teaching children how to think more effectively. Seymour Papert [1980] complains that our tendency is to categorise children into smart and dumb people when, in fact, it is often a question of context and experience. Systematically questioning data bases, working out flow charts, developing habits of precision and discipline, building in checks, carrying out sub-routines in order to build larger structures, all of these foster intellectual qualities which are not produced same way in the present system. We know that handicapped children have shown substantial improvements in I.Q. tests when given the proper tools. This principle will be found applicable to virtually all children. The human mind is an exquisite information processing device reflecting the evolution of intelligence over a period of 10^8-10^9 years. Chris Evans (personal communication) believed that the scale of intelligence should begin with a rock or some other inert matter which has zero intelligence, then work up from an amoeba which clearly has enough intelligence to move away from an undesirable environment and towards a more desirable one, up through a variety of invertebrates to fish, amphibians, etc, up to the mammals. Finally we look at our closest relative, the chimp, which one can teach the rudiments of logic with no difficulty whatsoever.

The high motivational state induced in children working with good education software coupled to the emergence of a global network of databases which allow the child access to information with unprecedented ease, must have an impact on the understanding children develop of the world they live in, and for that matter, in understanding themselves. Furthermore, as indicated above, children encouraged to create their own data bases, perhaps write their own programs, will develop intellectual skills of precision, logic, a systematic and orderly method for producing work, and a much more sophisticated approach to problem solving. The cumulative improvements in intellectual skills coupled to their markedly expanded understanding of the world, will differentiate such children almost to the extent of being a new sub-species: Homo sapiens cerebrus, or some such.

The matter is analogous to a situation sometime probably between five and ten million years ago, when our pre-human hominid ancestors began to use weapons, both to ward off predators and to subdue prey. That earliest of all technological revolutions differentiated the hominid stock from the rest of the primates. The hominids were able to extend their econiche

to hunting large game. In due course as they mastered fire, they were able to extend their geographic range more successfully than any other primate. In human history it was always those who were able to develop and use new technologies adroitly, who in the long run not only survived better, but came to dominate the others. Homo sapiens cerebrus will survive, prosper, and in due course dominate all those who do not partake of the new intellectual technology. Among higher organisms, new behaviour patterns rather than new anatomical features, set the stage for new patterns of evolution. The computer is setting the stage for a revolution as profound as the hominid revolution of several million years ago. Will we be able to cope with it?

References

Evans, C. The Mighty Micro Victor Gollancz (London, 1979).

Papert, S. Mindstorms Basic Books, New York (1980).

Stonier, T. Changes in Western Society: Educational Implications in World Yearbook of Education 1979: Recurrent Education and Lifelong Learning T Schuller and J Megarry (Ed) Kogan Page, London, (1979) pp31-34

Stonier, T. The Wealth of Information: A Profile of the Post-Industrial Economy Thames/Methuen, London (1983).

Stonier, T. and Conlin, C. The Three Cs: Children, Computers and Communication John Wiley & Sons, Chichester (1985).

Stonier, T. The Computer: Most Powerful Technology Ever?" in New Directions in Education and Training Technology B S Alloway and G M Mills (Eds) Kogan Page, London, (1985) pp 13-21

Stonier, T. Education: Society's N⁰ 1 enterprise" in Open Learning in Transition: An Agenda for Action National Extension College 25th Anniversary Book, Nigel Paine, ed, Glasgow (1988) (in press)

AUTHOR INDEX